W 20.00

Thurs. → 5:30

MARKETING MANAGEMENT
Text and Cases

MARKETING MANAGEMENT
Text and Cases

John A. Quelch

Robert J. Dolan
Both of Harvard University

Thomas J. Kosnik
Stanford University

IRWIN

Burr Ridge, Illinois
Boston, Massachusetts
Sydney, Australia

Senior sponsoring editor:	Stephen M. Patterson
Editorial coordinator:	Lynn Nordbrock
Marketing manager:	Scott J. Timian
Project editor:	Paula M. Buschman
Production manager:	Bette K. Ittersagen
Designer:	Larry J. Cope
Art coordinator:	Mark Malloy
Compositor:	Carlisle Communications, Ltd.
Typeface:	10/12 Sabon
Printer:	The Maple-Vail Book Manufacturing Group

Library of Congress Cataloging-in-Publication Data

Quelch, John A.
　　Marketing management : text and cases / John A. Quelch, Robert J.
Dolan, Thomas J. Kosnik.
　　　　p.　　cm.—(The Irwin series in marketing)
　　Includes index.
　　ISBN 0-256-10955-9
　　　1. Marketing—Management.　　2. Marketing—Management—Case studies.
　　I. Dolan, Robert J.　II. Kosnik, Thomas J.　III. Title.　IV. Series.
　　HF5415.13.Q45　1993
　　658.8—dc20　　　　　　　　　　　　　　　　　　　　　　　　　92–31499

Printed in the United States of America
1　2　3　4　5　6　7　8　9　0　MP　9　8　7　6　5　4　3

John A. Quelch is Professor of Business Administration, Graduate School of Business Administration, Harvard University, where he oversees the introductory MBA Marketing course taken by all 800 students each year and chairs the first year MBA curriculum committee. Professor Quelch has published articles in journals ranging from *Harvard Business Review* to *Marketing Science*. He is the (co)author of 10 books including *Ethics in Marketing* (1993), *Global Marketing Management* (1992), and *The Marketing Challenge of Europe 1992* (1990). He serves as a director of Reebok International Ltd. and WPP Group plc. He is a graduate of Oxford University (BA), University of Pennsylvania (MBA), and Harvard University (MS and DBA).

Robert J. Dolan is the Edward W. Carter Professor of Business Administration and Marketing Area Chairman at the Graduate School of Business Administration, Harvard University. He is editor of the Field Studies section of *Marketing Science*. An expert on product policy and pricing, his work has appeared in leading journals such as the *Bell Journal of Economics, Marketing Science,* and the *Journal of Marketing*. His latest book is *Managing the New Product Development Process* (1993). He is a graduate of Boston College (BA) and the University of Rochester (MS and PhD).

Thomas J. Kosnik is a lecturer at Stanford Graduate School of Business and in the Stanford Engineering Management program. From 1985 to 1989, he was an assistant professor at Harvard Business School. Kosnik's research focuses on the design and marketing of information technology-based products and services for global markets. He has worked in design, sales, and marketing roles in the computer software and systems integration industries. He is a graduate of Duke University (BA), University of Virginia (MBA), and Stanford University (PhD).

THE IRWIN SERIES IN MARKETING

Levy & Weitz
RETAILING MANAGEMENT
First Edition

Mason, Mayer, & Wilkinson
MODERN RETAILING
Sixth Edition

Mason, Mayer, & Ezell
RETAILING
Fourth Edition

Mason & Perreault
THE MARKETING GAME
Second Edition

McCarthy & Perreault
BASIC MARKETING: A
GLOBAL-MANAGERIAL
APPROACH
Eleventh Edition

McCarthy & Perreault
ESSENTIALS OF MARKETING
Fifth Edition

Peter & Olson
CONSUMER BEHAVIOR AND
MARKETING STRATEGY
Third Edition

Peter & Donnelly
A PREFACE TO MARKETING
MANAGEMENT
Fifth Edition

Peter & Donnelly
MARKETING MANAGEMENT:
KNOWLEDGE AND SKILLS
Third Edition

Quelch & Farris
CASES IN ADVERTISING AND
PROMOTION MANAGEMENT
Third Edition

Quelch, Dolan, & Kosnik
MARKETING MANAGEMENT:
TEXT AND CASES
First Edition

Smith & Quelch
ETHICS IN MARKETING
First Edition

Stanton, Spiro, & Buskirk
MANAGEMENT OF A SALES
FORCE
Eighth Edition

Thompson & Stappenbeck
THE MARKETING STRATEGY
GAME
First Edition

Walker, Boyd, & Larréché
MARKETING STRATEGY:
PLANNING AND
IMPLEMENTATION
First Edition

Weitz, Castleberry, & Tanner
SELLING: BUILDING
PARTNERSHIPS
First Edition

This volume is a substantial departure from the concept on which most other marketing books are based. Here we cover not only the substance of marketing, but also the process of marketing—the activities that marketers perform to satisfy customer needs and to build an enduring, distinctive, competitive competence. Each activity such as strategy formulation, planning, programming and budgeting, and implementation is important in its own right and receives careful attention. We have also endeavored to demonstrate both the unity of the total process and the important relationships among the activities. Understanding the marketing process can leverage the effectiveness of marketing plans and programs.

Any learning process is based on a series of partnerships. Most important among these is the partnership between student and teacher. In the case method, the student assumes much of the responsibility for his or her own development, and the teacher provides the structure and support necessary to the process. A second equally important partnership involves all the students in a class; their interactions and respectful sharing of thoughts and testing of ideas are critical to their growth and development.

In this book, the integration of textual notes and cases represents an equally important partnership. The textual notes provide the structure and nomenclature, while the cases provide the opportunity to apply the principles described in the notes. We believe that the breadth, depth, and integrated nature of this material will ensure its relevance to the student and its rigorous application in the classroom.

Almost all books are cooperative efforts. Because this book contains so many cases, it is more of a cooperative venture than most. Thus, we want to extend our sincere appreciation to a wide range of people, including:

- The many people on the Harvard Business School marketing faculty who have, over the years, contributed to the development of the first-year MBA marketing course, the required course on which this volume is based. They provided us with a heritage of devoted teaching and a tradition of experimentation that enabled us to develop this material.
- Our colleagues in the marketing discipline who have labored to develop and explain important marketing skills and concepts. We are indeed indebted to

the academy for the knowledge we are attempting to disseminate in this volume.

- The administration of the Harvard Business School, and its supporters, particularly those companies who are members of the Associates of the Harvard Business School. Under the leadership of Dean John H. McArthur and the Directors of the Division of Research, the school provided us with the substantial financial resources needed to complete a field-oriented project of this magnitude.
- The editorial and word-processing support functions of the Harvard Business School, which are exceptional because of their competence, quality, and generosity. We are particularly appreciative of the assistance provided by Antoinette Prince and Elisa Morton Palter who were responsible for preparing the manuscript for submission.
- The many companies, anonymous and named, that provided case material. The case method stands and falls on the support of generous organizations who cooperate in the development process.
- Our colleagues in the first-year marketing course since September 1986 who, in our weekly, four-hour staff meetings, shared their thoughts and helped to develop ours. We are particularly indebted to Professor Robert D. Buzzell who developed the initial concept of the marketing process as used in this book. This concept was carefully and constructively nurtured and improved by many members of our teaching group.
- Our students who also shared their thoughts with us and who, in the process of their own education, added immensely to our development and to the evolution of the concepts and material in this book.
- The many research assistants and others who contributed to the development of the materials included in the book and who are noted with sincere gratitude in the table of contents and on the title pages of their individual works. No group of three people could have developed such a wide range of high-quality material alone.
- The authors also gratefully acknowledge the editorial support at Irwin of Steve Patterson, senior sponsoring editor, Lynn Nordbrock, editorial coordinator, and Paula Buschman, project editor. We also note the effort put forth by Thelma Prince, proofreader.
- Our loving families, and particularly Joyce Huntley Quelch, Kathleen Splaine Dolan, and Jill Summerbell, who provided us with the confidence to start and, more important, the patience to complete this work. We dedicate this volume to them with great and sincere appreciation.

John A. Quelch
Robert J. Dolan
Thomas J. Kosnik

CONTENTS

OVERVIEW

AN INTRODUCTION TO CASES

Management instruction involves the development of a set of philosophies, approaches, skills, knowledge, and techniques. Lectures and readings are the most efficient way to acquire knowledge and to become informed about techniques. Exercises or problem sets are an excellent way to begin to learn about the application and limitations of techniques. But the development of philosophies, approaches, and skills is best served by the case method, which can also help to provide knowledge and experience with techniques. The case method becomes a part of a broad gauge approach to management education and development. It is therefore generally used in well-orchestrated concert with other approaches.

Most students and executive program participants are quite familiar with lectures, readings, exercises, and problem sets, but the case method is often new to them. It is important to understand the basis for the case method and to have some idea of how to approach cases. That is the purpose of this brief note.

The case method is built around the concepts of *metaphors* and *simulation*. Each case is a description of a real business situation and serves as a *metaphor* for a particular set of problems. The situations which you face as a manager may differ from the metaphors we have chosen here, but taken together, the cases provide a useful and relevant set of metaphors for marketing situations. The cases were selected to include a wide variety of products and company types so that at least some of them would be relevant along those dimensions. The situations analyzed and skills developed in the cases are relevant to almost all marketing management situations. Thus they are relevant to students of marketing management.

The case method of management instruction is based upon the belief that management is a set of skills, rather than a collection of techniques or concepts. The best way to learn a skill is to practice in a *simulation*-type process. Thus, the swimmer swims and the pianist plays the piano. The swimming novice might drown if thrown into deep water after reading a set of books. And few of us would want to hear a concert pianist who had never before touched a piano, but who had attended many lectures on piano playing. Because it is impractical to have the student manager manage a company, the case provides a vehicle for simulation.

This note was prepared by Professor Benson P. Shapiro.
Copyright © 1984 by the President and Fellows of Harvard College.
Harvard Business School case 0-584-097.

The total case process consists of four steps ordered as follows:

1. Individual analysis and preparation.
2. Optional informal small group discussion.
3. Classroom discussion.
4. End-of-class generalization about the learning.

Each of these steps asks the participant to perform related but different activities.

While there is no "one ideal way to approach a case," some generalities can be drawn. The student gains the most by immersing him- or herself in the case and actively playing the role of the protagonist. The protagonist is usually one manager, but is sometimes a group. By actively studying the case, the student begins to learn how to analyze a management situation and develop a plan of action. By participating in an involved manner in the case discussion, the student learns to commit him- or herself to a position easily and to express that position articulately. The core of management decision making consists of the processes of analysis, choice, and persuasion.

The fourth step, generalization, is also part of good management practice. The smart manager steps back from each situation he or she has experienced and asks, "What did I learn?" and "How does the situation and the lesson relate to my whole experience?" The astute student will want to do the same thing on his or her own, building on the help provided by the instructor. An important part of that process is to relate the cases to the assigned reading material. The reading material generally provides the structure and techniques, and the case a simulated experience in the application of the structure and techniques. The cases also help to develop a generalized approach to business situations as well as a set of philosophies.

The case method is demanding of both teachers and students. Participants who are involved in each case analysis and discussion, and who attempt to generalize their learning across cases gain the most from the process.

Each person should strive to develop the ability to ask "the right questions" about each case. The instructor may provide specific questions for each case. The following questions are among those which are generally relevant to all cases:

- Who is the protagonist?
- What are his or her objectives (implicit or explicit)?
- What decisions (implicit or explicit) must I make?
- What problems, opportunities and risks do I, as the protagonist, face?
- What evidence do I have to help make the decision? Is the evidence reliable and unbiased? Can I improve it?
- What alternative courses of action are available?
- What criteria should I use to judge the alternatives?
- Are there ethical issues involved?
- What action should I take?
- How should I convince others in the company as well as customers, competitors, and channel members that my approach is best?
- What contingency plan do I have to respond to adverse reactions?
- What did I learn from this case?
- How does it relate to past cases and my own "live" experiences?

An Introduction to Marketing

Marketing is the function of the company, or nonprofit organization, with the responsibility for serving customers and for dealing with intermediaries and external support organizations such as distributors and advertising agencies. Many people who come to the study of marketing with little or no business experience picture it as the study of selling and advertising. While marketing certainly includes selling and advertising, it encompasses much more. Perhaps the best way to explain the scope and nature of marketing is to review a specific example of some of the decisions marketers make.

The Substance of Marketing

Assume for a moment that you have decided to enter the watch business. You must make a set of important marketing-related decisions which might include:

1. To which consumers should I sell my watches? How should I define the consumer I hope to serve? Should I think in terms of geography, perhaps the country or region of the country in which my consumer lives? Or maybe the consumer's income or sex or fashion orientation is more important.
2. What product or products should I offer? For example, should I offer digital or analog, ornate or simple, multifunction or single function?
3. How much should I charge for each watch? Should I offer discounts to people who pay cash or who buy in large volumes?
4. Should I sell direct to consumers or through stores, and if through stores, what type of stores? Watches are, after all, sold in drug stores, gift shops, department stores, jewelry stores, and a myriad of other outlets. Do I want to offer my product in several types of outlets or only in one type?

This note was prepared by Professors Benson P. Shapiro and John A. Quelch.
Copyright © 1984 by the President and Fellows of Harvard College.
Harvard Business School case 0-584-124.

And, how do I select and service the particular outlets I choose? Finally, how do I convince the store to carry my brand?

advertising

5. How should I communicate to the consumers to whom I wish to sell? Do I use advertising, and if so in what media? I could use television, radio, magazines, newspapers and many other media. And, how do I reach the stores? Do I use salespeople? Should the salespeople visit the stores or should they just telephone them?

These decisions help to explain two important marketing concepts. The first decision is perhaps the most important decision in marketing—*market selection*. Market selection is the choice of which customer needs to attempt to fill and which customer needs to *explicitly* not attempt to fill. Any given organization has a very finite set of abilities and resources and, thus, can serve only a certain group of customers and fill only a limited set of needs. It is impossible for any organization to succeed in being "all things to all people." The market selection theme will pervade this book just as it pervades good marketing practice.[1]

The other four decisions (items 2 to 5 as listed above) relate to the second key concept—the *marketing mix*. The marketing mix is the "tool kit" of the marketer and consists of four elements:

1. *Product policy*—all aspects of the product which the customer receives including the physical product and all of the service enhancements. Sometimes the "product" is purely a service.

2. *Price policy*—the total financial cost of the product to the customer including such things as discounts, rebates, and the like, and the price to the wholesalers or retailers, or both, who carry the product.

3. *Distribution policy*—which are the intermediaries through which the product flows to the consumers. They include retail stores, wholesalers, and industrial distributors as well as a wide range of other organizations.

4. *Communication policy*—which is the means by which the organization "talks to" its customers, prospective customers, and other people important to the organization such as distributors. This is the most visible part of marketing because it includes advertising and personal selling. Although it is the most visible, and thus the most recognized, it is only one element in the marketing mix.

The *four elements* of the marketing mix are so important that they are the organizing framework for the first part of this book. We will cover communications, pricing, product, and distribution policy in that order. Almost all marketing textbooks and courses use this framework. One easy way to remember the elements was popularized by J. E. McCarthy[2] and is called the *Four Ps:*

1. Product.
2. Price.
3. Place (distribution channels).
4. Promotion (communication).

---

[1]For more on this topic see E. Raymond Corey, "Key Options in Market Selection and Product Planning," *Harvard Business Review,* September–October 1975, *HBR* order no. 75502.

[2]E. Jerome McCarthy with Andrew A. Brogowicz, *Basic Marketing: A Managerial Approach,* 7th ed. (Homewood, Ill.: Richard D. Irwin, 1981), pp. 42, 261.

We prefer the term *distribution* because we think that the channel provides much more than a place to buy. We use *communication* instead of promotion because promotion also means a short-term cut in price usually accompanied by increased communication. But the four Ps is a useful mnemonic device.

Market selection and the marketing mix decisions are the key substantive issues in marketing. We now look at the "players," the participants who are involved with marketing.

The Participants

Just as there are 4 Ps, there are also 4 Cs. This is a useful mnemonic device to remember the participants in the marketing arena. They are:

1. Company—the protagonist organization which can be a nonprofit organization or a governmental entity.
2. Consumers—the person or people who use, buy, or influence the purchase of a product or service.
3. Channels—we spoke before about distribution channels. Distribution channel policy is an element of the marketing mix and the channels are participants.
4. Competitors—other organizations which attempt to satisfy the same consumer needs.

This book is devoted to business marketing so we focus on companies. But marketing is also practiced by nonprofit organizations and government agencies. Some nonbusiness programs have led to very visible advertising campaigns such as those against smoking and those to encourage young people to join the United States armed forces. Nonprofits, like businesses, have to look at all four elements of the marketing mix, and at market selection decisions. Since about 1970, there has been a great deal of study of nonbusiness marketing.[3]

The consumer is the *raison d'être* of all marketing. In fact, the idea that the key to marketing is to satisfy the consumer has been called the *marketing concept*.[4] Consumer is actually a catch phrase for a total purchasing unit which sometimes includes several or more individuals and is often referred to as a *decision-making unit* (DMU). To understand the DMU concept, we must look at the different types of marketing. Marketing that involves the sale to ultimate consumers of products which travel through a distribution channel in essentially unchanged form is called consumer or consumer-goods marketing. Industrial marketing, on the other hand, is the marketing of products to companies, institutions, and governments. Sometimes, the same product is sold as both a consumer good and an industrial good. Mattresses, for example, are sold to ultimate consumers, as well as to hotels (companies), hospitals (often nonprofits, but not always), and prisons (governments).

---

[3]See, for example, Benson P. Shapiro, "Marketing for Nonprofit Organizations," *Harvard Business Review*, September–October 1974, *HBR* order no. 74512; and Christopher H. Lovelock and Charles B. Weinberg, *Marketing for Public and Nonprofit Managers* (New York: John Wiley & Sons, 1984).

[4]B. McKitterick, "What is the Marketing Management Concept?" in *The Frontiers of Marketing Thought and Science*, ed. Frank M. Bass (Chicago: American Marketing Association, 1957), pp. 71–82.

The industrial DMU is often large and complex, sometimes involving over 10 people. It is not unusual for a large purchase to be made by a formal committee or task force or for many individuals to play important roles in a very complex *decision-making process* (DMP). Even consumer goods can involve multiperson DMUs. In the purchase of plumbing fixtures for a home, the actual purchaser may be influenced by users (perhaps children in the family), experts (an architect, for example), and installation personnel (the plumber). A more common case might be a vacation or automobile purchase in a family of four where each member has different needs and criteria.

By the end of the book, it should be clear that the consumer should be the focus of almost all marketing action and that consumer analysis is a difficult and endless, yet important, task. It is impossible to put too much effort into it.

The channel, the third participant, is viewed as a participant because it is an active player in the marketing process. Products often succeed or fail based on whether or not they can attract trade (or channel) support. The channel is typically presented with far too many products to carry, so some are carried, a smaller number receive active support, and some are not even carried. If the company's marketing plan assumes that the stores will carry a product, and they don't, the result is either failure or a change in the plan or execution of the plan. The channel justifies the same type of careful analysis as the consumer.

The fourth participant is competition. Few products face no competitors. Sometimes the competition is very direct as between Pepsi-Cola and Coca-Cola. At other times, it is more subtle as when trade associations for different fruits compete with one another. It is unlikely that consumers will simultaneously and for long periods increase their consumption of all fruits. Consequently, the trade associations for peaches and apples compete with one another for "share of stomach" as it is called in the food industry. At an even broader level, all uses of the consumer's funds compete with one another because both money and time are limited. If even the wealthy consumer has purchased a yacht, then a villa on the Italian Riviera is out of the question, at least for a while.

Generally, competition is viewed in terms of substitution for a given product need. Thus, gas ranges are viewed as competitive with electric ranges. But the competition among electric ranges may be viewed as more intense than between electric and gas ranges. The definition of competition is often an art in itself.

Marketing is a blend of science and art, and the conceptual structures we use are not perfect. They are good if they are useful; they don't have to be perfect. Marketing, furthermore, at this time does not have one overarching, unified theory. There are many concepts, but each is useful in only some situations. The art of marketing is to apply each concept (the science) to the right situation and only the right situation. That is one reason that the case study is so appropriate in marketing. It emphasizes the situation-specific nature of marketing without detracting from theory building and concept generation.

The Marketing Process

Traditional marketing management courses have focused on the substance of marketing, particularly the marketing mix. An equally important, but neglected, aspect of marketing is the *marketing process*—how marketers do their job. The process is equal in importance to the substance because the process determines the nature and quality of the decisions made. A good process is likely to lead to a good decision. On the other hand, a faulty process will produce a good decision only on a random or accidental basis. The study of process, unfortunately, is considerably harder than the study of substance, which is already difficult enough.

The marketing process can be divided in several different ways. As shown in Exhibit 1, conceptualization of marketing tasks is:

1. *Marketing research*—the deliberate and careful acquisition and examination of qualitative and quantitative data to improve decision making.
2. *Marketing strategy formulation*—the development of the broadest marketing/business strategies with the longest-term impact.
3. *Marketing planning, programming, and budgeting*—the development of longer-term plans and short-term programs which generally focus on integrated approaches for a given product, and on the allocation of scarce resources such as sales effort or product development time across various products and functions.
4. *Marketing organization and implementation*—the task of getting the marketing job done which typically involves skills such as organizing, allocating, interacting and monitoring.

It is important to note that:

1. Each part of the process is intimately related to the other parts of the process. Exhibit 1 is an attempt to capture the more important relationships.
2. The dividing lines between any two parts of the process are vague and unclear. This is particularly true of those elements of the process which are clearly connected. The distinction, for example, between a marketing plan and a marketing program is very "muddy" indeed. Different companies and different people place the "dividing line" in different places. The precise boundaries, however, are now as important as the general concept.
3. Each element can be divided into smaller subelements. Marketing planning, for example, includes market assessment, which is the evaluation and selection to serve specific product/customer markets. Product-line planning is another subelement of marketing planning.

One reason that the marketing process has not received more attention is the "fuzziness" of the definitions and the lack of clarity about the distinctions. The words used here are in general use, although some companies and people use others. No "supreme body of marketers" sets definitions, although from time to time the American Marketing Association has published glossaries. Indeed, the concepts themselves change to meet the needs of individual companies, people, and situations.

Marketing Research

All marketing decisions should be based upon careful analysis and research. The analysis and research need not be quantitative, but it should be deliberate and should be matched to the magnitude of the decision being made.

Much has been written about the formal analysis and research to support marketing decisions. None of it, however, replaces common sense and good judgment. The marketer's quiver has some very powerful analytical arrows; and the rapid development of computers, mathematics including statistics, and other supporting disciplines such as psychology and sociology ensure that the diversity and power of the arrows will continue to increase. All of the tools must be applied carefully and intelligently to the decision at hand. It is a fine line, indeed between healthy skepticism and arrogant neglect of useful tools. The right analytical tool well applied can substantially improve marketing decision making.

Marketing Strategy Formulation

Strategy formulation is the broadest, longest-term marketing activity. At this stage, complex and subtle integration with other corporate functions is required. All of the functional strategies must fit together into a business strategy.

Because marketing deals with customers and the competitive environment, it is an early part of the total strategy formulation process. When done well, it is impossible to separate the marketing strategy from the corporate strategy. The two meld together into a unified whole.

Many young executives are seduced by the glamour of strategy formulation. It is generally not the best place to learn about marketing. Strategy formulation skills develop generally after narrower skills such as implementation, and should not be stressed too early in one's career. Young managers also tend to benefit from the shorter activity-result-feedback cycle of implementation and programming more than the longer-term, more subtle feedback needed to monitor and audit strategy formulation.

Marketing Planning, Programming, and Budgeting

Still higher on the dimension of time impact is the marketing planning activity. It involves objectives and plans with a two- to five-year time horizon and is thus further from the day-to-day activity of implementation.

Because of their broader nature and longer-term impact, plans are typically developed by a combination of higher-level line managers and staff specialists. If the specialists take over the process, it loses the commitment and expertise of the line managers who are responsible for carrying out the plan. The planning process is probably more important than the final planning document. The process ensures that a realistic, sensible, consistent document is produced, and leads to important organizational learning and development in its own right.

The marketing plan typically includes details about the marketing programs that will be implemented to achieve the plan. The resources allocated to these programs and the overall pro forma budget give quantitative precision to the plan.

Programs can be related either to one element of the marketing mix such as distribution for one or more products, or to all elements of the mix for a single product or market. To some extent, the choice will be determined by the nature of the company's organization. The more functional the organization (i.e., separation of marketing functions such as advertising, sales, and the like), the more likely it is that the programs will focus on one aspect of the mix across all products and markets. On the other hand, companies which organize around products or markets tend also to develop programs for each of them.

Allocating is a necessary function because there is never enough of any scarce resource such as advertising dollars or distribution effort to meet the "needs" of all products, markets, and programs. In many ways, marketing is deciding what *not* to do: which prospects not to sell to, which products not to produce, and so on. Allocation is the formal process of choosing what to do and what not to do, as well as choosing how much to do. Because marketers tend to be optimists (who else would constantly go to the marketplace to compete for customer attention and purchases?), they often underestimate the amount of effort which will be required to accomplish a goal. Allocation requires the stark realism to separate the clearly feasible from the hopeful. It forces the marketer to set explicit priorities and to make hard decisions.

Budgeting reflects the programs and allocations in a set of quantitative forecasts or estimates which are important within and beyond the marketing function. The budgets generally include financial pro formas which are used by the control and finance functions to forecast cash flows and needs. They also generally include unit sales forecasts that are used by production scheduling personnel to "load the factory" or service operation. If the forecasts are too low, customer needs are unmet and sales are lost. If the forecasts are too high, capacity sits idle and costs are much higher than they should have been.

Marketing Implementation

Strategy formulation, marketing planning and budgeting all lead to marketing implementation as shown in Exhibit 1. This is the executional phase which, in part, produces the actual results. Poor implementation can ruin even the best strategies, plans, and programs. The total purpose of all that goes before implementation is to ensure excellent execution.

The separate note on implementation provides much greater depth, but, at this point, it is appropriate to highlight a few thoughts. First, implementation means different things to different people in the organization. To the salesperson, it means going through all of the steps of the selling process, while to the national sales manager, it might mean reorganizing the whole sales force. Second, because of the relatively short time frame involved in most implementation activities, monitoring and auditing are generally easier than for the longer-term strategies and plans. Third, implementation is very people oriented. The results of implementation are manifested in people doing things—buying, selling, training, reorganizing, etc. Marketing implementation is different from implementation in most other functional areas because the primary focus of marketing is outside the company. Thus, marketing implementation focuses on prospects, customers, distributors, retailers, centers of influence such as architects who specify but do not purchase building materials, advertising agencies, and so on. But marketing implementation also includes dealing with other functional areas to gain support and to develop coordination. Product managers, for example, must implement their plans and programs through product development, production, service, and logistics personnel in other functional areas.

Monitoring and Auditing

One reason to develop strategies, plans and budgets is to have a set of goals or standards against which to measure performance. If, for example, sales are 10 percent below the plan, we can examine the cause of the shortfall. Was it, perhaps, poor execution? Or a poor program? Or even an inflated goal?

Marketing audits usually include two parts. The first is an assessment of performance against quantitative goals. Note that just because the goals are quantitative (stated in units, dollars, or share points), they are not necessarily objective. Usually they are subjective but quantified—the numbers are still the result of human judgment. The second part of a comprehensive audit reviews the processes and other nonquantifiable aspects of the marketing operation. This is more difficult, yet probably more important.

Because marketing is a mixture of art and science, quantitative and qualitative, and because it involves so many interactive variables, it is hard to audit. If the advertising-to-sales ratio is above the industry average, for example, does this indicate good or poor performance? Standards are few, and comparisons difficult. Nonetheless, the marketing audit is important because it forces careful review of the past before new plans are developed.

The audit raises a variety of important topics:

1. Who should perform the audit? Can the planners, programmers, and executors audit their own performance without bias? If they cannot, who knows enough about the operation to perform the audit? Should outsiders such as consultants be involved, and in what capacity?
2. How often should the audit be performed? Should it be on a regular calendar basis (as every year) or only at certain important points (at a major change in strategic direction)?
3. How comprehensive should the audit be? Should it involve all aspects of marketing or just some?

While auditing normally refers to an activity which is done only on certain occasions, monitoring generally refers to a more day-to-day review activity. It also often refers more to a review of external data (e.g., market share reports) than internal activities. It, too, is an important part of the total marketing process because it provides a frequent check of progress against plans and programs.

Lateral Connections

The marketing process is not nearly as "clean and separated" as Exhibit 1 implies. The activities are, in fact, interrelated and contemporaneous. Programs flow into plans just as plans flow into programs. Implementation goes on all the time. Thus, Exhibit 1 provides intellectual guidelines, not real delineations.

The marketing process also has a second dimension—the lateral connection to other functional parts of the company, such as production and operations, finance, control, and human resources management. The marketing strategy thus becomes part of the total corporate strategy, which includes all functional areas. The marketing plan is often part of a broader corporate business plan. The marketing plan is usually the "front end" of the corporate plan, because it spells out the operational, human, and financial resources needed to support the corporation's approach to its markets.

Marketing programs and budgets are usually part of the company's fundamental operating documents. The sales forecasts in the programs and budgets, for example, become the production schedule for the manufacturing function. Those, in turn, became the staffing programs for the human resources function and indicate the working capital needs to be supported by the finance function. If, for example, finance cannot support such a high level of inventory and accounts receivable, the sales forecast, production schedule, and staffing program must be scaled down. In most companies great effort must be devoted to such lateral connections. The coordination needs are very high and the amount of conflict often great. Risk aversion and opportunity sensitivity differ among functions. Varying reward systems sometimes encourage different types of behavior.

The corporation must develop formal and informal ways to foster good, open lateral connections. That need compounds all the marketing-oriented topics and concerns raised in this note.

Summary

This book looks at marketing in a fundamentally different way from most other marketing books. While Part I is organized around the marketing mix (communications, distribution, pricing, and product policy decisions), Part II advances beyond fundamental knowledge of marketing elements to develop skills in operating effectively in the marketing function. Many of the cases in this volume have been developed specifically to provide exposure to the "how" of marketing as well as to the "what" so that skills in managing the marketing process can be developed.

Exhibit 1

The marketing process

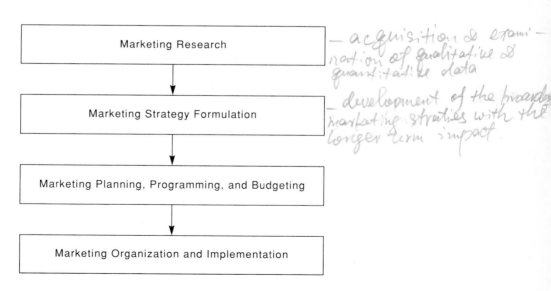

— acquisition & examination of qualitative & quantitative data

— development of the broader marketing strategies with the longer term impact

Basic Quantitative Analysis for Marketing

Simple calculations often help in making quality marketing decisions. To do good "numbers work," one needs only a calculator, familiarity with a few key constructs, and some intuition about what numbers to look at. This note has as its primary purpose the introduction of key constructs. The development of intuition about what quantities to compute can begin with this note, but is best accomplished by repeated analyses of marketing situations and application of the concepts and techniques presented here. Case study analysis provides that opportunity.

The organization of the note is as follows. First we define key constructs such as variable cost, fixed cost, contribution and margin. Following definition of these basic constructs, we discuss a most useful quantity: the "break-even" volume. We show how to calculate and use this quantity in marketing decision making.

Basic Terminology

As marketers, we are usually concerned with understanding the market or demand for the product or service in question. However, if we are to assess the likely profit consequences of alternative actions, we must understand the cost associated with doing business as well. For example, consider a firm choosing a price for its new videocassette tape. The manager estimates weekly sales for different prices to be:

Weekly Sales Estimate	Price
600 Units	$7.50
700 Units	6.00
1,000 Units	5.00

Which price is best for the firm? From the data given so far, we cannot answer the question. We can calculate the expected revenue generated by each pricing strategy,

This note was prepared by Professor Robert J. Dolan.
Copyright © 1984 by the President and Fellows of Harvard College.
Harvard Business School case 0-584-149.

but without cost information, it is not possible to determine the preferred price. This is the reason we begin this marketing note by considering key cost concepts.

The cost concepts we introduce are variable cost, fixed cost, and total cost. Second, we combine the cost information with price information to determine unit contribution and total contribution. Exhibit 1 shows the relationship between a typical firm's unit output and total cost of producing that output.

The first important feature of Exhibit 1 is that the total cost line (the solid line) does not go through the origin (i.e., for a zero output level, total cost is not zero). Rather, total cost is OA dollars as shown by the length of the double-headed arrow in Exhibit 1. We call OA the firm's "fixed costs." Fixed costs are those costs which do not vary with the level of output. An example of a fixed cost is the lease cost of a plant. The monthly lease fee is set and would be incurred even if the firm temporarily suspended production.

Although OA dollars are fixed, a second component of cost, called "variable cost," increases as output increases. As we have drawn Exhibit 1, total costs increase in a linear fashion with output produced. In reality, it is possible for the total cost curve to be as shown in either Exhibit 2 or Exhibit 3. Exhibit 2 represents a situation where each unit is cheaper to produce than the previous one. This would occur, for example, if the firm could buy raw material at lower unit prices as the amount it bought increased. Exhibit 3 shows the opposite situation (i.e., each unit is more expensive to produce than the previous one). This might happen if the firm faced limited supply of inputs and had to pay higher unit prices as its demand increased.

While many real world examples of Exhibits 2 and 3 type of situations exist, we will typically be making the assumption that Exhibit 1 is a good enough approximation of actual cost behavior. The total cost line drawn in Exhibit 1 is special because it represents the case of each unit costing the same. Thus, for Exhibit 1, we can write:

$$\begin{array}{l} \text{Total cost} \\ \text{for output} \\ \text{level } V \end{array} = \begin{array}{l} \text{Fixed} \\ \text{cost} \end{array} + \begin{array}{l} \text{Total variable} \\ \text{cost for} \\ \text{output level } V \end{array} \qquad (1)$$

$$= \text{Fixed cost} + [k \times V]$$
$$(OA)$$

In Equation 1, k is the cost of producing one more unit of output. It is the slope of the total cost curve in Exhibit 1 and does not change over the range of output shown. In summary, one can divide the firm's total cost into two parts: fixed cost and variable cost. Second, we will frequently assume that the cost of producing an additional unit of output does not change, so we can write the variable cost as $k \times V$ where V is total output.

Having defined total, variable, and fixed cost, we can now introduce the concept of contribution. If k is the constant unit variable cost and P the price received for the good or service, then we define

$$\begin{array}{l} \text{Unit contribution} \\ \text{(in dollars)} \end{array} = P - k \qquad (2)$$

If V is the total number of units the firm sells, then

$$\text{Total contribution} = (P - k)V \qquad (3)$$

That is, total contribution equals unit contribution times unit volume sold.

If we take the *V* in Equation 3 inside the parentheses, we obtain

$$\text{Total contribution} = \underset{\substack{\text{Total} \\ \text{revenue}}}{\overset{PV}{\text{Total}}} - \underset{\substack{\text{Total} \\ \text{variable} \\ \text{cost}}}{\overset{kV}{\text{Total}}} \tag{4}$$

Thus, total contribution is the amount available to the firm to cover (or contribute to) fixed cost and profit after the variable cost has been deducted from total revenue.

Let's solidify our understanding of these definitions by working through the videocassette tape pricing problem. Suppose the unit variable cost *k* is $4; then, assuming the sales forecasts for each price level given above are correct:

Price = $5

Unit contribution $= \$P - k = \$5 - \$4 = \$1$
Total contribution $= (P - k)V$
per week $= \$1/\text{unit} \times 1,000 \times 1,000 \text{ units/week}$
$= \$1,000/\text{week}$

Price = $6

Unit contribution $= \$6 - \$4 = \$2$
Total contribution $= \$2/\text{unit} \times 700 \text{ units/week}$
per week $= \$1,400/\text{week}$

Price = $7.50

Unit contribution $= \$7.50 - \$4 = \$3.50$
Total contribution $= \$3.50/\text{unit} \times 600 \text{ units/week}$
per week $= \$2,100/\text{week}$

Since, by definition, the fixed cost associated with each output level is the same, the firm is best off by charging $7.50 since of the three possible prices $7.50 maximizes the total contribution. Demonstrate to yourself that if the unit variable cost were $1, the firm would be better off at the $5 price.

Margin Calculations

The term *margin* is sometimes used interchangeably with *unit contribution* for a manufacturer. Margin is also used to refer to the difference between the acquisition price and selling price of a good for a member of the channels of distribution. For example, consider Exhibit 4, in which we have the videocassette tape manufacturer selling through a wholesaler, who in turn sells to retailers, who then sell to the public. Each of the three members of the channel of distribution (manufacturer, wholesaler, retailer) performs a function and is compensated for it by the margin it receives:

$$\underset{\text{margin}}{\text{Manufacturer's}} = \underset{\substack{\text{selling price} \\ \text{to distributors}}}{\text{Manufacturer's}} - \text{Manufacturing cost}$$

$$= \quad \$7.50 \quad - \$4.00 = \$3.50$$

$$\text{Wholesaler's margin} = \underset{\substack{\text{selling price} \\ \text{to retailers}}}{\text{Wholesaler's}} - \underset{\substack{\text{paid to} \\ \text{manufacturer}}}{\text{Price}}$$

$$= \quad \$8.70 \quad - \$7.50 = \$1.20$$

$$\text{Retailer's margin} = \begin{matrix} \text{Retailer's} \\ \text{selling price} \\ \text{to consumers} \end{matrix} - \begin{matrix} \text{Price paid to} \\ \text{wholesaler} \end{matrix}$$

$$= \quad \$10.00 \quad - \$8.70 = \$1.30$$

So the dollar margin is a measure of how much each organization makes per unit of goods sold.

The unit contributions and margins we have presented so far have all been in dollar terms. It is sometimes more useful to state margins in percentage terms. Consider the retailer in Exhibit 4, who makes a $1.30 margin for videocassette tapes. Are all items offering the retailer a $1.30 margin equally attractive to the retailer? For example, would the retailer be interested in stocking a color television that retails for $300 if he or she has to pay $298.70 for it? The color TV offers the same $1.30 margin. Yet, intuitively, it seems the retailer would not view the $1.30 on the color TV as acceptable, whereas he or she might view the $1.30 on the tape as acceptable. In short, items offering the same dollar margin are not necessarily equally attractive. Often, margins in percentage terms are more useful.

We define the retailer's percent margin as:

$$\begin{matrix} \text{Retailer's percent} \\ \text{margin} \end{matrix} = \frac{\begin{matrix} \text{Selling price} \\ \text{to consumers} \end{matrix} - \begin{matrix} \text{Purchase price} \\ \text{from wholesaler} \end{matrix}}{\text{Selling price to consumers}} \qquad (5)$$

$$= \frac{\text{Retailer's dollar margin}}{\text{Selling price to consumers}}$$

Note that in the denominator of Equation 5, we have the selling price to consumers. It would have been as logical to put purchase price from wholesaler there instead. It is only by convention that we divide by the selling price. For any member of the channel, we will always compute its percentage margin by dividing its dollar margin by the price at which it sells the goods. While this is the common definition and we will use it in all the cases and discussions, you should understand that this convention is not universal. Thus, you may encounter situations where an alternative convention is followed, and you must be alert to the distinction.

From Equation 5 and the numbers in Exhibit 4, we see that:

$$\begin{matrix} \text{Retailer's percent} \\ \text{margin} \end{matrix} = \frac{\$10.00 - \$8.70}{\$10.00}$$

$$= 13\%$$

Using similar logic, you should be able to show that manufacturer and wholesaler percent margins from Exhibit 4 are 46.67 percent and 13.79 percent respectively.

Break-Even Volume—Mechanics

Perhaps the single most useful summary statistic one can compute from quantities defined above is the break-even volume (BEV). The BEV is the volume at which the firm's total revenues equal total cost; below BEV, the firm has a loss; above BEV, the firm shows a profit. Exhibit 5 presents some example data. BEV calculation answers questions such as, if the firm charges $7.50, how many units must be sold to cover costs? We can obtain the answer by drawing a total revenue line as in Exhibit 6. The point at which the total revenue line cuts the total cost is BEV. For volumes below

BEV (to the left of BEV on Exhibit 6), the firm runs a loss; for volumes above (to the right on Exhibit 6), the firm shows a profit.

We can derive the BEV algebraically from the fact that at the BEV, total cost and total revenue are equal.

$$\text{Total revenue} = \text{Total cost} \qquad\qquad (6)$$

$$\text{Price} \times \text{BEV} = \text{Fixed cost} + (k \times \text{BEV})$$

Solving Equation 6 for BEV, we obtain:

$$\text{BEV} = \frac{\text{Fixed cost}}{\text{Price} - k}$$

$$= \frac{\text{Fixed cost}}{\text{Unit contribution}}$$

Hence, for the example of Exhibit 6,

$$\text{BEV} = \frac{\$2,000}{\$3.50/\text{unit}} = 571.43 \text{ units}$$

Break-Even Volume—Applications

So, the BEV calculation is simple. Simplicity plus relevance are the characteristics which make BEV so frequently warranted in case analysis. BEV can be of help in making decisions about unit contribution (through price or variable cost changes) or the appropriate level of fixed costs for a business. We now demonstrate each.

First, with respect to unit contribution, let us carry the videotape manufacturer example a little further. We have shown that at a price of $7.50, BEV is 571 units. Since

$$\text{BEV} = \frac{\text{Fixed cost}}{\text{Unit contribution}}$$

a price change impacts the BEV. For example, with price at $7, the BEV increases to 666.66 units. At $8, it decreases to 500 units. Exhibit 7 shows the BEV for various price levels. All price/volume combinations of the "iso-profit curve" offer the same profit (i.e., zero). From the perspective of a pricing decision, the decision maker may say: "Do I have a better chance of trying to sell 2,000 units at $5 or trying to sell 333.33 units at $10?" Notice that for our example cutting the price in half (from $10 to $5) would necessitate a six-fold increase in volume to be worthwhile for the firm. The reason for this, of course, is that this price cut would reduce the unit contribution from $6 ($10 − $4) to $1 ($5 − $4). Taken with some sense of the market size and competitors' positions, this analysis can be very useful in narrowing the feasible price range for the product.

Before considering fixed cost changes, we should note that this type of analysis can be done for any given level of profit as easily as the break-even level. For example, if the firm's goal is to make $1,000 per time period in addition to covering its fixed cost, then we can determine the volume required to achieve that goal given any particular price. All the points on the "iso-profit curve" in Exhibit 7 have the property that the (Price − V.C.) × Volume = $2,000, which is our fixed cost level. If the firm wants to make $1,000 per time period in addition to covering the $2,000 fixed cost, the relevant set of points becomes those satisfying (Price − V.C.) ×

Volume = $2,000 + $1,000 = $3,000. For any given price, the required volume is ($3,000)/(Price − V.C.). Exhibit 8 shows these points along with the "break-even" curve of Exhibit 7.

BEV is also useful in analysis of proposed changes in fixed costs. First, it can be used to aid in the decision of whether a new product should be marketed at all. For example, consider a firm which estimates the initial setup costs for plant and equipment and initial advertising outlays required to enter the market to be $3 million. The firm also believes that unit contribution from the product will be about $1,000. Should the firm enter the market? By BEV type of analysis, it is easy to see that the firm must sell 3,000 units just to cover its initial investment. Combined with some knowledge about total market size and competitive offerings, this analysis may suggest whether or not the $3 million investment should be made.

Second, the question of proposed changes in the fixed costs of marketing an existing product can be analyzed. For example, a proposition is made to the tape manufacturer that a $300,000 advertising campaign be undertaken. Should the firm do it? Following the BEV logic and assuming a $7.50 price, we can see

$$\frac{\text{Incremental volume required}}{\text{to justify expenditure}} = \frac{\text{Incremental expenditure}}{\text{Unit contribution}}$$

$$= \frac{\$300,000}{\$3.50/\text{unit}}$$

$$= 85,714 \text{ units}$$

So for the $300,000 advertising expense to be justified, the decision maker would have to believe that the expenditure will generate incremental volume of almost 86,000 units.

Using the Numbers

In this note we have shown how one can calculate a quantity given other quantities. Essentially, we showed how to translate some facts or estimates into other facts/estimates. This translation process is useful if the end result is a fact/estimate which is suggestive of what one should do as the manager. For example, we put together a fixed cost of $2,000 (is this good, bad, or indifferent?) and a unit contribution of $3.50 (is this good, bad, or indifferent?) to come up with a break-even volume of 571 units (is this good, bad, or indifferent?)—in the hope that the answer to the third question wouldn't be "indifferent" even though it's likely that's what the first two answers would be.

What makes one able to say if 571 units is good or bad? To be able to say it's good or bad, you have to have some other number in your head to compare it to. For example, if the total market for the product is estimated at 500 units, 571 is bad. If it's 50,000 units, 571 represents only a 1.14 percent share, so *maybe* 571 is good.

The key point is this: numbers have meaning only when there is some benchmark to compare them to. In marketing, such benchmarks are developed from understanding the market size, growth rate, and competitive activity. The finding BEV = 571 is, in and of itself, useless unless combined with other information to provide a meaningful context.

As noted at the outset, useful numbers work requires intuition about what quantities to calculate. This short note does little to develop that intuition. Our goals were more modest; for example, to specify terminology, mechanics, and suggest potential applications. The goal of the quantitative analysis must always be kept clear: to help in making marketing policy decisions.

EXHIBIT 1

Total cost as function of output

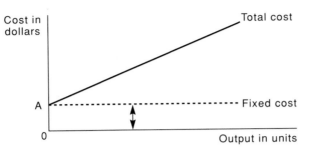

EXHIBIT 2

Cost increasing at decreasing rate

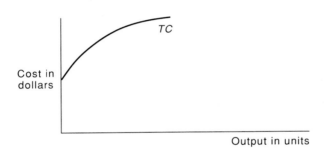

EXHIBIT 3

Cost increasing at increasing rate

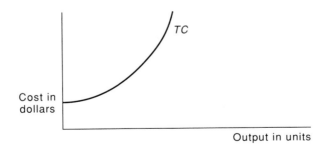

Exhibit 4

Price and cost at levels in the channel of distribution

Manufacturer cost: $4.00
Selling price to distributors: $7.50

Purchase price from manufacturer: $7.50
Selling price to retailer: $8.70

Purchase price from wholesaler: $8.70
Selling price to consumer: $10.00

Purchases from retailer at $10.00

Exhibit 5

Total cost line with fixed cost = $2,000 and unit variable cost = $4

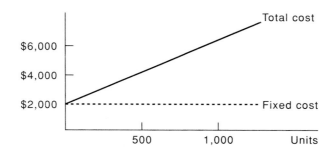

Exhibit 6

Cost, revenue, and break-even volume

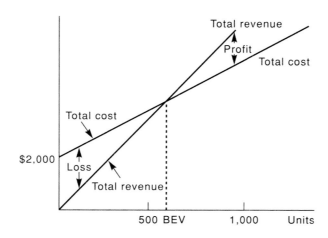

Exhibit 7

*Price and associated
break-even volumes*

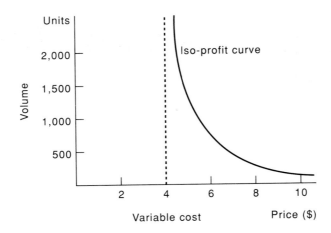

Exhibit 8

*Curves for break-even
and $1,000 profit*

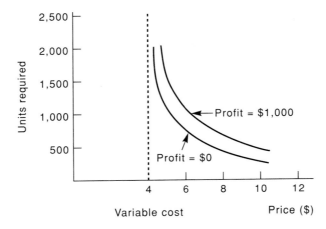

I THE MARKETING MIX

Introduction

THE MARKETING MIX

Components of the Marketing Mix

Ask any marketer: "What is the marketing mix?" You are likely to receive the cryptic reply: "The Four Ps." What are the Four Ps? Four variables that a marketer can use in different combinations to create value for customers: product, pricing, promotion (marketing communications), and place (distribution). Several of the subelements in each of the Four Ps that constitute the marketing mix are listed on the following page.

There are actually five Ps. The market mix can be designed, the people whom the marketer wishes to target must be specified. The clarity with which the target market is first defined often determines the ease with which decisions on the various elements of the marketing mix are made and, also, the internal consistency and robustness of the overall marketing program.

One of the most striking aspects of marketing is the great variety of marketing approaches different companies use. Of course, the marketing approaches of companies that offer toothpaste differ greatly from those that offer coal-fed boilers for electric generation. Major differences in the cost of the product, size of the market, amount of labor required in making a choice, and the overall significance of the purchasing decision are reflected in the approaches.

More surprising are the variations among marketers of the same product categories. Cosmetics, for example, are sold in a myriad of ways. Avon has a direct sales force of several hundred thousand people who call on individual consumers. Charles of the Ritz and Estée Lauder use selective distribution through department stores. Cover Girl and Del Laboratories market their products in chain drugstores and other mass merchandisers. Cover Girl does a great deal of advertising, while Del emphasizes personal selling and promotions, and Redken sells exclusively through beauticians. Revlon's strategy encompasses a wide variety of approaches. How do we understand all these variations?

This note was prepared by Professor Benson P. Shapiro.
Copyright © 1992 by the President and Fellows of Harvard College.
Harvard Business School case 9-584-125 (Rev. 4/2/92).

Major Elements of the Marketing Mix	Subelements
Product	Product design
	Product positioning
	Product name and branding
	Packaging
	Breadth and depth of product line
	Level and type of customer service
	Product warranty
Price	Manufacturer, wholesaler, and retailer selling prices
	Terms and conditions
	Bidding tactics
	Discount policies
	Skim versus penetrating pricing
Promotion (marketing communications)	Advertising
	Sales force policies
	Direct marketing (mail, catalog)
	Telemarketing (by telephone)
	Public relations
	Price promotions—consumer
	Price promotions—trade
	Trade shows and special events
Place (distribution channels)	Direct versus indirect channels
	Channel length
	Channel breadth (exclusive, selective, or intensive)
	Franchising policies
	Policies to ensure channel coordination and control

The purpose of this reading is to look at the marketing mix as an integrated whole, to provide tools that will explain why some programs prosper and others fail, and to improve readers' ability to predict, before the fact, which programs will succeed and which will not.

Marketing Programs

A marketing program is made up of the various elements of the mix and the relationships among them. A useful way to look at each element and subelement separately, and in pairs, is the sales response curve. In its simplest form, the curve shows the relationship between sales, usually measured in units but sometimes in dollars, and a marketing input measured in either physical or financial (e.g., dollars) terms, as shown in Exhibit 1.

The same relationship can be represented by a mathematical function or a chart listing unit sales and advertising expenditures. The graphical representation of the sales response curve is more meaningful to most people.

A more sophisticated sales response curve will have two independent variables with one dependent variable—sales. One might, for example, picture a graph of the relationship between the number of sales calls and advertisements as the independent (input) variables and unit sales as the dependent (output) variable.

Sales response curves enable a marketer to study the relationship between a given level of expenditure in one or more marketing areas and the likely level of sales. Even more powerfully, however, it demonstrates how sales are affected by changes in expenditure. Exhibit 1, for example, implies that as advertising expenditures increase, they have little impact initially, then a great deal of impact, and, finally, little impact again. Thus, the marketer can understand the dynamics of the relationships and interactions of the two elements.

The subject of interaction brings us naturally to the concept of the marketing mix itself, which emphasizes the fit of the various pieces and the quality and size of their interactions.

There are three degrees of interaction. The least demanding is consistency. Consistency is the lack of a poor fit between two or more elements in a mix. It would seem generally inconsistent, for example, to sell a high-quality product (product quality) through a low-quality retailer (distribution channels). Sometimes it is done successfully, but it is difficult to maintain such an apparent inconsistency over a long period of time.

The second level of positive relationship among elements of the mix is integration. While consistency is the lack of a poor fit, integration is the presence of a positive, harmonious interaction among the elements of the mix. For example, heavy advertising can sometimes be harmonious with a high price, because the added margin from the high price pays for the advertising and the high advertising creates the brand differentiation that justifies the high price. This does not mean, however, that heavy advertising and high price are always harmonious. Marketing is a very complex area, and each situation must be analyzed on its own merits.

The highest form of relationship is leverage, the situation in which each individual element of the mix is used to the best advantage in support of the total mix. A good example relates to the sales response curve introduced earlier. Even though it would not be sensible to invest additional advertising dollars in the flat part of the curve (upper end), it might be sensible to invest dollars in other elements of the mix at that time.

Once the elements of the marketing mix have met the internal tests of consistency, integration and leverage, the next step is to check that the proposed program fits the needs of the target *customers*, the core competencies of the *company*, and the likely responses of key *competitors*.

Program/Customer Fit

The concept of program/customer fit encompasses development of a program that fits the needs of the target-market segments. Such a program, in fact, builds solidly upon the concepts of consistency, integration, and leverage. Leverage, for example, involves choice of the most appropriate tools for a particular market segment over other, less efficient[1] tools. The price-sensitive but brand-insensitive consumer, for example, might be better approached with price promotions than with expensive advertising programs or packaging.

If the marketing program is to fit the customers it serves, the market must first be carefully and explicitly delineated. If the target has not been defined, it cannot be reached! One of the last steps before launching a program is a holistic analysis of the impact of each element and of the total mix on the people in the target market segment, emphasizing tests for consistency, integration, and leverage.

---

[1]Efficiency, in this sense, corresponds to the engineering concept of output per unit of input. Thus, we might look at unit sales generated per dollar of advertising or personal selling to determine which is more efficient or what combination of the two is most efficient.

Program/Company Fit

A good program/market fit and a consistent, integrated, and leveraged program are not enough for success. The program must also fit the company. When individuals with unique strengths and weaknesses work in formal organizations, the organizations themselves develop unique patterns of characteristics. These attributes relate to the human and cultural environment of the organization as well as to such material aspects as its financial strength and manufacturing prowess.

A marketing program must match the core competencies of the company or organization that is implementing it. An organization with extensive mass advertising experience and expertise, for example, is more likely to be able to carry out a program that leans heavily on advertising than an organization less strong in that particular area. Over time, these behavioral or cultural attributes can change, but the rate of change is limited. It takes quite a while for a company that does not understand advertising to develop a competence in that area. The ability to identify and recruit experts from other companies takes time and, often, several trial-and-error cycles. One person, furthermore, generally cannot change a whole culture, particularly of a large organization. Clearly, the behavioral fit between the program and the company must be carefully considered.

Behavioral aspects go beyond just marketing, to the company at large; a marketing program must fit the company's broader capabilities. For example, a company that stresses efficient manufacturing and distribution and administrative austerity may very successfully carry out a price-oriented strategy but fail miserably with an account-oriented marketing program that calls for a customer-oriented culture with responsive operating and logistics people.

As we look beyond marketing, we must also consider the tangible effects of other corporate strengths and weaknesses. The large plant with facilities for long production runs, for example, is well suited to a marketing strategy based on a narrow product line and intense price orientation. By the same token, a company with a strong balance sheet and low cost of capital can much more easily accommodate a marketing program requiring generous credit terms than can its more financially limited competitor.

Market position can also help to determine the most sensible mix for a marketing program. The market-share leader, for example, gains when its astute marketing mix of national advertising, company-owned distribution, and heavy research and development encourages the industry to compete on a fixed-cost basis. Its position enables it to spread fixed costs over the larger unit volume and realize a lower cost per unit sold than smaller competitors.

Small unit-share competitors or niche marketers, on the other hand, need marketing programs that stress variable costs so that their cost per unit sold equals that of the largest competitors. Smaller companies, therefore, often emphasize intensive price promotions, a commission sales force, and independent distributors.

Program/Competitor Fit

An effective marketing program must not only fit the company's own core competencies, it must also take account of competitors' programs. Discussion of three topics can clarify questions about marketing-program design as they relate to the competition.

1. The concept of competitor/program fit.
2. The "Why can't we emulate them?" question.
3. The competitive-response matrix.

Competitive/program fit can be defined as the characteristics of a marketing program that, while building on a company's strengths and shielding its weaknesses, protects it from competitors by capitalizing on *their* weaknesses, in the process creating a unique market personality and position. Accomplishing this set of tasks requires meticulous analysis and honest introspection. The most serious danger, other than that of neglecting the issue altogether, is underestimating both the strength of the competition and the weaknesses of one's own company.

Perhaps the height of disregard for the difference in situations is embodied in a question that is very frequently posed: "Why can't we emulate them?" The answer is twofold. First, the strengths of the leading competitor are almost certainly different from those of any other competitor. Second, in all likelihood, the leading competitor took command when the market was quite different. Most important, the market leader probably did not exist in its present form, nor was there another firm of equal stature and situation. Thus the leader expanded into a vacuum that no longer existed after it filled it. For these reasons, companies that blindly attempt to imitate the leader usually fail, often painfully.

The concept of the marketing mix can provide a powerful tool to view competitors as they compete with one another by emphasizing different elements and mixtures of those elements. A useful way to visualize alternative action/reaction patterns is the competitive-response matrix.[2] A simple matrix might include two companies and three subelements of the marketing mix, such as price, product quality, and advertising. The matrix would look like this:

		Company A		
		Price	*Quality*	*Advertising*
Company B	Price	$C_{p,p}$	$C_{q,p}$	$C_{a,p}$
	Quality	$C_{p,q}$	$C_{q,q}$	$C_{a,q}$
	Advertising	$C_{p,a}$	$C_{q,a}$	$C_{a,a}$

The coefficients (the Cs of the matrix) represent the probability of Company B responding to Company A's move. Thus the coefficient $C_{a,p}$ represents the probability of Company B responding with a price cut (top row of matrix) to Company A's increase in advertising (right-hand column of matrix). The diagonal ($C_{p,p}$, $C_{q,q}$, $C_{a,a}$) represents the likelihood of Company B responding to a move by Company A with the same marketing tool (e.g., meet a price cut with a price cut). The coefficients can be estimated by the study of past behavior and by management judgment.

The competitive response matrix is a flexible, analytical approach. For example, one can include many marketing tools and add more rows for delayed responses (e.g., will they cut price immediately or wait a month or a quarter?) and additional competitors.

---

[2]J. Lambin, *Advertising, Competition, and Market Conduct in Oligopoly over Time* (New York: American Elsevier, 1976).

The competitive response matrix can help develop a distinctive approach to the market by enabling a company to see how it can differentiate its program from the marketing program of competitors.

Such competitive analyses have proven useful to many companies and are particularly important for making major irreversible capital commitments. The essence of all these programs is role playing, in which executives and marketers take the parts of the major competitor or competitors. Some companies have even devised elaborate competitive games built around their industry, with one or several company executives representing each competitor. The response matrix can be usefully incorporated into programs of this kind.

Why bother to take the time to do competitor response matrices and role play the relations of key competitors? First, you will benefit from a reality-test of your plan's viability. Having a group of creative colleagues develop responses to your marketing mix as though their jobs depended on it is an excellent way to pinpoint blind spots in your analysis and generate responses that may surprise you. It is better to discover how an unanticipated competitor response might sabotage a marketing program before investing millions in attempting to implement it.

Second, by predicting likely competitor responses and their economic impact, your ability to predict the costs and benefits of your proposed marketing mix will increase. Each cell in a competitive response matrix can be tied to a forecast of unit sales, revenues, profits, and market share. This makes it possible to identify best case, worse case, and most likely economic performance outcomes for a marketing program. If the range of outcomes is unfavorable, the program can be modified or abandoned.

Third, asking regularly marketers and other company executives to anticipate competitive responses encourages all involved to learn more about the competition. The discipline of analyzing whether a competitor will respond to your proposed marketing mix with a price cut or a new product launch focuses attention on what that competitor has done in the past in response to various competitive challenges. As a company's executives come to know a competitor better, their ability to predict its response increases. Over time, a company may be able to shape the reactions of competitors through its own choice of tactics so that they respond in ways that do not negate its own marketing initiatives, and may even help them.

The Expanded Mix

Like most concepts, the marketing mix is an abstraction, and real marketing programs do not always fit perfectly the product, price, communication, and distribution paradigm. In fact, several parts of the mix—promotion, brand, and terms and conditions—fall at the interface of two elements.

Promotion, which is defined strictly as short-term price cuts to the trade and consumer incentives such as coupons, contests, and price allowances, actually shares characteristics with both price and communication.

Brand, which is often viewed as an aspect of product, is clearly also part of communications and can serve to help coordinate product policy and communication.

Terms and conditions relate to a myriad of contractual elements that, though closely related to price (payment terms, credit, leasing, delivery schedules, and the like), are so close to personal selling that they can be viewed as an interface between price and communications. Other elements, such as service support, logistical arrangements, and so forth, also relate to product policy. The important thing is to recognize their usefulness as marketing tools without worrying about categorizing them.

Conclusion

Implicit in this reading are several questions that, if answered through careful analysis, can help a company to focus on the most important aspects of the total marketing mix and their fit with the customers, company, and competitive situation.

1. Are the elements of the marketing mix consistent with one another?
2. Do the elements add up to a harmonious, integrated whole?
3. Is each element being used to its best leverage?
4. Does the total program, as well as each element, meet the needs of the carefully and explicitly defined target market segment?
5. Does the marketing mix build on the organization's culture and core competencies? Does it either avoid weaknesses or imply a clear program to correct them?
6. Does the marketing mix create a distinctive personality in the competitive marketplace and protect the company from the strongest competitors?

Exhibit 1

The sales response curve

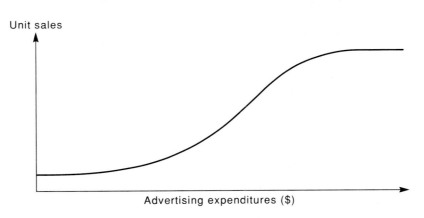

Hurricane Island Outward Bound School

Tell yourself, while 50 feet above a quarry on a one-foot-long, one-inch-wide cliff, being held up by a single rope, that you're not scared, but rather having fun. Capability becomes a state of mind, depending on how focused and committed you are. These are not challenges of you conquering the cliff, but of trust conquering fear. Do you trust the person holding your safety line? Or, rather, do you trust yourself?

—Student

I learned that I am a strong person, that even when I'm almost dead sure I can't do something, I can. Now I'm ready to hold out my hand—like my instructors held out their hands—and pull up someone who needs help. Ready to give my friend who is discouraged a hug. Ready to recognize the people I can rely on and those I can't.

—Student

To serve, to strive, and not to yield.

—Outward Bound motto

Philip Chin sketched out ideas in a notebook as the small commuter plane he had ridden from Boston approached Owls Head Airport. Behind Owls Head lay the town of Rockland, Maine (population 8,000), home to the headquarters of the Hurricane Island Outward Bound School (Hurricane), where Chin was director of marketing.

Hurricane was one of five U.S. schools in the Outward Bound movement. Outward Bound had pioneered a rigorous form of "experiential" education that placed groups of students in wilderness settings to develop self-confidence, teamwork, and respect for the environment.

In early October 1986, the summer crowds in Penobscot Bay were largely gone; the quiet waters below Chin's plane sported only a few fishing boats at anchor. Soon the fall weather would settle in, closing Owls Head two days out of

---

This case was prepared by Bruce H. Clark under the supervision of Professor Thomas V. Bonoma.

Copyright © 1987 by the President and Fellows of Harvard College.

Harvard Business School case 9-588-019.

three and thus requiring a two-hour drive to Portland for reliable air service. Now, operationally, the school was slowing down, while administratively the nonprofit organization's pace was quickening. The school was well into its 1987 planning process.

Chin had been at Hurricane for only eight months. He had been brought to Maine from New York City especially for his marketing experience. A Wharton MBA, he had worked in marketing management at General Foods, Doubleday Book Clubs, and PepsiCo. He had spent the last five years as a new-venture and marketing consultant. Except for the controller, Joe Adams, Chin was the only senior manager at Hurricane who had not risen from the course development and instruction side of the school.

As director of marketing, Chin was responsible for the organization's 1987 marketing plan. The 1987 plan would be his first for Hurricane. Aside from choosing the most productive tactics on which to spend a very limited marketing budget, Chin had to be certain that any marketing initiative would accurately reflect the unique character and concerns of Hurricane Island Outward Bound.

Outward Bound History

The first Outward Bound school was established by Kurt Hahn in 1941. Originally the headmaster of a German boarding school, Hahn was jailed in 1934 for his outspoken criticism of Adolph Hitler. He escaped to Scotland and continued his work in education, developing a system of interrelated athletic and educational standards for teenage boys. This system became the foundation for the first Outward Bound course and school, in Wales. During and after World War II, the Outward Bound concept spread rapidly; in 1986, there were more than 30 chartered Outward Bound schools around the world.

The first U.S. Outward Bound school was chartered in 1962 in Colorado, followed immediately by the Voyageur school in Minnesota. Hurricane was founded in 1964. In 1965, these three schools collaborated to found a national coordinating body—Outward Bound, Inc., also known simply as "National." National was a nonprofit institution responsible for chartering new schools and supporting the Outward Bound movement in the United States. While the schools were independently organized and managed, they agreed to abide by certain joint policies established by National. National also conducted fund-raising, publicity, and advertising campaigns for Outward Bound as a whole. To support these activities, each member school paid franchise and marketing fees to National. Franchise fees went toward safety and curriculum work; marketing fees paid for National's marketing campaign, and were based on the level of activity National conducted for each school. Beyond these activities, the confederation of schools was quite loose.

Each school was governed by a board of trustees, similar in function to a board of directors. The schools' trustee chairs comprised National's Outward Bound Executive Committee (OBEX), which ruled on issues of national concern to Outward Bound.

Hurricane Island Outward Bound School

Most of the Outward Bound schools, while offering a variety of courses, specialized in one area. Hurricane Island was the sea school. Founder and school president Peter Willauer's work in education and sailing led him to envision an outdoor classroom on the ocean. While working at a private high school, he began to piece together the philosophy, funding, and board members for Hurricane. After enlisting volunteers to construct the Hurricane Island site in the summer of 1964, Willauer enrolled and graduated the school's first group of students in 1965.

The early years of the school were lean. In the mid-1980s, Vice President for Development Pen Williamson recalled "a little summer sailing school" struggling for existence in Boston. In 1971, the school moved to new headquarters in Rockland. Over the next decade, Hurricane expanded dramatically, both in facilities and in number of staff and students. It was not until the 1980s, however, that rapid growth seemingly began to outstrip the ability of the organization to manage it. (See Exhibit 1 for a financial summary of Hurricane's performance.)

Through 1985, Hurricane had never broken even on an operating basis. Instead, the organization relied on contributions to make up the difference between tuition revenues and expenses. In the early 1980s, the trustees became concerned as the organization accumulated a series of large operating deficits. Peter Willauer seemed particularly stretched in his dual role as chief executive officer and chief fund-raiser. Hank Taft, formerly president of National, noted that burnout from this dual role was common for school directors; Willauer was the only school founder in the country who was still running his school.

Like most of the Outward Bound schools, Hurricane had a very active group of trustees. Thirty-six men and women sat on a half-dozen committees, which met monthly to monitor and aid the school's management. Most trustees were successful businesspeople, and all had been on at least one Hurricane course.

In late summer 1985, management and the trustees agreed on a new organizational structure, giving Willauer some relief on the operating side of the organization. They created the office of the vice president to take over day-to-day operating responsibilities. Vice presidents Bob Weiler and George Armstrong shared these tasks, freeing Willauer to focus on strategic direction and fund-raising. (See Exhibit 2 for Hurricane's organization chart.)

In 1985, the operating deficit became smaller, and 1986 found the school in the midst of its busiest year ever. By year's end, some 3,700 students would spend over 70,000 student program days (SPD)[1] in over 50 courses at any of 13 sites in Maine, Florida, New York, New Hampshire, and Maryland. Controller Joe Adams predicted that in 1986, the school would break even for the first time, and accumulate record revenues of just over $5 million. Still, finances were a high management priority. The school required a sound financial base to continue its growth.

Course Offerings

The mission of Hurricane Island Outward Bound is providing safe, challenging, educational experiences in a wilderness setting, carefully structured to improve self-esteem, self-reliance, concern for others, and care for the environment.

—Mission Statement

The school's offerings were divided into two segments: (1) special programs, administered by vice president George Armstrong, and (2) public courses, directed by vice president Bob Weiler. Special programs were courses that the school ran by contract for specific groups, often through government agencies. Among the populations served in this manner were Vietnam veterans, emotionally and developmentally handicapped youth, juvenile delinquents, and substance abusers. In 1985, special programs accounted for 23 percent of Hurricane's students, 32 percent of student program days, and 33 percent of tuition revenues.

All other students enrolled in public courses. The marketing department worked almost exclusively with public courses (special programs were more the result of contract negotiations). Public courses were divided into four segments by location and activity: Maine Sea, Florida Sea, Winter Land, and Summer Land. (See Exhibit 3 for descriptions of the segments and Exhibit 4 for recent attendance trends. Exhibit 5 gives the most recent projections for 1986 financial performance from the marketing department.)

Course length ranged from 3 to 101 days. All courses were carefully constructed to provide challenges while ensuring safety. Both the course directors and an active Trustee Safety Committee rigorously monitored course ac-

---

[1]One student program day: one student in a course for one day.

tivities and instructors. In addition, the school required U.S. Coast Guard certification for all sailing instructors, and land instructors were certified by the state of Maine as "Maine Guides." As a result, the school had never had a fatality despite the often strenuous nature of course activities.

In each course, participants were organized into "watches" of up to 12 students and one or two instructors. The watch was the basic unit of instruction; watch members performed most of their activities as a group. In the early part of a course, instructors concentrated on teaching the skills necessary for course activities; they assumed no prior experience. Once student skills were adequate, the instructors began allowing the group to perform activities with less direct supervision, intervening only in the event of trouble. The climax of most courses was Solo, when the watch broke up and individuals spent anywhere from several hours to three days alone in the wilderness, except for daily visits from an instructor.

Although learning wilderness survival skills was an important part of each course, more important was learning to work with a group under often trying circumstances and gaining self-confidence and the ability to trust fellow watch members. For this reason, the school had lately begun running short courses for groups of managers who desired this kind of experience. The courses, called the Professional Development Program (PDP), were very successful — 158 executives attended in 1985 — leading to expanded activities in 1986. Hurricane's marketing department was responsible for PDP in addition to regular public courses.

Marketing at Hurricane

For a long time, marketing consisted of opening our doors at the beginning of the summer and closing them at the end. More people came every year. Then in 1979 that didn't work anymore; our enrollment dropped. And 1980 was the same.

—Bob Weiler, Vice President

Marketing did not exist as a formal function at Hurricane before 1980. The school's major promotion tool then was group presentations: instructors and managers went out to schools and other institutions to talk about the Outward Bound experience. In most cases, Hurricane arranged presentations reactively. A request for a presentation would come in, and whoever wanted to go and give the talk would do so.

One result of the late 1970s' enrollment dip was the upgrading of the marketing function. In 1981, Hurricane hired Ted Rodman as the school's first marketing director. The Trustee Marketing Committee advocated and won a marketing budget equal to 10 percent of projected public course revenues. (The committee felt this percentage was an average figure for the business world.) The budget included salaries for the marketing and public relations departments, the National marketing fee, and funds for marketing and public relations (PR) campaigns.

Rodman had previously operated his own direct-mail and graphic design firm, and he transferred the skills he had developed there to Hurricane. He championed what he called "volume marketing," which consisted of major direct-mail campaigns whose yields could be accurately predicted. He concentrated on new advertising creative work, market segmentation, and positioning.

The primary direct-mail piece for marketing was the school course catalog. Produced once every two years, it was a glossy, 24-page, full-color magazine describing the school and the various programs it offered. Prospective students could get more information by writing the school or calling its toll-free number. In either case, they received an application and course schedule, which provided additional details about the courses and their exact dates. Students then applied for specific courses on specific dates, listed alternate preferences, and enclosed a nonrefundable $25 application fee. Upon receipt of the application, the admissions department sent the student an enrollment package that included comprehensive information on clothing, travel, and any other requirements for each course. The package also included a four-page medical form. All students were required to have a physical exam before being accepted in a course.

The admissions department encouraged students to return the enrollment forms as quickly as possible. Along with the completed forms, students sent a nonrefundable $100 enrollment fee. This fee reserved a spot for the student in a specific course. Tuition was due in full 60 days before the beginning of the course, or with the enrollment fee if the student was applying later. If a course was oversubscribed, the admissions department placed students on a waiting list. If a student was not admitted to the course by two weeks before the course's beginning, he or she was given the option of getting a tuition refund or having the money credited to a future course. Noting the length of the admission process, Chin remarked, "Enrollment is not an impulse buy."

Supplementing the Hurricane catalog was the National course catalog, which described all five schools' offerings, organized by activity. Inquiries to National were routed to the appropriate school.

In 1984 and 1985, Ted Rodman, controller Joe Adams, and the Marketing Committee began a re-evaluation of the school's pricing. As Adams put it, "We know we can always sell a course if the price is low enough. Can we sell it at a price where we cover our costs?" Public course tuition in 1986 ranged from $400 to $3,800 per student, depending on the length and nature of the course. Approximately 20 percent of students received substantial support from Hurricane's financial aid program as part of the school's commitment to serving the underprivileged. Marketing allocated financial aid to help support appropriate levels of female and minority participation in Outward Bound.

Marketing under Ted Rodman received mixed reviews from other Outward Bound managers. Public course enrollment did recover strongly in the 1980s, and the curriculum shifted to a more profitable mix of courses. Others also appreciated Rodman's feel for visuals; his catalogs featured stunning photography. They further credited him with developing an accurate forecasting system for overall public course enrollment.

Still, some staff members were uneasy with the idea of "marketing" the school. Most people who worked for Outward Bound did so because they were dedicated to the concepts behind and experiences offered in the courses. Those who ran the courses feared that marketing would "tell them what to do," or distort the concepts. When formal marketing first came to Hurricane, director of staffing Tino O'Brien recalled, "We spent a good deal of time educating our marketers in the reality of what Outward Bound was."

In September 1985, Rodman left to become marketing director for a local ski area. Vice president George Armstrong took over his duties until Philip Chin arrived in February of 1986.

1986 Marketing Efforts
The 1986 marketing plan was based on four strategic initiatives: (1) segmenting markets, (2) developing new pricing, (3) changing the course mix, and (4) assigning financial aid dollars to low-demand areas.

Hurricane made a concerted effort to segment the markets it served and assign priorities to the segments. Analysis of historic enrollment patterns revealed that some parts of the population dominated the school's student body. Given management beliefs that Hurricane's market penetration was low in all areas, the school decided to target those groups with which it had had the most success in the past.

Demographically, the organization identified 14- to 19-year-olds as its primary target, with 20- to 35-year-olds next. Geographically, the school gave first priority to the northeastern United States, which it defined as the six New England states and New York. Second priority went to the mid-Atlantic states (New Jersey, Pennsylvania, Delaware, and Maryland), plus Florida. In addition to these segments, the marketing department identified six buying groups within the demographic and geographic markets whom it felt the school could successfully address: (1) high school and college students, (2) "juniors" (ages 14 and 15), (3) municipal and agency contacts (for special programs), (4) young professionals, (5) corporations, and (6) Hurricane course alumni.

The school also developed a differential pricing scheme, both to maximize revenue and to smooth demand. Hurricane raised prices on introductory and adult courses, but tried to keep prices competitive on "mature" courses like Maine Sea. The school lowered prices on certain off-peak courses (September through May) to encourage enrollment at those times, although tuition differences between identical courses rarely exceeded 15 percent. (See Exhibit 6 for an example of a differential pricing schedule.)

Hurricane continued to examine the profitability and popularity of its courses, shifting the mix to build more revenue and better utilize existing facilities. In many cases this involved shortening less profitable courses or reducing the number of times they were offered. This increased capacity for other, more profitable courses.

Finally, the school used its scholarship program to support Maine Sea and to build off-season demand. Hurricane targeted scholarship-subsidized groups for such efforts, as this was more manageable than attempting to coordinate individual-aid programs.

Tactically, these strategic moves were translated into a number of marketing initiatives over the course of the year, including experimenting with two new sales tools. The first was a direct sales recruiter, who gave presentations to educational institutions, civic groups, trade associations, and business groups. The school especially hoped to increase high school student enrollments, and supported the recruiter, a former course director for Hurricane, with a direct-mail campaign to principals of public and private high schools.

The marketing department's second innovation was a telemarketing campaign aimed toward prospective students who had applied but not yet enrolled. Members of the admissions department staff called these students to discuss the Outward Bound experience as part of a larger effort to improve the school's response to inquiries about courses.

Following the 1985 PDP experience, Hurricane expanded its effort to reach corporations. Chin and Bob Weiler made most of the sales calls, as both had had experience working in major corporations. By summer's end, Hurricane had completed contracts with the Gillette Company, Citicorp, Corning Glass, MCI, Xerox, and General Electric, among others.

The school also continued its advertising and direct-mail effort in 1986, mailing over 35,000 pieces in four major campaigns and a series of smaller efforts, which included the high school mailing mentioned earlier.

1987 Considerations
Nobody's in this to make money. Everybody's involved in a tremendous educational process. Beyond that, you want to run it well.

—Hank Taft, former president, National; former Marketing Committee chair, Hurricane

The overall goals for the school were continued growth and financial stability. With those guidelines in mind and a very limited budget, Chin had to develop and support marketing tactics that would help the school realize two strategic objectives: (1) maintain school leadership within the Outward Bound system and (2) build off-season business.

Maintaining school leadership.   Defining Outward Bound's competition was extraordinarily difficult because of the diverse markets the school served. For juniors, the competition could be summer camp. Vacations, summer jobs, and other wilderness experience organizations beckoned college students. Corporate training was a fragmented, high-growth industry that was becoming more competitive.

The one constant in all of these markets was the presence of the other Outward Bound schools in the United States. Although National's policies restrained cutthroat competition on territory and advertising, there was a usually friendly rivalry among the five schools. Hurricane was the largest of the five in terms of SPDs, while Colorado enrolled the most students. Between them, the two schools controlled approximately 70 percent of the system's business. Leadership in the system was a source of pride to staff members, and the school strove to maintain it.

Building off-season business.   In talking with managers, it was apparent that marketing's most important objective was to build off-season business. Each year, Hurricane served well over half of its students in June, July, and August. Marketing Committee chair Bill End noted, "Selling the summer is not the trick for marketing. You could probably do nothing and sell out this period." Building business in the "shoulders" around the peak season, however, seemed to be where marketing could truly add value.

The dramatic seasonality of Hurricane's student population affected every aspect of the school's operations. The biggest problem was staffing the courses. Tino O'Brien, in an office wallpapered with huge charts depicting staffing requirements for every course at the school, spoke with feeling: "It's a totally untenable high-risk situation with staffing. We need fully trained, fully committed staff for two months." The school's inability to offer year-round positions to instructors hamstrung recruiting efforts. "It affects both quality and safety," added O'Brien. George Armstrong agreed. He noted that over half the school's expenses were labor-related, and that simply hiring people for the summer and then laying them off in the fall was not viable because the immediate labor supply was tight.

Results in this area had been unsatisfactory. Off-season pricing and skewing scholarship funds to off-peak courses had proven unable to offset the fact that most juniors, high school students, and college students were simply unable to attend courses during the academic year. And Hurricane's Florida base was too small to provide winter counterweight to courses based in the Northeast.

Marketing Options.   The 1987 marketing expense allocation was $308,000. Of this, $125,000 was dedicated to payroll for current staff; $40,000 covered the Outward Bound National marketing fee; $39,000 was for other marketing programs, including advertising and the school's direct-mail campaign; $15,000 was for public relations, trade shows, and other sales promotions; and $35,000 was for two new staff positions, an assistant marketing manager and a new public relations/production coordinator. This left $54,000 for discretionary 1987 marketing programs. Chin already had a number of proposals on which he could spend the money.

1. Expand "Alumni in Marketing" network.   Chin thought the "Alumni in Marketing" network (AIM) might prove the most cost-effective and least controversial of any of the proposals he was considering. More than 25,000 people had taken Hurricane courses in the last 20 years, and the school had a solid alumni mailing list that it used for fund-raising and public relations activities. Managers throughout Hurricane were enthusiastic about the network in principle, but were uncertain about how to use the alumni resource.

Chin identified two ways alumni could help marketing. The first was to identify interested groups and individuals to whom the school could direct its efforts. Alumni often had access to schools, professional associations, and other institutions through which they assembled audiences for group presentations. The second way alumni could help was to take part in the presentations by doing publicity, helping with logistics, and providing testimonials.

Experiments with alumni volunteers in 1986 had been very successful. Charlie Reade, the direct sales recruiter, had coordinated alumni efforts in the course of making his presentations. Two direct-mail campaigns for leads had been successful enough to warrant repeating them in 1987. But Chin was uncertain how enthusiastically he should push this network, as he had no clear idea of how many alumni would want to volunteer. If too few were interested, the effort in reaching them might be wasted. If too many were interested, administering the network would rapidly become complex. The latter situation seemed more likely than the former. If AIM took off, Chin might have to hire someone to manage it, which he calculated would cost at least $20,000 per year. Even with a manager dedicated to the network, coordination of effort among marketing, sales, and hundreds of alumni would be a substantial task. If volunteers were overutilized, they might tire or reduce donations on the grounds that they were already giving their time. If they were underutilized, they might lose enthusiasm for the network or even the school. Chin felt that careful management of both operations and volunteers' expectations would be critical.

If successful, the AIM network could be a great asset to all phases of marketing. In the future, selected alumni might be able to make their own presentations under Hurricane supervision. Some managers estimated that over half of all public course inquiries came from word of mouth; getting alumni talking about and working for Hurricane in a new way could boost these referral enrollments. And well-managed participation would be bound to generate renewed enthusiasm for the school, perhaps adding to the donor base and generating repeat business.

Unfortunately, Chin foresaw problems in tracing revenues generated by AIM. Like public relations, the benefits generated through AIM would mostly be intangible: better organization for presentations, more word-of-mouth advertising, greater enthusiasm.

Given the response to 1986 tests, Chin felt that expanding a network of volunteers would require hiring a manager over the course of the year. He did not want to cut into Charlie Reade's valuable sales time with extensive administrative duties. Assuming they hired someone in spring 1987, the cost would be about $15,000 for the 1987 budget.

2. Build corporate Professional Development Program (PDP).

"PDP raises emotions at the school," Chin commented. "It raises concern with the program [course development] people. It raises joy with Joe Adams."

In the early PDP work Hurricane had done, the school had presented itself as an alternative to traditional in-house training. The goal was to put managers together under adverse conditions and watch them respond. The PDP course focused on leadership, team building, stress management, communication, and goal setting. Usually, the Outward Bound experience was mixed with a more traditional training presentation. For example, General Electric's group came to Rockland for a seminar and a three-day course before reporting to GE's New York training center for four weeks of in-house work.

The 1986 experience with PDP had been very positive. Although there was no formal feedback mechanism to collect information from the companies involved, informal follow-up elicited numerous positive comments. Responses from human resource professionals at the companies suggested that managerial participants showed a greater sense of confidence, were better at meeting deadlines, and had stronger presentation and communication skills than they had had in the past.

In addition to benefiting the participants, the program could be extraordinarily profitable for the school. Chin felt that Hurricane could charge corporate clients more, perhaps as much as $200 per SPD, and that $75 per SPD was an appropriate overall goal for public courses. (Adams estimated that the direct cost to Hurricane of one SPD was $45. The remaining $30 in the goal covered fixed overhead.) Also, corporations were more likely to fill off-season courses because executives often took vacations in the summer.

Finally, Chin felt there was moral justification for expanding PDP. "Businesspeople need to learn compassion. We hide behind titles and systems rather than confronting emotional and moral issues." Chin noted feedback that suggested the experience of seeing peers surpass their limits was transferred to the workplace. Managers became more open and able to cope with emotions. Chin felt that such managers would be stronger assets not only to their companies, but also to their communities.

Other Hurricane managers had mixed feelings about the program. Vice president George Armstrong listed three criteria he considered when looking at new course proposals:

> First, does it fit what the organization is all about? Second, does it make money? Third, does it fit the schedule? If we can develop a three-day managers' course that meets those goals, I say let's do as many as we can.

Some felt that PDP was precisely *not* what the organization was all about. Former Marketing Committee chair Hank Taft remarked, "I think we owe it to the underprivileged to serve them, even though managers can benefit."

Tino O'Brien noted that staffing such courses was sometimes difficult. "We have a lot of young, idealistic instructors, and it's hard to get them excited about serving rich people." Still, he continued, "the objection to them is mostly theoretical. Once the instructors get out with them on a course, they usually enjoy it." Personally, Tino said, he felt the school should run some PDP courses as long as PDP did not drive the organization. He added dryly, "Executives are people, too."

In general, Chin felt, the school needed to strike a balance on PDP. The school could not go very heavily into corporate programs without endangering its donor base. Most managers believed that donors might contribute less to Hurricane if the school seemed to be moving away from its mission to serve youth and the underprivileged.[2] Also, PDP courses were not as operationally flexible as the average Hurricane offering. Once established, schedules could not be changed; groups of managers could not be shifted to different dates or courses. Chin recalled the time when a late-summer demand surge had hit the school, and Hurricane had to scramble to serve all of its students, particularly the corporate clients. He remembered painfully, "There were situations this summer where we mobilized an extra effort to serve the people who paid."

Chin thought the best way to expand PDP was to hire a recruiter specifically for the program. "In the past, we have

---

[2]In 1985, donors provided $732,000 in contributions for operations and $956,000 in contributions for property, plant, equipment, and other capital items.

been reactive. We want to put resources to our opportunities." Chin envisioned a coordinated marketing approach, beginning with a PDP-specific brochure. The brochure would be mailed to the vice presidents of human resources at Fortune 500 companies and other identified prospects in the Northeast, and followed up first by phone and then in person by the PDP recruiter.

The mailing alone would cost about $1,000; adding a PDP recruiter would cost as much as $30,000 once travel and other expenses were factored in. In return, Chin hoped to realize about $200,000 in gross revenue. In any case, it did not seem feasible for him and Bob Weiler to continue making these sales calls as the complexity of other parts of their jobs grew, so he would have to develop a staffing solution, anyway.

3. Expand direct sales recruitment.

In 1986, Hurricane's sales force consisted of two ex-instructors: Charlie Reade, who recruited for public courses, and Holly Miller, who was in charge of special programs. Previously, instructors and managers had gone out on an ad hoc basis, but the school felt that it would benefit from a more systematic approach to direct recruitment. Reade and Miller had begun full-time organized recruiting in 1986, with much success. The school projected that recruiting would generate 17 percent of 1986 applications and 20 percent of 1986 enrollments. Demand for group presentations was rising. The school estimated that it would make over 50 presentations in the first three months of 1987.

Many managers considered face-to-face presentations the most effective way for the school to approach prospective students. Presentations had changed with the advent of full-time recruiters. Chin explained that the biggest change management had made was to encourage recruiters to ask for applications or a contract on the spot, whereas in the past they had merely given the informational presentation and asked people to call if they were interested. Chin felt "asking for the order" had made a great difference in the success of the recruiters, but it had been controversial. Recruiters were unaccustomed to that style. Chin remarked, "It began to smack of commercialism to some people. That worried them."

Rather than add more full-time recruiters, Chin was considering expanding the use of "sub-recruiters." Sub-recruiters would address specific segments, such as high school students. They would work under short-term contracts with specific performance objectives like the number of presentations made or the number of organizations contacted. Hurricane managers hoped that they might be able to provide off-season work to course instructors by making them sub-recruiters; another leadership school put all its instructors "on the road" every fall. Hurricane's sub-recruiters would work under the supervision of the full-time recruiters. Chin estimated that adding two sub-recruiters would cost $9,000 in 1987.

4. Build telemarketing capabilities.

In 1986, the admissions department experimented with calling prospective students after they had applied but before they had enrolled. Students seemed to enjoy speaking with someone from the school, especially given the high levels of anxiety some had about course activities. Chin and others believed that students who were contacted would be more likely to enroll, although tracking on the initial experiment had been inadequate to determine this conclusively.

Unfortunately, the admissions department could not provide full-time telemarketers. Chin believed that hiring good telemarketers for Hurricane would be a tough job. Candidates needed to have both good selling skills and sufficient program knowledge to answer student's questions.

One alternative to full-time telemarketing would be an extended test. Chin envisioned calling 500 to 1,000 prospective students who had applied but not yet enrolled. By setting up a careful response-tracking system, the school could determine whether a further investment was warranted. It was difficult to determine the cost of all this. Even using part-time people to start, payroll and phone costs would escalate rapidly. Chin had tentatively allocated $6,000 for an extended test in 1987.

Alternatives: Pricing and the Course Mix

Given the amount of money Chin had available, he could not fund all four of the programs outlined above. One way of getting around this problem was to find ways to make the school's courses more profitable, thus providing more funds for marketing programs.

In addition to the differential pricing schedules developed in 1985 and 1986, the school's prices in general had increased at a pace of about 15 percent per year for the last two years. Raising prices again had been discussed in 1987 planning meetings. Joe Adams was in favor of another price increase; the school average was still below his goal of $75 per SPD. Others were not so sure. Hurricane had reached what Chin called "the $2,000 barrier" on a number of popular courses. He was uneasy about raising prices any higher for these courses. It was unclear how much selective or general price increases would affect demand, or what they might do to marketing's overall contribution to profit.

Another way to raise course profitability would be to alter the course mix or the range of sites at which the courses were offered. The effect would be easier to trace, though implementation would be more difficult. Course mix was the area in which course managers and the marketing department were most likely to clash. While it was relatively easy to expand activities in a profitable course, it was much more difficult to cut back on an unprofitable one. Because of the school's nonprofit mission, many managers believed firmly that profitability was not a valid criterion for judging the worth of a course. Courses were more likely to be eliminated for safety reasons or for lack of students. In addition, many courses had been championed by individuals who were dedicated to the segments their courses served. The Vietnam veterans' course in the special programs area, for example, had been created, funded, and marketed primarily through the efforts of an ex–Green Beret colonel. Further, certain courses were strongly identified with the organization as a whole. The Maine Sea courses, for example, were part of the school's history and original mission. Despite the significant overhead expense of maintaining the 18 large boats used in them, there was no question that Maine Sea would continue to be integral to Hurricane's operations.

Evaluating Marketing Tactics

Three numbers appeared at the head of virtually every planning document for marketing at the school: the number of students served, the number of SPDs, and total revenue. Different interested parties, however, placed different emphases on these numbers. On one side, the "business-oriented" managers and many of the trustees were most concerned with the revenues that public courses generated. The financial crisis of the early 1980s had convinced them, above all, that the school had to break even on its operating revenues and expenses. Two of their long-term goals were to reduce the school's debt burden and to purchase certain properties critical to its operations; therefore, a surplus of revenues over expenses would be even better.

On the other side, many of the "course-oriented" managers and donors were more concerned with serving as many deserving students as possible. They tended to focus on number of students and SPDs. For them, marketing's job was to "fill the courses." Beyond students and SPDs, these people watched such measures as the proportion of students receiving financial aid, and the demographic characteristics of students, including age, sex, and race. While they knew that obtaining funds was important, they were worried that marketing and finance concerns might drive the organization away from its from its original mission of serving youth and the disadvantaged. Growth seemed far more worthwhile than debt reduction.

Each of the four marketing initiatives proposed had strengths and weaknesses relative to the tension between financial concerns and service concerns. Direct sales and telemarketing, for example, were targeted approaches that allowed the school to solicit populations with desirable demographic traits, such as minority groups. They could also be used to concentrate on filling specific courses. AIM was less controllable and measurable—who the tactic reached depended on which alumni volunteered and what their contacts were. PDP was focused and profitable, but some felt it was aimed at the wrong target market.

Beyond all this, Chin was concerned about how accurately the school would be able to link results to *any* initiative. Despite the admissions department's heroic effort to organize student data, Hurricane often had no idea why a given student enrolled. (See Exhibit 7 for a rough forecast of 1986 results by marketing tactic.) Chin was dedicated to developing better marketing information systems at the school (which was one reason he wanted an assistant marketing manager aboard), but this would require changing procedures in marketing and admissions, and he was not sure what the financial or organizational costs of these changes would be.

Finally, there were the three marketing objectives staring at him from the front page of his notebook. With all the other plan goals, these were the real ones: delivering 2,700 students, 47,800 SPDs, and—perhaps most important—$3.4 million in revenues while staying within his budget and balancing the interests of management, donors, trustees, instruction staff, and, ultimately, the students.

On the one hand, Chin felt the school was slowly becoming more "businesslike" due to the demands of growth. On the other hand, as Hank Taft had remarked before he retired in September, "Nobody's in this to make money." Changing the way Outward Bound concepts were marketed could change other things about the organization as well. Chin wondered if there were other ways to reach his goals that he had missed. As his plane landed at Owls Head, he snapped his notebook shut, but the questions remained.

EXHIBIT 1   **Statement of Activity, 1982–1985 ($000)**

	1982	*1983*	*1984*	*1985*
Support and revenue				
Tuition:				
Public courses	$1,563	$2,013	$2,445	$2,672
Special programs	485	744	944	1,284
Subtotal	2,048	2,757	3,389	3,956
Outside support:				
Operating contributions	418	883	789	732
Support from National	0	68	85	66
Other	169	191	256	200
Subtotal	587	1,142	1,130	998
Total support and revenue	2,635	3,899	4,519	4,954
Expenses				
Cost of sales:				
Public courses	1,442	1,851	2,264	2,395
Special programs	425	644	793	1,054
Depreciation	95	138	73	84
Subtotal	1,962	2,633	3,130	3,533
Operating expenses:				
Administration	421	543	639	697
Marketing	346	319	293	319
Development	131	135	188	173
Student aid	333	467	486	323
Depreciation	49	51	63	71
Other	104	81	37	0
Subtotal	1,384	1,596	1,706	1,583
Total expenses	3,346	4,229	4,836	5,116
Operating surplus (deficit)	(711)	(330)	(317)	(162)
Net capital additions[a]	1,028	177	60	962
Excess (deficiency) to funds	317	(153)	(257)	800
Fund balances end of year	2,148	1,995	1,738	2,538
Balance sheet items				
Total assets	3,522	3,650	3,635	3,981
Total liabilities	1,374	1,655	1,897	1,443

[a]Includes capital contributions, gain (loss) on sale of property and equipment, and net investment activity.
SOURCE: Hurricane Island Outward Bound School.

EXHIBIT 2

Organization chart

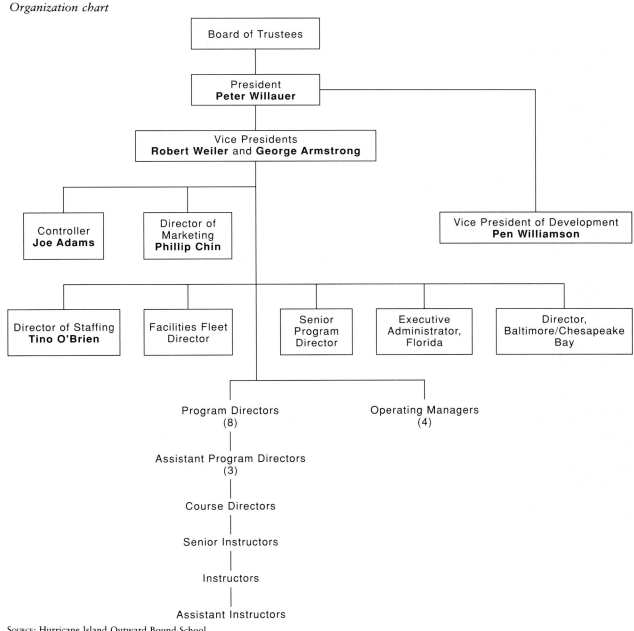

SOURCE: Hurricane Island Outward Bound School.

Exhibit 3

Course descriptions

I. Public Courses

Maine Sea Program

   Sailing courses run from May through September. A 30-foot open pulling boat becomes the base for lessons in seamanship, navigation, sailing, rowing, ecology, and survival on land and sea. Includes segments on rock climbing and the Hurricane Island ropes course. Based in Penobscot Bay, Maine.

Florida Sea Program

   Sailing courses run from November through April. Content similar to Maine Sea, but conducted in the tropical wilderness of the Florida Keys. Includes extensive swimming and snorkeling to explore the ecology of the Keys. Based in the Great Heron Wildlife Preserve, Florida.

Summer Land Program

   Canoeing, backpacking, white water rafting, bicycling, and "multi-element" courses run from May through September. Most courses include rock climbing, wilderness camping, and expedition-planning skills. Based in Maine and New York.

Winter Land Program

   Winter mountaineering courses run from December through March. Activities include cross-country skiing, snowshoeing, backpacking, and winter camping. Based in Maine and New Hampshire.

II. Special Programs and Populations

   Ongoing programs have been developed for a wide range of audiences, including Vietnam veterans, substance abusers, troubled youth, schools, and corporations. These customized programs use many of the facilities and activities of the public courses.

Source: Hurricane Island Outward Bound School.

Exhibit 4   Attendance by Course Area, 1981–1985

	1981		1982		1983		1984		1985	
	Students	*SPDs[a]*	*Students*	*SPDs*	*Students*	*SPDs*	*Students*	*SPDs*	*Students*	*SPDs*
Public Courses										
Maine Sea program	1,016	18,432	938	16,849	1,091	19,439	1,208	21,409	1,120	18,088
Florida Sea program	183	2,095	249	3,097	230	3,287	275	4,315	289	4,658
Winter Land program	120	1,017	244	2,711	231	1,970	184	1,612	190	1,611
Summer Land program	157	2,771	289	4,304	372	6,141	441	5,599	645	8,700
Other	92	1,343	236	5,724	319	7,824	366	8,056	363	8,169
Subtotal public courses	1,568	25,658	1,956	32,685	2,243	38,661	2,474	40,991	2,607	41,226
Special Programs	474	8,686	726	13,060	1,596	15,134	1,264	16,525	760	19,137
Total enrollment	2,042	34,344	2,682	45,745	3,839	53,795	3,738	57,516	3,367	60,363

[a]Student program days.

Source: Hurricane Island Outward Bound School.

EXHIBIT 5 **Projected 1986 Financial Performance by Course, Prepared September 1986**

Course	Student Capacity	SPD Capacity	Tuition	Students	SPD	Revenue
Maine Sea						
HI 26-day	100	2,600	$ 1,600	64	1,664	$ 102,400
HI 22-day	596	13,112	1,225/1,425	386	8,492	541,650
HI 11-day	240	2,640	900	152	1,672	136,800
HI 6-day	120	720	600	57	342	34,200
Sea Kayak 7-day	40	280	700	36	252	25,200
Sea Kayak 14-day	20	280	1,000	18	252	18,000
Contracts/Groups	90	990	809	85	935	68,765
Subtotal	1,206	20,622		798	13,609	$ 927,015
Florida Sea						
FL College 22-day	10	220	$ 1,200	8	176	$ 9,600
FL 22-day	10	220	1,200	8	176	9,600
FL 14-day	180	2,520	1,000	104	1,456	104,000
FL 8-day	200	1,600	800	72	576	57,600
Contracts/Groups	20	160	500	18	144	9,000
Subtotal	420	4,720		210	2,528	$ 189,800
Summer Land						
Maine Chall. 26-day	192	4,992	$ 1,600	128	3,328	$ 204,800
Long jrs. 28-day	144	4,032	1,700/1,800	126	3,528	223,400
Juniors 22-day	72	1,584	1,300	66	1,452	85,800
Rafting 6-day	105	630	600	90	540	54,000
Summerland 22-day	120	2,640	1,300	92	2,024	119,600
Summerland 9-day	160	1,440	800	105	945	84,000
Cycling 22-day	40	880	1,300	16	352	20,800
Cycling 9-day	100	900	800	46	414	36,800
Dynamy 22-day	48	1,056	700	42	924	29,400
Contracts/Groups	36	288	500	32	256	16,000
Subtotal	1,017	18,442		743	13,763	$ 874,600
Winter Land						
Winter College 22-day	12	264	$ 1,000	8	176	$ 8,000
Winter 22-day	12	264	1,000	6	132	6,000
Winter 9-day	60	540	800	24	216	19,200
Winter 6-day	100	600	600	34	204	20,400
Gould 8-day	84	672	400	72	576	28,800
Subtotal	268	2,340		144	1,304	$ 82,400
Managers						
Career Dev 4-day	96	384	$ 500	80	320	$ 40,000
Maine Sea 8-day	116	928	950	84	672	79,800
Land 6-day	20	120	750	16	96	12,000
Contracts/Groups	60	360	1,200	50	300	60,000
Subtotal	292	1,792		230	1,388	$ 191,800
Other						
Summer 64-day	24	1,536	$ 3,200	20	1,280	$ 64,000
Florida 78-day	24	1,872	3,800	16	1,248	60,800
Florida 80-day	24	1,920	3,800	17	1,360	64,600
Jrs. 15-day	180	2,700	900/950	162	2,430	150,400
Maine directive	154	4,312	1,800	127	3,556	228,600
Florida directive	110	3,080	1,800	82	2,296	147,600
Instructor training	36	3,612	3,800	21	2,107	79,800
Subtotal	552	19,032		445	14,277	$ 795,800
Public course total	3,755	66,948		2,570	46,869	$3,061,415

SOURCE: Hurricane Island Outward Bound School.

EXHIBIT 6   1986 Pricing, 22-Day Maine Sea Course

Starting Date	Ending Date	Tuition	Student Capacity	Actual Students
5/16/86	6/6/86	$1,225	72	12
5/26/86	6/16/86	1,225	72	12
6/12/86	7/3/86	1,425	72	48
6/14/86	7/5/86	1,425	48	46
7/9/86	7/30/86	1,425	48	46
7/11/86	8/1/86	1,425	72	70
8/5/86	8/26/86	1,425	68	64
8/8/86	8/29/86	1,425	72	70
9/5/86	9/26/86	1,225	72	18

SOURCE: Hurricane Island Outward Bound School.

EXHIBIT 7   Projected Results by Marketing Tactic, 1986

	National Marketing[a]	Direct Sales	Direct Mail	Other/ Unknown	Total
Applications[b]	1,100	600	340	1,500	3,540
Conversion rate	60%	85%	75%	75%	72%
Students enrolled	660	510	256	1,125	2,551
Revenues	$792,000	$612,000	$307,200	$1,350,000	$3,061,200
Direct cost	$ 39,000	$ 68,500	$ 26,250	NA	$ 295,000

[a]Inquiries about Hurricane courses generated by National (Outward Bound, Inc.) marketing.

[b]Approximately 1 of every 15 inquiries about all Outward Bound courses generated by National eventually converted to applications. Approximately 1 of every 8 inquiries Hurricane generated internally converted to applications. Hurricane received about 27% of all applications generated by National. NA means not available.

SOURCE: Hurricane Island Outward Bound School.

DOMINION MOTORS & CONTROLS, LTD.

Dominion Motors & Controls, Ltd. (DMC), had acquired over 50 percent of the available market for oil well pumping motors in the northern Canadian oil fields since they were discovered in 1973. Although the company was a large supplier of motors and control equipment in the Canadian market, and had an excellent reputation for product quality, DMC executives believed it had been especially successful in this market because of one salesperson hired in 1974. He was both aggressive and capable, and could "talk the oil people's language." He had gained experience in

This case was prepared by Professor E. Raymond Corey.
Copyright © 1989 by the President and Fellows of Harvard College.
Harvard Business College case 9-589-115(Rev. 6/28/91).

Texas in electrical equipment sales and oil field electrical application engineering. At that time, none of DMC's competitors had salespeople in the area with similar skills. The company, therefore, was able to establish an early foothold and develop a strong market position.

Early in 1985, however, DMC was threatened with the loss of this market because of tests performed by the Hamilton Oil Company. Hamilton was the largest oil company active in Canada; it owned and operated over 30 percent of the total producing wells. John Bridges, head of Hamilton's electrical engineering department, who was in charge of the motor testing program, had concluded that DMC's motor was third choice behind those offered by Spartan Motors, Ltd., and the Universal Motor Company of Canada, respectively. Thus, in March 1985, executives of DMC had to decide what action, if any, the company could take to maintain its share of the oil well pumping market.

Company Background

Dominion offered a line of motors ranging from small fractional horsepower (hp) units to large 2,000-horsepower motors. The company also produced motor control and panel-board units, which would automatically control and protect a motor. In 1984 DMC sales approximated $323 million and were distributed among the following product groups:

Product Group	Sales ($ millions)	Unit Sales
Control and panel boards	$ 72	NA
Fractional horsepower motors	126	500,000
1–200 hp motors	85	22,000
250–2,000 hp motors	40	700

About 80 percent of DMC sales were made directly by company salespeople to original equipment manufacturers (OEMs) and large industrial users, such as oil companies, paper mills, and mining concerns. Approximately 20 percent of sales were made to distributors for resale, primarily to small users (small drilling contractors and others) and small OEMs. DMC's discount schedule for various classes of purchasers appears below.

Purchaser	Discount (percent)	List Price Multiplier
OEM	45	0.55
Reseller	40	0.60
Large user	38	0.62
Small user	25	0.75

Oil Well Pumping Motor Market

Major oil fields were discovered in northern Canada late in 1973. By 1984, there were approximately 5,500 producing wells in these fields, of which 850 were started in operation in that year. Hundreds of oil companies were active in the area, but only about 25 owned 50 or more wells.

According to industry estimates, an average of 1,000 new wells would enter production each year for the next five years. Estimators were careful to point out, however, the difficulty of making such forecasts with any degree of accuracy. Actually, many people intimately acquainted with the young Canadian oil industry believed that this estimate might prove low. Because of rapid changes in world economic and political conditions and technology, forecasting

was most difficult. Sales to this market were seasonal; over 80 percent were made between April and September.

Dominion's competition consisted of other well-known Canadian motor manufacturers and a number of foreign competitors (particularly British, German, and Japanese firms).[1] All the Canadian manufacturers maintained closely competitive pricing structures. Foreign competitors, however, usually sold 10 to 20 percent below the Canadian's established prices.

Dominion salespeople attempted to sell a motor and control unit as a package. Frequently, however, oil field customers bought the motor of one manufacturer and the controls of another. The majority of DMC's competitors did not offer motor controls. The main sources of motor control competition were control manufacturers.

From 1973 to 1984, DMC sold about 15 percent of the control and panel-board units used in oil well applications. The average pump system installed to deliver oil from a proven well cost about $34,000. Approximately $5,000 of this was invested in electrification of the pumping installation (motor, controls, wiring, installation, and so forth). The motor itself accounted for approximately one third of this $5,000 investment and the control and panel-board units another 30 percent of this amount.

The Buying and Selling of Oil Well Motors

Large Canadian oil producers were typically organized so that production (removing petroleum from the ground) was separated from refining (making the petroleum into useable products, such as gasoline and lubricants) and marketing. The production organization in the larger companies typically included field operations people (who managed the rigs themselves), engineers, purchasers (who actually ordered the equipment), geologists (who assessed the likelihood of finding oil in different locations), and standard administrative functionaries, such as personnel and legal staff. Field operations were generally organized geographically with regional directors, district managers, rig supervisors, and also foremen for each shift and for the special functions, such as maintenance. Rig supervisors were in charge of operating the rig itself and were viewed as important people. They typically were experienced hands who had worked up from entry level positions. They played a major role in rig operations, and their opinions about machinery were respected by other oil company personnel. Engineering designed and specified equipment, such as the rotating drilling platforms, and included primarily mechanical and a few chemical engineers.

Normally, salespeople called on their customers to keep them abreast of changes in the line and to nurture the re-

---

[1] Many U.S. motor manufacturers operated Canadian subsidiaries, which were considered Canadian competition.

lationships they had developed over the years. The people they called on in the large companies varied; in some cases they were top executives; in others, engineers; and in still others, operations managers, rig superintendents, and a variety of related rig personnel. During these calls the salespeople often obtained leads on companies believed to be contemplating expansion or overhauls.

The smaller companies had simpler organizations. The very small ones often owned only a few rigs, sometimes only one. These operators did no refining, but sold their production to the large, integrated producers. Few small operators had separate engineering departments. They tended to comply more with industry standards in their buying and often followed the larger companies in purchasing policies and equipment choice.

Dominion's Advertising and Promotion Programs

Dominion had an advertising program that management considered of limited value in making sales but useful in helping the salespeople. Trade journals were used to reach the different buying influences.

Although management did not expect its advertising actually to produce sales, it was strongly opposed to a mere business card style of advertising in trade papers. It made every effort to present effective selling copy and layout. The advertisements often pictured actual installations with fairly long accompanying sales arguments.

Catalogs were important in DMC's promotional program. Each motor size was described in a general catalog distributed to purchasing and engineering personnel. This single-publication approach, in contrast to pamphlets describing each motor, was difficult to revise. But management believed that the catalog was lower cost and more efficient than individual pamphlets because the product line was quite small and the motor designs and specifications were seldom changed.

Factors Affecting Specifications of Oil Well Pumping Motors

Approximately 80 percent of the motors sold for oil well pumping applications since 1973 had been 10-hp NEMA[2] design C (high starting torque, low starting current), totally enclosed, fan-cooled units with moisture-resisting insula-

tion. The remaining 20 percent of sales were motors of the same type but with higher or lower horsepower ratings.

Such factors as drilling depth, oil viscosity, water content of pumped fluid, underground pressure, and the government-controlled production allowables in the northern Canadian fields had determined the type of motor best suited for this area.[3] One particularly important determinant had been the low winter temperatures, which required a motor with a high starting torque.[4] To be assured of sufficient starting torque, many oil companies were using 10-hp motors even though these were larger than was actually required to lift the oil to the surface. This practice was called "overmotoring."

During 1984, power companies serving the oil fields made two announcements that could affect the specifications of oil well pumping motors. First, their schedule of power rates was changed. The former flat rate, charged regardless of the horsepower of motors on a pumping installation, was replaced with a graduated schedule based on connected horsepower of an installation:

Horsepower of Installation		Monthly Base Charge per Horsepower
5	125. —	$25.00
7½	161.25	21.50
10	200. —	20.00

Second, power companies demanded that their customers stop overmotoring and improve the "power factors" of their installations.[5] They did not, however, indicate at the time what, if any, penalty overmotoring would incur.

---

[2]National Electrical Manufacturers Association was a nonprofit organization to which the great majority of electrical manufacturers in the United States and Canada belonged. It developed and promulgated standard specification for electrical equipment. Adherence to the standards was entirely voluntary; neither members nor nonmembers were precluded from manufacturing or selling products that did not conform to them.

[3]The characteristics of oil fields yet to be discovered could easily differ from those of existing fields, and, therefore, other types of motors might come to be required.

[4]Starting torque, expressed in pounds-feet, was the twisting or turning power of the motor, which enabled it to overcome initial load resistance.

[5]The power factor of an a.c. circuit was defined as the ratio of power-producing current to total current. In most a.c. circuits, both magnetizing current (which did no work) and power-producing current were conveyed. If no magnetizing current was present, the total current equaled the power-producing current and the power factor was unity or 100 percent. In motors working well below their rated capacity, much magnetizing current was present and the power factor was quite low. The lighter the load relative to the motor capacity, the lower the power factor.

The watt-hour meter used to determine a customer's power bill recorded only power-producing current, so when a utility system had to carry nonpower-producing current, its income and ability to carry payload, or power-producing current, were reduced. Consequently, more facilities were required to serve a low power-factor load than a high power-factor load of the same kilowatt (pay-load) demand.

Hamilton's Field Test Program

Following these announcements, John Bridges, Hamilton's chief electrical engineer, initiated field tests on oil well pumping motors. His objective was to define the specifications of a motor that could be used most economically. The tests, therefore, were to determine (1) the horsepower required to lift the fluid, and (2) the maximum starting torque required to start the pumping units at low winter temperatures.

min.

Although the tests were completed by early 1985, DMC executives only became aware of them in March through reports of a salesperson calling on Hamilton. Although the salesperson was unable to obtain a memorandum describing the test procedures and findings, DMC executives pieced together what they believed to be a fairly accurate picture of the conclusions.

According to their information, Bridges had determined the following: (1) fluid-lifting requirements dictated a 3- to 5-hp motor; (2) starting torques in excess of 70 pounds-feet would energize the pumping units at temperatures as low as −50°F; (3) this starting torque requirement would necessitate a 7½-hp motor; and (4) because the Spartan 7½-hp motor had the highest starting torque of the motors tested (see Exhibit 1) and the Universal 7½-hp motor had the second highest, these should be his company's first and second choices in the future. Dominion's 7½-hp motor would be the third choice. Management at DMC also learned that Bridges planned to report his findings formally to Hamilton's executives in May.

Dominion executives believed these tests had not produced data sufficient to define oil pumping requirement accurately. They did believe, however, that the findings had provided rather specific indications of pumping needs under a given set of operating conditions.

DMC personnel were extremely concerned, nevertheless, about the probable effect that Hamilton's endorsement of the Spartan and Universal motors would have on Dominion's market standing. Bridges was known to be very influential in establishing Hamilton's purchasing policy.[6] In addition, because Hamilton was the only firm operating in the Canadian oil fields that maintained an electrical engineering staff, Bridges's recommendations would probably carry great weight in the entire industry. Most DMC exec-

utives believed, therefore, that they could not hope to stay in the oil well pumping market unless they responded somehow to Bridges's challenge.

Possible Solutions to Dominion's Problem

Four courses of action were developed by Dominion executives:

1. Reduce the price of DMC's 10-hp motor to that of the 7½-hp motor.
2. Reengineer DMC's present 7½-hp motor to make its starting torque at least equal to that of the Spartan 7½-hp unit.
3. Undertake design of a definite-purpose motor for the oil well pumping market. This would ideally be a basic 5-hp motor with the starting torque of a 10-hp unit.
4. Attempt to persuade Bridges and Hamilton executives that the conclusions reached from their test results unduly emphasized obtaining the **maximum** starting torque available.

Alternative 1. Reducing the price of DMC's 10-hp motor to the level of its 7½-hp unit was advocated by several executives as a quick initial way to meet the problem. Such a move, they thought, could be taken either immediately or as late as May 1985. These executives pointed out that the oil well motor market was rapidly becoming active after its usual winter slump and that, if the company wanted to share in the 1985 sales, DMC must gain a competitive position immediately. They recognized that this would not be a long-run solution. It did appear, however, that a 10-hp motor could continue to be acceptable for the short run, because the savings from using a 7½-hp instead of a 10-hp motor were not large and because no oil company had yet been penalized for maintaining low power factors. (Exhibit 2 shows the cost and prices of the small motors in DMC's line.)

Some executives argued that there was no need to reduce the price of the company's 10-hp motor until Bridges delivered his formal report. They doubted that many oil companies would hear of the results until the formal report, so there might not be much effect on motor purchases for another two or three months. Dominion could continue selling its 10-hp motor at the usual price until it encountered objections and the market became aware of Hamilton's endorsement of the Spartan motor.

Executives who favored this alternative believed it would immediately combat Hamilton's endorsement of the Spartan motor. It would be a useful temporary competitive measure until they could obtain and completely study Bridges's test results. Then DMC could reach a more satisfactory and reasoned strategy decision. They believed that adequate ap-

---

[6]All oil well pumping motors used by Hamilton Oil Company were procured through its production department, and most of the motors this department purchased were for oil well pumping. Other departments independently purchased large numbers of motors either directly from manufacturers or through contractors. Motors used in refineries, for example, were typically acquired as original equipment through the contractors who built the refineries. Motors for an average oil refinery in Canada cost between $250,000 and $1,000,000.

praisal of Bridges's tests, results, and conclusions might require as much as one year, especially if company executives wanted to have DMC's own engineers make comparative tests.

Alternative 2.   Several company executives believed that DMC's best opportunity to stay in the oil well market lay in reengineering its existing 7½-hp motor to give it a starting torque equal to or greater than that of the Spartan 7½-hp motor.[7] Initial investigations revealed two ways of increasing starting torque.

First, at least 105 pounds-feet or starting torque could be obtained by modifying the existing 7½-hp internal motor components. This motor would have the same frame size (i.e., mounting dimensions) as the existing 7½-hp motor, but its temperature rise would be greater than NEMA standards. This departure would not, according to DMC personnel, significantly alter the safety or operating characteristics of the motor, because special high temperature insulation would be used. These executives were uncertain, however, how oil field users might react to an operating temperature above NEMA standards. A manufacturing cost of $790 would be incurred to produce this motor.

A second way to obtain the same starting torque was to use a larger motor frame. This motor would continue to meet or exceed all NEMA's minimum standard performance specifications, but not NEMA mounting dimensions for its rating. Executives at DMC believed, however, that standard motor mounting dimensions were not important in oil well pumping applications. They also believed that such a motor would meet less customer resistance than one that exceeded NEMA's maximum temperature rise. The manufacturing cost of this motor would be $867.

Neither of these methods would involve additional investment in plant or equipment. It would take approximately three months to begin shipment of the modified motor.

Advocates of altering the company's existing 7½-hp motor to increase starting torque believed this was the answer to the product problem. They pointed out that "souping-up" would give DMC a motor with the highest starting torque of any 7½-hp motor then available.

Not all DMC executives agreed that this alternative would be desirable, however. They pointed out that such a move would invite a torque war, which could lead to unbalanced motor designs.[8] This could confuse motor users and be detrimental to the motor industry as a whole. It had long been DMC's policy to support industry standards by not publicizing or claiming operating characteristics in ex-

cess of NEMA standards. The company had excellent testing facilities, which enabled engineers to design motors close to NEMA standards and, thus, reduce costs. One executive stated, "There is no point in building more margin into our motors than required by the NEMA standards. . . . Our better testing facilities allow us to design closer to NEMA standards than our competitors. . . . There is no point in building a large margin into our motors."

Alternative 3.   A number of DMC's executives supported a move to design a definite-purpose motor for the oil well pumping market. They felt this was the only way to regain effective product leadership. The Hamilton tests, they pointed out, indicated that the specific motor desired would have the running characteristics and rating of a 5-hp unit but the starting torque of a 10-hp motor. This motor would exceed minimum NEMA specifications. They reasoned that such a unit would have unquestioned competitive superiority in this market. Preliminary examination indicated that the motor could be produced at a manufacturing cost of approximately $665.

Executives believed that such a motor could be successfully sold at a net price of $1,045 to large users. They reasoned that the definite-purpose motor should be priced close to the 5-hp general-purpose motor, because it was actually a 5-hp motor. Also, it would be priced below the 7½-hp general-purpose motor to give DMC a price advantage over the competition's 7½-hp motors. Some managers, however, believed a definite-purpose motor could be sold for somewhat more than $1,045 and perhaps more than a current 7½-hp motor. An investment of $75,000 was believed adequate to provide the required engineering and testing. Executives believed only minor expenditures for plant and equipment would be necessary to produce the new motor. Engineers estimated that it would take four to five months for production to begin.

Those who favored this alternative summarized its merits by noting that DMC would be offering the market exactly what it wanted. Furthermore, they believed that the first manufacturer to offer a definite-purpose motor, tailored to the needs of the market, would have an important tactical advantage over competitors, which could be expected to last a long time. They felt that with such a motor DMC could increase its share of the oil well pumping market to approximately 60 percent.

With few exceptions the Canadian motor industry had adhered to general-purpose motors—designed to be acceptable for a number of applications. As a rule, their performance characteristics exceeded the specific requirements of any individual application. Some industry executives believed that this philosophy (based on NEMA standards) had been the salvation of the Canadian motor industry. They pointed out that the Canadian motor market was less than one tenth the size of the U.S. market, making it economically difficult to justify small production runs of

---

[7]Under this alternative DMC's present 7½-hp motor, with a starting torque of 89 pounds-feet, would continue to be manufactured and sold to customers who had no need or interest in high starting torques.

[8]This was described by one executive as technical inflation.

special-purpose motors. Manufacturers had concentrated on standard, general-purpose motors to achieve unit costs competitive with those of imported motors.

Alternative 4. Several members of DMC's management group believed that Bridges's conclusions were not completely accurate. They argued that, before considering changes in product and market strategy, they should attempt to persuade Bridges and the executives of the Hamilton Oil Company that another set of conclusions could be drawn from the test results. Several DMC executives knew Hamilton's purchasing vice president socially and believed that perhaps they could approach him.

These executives pointed out that all 7½-hp motors tested had starting torques in excess of 80 pounds-feet (see Exhibit 1) and, therefore, should have been satisfactory, because 70 pounds-feet of torque was deemed capable of "breaking" a pump in the most extremely cold weather. Apparently Bridges had reasoned that, because starting torque was the most important feature in oil well pumping motor applications, he should get as much of it as possible. The Spartan motor was his first choice, because it had the highest starting torque. Most DMC executives believed that the instances when 80 pound-feet of torque would not start a motor would be extremely rare, but, as one expressed it, "Engineers love big margins whether they use them or not."

Many company executives believed there was real reason for questioning Bridges's conclusions, but they did not know how to present different arguments. Bridges was scheduled to present his conclusions early in May to Hamilton's top management. Several DMC executives close to the situation reported that Bridges was convinced of the validity of his interpretations and showed an intense pride of authorship. They believed it would be very difficult to approach him directly. Some felt that nothing but ill will could be generated by any attempt to alter Bridges's recommendations.

Dominion executives were united in their concern that, although Bridges had begun his tests in October 1984, they had not known of them until March 1985. Most believed that the present problem would never have arisen had they known of Bridges's tests when they first started. Although most executives were not in favor of encouraging a trend to definite-purpose motors, they did feel that, when a customer was attempting to define its motor needs precisely, DMC personnel should work with the customer so the company could be in on the ground floor of subsequent developments.

Some executives believed that DMC personnel should go one step further and begin testing and defining the motor needs of the company's various market segments in preparation for when a customer (such as Hamilton) might conduct an investigation itself. Executives who supported this policy believed that such work could be looked on as a long-term investment in maintaining DMC's future market position. Company engineers, however, were already overburdened; and so a program such as this one would necessitate additional hiring.

Exhibit 1 Maximum Starting Torques of Motors Tested by Hamilton Oil Company (in pounds-feet)

| Horsepower | Starting Torque by Motor Manufacturer | | | Minimum Starting Torque Required by NEMA Standards |
	Spartan	*Universal*	*Dominion*	
5	68	65	60	57.7
7½	102	97	89	76.5
10	110	109	105	101.5

Exhibit 2 Costs and Prices of DMC's Small Integral Motors

Horsepower	Manufacturing Cost[a]	Total Cost[b]	List Price	Prices to Large Users
5	$ 511.53	$ 571.20	$1,685	$1,045
7½	663.51	714.00	1,940	1,200
10	816.00	907.80	2,550	1,580
15	1,229.10	1,371.90	3,725	2,310

[a]Manufacturing cost includes direct labor, materials, and other variable manufacturing costs.
[b]Total cost includes manufacturing cost and charges for fixed manufacturing overhead, engineering, transportation, sales service, advertising, administrative overhead, and depreciation. It does not include sales commissions (8 percent of net sales billed) or transportation costs (2 percent of net sales billed).

MEM Company, Inc.

In December 1980, Gay Mayer, president of MEM Company, Inc., was considering how to increase sales of the company's line of men's toiletries, which included the English Leather brand.[1] Sales had risen 10 percent in 1979 over the previous year but had flattened in 1980. Several options to improve sales growth existed, but the two that interested Mayer the most were expansion of distribution into food stores and introduction of a new brand.

Company Background

In 1883, Mark Edward Mayer opened a first-class women's perfume and soap store in Vienna. Exports to the United States began in 1920. Sales were so strong that the company moved to the United States in 1935. It began to shift emphasis to men's fragrances after one of its department store accounts accidentally displayed MEM cologne for women in the men's department, where it rapidly sold out. The company developed a more masculine-looking package, changed the fragrance formula slightly, and introduced a men's cologne under the generic name *Russian Leather*. In 1947, the name was changed to English Leather in response to the Cold War and a Fifth Avenue buyer's desire to merchandise MEM products in conjunction with high-quality English clothing.

Sales growth accelerated after the company went public in 1966, approaching $60 million in 1979. Approximately one third of these sales were derived from two subsidiaries, Tom Fields, Ltd. (which manufactured the Tinkerbell line

of children's toiletries), and Lebanon Packaging Company, acquired in 1969. Sixty percent of MEM sales were accounted for by six lines of men's toiletries: English Leather (introduced in 1947); Lime (1968); Timberline (1970); Wind Drift (1972); Musk (1975); and Racquet Club (1978). Lime and Musk had been developed in response to similar competitive fragrances. Timberline and Wind Drift appealed to men who enjoyed the outdoors and the sea; Racquet Club had been introduced to capitalize on the growing popularity of tennis and other racquet sports.

All six lines carried the English Leather name on product labels, and all were sold in similar packages. They covered three broad product categories: (1) face savers, including all-purpose lotion, after-shave, and shaving cream; (2) headliners, including shampoo and hair tonic; and (3) body guards, including cologne, deodorants, bath soaps, and talc. A breakdown of MEM men's toiletries by line and product category is shown in Table A.

During 1979, 39 percent of English Leather dollar sales were in face savers, 1 percent in headliners, and 14 percent in body guards. Of the remainder, 37 percent were accounted for by gift sets and 9 percent by mixed prepacks.[2] The breakdown was similar for the other five lines, except that gift sets accounted for, on average, only 20 percent of sales. Although individual slow-selling items were sometimes dropped, MEM had never discontinued an entire line.

The MEM company distributed under license the expensive John Weitz designer and Acqua di Selva lines of men's toiletries to about 1,000 department store and men's specialty store accounts. It also sold the Embracing line of

---

This case was prepared by Professor John A. Quelch.
Copyright © 1981 by the President and Fellows of Harvard College.
Harvard Business School case 581-154.

[1]Blondit, English Leather, Timberline, Tinkerbell, and Wind Drift were registered trademarks of MEM Company, Inc.

---

[2]A mixed prepack was a set of merchandise sold to the trade, sometimes at a discount, which included items from several MEM lines.

TABLE A   MEM's Toiletries for Men

	Face Savers	Headliners	Body Guards	Gift Sets	Total
English Leather	20	3	11	19	53
Lime	3	0	2	4	9
Musk	7	0	2	3	12
Timberline	5	0	2	4	11
Wind Drift	5	0	2	4	11
Racquet Club	6	0	3	5	14
Total	46	3	22	39	110

lower-priced women's spray and splash colognes, Blondit creme bleach for facial and body hair, and a variety of novelty and boutique soaps. In aggregate these products accounted for 5 percent of MEM sales in 1979.

Production Process

After-shaves and colognes are fragrances blended with varying quantities of other raw materials, principally water and alcohol. After-shaves contain more water, less alcohol, and less fragrance than colognes. Once packaged, both remain chemically stable unless exposed to heat and light. When applied to the skin, evaporation releases the fragrance. It is important to ensure that the ingredients evaporate simultaneously and that the chemistry of the reaction is constant among consumers despite differences in body metabolisms.

Like its major competitors, MEM did not develop or manufacture most of the fragrances in its toiletries; these were supplied by about 30 international companies, including Roure-Dupont, Givaudan, and International Flavors and Fragrances. Development of a fragrance involved skilled compounding by specialist chemists of as many as 50 raw materials, both natural and synthetic. Fragrance formulas were not usually divulged, in order to ensure the loyalty of buyers to their original suppliers.

Typically MEM would invite about six manufacturers to submit fragrance samples on a speculative basis. The company would specify a price range and target consumer group. Samples would be evaluated on a range of attitudinal dimensions by MEM employees, after which one or two would be chosen for testing in selected markets. Such research often proved inconclusive, so the judgment of senior management was usually paramount in the final selection of new fragrances.

The MEM company subcontracted manufacture of its shaving creams and some deodorant sticks. It compounded and packaged most of its products at its 205,000-square-foot Northvale, New Jersey, plant. Production efficiency was limited by the breadth of the product line, frequent need for short production runs, and seasonality of sales. Packaging, particularly of gift sets, remained labor intensive and largely unautomated. And although floor space was not fully utilized, much had to be devoted to storing over 200 lots of individual plastic, wood, paper, and glass packages and containers.

The Men's Toiletries Market

Data on the men's toiletries market were sparse, partly because of the fragmentation of the industry, partly because substantial male use of products targeted at women was believed to occur. Some 60 companies and 200 brands competed for consumer purchases of men's cologne and aftershave. Retail sales of those products through all classes of trade during 1979 were estimated at $224 million and $189 million respectively, up 10 percent and 4 percent over 1978 and six times greater in 1965 (see Exhibit 1). Retail sales of men's deodorants, shaving creams, and hairdressings were estimated at $330 million, $135 million, and $150 million, respectively.

Mayer divided the men's toiletries market into three groups, based on price point. (See Exhibit 2.) The exclusive group included designer-name brands, such as Pierre Cardin and Oleg Cassini, with retail selling prices over $10 for a 4-ounce bottle of cologne. These were distributed primarily through department stores and men's specialty stores and were advertised in men's, women's, and dual-audience magazines.

The MEM products competed principally in the *medium-priced* group, in which a 4-ounce bottle of cologne typically sold for between $4 and $10. English Leather's principal competitors were Old Spice, manufactured by the Shulton division of American Cyanamid; British Sterling, manufactured by the Spiedel division of Textron; Jovan, manufactured by Beecham, a major British pharmaceutical company; and Brut, manufactured by Fabergé, a public company with annual sales estimated at $250 million. Next to Old Spice, MEM had the broadest product line among these competitors. Mayer believed that English Leather users were typically somewhat younger than users of either British Sterling or Old Spice.

The third, *mass* group of brands, selling below $4, included Aqua Velva (manufactured by J. B. Williams Company), Mennen Skin Bracer, and Brut 33. These brands were also thought to appeal to an older age group than English Leather. They were distributed primarily through food stores, drugstores, and mass merchandisers and discount stores, such as Kmart.

Several trends were evident in the market during the late 1970s. Many independent manufacturers were acquired by large corporations attracted by their high profit margins. Further, many manufacturers were active in more than one segment. Shulton marketed both the Old Spice and the exclusive Pierre Cardin brands. Fabergé marketed Brut in the medium-priced segment and Brut 33 in the mass segment. Mennen marketed Mennen Skin Bracer in the mass segment and had recently introduced Millionaire in the medium-priced segment.

Many new products were introduced during the late 1970s. In the exclusive market segment, new brands with designer names were frequently launched, partly because national distribution and heavy advertising were not considered essential to success. More surprising to MEM executives was the number of new products in the medium-priced segment backed by substantial advertising expenditures. In 1979, for example, the Ralph Lauren division of Warner Communications introduced Chaps, Jovan introduced Oleg Cassini, and Lever Bros. introduced Denim. Combined advertising expenditures on these three brands approached $7 million in 1979.

Media advertising expenditures on men's after-shave and cologne in 1979 totaled $45 million, of which 80 percent was spent on television and 18 percent in consumer magazines. These represented a 30 percent increase over 1978, although media costs had increased only 15 percent. The top 12 brands accounted for 62 percent of expenditures in 1979, up from 52 percent in 1978. Shulton spent 50 percent more to advertise Old Spice than MEM spent on all six of its lines in 1979. In 1980, it appeared that English Leather would be outspent by Brut as well, as MEM's share of industry advertising declined. A consumer survey showed English Leather ranking second only to Brut in unaided advertising awareness (see Exhibit 3).

Sales and Distribution

MEM men's toiletries were distributed through a variety of channels representing about 24,000 retail outlets (see Exhibit 4). The percentages of sales by line and class of trade for 1979 and 1980 are reported in Exhibit 5. Although MEM's distribution penetration was less than that achieved by Old Spice, company executives believed that their current general merchandise, mass merchandise, and drug accounts were responsible for at least 80 percent of men's fragrance sales through these classes of trade. All shipments were made direct to retail stores or to the regional warehouses of retail chains. Wholesalers were not significantly involved in MEM's distribution.

In 1960, MEM products had been distributed primarily through department stores and men's specialty stores. However, changes in consumer shopping patterns, the broadening popularity of MEM products, and the substantial merchandising support required by department stores caused the company to expand distribution. By 1980, English Leather was the highest-selling line of men's toiletries carried by general merchandise chains, such as Sears, Roebuck & Company and J. C. Penney. Nevertheless, as indicated in Exhibit 6, English Leather placed second to Old Spice in dollar market share in drugstores and mass merchandise outlets. Distribution through food stores accounted for less than 2 percent of sales in 1980; however, MEM executives were receiving an increasing number of inquiries from food chains about carrying a limited selection of their faster-moving items.

The company's accounts were classified by sales revenue potential. Frequency of calls by MEM salespeople varied accordingly. Buyers at important headquarters accounts of major chains would be visited six times a year. Several thousand accounts bought in quantities too small to justify any sales call and were serviced through the mail. The MEM sales force of 50 was one of the largest in the industry. Each salesperson was responsible for all accounts in a geographic territory. Some salespeople were required not to call on the outlets of certain national accounts located in their territories. (For example, Kmart allowed no supplier salespeople

in its retail stores.) Because the sales force was able to visit and provide merchandising assistance to 14,000 retail outlets three times a year on average, MEM had achieved better distribution penetration than most of its competitors, particularly in independent drugstores.

The average salesperson compensation package of over $30,000 included 70 percent salary and 30 percent commission. (Most manufacturers of men's toiletries did not offer such a high commission component but, unlike MEM, they typically reimbursed expenses.) Partly as a result, MEM's sales force turnover was low and MEM salespeople were considered above the industry average in both quality and experience. They had to be versatile to sell in several classes of trade, which differed widely in merchandising objectives and practices.

Retail sales were concentrated around the Father's Day, graduation, and Christmas gift-giving periods. Over 40 percent of annual retail sales of MEM men's toiletries occurred during November and December, and three quarters of these were believed to be gift purchases. Because of this seasonality, MEM commonly held a cash surplus during the first half of each year, but had to borrow during the second half to finance its dating program. Under this program, the trade was not required to pay invoices on midyear orders for Christmas shipments until year-end. A sliding scale of discounts for prepayment of invoices before the dating deadline was also offered.

Pricing Policy

Products were shipped by MEM with freight prepaid and typically allowed the trade a 40 percent margin. Suggested retail prices were maintained in most outlets. Rapid increases in the cost of raw materials for fragrance compounding and packaging caused retail prices of men's toiletries to rise dramatically during the 1970s, and the industry became concerned that competitiveness of their products in the gift marketplace might be jeopardized. The MEM company had not raised its prices as fast as the industry, and, partly as a result, its line had become increasingly acceptable to more price-oriented classes of trade.

An income statement outlining the cost structure for MEM men's toiletries is presented in Exhibit 7. The contribution margin varied widely item by item; it was highest on colognes packaged in plastic containers. (Executives believed that the significant cost difference between glass and plastic packaging would not be credible to consumers if fully reflected in a retail price differential.) Margins were lower on more frequently used products, including after-shaves, deodorants, and shaving creams, and also on gift sets. Gift sets were priced as the sum of the prices of the component items, but because of incremental packaging and labor costs their percentage margins were lower than the average on the component items.

The MEM company sometimes offered its products to the trade at promotional prices. During 1980, about 10 percent of its men's toiletries were sold at prices that allowed 45 percent or 50 percent margins as opposed to the usual 40 percent. Trade interest was maintained through frequent prepacks shipped with counter or shelf display units and through gift-with-purchase, purchase-with-purchase, and self-liquidating premium consumer promotions.[3]

Less-expensive brands of men's toiletries typically offered more price-oriented consumer promotions, such as coupons and refunds. Promotions for MEM men's toiletries during 1980 are summarized in Exhibit 8. A merchandising tear sheet for one of these promotions is reproduced in Figure A.

Marketing Communications

As indicated in Exhibit 9, 20 percent of MEM men's toiletries sales dollars were spent on marketing communications, principally advertising and promotion. The vice president of finance hoped to maintain this ratio in 1981 even if the company introduced a new line.

Advertising for MEM men's toiletries was aimed at males and females, aged 18 to 34, in households with annual incomes over $10,000. Men in this age group were believed to be the heaviest users of men's toiletries and the most likely to switch brands. Since 1967, MEM had employed the theme "All my men wear English Leather, or they wear nothing at all." Some MEM executives believed this theme was becoming "tired," and "a less provocative approach might be better suited for the 1980s." Slogans used by competitive brands tended to emphasize either a macho or a success theme. (See Exhibit 10.)

Measured media advertising expenditures, summarized in Exhibit 11, emphasized national television and consumer magazines with support from network radio. Some MEM executives believed that the budget should be concentrated entirely in television. Advertising on television was devoted exclusively to English Leather and was aired primarily during prime time, late fringe, and late night.[4] Magazine advertising in 1980 covered all six lines of MEM men's toiletries and was placed primarily during June and the fourth quarter in a diverse group of 25 magazines, such as *People, Playboy,* and *Cosmopolitan.* Radio was used as a supportive medium immediately before the Christmas holiday; it afforded scheduling and copy flexibility and added to the frequency with which the advertising message was delivered. About 20 percent of advertisements in all media promoted gift sets.

In addition to national advertising, there were three other major areas of expenditure in the MEM communications budget. First, the company offered the trade a cooperative advertising program, under which it contributed toward the cost of store advertisements that prominently featured MEM merchandise (contribution was up to 5 percent of the value of store purchases from MEM). Second, MEM was a prominent and frequent sponsor, under the English Leather name, of championship sports events in tennis, skiing, and auto racing. The company also jointly promoted local events with retailers who carried MEM merchandise. Finally, MEM, like other manufacturers of men's toiletries, made substantial use of both free samples to be distributed by sales clerks, and of testers to be used by customers at the point of purchase.

Sales Growth

Mayer and other MEM executives believed that periodic new product introductions were essential in the men's toiletries market to maintain consumer and trade interest and to sustain sales growth. It had been over two years since Racquet Club had been introduced.

A new brand, tentatively named Cambridge,[5] was under consideration for introduction in 1981. A fragrance had been selected and focus group interviews with target consumers had been conducted.[6] (See Exhibit 12.) Reaction to the Cambridge name in association with a line of men's toiletries was favorable, so a preliminary marketing program was developed. (See summary in Exhibit 13.) It called for Cambridge to be targeted at men aged 18 to 34 and to sell at $10 retail for a 4-ounce bottle of cologne. Mayer believed Cambridge would gain sales primarily at the expense of British Sterling and other brands in the $7 to $10 range.

Yet, the level of advertising expenditures that would support a Cambridge introduction was still unresolved. The company's advertising agency had been asked to develop three media plans for high, medium, and low expenditure. (See Exhibit 14.) Mayer believed that the lowest expenditure level represented the minimum necessary to achieve his 1981 target of $3 million in factory sales.

Not all MEM executives were enthusiastic about the Cambridge program. Some argued that even the lowest of the media budgets was unaffordable and that the level of

---

[3]Gift-with-purchase (GWP) and purchase-with-purchase (PWP) promotions offered consumers either a free gift or a second item at a discounted price as incentives to purchase the promoted product at the regular price. A self-liquidating premium was an item offered at a price substantially below normal retail (usually 30 percent to 50 percent lower) in return for one or more proofs of purchase from the sponsoring manufacturer's products.

[4]Prime time is divided into early prime (7:30–9:00 P.M.) and late prime (9:00–11:00 P.M.); late fringe is 11:00–11:30 P.M. and late night, 11:30 P.M.–1:00 A.M.

[5]The MEM company had acquired a trademark on the name *Cambridge* for toiletries. The Philip Morris Company held a similar trademark for cigarettes and had recently spent $4 million launching its low-tar Cambridge brand.

[6]In a focus group, a trained interviewer typically spends one to two hours with 6 to 10 consumers probing product and brand meanings or seeking reactions to specific new product or advertising concepts.

advertising needed to launch the new brand could be greatly reduced if the well-known English Leather name was included both on the package and in the advertising. These executives wished to call the brand "Cambridge by English Leather."

Others believed that the potential of Racquet Club had not yet been exhausted and that another new product in the medium-price range would be wasteful. They pointed out that Racquet Club's initial sales were made largely at the expense of Lime, Musk, Timberline, and Wind Drift, because many retailers, especially chain drug buyers, had not been willing to provide additional shelf facings for MEM products.

Some of those who favored a product launch believed that MEM should give first priority to a low-priced brand to penetrate food stores. Although food stores had long carried men's toiletries, MEM had been reluctant to sell through this channel. The men's toiletries sections in many food stores had traditionally been serviced by rack jobbers.[7] The MEM company preferred to sell only direct to retail accounts to maintain consistent product margins. During the 1970s, however, many major food chains merged with or established their own drugstore chains. (For example, Medi Mart drugstores and Stop & Shop supermarkets were owned by the same company.) As a result, their direct buying from men's toiletries manufacturers increased. Mayer knew that food chains typically stocked only the high-turnover items in a product line and that they

pressed for frequent trade deals and year-round national television advertising. He wondered, however, whether the MEM sales force should now attempt to sell to the major food chains, particularly those that emphasized assortment and service, rather than low prices. If he proceeded in this direction, Mayer wondered which, if any, items in the six existing lines should be offered to the food chains or whether a new brand would be more acceptable.

Conclusion

On December 20, 1980, Mayer learned that Shulton was planning to launch its first new brand of men's toiletries since the introduction of Old Spice in 1936. Under the brand name Blue Stratos, an after-shave and cologne would be available for shipment to the trade in March 1981, to be followed by a bath soap, stick deodorant, shave cream, and body talc. The 4-ounce bottle of cologne would carry a suggested retail price of around $10. The trade press reported the advertising would feature the slogan "Unleash the spirit" and use a hang-gliding motif to symbolize the freedom and adventure of the sky. Shulton announced that the Blue Stratos national rollout would be supported by a $12 million communications budget. In addition to network television and full-page advertisements in *Playboy, People,* and *Sports Illustrated,* Shulton planned to mail 10.3 million samples of three-pack product wipes to reach one third of all men aged 18 to 34. Recognizing that Blue Stratos was targeted at the same market as Cambridge, Mayer wondered whether he should cancel or delay the Cambridge introduction and commit his entire 1981 communications budget to reinforcing the six existing lines.

---

[7]Rack jobbers are compensated on a percentage margin basis for stocking the shelves in retail outlets. They do not take title to the merchandise they handle.

EXHIBIT 1 Men's Toiletries for Three Classes of Trade, 1979 (dollars and unit sales in millions)

	Retail Dollar Sales				Unit Sales	
	After-shave	*Cologne*	*Total*	*Increase over 1978 (percent)*	*Total*	*Increase over 1978 (percent)*
Chain and independent drugstores	$ 78	$ 71	$149	15%	43	5%
Mass merchandisers and discount stores	38	26	64	15	23	5
Food stores	29	4	33	10	16	0
	$145	$101	$246	13%	82	3%

NOTE: Data for department stores and men's specialty stores were not available in this study.
SOURCE: Rosenfeld, Sirowitz & Lawson, Inc.

Exhibit 2 Retail Price Points for MEM Men's Toiletries and Competitive Brands, July 1980

	After-shave 2 oz.	Cologne 2 oz.	After-shave 4 oz.	Cologne 4 oz.	After-shave 8 oz.	Cologne 8 oz.
English Leather	$ 2.50	$ 3.00	$ 4.00	$ 6.00	$ 5.50	$ 8.00
Lime	2.50	3.00	3.50	5.50	5.00	7.50
Musk	3.00	3.50		6.00		
Timberline	2.50	3.00	3.50	5.50	5.00	7.50
Wind Drift	2.50	3.00	3.50	5.50	5.00	7.50
Racquet Club	3.00	4.50	5.00	6.50		
Acqua di Selva	7.50	8.40	11.00	13.50		21.00
	(1.75)	(1.75)	(3.50)	(3.50)		(7.00)
Aramis		8.50	9.00	12.50	15.00	22.00
British Sterling	3.50	4.00	7.00	7.00	7.50	9.50
Brut		4.50		9.00		15.00
		(1.50)		(3.20)		(6.40)
Brut 33			2.50	2.50		4.15
			(3.50)	(3.50)		(6.00)
Brut 33 Musk				4.15		
				(3.50)		
Cardin	6.00	8.00	8.50	12.50	15.00	22.50
Chaps		6.50	8.50	9.50	12.50	14.50
Denim	3.00		5.00	7.50		
Monsieur Jovan		3.50	7.00	7.50	10.50	11.00
Old Spice			3.00	4.50	4.75	6.50
			(4.25)	(4.25)	(8.50)	(8.50)
Oleg Cassini		7.00		11.50		

NOTE: Numbers in parentheses indicate different ounce-size package from that shown in column heading.

SOURCE: Company records.

Exhibit 3 Results of 1980 Consumer Survey (percent of respondents)

	Brand Awareness[a]		Advertising Awareness		Correct Slogan Identification	Brands Ever Used	Brands Now Used	Brand Used Most Often
	Unaided	Total	Unaided	Total				
Aqua Velva	13%	94%	2%	86%	NA	4%	NA	NA
Aramis	40	83	3	52	9%	28	22%	22%
British Sterling	NA	NA	NA	NA	NA	4	4	NA
Brut	52	96	28	84	80	24	8	6
Canoe	NA	NA	NA	NA	NA	22	14	10
Denim	9	62	4	57	21	4	2	NA
English Leather	41	96	27	85	45	30	12	4
Jovan	12	72	6	68	NA	8	4	4
Mennen Skin Bracer	19	88	1	77	NA	16	12	8
Old Spice	48	93	24	83	74%	30	20	20
Pierre Cardin	NA	NA	NA	NA	NA	6	4	NA
Royal Copenhagen	15%	50%	4%	43%	NA	10%	8%	6%

[a] To qualify as having unaided awareness of a brand or its advertising, a consumer had to name it in response to questions such as "What brands of men's after-shave or cologne can you name?" and "What brands of men's after-shave or cologne have you seen advertised?" Total awareness measures also included consumers with aided awareness who replied affirmatively to questions such as "Have you heard of brand X?" or "Have you seen advertising for brand X?" Correct slogan identification required a consumer to name the associated brand correctly when presented with a particular slogan.

NA means not available.

NOTE: Percent of respondents is based on telephone interviews with men and women purchasers of men's cologne and after-shave conducted in New York and Chicago during December 1980.

Source: Rosenfeld, Sirowitz & Lawson, Inc.

Exhibit 4   Account Penetration by Class of Trade, 1980

	Number of Headquarters Accounts Sold	Number of Retail Outlets Penetrated	Estimated Total Number of Retail Outlets
Department stores	17	900	3,000
General merchandise chains[a]	12	3,600	4,000
Chain drugstores[b]	56	6,000	9,500
Independent drugstores	NA	6,500	40,000
Mail-order catalogs	8	50	
Mass merchandisers and discount stores[c]	35	6,000	10,000
Armed forces stores	NA	700	
Men's specialty stores and other stores[d]	NA	1,000	
Export	NA	NA	NA

[a]Includes Sears, Roebuck & Company, J. C. Penney Company, and Montgomery Ward.
[b]Includes drug accounts with more than five retail outlets, such as Osco Drug and Medi Mart.
[c]Includes Woolco-Woolworth, Kmart, Zayre, and Service Merchandise.
[d]Includes college bookstores, gift shops, food stores, and so on.
NA means not available.
Source: Company records.

Exhibit 5   Percentages of Dollar Sales by Product Line and Class of Trade, 1979 and 1980

		English Leather	Lime	Musk	Timber-line	Wind Drift	Racquet Club	Mixed Prepacks	Other	Total[c]
Department stores	1979	2.6%[a]	0.1%	0.3%	0.1%	0.2%	0.3%	0.3%	[b]	3.9%
	1980	2.0	0.1	0.2	0.1	0.1	0.2	0.1	[b]	2.8
General merchandise chains	1979	8.2	0.3	1.1	0.5	0.5	1.1	1.0	0.1%	12.8
	1980	7.4	0.2	1.1	0.4	0.4	1.1	1.0	0.1	11.7
Chain drugstores	1979	21.3	1.0	3.2	1.6	1.1	2.0	2.9	0.1	33.2
	1980	22.5	1.0	3.4	1.5	1.1	1.4	2.7	0.1	33.7
Independent drugstores	1979	5.3	0.3	0.7	0.4	0.4	0.9	0.6	0.1	8.7
	1980	5.3	0.2	0.7	0.3	0.4	0.8	0.4	0.1	8.2
Mail-order catalogs	1979	0.9	[b]	[b]	[b]	[b]	0.1	[b]	[b]	1.0
	1980	0.4	[b]	[b]	[b]	[b]	[b]	[b]	[b]	0.4
Mass merchandisers and discount stores	1979	16.2	0.4	2.0	0.6	0.6	1.7	1.2	0.1	22.8
	1980	18.3	0.4	2.2	0.5	0.5	2.3	0.9	0.1	25.2
Armed forces stores	1979	3.6	[b]	0.6	[b]	[b]	0.4	0.1	[b]	4.7
	1980	4.0	[b]	0.7	[b]	[b]	0.3	0.2	[b]	5.2
Men's specialty/ other stores	1979	4.8	0.2	0.3	0.2	0.1	0.4	0.9	0.1	7.0
	1980	5.4	0.2	0.4	0.2	0.1	0.3	1.0	0.1	7.7
Export	1979	3.7	0.3	0.3	0.3	0.1	0.3	0.5	0.1	5.6
	1980	3.0	0.2	0.3	0.3	0.1	0.5	0.5	0.2	5.1
Total[c]	1979	66.6	2.6	8.5	3.7	3.0	7.2	7.5	0.6	100.0
	1980	68.3%	2.3%	9.0%	3.3%	2.7%	6.9%	6.8%	0.7%	100.0%

[a]That is, "2.6 percent of 1979 dollar sales of MEM men's toiletries were of English Leather sold to department stores."
[b]Sales volume less than 0.1 percent.
[c]Final columns and rows may not total 100 percent because of rounding.
Source: Company records.

EXHIBIT 6   **Market Shares of Major Men's Toiletries Brands for Three Classes of Trade, 1979**

	Independent and Chain Drugstores	Mass Merchandisers and Discount Stores	Food Stores
English Leather	14.5%[a]	12.7%	NA
Old Spice	16.4	20.5	20.8%
Mennen Skin Bracer	7.5	10.6	27.9
Brut	10.7	12.4	14.9
Four-brand share total	49.1%	56.2%	63.6%

[a]That is "14.5 percent of dollar sales of after-shaves and colognes through independent and chain drugstores in 1979 were of English Leather brands."
NA means not available.
NOTE: Data for general merchandise chains were not reported in this study.
SOURCE: Rosenfeld, Sirowitz & Lawson, Inc.

EXHIBIT 7   **1979 Income Statement for Men's Toiletries (percent)**

Gross sales	100.00%
Raw materials	37.55
Direct labor	7.17
Contribution margin	55.28
Manufacturing overhead	2.34
Real estate, taxes, insurance, utilities, depreciation	2.02
Shipping[a]	8.09
Advertising and promotion	20.52
Field sales force	7.52
General and administrative	7.17
Net pretax income from operations	7.62
Other income[b]	1.47

[a]Company prices include prepaid freight charges.
[b]Net interest income on seasonal cash flows.
NOTE: Income statement does not include Lebanon Packaging Company, Tom Fields, Ltd., and the Acqua di Selva and John Weitz lines.
SOURCE: Company records.

EXHIBIT 8   **Summary of 1980 Promotions and Trade Deals**

1. Prepack containing 24 English Leather Power Foam for the price of 22 (2 free with 22), providing the trade a 45% margin at suggested retail of $2.
2. Prepack of 12 four-piece gift sets containing cologne and after-shave in both English Leather and Musk. Tied into a SuperShooter consumer sweepstakes promotion, each package flagged "Regular $8.75 value, now $6.00."
3. Prepack containing 12 16-oz.-size English Leather Shampoo for the price of 11 of the regular 9-oz. size (1 free with 11), providing the trade a 45% margin at suggested retail price of $2.50 each.
4. Basket display prepack containing 1-oz. sizes of English Leather Cologne (72), Wind Drift and Musk (24 of each), and Lime and Timberline (12 of each), each priced at $1. Profit margin to trade—40%.
5. Prepack containing 12 English Leather Special Formula Deodorant Sticks for the price of 11 (1 free with 11), providing the trade a 45% margin at suggested retail price of $2.50 each.
6. Prepack containing 48 ½-oz. trial-size Musk Cologne for Men, priced at $1.50 each for impulse purchases. Profit margin to trade—40%.
7. Prepack containing 36 Pocket Mist-ers in six fragrances, priced at $2.50 each. Profit margin to trade—40%.
8. Prepack containing 36 1-oz. travel-size Racquet Club Cologne, priced at $1.50 each. Profit margin to trade—40%.
9. Prepack containing 6 4-oz. English Leather Cologne and 6 5-oz. Musk Cologne with new pump spray caps. Profit margin to trade—40%.
10. Prepack containing 12 5-oz. Musk Cologne for Men. Each package is flagged "Save $1.50, Regularly $6.50—Now Only $5.00." Profit margin to trade—40%.
11. A $6 value men's nail-care set offered for $3 with any $6 purchase of English Leather toiletries.
12. A $3 value English Leather gift set (containing after-shave, shave cream, and shampoo travel sizes) free with any $6 purchase of English Leather toiletries.
13. An executive briefcase plus a travel set of 1-oz. size colognes in English Leather, Lime, Wind Drift, and Timberline, valued at $29, priced at $10.

SOURCE: Company records.

EXHIBIT 9   Men's Toiletries Communications Budgets, 1977–1980 (dollars in thousands)

	1977	1978	1979	1980 Budget[a]
Media advertising, advertising production costs, and trade promotions:[b]				
English Leather	$2,135	$2,753	$2,755	$2,750
Lime	132	0	0	0
Musk	308	310	350	350
Timberline	300	220	250	150
Wind Drift	300	230	250	150
Racquet Club	NA	370	610	750
Subtotal	3,175	3,883	4,215	4,150
Co-op advertising	819	937	1,392	1,350
Sponsorships[c]	292	568	441	380
Point-of-sale samples, display fixtures	889	862	1,134	1,100
Sales sheets, flyers, brochures	107	133	140	150
Gift-with-purchase, purchase-with-purchase promotions	47	30	44	50
Public relations	40	50	46	50
Subtotal	2,194	2,580	3,197	3,080
Total	$5,369	$6,463	$7,412	$7,230
As % of sales	18.5%	19.5%	20.6%	20.0%

[a]As of December 1980, it appeared that actual expenditures would be close to budget.

[b]Figures for each line include cost of promotions and trade deals as well as cost of measured media advertising and production. Promotion costs allocated among lines on a prorated basis for cross-line events. Media advertising expenditures are reported in Exhibit 11.

[c]1980 budget includes approximately $150,000 in media advertising to promote sponsored events.

NA means not available.

NOTE: These figures exclude advertising and promotion expenditures for Acqua di Selva and John Weitz.

SOURCE: Company records.

EXHIBIT 10   Advertising Slogans of Men's Toiletries Brands

English Leather:	"All my men wear English Leather, or they wear nothing at all."
Old Spice:	"Put a little spice in your life with Old Spice."
Paco Rabanne:	"A cologne for men. What is remembered is up to you."
Denim:	"For men who don't have to try."
Chaps:	"It's the West. The West you feel inside of yourself."
Aqua Velva:	"It makes a man feel like a man."
Brut:	"Make every day your Brut day."
Pierre Cardin:	"For the man who gets the most out of life."
Aramis:	"The Aramis man. He expects everything."
Mennen Skin Bracer:	"For the man who takes care of himself."
Millionaire:	"Whatever you wear it with, you feel like a million bucks."

SOURCE: Rosenfeld, Sirowitz & Lawson, Inc.

EXHIBIT 11 **Measured Media Advertising Expenditures, 1979 and 1980 ($000)**

	Total	National TV	Network Radio	Consumer Magazines	Other[a]
1979 Actual	$2,036	$1,554[b]	$126	$318	$38
1980 Budget[c]	2,470[d]	1,816	266	369	19
Quarter 2	561	290	133	128	10
Quarter 4	$1,909	$1,526[e]	$133	$241	$ 9

[a]Includes spot TV and advertising in military publications.

[b]Comprises $1,064,000 advertising on network TV and $489,000 on syndicated sports programs.

[c]No advertising budgeted for the first or third quarters of 1980.

[d]Measured media advertising costs rose 15 percent in 1980 over 1979.

[e]Scheduled to deliver 640 household gross rating points (calculated as reach × frequency) during the five weeks before Christmas. During any four-week period, 92 percent of all U.S. households would be reached an average of 5.9 times.

NOTE: These figures exclude expenditures of Tom Fields, Ltd., Lebanon Packaging Company, and minimal advertising expenditures for Acqua di Selva and John Weitz.

SOURCE: Company records.

EXHIBIT 12 **1980 Focus Group Session: Summary of Findings**

During April 1979, in New York City 12 women (average age 25) participated in a focus group session conducted by one of the company's advertising agencies, Chalk, Nissen, Hanft, Inc. Key findings included the following:

- Respondents preferred clean, natural fragrances for men. Strong fragrances for men were disliked; they were associated with a woman reeking of perfume.
- Men favorably remembered English Leather as the fragrance of their youth—the brand "all the guys wore in college." Other fragrances were now perceived as more sophisticated.
- Old Spice was typically remembered as "the fragrance my father used."
- Respondents agreed that men lack knowledge of fragrances. When buying men's fragrances as gifts, some respondents stated that they would follow their own preferences; others would follow the perceived preferences of the recipient.
- Designer fragrances were expected to reflect the fashion images of the designers.
- Respondents were skeptical that a dual set of fragrances such as Jovan Man and Jovan Woman could succeed in satisfying the fragrance needs of the male and the female.
- The name *Cambridge* in association with a men's fragrance was seen as classic, understated, and dignified. Respondents would expect the package design to reflect the traditional quality of the name.

EXHIBIT 13   Proposed New Product Introduction Program

Brand name:	Cambridge.
Target customer:	Men, aged 18 to 34.
Product line:	After-shave, cologne, bath soap, deodorant stick, shaving stick, gift sets.
Retail price point:	$10 for 4-oz. cologne. Variable cost structure similar to other MEM men's toiletries.
Trade margin:	40 percent.
Introductory deals:	5 percent and 10 percent off-invoice allowances on small- and large-size prepacks. Sales of each prepack were expected to account for one third of 1981 Cambridge sales.
Sampling:	Production of one million ⅛-oz. samples to be distributed free at the point of sale at a cost of $200,000.
Merchandising aids:	Counter display materials, brochures, and testers at a cost in 1981 of $50,000.
Timing of launch:	First orders accepted in April 1981; first shipments in September 1981.
Sales target:	Gross factory sales of $3 million in 1981.

SOURCE: Company records.

EXHIBIT 14   Three Media Plans for Cambridge Introduction

	Plan 1	Plan 2	Plan 3
Network television	$249,180	$ 570,480	$1,140,960
Spot television	384,000	411,116	1,016,070
Consumer magazines	286,058	379,213	609,925
Trade magazines	9,900	13,000	26,000
Production	70,052	70,174	100,000
Reserve	—	56,017	107,045
Total	$999,190	$1,500,000	$3,000,000

NOTE: Reserve funds were used to finance one-time tie-in advertising efforts with individual retail accounts independent of co-op advertising.
SOURCE: Chalk, Nissen, Hanft, Inc.

COMMUNICATIONS POLICY

A. Mass Communications
B. Personal Selling

COMMUNICATIONS POLICY

Communications policy is a critical ingredient in virtually all marketing programs. Even a well-designed product or service intended to satisfy a pressing consumer need will have scant opportunity to do so if target consumers are unaware of its existence, do not understand what it can do for them, and have no idea of where to obtain it. Although communications policies frequently have far more complex objectives than providing this information, any marketing program must accomplish at least this minimum goal.

To develop an effective communications program for a product or products, the marketer must consider seven interrelated issues:

1. Objectives of the communications program.
2. Market segments to be targeted.
3. Choice of a push, pull, or hybrid communications strategy.
4. Message to be communicated.
5. Necessary intensity of communication.
6. Choice of media.
7. Economics of the proposed communications program.

Program Objectives

Management's first task is to specify clearly its communications objectives. These are often summarized as changing customer attitudes toward a product in terms of one or more elements of the awareness → knowledge → preference → trial → repurchase continuum known as the *hierarchy of effects*. The goal of a communications program might, for example, be to increase brand-name awareness from 40 to 70 percent of households or to increase the rate of brand trial from 10 to 25 percent of households. Though this hierarchy of effects may not be an appropriate model for all

This note was prepared by Professors Steven H. Star and John A. Quelch.
Copyright © 1992 by the President and Fellows of Harvard College.
Harvard Business School note 9-576-086.

products, it encourages marketers to examine in detail the effects of their programs in order to focus future efforts on the appropriate elements in the hierarchy.[1]

A second dimension of specifying communications objectives centers on the audience to be reached. For example, a marketer may wish to raise awareness for an office product among secretaries that have not tried it. What if the office products in that category are typically purchased by an office manager or purchasing agent who is not the ultimate user? In that case, the marketer may be better off targeting "purchasing agents and office managers who have not bought our brand," than "secretaries who have not tried our brand." To specify communications objectives clearly, management must understand the decision-making process for a product: who initiates the search, who influences the decision, who makes the purchase, and who uses the product.

A third dimension to the specification of communications objectives centers on the type of demand the firm is seeking to stimulate. As well as increasing selective demand for its own products, a company with a dominant market share in a particular product category may aim to increase demand for the category as a whole, knowing that it will reap a large portion of the incremental business.

A variety of other objectives may also be assigned to marketing communications programs. An advertising campaign by an airline, for example, may be designed to raise the morale and performance of service personnel, as well as to attract more travelers. So-called corporate advertising campaigns may be designed to raise the company's profile among the investment community, while advocacy advertising campaigns can be designed to present a political point of view often only indirectly related to sale of the company's products.

There is always a danger that too many objectives will be assigned to a communications program. In general, it is preferable to have a limited set of objectives set forth in sufficiently specific detail to permit performance measurement.

Target Market Segments

A market segment is a subgroup of consumers who share some common characteristic(s). These consumers may have the same demographic profile, (e.g., age, sex, and class distribution), live in the same region of a country, share a similar lifestyle, or be heavy users of a particular product or brand. The basic assumption underlying market segmentation is that consumers are heterogeneous and that different groups will respond to particular products and communications programs in different ways. The art of market segmentation is to identify the dimensions or the criteria on which it is most useful to segment actual and potential customers for the purposes of marketing. To be of value to management, a segment must be large enough in market potential to make tailoring a distinct marketing program economically worthwhile. Moreover, there should be enough media-audience information available to make media purchases cost effective.

---

[1]Some scholars suggest an alternative model in which a low-risk product trial *precedes* attitude change. See Herbert E. Krugman, "The Impact of Television Advertising: Learning without Involvement," *Public Opinion Quarterly,* Fall 1965, pp. 349–560.

Determining the appropriate audiences for a specific communications program generally depends on the target market segment(s) of the overall marketing program and the nature of the purchase-decision process in these market segments. Based on the understanding of their firms' marketing strategy, marketing managers select both the households or organizations to be reached and the individuals in those households or organizations who either make or strongly influence the purchase decision. Marketing managers will sometimes communicate a different message to each of several target segments at the same time. For example, in the case of the office product mentioned earlier, the marketer might decide to send different messages via different media both to secretaries who have not used the product and to office managers.

One segmentation approach of special value in developing communications policy is benefit segmentation. Different segments are identified according to the varying importance they attach to different product benefits. This benefit analysis can guide the communications messages to be targeted at different segments. For example, a manufacturer of printing presses found that book publishers are especially sensitive to production quality and consistency but not especially concerned about machine downtime; newspapers, on the other hand, are less concerned about quality but extremely time sensitive and very concerned about machine reliability and avoidance of downtime. The manufacturer developed different products and communications programs to address these two benefit segments.

Consider a second example, that of a specialized manufacturer of industrial instant adhesives used to bond metal and plastic surfaces. In selecting the appropriate audiences for its communications program, such a manufacturer might usefully develop a complete listing of all users of industrial adhesive in the United States, categorized by geographic location, capacity, size and nature of the firm, and (possibly) current purchasing behavior. Using these data, the adhesive manufacturer could determine which segment or segments of this market it should target with its overall marketing strategy and what priorities to assign to each market segment, or even to each potential customer.

Having decided which organizations are to be the targets of its marketing program, the marketing manager would then determine which individuals or positions in those target firms play significant roles in the purchase-decision process for adhesives. In this case, he or she might determine that purchasing agents play the decisive role but that production foremen have strong views regarding the ostensible advantages of competitive brands of adhesives and that senior executives regularly review supply arrangements for such items as adhesives in order to assure guaranteed availability during strikes or shortages. Under these circumstances, the adhesive manufacturer might decide that all these members of the purchase decision-making unit (DMU) should receive communications—to different degrees and with different messages.

Defining target audiences for consumer goods is also complex. The manufacturer of a new children's breakfast cereal, for example, might define new target segments in various ways: as households with children; as households with two or more children below the age of 12; as households with two or more children below the age of 12 who currently are or are not heavy users of children's breakfast cereals; or even as households that are currently heavy users of a competitive brand. After selecting one or more of these segments, the cereal manufacturer would then determine who makes or influences the decision to buy breakfast cereals. The purchase may be made by an adult member of the household; but young children, or their older brothers and sisters, may contribute to the decision process. Like the adhesive manufacturer, the cereal manufacturer might usefully include several members of the DMU in its communications program.

Demographics may not, however, always be an adequate basis for segmentation. A health and beauty aid manufacturer, for example, found that all demographic groups in all regions of the country were equally likely to use a particular product. In addition, a group of heavy users with outdoor lifestyles was identified; they were more price conscious and less brand loyal than lighter users and tended to buy larger sizes in discount stores, whereas lighter users usually purchased smaller sizes in drug stores. Further investigation revealed that heavy users were more frequent viewers of televised sports, which enabled the marketing manager to develop one communications campaign for light users and one for heavy users of the product—employing different media and focusing on different product uses.

Choice of Push versus Pull Strategy

Once the objectives and the target segment have been identified, an overall strategy for how best to direct the flow of marketing communications must be defined. Two options exist: *push* and *pull*.

With a *push* strategy, the manufacturer communicates with the final consumer indirectly, through the distribution channel. The manufacturer tries to encourage wholesalers and retailers to push its brand, rather than competing brands, through the channel to the ultimate customers. A push strategy must provide channel members with both the ability and motivation to promote the target brand. Push programs are often implemented via a combination of dealer training, sales support, point-of-purchase merchandising assistance, and trade promotions. The goal of a push strategy is to capture "share of mind" of the wholesale and retail sales personnel, so that they recommend or "push" the manufacturer's brand to customers who intend to buy but do not have a clear brand preference.

With a *pull* strategy, the manufacturer communicates direct to the final consumer, sending messages about the brand "over the heads" of channel members. The messages aim at encouraging consumers to pull the manufacturer's product through the channels by searching for it by name at the point-of-sale. This requires the consumer to establish both an intention to buy in the product category, and a preference for the manufacturer's brand before arriving at the point-of-purchase. Television ads, free samples, and consumer promotions, such as coupons in the Sunday newspaper, are examples of media used to implement a pull strategy. The goal of a pull strategy is to get the name of the brand (such as Pepsi or Right Guard) rather than the name of the product category (such as soda or deodorant) on to the consumer's shopping list.

Conventional wisdom suggests that push strategies may be more effective early in the product life cycle, when consumers need to be educated. Pull strategies may be more effective for more mature product categories with large numbers of customers who know about the product category and need merely to be told about alternative brands.

However, the choice between a push or pull strategy is not always that simple. Different manufacturers with similar products in the mature industries are often successful using pull strategies. For example, in the 1980s, Procter & Gamble placed relatively greater emphasis on pull communications programs for its Prell and Head & Shoulders brands of shampoo. Push strategies were successfully employed by high-priced niche competitors, such as Clinique, and lower priced "value" competitors, such as Helene Curtis with its Suave brand. What conclusions can be drawn? A winning communications program can be designed using either a push, pull, or hybrid strategy. The challenge is to select a strategy that best fits the information needs of the target customer and the relative competence of the marketing company, and that also takes into account the strategies of other leading competitors.

Message Delineation

Having identified the specific individuals to be reached through its communications policy, the company's next task is determining what message or messages it wishes to communicate to each of its audience segments. At a conceptual level, such messages may be viewed as satisfying each audience segment's need or desire for information relevant to the purchasing process. Once the message content is determined, the marketer can turn his or her attention to *how* to communicate it. An audience segment's need for information generally may be ascertained by answering such questions as:

- At what life-cycle stage is the product or service?
- At what stage is the audience segment along the awareness → trial → repurchase continuum?
- What is the product or service intended to do for members of the audience segment?
- How does it compare with available alternatives?
- What role does this audience segment play in the household or organizational purchase-decision process?

The position of the product in its life cycle often determines what information should be communicated. For a totally new product category (e.g., an optical scanner to be used in automated typesetting), the initial communications task may simply be to create awareness that it is now possible to do something not previously feasible. For a new entry in an existing product category (e.g., a new type of potato chip), however, it may be necessary not only to announce that the new product is available but also to describe its benefits relative to alternatives. In either case, the marketer developing a message strategy needs to distinguish between what consumers already know and what they need to know, since the frequent repetition of well-known facts may eventually generate a negative reaction, rather than a positive reinforcement.

Once the target audience is aware of a new product or service and knows, in general terms, what it is supposed to do, the next communications objective is often to encourage a trial or a closer look. For frequently purchased consumer goods (e.g., toothpaste or potato chips), it is generally enough to communicate convincing reasons why the customer should deviate from a well-established purchasing pattern. For infrequently purchased durable or capital goods (e.g., furniture or word processors), the most appropriate communications objective might be to convince members of the target audience to consider the product or service the next time they enter the market and to explain how to learn more about the product and locate a dealer.

Once the target audience has been directly exposed to the new product or service—whether through actual trial or, say, a supermarket or trade show demonstration—the marketer's communications objective may shift. At this point, he or she will try to ensure that the target audience is fully aware of the various uses and advantages of the product or service. At this stage in the communications cycle, the differing information needs of individual members of the DMU are especially significant. In the case of the optical scanner, for example, it may initially be critical to inform members of the target DMU that the new product exists, that it is made by the XYZ Company, that they can now get further information and observe the equipment in operation, and so on. Once these communications objectives have been accomplished, however, it is frequently necessary to convey different messages to potential customers' top management, technical staffs, production people, and procurement personnel.

In designing messages for specific audience segments, it is generally useful to know what the product or service will do for the intended recipient of the message. While it may be noteworthy that the instant adhesive described earlier is baked at an exceptionally high temperature and allowed to cool slowly, the relevance of this aspect of the production process is probably not immediately apparent to the firm's target audiences. However, the manufacturing process *may* be highly relevant to the purchasing agent, if it is related to fewer rejects at the time of delivery, or to the shop foreman, if it indicates high quality consistency and, therefore, fewer process problems.

In a similar vein, a consumer-products manufacturer will generally find it useful to focus on what its product will do for individual members of its target audience. A children's good-tasting nutritious cereal may, for example, provide a parent with a convenient way of preparing a quick, wholesome breakfast during the morning rush or simply with something a three-year-old will eat, rather than throw on the floor. For children, however, the salient message may be that the cereal tastes good, is fun to eat, or makes them feel like a big-game hunter, secure against childhood fantasies of rampaging lions and tigers.

Intensity of Communication

Given the target audiences and the clearly delineated messages to be communicated to these audiences, what level of communications effort will achieve the desired impact? To a considerable extent, the appropriate intensity of a communications program will be a function of:

- The nature of the message to be communicated.
- The number of targets to be reached.
- The receptivity of the audience to the message.
- The intensity of competitive communications activities.
- The amount of funds available for the communications effort.

Some messages simply require more time and effort to communicate than others. A new entry in an existing product category (e.g., a new flavor in an established line of soft drinks) requires no major behavioral change of the target consumer and generally calls for only a low level of communications intensity. In effect, all that is necessary is to inform the target consumer that the new flavor is available and is worthy of trial. At the other extreme, a complex industrial new product, such as the optical scanner cited earlier, may perform a new function in such a way as to necessitate major changes in the production process in which it is applied; it is, therefore, likely to require a very intensive communications effort to educate and convince customers about the new technology.

In general, a more intense communications effort is required when a product is introduced than later in its life cycle. At the time of introduction, it is often necessary to inform customers about the existence of a new product; its function, features, benefits, and costs; and where or how to buy it. As an increasing percentage of the target audience becomes aware of the product's existence and major attributes, it may only be necessary to remind them of these facts or to stress particular benefits.

The number, heterogeneity, and receptivity of members of the target audience have a significant influence on the necessary intensity of communications effort. In general, a greater level of effort is needed to reach a lot of people than to reach a few people, or to reach separate audiences with different messages than to reach a single audience with a single message. Similarly, it often requires less effort to communicate a message when the audience is actively seeking information of the kind being communicated (e.g., gasoline mileage data in the 1990s) than to communicate the same message to a relatively passive audience (e.g., gasoline mileage data in 1965). In general, a higher level of communications intensity is required for mundane, unimportant products than for those which more readily engage a customer. Nonetheless, marketers should remember that the importance of a product category varies from customer to customer and may be heightened by, for example, the introduction of new products.

In situations where the purpose of a communications program is to convince potential customers to purchase one brand, rather than another that promises similar benefits, the intensity of competitive communications efforts will often establish a minimum threshold that must be surpassed if a communications program is to achieve its desired effects. If, for example, one brand of analgesic communicates to target consumers the importance of "getting rapidly into the bloodstream" 10 times per week, it is unlikely that the message of a competitive analgesic emphasizing "gentleness to your stomach" will have much impact if it reaches the target only once a week. Similarly, even an exceptional salesperson will find the going tough if a buyer he or she visits twice a year has weekly lunches with the competition.

Ultimately, however, the intensity of a communications program depends largely on the extent of the target audience's need for information and the willingness of the purchaser to pay for the information. In the competition between private-label or generic grocery and advertised brands, for example, the higher price necessitated by the advertised brand's communications program will be paid only if the target consumer finds the information communicated worth the difference in price. Not surprisingly, private labels tend to do least well in product categories that present consumers with considerable perceived risk or in which it is difficult for them to determine the respective merits of competitive brands. Similarly, consumers who have the least confidence in their own purchasing ability are most likely to purchase more expensive, advertised brands, even at income levels that would most benefit from the savings from buying generic goods.

Although every company has limits to its communications budget, the prime determinant should be the nature of the communications task, rather than the spending level of the firm's principal competitor or the firm's historical advertising-to-sales ratio. There is usually no reason to believe that the competitor's budget-setting process is superior and, therefore, worthy of imitation. Moreover, the advertising-to-sales ratio approach is based on circular reasoning; it makes advertising a function of sales, rather than sales a result of advertising.

In addition to setting the absolute level of the communications budget, management must also decide on its allocation. This allocation may occur along several dimensions, according to products in the line, in which new products may receive proportionately more funds than mature products; target groups, in which current users who need merely to be reinforced will probably receive less emphasis than nonusers who need to be made aware of the product and induced to prefer it; and geographic regions, where low-share development markets may receive proportionately more funds than high-share markets. Communications expenditures must also be allocated among media types and specific vehicles. In addition, management must decide how to allocate funds over the planning cycle—for example, whether to have a constant level of media spending or periodic "blitzes." Finally, communications expenditures are sometimes allocated between the manufacturer and its channel intermediaries on a cooperative basis, particularly when consumers are as concerned about the quality of the distributors from which they buy the product as they are about the brands they select.

Choice of Media

Marketers can choose from a wide range of communications media to convey their messages to target audiences. They can employ, for example, such mass media as outdoor billboards, television, mass-circulation magazines, and newspapers; more selective media, such as FM radio, specialized magazines, or *The Wall Street Journal;* point-of-purchase advertising; direct mail; telemarketing; or personal selling. Moreover, the diversity of the communications mix available to consumer-goods and industrial marketers has increased greatly in recent years, partly in response to rapid escalation in the costs of network television advertising and the personal sales call. More and more often, consumer marketers are supplementing advertising efforts with point-of-sale merchandising and in-store sales promotions, particularly for products that are seen as impulse purchases. Even industrial marketers are supplementing the efforts of their salespeople with telemarketing and direct mail. As such new technologies as interactive videotex emerge, selecting the appropriate communications mix will become even more complicated.

In virtually all cases, personal selling is considerably more expensive than the various types of media and nonmedia advertising. In the 1980s, the typical industrial sales call cost almost $200. By contrast, the estimated cost of 20 minutes spent by a retail salesperson explaining the features of a major appliance to a consumer was about $5; a high-quality direct mail piece cost between $2 and $3 (including the cost of the mailing list); the selective media cost between 10¢ and 15¢ per impression; and the mass media cost as little as 1¢ per impression.

However, personal selling offers two principal compensatory advantages over advertising. First, communications can be precisely tailored to individual customer needs in a two-way process. The audience's attention can be held longer, and more complex messages can be more easily delivered. Second, salespeople provide valuable feedback to headquarters on new sales prospects, product performance, and competitive activity.

Before discussing media selection criteria further, it is important to stress three points. First, all elements of the marketing mix, intentionally or unintentionally, perform a communications function. The price at which a product is offered and the channels through which it is distributed tell the consumer as much about it as the advertising copy. Second, many communications about a product are outside the control of the marketer: word-of-mouth and friends' recommendations are highly valued as information sources, especially in the case of such high-risk purchases as automobiles and microcomputers. Third, only rarely will there be a single best medium to which all communications dollars should be allocated. Selecting a mix of media, however, requires the marketer to define carefully the role of each element and to send a consistent message across all media.

In choosing among communications media, a number of considerations are especially significant. First, it is necessary to ensure that the medium chosen will actually reach the target audience. Second, it is essential that it be appropriate for the message conveyed. Finally, because the relative costs of alternative communications media vary widely, cost differences must be taken into account in establishing an effective communications mix.

Generally, the marketer of a complex technical product (e.g., the optical scanner described earlier) has no choice but to rely principally on personal selling, despite its costs. Personal selling makes certain that the relevant decision makers and influencers are exposed to the message, allows for custom tailoring to the information needs of each customer, and gives the communicator the opportunity to respond to questions and objections and to convey feedback to the manufacturer. Even so, the salesperson's task can often be simplified—and sometimes made possible—by a media advertising campaign that establishes credibility and stimulates a need for information.

In the case of infrequently purchased, high-ticket goods for which the consumer shops around (e.g., major appliances, furniture), the bulk of the target audience's information needs will generally be satisfied in the retail store, through visual inspection, descriptive tickets and price tags, and personal selling. Under these circumstances, the marketer's media efforts will generally emphasize retailer "push," rather than direct consumer "pull." Even in these circumstances, however, media advertising may be used to stimulate primary demand, presell desirable product features, or draw consumers to outlets that carry a particular brand.

At the opposite extreme, marketers of frequently purchased, low-ticket convenience goods rely mostly on impersonal communications through print or electronic media. Package copy and in-store displays may communicate part of the message and reinforce or supplement media communications.

Depending on the targets of the communications program, the marketer may find it more economical to use mass media (intended to reach everybody) or selective media (intended to reach targets with specified characteristics). In making the choice of media, the marketer should consider the probability that a particular message will reach its target. This assessment requires an appreciation of (1) where target consumers expect, on the basis of experience, to obtain information about a particular product category; (2) the appropriateness of particular media for specific communications objectives (e.g., advertising to build awareness); and (3) the degree to which competitive advertising already dominates particular media. An additional critical factor is the comparative economics of reaching the target audience through different means. A marketer of disposable diapers, for example, may pay less per impression (cost per thousand readers or viewers) for a mass medium that reaches both mothers with infants and a lot of other people, or more per impression for a selective medium that reaches a higher concentration of mothers with infants.

The nature of the medium is also relevant to the selection of media. Certain products (e.g., food preparation gadgets), which require visual demonstration as part of their communication programs, are good candidates for television advertising. Other products (e.g., compact disk players) require a good deal more detailed descriptive copy, which makes magazine advertising the best medium. Supermarkets, which seek to communicate reduced prices on specific items for limited periods, find newspapers to be the appropriate vehicle because of their low-cost, mass audiences, large formats, and precisely timed impact on readers.

The Economics of Communications

With few exceptions, the types of communications efforts described here require the expenditure of funds and other scarce resources. Such expenditures can vary from a few hundred dollars for a small retailer who simply wishes to announce its existence, to many millions of dollars for firms with large sales forces or extensive advertising programs. Whatever the size of a firm's communications budget, however, its costs must ultimately be paid by the purchasers of the firm's products or services.

Alternative communications media differ significantly in the timing with which expenditures take place. A new product introduced with a pull advertising campaign, for example, requires a sizable up-front investment in communications that (it is hoped) will be recovered through subsequent purchases. Marketers employing a push strategy, conversely, can often compensate distribution channels for their communications efforts through extra discounts and pay salespeople on a commission basis for a—in effect—pay-as-you-go method of covering communications costs. Partly for this reason, push strategies are often favored by small companies with limited resources.

Whatever the timing of communications costs, they can be justified economically only if they lead to either a higher price (and unit contribution) or a greater unit volume than would occur without them. In either case, the product of incremental unit contribution (if any) multiplied by incremental volume (if any) must exceed the expenditure on communications. The appropriate time frame in which communications costs are to be recovered will, of course, depend largely on the objectives of the communications effort.

Management of Marketing Communications

The complexities of communications policy are such that many producers seek the assistance of outside specialist firms, most often advertising agencies. Though companies usually develop their own advertising objectives and strategy, they often leave the execution to the agency. Some companies use a similar approach to personal selling, hiring independent representatives, who sell their products on a commission basis, along with the products of other, noncompeting companies. Manufacturers with sufficiently broad product lines and the necessary resources generally prefer to have the control and leverage that comes from working through their own sales forces.

Five functions are involved in the management of a sales force. *First,* the appropriate type of salesperson, which varies according to the communications task, must be recruited. The selling skills required to make door-to-door cold calls selling encyclopedias are different from those required to solve information-processing problems and sell computer systems to a large account.

Second, salespeople must be trained, not only in general selling skills but also in the technicalities of their product lines and in how the products they are selling can benefit different types of customers.

Third, salespeople must be deployed; that is, they must be assigned to particular territories, products, or customer accounts. Relationships with an organization's larger customers, which may buy nationwide, rather than in a single sales territory, are frequently handled by national account managers. These managers not only sell but work with customers to solve problems and provide feedback to the vendor's headquarters, which may lead to the development of new or improved products or services.

Fourth, salespeople must be motivated and compensated in a manner consistent with the tasks defined for them. A salesperson whose responsibilities include solving customer problems is likely to be compensated on a straight salary basis. Conversely, a salesperson handling noncomplex products and acting primarily as an order taker is more likely to work on commission.

Fifth, a sales organization must be developed to manage these various tasks and to evaluate the performance of both individual salespeople and the entire sales force. As in the case of advertising, it is essential to set specific, quantifiable objectives against which performance can be evaluated.

Other communications activities, such as advertising, require similar careful management. However, because it involves fewer people, who usually work in a centralized setting, as opposed to the dispersion of the sales force, advertising management tends to be less complex.

Ethical Issues in Communications Policy

For decades, potential ethical problems in marketing communications have received scrutiny from government agencies, skeptical consumer advocates, and other interest groups. Despite the fact that millions of people earn a living as sales professionals, in most cultures around the world there exist negative stereotypes of salespeople as dishonest, manipulative hucksters who have no qualms about tricking customers into spending too much for products they don't really need.

In the United States, advertising has been viewed by many business executives as a healthy way to stimulate market demand, thereby fueling the growth of industries and prosperity of the national economy. However, advertising's critics have charged that marketing communications often violate ethical principles, by overstating the benefits of products, preying on consumer fears and emotions, manipulating the minds of children and socioeconomically deprived citizens, fostering sexist stereotypes that perpetuate prejudice and violence against women, and encouraging people to engage in dangerous habits, such as smoking cigarettes, drinking, and driving fast cars and motorcycles on mountain roads.

Any communication, marketing or otherwise, has the potential to violate ethical principles, if duplicity or manipulation is used to influence others to do things that are not in their best interests. Three guidelines must be followed to ensure that marketing communications honors the principles that are the foundation of ethical behavior:

- The *utilitarian principle:* Do not waste society's resources. For example, a sales program that uses extravagant perks and gifts to entice purchasing agents to spend more than is needed on industrial products violates this principle. So, too, might be an advertising program that encourages poor people to purchase lottery tickets, rather than the necessities that their families require.
- The *rights principle:* Marketers should treat customers and others in the market place in a way that they would want to be treated, if roles were reversed. Truthful advertising conforms to the rights principle. Duplicitous or exaggerated advertising claims do not.
- The *justice principle:* Treat equals equally; care for those less fortunate; and honor diversity. Ensuring that advertising does not take advantage of children or the poor reflects the justice principle. Advertising using sexual fantasy to encourage teens to smoke cigarettes, and high pressure sales pressure tactics against naive consumers, may also violate the justice principle.

The questions below are worth asking during the planning and execution of any marketing communications strategy, to set and maintain appropriate ethical standards:

- Are the claims about benefits true? Have we in our enthusiasm for our products or services gone too far in touting their advantages?
- Have we put incentive systems in place that encourage our sales force to engage in unethical practices toward customers?
- Are there certain customer segments we should avoid, because persuading them to spend scarce resources on our products is not in their best interests or in the interests of their families?
- Have we warned customers adequately about the potential risks of using our products?
- Are we using imagery in our communications that encourages treating women as sex objects?
- Does our communications program implicitly hurt any minority group by presenting negative stereotypes?
- If our communications program is to be implemented in multiple countries and cultures, have we learned enough about the values and mores in each target market to ensure that we are honoring local ethical practices?
- Where the ethics of different cultures are in conflict, are we willing to listen and learn, rather than judge and preach, in an effort to develop the appropriate communications strategy for each market?

The questions above are not all-inclusive, but illustrate the process of self-examination that must be undertaken to reinforce ethical practices in marketing communications.

Conclusion

Communications policy is critical to the success of any marketing program. An excellent product can never be successful in the marketplace if its benefits are not communicated effectively to target consumers. In the 1980s, an increasing diversity of communications approaches was available to marketers to reach end consumers, channel intermediaries, and other constituencies. In the 1990s, the formulation and implementation of communications policy promises to become even more complex and challenging.

A final note—We have presented the steps in the development of a communications policy in a fixed sequence, as if it were always appropriate for the marketer to begin with step 1 and proceed serially through to step 7. In actual practice, however, it is generally more fruitful to consider all seven steps more or less simultaneously, adjusting the various elements in the communications policy as the program is developed. In this way, consistency—the primary requisite of an effective communications program—can be achieved by integrating objectives, target, push or pull strategy, message, intensity, media, and economics.

SUNKIST GROWERS, INC.

In October 1972, executives of Sunkist Growers, Inc. (SGI), were considering their media strategy for the 1973 fresh lemon advertising campaign. They were debating a proposal to place the entire $1 million media budget in a single magazine, *Ladies' Home Journal*. They believed that the proposed media schedule of 30 double-page insertions represented an unprecedented level of advertising concentration in one publication.

Origins and Functions of SGI

SGI was a nonstock, nonprofit cooperative marketing association representing 8,000 citrus growers in California and Arizona. Membership had decreased during the 1960s due to consolidation of holdings, but the percentage of California and Arizona growers who were associated with SGI had held constant. The SGI organization provided processing, marketing, research, and procurement services to its member growers. Commercial packing houses independent of SGI's facilities could be used by member growers, but they had to be licensed by SGI in order for their fruit to carry the Sunkist trademark.

As well as handling sales of fresh grapefruit, oranges, lemons, tangerines, and limes, SGI manufactured over 1,600 citrus juice and peel products, including natural strength and concentrated juices, beverage bases, and purees. During 1971, SGI sales of fresh fruit and processed fruit products totaled $350 million. Of this amount, 52 percent was accounted for by domestic sales of fresh fruit, 26 percent by fresh fruit exports, and 22 percent by sales of processed fruit products.

The Market for Fresh Lemons

As indicated in the following chart, SGI growers were expected to produce 29.1 million cartons of lemons in 1972. SGI production represented 87 percent of the lemons grown in California–Arizona, 80 percent of those grown in the United States, and 23 percent of those grown worldwide.

This case was prepared by John Quelch under the direction of Professor Stephen A. Greyser.

Copyright © 1976 by the President and Fellows of Harvard College.

Harvard Business School case 9-577-051.

Note: SUNKIST and SK are trademarks of Sunkist Growers, Inc.

Lemon Production: 1969–1972
(millions of cartons)

	1969	1970	1971	1972 (est.)
SGI production:	25.2	25.8	26.9	29.1
Fresh fruit—domestic	10.4	10.3	10.3	10.1
Fresh fruit—export	4.4	5.5	5.9	6.7
Processed fruit products	10.4	10.0	10.7	12.3
Other California–Arizona	6.4	3.8	6.0	4.3
Other U.S. states	1.9	3.0	2.4	2.8
Other countries	87.0	90.8	89.7	90.1
Total world production	120.5	123.4	125.0	126.3

Between 1969 and 1972, SGI lemon production increased 15 percent. Executives believed that this growth would continue both in California–Arizona and in Florida, the other major production area in the United States. Production increases outside the United States were also forecast, leading some SGI executives to conclude that continued growth in SGI lemon exports would be hard to sustain. They concluded that fresh lemons would need to be more vigorously marketed in the United States during the 1970s.

Sales of fresh lemons in the United States declined throughout the 1960s, partly in response to the introduction of bottled lemon juices, such as Realemon (marketed by Borden), which many consumers apparently viewed as more convenient than fresh lemons. In addition, an increasing number of products were reaching the consumer with lemon flavor already added—such as instant iced tea with lemon, lemon pie mixes, and lemon soft drink mixes. As a result, an increasing percentage of lemon production was channeled into exports and into the manufacture of processed products. Demand growth in these two areas had enabled SGI to sustain modest increases in fresh lemon prices. However, because the gross margin on the sale of a fresh lemon was seven times the margin obtained if the same lemon were sold for processing, grower returns depended heavily on SGI's ability to maintain domestic demand for fresh lemons.

The prospect of a continuing increase in domestic lemon production raised two additional concerns. Although most of the Florida lemon crop was usually processed into concentrates and other products, SGI executives believed that increased production might encourage Florida growers to expand their fresh lemon sales in the major eastern markets. Florida growers could capitalize on their relative geographical proximity and consequent lower transportation costs to undercut SGI lemon prices in these markets. In addition, production forecasts indicated that increases in fresh lemon supplies in both California–Arizona and Florida would occur primarily during the winter months when fresh lemon consumption was traditionally lower.

SGI graded its fruit by size and quality. The premium grade fruit was stamped with the Sunkist trademark. Increased demand for Sunkist lemons from Japan during the 1960s caused the share of U.S. fresh lemon sales held by the Sunkist brand to decline in favor of SGI's unbranded choice grade of lemons. Some SGI executives believed that this trend enabled competitive lemons produced both in the United States and abroad to make inroads into SGI's U.S. market. The following table indicates the shares of SGI's domestic and export shipments accounted for by Sunkist brand and by unbranded choice lemons in 1961 and 1971:

	Sunkist Brand		Choice (unbranded)	
Shipments	*1961*	*1971*	*1961*	*1971*
Domestic	75%	62%	16%	34%
Export	16	58	74	36

Consumption Trends

Fresh lemon consumption in the United States had steadily declined from four pounds per person in 1950 to two pounds per person in 1971.[1] An even sharper drop in at-home consumption was partly cushioned by the strength of the institutional market. The growing trend toward eating away from home meant that fresh lemon demand by institutions, such as restaurants, was increasing significantly from year to year. By 1971, the institutional market accounted for between 20 percent and 30 percent of SGI domestic fresh lemon shipments.

There was substantial variation in per capita fresh lemon consumption across SGI sales districts. For example, the New York sales district—with 8.5 percent of the U.S. population—accounted for 16.4 percent of SGI domestic fresh lemon shipments in 1971. However, SGI's market share did not vary significantly from one sales district to another.

Data from the 1970 Brand Rating Index (BRI)[2] revealed that 13 percent of U.S. households consumed 74 percent of all fresh lemons. Moreover, as shown in the following chart, 28 percent of households did not use lemons at all:

[1]The U.S. population in 1971 was around 220 million, living in about 70 million households.

[2]The BRI was a market research service that measured household penetration and use of several thousand branded grocery items.

Frequency of Use	Percent of U.S. Households	Percent of Fresh Lemon Consumption	Number of Fresh Lemons Consumed
Heavy: more than one a week	13%	74%	2.2 lemons/week
Moderate: one to four times a month	29	22	1.3 lemons/month
Light: less than once a month	30	4	3.0 lemons/year
Nonuser	28	—	—

Further analysis of the 1970 BRI data indicated that heavy lemon users had few distinctive demographic characteristics. Exhibit 1 presents the percentages of at-home fresh lemon consumption accounted for by nine demographic groups.

A second study, which compared Market Research Corporation of America (MRCA) Menu Census[3] data for 1963 and 1968, showed there had been no significant shift in the demographic profile of lemon users during that five-year period. The study also compared the incidence of fresh lemon and bottled lemon usage for various applications. Results are reported in Exhibit 2. Some executives believed that SGI advertising for fresh lemons had, in fact, assisted the market development of the bottled substitute.

Exhibit 3 presents the results of a further market research study that compared the percentages of heavy, moderate, and light users who used fresh lemons in various ways. Executives concluded that heavy users applied fresh lemons to a wider variety of food, and that broader recognition of the diversity of lemon uses, therefore, should be a major goal of SGI fresh lemon advertising.

In 1971, SGI executives commissioned a nationwide psychographic survey of consumers to define the interests, attitudes, and opinions of heavy lemon users. Questionnaires were mailed to 800 homemakers on the MRCA national panel. Analysis of 500 returned questionnaires yielded three clusters of heavy fresh lemon users. These three groups were characterized as (a) artistic women, (b) women with an above-average interest in food preparation, and (c) experimenters. Exhibit 4 profiles the members of each cluster and summarizes the percentage of survey respondents falling into each group. Each cluster included over one third of the respondents. Some women were included in more than one cluster. Together, women who fell into at least one cluster accounted for 68 percent of all respondents.

[3]The annual MRCA Menu Census was based on menu diaries completed daily for two weeks by 4,000 U.S. households.

SGI executives were interested in whether these clusters might represent future target markets. An advertising campaign directed at the types of consumers included in the clusters might reinforce continued use among those consumers who were already heavy users, and additionally convert some light and moderate users to heavy users by increasing the frequency with which they used fresh lemons.

The same study also provided information on specific consumer attitudes toward lemons. The findings, reported in Exhibit 5, prompted some executives to conclude that light and moderate users had to be more strongly convinced that fresh lemons were convenient to use.

Promotion and Advertising through 1971

SGI executives were concerned about how the retailer viewed fresh lemons. Given the decline in per capita consumption, the trade had become increasingly reluctant to promote fresh lemons at feature prices. The only lemon promotions occurred during the summer, and they emphasized lemon uses for iced tea and lemonade. The trade cited unpredictable prices and unreliable supplies as constraints on their ability to plan fresh lemon promotions. Trade buyers also regarded fresh lemon prices as relatively high, especially when translated into cost per serving to the consumer. Price increases prior to 1971, coupled with slower movement off the shelf, caused the trade to view lemons increasingly as a specialty item. During 1971, however, in a test market in Cleveland, a combination of guaranteed prices, guaranteed supplies, performance contracts, and SGI advertising had prompted many retailers to feature lemons at promotion prices and to set up special displays. SGI executives concluded that the resulting sales increases indicated that promotions, if well organized, could stimulate impulse purchases of fresh lemons by consumers.

The trade's increasing interest in prepackaging of produce also concerned SGI executives. They believed that the visibility of the Sunkist brand name on fresh lemons at the point of purchase was being eroded by the prepackaging of fresh lemons in plastic bags and overwrapped trays. The trade favored prepackaging because it facilitated handling, stock rotation, and customer checkout. Some trade buyers also believed that prepackaging could stimulate larger quantity purchases by consumers. In response to the prepackaging trend, SGI was encouraging the use of plastic bags on which the Sunkist brand name was clearly imprinted.

SGI executives were concerned about the effectiveness of advertising as well as promotion. Traditionally, SGI advertising presented recipes that emphasized the versatility and convenience of the fresh lemon. Advertising was concentrated in women's magazines. Two typical advertisements from the 1971 campaign, promoting unusual uses for fresh lemons, are reproduced as Exhibits 6 and 7. The principal objective of advertising was to increase consumption among all user groups.

In evaluating advertising performance, executives paid particular attention to awareness measures. They believed that the usage patterns for fresh lemons reflected a low public awareness of the product. For example, in a 1966 study conducted in Baltimore and Chicago, homemakers had been asked to name 10 different kinds of fruit. Among a total of 18 fruits mentioned, 13 were named more frequently than the lemon. Only 22 percent of respondents mentioned the lemon.

Awareness measures were regularly gathered in the annual SGI advertising performance tracking study. The study conducted in late 1971 indicated that the 1971 campaign had minimal impact. Only 268 of 6,000 homemakers interviewed stated that they had seen SGI lemon advertising—a lower awareness level than that registered in the 1970 tracking study. Television was credited as the source of awareness of lemon advertising more than any other medium (by 47 percent of those who stated that they had seen SGI lemon advertising), even though SGI had not used television advertising during 1971. Magazines were cited as the source of advertising awareness by 29 percent of the group, followed by newspapers (19 percent) and retailer advertising (8 percent).

Consumer playback[4] of specific points from the 1971 SGI lemon advertising campaign was also disappointing. Although 60 percent of the 268 homemakers aware of SGI lemon advertising could correctly play back some elements of the advertising content, 17 percent only played back points from the 1970 advertising campaign. However, SGI executives were pleased with the responses to another question in the same tracking study: "If you wanted the highest quality lemons, which brand would you buy?" The answer "Sunkist" was given by 60 percent of those interviewed.

Executives partly explained the low awareness and recall results by the fact that SGI lemon advertising had to compete with millions of dollars of other food advertising to gain the consumer's attention. In addition, SGI had to contend with heavy advertising by manufacturers of frozen lemonade and bottled lemon juice. Borden reportedly spent $2.2 million in 1971 advertising and promoting Realemon bottled juice, with advertising concentrated in print media. And the Florida-based Minute Maid cooperative spent about $425,000 in 1971 on print advertising for its processed lemonade products.

Information on SGI fresh lemon advertising budgets from 1967 to 1972 appears in Exhibit 8. SGI media expenditures in the United States had increased modestly in real terms during this period. The SGI fresh lemon media budget in

---

[4]Playback measured the strength and accuracy of a consumer's recall of an advertising message.

the United States depended on the size of the crop, the per carton assessment for advertising negotiated between SGI and its growers, and the percentage of funds allocated to domestic advertising as opposed to development of export markets.

The 1972 Lemon Advertising Campaign

In view of the apparently weak impact of the 1971 campaign, SGI executives decided to test the effectiveness of greater advertising intensity in 1972. Hence, they pressed for and obtained an increase in the per carton advertising assessment from 16¢ to 17¢. The creative approach used in the 1971 campaign was continued.

The 1972 SGI fresh lemon advertising program included a national base campaign and a development campaign in three test markets. The national base campaign consisted of one advertisement every month from January to October in each of two women's magazines, *Ladies' Home Journal* (a monthly magazine covering fashion and homemaking for the younger woman), and *Family Circle* (a monthly magazine dealing with home management and family care). The development campaign provided advertising support at four times the weight of the national campaign over a four-month period in the Boston, Dallas, and Houston markets. In addition to the national base campaign, full-page advertisements were placed each month between March and June in relevant regional editions of five additional women's magazines (*American Home, Good Housekeeping, McCall's, Redbook,* and *Woman's Day*). Six advertisements were also placed in Sunday newspaper supplements in each market. After the end of June, advertising intensity in the development markets reverted to the national base campaign.

To evaluate the success of the development campaign, three control markets—Pittsburgh, Oklahoma City, and Memphis—with similar demographic and lemon usage profiles to the three development markets, were selected for comparative purposes. Consumers in the control markets were exposed only to the national base campaign.

During the six-month period from March to August, fresh lemon shipments to the development markets rose an average of 6 percent above the expected levels that executives had set on the basis of shipments during the previous seven years. Fresh lemon sales in the development markets during the six-month period were also 5 percent higher than during the immediate pretest period (January–February). These increases were viewed positively by SGI executives, given that sales in the control markets dropped 3 percent below expected levels between March and August.

Some SGI executives believed that the development campaign had more impact on increasing the frequency of use among existing users than on increasing the total number

of users. From the data presented in Exhibit 9, they concluded that frequency of use did not change in the control markets but did increase in the development markets. In addition, there was evidence of reduced use of bottled juice in both groups of markets, but only for the duration of the campaign.

Executives were also interested in comparing awareness and recall in the development and control markets. Measurements of unaided awareness, total awareness, and advertising recall in both control and development markets between March and August are presented in Exhibit 10. SGI executives concluded that the increased intensity of the development campaign did not generate the substantially increased awareness levels that they had hoped for. Both unaided awareness and total awareness hardly changed during the tracking period. As the development campaign progressed, total awareness improved; but, by the end of the 20th tracking week, one month after the end of the campaign, awareness had declined to its precampaign level of 7 percent. A similar pattern was evident for correct advertising recall, which was only slightly higher in the development markets compared to the control markets. Like awareness, correct recall increased during the development campaign, but decreased when it ended.

Some executives concluded from the 1972 tracking study that the weight of the national advertising campaign was too light to produce significant results. Furthermore, they believed that the shifts in awareness, attitudes, and sales in the development markets could have been greater had the impact of increased advertising intensity not been diffused by the number of print vehicles used in the campaign. They argued that concentration of fresh lemon advertising against a more limited audience would achieve a greater impact. The specific target audience might, they thought, be defined either on a regional basis, or as a demographic segment, or as the audience of a specific media vehicle.

The 1973 Lemon Advertising Campaign

After assessing the results of the 1972 tracking study, SGI executives set the following parameters for the 1973 campaign:

1. The campaign should present a series of ideas showing how fresh lemons can quickly and easily turn ordinary dishes into something unusual and creative.

2. The campaign should seek to increase demand for fresh lemons nationwide.

3. To achieve the necessary advertising weight with the available budget, the fresh lemon program should be concentrated against a limited media audience.

4. To ensure that fresh lemon advertising attracts consumer attention, the campaign should use multiple messages in a given medium to build frequency.

5. The campaign should be run on a year-round basis to ensure continuity of demand for the constantly available supply of fresh lemons.

SGI executives decided to concentrate advertising in a single media vehicle as the most appropriate way to obtain an increased weight of advertising against a limited target audience. Several SGI executives had concluded from the 1972 advertising program that developing the country several markets at a time would take too long to achieve. A standard national campaign had two further advantages. First, it meant that each sales district had an equal opportunity to benefit from advertising expenditures. Second, it facilitated a balanced distribution of fresh lemons nationwide.

Accordingly, SGI executives decided that they would place the entire 1973 media advertising budget in a single vehicle. They hoped, as a result, to be the dominant advertiser in the selected vehicle. Since magazines had been the traditional medium used by SGI for its fresh lemon advertising, it was decided that the single vehicle would be selected from a list of 25 magazines. The media budget available for fresh lemon advertising in 1973 was set at $1 million, too small to permit any meaningful television campaign.

Twelve new advertisements were created for the 1973 campaign. As in previous years, they presented a series of recipes emphasizing the versatility and convenience of fresh lemons. Recipes were selected on the basis of both how easily they could be prepared and how much fresh lemon juice or rind they required. Each of the new advertisements presented four or five complementary recipes involving fresh lemons within a particular food category, such as soups or salads; previous advertisements had each included only a single recipe. In addition, each new advertisement was the size of a double-page spread and consisted of two nearly identical photographs. The photograph on the left-hand page showed a group of relatively mundane dishes, while the right-hand page showed the same dishes dramatically enhanced by the use of fresh lemons. Two examples of advertisements created for the 1973 campaign are presented as Exhibits 11 and 12.

SGI executives noted that the 1971 psychographic study had gathered magazine readership information on members of each of the three psychographic clusters of fresh lemon users. The results of this portion of that study are presented in Exhibit 13. In addition, SGI executives believed that two criteria, reflecting the basic strategy of the campaign, had to be applied to the list of magazines under consideration. First, they decided that the chosen magazine had to reach at least 20 percent of women 18 years or older with a single issue. Second, magazines were eliminated if their advertising costs precluded a schedule of at least 18 double-page spreads within the $1 million budget. Based on these criteria, the list of contenders was narrowed to *Ladies' Home Journal, Better Homes and Gardens,* and *McCall's.*

The managements of these three magazines were asked to submit written proposals covering such issues as media discounts, promotional support, use of kitchens and photographic staff in the creation of advertising copy, and coordination of advertising placement with editorial recipe information. All three magazines submitted what executives considered equally acceptable proposals. In view of the size of the proposed media purchase, the level of assistance offered did not surprise SGI executives. However, the magazines differed somewhat in the media discounts that they were prepared to offer. The *Ladies' Home Journal* offered the largest discount in both absolute and relative terms—$1.7 million worth of undiscounted advertising space for $1.0 million. This sum would purchase 30 double-page color spreads (24 in regular national editions, and 6 in Prime Show Case editions distributed in zip code areas with above-average income levels) over a 12-month period. The proposed insertion schedule is presented in Exhibit 14.

Overall, the 30 insertions would achieve 355 million impressions on women aged 18 years or older. In any one month, the *Ladies' Home Journal* was believed to reach 20.7 percent of these women. And when the 12-issue campaign reach was considered, almost half of all adult women would see at least one issue carrying SGI fresh lemon advertising:

Twelve-Issue Campaign Reach—*Ladies' Home Journal*

Nine or more issues seen by	12.3% of women 18 years or older
Six or more	20.1
Three or more	30.8
At least one	45.6

Before committing to purchasing the *Ladies' Home Journal* package, SGI executives wished to evaluate the process by which this magazine had emerged as the leading prospect from among the 25 original contenders. In addition, they decided to once again review their objectives and program for the 1973 fresh lemon advertising campaign.

EXHIBIT 1 Demographic Characteristics of Fresh Lemon Users

Household Characteristics	Percent of U.S. Households	Percent of U.S. Fresh Lemon At-Home Consumption
Homemaker 35–49	32%	35%
Live in 1 million-or-over metro area	35	40
Live in central city of metro area	30	33
Have children 12–17 years old	25	29
College-educated homemaker	20	22
Household income $15,000 or over	15	18
Black households	9	16
Western region	17	19
Southern region	31	40

NOTE: To be read, for example: While 32% of U.S. households included homemakers aged 35–49, these households accounted for 35% of fresh lemon at-home consumption.
SOURCE: Brand Rating Index 1970.

EXHIBIT 2 Incidence of Fresh Lemon and Bottled Lemon Usage, 1963 and 1968

	Fresh		Bottled	
	1963	1968	1963	1968
Total usage	22%	19%	9%	12%

	Percent of Users		Percent of Users	
	1963	1968	1963	1968
Hot tea	27%	21%	16%	14%
Cold tea	26	33	14	21
On fish	17	16	10	15
Salad	12	11	11	9
Pie	16	11	10	7
Lemonade	17	9	5	6
Salad dressing	6	8	6	12
Sauces	7	8	8	9
Cakes/cookies	4	5	4	4
On vegetables	5	4	4	3
In juice	3	3	3	3
In alcoholic drinks	3	3	4	2
On meat	4	3	3	3
On fruit	5	3	4	2
Eaten as is	—	3	—	3
Other	13	10	11	10

NOTE: To be read, for example: Twenty-two % of respondents to the 1963 survey used fresh lemons at least once during the two-week reporting period. Of these respondents, 27% reported using fresh lemons in hot tea during the reporting period.
SOURCE: MRCA Menu Census.

EXHIBIT 3   **Incidence of Fresh Lemon Use by Type of User**

Ways Used	Heavy Users	Moderate Users	Light Users
In tea/drinks	91%	78%	80%
On fish	73	75	58
Cooking and baking	74	68	59
Lemonade	47	37	40
In salad dressing	48	21	12
On vegetables	44	24	11

NOTE: To be read, for example: Ninety-one % of heavy users used fresh lemons in tea/drinks.

Heavy users are defined more broadly in this study than in BRI reports. Whereas BRI limits heavy users to those using lemons *more* than once a week, this study includes once-a-week users in the heavy user group. BRI reports heavy users as 13% of respondents. Here, and in Exhibits 4 and 5, inclusion of once-a-week users increases the percentage of heavy users to 33%.

SOURCE: Foote, Cone & Belding Research Department.

EXHIBIT 4   **Profiles of Three Psychographic Clusters**

1. Artistic Women

Women in this cluster believe that they are more creative and artistic than others. They are interested in cultural events and activities and are apt to appreciate a trip to the art gallery or a night at the ballet. They are likely to have attended college and to be married to an executive. Age or income have little bearing on membership in this group.

2. Women with Above-Average Interest in Food Preparation

These women enjoy taking a lot of time and trouble in preparing food. They would rather bake from scratch than use a mix. Their sense of pride and feeling of accomplishment is rooted in the way the finished dish is prepared. They tend to be older than the members of the other two groups and to live in households with lower incomes.

3. Experimenters

These women are openly receptive to new, unique, or untested activities. It is immaterial whether the activity is viewed as a creative endeavor. The central benefit for these women is the experience of doing things a different way. They enjoy experimenting with new sauces for meat and with a wide variety of spices. They consider themselves adventurous eaters, willing to try the unusual dish. As a group, they are somewhat younger than the other women.

Cluster	Percent of Responding Homemakers	Percent of Cluster Members Classified as Heavy Users of Fresh Lemons
Artistic	33%	45%
Food preparation	40	45
Experimenters	42	44
Three clusters combined	68%	47%

SOURCE: Foote, Cone & Belding Research Department.

EXHIBIT 5   **Attitudes about Fresh Lemons among Heavy and Moderate Users**

	Percentage of All Respondents Agreeing	Percentage Agreeing among Those Who Are:	
		Heavy Users	Moderate Users
Total Sample	(100.0%)	(47.0%)	(23.0%)
Attitude Statement			
Fresh lemons add zest to food	50.4%	58.7%	43.3%
Fresh lemons bring out the flavor in food	52.4	60.0	41.7
Fresh lemons are pleasant	51.2	66.0	44.0
Fresh lemons have a nice shape and texture	54.8	61.1	43.6
Fresh lemons are attractive and decorative	50.0	61.5	41.0
Lemons are good for dieting	29.8	36.6	24.8
Fresh lemons smell clean	62.8	70.1	54.6
Many people do not know how to use fresh lemons	28.2	34.9	19.9
Fresh lemons are one of the best deodorizers around	30.0	41.0	22.0
You can use all of a fresh lemon	44.8	53.6	33.5
Fresh lemons are one of the best skin care products available	18.2	24.9	11.5
If your mother used fresh lemons, you will, too	23.4	30.7	17.9
Fresh lemon juice keeps you regular	18.2	25.4	10.7
Fresh lemons are refreshing	49.6	59.5	41.5
The most important use for fresh lemons is as a seasoning	21.0	22.3	20.0
Some lemons have too many seeds	24.2	27.4	21.8
Fresh lemons are the only things to use for making drinks	18.0	20.0	16.2
Fresh lemons are convenient to use	35.2	51.5	25.2
Fresh lemons are used only at certain times of the year	19.6	23.6	17.5
Fresh lemons are good for making salad dressing	42.4	51.3	34.1
I frequently cook with lemon rind	18.8	21.9	15.8
You should always have fresh lemons on hand	41.4	58.1	21.7

NOTE: To be read, for example: Among the 47.0% of survey respondents who were heavy users, 58.7% agreed that fresh lemons add zest to food.
SOURCE: Foote, Cone & Belding Research Department.

EXHIBIT 6
1971 print advertisement

Don Heller's friends thought he must be kidding when he volunteered to make hollandaise sauce. But he showed them. With a lemon trick and a blender.

A foolproof hollandaise you can make in five minutes. Thanks to fresh lemons. And your blender.

Hollandaise is a classic sauce. And for good reason. It tastes divine. Looks beautiful. And turns ordinary things like vegetables into the hit of the meal.

The trouble is, it's hard to make.

But not with this recipe. Here's a hollandaise that's simple, quick, and utterly foolproof. The blender and fresh lemons are the secret.

Fresh Sunkist lemons are the secret behind so many of the elegant touches that make great cooking. No wonder good cooks couldn't cook without them.

Don's Blender Hollandaise
(about 1 cup)

½ cup butter or margarine (1 stick)   4 egg yolks
2 to 3 tablespoons fresh squeezed lemon juice
¼ teaspoon salt   dash of pepper

Heat butter or margarine until bubbly. Meanwhile, place egg yolks, fresh lemon juice, salt and pepper in electric blender. Turn blender on and off quickly. Then turn to high speed and slowly add bubbly butter in a very thin but steady stream. Turn off blender and serve immediately over broccoli, asparagus, or grilled tomatoes. On fish. Or to make Eggs Benedict.

Sunkist.

In every great cook's bag of tricks, you find the fresh lemon.

EXHIBIT 7
1971 print advertisement

In every great cook's bag of tricks, you find the fresh lemon:

Sandy's Lemon-Mustard Sauce for Seafood. The trick is using fresh Sunkist lemon to turn canned soup into a great sauce.

This sauce is just as great on any fish casserole—tuna, mackerel, salmon. It makes frozen shrimp, fish cakes, even vegetables taste great too.

That's what fresh lemon does for you. It has the good looks and good taste to make ordinary food something special.

Lemon-Mustard Seafood Sauce.
In a saucepan, put
1 can undiluted cream of celery
* soup (or cream of mushroom)
¼ cup mayonnaise
2 teaspoons grated lemon peel
2 tablespoons fresh lemon juice
1 teaspoon prepared mustard
Stir it all together over medium heat until it's smooth and bubbly. What you don't use, cover and refrigerate.

Like some more good lemon tricks? Write to: Sunkist Growers, Inc. S-72-3, Box 7888, Van Nuys, California 91409. **Sunkist.**

EXHIBIT 8   SGI Fresh Lemon Advertising Budgets: 1967–1972

	1967	1968	1969	1970	1971	1972 (est).
Total domestic and international fresh lemon shipments (thousand cartons)	16,135	15,849	14,810	15,813	16,169	16,700
Assessment per carton	12¢	16¢	16¢	16¢	16¢	17¢
Total budget for U.S. and international fresh lemon advertising and promotion ($000)	$1,936	$2,536	$2,370	$2,530	$2,587	$2,839
Funds allocated for fresh lemon advertising in United States ($000)[a]	$746	$638	$738	$1,034	$818	$1,137
U.S. fresh lemon advertising share of total budget	39%	25%	31%	41%	32%	40%
Value of advertising dollar in 1967 dollars*[b]	$1.000	$.950	$.902	$.857	$.814	$.773
Value of U.S. fresh lemon advertising budget in 1967 dollars ($000)	$746	$606	$666	$886	$666	$879

[a]About 20% of the U.S. fresh lemon advertising budget was typically spent on administration and media production costs. In 1972, $910,000 was spent on *media advertising purchases.*

[b]Adjustments assume an annual inflation rate of 5%, incorporating annual cost inflation of 3.5% plus annual population growth of 1.5%.

SOURCE: Company records.

$$\frac{1}{1.137} = \frac{x}{100}$$

Percent   BUDGET

magazine   88% $1,000,000

BULK MAIL   8%   90,960

Recipes   4%   46,040

EXHIBIT 9   Fresh Lemon Usage: 1972 Control and Development Markets

	Weeks after Advertising Start							
	0	*1–4*	*5–8*	*9–12*	*13–16*	*17–20*	*21–24*	*25–28*
Interviewing dates	1/31 – 2/26	2/28 – 3/25	3/27 – 4/22	4/24 – 5/20	5/22 – 6/17	6/19 – 7/15	7/17 – 8/12	8/14 – 9/8
Control Markets	N=(300)	N=(300)	N=(300)	N=(300)	N=(300)	N=(300)	N=(300)	N=(299)
Use fresh lemon in home	74%	76%	80%	71%	66%	78%	80%	71%
Do not use fresh lemon in home	26	24	20	29	34	22	20	29
Use bottled lemon juice in home	65	60	64	55	57	60	65	63
Frequency of Use								
Almost every day	9%	12%	9%	13%	16%	20%	15%	14%
A few times a week	16	16	18	18	14	17	18	12
About once a week	9	9	9	12	8	9	10	11
Two or three times a month	15	13	14	8	9	14	12	10
About once a month	6	9	11	8	8	10	10	11
Less often	19	16	19	12	11	8	14	13

	Weeks after Advertising Start							
	0	*1–4*	*5–8*	*9–12*	*13–16*	*17–20*	*21–24*	*25–28*
Interviewing dates	1/31 – 2/26	2/28 – 3/25	3/27 – 4/22	4/24 – 5/20	5/22 – 6/17	6/19 – 7/15	7/17 – 8/12	8/14 – 9/8
Development Markets	N=(401)	N=(400)	N=(400)	N=(400)	N=(400)	N=(400)	N=(400)	N=(395)
Use fresh lemon in home	70%	71%	70%	71%	73%	74%	78%	74%
Do not use fresh lemon in home	30	29	30	29	27	26	22	26
Use bottled lemon juice in home	58	58	57	52	58	54	59	59
Frequency of Use								
Almost every day	14%	15%	11%	13%	15%	17%	16%	16%
A few times a week	18	18	20	18	19	21	20	18
About once a week	12	10	11	10	11	10	13	8
Two or three times a month	10	12	12	12	12	13	15	15
About once a month	7	6	6	6	5	6	7	8
Less often	9	10	9	12	10	7	8	10

SOURCE: 1972 SGI advertising tracking study.

EXHIBIT 10   Unaided Awareness, Total Awareness, and Advertising Recall Results: 1972 Control and Development Markets

Weeks after Advertising Campaign Start	19971 Control	Unaided Awareness[a]		Total Awareness[b]		Correct Advertising Recall[c]	
		1972 Control	1972 Development	1972 Control	1972 Development	1972 Control	1972 Development
0	4%	6%	5%	8%	7%	4%	3%
4	4	5	5	5	10	3	8
8	2	5	6	9	8	5	6
12	1	5	7	9	14	6	9
16	3	4	11	9	17	6	13
20	2	3	8	9	11	7	8
24	1	5	7	7	11	5	7
28	2	4	5	6	9	4	5

[a]The percentage of respondents who mentioned Sunkist lemon advertising when asked: "What advertisements have you seen lately?"
[b]The percentage of respondents with unaided awareness plus those with aided awareness who mentioned Sunkist lemon advertising when asked: "What advertisements for fruit have you seen lately?"
[c]The percentage of respondents who could correctly recall elements of the content of Sunkist's fresh lemon advertising campaign when asked to do so.
SOURCE: 1972 SGI advertising tracking study.

EXHIBIT 11

1972–73 print advertisement

EXHIBIT 12

1972–73 print advertisement

EXHIBIT 13 Index of Magazine Readership by Psychographic Cluster and Cost per Thousand Delivered Audience

Magazine	Artistic	Above-average Interest in Food Preparation	Like to Experiment	Cost per Thousand Delivered Audience
Harper's Bazaar	164	159	132	$14.72
Gourmet	147	145	169	20.80
Saturday Review	171	143	148	14.18
Mademoiselle	200	125	83	13.68
Vogue	140	156	129	14.59
Cosmopolitan	138	119	147	12.01
Glamour	173	134	102	12.21
New Yorker	191	141	178	14.68
Newsweek	139	194	133	9.82
U.S. News & World Report	111	98	108	11.20
Time	129	86	116	9.43
McCall's	113	110	105	13.36
Better Homes & Gardens	104	113	103	9.49
American Home	121	107	101	14.24
Sunset	113	120	96	21.54
Good Housekeeping	92	110	98	14.35
Redbook	90	84	118	11.49
Woman's Day	104	102	102	14.50
Look	102	100	103	15.60
National Geographic	115	89	103	24.89
Family Circle	94	100	101	13.30
Ladies' Home Journal	105	111	95	10.14
Reader's Digest	87	97	98	9.50
Life	125	88	91	17.10

NOTE: The higher the index number in each column, the greater the percentage of respondents who regularly read the magazine whose psychographic profiles matched those of the designated cluster.

SOURCE: Foote, Cone & Belding Research Department.

EXHIBIT 14   *Ladies' Home Journal* **Proposed Insertion Schedule for the 1973 Fresh Lemon Advertising Campaign**

	January	*February*	*March*	*April*	*May*	*June*
National issue	Sauces Desserts Hamburger	Condiments Vegetables	Fish Canned drinks	Salads	Hamburger Summer drinks Vegetables Convenience	Salads Condiments
Zip issue		Soup	Sauces	Desserts		Fish

	July	*August*	*September*	*October*	*November*	*December*
National issue	Summer drinks Fruit	Convenience	Soup Hamburger	Fish	Desserts Canned drinks	Soup Sauces
Zip issue	Hamburger					Vegetables

SOURCE: Company records.

REEBOK INTERNATIONAL LTD.

In June 1988 executives of Reebok International, Ltd.'s Reebok Footwear Division (RFD) met to review the company's U.S. marketing communications program for the second half of the year. In addition to category advertising to promote specific product lines, such as aerobic shoes, Reebok's vice president of advertising intended to pursue three multiproduct umbrella campaigns: television advertising during the 1988 Summer Olympics; television and print advertising with the tag line "Reeboks let U.B.U."; and print advertising to introduce Reebok's new performance feature, the Energy Return System.

In addition, Reebok executives had to review their marketing communications plan for the Human Rights Now! world concert tour. On March 29 Joe LaBonté, Reebok's president and chief operating officer, had announced that Reebok was joining Amnesty International (AI) in sponsoring this tour, which would celebrate the 40th anniversary of the United Nations' Universal Declaration of Human Rights. However, debate continued within Reebok about the merits of this sponsorship, about how aggressively Reebok should publicize its association with the tour, and about how the proposed communications program for the tour related to RFD's overall marketing communications plan.

Company Background and Strategy

Reebok's antecedent, J. W. Foster and Sons, was founded in England in 1895 as a manufacturer of custom track shoes that were marketed by mail worldwide. The company was renamed Reebok in 1958. In 1979 Paul Fireman bought the North American distribution rights. In 1984, he and his backers, principally Pentland Industries plc, bought the parent company.

Fireman's first imports into the United States were three styles of hand-stitched, high-priced running shoes. In 1982, convinced that interest in running would plateau and aerobics would become the next fitness craze, Fireman intro-

This case was prepared by Tammy Bunn Hiller under the supervision of Professor John A. Quelch.

Copyright © 1988 by the President and Fellows of Harvard College. Harvard Business School case 9-589-027.

duced the first aerobic/dance shoe, the Reebok Freestyle. The shoe was unique. It was made of garment leather. It was soft, supple, wrinkled at the toe, and comfortable to wear from day one. It was also more attractive than competitors' athletic shoes. Furthermore, it was the first athletic shoe specifically targeted at women.

With the introduction of aerobic shoes, Reebok began a period of phenomenal growth. Between 1982 and 1987, net sales grew from $3.5 million to $1.4 billion, and net income grew from $200,000 to $165 million. Reebok ranked first among major U.S. companies in sales growth, earnings growth, and return on equity for the years 1983 through 1987. Fireman's goal was for Reebok to become a $2 billion multinational by 1990.

Reebok's growth was accomplished through broadening of existing product lines, expansion into additional product categories, and acquisitions. Exhibit 1 presents a chronology of Reebok's new product line introductions and acquisitions. The company had five operating units: Reebok North America (which included RFD and the Reebok Apparel Division), Reebok International, Rockport, Avia, and Ellesse.

In 1987 RFD sold approximately 42.17 million pairs of shoes to its U.S. retailers. The shoes were sold to consumers for an average price of $43. RFD accounted for approximately 71 percent and 88 percent of Reebok's 1987 sales and operating profit, respectively. The division's sales and estimated operating income for 1983 through 1987 are shown in Table A.

In the 1980s RFD diversified its product offerings dramatically. In 1979 the division sold three shoes. In 1988 it sold more than 300 different shoes in 10 product categories. Aerobic shoes accounted for 56 percent of the division's sales in 1984. In 1987, they constituted only 29 percent.

The division sold its shoes direct to retailers through 17 independent sales organizations. This sales force sold only Reebok brand products and was paid on a commission basis. A staff of field service and promotion representatives, employed by Reebok, supported the sales force by traveling throughout the United States teaching retailers and consumers about the features and benefits of the division's shoes. RFD followed a limited distribution strategy. Its shoes were sold only through specialty athletic retailers,

sporting goods stores, and department stores. They were not sold in low-margin mass merchandiser or discount stores.

RFD, like other major athletic shoe companies, contracted out all of its manufacturing. The shoes were made in eight countries. Most of them, 71 percent in 1987, were produced in South Korea. The division's large-volume needs, combined with labor disruptions in South Korea, caused supply problems in 1987. In late 1987, RFD added sourcing capacity in Taiwan, China, Thailand, the Philippines, and Indonesia. It also contracted to take all of the production of H.S. Corporation, a large South Korean footwear manufacturer that produced approximately 30 million pairs of shoes annually.

The Athletic Footwear Industry

Growth of the Industry. Between 1981 and 1987, the U.S. athletic footwear market more than doubled in size. Wholesale sales of branded athletic footwear neared $3.1 billion in 1987. Nonbranded footwear added another $0.4 billion. Reebok held a 32.2 percent share of branded athletic footwear in 1987, up from 3.3 percent in 1984.

The industry's dynamic growth began in the early 1980s with the running craze. The running shoe was a new product that did not replace existing lines. Compared with the sneakers of the 1970s, it was made of different materials, was more performance oriented, and was more expensive. It also became a fashion item as Americans embraced more casual, health-conscious lifestyles.

In 1983 running shoe sales declined dramatically as Americans turned to other forms of exercise. New categories, such as aerobic and fitness shoes, however, continued to drive industry growth. The success of the aerobic shoe prompted many companies to develop women's shoes for traditionally male-dominated categories, such as basketball. By 1987, walking shoes, targeted largely at older females, were the fastest-growing line. Industry experts expected 8–12 percent growth in the U.S. athletic footwear market in 1988.

In 1987 Reebok also held a 4.4 percent share of the $4.5 billion foreign-branded athletic shoe market. Development of foreign markets lagged three or four years behind that of

TABLE A RFD Sales and Estimated Operating Income ($ millions)

	1983	1984	1985	1986	1987
Net sales	$12.0	$64.0	$299.0	$841.0	$991.0
Cost of sales	6.8	37.9	171.0	475.0	562.0
Gross margin	5.2	26.1	128.0	366.0	429.0
SG&A expense	4.0	14.0	52.0	131.0	169.0
Operating income	1.2	12.1	76.0	235.0	260.0

the U.S. market. In 1987 the aerobics boom was just taking off in Europe, and the women's athletic shoe market was largely untapped.

The Competition.   Nike, in second place, had an 18.6 percent market share, down from 31.3 percent in 1984. Founded in 1964, Nike rose to prominence in the late 1970s thanks to high-tech innovations in running shoes. In 1984, however, Nike ignored the aerobics trend, wrongly counting on its running shoes to sustain company growth. Its warehouses became overstocked with running-shoe inventory, which Nike had to sell off through discount stores. This action tarnished Nike's reputation with the trade. From 1983 to 1985, its sales rose by only 9 percent. However, in 1985, the Air Jordan basketball shoe, named for Michael Jordan of the Chicago Bulls, generated sales of $100 million. In 1986 sales fell as quickly as they had risen when Jordan broke his foot early in the NBA season. That year Nike lost its number-one U.S. market share position to Reebok.

In 1987 Nike closed excess plant capacity, slashed overhead, and spent $23 million to promote its new Air line with a "Revolution in motion" advertising campaign that featured the Beatles' original recording of "Revolution." It also took advantage of Reebok's supply problems to revitalize its dealer relations.

Nike's expressed goal was to recapture the number-one spot from Reebok. For 1988, according to *Advertising Age* magazine, Nike was stepping up advertising spending by 36 percent to $34 million. Ten million dollars would be spent on network television for its new "Just do it" campaign, which would break in mid-August. In February 1988, Nike introduced a fashion-oriented nonathletic brand for women in an attempt to penetrate a market in which it was historically weak. The shoes, called IE, did not carry the Nike name.

Converse held an 8.1 percent share of the U.S. market in 1987, down from 11.2 percent in 1984. The Converse name was closely identified with canvas athletic shoes for children and teens, particularly for basketball. In 1988, the company introduced the Evolo line of leather athletic shoes featuring upscale Italian styling and aimed at a more fashion-conscious customer.

Adidas, the world's largest athletic shoe company, had a 5.7 percent U.S. share and a 25 percent world share in 1987. Headquartered in West Germany, Adidas lost $30 million on its U.S. sales. Its 1988 U.S. advertising budget was estimated at only $3 million.

Avia, owned by Reebok, was the fifth-largest competitor in the U.S. branded athletic shoe market. Avia emphasized design technology and targeted active athletic participants who valued performance and functionality over other product features. With 1987 sales of $157 million, its share was 4.9 percent, up from 0.4 percent in 1984. Avia's 1988 advertising budget of $20 million was double 1987 expenditures.

Industry experts grouped Avia with LA Gear (2.3 percent share) and Asics Tiger (2.2 percent share) as small companies with innovative products and the potential to become significant players in the market. Twenty-five other companies competed in the branded athletic shoe market. Each had found a niche for itself, but none had been able to expand beyond it.

Competition remained keen in 1988. First, higher leather costs, increased labor rates, and a weakened dollar had increased the cost of Far East production by 10 percent in 1987. Further cost hikes, which would put pressure on the margins of all competitors, were expected in 1988. Second, to reduce inventory markdowns, retailers were narrowing their selections to only four or five brands and one or two lines of a few other brands. Third, athletic shoe product life cycles appeared to be shortening. By 1988, the life of a new model averaged only about nine months.

Consumer Attitudes and Behavior

Paul Fireman credited Reebok's success to an ability to stay close to the consumer. "Consumer preferences are constantly changing," he contended, "and future progress is linked to our skill in understanding the messages sent from the marketplace so we can deliver the right products."

Industry experts segmented athletic shoe consumers into serious athletes, weekend warriors, who used their shoes for sports but were not zealous athletes, and casual wearers, who used athletic shoes only for streetwear. The "pyramid-of-influence" model, traditionally used in marketing athletic shoes, posited that the serious athlete was a very small segment of the market but an important opinion leader for both weekend warriors and casual wearers. Casual wearers accounted for 80 percent of athletic shoe purchases, wanted both style and comfort, and were thought to select shoes based on what they saw serious athletes wearing.

The pyramid model led athletic shoe marketers to emphasize technological and performance superiority to appeal to serious athletes. New shoes were first introduced in exclusive sports shops and gradually expanded into wider distribution.

The validity of the pyramid-of-influence model was questioned by some Reebok executives, who believed that advertising directed at the serious athlete did not reach many consumers. They pointed to the results of a June 1986 survey that indicated that friends and relatives, not athletes, were the most important influence in athletic shoe users' brand decisions. Exhibit 2 shows the sources of information that athletic shoe purchasers used to decide which brand to buy. In addition, in a world where new athletic shoe styles could be knocked off in three months, the executives questioned the appropriateness of new product introductions not directed at the mass market.

In the 1986 survey, consumers were asked how important various attributes were when deciding which athletic shoes to buy. Fifty-eight percent of respondents rated comfort extremely important, followed by support/stability (43 percent), design (36 percent), quality (35 percent), price (30 percent), fashion (20 percent), and leadership (12 percent).

An October 1987 attitude and usage study indicated that 95 percent of athletic shoe owners were aware of Reebok shoes, up from 57 percent two years before. Ninety-eight percent of all teens, a segment that purchased more than three pairs of athletic shoes per year, were aware of Reebok brand. Moreover, unaided awareness of Reebok had doubled over the past two years, whereas that of Nike had dropped. Fifty-three percent of teenagers surveyed considered Reebok the "in" shoe, compared with 38 percent for Nike. Reebok was also rated superior to its major competitors in both quality and comfort.

The brand had high penetration. Fifty-two percent of all people surveyed and 70 percent of the teens surveyed had owned Reebok shoes. Two years before, only 18 percent of people surveyed had ever owned Reebok shoes. Reebok's current ownership was 45 percent of those surveyed, higher than for any other brand. In addition, Reebok shoes were currently worn in 61 percent of the households in which athletic shoes were purchased in 1987. The owners claimed to be loyal as well. Two out of three of those who last purchased Reebok intended to make Reebok their next purchase, a repurchase rate higher than that for any competing brand. Finally, Reebok owners were significantly more likely to buy athletic shoes at regular price than were nonowners.

The results of the attitude and usage study were positive. But a series of focus group interviews in October 1987 uncovered some disturbing qualitative information.[1] In past focus groups, when participants were asked to describe Reebok shoes, the most commonly used adjectives were *innovative, vivid, adventurous, experimental, special, vibrant,* and *new.* The October 1987 focus group members, however, used such words as *comfortable, youthful, energy, fun, diverse, clean, leader, a standard,* and *middle class.* Teens said they were still buying Reeboks, but the way they talked about them had changed. They used to brag about their Reeboks. Now some teens apologized for them. At the same time, participants insisted that Reebok was not a badge brand. In other words, wearing Reeboks did not brand one as a jock or a yuppie or any other "type." "My Reeboks" meant something different to each person.

Sharon Cohen, vice president of advertising and public relations for Reebok North America since 1984, concluded: "When Reebok was new, just being discovered, we

had a cult-like following. We were fresh and exciting and had brought new dimensions to the athletic shoe industry — style and comfort. Today we are a mass-appeal shoe, and this requires new strategic thinking. Now that everyone is wearing Reeboks, our job and the job of our advertising is to keep our brand exciting."

Marketing Communications

Before 1987. According to Cohen, Paul Fireman "always started with advertising. If he had only $100, he'd spend it on advertising." In the early years of the company, he made his own media buys. He bought astutely, making ad hoc print media purchases at low rates to make the brand as visible as possible even though sales were modest.

By the early 1980s, RFD's advertising program consisted of product-specific, sports-context print ads, heavy concentration in specialty periodicals targeted at serious athletes, lighter buys in related general-interest magazines, media-exposed use of the products by a select group of successful athlete endorsers, and a great emphasis on grassroots involvement.

Reebok paid star athletes to wear the Reebok label and to participate in Reebok-sponsored promotions, such as tennis clinics and autographing sessions. These athletes could also earn bonuses by winning specified tournaments/games/events or by winning specified honors within their sports, or both. In addition, lesser athletes, mostly promising youngsters, received free shoes and clothing from Reebok but were paid nothing. By supporting their training efforts in this way, Reebok increased the likelihood of signing them to endorsement contracts if they excelled later.

RFD's marketing of aerobic shoes exemplified its heavy grass-roots involvement in the sports addressed by its products. The division published aerobics newsletters, sponsored seminars and clinics, funded research on injury prevention, and created the sport's first certification program for instructors. It also offered aerobics instructors discounts on shoes and put Reebok shoes on the feet of many television aerobics instructors.

In addition, RFD communicated with its consumers through point-of-sale pieces and merchandising promotions in retail stores, outdoor advertising, radio, and, starting in 1986, television. RFD also advertised in trade publications, catalogues, and sales brochures to help its salespeople communicate better with their dealers.

As RFD's sales grew, so did its advertising, promotion, and public relations budgets. Combined, they grew from $2.7 million (4.2 percent of sales) in 1984 to $6.5 million (2.2 percent of sales) in 1985, $10 million (1.1 percent of sales) in 1986, and $34 million (3.4 percent of sales) in 1987.

---

[1] A focus group brings together 6 to 10 individuals for an open-ended discussion led by a moderator.

In 1986 RFD began testing new approaches to advertising. It ran the advertisement shown in Exhibit 3, which featured a couple wearing Reebok shoes riding a motorcycle to brunch and was the first ad to feature an athletic shoe advertised outside of a sports context. It was followed by an 18-month-long campaign with the theme "Because life is not a spectator sport." Each print ad, an example of which is shown in Exhibit 4, emphasized the participant and the joy of the sport, not the shoe and its attributes. The ads used an unusual technique called "prism color," in which photographs were transformed into pastel acrylic paintings. They ran in a balanced mix of 40 general-interest and specialty sport magazines.

The 1987 Program.   Each year, RFD developed a divisional marketing communications budget plus separate budgets for each category of sports shoe. Category managers were responsible for the decision making and management of their budgets, and Cohen was responsible for managing the divisional budget. Cohen and the category managers all reported to Frank O'Connell, the president of Reebok North America. Exhibit 5 presents the division's marketing organization in relation to the total corporation.

RFD's 1987 divisional advertising budget is outlined in Exhibit 6. In 1987, RFD advertised via print, radio, and television directed toward both the trade and consumers. Trade advertising, illustrated in Exhibit 7, emphasized that "Reebok is performance." Consumer advertising through July focused on the "Because life is not a spectator sport" campaign. In August, the division began a new multi-themed campaign with different television and print ads designed for each sports category. Depending on the sport, print ads addressed one or more of four themes: performance, new technology, "classic" styling, and fashion. Exhibits 8 through 11 show ads for four sports categories. Five television ads each sold a different sports shoe, but all dramatically employed motion and featured "real people," not high-profile athletes. Radio was used to reinforce the television message.

The variety in RFD's 1987 advertising effort was exemplified by contrasting the second-half advertising of shoes in two sports categories, tennis and basketball. Tennis shoe advertising was targeted at 18- to 49-year-old adults. The category manager's $975,000 advertising budget was split nearly equally between television and magazines. Both the magazine and television copy evoked tennis tournaments. The television ads were shown only during the U.S. Open. The print ads ran in nine tennis magazines, including *Tennis* and *Racquet Quarterly,* and three general sports magazines, including *Sports Illustrated.*

Men's basketball shoe advertising was targeted at 12- to 24-year-old males. Approximately $1.2 million was spent, 60 percent on television, 24 percent on print, and the rest on radio. Ads in all media showed amateur players in action on neighborhood playground basketball courts. Television ads ran on network prime time and late night and during sports events. Magazines used were *Sports Illustrated, Boys' Life,* and *High School Sports.*

Women's basketball shoe advertising was targeted at female teens. The $960,000 women's basketball shoe budget, like that for tennis, was split evenly between television and print. Unlike the tennis ads, however, the basketball ads were fashioned-oriented and did not show shoes being used in sports contexts. The television ad ran on early-fringe, weekend, and late-fringe network TV and on the MTV (music television) cable channel. The print ads ran in seven general-interest, fashion, and teen magazines, including *People, Glamour,* and *Seventeen.*

In addition to product-specific advertising, RFD sponsored a special insert in *Rolling Stone* magazine. The insert, titled "Artists of the Year 1967–1986," featured five Reebok shoe ads. These ads were one-offs; that is, they were used only once, in the *Rolling Stone* insert. Each ad featured someone giving a "Best performance in a pair of Reeboks" in a decidedly nonsports context. Exhibit 12 shows one of the ads.

Grass-roots promotions and athlete endorsements remained a large part of RFD's communications program in 1987, costing approximately $18 million. Promotional events included sponsorship of tennis tournaments for juniors and celebrities, the Reebok Teaching Pro Classic for tennis professionals, the Reebok Professional Aerobics Instructor Alliance, and the Reebok Racing Club. Shoe endorsers included basketball players Dennis Johnson, Danny Ainge, and Brad Daugherty, marathoner Steve Jones, tennis players Hana Mandlikova and Miloslav Mecir, aerobics expert Denise Austin, and the members of the U.S. National Cycling Team.

The 1988 Program

Category advertising.   The 1988 category budgets totaled approximately $22 million, $8 million of which was earmarked for category-specific print and television ads. The rest was allocated to athlete endorsements and grass-roots promotional events. The communications program for each category varied widely, as exemplified by the allocation of the 1988 budgets for tennis and basketball shown in Exhibit 13.

Almost 75 percent of the tennis category expenditures in 1988 were allocated to athlete endorsements and local and national tournament sponsorship. The objective was to maintain Reebok tennis shoes' credibility in the world of tennis. Reebok currently had a 40 percent share of the U.S. tennis shoe market and marketed the five best-selling tennis shoes in the world. Fewer than 10 percent of Reebok tennis shoes sold, however, were used on the tennis court; the rest were used for streetwear.

Tennis shoe print advertising in 1988 was geared toward casual usage. Thirty percent of the budget was allocated to hard-core performance-oriented ads. The rest was allocated to lifestyle/fashion-oriented ads, a departure from the strict performance orientation of the past.

Reebok basketball shoes, introduced in late 1985, were the best-selling basketball shoes in the United States. The category's 1988 television and radio ads featured people talking about the greatest basketball players they had ever seen, the "legends" of the old playgrounds. Print and outdoor ads showed "real" people engaged in playground basketball. Consumer promotions were of two types. First, a court-painting program sponsored renovation of basketball courts in low-income areas. Second, 10 local basketball tournaments, such as the Gus Macker 3-on-3 tournament in Belding, Michigan, were sponsored. Players under contract to Reebok attended the events to heighten their impact.

"U.B.U." umbrella advertising.   From the 1987 consumer research, Frank O'Connell concluded that RFD needed a new umbrella campaign to rekindle the vitality of the Reebok name while ensuring its continuity as a mainstream brand. He charged Chiat/Day with developing advertising copy that was "on the edge, far out, with a unique look that would be new not only to footwear advertising, but to the whole advertising industry." Chiat/Day recommended that the new campaign stress freedom of expression and the individuality that one could achieve wearing a pair of Reeboks, but at the same time maintain the brand's mass appeal.

The result was an offbeat campaign with the tag line "Reeboks let U.B.U." The ads featured zany vignettes of people expressing their individual styles in their Reebok shoes: a three-legged man strutting in a baseball cap and raincoat, a girl dressed like a princess emerging from a subway exit wearing her crown and her Reeboks, a bevy of wood nymphs tiptoeing through a forest glade, a room full of pregnant women aerobic dancing, and a young couple rolling on the grass. Throughout the television commercials, "U.B.U." flashed on the screen in large, jagged, typewritten-style letters. In the final seconds of each ad, "Reeboks let U.B.U." appeared across the screen. The ads would be targeted at 18- to 34-year-old adults, particularly women. They would be run on prime-time and late-night shows, such as "The Wonder Years," "Moonlighting," "LA Law," "thirty-something," and "Late Night with David Letterman" and on cable channels, such as MTV, ESPN, and WTBS.

The proposed "U.B.U." print campaign used a revolutionary new colorization process. A marriage of photography and illustration, its finished product resembled that of colorized videos. The print ads, like the television ones, featured self-expression in Reebok shoes and used the same tag line. Exhibit 14 shows a sample print ad. The ads would run in fashion magazines, such as *Esquire* and *Glamour,* entertainment magazines, such as *People,* and lifestyle/special-interest magazines, such as *Rolling Stone, Self,* and *New York Woman.* Insertions would begin in August issues and run at least through December. In addition, ads would appear in July editions of five athletic shoe trade magazines.

Olympics advertising.   RFD purchased $6 million worth of television advertising time during NBC's coverage of the 1988 Summer Olympics, which spanned the last two weeks of September. Although Reebok shoes were not "Official Products of the 1988 Summer Olympics," this media purchase represented the largest concentrated spending level in the history of the athletic footwear industry and ensured the Reebok brand exclusivity in athletic footwear advertising during NBC's coverage of the Summer Games. The Olympics advertising was expected to excite Reebok brand dealers, many of whom believed that the principal way to sell athletic shoes was through ads associating them with sports.

The next step was to finalize copy for both the Olympics campaign and the umbrella campaign. The copy proposed by Chiat/Day for the Olympics ads featured "real" people wearing Reebok shoes frantically engaged in street or front-yard sports. Commercials began with the tag line "Summer Games, Bronx, New York" (or Baltimore, Maryland, and so on). At the end of each commercial, one person stopped his or her action and stated, "And you thought all the excitement was in Seoul."

ERS.   Both the Olympics and "U.B.U." ads would be targeted at style-conscious 18- to 34-year-old adults. To reach active sports participants, RFD also planned to run a performance-based print campaign featuring Reebok's new Energy Return System (ERS). ERS shoes were designed to compete with Nike's Air line in the $75–$90 per pair retail price range. Compressed air—sandwiched in four brightly colored tubes visible through the sole of the shoe—cushioned the foot when it hit the ground, captured some of the energy released, and returned it to the foot for extra bounce. The proposed ERS ads would carry the slogan "The revolution is over" in response to Nike's successful 1987 "Revolution" campaign. Exhibit 15 shows a sample ad. The ads would run from June to December in sports magazines, such as *Runner's World, Outside,* and *Sports Illustrated.*

RFD's divisional marketing communications budget would cover the $17 million combined cost of the "U.B.U.," Olympics, and ERS campaigns through the end of 1988. Exhibit 16 provides a breakdown of the proposed ad spending by campaign and media.

The Human Rights Now! Tour

While O'Connell, Cohen, and Chiat/Day were developing copy for RFD's freedom-of-expression umbrella campaign, an opportunity arose to help finance a world concert tour conceived by AI. The objective of the tour, later named the

Human Rights Now! world concert tour, was to support AI's worldwide effort to develop awareness of the human rights guaranteed in the United Nations Universal Declaration of Human Rights.

Chiat/Day brought the idea to Reebok and suggested that it help underwrite the tour to reach young people with a positive message about the company. Before proceeding, Joe LaBonté commissioned a telephone survey of 1,000 U.S. adults to determine their awareness of and attitude toward AI. Awareness was highest (60 percent) among people 18 to 34 years old. Almost half of this age group (49 percent) had a favorable attitude toward AI, and only 7 percent had an unfavorable attitude. The rest were neutral or unaware.

Joe LaBonté decided to support the Human Rights Now! world concert tour because he believed in the tour's cause and because it offered the opportunity to give something back to the young people who were responsible for the company's success. After discussions with Paul Fireman, he committed Reebok as sole underwriter of the tour. He felt that the time it would take for AI to enlist several sponsors would likely delay the concert tour until 1989. In addition, being sole corporate sponsor would give Reebok a greater voice in tour promotion decisions than if the job were shared.

LaBonté announced Reebok's underwriting of the tour at a press conference in Los Angeles on March 29. At the same time, telegrams announcing the sponsorship were sent to all of Reebok's retailers. Soon thereafter, letters explaining Reebok's involvement with the tour and the Reebok Human Rights Award were mailed to all Reebok employees, U.S. Reebok sales agencies, and Reebok International Division distributors.

Once committed to the tour, LaBonté formed a task force consisting of himself; Linda Lewi, vice president of Cone Communications, Reebok's public relations agency; and Angel Martinez, vice president of business development, to handle the public relations and advertising surrounding Reebok's involvement with the tour. Among their most important tasks was the management of relations between Reebok and AI.

AI was a nonpartisan organization with a worldwide grass-roots network that tried to ensure respect for human rights, the release of nonviolent prisoners of conscience, fair and prompt trials for all political prisoners, and an end to torture and executions. AI was funded by 700,000 members in 150 nations. It strove to be independent and impartial. The organization did not support or oppose any government or political system and accepted no financial contributions from governments. AI's activity included letter-writing campaigns in which AI members sent letters, cards, and telegrams on behalf of individual prisoners to government officials; publicizing of human rights abuse patterns; and meetings with government representatives. Members also organized public awareness events, such as

vigils outside government embassies. Since its founding in 1961, AI had worked on behalf of more than 25,000 prisoners around the world. In 1987 more than 150 of the prisoners of conscience "adopted" by AI groups in the United States were released.

Human Rights Day, December 10, 1988, would mark the 40th anniversary of the Univeral Declaration of Human Rights. Adopted by the General Assembly of the United Nations in 1948, the declaration, based on the twin pillars of freedom from want and freedom from fear, proclaimed fundamental and equal rights for "all peoples and nations." On March 3, 1988, AI launched its most ambitious campaign ever, titled Human Rights Now! Its goals were to mobilize public opinion and pressure governments to honor the declaration. In March, AI circulated copies of the declaration and petitions in support of it around the world. The combined petition would be presented to the United Nations on December 10.

In 1986, AI had sponsored an American rock music concert tour that brought AI 100,000 new members, most of whom were high school and college students. This success led AI to view music as an important vehicle to spread its message. Hence the Human Rights Now! world concert tour was conceived and scheduled to begin in September 1988. Although the venues and artists were not all finalized, AI hoped to include countries on five continents, including some with records of frequent human rights violations. Eighteen concerts were planned in 16 countries. Firm venues included Los Angeles, Philadelphia, London, and Brazil. Possibilities included Zimbabwe, the USSR, India, Thailand, Yugoslavia, Japan, Argentina, Italy, Spain, France, the Ivory Coast, Costa Rica, and Canada. The six-week tour would feature both international artists and national artists of each country in which the tour played. All artists would play for free. Sting, Peter Gabriel, Youssou N'Dour, and Tracy Chapman had committed themselves to the whole tour. Bruce Springsteen was considering joining the tour. If he did so, he would headline the event.

AI estimated that the tour would cost $22 million to produce. It expected to raise $12 million via ticket sales and broadcast rights. This left a $10 million shortfall. Therefore, for the first time in its history, AI sought corporate assistance.

In an agreement signed on April 22, Reebok made a commitment to provide $2 million seed money immediately and to finance the tour deficit to a maximum of $8 million. In addition, the nonprofit Reebok Foundation decided to fund up to $2 million.[2] The tour deficit was defined as the tour receipts received by AI from all sources other than

---

[2]The Reebok Foundation was a nonprofit organization set up in 1987 to seek out grant opportunities. In its first year, the foundation awarded grants to 32 organizations in the fields of education, arts/culture, human/social services, health, and religion.

Reebok and charitable contributions to AI minus all tour expenses.

AI had to consult with Reebok on all tour matters but had the final say on most aspects of the tour. Tour logo, name, and the design of tour merchandise required mutual approval. Reebok had certain rights to the tour name and logo as well as to photographs of the artists and audio and visual material created by AI and Reebok during the tour. Reebok could participate in the negotiation of the sale of television, radio, theatrical, and home video rights for any tour concert. The company could also create its own advertising with respect to the tour and its purposes. In addition, Reebok had the exclusive right to manufacture all tour merchandise, including clothing, posters, buttons, programs, videos, and books. The tour logo, advertising, promotional materials, and merchandise would all carry "Made possible by the Reebok Foundation" as a tag line. AI would be responsible for selling tour merchandise on the grounds of the concert on concert days. Reebok had the exclusive right to sell it through all other channels. Net profits from the sale of tour merchandise were considered tour receipts. In the unlikely event that merchandise net profits exceeded the tour deficit, the balance would be donated to AI.

To further emphasize Reebok's interest in human rights, the task force decided to establish the Reebok Human Rights Award, which was independent of AI. The $100,000 annual award, to be funded through the Reebok Foundation, would be split between two young people under 30 years of age, one male and one female. It would honor young people who, by circumstance or choice, acted against great odds to raise public awareness of and thereby help protect freedom of expression, or who suffered in their attempts to exercise their own freedom of expression.

In early June, the task force met to finalize a marketing communications program for the tour. Lewi proposed the $5 million plan shown in Exhibit 17. This expense would be in addition to the cost of underwriting the tour. The plan consisted of pre-event, event, and postevent advertising, promotions, and public relations.

The proposed pre-event plan included the following: advertising the tour on national and spot radio; advertising on network and cable television stations via 20 public service announcements featuring celebrities talking about human rights abuses; advertising with spreads emphasizing a human rights theme in *Rolling Stone, Spin, L.A. Style, Details,* and *Interview* magazines and in the campus newspapers of the top 60 colleges and universities; speaking engagements by Reebok and AI executives before college leadership groups; interviews of AI executives and Human Rights Now! tour artists on "Good Morning America" and similar programs to explain the tour and the award; newsletters and information meetings for employees, sales agencies, and international distributors; and premiums such as

T-shirts with the tour logo to be given to retail store clerks to stimulate their awareness of and excitement about the tour. The radio and magazine ads would break on August 1, followed by the television ads in mid-August and the campus newspaper ads in early September.

Tentative plans for the event communications included the following: broadcasting at least one of the concerts via network television or cable; interviews to be given by the artists and by AI and Reebok executives on "Good Morning America" and similar shows; a radio petition drive to affirm support for the Universal Declaration of Human Rights; promotions through bookstores and record stores offering free concert tickets and tour merchandise to winning consumers; employee and retailer sweepstakes, with winners to be given free trips and tickets to concerts in Los Angeles or London; free tickets to be given to VIP customers in each country with a venue; hospitality suites set up at venues to entertain VIP customers; use of Reebok athletes to attend event parties and to give third-party endorsements of Reebok's underwriting of the tour; and invitations to all RFD employees to a closed-circuit viewing of one of the concerts.

The postevent plan included the following: stories released to leading newspapers, trade publications, and entertainment, lifestyle, and business magazines describing the tour's success and Reebok's charitable contribution to that success; sales of a tour documentary video and book; use of the video and book as retailer premiums; and the Reebok Human Rights Award ceremony.

The task force had to decide what changes, if any, to make to the proposed communications plan. Other Reebok executives were consulted before the meeting. Several sales managers queried, "How will this sell shoes?" They wished to explore opportunities for promotional tie-ins at the point of sale and advocated running "U.B.U." ads during the television broadcasts of the concerts. They thought that every opportunity to exploit Reebok's association with the tour should be used to sell more shoes.

Other executives disagreed. They cited risks to Reebok from association with the tour and advised that the company keep its involvement with the tour low-key in its retail outlets. Some executives were also wary of involving Reebok's athletes in the tour communications program. They feared that any negative tour publicity could rub off on the athletes and damage their influence as opinion leaders.

At the outset of the meeting, LaBonté stated: "The Human Rights Now! concert campaign promises to be the most exciting event this year in the athletic footwear industry. Our involvement with the tour must be perceived positively by our consumers, dealers, distributors, and employees. We must also ensure that the tour's advertising and promotion mesh with RFD's overall 1988 communications program."

EXHIBIT 1 **New Product Line Introductions
and Acquisitions**

Introductions

Year	Product Line Introduced
1979	Reebok running shoes
1982	Reebok aerobic shoes
1983	Reebok tennis shoes
1983	Reebok fitness shoes
1984	Reebok children's athletic shoes
1985	Reebok apparel
1985	Reebok basketball shoes
1986	Reebok walking shoes
1987	Reebok volleyball/indoor court shoes
1987	Reebok sports conditioning shoes
1987	Reebok infants' and children's shoes
1987	Metaphors (women's casual comfort shoes)
1988	Reebok golf shoes
1988	Reebok cycling shoes

Acquisitions

Date	Company Acquired	Product Line
October 1986	The Rockport Company	Casual, dress, and walking shoes
April 1987	Avia Group International, Inc.	Athletic footwear for aerobics, basketball, tennis, running, walking, fitness/sports conditioning, and volleyball
	Donner Mountain Corporation (subsidiary of Avia)	Walking and casual shoes and hiking boots
May 1987	John A. Frye Corporation	Leather boots and casual and dress shoes
June 1987	ESE Sports, Ltd.	Reebok's Canadian distributor
January 1988	Ellesse USA, Inc.: exclusive rights to the Ellesse trademarks for the United States and Canada	Sportswear and athletic footwear

EXHIBIT 2 **Sources of Information Used by Athletic
Shoe Purchasers**

		Reebok	
Information Source	Total	Users	Nonusers
Friend or relative	72%	69%	74%
Coach or instructor	65	64	65
Salesperson	54	53	54
Article in magazine	50	52	48
Advertisement	45	43	47

NOTE: All people included in the survey had bought athletic shoes for
their own use within the 12 months prior to the survey and were aware
of the Reebok brand. Reebok users were people who claimed to own and
wear Reebok shoes fairly regularly. Reebok nonusers were people who did
not.

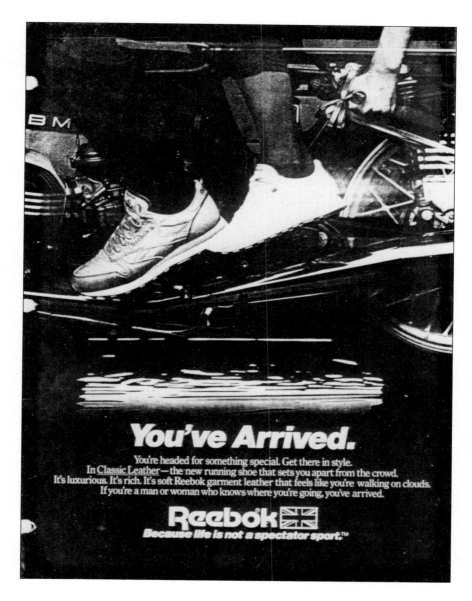

EXHIBIT 5

Reebok footwear division marketing organization

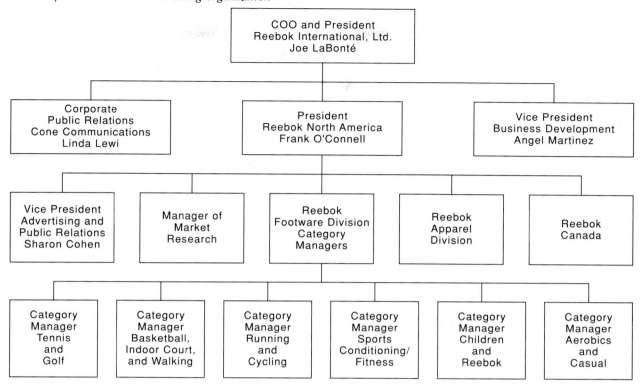

**EXHIBIT 6   Reebok Footwear Division 1987
             Advertising Budget ($000s)**

Television:	
Network	$ 6,354
Spot	2,107
Cable	222
Total TV	8,683
Radio spot	179
Print:	
Magazines	7,475
Newspapers	166
Total print	7,641
Outdoor and other	350
Total	$16,853

EXHIBIT 7
1987 Reebok trade advertisement

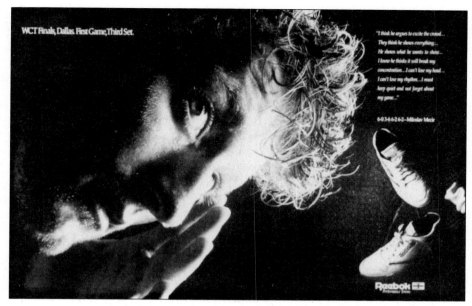

EXHIBIT 10

*1987 Reebok running
shoe print ad*

EXHIBIT 11

*1987 Reebok aerobic
shoe print ad*

Exhibit 12

Reebok Ad from 1987
Rolling Stone *magazine*
insert

Best Performance in a pair of Reeboks February 12, 1982

EXHIBIT 13   **1988 Tennis and Basketball Category Allocation of Marketing Communications Budgets**

Communications Program	Basketball	Tennis	
Athlete endorsements	32%	59%	*peer influence*
Magazine ads	3	15	
Television ads	37	—	
Newspaper ads	4	—	
Radio	5	—	
Consumer promotions	8	12	
Associations and clubs	—	7	
Outdoor	5	—	
U.S. Open sponsorship	—	7	
Merchandising aids	6	—	
Total	100%	100%	

EXHIBIT 14

1988 "Reeboks Let U.B.U." print ad

REEBOKS LET U.B.U.   Reebok ✚

The revolution is over.

Introducing the Reebok Energy Return System.

While Nike is singing the praises of their revolution, let us introduce you to something that really deserves the term: The Energy Return System from Reebok: E.R.S.

This system actually saves a significant amount of the energy you put into running, and then returns it to you just when you need it most.

No other shoe has ever been designed to do this. That's why the Reebok World Trainer with E.R.S. actually returns up to 30% more energy per milliliter of compression than either the Nike Air Max or the Tiger Gel 100.

What's more, this energy return is accomplished with no loss in either cushioning or stability. In

fact, the World Trainer surpasses most shoes on both counts.

But no running shoes did. The challenge was to put such a system into a running shoe that would propel the runner on his way.

Our Energy Return System is basically a series of tubes in the midsole. Six tubes under the ball of your foot. Four under your heel.

These tubes are made of one of the most resilient materials on earth: DuPont Hytrel.® It's the same stuff they make car bumpers out of.

Lots of every day objects have natural energy return systems. Springs. Pogo sticks. Diving boards.

When your foot strikes the ground, the Hytrel tubes store up the energy. As your foot rolls forward, the tubes return to their original shape and

release the energy. Kind of like a spring being sprung.

A RUNNING SHOE AS FINELY TUNED AS A RACE CAR

Timing is everything. In a high-performance engine. In a running shoe.

Fortunately, Reebok's E.R.S. can actually be 'tuned.' By regulating the size and position of the Hytrel tubes, we can make sure the energy release

is exactly synchronized with the forward motion of your foot. Your energy is used instead of lost. Your running is more efficient because your shoe is more efficient. Imagine. A running shoe as efficient as a race ready Porsche. It kind of deflates all that talk about Air.

E.R.S. IS THE NEXT LOGICAL STEP IN SHOE DESIGN.

Which means others will surely follow.

But leading the race is not an unfamiliar position for Reebok. For the first half of this century, the family that founded Reebok made the running shoe to beat. It was their shoe that went to the 1924 Olympics dramatized in "Chariots of Fire."

But we're not so foolish as to think we could create a revolution out of thin Air. Revolutions require bigger ideas. Like giving power back to the people. Or in this case, energy back to the runner.

AIR, GEL AND E.R.S. EACH HAVE THREE LETTERS. THAT'S WHERE THE SIMILARITY ENDS.

ENERGY RETURNED

The Reebok World Trainer.
The first running shoe with E.R.S.

Reebok
Running Shoes

EXHIBIT 16 **Reebok Footwear Division, Proposed 1988 Advertising Budget Spending by Campaign ($000s)**

Campaign	Television	Magazines	Outdoor	Total
"U.B.U."	$ 8,000	$1,900	$700	$10,600
Olympics	6,000	0	0	6,000
ERS	0	600	0	600
Total	$14,000	$2,500	$700	$17,200

NOTE: Budget excludes individual category communications budget and Human Rights Now! tour budget.
An additional $1 million in sports-specific ERS print ads would be paid for out of individual category manager budgets.

EXHIBIT 17 **Proposed Marketing Communications Budget for Human Rights Now! Concert Tour and Reebok Human Rights Award**

Marketing Unit	Proposed 1988 Budget
Advertising:	
Media production	$ 50,000
Radio and campus media	1,575,000
Logo development	15,000
Merchandising brochures	25,000
Tour posters	100,000
Satellite network	375,000
Promotional materials	125,000
TV/video animated logo	15,000
Total advertising	$2,280,000
Public relations:	
Press kits	$ 6,325
Clerk program/newsletter	65,000
Media relations	215,000
Parties	30,000
Ticket purchases	187,500
Press conferences	220,000
Radio	50,000
Human Rights Award	190,000
PR fees	250,000
Human rights education/campus program	251,000
Total public relations	$1,464,825
Promotions:	
Retail clerk premiums/contests	$ 200,000
Athletes program	60,000
Celebrity network TV, etc.	100,000
Internal support program	50,925
Distributors	3,000
Total promotions	$ 413,925
Merchandising:	
Product for tour musicians and VIPs	$ 92,650
Staff	175,000
Other:	
Contingency	250,000
Legal and accounting	260,000
Total other	$ 510,000
Total budget	$4,936,400

THE MASSACHUSETTS LOTTERY

"It's a chance to make your dreams come true."

The Massachusetts State Lottery was created by a legislative act in September 1971, "to provide a source of revenue for the 351 cities and towns of the Commonwealth." Its first lottery product, a 50-cent weekly game, was introduced the following year and referred to as "The Game" to establish the image of the lottery as being "fun," rather than gambling. The Game realized total revenues of $56 million in 1972, and, in its first full calendar year of operation, $72 million in 1973. In subsequent years, the lottery continued to grow, increasing its revenues and offering a variety of games. By 1988, total revenues were $1,379.2 million, around $235 per capita, generating net revenues distributed to the state of $434.8 million. Chairman Robert Crane, in the lottery's 1987 annual report, commented: "Modern marketing techniques and the most up-to-date electronic equipment enable Massachusetts to be the leader among state lotteries." The lottery had become one of the largest commercial enterprises in the state. Yet state lotteries, and particularly their advertising, were subject to criticism. An editorial in *The Economist*, July 1989, observed:

> Governments have no duty to stop people from spending their money foolishly. But they do have a duty not to encourage people to spend their money in that fashion. On both counts,

the role of government in America's current state-lottery frenzy is wrong. Egged on by $400 million a year in fantasy-inducing government-paid advertisements, Americans now spend more than $15 billion a year—up from $2 billion a decade ago—on ever-smaller chances of winning ever-larger sums of money.

State Lotteries

In 1988, 29 states were operating lotteries, generating total revenues of $15.6 billion, $93.73 per capita; with 48 percent distributed as prizes, 15 percent covering operating costs, and the remaining 37 percent, $5.74 billion, constituting total net revenues to the states. As Table A shows, California had the highest total revenue, with Massachusetts ranked fifth, though having the highest per capita revenue. On average, 3.3 percent of own-state revenues were generated by lotteries.[1] Half of the states operating lotteries earmarked net revenues entirely for specific public services (education in 50 percent of cases), the remainder added the revenues to general funds.

As well as generating revenue, state lotteries were also intended to provide an alternative to illegal gambling and hence help curb the associated organized crime. A 1972 report by the Fund for the City of New York recommended legalization of the numbers game and betting on sports. Noting that the illegal numbers game was widely played by the poor, the fund concluded:

This case was prepared by Professor N. Craig Smith and Ron Lee with assistance from Professor John A. Quelch.

Copyright © 1989 by the President and Fellows of Harvard College.

Harvard Business School case 9-590-009.

---

[1]Own-state revenues exclude state borrowings and federal grants and reimbursements.

TABLE A   The Lottery Industry
The Leading Players, State by State, Ranked in Order of Their Annual Revenues

State/Year Started	Total Revenues ($ mil)	Percent Change ('88–87)	Revenues per Capita	Prize as Percent of Total Revenues	Operating Expense as Percent of Total Revenues	Net Income ($ mil)	Percent of Revenues to State
California/1985	$2,106.4	49%	$ 74.78	49%	13%	$804.0	38%
New York/1967	1,632.0	8	91.17	47	9	725.6	44
Pennsylvania/1972	1,461.0	9	121.48	50	10	592.9	40
Ohio/1974	1,411.0	31	129.78	48	14	545.6	38
Massachusetts/1972	1,379.2	8	234.92	59	10	434.8	31

SOURCE: "Lottomania," *Forbes*, March 6, 1989.

1. The primary objective of any legalized gambling should be the elimination of illegal operations.
2. Legal gambling should be seen as a tool of law enforcement rather than a substitute for law enforcement.
3. The purpose of the legal game should be to attract current players, not to create new players.

Yet, in 1989, *The Economist* was urging the privatization of lotteries: "legal private competition would help the consumer. It would quickly drive up the prizes on lottery tickets beyond the current chintzy 48 cents on the dollar. Private lotteries could well put state lotteries out of business completely." Unlike state lotteries, private lotteries and their advertising would also come under Federal Trade Commission jurisdiction.

In December 1988, when the prize for the New York Lotto had reached $45 million, the largest in the lottery's history, 80 percent of the state's adult residents bought tickets. Massachusetts claimed more than 60 percent of its adult population regularly bought lottery tickets. Yet research findings suggested a small proportion of participants accounted for most lottery sales. *The Wall Street Journal* cited a study by Duke University economists Charles Clotfelter and Philip Cook, which found that the 10 percent betting most frequently accounted for around 50 percent of the total wagered, with the most frequent 20 percent accounting for 65 percent. Characteristics of lottery players and participants in other types of commercial gambling (legal and illegal) were also reported:

- Sex: men generally gamble more than women, but almost equal numbers play lotteries.
- Age: generally young people gamble the most, but in lotteries the under-25 and over-65 age groups play less frequently and less heavily than the in-between ages.
- Education: gambling generally rises with education, but lottery play falls steadily as formal education increases.
- Occupation: laborers play the lottery the most and professionals the least.
- Race: blacks and Hispanics outplay non-Hispanic whites.
- Income: dollar amount wagered is fairly constant at all income levels, but proportionately higher amounts of household income are, therefore, wagered by lower-income players.

A California survey reported in *US News and World Report* found that "the poor" wagered 2.1 percent of their income on lotteries, compared with the 0.3 percent expenditure of "the rich." *Money* calculated that the typical player's household income was $25,000. Some poor had become rich, with 800 people winning at least $1 million in 1987, though they represented only 0.000008 percent of the 97 million who played the lottery annually. Sheelah Ryan, a 63-year-old mobile home resident in Florida won the biggest lottery jackpot in North American history in 1988. She commented: "This is the first time I've ever won $55 million!" However, the odds of winning were greater in other forms of commercial gambling. In comparison to the 50 percent payout in lotteries, prizes averaged 81 percent of the total amount wagered in horse racing, 89 percent in slot machines, and 97 percent in casino table games.

Lottery Marketing[2]

In *Selling Hope*, Clotfelter and Cook questioned whether the businesslike orientation of state lotteries was in the public interest. They attributed much of the success of state lotteries to the use of sophisticated marketing:

> Unlike virtually every other operation of government at any level, but very much like most suppliers of consumer products, lottery agencies pay attention to details of product design, pricing, and promotion. This marketing is motivated by the lotteries' objective of maximizing revenue and made possible by their unusual degree of independence. . . . With the help of . . . specialists and experienced advertising agencies, the lotteries have set about to increase their revenues by stimulating the demand for their products.

State lottery marketing was "not as an afterthought but as a deliberate policy." Clotfelter and Cook quote one lottery director as having commented: "To survive and prosper, it is essential that lotteries practice the business techniques of the private sector, particularly in the area of marketing."

As monopoly suppliers of legal lottery games, the state lotteries realized their objective of maximizing revenue by strategies of recruiting new users or stimulating increased usage, rather than growing market share. Increasing usage was the dominant strategy, so, for example, Maryland lottery's advertising plan stated: "All advertising programs for the lottery must develop regular participants of the games, not casual impulse sales." Accordingly, target marketing, based on regular marketing research to identify the characteristics and preferences of market segments, was well established. So Arizona, using data collected from winners, found that games involving future drawings were more attractive to older people than to younger ones. Heavy users were targeted in particular, with market segments often geographically defined so that neighborhoods were identified with the highest relative rates of participation for each

---

[2]This section is based on Charles T. Clotfelter and Philip J. Cook, *Selling Hope: State Lotteries in America* (Cambridge: Harvard University Press, 1989).

lottery game. Lottery advertisements in Spanish were commonplace in California and New York, though the targeting of minority groups had become controversial in some states. There had even been a boycott organized of the Illinois lottery, following charges that it devoted special attention to sections of Chicago populated by poor blacks.

According to lottery consultant John Koza, psychographic segmentation as well as demographic segmentation was important. "Belongers," one of nine distinct lifestyle groups in the VALS (Values and Lifestyles) typology, although not inherently attracted to gambling activities, was a substantial group of participants in lotteries, because they were government-sanctioned. As Koza put it, for this segment, "If the government says 'it's ok,' then it's ok." The "societally conscious" group, however, gambled considerably less than average and, accordingly, was less likely to be targeted. Having segmented the market, lotteries would then put together appropriate marketing mixes.

Product design encompassed play value, prize structure, the variety and the complexity of games. Instant "rub-off" games, for example, added play value to an otherwise passive game by incorporating elements of choice and suspense.[3] A mix of prize structures often was used to appeal to different players; though a study showed that neither players nor nonplayers knew the odds of winning the Washington state's lotto game, the awareness of large prizes, rather than the odds, was the overriding concern. Price considerations not only included the ticket price but also the expected value of prizes. However, lottery managers often were constrained by state legislation specifying payout rates or setting minimum rates, though some states, such as Massachusetts, provided the flexibility to vary the payout rates among games. Yet awareness of this variation was often low, as Clotfelter and Cook conclude: "players generally appear to be ignorant about basic parameters of the lottery games in which they participate."

Convenience of purchase was important in reaching impulse buyers, especially for instant games. Convenience stores, supermarkets, liquor stores, drugstores, newsstands, and lottery ticket kiosks were the main outlets used. Vending machines were sometimes utilized in high traffic areas. Enlisting the support of retail agents was an important place consideration, as Clotfelter and Cook suggest: "A cashier who asks, 'Would you like a lottery ticket with that quart of milk?' may have a significant role in determining a lottery's success in maximizing sales." Promotion considerations encompassed advertising, sales promotions, publicity, and personal selling. Sales promotions included "buy one, get one free" offers; free ticket coupons in newspapers, which achieved high redemption rates; and joint

promotions with retailers, such as McDonald's. Lottery sales representatives played an important role—in dealing with retail agents—as well as favorable publicity. Clotfelter and Cook write: "Imagine how delighted most companies would be if their main product were featured on television news shows and newspaper front pages. For lotteries this kind of publicity has become routine." All lotteries employed public relations specialists.

Advertising was largely on television (an estimated 57 percent of state lottery budgets allocated to specific media in 1988), but radio (16 percent) was also important, as were point-of-sale advertisements (11 percent), print advertisements (7 percent), and transit signs and billboards (5 percent). Selective data analyzed by Clotfelter and Cook suggested the time devoted to lottery advertising was about three fourths the total amount for all state advertising, such that "most state citizens see lottery ads far more often than virtually any other message put out by the state." A survey by Maryland found that those most likely to be aware of lottery advertisements were young adults, blacks, television watchers, and lottery players. Attention was paid to the timing of advertising, particularly to coincide with paydays. The advertising plan for Ohio's Super Lotto specified: "Schedule heavier media weight during those times of the month when consumer disposable income peaks."

Clotfelter and Cook's content analysis of a sample of advertisements provided by 13 of the largest lotteries identified 8 primary messages, split equally between the "largely informational" and the "basically thematic." Informational advertisements included announcements of a new lottery game; direct appeals to buy tickets (in California: "Watch it grow! Play Lotto 6/49"); information about how to play a lottery game; details about winners; and, notably in brochures, information on rules of the game, prize structures, and the odds of winning. Many advertisements featured a reminder of the lottery's contribution to the state: "Thanks to you, everybody wins" (District of Columbia), "Our schools win, too" (California). Only a few advertisements were devoted to this purpose, though a series on this theme was developed by Maryland:

> One of the most dramatic of these was a television spot depicting a little boy wandering away from his family's campsite in the woods. In the gathering darkness the frightened boy wanders through the woods crying for his mother and father while the worried parents describe their son to police officers. A state police helicopter spots the boy with a searchlight, and a voice-over points out that the state lottery contributed $300 million in funds for public service, part of which was set aside for this police helicopter. As a sobbing mother is notified that her son is safe, the ad intones: "The Maryland state lottery pays off in ways you may not even know about."

Thematic advertisements employed humor and fantasy, with themes of the fun and excitement of the lottery; the

---

[3] "Rub-off" games had hidden symbols revealed by rubbing a coin over the surface of the card.

dual message that anyone can win and that winning can change your life, such as "before-and-after" advertisements; a focus on wealth and luxury, "The rich. Join them" (Michigan); and a focus on money itself, such as coins being minted. Clotfelter and Cook reported that many advertisements portrayed wealth, leisure, gracious living, excitement, romance, and fame. A California advertisement featured dreams of possibilities created by winning, from a carefree retirement to establishing a father-son business. Advertisements tended to show wholesome surroundings and players younger and more affluent than the typical lottery player. Clotfelter and Cook described lottery advertisements as "among the most clever and appealing shown on television today."

Omissions from lottery advertisements formed the basis of some of the strongest criticisms. A consistent overstatement of the true value of prizes was said to result from not disclosing that large prizes were typically paid out over a 20-year period, and that the stated prize was the sum of the payments not its present value, that large prizes only applied to single winners, and that jackpots were subject to taxation. Clotfelter and Cook found only 20 percent of the advertisements in their sample gave any information on the odds of winning, and usually only the probability of winning any prize as opposed to the grand prize. They suggested that, with over 50 percent of the advertisements mentioning the dollar amount of prizes, there was an emphasis on prizes over probabilities giving a distorted impression of the probability of winning and increasing players' "subjective probability" of winning.

Missouri, Virginia, and Wisconsin attempted to restrict lottery advertising, viewing it as an inducement to gamble. This was in keeping with a wide-ranging National Association of Broadcasters code of conduct which, if it had not been ruled anti-competitive, would have questioned many lottery advertisements because of specific provisions on lottery advertising practice which, for example, said advertisements should not "indicate what fictitious winners may do, hope to do, or have done with their winnings."

Clotfelter and Cook believed that, while those running the lottery were well-intentioned and professional, there were legitimate concerns about their marketing practices, notably the use of misleading advertising and, largely as a consequence, the undermining of the credibility of state government. As California's attorney general commented, "People look to the government to be honest and straightforward and not to be using suckering kinds of techniques."

The Massachusetts Lottery

The legislation governing the Massachusetts lottery specified revenue distribution such that a minimum of 45 percent was to be paid out in prizes, operating expenses were not to exceed 15 percent (from this amount a 5 percent

commission and 1 percent bonus was paid to the sales agents who sold the tickets), and the balance was to be distributed to the Local Aid Fund for the benefit of the 351 towns and cities of the Commonwealth. The lottery itself assumed no responsibility for determining how much each city or town was to receive. The Department of Revenue was responsible for disbursement of revenue, according to each city or town's population. The cities and towns were then free to use their share of the revenue as they saw fit. The lottery produced around 3.8 percent of Massachusetts' revenues generated within the state.

After the The Game was established in 1972, the Massachusetts State Lottery Commission pioneered the Instant Game. In this game, the player purchased a rub-off ticket with a preprinted prize structure, which allowed the buyer to know immediately if he or she was a winner. Prizes ranged from a free Instant lottery ticket to $100,000 a year for life. Despite its initial success, the Instant Game suffered a decline in popularity in 1977 and 1978. To encourage sales, the prize structure was readjusted to devote a greater portion of the prize money to the lower tier prizes, which could be paid "instantly" by the sales agents. In 1987, sales were over $425 million and the Instant Game became Massachusetts' most popular lottery. In 1976, the Lottery established the Numbers Game to allow players to participate more actively through selection of their own four-digit number, type of bet (with variation of the amount and which combination of digits in the four-digit number were bet on), and length of time they wished to play (between one and six days). The second objective of the Numbers Game was to challenge illegal gaming through an attractive and honest numbers game.

Megabucks, a number selection game whose jackpot grew until it was won, was established in 1982. Six numbers were to be chosen from a field of 30, which was later increased to a field of 36. In 1984, three drawings that failed to produce a winner ended by producing a jackpot of $18.2 million. Megabucks was the fastest-growing game in the history of the Massachusetts State Lottery, beginning with weekly sales of $50,000 in 1982 and growing to over $7 million a week in 1987.

Exhibit 1 shows an advertisement for Mass Millions. Launched in 1987, this game was designed to respond to public interest in very large jackpots. Though the Megabucks game routinely produced jackpots of $2 to $6 million, the jackpot did not reach $10 million or more unless no one won the jackpot for three or four drawings. Mass Millions was structured to produce larger but less-frequent jackpots than Megabucks. Players selected six numbers out of a field of 46, with each bet costing $1. Players matching all six numbers were guaranteed a minimum jackpot of $1 million. Players who matched five of the six winning numbers plus the "bonus" (or seventh) number won $50,000. The odds of winning the smallest prize ($2) were one in 47, the odds of winning the jackpot were one in over 9 million.

Massachusetts Lottery Advertising

Massachusetts lottery advertising and promotion expenses in 1988 were just under $11.5 million, with around 38 percent on television advertising, 38 percent on radio, 20 percent on press, and 4 percent on point-of-sale materials. Agents selling lottery tickets provided flyers giving information on the odds and prize structures for games. Exhibit 2 shows an example of a flyer for a $1 instant game. Around 250,000 flyers were produced for each instant game (there would typically be seven different games in a year).

Criticism of lottery advertising was not uncommon. Writing in *Adweek* in March 1989, John Carroll suggested the advertising by the Massachusetts lottery "rivals professional wrestling in its egregious manipulation of people's baser instincts." He referred, for example, to the "ESP" campaign:

> Remember the "ESP" campaign? The television spot asked you to pick a number from one to five, then superimposed a number on the screen. (I think there were five versions of the spot.) If you were right, the spot went on to say, you *might* have ESP. Admittedly, that would come in handy when filling out your lottery slip. Unfortunately, though, there are no lottery games in this state that have one-to-five odds. If you really did have ESP, you'd probably have a better chance of making money from the *National Enquirer.*

Exhibit 2

The Massachusetts Lottery: Instant game point-of-sale flyer

Front

Rear

With over $66 million in total cash prizes, this game is The New Green Monster.

Play the game like the pros—for money. It's Grand Slam, The Lottery's newest instant game. Scratch out a hit and you could win up to $1,000 instantly.

You could really clean up playing Grand Slam because it's the game of extra winnings—over 16,500 prizes at $500 or more and over $66 million in total cash prizes plus a chance to win up to 4 times on a ticket.

Grand Slam—all the excitement of the big leagues with a chance to come home a winner.

PRIZE STRUCTURE FOR GRAND SLAM

PRIZE AMOUNT	PRIZES IN GAME	PROBABILITY OF WINNING
$1,000	300	1:336,000.0
$1,000+$500+$500	400	1:252,000.0
$500	16,100	1:6,236.9
$40	118,500	1:852.1
$40+$10+$10+$10+$10	238,500	1:423.5
$10	112,000	1:900.0
$10($5+$5)	224,000	1:450.0
$10($4+$4+$2)	336,000	1:300.0
$10($4+$2+$2+$2)	336,000	1:300.0
$5	112,000	1:900.0
$5($2+$2+$1+$1)	224,000	1:450.0
$4($2+$2)	336,000	1:300.0
$4($2+$1+$1)	672,000	1:150.0
$4($1+$1+$1+$1)	672,000	1:150.0
$2	3,696,000	1:27.3
$2($1+$1)	3,696,000	1:27.3
$1	8,400,000	1:12.0
CASH PRIZES	19,525,100	1:5.2

Prize Structure based on the sale of approximately 100,800,000 tickets.

All winners, tickets and transactions subject to Lottery Commission rules as published in the code of Massachusetts regulations.

THE LOTTERY

British Airways

On Sunday, April 10, 1983, a six-minute commercial for British Airways (BA) was aired in the middle of a weekend talk show. The commercial included a statement by Lord King, BA's chairman, and highlighted BA's achievements during the previous two years. The commercial also included the inaugural showing of a 90-second advertisement known as Manhattan Landing. This advertisement and three others formed the basis of an unprecedented £31 million advertising campaign designed to promote BA's brand name and corporate image worldwide.[1]

British Airways

By many criteria, BA was the largest international airline in the world. In 1982–83, BA carried 11.7 million passengers on 130,728 international departures, well ahead of Air France, which carried 9.6 million international passengers. In terms of international passenger miles, BA's 37 billion a year comfortably surpassed Pan Am. BA flew to 89 cities in 62 countries outside the U.K. (United Kingdom) during 1982–83. Forty-two percent of BA sales were made in the U.K., 25 percent in the rest of Europe, and 33 percent in the rest of the world.

BA was a state-owned enterprise, formed as a result of the 1972 merger of British European Airways and British Overseas Airways Corporation. The economies of scale in the work force, which many expected from the merger, were slow to materialize. Partly as a result, BA continued to record annual losses throughout the 1970s. BA's financial performance was aggravated by increases in the price of fuel oil stemming from the 1973–74 energy crisis. In addition, greater price competition, especially on transatlantic routes, resulted from the deregulation of international air fares. An example of this trend was the advent of the low-price, no-frills Laker Airways Skytrain service on the lucrative transatlantic route in 1979.

The election of a Conservative government in the U.K. in 1979 prompted a change in approach toward the management of BA. The new administration was determined to reduce the losses that almost all state enterprises showed each year and, in many cases, to restore these enterprises to private ownership. A new chairman, Sir John (later Lord)

King, was appointed to head BA in 1980. He initiated programs to improve BA's products and services along with a hiring freeze and an early retirement program to reduce the size of the work force. By March 1983, BA's work force had been reduced to 37,500 people from 59,000 just three years earlier. In addition, BA showed a profit in 1982–83 for the first time in 10 years, compared to a £500 million loss in 1981–82 (see Exhibit 1).

Industry observers believed that BA would have to sustain this improved performance if stock was to be offered to private investors by the end of 1984. So the programs of product and service improvement continued, together with further labor cutbacks. Recently introduced Boeing 757s were added to the fleet in 1983, a quality control division was established, and the U.K. Super Shuttle was introduced.[2]

The turnaround in performance was recognized when BA received the 1983 Airline of the Year award, based on a survey of business travelers. However, although costs were reduced and the quality of service improved, BA's public image remained weak. Along with other nationalized industries, BA continued to share a reputation for inefficiency and incompetence. Accordingly, Lord King stated that one of his main objectives was "to make the airline proud again."

Advertising during the 1970s

During the 1970s, BA country managers had revenue responsibility for BA's marketing and operations in their individual markets. The advertising agencies with which they dealt were appointed by BA headquarters. Foote, Cone & Belding (FCB) had held the BA account in the U.K. since 1947 and, as a result, many country managers outside the U.K. also used FCB subsidiaries or affiliates.

In 1978, British Airways appointed FCB as its worldwide agency, meaning that all country managers *had to* deal with FCB subsidiaries or affiliates in their countries. The purpose was to achieve a more favorable commission rate from FCB, rather than to increase centralized control of advertising content around the world. Indeed, in the United States, where the BA account moved from Campbell Ewald to FCB, the BA advertising theme built around Robert Morley and the slogan "We'll take good care of you" was re-

---

[1]BA's fiscal year ran from April 1 to March 30. At the time of the case, £1 was equivalent to about $1.50.

---

[2]Four shuttles operated between London and Manchester, Glasgow, Edinburgh, and Belfast. Tickets could be purchased in advance or on board, and flights typically left every hour during the day.

tained intact, since it had only recently been launched (see Exhibit 2). Although the Morley campaign was considered a success, building as it did on Britain's favorable reputation in the United States for old-fashioned hospitality, the campaign nevertheless caused problems for BA executives in the United States. In the words of one, "It overpromised on customer service; every time something went wrong, my phone would ring off the hook."

Prior to the appointment of FCB as the worldwide agency, BA country managers were not required to submit their proposed advertising copy to headquarters for approval. There were certain loosely defined guidelines governing the presentation of the BA logo; but, beyond that, local country managers and their agencies were free to determine their own advertising copy. Major advertising campaign concepts did, however, require headquarters approval. Following the appointment of FCB as the worldwide agency, this procedure changed. Each December, BA country managers would submit to headquarters requests for advertising funds for the following fiscal year as part of the annual planning process. Once the commercial director at headquarters had allocated these funds, each country manager would then brief the local FCB agency or affiliate, and develop the advertising copy for the coming year. Country managers in the larger markets would submit their advertising copy to the commercial director in London more as a courtesy, while the smaller countries were required to submit their proposed copy for approval. Headquarters required changes in about 5 percent of cases, typically on the grounds that the advertising overstated claims or was inconsistent with the image BA wished to project.

Whatever the intent, the result of this process was inconsistent advertising from one country to another. First, campaigns varied across markets. The Robert Morley campaign was only considered suitable for the United States. And a recently developed U.K. campaign in which a flight attendant emphasized the patriotism of flying the national flag carrier could likewise not be extended to other countries. Second, commercials and advertising copy promoting the same service or concept were developed in different markets. There were limited procedures within BA and the agency for ensuring that the best ideas developed in one market were transferred to other markets. Finally, the quality of FCB's subsidiaries and affiliates varied significantly from one country to another, aggravating the problem of inconsistency.

BA advertising during this period, like the advertising for most other major airlines, tried to persuade consumers to choose BA on the basis of product feature advantages. Rather than attempting to build the corporate image, BA advertising emphasized superiority and differentiation in scheduling, punctuality, equipment, pricing, seating, catering, and/or in-flight entertainment. Advertising typically focused on particular products, such as the air shuttle, BA tour packages, route schedules, and classes of service (such as Club[3]). The impact on sales of many of these product-specific and tactical advertising efforts could be directly measured. In addition, the commercial director responsible for BA advertising worldwide insisted that a price appear in all advertisements in all media. Frequently, BA advertisements compared the prices of BA services to those of competitors. The commercial director's insistence on including price information in each advertisement frequently caused problems. For example, in the United States, the APEX fare[4] to London from New York differed from that from Boston or Chicago, so different commercials had to be aired in each city.

The 1982–83 advertising budget of £19 million was allocated almost entirely to advertising of a tactical or promotional nature. Only the patriotic "Looking Up" campaign in the U.K. made any effort to develop BA's corporate image. About 65 percent of the 1982–83 budget was allocated by the commercial director to the International Services Division (ISD); about 30 percent to the European Services Division (ESD), and about 5 percent to the Gatwick Division, which handled BA air tours, package holidays, and cargo business in the U.K.[5] BA advertising expenditures during 1982–83 for 14 representative countries are listed in Exhibit 3 together with other comparative market information.

Saatchi & Saatchi Appointed

In October 1982, the Saatchi & Saatchi (S&S) advertising agency was asked by Lord King to explore the possibility of developing an advertising campaign which would bolster BA's image and which could be used on a worldwide basis. S&S was one of the first agencies to espouse the concept of global brands. In newspaper advertisements such as that shown in Exhibit 4, S&S argued that demographic and cultural trends, and, therefore, the basic factors underlying consumer tastes and preferences were converging. In addition, S&S noted a growing spillover of media across national borders, fueled by the development of satellite television. Given these trends and the increasing level of international travel, S&S viewed the concept of global brands employing the same advertising themes worldwide as increasingly plausible.

Following its appointment, S&S set up a Central Policy Unit (CPU) to plan and coordinate work on the worldwide BA account. This unit included a director aided by special-

---

[3]The BA equivalent of Business Class.
[4]Advance purchase excursion fare.
[5]The geographical coverage of the ISD and ESD mirrored that of the old BOAC and BEA.

ists in research, planning, and budgeting. Over a two-month period, the CPU developed into a complete account team, one section of which handled advertising in the U.K. and Europe, while the second handled advertising in the rest of the world. The account team included a creative group and a senior media director with international experience.

After winning the BA account, S&S had to resign its business with British Caledonian, Britain's principal private airline. This business amounted to £3.5 million in media billings in 1982. Three S&S offices in other countries had to resign competitive airline accounts. Of the 62 countries in which BA had country managers, S&S had wholly owned agencies in 20 and partly owned agencies in 17. In the remaining countries, S&S retained a local agency, in some cases an FCB affiliate, to continue to handle the BA account. S&S did not permit its overseas affiliates to collect commissions on locally placed media billings as compensation for working on the local BA account. Rather each affiliate received a fee or share of the commission for the services it performed from S&S headquarters in London. S&S billed BA headquarters for all of its services worldwide, except in the case of such markets as India, where legal restrictions inhibited currency transactions of this nature.

The relationship between S&S affiliates and headquarters was closer than it had been when FCB handled the BA account. A BA country manager would work with the local S&S agency to develop an advertising copy proposal, which would be submitted to BA headquarters in London on a standard briefing form. The BA headquarters advertising manager would then decide whether to approach the S&S account team in London to develop a finished advertisement to be sent back to the BA country manager. Under this system, neither BA country managers nor their local agencies were involved in the design of advertising copy, except in terms of working requests, stating objectives, and suggesting content. According to S&S executives, the frequency with which certain types of advertisement were requested meant that it might, in the future, be possible to develop standard "ad mats." BA country managers and their local agencies would simply fill in the relevant destination and fare information on these ad mats and would not have to submit them to London for approval.

The system described above varied somewhat from one country to another. BA country managers and their local agencies in the five most important long-haul markets (United States, Canada, Australia, South Africa, and Japan) had slightly more autonomy than their counterparts in less important markets. Although all advertising had to be approved in London prior to use, finished copy could be developed in the local market by the local agency in conjunction with the BA country manager.

An early example of how commercials might be developed for use in more than one country under the S&S

approach occurred at the end of 1982. The U.S. country manager developed an advertising proposal for the "Inbound" line of package tours from the United States to the U.K. Members of the U.S. agency creative team and BA executives from New York came to London to develop proposed scripts for the commercials. These were then approved by the U.S. country manager, but the commercials were shot in the U.K. so British scenery could be included. These same commercials were subsequently used in South Africa and the Caribbean with different voiceovers; these countries' budgets could not be stretched to fund their independent production of television commercials of this quality.

Meanwhile, organization changes occurred at BA. Following the appointment of Mr. Colin Marshall as managing director in February 1983, the three divisions were replaced by eight geographic market centers, which handled BA's basic passenger business and three additional business units handling cargo, air charter services, and package tours. These 11 profit centers reported to Mr. Marshall through Mr. Jim Harris, marketing director.[6] Mr. Harris also supervised a central marketing services staff involved with strategic planning, advertising, market analysis, and market research. An advertising manager who reported to the general manager for marketing services was responsible for agency relations and for the review and implementation of advertising by BA country managers. One of his assistants handled relations with the U.K. and European country managers; a second handled relations with the remaining country managers.

Under this new organization, BA country managers submitted their annual marketing plans, including proposed advertising and promotion budgets, to the appropriate market center manager in London. The country managers were informed in 1983 that their future budget proposals would have to provide detailed objectives and research support. In particular, country managers would have to forecast how their overall sales and profits would be impacted by particular advertising and promotion programs. The total advertising budget would be allocated among the country managers according to the quality of the proposals and according to which markets were designated for maintenance or development spending levels.

If a country manager required additional funds during the fiscal year or wished to offer special consumer price deals and travel agency commissions above the norm applicable to the countries in his or her market center, that manager could apply to the market center manager in London. The marketing director held a reserve fund to deal with such contingencies. He or she also reserved the right to

---

[6]The marketing director performed the tasks previously undertaken by the commercial director. The latter title was no longer used.

reallocate funds designated for one market to another during the fiscal year if, for example, foreign currency fluctuations altered the attractiveness of one market versus another as a holiday destination.

Development of the Concept Campaign

The S&S creative team was charged with developing an advertising campaign that would restore BA's image and prestige, and not necessarily by focusing on specific BA products, services, and price promotions. The agency described the qualities of the ideal advertising concept for the campaign: "It had to be simple and single-minded, dramatic, and break new ground, instantly understood throughout the world, visual rather than verbal, long-lasting, likable, and confident." S&S executives believed that the type of product-feature-based advertising used by BA and traditional in the airline industry could not satisfy these objectives. First, an airline competitor could easily match any product-based claim BA might make. Second, such advertising only impacted that portion of the target market who viewed the benefit on which superiority was claimed (e.g., seat width) to be particularly important. The agency believed that only a brand concept campaign could focus consumers on the permanent and essential characteristics of BA, which transcended changes in product, competitive activity, and other market variables.

The agency established five objectives for the worldwide BA concept campaign:

- To project BA as the worldwide leader in air travel.
- To establish BA as the world's most successful airline.
- To demonstrate the superiority of BA products.
- To add value in the eyes of passengers across the whole range of BA products.
- To develop a distinctive, contemporary, and fashionable style for the airline.

The account team had the benefit of consumer research that S&S had conducted in July 1982 with business and pleasure travelers in the U.K., United States, France, Germany, and Hong Kong to understand better attitudes toward, and preferences for, particular airlines. Based on these data, S&S executives concluded that consumers perceived most major airlines as similar on a wide array of dimensions. To the extent differences existed, BA was viewed as a large, experienced airline using modern equipment. However, BA was rated poorly on friendliness, inflight service, value for money, and punctuality. In addition, BA's image varied widely among markets; it was good in the United States, neutral in Germany, but weak in France and Hong Kong. The name of the airline and the lack of a strong image meant that consumer perceptions of its characteristics were often a reflection of their perceptions of Britain as a country.[7] BA was often the carrier of second choice after a consumer's national flag airline, particularly among consumers taking a vacation trip to the U.K.

By November 1982, BA had developed in rough form a series of 11 television commercials around the theme "The world's favorite airline." The lead commercial of the concept campaign, known as "Manhattan Landing,"[8] was to be 90 seconds long with no voiceover during the first 40 seconds and with a total of only 35 words of announcer copy. It would show the island of Manhattan rotating slowly through the sky across the Atlantic to London accompanied after 70 seconds by the statement that "every year, we fly more people across the Atlantic than the entire population of Manhattan."[9] Ten other commercials known as the "preference" series showed individuals (from an Ingrid Bergman look-alike in Casablanca to members of a U.S. football team) receiving airline tickets and being disappointed to find that they were not booked on BA. International celebrities, such as Peter O'Toole, Omar Sharif, and Joan Collins, were shown at the end of each commercial checking in for a BA flight. The announcer copy for all the preference commercials was identical. Storyboards for Manhattan Landing and one of the preference commercials are presented as Exhibits 5 and 6. The intention was to air these commercials in all BA markets worldwide with changes only in the voiceovers.

In November, the BA board of directors approved production of Manhattan Landing and three of the preference commercials. Production costs for these four commercials were estimated at £1 million.[10] S&S executives were asked to have the finished commercials ready for launch by April 1983—a very tight schedule given the complexity of the executions.

While the commercials were being produced, members of the S&S account team and BA headquarters advertising executives traveled to each BA market. Their purpose was to introduce and explain the worldwide concept campaign at meetings attended by each BA country manager and his or her staff along with representatives of the local BA ad-

---

[7]In addition, some BA executives believed that BA was perceived more favorably in countries that had previously been served by BOAC than those previously served by BEA.

[8]The Manhattan Landing commercial was originally conceived as a corporate advertisement to be shown exclusively in the U.K. to support BA's privatization effort. When it became clear that the offering of BA stock to the public would be delayed until at least the end of 1984, it was decided to include it in the worldwide concept campaign.

[9]BA flew 1.5 million passengers across the Atlantic to the U.K. in 1982–83, more than Pan Am and TWA combined. The population of Manhattan was 1.4 million.

[10]Recent BA television commercials had cost about £75,000 to produce.

vertising agency. These visits occurred during January and February 1983 and involved the presentation of storyboards, rather than finished commercials.

Reactions to the Concept Campaign

Reactions varied. The concept campaign was well received in the United States, although the BA country manager was concerned about its dissimilarity from the existing Robert Morley campaign, which emphasized traditional British values. In India, there was some question about whether Manhattan would hold any significance for the local audience. In other countries, including former British colonies, the claim "the world's favorite airline" was met with such reactions as "you must be joking!" The claim seemed to lack credibility particularly in those markets where BA was in a relatively weak share position versus the national flag carrier. In other markets, such as France and Kuwait, only the state-owned airline was allowed to advertise on television, so the BA concept commercials could only be used in cinema advertising.

Questions about the proposed campaign were also raised by S&S affiliates. Since the parent agency had built its reputation on the importance of developing clear-cut positioning concepts, the proposed commercials seemed inconsistent with the philosophy of the agency. Even though the preference commercials were each planned to be 60 seconds long, some agency executives argued that they were too cluttered and tried to achieve too many objectives.

In particular, the 90-second Manhattan Landing commercial was greeted by some with amazement. One agency executive commented: "The net impact of three 30-second commercials would surely be greater?" The South African agency requested a 60-second version of the commercial because the South African Broadcasting Company would not sell a 90-second piece of commercial time. S&S management had to decide whether to accommodate this request.

Other BA country managers were concerned that the concept campaign would reduce the funds available for local tactical advertising presenting fare and schedule information specific to their particular markets. One BA manager, after seeing the proposed campaign commented, "Where are the smiling girls, the free cocktails, and the planes taking off into the sunset?" Another asked, "Will this campaign sell seats?" The BA proposal to spend half of the worldwide 1983–84 advertising budget of £26 million on the concept campaign meant that the amount available for local tactical advertising would fall from £19 million to £12 million. Preliminary BA concept and tactical advertising budgets for 14 representative countries are presented in Exhibit 7. Partly in response to the country managers' concerns, the total budget was raised to £31 million in April when BA's 1982–83 operating results were known. Forty percent of the new budget was allocated to the worldwide

concept campaign, 60 percent to tactical local market advertising.

Some country managers complained that their control over advertising would be reduced and that a corporate advertising expenditure in which they had no say would be charged against their profits. BA headquarters executives responded that, while the country managers were required in 1983–84 to spend 40 percent of their budgets against the concept campaign, they were free to determine the media allocation of concept campaign expenditures in their markets and the weight of exposures given to each of the four executions. They were also free to spend more than 40 percent of their budgets on the concept campaign if they wished.

Despite such concessions, the Japanese country manager remained adamantly opposed to adopting the concept campaign. On the London–Tokyo route, Japan Air Lines held a 60 percent market share, compared to BA's 40 percent. Of the traffic on the route, 80 percent originated in Japan, and 80 percent of those on board BA flights were tourists on package tours. The Japanese country manager rejected the concept campaign as inappropriate. He presented market research evidence showing that his main challenge was selling Britain as a destination, rather than developing consumer preference for BA.

The April 10 Launch

Some S&S executives had hoped that BA would commit almost all of its 1983–84 advertising budget to the concept campaign. However, local marketing requirements highlighted by the country managers necessitated the continuation of tactical advertising, albeit at a reduced rate. The logo and slogan from the concept campaign were, however, to be incorporated in BA tactical advertising, and the requirement that tactical creative copy be developed by S&S in London ensured that this would be the case.

Despite all the reservations they had encountered, BA and S&S executives in London felt that they had sold the campaign effectively to most of the BA country managers. Thus, an invitation was mailed by Lord King to all BA employees in the U.K. to view the introductory television commercial on April 10. Videocassette copies of this six-minute commercial were mailed to BA offices around the world. BA country managers invited representatives of the travel industry to attend preview parties timed to coincide with the launch of the new concept campaign in their respective countries.

The campaign was launched in the U.K. on April 10 as planned and, within two weeks, was being aired in 20 countries. For two reasons, few country managers adopted a "wait and see" attitude. First, the marketing of package tours for the summer season had already started (in the northern hemisphere). Second, many country managers had exhausted their 1982–83 advertising budgets by the end of January, with the result that consumers had not been exposed to any BA advertising for several months.

The Concept Campaign in the United States

The United States was one of the countries in which the concept campaign was launched on April 10. The BA country manager welcomed the campaign since consumer research indicated that BA's size was not recognized by most consumers in a country where, for many, bigger meant better. When asked to name the airline that carried the most passengers to the U.K., more respondents cited Pan Am and TWA than BA. The results of the survey, conducted in New York and Los Angeles in March 1983, also showed:

- Unaided awareness of BA as a leading international carrier was 41 percent in New York (Pan Am—85 percent; TWA—74 percent) and 33 percent in Los Angeles (Pan Am—76 percent; TWA—74 percent).
- Unaided recall of BA advertising was 21 percent in New York and 17 percent in Los Angeles.
- BA was mentioned as one of the three largest airlines in the world by 15 percent of New York respondents and 13 percent in Los Angeles.
- BA was mentioned as one of the three best international carriers by 11 percent of New York respondents and 9 percent in Los Angeles.

The BA country manager viewed the concept campaign as a means of addressing some of these deficiencies. Since the claim "the world's favorite airline" was well documented, the U.S. country manager did not anticipate a legal challenge from Eastern Airlines, which used the slogan "America's favorite way to fly."

The media plan for the concept campaign (Exhibit 8) called for a combination of spot television in BA's six key gateway cities, national network television, and commercials on Cable News Network. The Manhattan Landing commercial was scheduled to be shown four times on national network television. Management argued that this would provide BA with exposure in important markets near gateway cities and would also excite the BA sales force and the travel industry. Four exposures were deemed sufficient given the commercial's creative originality. They would reach 45 percent of the U.S. adult population an average of 1.2 times.

The budget for the concept campaign from April to June was $4 million. Nevertheless, during this period, the BA country manager expected to be outspent by Pan Am and TWA in BA gateway cities. In 1982–83, Pan Am and TWA advertising expenditures for domestic and international routes combined approximated $65 million and $50 million, respectively.

In addition to the concept campaign, the BA country manager had also developed a business campaign and a leisure campaign for 1983–84.

Business campaign. Recent consumer research indicated that Pan Am and TWA were perceived as superior to BA on attributes important to business flyers. BA advertising directed at business people had not significantly improved these perceptions (BA and TWA advertisements targeting the business traveler are presented in Exhibits 9 and 10). However, the perceptions of BA among its business passengers were much more positive than those of non-BA passengers, indicating significant customer satisfaction. BA's U.S. marketing director concluded that BA had a substantial opportunity to increase its share of the transatlantic business travel market.

The following three objectives were established for the 1983–84 business advertising campaign:

1. Increase awareness of the name "Super Club" as a service comparable to (or better than) TWA's Ambassador Class and Pan Am's Clipper Class.
2. Increase the business traveler's awareness and knowledge of the features of all three BA business travel services: Concorde, First Class, and Super Club.
3. Maximize the "halo" benefits of BA's Concorde in marketing efforts directed at First Class and Super Club consumers.

The media schedule for the business campaign (Exhibit 11) emphasized national magazines and both national and local newspapers. Magazines were selected that had higher than average percentages of readers in BA's gateway cities. Newspapers with strong business sections were given preference.

Leisure campaign. BA advertising targeting the leisure traveler had traditionally focused on BA's hotel, car rental, and package tour bargains. Despite high consumer recall of these "bolt-on" features, consumer perception research indicated that BA lagged its competitors on such attributes as "good value for money" and "good deal for leisure travelers." Accordingly, BA's advertising agency suggested that these bolt-on features be subordinated to the objective of creating a general impression of value for money through advertising an airfare bargain along with BA's expertise in things British.

The objectives for the 1983 summer campaign were:

1. Capitalize on BA's reputation as a marketer of good vacation buys, reinforcing consumers' willingness to arrange their European vacations with BA.
2. Promote awareness of and demand for BA's summer transatlantic leisure-oriented fare of $549 roundtrip.

A BA summer campaign newspaper advertisement and a Pan Am advertisement targeting the leisure traveler are reproduced as Exhibits 12 and 13. BA executives were planning on developing print advertisements targeting the leisure market, which would mirror the commercials in the concept campaign if it proved successful.

The media schedule for the leisure campaign (Exhibit 14) emphasized spot television and the travel sections of local newspapers. Their late advertising deadlines meant that fare changes could be quickly communicated to consumers.

Conclusion

As BA and S&S executives implemented the worldwide concept campaign and the biggest advertising effort in BA history, they contemplated several issues. First, if awareness, recall, and sales data indicated that the campaign was not having the desired impact in a particular market, would BA headquarters permit the country manager to curtail the concept campaign? Second, if the campaign was successful, how long could it be sustained before becoming "tired?"

A third issue was how competitive airlines would respond to the BA concept campaign. Believing that the major carriers wished to avoid a new worldwide competitive price war, BA executives believed that they would adopt a "wait and see" attitude. However, market share losses would make retaliation inevitable, particularly in markets like the Far East, where Singapore Airlines and Cathay Pacific held high market shares and were extremely price-competitive. In such a situation, should BA steadfastly continue to spend 40 percent of its advertising budget on the concept campaign or should some of these funds be diverted to tactical advertising in particular local markets? The probability of such diversion of funds depended partly on the emerging profit picture during the fiscal year and partly on the level of unspent tactical advertising funds. It was, therefore, more likely to become an issue toward the end of the fiscal year.

A further related issue was the appropriate budget split between the concept campaign and tactical advertising in 1984–85. Some BA executives argued that, if the concept campaign were successful, it would be possible to reduce expenditures on the campaign to a maintenance level and proportionately restore tactical advertising. They maintained that such a move would shift control of the advertising budget from S&S back to BA. But agency executives argued strongly that the concept campaign should be centrally administered from BA headquarters and that expenditures on the campaign in each country should not, unlike tactical advertising, be regarded as a route operating cost. They also argued that the concept campaign was essential to BA's long-term effectiveness and should not be sacrificed to short-term operational requirements.

EXHIBIT 1   **British Airways: Income Statement,
April 1, 1982 to March 31, 1983**

	Million £
Sales revenues	
Passengers on scheduled services	1,771
Passengers on charter services	86
Freight	151
Mail	36
Ground arrangements for package tours	100
Total	**2,144**
Expenses	
Staff	593
Aircraft	101
Engineering	107
Operations	863
Marketing	205
Accommodation, ground transport, and administration	159
Recoveries	(158)
Ground arrangements for package tours	102
Total	1,972
Operating surplus	172
Plus: Operating surplus from nonairline activities[a]	18
Plus: Other income[b]	20
Total	210
Less: Cost of capital borrowings and tax	149
Profits before extraordinary items	51
Plus: Profit on sale of subsidiaries	26
Profit	77

[a]Including BA helicopters, BAAC, and IAC.

[b]Investments in other companies, interest earned on cash deposits, surplus from disposal of assets.

"We're up in the air
before most airlines
even wake up!"

We can beat the experience

British Airways beats Pan Am's experience five times a day. After all, we have more business seats to London than Pan Am and TWA combined.

You'd like a 10 a.m. flight? Of course we have it…we've had it for years. And British Airways offers something really special on it. First Class and Super Club® passengers receive a voucher worth £20 (about $33) for dinner in any one of four exclusive restaurants. Tourist passengers receive a voucher for a choice of one of five evenings of cabaret entertainment with dinner.*

British Airways has the very first flight out daily (9:30 a.m. Concorde). So we're up in the air before most airlines even wake up. We also have the last daily flight out (10:00 p.m.) and three flights in between. And British Airways Super Club seats are by far the world's widest business class seats.

Need we go on? We could mention our free helicopter service,** or our preferred hotel and car rental rates for business travelers, or our longstanding commitment to our 10 a.m. flight. And you'll be pleased to note that your flight miles between the U.S. and London will count as credit toward the A Advantage® travel award plan.

So you see, British Airways has no trouble beating the experience. It's experience like ours that makes us the world's favourite airline. That's why British Airways flies more people to more countries than anyone else. See your travel agent or corporate travel department.

*Offer valid April 15-October 31, 1983 and subject to government approval. For full fare USA originating passengers only. See vouchers for details.
**Helicopter service free for Concorde, First Class and Super Club passengers.

DEPARTURE	AIRCRAFT	FREQUENCY
9:30AM	Concorde	Daily
10:00AM	TriStar/747	Daily
1:45PM	Concorde	Daily
7:00PM	747	Daily
10:00PM	747	Daily

British airways
The World's Favourite Airline™

EXHIBIT 3   Comparative Data for 14 Markets

	Percent BA 1982–83 Worldwide Passenger Revenues	1982–83 Advertising Expenditures (£000)	Principal BA Competitors	BA's Market Share versus Principal Competitor	Percent Business/Percent Pleasure BA Passengers
United Kingdom	42.0%	6,223	British Caledonian[a] Pan American	Similar	42/58
United States	14.0	5,773	Pan American TWA	Lower	26/74
Germany	5.0	228	Lufthansa British Caledonian	Lower	50/50
Australia	3.0	967	Qantas Singapore Airlines	Similar	6/94
France	3.0	325	Air France British Caledonian	Lower	52/48
Japan	3.0	393	Japan Airlines Cathay Pacific Airways	Lower	30/70
Gulf States	2.0	134	Gulf Air Kuwait Airlines	Lower	12/88
Canada	2.0	991	Air Canada Wardair	Lower	11/89
South Africa	2.0	331	South African Airways TAP (Air Portugal)	Lower	15/85
Italy	2.0	145	Alitalia Dan Air	Lower	50/50
New Zealand	1.0	125	Air New Zealand Singapore Airlines	Similar	3/97
Egypt	0.5	53	Egyptair Air France	Similar	26/74
Zimbabwe	0.4	41	Air Zimbabwe KLM	Higher	8/92
Trinidad	0.3	77	BWIA	Higher	7/93

[a]These are BA's principal competitors on international routes. BA's main competitors on domestic United Kingdom routes were British Midland Airways and Dan Air.

Exhibit 4
Saatchi & Saatchi newspaper advertisement

THE OPPORTUNITY FOR WORLD BRANDS.

Nowadays, life for branded goods manufacturers is not as straightforward as it once was.

Many years ago manufacturers first recognised that advertising could provide a key foundation for their business growth.

They realised that while their customer was the retailer, the actual 'consumer' was the public; that advertising could enable them to build a solid position in their market by building the goodwill of their real customer – the 'consumer.'

They also saw that if they, the manufacturers, did something to move their goods from retailers' shelves as quickly as they arrived on them, trade would be brisk and everyone would be satisfied.

Thus the manufacturer became the advertiser of 'branded' products, the retailer became the purveyor of 'brands' and advertising became a conspicuous feature of the age.

This happy cycle produced 'brands' of startling endurance and longevity, as the table below shows.

US BRAND LEADER

1923	CURRENT POSITION
SWIFT PREMIUM, BACON	NO. 1
EASTMAN-KODAK, CAMERAS	NO. 1
WRIGLEY, CHEWING GUM	NO. 1
NABISCO, BISCUITS	NO. 1
EVEREADY, BATTERY	NO. 1
GOLD MEDAL, FLOUR	NO. 1
LIFE SAVERS, MINT CANDIES	NO. 1
SHERWIN-WILLIAMS, PAINT	NO. 1
GILLETTE, RAZORS	NO. 1
SINGER, SEWING MACHINES	NO. 1
COCA-COLA, SOFT DRINKS	NO. 1
CAMPBELL'S, SOUP	NO. 1
IVORY, SOAP	NO. 1

SOURCE: ADVERTISING AGE

Brand Character

Nowadays, when probed deeply, consumers describe the products they call brands in terms that we would normally expect to be used to describe people. They tell us that brands can be warm or friendly; cold or modern; old-fashioned; romantic; practical; sophisticated; stylish and so on.

They talk about a brand's persona, its image and its reputation – and this 'aura' or 'ethos' is what characterizes a brand.

It follows that all brands, like all people, have a 'personality' of one kind or another. But like the strongest individuals, the strongest brands have more than mere personality – they have 'character' – more depth, more integrity, they stand out from the crowd.

Note the importance that one major marketer attaches to this concept.

> *"My acid test on the issue is whether a housewife intending to buy Heinz Tomato Ketchup in a store, finding it to be out of stock, will walk out of the store to buy it elsewhere or switch to an alternative product."*
> A.J. O'REILLY, PRESIDENT & CEO, H.J. HEINZ

This explains why the best marketers try to develop powerful brand characters. They make them less vulnerable in the market-place. They help a higher quality product to be perceived as such by consumers.

Today, the establishment of such strong and enduring brands is rather more difficult.

- ☐ Static populations mean static markets which means increased competition for market share.
- ☐ Product quality is converging, with increasing technological parity among major marketers.
- ☐ The influence of the retailer and retailers' own store brands is growing in many parts of the world.
- ☐ Marketing expenses are growing, as manufacturers respond to the ever-higher cost of reaching the consumer.

All in all, the pressures on manufacturers' brands are immense.

Superior Product Quality

Serious marketers know that in the face of these pressures the success of their brands can only rest on superior product quality.

They know that as the consumer views more products as commodities, it becomes harder to establish a meaningful point of difference for their products. They know that clever marketing and promotion of cosmetic differences cannot paper over this.

They know that the longevity of their brands is helped by good marketing, but is founded on superior product performance and this in turn is founded on their ability to produce a *higher quality product at a lower cost.*

Which is why market leaders' priorities are now focusing on a common objective which was not among their priorities in previous decades – to work diligently to be the *low-cost producer* in their market.

Low costs provide the means to achieve that happiest of all situations – higher product quality ... fewer price increases ... and more advertising.

Low costs are the priority as a sound base for all the other steps needed to build growth.

Thus, the competitive intensity of maturing packaged goods markets around the world has brought to the fore the economic logic of world brands – *the opportunity for international economies of scale as the basis of long-term strategic security.*

Today, the most thoughtful companies are adopting a new approach to international marketing.

These companies are moving through the five basic stages in the life of a multinational corporation as seen in the chart below.

And as they pass through stages 4 and 5 the need for pan-regional and world marketing is emerging at the heart of their business strategy.

> *"The globalization of markets is at hand. With that, the multinational commercial world nears its end, and so does the multinational corporation.*
>
> *The global corporation operates as if the entire world (or major regions of it) were a single entity; it sells the same things in the same way everywhere.*
>
> *Corporations geared to this new reality can decimate competitors that still live in the disabling grip of old assumptions about how the world works."*
> PROFESSOR THEODORE LEVITT, HARVARD UNIVERSITY

A New Approach

After the vicissitudes of the 1950s and 1960s, more companies are now reaching the status of having acquired 'critical mass' in various regions of the world. They are now starting to turn from primary concern about 'return on acquisition investment' and 'overhead recovery' towards getting to grips with long-term franchise building across each world region.

At the same time the progressive harmonization of 'headquarters' and 'local' management culture and style, evolving from more frequent two-way movement of personnel, is enhancing the likelihood of successful adoption and execution of pan-regional business strategies.

And meanwhile in Europe, management's strategic thinking is beginning to broaden to match the dimensions of the Common Market as legislative harmonization focuses attention on pan-European issues.

International Growth Priority

Companies have passed through the bygone age when many of them treated 'Overseas Division' as the poor cousin of the organisation, struggling to compete in foreign markets with strongly established indigenous competitors.

The international divisions of many companies are now beginning to 'come of age' and receive their rightful allocation of corporate resource, if only for the practical reason that corporate earnings growth in many multinationals is today often provided by non-domestic markets.

Business System Economics

The strategic value of pan-regional branding lies in the scale economies it affords across the company's business system – to help make the company the low-cost producer.

Where the economies arise will vary by product category, and may include research and development, materials purchasing, manufacturing, distribution and advertising.

The optimum business system for a European beer, for example, is markedly different to that for chewing gum, but the principle is the same. Secure, franchise-protected volumes at the regional scale can allow a company to *build a price/cost/value structure which will eventually put it out of reach of competition.*

All these factors set the conceptual framework within which a truly pan-regional brand can exist in the years ahead. The international need is the starting point. Research will be conducted to look for market similarities between countries, not to seek out differences. Similarities will be the new fuel for growth.

The creative process will still be as vital as ever; marketers in each location will still be dependent on the intuitive creative judgement of locally based creative management, but this effort will be marshalled to a single-minded overall advertising strategy.

Marketing Learning Curve

There is then a real marketing learning curve that allows the progressive refinement of a success formula, as the pan-regional brands broaden their experience country by country.

The best creative brains are given an opportunity to develop advertising for an entire region of the world, and not simply for one market – to find a real advertising idea *so deep in its appeal* that it can transcend national borders previously thought inviolate.

Consumer Convergence

In the past, the successes in world branding have been few, and have been achieved by virtue of the sheer will and far-sighted commitment of managements who stayed consistently with a long-term vision for the business. Procter & Gamble is a company in this category that comes to mind.

In the future, the only winners in cross-country branding will be companies who have seen that social developments are making redundant the old idea that differences between nations are decisive in framing marketing strategy.

The most advanced manufacturers are recognising that there are probably more social differences between Midtown Manhattan and the Bronx, two sectors of the same city, than between Midtown Manhattan and the 7th Arrondissement of Paris. This means that when a manufacturer contemplates expansion of his business, consumer similarities in demography and habits rather than geographic proximity will increasingly affect his decisions.

Demographic Convergence

Trends of vast significance to consumer marketing, such as ageing populations, falling birth rates, and increased female employment are common to large segments of the modern industrial world.

Consumer convergence in demography, habits and culture is increasingly leading manufacturers to a consumer-driven rather than a geography-driven view of their marketing territory.

Decline of the Nuclear Family

Some of the most telling developments spring from the same source – the decline of the nuclear family. Observers have attributed this to various causes – the rapid pace of technological development; higher labour productivity which reduces hours of work; and other more metaphysical notions such as the emergence of a 'liberal' philosophy, which increasingly recognizes that a woman's role can exist outside the home.

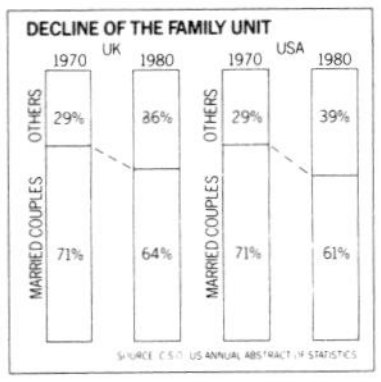
DECLINE OF THE FAMILY UNIT
UK
USA
1970
1980
1970
1980
OTHERS
MARRIED COUPLES
29%
36%
29%
39%
71%
64%
71%
61%
SOURCE: C.S.O. US ANNUAL ABSTRACT OF STATISTICS

Whatever the causes, the effects in terms of household composition have been dramatic. There are now less children per household, and a declining proportion of households which conform to the two-adult-two-children pattern.

The result is the erosion of the traditonal family unit and its clarity of role and relationship. The effects have been illustrated by the decline of formal meal-taking and the corresponding increase in the sales of 'instant' and 'convenience' foods. The multinational expansion of fast-food franchises like McDonalds is another manifestation of the same trend.

Changing Role of Women

The table below shows the change in the role of women in the working population over the past decade. The fact that the majority of women in most modern societies now have a job requires a major adjustment to current ideas on communicating with a consumer group that no longer conforms to the home-centred stereotype of yesteryear.

MORE WORKING WOMEN

	%CHANGE 1970–1979 WORKING POPULATION	WORKING WOMEN
USA	+ 24.4	+ 37.6
BELGIUM	+ 8.3	+ 24.7
NETHERLANDS	+ 10.1	+ 24.6
ITALY	+ 8.1	+ 22.8
FRANCE	+ 7.7	+ 17.3
UK	+ 4.5	+ 15.1
GERMANY	− 1.6	+ 3.5

SOURCE: EUROSTAT

Associated with this change, there has been a well documented trend to lower marriage rates and higher divorce rates. This trend has led one group of social scientists to invent the phrase "serial monogamy" to describe what they forecast to be the nature of relationships in the 1980s and beyond. They suggest that there will be an increasing tendency for couples to live together for a number of years, then to change their partners and set up home afresh, changing again after a few years, and so on. This discontinuity in formal relationships, especially where children are involved and re-marriages occur, will have profound effects on family relationships.

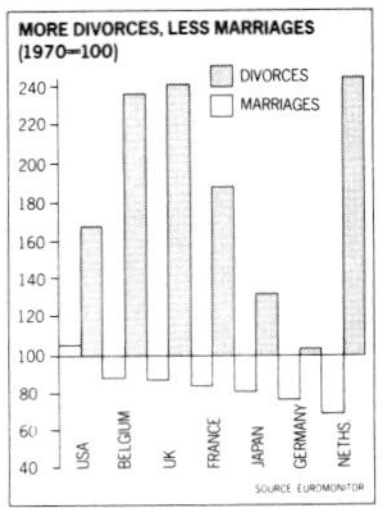
MORE DIVORCES, LESS MARRIAGES (1970=100)
DIVORCES
MARRIAGES
240
220
200
180
160
140
120
100
80
60
40
USA
BELGIUM
UK
FRANCE
JAPAN
GERMANY
NETHS
SOURCE: EUROMONITOR

Static Populations

Population growth is now almost zero in the western world. All modern industrial countries are forecast to produce population growth of much less than 1% per annum over the next 20 years. It is hardly surprising that within this static population, the age structure is undergoing a transformation. The over 65s are a growing group relative to the 25–65s, and that group is growing relative to the fourteen and unders.

STATIC POPULATIONS

	% GROWTH PER ANNUM 1960–70	1980–2000 ESTIMATE
AUSTRALIA	2.0	0.8
CANADA	1.8	0.8
USA	1.3	0.7
SPAIN	1.1	0.7
JAPAN	1.0	0.6
FRANCE	1.0	0.4
ITALY	0.6	0.3
UK	0.5	0.2
GERMANY	0.9	0.1

SOURCE: WORLD DEVELOPMENT REPORT

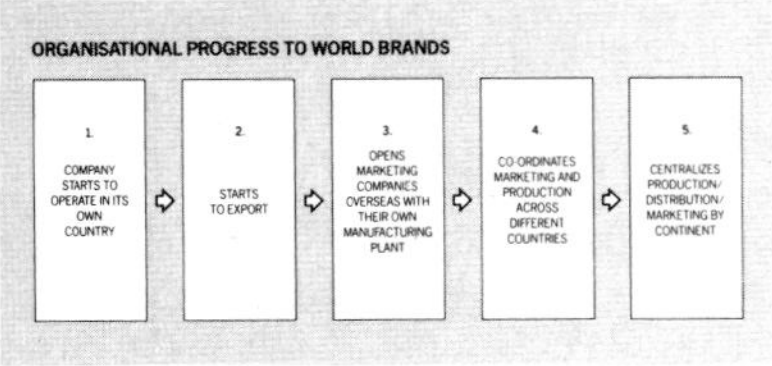
ORGANISATIONAL PROGRESS TO WORLD BRANDS
1. COMPANY STARTS TO OPERATE IN ITS OWN COUNTRY
2. STARTS TO EXPORT
3. OPENS MARKETING COMPANIES OVERSEAS WITH THEIR OWN MANUFACTURING PLANT
4. CO-ORDINATES MARKETING AND PRODUCTION ACROSS DIFFERENT COUNTRIES
5. CENTRALIZES PRODUCTION/ DISTRIBUTION/ MARKETING BY CONTINENT

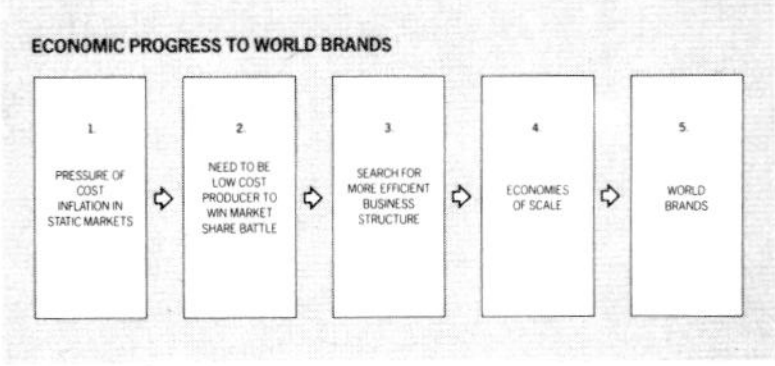
ECONOMIC PROGRESS TO WORLD BRANDS
1. PRESSURE OF COST INFLATION IN STATIC MARKETS
2. NEED TO BE LOW COST PRODUCER TO WIN MARKET SHARE BATTLE
3. SEARCH FOR MORE EFFICIENT BUSINESS STRUCTURE
4. ECONOMIES OF SCALE
5. WORLD BRANDS

EXHIBIT 4
(concluded)

Higher Living Standards

In most western countries, improvements in the material standard of life have resulted in a growing demand for consumer durables and for more leisure. This is reinforced by shorter working weeks that accompany technological progress and productivity growth.

The entry of women into the labour market itself creates a demand for consumer durables to ease the strain of 'keeping house'.

HIGHER LIVING STANDARDS

	GROWTH IN REAL PERSONAL CONSUMPTION 1970–82
USA	+ 42%
UK	+ 26%
FRANCE	+ 60%
GERMANY	+ 34%
JAPAN	+ 65%

SOURCE: HENLEY CENTRE

Cultural Convergence

At the same time as demography is converging, television and motion pictures are creating elements of shared culture. And this cultural convergence is facilitating the establishment of multinational brand characters. The worldwide proliferation of the Marlboro brand would not have been possible without TV and motion picture education about the virile rugged character of the American West and the American cowboy – helped by increasing colour TV penetration in all countries.

Observers believe that cultural convergence will proceed at an accelerated rate through the next decade – particularly with the deployment of L-SAT high-power TV satellites throughout Europe.

EUROPE'S NEW SUPER STATIONS

These developments will reduce cultural barriers as countries exchange their media output through satellite networks – for the first time allowing viewers freer access to international television without the barrier of language.

Marketing Timetables

Analysis of all these demographic, cultural, and media trends is allowing manufacturers to define market expansion timetables. Essentially, marketers will be tracking trends which indicate when a region is ready for attack via programmes they have tested elsewhere.

For example, current changes in European laundry practices were foreshadowed by similar trends in the US during the late '60s and early '70s. Thus a US manufacturer of low-suds detergent would examine the growth in the penetration of front-loading washing machines in the UK to assess the ripening potential for his own product.

MARKET EXPANSION TIMETABLES
% OF HOUSEHOLDS OWNING FRONT LOADING WASHING MACHINES

'76 '77 '78 '79 '80 '81 '82 '83

SOURCE: COMPANY RESEARCH

Consider also Europe's soap powder manufacturers. Driven by improved washing machine technology and the increased popularity of relatively fragile synthetic and coloured fabrics, European laundry habits have converged. Every major nation now washes a majority of its wash loads in under 60°C water. This has created a common need for a product which performs well under these circumstances.

The result has been the marketing of single brands with a common brand name, product formulation, and positioning across the whole of Europe.

In the future, the only winners in cross-country branding will be companies who do a lot of things right and synthesise their efforts effectively around three golden rules:

1. To market clearly differentiated products that either drive, or capitalize on, real convergences in consumer habits and tastes.

2. To create a dedicated management value system that mirrors the vision of a pan-regional branded business.

3. To monitor their brands' character on a consistent, continuous, comparable basis across geography and over time.

The opportunity for world brands is there to be seized but only for those companies with the long-term determination to meet these stringent requirements.

Here are two other examples of the global approach in action – for British Airways and Procter & Gamble's Pampers. The Pampers brand was introduced in the US in the late 1960s. Pampers created the disposable diaper market by providing a product that was more convenient and more absorbent than cloth diapers at a price consumers were willing to pay. Pampers is now Procter & Gamble's largest brand and is sold on a similar strategy almost all over the world. If the Pampers business was a separate company, it would rank in the top one-third of the 'Fortune 500' list.

Does a global advertising campaign have to be bland? Not according to the South China Morning Post which described B.A.'s new worldwide campaign as *"unique and imaginative"*; or the Sydney Morning Herald – *"a radical departure from the usual formula"*; or Newsweek – *"a tour de force"*; or the Wall Street Journal – *the most audacious attempt so far . . . in an all-new world campaign"*; or the London Sunday Times – *"a flash of inspiration."*

The Agency is now working on a similar exercise on Silk Cut for American Brands/Gallaher – a Company whose marketing was recently described by the Financial Times as *"an object lesson for its competitors on the rewards of brand discipline."*

65 OFFICES IN 38 COUNTRIES.

THE UK AGENCY WORKS WITH 6 OF BRITAIN'S TOP 10 ADVERTISERS.

THE US AGENCY HANDLES MORE No. 1 BRANDS THAN ANY OTHER AGENCY IN AMERICA.

THE INTERNATIONAL NETWORK WORKS WITH 44 OF THE WORLD'S TOP 200 ADVERTISERS.

Impact on Agency Structure

What are the implications of these trends for the advertising industry?

Business service companies, such as agencies, benefit from the increasing complexity of problems in their areas of expertise. Knowledge has value, and there is a greater 'value-added' during periods of turmoil and change in the business environment.

Most observers believe that the trend to pan-regional or global marketing will have a marked impact on the structure of advertising agencies... because world brands require world agencies.

A HANDFUL OF WORLDWIDE AGENCY NETWORKS WILL HANDLE THE BULK OF $125 bn WORLD ADVERTISING EXPENDITURE FOR MAJOR MULTINATIONALS.

Many expect to see the advertising industry moving in the same direction as accounting, banking, financial services, etc. – a polarization between worldwide networks servicing global corporations, and strong local firms handling domestic clients in their own country.

SOME OF THE AGENCY'S CLIENTS IN 3 OR MORE COUNTRIES

ALLIED LYONS	IBM
AMERICAN BRANDS	JOHNSON & JOHNSON
AMERICAN MOTORS	NABISCO BRANDS
AVIS	NESTLE
BLACK & DECKER	PEPSICO
BRITISH AIRWAYS	PROCTER & GAMBLE
BSN-GERVAIS DANONE	PLAYTEX
CADBURY SCHWEPPES	ROWNTREE MACKINTOSH
CHESEBROUGH-POND'S	TIMEX
DU PONT	UNITED BISCUITS

This is pleasant for the business prospects of those agencies who can serve this global requirement, but leaves open one important question – whether this trend will result in *better* advertising? On this question opinions differ.

Some agency managers are fond of saying that they would rather operate a solid, disciplined international network than run the best creative agency in the world.

Meanwhile, others declare that they would rather have high creative standards than succumb to the arthritis of international management structures.

Both these viewpoints ignore the possibility of combining discipline and creativity in one international organisation. This is because is it hard to do.

IN 1982, OUR UK AGENCY WON MORE TOP UK ADVERTISING AWARDS THAN ALL THE OTHER MAJOR MULTINATIONAL AGENCIES PUT TOGETHER.

SOURCE: GOLD AND SILVER AWARDS IN THE CAMPAIGN PRESS AWARDS, D&AD AND BRITISH TELEVISION ADVERTISING AWARDS

The Company has always aimed to create *the one type of agency which has somehow eluded the group of those few men and women who have tried to achieve it* – a large agency, certainly, with all the stability that gives to employees, and all the back-up that provides for clients – but one which at the same time also succeeds in being progressive, youthful and innovative in approach.

The fact that this combination has so rarely been achieved in our industry increases the sense of purpose with which we continue to pursue it as our goal.

This has been the fundamental spur to our growth over the years.

HIGH CREATIVITY ACROSS A DISCIPLINED WORLD NETWORK. THE COMPANY'S CONSISTENT STRATEGIC GOAL.

Last month Saatchi & Saatchi Company PLC, the parent company of the worldwide agency network, announced its results for the year ended September 30th 1983. It was the Company's 13th successive year of profit growth. In the year pre-tax profits rose by 103%, earnings per share by 40%, dividends per share by 45%.

Over the last five years the Company has shown a compound average growth of 43% in pre-tax profits, 33% for earnings per share, and 37% for dividends per share.

If you would like a copy of the Chairman's Statement on these results please write to the Company Secretary, Saatchi & Saatchi Company PLC, at 80 Charlotte Street, London W1A 1AQ, or 625 Madison Avenue, New York, New York 10022.

SAATCHI & SAATCHI
COMPTON WORLDWIDE.

EXHIBIT 5

Manhattan Landing storyboard

EXHIBIT 6

Casablanca Preference Campaign storyboard

EXHIBIT 7 BA Concept and Tactical Advertising Budgets: Initial 1983–84 Plan (£000)

	Concept Campaign			Tactical Campaigns	Row Total
	April–September	*October–March*	*Total*		
United Kingdom	4,700	1,200	5,900	3,200	9,100
United States	2,600	750	3,350	2,450	5,800
Germany	450	450	900	607	1,507
Australia	500	100	600	350	950
France	150	200	350	269	619
Japan/Korea	200	70	270	400	670
Gulf States	0	35	35	190	225
Canada	900	200	1,100	400	1,500
South Africa	300	75	375	250	625
Italy	150	100	250	225	475
New Zealand	100	0	100	100	200
Egypt	50	0	50	30	80
Zimbabwe	32	0	32	25	57
Trinidad	18	0	18	27	45
Other	NA	NA	860	3,220[a]	4,080
Total	10,150	3,180	14,190	11,740	25,930

[a]Includes contingency fund.
NA means not available.

EXHIBIT 8 Media Budget and Schedule of the British Airways Concept/Brand Campaign in the United States ($000)

	April–June 1983		September–October 1983	
	No. Spots	*Expenditures*	*No. Spots*	*Expenditures*
Spot television (in 6 gateway markets)[a]	686	$2,900	175	$572
Network television[b]	4	1,040	—	—
Cable television	40	104	25	58
Total	730	$4,044	200	$630

Reach/Frequency

Gateway cities	86%/8.7 times	63%/3.3 times
Remainder of United States	45%/1.2 times	—

Audience Composition	*Percent of Those Reached*	*Index[c]*
Adult men	48%	102
Adult women	52	99
Age 25–54	73	137
Household income $30,000 +	47	169

[a]New York, Washington, Boston, Miami, Chicago, and Los Angeles.
[b]Only the Manhattan Landing execution was shown on network television. It was targeted at the 78% of U.S. households not reached by the spot television advertising.
[c]Each index figure represents the percentage degree to which the audience reached included more or fewer people than the U.S. population at large.

EXHIBIT 9

BA business campaign magazine advertisement

EXHIBIT 10

TWA business segment magazine advertisement

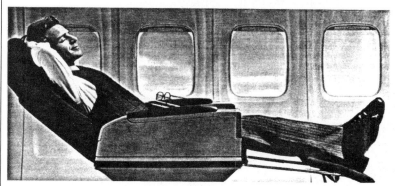

TWA.
Our First is foremost.

Only TWA has First Class Sleeper-Seats℠ on every widebody. For First Class comfort.

First and foremost, there are our First Class Sleeper-Seats.

They are available on every 747, every L-1011, and every 767, everywhere we fly in the U.S., Europe and the Middle East. So you can rest easy every time you fly TWA.

Just settle into a Sleeper-Seat, and you'll be impressed with its incredible comfort and legroom. Then settle back—the seat stretches out with you.

Royal Ambassador℠ Service. First Class service in a class by itself.

TWA's Royal Ambassador Service is available on every transatlantic and transcontinental route we fly, as well as selected shorter domestic flights.

We offer a gourmet menu with a choice of entrees like Chateaubriand. Vintage wines from California and France. A selection of fine liqueurs and cognac. All cordially offered to you in a warm, personal manner.

We even cater to your needs before you take off. In major airports, you'll find a special First Class desk to speed you through check-in. And a special lounge for transatlantic passengers to relax in before flight time.

So call your travel agent, corporate travel department, or TWA.

Because for First Class service that's second to none, there's only one choice. TWA.

You're going to like us ◢TWA

Source: *New York Magazine,* March 7, 1983.

EXHIBIT 11   Media Budget and Schedule of the British Airways Business Campaign in the United States ($000)

	December 1982–March 1983[a]		April–June 1983		September–October 1983	
	No. Insertions	Expenditures	No. Insertions	Expenditures	No. Insertions	Expenditures
22 magazines	8	$121	30	$ 745	22	$674
3 newspapers (*The Wall Street Journal, New York Times, L.A. Times*)	9	563	13	371	17	276
Total	17	**$684**	43	**$1,116**	39	**$950**

Reach/Frequency: Men 25–54

Gateway cities	73%/7.4 times[b]	65%/5.4 times
Remainder of United States	67%/6.3 times	55%/3.5 times

Percent Reach to Those Planning Foreign Travel for Business

Audience Composition		Index
Adult men[c]	72%	147
Age 25–54	69	126
Attended/graduated college	64	197
Household income $35,000+	55	284

[a]No insertions prior to February 1983.
[b]Figures for December 1982 through June 1983.
[c]In 1982–83, about 10% of transatlantic business travelers were women.

Great Britain Great Price

$549

round trip
(and only $18 a day for a hotel*)

With British Airways' fantastic fares and today's incredible dollar exchange rate, there's never been a better time to visit Britain. Plus, British Airways offers "London Hotel Bargains" including the modern, convenient Kennedy Hotel for only $18 per night (includes private bath and continental breakfast); the Regent Palace for $13 a day (without private bath but a stone's throw from Piccadilly); and "Britain Car Rental" offering a Ford Fiesta with unlimited mileage for only $17 a day. Call British Airways or your travel agent for more information on these and other great deals now!

"Good show"

Britain Salutes
New York 1983

British airways

Airfare valid for travel through September 14. Tickets must be purchased 21 days in advance. Minimum stay 7 days. Maximum stay 6 months. There is a weekend surcharge. Car and hotel rates valid through October 31. Petrol and tax not included with car.
*Hotel rates per person, double occupancy and include VAT and tax.

British Airways, P.O. Box 10010,
Dept. H.T. Long Island City, NY 11101
Dear Mr Morley,
Please send me the following brochures.
☐ DollarSaver™ Holidays in London
☐ Fly/Drive Holidays in Britain

Name
Address
City
State   Zip

EXHIBIT 14   **Media Budget and Schedule of the British Airways Leisure Campaign in the United States ($000)**

	December 1982–March 1983		April–June 1983		September–October 1983	
	No. Spots, Insertions	*Expenditures*	*No. Spots, Insertions*	*Expenditures*	*No. Spots, Insertions*	*Expenditures*
Spot television (10 markets)	—	—	450	$795	—	—
Local newspapers (11 markets)	3–4/market	$641	3–7/market	620	4–6/market	$550
Reach/Frequency Average market	40%/2.0 times		75%/5.0 times		47%/2.9 times	

	Percent Reach to Those Planning a Foreign Vacation	*Index*
Audience Composition		
Adult men	45%	96
Adult women	55	105
Age 25–54	60	114
Household income $30,000 +	49	175

WATERS CHROMATOGRAPHY DIVISION: U.S. FIELD SALES (A)

The cornerstone of our business—and a big part of the Waters culture—is "The Waters Difference."

William (Bill) Shippey, president of the Waters Chromatography Division of the Millipore Corporation, explained further:

> Waters was considered a pioneer in high-performance liquid chromatography [HPLC], which is a relatively new technique for separating complex chemical mixtures into their individual components. In the early years, there was limited expertise in the industry, and many of the people who knew HPLC worked at Waters. We built our business by helping customers with their separation problems. We would send in application specialists to show them how to use HPLC—and our products—for their particular task. With this application-oriented approach, Waters essentially created the market for HPLC.

Chane Graziano, vice president of worldwide business operations, agreed: "Technical expertise and strong customer support are the basis of our differentiation in the marketplace, and our premium price. That's why our field organization is staffed by expert chemists with experience in HPLC—not typical sales representatives."

Rod Bretz, regional sales manager for New England, interjected:

> It's not always that easy to make a technical person into a salesperson. They sometimes get caught up with the technology and don't close the order as soon as they might. Also, a salesperson must be flexible, and highly technical people sometimes tend to be inflexible and thus not responsive to customer needs. Selling, though, is a skill that can be learned. Salespeople with a technical background have a much better chance for success because we sell solutions to problems, and a technical background very often is needed to deal with our customers' problems.

Industry Background

HPLC Technology. The objective of HPLC was to separate a complex chemical mixture into its individual components. Essentially, an HPLC system consisted of a reservoir of solvent, a pump, an injector, a steel or plastic column tightly packed with microscopic particles, a detec-

tor, and a recorder. The HPLC separation process involved a three-way chemical interaction among the sample, the solvent, and the column packing material. Depending on the nature of the sample, specific solvents and column packings were selected from the wide array of available HPLC chemical products. (Exhibit 1 shows the basic components of a system for performing HPLC, and describes the separation process.)

Competitive Environment. The worldwide market for HPLC was estimated at approximately $350 million in 1984, and was expected to grow 15 percent annually through the rest of the decade. Waters was the world leader in HPLC, with a market share at least double that of its nearest competitor. Competitive pressures varied by geographic area, as reflected in Waters's regional business performance (see Table A).

The HPLC market could be divided into two broad segments: (1) instruments, which included pumps, injectors, detectors, and data and control units; and (2) chemical products, which included the packed columns and other disposable supplies and accessories used in HPLC systems. Both market segments were dominated by Waters, which competed directly against other premium-priced vendors (Hewlett-Packard, Varian, Perkin Elmer, Beckman, and IBM in instruments; Du Pont and Altex in columns) and also faced growing pressure from smaller, low-cost manufacturers.

Company Background

History. Waters was founded in 1962 to develop, manufacture, and market HPLC-based products used for the analysis and purification of fluids in critical applications. A 10-year "boom period" of fast growth and big profits

This case was prepared by Research Associate Shirley M. Spence and Professor Thomas V. Bonoma.

Copyright © 1985 by the President and Fellows of Harvard College.

Harvard Business School case 9-586-011.

TABLE A   **Waters Regional Business Results, 1984 Forecast ($ in millions)**

	U.S.	Canada	Europe	Pacific	Total
Sales	$70.0	$5.7	$40.8	$25.5	$142.0
Market share (%)	48%	60%	36%	30%	40%

ended in the mid-1970s as competitive pressure mounted. Sold by founder James Waters in 1980, the company became a largely autonomous operating unit of the Millipore Corporation—the world leader in membrane separation technology. Projections for 1984 showed worldwide sales of the Waters Chromatography Division at $142 million, which represented approximately 43 percent of Millipore's total net revenues. (Exhibit 2 shows the Waters income statement.)

Products.   Waters offered a complete line of HPLC instruments, accessories, columns, and supplies. In 1984, instrument sales represented over 62 percent of total Waters revenues, with the balance largely accounted for by sales of chemical products and revenues from spare parts and service (i.e., preventive maintenance contracts, repair fees, customer "HPLC Schools"; see Table B).

A Waters instrument system was assembled from a choice of standard modules (pumps, injectors, detectors, and other accessories), as shown in Exhibit 3. Modules could be facility-installed as part of a complete new system, added to an existing system, or sold separately to customers wishing to assemble their own system. A complete system cost between $10,000 and $40,000, depending on the choice of modules. Waters also offered dedicated systems tailored for specific applications (e.g., the Sugar Analyzer I for analyses of corn, beet, and cane sugars).

The Waters chemical products line encompassed a total of 380 items, including a variety of packed columns for use in Waters or competitive instrument systems. Chemical products prices ranged from $175 to $750 per item, with an average customer order amounting to $900.

Customers.   Waters served a technical customer base in a variety of research and industrial settings, focusing on specific application niches within each customer market. In 1984 the company's largest markets were (1) pharmaceuticals, a large and mature business base; and (2) life sciences/biotechnology, a new and rapidly growing segment. Other important markets included polymers, industrial chemicals, food/agriculture, and electronics. The four broad application areas targeted by Waters were analytical laboratories, research laboratories, clinical laboratories, and quality control laboratories. Virtually all Waters sales were made directly to end users by the division's own sales force.

Marketing Strategy.   Waters's overall marketing objective was to grow the business at least 20 percent annually by maintaining market share in existing markets and by developing new market areas via the aggressive marketing of existing products, the timely introduction of new products, and a broadened applications emphasis.

Organization and Management.   The Waters Chromatography Division, which employed 1,485 people in 1984, was organized into functional departments: manufacturing, human resources, marketing, research and development, and worldwide business operations (field sales and service). Department heads were based at the divisional headquarters in Milford, Massachusetts, and reported directly to Bill Shippey. Shippey, who held an engineering degree and had a background in sales, joined Waters in 1981 as general manager of U.S. business operations and was named president in 1983.

Waters Sales and Service Organization

As vice president of worldwide business operations for Waters, Chane Graziano was responsible for the company's domestic and foreign field organizations, and also supervised three staff groups located at divisional headquarters. (See Exhibit 4 for a partial organization chart.) Graziano, whose background included a position as a laboratory chemist at Procter & Gamble as well as 10 years in sales management with a major HPLC competitor, had been recruited by Waters in 1979 for a U.S. sales management position. In his current role, he had profit and loss responsibility for Waters's U.S. business and its foreign subsidiaries.

Headquarters Staff.   Headquarters staff for worldwide business operations consisted of a national accounts manager, two worldwide sales training personnel, and a 31-person customer support group.

National accounts manager (NAM).   The NAM position involved the management of 40 U.S. customers who collectively represented about 45 percent of Waters's total dollar volume. These included U.S. government agencies (e.g., the

---

TABLE B   **Waters Sales by Product Line**
($ in millions)

	1983 — Actual		1984 — Forecast	
	Amount	Percent Change	Amount	Percent Change
Instruments	$ 75.7	7.2%	$ 88.5	16.9%
Chemical products	23.1	1.8	26.3	13.9
Spare parts and service	18.7	28.1	22.6	20.9
Other[a]	2.5	78.6	4.6	84.0
Total sales	$120.0	9.8%	$142.0	18.3%

[a]Products purchased from original equipment manufacturers for resale to Waters customers

Food and Drug Administration) and major university and industrial accounts, such as Hoffman LaRoche, Eli Lilly, Dow Chemical, the Massachusetts Institute of Technology, Procter & Gamble, and Monsanto. With each of these accounts, Waters conducted annual contract negotiations in which customer spending commitments were made in exchange for special terms. Waters management tried to institute high visibility programs that provided value to the end user, as opposed to price discounts seen only by the purchasing agent. As an example, for the $2 million Monsanto account, Waters offered a $200,000 package that included a full-time service engineer plus a 5 percent discount, rather than an equivalent cost 10 percent discount.

The NAM position had evolved over time. Until recently, contract negotiations, order monitoring, and the handling of other major account program details had been assigned to a trained national accounts administrator. In 1984, Graziano decided to convert the job to a training position for senior sales representatives on track for regional management posts. Responsibilities would include managing Waters's existing base of national accounts and establishing 10 to 20 high-potential target accounts. Graziano was considering restructuring the NAM compensation package—which offered a flat salary of $40,000—to include a base salary plus a commission linked to growth within target accounts. As of late 1984, the new NAM position had not yet been filled.

Worldwide sales training. The director of worldwide sales training was responsible for planning and implementing Waters's standardized training program for new field sales personnel. The program consisted of six week-long courses designed for 20 to 25 participants each. Course topics were (1) chemistry, (2) chromatography, (3) HPLC hardware, (4) basic selling, which taught a consultant-style approach, (5) competitive selling, and (6) S-4, which described four basic social styles (expressive, amiable, driver, analytical) and taught sales representatives to recognize and adapt to the individual customer's preferred style. A new sales recruit was sent immediately to the first four courses of the series, and then attended the remaining two courses sometime over the next few years.

Customer support. The primary goal of the customer support group was "to get the right people doing the right thing when a customer calls."[1] This effort occupied a staff of 31 people, and involved three major activities: (1) telephone support for customers needing technical assistance with application or equipment problems, (2) response to customer requests for information, and (3) telephone

order-taking. Management estimated that 75–80 percent of instrument orders and virtually all chemical products orders were placed by mail or telephone. Instrument orders usually were based on a quotation prepared by a field sales representative, whereas chemical products and small parts typically were ordered by the purchasing agent from Waters's published price list. Field sales representatives received weekly order reports for their respective territories.

The customer support department also included a six-person telephone-lead screening group staffed by sales trainees. Prospective customers requesting information were taken through a series of questions listed on a "qualifier" sheet, which then was forwarded to the appropriate field sales representative for follow-up.

U.S. Field Operations. Since 1981, U.S. field operations had been divided into three areas (Midwest, West/South, East), each operating as a profit center. Each area had its own branch sales office and applications laboratory facilities for running customer samples. Overall responsibility for each area rested with its general manager, who reported directly to Chane Graziano. Area general managers earned approximately $75,000 in salary and were eligible to participate in company stock benefit plans.

In addition to the three area general managers, the 1984 U.S. field organization included a total of eight regional managers, 57 sales representatives, 53 service representatives, and 26 sales support personnel. The Eastern area's reporting structure (see Exhibit 4) was similar to that of the two other areas. Its general manager, J. Sweeney, directly supervised an applications laboratory manager, three field marketing managers,[2] and three regional managers. Each regional manager, in turn, directly supervised seven or eight sales representatives and also was responsible for seven service representatives and a technical support person.

The Regional Manager. The regional manager (RM) typically had come up through the sales ranks, where he or she had demonstrated good selling skills and the ability to manage a territorial business effectively. The RM was charged with maximizing revenues from an assigned geographic region, and managed a regional budget that included service as well as sales expenses. RM compensation consisted of a salary of $40,000–50,000 plus $10,000–20,000 in commissions, based on regional sales volume growth.

The RM was considered a "front line manager" whose primary responsibility was managing the sales force. The

---

[1]This group also provided secretarial support for special field sales activities (e.g., a mailer for a seminar).

[2]Field marketing managers, who focused on specific products or markets according to the area's needs, conducted promotional activities (e.g., seminars, direct-mail campaigns) designed to generate leads for sales follow-up.

RM was expected to spend at least 60 percent of his or her time in the field, helping sales representatives with skills development and customer calls. At the beginning of every year, the RM worked with each salesperson to construct a territorial business plan, which they reviewed together on a quarterly basis. The RM also conducted annual performance reviews, which included career development planning. Hirings and terminations were handled by RMs, with the approval of the area general manager.

In performing their sales supervisory duties, regional managers relied primarily on personal observation of salespeople's activities and on quote conversion rates (i.e., a comparison of quotations issued versus actual orders, which afforded a measure of lost business). Chane Graziano explained his views on performance standards as follows:

> I leave it up to the regional managers, some of whom are interested in calls per day. I'm not. I believe you should concentrate on the input (i.e., skills development) and the output (i.e., quotations and orders), not the number of calls. The key thing is productive time. If I know the number of leads sent to a rep, how many prospects he or she has, the dollar value of quotations issued, and the actual order figures, then I can calculate productive time and the success of the individual.

The regional manager's direct supervision of field service and technical support personnel was limited. The service group was managed internally by a regional service manager.[3] Field service representatives were responsible for prepurchase demonstrations, installation of equipment, customer training on new instruments, preventive maintenance for service contract customers, and repair work. Service representatives received about $24,000 in base salary, and could earn $3,000–5,000 extra through an incentive plan based on service billings and contracts, and sales of spare parts, accessories, and chemical products. Technical support staff, who handled customer training programs ("HPLC schools") and provided service for customers' technical problems, earned $25,000–35,000 per year, with no incentive plan.

When not working directly with the sales force, the regional manager was occupied with administrative duties, such as signing expense accounts, tracking quotations and orders, preparing sales forecasts, and writing reports monthly. The RM, who was authorized to discount prices up to 8.9 percent in competitive situations, also was responsible for good business practices on the part of Waters field personnel.

The Sales Representative.   Field sales representatives sold all Waters products to all customer markets in their assigned geographic territories and also conducted technical seminars on various HPLC topics. Each salesperson had a dollar-volume quota and was expected to devise and implement a business plan to achieve that goal. In 1984, a salesperson managed from 2 to 100 customer accounts (the average was 40 accounts) and generated $1.3 million in total sales.

Over the 1980–84 period, Waters added 27 new field sales positions to meet the needs of its rapidly growing business. The typical new recruit was 25 to 30 years old, with two or three years of laboratory experience. Waters management explained that there had been a shift first away from and then back to the tradition of fielding a technically trained sales force:

> By the mid-1970s, the HPLC market had matured to the point where there was a substantial base of experienced chromatographers who were more interested in instrument features and options than in application support. Our competitors were quick to capitalize on this, taking the approach: "You already know how to use HPLC, customer; now buy this fancy new gear." We were losing hardware business because we couldn't sell competitively. Our technically trained reps just couldn't handle it and began to fall out, so we hired the competition to fill the gaps. When we did a study on the backgrounds of our top-performing salespeople, we found that the competitive hires were the most productive over the short term, but generally stayed only 12 to 18 months. Part of the problem was that they were from companies where HPLC was just one of five or six product lines sold, so they weren't expected to be expert in HPLC. Also, they liked to get the order and move, and didn't want to spend a lot of time with each customer. In the early 1980s, we returned to our policy of recruiting expert chromatographers for field sales.

New field sales representatives usually were drawn from the telephone-lead screening group at Waters headquarters, or were recruited directly from Waters application laboratories and from among Waters customers. New sales hires usually spent their first month attending sales training courses in Milford and then moved to the field. The regional manager would help the new salesperson develop a territorial business plan and set up a call schedule and usually spent a minimum of one week making calls with the representative.

The sales representative's compensation package included a base salary, a sales incentive program, an expense account, and the use of a company car. In 1983, the average Waters salesperson earned $34,000 in salary and commission, while about 10 percent of the sales force earned $60,000 or more. In addition, Graziano accompanied 40 salespeople and their spouses to Hawaii on a vacation trip earned by increasing territorial volume by $300,000 or more.

---

[3]Regional service managers indirectly reported to the vice president of products, projects, and services, who was part of the Waters marketing department.

In 1984, base salaries, which included an annual merit increase tied to U.S. inflation rates, ranged from $24,000 for a new hire to $42,000 for a salesperson with 10 years of experience. The Waters 1984 incentive program was linked to achievement of territorial sales quota and had two broad components: (1) an annual plan linked to a 12-month quota calculated by adding $300,000 to the territory's base business (i.e., the previous year's volume) and (2) a quarterly plan linked to quarterly goals, which were seasonally adjusted percentages of the annual quota. (Incentive plan descriptions and a sample calculation of a salesperson's 1984 bonus appear in Exhibit 5.)

At the time of hire, 70 percent of sales representatives did not plan a career in sales but rather saw it as a route to a marketing position at the home office. In reality, only 10 percent eventually did follow that path, while the others decided to remain sales representatives, opted for a sales management track, or left the company. Management estimated annual field sales turnover at 10–20 percent, and the cost in lost orders of each turnover at $260,000.

Waters Sales — A Day in the Field

On November 14, 1984, a casewriter spent a day making customer calls with Ray Burnett, a Waters field sales representative. An accounting of this day follows background descriptions of Ray Burnett and his supervisor, Rod Bretz. (A summary of the day's activities is also provided in Exhibit 6.)

Ray's Background. Ray grew up in New England and also attended college there, earning a degree in biology. He joined Waters in 1975 as an applications laboratory chemist and subsequently moved to the position of telephone-lead screener at the Milford home office. In 1977, he was assigned to a sales territory in St. Louis, Missouri, where he built up a successful sales record over the next three years. Ray then decided to return to New England and requested a transfer, which was granted. He purchased a home in a seaside Massachusetts town about 40 minutes by car from downtown Boston and 60 minutes from Milford. Ray, his wife, and two young children were still living there in 1984.

Since returning to the New England region, Ray had managed three different sales territories. Upon his arrival in late 1981, he had been given a choice of two territories: (1) an industrially oriented area that was enjoying good growth or (2) Boston, where Waters business was biology-based and less strong. Ray chose Boston, and had a relatively poor year in 1982. In 1983, Ray was assigned a new territory that included downtown Boston and the Massachusetts Medical Center. That year he generated $1.4 million in sales, earning $26,000 in commissions. In 1984, territorial boundaries shifted once again. Ray's new territory included part of his previous area plus some new accounts.

Ray's Supervisor. Ray reported directly to Rod Bretz, the New England regional manager. Bretz, who held a business administration degree, had come from a regional sales manager's position at a pharmaceutical company to be a field sales representative for Waters in 1973. In 1975, he was transferred from his Louisiana territory to a management position at Waters headquarters. Five years later, he decided to return to field sales: "It wasn't any fun inside anymore. For a salesman, getting the order is all the fun, and I'm a salesman."

During Bretz's subsequent four years as regional manager for New England, that region's sales climbed from $2.4 million in 1980 to $9.5 million in 1984, its field organization grew from 6 people to 16, and the number of sales territories doubled. To Bretz, establishing territorial boundaries had been an immediate and ongoing challenge. He explained:

> When a territory's volume base gets too big, you have to divide it up. The big question, though, is: Who divides it? When I took over New England, I could see there had been gerrymandering: people had been setting up territory boundaries so as to get and keep the best accounts. I believe in fair play, though, so each time there was a personnel shift, I'd readjust the territories with the objective of giving each salesperson a business base that would allow him or her to be successful.

According to Bretz, the salesperson's job was "to go out and get orders." Noting that new recruits typically had strong chemistry backgrounds but no field sales experience, he added:

> A lot of people here think of salespeople as used-car hucksters. We're always arguing over what's more important—technical or selling skills. I say its a 49–51 percent split, with the extra 2 percent going either way. You don't have to be a Ph.D. in chemistry, though it makes it easier. I believe the salesperson must know a certain amount about the product but that, essentially, he or she is a broker for the technical know-how of our applications laboratory people and service engineers. It's my job to make sure my salespeople get that technical support . . . and anything else they need to be successful.

Bretz maintained substantial contact with customers through his frequent participation in sales representatives' calls and his involvement in service management issues. On average, Bretz spent three days a week in the field and two days at home, where he had an office. He prioritized his field time against inexperienced salespeople but had frequent telephone interaction with all his sales representatives. Bretz estimated that over the past year he had spent 12 days in the field with Ray and had spoken with him by telephone at least once a week.

conflict with

Ray Burnett's Job.   Ray defined his field sales position as "using my technical background to help people solve their problems." He also compared his job to "running my own little business." He had full responsibility for building volume in his territory and a large measure of control over his time and activities. He estimated that 25–30 percent of his time was spent on direct selling, with much of the balance devoted to customer service and the conducting of seminars on various HPLC topics. Ray said he usually got home around 8:00 P.M., often because he would "get stuck helping someone in a lab." He did weekly call reports only sporadically, preferring to spend the time on call planning.

Ray covered a geographic area that included parts of downtown Boston, some northern suburbs, and central Massachusetts. In 1983, about 80 percent of that territory's $1.4 million business had been generated by only 20 percent of its accounts: the Massachusetts General Hospital, the Massachusetts Institute of Technology, the University of Massachusetts medical area, the New England Nuclear Corporation, and the Polaroid Corporation. In planning his calls, Ray concentrated first on his existing customer base. He allocated calls roughly according to the percentage of business represented by each account but tried to see each customer at least twice a year.

Ray also tried to allocate some time to new business development. For instance, if time permitted, he could "cold call" any one of a number of companies along his route—that is, get into its research and development or quality control laboratory, speak with someone about potential applications for HPLC, and get a sample for a "trial run" at a Waters laboratory. Ray felt there were many new business opportunities in his territory, but found he had little time to pursue them.

Ray's sales quota for 1984 was $1.7 million, which represented a 21 percent increase over his 1983 base business. He expected to sell 26 instrument systems and generate about $1.5 million in total sales in 1984. In general, Ray felt he did "pretty well" financially as a Waters sales representative, but he had some concerns about the company's sales incentive program:

> When I started with Waters there was no bonus plan. They started one in 1980 and have changed it every year since then. The current program is largely based on volume growth. The problem with this program, I think, is that it encourages a "sell and run" attitude. It says, "Don't worry about support and service"—which is not how this company became successful. I personally feel that we ought to have an uncommissioned sales force.

Recently, Chane Graziano had contacted Ray to set up a meeting to discuss an opening for the position of national accounts manager. Ray had mixed feelings about the idea of leaving field sales for a home office position. On the one hand, he was tired from the long hours and hectic pace of his field sales job. On the other hand, he would miss the freedom of working out of his home, and he also had some questions about the financial implications of the move.

Ray was looking forward to the next day's meeting with Graziano, both to learn more about the NAM position and to see whether his field-based perceptions of the business matched those of management. Ray felt that, in general, HPLC customers made their instrument purchase decision based on three considerations: (1) equipment capabilities (i.e., instrument features), (2) service and support, and (3) price. Ray had noticed an increasing price sensitivity in the market and found that Waters was perceived as high priced: "Some of our instrument systems are less expensive and more capable than the competition, yet customers don't call because they think they can't afford us." Ray also found that, whereas Waters once dominated the chemical products business, the impression now among customers was that Waters had not "kept up."

Ray Burnett's Customer Calls, November 14, 1984.
Teddie Peanut Products, Inc. (Everett, Massachusetts).   Ray's first appointment was at 11:00 A.M. with the quality control (QC) manager at the Teddie Peanut Products processing plant. In the car, Ray explained to the casewriter that Teddie Peanut Products was a marketing-generated lead. Joe, Teddie's QC manager, had seen some Waters promotional materials and had called the company for more information on HPLC systems to be used for aflatoxin analysis.[4] His name had been forwarded to Ray, who had followed up by telephoning for an appointment and mailing some informational materials: a 12-page color brochure on Waters instrument systems, a Waters technical bulletin on "Rapid, High Sensitivity Determination of Aflatoxins in Peanut Products by HPLC," and a sample chromatogram from an aflatoxin analysis.

The factory was off the highway but relatively easy to find. The otherwise nondescript building was topped by a huge billboard cutout of a teddy bear. At 10:55 A.M., Ray asked the receptionist in the front lobby to tell Joe that "Ray from Waters" had arrived. In a few minutes, Joe came down to escort his visitors up to a small, crowded office on the second floor.

Ray first asked Joe how he had heard about Waters. In response, Joe pulled out a magazine to show Ray the Waters advertisement that had prompted his call. Joe then explained that his monitoring of aflatoxin levels involved testing incoming batches of raw peanuts as well as samples of the processed product. At present, the samples were sent

---

[4] Aflatoxins were carcinogenic compounds produced naturally by fungi in many agricultural products, including peanuts. In the United States, the Food & Drug Administration (FDA) had established maximum aflatoxin levels for raw and finished peanut products.

to a local laboratory and the results telephoned to Joe, who logged them in a book and used them for quality control decisions.

Joe said he was interested in in-house alternatives to the laboratory contract service. When probed about his specific needs, he indicated that speed and cost were important factors. He also asked about help with equipment installation. Ray assured him that Waters would provide assistance in installing the system and "debugging" his application.

When asked if he was familiar with HPLC techniques, Joe said he had a basic understanding from his university studies but had never used the method himself. Ray then reviewed the sample chromatogram with Joe, who seemed a little puzzled. Upon asking about Joe's staffing situation, Ray learned that doing the aflatoxin analysis work in-house would require hiring a new, technically qualified person.

Ray brought out the quotation sheet he had prepared the previous evening and reviewed it in detail with Joe. For Joe's needs, there were two instrument system options: (1) a less expensive ($13,000) basic package that could be automated at an incremental cost and, if desired, could be expanded to provide additional application capabilities, or (2) a dedicated system ($21,000) that was easier to operate but was specific to aflatoxin analysis. Joe seemed most interested in the basic package option, since he was anticipating FDA regulations that would require the monitoring of additional substances. He said that he would, however, need to look at cost considerations more closely and present the issue to his management. Joe accepted Ray's offer to telephone in a few weeks for further discussion, and the meeting ended.

Back in the car at 11:30, Ray commented that the promise of technical support by Waters was especially important to new HPLC users like Joe. Following up on that promise, however, was the challenge. In Joe's case, Ray probably would get a sample from him and take it to the Waters laboratory for analysis. There was supposed to be support staff for running samples, but Ray found the turnaround time slow and often did it himself. If Joe ultimately did buy a system, Ray would have to get an already overextended Waters service person to do the installation and initial training, or do the two-day job himself. The danger, though, was that the salesperson could easily end up "doing it all": finding the customer, running samples, selling instruments, starting up equipment, training, and servicing.

Otis Clapp (Cambridge, Massachusetts). At noon, Ray arrived at Otis Clapp, a medical supply company located in the warehouse district. Otis's laboratory manager had called Ray about an instrument breakdown, and Ray wanted to drop off a replacement part. Ray told the casewriter:

> Customer loyalty depends on rapport. They'll remember me at Otis. It takes one to three years to build up a relationship but eventually it pays off. Yet, I've changed territories every year,

because business growth calls for splitting one territory into two or because the company wants to vary reps' mix of accounts. I think continuity is critical, but we've had pretty high turnover in field sales over the past three years.

After climbing the two flights of stairs to the main office, Ray was told that the laboratory manager was at lunch but should be back in 20 minutes. Ray asked if he could use the telephone to catch up on calls, but was told that all telephones were out of order. About five minutes later, Ray decided to leave the part, along with a note telling the laboratory manager to call if the replacement piece didn't fix the equipment problem.

Massachusetts General Hospital, Cardiac Research Laboratory (Cambridge, Massachusetts). In the elevator, on the way to a 3:00 P.M. appointment with Dr. Michael Margolis, chief of cardiac surgery, Ray encountered a Waters customer from another laboratory area. The technician had a question about a new Waters instrument. Her question was only partially answered by the time her floor was reached. Ray offered to stop by later to see her, but she said she could get any other needed information from the Waters brochure on the instrument.

Dr. Margolis had been a Waters customer for a number of years. He had called Ray to ask him to stop by but had not specified the purpose of the meeting. Since Ray was a few minutes early, he made a quick tour of the cardiac research laboratory and chatted briefly with the laboratory research assistant. The laboratory had three Waters HPLC systems, one of which was very old and one of which included some components from other manufacturers. The laboratory assistant subsequently joined Dr. Margolis and Ray in a meeting held in the doctor's office.

Dr. Margolis began by explaining that he recently had attended a Waters symposium and had some questions about Waters's new data and control system and its amino acid analyzer. The ensuing discussion was lively, relaxed, and technically detailed. Dr. Margolis clearly was knowledgeable not only about HPLC technology but also about various competitors' products and services. He took notes throughout the meeting, and frequently asked his laboratory assistant for his opinions. Ray handled questions about cost and instrument capability easily and without referring to technical publications.

Dr. Margolis first asked Ray to tell him about the Waters 840 Work Station. Ray explained that the system, which included a Digital benchtop computer plus Waters software plus instrument interface units plus a printer, could handle the data management and system control needs of up to four HPLC instruments. Ray estimated the cost of a Waters 840 capable of handling the cardiac research laboratory's three instruments at about $30,000. He also advised Dr. Margolis that the next availability date for the Waters 840 would be in March of 1985.

There was considerable discussion of the logistics and cost of incorporating the Waters 840 into the laboratory's existing facilities. For instance, Dr. Margolis wanted to know if Waters would give a trade-in allowance on the laboratory's present data and control system.[5] He also had concerns about who would be responsible for repairs, citing problems in the past with two vendor-warranty arrangements. Ray explained that Digital would be responsible for servicing the computer hardware but assured him that Waters would stand behind the equipment. Last, Dr. Margolis asked where he could see a Waters 840; Ray told him that there was one presently in use in the radiation biology laboratory.

Dr. Margolis then turned to the subject of the new Waters amino acid analyzer, asking Ray who was using it and what had been published about it. Ray answered, "Ever since the *Science* magazine blurb about it, the phones have been ringing off the hook." He invited Dr. Margolis to come to see the new system at Waters in Milford.

As they walked to the elevator, Dr. Margolis advised Ray that the Waters 840 purchase was a long-term issue, and that in 12 months or so he would be ready to buy. He had raised the issue with Ray now because he was trying to decide whether or not to sell his existing Waters data and control module to an interested buyer. In the elevator, Ray explained that this situation was not unusual: research customers usually first decided to buy the instrument and then found the money.

Massachusetts General Hospital, Radiation Biology Laboratory (Cambridge, Massachusetts). At 5:00 P.M., Ray was scheduled to see Bill, a radiation biology researcher who had come to the Massachusetts General Hospital to work with his present supervisor. One of Bill's responsibilities was to start up a newly purchased Waters HPLC system. Ray had been working with him on that task and the two had become quite good friends, sometimes going out for a drink after work.

When a problem with the new system had arisen, Ray had brought in his own instrument as a temporary substitute. That replacement was now malfunctioning, and Bill had called Ray for help. Ray spent about 15 minutes poking around the system before identifying the problem. He also checked another Waters instrument, which was awaiting a spare part from Service. Ray promised to follow up on the replacement part. He also offered to come in and explain to Bill's supervisor why the new system start-up had been delayed. The offer was accepted by Bill, who then escorted Ray to the parking lot. At 5:30, Ray headed home.

Telephone calls.   Between personal calls, Ray would find a pay phone, usually in the lobby of his last or next appointment, and make as many calls as possible. In the hour between lunch and the meeting with Dr. Margolis, for example, Ray made nine telephone calls and talked to 15 people on a range of topics: a customer interested in a rental program needed help with financing, and Ray was trying to make the necessary arrangements through a bank in Chicago; another customer had an instrument problem; one prospect was almost ready to buy and wanted to talk to Ray; Romicon offered him a job in marketing. A large percentage of Ray's calls involved problem solving. Ray's favorite calls, however, were those that occurred late in the afternoon and culminated in a customer commitment to buy a $60,000 instrument system.

_____

[5]Waters had a buy-back policy based on 20 percent depreciation per year of use.

EXHIBIT 1

Liquid chromatography; components of an HPLC system

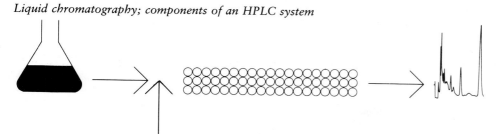

Solvent   Pump   Injector   Column   Detector   Recorder

Separation Process

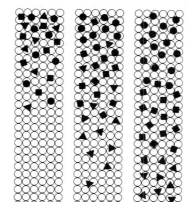

When a sample is injected into a liquid chromatography column, its various components are uniformly distributed.

The components move at different speeds through the column packing material.

Their different rates of progress tend to separate the components into bands in the column which exit separately. As they exit, the components of the sample can be detected and quantified.

Chromatogram

The chromatogram at right results from the HPLC separation of a common headache tablet. A comparison of the positions and heights of the peaks with the positions and heights of peaks derived from known standards allows an identification and quantitation of the four components of the tablet.

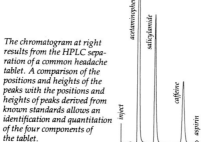

SOURCE: Waters Chromatography Division.

EXHIBIT 2   **Waters Income Statement ($ in millions)**

	1983 (Actual)	*1984 (Forecast)*
Sales	$120.0	$142.0
Gross margin	72.0	85.2
% of sales	60.0%	60.0%
Selling, general and administrative	48.0	54.0
% of sales	40.0%	38.0%
Research and development	9.0	10.7
% of sales	7.5%	7.5%
Operating expense	57.0	64.7
% of sales	47.5%	45.6%
Corporate contribution	$ 15.0	$ 20.5
% of sales	12.5%	14.4%

SOURCE: Waters Chromatography Division.

Exhibit 3

Waters instruments

Begin with your basic starting system then add capability as your needs change.

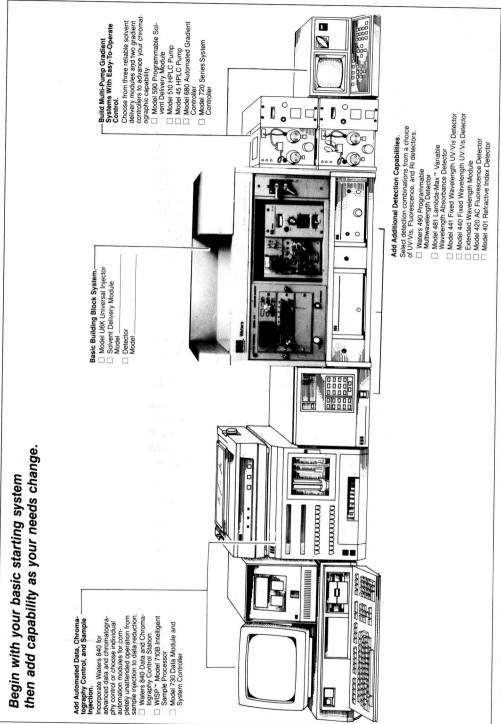

Add Automated Data, Chromatography Control, and Sample Injection.

Incorporate Waters 840 for advanced data and chromatography control or choose individual automation modules for completely unattended operation from sample injection to data reduction.

☐ Waters 840 Data and Chromatography Control Station
☐ WISP™ Model 710B Intelligent Sample Processor
☐ Model 730 Data Module and System Controller

Basic Building Block System.

☐ Model U6K Universal Injector
☐ Solvent Delivery Module
Model _____
☐ Detector
Model _____

Add Additional Detection Capabilities.

Select detection combinations from a choice of UV/Vis, Fluorescence, and RI detectors.

☐ Waters 490 Programmable Multiwavelength Detector
☐ Model 481 Lambda-Max™ Variable Wavelength Absorbance Detector
☐ Model 441 Fixed Wavelength UV/Vis Detector
☐ Model 440 Fixed Wavelength UV/Vis Detector Extended Wavelength Module
☐ Model 420 AC Fluorescence Detector
☐ Model 401 Refractive Index Detector

Build Multi-Pump Gradient Systems With Easy-To-Operate Control.

Choose from three reliable solvent delivery modules and two gradient controllers to advance your chromatographic capability.

☐ Model 590 Programmable Solvent Delivery Module
☐ Model 510 HPLC Pump
☐ Model 45 HPLC Pump
☐ Model 680 Automated Gradient Controller
☐ Model 720 Series System Controller

Source: Waters Chromatography Division.

EXHIBIT 4
Waters 1984 partial organization chart

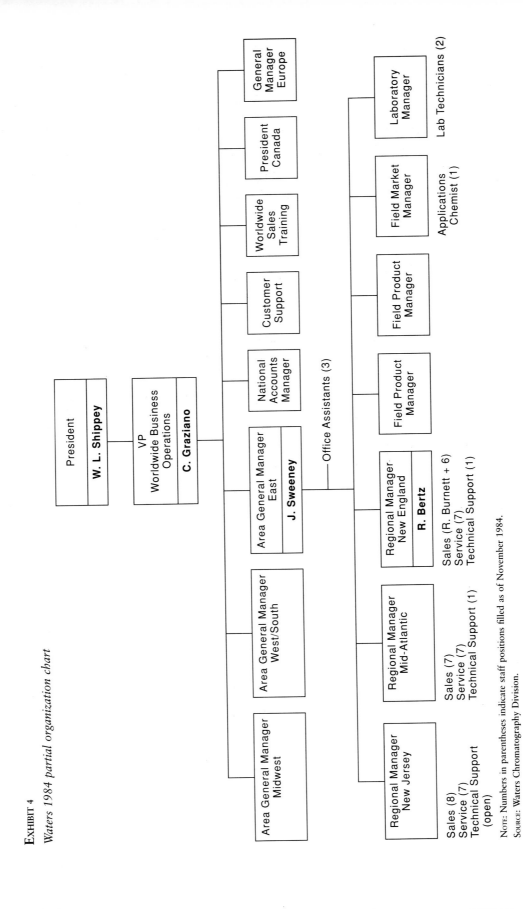

NOTE: Numbers in parentheses indicate staff positions filled as of November 1984.

SOURCE: Waters Chromatography Division.

EXHIBIT 5   Waters 1984 Sales Incentive Program

Program Description

Under the *annual plan,* sales representatives were paid a 4 percent commission on the first $300,000 in territorial growth versus base business and a 10 percent commission on any sales in excess of that quota figure. Under the *quarterly plan,* Waters paid a $500 bonus for achieving the quarterly volume goal plus approximately $300 commission on each instrument system sold. (For purposes of the incentive program, Waters defined an instrument system as either *pump plus injector plus detector* or *two pumps plus control unit.*)

Quarterly plan earnings were paid at the end of each three-month period, and were retained whether or not annual plan quotas were met. For sales representatives who did achieve their annual plan quotas, these quarterly plan payments were considered a draw against the annual plan (i.e., total earnings from the quarterly plan were deducted from the sum earned under the annual plan). Earnings from the 1984 annual plan (minus quarterly draw) would be paid to sales representatives in a single sum in February of 1985.

Sample Calculation of Sales Representative's 1984 Bonus

Performance:	Base business (1983) sales = $1.0 million		
	1984 quota = $1.3 million		
	1984 actual sales = $1.4 million		
	Sold 20 systems (5 per quarter)		
	Met all quarterly goals		
Annual plan earnings:	4% on $300,000	=	$ 12,000
	10% on $100,000	=	10,000
	Total		$ 22,000
Quarterly plan earnings:	By quarter:		
	5 systems @ $300	=	$ 1,500
	Goal @ $500	=	500
	Total		$ 2,000
	Total year		$ 8,000
Total 1984 bonus:	Annual plan earnings	=	$ 22,000
	Less quarterly draw	=	−8,000
	Net earnings		$ 14,000

SOURCE: Waters Chromatography Division.

EXHIBIT 6   Ray Burnett's Schedule: November 14, 1984

A.M.

9:00–10:00[a]	Drove from home to the Harvard Business School (HBS) for 10 A.M. pickup of casewriter. Arrived early so made phone calls from pay phone for about half an hour.
10:00–10:30	Drove to Everett, Mass., for an 11:00 A.M. appointment with the Quality Control/Assurance manager at the Teddie Peanut Products, Inc., factory.
10:30–11:00	Talked with casewriter.[b]
11:00–11:30	First personal call.
11:30–12:00	Drove to Cambridge, Mass., to drop off replacement instrument part at Otis Clapp (second personal call).

P.M.

12:00–12:15	Left part and note at Otis Clapp.
12:15–12:30	Drove to Massachusetts General Hospital where had a 3:00 P.M. appointment with Chief of Cardiac Surgery. Parked at hospital and walked to nearby restaurant.
12:30–1:45	Lunch.[c]
1:45–2:45	Made phone calls from restaurant pay phone.
2:45–3:00	Walked back to Massachusetts General Hospital for appointment, and went to Cardiac Lab. Brief conversation with another hospital staff client on elevator.
3:00–4:00	Third personal call.[d]
4:00–4:45	Made phone calls from hospital lobby pay phone.
4:45–5:00	Walked to another Massachusetts General Hospital building for appointment with Radiation Lab technician to check equipment breakdown.
5:00–5:30	Fourth personal call.
5:30–6:30	Drove casewriter to HBS, and headed home.

[a]Ray had spent approximately an hour the previous night planning calls.

[b]Normally, Ray would have used this time to make phone calls.

[c]Lunch was longer than usual due to the presence of the casewriter.

[d]Call was probably longer than would have been in the absence of the casewriter since the customer was interested in discussing Waters with the casewriter.

MCI TELECOMMUNICATIONS CORPORATION: VNET (A)

In April 1987, Ms. Barbara Voigt, a national accounts manager at MCI Pacific, was preparing a formal proposal for Mr. Brian Kelly, director of telecommunications at the Seaboard Insurance Company. The proposal was to sell Seaboard MCI's new network product, Vnet. Mr. Kelly and several of his staff had recently attended a presentation of the product's capabilities at MCI, and he had requested a follow-up from Ms. Voigt.

Vnet had been introduced in September 1986. It was MCI's entry in a new category of network products, which included AT&T's SDN and US Sprint's VPN, all introduced within the past year. These products shared the fundamental innovation that each reduced the customer's need for expensive equipment by using a sophisticated computer system to allocate the customer's traffic over the public carrier's lines; all the customer's traffic could be integrated in a single communications system without the customer owning or leasing expensive equipment on premises to handle the coordination. In addition, customers without existing networks could gain services previously unavailable to them.

Private Telecommunication Networks

In the 1950s, AT&T introduced a private-line service called Telpak, which provided discounts to heavy users of long-distance transmissions. AT&T would provide a "trunk" (transmission cable) between two points for the exclusive use of a single institution. Price was based strictly on the length of the line, so the customer paid a flat rate each month, regardless of call volume. Private lines were typically leased between locations with very heavy telecommunications traffic, since the flat fee made the costs very efficient: If the trunk was in constant use, the monthly charge was a fraction of the alternative per-minute pricing. However, customers soon needed communications engineers to optimize their systems: If a private line were overutilized, users would be annoyed by line noise or delayed by busy signals; if it were underutilized, the monthly charges might exceed the charge-per-minute alternatives.

As more locations in a given firm required interconnection, switching systems became necessary for integrating individual lines. Thus, private-line systems gradually became private-network systems. Customers were usually

large institutions requiring extensive, continuous, and exclusive access to voice or data transmission facilities, or both. The trend toward private networks increased in the 1960s and 1970s as more sophisticated switching hardware offered expanded network control capabilities, such as automatic least-cost call routing and one-digit speed dialing for frequently used numbers. Network customers either purchased switching equipment or leased it from AT&T.

By the mid-1970s, AT&T's private-line revenues were reportedly $1.2 billion annually; but, for it and other long-distance companies, private-line services were not as profitable as standard switched services, due to the heavy discounts involved. Private lines also required more expensive preventive maintenance by the vendor, because, if the line were to become inoperative, there was generally no backup capacity for the customer; public switched networks had enough capacity that they could easily compensate for a single line going down. In the 1970s, state utilities commissions also raised taxes on intrastate private lines, further depressing margins on private-line services.

In response, AT&T discontinued its Telpak pricing in 1981 and raised prices for private-line services. Consequently, many customers that had installed expensive switches for their private lines were actively looking for alternatives. Meanwhile, Satellite Business Systems and AT&T began offering integrated packages of lines and switches. These fixed-facility, private-network systems were sold at significantly higher rates than Telpak, even considering the inclusion of the switching hardware. One MCI manager noted, "AT&T wanted to own the customer's network business. By providing dedicated systems, they built up customers' aversion to risking everything on an untried competitor."

By 1984, AT&T's private-line/private-network annual revenues had reportedly grown to $2.4 billion, while the U.S. Bureau of Labor Statistics reported that interstate private-line charges had increased 68 percent from 1975 to 1985, with additional increases of 50 percent or more from 1985 to 1987.

Virtual Networks

In the mid-1980s, three long-distance companies announced the development of software-defined virtual networks. These virtual networks required no equipment leases or purchases by the customer, because transmission and switching capacity was automatically partitioned from the vendor's public network. Rather than laying a physical trunk between two points (as with fixed networks), the carrier's computer system made transmission capacity

This case was prepared by Research Associate Jon E. King under the supervision of Assistant Professor Frank V. Cespedes. Copyright © 1988 by the President and Fellows of Harvard College.

Harvard Business School case 9-588-068.

available on demand. Exhibit 1 shows a simplified diagram of the hardware comprising and interacting with Vnet, not including the computer systems.

This type of a system required a carrier to establish a complex high-speed database. But since a carrier's public network was largely a fixed-cost system, more traffic over such a system would help to leverage the carrier's investment by utilizing existing capacity.

Beyond this basic similarity among the three virtual network offerings, there was significant divergence in design and strategy. Vnet, for example, utilized a centralized database system, which stored all the customers' parameters in two computer banks, east and west. AT&T's SDN system included several separate databases, with each customer's data being stored on only one. In US Sprint's VPN architecture, every piece of data for every customer was stored in every switch. These and other design differences defined and limited the features that could be offered by each product. For instance, because of its centralized architecture, MCI offered customers immediate data updating, which US Sprint could not provide since there were too many databanks to revise in a short time.

One MCI manager involved in Vnet's development explained:

> Virtual networks can provide more flexibility and reliability than a fixed facility network. Private networks demand hardware; the owner must consider purchasing, obsolescence, demand fluctuation, operations, and maintenance. Staff requirements are extensive, and switching equipment requires space; if a building (or a subsidiary) housing the switches is sold, the entire network must be refit. Many corporations have certain branch offices too small or too remote to justify leasing cable for it; these remote locations would, therefore, not be integrated with the rest of the system, and could only be reached through the public network. This becomes a serious concern as "intelligent" switches provide networks with advanced features that the remote sites cannot enjoy. Virtual networks can relieve these problems by eliminating hardware-oriented concerns and by integrating remote locations with the rest of the customer's system.

Each vendor also offered an array of customization options. Vendor engineers would work with the customer's telecommunications staff to so design the system that all locations were covered and desired services included. The net intended effect was to provide users with a service that duplicated or exceeded the sophistication of a fixed network, yet eliminated the operation's constraints.

An independent technical analyst reported on the value of virtual networks for various types of customers:

> For corporations without heavy, concentrated traffic, virtual network offerings are probably the only practical method of achieving a corporate network. Fixed facility overhead and fixed line rates just don't make sense for these customers. Concentration is a big issue: If a customer's locations are dispersed, virtual networks are justifiable.

Corporations with significant evening and weekend traffic will generally justify more traditional fixed facilities; since demand will fluctuate less, capacity of private lines can be used very effectively. Conversely, customers with primarily business-hour traffic will more easily justify virtual networks, since they don't want to pay for round-the-clock availability when they're not using it.

Finally, single vendor responsibility for end-to-end network service is very desirable, since bookkeeping, service, and management are simplified for the customer; pinpointing the problem is the vendor's responsibility, not the customer's. This kind of arrangement is difficult to find in the post-divestiture environment.[1]

Prices and Services.   MCI voluntarily followed AT&T's federally mandated practice of filing a public price schedule or "tariff" for each of its services. Tariffs were filed with the Federal Communications Commission and could only be changed with FCC approval. In the mid-1980s, tariffs for many products were lowered and refiled within a few months of the previous filing; this was true of virtual network services in 1986 and 1987. One reason was that the FCC limited AT&T profit levels, forcing prices down; another was the increase in industry competition. MCI often followed AT&T's format for its tariffs where applicable, so competing services could be quickly compared by price. But one MCI manager noted, "This was only partially true of Vnet's tariff, since it differed from AT&T's SDN product in many features, and also because MCI is determined to exhibit market leadership with this product. This is not a 'me-too' product, and we don't want to give any impression that it is."

Vnet was tariffed similarly to WATS-like[2] products, in that calls were charged per-minute at five different rates, depending on the call's distance. These five bands, and the

---

[1] Single vendor responsibility meant having all telecommunications services provided by one firm; this was seen as an advantage by some analysts, because it simplified interconnection and coordination. Others felt that using multiple vendors for different services was necessary to compile the exact set of services the customer desired. Some customers also valued having several vendors for the same reason many firms avoided single-sourcing an essential product: If one vendor failed, the customer would have a backup, and each vendor might feel more pressure to perform better if there were an active competitor. Before its divestiture, AT&T had provided "end-to-end service" to its customers, including local calls.

[2] Dial-1 was basic long-distance service available to commercial and residential customers; charges were per-minute and increased with the distance of the call. Wide-area telephone service (WATS) was similar to Dial-1 except that it was only for businesses, could be limited to a certain maximum distance, and had lower per-minute charges. There were many other services that were similar to WATS, referred to here as "WATS-like."

typical distribution of commercial long-distance calling in each band, were as follows:

Band	Distance (miles)	Percent of calls
1	0–292	41%
2	293–430	8
3	431–925	21
4	926–1,990	16
5	1,991–3,000	14
Total		100%
Business hours		85%
Evenings		10
Nights and weekends		5
Total		100%

Intracompany, or "on-net" calling (the traffic that would be carried by a private network), typically accounted for 20 percent of a company's total telecom usage. For a company with a fixed network, off-net calls would be handled by a public commercial offering, such as WATS or Dial-1. Virtual networks carried all calls on the vendor's public lines, and the product software merely billed the call differently if it terminated outside the customer's premises. Vnet ran approximately 20 percent lower than SDN for intracompany calls, and 8–12 percent less than SDN for off-net calls; the weighted average showed a 13 percent difference.

Per-minute rates for both Vnet and SDN increased as call mileage increased (see Exhibit 2). Per-minute rates also decreased as call duration increased. Assuming the typical mileage distribution above, average per-minute call costs were as follows:

Minutes	Vnet (MCI) On-Net/Off-Net	SDN (AT&T) On-Net/Off-Net
1	$0.1227/$0.1800	$0.2155/$0.2605
2	0.1186/ 0.1760	0.1679/ 0.2125
3	0.1173/ 0.1746	0.1520/ 0.1965
4	0.1166/ 0.1739	0.1440/ 0.1885

AT&T offered a 25 percent discount on calls outside business hours; MCI, 30 percent. MCI also offered a discount of up to 5 percent for high volume; AT&T had no volume discount. MCI charged a setup fee of $5,000 (which was waived until 9/87); AT&T's setup fee was $60,000, recently lowered from $105,000.[3] Special features were hard to compare without specific customer information, but MCI offered many that AT&T did not. Moreover, MCI sold most features as systemwide packages,

while AT&T generally installed and charged for options individually at each customer location. Thus, without knowing how many locations were being considered, and which options were needed where, total monthly service fees (not including per-minute charges) were impossible to compare. On standard features for which prices were easily compared, Vnet's rates were 10–20 percent below SDN's.

Vnet Options. Vnet offered several service options and more were planned as demand for the product grew. Certain options were oriented toward end-users, such as single-digit dialing or credit-card calling from off-net. Other services, such as rerouting a call to avoid busy lines, were automatic, spanned only fractions of a second, and did not notify or interrupt the user although reports were generated for the telecom staff. One MCI technical manager noted, "Many of these features don't even come out in the sales process, but in fact end up impressing the customer after installation. On the other hand, customers without existing networks may not appreciate some of Vnet's features, since they have never had the problems those features solve."

Some of the MCI options not offered by AT&T were international calls, off-site access, dedicated trunks between the vendor's switches, and an automatic number conversion system, which routed an on-net call cheaply, even if it were dialed as an off-net call (with 10 digits, rather than 7). MCI also provided a range of billing data broken down by location or operating unit; this allowed customers to allocate telcom expenditures to different profit centers. Previously, most companies' networks had operated as cost centers, since it was difficult to pass financial responsibilities to the appropriate users.

An important Vnet design option was "hybridizing" with the customer's existing facilities. The customer could retain any part of its existing network, including all lines and numbering systems, and Vnet would provide the additional services the customer needed to fill out the system. While this was very demanding for Vnet engineers (since integrating with customer equipment was a detailed customization process), the customer could integrate every branch location with the network while utilizing existing facilities at full capacity. Ms. Peggy Knight, product manager for Vnet, noted:

We designed Vnet with hybridizing in mind, so it is probably easier for us than for AT&T: they usually have a "rip-it-out" attitude toward existing networks. We realized that MCI does

---

[3]US Sprint did not publish a tariff for VPN, so charges varied from customer to customer and might be adjusted dramatically from month to month. Although AT&T and MCI had published tariffs, each could offer limited promotions to individual customers.

not have the clout in the business community to demand tearing out an existing system. We have succeeded by asking customers to try us out a little at a time, and grow their Vnet usage as capacity needs increase and as existing fixed facilities obsolesce. The largest customers can justify fixed networks, because they can use their equipment at capacity and because a fixed-facility network offers unparalleled security. So the 200 largest users will probably retain their existing networks for the time being.

Since virtual networks are new services, AT&T will probably continue to add functions just as MCI will, though not necessarily the same ones. Thus, AT&T may include at some later date the functions we've included in Vnet.

Mr. Gene Eidenberg, president of MCI Pacific, commented:

The telecom industry is fast-paced, and the advantages of technical innovations don't last long as competitors adopt those technologies. Therefore, lasting advantages will only be derived from customer service and problem solving.

AT&T's position is very different from ours. They have no motivation to cannibalize their installed base of hardwired network services, which are annuities. Selling SDN for them may entail large deconstruction and installation costs, only to replace a large current revenue stream with a smaller one. On the other hand, AT&T does not like to lose large national business and typically reacts immediately to inroads.

MCI does not have a big installed base of private network business and has been able to move aggressively. But MCI can't afford to damage its credibility with large accounts and, therefore, can't move too fast. One has to remember that telecom managers themselves are "vendors" to their internal users. The sales cycle for large customers can be two years; it requires good people, patience, and customer confidence.

MCI Organization

When AT&T divested its regional telephone companies in 1984, MCI decentralized its operations to work more closely with the seven newly independent regional telephone companies. Seven MCI divisions were set up to perform marketing, installation, and service within geographical regions. Concentrating on telco relations was important, since MCI needed hardwired interfacing with local telephone companies to provide customers with MCI's long-distance services. The years 1984–86 were an especially crucial period, because most residential phone customers in the nation were asked to decide on a long-distance carrier, and MCI focused most of its attention and resources on this opportunity. (See Exhibit 3 for financial information.)

The National Accounts Program (NAP) was started in late 1984 to coordinate selling efforts to the nation's largest users of telecommunications services. Although the program was managed at headquarters, each MCI division had a vice president of national accounts responsible for dedicated NAP sales efforts. This person was responsible to the division president, but also coordinated efforts with headquarters. Headquarters monitored account development, reviewed recommendations to add new accounts to the NAP list of about 225 firms, and coordinated interdivisional sales and service needs for these large, multilocation accounts. NAP headquarters organization in early 1987 is shown in Exhibit 4.

One headquarters manager pointed out that different divisions put different levels of emphasis on Vnet, because of local conditions:

Some divisions still have great growth potential in basic services and focus there. Eastern and central corporate customers often have widespread national network needs, but western networks are typically longitudinal down the coast, and comparatively few southeastern and southwestern companies have major branches outside their regions.

Mr. Bill Gallagher, MCI Pacific's VP of national accounts, added:

This division is three time zones away from headquarters in Washington, D.C., so we must be very independent here. The California Public Utilities Commission is one of the toughest in the country, so we have our own local constraints and challenges. I wanted to make sure we had a full-service organization out here, because I knew we couldn't hope for frequent visits from East Coast product specialists. Further, AT&T has the resources to move mountains, so we must secure the mountains quickly before AT&T gets to them.

Since existing WATS lines can be converted to Vnet access lines, Vnet is a simple product to the user, perhaps too simple, since it can be a threat to a corporation's telecom staff with obsolete jobs. In addition, customers like playing competitors off one another. It is, therefore, important to be positioned at all executive levels in the customer organization and to know top management at our national account customers. But the telecom managers are the ones who make the decisions (even if they need board approval), and top-down selling can alienate these important middle managers. Brian Kelly, for instance, has reportedly been very unhappy about AT&T people going around him and dealing directly with business unit managers at Seaboard.

National accounts did not have a dedicated technical operations staff, although individual accounts had dedicated operations personnel, and NAP headquarters did run a central service center to expedite work on account problems. The National Accounts Program had a separate product management group responsible for product definition, development, implementation, and training. NAP also had a division sales support staff, which developed sales tools, helped prepare proposals, and assisted NAMs during difficult stages of a sale.

An important event for MCI in 1986 was the acquisition of Satellite Business Systems (SBS) from IBM. SBS provided voice and data transmission primarily for businesses with large telecommunication volumes. Although SBS customers (and employees) were free to change vendors, many stayed with MCI. MCI and IBM also set up a limited set of joint marketing efforts.

MCI network operations (installation, maintenance, technical service) had been decentralized with the rest of the company in 1984, but was reorganized in early 1987 into three large units: east, central, and west. Responsibility for operations was moved out of the divisions and added to the engineering organization at headquarters.

Customers

Private lines used for voice transmission in the daytime were often used for data transmission at night. During the 1980s, as telecommunications devices incorporated more computing functions and computers demanded more communications facilities, the telecom and data processing groups in large corporations were brought closer together under the aegis of management information systems (MIS) departments. The telecom manager's role in many companies was changing into that of an information manager who had to assess the company's transmission requirements and sell significant investment decisions to top management. Conversely, as computers and software became more important in telecommunications, DP/MIS managers became more important in telecom purchase decisions. Whereas telecom managers' backgrounds generally involved dealing with the old Bell System (many were former Bell employees), DP managers were often computer programmers who had risen to managerial positions and came from environments dominated by IBM and other mainframe manufacturers. Exhibit 5 outlines the organization of the telecom unit at Seaboard.

MCI provided 5–10 percent of the telecommunications services of many Fortune 500 companies but had few deeply penetrated accounts. Mr. Jonathan Crane, vice president of national accounts, stated:

> MCI could not expect serious commitment from national account customers without a product such as Vnet. It is the flagship of our newly developed products, and is aimed at convincing prestige accounts that MCI is innovative, responsive, and effective. It was designed for the largest, most widely dispersed users of telecom services; these are obviously targets of competition in the industry.
>
> It was also designed to be sold to headquarters: selling at headquarters requires fewer resources, less time, and headquarters staffs have the technocratic clout to impress branch locations with their expertise. So even in a decentralized company, selling to headquarters first has influence on branch decisions. MCI's tariffs reward consolidation of traffic, allowing corporate headquarters the benefit of volume discounts unavailable to an individual branch.

MCI sold Vnet through both its National Accounts Program and Major Accounts sales forces, although support staff at MCI headquarters focused on national accounts. Every national account received a brief presentation on Vnet sometime in 1986 or 1987, and about half were given hour-long introductions to the system. By April 1987, 12 customers had fully functioning Vnet systems, 15 more were in the process of installation, and another dozen were in the final phases of their decision process. National accounts headquarters staff formed a Vnet "swat team" for advanced presentations to customers at a national accounts manager's (NAM) request. Sales of Vnet to major accounts were exceptions, usually initiated at the request of the customer.

Vnet Buying Process.   Mr. Carl Vorder Bruegge, MCI's senior vice president of sales and marketing, stated:

> Vnet is not an easy product to sell: customers and this new product are both technologically sophisticated, and salespeople must understand both. Unlike most of MCI's products, Vnet requires extensive customer education, lengthy feasibility studies, and coordination within large multiregional accounts.

Some MCI managers were concerned that the traditional orientation of MCI's selling efforts would hinder Vnet's acceptance in the marketplace. One executive commented, "MCI will have to undergo a substantial change to sell Vnet; I think our salespeople are so accustomed to selling whatever AT&T sells, but at a lower price, that it will be hard for them to think and act differently." Ms. Knight pointed out that, "Although MCI never marketed a network product before Vnet, SBS people sold only private network services; they are educating the rest of the sales force."

Mr. Vorder Bruegge distinguished between two types of customers:

> At companies that don't presently have private networks, our most likely ally is the executive with financial responsibility for communications costs. This person probably has little or no communications staff and is likely confused about current communications costs at his company. There is probably decentralized decision making for telecom services at various locations, and some of the sites may already be using MCI long-distance service.
>
> At companies that do have networks, the director of telecommunications is the decision maker. This person may not be a serious prospect for Vnet: a very large, sophisticated network, which is already in place, may be perfectly suited to the customer's needs.
>
> We also run straight into an installed base of AT&T services; it has traditionally been much easier for telecom managers to buy AT&T services, since most have never looked at the financial bottom line of their telecommunications. If there's a dial tone and the call goes through, most companies are satisfied and tend to ignore the costs. As a result, from the point of view of many telecom managers, "no one ever got fired for buying AT&T."

Ms. Knight offered another perspective:

The corporate telecom managers are the people to sell to; they want to hear about Vnet, because they want to improve their private networks. These managers also have internal turf-fights to deal with: different site managers have different needs and cost levels. If we can help the VP of communications satisfy various local managers through Vnet, that VP will help us sell.

Vnet can't offer the best savings in a heavy-traffic area, but it can offer features across the entire system that would be prohibitive for a fixed network. For instance, Vnet can lower costs for a customer's remote location, but we can't improve costs for a central location with private trunks used at capacity 24 hours a day. Yet the headquarters manager wants a consistent system and consequently is looking for a package which will integrate all his locations. So if total costs can be lowered with Vnet, the HQ manager will likely subsidize a central location so that it will come onto Vnet instead of buying into a separate fixed-facility system.

We did not specifically target any accounts at the start: there was no standard profile or checklist circulated to highlight likely customers. A "typical" profile is a customer whose network has long, inefficient lines for several branches. The obvious alternative is shutting down those lines and signing those branches up for WATS service; but then those locations are lost from the network: WATS can't be integrated. This upsets the telecom manager, who often is torn between the desire for control over one centralized system and the need for cost-effective telecommunications.

It helps if the customer has confidence in MCI already, and dislikes AT&T for its perceived arrogance. It is also best if the telecom manager wants to aggressively manage the network to solve the company's problems; these people are the risk-takers.

MCI Pacific

The MCI National Account Team for Seaboard consisted of Ms. Voigt, the national account manager; Ms. Kathy Doll, national account service specialist; and Mr. Joe Somerville, national account technical specialist.

Ms. Voigt took over the Seaboard account in early 1987; before that, the account was managed by a NAM, who also had responsibility for one of MCI Pacific's biggest accounts. She had joined MCI in 1983 as a commercial sales rep and soon moved to major accounts. When national accounts was founded at the end of 1984, she became a NAM. Besides Seaboard, Ms. Voigt had responsibility for another account that took up approximately two days of her time each week.

Since assuming responsibility for the Seaboard account, she had leased Seaboard a new transatlantic trunk and sold a package of discount Dial-1 services called CAS (corporate

accounts service). She was meanwhile trying to replace other vendors' WATS services with Prism[4] at several Seaboard locations.

Her immediate goal for Vnet was to convert some of the 16 Seaboard locations that MCI already served with Prism services, so Mr. Kelly (Seaboard's telecom director) could "try it out." Ms. Voigt's other account was already on Vnet, so she had experience with all stages of the sale; however, that firm had very little in common with Seaboard.

Ms. Doll had been with MCI for three years and had been on the Seaboard account since early 1986. As a service specialist, she was responsible for maintenance issues, billing, order taking, tracking implementation, expediting work orders, and general preventive precautions. Every several weeks she reported her findings to Mr. Kelly, including charts of Seaboard's continuing improvement in cost control. She developed a users' survey in 1987, which Ms. Paige Manning, Seaboard's voice services manager, distributed to the 16 locations MCI served. She also helped develop a database on Seaboard's customers. Ms. Doll also worked on another account, but she spent one or two days each week on-site at Seaboard.

Mr. Somerville, the account's technical specialist, also had responsibilities for another account but spent half his time at Seaboard. His tasks included technical specifications, engineering, and training the Seaboard telecom staff.

In addition to selling Vnet, Ms. Voigt had several other items on her agenda with the account. She had set up a presentation for higher management to consider subscribing to MCI Mail, an electronic mail service with which employees could send messages to one another (and to other subscribers) using their personal computers. She was also interested in selling data services (since Mr. Kelly was planning to modernize the data network), and was offering Seaboard a "co-location" service. This involved Seaboard placing its IBM data processing equipment at MCI switch sites, where MCI would contract to maintain the equipment. This would relieve Seaboard personnel from such operations. Ms. Voigt felt this would be hard for AT&T to counter, because it was their policy not to install competing (IBM) equipment on their premises. Through MCI's relationship with IBM, MCI was also considering joining a consortium of data processing vendors (called Insurance Value Added Network Systems) which provided data services at a discount to member insurance companies.

Seaboard Insurance Company

Seaboard was among the 10 largest insurance companies in the United States, specializing in property and casualty insurance, predominantly for businesses. It had been owned by a larger financial services organization from 1968 until early 1985, when it was spun off as an independent com-

---

[4]Prism was a WATS-like series of products offered by MCI, which included more flexibility than the standard WATS service.

pany. At the time of the sale, property-casualty insurance was in a severe downturn, and Seaboard reported an $87 million loss for 1985. One industry observer reported, "Seaboard was trying to increase its share of the highly competitive U.S. commercial insurance market and, as a result, didn't charge enough for many policies." Yet, as recently as 1980, Seaboard had provided more than half of its parent's net income.

In 1987, Seaboard employed 12,000 people in 65 offices across the country. Additionally, 9,000 independent insurance agents sold Seaboard policies, although most sold competing policies as well. Seaboard's president enumerated the following goals for the company: to be the largest provider of community, personal, and specialty insurance in the United States; to maintain profitability; and to improve distribution of services and create efficiencies through information systems.

At the end of 1985, Seaboard's three-year-old fixed voice services network (which had been leased from AT&T) was dismantled, because of its high cost. Replacement long-distance services were then provided by different vendors at its 65 PBX locations across the nation.[5] MCI provided Seaboard with Prism services at seven sites, and it took over service at nine more sites in 1986 after acquiring SBS. AT&T served the other 49 sites with WATS. Dial-1 services were provided by AT&T at all but five locations: those were contracted to MCI in 1987 as a test. MCI also installed a high-speed private line to London for Seaboard in 1987. All "800" (reverse-charge) lines and data lines were provided by AT&T, and all data processing equipment was IBM. For credit-card calling, Seaboard used American Express cards. MCI's 1986 revenues from Seaboard were $725,000 out of a total long-distance budget of about $6 million (Seaboard's total telecommunications budget in 1986, including equipment and personnel, was $16 million.) Account revenues for 1987 were expected to reach $900,000 for MCI.

Mr. Kelly had responsibility for all voice and data communications at Seaboard. According to the previous NAM, Mr. Kelly's key criteria for selecting telecommunications services were cost, service, and transmission quality (lack of noise, and so on), and his current goals were (a) to improve the efficiency of Seaboard's telecommunications system, (b) to reduce operating expenses without sacrificing quality, and (c) to enhance his staff's knowledge of the available range of products, services, and vendors in the telecommunications industry.

Mr. Kelly, 42, had joined Seaboard in 1985 after six years as telecom director at Arpac Corporation, a large

West Coast conglomerate. In 1983, he had canceled all MCI services at Arpac because of unsatisfactory service quality (notably call cut-offs). While at Arpac he had also canceled a new product from AT&T that had performed poorly.

At Seaboard he reported to Mr. Don Dowling, vice president of operations, and directed a staff of 14. Two recently hired senior analysts reported directly to him for special projects involving modernization, expansion, and "strategic design." Two managers ran voice and data services, respectively. Ms. Paige Manning, 37, had recently joined Seaboard as manager of voice services and coordinated six voice analysts. Her function was to allocate current work orders from the various Seaboard offices to the voice analysts. Ms. Doll noted, "Before Paige was hired, each analyst had covered a specific territory, and work flow tended to be high or low in different regions at different times. Brian felt that was wasteful, so he brought in Paige to coordinate."

The analysts' jobs were to make sure that the individual Seaboard locations had the facilities and services they needed: those offices had no one locally responsible for telecommunications. Analysts ranged in age from late 20s to late 30s.

Mr. Mike Carey headed the data services function and directed four analysts. Responsibilities were roughly parallel to those of the voice group, but the data group maintained a fixed facility data network, which included high speed "backbone" circuits between the six major offices (San Francisco, Dallas, Los Angeles, Atlanta, Omaha, and Trenton), lower capacity links to the other 59 branches, and the data processing equipment linked by the network.

Depending on the service required, a telecom vendor decision at Seaboard could be made by an analyst or by the board of directors. For instance, WATS service had been primarily up to the analysts when they had set up each office's services. All purchases required Mr. Kelly's acquiescence. However, with the advent of Ms. Manning's position, vendor choices were increasingly brought to her. For corporatewide projects, such as a network installation, the board would ultimately decide on the capital investments and vendors required. In such cases, Mr. Kelly would go to the board with a proposal for the project, and present the vendors' alternatives. He would typically recommend one vendor over others.

Decision levels were harder to predict for decisions of medium scope. A pilot test of a new service that required expenditures would need to be reviewed by Mr. Kelly's superior, Mr. Dowling, and possibly by the executive vice president of systems and operations, Mr. Richard Cabell. However, if a trial or feasibility study required no significant outlay, Mr. Kelly could authorize such a test himself. The recent decisions for buying MCI's Dial-1 services and London cable were made by Mr. Kelly on his authority.

---

[5] A private branch exchange (PBX) was the electronic switchboard unit that coordinated all the telephone traffic at a single customer location.

April 23 Presentation.   On Thursday, April 23, Mr. Kelly, Ms. Manning, two voice services analysts, and two data services analysts visited MCI Pacific's headquarters in San Francisco for an in-depth presentation on Vnet from 1 P.M. to 4 P.M. (While the other Seaboard attendees arrived on time, Mr. Kelly arrived 40 minutes late.) Ms. Voigt had secured Mr. Roger Naff, senior manager of technical support at MCI Pacific, to lead the presentation; Mr. Naff had worked at Bell Labs and Western Electric before joining MCI in 1984. He brought two technical specialists with him from the Los Angeles office. Also present was Pacific's operations manager, Mr. Harry Sells, who had covered the Seaboard account when he had worked for AT&T. Ms. Linda Starek, an MCI senior sales manager, and Ms. Doll were also in attendance.

Mr. Naff started with an overview of current trends. Seaboard had been displeased with its previous network, because of rising costs; high-capacity trunks were becoming more efficient due to new data compression and multiplexing technologies, as well as the widespread use of optical fiber; and local access charges were rising, because of local telcos and state utilities commissions, especially California's. Average per-minute costs in 1987 ranged from 20 cents per minute for high-capacity digital trunks to 42 cents per minute for standard Dial-1 service.

He then covered the idea of network hybridization. He noted that an independent consultant had developed software for optimizing Vnet layout when integrated with an existing system. The current parameters of the customer's existing system were entered into the computer, which would analyze traffic patterns and any specifications the customer demanded. Mr. Kelly mentioned that he knew of the consultant and liked his work. Mr. Naff mentioned that most Vnet customers were hybrids, but that AT&T resisted the notion of hybridization.

One Seaboard voice analyst noted that, "Although SeaNet, our private voice network, had been cost effective when set up in 1982, the cost structures changed so dramatically that in three years it was not competitive. What sort of failsafe pricing is available with Vnet to ensure that it is still economical for us in several years? You probably insist on a long-term contract to protect yourselves from falling prices." Mr. Naff responded, "MCI only asks for 30-day contracts, so the tariff can drop from month to month in a volatile market. We understand that customers aren't interested in an all-or-nothing commitment."

Mr. Naff then covered service options. Credit-card services could be integrated with Vnet, since they shared the same database, and Vnet could be accessed through dedicated trunks or through the local telcos. Seven-digit dialing was available for the entire network; one analyst mentioned, "That was the one significant feature lost when SeaNet was disassembled."

Mr. Naff outlined MCI Pacific's experience in designing and installing Vnet for customers, and he mentioned that the 16 Prism lines already being used at Seaboard could be immediately changed into Vnet lines without any adjustment required of the customer. MCI could also provide direct termination overflow, so, if any access line was full, an incoming call would automatically be routed through the local telco, rather than meeting a busy signal. One- or two-digit speed calling would be available by December.

The next topic was Vnet's interactive features, none of which were currently being offered by competitors. The customer information manager allowed the customer's telecom staff direct and immediate access to the central memory bank of the Vnet system. Any changes the customer wished to make in range privileges, calling cards, ID numbers, and the like, could be implemented by the customer in 15 minutes. Mr. Naff contrasted this system with US Sprint's VPN architecture, which required lengthy vendor updating of each switch, and with AT&T's system, which did not offer direct customer control.

Another interactive Vnet feature, the network information management system, would provide traffic-flow information to the customer for fine-tuning the design as the network grew. This included utilization figures, failure reports, call counts, and other statistics. IBM also offered a complementary system called Netview, which provided further network data. MCI could also provide multiple invoices, breaking down charges as the customer directed, so they could be allocated to specific sites or individual operating units. One Seaboard analyst noted that several locations without "intelligent" PBXs could benefit from that information.

Discussion then moved to pricing. SDN charged $60,000 for initial setup, while Vnet was only $5,000 and MCI charges were waived until autumn to encourage sampling. With maximum savings, a Vnet call could cost as little as 15 cents per minute, end-to-end; the average was 20 cents. A Seaboard analyst noted that their calls currently averaged 24 cents per minute. Mr. Naff mentioned that Vnet favored customers with short calls, since AT&T's charges were significantly higher in the early minutes of a call. Ms. Voigt noted that Vnet was slightly more expensive per minute than Prism, but the integrated features were incomparable.

Mr. Kelly stated, "We need more chats about voice-data integration, but for us, that's still far down the road. Our data network needs an overhaul, but that is separate from our consideration of Vnet." Mr. Naff noted that, "Vnet can be used to make the datanet more efficient: excess capacity can be used for voice traffic, and data overflow could be handled by Vnet." A Seaboard data analyst pointed out that, "Only seven or eight of our locations have enough combined traffic to warrant that kind of piggybacking. And by the way, Seaboard is firmly entrenched with IBM and, therefore, would demand compatibility." Mr. Naff responded, "We do business with IBM: they are our biggest customer and our largest stockholder."

Mr. Kelly asked about including independent agents on the net and invoicing them the bills, and then he asked about putting agents on and allowing them to place free calls to Seaboard. Mr. Naff answered that either option could be worked into the hybridization program. Mr. Kelly then wrapped up the meeting:

> Seaboard has no established plan for network integration. For now, we in this room are just meter readers, not traffic managers. Our immediate concerns are grades of service, quality, features, and subsidization of smaller locations. For our next meeting, I'd first like to know: Why does Seaboard need a network at all? Secondly, I'd like a detailed comparison with SDN; Sprint's VPN is not a consideration.
>
> The management tools in a network are worth something to us. We want to move away from cost considerations to strategic enhancements and modernization. This project won't fly if we're only saving money. How will you make us more effective in the marketplace? For example, airlines use their telecommunications systems to make themselves more competitive. Be creative: our habits can change. We want to be the innovator; everyone else will have to catch up. If you can do this, I'll be very happy, because I'll probably get a big raise.
>
> Barbara, let's set up an initial meeting for next week, and the full proposal can be presented next month.

After the Seaboard staff had left, the MCI team met to discuss the meeting and what the next steps should be.

EXHIBIT 1

MCI Telecommunications Corporation: Vnet (A)

Elements Involved in Vnet System, Including Off-net Calls (Diagrams simplified; typical systems would involve dozens of switches, access points, PBXs, and the like)

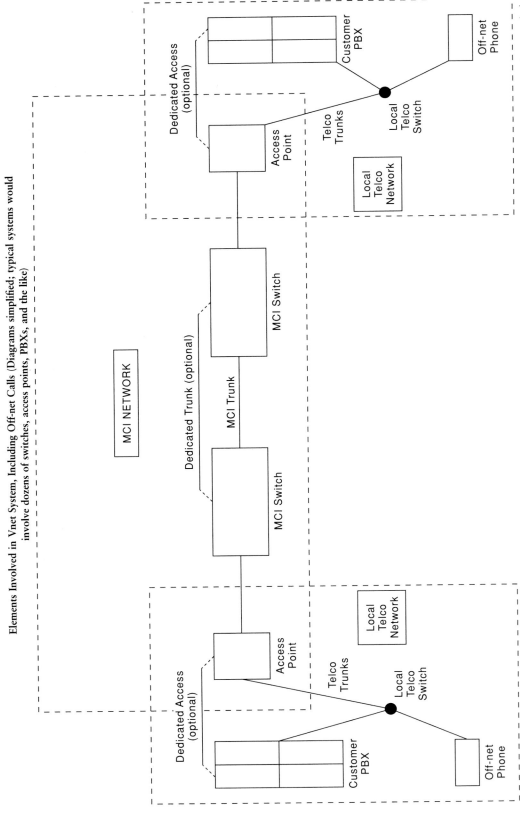

NOTE: Dedicated lines were private lines integrated into Vnet's software, but leased separately by MCI or the local telephone company. Such lines reduced or eliminated certain per-minute charges, and, if used at capacity, could reduce total monthly costs.

EXHIBIT 2

*MCI
Telecommunications
Corporation: Vnet (A)*

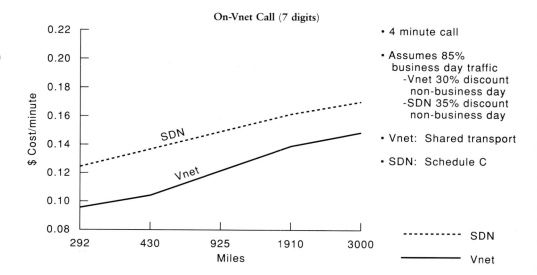

On-Vnet Call (7 digits)

• 4 minute call

• Assumes 85%
  business day traffic
  -Vnet 30% discount
   non-business day
  -SDN 35% discount
   non-business day

• Vnet: Shared transport

• SDN: Schedule C

----------- SDN

——————— Vnet

EXHIBIT 2

(concluded)

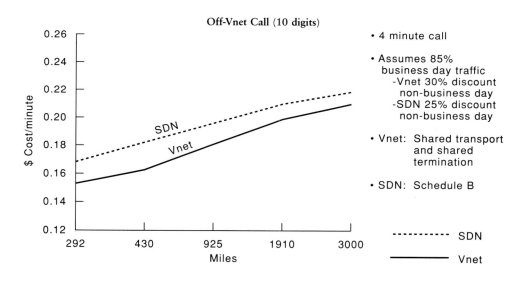

Off-Vnet Call (10 digits)

• 4 minute call

• Assumes 85%
  business day traffic
  -Vnet 30% discount
   non-business day
  -SDN 25% discount
   non-business day

• Vnet: Shared transport
  and shared
  termination

• SDN: Schedule B

----------- SDN

——————— Vnet

Exhibit 3   MCI Telecommunications Corporation: Vnet (A)

Income Statement: MCI (1984–1986)

	Year Ended December 31 (In millions, except per share amounts)		
	1986	*1985*	*1984*
Revenue:			
Sales of communications services	$3,592	$2,542	$1,959
Operating expenses:			
Local interconnection	1,636	874	480
Leased communications system	267	280	343
Sales, operations and general	1,097	835	696
Depreciation	451	347	265
Restructuring charges and asset write-downs	585	154	50
Total expenses	4,036	2,490	1,834
(Loss) income from operations	(444)	52	125
Interest (expense)	(187)	(201)	(189)
Interest income	63	86	115
Portion of antitrust settlements, net	39	207	
Gain on sales of assets	65	18	
Other income (expense), net	1	6	(1)
(Loss) income before income taxes and extraordinary item	(463)	168	50
Income tax (benefit) provision	(32)	28	(9)
Extraordinary loss on early debt retirements, less applicable income tax benefits ($17 and $26)	17	27	
Net (loss) income	($ 448)	$ 113	$ 59
(Loss) earnings per common share:			
Primary and assuming full dilution:			
(Loss) income before extraordinary item	($1.57)	$0.59	$0.25
Net (loss) income	($1.63)	$0.48	$0.25
Circuit miles	485	322	198
Billable calls	2,812	1,760	1,232
Number of employees	13,650	12,445	9,870
Average revenue per minute per call	$0.242	$0.266	$0.281
— Local interconnection	0.111	0.091	0.069
— Leased communications system	0.018	0.029	0.049
— Gross margin	0.113	0.146	0.163

EXHIBIT 4

MCI Telecommunications Corporation: Vnet (A)

National Accounts Organization (April 1987)

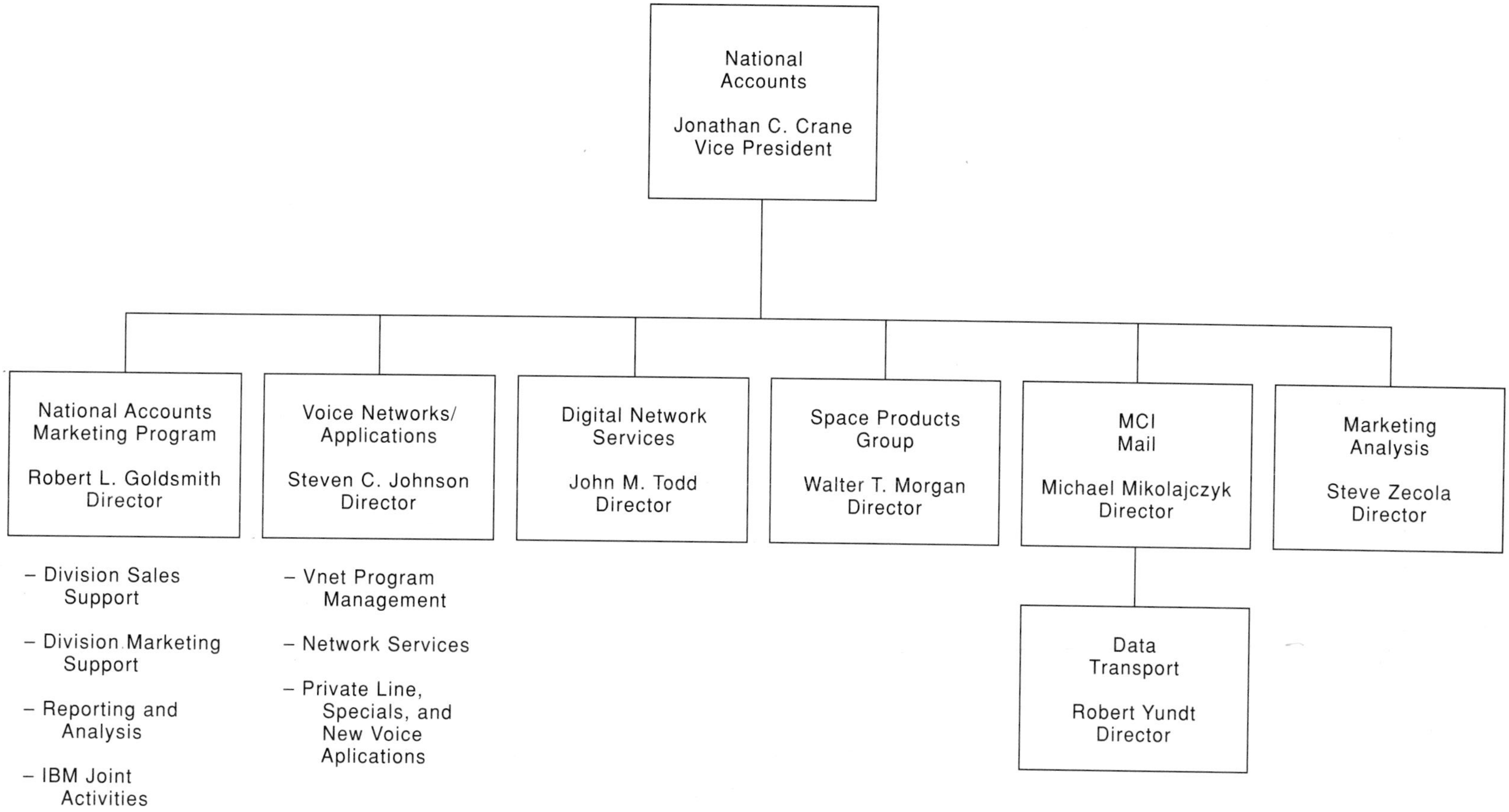

```
                    ┌──────────────────┐
                    │ National         │
                    │ Accounts         │
                    │                  │
                    │ Jonathan C. Crane│
                    │ Vice President   │
                    └────────┬─────────┘
                             │
   ┌──────────┬──────────┬───┴──────┬──────────┬──────────┐
   │          │          │          │          │          │
┌──┴───┐  ┌───┴───┐  ┌───┴───┐  ┌───┴───┐  ┌───┴───┐  ┌───┴───┐
│Nat'l │  │Voice  │  │Digital│  │Space  │  │MCI    │  │Market-│
│Accts │  │Net-   │  │Network│  │Products│ │Mail   │  │ing    │
│Mktg  │  │works/ │  │Services│ │Group  │  │       │  │Analysis│
│Program│ │Applic.│  │       │  │       │  │       │  │       │
└───────┘ └───────┘  └───────┘  └───────┘  └───────┘  └───────┘
```

National Accounts Marketing Program	Voice Networks/ Applications	Digital Network Services	Space Products Group	MCI Mail	Marketing Analysis
Robert L. Goldsmith Director	Steven C. Johnson Director	John M. Todd Director	Walter T. Morgan Director	Michael Mikolajczyk Director	Steve Zecola Director

Under **National Accounts Marketing Program**:
– Division Sales Support
– Division Marketing Support
– Reporting and Analysis
– IBM Joint Activities

Under **Voice Networks/Applications**:
– Vnet Program Management
– Network Services
– Private Line, Specials, and New Voice Applications

Under **MCI Mail**:
Data Transport
Robert Yundt Director

EXHIBIT 5

*MCI
Telecommunications
Corporation: Vnet (A)*

Seaboard Insurance Company Organization

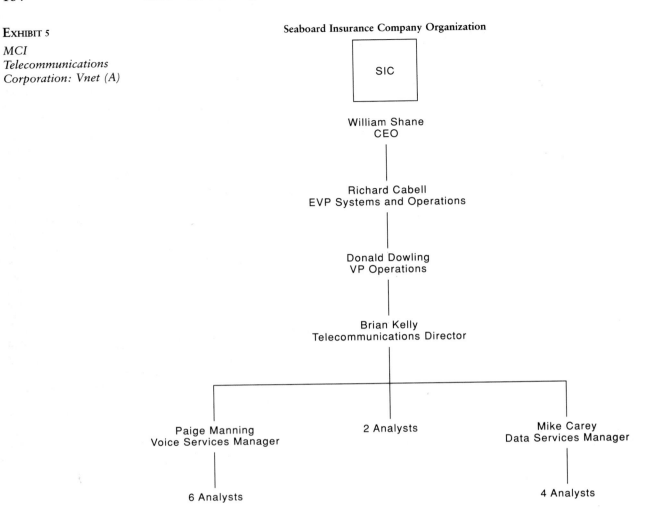

PETITE PLAYTHINGS, INC., 1984 (A)

After Harold Cassady received his MBA in June 1984, he joined Petite Playthings, Inc., of New York City. He expected to work for six months as a marketing analyst and then to be assigned to a sales territory for one to two years. Following that, he would return to New York in a sales or marketing management position.

Petite Playthings—a large children's-wear manufacturer by industry standards, with sales of $50 million—employed 25 salespeople who were paid a straight commission of 4 percent of sales. As was typical in the industry, all salespeople reported to the national sales manager, Fred Rodgers.

In early September 1984, Ed Autry, the salesperson who covered Texas, died suddenly. During the fiscal year July 1983 to June 1984 the territory had shipped slightly over $1,750,000 in sales. Ed had been a long-term employee of Petite Playthings and had a good reputation within the sales force for sales skill and servicing ability.

When news of Autry's death reached headquarters, Fred Rodgers asked Cassady to take Autry's territory. Hal Cassady perceived this as an excellent opportunity. First, it

This case was prepared by Professor Benson Shapiro.
Copyright © 1984 by the President and Fellows of Harvard College.
Harvard Business School case 9-584-080 (Rev. 8/15/90).

shortened his training period. Second, it gave him a territory considerably better than most new hires, since the commissions for the past year had been over $70,000. Third, it was a territory with good potential for growth.

Fred Rodgers explained that, since he was about to leave for a two-week trip to Europe, Hal Cassady would have to introduce himself to the territory. This was regrettable since he preferred to introduce Cassady to the major accounts.

On Sunday, September 9, Cassady flew to Texas to get settled and to begin covering the territory. On Monday and Tuesday he traveled the suburban and exurban areas around a large city. He had arranged to meet his second-largest customer—the children's-wear buyer for a large department store—for dinner on Tuesday evening. In reviewing his orientation to the territory on his way to dinner, Cassady was pleased with the approach he had taken. He had begun to learn about his accounts, and in these early stages he had been successful in developing rapport with some smaller accounts. These experiences made him feel confident about meeting Jim Carson, the buyer, who had purchased over $200,000 worth of merchandise from Petite in the 1983–84 fiscal year—accounting for $8,000 in commissions to Autry.

Cassady was anxious to discuss the upcoming winter line as well as to find out how the fall line was selling. Although he wanted to discuss business, he did not want the dinner conversation to become too "weighty."

PRICING POLICY

PRICING POLICY

Fred Jr., a college senior about to begin job interviews, goes to the local specialty shop to investigate the purchase of a suit. Having recently seen advertisements of Hart, Schaffner & Marx suits in major men's magazines, Fred asks the clerk to see the HSM brand in grey pinstripe cloth. The suit looks fine, but Fred is stunned by the $495 price tag. The salesperson explains the quality of HSM cloth and the amount of hand-tailoring in HSM suits. For comparison, Fred tries on a $315 unadvertised brand. The salesperson reinforces the message of the magazine advertisement of the HSM suit for job interviews and that the suit's conservative style makes it a "good investment." Fred Jr. decides to buy the HSM suit and charges the purchase on the specialty store's own credit card.

Fred Sr., the chief executive officer of a small regional airline, studies the projected load factors once again. He has been to the aircraft manufacturer's plant and taken a number of demonstration rides. The aircraft company representative is shown into his office. The representative presents the rationale for selecting his company's plane as the one to expand the fleet. The representative presents the delivery schedule, stresses the support offered by the company and the financing offered. Fred Sr. is impressed with the quality of the manufacturing, the thoroughness of the sales presentation, and the support services. He decides, "I'm sorry but with the load factors we project on that route right now, the economics don't make sense. I just can't justify buying right now."

So Fred Jr. buys the suit, and Fred Sr. does not buy the plane. In making their decisions, father and son go through a similar process, albeit one more rigorously than the other. Both balance the benefits they perceive in the product against price. Fred Jr. bought the suit because his perceived value exceeded the $495 price. Fred Sr. did not buy the plane because the stream of benefits he expected (given the projected load factors) did not exceed the cost.

These two scenarios demonstrate the relationship between price and other elements of the marketing mix. Fred Jr.'s purchase of the suit shows that the marketing activities of the firm created a bundle of product and services, which justified the

This note was prepared by Professor Robert J. Dolan.
Copyright © 1984 by the President and Fellows of Harvard College.
Harvard Business School case 9-585-044 (Rev. 4/2/92).

$495 expenditure. Fred Jr. probably would not have bought the HSM suit if he had not seen an advertisement for HSM and received the reinforcing message from the salesperson at the point of purchase. Thus, the product, promotion, and place elements of the mix created a perceived value greater than the price, resulting in a sale.

Proper pricing is, thus, a function of the other elements of the marketing mix. In general, the major factors affecting the price decision are the internal and external factors shown in Figure A.

FIGURE A

Pricing Consideration

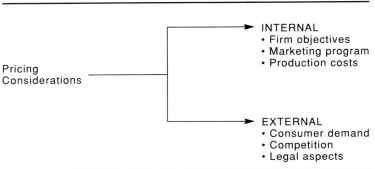

Internal Factors

General Foods' corporate objective is to have brands in the number one market share position at "fair prices." Think of how the price-setter for Jello Pudding Pops is affected by this statement of objectives. Would the price of the pops be different if the GF objective was to "maximize contribution to corporate overhead and profit in next fiscal year?" Most likely it would, and, thus, a key guide to price-setting is the firm's goals:

- Desired return on investment (ROI).
- Market share position.
- Image in consumer's mind (e.g., premium priced, fair value).
- Short-run cash flow.
- Stability of contribution.
- Firm growth rate.
- Penetration of certain market segments.

In the case of GF, for example, the corporate directive is quite clear on price being a part of a marketing mix that delivers what a majority of consumers perceive to be good value on an enduring basis.

As suggested in the scenarios above, a second major internal factor is the other elements of the marketing mix (i.e., the overall marketing program, of which price is a part). IBM, for example, provides substantial value, added on mainframe computer purchases in the form of benchmark testing, briefings for senior management on trends in data processing, and on-site technical assistance. The IBM strategy then might be depicted as the coordinated strategy of where the high service creates high value, permitting high prices, creating good margins, which fund the high service. Other computer manufacturers have taken the fundamentally different approach of little augmentation of basic product with services, meaning low cost and lower prices.

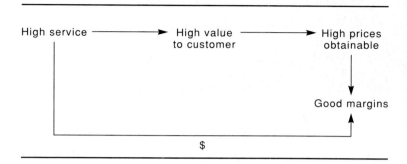

The third element in the pricing framework is cost. In some companies, this is the *only* factor considered in pricing, as price is just cost plus some standard markup. Obviously, cost is a key consideration in that it usually gives a lower bound on price. (A firm may sell below cost for a time if the goal is to penetrate a market in anticipation of future profitable sales.) Cost data are not unambiguous, however. Careful consideration must be given not only to current cost but also to projected future cost as affected by price and volume sold.

External Analysis

Once the internal analysis is completed, and the firm has specified its objective, formulated an overall marketing strategy, and determined the cost of operations, the next step in pricing is to look out to the market. The major external factor is consumer demand or the value consumers place on the services. The following diagram shows the relationship of customer value to other parts of the pricing framework.

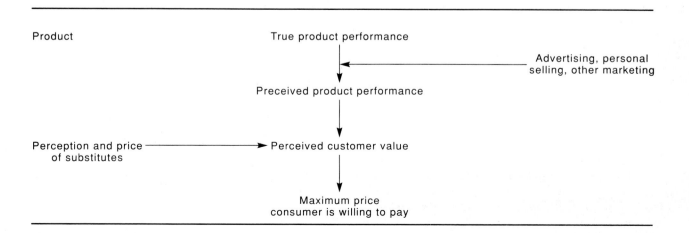

The product has some true performance associated with it, which is transformed into perceived product performance by the advertising, personal selling, and other activities of the firm. Given customer wants, perceived product performance is evaluated against the perceived performance of substitutes. Given the price of these substitutes, the perceived customer value is created, which is the maximum price the consumer will pay. Thus, in the Fred Sr. plane-purchasing scenario, the aircraft manufacturer demonstrated the performance of its plane to create a favorable perception of product performance in Fred Sr.'s mind. However, the load-factor studies defined Fred Sr.'s wants, and the lack of fit of the perceived product performance to his wants created a perceived customer value less than the price and hence "no sale."

There are several important features of perceived customer value:

1. It varies across customers.
2. For a given customer, it will vary over time as perceptions of the product and competitive price change.
3. It is to some extent controllable by the marketer.

The above schematic shows how competition is part of the pricing equation. Since one firm's price influences the other firm's perceived value, we have a relationship, such as:

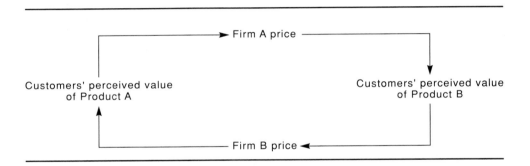

For example, if Firm A is Pan American Airlines, Pan Am's April 1990 $119 price for the shuttle between New York and Boston influenced customers' perceived value of a similar flight on the Trump Shuttle (Product B). This was a key input to Trump's pricing. In May 1, 1990, Trump dropped its price to $79, affecting the perceived value of Pan Am's shuttle (Product A). This decrease in perceived value of its product forced Pan Am to lower its price.

The popular press contains many discussions of the "cutthroat" competition in the airline industry. What makes some industries more price-competitive than others? Intensity of competition is a function of the extent of product differentiation and the cost structure. The airline industry has very little product differentiation (e.g., while Pan Am and Trump claimed differentiation in terms of on-board ticketing, snacks, "attendants who attend," frequent-flyer plans, etc., the differences were, in most consumers' views, quite small). Second, the airline industry is a high-fixed/low-variable cost industry; profits are very volume sensitive. An indicator of the cost structure of an industry is the relationship between price perceived and variable cost. This relationship is captured in the marginal income ratio (MIR). The MIR is the percent of revenue available for contribution to fixed costs and profit after variable costs have been covered. MIR is given by:

$$\text{MIR} = \frac{\text{Price} - \text{Variable cost}}{\text{Price}}$$

For the airline business with its very high per-flight fixed cost (e.g., capital equipment, crew wages, landing fees), the MIR is high. For the Pan Am shuttle, for example, the cost of an incremental passenger is quite small relative to the $119 price. The incremental passenger increases ticket processing and fuel consumption. But these costs are quite small. If we estimate at $6, we see Eastern's business is characterized by an MIR of

$$\text{MIR} = \frac{\$119 - \$6}{\$119} = 95\%$$

On the other hand, some industries are characterized by low capital investment, but a high raw materials cost. For example, a metal fabricator engaged in shaping purchased raw materials might incur variable costs of $90 on a $100 job. The resulting MIR is:

$$\text{MIR} = \frac{\$100 - \$90}{\$100} = 10\%$$

The importance of MIR in understanding the competitiveness of an industry can be seen by examining the economics of a price change in these two markets. Suppose each of the two firms above were contemplating a price increase of 10 percent. Generally, as price increases, one expects volume sold to decrease. How much volume could be lost in each case and still have current contribution increase?

Since total contribution is the unit contribution (price minus variable cost) times unit volume, current contribution increases if:

$$(P - VC)X \leq [(1.1)P - VC]Y$$

where X is the current volume and Y is the volume after the price increase. This implies that:

$$\frac{P - VC}{1.1P - VC} \leq \frac{Y}{X}$$

or multiplying the left-hand side by $[(1/P)/(1/P)]$,

$$\frac{[(P - VC)/P]}{0.1 + [(P - VC)/P]} \leq \frac{Y}{X} = \frac{MIR}{0.1 + MIR} \leq \frac{Y}{X}$$

Thus, the new volume, as a percent of the old, must be greater than MIR/(0.1 + MIR). Consequently, for Pan Am with an MIR of 0.95, unit sales cannot drop below 90.28 percent of present volume. For the metal fabricator with MIR = 0.1, the contribution is much less sensitive to volume, and unit sales can drop to 0.1/(0.1 + 0.1) = 50 percent before the price increase is not justified. From the formula, we see that the higher the MIR, the more sensitive the business is to volume and the more ready firms will be to protect their volumes. Thus, competitive reaction to share-gaining attempts is likely to be strong in high MIR industries, such as airlines.

The final external consideration is legal aspects. A series of antitrust laws is in force in the United States, which attempts to prohibit any pricing practices that would reduce competition. For example, if a firm's very low prices would be viewed as an attempt to force a competitor out of business, court action may result.

We can combine and expand the two diagrams above to capture the complexity of pricing decisions.

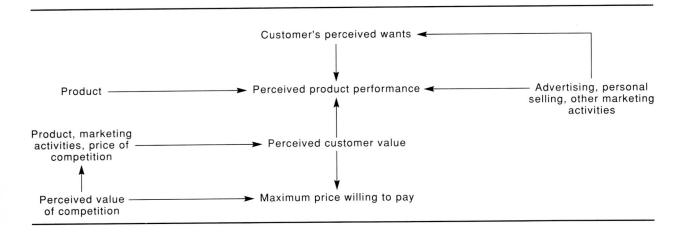

This diagram shows the impact of the other elements of the marketing mix and also the interrelationship between value and price for competitive products. Couple this with the fact that perceptions of wants, perceptions of performance, competitor prices and objectives, and own cost are changing over time, and we see that pricing is a complex decision.

Some Special Issues—Price Dynamics

The above framework is intended to give broad guidelines on how to make pricing decisions for a given product, at a given stage of the life cycle. Two special topics on the dynamics of price warrant discussion here: new product pricing and temporary price reductions (i.e., price promotions).

New products that are major innovations present difficult pricing problems because customer value is often difficult to assess. Two basic strategies are available to the firm: skim pricing and penetration pricing. In skim pricing, the firm sets a high price initially to obtain high unit contributions. Price is lowered as time goes on. This initial high-price strategy is effective in segmenting the market (i.e., those who place a high value on the good buy initially at the high price). Price is then lowered to pick up those with lower evaluations. The most well-known skimming strategy is with books—first coming out in hardcover, then in the same generic product in paperback form later to tap the more price-sensitive segment.

Penetration pricing is a strategy of low entry prices to get to the mass market quickly. When there are substantial economies of large production, the low-price/high-volume strategy has very favorable production cost effects and may be an effective barrier to competitive entry. A major risk in penetration pricing is that, with a new product, demand is very difficult to predict. Consequently, a low initial price may swamp the firm with orders many times its production capacity.

In general, a skim policy is good for markets where consumers are relatively price insensitive, but consumer education to the product is required. On the other hand, penetration pricing that sacrifices short-term profit for volume is appropriate when there are economies in production and competitors may enter.

A second dynamic in pricing is the short-term price reduction or price promotion. This has become a very common practice, particularly among manufacturers of products sold through grocery stores. In a price promotion, the manufacturer announces that, for a fixed time, his or her good will be offered at a discount. After the promotional period, the good returns to its regular price. Often, instead of being stated as a direct price reduction, the offers are made in a "free-goods" form, (i.e., instead of saying price is reduced 10 percent, the offer might be "buy nine cases, get one free"). Price promotions can serve to clear excess inventories of a brand and, perhaps, to gain the attention of the trade. Promotion policy is very difficult to manage, however, because there is a danger that, if the device is used too often, buyers will just delay their purchases until a promotion period.

Ethical Issues in Pricing Policy

In virtually every country, pricing policy is subject to regulations that constrain the options open to marketers. For example, in the United States, it is illegal to collude with other competitors to "fix" prices, or for a manufacturer to try to control retail prices by threatening to withdraw support from retailers that discount its products excessively. There are also laws prohibiting foreign manufacturers from dumping products at prices below their production costs. It is imperative that marketers learn the laws regarding pricing in each of the countries where they operate. Given the differences among countries and the complexity of the regulations, this is an area requiring serious and continuous attention.

There are also ethical issues in pricing policy. That is, there are situations where pricing practices may not be illegal but are questionable on ethical grounds. Examples include:

- The semiconductor industry experiences a capacity shortage for a particular semiconductor chip critical to the manufacture of microcomputers. Some firms decide to raise prices significantly and to delay shipments to long-term customers who have standing orders for the chips at lower prices.

- A pharmaceutical manufacturer with a patented product for the treatment of a deadly disease is able to charge extremely high prices for its product, because patients have no alternative.

- A university is allowed some discretion in allocating indirect costs to an overhead pool that will be charged to research contracts paid by the federal government. There are some items that are "perfectly legal" to include in the overhead pool, although they seem to stretch the definition of what is allowable. University accounting personnel decide to include them anyway, since the auditors are unlikely to challenge them. Besides, even if the questionable costs are included, the university's overhead rates are lower than those of defense contractors with whom the government does business.

- A retail shopkeeper in a jewelry store routinely marks up merchandise well above the suggested retail prices of manufacturers. This allows him to appear to offer deep discounts to customers who haggle aggressively over prices. When he encounters inexperienced buyers who do not know to ask for a discount, he gleefully charges the full price, saying, "If they are willing to pay that much, then the product must be worth it to them. Isn't that the essence of value-based pricing?"

Managers in every industry have to confront both legal and ethical issues in pricing. The first challenge is to know the laws in all their complexity and obey them. The second, subtler, challenge is to recognize that some practices, while not illegal, are still questionable on ethical grounds. The third challenge is to show restraint in situations that might allow a marketer to charge excessive prices to customers who are not able to discern fair market value, or who are so desperate that they will pay any price for the product.

Summary

Pricing is a complex, dynamic process. This note serves only to raise considerations in the pricing decision. No magic pricing formula exists. Some companies adopt formulas as a way to cope with the uncertainty and complexity (e.g., price is cost plus 25 percent markup). This clearly results in less than optimal decisions, however, as important considerations are ignored. The quality of pricing decisions (like most marketing decisions) improves with one's clarity of objectives and understanding of consumer and competitive behavior.

Computron, Inc., 1978

In July 1978, Thomas Zimmermann, manager of the European Sales Division of Computron, was trying to decide what price to submit on his bid to sell a Computron 1000X digital computer to König & Cie., AG, Germany's largest chemical company. If Zimmermann followed Computron's standard pricing policy of adding a 33⅓ percent markup to factory costs and then including transportation costs and import duty, his bid would amount to $311,200; he feared, however, that this would not be low enough to win the contract for Computron.

König had invited four other computer manufacturers to submit bids for the contract. A reliable trade source in Zimmermann's opinion indicated that at least one of these competitors was planning to name a price in the neighborhood of $218,000. This would make Computron's normal price of $311,200 higher by $93,200, or approximately 43 percent. In conversations he had had with König's vice president in charge of purchasing, Zimmermann was led to believe that Computron would have a chance of winning the contract only if its bid was no more than 20 percent higher than the lowest bid.

Since König was Computron's most important German customer, Zimmermann was particularly concerned over this contract and was wondering what strategy to employ in pricing his bid.

Background on Computron and Its Products

Computron was an American firm that had, in the winter of 1976, opened a European sales office in Paris with Thomas Zimmermann as its manager. The company's main product, both in the United States and Europe, was the 1000X computer, a medium-sized digital computer designed specifically for process control applications.

In the mid-to-late 1970s the market for digital process control computers was growing quite rapidly. These were substantially different from computers used for data processing and engineering calculation. They were generally produced by specialized companies, not by the manufacturers of office and calculation-oriented digital computers. These companies also were different from those that produced analog process control computers (the units traditionally used for process control).

Digital computers were classed as small, medium, or large, depending on their size, complexity, and cost. Small computers sold in the price range up to $80,000, medium computers from $80,000 to $600,000, and large computers from $1,000,000 to $6,000,000.

The Computron 1000X was designed specifically for process control applications. It was used in chemical and other process industries (oil refining, pulp and paper, food manufacture, and so on) as well as in power plants, particularly those for nuclear power.

In addition to its 1000X computer, Computron manufactured a small line of accessory process control computer equipment. This, however, constituted a relatively insignificant share of the company's overall sales volume.

During its first six months the European sales office did only about $1 million worth of business. In the 1977–78 fiscal year, however, sales increased sharply, totaling $5 million for the year.[1] Computron's total worldwide sales that year were roughly $44 million. Of the European countries, Germany constituted one of Computron's most important markets, having contributed $1,200,000, or 24 percent, of the European sales total in 1977–78. England and Sweden were also important, having contributed 22 percent and 18 percent, respectively. The remaining 36 percent of sales was spread throughout the rest of Europe.

Computron computers sold to European customers were manufactured and assembled in the United States and shipped to Europe for installation. Because of their external manufacture, these computers were subject to an import duty, which varied from country to country. The German tariff on computers of this type was 17.5 percent of the U.S. sales price.

Prompted primarily by a desire to reduce this import duty, Computron began constructing a plant in Frankfurt. It would serve all the European Common Market and was scheduled to open September 15, 1978. Initially it was to be used only for assembly of 1000X computers. This would lower the German import duty to 15 percent. Ultimately the company planned to use the plant to fabricate component parts as well. Computers completely manufactured in Germany would be entirely free from import duty.

The new plant was to occupy 10,000 square feet and employ 20 to 30 people in the first year. Its initial yearly overhead was expected to be approximately $300,000. As of July 1978, the European sales office had no contracts on which the new plant could begin work, although training of employees and the assembly and installation of a pilot model 1000X computer could keep the plant busy for two

This case was prepared by Professor Benson P. Shapiro. The original version, entitled *Computron, Inc.,* was written by Ralph Sorenson for l'Institut pour l'Etude des Méthodes de Direction de l'Entreprise (IMEDE), Lausanne, Switzerland, copyright 1965. Copyright © 1978 by the President and Fellows of Harvard College.
Harvard Business School case 579-031 (Rev. 7/15/91).

[1]Computron's fiscal year was July 1 to June 30.

or three months after it opened. Zimmermann was somewhat concerned about the possibility that the new plant might have to sit idle after these first two or three months unless Computron could win the König contract.

Company Pricing Policy.   Computron had always concentrated on being the quality, blue-chip company in its segment of the digital computer industry. The company prided itself on manufacturing what it considered the best all-around computer of its kind in terms of precision, dependability, flexibility, and ease of operation.

Computron did not try to sell the 1000X on the basis of price. Its price was very often higher than that for competing equipment. In spite of this, the superior quality of Computron's computers had, to date, enabled the company to compete successfully both in the United States and Europe.

The European price for the 1000X computer was normally figured as follows:

U.S. cost (includes factory cost and factory overhead)
+ Markup of 33⅓% on cost (covers profit, R&D allowances, and selling expenses)
+ Transportation and installation costs
+ Import duty

Total European price

Prices calculated by this method tended to vary slightly, because of country-to-country differences in tariffs and differences in components between specific computers.[2] For the König application, Zimmermann had calculated that the "normal" price for the 1000X computer would be $311,200:

Factory cost	$192,000
33⅓% markup on cost	64,000
Quoted U.S. price	$256,000
Import duty	
(15% of quoted U.S. price)	38,400
Transportation and installation	16,800
Total "normal" price	$311,200

The 33⅓ percent markup on cost was designed to provide a before-tax profit margin of 11 percent of the quoted U.S. price, an R&D allowance of 8 percent, and a selling and administrative expense allowance of 6 percent. The stated policy of top management was clearly against cutting this markup to obtain sales. Management felt that cutting prices "not only reduced profits but also reflected unfavor-

ably on the company's 'quality' image." Zimmermann knew that Computron's president was especially eager not to cut prices at this particular moment, because Computron's overall profit before taxes had been only 6 percent of sales in 1977–78, compared with 17 percent in 1976–77. Consequently, the president had stated that not only did he want to maintain the 33⅓ percent markup on cost, but he was eager to raise it.

In spite of this policy, Zimmermann was aware of a few isolated instances when the markup had been dropped to the neighborhood of 25 percent to obtain important orders in the United States. In fact, he was aware of one instance when the markup had been cut to 20 percent. In the European market, however, Computron had never yet deviated from a 33⅓ percent markup on cost.

The Customer

König & Cie., AG, was the largest manufacturer and processor of basic chemicals and chemical products in West Germany. It operated a number of chemical plants throughout the country. To date it had purchased three digital computer process control systems, all from Computron. The purchase was made during 1977–78 and represented $1 million worth of business for Computron. Thus König was Computron's largest German customer and alone constituted over 80 percent of Computron's 1977–78 sales to Germany.

Zimmermann felt that the primary reason König had purchased Computron systems was their proven reputation for flexibility, accuracy, and overall high quality. So far, König officials seemed well pleased with their Computron computers.

Looking ahead, Zimmermann felt that König would continue to represent more potential business than any other single German customer. He estimated that during the next year or two König would need another $1 million worth of digital computer equipment.

The computer on which König was then inviting bids was to be used in training operators for a new chemical plant. The training program was to last approximately four to five years, after which the computer would either be scrapped or converted for other uses. The calculations the computer would have to perform were highly specialized and would require little machine flexibility. In the specifications published with the invitations to bid, König management had stated that it was primarily interested in dependability and a reasonable price. Machine flexibility and pinpoint accuracy were of very minor importance, because the machine was not to be used for on-line process control.

Competition

In Germany, approximately nine companies were competing with Computron in the sale of medium-priced digital

---

[2]Depending on the specific application, the components of the 1000X varied slightly, so each machine was somewhat different.

process control computers. Four companies accounted for 80 percent of sales in 1977–78 (see Table A).

Zimmermann was primarily concerned with competition from the following companies:

Ruhr Maschinenfabrik, AG: a very aggressive German company which was trying hard to expand its share of the market. Ruhr sold a medium-quality, general-purpose digital computer at a price roughly 22.5 percent lower than Computron charged for its 1000X computer. Because the Ruhr machine was manufactured entirely in Germany, the absence of import duty accounted for 17.5 percent of the price differential. To date, Ruhr has sold only general-purpose computers, but reliable trade sources indicated that it was then developing a special computer for the König bid. Ruhr's planned price for the special-purpose computer was reported to be about $218,000.

Elektronische Datenverarbeitungsanlagen, AG (EDAG): a relatively new company, which had developed a general-purpose computer of comparable quality to the Computron 1000X. Zimmermann felt that EDAG presented a real long-range threat to Computron's position as the blue-chip company in the industry. To get a foothold, this firm had sold its first computer almost at cost. Since that time, however, it had undersold Computron only by the amount of the import duty to which Computron's computers were subject.

Digitex, GmbH: a subsidiary of an American firm, which had complete manufacturing facilities in Germany and produced a wide line of computer equipment. The Digitex computer that competed with the Computron 1000X was only of fair quality. Digitex often engaged in price-cutting tactics, and in the past the price of its computer had sometimes been as much as 50 percent lower than that of Computron's 1000X. In spite of this difference, Computron had usually competed successfully against Digitex because of technical superiority.

Zimmermann was not overly concerned about the remaining competitors; he did not consider them to be significant factors in Computron's segment of the industry.

The German Market

The total estimated German market for medium-priced digital process control computers of the type manufactured by Computron was running at about $4 million per year. Zimmermann thought this could be expected to increase at an annual rate of about 25 percent for the next several years. For 1978–79 he already had positive knowledge of about $1.3 million worth of new business, broken down as follows:

König & Cie., AG:	
Frankfurt plant	$ 300,000
Düsseldorf plant	250,000
Mannheim plant	150,000
Central German Power Commission	440,000
Deutsche Autowerke	160,000
Total	$1,300,000

This business was in addition to the possible computer sale to König; however, none of this already known business was expected to materialize until late spring or early summer.

Deadline for Bids. The deadline for submission of bids to König was August 1, 1978—then less than two weeks away.

TABLE A   **Market Shares for Companies Selling Medium-Priced Digital Computers to the German Market, 1977–78**

Computron, Inc.	$1,200,000	30.0%
Ruhr Maschinenfabrik, AG	800,000	20.0
Elektronische		
Datenverarbeitungsanlagen, AG	500,000	12.5
Digitex, GmbH	700,000	17.5
Six other companies (combined)	800,000	20.0
Total	$4,000,000	100.0%

Cumberland Metal Industries: Engineered Products Division, 1980

Robert Minicucci,[1] vice president of the Engineered Products Division of Cumberland Metal Industries (CMI), and Thomas Simpson, group manager of the Mechanical Products Group, had spent the entire Wednesday (January 2, 1980) reviewing a new product CMI was about to introduce. (See Exhibit 1 for organization charts.) The room was silent, and, as he watched the waning rays of the sun filtering through the window, Minicucci pondered all that had been said. Turning toward Simpson, he paused before speaking.

> Curled metal cushion pads seem to have more potential than any product we've ever introduced. A successful market introduction could as much as double the sales of this company, as well as compensate for the decline of some existing lines. It almost looks too good to be true.

Simpson responded, "The people at Colerick Foundation Company are pressing us to sell to them. Since they did the original test, they've been anxious to buy more. I promised to contact them by the end of the week."

"Fair enough," Minicucci said, "but talk to me before you call them. The way we price this could have a significant impact on everything else we do with it."

The Company

Cumberland Metal Industries was one of the largest manufacturers of curled metal products in the country, having grown from $250,000 in sales in 1963 to over $18,500,000 by 1979. (Exhibit 2 shows CMI's income statement.) It originally custom fabricated components for chemical process filtration and other highly technical applications. Company philosophy soon evolved from selling the metal as a finished product to selling products that used it as a raw material.

The company's big boost came with the introduction of exhaust gas recirculation (EGR) valves on U.S. automobiles. Both the Ford and Chrysler valve designs required a high temperature seal to hold the elements in place and prevent the escape of very hot exhaust gases. Cumberland developed a product that sold under the trademark *Slip-Seal*. Because it could meet the demanding specifications of the automakers, the product captured a very large percentage of the available business, and the company grew quite rapidly through the mid-1970s. Company management was not sanguine about maintaining its 80 percent market share over the long term, however, and moved to diversify away from a total reliance on the product and industry. Thus, when a sales representative from Houston approached CMI with a new application for curled metal technology, management examined it closely.

The Product

Background.   The product that Minicucci and Simpson were talking about was a cushion pad, an integral part of the process for driving piles.[2] Pile driving was generally done with a large crane, to which a diesel or steam hammer inside a set of leads was attached. The leads were suspended over the pile for direction and support. The hammer drove the pile from the top of the leads to a sufficient depth in the ground (see Exhibit 3).

The cushion pads prevented the shock of the hammer from damaging hammer or pile. They sat in a circular "helmet" placed over the top of the pile and were stacked to keep air from coming between striker plate and ram, as shown in Exhibit 3. Of equal importance, the pads effectively transmitted energy from the hammer to the pile. A good cushion pad had to be able to transmit force without creating heat and still remain resilient enough to prevent shock. With an ineffective pad, energy transmitted from the hammer would be given off as heat, and the pile could start to vibrate and possibly crack.

Despite the importance of these pads to the pile-driving process, little attention had been paid to them by most of the industry. Originally, hardwood blocks had been used. Although their cushioning was adequate, availability was a problem and performance was poor. Constant pounding quickly destroyed the wood's resiliency, heat built up, and the wood often ignited. The blocks had to be replaced frequently.

Most of the industry had shifted to asbestos pads (normally ¼-inch thick) which were used most often and seemed to perform adequately, or stacks of alternate layers

---

This case was prepared by Jeffrey J. Sherman (under the direction of Professor Benson P. Shapiro).
Copyright © 1980 by the President and Fellows of Harvard College.
Harvard Business School case 580-104.
    [1]Pronounced Minikuchi.

---

[2]Piles were heavy beams of wood, concrete, steel, or a composite material, which were pushed into the ground as support for a building, bridge, or other structure. They were necessary where the geological composition could shift under the weight of an unsupported structure.

of ½-inch-thick aluminum plate and 1-inch-thick micarta slabs. (These were not fabricated, but simply pieces of micarta and aluminum cut to specific dimensions.) Both pads came in a variety of standard diameters, the most common being 11½ inches. Diameter was determined by the size of the helmet, which varied with the size of the pile.

Curled Metal and the CMI Cushion Pad. Curled metal was a continuous metal wire that had been flattened and then wound into tight, continuous ringlets. These allowed the metal to stretch in both length and width and gave it three-dimensional resiliency. Because it could be made of various metals (such as copper, monel, and stainless steel), curled metal could be made to withstand almost any temperature or chemical. Stacking many layers could produce a shock mount, an airflow corrector, or a highly efficient filter. Tightly compressed curled metal could produce the Slip-Seal for exhaust systems applications or, when calendered and wound around an axis, a cushion pad for pile driving.[3]

Cumberland purchased the wire from outside vendors and performed the flattening and curling operations in-house. The CMI pad started with curled metal calendered to about one inch thick and wound tightly around the center of a flat, metallic disk until the desired diameter had been reached. A similar disk was placed on top, with soldered tabs folded down to hold it all together. The entire structure was then coated with polyvinyl chloride to enhance its appearance and disguise the contents (see Exhibit 4).[4]

The advantage of this manufacturing process was that any diameter pad, from the standard minimum of 11½ inches to over 30 inches for a custom-designed application, could be produced from the same band of curled metal.

Comparative Performance

The Colerick Test. After struggling to find a responsible contractor to use the product and monitor its performance, CMI persuaded Colerick Foundation Company of Baltimore, Maryland, to try its pads on a papermill expansion in Newark, Delaware. The job required 300 55-foot piles driven 50 feet into the ground. The piles were 10-inch and

14-inch steel H-beams; both used an 11½-inch helmet and, thus, 11½-inch cushion pads. The total contractor revenue from the job was $75,000 ($5 per foot of pile driven).

Colerick drove a number of piles using the conventional ¼-inch thick asbestos cushion pads to determine their characteristics for the job. Eighteen were placed in the helmet and driven until they lost resiliency. Pads were added, and driving continued until a complete set of 24 were sitting in the helmet. After these were spent, the entire set was removed and the cycle repeated.

The rest of the job used the CMI pads. Four were initially installed and driven until 46 piles had been placed. One pad was added and the driving continued for 184 more piles. Another pad was placed in the helmet, and the job was completed. Comparable performances for the entire job were extrapolated as follows:

	Asbestos	CMI
1. Feet driven per hour while pile driver was at work (does not consider downtime)	150	200
2. Piles driven per set of pads	15	300
3. Number of pads per set	24	6
4. Number of sets required	20	1
5. Number of set changes	20	1
6. Time required for change per set	20 mins.	4 mins.
7. Colerick cost per set	$ 50	Not charged

Although the CMI pads drove piles 33 percent faster than the asbestos and lasted for the entire job, Simpson felt these results were unusual. He believed that a curled metal set life of 10 times more than asbestos and a performance increase of 20 percent were probably more reasonable, because he was uncertain that the CMI pads in larger sizes would perform as well.

Industry Practice. Industry sources indicated that as many as 75 percent of pile-driving contractors owned their hammers, and most owned at least one crane and set of leads. To determine the contractors' cost of doing business, CMI studied expenses of small contractors who rented equipment for pile-driving jobs. These numbers were readily available and avoided the problem of allocating the cost of a purchased crane or hammer to a particular job.

Standard industry practice for equipment rental used a three-week month and a three-day workweek.[5] There was

---

[3]In calendering, curled metal ringlets were compressed between rollers to make a smooth, tight band.

[4]The managers at CMI were concerned that other manufacturers might discover this new application for curled metal and enter the business before CMI could get patent protection. The company had a number of competitors, most of whom were substantially smaller than CMI and none of whom had shown a strong interest or competence in technical, market, or product development.

[5]This means that a contractor who rented equipment for one calendar month was charged only the "three-week" price but had the equipment for the whole calendar month. The same was true of the "three-day week." Contractors generally tried to use the equip-

TABLE A   **Equipment Rental, Labor, and Overhead Costs**

	Per Standard			
	Month	*Week*	*Per Hour*	*Average Cost per Real Hour[a]*
1. Diesel hammer	$ 4,500–7,200	$1,500–2,400	$62.50–100.00	$ 34
2. Crane	8,000–10,000	2,667–3,334	111.00–140.00	52
3. Leads @ $20 per foot per month (assume 70 feet)	1,400	467	19.44	8
4. Labor[b] — 3 laborers			18.00–24.00	21
at $6–8 per hour each			8.00–12.00	10
1 crane operator			12.00–14.00	13
1 foreman				
5. Overhead[c]			100.00	100
(office, trucks, oil/gas, tools, etc.)				

(Casewriter's note: Please use average cost per real hour in all calculations, for uniformity in class discussion.)

[a]These costs were calculated from a rounded midpoint of the estimates. Hammer, crane, and lead costs were obtained by dividing standard monthly costs by 4.33 weeks per month and 40 hours per week.

[b]Labor was paid on a 40-hour week, and a 4.33-week month. One-shift operation (40 hours per week) was standard in the industry.

[c]Most contractors calculated overhead on the basis of "working" hours, not standard hours.

no explanation for this, other than tradition, but most equipment renters set their rates this way. The cost of renting the necessary equipment and the labor cost for a job similar to that performed by Colerick were estimated as shown in Table A.

Hidden costs also played an important role. For every hour actually spent driving piles, a contractor could spend 20 to 40 minutes moving the crane into position. Another 10 to 15 percent was added to cover scheduling delays, mistakes, and other unavoidable problems. Thus, the real cost per hour was usually substantially more than the initial figures showed. Reducing the driving time or pad changing time did not usually affect the time lost on delays and moving.

All these figures were based on a job that utilized 55-foot piles and 11½-inch pads. Although this was a common size, much larger jobs requiring substantially bigger material were frequent. A stack of 11½-inch asbestos pads weighed between 30 and 40 pounds; the 30-inch size could weigh seven to eight times more. Each 11½-inch CMI pad weighed 15½ pounds. The bigger sizes, being much more difficult to handle, could contribute significantly to unproductive time on a job. (See Exhibit 5.)

Most contracts were awarded on a revenue-per-foot basis. Thus, contractors bid by estimating the amount of time it would take to drive the specified piles the distance required by the architectural engineers. After totaling costs

ment for as much time per week or per month as possible. Thus, they rented it on a "three-week" month but used it on a "4.33-week" month.

and adding a percentage for profit, they submitted figures broken down into dollars per foot. The cost depended on the size of the piles and the type of soil to be penetrated. The $5 per foot that Colerick charged was not atypical, but prices could be considerably greater.

Test Results. The management of CMI was extremely pleased by how well its cushion pads had performed. Not only had they lasted the entire job, eliminating the downtime required for changeover, but other advantages had become apparent. For example, after 500 feet of driving, the average temperature for the asbestos pads was between 600°F and 700°F, which created great difficulty when they had to be replaced. The crew handling them was endangered, and substantial time was wasted waiting for them to cool. (This accounted for a major portion of the time lost to changeovers.)

The CMI pads, in contrast, never went above 250°F and could be handled almost immediately with protective gloves. This indicated that substantial energy lost in heat by the asbestos pads was being used more efficiently to drive the piles with CMI pads. In addition, the outstanding resiliency of the CMI product seemed to account for a 33 percent faster driving time, which translated into significant savings.

In talking with construction site personnel, CMI researchers also found that most were becoming wary of the asbestos pads' well-publicized health dangers. Many had expressed a desire to use some other material and were pleased that the new pads contained no asbestos.

The CMI management was quite happy with these results; Colerick was ecstatic. Understandably, Colerick became quite anxious to buy more pads and began pressing Tom Simpson to quote prices.

A Second Test. To confirm the results from the Colerick test, CMI asked Fazio Construction to try the pads on a job in New Brighton, Pennsylvania. This job required 300 45-foot concrete piles to be driven 40 feet into the ground. Asbestos pads (11½ inches) were again used for comparison. Total job revenue was $108,000, or $9 per foot, and Fazio would have paid $40 for each set of 12 asbestos pads used. The results from this test are shown as follows:

	Asbestos	CMI
1. Feet driven per hour while pile driver was at work (does not consider downtime)	160	200
2. Piles driven per set of pads	6	300
3. Number of pads per set	12	5
4. Number of sets required	50	1
5. Number of set changes	50	1
6. Time required for change per set	20 mins.	4 mins.
7. Fazio cost per set	$40	Not charged

The Market

Projected Size. There were virtually no statistics from which a potential U.S. market for cushion pads could be determined, so Simpson had to make several assumptions based on the information he could gather. A 1977 report by *Construction Engineering* magazine estimated that approximately 13,000 pile hammers were owned by companies directly involved in pile driving. Industry sources estimated that another 6,500 to 13,000 were leased. He assumed that this total of 19,500 to 26,000 hammers would operate about 25 weeks per year (because of seasonality) and that they would be used 30 hours per week (because of moving time, repairs, scheduling problems, and other factors).

Simpson further assumed that an average actual driving figure (including time to change pads and so on) for most jobs was 20 feet per hour, which amounted to between 290 million and 390 million feet of piles driven annually. To be conservative, he also assumed that a set of curled metal pads (four initially installed, plus two added after the originals lost some resiliency) would drive 10,000 feet.

Purchase Influences. In the pile-driving business, as in other parts of the construction industry, a number of enti-ties participated in purchases. The CMI management was able to identify six types of influences.

1. *Pile hammer manufacturers.* A number of manufacturers sold hammers in the United States, although many were imported from Western Europe and Japan. The leading domestic producer in 1979 was Vulcan Iron Works of New Orleans, whose Model #1 had become the standard used by architectural engineers specifying equipment for a job. Simpson did not feel these manufacturers would purchase a large dollar volume of cushion pads, but they could be very influential in recommendations.

2. *Architectural/consulting engineers.* Pile driving required significant expertise in determining the needs of a construction project. Thorough stress analysis and other mathematical analyses were necessary. Because of the risks in building the expensive projects usually supported by piles, the industry looked to architectural/consulting engineers as the ultimate authorities on all aspects of the business. Consequently, these firms were very detailed in specifying the materials and techniques to be used on a project. They always specified hammers and frequently mentioned pads. The CMI management felt that, although no sales would come from these people, they could be one of the most important purchase influences.

3. *Soil consultants.* These consultants were similar to the architectural/consulting engineers, but were consulted only on extraordinary conditions.

4. *Pile hammer distributing/renting companies.* This group was an important influence, because it provided pads to the contractors. In fact, renting companies often included the first set of pads free. CMI management felt that these companies would handle the cushion pads they could most easily sell and might even hesitate to provide pads that enabled a contractor to return equipment faster.

5. *Engineering/construction contractors.* The contracting portion of the industry was divided among large international firms and smaller independents. The former almost always participated in the bigger, more sophisticated jobs. Companies like Conmaco and Raymond International not only contracted to drive piles but also designed jobs, specified material, and even manufactured their own equipment. It was clear to Simpson that, if he was to succeed in getting CMI pads used on bigger, complex construction projects, CMI would have to solicit this group actively on a very sophisticated level.

6. *Independent pile-driving contractors.* These contractors represented the "frontline buying influence." Their primary objective was to make money. They were very knowledgeable about the practical aspects of pile driving, but not very sophisticated.

No national industry associations influenced this business, but some regional organizations played a minor part. Contractors and others talked freely, although few were willing to reveal competitive secrets. The company was unsure how important word-of-mouth communication would be. Very little was published about the pile-driving industry, although construction-oriented magazines like *Louisiana Contractor* occasionally reported on pile-driving contractors and their jobs. These magazines featured advertising by suppliers to the trade, mostly equipment dealers and supply houses. One industry supplier, Associated Pile and Fitting Corporation, sponsored professional-level "Piletalk" seminars in various cities, bringing designers, contractors, and equipment developers together "to discuss practical aspects of installation of driven piles."

Another potential influence was Professor R. Stephen McCormack of Pennsylvania A&M University. He had established a department to study pile driving and had become a respected authority on its theoretical aspects. Sophisticated engineering/construction firms and many architectural consultants were familiar with his work and helped support it. Cumberland management felt that his endorsement of the operational performance of CMI cushion pads would greatly enhance industry acceptance. The company submitted the pads for testing by Dr. McCormack in the fall of 1979, and, although the final results were not yet available, he had expressed considerable enthusiasm. Final results were expected by early 1980.

Competitive Products and Channels of Distribution.   The pile-driving industry had paid very little attention to cushion pads before CMI's involvement. Everyone used them and took them for granted, but no one attempted to promote pads. No manufacturers dominated the business. In fact, most pads came unbranded, having been cut from larger pieces of asbestos or micarta by small, anonymous job shops.

Distribution of pads was also ambiguous. Hammer sales and rental outlets provided them, heavy construction supply houses carried them, pile manufacturers sometimes offered them, and a miscellaneous assortment of other outlets occasionally sold them as a service.[6] The smaller pads sold for $2 to $3 each; larger ones sold for between $5 and $10. Three dollars each was typical for 11½-inch pads. The profit margin for a distributor was usually adequate—in the area of 30 to 40 percent—but the dollar profit did not compare well with that of other equipment lines. Most outlets carried pads as a necessary part of the business, but none featured them as a work-saving tool.

The CMI management felt it could be totally flexible in establishing an organization to approach the market. It toyed with the idea of a direct sales force and its own distribution outlets, but eventually began to settle on signing construction-oriented manufacturers' representatives,[7] who would sell to a variety of distributors and supply houses. The company feared an uphill struggle to convince the sales and distribution channels that there really was a market for the new pad. Management expected considerable difficulty in finding outlets willing to devote the attention necessary for success; but it also felt that, once the initial barriers had been penetrated, most of the marketplace would be anxious to handle the product.

The Pricing Decision

Simpson had projected cost data developed by his manufacturing engineers. Exhibit 6 shows two sets of numbers: one utilized existing equipment; the other reflected the purchase of $50,000 of permanent tooling. In both cases, the estimated volume was 250 cushion pads per month. Additional equipment could be added at a cost of $75,000 per 250 pads per month of capacity, including permanent tooling like that which could be purchased for $50,000.

Both sets of numbers were based on the assumption that only one pad size would be manufactured; in other words, the numbers in the 11½-inch size were based on manufacturing only this size for a year. This was done because CMI had no idea of the potential sales mix among product sizes. Management knew that 11½ inches was the most popular size, but the information available on popularity of the other sizes was vague. CMI accounting personnel believed these numbers would not vary dramatically with a mix of sizes.

Corporate management usually burdened CMI products with a charge equal to 360 percent of direct labor to cover the overhead of its large engineering staff. Simpson was uncertain how this would apply to the new product, because little engineering had been done and excess capacity was to be used initially for manufacturing. Although it was allocated on a variable basis, he thought he might consider the overhead "fixed" for his analysis. Corporate management expected a contribution margin after all manufacturing costs of 40 to 50 percent of selling price.

Simpson was enthusiastic about the potential success of this new product. The Engineered Products Division was particularly pleased to offer something with such high dollar potential, especially since, in the past, a "large cus-

---

[6]Supply houses were "hardware stores" for contractors and carried a general line of products, including lubricants, work gloves, and maintenance supplies. Distributors, in contrast, tended to be more equipment oriented and to sell a narrower line of merchandise.

[7]Manufacturers' representatives were agents (sometimes single people, sometimes organizations) who sold noncompeting products for commission. They typically did *not* take title to the merchandise and did *not* extend credit.

tomer" of the division had purchased only about $10,000 per year.

He was still uncertain how to market the pads and how to reach the various purchase influences. Advertising and promotion also concerned him because there were no precedents for this product or market.

For the moment, however, Simpson's primary consideration was pricing. He had promised to call Colerick Foundation Company by the end of the week, and Minicucci was anxious to review his decision with him. He hoped other prospects would be calling as soon as word about the pads' test performance got around.

EXHIBIT 1

Engineered products division organization chart

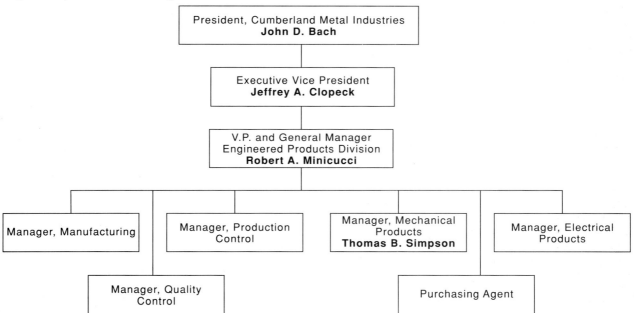

Exhibit 1

(concluded) **Mechanical products group organization chart**

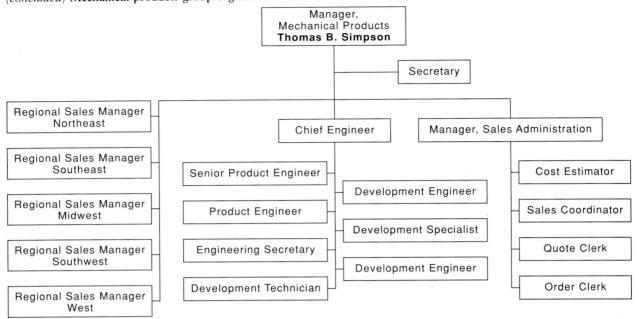

Exhibit 2   Income Statement

December 31	*1979*	*1978*
Net sales	$18,524,428	$20,465,057
Costs and expenses:		
Cost of sales	11,254,927	11,759,681
Selling expenses	2,976,396	2,711,320
General and administrative expenses	2,204,291	2,362,528
	16,435,614	16,833,529
Income from operations	2,088,814	3,631,528
Other income (expense):		
Dividend income	208,952	—
Interest income	72,966	186,611
Interest expense	(40,636)	(31,376)
	241,282	155,235
Income before income taxes	2,330,096	3,786,763
Provision for income taxes	1,168,830	1,893,282
Net income	$ 1,161,266	$ 1,893,481
Net income per share	$1.39	$2.16

EXHIBIT 3

Typical steam- or air-operated pile driver with helmet and cushion pad

Steam or Air Cylinder

Guide Rods, or "Leads"

Rising and Falling Weight (Ram)

Piledriver Ram Point

Piledriver Base

Striker Plate

CMI Cushion Pads

Helmet (or Cap Block)

Pile

A schematic diagram of typical pile driver

Pile hammer inside leads driving a steel H-beam into the ground

CMI pile-driving pad in position in helmet

Close-up of hammer driving pile (most of the pile is already in the ground)

EXHIBIT 3
(concluded)

188

EXHIBIT 4

Close-up of CMI curled metal cushion pad for pile driving

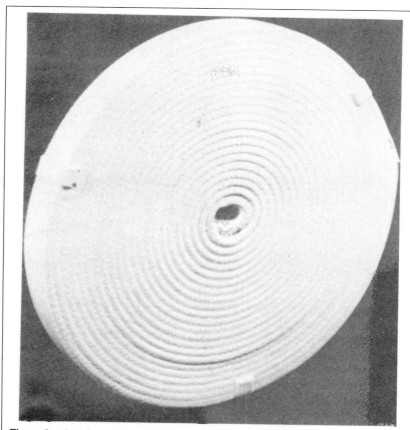

The calendered curled metal is wound tightly around the central point of a flat metallic disk. (The disk is on the back side of the pad from this view.) Soldered tabs secure the curled metal to the disk. The entire structure is coated with polyvinyl-chloride.

EXHIBIT 5   Curled Metal Cushion Pad Standard Sizes

Diameter (inches)	Thickness (inches)	Weight (pounds)
11½	1	15½
14	1	23
17½	1	36
19¾	1	48
23	1	64
30	1	110

EXHIBIT 6   Two Sets of Projected Manufacturing Costs

			Size			
	11½"	*14"*	*17½"*	*19¾"*	*23"*	*30"*
Estimates per Pad with Existing Equipment						
Variable:						
Material	$ 15.64	$ 20.57	$ 31.81	$ 40.39	$ 53.16	$ 95.69
Labor	28.80	33.07	50.02	57.07	69.16	118.36
Total variable	44.44	53.64	81.83	97.46	122.32	214.05
Fixed factory overhead:						
At 360% direct labor	103.68	119.05	180.07	205.45	248.98	426.10
Total manufacturing cost	$148.12	$172.69	$261.90	$302.91	371.30	$640.15
Estimates with Purchase of $50,000 of Permanent Tooling						
Variable:						
Material	$ 15.64	$ 20.57	$ 31.81	$ 40.39	$ 53.16	$ 95.69
Labor	11.64	15.25	21.85	26.95	30.57	56.09
Total variable	27.28	35.82	53.66	67.34	83.73	151.78
Fixed factory overhead:						
At 360% direct labor	41.90	54.90	78.66	97.02	110.05	201.92
Total manufacturing cost	$ 69.18	$ 90.72	$132.32	$164.36	$193.78	$353.70

NOTE: Estimated volume was 250 cushion pads per month.

FEDERATED INDUSTRIES (A)

In July 1984, Thomas Connors once again studied the internal consulting staff's report, "Federated Pricing in the Capacitor Market." Appointed manager of Federated's Capacitor Division in June 1983, Connors had completed a rough inaugural year. While Federated held the dominant market-share position in this low-growth industry, its performance hardly mirrored the descriptions of "cash cow" operations Connors had often read in the popular press. In fact, the division had lost more than $1 million in 1983. (See Exhibit 1.)

As part of a 1983 year-end review, Connors had funded an in-house consulting group's comprehensive history of Federated's pricing and product policy in the capacitor market. Using this information, he set policy for the first six months of 1984. Now, in July 1984, industry capacity utilization was about 40 percent, and prices were at a new low. Connors hoped that in reviewing the report he might devise a plan for stopping industry price erosion and for returning the Capacitor Division to a profitable status for

This case was prepared by Professor Robert J. Dolan.
Copyright © 1984 by the President and Fellows of Harvard College.
Harvard Business School case 9-585-104.

the first time in several years. However, Connors could not dismiss the possibility that the best plan might be withdrawal from the market. In the short term, he faced an important decision on a bid for Southern Valley Authority, due August 6. Should Federated bid, and, if so, what price?

When Connors took the manager's position, his boss, Joe Meehan, general manager of the Electrical Equipment Group, had clearly outlined his goals for the Capacitor Division:

1. Obtain more profitable price levels.
2. Restore Federated's share to its 1977 level of 50 percent versus the current 36 percent.
3. Stabilize prices.

Events of the last year hardly fit this description.

Federated Industries Background

Federated's Electrical Equipment Group contained three product divisions. (See Exhibit 2.) The Transformer, Switchgear, and Capacitor divisions had 1983 sales of $75.7 million, $31.2 million, and $8.4 million, respectively. All products were sold by a common sales force of 50 people, organized into 10 geographic districts. Customers for the group's products were the 3,500 electrical utilities in the United States.

Federated's products enabled utilities to distribute power more efficiently. Transformers were basically of two types. Step-up transformers took electricity from generators and raised it to higher voltages for transmission over long-distance lines. The transmission voltage, up to 500,000 volts, required reductions as low as 120 or 240 volts for home or factory use. Step-down transformers performed this function. Switchgear protected electrical circuits by switching loads to alternative lines or breaking the circuits when necessary. Capacitors increased utilities' power factors by boosting the useful current in a line as a percentage of the total current.

Of the 3,500 U.S. utilities, only 1,000 both generated and distributed power. The other 2,500 bought electricity from a generating firm and sold it to users. For marketing purposes, utilities were categorized as:

1. Large Public, such as the federally run Tennessee Valley Authority, Bonneville Power Authority, and Southeast and Southwest Power Authority.
2. Small Public, such as municipalities and rural electrification authorities, serving sparsely populated areas.
3. Investor Owned, such as Consolidated Edison and Houston Power and Light.

The Investor Owned group, consisting of only 435 firms, accounted for 65 percent of demand for electrical equipment. Prices for this group were negotiated; the buyers were sophisticated and price-oriented. Some manufacturers maintained published prices that served as a starting point for negotiations. Large users expected negotiated discounts off list or "book" prices.

The Large Public utilities bought via sealed bid. Tight specifications made the products of qualifying suppliers essentially equivalent. The lowest bid won the order, and all bids were a matter of public record after the opening. These utilities accounted for 20 percent of demand.

Municipalities and rural electrification authorities were small operations and quite unsophisticated in their buying procedures. Typically, these buyers did not plan ahead, delivery was more important than price, and they usually stayed with the same supplier for a long time. This group accounted for the remaining 15 percent of total demand.

Of the three products sold by the Electrical Equipment Group sales force, capacitors were by far the simplest. Essentially a metal box filled with foil and paper insulation, a capacitor had no moving parts. Many buyers viewed the capacitors of various suppliers as equivalent. Despite their simplicity, capacitors were very valuable to the utilities. Without capacitors, the typical power loss at a primary feeder station (i.e., the difference between the kilowatt

hours produced or purchased by a utility and the kilowatt hours sold to customers) was 8 percent. Capacitors could reduce this power loss to 2 to 3 percent by bringing the voltage and current into phase. In short, the increased efficiency in electrical power transmission was worth many times the cost of capacitors. The standard measure of capacitor size was kilovars (KVAR). A large public utility might order 10 or more banks of 20,000 KVAR capacitors that cost approximately $40,000 each in 1983. About one third of the utilities made a capacitor purchase in a given year.

Capacitor Industry

Suppliers. For more than 15 years, the capacitor industry had been dominated by three suppliers: Federated, Midland Electrical, and Brice. At various times, three or four other firms competed for business, but none of these fringe firms directed their primary attention to the capacitor market. Some offered capacitors merely to legitimize their full-line supplier claims. Others came into the market on a seasonal basis as demand for their other product lines slowed. Total capacity in the hands of this collection of marginal participants had never exceeded 30 percent of industry capacity. (Exhibit 3 shows three-shift manufacturing capacity in KVARs by firm for 1971–83 and industry shipments in units.)

Midland Electrical was a large, diversified manufacturer of consumer, defense, and industrial products, with 1983 sales of $1.27 billion. Midland and Federated were the original market suppliers. Brice, considerably smaller than either Federated or Midland, with $57 million in 1983 sales, specialized in electrical transmission and distribution equipment. In 1980, new management in Brice's capacitor division took an aggressive tack, significantly increasing capacity and introducing a lower-quality, lower-price capacitor line. (See Exhibit 4 for market and industry capacity shares of the three major competitors for 1977 to 1983.)

Trends. As Exhibit 3 shows, the industry historically suffered from overcapacity. Participants seemed too quick to respond to upswings in demand with capacity increases. For example, increased demand in 1975–76 promoted capacity additions by each of the players in the market, only to see an easing of demand through 1979. Average price per kilovar dropped from $6.52 in 1975 to $3.90 in 1978. (See Exhibit 5 for the history of: (1) industry shipments in units, (2) industry revenues for capacitors, and (3) average price per kilovar for the period 1971–83.)

Federated Capacitor Experience

History. Federated's Capacitor Division had operated at a loss since 1980. Universally regarded as the industry leader,

Federated offered top-quality products and as recently as 1977 had held a 48 percent share. Although its share dropped as low as 30 percent in 1981, Federated always maintained market leadership.

Federated's average sales price was usually 5–10 percent above the industry average, but followed the industry trend shown in Exhibit 5. Naturally, the price erosion put pressure on the manufacturing group to reduce costs, which it accomplished as follows:

Capacitor Direct Manufacturing Cost per Kilovar

1977: $2.70	1980: $2.18
1978: 2.02	1981: 2.00
1979: 1.98	1982: 1.94
	1983: 1.96

Connors commented on the situation in July 1984:

> It's a little hard to understand how an industry gets itself in a position like this. Part of our problem has been that the capacitor market always seems to get tied up with what's going on in the big heavy equipment market. Somebody starts cutting prices in transformers and, next thing you know, it's dragged over into the capacitor market. But still, we're not making any money and I'm sure nobody else is, but how do we get the price level back up to a reasonable level? I've budgeted a loss of $860,000 for capacitors this year [1984]; but if this $1.98 price level sticks, the loss will be a lot more than that.

Recent Pricing in the Capacitor Market

The $1.98 price level to which Connors made reference was a competitive bid made by Midland Electrical on May 11, 1984. Southern Valley Authority announced the award and price on May 21, 1984. Connors had bid $2.08 on the approximately $600,000 procurement to "be sure we'd get the business." Prompted by this and later events, Connors decided to restudy the market and consider the possibility of withdrawing.

Consultant's Report, December 1983.   In December 1983, Connors recognized the need for a comprehensive, systematic review of past pricing policies if he were to lead Federated and the industry out of its problems. Federated's internal consulting group had a good reputation for unbiased reports of this type, so Connors commissioned a study. Since the team would only examine internal Federated documents, the fee to the Capacitor Division was small and the job would be completed in one month.

Excerpts from the report follow:

> We have examined price movements in the capacitor industry for the previous six years. During this time, the market price has fallen from over $6.00 to below $2.50. The following graph [see case Exhibit 6] shows the trend of: (1) Federated's

Book Price, (2) Federated's Average Price Obtained, and (3) Federated's Direct Cost averaged over calendar years. Superimposed on the graph is the time line for the five pricing policies Federated has employed from January 1978 to December 1983:

1. Ad hoc Pricing, pre-January 1978–March 1980.
2. Strict Book Pricing, March 1980–April 1982.
3. Controlled Opportunistic Pricing, May 1982.
4. Selective Pricing, June 1982–November 1983.
5. No Book Price, December 1983.

We now review market performance under each of the five pricing policies:

Policy 1: Ad hoc Pricing, pre-January 1978 to March 1980.   We use the term *ad hoc* to refer to this period, because, although book prices[1] did exist, they became meaningless in early 1978, due to low industry capacity utilization and price-cutting by small suppliers in particular. With no realistic book price to guide individual bids or negotiations, Federated policy was essentially ad hoc. In the second half of 1978, Federated share dropped to 39 percent (from 45 percent a year previously). By the end of 1979, there was widespread recognition that Federated must formulate a policy. Mr. Meehan, general manager of the Electrical Equipment Group, directed Mr. Splaine, manager of the Capacitor Division, to slow down the price erosion, bring market stability, and eventually lead market prices to a level that would again permit operations at an acceptable profit level.

Policy 2: Strict Book Pricing, March 1980 to April 1982.   Mr. Splaine announced the division's new Book Price Policy in a memorandum to the sales force [see case Exhibit 7]. During the 26 months the Book Price Policy was in effect, Federated made 28 price changes—22 increases, six decreases. Average price declined from $4.25 (March 1980) to $3.50 by December 1981. Federated market share for 1981 reached an all-time low, 30 percent. A major cause of the share loss was Federated's loss of all large, public bid business. Since competitors knew the Federated bid would be the published book price, they consistently undercut Federated by 1 to 2 percent.

Policy 3: Controlled Opportunistic Pricing, May 1982.   In reaction to the problems with the Book Price Policy, Federated introduced Controlled Opportunistic Pricing. The major features of this policy were: (1) the frequency of book price changes was restricted to once a month and (2) price cuts of up to 6 percent off book would be permitted. According to Mr. Splaine's memorandum to the sales force, the objective of this policy was "to allow greater flexibility and selectivity in securing the most desirable jobs; to allow Federated to meet competitive prices, as long as they were within 6 percent of book prices." This policy was in place only one month and then revised to become Selective Pricing Policy because of lack of ability to compete on large jobs.

---

[1]Casewriter's note: Book prices were widely published and disseminated throughout the industry. Generally, they represented the price level that the industry leader judged fair given costs. Book price was an upper bound to market price, and buyers typically expected some percentage reduction off book price.

Policy 4: Selective Pricing, June 1982–November 1983. This policy revised the Controlled Opportunistic Policy per Mr. Splaine's memorandum to the sales force [see case Exhibit 8]. The main changes were that price cuts of more than 6 percent off book were permitted on sealed bids of over $200,000 and, if competitive prices were known conclusively, Federated would match the price. Prices continued to decline throughout the remainder of 1982, after the institution of Selective Pricing in June. The policy was severely criticized in the December 1982 review meeting. However, Mr. Splaine retained the policy, increasing book price from $3.80 to $3.95. However, this had no impact on the market price. In early 1983, the intensity of the price-cost squeeze induced both Midland and Brice to lower their product quality in an effort to lower their manufacturing cost. By Federated testing procedures, Midland and Brice capacitors would now cost the utilities significantly more in repair and maintenance cost over a 25-year period.

By June 1983, Federated's average received price was $2.80, and book price was $3.95. Consequently, the situation was much like that in 1978 when book price became meaningless. Mr. Connors replaced Mr. Splaine as manager of the Capacitor Division.

Policy 5: No Book Price, December 1983. Mr. Connors's first action in July 1983 was to attack the quality of Midland and Brice capacitors in an intense personal selling effort. Customers were told that Federated would never lower its quality. Midland and Brice effectively countered Federated claims by extending the warranties on their products. Federated refused to offer extended warranties. In November 1983, Federated attempted to reestablish a meaningful book price at $3.12, approximately 10 percent above the average price being received at that time. Federated stated publicly that it would quote only book prices. This effectively was a return to Policy 2, Strict Book Pricing. However, when competitors continued to take business at the $2.80–$2.85 level, Federated responded by withdrawing book prices in a press release through Mr. Meehan's office [see case Exhibit 9].

Events Since December 1983. Connors related events since Federated's withdrawal of book prices in December 1983:

In November, I tried to get market prices up by quoting a reasonable book price at $3.12 and saying we'd stick to it, but those other guys just wouldn't come up. So, I thought maybe it would be better for everybody if somebody else took the lead for a while.

On January 3, Midland tried to take over the leader role, quoting the book price we had just abandoned, $3.12. We found out about this in mid-February when one of our salespeople picked up a copy of the new Midland price list from a customer.

Encouraged by the Midland announcement, Federated reestablished book prices at $2.80, lower than Midland's book of $3.12, but above market. One day before, however, and unknown to Federated, one of the fringe firms announced a book price of $2.68. Midland responded with a $2.50 book price effective March 12. Federated then matched this $2.50 book price, effective March 26. This set the stage for the SVA bids, which eventually resulted in the $1.98 price level.

SVA Bidding. Southern Valley Authority, a large public utility operating under a sealed bid procedure, divided its 1984 procurement into three stages as shown in Table A. Connors recalled the Stage 1 and Stage 2 bidding:

For Stage 1, SVA qualified only Midland and us on a prebid test. I was running at 27 percent share for the first quarter of 1984. I had budgeted 36 percent—so I needed the business. We had a lot of debate on Stage 1 pricing, which revolved mostly around how different things set you up for Stage 2 since there was 10 times as much business there.

At the time, we both [Federated and Midland] had $2.50 book prices. I felt we had to quote book because, if we got aggressive, we might push prices down to $2.10–$2.20 for the rest of the year. So we went in at $2.50 per kilovar, the book. So did Midland, but they knocked nickels and dimes off the accessories so they beat us out by $200 on a $60,000 order!

By April, when it was time to prepare our Stage 2 bid, price cutting was all over the place, down as low as $2.10. The market was really unstable and some people here actually thought we should pass. SVA had added Brice and one of the small guys, Astor Electrical, to the qualified list for this round. But, here's $600,000 worth of business and I've got a market share goal of 36 percent for 1984, which I can't make without this realistically. So, we decide: let's get the business—we go at $2.08; it's low but we want to be sure to get it.

TABLE A 1984 Procurement

	Closing Date for Bid	Award Announced	Requirements (Number)–Type
Stage 1:	March 19, 1984	April 9, 1984	(2)–12,000 KVAR Banks (10)– 100 KVAR Spares
Stage 2:	May 11, 1984	May 21, 1984	(24)–12,000 KVAR Banks (100)– 100 KVAR Spares
Stage 3:	August 6, 1984	August 20, 1984	(16)–12,000 KVAR Banks (64)– 100 KVAR Spares

Well, you know the rest—Brice was out of it at $2.56, which we expected, Astor at $2.04, and Midland at $1.98—the first time anybody booked anything below $2.00.

Aftermath of SVA Stage 2 Bidding.   Many private utilities waited on the sidelines for the results of the SVA Stage 2 bidding. Connors reacted to Midland's $1.98 bid by accepting business at $1.98 per KVAR for any requirements on which customers would accept delivery by May 1985. Between May 21 and 24, 19 Federated's sales engineers were told to take this offer first to those customers who seemed likely to accept. The sales force was told to prevent leaks of these offers to the competition. On May 25, however, Midland telephoned major utilities stating that their capacitor prices had been withdrawn for review and urging them not to make long-term commitments.

By the end of June, 44 utilities had been approached with the $1.98 offer by Federated, Midland, or Astor. An estimate of total business placed is shown in the table at the top of the next column.

With these orders, capacitor orders booked for the first six months of 1984 totaled $13.8 million.

Connors's Decisions.

The May–June selling blitz put $1.5 million worth of orders on Federated's books at $1.98. Direct manufactur-

	Number of Customers	KVAR Sold	Dollar Value
Federated	15	760,000	$1,505,800
Midland	4	536,000	1,061,200
Astor	2	222,000	439,560

ing cost for 1983 was $1.96. While history suggested some manufacturing price reductions in 1984, this $1.98 business hardly seemed in keeping with Meehan's first goal of "more profitable price levels." On the other hand, Connors thought, without the $1.98 offer, there was no way Meehan's second goal of market share increase could be attained.

Connors studied the consultant's report, hoping to improve his understanding of how the market worked. Stage 3 SVA bids were due on August 6. SVA had qualified the same four suppliers as for Stage 2. Again, there was more than $500,000 in business at stake. As he thought, a telephone call relayed the news that Midland had just cut its book price to $2.30. Connors wondered, were Meehan's goals attainable, or should Federated get out of the capacitor market?

EXHIBIT 1   1983 Capacitor Division Income Statement (dollars in 000s)

	Dollars	Percent
• Sales:		
Capacitors	$6,534	78%
Accessories	1,866	22
Total sales	$8,400	100%
• Costs,		
direct:		
Materials	$4,200	50%
Direct labor	420	5
Other variable	1,008	12
Total costs	$5,628	67%
Overhead[a]:		
Manufacturing overhead	$1,008	12%
Engineering	420	5
Marketing	1,260	15
General and administrative	1,344	16
Total overhead	$4,032	48%
• Profit:		
Profit before tax	($1,260)	(15%)

[a]Overhead was allocated among the three product divisions of the Electrical Equipment Group based on sales volume. Connors estimated that Federated's withdrawal from the capacitor market would actually reduce the group's overhead by about $2 million per year.

EXHIBIT 2

Electrical Equipment Group organization chart, May 1983

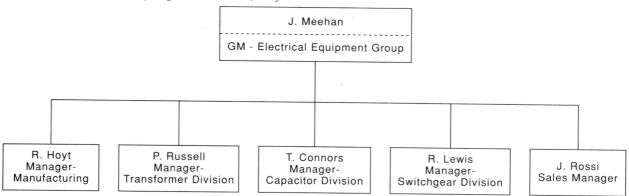

EXHIBIT 3

Industry shipments and total three-shift manufacturing capacity

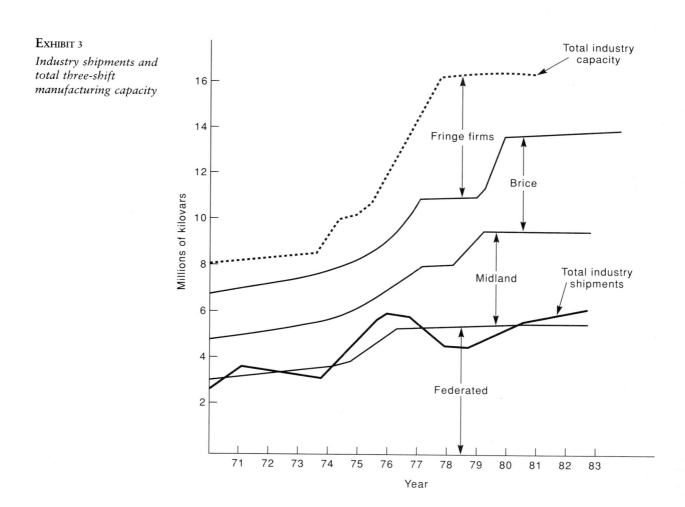

EXHIBIT 4   **Market and Capacity Shares**

Market Shares, 1977–1983

	Federated	*Midland*	*Brice*	*Fringe Firms*
1977	48%	13%	25%	14%
1978	45	10	19	26
1979	39	18	16	27
1980	34	25	18	23
1981	30	27	18	25
1982	36	30	12	21
1983	36	28	16	20

Capacity Shares, 1977–1983

	Federated	*Midland*	*Brice*	*Fringe Firms*
1977	37%	20%	19%	24%
1978	34	16	19	31
1979	33	20	18	27
1980	33	24	21	22
1981	33	24	21	22
1982	35	20	22	23
1983	35	20	22	23

EXHIBIT 5   **Industry Demand and Price History, 1971–83**

	(1) *Industry Shipments in KVAR (millions)*	*(2)* *Industry Revenues for Capacitors[a] (millions of $)*	*(3)* *(2) ÷ (1) Average Price per KVAR ($)*
1971	3.1	$23.25	$7.50
1972	3.9	29.85	7.65
1973	3.8	28.20	7.42
1974	3.5	23.70	6.72
1975	4.9	31.95	6.52
1976	6.0	27.30	4.55
1977	5.8	23.85	4.11
1978	4.5	17.55	3.90
1979	4.5	19.35	4.30
1980	5.2	22.80	4.38
1981	5.7	21.60	3.78
1982	5.9	19.50	3.30
1983	6.2	18.15	2.92

[a]Omits sales of accessories, such as racks and pole mounting devices. Typically, these would amount to 25 percent of capacitor sales.

E<small>XHIBIT</small> 6

Federated Book Price, average price received, direct cost (1978–1983)

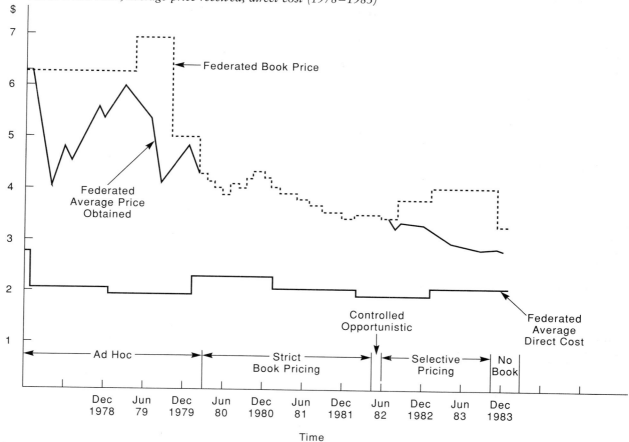

NOTE: Under Strict Book Pricing (March 1980–April 1982), Federated Book Price and Federated Average Price Obtained were identical.

EXHIBIT 7   Letter Announcing Book Pricing Policy

TO: Electrical Equipment Group Sales Representatives

FROM: D. Splaine, Manager, Capacitor Division

DATE: March 7, 1980

SUBJECT: Capacitor Pricing

Given developments in the electrical market, of which you are all well aware, the Capacitor Division has revised its pricing policy. Our new policy, "Book-Price Policy" is as follows:

1. We will publish a Book Price to be quoted to all electrical utilities. There are no exceptions.
2. The Capacitor Division will adjust Book Prices to keep them competitive with the market level.
3. If Book Prices are reduced, the price of unbilled previously booked business will be adjusted to the lower price.
4. All price changes will be announced to you and the press 48 hours before they take effect.

We believe this policy to be realistic and fair. All customers can have confidence that they will receive the same price from us and they will all receive the benefits in their billings of any reduction in price.

We want you to communicate all changes in capacitor market conditions to us promptly and accurately. Our ability to adjust our published prices to the market level quickly and to keep competitive depends on you.

Enclosed is a copy of the booklet "A Pricing Policy Which Offers You Fairness, Consistency, and Simplicity, in Addition to Better R&D and Better Products." Please use this booklet to communicate this program to our customers.

EXHIBIT 8   Letter Announcing Selective Pricing Policy

TO: Electrical Equipment Group Sales Representatives

FROM: D. Splaine, Manager, Capacitor Division

DATE: May 29, 1982

SUBJECT: Capacitor Pricing

Our one month of experience with our Controlled Opportunistic Policy indicates desirable modifications to this policy. Our new Selective Pricing Policy effective immediately is as follows:

1. Sales reps are given authority to negotiate within the 6 percent range of published prices.
2. On sealed bids of $200,000 or more, the 6 percent limit need not apply but concurrence of the Capacitor Division must be obtained.
3. In the event that a conclusive reading is obtained on competitive price, the Capacitor Division will meet the competitive price.

This policy enables us to select those jobs offering attractive margins and having low engineering and drafting expense per unit, while we maintain our market position and meet our sales budgets.

Exhibit 9   **Trade Press Release, December 1983**

FOR IMMEDIATE RELEASE:

December 4—Federated Industries Capacitor Division announced that, effective immediately, published prices on Federated's high-voltage power capacitors are to be used for estimating purposes only. This, in effect, withdraws the price increase announcement of July 9, and Federated's prices which became effective on November 13, 1983.

The general manager of Federated's Electrical Equipment Group, Joseph Meehan, stated that it has become evident that competitive activity has caused Federated's price of July 9 ($3.90 per kilovar) to become out of line with the market. Meehan stated that he believes the published prices adopted by Federated on November 13 ($3.10 per kilovar) are realistic and fair for high-quality products. He hopes the market will strengthen within a reasonable period. In the meantime, Federated plans to remain fully competitive with other quality suppliers.

Hartmann Luggage Company: Price Promotion Policy

In January 1981, Ira Katz, president of the Hartmann Luggage Company, was evaluating past price promotions and considering whether to continue offering them in the coming year. A consultants' study endorsed by the company's chief financial officer had concluded that one of Hartmann's price promotions, though it increased sales, had generated a contribution below what would have been obtained if the promotion had not been run. On the other hand, Thomas Schuster, Hartmann's recently appointed vice president for sales and marketing, questioned several key assumptions of this study. He believed price promotions could increase trade interest in Hartmann, attract new customers, and encourage current customers to add new pieces to their existing Hartmann collections.

Katz remained dubious, commenting to Schuster:

I think price promotion hurts the Hartmann image. We can do other exciting things to get dealer support, increase sales, and still maintain suggested retail prices. Remember, we increased sales by 20 percent in the year just ended with only a minor promotion by significantly more advertising. However, I'm open to persuasion. Let's reassess all our past promotions and review the consultants' study. In addition, let's consider how price promotion policy will fit with our future marketing strategy and, in particular, with the product line additions we're considering for 1981–82.

Company Background

The Hartmann Luggage Company was founded in Milwaukee in 1877 to manufacture trunks; it began producing luggage in 1930. Katz became president in 1957, not long after his father purchased the company; in 1960, he moved both the corporate offices and manufacturing plant to Lebanon, Tennessee.

From the outset Hartmann's products were among the most expensive in the industry, designed for customers who demanded the highest quality and durability in luggage. The company distributed its merchandise only through leading department stores and luggage specialty shops, and until 1955 it restricted distribution to one carefully selected dealer in each market area. Under Katz's leadership, Hartmann widened its distribution, reduced its product line, and developed a comprehensive training program for retail salespeople.

During 1980, Hartmann's revenues totaled $33 million, with pretax earnings of about 12 percent. Company sales grew at an average annual rate of 22 percent between 1974 and 1980, compared with 5 percent for the luggage industry as a whole. Katz wanted Hartmann to achieve an earnings growth rate of 25–30 percent annually, maintain a prestigious image, and increase its share of the high-quality luggage market.

The Product Line.   Hartmann's manufacturing process was relatively labor intensive. Among the distinctive features common to all framed Hartmann luggage were wooden frames, build square to allow extra space in packing, and 24-carat gold-plated Touch-O-Matic locks, recessed behind distinctive flaps and designed for easy opening. Handles were hand-sewn double loops bolted through

---

case frames. All framed case interiors were lined with fabric specially treated with Zepel stain repellent.

All luggage was sold under the Hartmann name. Katz had considered manufacturing private-label luggage, but believed it might jeopardize the firm's quality image without increasing consumer recognition of the Hartmann brand. The product line included four series of luggage in both framed and soft-sided pieces. Models and styles were similar from one series to another, but prices differed within models on the basis of variations in outside covering. Exhibit 1 shows comparative retail selling prices and pieces available for the four series, with a summary of trade orders.

The most expensive series was the 4700, illustrated in Figure A, a collection of men's luggage made from industrial belting leather. Prices on this line had increased 100 percent since 1975 because of the rising cost of leather. The 4800 series, available in both men's and women's models, was manufactured in two colors of Ultrasuede, a fabric (made popular by the fashion designer Halston) that looked like expensive suede but could be wiped clean with soap and water. The 4400 series was made of a durable synthetic fiber that resembled tweed and was trimmed with belting leather. Finally, the 4200 series was manufactured in both vinyl and fabric with vinyl trim.

As soft-sided, flexible, lighter-weight luggage became more popular in the 1960s and 1970s, Hartmann had developed the Nouveau Hobo line. It was available in belting leather (4700) and Ultrasuede (4800), but sold most widely in a strong nylon fabric trimmed with belting leather (4400), shown in Figure B. Nouveau Hobo bags were for the most part highly flexible carry-ons and totes, built on a patented "Featherflex" skeleton frame to keep their shape. In the spring season of 1980, about 13,000 Nouveau Hobo pieces were ordered.

Katz was considering several changes to Hartmann's product line in 1981. Sales of the Ultrasuede line were weakening, and he was considering replacing it. Hartmann could also introduce an additional line of designer luggage at a price point 10 to 15 percent below that of the 4200 line. The firm's advertising agency believed that this brightly colored casual luggage designed by Gloria Vanderbilt could be distributed through women's specialty stores as well as department and luggage stores; it recommended that Hartmann budget $725,000 in 1982 to introduce the new line. Agency executives argued that the line would enable Hartmann to broaden its customer base to include women aged 25 or older from households with $25,000 or more in annual income. Management characterized its present customers as aged 35 or older and living in households with at least $35,000 annual income.

The Luggage Industry.   The dollar value (at manufacturers' prices) of all luggage products sold in the United States in 1980 totaled $664 million.[1] Sales were forecast to increase 9 percent in 1981—to $724 million. Imports, whose dollar value had risen at a compound annual rate of 34 percent since 1974, accounted for 29 percent of 1980 sales. During the 1970s, most imports had been low-quality, non-leather items, but, by 1980, many retailers were praising the quality and construction of the leather and leather-trimmed luggage from Italy and South America.

Government statistics listed 293 luggage manufacturers in the United States; only 124 had more than 20 employees. Two firms dominated the luggage market: Samsonite Corporation (a subsidiary of Beatrice Foods, Inc.), with estimated 1979 sales of $140 million (including some folding furniture), and American Tourister (a subsidiary of Hillenbrand Industries, Inc.), with 1979 sales of about $85 million. Both brands were priced about 75 percent below Hartmann's 4700 line. According to Katz, Hartmann's most significant direct competitors were Lark (a subsidiary of General Mills, Inc.), and French—both of which produced fashionably designed, durable, and expensive luggage of high quality. Katz estimated Lark's 1979 sales at $20 million and French's at $6 million. Louis Vuitton, an imported line priced 25 percent above Hartmann's 4700 series, sold an estimated $8 million in 1979; Katz believed this brand competed primarily with Hartmann's Ultrasuede.

In 1963, only 36 percent of all manufacturers' unit shipments of luggage were soft-sided; by 1979, the share had risen to 71 percent. (Hartmann's framed luggage was considered hard-sided luggage.) Such items as totes and garment bags were increasingly viewed by the trade as likely impulse purchases, so they were often displayed by retailers outside the traditional luggage department.

A further trend was the increasing percentage of luggage purchases by women. As a result, manufacturers were thought to be paying more attention to fashion and style in product development. Although some luggage retailers were skeptical about the growth potential of designer-name luggage, they welcomed increased fashion orientation because it permitted more exciting merchandising at the point of sale.

The dollar sales of luggage through various distribution channels in 1980 were:

Specialty stores	16%
Department stores	30
General merchandise chains (e.g., Sears)	18
Catalog showrooms	21
Discount stores (e.g., Kmart)	11
Mail order	5

---

[1]The U.S. Commerce Department's definition of luggage products included, in addition to suitcases and travel bags, briefcases, bags for sports and hobby equipment (golf, photography, shooting), physicians' bags, and salespeople's sample cases.

FIGURE A

Hartmann's most expensive luggage (4700 Series)

For That Extra Touch

When traveling for business or pleasure, why shouldn't you have the ultimate in luggage? Natural Belting Leather - by Hartmann.
This three piece "carry-on" luggage group consists of - Hanger garment carrier, made of strong, durable nylon and belting leather; may be carried open or folded. Capacity 3 suits, 6 shirts, etc.
The carry-on single suiter has ample space as an over-nighter. All Belting Leather.
The attache case, also in Belting Leather, is attractive, spacious, with desk and three-pocket file. Even the interior trim is Belting Leather.
One or all three make you feel like a Special Person.

hartmann luggage

- Handcrafted.
- Flexible frame.
- Soft expanding sides.
- Rugged hand sewn leather handle.
- Touch-O-Matic locks cover flaps for neatness and safety.
- Zepel stain repellent.
- Removable desk and file section (attache case only).

SOURCE: Merchandising sheet.

Hartmann presents Nouveau Hobo.

How to keep yourself together while you let yourself go.

A new concept in luggage design with ingenuity and craftsmanship found in all Hartmann luggage for men and women.

Designed with square corners so you can pack it full without wasted space.

Hobo Casuals are treated with Zepel® stain repellent to resist dirt, grease, and water.

Features

- Tough and Light Weight—100% nylon Fishermans Pack Cloth —with natural Industrial Belting Leather Trim.
- Classic look.
- Multi-zippered Pockets on every model.
- Adjustable Shoulder Straps on models NH2, 3 and 4.
- Featherflex Frames on models NH5, 6 and 7 hold case in shape.

1. NH2—Toutes Les Choses
2. NH4—Suspense
3. NH3—The Harvard Club
4. NH1—Executote
5. NH5—Packhorse
6. NH6—Transcontinental 24˝
7. NH7—Le Tour Du Monde

hartmann luggage

SOURCE: Merchandising sheet.

Katz considered luggage a postponable purchase and noted that sales were highly seasonal. The industry's retail year was divided into spring (February–July) and fall (August–January) seasons. Retail sales of Hartmann luggage by month in 1979 reflected this industry pattern:

January	6.8%	July	7.0%
February	5.0	August	7.0
March	5.4	September	7.7
April	6.5	October	6.8
May	9.4	November	8.8
June	9.8	December	19.8

The Luggage Consumer. Publicly available research on the luggage consumer was sparse. The latest reported survey had been conducted by *Luggage and Travelware* magazine in 1977. Questionnaires mailed to recent luggage purchasers in 10 states generated a 47 percent response. Key findings are summarized in Exhibit 2.

Like most other firms in the industry, Hartmann had conducted little market research. In 1976, a questionnaire mailed to a sample of 1,000 Hartmann owners drawn from warranty cards generated a 57 percent response. It revealed that over 70 percent of Hartmann owners were aged 26–55; 49 percent shopped for luggage in traditional department stores; 36 percent shopped in luggage specialty stores; and 31 percent had received their luggage as gifts. Durability and style were considered the most important features in selecting luggage. (Price was not an option on the questionnaire.) Katz believed that four years later the profile of the typical Hartmann owner had not changed.

In 1979, Hartmann conducted a telephone survey of consumers over 25 years old with household incomes greater than $25,000. When presented with a list of names of luggage manufacturers, 17 percent recognized the Hartmann brand name; the overall aided awareness level ranged from 28 percent for respondents with over $35,000 in household income to 9 percent for respondents with $25,000–$35,000. Comparable awareness levels for American Tourister and Samsonite were over 90 percent. Only 5 percent of respondents recalled having seen any Hartmann advertising.

Sales and Distribution. Hartmann's sales force consisted of 16 territory managers, who reported to four regional vice presidents. The vice presidents reported to Schuster and spent two thirds of their time selling to their own accounts. Territory managers averaged $35,000 in annual earnings, typically receiving 60 percent of their compensation as salary and 40 percent as a bonus on dollar sales in excess of individual quotas. They averaged $1.5 million in annual sales and visited their major accounts several times a month. The salespeople of many luggage manufacturers

with broader distribution or smaller sales forces visited their accounts only twice a year and acted primarily as order takers.

Hartmann luggage was sold through 100 department stores and 485 specialty luggage stores throughout the United States, representing just over 1,600 separate outlets. Each class of trade accounted for 50 percent of Hartmann's dollar volume. These stores accounted for approximately 40 percent of the dollar value of all U.S. luggage sales.

In choosing retailers, the company looked first for a reputation for carrying fine merchandise. Katz preferred stores to carry at least one other high-quality brand, such as Lark or French, because such a selection facilitated trade-up selling (i.e., retail clerks encouraged customers who asked for relatively lower-priced merchandise to buy more expensive goods, stressing their product benefits and higher quality). The company expected its retailers to display all four series of Hartmann luggage and to stock a minimum inventory of $11,000 per outlet at suggested retail prices.

Retail Merchandising Program. New accounts with at least three branches were required to participate in Hartmann's retail merchandising program. As of January 1981, 94 accounts representing 482 retail outlets and about 50 percent of Hartmann's sales dollars were involved in the program, which Katz believed was unique in the industry. He noted:

> Most stores frown on incentive programs, but we felt we had to reward the sales clerks for their efforts, and we thought we could make the program stick if we stressed that its purpose was to help the entire luggage department. We've always stressed trade-up selling, but we tell retail salespeople to focus on any trade-up line—Lark, French, or Hartmann. That way our program appears less obviously self-interested to the retailer. Frankly, I would welcome more competition at the higher-priced end of the market. Hartmann sales could grow more rapidly if aggressive competitors helped to make the consumer more conscious of the advantages of better-quality, higher-priced, more-fashionable luggage.

A key feature of Hartmann's retail merchandising program was a weekly sales goal for Hartmann merchandise for each store, determined jointly by the Hartmann sales force and retail management. Assuming satisfactory performance, sales goals for each store were raised about 25 percent in dollars and about 15 percent in units each year. Branches reaching and exceeding goals were recognized with awards and trophies. In addition, a sales-incentive point system rewarded outstanding individual sales clerks with free Hartmann luggage. A clerk could earn enough points to receive a $300 suitcase by selling $30,000 of luggage at retail. Katz estimated the cost of the incentive program at about 0.25 percent of Hartmann's factory sales.

The second major feature of Hartmann's retail merchandising program was training retail salespeople. Through breakfast seminars, films, and promotional handbooks, the Hartmann sales force taught salespeople first to approach each customer with a detailed description of one of the store's top luggage lines, usually Hartmann's belting leather. This presentation emphasized the high-quality construction, patented locks, and unique handles common to every Hartmann product. If, after this demonstration, the customer viewed the belting leather line as too expensive, the salesperson presented a similar Hartmann model in the second most expensive series, noting the similarities in design and quality of construction despite the different exterior. Katz described this approach as "selling up by stepping down."

The program was well received by retailers. During 1979, 25 new outlets had joined the program and none had withdrawn. To demonstrate the higher profitability of more expensive luggage to department and specialty store buyers, Hartmann developed a chart in August 1979 (see Exhibit 3). Net profits before taxes to the retailer on Hartmann luggage sales ranged from 21 percent on the 4200 line to 36 percent on the 4700 line, compared with 13 percent on Samsonite's Silhouette line and an average 8 percent on all luggage. By May 1980, Hartmann's suggested retail prices offered retailers a margin of 54 percent, compared with a 51 percent average margin for luggage sold in department and specialty stores, and a 46 percent average margin for the luggage industry as a whole.

Pricing.   Katz stated that the goal of Hartmann's pricing policy "was to make each piece stand on its own two feet." Between 1976 and 1980, Hartmann had increased prices each year, partly in response to the rapidly rising cost of leather. The average annual increase, weighted by sales volumes for each product, ranged from 10 percent in 1976 to 13 percent in 1980.[2] Katz gave advance notice of each increase to Hartmann's trade accounts through a personal letter. Schuster estimated the company's overall contribution margin at 44 percent. The average for the luggage industry as a whole was 25 to 30 percent.

Hartmann attached price tags to all its luggage before shipment. Before resale price maintenance ended in 1975, the company had insisted that all retailers sell its luggage at only the full recommended retail price.[3] Hartmann set its suggested retail prices in round numbers, such as $100,

rather than at price points, such as $99.95, and its executives believed that few trade customers substituted new price tags. Some high-quality retailers, however, periodically offered up to 25 percent off the price tags, either on all luggage items in their stores or on selected lines, to stimulate consumer purchases during slow selling periods. In addition, retailers occasionally negotiated price with customers: for example, a 10 percent discount might be offered on the purchase of five pieces of luggage. Hartmann's executives discouraged such negotiation, and it was believed to be least prevalent in the types of outlets that carried Hartmann luggage.

Advertising.   Hartmann spent approximately 5 percent of sales on a national advertising program, cooperative advertising, trade advertising, merchandising sheets, and other selling aids. Media expenditures for the national advertising program during 1977–80 were reported by the company as follows:

	Number of Publications	Cost of Media Space
1977 Spring	6	$286,596
Fall	7	390,935
1978 Spring	6	416,095
Fall	6	487,280
1979 Spring	10	478,030
Fall	9	725,470
1980 Spring	10	708,840
Fall	6	941,160

Katz estimated that Lark spent about 3 percent of sales on advertising; French placed no national advertising. In the industry as a whole, Hartmann was the third-largest advertiser—behind Samsonite and American Tourister, both of which used television as well as print media and spent about 2.5 percent of sales on national advertising. A typical Samsonite magazine ad is reproduced in Figure C.

Hartmann's advertising for 1980 appeared in executive *Newsweek,*[4] *Time, Business Week, Glamour, Vogue, New Yorker, Town and Country, Travel and Leisure,* and the *New York Times Magazine.* Traditionally, advertising had focused on the differentiating features of Hartmann luggage, particularly the more casual lines (see Figure D). During 1980, the company also placed a series of smaller advertisements in *The Wall Street Journal;* these stressed

---

[2]The consumer price index rose 6.5 percent in 1977 over 1976, 7.7 percent in 1978, 11.3 percent in 1979, and 14.4 percent in 1980.

[3]Resale price maintenance (or fair trade) laws permitted manufacturers or distributors of trademarked products to determine their resale prices. They had initially been advocated by small, independent retailers seeking protection from price-cutting by large chains. National resale price maintenance legislation regulating interstate commerce, passed in 1938, was terminated in 1975 by the Consumer Goods Pricing Act.

---

[4]Executive *Newsweek* was sent to 550,000 subscribers selected from the magazine's total circulation of 2,950,000. Advertisers paid a premium to reach this group of professionals, managers, and executives earning over $20,000 annually. The editorial content of executive and standard editions was identical.

FIGURE C

1980 Samsonite magazine advertisement

Hartmann's name and reputation, rather than particular models of luggage.

Unlike Samsonite and American Tourister, Hartmann did not aggressively promote its co-operative advertising program to its retailers. The company required that all pro-posed co-op advertising be approved by Hartmann in advance and feature its name in the headline. Acceptable media were limited to individual retailer catalogs (such as Christmas catalogs), direct mail promotions (including retailer statement stuffers), the national magazines in the

FIGURE D

1979 Hartmann magazine advertisement

company's current corporate campaign, and city magazines (such as *Boston Magazine*) whose readership met Hartmann's upscale demographic criteria. Newspaper advertising that mentioned Hartmann did not qualify. Retailers could accumulate co-op allowances at the rate of 2.5 percent of their dollar purchases of full-priced in-line Hartmann luggage.[5] These funds could be used to cover 50 percent of the cost of eligible co-op advertisements. Allowance money could not be accumulated on purchases of promoted or discounted merchandise. The co-op advertising program cost Hartmann an estimated $130,000 for fiscal year 1981.

Because Hartmann funded no co-op advertising in newspapers, its price promotions were advertised only locally by larger retailers. Samsonite and American Tourister both permitted newspaper co-op advertising, so their price promotions were featured more extensively in local than in national media. By contrast, advertisements for Hartmann's price promotions in 1976, 1977, and 1979 were incorporated in the national advertising campaign. Some Hartmann executives believed the company should advertise its price promotions in newspapers or perhaps transfer the money spent on advertising the price promotions into a special co-op account against which retail accounts could draw if they wished to advertise them.

Price Promotion in the Luggage Industry. Price promotion strategies in the luggage industry varied widely. Dominant, popularly priced brands like Samsonite and American Tourister held several promotion events a year. Typically, a temporary price discount would be announced to the trade in advance, and an order placed during a specified period would be invoiced at a discount price. Usually only one order was allowed per promotion. Schuster believed many of these promotions were held to clear a manufacturer's surplus inventory, rather than to increase long-term market share.

Price promotions typically were offered on some or all of the pieces at one price point in a manufacturer's standard product line. They rarely covered either all pieces at all price points or one piece across several price points. Schuster believed that, in general, more frequent promotions on narrower selections of luggage targeted at specific consumer segments would prove more profitable. Although some luggage manufacturers promoted either their lowest price points or their slower-selling pieces, Hartmann preferred the idea of promoting its most popular lines. "If and when we promote, we would emphasize a strength, not a weakness," Katz explained.

---

[5] In-line merchandise was the most recent, prevailing product line, as distinct from items manufactured especially for promotions or discontinued items being sold off through promotions.

Among the more expensive brands, Lark ran no price promotions, except occasional clearances of discontinued merchandise. French ran no national price promotions and never promoted in-line merchandise. However, French often bought closeout leather or fabrics at a discount and made up three- or four-piece sets of luggage in one of its standard designs. These then were offered to the trade at a price lower than that of similar in-line merchandise.

Most price promotions on luggage coincided with seasonal sales peaks, either before Christmas or during the late spring wedding and graduation period. Traditionally, Samsonite and American Tourister both ran a major promotion in May and June. Retail buyers, seeking to ensure a steady stream of promotion-generated traffic, preferred consecutive, rather than concurrent, promotions. Overlaps were becoming unavoidable, however, as the number of manufacturers running promotions, along with the frequency and average duration of the events, all increased. To appeal to retail buyers, some smaller manufacturers had begun to offer their promotions in February and March.

Hartmann's Gift-with-Purchase and Purchase-with-Purchase Promotions. In 1972 and between 1975 and 1977, Hartmann ran one promotion yearly that typically offered consumers either a gift or discounted merchandise with a specified purchase of in-line merchandise at the regular price. Discounts on in-line merchandise were not offered during this period. In 1972, a gift-with-purchase (GWP) promotion offered a free "hanger" (garment bag) to customers purchasing three pieces from Hartmann's 4200 line. In 1976, one of four vinyl carry-ons, variously valued at $50 and $55, was offered between May 1 and June 20 at $12.50 or $13.75 to customers purchasing two matching pieces in the 4200 line. An advertisement for this promotion is reproduced in Figure E. Approximately 9,800 of these purchase-with-purchase (PWP) carry-ons were sold. The focus of the 1977 promotion, which ran from May 2 to June 19, was also a PWP item, a "pancake" or flat-folding bag. Five insertions in national magazines, illustrated in Figure F, advertised this promotion. The pancake, a $75 value, was offered for $18.95 to customers purchasing $200 worth of Hartmann luggage; about 13,000 pancakes were sold.

These gifts or discounted pieces were all specially manufactured for the promotions. Although some were similar in style to in-line merchandise, none matched exactly. Hartmann's efforts to sell these pieces later at full price were unsuccessful. "Any item that started out on promotion," one Hartmann executive noted, "was automatically killed when we tried to sustain it as a regular full-priced item in the line."

Retailers grew increasingly unenthusiastic about GWP and PWP promotions. Because of lack of experience with such promotions, Hartmann did not know how many of

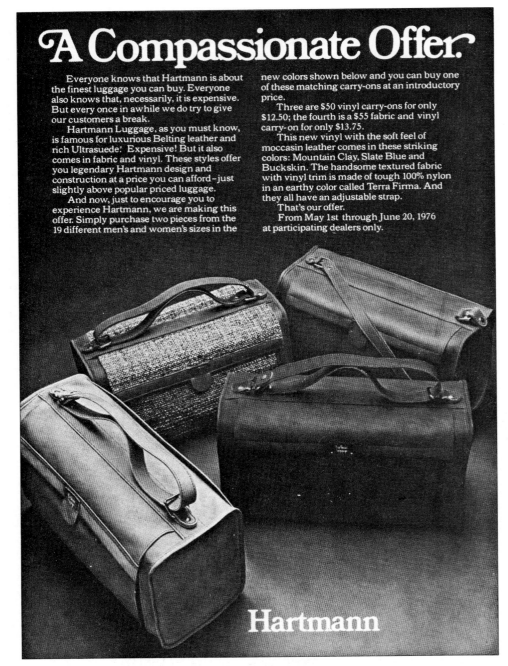

FIGURE F

Magazine advertisement for 1977 promotion

HARTMANN INTRODUCES "THE PANCAKE."

The Pancake is one of the most ingeniously designed casual cases ever made by Hartmann. It's light, easy to carry, goes anywhere anytime, and is as durable as any luggage Hartmann has created.

And the Pancake folds flat as a pancake to fit inside your suitcase so you can take it away empty and bring it back full. It stores flat in your closet when you return from your trip.

HOW TO BUY THE $75 PANCAKE FOR ONLY $18.75.

For every $200 worth of Hartmann Luggage that you buy, you can own a Pancake for only $18.75. Remember, Hartmann cases retail from $450 to $100 and less. In a full range. From rugged industrial belting leather, to luxurious Ultrasuede,® durable fabric, or vinyl.

The Pancake itself is constructed of our genuine industrial belting leather and durable Zepel® stain-resistant nylon pack cloth. The Pancake is Hartmann quality all the way: a gutsy nylon zipper, brass rings, and the classic Hartmann look. Yet it weighs under two pounds. You carry it over-the-shoulder, by hand, or on your arm, with genuine belting leather straps that change with your needs. And the zipper pocket holds your passport and all your important papers.

Take advantage of this limited time offer at once. It runs from May 2 to June 19, 1977. See The Pancake at a participating Hartmann dealer today.

Hartmann Luggage available also in four price points: (series 1) industrial belting leather: (series 2) Halston designed Ultrasuede® fabric: (series 3) tough woven fabrics with belting leather trim: (series 4) nylon fabric with vinyl trim or all vinyl. Each Hartmann can be matched to other pieces for complete sets. For brochure write: Hartmann, Dept. P2, Lebanon, Tennessee 37087.

each gift or discounted item to manufacture, and retailers did not know how many to order. The trade could place only one order for each promotion. At the end of the promotion period, retailers who had overordered were left with inventory that did not match the existing lines, and Hartmann refused to take back merchandise once it was shipped. Moreover, retailers complained that promotion merchandise occupied valuable floor and shelf space without adequate dollar returns. They argued that only price-off promotions on in-line merchandise could substantially increase store traffic and sales. Rather than absorb the cost of such price promotions themselves, they looked to manufacturers to cover the margin lost.

Hartmann's Price-Off Promotions.   In 1978, Hartmann ran its first price-off promotion on in-line merchandise. The promotion was announced on January 1; the trade was permitted to place orders at promotion prices during the first quarter for delivery on March 25. From April 12 to May 6, all 4200 pieces were sold at a 20 percent discount by participating retailers, who took a 48 percent margin on the promoted line instead of their normal 52 percent. The promotion was not featured in Hartmann's national advertising, but many participating stores ran local newspaper advertisements to announce it. A total of 75,788 units of 4200 luggage was sold to the trade during March–May 1978, of which 75,174 were sold at promotion prices.

From April 22 to May 6, 1979, Hartmann offered an in-line, 20 percent price-off promotion featuring three popular carry-on pieces in all four luggage series. These items were selected because of the increasing popularity of carry-on luggage; management believed that this promotion would enhance Hartmann's fashionable, up-to-date image. Five insertions of the advertisement shown in Figure G in national magazines announced the promotion. Once again, participating retailers took a 48 percent margin. Although this promotion ended in early May, order backlogs resulted in deliveries of promoted merchandise as late as June. Katz noted that, to avoid adding a second shift to the soft-sided production line, Hartmann had to begin producing inventory for a promotion at least six months in advance.

Orders for the three carry-on items fell significantly below 1978 levels following the promotion period. Hartmann's territory managers, however, assured Katz that dealers were simply selling off their delayed shipments. Schuster commented:

> Assuming you don't restrict the quantity of promoted merchandise each dealer can buy, a 30 percent discount ensures that all promoted merchandise will be sold through to the end consumer. At only a 20 percent discount, you run the risk of just giving away margin. The trade loads up and the merchandise sits in inventory, stealing from future sales at full price.

Katz, however, opposed large discounts. He was disturbed by the trade's tendency to overbuy when Hartmann lowered its price during a promotion and then to sell promoted merchandise at full retail price after the promotion ended.

Hence, for its 1980 promotion (which ran during the first two weeks of June), Hartmann reverted to a promotion of specially manufactured pieces in nylon trimmed with leather, which sold at a 20 to 25 percent discount from similar models in the strong-selling 4400 series. To announce this promotion, Hartmann used merchandising sheets that described the items in the Hartmann product line (see Exhibit 4); these were distributed to retail accounts by Hartmann's salespeople or through the mail. Katz knew this would be less popular with retailers than a promotion on in-line merchandise; he viewed it as a step toward discontinuing promotions in 1981. About 14,400 of the 1980 promoted items were sold—only half of those forecast. Katz concluded that retailers would not oppose a decision to discontinue promotions.

Consultants' Study of the 1978 Promotion

Uncertainty about the profitability of Hartmann's promotions led the company to commission an investigation of the issue. Consultants assessed the profitability of Hartmann's first price-off promotion on in-line merchandise, run in 1978.

They first assembled pricing data for the 4200 line (see Table A). On the basis of a computer-assisted time-series analysis of previous sales of the line, the consultants estimated that Hartmann's 4200 factory sales during the same period without promotion would have totaled 48,960 units, or 65 percent of the actual unit total. Using the formula shown in Table B, they estimated that the 1978 promotion cost Hartmann $132,000 in lost contribution (excluding the contribution from 614 units in the 4200 line that sold at regular prices).

The study also concluded that sales of the 4400 line had been cannibalized: 4400 unit sales for March–May 1978 totaled 15,130—short of the forecast 17,070 units—for a contribution loss of $40,366. Had Hartmann not run the promotion, it could have maintained inventory at a normal level. Instead, the company fell behind schedule on production, and inventory levels dropped below normal. As a result, Hartmann saved $16,068 in inventory costs. No additional costs were incurred in financing receivables; Hartmann "factored" receivables as soon as they were billed, at a variable cost of 0.85 percent of invoiced sales (i.e., an independent factoring agent took title to Hartmann's receivables at a discount from the invoice value and assumed responsibility for their collection. In return, Hartmann received the invoice value less discount from the agent immediately upon billing).

The consultants concluded that Hartmann had suffered a net loss from the 1978 promotion. In their opinion, the company could not expect to achieve rapid sales growth

TABLE A   **Pricing Data for Hartmann's 4200 Line**

Per Unit	Nonpromoted	20% Promotion
Average retail selling price[a]	$100.00	$80.00
Average manufacturer's selling price[b]	48.00	41.60
Variable costs[c]	34.70	34.70
Average contribution[d]	13.30	6.90

[a]An average of the per-unit suggested retail selling price of each model in the 4200 line.

[b]Retailers shared cost of promotion with Hartmann by taking a 4% reduction in margin.

[c]Includes allocated general and administrative expenses and manufacturing overhead, 7% selling expenses, 5% advertising/promotion allocation, and direct labor and raw material costs.

[d]An average of the per-unit contributions of each model in the 4200 line. (This equals manufacturer's selling price minus all variable costs per unit, including share of general and administrative expenses as well as direct labor and raw material costs.)

and high earnings growth simultaneously. They recommended that Hartmann discontinue its annual price promotions and concentrate on building brand awareness among target consumers by increasing advertising.

Debate over the Study.   After reviewing the sales history of the 4200 line (see Exhibit 5), Schuster questioned the conclusions of the study on two grounds. First, he believed that the forecast of nonpromoted volume based on the time-series analysis (48,960 units) had been too optimistic; 4200 sales had totaled only 31,742 in March–May 1977. Noting further that 4200 sales in January–February 1978 had run 22 percent behind 1977 sales in that period, Schuster set his forecast for normal March–May sales 22 percent below the corresponding 1977 sales level and

argued that the promotion had generated 49,760 incremental unit sales, not 26,214. Second, he believed that no additional fixed costs had been incurred from the promotion and that assigned overhead should not be included in the variable cost figure. His estimates of average unit variable costs were lower ($25.76)[6] and unit contribution higher than those of the consultants. Under his assumptions, a lower percentage increase in sales was required to compensate for the contribution loss of sales at the promoted price. Without considering cannibalization effects or savings on inventory carrying costs, Schuster concluded that the promotion had generated over $600,000 in incremental contribution.

Katz disagreed with Schuster's analysis for three reasons: (1) he viewed the consultants' assignment of fixed overhead before calculating unit contribution as more consistent with Hartmann's conservative accounting practices; (2) he believed that cannibalization effects and savings on inventory-carrying costs should not be ignored; and (3) he pointed out that, because the April–May 1978 promotion had been announced on January 1, Schuster should not have based his forecast of normal March–May 1978 sales of 4200 units on the fact that January–February 1978 sales at regular prices were 22 percent lower than in 1977. Indeed, Katz believed that a sales decrease of only 22 percent indicated the strength of 4200 sales at regular prices, considering that the trade had been able to place orders at promotion prices during January and February.

Although Katz respected Schuster's intelligence and strong background, he still wondered whether Hartmann's ability to achieve 1981 sales and earnings objectives would be helped or hindered by a price promotion. If a promotion was offered, he and Schuster would have to decide what merchandise should be featured, on what terms, when, and for how long.

---

[6]Includes direct labor and raw material costs only.

TABLE B   **Consultants' Formula for Estimating Hartmann's 1978 Promotion Cost**

$$\text{Incremental dollar gain (loss) from promotion} = \left\{ \begin{array}{c} \text{Promoted} \\ 4200 \\ \text{Units} \end{array} \times \begin{array}{c} \text{Promoted} \\ 4200 \text{ Unit} \\ \text{Contribution} \end{array} \right\} - \left\{ \begin{array}{c} \text{Forecast} \\ 4200 \\ \text{Units} \end{array} \times \begin{array}{c} \text{Normal} \\ 4200 \text{ Unit} \\ \text{Contribution} \end{array} \right\}$$

EXHIBIT 1 Retail Prices, Pieces Available, and Unit Orders by Series, 1976–1980

	1980 Retail Prices[a]	1980 Pieces Available	Unit Orders[c]									
			1976		1977		1978		1979		1980	
			Spring[b]	Fall	Spring	Fall	Spring	Fall	Spring	Fall	Spring	Fall
Men's Styles												
Belting Leather (4700)	$415	10	5,940 (100)	5,914 (100)	7,012 (118)	6,670 (113)	8,258 (139)	8,300 (140)	9,044 (152)	6,116 (103)	4,720 (79)	6,968 (118)
Ultrasuede (4800)	315	10	6,796 (100)	4,758 (100)	3,580 (53)	2,950 (62)	3,622 (53)	4,832 (102)	6,678 (98)	4,086 (86)	3,384 (50)	3,956 (83)
Fabric (4400)	215	17	14,120 (100)	21,232 (100)	19,912 (141)	19,426 (91)	22,278 (158)	21,916 (103)	43,298 (307)	27,080 (128)	37,692 (267)	35,656 (168)
Fabric/Vinyl (4200)	150	9	1,652 (100)	996 (100)	—	—	—	—	—	—	—	750 (45)
Vinyl (4200)	140	10	21,994 (100)	21,556 (100)	36,652 (167)	46,116 (214)	59,164 (269)	42,404 (198)	50,892 (231)	40,022 (186)	40,938 (186)	49,060 (228)
Women's Styles												
Ultrasuede (4800)	$295	9	4,052 (100)	6,532 (100)	5,240 (129)	4,076 (62)	4,968 (123)	3,102 (47)	5,182 (129)	3,004 (46)	2,364 (58)	3,038 (47)
Fabric (4400)	185	12	12,338 (100)	6,974 (100)	16,696 (135)	21,114 (303)	22,110 (179)	22,782 (327)	31,374 (254)	20,962 (301)	34,616 (281)	27,518 (395)
Fabric/Vinyl (4200)	130	8	8,254 (100)	6,742 (100)	10,822 (131)	12,853 (191)	26,266 (318)	12,652 (188)	13,828 (168)	6,902 (102)	5,190 (63)	10,566 (157)
Vinyl (4200)	120	8	19,364 (100)	23,608 (100)	22,904 (118)	23,750 (101)	28,414 (147)	18,356 (78)	22,692 (117)	14,100 (60)	17,780 (92)	29,130 (123)

[a]Prices are for a man's and a woman's under-seat carry-on.

[b]Spring 1976 index = 100.

[c]Unit orders of in-line merchandise only. For example, spring 1980 figures do not include orders of the specially manufactured promotion pieces similar to the 4400 series.

SOURCE: Company records.

EXHIBIT 2   Selected Findings of *Luggage and Travelware* Market Research, June 1977 Study

- 51 percent of respondents owned three or four pieces of luggage, and 27 percent owned five or more.
- 47 percent of respondents had purchased their luggage in a department store, 28 percent in a luggage store, and 9 percent at a discount or variety store; 7 percent had purchased some pieces at sporting goods stores or specialty clothing shops; 41 percent had received luggage as a gift.
- 53 percent of respondents preferred a standard hard-sided suitcase (or set of these) in packing for a trip; 34 percent preferred a garment bag, either alone or with another piece, such as a tote; 7 percent preferred a duffel bag.
- 69 percent of respondents would be motivated to buy new luggage because their present pieces were the wrong size. The least important reasons for buying new luggage were "out-of-date appearance of present luggage" and "the pieces I own don't match."
- 31 percent of respondents cited price as the most important criterion in selecting luggage; 21 percent cited it as the least important criterion.
- 48 percent of respondents believed they would favor a brand of luggage they recognized or had seen advertised; 38 percent said they would not.
- 47 percent of respondents stated that in deciding where to shop for luggage, they would be drawn to stores with attractive displays; 45 percent favored a full-service store with an informed sales staff; 26 percent would "wait for a sale, then go there to buy"; 13 percent said they might respond to TV, radio, magazine, or newspaper advertising.

NOTE: A questionnaire was mailed to a random sample of approximately 1,000 consumers nationwide; 47% of the questionnaires were completed and returned.

EXHIBIT 3

Luggage retailer cost structures for Hartmann and competitive products, August 1979

	Department Average		Samsonite Silhouette		Hartman 4200 (vinyl)		Hartman 4400 (fabric & leather)		Hartman 4800 (ultrasuede)		Hartmann 4700 (belting leather)	
	$	%	$	%	$	%	$	%	$	%	$	%
Average retail price	76.00	100.0	86.70	100.0	115.31	100.0	183.46	100.0	287.88	100.0	386.11	100.0
Merchandise cost[a]	38.00	50.0	42.48	49.0	55.35	48.0	88.06	48.0	138.18	48.0	185.33	48.0
Retail reductions[b]	3.88	5.1	4.42	5.1	5.88	5.1	9.36	5.1	14.68	5.1	19.69	5.1
Selling cost[c]	6.31	8.3	6.75	7.8	7.94	6.9	10.76	5.9	15.10	5.2	19.17	5.0
Fixed cost[d]	21.74	28.6	21.74	25.1	21.74	18.9	21.74	11.8	21.74	7.6	21.74	5.6
Net profit before taxes	6.07	8.0	11.31	13.0	24.40	21.1	53.54	29.2	98.18	34.1	140.18	36.3
Profit % of Sales	8%		13%		21%		29%		34%		36%	

[a]*Merchandise cost:* Beginning cost inventory plus net purchases plus inward transportation minus ending cost inventory minus cash discounts earned on purchases plus net alterations and workroom costs.

[b]*Retail reductions:* Include markdowns, employee discounts, and inventory shortages (the excess of book inventory over physical inventory).

[c]*Selling cost:* Includes direct and indirect compensation for salespeople, checkout and stock replenishment personnel.

[d]*Fixed cost:* Includes all other expenses.

SOURCE: Financial and operating results of department and specialty stores, National Retail Merchants Association, 1978.

EXHIBIT 4

Merchandising sheet for 1980 promotion

SUGGESTED PRICE LIST FOR HARTMANN FASHION INVESTMENT PROMOTION 4400 SERIES				
WOMEN'S SIZES	SUGGESTED REGULAR RETAIL (4400)	PERCENTAGE DISCOUNT	SUGGESTED SALE RETAIL (4400)	PROMOTION WHOLESALE
747 UW The Under	165.00	20%	132.00	68.65
W24 Jr. Pullman	195.00	20%	156.00	81.15
W26 Pullman	217.00	25%	162.75	84.65
W29 Jumbo Pullman	240.00	25%	180.00	93.60
W17 Fashion Tote	138.00	25%	103.50	53.80
MEN'S SIZES				
A4 Deluxe Slender Dispatche	172.00	25%	129.00	67.10
A9 Deluxe Commute-taché	195.00	22%	152.00	79.10
747UM The Under	195.00	25%	146.25	76.05
M/S Men's Suiter	240.00	25%	180.00	93.60

Fashion Investment Promotion
by hartmann

25% to 20% OFF PROMOTION of Hartmann's
Most Popular Price Point

4400 Special Promotion
(strong fashion fabric trimmed in full-grain leather)
STARTING JUNE 1st, 1980.

EXHIBIT 5   4200 Series Trade Orders, 1976–1978

	1976	*1977*	*1978*
January	4,536	18,616	10,706
February	4,012	8,166	10,124
March	5,606	11,168	19,334[a]
April	15,120	10,066	36,636[a]
May	14,768	10,508	19,818[a]
June	8,222	11,854	16,226
Total spring season	51,264	70,378	113,844
Total fall season	52,902	82,720	73,412
Year total	104,166	153,098	187,256
Year index	100	146	178

[a]All except 614 units, shipped during March–May 1978, were sold at promotion prices.

Workbench Pricing Strategy*

In late June of 1988, Bernice Wollman, vice president of planning and development for Workbench, a chain of contemporary furniture stores, sat at her desk looking over two and a half years of sales results for Workbench's New York City and Long Island stores. An alarming trend had developed in that market area, one that was also occurring in Workbench's other market areas (New England, Chicago, New Jersey, Philadelphia, and Ohio)—it had become more difficult to maintain sales levels and achieve an average gross margin of 60 percent while at the same time offering a large proportion of merchandise at *reduced prices*. In 1987, approximately 80 percent of Workbench's sales in Long Island and New York City were of reduced price merchandise. To maintain average gross margin at approximately 60 percent, the list price gross margin had been raised in March of 1988 from 64 to 66 percent. In the first half of 1988, reduced price sales were still 80 percent of net sales, with net sales in New York City somewhat above the sales during the same period in 1987. However, sales in Long Island in the first half of 1988 were 10 percent below sales in the first half of 1987!

As Wollman reviewed the sales results, she thought about her upcoming meeting with Warren Rubin, founder, chairman, and CEO of Workbench. He had asked her to investigate possible changes in Workbench's pricing strategy for its original and strongest market, New York City and Long Island stores. One interesting alternative was *Everyday Fair Pricing*. To prepare for this meeting, Wollman had assembled all of the consumer and competitor data that had been collected over the past two years. Wollman wondered what the data would tell her about Workbench's pricing strategy—should the strategy be changed, and, if so, how?

Background on Workbench

Workbench was founded by Warren Rubin in 1955. In 1988, the chain consisted of 36 stores in six regional areas, New York City, Long Island, New Jersey/Philadelphia, New England, Chicago, and Ohio. The stores in each major trading area in New York City and Long Island are listed in

Table A, along with the approximate selling space for each. Major competitors in each trading area are also listed.

Workbench's Park Avenue store, in the Lower Midtown trading area, was also the site of the corporate headquarters. This store carried the same styles as the other stores but had the space to show more than one finish for the wood pieces and more than one configuration on desk and storage systems.

Workbench sold a wide selection of contemporary furniture in the medium to high quality and price range. For example, Workbench's discounted prices for sofas ranged from $649 to $900. In general, contemporary furniture was unbranded or carried brands that were not widely known, in contrast to more traditional furniture, which included such strong brand names as Henredon and Drexel. Examples of the furniture sold in Workbench stores are shown in Exhibits 1–3, which are representative advertisements run by Workbench during the first six months of 1988. The store had kept some of the same product line of butcher block tables, platform beds, chairs, tables, desks, bookcases, couches, and so on as imitators that had entered the market, often with lower-priced and lower-quality goods. As a result, some of Workbench's lines resembled lower-quality merchandise in other stores, while others, such as their desk and storage systems, were distinctive.

Workbench was known throughout the furniture industry for having exceptionally well-trained salespeople. In "Champions of Customer Service," an article in National Home Furnishings Association's *Competitive Edge* magazine, Workbench was cited as an example of superior customer service by executives of NHFA's affiliated organizations and other industry sources:

> Well-educated customers are easier to serve, so Workbench goes the extra mile to correct misinformation and provide facts to facilitate customers' decision making. Salespeople know Workbench products inside and out; full-color, take-home leaflets provide product dimensions; and a Furniture Shopper's Handbook details the "secrets" of selecting furnishings to best suit the customer's needs. Delivery personnel are instructed to offer the latter publication to all customers if they haven't already received one from a Workbench salesperson.

Workbench salespeople were also known for their low-key approach to selling. They were friendly and knowledgeable, yet not overly aggressive. Workbench's laid-back selling approach was also reflected in the way the furniture was displayed. The displays were simple and understated, usually featuring room set arrangements. In contrast to many of its competitors, such as Scandinavian Design,

---

This case was prepared by Professors Gwen Ortmeyer and Walter J. Salmon.

Copyright © 1990 by the President and Fellows of Harvard College.

Harvard Business School case N9-590-115 (Rev. 7/5/91).

*Workbench Pricing Strategy is an abridged version of Workbench.

TABLE A   Store Locations of Workbench and Its Competitors

New York City Trading Areas

Downtown	Lower Midtown	Midtown
Workbench (3,000 sq. ft.)	Workbench (15,000 sq. ft.)	Conran's
The Door Store	The Door Store (2 locations)	Scandinavian Gallery
Conran's	Scandinavian Gallery	
	Macy's	**Upper East Side**
Upper West Side	B. Altman's	Workbench (3,000 sq. ft.)
Workbench (8,000 sq. ft.)		The Door Store
Conran's		Bloomingdale's

Long Island Trading Areas
Nassau County

North Shore	Middle Island	South Shore
Workbench (6,000 sq. ft.)	The Door Store	Seaman's
Conran's	Macy's	
Scandinavian Gallery	Bloomingdale's	
B. Altman's	Seaman's	
Abraham & Strauss		

Suffolk County

Smith Haven	Huntington/Farmingdale
Workbench (4,000 sq. ft.)	Workbench (4,000 sq. ft.)
Macy's	Macy's
Abraham & Strauss	Abraham & Strauss
Seaman's	Seaman's

Workbench did not typically carry accessory items, other than lamps.

The Workbench showroom was uncluttered, well-lit, and carpeted. Within each furniture category (tables, upholstery, wall systems, and so on) Workbench carried from 4 to 10 different styles. In upholstery, for example, seven to nine styles were displayed. Upholstery pieces were usually displayed in one or two fabrics; most of the fabrics were solid off-white or beige in tone. In addition, most of the upholstered pieces could be custom ordered in up to 100 different fabrics. Wood pieces were stocked in at least two finishes, oak and teak. Some pieces were carried in three finishes. Workbench was probably the least "trendy" contemporary furniture retailer. A consistent set of basic styles was maintained with the focus being on clean simple lines and good quality.

Workbench's salespeople received a base salary plus sales commission. Each full-time salesperson received $140 per week as a base salary; part-time salespeople, who worked an average of 20 hours per week, received $70. The commission rate varied by store and over time. The sales force expenditures presented in Exhibit 4 (Contribution Analysis for Long Island and New York City Workbench Stores) show, for each region, the average number of full-time and part-time salespeople and the average commission rate for six month periods from July 1986 to June 1988.

For the most part, Workbench's leases in New York City and Long Island specified flat rent per month. In general, Workbench's stores were in nonregional mall locations (often referred to as strip malls) similar to those of one of its specialty store competitors, Conran's.[1]

Workbench offered its customers the option of picking up their furniture in assembled form at any of Workbench's stores, but the majority chose to have their purchase delivered and assembled for a fee of $30 to $50 (1986 figures). Delivery usually took place within two weeks. Some lower-priced contemporary furniture stores, the Door Store most notably, sold furniture in unassembled form. Workbench accepted major credit cards, such as MasterCard, Visa, and, as of April 1988, American Express. The store also

---

[1] A regional mall is a shopping center that typically includes two or more department stores as major tenants, along with numerous specialty shops. Regional malls usually exceed 400,000 square feet and are often enclosed. Strip malls are much smaller than regional malls and are usually not enclosed shopping centers. A strip mall has fewer specialty stores than a regional mall and does not typically contain a major department store.

offered its own Workbench credit card. Credit approval, collections, and receivables, however, were the responsibility of a third party, which charged Workbench according to the percentage of the sales charged to the Workbench credit card.

Exhibit 4 shows an historical analysis of sales and certain expense categories for the last half of 1986, all of 1987, and year-to-date 1988 for the three Long Island and four New York City stores. Over the past three years, Workbench management had found it increasingly difficult to achieve its *average gross margin* goal of 60 percent and, at the same time, maintain growth in net sales.[2] Sale-priced merchandise continued to be a large percentage of the merchandise sold at Workbench, largely because "sale" merchandise constituted an increasing percentage of Workbench's net sales during nonsale months (all sales were at discount during sale months). Thus, the percentage of net sales sold at discounted prices was over 82 percent by December of 1987. To maintain average gross margin, Workbench executives had raised this list price gross margin from 64 percent to 66 percent in March of 1988.

In June of 1988, the Tannen Agency was brought in as Workbench's new advertising agency. It was hoped that Norman and Eileen Tannen, who had developed very visually appealing advertisements for the Crate and Barrel furniture store in Boston, could create similar image-based advertising copy for Workbench. In the first six months of 1988, Workbench weekly newspaper ads, typically run in Sunday magazines, such as the *New York Times Sunday Magazine,* promoted sale-priced merchandise, either in the form of a discount offered on all merchandise (Exhibit 1) or a discount on selected items (Exhibit 2). During the months of January and August, the store ran its storewide sale, in which all merchandise in the store was offered at a discount. The store also ran a warehouse sale in the store (Exhibit 3) for one week each in May and November, which featured certain excess quantities and out-of-style merchandise at up to 40 percent off the list price.

---

[2]When net sales (sales at actual prices) consist of sales made at list prices together with sales made at discounted prices, the *average gross margin* is equal to:

$$\frac{\text{(Net sales} - \text{Cost of goods sold)}}{\text{Net sales}}$$

List price gross margin, typically referred to as *percentage markup* by retailers, is equal to:

$$\frac{\text{(List price sales} - \text{Cost of goods sold at list prices)}}{\text{(List price sales)}}$$

Discount price gross margin is equal to

$$\frac{\text{(Discount price sales} - \text{Cost of goods sold at discounted prices)}}{\text{(Discount price sales)}}$$

Everyday Fair Pricing

Retailers like Workbench, which sold the bulk of their merchandise at reduced prices, faced a number of problems. Most important was the erratic sales pattern associated with a highly promotional pricing policy. Sales per period usually peaked, but at a level difficult to predict during sale periods, as consumers took advantage of reduced prices. Following a sale event, sales then declined as consumers waited for the next sale. This pattern of sales required more merchandise in inventory as a buffer against the high demand created during sale periods. Consequently, inventory carrying costs were higher. Furthermore, since more inventory was purchased and held in anticipation of a sale event, there was a greater likelihood of overbuying merchandise. Excess merchandise, typically referred to as residuals, was then sold at reduced prices.

The reverse of overbuying, referred to as stockouts, was also more likely to occur with a policy of frequent sale events. Given the difficulty of predicting the impact of a sale, insufficient merchandise was sometimes ordered for a sale event. Stockouts often resulted in lost sales and goodwill.

A policy of frequent sales had other negative consequences. First, it often resulted in diminished customer service. Sales aggravated the peaks and valleys of customer traffic. The result was less service at peaks and more salespersons idle time in valleys. Furthermore, it was difficult for the salesperson to determine whether a customer should receive an immediate discount on an item that was not on sale if that item was slated to go on sale soon.

Second, a policy of frequent sales often resulted in higher advertising costs. Department stores, for example, focused their advertising budgets primarily on sale-oriented messages. As sale events became more frequent, advertising budgets increased to announce the sales. Workbench's current sale-oriented advertising focus was of particular concern to Wollman. She felt that it had interfered with conveying a consistent image and style to the customer.

Finally, both Wollman and Rubin felt that the promotional prices offered by Workbench and most of its competitors were unfair to consumers. As Rubin put it, "most 'regular' prices around furniture stores today are fakes. They are inflated numbers created to allow for artificial reductions."

Everyday Fair Pricing was an alternative to the promotional pricing strategy currently in place at Workbench. With an EDFP policy, Workbench would reduce its prices on all merchandise and would hold clearance sales only for discontinued or damaged merchandise. If the new list price gross margin were so set as to maintain average gross margin, consumers would pay regular prices close to the previous sale prices. These new prices would be close to competitors' sale prices. Consumers would benefit: by not having to wait for a sale event for fair prices, by receiving better service, and by experiencing fewer stockouts.

Competition

Workbench had a variety of competitors in the New York City and Long Island areas, ranging from department stores like Macy's, Bloomingdale's, B. Altman's, and Abraham and Strauss, to other contemporary furniture stores like the Scandinavian Design/Gallery stores and the Door Store. Workbench also competed with Conran's, a store selling contemporary furniture as well as dishes, linens, and a variety of other household items. What follows are descriptions of what Wollman considered the most direct competitors.

Department Stores.   Bloomingdale's, Macy's, B. Altman's, and Abraham and Strauss each carried contemporary furniture among the wide range of furniture styles they offered. These stores carried medium- to high-quality furniture at a wide range of price points. In these stores, the furniture department typically occupied an entire floor. Nearly all of their furniture was sold "on sale." For example, sofa prices in these stores ranged from a low sale price of $499 to a high sale price of $1,600. The bulk of their sofa sales was in the $499 to $899 sale price range.

Wollman considered the upholstery category to be the main strength of the department stores. They carried a much broader range of styles and fabrics. Workbench dominated in the wood and storage system categories. Furthermore, Workbench offered better service than the typical department store. In particular, salespeople were more available, friendlier, and more knowledgeable at Workbench.

Bloomingdale's, in particular, had been known as a fashion leader in furniture. In recent years, however, as Bloomingdale's became more sale oriented, its fashion leadership had deteriorated. Currently, Bloomingdale's primary furniture supplier was a particularly promotional manufacturer. As a result, Bloomingdale's furniture lines were no longer considered so distinctive.

Each of the department stores typically ran a weekly newspaper advertisement featuring furniture, usually presenting a mix of styles. The furniture in the advertisements, 75 percent of which was upholstered pieces, was almost always listed at sale or discounted prices. Contemporary pieces usually were included in these general advertisements. About every other week, the department store ads would focus specifically on contemporary furniture. Macy's and Abraham and Strauss were known to include furniture in their monthly mailings. These six- to eight-page color mailings always featured sale-priced merchandise. The two stores sent out mailings entirely devoted to furniture about twice a year.

All of the department stores offered their own store credit cards. The stores delivered to the customer's home for a fee averaging $32.50 (1986 figures), with a delivery lead time ranging from two weeks to a month for in-stock items.

The Door Store.   The Door Store carried some merchandise—butcher block tables, for example—that was similar to Workbench's, but at a lower price point and of lesser quality. Their sofa prices ranged from $499 to $799, with the bulk of sales being in the $499 to $599 range. Of Workbench's specialty store competitors, the Door Store tended to have smaller locations and the smallest assortment of styles and finishes. It also carried a very limited collection of accessory pieces. Its showrooms were somewhat cluttered with less attractive displays than Workbench and other specialty stores. Door Store ads, run weekly in the *New York Times Sunday Magazine,* usually featured promoted merchandise (see Exhibit 5). The Door Store offered limited delivery and assembly at an extra charge. Most furniture was picked up by the customer in unassembled form, however. The Door Store accepted all major credit cards.

Conran's.   Conran's, a subsidiary of the British home furnishing retailer Habitat, with its four stores in the New York metropolitan area, offered a wide range of contemporary furniture and home furnishings. Customers could purchase almost anything for their home, except major appliances, including furniture, dishware and crystal, bed and bath linens, and cookware. Conran's stores were larger than Workbench's. The store on East 54th Street, for example, had about 40,000 square feet of selling space, half of which was devoted to furniture. Conran's upholstered furniture was distinctive, largely because it used fabrics exclusive to Conran's instead of the manufacturer's standard line. The sofa prices ranged from $499 to $1,000, with most in the $699 to $899 price range. Wollman considered Conran's to be Workbench's most fashion-oriented competitor. It often carried occasional pieces like lamps or end tables that were highly distinctive and were meant to sell only in that season. The displays at Conran's were a mix, with some displays being well accessorized and very visually appealing. Other displays, however, were more cash and carry in approach, with the furniture piece—a desk, for example—being shown next to the stack of boxes containing the unassembled product.

Conran's advertising efforts focused heavily on the store catalog. The catalog, a page of which is reproduced in Exhibit 6, printed four times per year and showed all of the retailer's furniture lines. Much of Conran's furniture could be picked up by the customer at the store. Many items—television stands, dressers, and some end tables, for example—were offered in unassembled form. Delivery of larger items like sofas was offered at an extra charge, averaging $45 (1986 figures), and took anywhere from four to six weeks.

Scandinavian Design/Gallery.   Scandinavian Design, or Scandinavian Gallery as it was called in some locations, was Workbench's closest competitor. It carried some of the same merchandise, in particular upholstered furniture and bookcases, but carried a larger assortment. There were, however, some differences. Scandinavian Design sold mostly teak and some rosewood, while Workbench tended to sell oak and teak furniture that was simpler in design and more classically contemporary. Scandinavian Design's sofas were sale priced from $499 to $899; sales were evenly distributed across the price range. Scandinavian Design advertised more aggressively than Workbench. It frequently ran a *free-standing insert* in the Sunday *New York Times*. This three–four-page full-color insert showed various furniture lines, typically at promotional prices (see Exhibit 7 for sample pages). Scandinavian Design offered delivery and assembly for an extra charge of $35 (1986 figures). Major credit cards were accepted, as well as the store's own credit card. Workbench and Scandinavian Design differed in their store sites, particularly on Long Island. Workbench tended to be located in strip malls, whereas Scandinavian Design was more concentrated in regional malls. On average, Scandinavian Design stores tended to be larger than Workbench stores.

Robert Darvin, the president of Scandinavian Design, had announced a new look for the retailer in April of 1988, called Freestyle. Freestyle represented a 40 percent change in Scandinavian Design's product line. It would incorporate four styles, Italian Modern, American Casual, Ecclectic Accents, and Scandinavian Classics, the latter being the product line most like Workbench's. Scandinavian Design, however, had been experiencing problems. In fact, it was common knowledge in the industry that vendors were no longer taking orders from Scandinavian Design and that bankruptcy might be imminent. Wollman was not certain, however, that the customers were aware of Scandinavian Design's current status. In fact, stores in the New York and Long Island area were still open and Scandinavian Design was still advertising, though stockouts were naturally a severe problem.

The Workbench Customer

Wollman felt there were three general categories of Workbench customers. One segment consisted of affluent, well-educated individuals or households who used Workbench as the basic furniture resource for their entire home. These households often could afford more expensive furniture for their living room, for example, but chose Workbench for its simple style and good quality. Workbench's most affluent customer, on the other hand, consisted of very wealthy households that bought Workbench pieces to furnish the children's room or apartment, the maid's quarters, or a vacation home. These households purchased much more expensive furniture for the living or dining rooms. A third segment of customers included younger, well-educated, but less-affluent households. These households often used Workbench furniture for their first apartment. For this seg-

ment, in contrast to the other two, the purchase of a sofa, for example, was considered a major allocation of funds.

The New York City customers and the Long Island customers differed in a couple of ways. New York City customers tended to live in upscale apartment buildings in some of Manhattan's better neighborhoods. Since most Manhattan customers either walked or took a cab to the nearest Workbench, the New York City stores had substantial walk-in trade. Furthermore, the customers, at any particular store in New York City, tended to come from the immediate neighborhood surrounding the store. Thus, the Spring Street store attracted customers from Greenwich Village, the Broadway store from the upper West Side, the Third Avenue store from the upper East Side, and the Park Avenue store from Midtown. Wollman had noted that customers who lived in the 10021 zip code area, Manhattan's most exclusive area located on the upper East Side, tended to shop at both the Third Avenue and the Park Avenue stores. Because most customers did not drive their own car to shop at the Manhattan stores, customer pickup was difficult.

Long Island customers generally owned homes with high property values. They drove, rather than walked, to a Workbench store; thus, they were less likely to live in close proximity to one of Workbench's stores. Wollman had found that the Long Island stores tended to pull customers in from a surrounding seven-mile radius. In Long Island, customer pickup was more prevalent.

In addition to Wollman's general impressions of Workbench's customer profile, she had various other pieces of information:

1. The average dollar purchase, calculated from sales slips at the Park Avenue store, was about $525. Furthermore, the average dollar purchase was about the same in a storewide sale month as in other months.

2. A survey of 322 of Workbench's upholstery customers had been conducted in August and September of 1987. Customers were surveyed from all Workbench stores, not just the Long Island and New York City stores. The result of this survey are summarized in Exhibit 8.

3. Recently, a survey had been done with customers, right after they had made a purchase. As the salesperson was writing up the order, he or she asked the customer what had brought them into the store and whether they had seen Workbench's newspaper ad or mailer. The responses to this survey, split by area and by store, are given below in Table B.

4. In December of 1987 (nonsale period) and January of 1988 (storewide month) Wollman had charted the sales of the Park Avenue store according to how close the customer lived to the store. These data are given below in Table C.

TABLE B   In-store Survey

Question: What brought you into the store today?

	Long Island (n = 1,191)	New York City (n = 3,805)
Newspaper ad	28.71%	17.45%
Mailer	2.85	2.96
Friend	4.36	3.10
Phone order	3.77	7.51
Walking by	12.42	26.54
Repeat business	39.71	34.53
Customer refuse	2.35	2.31
Came in to modify an order	5.79	5.57

Question: Did you see our newspaper ad or mailer?

	Long Island (n = 1,191)	New York City (n = 3,805)
Mailer	9.99%	12.01%
Newspaper ad	24.51	18.10
Both	2.93	6.78
Neither	54.07	54.03
Customer refuse	2.85	2.57
Rewrite an order	5.62	6.49

TABLE C   Park Avenue Store Sales for December 1987 and January 1988, by Address

	Customers within 1.5 Miles of Park Avenue Store	Other Manhattan Areas	Outside Manhattan
December: Nonsale month[a] (n = 277)	43%	22%	35%
January: Storewide sale month (n = 294)	47	27	26

[a]However, there may have been merchandise sold at reduced price.

5. In addition to the other sources of consumer data, Wollman had commissioned a telephone survey of recent Workbench customers in New York City and Long Island. This survey provided information about why current customers shopped at Workbench, the other furniture stores their customers visited, and the factors their customers considered important when buying furniture. In addition, current customers were asked about their expectations of a furniture store that offered everyday fair pricing. Wollman had hired a market research agency that specialized in telephone surveys to conduct the interviews. Since customer delivery required the customers' address and phone number, the sample could be constructed from Workbench's delivery records. Approximately 1,300 customers were telephoned to generate 190 completed surveys for a response rate of 14.5 percent. A summary of the results of the survey is provided in Exhibit 9.

Projected Impact of a Change in Pricing Strategy

Wollman knew that a change in strategy would be judged by its projected impact on key elements of Workbench's business—net sales, expenses, and contribution. Exhibit 4 shows an historical analysis of the income and expense categories that she felt might be impacted by a change in pricing strategy. Wollman felt that a major shift in strategy should be evaluated by its net contribution after considering the change in relevant income and expense figures. In particular, Wollman wanted to compare a forecast of financial results, given no change in pricing, to a projection of results, given a revised pricing policy. Wollman was most interested in projecting the impact of a change to Everyday Fair Pricing. Such a change was likely to affect contribution in the following ways:

1. *Customer acceptance.* A predicted pattern of *sales growth* under an Everyday Fair Pricing strategy was initial customer resistance and eventual acceptance as consumers become accustomed to the more stable pricing.

2. *Stockouts.* Wollman had asked the vice president of merchandising, Marty Brantley, for an estimate of the *net sales* lost due to stockouts. Brantley felt that Workbench could realize 5–6 percent greater net sales if all stockouts were eliminated. This estimate included merchandise out of stock for as little as two weeks, a stockout that didn't usually result in a lost sale. It also included more serious stockouts of 12 to 16 weeks. Nearly half the stockouts of a longer duration like 12 weeks resulted in a lost sale. While Wollman and Brantley felt that the improved predictability of sales levels associated with Everyday Fair Pricing might lead to more accurate buying and fewer stockouts, they were perplexed about the net sales impact they should expect.

3. *Residuals.* Wollman also had asked Brantley to estimate the impact of residuals on *net sales*. He estimated that between 3–5 percent of net sales was of residual merchandise sold at reduced prices averaging a 25 percent discount during the semiannual in-store warehouse sale. With a move toward Everyday Fair Pricing, a decrease in the percent of merchandise sold during the warehouse sale might be expected. Wollman and Brantley were uncertain about the magnitude of the improvement, however.

4. *Percentage of net sales at reduced prices* also was expected to decrease, due to the generally lower incidence of marked-down merchandise. Clearance sales, such as the Warehouse sale, were still anticipated, though they were expected to constitute a smaller proportion of net sales.

5. *Discount gross margin* was expected to change, along with the lower incidence of sales. Currently discount gross margin was high because the discount offered (approximately 13 percent across both regions from July 1987 to June 1988) was small but was offered on a large proportion of the merchandise sold. With Everyday Fair Pricing, less would be sold at reduced prices; but the remaining clearance sales would offer a higher discount and, therefore, generate a correspondingly lower gross margin.

6. *List price gross margin.* Since regular prices under an Everyday Fair Pricing strategy would be lower, the list price gross margin would be reduced. Wollman wondered, however, if retaining a 60 percent average gross margin target was realistic, particularly since the success of the Everyday Fair Pricing strategy relied on convincing the consumers that the price offered was *fair* relative to other retailers.

7. *Inventory turns.* Inventory turns currently averaged 3.7 for merchandise at the warehouse and 2.5 if store samples were included. If Everyday Fair Pricing were implemented, it was likely that less inventory would be needed; thus, inventory turns might increase with a corresponding decrease in inventory carrying costs. The best performers in furniture retailing averaged inventory turns up to six times per year. How close Workbench could come to such a figure by adopting Everyday Fair Pricing was unclear. Workbench financed 75 percent of its inventory through short-term debt with an 8 percent interest rate. Since carrying inventory was a long-term commitment for Workbench, Wollman thought that an argument could be made for a pre-tax weighted average cost of capital inventory carrying charge of 15 percent.

8. *Sales force expenditures.* Given Workbench's compensation structure for full- and part-time salespeople, a decrease in net sales during the introduction of Everyday Fair Pricing could impact their take-home pay quite seriously. Wollman, therefore, felt adjustments would need to be made to the compensation structure if a short-term drop in sales was expected.

9. *Advertising.* It was anticipated that an intensive advertising campaign would be needed initially to inform consumers of Workbench's new pricing strategy. New advertising copy would need to be developed, and an initial burst of print advertising and direct mail would be necessary to announce the change. However, many industry experts felt that, once customer acceptance had been won,

advertising expenditures would fall below the expenditure level prior to the change. Thus, over the long term, expenditures would be lower with an Everyday Fair Pricing strategy, because weekly sale announcements would no longer be required. One advertising agency expert had estimated that advertising expenditures might be over one and one-half times greater during the first year of Everyday Fair Pricing. Second-year expenditures were estimated to be 75 percent of those in the first year, and the years thereafter about 50 percent.

The analysis in Exhibit 4 contained only those income and expenditure categories that Wollman felt might be impacted by a change in pricing strategy. Other categories like rent, for example, therefore, were not included in the analysis. Similarly, warehousing expense was not considered relevant, because Workbench's warehouses were operating at a low level of capacity and, therefore, could absorb any change in sales and inventory resulting from Everyday Fair Pricing.

Conclusion

Wollman looked at the stack of consumer and competitor data sitting in front of her. It was hard to believe that only 50 of the 190 people contacted for the telephone survey had bought at regular price, but this trend was certainly reflected in Workbench's sales data as well. She wondered whether it made sense for Workbench to continue its promotion policy and, if so, whether another increase in the markup was needed. She was intrigued by the notion of Everyday Fair Pricing and felt that it was more in tune with the culture Warren Rubin had instilled at Workbench. But how, she wondered, would customers and competitors respond to such a drastically different approach? With the meeting with Rubin approaching, Wollman knew she had to answer three questions: Should Workbench change its pricing policy? Why, or why not? And finally, How will it be implemented?

Exhibit 2

Sample Workbench advertisement

EXHIBIT 3

Sample Workbench advertisement

WAREHOUSE SALE IN OUR STORES

Memorial Day Weekend, Thurs., May 26–Mon., May 30.

SAVE 20%-50% & MORE

ON A WIDE RANGE OF DISCONTINUED, SLIGHTLY DAMAGED, AND OVERSTOCKED PIECES

You'll find fantastic savings on sofas, loveseats, chairs, wall systems, modular cabinet systems, bookcases, dining tables and chairs, bedroom furniture, kid's stuff and more. So come to any of our Workbench stores and save.

LISTED BELOW ARE SOME EXAMPLES OF SPECIAL SAVINGS AT OUR STORES.

Our pine veneer drop leaf dining table—your choice 39" wide or 47" wide. **$99** reg. $190 or $225	23" Breuer-style barstool with upholstered seat and cane back. **$69** reg. $125	Our best selling kid's desk in choice of white lacquer, oak or teak veneer. **$179** reg. $325
Solid beech, slat dining chair in natural finish. **$45** reg. $95	Our entire TIVOLI Wall System inventory at 40% off regular prices (pieces reg. $50 to $300). For example, wide tall cabinet in oak or teak. **$180** reg. $300	Twin size platform bed with headboard in teak veneer. **$175** reg. $350
Computer desk and bridge in white melamine with adjustable keyboard shelf. **$199** reg. $440	Black leather casual chair and ottoman on teak frames. **$399** reg. $750	Kid's bunkbed in white lacquer. Includes guardrail. (Mattresses not included) **$499** reg. $800

5 DAYS ONLY— SO HURRY IN FOR SAVINGS!

Sale conditions include: Some items cash & carry only • Some items limited to store stock • Assembly not included on all items • Cash, checks, Workbench Credit Card, MasterCard, The American Express Card, VISA, accepted • Delivery available at additional charge.

workbench.

OPEN SUNDAYS

CHICAGO 158 W. HUBBARD STREET (312) 661-1150
CHICAGO 556 W. DIVERSEY EAST OF CLARK ST. (312) 327-1919
DOWNERS GROVE CORNER OF FINLEY RD. & BUTTERFIELD RD. MAIN ST. SQUARE SHOPPING CTR. (312) 495-1090
SKOKIE FASHION SQUARE, SKOKIE BLVD. SOUTH OF GOLF RD. (312) 673-5430
ARLINGTON HEIGHTS 39 WEST RAND RD. ARLINGTON ANNEX SHOPPING CTR. (312) 394-1665

VISIT OUR CLEARANCE CENTER—5151 KEYSTONE CT. AT ALGONQUIN RD., ROLLING MEADOWS (312) 577-5875

OPEN SUNDAYS ALSO 60 STORES THROUGHOUT THE U.S

© Workbench Inc., 1988

EXHIBIT 4 Contribution Analysis for Long Island and New York Workbench Stores

Workbench—New York City Region

	July–Dec. 1986	Jan.–June 1987	July–Dec. 1987	Jan.–June 1988
Sales growth			11.0%	1.5%
Sales breakdown:				
% list price	15.5%	21.9%	17.1%	19.2%
% discount	84.5%	78.1%	82.9%	80.8%
Gross margin as % of sales:				
List price	63.0%	64.0%	64.0%	65.7%
Discount	57.0%	57.6%	58.3%	59.9%
Discount received by customer as percent of list price	14.0%	14.1%	12.7%	13.5%
Sales force expense:				
FT people	13	13	13	14.5
PT people	5	5	5.5	5
FT salary ($140/wk)	3,640	3,640	3,640	3,640
PT salary ($70/wk)	1,820	1,820	1,820	1,820
Sales commission	3.2%	2.8%	3.6%	2.8%
Credit expense (% sales)	0.77%	0.62%	1.00%	1.31%
Advertising expense	243,000	164,248	215,231	272,247
Annual inventory turns	3.0	3.0	3.0	3.0
Annual WACC	15.0%	15.0%	15.0%	15.0%

Contribution Analysis

Workbench—New York City Region

	July–Dec. 1986	Jan.–June 1987	July–Dec. 1987	Jan.–June 1988
Net sales	4,073,238	4,446,162	4,519,825	4,513,576
List price	631,352	973,709	772,890	866,607
Discount	3,441,886	3,472,453	3,746,935	3,646,969
COGS	1,714,677	1,823,653	1,842,370	1,760,284
Gross margin	2,358,561	2,622,509	2,677,455	2,753,292
Commission expense	131,980	124,831	161,284	125,171
Investment carry cost	85,734	91,183	92,119	88,014
Contribution	2,140,847	2,406,495	2,424,053	2,540,107
Other relevant expenses:				
Salary FT & PT	56,420	56,420	57,330	61,880
Credit	31,184	27,689	45,275	59,037
Advertising	243,000	164,248	215,231	272,247
Contribution after changes in relevant income and expense	1,810,243	2,158,138	2,106,217	2,146,943

Workbench—Long Island Region

	July–Dec. 1986	Jan.–June 1987	July–Dec. 1987	Jan.–June 1988
Sales growth			-9.5%	-10.0%
Sales breakdown:				
% list price	19.4%	17.6%	17.6%	19.7%
% discount	80.6%	82.4%	82.4%	80.3%
Gross margin as % of sales:				
List price	63.0%	64.0%	64.0%	65.6%
Discount	57.0%	56.9%	58.1%	59.3%
Discount received by customer as percent of list price	14.0%	16.5%	13.5%	15.5%
Sales force expense:				
FT people	5	6.5	7	6
PT people	4	3	4	5
FT salary ($140/wk)	3,640	3,640	3,640	3,640
PT salary ($70/wk)	1,820	1,820	1,820	1,820
Sales commission	3.3%	3.0%	3.1%	3.1%
Credit expense (% sales)	0.57%	0.82%	0.92%	1.03%
Advertising expense	133,300	80,388	131,756	156,646
Annual inventory turns	3.0	3.0	3.0	3.0
Annual WACC	15.0%	15.0%	15.0%	15.0%

Contribution Analysis

Workbench—Long Island Region

	July–Dec. 1986	Jan.–June 1987	July–Dec. 1987	Jan.–June 1988
Net sales	1,980,826	1,943,663	1,793,326	1,748,922
List price	384,280	342,085	315,625	344,538
Discount	1,596,546	1,601,578	1,477,701	1,404,384
COGS	829,556	814,441	732,915	690,615
Gross margin	1,151,270	1,129,222	1,060,411	1,058,307
Commission expense	65,820	58,310	55,979	53,779
Investment carry cost	41,478	40,722	36,646	34,531
Contribution	1,043,972	1,030,190	967,786	969,997
Other relevant expenses:				
Salary FT & PT	25,480	29,120	32,760	30,940
Credit	11,241	15,936	16,522	17,946
Advertising	133,300	80,388	131,756	156,646
Contribution after changes in relevant income and expense	873,951	904,746	786,748	764,465

Exhibit 5

Sample Door Store advertisement

EXHIBIT 6

*Sample Conran's
advertisement*

SYSTEM:
A GROUP OF
ITEMS THAT
FORM A UNIFIED
WHOLE, AS IN
INTERMODE.

a.VARANASI RUG
*A bold zigzag patterned rug,
handwoven of high quality
5-ply yarn in contrasting black
and natural. 100% wool on a
cotton warp. Imported.*
4'8"x7'8"
P360058   10 lbs.   **$175.00**

**b.GARDEN
AXMINSTER RUG**
*Woven in England in a muted
palette of green, gold,
periwinkle, and rose. 80%
wool with 20% nylon for added durability.*
4'x6'
P394629   10 lbs.   **$175.00**

a.PROFILE BEDROOM
*Sleek and streamlined, our
Profile Collection provides
roomy, attractive storage,
equally suitable for contemporary and traditional interiors.
In addition to the ample chests
there is a blanket box and
nightstand. Because each
piece is sold individually, you
can plan for your specific
space and storage requirements. Made in Sweden, the
collection is available in black
stained or natural ash veneer
with solid ash edge detailing.
Imported. QA*®

Nightstand
H20"xW20¹/2"xD17"
Black   *F776432*   *45 lbs.*
Natural *F443980*   **$199.00**

5-Drawer Chest
H44"xW29¹/2"xD17"
Black   *F776416*   *117 lbs.*
Natural *F443484*   **$399.00**

3-Drawer Chest
H28"xW29¹/2"xD17"
Black   *F776483*   *75 lbs.*
Natural *F443476*   **$259.00**

Double Dresser
H28"xW59"xD17"
Black   *F776424*   *132 lbs.*
Natural *F443492*   **$499.00**

Blanket Box
H20"xW40¹/4"xD17"
Black   *F776440*   *40 lbs*
Natural *F443972*   **$259.00**

INTERMODE

1.

2.

3.

4.

5.

6.

7.

EXHIBIT 7

*Sample Scandinavian
Design advertisement*

(from the cover)
The Piazza Leather Sofa.
$799.95 Reg. $1,099.95. One of our
finest leather values! Imported from
Italy exclusively for us, the Piazza is
79″ long and is available in your choice
of tan or cream. Matching loveseat
and armchair also available.
Brass & Glass Bunch Table.
$179.95 Reg. $229.95
Brass & Glass Lamp Table.
$299.95 Reg. $349.95
4′3″ x 6′3″ Wool Rug.
$219.95 Reg. $299.95
Casa Luce Table Lamp.
$299.95 Reg. $349.95

A. The Palm Springs Sofa.
$549.95 Reg. $699.95. A contem-
porary classic. 85″ long. Upholstered
in a soft cream-colored cotton-blend
fabric. Matching loveseat also on sale.
4′3″ x 6′3″ Wool Rug.
$219.95 Reg. $299.95

B. Teak Expando Set.
$449.95 Reg. $549.95. It's an
entertainment center. Bookcase.
Wall system. Room divider. Whatever!
Sold in pairs as shown. Available in
rosewood at additional cost.

C. Teak Entertainment Center.
$799.95 Reg. $899.95. Organize
your audio/video system with this
efficient entertainment center from
Denmark. Features solid teak edging, smoked glass door, and pull-out
shelves for turntable & VCR.
57¼″l x 18″d x 54″h.

D. Teak Utility Cart.
$249.95 Reg. $299.95. Use it for the
microwave, or as TV/Video cart. On
castors for easy movement. Imported
from Denmark.

E. Teak Video Trolley.
$169.95 Reg. $199.95. Now you can
move your TV and VCR easily from
room to room! On castors with handy
tape storage drawer. Imported from
Denmark.

Connecticut
Orange, Route 1 203-795-0703
Stamford Town Ctr. 203-964-9009
Westfarms Mall 203-521-3670
Crystal Mall 203-442-7019
New York
Broadway & 63rd, NYC 212-307-5360
Madison & 34th, NYC 212-689-6890
Queens Center 718-699-5600
Roosevelt Field Shpg. Ctr. 516-248-5205
Walt Whitman Mall 516-351-1327
Smith Haven Mall 516-360-8505
Manhasset, Northern Blvd. 516-627-4424
Scarsdale, Central Ave. 914-472-0210
Staten Island Mall 718-983-1300
White Plains/The Galleria 914-997-8262
New Jersey
Paramus Park Mall 201-967-7446
The Mall at Short Hills 201-467-4115
Totowa, Route 46 201-256-1222
Union, Route 22 201-964-5240
Woodbridge Center 201-636-5530

scandinavian gallery

Ask about our Price Guarantee: your assurance of receiving the best price anywhere on everything we sell. Major credit cards accepted. The American Express® Card is always welcome. The Scandinavian Design/Gallery Credit Card is the easiest way to shop with us. Not all items in stock or on display in showrooms. Quantities subject to availability from manufacturer. Delivery extra. In some instances, assembly extra. Wood products feature selected solid hardwoods and wood veneers. Prices good through March 31, 1987. Not applicable to prior or pending orders. Advertising supplement to: New York Times, Long Island Newsday, Newark Star Ledger, Connecticut Newspapers, Bergen County Record, Staten Island Advance, New Brunswick Home News.

EXHIBIT 7
(concluded)

A. The Mandy Navy Sofa.
$549.95 Reg. $649.95.
Contemporary, with a special touch of country! 84″ long. Coordinating pillows included. Matching loveseat and queen-size sleeper also on sale.

B. The Caravelle Apartment Sofa.
$549.95 Reg. $649.95. The perfect sofa when living space is at a premium! 81″ long, upholstered in a deep beige textured fabric. Coordinating pillows included. Matching loveseat & full innerspring sleeper also on sale.

C. Elegant Teak Dining Table.
$1,299.95 Reg. $1,499.95. Solid teak edging enhances one of our finest teak dining tables from Denmark. 42″ x 65,″ extends to 105″ with two self-storing leaves. Lacquered finish.
Teak Buffet.
$899.95 Reg. $1099.95
Lighted Hutch.
$899.95 Reg. $1099.95
Teak Arm Chair.
$349.95 Reg. $399.95
Teak Side Chair.
$299.95 Reg. $349.95
6′ x 9′ Wool Rug: "Village Life."
$599.95 Reg. $699.95

D. The Pisa Leather Collection.
Graceful lines, combined with matchless comfort, highlight this leather living room from Italy. Available in white (shown), or cream.
81″ Sofa.
$1,399.95 Reg. $1,599.95
59″ Loveseat.
$1,199.95 Reg. $1,399.95
Armchair.
$899.95 Reg. $999.95
Glass Top Swivel Cocktail Table.
$599.95 Reg. $699.95
4′7″ x 67″ Wool Rug: "Innovation."
$399.95 Reg. $449.95
Casa Luce Table Lamp.
$349.95 Reg. $399.95

E. Cozy 5-Piece Dining Set.
$749.95 Regularly $899.95.
A wonderful value in contemporary dining! Table measures 57″ x 35½,″ extends to 97″ with two self-storing leaves. Solid teak legs and edges. Four solid teak side chairs upholstered in a wool-blend fabric.
4′ x 6′ Dhurrie Rug (Many styles).
$119.95 Reg. $149.95

F. Travertine & Glass Dining Table.
$899.95 Reg. $999.95. Clearly beautiful. Imported from Italy. Measures 78″ x 39¼,″ with 1/2″ thick bevelled glass top supported by two travertine bases.
Fully Upholstered Arm Chair.
$249.95 Reg. $299.95
Fully Upholstered Side Chair.
$199.95 Reg. $249.95
Package: Table, 2 arm & 2 side chairs.
$1,699.95 Reg. $1,999.95
6′ x 9′ Wool Rug: "Plaza."
$1,299.95 Reg. $1,499.95

EXHIBIT 8 Key Results from Upholstery Survey (Sample Size = 322)

- Over ⅔ of the upholstery customers surveyed waited or shopped, or both, over three weeks before purchasing.
- Workbench benefited from walk-by traffic, with 26 percent of the repeat purchasers and 42 percent of the first-time buyers at Workbench reporting that they came to Workbench to shop for upholstery because they were "passing by."
- When asked if there was anything Workbench could do to improve its service, 75 percent of all surveyed responded no. Of those who responded yes, 60 percent (or 15 percent of all surveyed) said Workbench could improve its delivery times. It should be noted that, in New York City, 78 percent of the stock merchandise (i.e., nonspecial order) was delivered within two weeks; outside New York, 53 percent within two weeks.
- Seventy-five percent of the previous Workbench shoppers and 90 percent of the first-time buyers had shopped elsewhere before making their purchase at Workbench.
- When asked why they had come to Workbench to shop, 31 percent of the New York City and 44 percent of the New York suburb respondents said they had noticed Workbench's ads or had read about a Workbench sale. First-time buyers, in particular, seemed to come to Workbench because of its advertising, with 34 percent saying they had noticed Workbench's ads or had read about a sale.
- Fifty-two percent of the New York and 61 percent of the New York suburb customers had bought Workbench furniture previously.

EXHIBIT 9 Key Results from Telephone Survey (Sample Size = 190)[a]

- Approximately 50 percent of those surveyed had purchased from Workbench before.
- Seventy-four percent of those surveyed had purchased sale-priced merchandise. Seventy-nine percent of the repeat buyers and 69 percent of the first-time buyers purchased sale-priced merchandise. Seventy-nine percent of the Long Island customers and 69 percent of the New York City customers bought on sale.
- When asked why they had purchased from Workbench, 65 percent cited the attractiveness of the furniture styles, 15 percent cited the quality and durability of the furniture, 22 percent said the reasonable and fair prices offered by Workbench, and 12 percent said because the merchandise was on sale. An additional 11 percent cited Workbench's convenient location, and 12 percent said they had purchased at Workbench before and had been satisfied.
- Workbench's principal competitors differed across regions, with Scandinavian Gallery, Abraham and Strauss, Macy's, Levitz, Conran's, and Seaman's being mentioned by Long Island customers, and Macy's, Conran's, Bloomingdale's, and the Door Store being cited by New York City customers.
- Customers considered the attractiveness and durability of the furniture and getting "good value for the money" as being more important to their purchase decision than low prices, good sales assistance, good selection, and having the desired item in stock.
- When asked to compare Workbench to competitors on a number of dimensions—including lowest prices, attractive furniture, selection, sales assistance, durability, and value—Workbench scored well across all dimensions, but did particularly well with respect to sales assistance and best value. New York City respondents tended to rate Workbench higher relative to competitors than Long Island customers.
- Respondents were split in their expectations of the prices of an Everyday Fair Price retailer; 25 percent expected an Everyday Fair Price retailer's prices to be lower than the prices of other stores they shopped, 25 percent expected higher prices, and 50 percent expected their prices to be the same.
- Respondents, when asked the *advantages* they'd expect from an Everyday Fair Price furniture store cited quality (27 percent of the sample), service (43 percent), in stock and delivery (34 percent), selection (15 percent), and good exchange return policies (11 percent). Low regular prices were cited as an advantage by 6 percent of the respondents and good value by 8 percent. When asked to cite the *disadvantages* of shopping at an Everyday Fair Price furniture store, respondents offered primarily price dimensions, including higher prices (37 percent) and no sales or bargains (10 percent).

[a]Respondents had purchased from Workbench in the previous six months, half purchasing in New York City stores and half in Long Island stores.

PRODUCT POLICY

PRODUCT POLICY

The determination of product policy is central to an organization's marketing effort. A firm's choice of products influences all other elements of its marketing program and has significant implications for such other functional areas as finance, production and operations, and human resources management. So important is product policy that many firms structure their organizations around products, with individual product managers responsible for the marketing and profitability of each product or product line.

The word *product* connotes a physical good; however, in its marketing sense it also includes intangible services offered before, at, or after the time of sale. The entire package is sometimes referred to as the augmented product. The mix of tangibles and intangibles in the augmented product varies from one product or service to another. A manufacturer of canned vegetables is required to deliver few incremental services to the consumer beyond the physical product. On the other hand, a passenger airline's reason for being is the delivery of the service; its planes are tangible goods that permit it to do so and act as visual symbols of the service organization. Although this chapter emphasizes product policy formulation from the standpoint of profitmaking private firms, nonprofit and government organizations are faced with similar decisions.

The following issues are typical of the varied product policy decisions faced by managements of different organizations:

- A major automobile producer considers dropping its line of large luxury sedans and broadening its small-car line.
- A well-known ski equipment firm debates purchase of a company that makes scuba and diving gear.
- A liberal arts college reviews the feasibility of adding a professional degree program to its curriculum.
- A manufacturer of high-quality electric motors considers developing an inexpensive utility model with lower performance characteristics.

This note was prepared by Professor John A. Quelch.
Copyright © 1985 by the President and Fellows of Harvard College.
Harvard Business School case 9-585-022 (Rev. 4/2/92).

- A manufacturer of private-label socks wonders whether to introduce its first branded line.
- A toy company evaluates whether to withdraw a recently introduced product after a safety hazard is uncovered.
- A manufacturer of health and beauty aids examines the implications of altering package sizes in its line of denture adhesives.

For many companies, appraising the need for changes in the product line is a continuing process, reflecting the dynamic nature of the marketplace as well as changes in the nature and resources of the firm itself. One objective should be to eliminate or modify products that no longer satisfy consumer needs or fail to contribute significantly (directly or indirectly) to the well-being of the firm. Another set of objectives relates to the addition of new products or product features that will better meet consumer needs, enhance the company's existing product line, or improve utilization of resources.

Product Decisions

Most companies are multiproduct organizations, often producing a variety of different product lines. This means that policy decisions may be made at the level of individual products, product lines, or the company's entire product mix.

Individual product items have separate designations on the seller's list and include different flavors or colors, different forms of the same product, and different sizes.

Product lines are a group of different products that are related in the sense that they satisfy a particular class of need, are used together, and possess common physical or technical characteristics. They are sold to the same customer groups through the same channels, and they fall within specific price ranges.

The product mix is the composite of products offered for sale by a firm. Although a particular product item—or even an entire product line—may not be profitable in itself, it may contribute to the well-being of the firm by enhancing the overall product mix, particularly among customers who wish to deal with a full-line supplier. Some large corporations produce several thousand product items, grouped into a wide variety of different product lines, which together constitute the firm's product mix.

Closely associated with these three levels of product decisions are the concepts of breadth, depth, and consistency of product mix. Breadth of product mix refers to the number of different product lines marketed by the company. Depth of product mix designates the average number of items (e.g., sizes, weights, colors) offered in each product line. Consistency of product mix alludes to the degree of similarity between product lines in end use, technology and production techniques, distribution channels, and so forth.

Product-mix decisions tend to reflect not only the nature of the market and the resources of the firm but also the underlying philosophy of company management. Most firms are faced with several options over time. Some pursue a policy of diversity, while others prefer to concentrate efforts on a narrow product mix, offered in a limited number of sizes and varieties.

A firm's choice of product strategy should be determined by management's long-run objectives for profit levels, sales stability, and growth, as modified by personal values and attitudes toward risk. Market opportunities for the firm's product mix determine the upper limits for potential corporate profitability, while the quality of the marketing program tends to determine the extent to which this potential is achieved.

While the ideal product mix is likely to vary from firm to firm and may be hard to define, certain situations suggest a suboptimal mix:

1. Chronic or seasonally recurring excess capacity in the firm's production, storage, or transportation facilities.
2. A very high proportion of profits coming from a small percentage of product items.
3. Inefficient use of the sales force's contacts and skills.
4. Steadily declining profits or sales.

When the product line is narrower than optimum, there is a loss in economies of scale. On the other hand, when the product line is broader than optimum, the firm suffers from excessive costs in manufacturing changeovers, order processing, and inventory management.

Adjustments to the Product Mix

Changes in product policy designed to correct any of the above situations or otherwise enhance the firm's ability to meet established objectives can take one of three basic forms.

Product abandonment. This step involves discontinuing either individual items or an entire line. Candidates for elimination include products for which demand is so low that uneconomically short production runs or uneconomically frequent price and inventory adjustments are required; products that absorb excessive management time relative to their profit contribution; and products that are out of date and, therefore, detract from the company's image.

Product modification. Changes may involve either tangible or intangible product attributes and may be achieved by reformulation, redesign, changing unit sizes, and adding or removing features.

New-product introduction. Besides developing, test marketing, and commercializing new products or product lines, this might include an addition or extension to one of the company's existing product lines or a me-too imitation of a competitor's product line. In all cases, management must decide what brand name the new item(s) should carry. Frequently, there is a trade-off between the advertising economies of scale associated with extending an existing brand name and the higher costs of cannibalization—when new products "steal" sales from existing products.

The New-Product Development Process

New-product development is widely viewed as a six-stage process:

1. Idea generation.
2. Concept screening.

3. Business analysis.
4. Prototype development.
5. Test marketing.
6. Commercialization.

The purpose at each stage is to increase the information available to management to reduce the risk of a wrong decision—to either continue or abandon a product. Note, however, that the process described here is highly stylized. In practice, steps overlap, are skipped or repeated, or are performed in a different order, depending on the realities of the situation, the urgency of the opportunity, competitive pressures, the judgment and whims of managers, and luck. In addition, the farther a new product moves through the process, the harder it is to cancel, because management develops a commitment to its success.

At the idea-generation stage, creativity is paramount, and the most frequent error is to generate too few ideas, not too many. Typical sources of new ideas are competitive products, implicit or explicit customer requests, ideas from salespeople and distributors, and special idea-generation meetings and committees including marketing, R&D, and manufacturing personnel. Once generated, ideas must be screened to reject clear losers. A set of screening criteria consistent with the company's goals must be established. It is important to identify the highest-priority projects and speed them through the process with special attention and extra resources.

Business analysis requires the development of a preliminary product description. The analysis should specify the target market, financial impact on existing items, opportunity for market development, likelihood of technical success, impact on manufacturing and service operations, and projected financial performance.

If prototype development is warranted, the concept must be carefully transferred from the marketing people to the technical developers. This is often a difficult transfer, as the cultural difference between the marketing department and the laboratory is often great. Each side must understand the other's role, perspective, and limitations.

The product emerges from the laboratory or engineering department as a prototype ready for test marketing. Consumer–packaged-goods test marketing is a precise art. The product is distributed in selected markets supported by the marketing program management expects to use in a national launch. Often, elements of the marketing program, such as the advertising and promotion budget, are the object of experimentation in the test markets. Because test marketing is expensive and broadcasts a company's intentions, a competitor may reach national distribution with an imitation product before an innovator has even finished analyzing its test-market data.

In the industrial arena, test marketing is different. Products often are shown to a few selected friendly customers for evaluation. These customers, known as beta test sites in electronics and related industries, report their experiences with the prototype. Good marketers send personnel to the test sites to monitor the units' performance and ensure that all relevant test data are carefully gathered and analyzed.

Toward the end of the test-market phase, a revised marketing program is developed. Volume and price forecasts are refined so that production and service capacity can be added.

Finally, the product is introduced into the commercial marketplace in a major national or international launch, a region-by-region rollout in the case of consumer goods, or a customer-by-customer or market-segment-by-market-segment rollout for industrial goods.

Few concepts that are generated in the first step of the process make it to prototype development. Fewer still reach commercialization, and even fewer succeed as established products.

The nature and length of the process and of each step and the relative importance of the steps vary by type of product, degree of newness, and the size of the company. A new flavor added to a line of food products may require more marketing investment than R&D effort and be executed within a year. Such a line extension is easily understood, fits into the established product line, and involves little risk. On the other hand, a new drug might require over a decade to be developed and to receive necessary government approval, and marketing costs would be much less than the R&D investment.

Such a discontinuous process of new-product development involves a great many risks: technological risk (Can we make a prototype?); marketing risk (If we can, will anyone buy it?); manufacturing and operating risk (Can we make it in volume?); and financial risk (Can we sell it at a price that will generate enough revenue to amortize the development process?).

Smaller companies with more limited resources tend to be more entrepreneurial and to commercialize an idea much more quickly than larger companies. In the latter, projects require many layers of executive approval in corporate cultures that generally discourage risk taking. Since the 1970s, large companies have attempted to foster more entrepreneurship and faster product development through new-product venture teams, while smaller companies often have been better funded because of the development of the venture capital marketplace. In addition, industries accustomed to rapid technological change tend to be more adept at managing the process. For example, electronics companies of all sizes innovate more quickly and easily than steel companies.

A good product-development process leads to successful products, while a poor one is unlikely to generate success. Unfortunately, the lag time between idea generation and commercialization is often so long that monitoring the process is a difficult task. Perhaps the best insurance a company can have is a portfolio of products at various stages of development. It is also worth noting that a process that produces few failures is probably too conservative and will not lead to major new-product successes. More than likely it will produce only safe but minor product modifications.

Product Positioning

Positioning is management's concept of where a product or service should stand in the marketplace relative to competitive products and services. An organization's ability to compete effectively in any given market is determined in large measure by its ability to position its product(s) appropriately relative to (1) the needs of specific market segments and (2) the nature of competitive entries. Product positioning, therefore, requires a synthesis of consumer analysis and competitor analysis.

In developing a position for a new product, management first discovers the range of benefits or attributes consumers use to make choices in the product category. Second, it identifies key consumer segments within the overall market for the product. Third, management evaluates, on the basis of experience or market research data, or both, the relative importance of each benefit to each segment.

In addition to this consumer analysis, management must consider how existing products perform in each area of interest to consumers. In choosing a position for a new product, management matches an appropriate package of benefits, clearly differentiated from competitive offerings on important dimensions, with a specific target segment whose needs are not fully satisfied by existing products. Positioning permits a firm to finesse the competition instead of competing head on.

Product positions often reflect not only intrinsic product characteristics but also the image created by promotional strategies, pricing decisions, and choice of distribution channels. Selective use of alternative brand names in multibrand companies also may help to achieve the desired image. For instance, the Mercury name, owned by Ford, carries different connotations for car buyers than does the Ford brand itself.

Effective positioning is essential to a product's success. If management does not consciously position a product, consumers will be confused, and competitive products that are precisely positioned will enjoy an advantage. At the same time, a product's positioning must be flexible enough to adjust to changes in competitive products and consumer needs.

Repositioning

Instead of physically modifying an existing product, firms sometimes elect to reposition the product by revising such elements of the marketing mix as advertising and promotion, distribution strategy, pricing, or packaging. However, a revision of the entire mix, including product features, also may accompany a repositioning strategy.

Sometimes repositioning represents a deliberate attempt to attack another firm's product and eat into its market share. In other instances, the objective is to avoid head-to-head competition by moving into alternative market segments with good potential whose needs are not presently well served.

Analysis of competitive offerings involves not only a review of product features and other marketing-mix strategies but also an evaluation of competitive advertising content. The image generated by advertisements and the nature of the slogans employed may constitute a major positioning tool, especially for such image-intensive products as cosmetics, liquor, and apparel.

Repositioning along price and quality/functionality dimensions is generally referred to as trading up or trading down. However, repositioning also may involve sideways moves, in which price and quality remain basically similar but modifications are made to a product's tangible benefits or image to enhance its appeal to different types of consumers or for alternative end uses.

Examples of repositioning existing products include advertising a deodorant formerly promoted only to men as "the deodorant for all the family"; reducing the price of a felt-tip pen to take advantage of a perceived market need for a cheaper model; modifying the assortment at a supermarket chain to improve its appeal to family groups; and giving an airline a more exciting image through changes in aircraft color schemes and uniforms and addition of on-board service frills—then promoting these in a glamorous advertising campaign.

Evaluating Product/Company Fit

The fact that good opportunities exist in the marketplace for a new or repositioned product does not necessarily mean that the organization should proceed with such a product. Unless there is a good fit between the proposed product and the firm's needs and resources, the net result of a decision to proceed might be harmful, or at best, suboptimal.

Among the dimensions to consider when evaluating product/company fit are:

1. Technological skills of labor and management.
2. Size of work force.
3. Financial resources.
4. Production resources and capacity.
5. Logistics facilities.
6. Feasibility of using existing sales force and distribution channels.
7. Needs and behaviors of existing consumers.
8. Impact on the market position of the firm's other products.
9. Consistency with the organization's existing image.
10. Seasonality of demand patterns for existing products. (Will the new product exaggerate existing fluctuations, or will it counterbalance them?)

If a proposed product is not consistent with one or more of the above dimensions, the company should not necessarily drop the idea. Companies in maturing markets, under pressure to diversify, often find that product options with a good product/company fit lack the necessary market-growth potential, and vice versa. In such cases, product/company fit may be sacrificed for the need to diversify. However, the poorer the fit, the larger the financial resources that may be needed either to purchase or to develop internally the requisite skills, production facilities, and market relationships.

Ethical Issues in Product Policy

Product policy decisions often require subtle and rigorous analysis of ethical issues. There may be side effects during the production, delivery, and use of a product that create costs and risks for the customer or for society at large. A few common questions that can be used to surface potential ethical issues include:

- Does the product function as promised? Does it adequately and reliably meet the needs it was designed to satisfy? Diet plans and self-help seminars are two examples of familiar product categories where unethical practices may result in customers not getting what they paid for.
- Have the product and its usage instructions been developed with a strong emphasis on consumer safety? This is particularly important if the product is intended for use by children, or by consumer segments with low literacy rates who may be unable to read or follow product usage instructions.
- Does the positioning of the product encourage customers to abuse the product in ways that may be dangerous for themselves or others?
- Are the product and its packaging environmentally friendly? Does either lead to toxic environmental impact, or to waste that is not biodegradable?
- If the product is a food, drug, or personal care item, does its packaging adequately protect consumers from the threat of tampering?

- Does the process used to produce or distribute the product threaten the ecology through water or air pollution, endangering wildlife, toxic rain, damage to the ozone layer, or other harmful side-effects?

Ethical analysis involving questions like these is important to ensure that principles are not sacrificed for profits in product policy decisions.

Conclusion

Product policy determination as an ongoing task reflects the changing nature of the marketplace. Because an organization's choice of products has such important implications for every facet of the business, it tends to be of great concern to top management.

Key considerations in the formulation of product policy are the skills, contacts, and other resources of the firm, its existing product mix, the corporate objectives established by management, the characteristics of existing and potential markets, the nature of the competition, and ethical considerations. The process of evaluating product-policy decisions, therefore, involves all the analytical modes employed in marketing—namely, environmental, market, consumer, trade, competitive, economic, and ethical analyses.

Suzuki Samurai

In June 1985, Leonard Pearlstein, president and CEO of keye/donna/pearlstein advertising agency, and his colleagues were finalizing the presentation that they would make the next day to Douglas Mazza, vice president and general manager of American Suzuki Motor Corporation (ASMC). Pearlstein's agency was competing with a half-dozen other advertising firms to represent Suzuki's new entrant into the U.S. automobile market, the Suzuki Samurai. Mazza had asked each agency the question: "How do you feel this vehicle should be positioned?" He had given keye/donna/pearlstein eight days to prepare an answer.

Company Background

Suzuki Loom Works, a privately owned loom manufacturing company, was founded in 1909 in Hamamatsu, Japan, by Michio Suzuki. In 1952, the company began manufacturing and marketing a 2-cycle, 36 cubic centimeter (cc) motorcycle, which became so popular that in 1954 the company introduced a second motorcycle and changed its name to Suzuki Motor Company, Ltd. (Suzuki).

During the late 1950s, lightweight vehicle sales boomed in Japan. Suzuki's motorcycle business grew, and in 1959 it introduced a lightweight van. The van's success encouraged Suzuki to develop lightweight cars and trucks. In 1961, it introduced its first production car, the "Suzulight," the first Japanese car with a 2-stroke engine.

In 1964, Suzuki began exporting motorcycles to the United States, where it established a wholly owned subsidiary, U.S. Suzuki Motor Company, Ltd., to serve as the exclusive importer and distributor of Suzuki motorcycles. Suzuki quickly established itself as a major brand in the U.S. motorcycle industry.

By 1965, Suzuki's product line included motorcycles, automobiles, motorized wheelchairs, outboard motors, general-purpose engines, generators, water pumps, and prefabricated houses. The company concentrated, however, on producing and marketing lightweight vehicles. Until 1979, Suzuki cars and trucks were sold only in Japan, where they were popular as economical transportation. In 1979, Suzuki automobiles were introduced into foreign

This case was prepared by Research Assistant Tammy Bunn Hiller (under the direction of Professor John A. Quelch).
Copyright © 1988 by the President and Fellows of Harvard College.
Harvard Business School case 9-589-028 (Rev. 8/15/90).

markets, and by 1984 they were available in over 100 countries and Hawaii.

In 1983, General Motors (GM) purchased 5 percent of Suzuki and helped the company develop a subcompact car for the U.S. market. The car, named the Chevrolet Sprint, was introduced on the West Coast in mid-1984 and was sold exclusively by Chevrolet dealers. The Sprint was Suzuki's first entry into the continental U.S. automobile market. The Sprint was subject to Japan's "voluntary" restraint agreement (VRA) on car shipments to the United States. The VRA, in place since 1981, limited the number of cars that each Japanese automobile manufacturer could ship to the United States in a given year. In 1984, Suzuki's total VRA quota of 17,000 cars went to GM as Sprints. GM quickly sold out its allotment even though Sprint's distribution was limited to its West Coast dealers.

American Suzuki Motor Corporation (ASMC)

GM's success with Sprint showed Suzuki that a market existed for its cars in the continental United States. Suzuki, which called itself "the always something different car company," planned to introduce several unique vehicles into the U.S. market over time. Suzuki had no guarantee, however, that GM would be willing to market the vehicles. Therefore, Suzuki decided to establish its own presence in the U.S. automobile industry.

Japan's VRA quotas made it impossible for Suzuki to export any cars other than the Sprint to the United States in the foreseeable future. Consequently, in 1985, Suzuki and GM began negotiations with the Canadian government to build a plant in Ontario that could produce approximately 200,000 subcompact cars per year. Suzuki management expected the plant to be on-line by early 1989, and the company could then begin selling cars in the United States under its own name.

Market forces, however, made Suzuki loath to wait until 1989. In 1984, Japanese imports achieved a record 17.7 percent share of U.S. new-car and truck sales. Based on first-quarter sales, industry experts predicted that Japanese imports would command a 19.2 percent share of the U.S. market in 1985. Total U.S. automobile sales were expected to grow by 10 percent in 1985, and this rapid growth made dealers optimistic and willing to invest money in new car lines, especially Japanese brands.

In addition, two other car companies, Hyundai Motor Company of South Korea and Zavodi Crvena Zastava

(Yugo) of Yugoslavia, were expected to enter the U.S. car market in 1986. Suzuki managers believed that brand clutter might limit their success if they waited until 1989 to introduce the Suzuki name into the continental United States.

Suzuki management was convinced that the time was right to enter the continental United States and that Suzuki had the right product to do so, the SJ413. Its forerunner, the SJ410, was a mini-four-wheel drive off-road vehicle with a 1,000 cc engine that Suzuki had introduced in 1960. By 1985, the SJ410 was sold in 102 countries and Hawaii. In 1985, Suzuki introduced the SJ413, an upgraded model that featured a 1,324 cc engine and was designed with the U.S. market specifically in mind. The SJ413 was more powerful and more comfortable than the SJ410. The upsizing of Suzuki's vehicle, combined with the downsizing of U.S. consumer automobile preferences, made the SJ413 a viable continental U.S. product.

If the SJ413 was imported without a back seat, the U.S. government classified it as a truck, for customs purposes. Trucks were not subject to Japanese VRA quotas; instead, they were subject to a 25 percent tariff versus a 2.5 percent tariff on cars. The tariff was high, but Suzuki management believed that it was worth paying.

On May 10, 1985, Suzuki hired Douglas Mazza to organize and head its new subsidiary, ASMC. Mazza was charged with developing a Suzuki dealer network to begin selling the SJ413 by November 1985. He also was responsible for creating the marketing plan for the SJ413, which would be named the Suzuki Samurai in the United States, as it was in Canada. Suzuki planned to market two versions of the Samurai in the United States, a convertible and a hardtop.

Samurai Dealer Network.   Mazza's goal was to establish ASMC as a major car company in the United States. To achieve this goal, he believed that he had to convince prospective dealers to build separate showrooms for the Samurai. If ASMC allowed a dealer merely to display the vehicle in an existing showroom, the dealer would invest little in the Samurai, monetarily or emotionally, and probably would sell only a few Samurais each month. Low Samurai sales per dealer and lack of facility and management commitment could jeopardize Suzuki's plan to introduce other cars into the United States, starting in 1989.

Therefore, Mazza drafted a dealer agreement that required prospective Samurai dealers to build an exclusive sales facility for the Samurai. The facility had to include a showroom, sales offices, and a customer waiting and accessory display area. Service and parts could share a facility with a dealer's other car lines, but a minimum of two service stalls had to be dedicated to Suzuki and operated by Suzuki-trained mechanics. Furthermore, Suzuki dealerships had to display required signs outside the sales office and in the service stalls. A minimum of three salespeople, two

service technicians, one general manager, and one general office clerk had to be dedicated to the Suzuki dealership.

The prospectus also explained that, as the product line grew, dealer requirements would expand to include a full, exclusive facility complete with attached parts and service. This up-front expansion plan was a first in the industry and was based on the belief that quick dealer profitability would be key to success—as a dealer's sales opportunities grew so, too, would the financial commitment and overhead.

ASMC's planned suggested retail price for the basic Samurai was $5,995. The planned dealer invoice price was $5,095, only 7.5 percent higher than ASMC's own landed cost for the vehicle. ASMC planned to offer about 50 dealer-installed options, the sale of which would boost a dealer's average unit profit. Mazza estimated that each dealership would need to sell approximately 30 Samurais per month to cover its monthly operating costs plus the finance charges on its initial investment.

To attract good dealers, Mazza knew that he must make the opportunity match the investment requirements. He, therefore, planned to limit the number of Samurai dealers so ASMC could guarantee a minimum supply of 37 units per month to each one. Thus, each dealership could earn a profit every month if it sold its total allotment. Suzuki had set Mazza the goal of selling 6,000 Samurais in the first six months of U.S. distribution, but Mazza and his new management team convinced the Japanese management that the U.S. opportunity was far greater. Suzuki raised its commitment to ASMC to 10,500 vehicles for the same time period. Consequently, Mazza decided to limit his initial dealer network to no more than 47 dealers. This small network implied rolling out the Samurai in only two or three states in November 1985. Mazza chose to introduce the Samurai into California, the nation's largest automobile market, and Florida and Georgia, where Japanese import sales were higher than the U.S. average.

Before Mazza could enlist dealers, he had to decide how to position the Samurai to consumers. The position he chose would help define the vehicle's target market, which, in turn, would influence ASMC's preferred dealer locations. By combining car registration data and census information, the concentration of owners of imported vehicles or owners of sport utility vehicles, for example, could be pinpointed by zip code. Dealerships could be selected with trading areas that encompassed zip codes with high concentrations of households that fell into Suzuki's target market.

Samurai Positioning

The keye/donna/pearlstein advertising agency had no experience in developing campaigns for automobiles. This appealed to Mazza, because he believed that a fresh approach was needed for his company's new product. After accepting Mazza's offer to compete for the Samurai account, Pearlstein and his associates quickly scanned automobile advertising of other manufacturers. They concluded that industry practice was to position vehicles according to their physical characteristics as, for example, subcompact cars versus compact cars versus luxury sedans. Most advertising was feature/benefit- or price-oriented. A typical ad noted that a vehicle was of a specific type and emphasized differentiating features and/or superior value for the money.

If they followed industry practice, Pearlstein's group had three options for positioning the Samurai based on its physical characteristics—as a compact sport utility vehicle, as a compact pickup truck, or as a subcompact car.

Exhibit 1 shows pictures of the Samurai. The most obvious position for the Samurai was as a sport utility vehicle. It looked like a "mini-Jeep," had 4-wheel drive capability, and was designed to drive well off-road. Such a position would be consistent with the Samurai's heritage and its positioning in the 102 countries where the SJ410 and SJ413 were sold. Foreign owners praised the Samurai's reliability, ability to go places where larger utility vehicles could not, and ease of repair.

The Samurai's size and price distinguished it from all other sport utility vehicles sold in the United States in 1985. The Samurai was smaller and lighter than the other vehicles, and its $5,995 suggested retail price was well below the other vehicles' $10,000 to $13,000 price range.

Pearlstein believed that, if the Samurai were positioned as a sport utility vehicle, it should be advertised as a "tough little cheap Jeep." Advertising copy would show the Samurai in off-road wilderness situations, squeezing through places where bigger sport utility vehicles could not go. Ads also would emphasize that the Samurai cost only half the price of an average Jeep.

Pearlstein was unsure, however, whether a compact sport utility positioning could generate the sales volume that Mazza envisioned for the Samurai. The market for sport utility vehicles was relatively small. As Exhibit 2 shows, total 1984 compact sport utility vehicles sales in the United States were less than 3 percent of total automobile industry sales. Mazza's goal was to build annual U.S. Samurai sales to 30,000 units within two years of the vehicle's introduction. To achieve this objective, annual Samurai sales would have to exceed the combined 1984 sales of all imported compact sport utility vehicles.

The second option, positioning the Samurai as a compact pickup truck, would tap a market that was two and one-half times the size of that for compact sport utility vehicles. Moreover, Japanese import trucks sold well in the United States, accounting for 54 percent of total 1984 compact pickup truck sales. The Samurai could be used as a truck when purchased without a back seat or when its back seat was folded up. Therefore, positioning it as a truck seemed feasible.

ASMC set the Samurai's suggested retail price at $5,995 in order to price it comparably with Japanese import compact pickup trucks, which had a high level of U.S. consumer acceptance. Therefore, in Pearlstein's view, if advertised as a truck, the Samurai's price would not be emphasized but mentioned only to indicate parity with other truck prices. Advertising copy would probably be serious, practical, male-targeted, and designed to portray the Samurai as a tough truck.

The third option, to position the Samurai as a subcompact car, would open up the largest of the three possible markets. Although the Suzuki SJ413 was not positioned as a car in Europe, a trend was developing in which professionals, especially doctors and lawyers, drove their SJ413s to their offices in the city and left their Mercedes at home. Similarly, in the United States, especially in California, sport utility vehicles were sometimes driven in town, although none had hitherto been positioned as a car.

The Samurai boasted an average 28 miles per gallon in combined city and highway driving, was priced lower than many subcompact cars, and offered more versatility. Therefore, it could reasonably be considered by those who were shopping for an economy car. If positioned against subcompact cars, Pearlstein believed that Samurai advertising copy should emphasize the vehicle's looks. The message to consumers would be "Why buy a Toyota Tercel or a Nissan Sentra when, for the same amount of money, you can buy a much cuter vehicle, the Samurai?" However, the vehicle might not meet consumers' expectations if it was positioned as a car. Because the Samurai was built on a truck platform, its ride was stiffer and less comfortable than even the least-expensive subcompact.

Market Research. Pearlstein defined positioning as "the unique way we want prospects to think about a product." Before choosing a position for the Samurai, he asked Don Popielarz, director of research and planning, to conduct research in order to gain a thorough understanding of not only the attributes that prospective buyers ascribed to the Samurai versus other vehicles but also the profile and characteristics of potential buyers. This information would help Pearlstein decide how to position the vehicle. Then his team could develop advertising copy and choose the media that would be most efficient in delivering the Samurai's message to its consumer target.

Popielarz started by reviewing the latest research available from outside sources. A demographic segmentation study conducted by J. D. Power and Associates divided new-car buyers into demographic segments based on the size/style of the car that was purchased. The "basic small-car" segment included such cars as the Chevrolet Sprint, Ford Escort, Honda Civic, Toyota Tercel, and Mazda 323. Most (54 percent) of the car purchasers in this segment were men, but only 43 percent of the principal drivers were male. The median age of the buyers was 38. The average domestic car buyer was 41, while the average import car buyer was 36. Sixty percent of the car buyers were married;

over one third had executive/professional/technical careers, and 43 percent were college graduates. The median household size was 2.69 people, and the median household income was $34,240.

From a survey conducted by *Newsweek* for use by pickup truck and sport utility vehicle manufacturers, Popielarz learned how consumers perceived sport utility vehicles versus pickup trucks. Consumers were asked to rate 29 vehicle features of domestic and imported pickup trucks and sport utility vehicles. The features were aggregated into seven factors that were then plotted on two-dimension perceptual maps. The seven factors were everyday driving, off-road/snow driving, passenger comfort, quality/durability, styling, capacity, and gas mileage. Exhibit 3 lists the vehicle features that made up each of the seven factors. Exhibits 4–7 show four maps that summarize consumers' perceptions of pickup trucks versus sport utility vehicles on the seven factors.

After reviewing research from outside sources, Popielarz studied a survey that Suzuki had recently conducted in Canada, where it sold approximately 4,000 Samurais in 1984. Suzuki randomly surveyed 374 Canadian Samurai owners. The majority (75 percent) of the Samurai buyers were male, and 62 percent were between the ages of 18 and 34. The average age of the buyers was 33. The most frequently mentioned occupation was skilled tradesperson (32 percent). Only 21 percent were college graduates, and only 1 percent were currently students. Fifty-one percent of the buyers lived in two-person households, and the average household income was $43,800.

When asked "When you hear the name Suzuki, what do you think of," 40 percent of the Samurai owners responded "motorcycle." Other answers included 4 × 4/4-wheel drive (23 percent), Jeep (16 percent), Japanese product/efficiency (14 percent), quality/well-made (11 percent), dependable/reliable (10 percent), versatility/work/play/goes anywhere (10 percent), small (9 percent), pleasure vehicle/fun (8 percent), my car (7 percent), and economical (6 percent). When the owners were asked to describe the Samurai using only one word or phrase, the word most often mentioned was "fun." Exhibit 8 lists all the words that were volunteered by five or more owners.

As Exhibit 9 shows, design/appearance was mentioned most frequently by owners as their main reason for purchasing the Samurai. When asked "Before making your purchase, what other automobiles did you consider," 29 percent mentioned various models of Jeep. Other vehicles mentioned included Ford Bronco and Ranger (24 percent), GMC Chevrolet Jimmy (7 percent), GM Chevrolet S-10 Blazer (8 percent), Toyota 4 × 4 pickup truck and Landcruiser (12 percent), and Nissan 4 × 4 pickup truck (4 percent). No other model was mentioned by as many as 4 percent of the respondents. When asked why they selected the Samurai over their "first alternative" vehicle, the overwhelming response was economy/value (59 percent) followed by design/appearance (29 percent).

Popielarz was unsure how to interpret the data from the Canadian study, given climatic and cultural differences between the United States and Canada. Furthermore, the Samurai was positioned as a rugged utility vehicle in Canada, where it was priced higher than was planned in the United States. In Canada, the Samurai was priced similar to the least-expensive sport utility vehicles and substantially higher than both light trucks and subcompact cars.

Fortunately, there was one continental U.S. market where Suzuki SJ410s were being sold, albeit unauthorized by Suzuki. In Florida, a "gray market" existed for Suzuki SJ410s. Since 1984, approximately 3,000 had been sold there by dealers who imported them from other Suzuki markets, including Puerto Rico, Guam, the U.S. Virgin Islands, and Panama.

Popielarz and Tim O'Mara, one of the agency's account supervisors, decided to conduct face-to-face interviews with five sales managers and sales representatives at three Florida dealerships that sold SJ410s. They asked the salespeople four questions. The first question was "Who is the buyer?" The dealers said the SJ410 buyer was young, on average between 18 and 30 years old, often single, often a first-time car buyer, and often a student. Young women seemed to like the vehicle, and many sales involved fathers buying SJ410s for their children. Additionally, there was an important secondary buyer group comprising people over 30, both single and married, who bought the Suzuki to use as a third or fourth vehicle.

The second question, "What does the buyer see as competition?" elicited a unanimous response from the dealers. There was no direct competition. Indirect competition included four-wheel drive vehicles, small cars, and convertibles. The SJ410 was less expensive than other convertibles and four-wheel drive vehicles, however, and was more "fun and [had more] style than small cars."

"Why does the buyer want this vehicle?" was the third question the dealers addressed. The "most fun for the dollars" was usually mentioned. As one sales manager stated, "I don't see too many people driving down the road in Chevettes and having a blast." Other replies included convertible top; versatility; utility; gas mileage; durability; cute and unique; handles in rain, snow, and off-road; and great for fishing, camping, and skiing.

The final question, "How are they selling?" prompted smiles from the salespeople, who typically responded, "People were just lining up to get them. Just couldn't get enough of them in." The SJ410s sold for an average price of $8,500 at the three dealerships.

One of the dealerships, King Motors in Fort Lauderdale, routinely surveyed its automobile buyers. The dealership had surveys completed by 150 recent Suzuki SJ410 buyers, which it allowed Popielarz and O'Mara to study. The vehicle buyer filled out the questionnaire; however, in many instances, the buyer was not the ultimate driver. Information on age was incomplete; but, of those who gave their age, 56 percent of the buyers were between 18 and 30; the rest were over 30. One third of the purchasers were women.

Exhibit 10 tabulates the King Motors survey responses. The majority of buyers learned about the Suzuki through word of mouth or seeing it when driving by the dealership. Most buyers came to King Motors planning to buy the Suzuki, rather than the AMC Jeep line, which also was sold there. Fewer than half of the buyers considered buying another vehicle but, when other automobiles were considered, they included both new and used Jeeps, small imported cars, and large used American convertibles.

Four-wheel drive was not the principal feature generating interest in the Suzuki. Only 45 percent of the men and 32 percent of the women surveyed said that it was an important factor in their purchase decision. The attributes that buyers rated as most important were price and the fact that it was a convertible model.

Popielarz knew that the Florida buyers who participated in the survey might not be typical of the kinds of people who would buy the Samurai once it was introduced nationwide. He did believe, however, that the survey results gave clues about who the early adopters were likely to be.

After interviewing the Florida dealers, Popielarz and O'Mara conducted focus group interviews in California with a group of women aged 25 to 33, a group of men aged 18 to 24, and another group of men aged 25 to 35. All of the participants were actively shopping for a new vehicle that was either a sport utility vehicle, a subcompact car, or an imported pickup truck. All had visited at least one dealer showroom within the previous two months.

During the sessions, focus group members viewed pictures of both the convertible and hardtop Samurais that would be sold in the United States, pictures of a variety of people who might drive the Samurai, a five-minute videotape showing the Samurai in action, and pictures of several vehicles with which the Samurai might compete. Respondents reacted favorably to the Samurai's appearance, describing it as "cute," "neat," and "fun." The Samurai's size invoked mixed reactions. Some believed its size would add to its driveability and maneuverability; they said it looked easy to drive around town and in the country. For others, especially those with children or pets, the small size was a drawback. Also, those who planned rugged off-road use said the Samurai was too small.

Group members who needed occasional four-wheel drive capability readily accepted the Samurai as a viable alternative to other four-wheel drive vehicles. Those people who did not need the four-wheel drive feature said that it did not reduce their acceptance of the vehicle.

Some people said that the Samurai was exactly what they were looking for in a vehicle. They saw it as a symbol of their independence to do something different and their practicality to drive a versatile vehicle. Interest in the Samurai among focus group members appeared to be linked more to attitude than to age. When asked to choose potential Samurai buyers from the pictures that were shown to them, the interviewees chose the younger, more active people.

Most of the interviewees recognized the Suzuki name and associated it with motorcycles or the attributes of Japanese automobile manufacturers—that is, higher quality and better engineering than the domestic competition. Their price expectations were between $8,000 and $12,000, significantly higher than the planned $5,995 price tag. They were quite knowledgeable, however, about the prices of the competitive vehicles discussed. When told the Samurai's actual price, most people expressed surprise and pleasure. A few expressed suspicion about the vehicle's quality at that price.

Conclusions. Popielarz and O'Mara reviewed the market research findings with Pearlstein and Spike Bragg, the agency's executive vice president. They concluded that any young or young-at-heart person considering the purchase of a small car, small truck, or sport utility vehicle was a prospect for the Samurai. Suzuki should, therefore, avoid positioning the Samurai as a specific type of vehicle so as not to exclude large groups of potential buyers.

Furthermore, they reasoned that Suzuki should not "overdefine" the vehicle. The Samurai appeared to represent different things to different people. Therefore, Suzuki should try to develop a position with broad enough appeal to attract a wide range of consumers, so each person could define the Samurai in his or her own way and rationalize the purchase decision in his or her own terms. Moreover, the ad agency thought that, if each consumer was allowed to personally define the Samurai, this would lead to greater congruence between the vehicle's promise and its delivery than if Suzuki tried to tell consumers what the Samurai was.

Bragg suggested that the Samurai be positioned as "the alternative to small-car boredom." He reasoned that sport utility buyers could be attracted to the Samurai just by looking at the vehicle, but that small-car buyers would need to be told that the Samurai was a fun alternative to dull automobiles. Furthermore, he believed that many purchasers of small trucks were buying them to use as cars, because compact import pickup trucks were less expensive than import subcompact cars and offered more versatility. An "alternative to small-car-boredom" positioning could, therefore, attract buyers from all three vehicle segments.

Pearlstein liked Bragg's idea but expanded on it. He thought that the Samurai should be positioned as the "antidote to traditional transportation." It was important that the Samurai not be labeled as any type of vehicle. No ads should refer to it as a car, truck, or sport utility vehicle.

Final Preparations for Presentation to Mazza

Pearlstein and his associates had to present their positioning recommendation to Mazza the following day. Although Mazza had not asked to be shown any creative execution of the position, the four men had developed copy that they believed would help to explain the "antidote-to-traditional-transportation" position that they had chosen. Exhibits 11 through 16 show examples of their proposed advertising copy.

Mazza had told Pearlstein that he planned to spend $2.5 million on advertising and promotion during the first six months after the Samurai's introduction. For 1985, estimated Jeep advertising was $40 million for the American market. Industry experts expected total 1985 car, truck, and sport utility vehicle advertising expenditures in the United States to approximate $4.25 billion. Traditionally, automobile manufacturers spent between $200 and $400 per vehicle on advertising and up to an additional $500 per vehicle on incentives, such as rebates and extended warranties.

Pearlstein and his group had to recommend how the Samurai's advertising budget should be spent. A typical automobile manufacturer spent 77 percent of its advertising dollars on television ads, 10 percent on radio commercials to add frequency to the television schedule, 10 percent on print ads, and 3 percent on highway billboards. The print ads were run in both general-interest magazines and enthusiast magazines—depending on the vehicle's positioning as a car, truck, or sport utility vehicle.

Pearlstein addressed his colleagues:

If we are to win the ASMC account, tomorrow we must sell our Samurai positioning strategy to Mazza. To sell it to him, we must be convinced that it is the best positioning for the Samurai. Let's now discuss the pros and cons of the "unposition" we are proposing versus the three options we originally considered. We must be able to back up our positioning recommendation with sound market research data. We must address any risks associated with our recommended positioning. Finally, we must develop a recommendation on how to spend the $2.5 million six-month advertising budget. We should discuss how our budget allocation recommendations would vary according to the positioning strategy chosen.

EXHIBIT 1

Samurai convertible and hardtop

EXHIBIT 2   **U.S. Automobile Industry Unit Sales**

Make	1984 Unit Sales	Projected 1985 Unit Sales
Compact Sport Utility Vehicles		
Suzuki SJ410 (Hawaii)	2,124	2,500
Mitsubishi Montero	2,690	2,800
Toyota 4Runner	9,181	19,300
Toyota Landcruiser	4,170	4,400
Isuzu Trooper	6,935	25,400
Total Japanese import	25,100	54,400
Ford Bronco II	98,446	104,500
GM Chevrolet S10 Blazer/GMC S15 Jimmy	175,177	225,200
Jeep CJ/YJ series	41,627	40,100
Jeep Cherokee/Wagoneer	84,352	113,900
Total domestic	399,710	483,700
Total compact sport utility	424,810	538,100
Compact Pickup Trucks		
Mitsubishi P/U	11,102	21,900
Toyota P/U	144,675	171,500
Nissan P/U	140,864	188,700
Mazda P/U	115,303	114,600
Isuzu P/U	32,372	46,200
Total Japanese import P/U 2WD	444,316	542,900
Jeep Comanche P/U	0	3,800
Ford Ranger P/U	173,959	185,800
Chevy/GMC S10/S15 P/U	181,692	200,200
Dodge Ram 50 P/U	37,356	56,100
Total domestic P/U 2WD	393,007	445,900
Total compact P/U truck 2WD	837,323	988,800
Mitsubishi P/U 4 × 4	2,156	1,900
Toyota P/U 4 × 4	81,904	101,400
Nissan P/U 4 × 4	51,082	65,400
Isuzu P/U 4 × 4	3,537	4,900
Total Japanese import P/U 4 × 4	138,679	173,600

EXHIBIT 2 *(concluded)*

Make	1984 Unit Sales	Projected 1985 Unit Sales
Jeep Comanche 4 × 4	0	4,800
Ford Ranger 4 × 4	48,110	56,400
Chevy/GMC S10/S15 4 × 4	47,409	51,200
Dodge Ram 50 P/U 4 × 4	12,499	12,500
Total domestic P/U 4 × 4	108,018	124,900
Total compact P/U truck 4 × 4	246,697	298,500
Total Japanese import P/U 2WD and 4 × 4	582,995	716,500
Total domestic P/U 2WD and 4 × 4	501,025	570,800
Total compact P/U 2WD and 4 × 4	1,084,020	1,287,300
Subcompact Cars		
Toyota Starlet	781	0
Toyota Tercel	107,185	95,400
Toyota Corolla	156,249	173,900
Nissan Sentra	194,092	225,700
Nissan Pulsar	39,470	51,400
Mitsubishi Mirage	2,354	12,400
Honda Civic	173,561	196,800
Mazda 323/GLC	43,641	60,000
Isuzu I-Mark	4,822	13,000
Total Japanese import	722,427	828,600
Volkswagen Rabbit/Golf	85,153	71,300
Chevrolet Spectrum	1,646	51,700
Chevrolet Sprint	9,464	29,700
Dodge/Plymouth Colt	82,402	96,100
Total domestic	944,668	1,112,900
Total subcompact	1,752,248	2,016,095
Total Car and Truck		
Total Japanese car	1,846,398	2,139,500
Total Japanese truck	664,813	849,800
Total Japanese car and truck	2,511,211	2,989,300
Total industry car	10,128,318	10,888,600
Total industry truck	4,048,998	4,675,200
Total industry car and truck	14,177,316	15,563,800

SOURCE: R. L. Polk & Company market area report.

NOTE: Sums of individual vehicle makes do not always equal total since only the top-selling makes are listed.

EXHIBIT 3   *Newsweek* **Study: Factors and the Features That Constitute Them**

Factor	*Feature*
Everyday driving	For highway driving
	Acceleration/power
	Riding comfort
	Ease of handling
	Quietness
	Maneuverability in traffic
	For long-distance vacations
	Safety features
	Seating comfort
	Towing capacity
Passenger comfort	Passenger seating capacity
	As a family vehicle
	Interior roominess
	For long-distance vacations
	Seating comfort
	Level of luxury
	Riding comfort
Quality/durability	Quality of workmanship
	Durability/reliability
	Quality of materials
	Tough, rugged
Styling	Interior styling
	Exterior styling
	Design of instrument panel
	Level of luxury
	Ground clearance
Off-road/snow driving	Off-road capability
	For driving in snow
	Ground clearance
	Fun to drive
	Tough, rugged
Capacity	Ability to carry large items
	Cargo capacity
	Towing capacity
Gas mileage	Gas mileage/fuel economy

EXHIBIT 4

Perceptual map from Newsweek *study: Off-road/snow driving versus everyday driving*

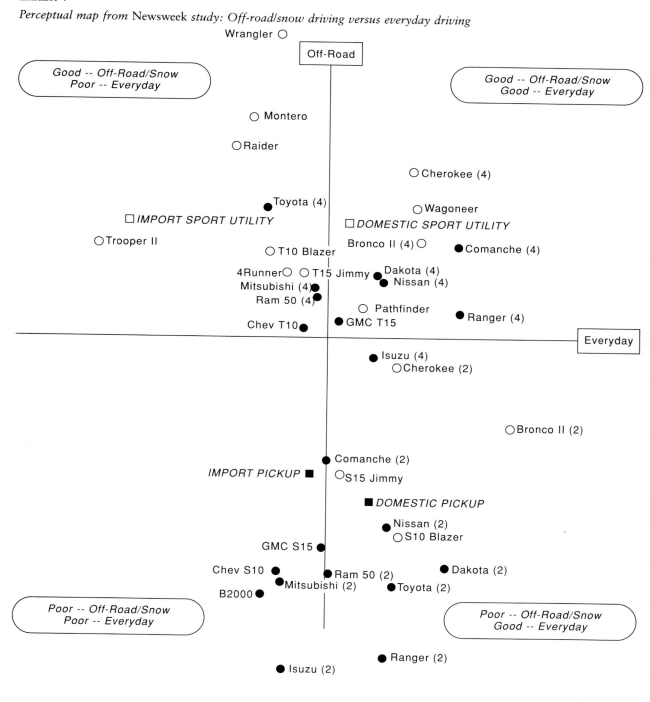

● Perceptions of *specific* brands/models of *pickup trucks*
○ Perceptions of *specific* brands/models of *sport utility vehicles*
■ Perceptions of the *category* of pickup trucks
□ Perceptions of the *category* of sport utility vehicles

Exhibit 5

Perceptual map from Newsweek *study: passenger comfort versus styling*

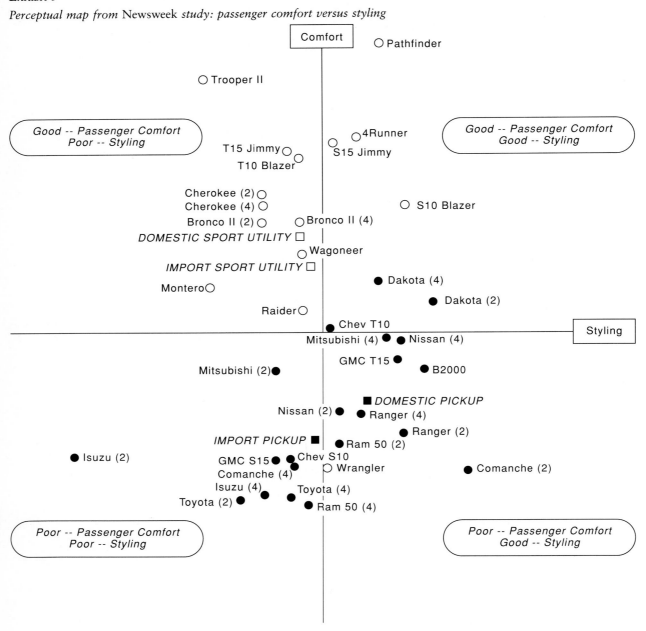

● Perceptions of *specific* brands/models of *pickup trucks*
○ Perceptions of *specific* brands/models of *sport utility vehicles*
■ Perceptions of the *category of pickup trucks*
□ Perceptions of the *category of sport utility vehicles*

EXHIBIT 6

Perceptual map from Newsweek *study: gas mileage versus everyday driving*

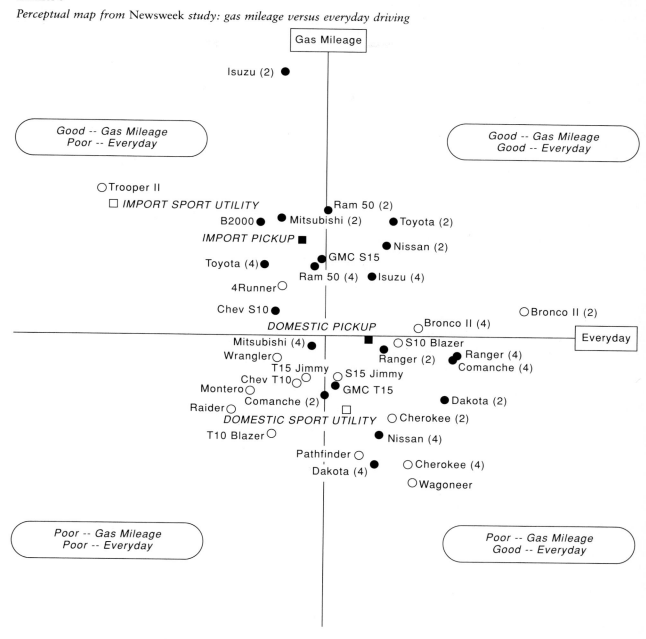

● Perceptions of *specific* brands/models of *pickup trucks*
○ Perceptions of *specific* brands/models of *sport utility vehicles*
■ Perceptions of the *category* of pickup trucks
□ Perceptions of the *category* of sport utility vehicles

EXHIBIT 7

Perceptual map from Newsweek *study: quality/durability versus passenger comfort*

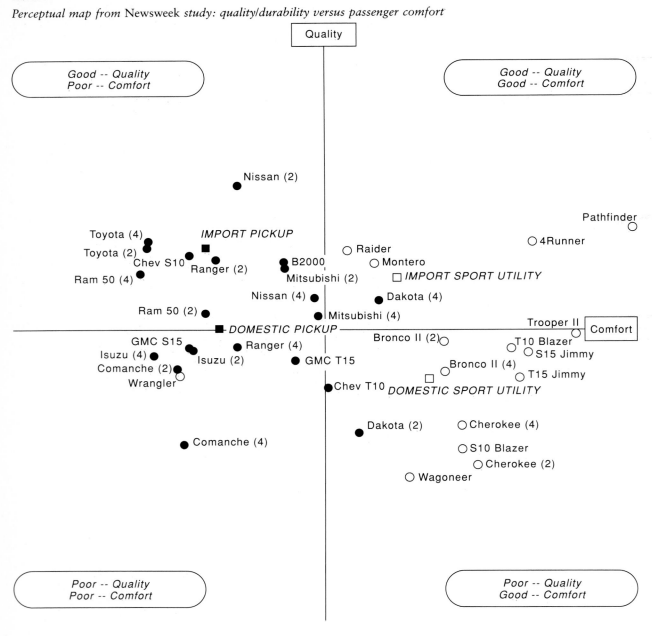

● Perceptions of *specific* brands/models of *pickup trucks*
○ Perceptions of *specific* brands/models of *sport utility vehicles*
■ Perceptions of the *category of pickup trucks*
□ Perceptions of the *category of sport utility vehicles*

EXHIBIT 8   Canadian Samurai Buyer Survey:
Suzuki Samurai One Word/Phrase Description

Word/Phrase Mentioned	Number of Mentions
Fun	41
Jeep	15
Great	13
Goes everywhere	11
Good	11
Economical	10
Practical	9
Reliable	8
All-terrain	7
Fantastic	7
Pleasure	7
Tough	7
Four-wheel drive	6
Four-by-four	5
Sporty	5
Versatile	5

NOTE: Samurai buyers were asked, "If you had to describe the Suzuki Samurai using only one word or phrase, what would you say about it?"

EXHIBIT 9   Canadian Samurai Buyer Survey: Reasons for Purchasing Samurai

Main Reason for Purchasing	Percent Mentioning
Design/appearance (net)	64%
4 × 4/4-wheel drive/jeep	39
Appearance/good-looking/sporty-looking	22
Convertible	19
Size/small/compact	8
Economy/value (net)	55
Economy/economical	18
Good mileage/fuel savings	18
Cost/reasonable price	18
Inexpensive/low price	10
Performance (net)	51
Traction/can go anywhere	19
All-season vehicle/functional	17
Fun/fun to drive	11
Ease of driving/handling/parking	7
Reliable/service (net)	19
Dependable/reliable	13
Quality/well-made/good	7
Need for jeep/second vehicle	8
Suits my life-style/needs/I like it	5%

NOTE: Samurai buyers were asked, "What are your main reasons for purchasing this vehicle?"

EXHIBIT 10   **King Motors' Suzuki SJ410 Buyer Survey**

	Total	Total Men	Total Women
Where Heard about Suzuki			
Word of mouth	41%	41%	42%
Dealer location	30	36	22
Ft. Lauderdale newspaper	20	17	24
Radio	6	5	7
Pompano Shopper	3	1	5
Came to Dealer to See			
Suzuki	76	75	77
AMC Jeep	17	21	14
Encore	1	0	2
Alliance	0	0	0
Wagoneer	0	0	0
Other	5	4	7
Considered Other Vehicle			
Yes	40	42	37
No	60	58	63
Considered AMC Jeep First			
Yes	28	30	25
No	72	70	75
Important Purchase Factors			
Price	76	72	80
Convertible	62	59	66
Gas mileage	46	46	45
Four-wheel drive	40	45	32
Size of vehicle	39	37	41
Color	22	26	18
Driving and handling	20	22	16
Other	7	9	5

The end of dull. The start of Suzuki.

Introducing the Suzuki Samurai.™ The end of dull, point and steer, econo-box driving. The start of 4x4 versatility in a new compact size all its own, convertible or hard top. With a nifty 1.3 liter, SOHC, 4-cylinder engine, 5-speed stick, and room for four. The price? Low. The place? Where there's never a dull moment. Your Suzuki automotive dealer. See him for a Samurai test drive today.

EXHIBIT 12

"Dull Barrier"
proposed print ad

Stop suffering the heartbreak of econo-box boredom. Get quick relief where there's never a dull moment. Your Suzuki auto dealer.

Take one test drive in a Suzuki Samurai™ and you, too, will break the dull barrier. The Samurai handles differently than an ordinary passenger car. Avoid sharp turns and abrupt maneuvers, and always wear your seat belt. For specific details, read your owner's manual.

SUZUKI SAMURAI BREAKS

THE DULL BARRIER

(DEALER NAME)

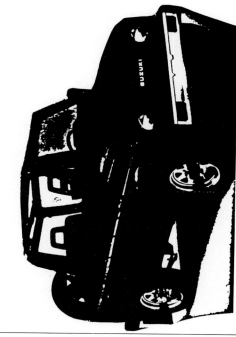

EXHIBIT 14   **Copy for Proposed Television Ad**

Setting:	A road leading from awesome mountains.
Atmosphere:	Dawn. Mysterious electrical storm flashes over the mountains. Something is about to happen. Something strange or wondrous.
What happens:	We see headlights approaching camera. From the dramatic music and overblown announcer, whatever's coming must be magnificent. Then the little Suzuki drives by at a casual speed. People inside wave to camera, giggle, car drives out of frame. Camera does double take, then watches car drive away.
(Dramatic music begins)	
Voice over:	"Prepare for the most extraordinary event of your lifetime . . ."
(Music builds)	
	"An event that will forever alter the course of mankind and womankind . . ."
(Music builds)	
	"The next major turning point in the history of all civilization."
(Music crescendos, then stops)	
(Beep, beep)	
People in the car:	"Hi!"
(Music continues)	
Voice over:	"Introducing the new Suzuki Samurai 4 × 4.
(Fades)	The beginning of the universe was dull by comparison. . . . The discovery of fire pales in significance."
(Live announcer dealer tag)	

EXHIBIT 15

Storyboard for proposed "Dull Barrier" television ad

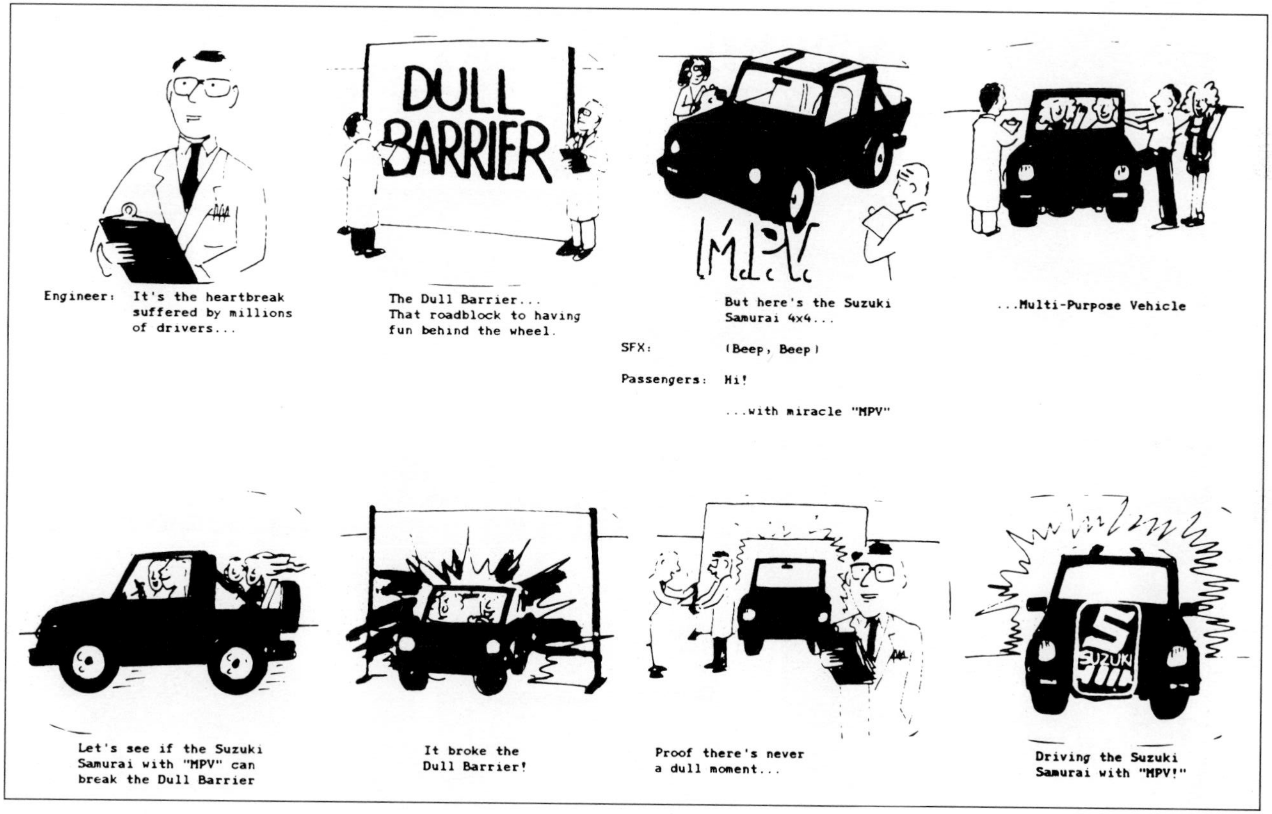

Exhibit 16
Storyboard for proposed "Amusement Park" television ad

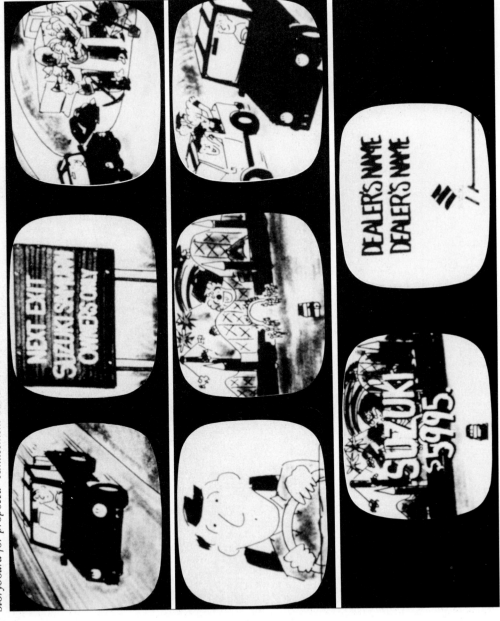

FORD MOTOR COMPANY: THE PRODUCT WARRANTY PROGRAM (A)

On Friday, January 23, 1987, Ford Motor Company executives, in a special meeting, held a lengthy discussion about warranty program alternatives. The meeting was organized to identify the best possible response to General Motors' (GM) change in its warranty policy. At a press conference the previous day, GM had announced improved warranty coverage to back its contention that the quality of its cars had reached an unprecedented high. Industry analysts expected the new warranty to increase GM's market share.

The Ford executives—from various departments, such as marketing, sales, manufacturing, product quality assurance, engineering, after-sales service, parts, warranty, and extended service plans—considered several warranty program alternatives and had to make recommendations to Donald E. Petersen, Ford's chairman of the board and chief executive officer.

The U.S. Car Market

Two important external events—the oil shocks of the 1970s and the U.S. economic recession—had both sent the U.S. car market into a sharp depression in the early 1980s. New-car sales declined dramatically, from 11.3 million units in 1978 to 8 million in 1982. In addition, foreign competitors were rapidly gaining market share (see Exhibit 1). Profitability of the four U.S. manufacturers—Ford, GM, Chrysler Corporation, and American Motors Corporation (AMC)—also had fallen sharply to an aggregate loss of $1.8 billion per year during 1980–82.

In 1983, however, the industry began a swift recovery that industry analysts attributed to increased efficiency, quality, and commitment. By 1986, sales of new cars had reached a record level, and the aggregate profit of the four U.S. automakers was $7.5 billion. The domestic share of the U.S. car market, however, reached an all-time low, while imported car sales and market share were both at record high levels in 1986 (see Exhibit 1).[1] Japanese import sales remained strong, despite Japan's continuation of voluntary restraints and the rise in the yen's value vis-à-vis the U.S. dollar. The Japanese automakers had moved up into the middle of the market with new, more upscale models that sold well. New models from Korea and Eastern Europe also helped to bolster import sales.

The U.S. car market was mature, global, high-technology, intensely competitive, and largely a replacement market. It was divided into five broad categories based on car size (see Exhibit 2). Stabilized fuel prices and the popularity of Ford's new Taurus and Sable models accounted for the intermediate category's success.

Outlook. For 1987, the forecast for new-car sales in the United States was 10.4 million units, 9 percent below the 1986 sales level. The predicted drop in sales was partly a result of the 1986 year-end sales boost, as buyers hurried to take advantage of sales-tax deductions that were to be phased out in 1987. The domestic automakers' sales were expected to decline by 12 percent, while the market share of imported cars was expected to rise.

The challenges facing U.S. automakers included:

1. Increased competition from cars produced in countries new to the U.S. market (e.g., Korea and Yugoslavia).
2. The growing array of higher-priced imported models.
3. Intensified price competition as new entrants sought their share of a mature market.
4. The anticipated increased production of cars produced in the United States by foreign companies.
5. Substantial overcapacity, both in the United States and abroad.

In addition, U.S. domestic car production was coming under increased pressure. In 1986, domestic production declined 4.8 percent from its 1985 level, even though sales increased 4.5 percent; record sales did not mean record production. Several foreign automobile manufacturers announced plans to build new production capacity in the United States, and output from these plants was projected to grow from 400,000 units in 1986 to between 1.5 and 2 million by 1990.

Domestic manufacturers prepared by increasing their efforts to achieve a slimmer work force, higher productivity, more efficiency, and leaner managerial staffs. They instituted massive capital expenditure programs for upgrading and building new plants as well as installingrobots and other state-of-the-art, labor-saving equipment. Computer-aided design of new models contributed to parts standardization and cost control. The increased adoption

---

This case was prepared by Professor Melvyn A. J. Menezes. Copyright © 1988 by the President and Fellows of Harvard College. Harvard Business School case 9-589-001 (Rev. 5/15/90).

[1]*Domestic cars* refer to cars built in the United States by the four U.S. automakers and three non-U.S. manufacturers (Honda Motor Company, Nissan Motor Corporation, and Volkswagen of America). *Imported cars* refer to cars sold in the United States but built elsewhere.

of just-in-time delivery systems for components and supplies reduced inventory and operating expenses.

Company Background

Founded by Henry Ford in 1903 and headquartered at Dearborn, Michigan, Ford Motor Company grew rapidly into a worldwide leader in automotive and automotive-related products and services. By 1986, Ford was one of the world's largest manufacturing enterprises, was the world's second-largest automaker, and was America's third-largest industrial corporation with 382,300 employees. In 1986, both sales ($62.7 billion) and net income ($3.3 billion) were the highest in the company's history, and Ford's profits topped GM's for the first time since 1924. In the U.S. market, Ford's 1986 sales and net income were $50 billion and $2.5 billion, respectively—up 14.9 percent and 23.6 percent, respectively, from the previous year. This was a spectacular turnaround from its poor 1980–82 performance, when cumulative net losses amounted to $3.5 billion.

Ford had two major lines of business—automotive and nonautomotive. The automotive line, which accounted for 93 percent of the company's revenue and 105 percent of the company's operating income, had two main operations:

- The North American Automotive Operations (NAAO) designed, engineered, developed, produced, and marketed cars, trucks, industrial engines, vehicle components, and replacement parts in the United States and Canada.
- The International Automotive Operations (IAO) handled the same functions as NAAO on six continents in nearly 200 countries and territories.

Management Philosophy. Ford's mission was "to improve continually our products and services to meet our customers' needs, allowing us to prosper as a business and to provide a reasonable return for our stockholders, the owners of our business." In 1980, management established six guiding principles to accomplish this mission. "Quality comes first" was the first principle. The company emphasized quality in every aspect of its functioning, and "Quality is Job One" was much more than an advertising slogan; it was a way of life. As one Ford executive stated, "Quality drives everything we do—more so than profitability does. It's because we believe that better quality leads to greater productivity, reduces the cost base, and results in higher profitability."

The importance given to quality and customers throughout the organization was strongly influenced by top management. As chairman and chief executive officer, Petersen stressed quality and commitment to customers in every aspect of the business. This philosophy guided Ford executives during 1980–82, when they faced increasing losses

and declining market share. Management's short list of priorities included quality, investing in new products and research and development, and bringing costs into line. Between 1980 and 1984, Ford spent almost $14 billion on new products, processes, machinery, and equipment, and another $9 billion on research and engineering development. The 1985 and 1986 results seemed to indicate that these priorities had paid off.

North American Automotive Operations (NAAO). Ford's performance was linked strongly to that of NAAO, which had three major U.S. divisions—the Ford Division, the Lincoln-Mercury Division, and the Ford Parts and Service Division (FPSD). In 1986, NAAO sold 2.28 million cars and 1.53 million trucks, and the gross contributions per unit (after considering warranty costs) were $500 for subcompact and compact cars; $1,000 for intermediate and full-size cars; $2,000 for luxury cars; and $1,500 for trucks.

During 1986, Ford stressed quality and productivity, not market share; in fact, the company's car market share declined slightly, from 18.8 percent in 1985 to 18.2 percent in 1986. With high industry sales volumes, capacity constraint was an important factor in the decline of Ford's car market share. By the end of 1986, the company had been producing at maximum capacity for 29 consecutive months.

Main Competitors

The automobile industry comprised four major U.S. manufacturers and several foreign competitors (see Exhibit 3). Ford management believed that its principal competitors were GM, Chrysler, and, more recently, the Japanese manufacturers as well.

GM dominated new-car sales. During 1979–85, GM invested $41.5 billion in reconstruction and expected it to pay off in the long run with greater profitability, quality, and productivity. GM's share of the U.S. car market declined, however, from 44.3 percent in 1984 to 41 percent in 1986. This decline caused several new high-tech assembly plants to run below capacity, slashing profitability.

Chrysler's share of the U.S. car market had improved for the sixth consecutive year, and its divisions were the fastest growing in the U.S. auto industry. Chrysler's strategy, starting in 1986, was to introduce a proliferation of models, which included small sedans (Dodge Shadow and Plymouth Sundance) and a midsize pickup truck (Dodge Dakota).

The Automobile Consumer

In the United States, an automobile was considered a necessity, and there was at least one vehicle on the road for every adult. In 1986, of the 88.5 million U.S. households, 53 percent owned two or more cars, and over 33 percent owned one car. Over 70 percent of all work-related commutes and over 80 percent of all travel from city to city were by car.

Ford conducted continuous market research on new-car buyers' shopping habits, buying processes, and ownership experiences. (Some general demographic and psychographic data on new-car buyers appear in Exhibit 4.) The research also indicated that consumers had become increasingly deliberate about the shopping process. On average, consumers visited five dealers before purchasing a car, and approximately half of those visits were to dealers selling the make that the consumer bought.

Ford tracked customers' purchase reasons, using a list of over 20 criteria. The most important criterion for buyers of all car categories was quality, measured by reliability and customers' perceptions of how well a car was made. The importance of all other purchase criteria varied substantially by car category. For example, warranty coverage was more important to buyers of compact and subcompact cars than to luxury-car buyers (see Table A).

In 1986, research on the buying process indicated the following:

- The new-car ownership cycle (i.e., the average age of the car that is replaced by the original owner when buying another new car) had increased steadily from 3.7 years in 1975 to 5.4 years. Availability of extended-length financing was a significant contributing factor.

- Of the 72 percent of buyers who financed their car purchase, the vast majority (80 percent) bought on a four- to five-year loan period.

- Loyalty among Ford owners (i.e., the percentage of Ford owners who purchased another new Ford) was 46 percent. This was the highest level Ford had achieved in the 1980s, approaching the level attained in the 1970s.

- The percentage of competitive-make owners who switched to Ford had increased in the 1980s. For example, 12 percent of the GM owners purchasing a new car in 1986 bought a Ford, compared with 8 percent in 1980.

- Ford's gain/loss ratio (the ratio of new buyers gained through switching sales to sales lost through disloyalty) had increased substantially, from 0.6 in 1980 to 1.1 in 1985. Corresponding competitive figures were as follows: GM, 1.3 and 0.8; Chrysler, 0.8 and 1.5; and imports, 3.6 and 2.1

Exhibit 5 shows how the various aspects of the buying process differed by category.

An owner's satisfaction with a new car was strongly influenced by the car's quality—for example, its driveability, engine, and transmission. Satisfaction was critical because it affected customer loyalty to the company (see Table B).

Product Policy

Ford's product policy had changed from its early focus on standardization and a narrow product line to challenging GM in the 1950s through several new product introductions. Throughout the 1960s, Ford had so proliferated and upgraded its models that, in 1970, it offered 88 variations of basic models, compared with 44 in 1960 and 15 in 1946.

Introducing successful new models had become a key to success in the industry. The total investment in a truly new product, however, was becoming extremely high, exceeding $500 million. The lengthy production process involved three main stages—design and development, manufacture of parts

---

TABLE A **Ranking of Top 12 Purchase Criteria after Quality**

	Overall	Subcompact	Compact	Intermediate	Full-size	Luxury
Value for money	1	2	1	2	4	7
Ease of handling	2	5	3	1	2	2
Price/deal offered	3	3	4	4	6	12
Riding comfort	4	9	6	3	1	1
Warranty coverage	5	4	5	5	7	8
Fuel economy	6	1	2	9	16	18
Safety features	7	7	7	6	5	3
Dealer service	8	6	8	8	8	6
Quietness	9	10	10	7	3	4
Cost of service/repair	10	8	9	10	11	17
Exterior styling	11	13	11	11	11	5
Interior styling	12	14	13	12	14	10

NOTE: Other criteria included future resale/trade-in value, power and pickup, fun to drive, technical innovations, large trunk/cargo area, passenger seating capacity, prestige, and dealer-assisted financing.

TABLE B   Impact of Owner Satisfaction on Loyalty

Satisfaction with Prior Ford Car	Loyalty Rate
Completely satisfied	55%
Very satisfied	51
Fairly satisfied	43
Somewhat dissatisfied	37
Very dissatisfied	31
Overall average	46

and subassemblies, and assembly. The design phase typically began five to seven years before product introduction and involved developing general product concepts, sketches of concepts, full-size models, and production cost targets.

Product quality at Ford was a corporate philosophy. As one executive said, "Quality includes every aspect of the vehicle that determines customer satisfaction and provides fundamental values. This means how well the vehicle is made, how well it performs, how well it lasts, and how well the customer is treated by both the company and the dealer." The importance of product quality was expected to become even greater in the years ahead, because the market was growing more competitive, and customers were increasingly emphasizing quality. To pursue the quality philosophy, Ford implemented several changes with its suppliers, dealers, and employees.

Ford set tougher standards for suppliers, assisted them to achieve those higher standards, made quality considerations a critical factor in every supplier selection decision, and established awards for suppliers that contributed to an improvement in Ford's quality performance. Award winners received preferential consideration for new business and for long-term contracts. In 1985, customer service introduced Quality Care, a joint program with Ford dealers, to improve predelivery and delivery procedures. Besides the Quality Care program, dealers offered customers a lifetime service guarantee with no recharge for repairs. For its internal operations, Ford established Quality Responsible Teams, linking their formal performance evaluation and bonuses to quality that was measured by customer reports of "things gone wrong" (TGW) per 100 cars. A TGW was whatever caused a customer to complain to the dealer—anything from a blemish in the paint to a broken transmission.

Customer research showed that the quality of Ford's 1986 cars, measured by TGW, was over 50 percent better than that of its 1980 models. For six consecutive years (1981–86), nationwide respondents to Ford's surveys judged it to be the best American manufacturer of high-quality cars and trucks. The quality ratings, which were supported by surveys conducted by independent firms, narrowed the gap with Japanese manufacturers.

Product Warranty

Most new cars in the United States were covered by four different types of warranty coverage:

1. Basic warranty (covering most parts except tires and maintenance items, such as filters and spark plugs).
2. Powertrain warranty (covering the engine, transmission, front- or rear-wheel drive shaft).
3. Corrosion warranty (generally applying to outer body rust-through).
4. Emissions warranty (be federal law, every car manufacturer had to provide a warranty on the emission control system for at least 5 years/50,000 miles, whichever occurred first).[2]

Both American and Japanese manufacturers tended to offer "partitioned" warranties, with separate coverage assigned to specific parts of the car. Most European manufacturers covered nearly all components of a car for a specified time or mileage (see Exhibit 6).

Over the past two decades, the role of warranties and the coverage they provided had varied considerably. Until 1960, Ford and the other auto manufacturers had offered a basic warranty of 3 months/4,000 miles, primarily to limit their liability. In 1960, this was increased to 1 year/12,000 miles.

Ford first used warranties as a marketing variable in the mid-1960s, when it offered a longer warranty on its Lincoln cars. This move met with great success, and Lincoln sales increased substantially. As a result of that success and the then-growing emphasis on consumerism, the Mercury and Ford divisions also offered longer warranties. By 1967, the basic warranty was 2 years/24,000 miles, and the powertrain warranty was 5 years/50,000 miles.

The auto industry's downturn in 1969–70 led to intense efforts at cost reduction. Analyses revealed that warranty costs had become extremely high, because of both the high frequency of product failure and the longer warranty period. Consequently, the basic warranty was reduced in 1970 to 1 year/12,000 miles, and the additional powertrain warranty was made optional. By 1980, the improvement in quality permitted Ford executives (in marketing, manufacturing, and quality assurance) to convince top management and members of the board that the costs of increasing the powertrain warranty to 2 years/24,000 miles would be significantly lower than in the late 1960s.

Ford, GM, and Chrysler were usually fiercely competitive on warranties. Through the 1980s, however, Chrysler had been the most aggressive warranty marketer in the

---

[2]The warranty period is usually defined in time and mileage and restricted to whichever occurs first. Throughout the rest of the case, the phrase "whichever occurs first" will be implied (unless otherwise stated) whenever the warranty period is mentioned.

industry. Chrysler placed enormous marketing emphasis on product warranty, and, in 1981, the company increased the powertrain warranty on all its domestic cars from 2 years/24,000 miles to 5 years/50,000 miles. Chrysler used its chairman, Lee Iacocca, as the pitchman in national television commercials, proclaiming that Chrysler had improved its car quality and was prepared to stand behind it and that the company's powertrain coverage was the best in the industry. Chrysler began to gain market share. Industry analysts estimated that the automaker's superior warranty coverage accounted for at least one of the approximately three percentage points that Chrysler gained in market share between 1980 and 1985. Ford and GM had lost 0.5 percent market share each. Consequently, they increased their powertrain warranties on nonluxury cars to 3 years/unlimited miles in January 1986 (see Exhibit 6 for various manufacturers' warranty coverage).

To invoke a warranty, a customer had to take the car to a dealer, who carried out the repair at no charge if the part or component that failed was still under warranty. Although most Ford dealers would honor the warranty, most customers returned to the dealer from whom they had purchased the car because they expected to receive preferential treatment from that dealer.

Ford dealers fulfilled an important role concerning warranties. They were required to explain the warranty coverage to a buyer at the time of sale, and they had to provide warranty repair service, whenever needed, according to the provisions of a sales and service agreement and Ford's warranty policy. On average, dealers were reimbursed for warranty work 26 days after they informed Ford.

Many dealers were concerned that their gross margins on warranty repairs were only 35 percent, compared with 50 percent on customer-paid repairs. This happened because of the automakers' reimbursement policies, which had two components—parts and labor. For parts, dealers generally charged dealer price plus 50 percent for customer-paid work but received only dealer price plus 30 percent from manufacturers for warranty work. Reimbursement of labor costs for any given repair was based on the dealer's approved labor rate multiplied by the manufacturers' standard labor time allowed for that particular repair job. Many dealers believed that the commercially available labor time standards (used for customer-paid work) exceeded the manufacturers' recommended time standards (used for warranty work) by about 30 percent.

The total cost of Ford's warranty program, approximately $1 billion in 1986, had three components. The first and largest was claims—parts and labor. This cost was related to product repair frequency as well as to labor rates and parts costs. Over the past few years, repair frequency had declined, but labor rates and parts costs had increased. The claims costs associated with each type of coverage are shown in Exhibit 7. A second component was the cost incurred on the warranty payment and administration de-

partment, which had 94 people in five sections: (1) warranty and policy, (2) parts return and inspection, (3) claims review, (4) dealer claims and supplier accounting, and (5) special processing. The final component—communication expenses—was minor, because most of it was accounted for under Ford's advertising expenses.

Some Ford managers believed that Iacocca's punchy "best-built, best-backed" Chrysler television commercials, which attracted much attention, may have goaded GM into increasing its warranty. GM's new warranty policy, announced on January 22, 1987, upgraded the powertrain warranty from 3 years/unlimited miles to 6 years/60,000 miles, and the corrosion warranty from 3 years/unlimited miles to 6 years/100,000 miles. The new warranty program, which applied retroactively to all GM's 1987 cars built in North America, covered the first buyer only. The second owner could buy the new warranty terms from GM for $100. Third and any successive owners would be entitled to a powertrain warranty of 2 years/24,000 miles. GM's new warranty policy, like Chrysler's, marked a change in philosophy. The focus shifted from the vehicle to the owner.

To remain competitive, Ford's marketing and sales executives believed that they had to respond quickly to GM's new warranty policy. For various alternative Ford powertrain warranty terms, industry experts' estimates of the effect of GM's powertrain warranty of 6 years/60,000 miles on Ford's domestic car market share (m.s.) points are shown in Table C.

Ford usually made its product warranty and pricing decisions in the summer for the following year's models, which were normally introduced in the fall. The warranty decision-making process was complex because the warranty program affected various departments with differing perspectives and often conflicting interests, and because the decisions were made at the highest levels. Changes in the warranty program needed to be approved by Chairman of the Board and CEO Donald Petersen; President and COO Harold Poling; and the Policy and Strategy Committee. The departments that recommended and influenced changes in the warranty program were sales, marketing, parts and service, product development, manufacturing, quality assurance, and extended service plans. Because of the warranty program's high financial implications, the controller's office scrutinized warranty costs.

Extended Service Plans

A program closely related to product warranties was the Extended Service Plans (ESP) program. Sold as a separate, stand-alone product, an extended service plan provided for long-term protection against certain unexpected repairs beyond the warranty period.

In the 10 years since its introduction in 1977, ESP had grown rapidly and increased in complexity. Various plans

TABLE C   Estimated Effect of Alternatives on Ford's Market Share (m.s.) Points

Ford's Powertrain Warranty Alternatives	Estimated Effect on Ford's Market Share Points	
	Nonluxury Cars	Luxury Cars
3 years/36,000 miles	1.75% m.s. loss	—
4 years/50,000 miles	1.5% m.s. loss	—
5 years/50,000 miles	1.0% m.s. loss	0.5% m.s. loss
6 years/60,000 miles	No change	No change
7 years/70,000 miles	0.75% m.s. gain	0.25% m.s. gain
Cover all Parts ("European")		
3 years/36,000 miles	1.5% m.s. gain	1.0% m.s. gain
4 years/50,000 miles	2.0% m.s. gain	1.5% m.s. gain

had been added, and support for ESP had grown substantially. By the end of 1986, 84 people worked full-time on ESP, and 350 service representatives spent approximately 8 percent of their time on ESP. The rest of their time was spent on other activities: 50 percent on owner relations, 25 percent on warranty administration, and 17 percent on equipment and technical administration.

Nearly 45 percent of Ford's new-car retail buyers bought a service contract. Approximately 60 percent of these bought a Ford service contract, and the others bought one from the over 200 companies operating in the automobile service contract industry. Most service contracts were purchased with the new vehicle (80 percent) or when the basic warranty of 1 year/12,000 miles expired (20 percent).

In January 1987, to meet different customer needs, Ford offered four different types of service plans: ESP BASE, ESP PLUS, ESP TOTAL, and ESP CARE (see Exhibit 8). Ford had over 100 different plans, because each of these four types of contracts was available in a variety of time (3, 4, 5, or 6 years) and mileage (36,000, 48,000, 60,000, 100,000, or unlimited miles) combinations, and for different types of vehicles (nonluxury car, luxury car, light truck, or heavy truck). The consumer prices of these plans ranged from $200 to $1,250 and averaged $415. Repairs covered by ESP were carried out on about 35 percent of the cars that had an ESP, and Ford's expense averaged $330 per car that needed repair. On each plan, Ford and the dealers got gross margins of $100 and $200, respectively. Although dealers sold ESP for new and used Fords as well as other makes, their margins on ESP were lower than those on competitors' service contracts.

The ESP department focused its communication on two broad target markets, trade and consumer. The strategy for the trade market (dealers) was to use the credibility of dealer testimonials to communicate the benefits of ESP. Ads were placed in leading automotive trade publications. The strategy for the consumer market (all potential purchasers

of new Ford cars) was to create an awareness of Ford's ESP and a consumer predisposition to purchase ESP by emphasizing peace of mind and the avoidance of expensive repairs with ESP coverage. Ads were placed in prominent national weekly news magazines, especially in the spring and fall.

Ford management believed that the ESP program was successful because 80 percent of Ford's dealers sold ESP—a higher percentage than that of any other domestic manufacturer (GM, 66 percent; Chrysler, 67 percent; and AMC, 71 percent). More important, ESP contributed significantly to Ford's profits (see Exhibit 9), resulting in additional parts profits of $3.6 million and a cumulative cash flow from 1976 through 1986 of about $300 million. As one Ford executive noted, "ESP by itself would equal or exceed the profitability of many consistently profitable company activities."

ESP managers worried that an increase in the warranty period would reduce ESP's attractiveness and consequently would cut into the department's sales and profits. Ford dealers disagreed on the salability of service contracts with longer warranties. A majority of the dealers believed that longer warranties would lower ESP sales; a few dealers felt that ESP sales would be unaffected.

Distribution

In the United States, cars were sold through an elaborate network of franchised dealers. The franchise agreement detailed clearly both the manufacturer's and the dealer's sales and service responsibilities. Over the years, the number of new-car dealerships had declined steadily; the average size of the dealerships had increased (due primarily to the closing of smaller-volume dealers); and there was a growing trend toward one dealer principal operating more than one dealership. In 1950, there were 50,000 retail outlets or dealerships, each run primarily by a different dealer principal. In 1986, however, there were 25,156 dealerships, with only 17,000 dealer principals. Another change was the increased concentration of the dealer network: in 1986, 20 percent of the dealerships (5,155) accounted for 80 percent of the sales. As the size of the dealerships grew, the balance of power began to shift from the manufacturers to the dealers. In 1986, the average dealership's sales and gross profit were $11.27 million and $1.6 million, respectively (see Table D).

Service and parts (S&P) comprised warranty work (18 percent of S&P sales), customer-paid work (43 percent), and wholesale and counter sales (39 percent). Four successive years of strong new-car sales led to substantial increases in warranty work—an 18 percent increase in 1986. However, car owners typically abandoned dealers after the warranty period. Dealerships' share of customer-paid (non-warranty) work dropped from 40 percent during the warranty period to 15 percent after the warranty period for those without an ESP, and to about 30 percent for those with an ESP. Overall, dealerships accounted for only 33 percent of the total warranty and customer-paid automobile service and parts business.

Advertising and Promotion

The automobile industry was one of the most heavily advertised in the United States. In 1986, nine auto manufacturers were among the nation's 100 leading advertisers, with GM (fifth) and Ford (sixth) in the top 10.

From 1986 onward, Ford's ads emphasized warranties. Corporate ads stressed warranties, and all the divisional ads ended with a warranty message. Ford's advertising appeared primarily on television (49 percent), although newspapers (16 percent) and magazines (25 percent) also were used extensively. To develop distinctive brand identities, Ford and other automakers created ad themes by brand. For example, Ford Division ads used the theme "Have you driven a Ford . . . lately?"; Lincoln ads had the "What a luxury car should be" theme; and Mercury ads used "The shape you want to be in" theme. GM's Pontiac division used "We build excitement," and its Chevrolet division proclaimed the "Heartbeat of America" theme.

TABLE D   Sales and Profits of Average Dealership by Department, 1986 ($000s)

	Sales	Gross Profit
New-car department	$ 7,325.7	$ 720.4
Used-car department	2,242.7	223.9
Service and parts	1,442.5	551.1
Finance and insurance	258.8	103.8
Total	$11,269.7	$1,599.2

Auto marketers also offered consumer promotions through cash rebates and low finance rates. In 1986, Ford spent over $100 million on consumer promotions. Industry analysts attributed the record 1986 car sales partly to the biggest consumer incentive promotion in automotive history. In the fall of 1986, GM announced a low financing rate of 2.9 percent. Ford matched that offer; Chrysler announced a 2.4 percent rate; and AMC introduced 0 percent financing. All these promotions lured unprecedented numbers of buyers into the marketplace. Some industry analysts believed that, despite their impact on sales, such consumer promotions were not good for the manufacturers in the long run, because competitors easily matched them, and because many consumers would not buy cars without them.

The Decision

During the discussions at the January 23 meeting, managers from various departments expressed different views on Ford's warranty position, and they proposed and supported several courses of action. Five alternatives were identified and discussed:

1. Do not respond. Maintain the existing warranty terms.
2. Match GM's terms. Offer a powertrain warranty of 6 years/60,000 miles, a corrosion warranty of 6 years/100,000 miles, and change from a vehicle warranty to an owner warranty. Have a $100 deductible and a transfer fee, but do not advertise those restrictions.
3. Exceed GM's terms. Offer a powertrain warranty of 7 years/70,000 miles. Also offer a corrosion warranty of 7 years/unlimited miles for all coastal states and 6 years/100,000 for inland states.
4. Offer less than GM but equal to Chrysler's coverage—5 years/50,000 miles.
5. Adopt a "European" approach. Offer a basic warranty (including powertrain) of 3 years/36,000 miles (for nonluxury cars) or 4 years/50,000 miles (for luxury cars) and a corrosion warranty of 6 years/100,000 miles.

One executive urged that the five options be compared in terms of expected market share, sales, contribution per unit, and total contribution. The executive wondered what would have happened if all manufacturers (including GM) had retained the warranty terms that existed on January 21.

When to implement the warranty policy change also was discussed. Some managers felt that a new warranty policy should be retroactive to all 1987 Ford cars, others felt that it should be effective immediately, and a few felt that the change should be announced and implemented for 1988 models.

Considerable debate arose over whether the warranty terms ought to be the same for all cars. Some managers argued for better warranty terms for nonluxury cars, other managers felt that luxury cars ought to have the better warranties. Yet others felt that all Ford cars should have the same warranty terms. This last group argued that different warranty terms for different categories of cars would con-fuse everyone. Some managers expressed strong concern about the impact that an increase in the warranty coverage would have on ESP profits and dealer profitability.

Despite the disagreement on the best response to GM's new warranty policy, the executives at this meeting realized that they had to decide on a course of action to recommend to Petersen.

EXHIBIT 1   U.S. New-Car Production, Sales, and Market Shares (millions of units)

| | | Retail Sales | | | | |
| | | Domestic | | Imports | | |
Year	Domestic Production Units	Units	Percent of Total	Units	Percent of Total	Total Units
1973	9.7	9.7	85.1%	1.7	14.9%	11.4
1974	7.3	7.4	84.1	1.4	15.9	8.8
1975	6.7	7.0	81.4	1.6	18.6	8.6
1976	8.5	8.6	85.1	1.5	14.9	10.1
1977	9.2	9.1	81.3	2.1	18.7	11.2
1978	9.2	9.3	82.3	2.0	17.7	11.3
1979	8.4	8.3	78.3	2.3	21.7	10.6
1980	6.4	6.6	73.3	2.4	26.7	9.0
1981	6.3	6.2	72.9	2.3	27.1	8.5
1982	5.1	5.8	72.5	2.2	27.5	8.0
1983	6.8	6.8	73.9	2.4	26.1	9.2
1984	7.8	8.0	76.9	2.4	23.1	10.4
1985	8.2	8.2	74.5	2.8	25.5	11.0
1986	7.8	8.2	71.3	3.3	28.7	11.5

SOURCE: *Ward's Automotive Yearbook*, various years.

EXHIBIT 2   U.S. Domestic Car Sales and Market Share by Size Category

	Subcompact	Compact	Intermediate	Full-Size	Luxury	Overall
1985 unit sales	1,296,701	2,562,588	2,463,556	1,077,308	804,389	8,204,542
1985 share of industry	15.8%	31.2%	30.0%	13.2%	9.8%	100.0%
1986 unit sales	1,325,325	2,461,192	2,540,491	1,115,789	772,091	8,214,888
1986 share of industry	16.1%	30.0%	30.9%	13.6%	9.4%	100.0%
1987 unit sales[a]	1,150,000	2,300,000	2,200,000	940,000	650,000	7,240,000
1987 share of industry[a]	15.9%	31.7%	30.4%	13.0%	9.0%	100.0%
Breakdown of 1986 Sales by Competitor						
Ford	35.7%	20.9%	25.9%	23.1%	23.0%	25.3%
General Motors	25.0	51.8	64.0	62.7	77.0	55.1
Chrysler	22.5	18.7	9.8	14.2	—	14.2
American Motors	5.0	—	0.3	—	—	0.9
Volkswagen	5.5	—	—	—	—	0.9
Nissan	4.0	—	—	—	—	0.6
Honda	2.3	8.6	—	—	—	3.0
	100.0%	100.0%	100.0%	100.0%	100.0%	100.0%

[a]Expected.

EXHIBIT 3 Competition in the U.S. Car Market

| | Sales[a] ($ billions) | | Net Income[a] ($ billions) | | U.S. Car Sales (000s of units) | | Share of U.S. Car Market (%) | | Advertising Expenses ($ millions) | Number of Dealers | Customer Profile, 1986 | | |
| | | | | | | | | | | | Loyalty[b] Levels | Mean Family Income | Female Buyers |
	1985	1986	1985	1986	1985	1986	1985	1986	1986	1986	(percent)	($000s)	(percent)
Ford	$52.77	$62.71	$2.51	$3.33	2,079	2,081	18.8%	18.2%	$648.5	5,460	46%	$30.7	41%
General Motors	96.37	102.81	4.00	2.93	4,692	4,693	42.5	41.0	839.0	9,680	61	34.6	41
Chrysler	21.26	22.59	1.64	1.40	1,245	1,309	11.3	11.4	426.0	4,023	45	30.6	43
AMC	4.04	3.46	(0.13)	(0.09)	131	77	1.2	0.7	116.2	1,349	NA	NA	NA
Toyota	24.35	38.21	1.24	1.55	620	634	5.6	5.5	208.8	1,079	35	36.3	50
Nissan	14.47	22.75	0.30	0.39	575	546	5.2	4.8	180.1	1,113	29	33.6	47
Volvo	13.58	13.24	1.02	1.02	104	113	0.9	1.0	NA	407	18	53.4	39
Honda	10.59	16.36	0.52	0.82	552	694	5.0	6.1	205.1	862	44	34.2	48
Mazda	6.28	9.85	0.13	0.49	211	222	1.9	1.9	156.8	764	27	34.9	48
Hyundai	—	NA		NA	—	169	—	1.5	NA	75	NA	NA	NA
Volkswagen	21.01	30.75	0.31	0.36	218	215	2.0	1.9	$152.2	878	21	41.3	34
BMW	6.16	7.81	0.13	0.18	88	97	0.8	0.8	NA	422	27	55.3	32
Mercedes-Benz	22.68	34.11	0.73	NA	87	99	0.8	0.8	NA	417	42%	80.0	33
Subaru	$ 2.69	$ 4.74	$ 0.60	$ 0.76	178	183	1.6	1.6	NA	809	NA	NA	NA
Others	NA	NA	NA	NA	258	319	2.4	2.8	NA	NA	NA	NA	NA
Total					11,038	11,451	100.0%	100.0%				$ 33.8	43%

[a]Sales and net income have been converted to U.S. dollars at the following rates:

	1985	1986
Toyota, Nissan, Honda, Mazda, Subaru	Y250 = $1	Y165 = $1
Volkswagen, BMW, Mercedes-Benz	DM 2.31 = $1	DM 1.92 = $1
Volvo	SEK 6.35 = $1	SEK 6.35 = $1

[b]Percentage of owners who repurchase a new car from the same corporation.

NOTE: NA means not available.

EXHIBIT 4   New-Car Buyer Profile, 1986

	Domestic Cars	Imported Cars	All Cars
Purchasing Characteristics			
Replaced previous car	85.0%	76.5%	82.5%
Plan to keep new car:			
0–1 years	3.9%	2.2%	3.4%
2–3 years	28.1	20.1	25.8
4–5 years	41.3	39.3	40.7
6–9 years	14.3	17.0	15.1
10+ years	12.4%	21.4%	15.0%
Median time	5.2 yrs.	5.5 yrs.	5.4 yrs.
Average price of car	$12,459	$12,978	$12,608
Demographic Characteristics			
Gender: Male	59.0%	57.2%	58.5%
Female	41.0%	42.8%	41.5%
Age:			
Under: 24	9.8%	14.0%	11.0%
25–34	21.0	38.1	25.9
35–44	19.1	22.2	20.0
45–54	15.9	11.1	14.5
55–64	16.9	9.1	14.7
65 and over	17.3%	5.5%	13.9%
Median age	45.7 yrs.	34.2 yrs.	43.0 yrs.
Median family income	$33,500	$37,000	$34,000

Vehicle Ownership by Household Income

Number of Vehicles	Under $10,000	$10,000–$19,999	$20,000–$29,999	$30,000–$39,999	$40,000 and over	All Households
0	39.5%	8.8%	2.3%	1.5%	1.1%	13.5%
1	42.8	46.2	30.4	17.7	12.2	33.7
2	13.6	31.6	44.8	49.7	43.8	33.6
3	3.1	10.2	15.2	20.5	25.5	12.8
4 or more	1.0	3.2	7.3	10.6	17.4	6.4
Total	100.0%	100.0%	100.0%	100.0%	100.0%	100.0%

EXHIBIT 4 *(concluded)*

	1981	1985
Psychographic Categories		
Driving enthusiast	10%	15%
Loves cars	15	18
Conspicuous consumer	12	12
Socially aware	13	7
Value conscious	19	18
Economy-minded	16	10
"American First"	15	20
Total	100%	100%

NOTE: The psychographic categories and the attitudes of the people they comprise are as follows:

Driving enthusiast: Enjoys cars, especially the driving experience. Thinks imports have good quality and would not go out of his or her way to "Buy American." Has the strongest import orientation, particularly toward European cars, of any psychographic group.

Loves cars: Regards his or her car as a possession to take pride in, rather than as a driving experience. Considers car's styling extremely important. Tends to be outgoing.

Conspicuous consumer: Engages in frequent trade-ins and brand switching. Likes to be the first to try new things and have all the latest options. Tends to like big, roomy, comfortable cars.

Socially aware: Considers social issues important, tends to be politically liberal. Desires fuel-efficient cars and has no empathy for big Detroit cars. Favors inexpensive cars and believes imports are good.

Value conscious: Tends not to be involved emotionally with cars or interested in them functionally. Appreciates a good value and favors Japanese cars.

Economy-minded: Is interested in inexpensive and economical transportation. Tends to have conservative lifestyle.

"America First": Says he or she will keep buying big, roomy cars as long as Detroit keeps making them. "Buys American" whenever possible. Does not think Japanese and German cars have better quality than U.S. cars. Has great interest in comfort and little interest in sports cars.

EXHIBIT 5 **Buying Process, 1986**

	Subcompact	Compact	Intermediate	Full-Size	Luxury	Overall
Ownership cycle (years)	5.0	5.3	5.7	6.3	4.8	5.4
Median income ($000)	30	34	34	39	58	34
Median age (years)	32	42	60	61	59	43
Ford's loyalty rates	47	36	40	64	56	46
Major other brand(s): Bought by Ford Owners	Japanese (28%) Chrysler (13%)	GM (32%) Japanese (18%)	GM (43%) Chrysler (9%)	GM (30%) —	GM (30%) European (14%)	GM (25%) Japanese (15%)
Owners of Other Makes Switching to Ford (%)						
GM	19[a]	10	8	10	10	12
Chrysler	13	11	16	22	18	14
Japanese	10	9	7	18	5	9
European	7	11	4	27	2	9

[a]To be read: "Of GM owners buying a subcompact in 1986, 19% bought a Ford."

EXHIBIT 6   1987 New-Car Warranties as of January 21, 1987 (time in years/miles in thousands)

	Basic	Powertrain	Corrosion	Emissions Defect
		Type of Warranty		
Nonluxury Cars				
Ford[a]	1/12	3/U[b] ($100)[c]	3/U	5/50
GM	1/12	3/U ($100)	3/U	5/50
Chrysler	1/12	5/50[d] ($100)	5/50	5/50
AMC	1/12	3/36 ($100)	3/U	5/50
Toyota	1/12.5	3/36	5/U	5/50
Nissan	1/12.5	3/36	3/U	5/50
Hyundai	1/12	3/36	3/U	5/50
Honda	1/12	2/24	3/U	5/50
Mazda	1/U	2/24	3/U	5/50
Volkswagen	2/U	2/U	6/U	5/50
Luxury Cars				
Ford	1/12	5/50 ($100)	5/100	5/50
GM	1/12	5/50 ($100)	5/100	5/50
Chrysler	1/12	5/50[e] ($100)	5/50	5/50
Mercedes	4/50	4/50	4/50	5/50
BMW	3/36	3/36	6/U	5/50
Volvo	3/U	3/U	8/U	5/50

[a]Of the 2.081 million Ford cars sold in the United States in 1986, 1.903 million (91%) were nonluxury cars.

[b]U signifies unlimited.

[c]$100 deductible charge for each repair visit.

[d]Limited to first retail owner; subsequent owners received 2/24.

[e]Limited to first retail owner. Second owner could obtain coverage for $25; otherwise, coverage reverted to 2/24.

EXHIBIT 7   Estimated Claims Costs of Warranties

Warranty Terms (years/miles)	Basic[a]		Powertrain[b]		Corrosion[b]		Emissions Effect	
	N[c]	L[d]	N	L	N	L	N	L
1/12,000	$157	$229						
2/24,000	325	445						
3/36,000	407	564						
3/Unlimited	435	609	$33		$1	$1		
4/50,000	467	653	49		2	2		
5/50,000	508	716	51	$62	2	3[e]	$93	$93
6/60,000	598	829	66	96	2	4	107	117
6/100,000	650	890	77	117	3	5	118	129
6/Unlimited	661	905	79	120	3	5	120	142
7/70,000	695	940	86	135	4	6	130	157
7/Unlimited	$760	$1,018	$100	$160	$5	$7	$145	$183

[a]The figures under basic correspond to all warranty costs (except emissions effect). For example, for nonluxury cars, $157 is the cost of the warranty for basic, powertrain, and corrosion for one year.

[b]The figures under powertrain and corrosion correspond to the warranty costs associated with them after the 1 year/12,000 miles basic coverage expires.

[c]N signifies nonluxury.

[d]L signifies luxury.

[e]Corresponds to 5 years/100,000 miles.

NOTE: Figures in boxes are values as of January 23, 1987.

EXHIBIT 8   Types of Extended Service Plans (ESPs), 1987

Features	ESP	ESP PLUS	ESP TOTAL	ESP CARE
Number of major components covered	81	113	All[a]	113
High-tech coverage	No	Yes	Yes	Yes
Scheduled maintenance	No	No	No	Yes
Wear-item coverage	No	No	No	Yes
Protection while traveling	Yes	Yes	Yes	Yes
Deductible per repair visit	$50	$25	$25	None
Prior approval	No	No	No	No
Transportation reimbursement	No	$20/day[b]	$20/day[b]	$20/day[c]
Towing reimbursement	No	$45 max.	$45 max.	$45 max.

[a]With a few exceptions.
[b]Maximum of 5 days.
[c]Maximum of 10 days.

EXHIBIT 9   Extended Service Plans (ESPs): Sales and Profits ($ millions)

	1984	1985	1986
Gross sales	$140.2	$195.0	$265.4
Lifetime profit before taxes	47.8	82.0	117.5
Added parts profits	$ 1.6	$ 2.5	$ 3.6
Contract Volume (000s)			
New:			
Ford	417	540	669
Competitors	5	7	12
Used:			
Ford	120	160	210
Competitors	63	83	110
Others	209	239	214
Total	814	1,029	1,215

THE BLACK & DECKER CORPORATION
HOUSEHOLD PRODUCTS GROUP: BRAND TRANSITION

In April 1984, Black & Decker Corporation (B&D) acquired the Housewares Division of General Electric Company (GE), combining the GE small-appliance product line with its own household product line to form the Household Products Group. The terms of the acquisition set the stage for a unique marketing challenge. B&D was permitted to manufacture and market appliances carrying the GE name, but only until April 1987. During the intervening three years, B&D would have to replace the GE name on all the acquired models with its own brand name.

Immediately after the acquisition, Kenneth Homa, B&D's vice president of marketing, was assigned responsibility for the brand transition. Homa had to design a marketing program to transfer the B&D name to the GE small-appliance lines without losing market share. Specifically, he had to determine the timing for the transition of the various GE product lines and the roles that advertising and promotion should play in the transition. Homa had been asked to have the proposal for the brand transition completed by June 1—only a week away. Before he began to formulate the proposal, Homa reviewed the acquisition and the challenges it presented.

The Acquisition

With 1983 sales of $1,167 million, B&D was the leading worldwide manufacturer of professional and consumer hand-held power tools. Over 100 products were produced in 21 factories around the world. By the late 1970s, B&D was confronting two important problems—a slower growth rate for the power tool market worldwide together with increasing foreign competition. At the same time, management realized that the American housewares market presented a significant opportunity. Capitalizing on its expertise in small-motor production[1] and cordless appliance technology, B&D introduced the Dustbuster® in 1979, a rechargeable hand-held vacuum cleaner. The Dustbuster Vac "moved B&D from the garage into the house"; 60 percent of Dustbuster purchases were made by women. The

Dustbuster's success prompted the launch of two other rechargeable products, the Spotliter™ rechargeable flashlight and the Scrub Brusher™ cordless scrubber. In 1983, these three products generated revenues of over $100 million, almost one third of B&D's U.S. consumer product sales. Pretax profit margins on these products were estimated at a healthy 10 percent. Sales of the three products were expected to increase by 30 percent annually between 1983 and 1985.

Consumer demand for these three innovative products led B&D executives to conclude that further penetration of the housewares market could generate substantial sales and profits for the company. They resolved to develop a family of products that could address consumer needs "everywhere in the house, not just in the basement or garage." However, a significant impediment to growth was B&D's limited access to housewares buyers in the major retail chains. B&D's three housewares products were sold along with B&D's power tools through hardware distributors to hardware buyers and were typically stocked in the hardware sections of retail stores. B&D sought to gain access to housewares buyers through the acquisition of a competitor, the GE Housewares Division.

With 1983 sales of $500 million (GE's total sales in 1983 were $26.79 billion), GE's Housewares Division was the largest competitor in the U.S. electric housewares or small-appliance market. (GE sales of small appliances outside the United States were limited. By contrast, 40 percent of B&D's total sales were made in Europe.) GE sold almost 150 models of products in 14 categories covering food preparation, ovening, garment care, personal care, and home security. (The categories were food processors, portable mixers, electric knives, can openers, drip coffee makers, toaster ovens, toasters, electric skillets, grills and griddles, irons, hair dryers, curling brushes/irons, scales, and security alarms.) In all the appliance categories in which it competed—except food processors, hair care products, and toasters—GE ranked first or second in market share. GE's success largely resulted from continuing attention to product innovation. For example, the GE product line included the recently introduced Spacemaker™ series of premium-priced under-the-cabinet kitchen appliances. The division's 150-person sales force called on housewares buyers in all channels of distribution.

Discussions between GE and B&D culminated in an agreement, announced in February 1984, whereby B&D would acquire the GE Housewares Division for $300 million, comprising $110 million in cash, a $32 million three-year note, and 6 percent of B&D stock. In return, B&D

This case was prepared by Research Assistant Cynthia Bates under the direction of Professor John A. Quelch. Professor Minette E. Drumwright prepared this version of the case.
Harvard Business School case 9-588-015 (Rev. 1/90).

[1]In 1983, B&D produced 20 million small motors, four times as many as its closest competitor.

acquired seven plants in the United States, Mexico, Brazil, and Singapore; five distribution centers; 16 service centers; and the Housewares Division's sales and management team. GE retained rights to the accounts receivable at the time of the transfer. Finally, B&D negotiated the right to continue to use the GE name on appliances in the Housewares Division product line for three years from the signing of the acquisition papers in April 1984. However, B&D could not use the GE name on any new appliances introduced after the acquisition. At a stroke, the acquisition transformed B&D from a specialist housewares manufacturer into the dominant full-line player in the housewares market.

The Housewares Market

Product Lines and Pricing.   After acquiring the GE division, B&D participated in five more broad housewares categories with aggregate industry sales of $1.4 billion divided as follows:

Food preparation	$275 million
Beverage makers	$325 million
Ovening	$250 million
Garment care	$200 million
Personal care	$350 million

The housewares market was mature and fragmented. Industry growth depended primarily on the rate of household formation and the pace of new product development. About one tenth of all small appliances in use were replaced each year. The timing of replacement purchases could be accelerated if manufacturers could persuade consumers to trade up to more highly featured, higher-priced, higher-margin models of a particular appliance.

The new B&D offered one of the broadest lines of any manufacturer, competing in 17 product groups. Market performance data for the principal product lines are summarized in Exhibit 1. In all these groups, B&D marketed multiple models that covered almost all price points and product feature configurations. For example, the B&D line included 18 different irons, with suggested retail prices from $14.76 to $25.89. The range included promotional, step-up, and premium models. Proctor-Silex, B&D's closest competitor in this category, offered 12 models.

B&D's models were priced competitively within each price/feature segment but, overall, B&D's share tended to be stronger in the medium and upper, rather than the lower, price ranges. In the fall of 1984, the average retail price of a B&D small appliance was 16 percent higher than the average retail price of its competitors' appliances. The B&D retail price premium varied across product categories as follows:

Food preparation	8%	Cleaning (Dustbuster,	
Ovening	26%	Scrub Brusher)	10%
Garment care	5%	Lighting (Spotliter)	6%
Personal care	16%	Smoke alarms	9%

Some B&D executives were concerned that the price premium in certain categories left B&D vulnerable to lower-priced competition. They advocated price decreases on some models for 1985. Other executives, noting that B&D/GE housewares prices had increased on average by only 10 percent between 1980 and 1984, believed that price increases were necessary to maintain margins. (The contribution margin on B&D small appliances, after variable costs, averaged 40 percent. The percentage margin was higher on premium models, such as the Spacemaker products.) However, all agreed that, despite B&D's share leadership position, competitive brands did not appear to set their prices in relation to B&D's prices.

B&D's price premium in the food preparation category was largely due to the premium-priced Spacemaker line of under-the-cabinet kitchen appliances. Launched in 1982 with a can opener, the Spacemaker line was expanded in 1983 to include a toaster oven, drip coffee maker, mixer, and electric knife. The Spacemaker line attracted some first-time purchasers into these five categories but, more important, persuaded current owners to trade up. Although the Spacemaker line at first reversed GE's share erosion in these categories, lower-priced imitations soon appeared. GE's standard countertop version of the Spacemaker appliances lost share as GE's competitors slashed prices to maintain their sales volumes in countertop models. Nevertheless, Spacemaker models were expected to account for about 40 percent of B&D's 1984 unit sales in the five product categories in which they competed.

Competition.   B&D's principal competitors in the housewares market were Sunbeam (a subsidiary of Allegheny International), Proctor-Silex (Wesray), Hamilton Beach (Scovill), and Norelco (Philips). Few offered as broad a line as B&D, but all four competed with B&D in at least six categories. In addition, B&D had to contend with specialist competitors in each product category. For example, Cuisinart was the market share leader in food processors as was Mr. Coffee in drip coffee makers. European manufacturers, such as Krups, were increasingly penetrating and helping to expand the premium price segment in some categories. Their higher-margin products were welcomed by department stores that sought to continue to compete with mass merchandisers in housewares. Japanese manufacturers were not a factor in the U.S. small-appliance market except for dual-voltage travel irons.

Following the acquisition announcement, B&D's housewares competitors saw the imminent demise of the strongest brand name in the housewares market (i.e., GE) as an opportunity to increase their market shares. Hence, prices on some existing models were reduced; price increases announced for 1985 were minimal, and promotional and merchandising allowances escalated. The timing of new product introductions accelerated and, in some instances, manufacturers decided to enter new product categories. Norelco and West Bend, for example, both announced that they would launch a line of irons.

Sunbeam was especially aggressive and heavily advertised two new products in the fall of 1984: the Monitor automatic shut-off iron and the Oskar compact food processor. Both were introduced at premium, rather than penetration, price levels. In addition, Sunbeam announced a $43 million marketing budget for 1985, including $25 million for national advertising, $10 million for cooperative advertising, and $8 million for sales promotion. The 1985 budget was more than Sunbeam had spent in the previous five years combined. Some analysts doubted that Sunbeam would follow through with this level of spending, however.

Besides GE's long-standing competitors, B&D also had to contend with imitators of its cordless vacuums and lights. Believing that the newly acquired product lines would divert B&D's management attention and resources, these imitators redoubled their efforts to capture more market share.

Distribution.   Small electric appliances were distributed through various channels. Table A shows the percentages of industry dollar sales accounted for by each of seven channels.

Mass merchandisers, such as Montgomery Ward, and discount stores, such as Kmart, had gained share in recent years, mainly at the expense of department stores. Catalog showrooms, such as Service Merchandise, carried the broadest line of small appliances, whereas other channels tended to cherrypick the faster-moving items. GE had built a disproportionately strong share position with volume retailers, notably catalog showrooms and mass merchandisers. B&D was traditionally strong in hardware stores. In the fall of 1984, B&D accounts carried, on average, 30 B&D stockkeeping units (SKUs). (An SKU is an individual model or item in the product line.)

TABLE A   Breakdown of Industry Dollar Sales by Channel (percent)

Catalog showrooms	15%
Mass merchandisers	28
Department stores	9
Hardware stores	5
Discount stores	8
Other[a]	29
Total	100%

[a] Includes sales through stamp and incentive programs, premiums, and military sales.

Most retailers did not view small appliances as especially profitable. Retail margins averaged 15 to 20 percent, though promotional merchandise was typically sold near cost. Hence, the space allocated to housewares by most chains remained stable, despite an increasing proliferation of new products. As a result, manufacturers were under more pressure than ever to secure shelf space through merchandising and promotion incentives.

Housewares and hardware buyers at B&D's major accounts determined twice a year which models they would specify as "basics." These selected models were carried in distribution for the following six months, usually in all the stores of a chain. Other models not specified as basics might occasionally be stocked but only in response to temporary promotion offers.

Basics were typically specified in January and May. Retail sales of small appliances peaked before Mother's Day and Christmas. Twenty-one percent of retail sales occurred in the first calendar quarter, 21 percent in the second, 17 percent in the third, and 41 percent in the fourth. Manufacturers and retailers scheduled their advertising and promotion efforts accordingly.

Consumer Behavior.   Consumers shopping for small appliances often were characterized as having low information needs, low perceived interbrand differentiation, and high price sensitivity. A 1984 B&D survey drew the following conclusions:

- Two out of three consumers bought their last housewares appliance on sale and/or with a rebate. The highest percentages bought on sale were the countertop drip coffee makers, mixers, and can openers.
- Two out of three consumers compared the prices of different brands and checked to see which brands were on sale.
- Fewer than one out of three consumers would wait until a specific brand went on sale.
- Almost three out of four consumers were willing to switch from their current brands when they purchased replacements. However, fewer than one out of four consumers were indifferent to brand names.

A follow-up study of buying behavior for irons found that most consumers, when they needed a replacement, would not wait for a sale but would check to see if a store was having a sale. Fifty percent bought a replacement within seven days. Only 10 percent of the irons were bought as gifts. Forty-two percent of the purchasers had a specific brand in mind when they set off for the store, and 85 percent ended up buying that brand. Thirty-eight percent were attracted to a particular store by its advertisement, and most bought at the first store in which they shopped. Half of all purchasers bought their irons on sale or with a rebate, or both.

Planning the Brand Transition

Consumer Research. To aid transition planning, B&D surveyed 600 men and women 18 to 49 years old in four geographically representative cities during July 1984. The survey first probed consumers' awareness of 10 housewares manufacturers, their ownership of small appliances by each manufacturer, and the degree to which their overall image ratings of each manufacturer were favorable or unfavorable. These results are summarized in Exhibit 2.

Next, respondents were asked to rate each manufacturer on various attributes using a 100-point scale. Averaging all responses, the researchers identified B&D's strengths and weaknesses compared with its main housewares competitors (GE excluded) and then with GE (see Table B).

The survey asked respondents whether they currently perceived B&D favorably or unfavorably as a manufacturer of each of 16 products. The percentages answering "very favorably" on a four-point scale were as follows:

Smoke alarms	62%	Irons	18%
Flashlights	60	Portable mixers	17
Vacuums	48	Toasters	17
Grills/griddles	29	Food processors	16
Electric knives	25	Coffee makers	13
Can openers	24	Skillets	12
Scales	22	Curling irons	11
Toaster ovens	21	Hair dryers	9

Qualitative research indicated that consumers considered B&D a suitable manufacturer of these products, but that they were largely unaware that B&D already made them.

Product Plans. Homa knew that B&D executives disagreed concerning both the timing and the manner in which the B&D name should be transferred to the GE small-appliance line. In talking with other executives, he had identified five points of view.

One group of executives argued that the name change should be executed across the entire product line as soon as possible to demonstrate B&D's commitment to the trade. At the other extreme, a second group, skeptical about the likely pulling power of the B&D brand in housewares, proposed that B&D delay the name transfer until the end of the three-year period.

A third group of executives supported a gradual transition whereby all the items in one or two product categories would be reintroduced under the B&D name in successive six-month periods. A fourth group wanted to execute the name change first on the premium quality items in several product categories to be followed later by the remaining lower-priced items in each product line. A fifth group argued that the transition schedule should be linked to a new product development program. Through such a program, the name change would be implemented in a product category only after the product line and packaging had been redesigned and/or when B&D could offer a new product with enhanced features.

As he planned the transition program, Homa also had to consider proposals for new or revised products that B&D

TABLE B B&D's Strengths and Weaknesses

	B&D Advantage versus Closest Competitor[a]	B&D (Dis)Advantage versus GE
B&D Strengths		
Has high-quality workmanship	+24	+5
Makes durable products	+23	+4
Makes reliable products	+20	+1
Leader in making innovative products	+18	(7)
B&D Vulnerabilities		
Makes products that can be easily serviced	+7	(17)
Makes products most people would consider buying	+7	(12)
Makes attractive, good-looking products	+6	(8)
Makes products that are generally priced lower	+5	(9)
Makes products that are easily found	+2	(9)

[a] Other than GE.

product managers had submitted. The proposals included the following:

- The Spacemaker line of under-the-cabinet appliances, which had been acquired from GE, could be redesigned by B&D to look sturdier and more compact. The edges could be rounded for additional safety.
- B&D could develop Black Tie™, a line of "men's grooming tools," which would be priced at a 15 percent premium over the hair care line acquired from GE.
- Plans had been developed for the Stowaway line of dual-voltage travel appliances. The line would include a folding iron, hair dryer, and curling irons.
- The Handymixer cordless beater, the first extension of B&D's cordless technology into the kitchen, had been proposed.
- An automatic shut-off iron had been designed by B&D. Unlike the Sunbeam model, the B&D iron would beep to let the consumer know that it had been left on.

Communications. An effective communications plan would be integral to the brand transition. Historically, B&D and GE had implemented communications programs with fundamental differences. Specifically, GE had emphasized push programs (e.g., volume rebates, purchase allowances), which were aimed at the trade, while B&D had emphasized pull programs (e.g., advertising, consumer rebates), which targeted consumers. These differences are reflected in Exhibits 3 and 4, which summarize the advertising and promotion expenditures for GE and B&D before the acquisition. Homa's tentative recommendations for 1985 communications expenditures also are included in Exhibits 3 and 4.

Advertising. Increased advertising expenditures would be necessary to bolster consumer brand loyalties in the face of more aggressive competition. Homa estimated that media expenditures of $100 million would be needed for the brand transition.

The issue of how to handle the brand transition in advertising was much debated. Some executives believed that explicit references to GE in B&D's advertising were necessary to maintain market share during the transition, especially in categories where GE's brand name equity was strong. These executives wanted a transition statement, such as "designed by GE, built by B&D," to be included in advertising. They also wanted hang tags on B&D products at the point of sale to indicate that the products had formerly been made by GE. Critics of this dual-branding approach, which included B&D's advertising agency, argued

that it would confuse consumers and simply sustain the GE franchise. Exhibits 5 and 6 present television advertisements proposed by B&D's advertising agency.

Promotional Programs. Homa had to determine whether or not to maintain GE's more generous support of promotional programs. Some trade accounts already had expressed concern about potential cutbacks that B&D might implement. Competitive housewares manufacturers did all they could to cultivate this concern in an effort to secure additional basics listings and shelf space for their own products.

At the time of the acquisition, GE's promotional programs for the trade included purchase allowances, volume rebates, dating discounts, and cooperative advertising. Promotional programs for consumers focused on consumer rebates.

Purchase allowances. During the 1970s, GE initiated purchase allowance (PAs) on selected models against orders paid for during the first two months after Christmas and Mother's Day, the peak retail selling periods. Over time, PAs came to be offered on orders placed beyond these two-month periods. By 1983, 90 percent of shipments included an off-invoice PA.

Volume rebates. GE operated a volume rebate program that offered trade accounts a year-end refund of up to 4.5 percent of their net purchases during the year. Accounts qualified for various percentage rebates according to the degree to which their purchases increased over those of the previous year. There were two other features of the program. First, the rebates were computed on an account's total purchases rather than separately for each shipping point. Second, the program attempted to maintain the total number of SKUs by requiring a dealer to have incremental sales in four of six defined product categories to earn the minimum rebate.

Dating discounts. Dating allowed customers to pay for goods after they were shipped and received. Dating encouraged trade accounts to place early orders for goods that they did not have to pay for immediately. The seasonality of retail sales and the desire of trade accounts to avoid holding high bulk-to-value small appliances in their own warehouses made dating programs a necessity in the small-appliance industry. Production planning and scheduling could become more efficient if a trade account placed early orders at the same time that it decided which SKUs to specify for its basics lineup.

GE Housewares Division's standard terms required full payment by the tenth of the month following an order, plus 45 days. The dating program permitted an account to place an order in May and June for shipment before September 1 and payment by December 10. A second dating program required payment by May 10 on orders placed in December and January. A schedule of early-payment allowances rewarded accounts for payment of invoices before the dating program due date. GE's purchase allowance and dating programs together permitted accounts to pay less and pay later.

Cooperative advertising. GE's Housewares Division had long offered trade accounts a cooperative advertising program. Accounts accrued 3 percent of their net purchases in a rolling 12-month cooperative advertising fund. (Allowance accrued more than 12 months previously that had not been spent were forfeited.) Accounts could draw on these accruals to subsidize the cost of retail advertising that featured GE products. GE paid the full cost of qualifying advertising but sometimes only partially charged accounts' accrual funds if they featured particularly profitable premium-priced products, such as items in the Spacemaker line, if they ran advertisements featuring multiple GE items, or if they timed their advertising to coincide with flights of GE national advertising.

Consumer rebates. Initiated in the 1970s to help sell slower-moving models, consumer rebates had become endemic to the housewares category by the early 1980s. By 1983, almost all list price increases were cushioned with rebates, and three quarters of all feature advertisements for GE housewares included references to manufacturer rebate offers. The average value of housewares manufacturers' consumer rebates escalated as each tried to outdo the other. In an effort to lead the industry toward more realistic list pricing, GE in 1983 curtailed rebates on irons and toaster ovens, two categories in which it was the market share leader. Far from following GE's lead, competitors increased their rebate offers. As a result, GE's share declined six points in both categories within six months.

Conclusion

Homa had two main concerns. How could the B&D brand name be transferred most effectively to the GE small-appliance line? What kind of communications program would facilitate the transfer?

EXHIBIT 1   Market Performance Summary for Selected Product Lines

Product	Year	GE/B&D Unit Share (percent)	Feature Ad Share (percent)	Average Retail Price ($)	GE/B&D Share Rank in 1984	Major Competitors (Share and Rank)		
Food processors	1983	16%	9%	$55.00	3	Cuisinart	25%	(1)
	1984	13	7	72.00		Hamilton Beach	21	(2)
	1985[a]	15	8	NA		Moulinex	11	(4)
						Sunbeam	7	(5)
Mixers	1983	31	22	16.00	2	Sunbeam	28	(1)
	1984	26	20	15.40		Hamilton Beach	21	(3)
	1985[a]	35	16	NA				
Can openers	1983	28	25	17.65	1	Rival	30	(2)
	1984	34	23	20.52		Sunbeam	8	(3)
	1985[a]	30	26	NA		Hamilton Beach	6	(4)
Toasters	1983	13	16	16.63	3	Toastmaster	32	(1)
	1984	12	10	21.01		Proctor-Silex	30	(2)
	1985[a]	11	10	NA				
Toaster ovens	1983	56	49	45.51	1	Toastmaster	25	(2)
	1984	52	39	47.85		Proctor-Silex	8	(3)
	1985[a]	50	40	NA		Norelco	4	(4)
Drip coffee makers	1983	17	13	34.48	2	Mr. Coffee	19	(1)
	1984	18	15	37.63		Norelco	17	(3)
	1985[a]	17	16	NA		Hamilton Beach	9	(4)
						Proctor-Silex	8	(5)
Electric knives	1983	39	NA	13.54	2	Hamilton Beach	47	(1)
	1984	37	NA	17.28		Moulinex	8	(3)
	1985[a]	39	NA	17.65				
Irons	1983	52	39	20.44	1	Proctor-Silex	18	(2)
	1984	46	29	21.83		Sunbeam	13	(3)
	1985[a]	45	29	NA		Hamilton Beach	11	(4)
Hair care	1983	8	8	17.74	4	Conair	22	(1)
	1984	6	4	15.37		Clairol	12	(2)
	1985[a]	5	3	NA		Sassoon	8	(3)
Cordless vacuums	1983	NA	NA	NA		Douglas	8	(2)
	1984	NA	38	NA	1	Sears	8	(2)
	1985[a]	NA	38	25.70		Norelco	7	(4)
Lighting products	1983	65	NA	NA	1	First Alert	25	(2)
	1984	57	44	NA		Sunspot	5	(3)
	1985[a]	38	36	21.10		Norelco	4	(4)

[a] Figures for 1985 are estimated.

NOTE: NA means not available.

EXHIBIT 2   Consumer Research on Major Housewares Manufacturers

	Aided Corporate Awareness (percent)	Product Ownership (percent)	Corporate Image Ranking	
			Men	Women
General Electric	100%	91%	2	1
Black & Decker	99	67	1	2
Mr. Coffee	99	51	4	5
Conair	79	43	9	8
Hamilton Beach	93	43	5	6
Norelco	98	54	3	4
Proctor-Silex	80	28	8	7
Rival	56	19	10	10
Sunbeam	96	48	6	3
Toastmaster	92	41	7	9

(handwritten annotation next to Corporate Image Ranking column: "1 – house", "2 – garage")

EXHIBIT 3   Advertising and Merchandising Expenditures for GE Housewares (in millions of dollars and percentage of net sales billed)

	1983		1984		1985[a]	
	Dollars	Percent of Sales	Dollars	Percent of Sales	Dollars	Percent of Sales
Push Programs						
Purchase allowances	$17.5	3.5%	$22.5	4.5%	—	—
Volume rebates	14.0	2.8	14.5	2.9	$ 12.5	2.5%
Cash discounts	—	—	—	—	—	—
Subtotal	31.5	6.3	37.0	7.4	12.5	2.5
Pull Programs						
National advertising	8.5	1.7	16.5	3.3	34.0	6.8
Co-op advertising	26.0	5.2	25.5	5.1	32.0	6.4
Consumer rebates	13.0	2.6	9.5	1.9	15.0	3.0
Consumer promotions	1.5	0.3	1.0	0.2	0.5	0.1
Sales promotion materials	3.0	0.6	1.5	0.3	3.5	0.7
Press relations	1.0	0.2	1.0	0.2	1.0	0.2
Exhibits	1.0	0.2	1.0	0.2	1.0	0.2
Functional support expenses	1.5	0.3	1.5	0.3	2.0	0.4
Corporate promotion assessment	—	—	—	—	—	—
In-store merchandising	—	—	—	—	3.5	0.7
Subtotal	55.5	11.1	57.5	11.5	92.5	18.5
Total merchandising expenditures	$87.0	17.4%	$94.5	18.9%	$105.0	21.0%

[a] Estimated.

NOTE: 1984 and 1985 figures continue to separate the former GE housewares line from the former B&D household products line for ease of comparison. Total 1985 B&D Household Products Group expenditures can be calculated by summing the last columns in Exhibits 3 and 4.

EXHIBIT 4   **Advertising and Merchandising Expenditures for Black & Decker Household Products (in millions of dollars and percentage of net sales billed)**

	1983		1984		1985[a]	
	Dollars	*Percent of Sales*	*Dollars*	*Percent of Sales*	*Dollars*	*Percent of Sales*
Push Programs						
Flexible funds (off-invoice)	—	—	—	—	—	—
Retail incentive plan	—	—	—	—	$ 1.0	0.6%
Cash discounts	$ 0.9	0.9%	$ 1.2	0.9%	1.5	0.9
Subtotal	0.9	0.9	1.2	0.9	2.5	1.5
Pull Programs						
National advertising	8.9	8.9	12.0	9.2	18.6	11.0
Co-op advertising	2.0	2.0	3.1	2.4	7.3	4.3
Consumer rebates	—	—	2.2	1.7	11.7	6.9
Consumer promotions	—	—	—	—	—	—
Sales promotion materials	0.5	0.5	1.6	1.2	1.4	0.8
Press relations	—	—	—	—	—	—
Exhibits	—	—	0.1	0.1	0.3	0.2
Functional support expenses	—	—	0.1	0.1	0.3	0.2
Corporate promotion assessment	—	—	1.0	0.8	2.0	1.2
In-store merchandising	—	—	—	—	—	—
Subtotal	11.4	11.4	20.1	15.5	41.6	24.6
Total merchandising expenditures	$12.3	12.3%	$21.3	16.4%	$44.1	26.1%

[a] Estimated.

NOTE: B&D household products: Dustbuster Vac, Spotliter, and Scrub Brusher.

EXHIBIT 5

Proposed 1985 Spacemaker Advertisement

(SFX: TRAFFIC)
ANNCR: (VO) One of the most densely populated places on earth

is your kitchen counter. So crowded, the only place to go is up.

Presenting Black & Decker Spacemaker Appliances.

Coffeemaker,

mixer,

toaster oven,

electric knife

and can opener. The only completely coordinated line of under-the-cabinet appliances.

(SFX: BIRDS CHIRPING)
They return your counter

to a more natural state.

The Spacemaker line

from Black & Decker. Ideas at work.

EXHIBIT 6

Proposed 1985 Spotliter Advertisement

(SFX: Electronic High Tension) ANNCR: (VO) It splits the dark with a powerful beam.

Spotliter rechargeable light from Black & Decker.

A light built so strong

it can survive a drop of 6 feet.

Spotliter stores all the power you need in its own recharging base.

So on a moment's notice

it gives you light.

Light for your safety. . .and peace of mind.

It's one utility light that does more than just shine.

Spotliter.

One of the many lights

in the lighting series. From Black & Decker. Ideas at work.

THE PROCTER & GAMBLE COMPANY: LENOR REFILL PACKAGE

In July 1987, Kathy Stadler, assistant brand manager for Lenor, Procter & Gamble GmbH's (P&G Germany) profitable fabric softener brand, was preparing for an upper-level management meeting to discuss a proposal for the national launch of a Lenor refill package. The refill package represented an innovative solution to West Germany's growing environmental concerns by promising to reduce by 85 percent the packaging materials used in Lenor's standard plastic container. Management hoped that this line extension would help stem Lenor's eroding sales volume and market share.

Stadler recalled a memo written two years earlier by Rolf Kunisch, the general manager for P&G Germany, in which he advocated "moving the company's attitudes from defensive thinking in environmental terms toward proactive and successful approaches." While Stadler felt that the Lenor refill package met this mandate, she was uncertain about the consumer response. Stadler knew that the refill package would not address many German consumers' concerns that fabric softeners were "superfluous" products. A biodegradable version of Lenor still needed three years of development. The refill package seemed to offer an interim response to consumers. Would the public hail it as an attempt to protect the environment? Or would they view it as an effort to avoid addressing the public's underlying concern with Lenor's product formula?

Stadler's brand manager, Leonard Phillippe, felt that an aggressive promotion of an existing concentrated formula of Lenor, which used less packaging materials than the more popular, fully diluted version, would be less risky than the refill package introduction. Stadler, however, believed that this strategy would not stem Lenor's eroding sales volume. Nevertheless, she knew that both options would be hotly debated at the forthcoming meeting with Rolf Kunisch.

The Procter & Gamble Company

In 1987,[1] the Procter & Gamble Company (P&G), a leading consumer products company, had more than $13.7 bil-lion in assets, generated $17 billion in worldwide revenues, and delivered $617 million in pretax earnings. P&G sold products in 125 countries, marketing more than 100 brands of laundry, household cleaning, personal care, food, and beverage products. International operations, which included Europe, South America, and Asia, accounted for over 30 percent of P&G's 1987 sales and earnings. In 1987, international sales grew 38 percent, almost five times as much as U.S. domestic sales.

P&G had a long-standing reputation for superior products, marketing expertise, talented employees, conservative management, and high integrity in its business dealings. A strong corporate culture pervaded the firm. The 1987 annual report stated the company's philosophy as follows:

> We will provide products of superior quality and value that best fill the needs of the world's consumers. We will achieve that purpose through an organization and a working environment which attracts the finest people; fully develops and challenges our individual talents; encourages our free and spirited collaboration to drive the business ahead; and maintains the Company's historic principles of integrity and doing the right thing. Through the successful pursuit of our commitment, we expect our brands to achieve leadership share and profit positions and that, as a result, our business, our people, our shareholders, and the communities in which we live and work, will prosper.

To develop these superior products, P&G relied on continual product development. In 1987, more than 3.3 percent of its revenues were spent on research. In addition, P&G believed in extensive product and market testing. P&G frequently took two to three years to test a new product and its marketing strategy before a major launch.

Procter & Gamble GmbH. Procter & Gamble GmbH was established in 1963 following the acquisition of a local detergent manufacturer. By 1987, P&G Germany generated DM 1,037 million in revenues.[2] P&G Germany sold more than 30 brands, including Ariel, a top-selling detergent, and Lenor, West Germany's leading fabric softener. Seventy-seven percent of its revenues and 60 percent of its earnings came from the Laundry and Cleaning Division, which included detergents, cleaners, and fabric softener.

P&G Germany's 6,700-person subsidiary comprised four divisions: Laundry and Cleaning, Paper, Beverages, and Health and Beauty Care. Each division had sales, finance, manufacturing, and product development organizations. Every major P&G Germany product also had its own brand management team, which developed and imple-

---

This case was prepared by Julie L. Yao under the direction of Professors John A. Quelch and Minette E. Drumwright. Certain data and names have been disguised.
Copyright © 1991 by the President and Fellows of Harvard College.
Harvard Business School case 9-592-016 (Rev. 6/22/92).

[1]P&G operated on a July 1 to June 30 fiscal year basis; at the time of this case, P&G had just entered its 1988 fiscal year. Unless otherwise specified, all P&G company data are on a fiscal year basis.

---

[2]One U.S. dollar was equivalent to 1.9 deutschmarks (DM).

mented the brand's marketing strategy against sales and profit targets approved by top management. A brand team generally consisted of a brand manager, an assistant brand manager, and one or two brand assistants, who all worked closely with the division's other departments as well as with staff groups specializing in advertising services, management information systems, and personnel.

A 320-person sales force marketed P&G Germany products to the retail trade. Key account managers called on the headquarters of the large retail grocery chains year-round, while field salespeople serviced both independent stores as well as chain outlets.

P&G Germany manufactured most of its products locally. While some production was outsourced, P&G Germany generally preferred to manufacture its own products to ensure the highest level of quality control.

The Fabric Softener Industry

Fabric softener products first appeared during the 1950s to combat the perceived harsh effects of detergents; when added to the wash, fabric softener produced soft, scented, and static-free clothes. It was particularly popular in Europe where hard water washing conditions were common. In 1987, consumers could purchase fabric softener in one of three forms: a diluted liquid; a concentrated liquid, three times stronger than the dilute; and woven sheets that were used while machine drying. The regular user's average purchase cycle was two months. Dosage varied according to the type and volume of laundry, but an average washload required 100 milliliters of dilute or 35 ml of concentrate.

Fabric softener liquids combined 5 percent softening ingredients, called *cationic tensides*, with 95 percent water. Fabric softener concentrates included 15 percent softening ingredients. Fabric softeners were packaged in hard, high-density polyethylene (HDPE) plastic containers. Users added liquid fabric softener during a washing machine's wash cycle or poured it into a convenient special dispenser built into the machine before the start of the wash.

Like many other household chemical products, fabric softeners, with 2 percent inert nonbiodegradable ingredients, were considered by some environmentally conscious consumers to be unnecessary. An increasing number of consumers believed that a buildup of nonbiodegradable chemicals could affect their water supply. Many felt that the benefit delivered by fabric softener was superfluous.

Environmental Concern.   In the mid-1980s, public anxiety about environmental problems escalated in Europe. A 1986 survey of 11,800 Western European consumers revealed that 72 percent were "somewhat" or "very" concerned about ecological problems such as acid rain, toxic waste, landfill capacity, and the greenhouse effect. The media attributed these concerns to Europe's high population density and its centuries-old exploitation of natural resources.[3]

West German attitudes were consistently "greener" than those of neighboring countries. In 1987, an opinion poll entitled "Sorrows of the Nation" found that 53 percent of West Germans surveyed were concerned with the protection of the environment, up from 16 percent four years earlier. Concern for the environment ranked as their second most common concern, behind unemployment. Environmental issues also affected the German political arena, as evidenced by the rising popularity of the proenvironment Green Party.

A 1987 opinion poll showed that 47 percent of German households agreed that they used fewer environmentally problematic goods than previously, versus 21 percent who agreed with the same statement in 1985. Both consumer awareness of environmental issues and the percentage of consumers claiming a willingness to pay more for environmentally friendly packaging had increased. In practice, however, consumers traded off price against environmental safety; there was a limit to the price premium they were prepared to pay. In addition, many consumers indicated that they were not willing to give up product quality for the environment. Nevertheless, environmentally uncontroversial products, such as phosphate-free detergents, had become increasingly popular.

In 1984, a West German federal government agency publicly denounced allegedly environmentally harmful products, including P&G Germany's laundry booster, Top Job. A consumer boycott to force the removal of these products from the market caused Top Job's sales volume to drop by 50 percent in the following year. In 1986, the government passed the Waste Avoidance, Utilization, and Disposal Act, which gave authorities the power to restrict or even ban materials with problematic toxicity or waste volume.

The West German government also supported a nationwide eco-labeling initiative, called the Blue Angel program, to promote environmentally compatible products through labeling. By 1987, more than 2,000 products in 50 categories bore the Blue Angel seal; fabric softener products had never qualified. By 1987, the Blue Angel seal was recognized by 80 percent of West German consumers.[4] Industry experts believed that products "blessed" with the Blue Angel seal enjoyed increased sales of up to 10 percent.

Though public and media attention centered more on a product's contents and less on its packaging, the issue of

---

[3]A. Hussein, *Eco-labels: Product Management in a Greener Europe* (Environmental Data Services, Ltd. Finsbury Business Center), p. 53.

[4]Lori K. Carswell, *Environmental Labeling in the United States—Background Research, Issues, and Recommendations,* draft report, Applied Decision Analysis, 1989, p. 10.

solid waste reduction was rapidly capturing the German public's attention. Land was scarce; West Germany burned 34 percent of its trash, compared to only 3 percent in the United States. In some German communities, there was a social stigma associated with a household's use of larger trash bins. Some municipalities charged citizens for garbage collection based on volume. By 1985, West Germans recycled more than one third of their paper, glass, and aluminum waste; however, plastic recycling was limited. Focus group research indicated consumers would be receptive to products with reduced packaging.

Market Size and Trends. The average West German homemaker used eight different products, such as bleach and fabric softener, for washing and cleaning. The German fabric softener consumer enjoyed "fresh" clothes, which combined the characteristics of a soft touch, "clean" smell, and bright appearance. A 1986 P&G Germany market research study concluded that fabric softener usage and dosage were relatively uniform across all age groups, irrespective of brand. Fabric softener users, however, spent more effort on pretreating and prewashing their laundry than nonusers.

In 1987, West Germany was the largest fabric softener market in Europe, with retail sales totaling DM 346 million ($182 million), compared to almost $1 billion in the U.S. market, with a population four times West Germany's. Although the value of retail sales had increased due to price rises, market volume had fallen from a peak of 18,200 MSUs in 1983 to 16,700 MSUs in 1987.[5] Forecasters predicted further volume decreases of 1 percent to 3 percent per year.

Research had shown that this decline was attributed to a shrinking base of fabric softener users. Table A shows usage trends from periodic diary studies.[6]

Results from a 1986 telephone survey found that many consumers had ceased using fabric softener due to environmental concerns highlighted by the news media. Research revealed that West German consumers were more concerned about the environmental effects of using supplementary household products such as fabric softener than consumers in other West European countries. Exhibit 1 presents key results from this study.

---

[5]An MSU, or thousand statistical units, was a standardized P&G measure that permitted comparison of products on the basis of an equal number of uses. Consequently, a 1-liter bottle of 4:1 Lenor concentrate and a 4-liter bottle of Lenor dilute were equivalent on an MSU basis because both gave the consumer the same number of uses. Costs and unit volumes are presented per SU (abbreviation for statistical unit) for comparison purposes.

[6]Each participant was asked to keep a diary of his or her usage habits during a two-week time period, from which results were tabulated.

TABLE A   Fabric Softener Usage Trends
(percentage surveyed)

	1982	1984	1986
Fabric softener users	89%	84%	72%
Total wash loads softened[a]	72	67	57
Wash loads softened among users[b]	75	73	74

[a]Percentage of all wash loads recorded in diary study that had fabric softener added.

[b]Among fabric softener users, average percentage of wash loads per user that had fabric softener added.

Competition. In 1987, four competitors sold 78 percent of the volume in the West German fabric softener market.[7] P&G Germany's Lenor led the market with a 37 percent volume share, followed by Colgate-Palmolive's Softlan (20 percent), Unilever's Kuschelweich (Snuggle) (13 percent), and Henkel's Vernel (8 percent). Generic and private-label brands accounted for the remaining 22 percent of the market.

All four multinationals sold their fabric softener brands throughout Western Europe. Each competitor promoted similar product benefits: freshness, softness, ease of ironing, and elimination of static cling. Lenor's distinctive, 4-liter blue container appeared in the mid-1970s and quickly became the standard package size and shape imitated by competitors. By 1987, all brands were sold in both diluted and concentrated formulas, in 4-liter and 1-liter sizes, respectively. In addition, in 1987 Henkel and P&G introduced dryer sheets, which accounted for less than 1 percent of market volume. All brands were broadly distributed throughout the retail trade.

Vernel followed a low-budget advertising strategy. Softlan, on the other hand, was aggressively advertised through the media. Kuschelweich gained high consumer awareness through its "stuffed bear" advertising mascot. Lenor emphasized its "Aprilfrisch" scent. In newspaper and handbill copy, Lenor led in share of fabric softener features (42 percent for May/June 1987), followed by Softlan (21 percent), Kuschelweich (15 percent), and Vernel (5 percent).[8]

The materials cost for each brand varied due to different chemical formulations. Table B shows selected relative costs and pricing for the top four brands of diluted fabric softener in 1987.

---

[7]All market share figures were based on statistical unit (MSUs) volume.

[8]Feature share, calculated from a survey of 200 West German newspapers and 2,000 grocery handbills, represented the percentage of times a particular brand was featured in retail trade promotions for fabric softeners.

TABLE B   **1987 Indexed Costs and Prices for Leading German Fabric Softener Brands**

	P&G	*Colgate*	*Lever*	*Henkel*
Brand name	Lenor	Softlan	Kuschelweich	Vernel
Packaging	100	106	106	106
Chemicals	100	85	93	92
Media expenses	100	136	85	40
Total costs	100	105	94	82
Recommended retail price	100	87	88	85

NOTE: The index is based on a 4-liter package of dilute.

Consumers perceived little differentiation among fabric softener brands except on the basis of price and scent. Consequently, fabric softener brands were frequently involved in price and promotion wars to defend or capture market share, which depressed manufacturer and trade margins. For example, the average profit margin realized by retailers on Lenor declined from 12.7 percent in 1984 to 2.5 percent in 1986.

Henkel, a prominent German household products company with 1987 sales of DM 9.9 billion, rapidly imitated innovative product ideas and marketed them globally. Henkel also strongly emphasized environmental protection, spending nearly 25 percent of its DM 285 million research budget on this issue in 1987. Colgate-Palmolive (DM 10.6 billion in 1987 sales) and Unilever (DM 57 billion) devoted less than 2 percent of their revenues to R&D.

In early 1987, Henkel acquired Lesieur-Cotelle S.A., a French detergent manufacturer that produced Minidou, a fabric softener concentrate that, since the early 1980s, had been sold in 250-ml flat, plastic pouches. Minidou users emptied the pouch's contents into any 1-liter container and then diluted the concentrate with water. Some P&G executives suspected that Henkel might try either to extend the successful Minidou concept, which had captured 29 percent of the French market by 1987, to other markets or to license the use of the technology to Colgate-Palmolive, which was pursuing lower-cost packaging alternatives.

Distribution.   Fabric softener was sold through West Germany's highly concentrated retail market; five major chains together controlled more than 75 percent of total grocery sales (DM 127 billion in 1987). Manufacturers sold their products through several classes of trade: mass merchandisers (more than 53,800 sq. ft. in size), hypermarkets (16,100–53,800 sq. ft.), supermarkets (8,600–16,100 sq. ft.), convenience stores (under 8,600 sq. ft.), and discounters (various sizes). West German consumers shopped for fabric softener in all types of stores, although it was less likely than other grocery items to be purchased in convenience stores.

Fierce competition meant that grocery retailers achieved total after-tax profit margins of only 1 to 1.5 percent. Because they focused increasingly on the direct product profitability (DPP) of their stock per linear foot of shelf space, retailers were especially keen on high-margin, space-efficient products with rapid turnover. The emphasis placed on DPP resulted in a selective product assortment; only the large mass merchandisers and hypermarkets maintained a complete selection of brands and package sizes for any product category. Supermarkets kept a full range of brand names, but with limited size selection, whereas convenience stores and discounters sold only one or two brands. All classes of trade, except for convenience stores, also sold their own private-label brands in many high turnover categories.

Every August, manufacturer account representatives negotiated with each major retailer the following year's major target purchase levels, volume discounts, and new product listing agreements. Manufacturers needed a retailer's listing for each new product, even for product line extensions; individual retail stores could purchase products only from their chain headquarters' approved list. Although manufacturers could introduce new products throughout the year, listing agreements were easier to obtain during the August meetings. Approved products generally reached store shelves within two weeks of an order being placed. In addition to account representatives, each manufacturer also had field salespeople who serviced individual stores, both chain-owned and independents, by taking stock orders, suggesting shelf arrangements, and implementing local sales promotions.

To minimize handling and reshelving costs, many retail stores sought to display products in their original shipping cartons and stressed convenient packaging to the manufacturers. A set of product packaging guidelines, known as the "ten commandments," was developed by a retail trade association for manufacturers. These guidelines defined the dimensions, weight, and appearance of the shipping cartons that retailers preferred. Few products met all 10 guidelines.

Advertising and Promotion. In 1987, most television advertising reached German consumers via the two state-run national channels. Each September, manufacturers reapplied for time slots; the television stations then allocated specific commercial spots to each firm for the upcoming year. P&G Germany would then allocate the time slots it had been granted among its brands.

Regulations limited the consumer promotions that West German manufacturers could use. Coupons and refund offers were not permitted; the value of on-pack and in-pack premiums (gifts attached to or included in product packages) could not exceed DM 0.30 in value. Bonus packs, which gave consumers extra volume of product for the same price, were difficult to implement on liquid products such as Lenor. Price packs (products with a lower-than-normal recommended retail price preprinted on the package) were allowed but were rarely used due to trade opposition. Some manufacturers did run sweepstakes and contests though they were tightly regulated by government agencies.

Volume discounts and trade promotion allowances for each product were traditionally negotiated with individual retailers. P&G Germany instituted account-specific promotion plans based on total sales volume rather than the sales of each brand. This approach was considered more effective in building trade relationships because it gave retailers more flexibility in what they promoted.

Lenor Fabric Softener

Lenor, launched in West Germany in 1963, was the first nationally marketed brand of fabric softener. By 1987, Lenor had achieved 98 percent store penetration. More than half of Lenor's total volume was sold through mass merchandisers, as indicated in Exhibit 2. Sales revenue and unit volume in 1987 were DM 180 million and 6,200 MSUs, respectively.

At first, Lenor was sold as a specialty item in small, 500 ml containers, at a price nearly 10 times higher than the 1987 inflation-adjusted price for the same quantity. In 1965, P&G Germany broadened Lenor's appeal by lowering its price and developing a highly successful advertising campaign that remained in use for the following 18 years.

The 1-liter Lenor concentrate (Lenor CT) joined Lenor dilute on retail shelves in 1983. By 1987, 30 percent of Lenor's volume was sold in this 3:1 concentrated form. The package cap doubled as a measuring cup that the consumer could use to determine how much liquid to add, in undiluted form, to the wash. Brand management believed that some fabric softener users regarded the concentrate's performance as inferior to the dilute's, although laboratory tests demonstrated no difference in efficacy. These users questioned whether "so little could perform as well." One P&G executive explained, "Although the concentrate is less awkward to carry home from the store, many consumers are wedded to the 4-liter package." Advertising for Lenor concentrate stressed the number of wash loads that could be softened with the contents of the small, one-liter, package. Dryer sheets, introduced in the spring of 1987, sold to a limited market (0.4 percent of Lenor's 1987 sales volume) because 75 percent of West German households line-dried their laundry rather than using electric clothes dryers.

P&G Germany promoted Lenor heavily to the retail trade and consumers, spending 20 percent of the product's yearly manufacturer's sales on television and radio advertising, consumer promotions, trade promotions, and indirect brand support.[9] Table C indicates the percentage breakdowns of Lenor's advertising and promotion expenses for 1986 and 1987. Approximately 30 percent of the brand's total marketing budget was allocated to the concentrate.

In 1987, liquid Lenor was available in the package sizes and prices shown in Exhibit 3. Recommended retail prices

---

[9]Indirect brand support included development costs for advertisements and commercials, production expenses associated with store displays, and other expenses incurred for consumer and trade promotions.

TABLE C Percentage Breakdown of Advertising and Sales Budget

	Dilute 1986	*Dilute 1987*	*CT[a] 1986*	*CT[a] 1987*
Media	20%	23%	20%	21%
Consumer promotion	4	1	1	1
Trade promotion	74	74	77	75
Indirect brand support	2	2	2	2
Total	100%	100%	100%	100%

[a]CT stands for the 1-liter Lenor concentrate.

were at least 10 percent higher than those of its competitors. However, Lenor was a popular loss leader among retailers.[10] Ninety percent of Lenor dilute volume and 25 percent of concentrate volume were sold by retailers at feature prices in 1987.

Between 1984 and 1986, Lenor's sales volume had declined by 7.5 percent annually, with an actual loss of more than 1,000 MSUs. Sales volume in 1988 was predicted to decline similarly if nothing was done to revive the brand. Brand management attributed this loss to increasingly aggressive competitive price promotion, which eroded Lenor's market share, and to a shrinking market due to unfavorable consumer sentiment. Lenor brand management had to develop a marketing strategy that would combat Lenor's eroding sales and market share in the face of consumers' increasing environmental concerns.

Lenor's Strategic Options

Stadler reviewed the strategic options her brand management team had developed in the last few months.

Relaunch the 3:1 Concentrate.   One option explored was the aggressive relaunch of Lenor concentrate, promoting waste reduction benefits similar to those of a refill package. The 1-liter concentrate used approximately 45 percent less packaging materials than the 4-liter bottle on an equivalent use basis. Lenor's 1988 advertising and promotion budget (DM 45.2 million) could be increased by DM 2.9 million and be reallocated so that 40 percent would be spent on the dilute and 60 percent on the concentrate. Brand management estimated that this change would increase the concentrate's sales by 780 MSUs, 400 MSUs of which would result from cannibalization of the dilute. The finance department felt that the cannibalization rate would be even higher, with up to 480 MSUs of lost dilute sales.

The Lenor Refill Package.   A second option was introducing a new, more potent form of Lenor concentrate in a refill package. With the 4 from 1 concentrate, consumers would pour 1 liter of the concentrate into an empty 4-liter Lenor dilute bottle at home and add three liters of water to produce the original Lenor dilute formula. The Lenor brand group believed that the waste reduction benefits gained both from packaging reduction and bottle reuse would appeal to environmentally conscious consumers. The refill idea was not new to West Germans; many shoppers purchased milk packaged in flat, plastic bags that were then slotted inside a permanent container at home. Stadler also felt that "German consumers were ready to

bear the extra trouble associated with refilling to help their environment."

Preliminary research.   In the fall of 1986, P&G conducted two focus group interviews of 8 to 12 fabric softener users to explore their attitudes toward a refill concept and determine how to market such a product. Several users expressed interest in trying a refill product that they felt would reduce waste through container reuse. When asked how they would sell this idea to their neighbors, many said that they would stress waste reduction.

Next, a consumer panel test explored the acceptance of specific refill package ideas. Participants used different types of trial refill Lenor packages for four weeks, and afterward answered a survey about their likes, dislikes, and purchase intentions. From the results, researchers concluded that the refill concept had significant business-building potential.

Package design.   In the spring of 1987, P&G Germany explored two specific refill package options. Technical researchers suggested two designs: (1) a laminated cardboard carton, similar in design to a milk carton, and (2) a stand-alone, soft plastic package, known as a "doypack" pouch, already used in West Germany to sell single servings of fruit juice. The technical staff believed that it could expand the size of this package to hold fabric softener concentrate.

In March 1987, P&G Germany tested these refill options in a consumer panel test. Participants were asked to test one of two package designs for Lenor concentrate: a one-liter laminated "milk" carton and a one-liter doypack pouch. Users rated the laminated carton highest for its environmental compatibility, ease of use, and convenience; the doypack pouch ratings followed closely behind. Messiness was also a significant factor in preference for either package; participants who spilled the product when transferring it into the larger container rated both packages lower in terms of handling. Exhibit 4 summarizes the test results.

Laminated cartons versus doypack pouches.   Brand management investigated further the advantages and disadvantages of the two refill package designs. Both designs promised the same 85 percent reduction in package materials volume. In either case, P&G Germany had no facility that could produce the new packaging and would, therefore, need to hire subcontractors to meet a September launch date. This posed additional costs and risks. P&G Germany had not worked with any of the potential packaging suppliers before; consequently, Lenor's management did not have first-hand experience with their reliability in terms of delivery or quality. In addition, Lenor's product development group felt that there might be future capacity problems, since none of the potential subcontractors had ever handled the quantity of product P&G Germany was asking for.

---

[10]Loss leaders, products retailers sold at prices below cost to attract consumers, were usually popular brands in frequently purchased product categories.

Laminated cartons. Laminated carton technology had existed for 20 years. The cartons rarely leaked and consumers spilled a minimum of product during refill tests. Retailers could easily display the rigid carton on their shelves; the product would not require a customized shipping case. Each case would hold ten 1-liter cartons of Lenor.

West German safety regulations, focusing on the potential for accidental misuse of products, strongly discouraged packaging nonfood substances in containers generally used for food items. Consequently, P&G Germany ran some risk of government intervention if it used the laminated carton for its refill package. In addition, although the general public considered the carton as environmentally friendly, environmental experts regarded the wax-coated cardboard material as difficult to recycle.

Doypack pouch. Adapting the doypack pouch to Lenor's requirements proved difficult; the largest pouch size previously produced was 500 ml, half the size needed for Lenor. The first prototypes leaked and more than 10 percent of the packages burst when dropped. Lenor's product development group, felt optimistic, however, that these issues would be resolved within two months. Furthermore, a product-handling test in June 1987 revealed spillage difficulties. Participants in studio tests were asked to open the pouch and pour its contents into a 4-liter Lenor container. Although the least spillage occurred after the doypack's entire top was cut off with scissors, researchers found that users preferred to clip off only a corner of the package top. Lenor's brand management was concerned that the refill package would prove to be too messy for many consumers.

P&G Germany would need to produce customized shipping containers that would display the product attractively while following the stringent criteria determined by retailers. A picture of the doypack and the proposed case design are presented in Exhibit 5.

Comparative production costs. The laminated carton and doypack pouch would achieve respectively 5 percent and 14 percent cost savings per SU over Lenor dilute, due to reduced package materials and lower delivery costs.

Exhibit 6 shows a detailed cost breakdown for the proposed and existing Lenor product line. Lenor's allocated fixed costs were approximately DM 68 million per year.[11] The first 400 MSUs would cost an extra 33 percent and 41 percent for the carton and doypack, respectively.

Pricing. Exhibit 7 shows the breakdown of 1987 proposed prices and trade margins for the Lenor product line. Brand management wanted the suggested retail price for the refill package to be at least DM 1.5/SU lower than that for the 4-liter dilute to reflect packaging cost savings. This would provide the price incentive needed to motivate consumers to buy the refill packs. The savings were 5 percent of manufacturer's list price.

Volume forecasts. The brand group forecast a 1988 sales volume of 1,500 MSUs for the refill pouch; however, the team predicted that 60 percent of the refill package sales would come from cannibalization of existing Lenor sales. The finance department was less optimistic, forecasting an 80 percent cannibalization rate and a sales volume of 750 MSUs, resulting in only a 150 MSU net increase in total sales. For the launch, P&G would need 400 MSUs to stock 70 percent of West Germany's retail chain stores.

Promotion and advertising. Brand management proposed a 6.5 percent increase over its original 1988 advertising and promotion budget, with DM 6.5 million to be allocated specifically to the refill package relaunch. At estimated refill sales of 1,500 MSUs, this budget equaled DM 4.31/SU. Table D breaks down the Lenor marketing budget with and without the refill package introduction.

The Lenor brand group proposed to focus all Lenor advertising on the refill package for the first three months after launch. P&G Germany's advertising agency developed and tested two commercials called *Splish-Splash* and

---

[11]Fixed costs included general sales/marketing, administrative, and distribution costs (80 percent of total), fixed manufacturing (17 percent), and product research and development costs (3 percent).

TABLE D   **Alternative 1988 Advertising and Promotion Budgets**

	Without Launch	*With Launch*	*Difference*
Media	DM 10,849	DM 12,227	DM 1,378
Consumer promotion	1,957	1,976	19
Trade promotion	29,830	31,350	1,520
Indirect brand support	2,546	2,565	19
Total	45,182	48,118	2,936

Perspectives, based on the doypack pouch option (see Exhibits 8 and 9). *Splish-Splash* and *Perspectives* achieved unaided recall ratings of 37 percent and 47 percent, respectively, exceeding P&G Germany's 35 percent average unaided recall score for acceptable new copy.[12] Product labeling would highlight the environmental benefits of the packaging, in particular the 85 percent volume reduction in packaging materials, and would carry the phrase *refill pack*. Stadler hoped that the refill package would qualify for a Blue Angel label, which could help increase Lenor's sales, but felt uncertain that the improved packaging alone would gain the Blue Angel program's endorsement.

Proposed sales literature emphasized reductions in the retailer's warehousing (48 percent less), transportation (72 percent), and handling costs (70 percent) compared with the 4-liter Lenor dilute. The case container designs for both the carton and the doypack met 8 of the trade's 10 commandments, more than did any existing P&G Germany product. Finally, brand management felt that the opportunity to realize higher retail margins than could currently be obtained on the heavily promoted 4-liter dilute (9 percent versus 0 percent) would also appeal to the trade.[13]

An Integrated Marketing Option.   As Stadler pondered the pros and cons for the refill package, Daniel Knower, the assistant brand manager for Vizir, P&G Germany's liquid detergent brand, stopped by her office to discuss a new marketing concept he wanted to pursue. He said, "You know, we are struggling with the same environmental issues. I think that this refill concept is great and could be expanded to other brands, such as Vizir. We could market the products more efficiently under a new brand name, such as *Eco-pak.* Advertising copy could focus on the refill package as a product form that spanned multiple brands—Lenor, Vizir, and other liquid products." Realistically, both

Stadler and Knower speculated that the manufacturing complications, larger marketing scope, and increased coordination associated with such a strategy would add at least three months to the Lenor refill package's September introduction date. However, both felt that the idea merited discussion with their respective brand managers.

Conclusion

At the next day's meeting, Rolf Kunisch discussed several issues with the Lenor brand management team. First was the possibility that any effort P&G made to address environmental issues could backfire. The public relations department had warned of "waking a sleeping dog." P&G had many highly visible products that might attract opposition from environmentalists. Although the Lenor refill package might raise the firm's profile as an environmentally conscious corporate citizen, it might also draw attention to other P&G products for which environmental and cost-effective improvements were not readily available.

Kunisch was also concerned about the rapidity with which brand management had developed the refill package proposal. Had the product been tested enough? Were there hidden issues that might have been missed in the rush to launch? Was there really an urgent need for action? No other German consumer goods company had addressed environmental issues through innovative packaging. With such a novel and relatively untested idea, what risks would P&G Germany run as the first to market?

Several other P&G country managers in Europe had scoffed at the "crazy German ideas about the environment," seeing little applicability of the refill package idea to their own markets. Kunisch wondered if P&G Europe headquarters would also conclude that P&G Germany was overreacting to the environmental concerns of some West German consumers. Stadler left the meeting, uncertain of the final outcome for the refill package's future.

After the meeting, Lenor's brand manager, Phillippe, asked Stadler to prepare a revised set of recommendations for Lenor, addressing some of Kunisch's concerns. Stadler continued to be positive about the new packaging concept; however, she realized that the internal sell would be tougher than she had anticipated.

---

[12]Day-after recall testing measured communication effectiveness. Consumers who had watched television at the time when a test commercial spot was being shown were interviewed by telephone the following day. Unaided recall occurred when a consumer remembered the brand and message content of the test commercial without prompting. Aided recall involved prompting.

[13]Retail trade margins of 0 percent were due to the frequent use of the Lenor 4-liter dilute as a loss leader. Retail margins on Lenor sold at feature prices were often negative.

EXHIBIT 1   Selected Results from Fabric Softener Usage Monitoring Studies

	June 1985	*February 1986*
Percentage of respondents who were		
Fabric softener users[a]	60.0%	60.0%
Nonusers	40.0	40.0
Homemakers aware that fabric softener allegedly harms the environment		
Fabric softener users	55.0%	74.0%
Nonusers	66.0	70.0
Fabric softener users claiming to[b]		
Use less fabric softener per load	18.0%	24.0%
Soften fewer loads	16.0	14.0
Total (unduplicated)	26.0	27.0
Reasons nonusers never used/stopped using fabric softener		
Environmental reasons	42.0%	48.0%
Softness dissatisfaction	26.0	13.0
Effects on skin	29.0	23.0
Drying on clothesline	20.0	29.0

[a] Fabric softener users had used the product at least once in the previous three months before the interview; nonusers had not.

[b] Seventy-two percent of the users who used less softener or softened fewer loads claimed to be doing so for environmental reasons.

EXHIBIT 2   Lenor Sales Volume by Store Type in 1987

Store Type (by size)	Number of Stores	Percent Number of Stores	Grocery Market Turnover[b] (billion DM)	Percent Market Turnover	Lenor Volume Breakdown[a]	
					4-Liter Dilute	1-Liter Concentrate
Mass merchandisers	412	0.6%	17.2	13.6%	62.0%	36.0%
Hypermarkets	1,195	1.6	17.2	13.6	20.0	20.0
Supermarkets	2,542	3.5	18.6	14.7	9.0	13.0
Convenience stores	64,409	88.2	59.9	47.3	6.0	16.0
Discounters	4,442	6.1	13.8	10.9	3.0	14.0
Total	73,000	100.0%	126.7	100.0%	100.0%	100.0%

[a] Market turnover is defined as sales volume times retail value. 1.9 DM = US$1.

[b] Percentages are based on statistical unit volume for the first six months of 1987.

Exhibit 3   Lenor Liquid Package Sizes and Prices, 1987

Formulation	Size	Number of Units per Case	Number of Statistical Units per Case[a]	Suggested Retail Price (DM)	Average Feature Price (DM)	Suggested Retail Price Per SU (DM)	Average Feature Price Per SU (DM)	Percent Lenor Sales Volume
Dilute	4 L.	4	0.68	5.53	4.64	32.53	27.29	70%
Concentrate (3:1)	1 L.	16	2.01	4.75	4.08	37.81	32.48	30%

[a] Statistical units (SUs) convert different sizes and products to an equivalent use basis. Thus, two items with the same number of SUs will deliver an equivalent number of uses to the consumer.

Exhibit 4   Consumer Panel Results: March 1987

	1-Liter Carton	1-Liter Doypack
Number of users	205	205
Participants who would buy the alternative regularly at 4.98 DM	53%	49%
Favorable/unfavorable comments on handling	88%/33%	88%/41%
Percentage of reused containers that were "smeary" after transfer	10%	28%
Packaging ratings		
Ease of opening	57%	52%
Transferability of product	63%	46%
Environmental friendliness	74%	65%
Ease of disposal	79%	75%
Incidence of spillage	8%	25%

Exhibit 5

Case of doypack refill pouches

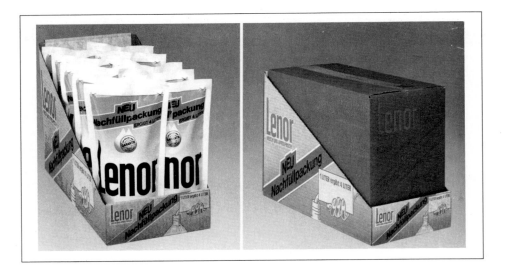

EXHIBIT 6 **1988 Breakdown of Direct Materials and Manufacturing Costs (DM per statistical unit)**

	1-Liter Carton[a]	1-Liter Doypack[a]	4-Liter Dilute	1-Liter Concentrate
Fabric softener chemicals	DM4.60	DM4.60	DM4.69	DM4.77
Packaging materials	1.84	1.82	3.40	2.72
Manufacturing	3.33	3.19	2.93	2.60
Delivery	0.86	0.76	1.79	1.01
Contractor expense	1.52	0.65	—	—
Total direct costs (DM)	12.15	11.02	12.81	11.10
Cost index (Lenor dilute = 100)	95	86	100	87
SU per container	0.17	0.17	0.17	0.126
Total costs/container (DM)	2.06	1.87	2.18	1.40

[a] P&G Germany expected that the first 400 MSU produced would cost 33% and 41% more for the carton and doypack, respectively, due to initial start-up costs.

EXHIBIT 7 **1988 Proposed Retail Price and Trade Margins**

	1-Liter Refill	4-Liter Dilute	1-Liter Concentrate
Expected retail price (DM)	5.49	5.79	4.89
Expected retail margin	9%	0%	9%
Manufacturer's selling price (DM)	5.04	5.79	4.49
SU per container	0.17	0.17	0.126
Retail revenues (DM/SU)	32.29	34.06	38.81
Manufacturer's revenues (DM/SU)	29.65	34.06	35.64

**EXHIBIT 8   Advertising Copy for Lenor Pouch:
Splish-Splash Commercial**

(Music begins, with young male and female dancers, brightly
dressed, dancing while holding Lenor containers and the Lenor
pouch.)

Singing to the 1960's tune of *Splish-Splash:*

Splish, Splash,
We're up-to-date,
Use Lenor in the refill pouch.

Just take your empty bottle,
Refilling is not difficult.
Just add water

Splish, Splash,
You feel it immediately,
Everything April-fresh and soft.
New Lenor in the
Environmentally safe refill pouch.

Splish, Splash,
The pouch is great,
Makes itself really small for the garbage

Splish, Splash,
Be up-to-date,
Use Lenor in the refill pouch.

EXHIBIT 9

Storyboard for
Perspectives *commercial*

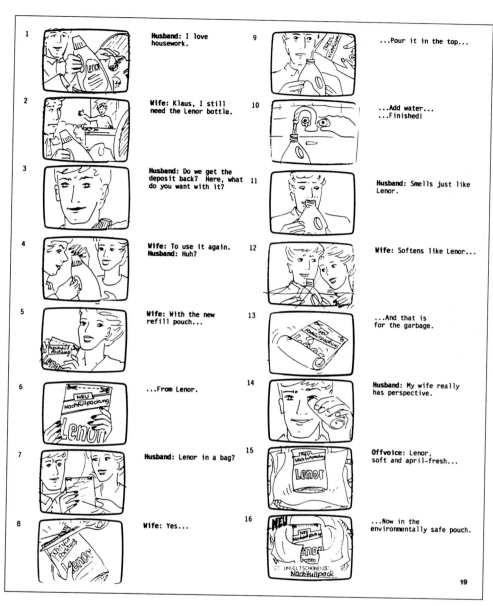

1 **Husband:** I love housework.

2 **Wife:** Klaus, I still need the Lenor bottle.

3 **Husband:** Do we get the deposit back? Here, what do you want with it?

4 **Wife:** To use it again. **Husband:** Huh?

5 **Wife:** With the new refill pouch...

6 ...From Lenor.

7 **Husband:** Lenor in a bag?

8 **Wife:** Yes...

9 ...Pour it in the top...

10 ...Add water... ...Finished!

11 **Husband:** Smells just like Lenor.

12 **Wife:** Softens like Lenor...

13 ...And that is for the garbage.

14 **Husband:** My wife really has perspective.

15 **Offvoice:** Lenor, soft and april-fresh...

16 ...Now in the environmentally safe pouch.

19

CHIPMAN-UNION, INC.: ODOR-EATERS SOCKS

It's tough for a small company like ours in a highly price-competitive industry to reduce its dependency on private label business.

Carl Hagen, vice president of sales at Chipman-Union, Inc. (CU), was discussing why his company had decided in March 1980 to investigate the introduction of a nationally promoted, branded sock. Chipman-Union primarily manufactured men's and boy's casual and athletic socks, which were sold to the trade unbranded as private label merchandise. To improve gross margins, CU was contemplating a line of deodorizing socks carrying the brand name Odor-Eaters.

Hagen, along with William Chipman, CU chairman, and Sibley Bryan, CU president, were evaluating a preliminary marketing program for Odor-Eaters. They had to decide whether to proceed further with the project.

Chipman-Union and Its Market

Chipman-Union was established in 1972 by a merger of the Union Manufacturing Company with Charles Chipman's Sons Company, Inc., a textile sales organization representing several mills, including Union. At the time, CU produced men's dress hosiery and men's, boys', girls', and misses' casual and athletic socks.

Chipman-Union's potential number of SKUs[1] was almost limitless, because of variations in style, size, color combination, yarn, and packaging. In deciding on the breadth of the product line, management had to weigh the advantages of being a full-line supplier against the high costs of short production runs. In 1979, the oldest of CU's three mills was closed, because of production inefficiencies. Partly as a result, Bryan and Hagen decided to narrow the product line. They first dropped all styles that had not generated an average 5,000 dozen pairs in annual sales over the previous three years. Next they cut all remaining styles that could not be manufactured on 108-needle machines.

By early 1980, CU's two mills were producing only 67 styles, in contrast to 350 styles two years previously, with-

out any reduction in capacity utilization. These styles were almost all cushioned socks[2] manufactured for the men's and boys' casual/athletic market in anklet, midcalf, and knee-high lengths. Industry shipments of such socks totaled 37 million dozen pairs in 1979, representing about $250 million in factory sales and $400 million in retail sales. CU's market share was estimated at 10 percent of units and 11 percent of factory sales.

Direct competitors of CU were companies that manufactured private label socks for general merchandise chains, such as Sears, Roebuck & Company and J. C. Penney; discount chains, such as Kmart; and food and drugstore chains. Abut 75 percent of 1979's dollar sales of men's and boys' casual/athletic hosiery was private label merchandise; no one company held more than a 20 percent share of this business. Sales of branded socks—casual and athletic—by Burlington and Interwoven were estimated at $15 million and $35 million, respectively, in 1979.

The Hosiery Industry

United States hosiery shipments in 1979 totaled 289 million dozen pairs, of which 25 percent or 72 million dozen pair were men's socks.[3] The percentages of 1979's dollar and unit sales for various types of socks are reported in Table A.

Per capita consumption of men's hosiery remained stable through the 1970s at about 10 pairs annually; however, the share of tube socks (these were socks with no shaped heel and, therefore could fit feet of many sizes) rose dramatically from fewer than 1 percent of shipments in 1970 to over 50 percent by 1979. Several factors contributed to this trend: increased athletic activity, as well as a desire to emulate the look of professional athletes; consumer perception of a better fit with no shaped heel; and relatively slower price increases, resulting from the manufacturing efficiencies of producing socks that were all the same size.

The branded hosiery industry was dominated by two large manufacturers, Burlington Industries and the Inter-

---

This case was prepared by Penny Pittman Merliss under the direction of Assistant Professor John Quelch.

Copyright © 1981 by the President and Fellows of Harvard College.

Harvard Business School case 581-073 (Rev. 1/87).

[1]An SKU is a stockkeeping unit, defined as a single item of merchandise for which separate sales and stock records are kept. One style of sock in a particular yarn and a particular color constitutes one SKU.

---

[2]Socks with some terry cloth or cushion construction. About 55 percent of socks sold in the United States (including most athletic and many casual socks) in 1979 were cushioned.

[3]National Association of Hosiery Manufacturers, *1979 Hosiery Statistics: 46th Annual Report.*

TABLE A Men's Hosiery Dollar and Unit Sales by Type, 1979

Type of Men's Hosiery	Percent of Dollar Sales	Percent of Unit Sales
Dress	34.9%	34.3%
Casual	21.9	23.6
Athletic	20.9	20.6
Work	13.7	16.0
Support	4.2	1.6
Other	4.4	4.0

NOTE: Dress socks were closely knit and sold primarily in dark colors suitable for semiformal or formal wear. Casual socks were typically coarser in texture and available in a broader range of colors. Athletic socks were always white, usually with stripe combinations.

SOURCE: Annual Consumers Report on Hosiery, *Men's Wear* magazine, 1980.

woven Division of Kayser-Roth, Inc., a subsidiary of Gulf & Western Industries, Inc. In 1979, there were 319 hosiery manufacturers in the United States, down from 457 in 1972. These companies operated 438 knitting mills, 93 percent of which were located in the southern United States. One reason for industry fragmentation was that entry required little capital investment. A knitting machine capable of producing eight dozen pairs of tube socks per hour cost about $4,500. Machines for knitting tube socks required less frequent and less expensive servicing than the finer-gauge machines needed for knitting dress hosiery.

Hosiery Distribution. The distribution of all men's hosiery, including dress socks, by class of trade is summarized

in Table B. As indicated, sales through discount chains, such as Kmart, increased dramatically between 1974 and 1979, mainly at the expense of general merchandise chains.

Most large retailers had two hosiery buyers, one for women's sheer hosiery (including nylons and panty hose) and one for all other hosiery products. These accounts typically divided their business among several manufacturers to ensure continuity of supply. Smaller accounts usually gave all their business to a single manufacturer providing a broad range of styles, for reasons of convenience and buying power.

Manufacturers competed for retailer business on the basis of price, assortment, and prompt delivery. With rising interest costs, buyers cut back on store inventories and demanded that manufacturers ship with shorter lead times.

Over 90 percent of CU's production was sold to 33 retail chains as private label merchandise. Of these, the three largest customers accounted for over 60 percent of sales. In 1979, about 1.0 percent of CU's production was sold to food and drug chains, a further 1.0 percent was sold to catalog showrooms, and 1.5 percent was exported.

Chipman-Union's principal accounts were handled by six salespeople based in New York City. They sold only CU merchandise. Annual sales and profit targets for each account were set by Hagen. Salespeople were compensated with salary plus bonus based on achievement of performance targets. In addition to its own sales force, CU used manufacturers' representatives to sell to catalog showrooms, military post exchanges, and the export market. (Manufacturers' representatives were independent salespeople who sold a range of complementary but noncompeting products of several companies. They did not warehouse or take title to merchandise and were typically

TABLE B Distribution of Men's Hosiery, 1974 and 1979

Outlet	Pairs		Dollars	
	1974	1979	1974	1979
General merchandise chains	29.4%	20.9%	29.4%	21.9%
J. C. Penney	10.6	8.3	10.7	8.2
Sears, Roebuck & Co.	6.9	6.2	7.1	7.1
Department	17.1	15.6	20.6	19.6
Speciality	6.0	4.8	8.6	6.9
Discount	26.5	36.5	21.1	29.3
Kmart	7.9	15.9	6.1	12.3
Variety	8.1	7.0	6.6	5.8
Supermarket	2.7	3.1	2.6	2.9
Drugstore	1.2	1.6	0.9	1.6
Other	9.1	10.5	10.2	12.0

NOTE: Men's hosiery is defined here as dress and casual hosiery to be worn by males aged 14 and over.

SOURCE: Market Research Corporation of America consumer purchase diary.

compensated on a commission basis by the manufacturers they represented.)

Hosiery Pricing.   As shown here, retail prices of men's hosiery had risen steadily with raw material cost increases, and price trends in the casual/athletic segment of the market were believed to follow the overall pattern.

Retail Price Point	Percentage of Pairs Men's Hosiery		
	1969	*1974*	*1979*
$0.00–$0.69	56%	38%	25%
$0.70–$1.00	30	33	40
$1.01 or more	14	29	35

Manufacturers' selling prices to the trade for a single style could vary widely because customers not only purchased in different quantities but also required different packaging. Hagen estimated the average manufacturer's gross margin on private label men's hosiery at 10 to 20 percent, as compared with 40 to 50 percent on such brands as Burlington and Interwoven. About 25 percent of men's branded hosiery was sold to the trade on deal at a discount from the regular price.

Manufacturers' suggested retail prices typically offered retailers a 50 percent margin on branded socks and a 40 percent margin on private label merchandise. Retailers relied heavily on price promotions to move unbranded men's hosiery. These usually coincided with back-to-school and Christmas storewide sales; 50 percent of annual retail sales of men's hosiery was typically made during these periods. Occasionally, manufacturers and retailers cooperated in designing special packaging for branded socks to serve as Christmas or Father's Day gifts.

Pricing policy at CU was set by Bryan and Hagen. Although CU averaged a 15 percent gross margin in 1979, management hoped to achieve an average 20 percent margin in 1980 from manufacturing efficiencies gained by narrowing the product line. Chipman-Union calculated gross margin as manufacturer's selling price less materials (49 percent), labor (10 percent), variable overhead (12 percent), fixed overhead including depreciation (8 percent), losses on imperfects (3 percent), and trade discounts (3 percent).

Product Differentiation.   The high level of private labeling and price sensitivity in the sock industry was partly attributable to limited opportunities for product differentiation. Retailers regarded socks as an unexciting product category. Unlike many fashion accessories, men's socks varied little in style or color by season. Consumer adver-

tising was minimal and appeared primarily in print media. Interwoven used the slogan "Sox Appeal" and stressed fit and durability. Burlington advertising for men's hosiery focused on odor protection and was targeted at women, who bought approximately two thirds of all men's and boys' socks.

Deodorizing or antimicrobial socks had been available throughout the 1970s, but only Burlington had attempted to promote odor control as a product feature. Since 1976 most Burlington socks, both branded and private label, were treated with an antimicrobial chemical developed by Dow Corning Corporation, which Burlington called Bioguard. By 1979 Burlington had spent about $2 million in promoting the "odor controller that keeps socks fresh all day."

Burlington licensed other hosiery manufacturers to use the Bioguard name. For example, in 1979 CU manufactured 200,000 dozen pairs of socks treated with Bioguard for J. C. Penney. About 75 percent of all men's and boys' socks sold by J. C. Penney under its label were believed to carry the name Bioguard.

Other deodorizing treatments included a process called Sanitized (a trademark of Sanitized, Inc., manufacturer of bacteriostatic chemicals), and Ultra-Fresh (a trademark of Betty Jean Hilton Sales Company, Inc.). The Sanitized process cost 10 cents per dozen pairs; the Dow Corning chemical treatment (Bioguard) cost 40 cents. Dow Corning's product was more concentrated and was thought to be longer lasting.

Manufacturers usually produced deodorizing socks only at the request of trade buyers; the incremental treatment cost was simply passed on in the factory price. Hagen estimated that 10 percent of all CU socks manufactured in 1979 were antimicrobially treated. By 1979, 30 percent of all men's and boys' casual/athletic socks were deodorizing, and Kayser-Roth was test marketing a branded deodorizing sock called Sock Sense. Kayser-Roth aimed to distribute this brand through food outlets, drugstores, and mass merchandisers, using self-service display racks containing 48 SKUs each. (Kayser-Roth had used food and drugstore outlets since 1973 for its No Nonsense brand of women's hosiery.)

Controlled Labels.   Chipman-Union management considered the private label market to be extremely price sensitive, offering little opportunity for product differentiation or for gross margins higher than 20 percent. Accordingly, CU had introduced several controlled label product lines. Controlled label merchandise carried a brand name but was marketed without consumer advertising or promotional support. Controlled labels were typically targeted at trade accounts that did not already purchase similar private label merchandise from the manufacturer. Although consumer awareness of controlled label brand names was low, manufacturers believed that merchandise offering even the appearance of a national brand could command a higher margin than private label goods.

The first controlled label, Just Socks, was test-marketed in food chains in 1975. It proved unprofitable, because of the costs of hiring personnel to check and restock retail displays. The product was never introduced beyond the test market.

Rabbit's Foot, a line of sports socks for men and women, also was launched in 1975 and targeted at sporting goods departments in department stores, independent sporting goods stores, and school team dealers. The average gross margin approached 30 percent, but the line was sold by manufacturers' representatives who received an 8.5 percent commission. In addition, CU underforecast the number of SKUs and level of inventory necessary to support the line.

Chipman-Union executives considered investing $5 million to $8 million to build Rabbit's Foot into a national brand. The idea was rejected because Rabbit's Foot lacked sufficiently distinctive product features. Annual sales never exceeded $800,000, and by August 1979 the label was being targeted primarily at military post exchanges.

A third controlled label, Show-offs, was a line of misses' knee-high socks introduced in 1978. Initially, Show-offs were targeted at discount chains, but CU later accepted offers from the manufacturers of women's branded socks to make Show-offs for sale under their brand names. Because Show-offs were shaped socks with knitted heels made of an expensive predyed yarn, inventory and manufacturing costs were above normal. During a two-year period before being phased out in the reduction of CU styles, Show-offs generated $750,000 in sales at a 25 percent gross margin.

A further effort to obtain higher gross margins involved a tie-in promotion with Life Savers, manufacturer of the well-known multicolored candy. In 1979, CU sold under license 60,000 dozen "Life Savers Fun Socks" packages, each containing two pairs of white tube socks with multicolored ankle stripes, along with a roll of Life Savers candy. Because Life Savers received a 3 percent royalty on dollar sales plus additional brand name exposure and consumer sampling, the company was willing to sell each candy roll to CU for 3 cents instead of the normal 15 cents. Fun Socks packages were sold primarily through regional discount chains at a retail price of $2.49 each and provided CU with a 27 percent gross margin. Hagen believed sales could have been much greater if there had been time to promote Fun Socks to other classes of trade, especially food and drug chains.

The Odor-Eaters Project

Chipman-Union management concluded in 1979 that neither controlled labels nor tie-in promotions could ever provide a margin over 20 percent on a large enough proportion of CU sales to warrant the required investment of manage-

ment time and manufacturing resources. The company next turned to a management consulting firm, Gunn, Fish and Mead (GFM), to assess the viability of a new national brand of high-quality men's and boys' deodorizing socks in casual and athletic styles. Although optimistic about the market potential, GFM concluded that marketing expenditures of $8 million to $10 million would be necessary to build 50 percent national unaided awareness of this new brand of socks[4] Some CU executives concluded that such an investment was beyond the company's financial capacity.

An opportunity arose, however, to negotiate a licensing agreement with Combe, Inc., manufacturer of Odor-Eaters® deodorizing shoe insoles, that would permit CU to use the Odor-Eaters name on a line of deodorizing socks. Combe (who also manufactured proprietary drugs, toiletries, and veterinary products, and who reported 1979 sales of about $50 million) introduced Odor-Eaters patented insoles in 1974. The insoles (loose inserts cut to fit the interior side of a shoe's sole and designed to provide warmth and comfort) were made from a latex foam containing activated charcoal for odor protection. Odor-Eaters insoles had been introduced under the Johnson's name to take advantage of the consumer and trade equity Combe had developed in Johnson's foot soap. Between 1974 and 1979, Combe spent almost $20 million on advertising Johnson's Odor-Eaters. By 1979 the brand had achieved 95 percent distribution in drugstores, 60 percent in supermarkets, and 50 percent in mass merchandisers.

Because unaided awareness of Odor-Eaters insoles had exceeded 50 percent nationwide, GFM estimated that Odor-Eaters socks treated under license with the Dow Corning's deodorizing chemical could be successfully introduced with marketing expenditures of $3.5 million. Chipman-Union executives were sufficiently interested in Odor-Eaters deodorizing socks to commission GFM to conduct consumer research studies and develop a preliminary plan for market introduction. Simultaneously, negotiations for possible licensing agreements were initiated with Combe and Dow Corning.

Consumer Research

During September 1979, four focus group interviews were conducted in New York and Chicago to review sock-buying habits and gauge reaction to the Odor-Eaters sock concept. Each group comprised consumers who were assembled and led by market research professionals into free discussion.

---

[4]Unaided awareness of a brand means a consumer would have to name the brand in response to a question, such as "What brands of socks can you name?" The aided awareness measure includes all consumers who reply affirmatively to a question, such as "Have you heard of Brand X?"

To qualify as a participant, a consumer had to be either a female head of household who purchased socks for male household members, or a male aged 18–35 who purchased his own socks. Key findings of the research are summarized in Exhibit 1.

During October 1979, mall intercept interviews were conducted in four locations with a total of 200 men and 400 women, recruited on the same basis as the focus group participants. Consumers were approached in a shopping mall and invited to participate in brief interviews, usually inside a booth or storefront within the mall. Interviewees were presented with a description of the product concept and then exposed to one of four cards (see Table C), after which they were questioned regarding their purchase intentions for each of the four styles. Purchase intentions are reported in Exhibit 2.

During the mall intercept interviews, 185 consumers agreed to take part in a home-use test for four weeks. Each consumer could select for the test the Odor-Eaters sock style he or she preferred. The purchase intentions of participating consumers at the end of this test are summarized in Exhibit 3.

Marketing Program Development

By March 1980, Combe and CU had drafted a possible licensing agreement (summarized in Exhibit 4). It presumed that CU would begin marketing Odor-Eaters socks in June 1980.

Chipman-Union and GFM executives had concurrently developed a marketing program for launching the product. All four styles of Odor-Eaters socks, previously tested in consumer research, would be included in the product line. Each was currently manufactured by CU and believed to be of equivalent quality to the best branded socks on the market. On the basis of the consumer research, it was decided that Odor-Eaters socks would be sold only in packages of three pairs. They would not be packed in plastic bags but would be held together by pressure-

sensitive bands so consumers could feel their quality at the point of purchase.

Odor-Eaters socks would be sold through special display units, as illustrated in Figure A. Each would include 16 SKUs, four styles each in four colors. A free unit would be provided to each store that placed an initial order for 24 dozen pairs across all four styles (the capacity of the unit), plus another 12 dozen pairs for back-up inventory. Each unit would cost CU approximately $100. A patent was pending on the unit, which was specially designed to accommodate only Odor-Eaters socks hangers.

The name Odor-Eaters was prominently featured on each display unit and package label in the same orange and black colors used to promote Odor-Eaters insoles. A claim of "all day protection against foot and sock odor" was backed by an unconditional one-year guarantee. The CU name was not used, because management believed that Burlington had confused consumers by simultaneously promoting both Bioguard and its corporate name.

The pricing schedule (see Exhibit 5) suggested retail prices for Odor-Eaters socks that would be equivalent to those for other national brands and would allow the trade a 45 percent margin. Hagen expected that some discounting would occur among large food and drug chains. He also discovered that one major specialty shoe store chain viewed a 45 percent margin as insufficient. This retailer suggested that CU manufacture the socks to be sold as private label merchandise under the store's name.

Chipman-Union intended eventually to sell Odor-Eaters socks to its existing customers. Initially, however, the brand would be targeted at food and drugstore chains (most did not carry any branded line of men's hosiery) and at discount chains. The consultants projected that, two years after introduction, CU could have 15,000 displays in place, of which 50 percent would be in food stores, 25 percent in drugstores, and 25 percent in discount stores. (This distribution level represented penetration of outlets accounting for 50 percent of all retail sales through each of the three classes of trade.) They further estimated that the inventory

TABLE C   Four Card Choices with Varying Style/Price Offerings

Odor-Eaters Sock Style	Card 1 1 pair	Card 2 1 pair	Card 3 3 pairs	Card 4 3 pairs
24-in. Athletic tube sock at	$1.99	$2.49	$5.99	$6.49
18-in. Athletic tube sock at	1.79	1.99	5.49	5.99
Athletic crew sock[a] at	1.79	1.99	4.99	5.49
Casual crew sock[a] at	1.89	1.99	5.49	5.99

[a]The term *crew* was a measure of sock length; when worn, a crew sock reached midway between the calf and the ankle. Both the athletic crew and casual crew socks had fitted heels.

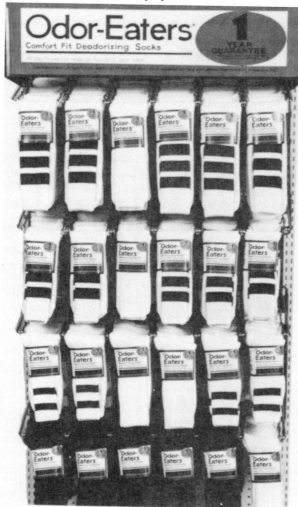

FIGURE A *Odor-Eaters display unit*

in each display unit would turn, on average, 2.54 times annually.[5]

Hagen noted that national food and drugstore distribution would require about 50 brokers or sales agents, who commonly charged a 5 percent commission on sales. Because CU had not previously dealt with brokers, Hagen was concerned about the company's ability to control them and ensure sufficient attention to servicing and restocking

the displays. Hence, he had investigated the possibility of employing the underutilized sales force of another manufacturer to distribute Odor-Eaters socks, but none was available.

Assuming that national distribution could be achieved, three additional salespeople would be required at an annual cost in salary and expenses of $70,000 each. Each would be exclusively responsible for sales of Odor-Eaters socks and supervision of CU's brokers in one of three regions of the country.

Communications Policy.   Television and print advertising would be targeted at female heads of households that included male family members aged 13 or older. This target represented about 65 million men living in 46 percent of the 71 million households in the United States. (A television commercial storyboard developed for the Odor-Eaters program is summarized in Exhibit 6.) Gunn, Fish and Mead estimated that advertising expenditures of $1 million over two years would be necessary to produce a 25 percent unaided awareness of Odor-Eaters socks among the target market in the United States. Hagen wondered how he could use the previous consumer research to project trial and repeat purchase rates and dollar sales at this level of audience awareness. The consultants estimated that triers converted to repeat purchasers would buy three packages (nine pairs) of Odor-Eaters socks annually.

Advertising could be supplemented with one or more consumer promotions. For example, a $1 cash refund offer could be promoted at the point of purchase by means of take-one pads, each with 50 refund request forms, attached to display units. The refund would be sent to any customer who mailed in a form plus a proof of purchase for one three-pair pack of socks. Based on a 7 percent redemption rate, the design, distribution, and redemption costs for this promotion would total $75,000 if it was offered on 15,000 displays. (The redemption rate for each consumer promotion was estimated on the basis of past experience with the specific type of offer.) Another option was a 25-cent coupon, to be distributed through free-standing inserts in Sunday newspapers with a combined circulation of 10 million. (Free-standing inserts were advertisements for one or more manufacturers, often in color and including coupons, delivered loose in newspapers and magazines.) Based on a 2.5 percent redemption rate, the total design, distribution, and redemption costs for this promotion were estimated at $136,500.

Gunn, Fish and Mead also suggested a trade promotion deal on opening orders to encourage retailers to set up display units. They noted that a 20 percent off-invoice allowance was commonplace on opening orders for new products aimed at food and drugstores. In addition, GFM suggested an advertising allowance, by which CU would repay a retail account a percentage of the opening order

---

[5]Gunn, Fish and Mead believed that the number of turns would be stable within the range of alternative retail prices for Odor-Eaters socks being considered by CU executives. They also anticipated a higher number of turns in food stores than in drugstores.

invoice on receiving evidence that Odor-Eaters socks were featured in the retailer's advertising. The consultants estimated that a 5 percent advertising allowance would be taken up by 55 percent of retailers placing opening orders. They further noted that the trade would expect CU periodically to offer similar off-invoice and advertising deals beyond the introductory offer.

Conclusion

By March 1980, CU had invested over $100,000 in consulting and marketing research fees plus considerable management time in investigating the Odor-Eaters project. Now management had to decide whether to adopt the GFM marketing program, launch the new product, and aim to place 15,000 display units in retail outlets within two years.

EXHIBIT 1   Results of Focus Group Interviews on Odor-Eaters Socks

General Sock-buying Patterns
Low interest category.
Low brand awareness.
Unplanned purchasing.
Heavier buying at back-to-school season.

Odor-Eaters Socks Concept
Smelly socks identified as laundry-handling problem.
Overall positive reaction to socks.
High rate of purchase intention.
Willingness to pay more for deodorizing feature.
Concern about whether sock meets its claim of maintaining all-day protection against foot odor through repeated washings for its entire life.

Packaging Preferences
Preference for packaging that allowed shoppers to feel the product.
Belief that socks packaged in plastic bags were relatively low in quality.

SOURCE: CU market research.

EXHIBIT 2   Results of Mall Intercept Tests

| | Purchase Interest by Type of Sock[a] | | | | | | | | | | | | | | | |
| | 24-in Tube | | | | 18-in. Tube | | | | Athletic Crew | | | | Casual Crew | | | |
	1L	1H	3L	3H	1L	1H	3L	3H	1L	1H	3L	3H	1L	1H	3L	3H
Definitely would buy[b]	18%	13%	13%	11%	5%	9%	10%	5%	9%	19%	9%	10%	22%	25%	24%	25%
Probably would buy	22	13	21	23	27	21	18	27	24	19	23	20	25	28	29	30
Might or might not buy	18	7	13	12	14	14	13	10	10	13	14	15	8	10	14	7
Probably would not buy	14	21	19	23	20	15	24	15	17	17	20	14	12	8	10	10
Definitely would not buy	28	44	34	30	34	40	35	43	40	33	34	41	34	28	22	27

[a]Based on respondent base of 150 each.
[b]That is, 18% of the 150 respondents exposed to the option of buying one pair of 24-in. tube socks at the low price stated that they definitely would buy.
NOTE: 1L = one pair at low price; 1H = one pair at high price; 3L = three pairs at low price; 3H = three pairs at high price.
SOURCE: CU market research.

EXHIBIT 3   Likelihood of Purchasing Odor-Eaters

	Total Respondents	24-in. Tube Sock	18-in. Tube Sock	Athletic Sock	Crew Sock	Price Groups			
						1 Pair at $1.79–1.99	1 Pair at $1.99–2.49	3 Pairs at $4.99–5.99	3 Pairs at $5.49–6.49
Respondent base[a]	(185)	(60)	(22)	(34)	(69)	(53)	(42)	(42)	(48)
Definitely would buy	38%	43%	45%	42%	29%	42%	45%	31%	33%
Probably would buy	44	47	27	35	51	38	40	48	50
Might or might not buy	14	7	23	15	16	13	10	19	13
Probably would not buy	3	3	5	6	1	4	5	—	4
Definitely would not buy	2	—	—	3	3	4	—	2	—

[a]Based on four-week consumer home-use test.
SOURCE: CU market research.

EXHIBIT 4   Summary of Draft Licensing Agreement between Chipman-Union and Combe

Chipman-Union received exclusive licensing rights to use the Odor-Eaters trademark on and in connection with hosiery products sold in the United States, Canada, and Mexico, so long as the hosiery met stipulated quality standards.

Chipman-Union pledged to "use its best efforts" in marketing Odor-Eaters hosiery. January–December 1980 was designated a test period during which Combe's licensing fee would be $60,000. From January 1981, Chipman-Union would pay a royalty to Combe Inc. of 5 percent of net sales[a] of Odor-Eater socks.

Chipman-Union's Odor-Eaters hosiery was required to meet a series of steadily increasing annual net sales goals over the first four years of the agreement. The sales goal for the fourth year also had to be met in each subsequent year.

The Odor-Eaters trademark could be displayed on CU's private label hosiery, so long as the hosiery met stipulated quality standards.

All advertising and promotional material for Odor-Eaters hosiery required written approval from Combe before publication or use. The trademark "Odor-Eaters" was to be prominently displayed in all advertising, printed in the typeface currently used on the logo for Odor-Eaters insoles.

Combe could terminate the agreement during 1980 if, in Combe's sole judgment, sales of Odor-Eaters hosiery were adversely affecting sales of Odor-Eaters insoles. In the event of such termination, the licensing fee paid by CU to Combe for test marketing would be refundable.

[a]Net sales were gross sales exclusive of returns and prepaid freight.
SOURCE: Company records.

Exhibit 5   **Pricing and Cost Structure**

	Description and Fiber Content							
	Men's Over-the-Calf Tube (80% cotton, 15% nylon, 5% elastic)		Boys' Over-the-Calf Tube (80% cotton, 15% nylon, 5% elastic)		Athletic Crew (85% cotton, 15% nylon)		Casual Crew (75% orlon acrylic, 25% nylon)	
	Package	*Dozen*	*Package*	*Dozen*	*Package*	*Dozen*	*Package*	*Dozen*
Retail price	$6.49	$25.96	$5.99	$23.96	$5.49	$21.96	$5.99	$23.96
Manufacturer's selling price ($)	3.57	14.27	3.29	13.18	3.02	12.07	3.29	13.18
Trade margin ($)	2.92	11.69	2.70	10.78	2.47	9.89	2.70	10.78
Trade margin (%)	45%	45%	45%	45%	45%	45%	45%	45%
Cost of goods ($)	2.23	8.92	1.89	7.57	1.78	7.11	1.94	7.76
Gross margin ($)	1.34	5.35	1.40	5.61	1.24	4.96	1.35	5.42
Gross margin (%)	37.5%	37.5%	42.6%	42.6%	41%	41%	41.0%	41.1%

NOTE: All socks were to be sold three pairs to a package, 24 packages to a case. Average per-package numbers across the four styles for use in calculations were $6.00 retail selling price, $3.30 manufacturer's selling price, $2.70 trade margin, $2.00 cost of goods, and $1.30 gross margin.

SOURCE: Company records.

Exhibit 6   **Summary of Possible Odor-Eaters Television Commercial**

Video	Audio
Open on a spokesman in a sporting goods store. He holds an old-fashioned sneaker in one hand and a sweat sock in the other.	Remember when sneakers were just sneakers . . . and socks were just socks?
He gestures to a display of flashy athletic shoes.	You think sneakers have changed?
He walks past a display of athletic equipment toward the Odor-Eaters socks rack.	Socks have really come a long way.
He picks some socks off the display.	Look . . . new Odor-Eaters deodorizing socks. That's right—Odor-Eaters *socks.*
He squeezes the socks, close-up.	They're cotton cushiony. . . .
He stretches the socks.	Keep their fit and won't fall down.
He points to the special treatment copy, close-up.	But here's the big difference. . . . Odor-Eaters socks are treated to control sock and foot odor . . . to stay fresh.
Go to the spokesman opening a clothes hamper and sniffing.	That means fresher hampers . . .
He opens a locker door and sniffs.	Fresher lockers . . .
He lays a pair of Odor-Eaters on a pair of athletic shoes.	. . . and fresher sneakers.
He holds a pair of Odor-Eaters socks and points to the guarantee.	Odor-Eaters socks will keep their fit and freshness one full year . . . guaranteed.
Move back as he puts the socks back on the rack.	Get cushiony, comfortable Odor-Eaters deodorizing socks.

DISTRIBUTION POLICY

DISTRIBUTION POLICY

The delivery of a good from its manufacturer to its user often involves other parties as well. For example, in buying a textbook, we typically buy from an independent bookstore (such as the college bookstore), not the publisher. Different manufacturers have made fundamentally different decisions on channels. For example:

- Avon sells through its own sales force directly to individual consumers in their own homes.
- Tupperware sells directly to end consumers but with a "party-plan" approach.
- General Motors Corporation sells cars to franchised dealers, who in turn sell to consumers.
- Clairol sells its small appliances, such as hair dryers and makeup mirrors, to wholesalers, who then sell to retail outlets.

Thus, some manufacturers sell direct to consumers (Avon, Tupperware), others involve one intermediary (General Motors), and still others, two or more (Clairol). While these examples are all of consumer goods, the same is true for industrial goods.

Why do these "middlemen" exist? How many intermediaries should there be at each level—for example, how many franchised dealers should General Motors have? How can the manufacturer make the other members of the channel do what it wants them to do? These are the questions we take up in this chapter. First, the "Key Decisions" section examines the channel design questions more closely. Then the "Factors Influencing Optimal Design" section describes the characteristics of manufacturers and markets influencing channel design. Finally, the "Channel Conflict and Control" section considers issues in managing the existing channel to achieve objectives.

This case was prepared by Professor Robert J. Dolan.
Copyright © 1984 by the President and Fellows of Harvard College.
Harvard Business School case 9-585-045 (Rev. 4/2/92).

Key Decisions

Figure A shows the set of activities linking a manufacturer and a customer-user.

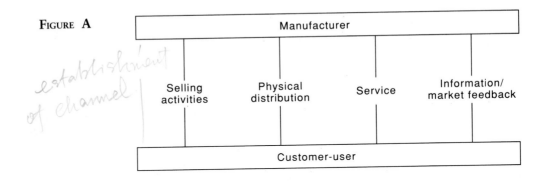

FIGURE A

establishment of channel

An efficient system provides for the following:

1. Selling activities: These can include providing information to the consumer through advertising, point-of-purchase displays, and personal selling.
2. Physical distribution: The goods must be transferred from the place where they are manufactured to the place where the consumer can conveniently buy them.
3. Service: For some products (e.g., home computers and many industrial goods), after-the-sale service must be provided.
4. Information/market feedback: To be effective in the long run, the manufacturer must have information from the marketplace. *Detailed* information from the marketplace. Detailed information on consumer reaction to certain attributes, acceptance of the product by specific classes of customer, and so on is required as input to the tailoring of the marketing program.

The channel design decision begins with the question: "What needs to be done to get my product sold?" Suppose a watch manufacturer has decided to compete in the mass market in the $15 price range. What specific tasks must be accomplished? Success in this type of market requires that the firm have:

1. An established brand name.
2. Distribution in a large number of convenient outlets.
3. Good display in those outlets.
4. An efficient means of restocking retail outlets.

Due to the low price positioning of the product, knowledgeable personal selling at the point of purchase is not necessary or feasible. After-the-sale service is not a major issue. Note how different the tasks would be if one were selling at the Rolex level ($300 and up), rather than at the Timex level. At high price points, personal selling at the point of purchase becomes crucial.

Once the tasks to be accomplished have been specified, the next question is: Who is to do each task? That is, Should the company perform the function or delegate it to an intermediary? This is a question of "channel length." For example, consider the good display in a large number of outlets, for our $15 watch. Theoretically, the manufacturer can perform this function by opening a large number of watch stores. However, existing retailer outlets, such as department stores and drugstores, evidently accomplish this task more efficiently than the manufacturer since we do not see Timex watch stores in major U.S. cities.

In general, a task will be the responsibility of one of the following:

1. Manufacturer.
2. Manufacturer's representative: A "rep" generally works with the manufacturer on a long-term basis. He is not an employee of the manufacturer but is usually granted exclusive territorial rights and paid on a commission basis (i.e., as a percentage of the manufacturer's sales he or she generates). The rep may sell noncompeting products. He or she does not take title to the goods and, consequently, has very limited authority on pricing and terms of sale.
3. Merchant middlemen: The key feature distinguishing these intermediaries from manufacturers' reps is that merchant middlemen buy and take title to the merchandise. They then resell the merchandise under the terms they desire, the manufacturer having given up control of the product with the sale to the merchant middleman. The most common merchant middlemen are:

   • Wholesalers (sometimes called "distributors") who resell to other merchants (e.g., retailers) or industrial users.
   • Retailers, who resell to consumers.

The rule on who should perform what functions is very simple: The most efficient organization for the task should do it.

Despite some popular notions to the contrary (best exemplified in such advertisements as "we've eliminated the middleman and passed the savings on to you!"), intermediaries exist because they make the marketing system more efficient. If the manufacturer can perform a task more efficiently, the manufacturer should perform it. Tasks are delegated only when there is an economic reason to do so. In the next section, we discuss factors that influence the economics of operating through manufacturer's reps and merchant middlemen.

Along with this "channel length" issue, there is the issue of channel breadth (i.e., how many firms of each type does the manufacturer want to have?). The basic alternatives with respect to channel breadth or intensity of market coverage are:

1. Exclusive distribution
2. Selective distribution
3. Intensive distribution

In exclusive distribution, the manufacturer establishes only one reseller in each region to carry the product. Yamaha pianos are an example of this policy. Exclusivity is granted by the manufacturer in the hope that it will induce strong selling support by the reseller. The cost is that, with an exclusive policy, the consumer must be willing to seek out the one outlet in his or her area carrying the brand.

The middle ground between exclusivity and seeking the maximum coverage possible is selective distribution. In selective distribution, there is more than one but a limited number of resellers in each market. Selective distribution is practiced by some clothing manufacturers, such as Perry Ellis, Hathaway shirts, Bally shoes, and is common in video equipment. The purposive limiting of the number of outlets is intended to increase the support the reseller provides the brand over the case of intensive distribution. Having more than one outlet is intended to increase shopping convenience over exclusive distribution.

Finally, many manufacturers try to place their products with as many resellers as possible. For some markets, it is believed that "share of space" (i.e., retail shelf space) equals "share of market," and, thus, the objective is to be as widely and intensively distributed as possible. Gillette razor blades, Kodak film, and Budweiser beer are examples of intensive distribution at the retail level.

It is sometimes thought that the more outlets the product is in, the better off the manufacturer is. However, since some manufacturers choose exclusivity, this is not generally the case. As suggested above, moving from exclusive to intensive trades off reseller support for easier availability of goods for the consumer. The next section discusses characteristics of the market situation to be considered in deciding if this trade-off is warranted.

Factors Influencing Optimal Design

Summing up the above section, the principal channel design questions are:

1. Channel length.
2. Channel breadth.

As is usually the case in marketing, an analysis of consumer behavior is the primary input into the resolution of these questions. Consider three examples to illustrate issues in channel breadth.

1. Shaving cream: Shaving cream is a frequent purchase for the majority of adult males. The acquisition of a new can is a routine and unexciting event. Since the buyer most likely thinks shaving creams are not very different from one another in quality or price, the manufacturer must be certain that the product is conveniently available to the prospective purchaser.
2. Television set: A television set is a relatively infrequent purchase of considerably greater expense than shaving cream. When the decision is made to buy a television set, several members of the family get involved—checking *Consumer Reports* and newspaper ads, shopping around, and generally gathering information appropriate to the importance of the decision. Since consumers do shop around, rather than just visit the most convenient outlet and buy there, there is no need for the manufacturer to be in every outlet. In fact, being in every outlet would be a mistake if the family relied on the retail clerk for information. Intensive distribution is justified for the shaving cream because the only retail support required is shelf space. However, when strong, point-of-purchase personal selling is required, going beyond selective distribution would jeopardize the required support. Hence, selective distribution is required.

3. Automobile: For some makes, the consumer behavior would be like that just described for television sets. However, for a speciality item, such as a Porsche 944, it is likely that the purchaser has a very strong brand preference even before the acquisition process begins. Thus, convenience of outlet is not a consideration, and the buyer will go just about anywhere to get the brand he or she insists on. Since the car is purchased infrequently and is an extremely important purchase, the buyer can behave this way. In this event, the permissibility of relatively inconvenient outlets indicates exclusive distribution. (Note that some provision may have to be made for less than exclusively distributed warranty servicing of the car.)

These three examples illustrate a frequently used categorization of goods used in marketing. Our shaving cream, television, and exotic car represent a "convenience good," a "shopping good," and a "specialty good," respectively.[1] Of course, no item can be definitely classified as any one of these three types for all consumers. However, the following is a useful guideline:

Convenience good	$\longrightarrow$	Intensive distribution
Shopping good	$\longrightarrow$	Selective distribution
Speciality good	$\longrightarrow$	Exclusive distribution

Once the channel breadth issue is decided, the manufacturer can consider who is to provide the coverage. A common first argument in favor of going direct (i.e., manufacturer performing all services) is that it is easier to guide and control one's own employees than it is to motivate independent parties. Second, in the early stages of a product's life, a very knowledgeable sales presentation may be required because of the educational needs of the consumer. Generally, a manufacturer's employee specializing in selling that manufacturer's products will be more knowledgeable than a distributor selling many products. Selling direct is important in many industrial settings, because buyers value a direct relationship with the company to ensure good service and supply in times of a shortage.

With respect to utilizing intermediaries, the first argument is usually that the sales volume of the product does not justify direct selling. In direct selling, the manufacturer performs all required activities, and, hence, this is the most expensive form. This cost is seldom justified if the good is a convenience good and the customer base is geographically dispersed.

As with channel breadth, consumer behavior has a direct impact on the channel length issue. For example, consumers wanting quick delivery (necessitating the maintenance of local inventories), one-stop shopping (i.e., being able to buy a variety of products at one outlet), or valuing an association with a local firm to whom their business is important all indicate the use of middlemen rather than direct distribution.

Thus, as in most marketing decisions, both company and customer issues affect the channel design decision. Competitive considerations can have an influence as well. For example, in the home computer market, firms have been forced to seek "unconventional" modes of distribution, because the traditional channels were already "clogged" with competitive makes. The distribution channel can be an effec-

---

[1]For details, see R. H. Holten, "The Distinction between Convenience Goods, Shopping Goods, and Specialty Goods," *Journal of Marketing,* July 1958; and L. P. Bucklin, "Retail Strategy and the Classification of Consumer Goods," *Journal of Marketing,* January 1963.

tive means of product differentiation. For example, L'eggs pantyhose opened up new channels in supermarkets and designed an efficient system for delivery. By moving into grocery stores, L'eggs effectively made pantyhose purchasing a convenience purchase for many women.

Channel Conflict and Control

Once the manufacturer delegates a task to a middleman, an inevitable pattern of conflict and cooperation begins. The manufacturer and the middleman cooperate because their joint efforts produce the sales of the product. However, there is conflict, because each wishes the other would do more to stimulate sales. For example, having sold the product to a merchant middleman at a given price, the manufacturer would like low retail prices to stimulate sales. For its part, the retailer would like a higher price than that which maximizes profits for the channel. And, similarly, the downstream firms wish the manufacturer would do more to stimulate sales (e.g., through national advertising).

In order to try to maximize the coordination and reduce the conflict, some relationships between manufacturers and middlemen are spelled out in contracts. These franchise agreements (e.g., McDonald's, Dunkin' Donuts, most gas stations, and automobile dealers) bind the parties to perform certain activities, rather than to seek their own profit maximization. These systems are sometimes called "contractual systems," as opposed to "conventional systems," in which parties operate independently.

Ethical Issues in Distribution Policy

Because channel management requires balancing the interests of manufacturers, middlemen, and customers, there are numerous situations when ethical issues may arise.

One class of situations involves ensuring fair dealings between manufacturers and distribution channels when one side has considerably greater bargaining power than the other. For example, a manufacturer with an extremely popular product line might be tempted to squeeze the channel's profit margins by encouraging competition among retailers to drive retail prices down and stimulate demand, while not lowering its own price to the trade. The channel then bears a disproportionate share of costs, and the manufacturer reaps a disproportionate share of the benefits. While not illegal, the manufacturer's behavior might be questionable on ethical grounds if the manufacturer drives the channel into a loss situation. The balance of power is sometimes reversed, with a critical channel member exerting extreme pressure on a manufacturer's profits through aggressive bargaining. This is not to say that tough price negotiations are unethical. However, there are times when hard bargaining tactics can be carried to an unethical extreme.

A second class of situations involves relations with international distribution channels that may be following ethical and legal standards different from those of the manufacturer. For example, the U.S. Foreign Corrupt Practices Act forbids payment of bribes or other inducements to facilitate sales in other countries, while the laws of the land in many countries do not prohibit such payments. A U.S. manufacturer may then be caught in a dilemma. If it refuses to make the side payment, it will obtain no business. If it makes the payment directly, it violates the U.S. law. Some manufacturers respond to this dilemma by selling their products to local distributors who do whatever is necessary (including making side payments that are legal in the country but illegal in the United States) to make the sale. Others refuse to do business in the country, thereby foregoing revenues and profits. Is the former practice ethical? Is the latter practice too provincial, expecting the rest of the world to follow one country's standards?

The above examples are just two among many ethical problems that arise in channel management. The questions below should help a marketer to identify when an ethical issue may be involved in a distribution decision:

- Is either the manufacturer or the distributor abusing its power, taking unfair advantage of the other partner?
- Has the manufacturer unwittingly put distribution incentive systems in place that encourage the channel members to engage in unethical practices toward end customers?
- Are distributors using the good name of the manufacturer to persuade customers to do things that are not in their best interests?
- Has the manufacturer tried to ensure that distributors provide the education and point-of-purchase communication necessary to ensure safe use of its products?

Ethical issues inevitably arise when multiple parties are involved in marketing exchanges. In many instances, the interests of manufacturer, wholesaler, and retailer may be in conflict. However, the marketing concept provides common ground for channel members to discuss their differences. According to Theodore Levitt, the purpose of marketing for all channel members is: "Satisfying the needs of the customer by means of the product and the whole cluster of things associated with creating, delivering, and finally consuming it."[2] A corollary of the marketing concept is that each organization in the marketing chain is entitled to a reasonable profit in exchange for its contribution to consumer value. With this in mind, the practices of each member of the distribution channel from manufacturer to retailer can be examined to see if they create value for customers, and to see if the rewards for delivering that value among channel members are allocated fairly.

Summary

Channel management involves a complex web of personal, economic, and legal relationships. As such, the channel decision, once implemented, is the most difficult to change in marketing. For example, it is much easier to cut the advertising budget in half than it is to drop half the firm's retailers if it is decided to shift from intensive to selective distribution. Managing change presents a challenge. We argued above that the optimal channel design was dependent upon consumers (e.g., their familiarity with the good, need for technical service, and so on), company resources, and competition. These factors all change over time. Consequently, the optimal channel design also changes over time. Given the high cost of change, marketing system design must not only consider current market conditions but also anticipate future changes in the marketplace.

---

[2]Theodore Levitt, (1960), "Marketing Myopia," *Harvard Business Review,* Reprint #75507, p. 6.

Lotus Development Corporation

Channel Choice: Direct versus Distribution

Lotus Development Corporation's director of sales operations, John Shagoury, stood at his office window staring across the Charles River at a breathtaking view of downtown Boston. But on this January 1986 morning, the view was lost on Shagoury. He was preoccupied with a major decision facing his young company—whether Lotus should bypass its distributors and dealers and have its own sales force sell directly to its large corporate users. Currently, Lotus's 90-person sales force called on several of these large accounts and took them through the complete selling cycle except for the final exchange of products for money. The company's local retail dealers drew up the final contract and effected delivery and after-sales service.

The evolving sophistication of these corporate buyers was starting to demand direct servicing, but this would mean the cannibalization of the dealers' highest-volume accounts. Indeed, dealer pressure had forced Lotus to discontinue direct selling when the company had tried it three years earlier. Lotus wanted to maintain its good relationship with dealers and distributors because under any scenario they would continue to be a primary sales channel. They would be particularly important for future products the company was planning to roll out.

Shagoury described the difficulty of making decisions in this new and rapidly changing industry.

> One of the things companies have going for them in other industries is history—growth trends, buying trends, and so on. We don't have any of that. There's not enough reliable data on which to base any analysis or decisions. Then if you do get something figured out, it changes the next day. Three years ago, software was being distributed in zip-lock bags with mimeographed documentation. Now we spend hundreds of thousands of dollars on packaging and creating user-friendly tutorials. Five years from now, software may be burned into ROM chips[1] and the integrated packages distributed by the hardware manufacturers. Who knows?

This case was prepared by Professor V. Kasturi Rangan and Douglas R. Scott with the assistance of Professor Thomas V. Bonoma. Copyright © 1986 by the President and Fellows of Harvard College.
Harvard Business School case 9-587-078 (Rev. 5/21/91).

[1]ROM stands for read-only memory—the silicon chip inside a computer that contains the basic operating instructions for the computer. Technological advances in silicon chip design and manufacture were expected to so increase the capacity of the ROM chip that it could also hold large operating systems and applications programs.

Industry Background

During the 1970s, technical and manufacturing advances in the semiconductor and magnetic memory fields greatly increased microprocessor and memory capabilities and greatly reduced their costs. This precipitated the development of the microcomputer (otherwise known as the personal computer), which could store, access, and process significant amounts of data and solve problems at a low cost.

The microcomputer created a demand for software that would address the needs of a vast new group of users. Entrepreneurial software programmers recognized this opportunity, and many individuals (often working out of their homes) developed functional packages. Low entry barriers soon gave rise to a small, highly fragmented market. Then, in 1982, a start-up company, Lotus Development Corporation, changed the rules of the game. The company's founder obtained $1 million in venture capital and used it to finance a blitz of advertising and marketing support programs to promote a new spreadsheet package for businesses—Lotus 1-2-3. This bold move expanded the market and greatly raised entry hurdles in the industry. A high-powered marketing program became the price that a software developer had to pay to be heard above the crowd of new product offerings. The "Lotus-style launch" was necessary to get distributors and dealers to carry a product, to get the computer magazines to review it, and to generate crucial word-of-mouth referrals.

By the end of 1983, the market stabilized somewhat as various one-product firms, such as Lotus (with 1-2-3), Ashton-Tate (with dBase II), and Microsoft (with MS/DOS) established their products as industry standards in their respective market segments. By 1985, the microsoftware industry was estimated to be about $5 billion (inclusive of an estimated 45 percent channel margin), with 14,000 companies and 27,000 different products.[2]

Included in the $5 billion figure was a $2 billion to $2.5 billion market for *special-purpose software and services.* These software programs were written for the unique requirements of an industry or a client (e.g., computer-aided instruction programs for educational institutions, order-entry systems for distribution warehouses, and medical-diagnosis bibliographies for physicians). The special-purpose segment of the industry was fragmented by many players and products.

---

[2]"Software: The Growing Gets Rough," *Business Week,* March 24, 1986.

The $2.5 billion *general-purpose software market* was divided into two major segments: operating systems and application software. Operating systems organized and managed the activities of the computer hardware and peripheral equipment; they got the hardware into a ready-to-think mode and, hence, were integral to the use of every microcomputer, regardless of the ultimate application. In 1985, the operating systems market was estimated to be about $250 million (in retail sales). Application software made up the rest of the general-purpose market. These were programs written to accomplish general problem-solving tasks, such as (1) mathematical computations (spreadsheet programs), (2) writing reports (word processing programs), and (3) organizing data files (database management programs). These three application segments were nearly equal in size and together accounted for 75 percent of all general-application software sales. Several other application pieces, such as electronic mail programs, made up the other 25 percent.

About 50 percent of the general-purpose software market was shared by seven companies: Lotus was the clear leader, with 1985 sales of $225 million, followed by Ashton-Tate and Microsoft, each with sales of about $100 million to $125 million. IBM, the industry leader in microcomputer hardware (with sales of about $6 billion to $7 billion) was a minor but not unimportant player in the microsoftware industry. IBM's sales of microsoftware in 1985 were estimated to be about $75 million. Apple Computer, the number two company in microcomputer hardware, also marketed software but to a lesser extent than IBM. Finally, other important participants, such as Software Publishing and MicroPro, with sales of about $40 million each, were constantly challenging Lotus, Ashton-Tate, and Microsoft.

By early 1986, new challenges arose for all participants as the demand for microcomputers slowed significantly. The growth rate for microcomputer sales went from 101 percent in 1982 to 55 percent in 1984, and to 22 percent in 1985. This slowdown seemed to signal that the sales to the "early adopters" had approached saturation and that product modifications would be required to develop other potential markets. The microsoftware industry, which had grown at a rate of 55 to 60 percent from 1982 to 1983, slumped to 20 percent in 1985. An article on the industry summed up the situation.

It wasn't long ago that computer software makers were the sexiest, craziest, glitziest members of corporate America. They possessed money and magic and a seemingly limitless future. . . . But almost overnight the industry changed. Slumping sales, a jaded public, and some spectacular failures forced the nation's computer software industry to grow up in a hurry. It skipped puberty, shed its flash and dazzle, and donned a business suit.[3]

The article went on to discuss the basic dilemma facing microsoftware companies:

Some software executives continue to believe that improvements in technology will restore an edge of excitement to what has suddenly become a mundane business. Salvation for them lies in speedier microchips and bigger electronic brains.

Others, however, have started to de-emphasize the technical aspects of their business and have adopted more fundamental, long-term strategies for improving market share. These include establishing closer relationships with customers and better addressing their needs.

Company Background

In the 1960s, Mitch Kapor, eventual founder of Lotus Development Corporation, was a drifter. During the 1970s, he worked as a disk jockey, a stand-up comedian, and a teacher of transcendental meditation. In 1986, as founder and chairman of the nation's leading microsoftware firm, Kapor was considered an industry visionary and an entrepreneurial legend.

It was on New Year's Day, 1979, that Kapor decided to get into the personal computer business. This decision first took him to Visicorp, producer of Visicalc, the first financial spreadsheet package in the market. He wrote a pair of program enhancements for Visicorp but quit after five months and teamed up with a former Data General programming wizard, Jonathan Sachs, to create an integrated business spreadsheet for the newly announced IBM PC.[4] Kapor devised a business plan, with projected first-year revenues of $3 million to $4 million, and approached Ben Rosen, a venture capitalist with a reputation for near-clairvoyance in high-technology areas. Rosen was skeptical but came up with $1 million. Kapor used the money to finance an intensive marketing effort, and the company went on to earn $53 million in revenues in its first year of operation (see Exhibit 1).

One of the company's goals in 1986 was to become the first software house to grow into a major corporation. Thus far, with every new generation of microcomputer hardware, major software companies had failed and new ones had moved in to take their places. Lotus was attempting to stay on top and grow by (1) diversifying beyond business spreadsheets and (2) becoming the worldwide leader in a

---

[3]"Where Is That Old Software Magic?" *Boston Globe*, May 20, 1986.

[4]The word *integrate* is used to describe software in which functions that were originally sold as separate applications programs (such as financial spreadsheets and word processing programs) have been combined onto one program. In the integrated 1-2-3, the financial spreadsheet was tied into graphics and database management capabilities.

full range of high-productivity microsoftware and services for the business and professional market.

Industry analysts felt that the company's superior sales organization, customer support programs, enormous installed base (estimated to be 1.7 million users worldwide), and dominant advertising presence would enable it to continually roll out new products, companion products, and product enhancements.

To keep the pipeline full of new products, Lotus followed a strategy of spending heavily on R&D, acquiring promising but underfunded software firms, forming joint ventures with hardware and other software vendors, and using innovative arrangements to retain proven independent developers.

Lotus Products 1-2-3.   This integrated spreadsheet program was the 1982 brainchild of Mitch Kapor and Jonathan Sachs that gave birth to the company called Lotus. The company's $4 million product launch in 1983 has been identified by many industry experts as the starting point in the creation of an entire industry. Lotus backed 1-2-3 with an intense sales support and advertising program. Its marketing budget was split 70:30 between dealer support and print advertising. The company's very first product brochure summarized Lotus's marketing strategy as follows:

> At the heart of our product philosophy is a recognition that it is not enough in today's marketplace to merely provide top quality productivity software. A software manufacturer in business for the long term must also fully document and support its products and consistently back its dealers with a full range of services—services that will make the products uniquely easy, painless, and profitable to sell.

In keeping with this philosophy, the company backed up its advertising campaigns (see Exhibit 2) with intensive dealer support, such as:

- Training seminars to provide dealers and their staff with extensive hands-on experience using 1-2-3 in an office environment.

- Special telephone support to answer specific product-related questions and provide on-the-spot advice.

- Promotions called "Dealer Demo Days" in which a Lotus retail sales representative organized site demonstrations of the product to dealer-invited prospects.

- Assistance in designing and managing direct-mail campaigns.

- Cooperative advertising allowances of up to 3 percent on net purchases.

- Product brochures, banners, counter cards, and shelf hangers.

1-2-3's extraordinary success was unparalleled in the microsoftware industry. It had stayed on top of the Softsel Hot List since March 1983.[5]

Reluctant to rest on the success of the original program, Lotus was committed to maintaining 1-2-3 as a state-of-the art product. The two revised releases (2.0 in September 1985 and 2.01 scheduled for September 1986) and the 1-2-3 Report Writer companion product increased the package's size, speed, and functions. Enhancements were planned to further improve the program's efficiency, user friendliness, and compatibility with other programs and possibly to give it a more flexible data structure.

A variety of competitive threats were expected to challenge 1-2-3. Products known as "1-2-3- clones," with retail prices as low as $99 (versus 1-2-3's price of $495), were one such threat. Industry analysts believed that 1-2-3's continuing enhancements would make it difficult for other products to completely duplicate its functions, and, unlike 1-2-3, documentation and customer support for the clones was expected to be sparse. It remained to be seen, however, whether the market would continue to pay $495 for 1-2-3 if a functional spreadsheet could be purchased for $99.

Javelin, a financial program (from a start-up company of the same name) released in late 1985, was another potential challenger. Javelin boasted a radically new data structure that greatly facilitated the handling of larger and highly interrelated spreadsheets, and several experts predicted considerable success for it.

A third challenge was expected from Microsoft: it had announced that Excel, an integrated spreadsheet developed for Apple hardware, would be adapted to IBM and IBM-compatible PCs by late 1986. The IBM version of Excel would feature a spreadsheet tied into a sophisticated, graphical user interface and a mouse-based entry system—features that both 1-2-3 and Symphony lacked.[6]

Symphony.   The success of 1-2-3 set off an industrywide race to produce integrated software. The market opportunities for such products seemed as broad as the microcomputer industry itself, since integrated software appeared

---

[5]Softsel was the largest microsoftware distributor, carrying over 4,000 software programs from vendors. Softsel's "Hot List" was its weekly listing of best-selling programs.

[6]The graphical user interface employed pictorial symbols to represent certain function alternatives instead of the one-word menus that the Lotus products used. A "mouse" was a small, hand-held device that allowed entries to be made by moving the mouse across the computer screen instead of using the keyboard. Excel would allow users to select functions by pointing to the function symbols with a mouse. Lotus believed that the programming required to run this system on current hardware used too much memory and made the computer too slow to be attractive to consumers.

likely to make single-purpose programs obsolete. Almost overnight, dozens of software companies fell under integration's spell; many made splashy announcements of products that did not even exist. The stronger the integration fever became, the more vulnerable Lotus looked. Industry experts believed that, as soon as a five- or six-function program came along, 1-2-3 would be superseded. Kapor, who believed in integration as much as anyone, was determined not to be leapfrogged. Lotus poured about $14 million into Symphony (its own five-function successor to 1-2-3) and Jazz (a similar package for Apple's Macintosh computer).

Symphony debuted in the summer of 1984 with the biggest advertising fanfare in software history—an $8 million campaign that included television spots during the Los Angeles Olympics (see Exhibit 3). In addition to the 1-2-3 functions, Symphony (priced at $695) enabled users to do word processing and manage telephone communications with other computers. Symphony played to mixed reviews. Computer magazines hailed it as a technical achievement, but they complained that it was too complex and that its commands were different from 1-2-3's.

Yet instead of catastrophe, there was anticlimax. The integration craze evaporated, and 1-2-3 regained its position as the number one selling program in the market. The integrated software market turned out to be much like the stereo component market: although some users on the low end of the market preferred the multifunction packages, most preferred to own the more sophisticated, single-purpose programs.

Even though Symphony did not live up to the industry's expectations, it was nevertheless quite successful. Of the multifunctional packages, it was by far the dominant leader, generating an estimated $30 million in revenues in its first year. Although Ashton-Tate's Framework, with its more sophisticated database and word processing functions, won several "performance showdowns," Symphony outsold Framework 5 to 1. Many industry observers felt that this demonstrated the benefits of being associated with Lotus 1-2-3 and the strength of the Lotus marketing organization. Symphony was evolving through an upgrade program similar to the one for 1-2-3, and Lotus had already introduced several companion products, such as Symphony Spelling Checker and Text Outliner.

Jazz. Jazz, programmed for the Apple Macintosh personal computer, was the equivalent of the Symphony program for IBM PCs. Apple was banking on Jazz to help it break IBM's (and 1-2-3/Symphony's) domination of the corporate microcomputer market. It did not turn out that way: individual hobbyists, not corporations, bought Macintoshes; unlike corporations, they did not need high-powered financial spreadsheets. Jazz apparently did not meet a need for many users, and its sales were disappointing.

Future product offerings. In addition to its three leading products (1-2-3, Symphony, and Jazz), Lotus worked toward broadening its product line outside the spreadsheet segment with such additions as Spotlight (for desktop organizing) and Signal (for stock market prices). Despite the company's attempts at diversification, 1-2-3 was projected to continue to provide more than half of the company's revenues in 1986 (see Exhibit 4).

Lotus hoped to create another sales boom by exploiting the neglected market for engineers and scientists. The company estimated that a half-million people were using 1-2-3 for technical purposes and believed the right product offerings could provide access to this huge market. In 1985, Lotus established an Engineering and Scientific Products Division to explore this market.

Lotus's strategy centered on two approaches: (1) to enhance 1-2-3 through expanded statistical functions, enhanced logic capabilities, improved graphics, and the development of direct data acquisition capabilities, so it was much more useful as a technical calculation aid; and (2) to develop a technical word processor that could handle the complex character demands of mathematical and scientific equations. Lotus committed significant programming talent to this challenge in hopes of creating another hot-selling package within one to three years.

Main Competitors

Ashton-Tate. In 1985, Ashton-Tate was the second-largest microcomputer software company in terms of applications programs revenues and the third-largest in terms of total revenues. With the introduction of dBase II in 1981, Ashton-Tate emerged as the leader in microcomputer database management technology. In June 1984, that company came out with a successful upgrade, dBase III, which was easier to use and had greater storage capacity, speed, and power. For the fiscal year ended January 31, 1985, dBase II provided 30 percent and dBase III provided 46 percent of the company's revenues.

Ashton-Tate's strategy for the future was to become a one-stop shopping center for corporate applications software. Like Lotus, it had started to explore the market for information services—including possible arrangements with such information suppliers as Dun & Bradstreet, Dow Jones, and McGraw-Hill. The company's overriding goal was to become the leading software company for corporatewide systems that linked microcomputers into mini and mainframe computer systems. Ashton-Tate's 45-person sales force sold through dealers and distributors; unlike Lotus, Ashton-Tate did not call on corporate accounts.

Microsoft. Microsoft, like Lotus, got its start from a single hit product. By the middle of 1983, the company had earned $50 million in royalties from its MS/DOS operating system ("the software that tells the IBM PC how to think"). By 1986, this operating system had become standard on nearly every IBM PC or compatible computer used in business. Microsoft also was making a push to become the "total microsoftware company" by expanding into the rapidly growing applications market, and, by 1986, it offered a very large range of programs (19) and ranked third in microsoftware applications revenues, behind Lotus and Ashton-Tate.

Microsoft had a smaller sales force (45 people) than Lotus, and its efforts were spread over three times as many products—directed primarily at retail accounts instead of corporate users. Because of this and other marketing disadvantages, Microsoft had traditionally been weaker than Lotus in serving the large corporate accounts. On the other hand, the company had channeled all of its applications sales through distributors and dealers; its exclusive use of distributors and dealers (who were annoyed by Lotus's attempts to sell directly to large corporate accounts) endeared it to the trade.

IBM.   For some time IBM had limited its participation in the microsoftware business to selling "vendor logo" software (products developed to IBM specifications by third parties). But in September 1984, IBM struck out on its own with a splashy announcement of 31 programs that either had been developed internally or had been obtained through purchase of marketing rights. For the business market, it offered the Personal Decision Series: five programs centered on a data management system that was positioned to compete with Lotus products and Ashton-Tate's dBase II. The prices of these five modules ran from $150 to $250 per module.

In May 1985, IBM caused a stir in the microsoftware industry by running a temporary promotion that included free software with the purchase of a PC XT (a special version of the IBM PC). If IBM were to permanently pursue this hardware/software bundling strategy for its entire PC

product line, it would radically change the character of the microsoftware business. IBM's microsoftware, however, did not make inroads into many market segments; its products were not technically outstanding; and many industry experts claimed that IBM's large organization prevented it from effectively transferring its technological and marketing skills to small-ticket items like microsoftware and from bringing these products to market on a timely basis. All the same, and probably because of similar products in wide use on dedicated IBM office equipment, IBM emerged as a major player in the word processing market segment, with a share of about 20 percent.

Distribution Channels

Table A presents an outline of the Lotus distribution system. As of 1985, 47 percent of the company's sales were made to distributors who then sold to retail dealers authorized by Lotus. Approximately 30 "house accounts" (very large retail dealers) bought directly from Lotus and accounted for an additional 19 percent of the company's sales. A large portion (about 70 percent) of house account sales were to large and medium businesses as opposed to individual customers. The remaining sales were made through hardware manufacturers (15 percent), educational institutions (11 percent), and others (8 percent).

Distributors.   Although the microsoftware distribution industry was less than seven years old, it had become the primary channel for all microsoftware products. Distributors received publishers' shrink-wrapped diskettes and documentation by the case, warehoused them, split them into smaller orders, and then delivered them to the retail dealers as needed.

Distributors provided dealers with many benefits. One advantage was price: they bought in such large lots that they could pass quantity discount savings on to dealers (see Exhibit 5 for the volume-purchasing discount structure). Distributors always had products in stock and could usu-

Table A   *Lotus distribution system*

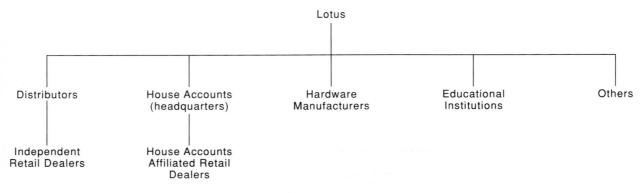

ally make shipments to local dealers much faster than the average publisher, and their broad exposure to many products enabled them to serve as the dealers' objective, one-stop source of technical advice. Many distributors furnished retailers with catalogs and product guides that described various packages and the differences among them. Selling on credit, distributors were often a critical source of financing for thinly capitalized dealers; also, they allowed dealers to return slow-moving packages and exchange them for other products.

At one point Lotus had five distributors: Softsel, Micro D, Softeam, First Software, and Software Distribution Services. Software distributors averaged a gross margin of about 10 percent on the sale of Lotus products and incurred total selling, handling, and transportation costs of about 5 percent on sales. The 1985 industry slowdown was interpreted by Lotus management to indicate that Lotus had too many competing distributors; price wars prevented any of them from achieving profitable margins. In April of that year, the company dropped Softeam and Software Distribution Services. These two distributors had sold the smallest volumes, and their weak financial positions had often made them a significant credit risk.

Microsoft used five distributors and Ashton-Tate used six; both companies used the three distributors that Lotus used. IBM did not use distributors but, instead, sold directly to retail dealers through its sales force.

Dealers. Unlike the distributors, who specialized in software, dealers typically carried both hardware and software products. Microsoftware on the average made up only 7 percent of dealer revenues, but it was felt that software capabilities often drove the sale of a hardware configuration.

To avoid oversaturating the market, Lotus capped the number of its authorized dealers at 4,000 in 1984. IBM had approximately 3,500 authorized dealers, and Ashton-Tate had 2,000. Microsoft, on the other hand, did not require dealers to be authorized; the number of Microsoft dealers was estimated to be more than 6,000.

Based on list prices, retail dealers theoretically could make a 35 percent gross margin on sales. Intense competition for the large accounts, however, had often lowered this to about 8 to 10 percent, leaving retailers with little or no margin on direct costs, and even losses on total costs, for such accounts (see Table B).

One industry analyst divided the dealers into three classes:

First, there are the traditional storefronts, dealing with walk-in business, largely the low-end, price-sensitive sort. These resemble stereo stores in a number of ways, and indeed sometimes were run by people with a stereo-selling background. Second, there are the high-end dealers, often with a number of outside salespeople who call on business accounts; these dealers usually

TABLE B Dealer Costs

Direct Costs	
Customer service, installation, and training	3– 5%
Order processing/invoicing	2– 3
Inventory support	2– 3
Credit	1– 2
Subtotal	8–13
Allocated Costs	
Salesperson salary	3– 5%
Sales promotion and advertising	3– 5
Administrative expenditure	6– 7
Subtotal	12–17
Total	20–30%

emphasize support and systems integration. Finally, there are the pure discounters, largely mail order but also storefront operations, such as the 47th Street Photo.

One Lotus manager estimated that, of Lotus's 4,000 retail dealers, approximately 15 percent were storefronts, 70 percent were full-service retailers, and the balance (15 percent) were discounters. In terms of dollars, however, the discount stores accounted for 25 percent of sales, while the storefronts accounted for only 10 percent of the company's retail sales.

In August 1984, Lotus targeted 30 of its largest retail dealers (mostly large retail chains, such as Computerland and Sears) to participate in its House Account program. These retailers were offered the opportunity to bypass the distributors and purchase directly from Lotus. Most of these accounts did not actually come on board until five months later when Lotus reduced the distributors' margins by 5 percent across the board, thereby enabling the House Accounts to buy at a lower price than their distributors (see Exhibit 6 for the volume-purchase discount structure).

Computer manufacturers. IBM, DEC, and Wang were authorized to sell Lotus products to their corporate accounts along with their hardware configurations. Lotus sold directly to these manufacturers at 40 percent off the suggested retail price.

Educational institutions. Lotus also sold directly (and offered its greatest discounts— 50 percent off the retail price) to colleges and universities. Its objective was to familiarize the student population with Lotus products to develop a loyalty that would endure when the students entered the work force.

Lotus's Sales force

By January 1986, Lotus had a 90-person national sales organization that consisted of both account representatives (reps) and systems engineers. The 75 account reps handled the traditional sales responsibilities, whereas the 15 systems engineers served as technical consultants to end users and potential buyers. The account reps tended to specialize by channel, either selling to corporate accounts or working with national retailers to develop sales programs. About 50 to 60 account reps called directly on large corporate users. On an average, each direct rep had about 10 to 15 corporate accounts.

When Lotus first started shipping 1-2-3 in 1983, it made sales through both the distributor/dealer channel and directly through its own sales force. However, as the industry evolved and 1-2-3 gained wider penetration, dealers often found themselves competing with Lotus's sales force for the high-volume accounts. As a result, in May 1984, Lotus discontinued direct selling through its sales force, under pressure from its dealers and distributors. Commenting on this decision, a company manager explained:

> Clearly, sensitivity to our dealers' requests was a major factor. But customer buying behavior was an equally important factor. Corporate America did not purchase microsoftware centrally. Decisions to use and support personal computers were by and large made by individual departments or managers. Order sizes were small and irregular. Frankly, I doubt if direct selling was a viable option at all under those circumstances.

After May 1984, the Lotus salesperson took a potential corporate buyer through the entire sales cycle until the buying decision was reached (at list price). At that point, the customer was given a list of authorized dealers in the area and encouraged to negotiate the best deal for price and support. The buyers, seeking a low price in return for a large purchase order, typically solicited bids from several dealers. This arrangement became an industry standard and was considered the best way to ensure maximum penetration of major corporate accounts without cannibalization of the dealers' highest-volume buyers. Because of competitive bidding, dealers did not make high margins on these large accounts, but they used this volume to achieve higher discount levels with Lotus.

Customer Buying Behavior

Financial spreadsheet packages usually were purchased for business use. The market was divided by type of business into two major segments: large corporate users and medium and small business users. The large corporations (loosely referred to as the Fortune 2000) accounted for approximately one half of the Lotus spreadsheets in use. The buying process within this segment, however, varied significantly and continued to change. Financial spreadsheet packages initially were purchased by individual employees or departments within a corporation and charged as expense items. Eventually, as the corporation became aware of its significant microcomputer needs and expenditures, someone (often a data processing manager) was given responsibility for consolidating microcomputer purchases in an attempt to ensure compatibility and to gain discounts from high-volume purchase arrangements. Consequently, the purchase of microcomputer capabilities was evolving from an individual expense item decision to a corporate capital budget proposal that had to be sold to various levels of decision makers. In other related industries, such as personal computers, similar buying patterns generally were better served by a manufacturer's direct sales force than a distributor organization. Also, since buyers received both purchase and usage guidance from their data processing departments, they were not completely dependent on the dealers' services. This reduced dependence usually meant that these customers aggressively shopped around for low prices, which often took them directly to manufacturers in search of a price deal for a committed large quantity.

A related buying trend was further increasing pressure on microsoftware companies to sell directly. While divisions or even departments of large corporations bought individually in the past, more recently there was an increased sensitivity toward standardization and aggregation of software purchases. This not only helped administrative uniformity but also achieved purchasing efficiencies. Generally called National Accounts, these large corporations bought centrally but requested delivery and service at various locations. Lotus's managers were aware of the trend but were helpless for the time being, because the company's distribution logistics were not geared to shipping small lots of a large order efficiently to several locations. Lotus's warehouse staff preferred to dispatch in pallet loads of 500 units, whereas dealers could effect dispatches in case loads (20 units) or even less. As a result, Lotus's retail dealers were allowed to accept orders for multilocation dispatches regardless of where the deal was originally negotiated. The only requirement was that the sale be negotiated face-to-face and not by mail order. Thus, the company's Boston dealer, for instance, could book orders at the Boston headquarters of a large corporation for delivery anywhere in the United States.

The medium/small business segment and individual users that accounted for the other half of Lotus spreadsheet sales were expected to be the source of most of the market's growth over the next 5 to 10 years. One microcomputer hardware maker estimated that there were 5 million to 7 million medium and small businesses in the United States (and a similar number of individuals) that could use microcomputers to improve job productivity. Without the aid of in-house expertise, this segment was much more dependent on the dealer's guidance. Consequently, these customers were more dealer-loyal and less price-sensitive; their decreased sensitivity was further aided by the fact that the software cost was usually overshadowed by an accompanying $2,000 to $12,000 hardware purchase.

The Decision

John Shagoury returned to his desk to grapple with the "direct versus distributor" decision. As he leaned back in his leather chair, his thoughts bounced back and forth over the pros and cons of the issue.

There was absolutely no doubt in Shagoury's mind that customer buying behavior demanded a direct selling relationship between Lotus and the company's larger corporate accounts. Shagoury was aware of dealer limitations in servicing such accounts.

> The problem with most of the dealers is that, if they do call on a large corporate account, they typically only get to the purchasing manager, and their sales effort is diluted across several hardware and software products.
>
> Now that microcomputer purchase decisions are being put into the capital budgeting process, the sales effort has to go way beyond the purchasing manager. We also have to sell aggressively to the information managers and actual users within the company.

If the company sold direct, in spite of 1-2-3 street prices, which were as low as $360 in many cases, it would be able to capture an additional $60 in margin, because its current average selling price to distributors and house accounts was only $300. Shagoury estimated that the fully loaded cost (including expenses) of a salesperson currently averaged about $150,000 per year. Lotus's sales managers often had told him that, as a rule of thumb, a salesperson had to invest an average of 20 hours on a corporate account for every 100 programs sold. In practice, however, it required double that time, because a salesperson usually spent 50 percent of his or her time traveling. Shagoury wondered about the margin implications of the two approaches.

Regardless of the numbers, a direct selling approach could have significant potential side benefits for the company. The challenge of direct selling responsibility combined with an appropriate commission plan could possibly provide its sales force the right motivation to consolidate the company's relationship aggressively with its large accounts.

On the downside, a return to direct selling would make Lotus the only major microsoftware publisher to compete with its dealers. The company did not want to upset its distributors and dealers and forfeit this primary channel to a competitor like Microsoft. The channel would be critical to Lotus's future; the company's planned engineering and scientific products would be sold to a fragmented and unknown market that could only be served effectively through a widespread network of local dealers. The medium and small business users who represented nearly half of Lotus's current revenues also would continue to be dependent on local service. Shagoury valued the dealer's marketing role:

> The problem is not so much getting dealer shelf space; our market presence will get that. The problem is getting dealer "mind space." We want the dealers to invest the time in getting to know us and our products so they will sell them over products they don't feel so good about.

He also felt that it would be impossible for Lotus's small sales force to provide direct service to all of the large corporate accounts:

> There is no way that our 90-person sales force can serve all of the Fortune 2000. We can probably do 500 very well and maybe 1,000 adequately. But what can we do for a corporation like Gillette, which is too sophisticated to buy from a retail dealer, yet not big enough to be serviced by a Lotus salesperson? We run the risk of offending them and losing their business.

As John Shagoury sat tugging at his beard, one of Mitch Kapor's favorite Zen quotes was running through his mind: "When standing, stand. When sitting, sit. But above all, don't wobble."

In an industry that had often extracted a fatal price for strategic errors, Shagoury knew that Lotus had to announce its decision soon. Procrastination—just as much as a poor decision—could cost Lotus its market leadership.

EXHIBIT 1   **Channel Choice: Direct versus Distribution, Consolidated Operations Statements, through December 31 ($000s, except per-share data)**

	1983	*1984*	*1985*
Net sales	$53,007	$156,978	$225,526
Costs and expenses:			
Cost of sales	6,798	24,459	42,893
Research and development	2,201	14,752	21,192
Sales and marketing	12,086	43,139	73,046
General and administrative	5,923	15,941	27,464
Total operating expenses	$27,008	$98,291	$164,595
Income from operations	25,999	58,687	60,931
Interest income	944	3,826	3,932
Other income	489	3,025	2,540
Total income	$27,432	$65,538	$67,403
Tax provisions	13,715	29,492	29,253
Income before extraordinary item	13,717	36,046	38,150
Extraordinary item: utilization			
of net operating loss carryforward	600		
Net income	$14,317	$36,046	$38,150
Net income per share:			
Income before extraordinary item	0.98	2.24	2.31
Extraordinary item	0.04	—	—
Net income per share	$1.02	$2.24	$2.31

Exhibit 2
(concluded)

It's a fact. Ninety percent of the business executives in this country suffer anxiety, insecurity and sweaty palms at the mere thought of using a personal computer.

Even though they know a personal computer can increase their productivity.

Enter a remarkable new software program that makes a personal computer so easy to run that we've named it 1-2-3. All those horror stories you've heard about how long it takes to learn to use a computer, how the commands are all in code, etc., you can now safely forget.

With 1-2-3, you can be using a personal computer in a surprisingly short time. Even if you've never been near one before. 1-2-3 instructs you right on the computer's screen in a friendly, helpful way, so you learn as you go along. Everything is in English, not code, so there's no new language to learn.

And there's a special HELP key you can press to put special instructions on the screen if you can't remember what to do next.

But for all its comforting ease of use, 1-2-3 is one of the most powerful programs available for the personal computer. It combines spreadsheet, information management and graphics all in one. It can look at more information in more different ways and do it faster than anything else you can buy. As a result, your productivity increases dramatically.

So there it is. Powerful. Easy to learn and use. Doesn't that sound like the perfect answer for you?

So put down your blankie and pick up the phone and call us at 1-800-343-5414. We'll give you the name of the dealer nearest you, who will give you a complete demonstration.

Once you see 1-2-3 in action you won't have a worry in the world. Except what to worry about next.

© Lotus Development Corporation,
Cambridge, MA 02138. (617) 492-7171
All rights reserved.

1-2-3 currently operates on the IBM and COMPAQ personal computers.
1-2-3 and Lotus are trademarks of Lotus Development Corporation.

EXHIBIT 3

Channel choice: Direct versus distribution, Symphony, TV advertising

Lotus "Talk of the PC World" :30 sec.

Lotus' exciting new commercials will be seen on major television networks throughout the year.

(SFX ROCK MUSIC)
VO When Lotus introduced

1-2-3 software

it rocked

the business world

And 1-2-3 is still

the number one selling PC software

But people said

NEWSCASTER What will Lotus do for an encore?

(SFX CLASSICAL MUSIC)
VO Lotus announces

Symphony
(SFX CLASSICAL MUSIC BUILDS)

VO 1-2-3 and new Symphony software from Lotus

One great idea after another

Source: Company materials

EXHIBIT 4   **Channel Choice: Direct versus Distribution, Projected Sales by Product ($000s)**

	1986	1987
1-2-3	$160	$188
Symphony	41	44
Upgrades and add-ins	33	43
Jazz	8	8
Word processing	—	14
Business products (new)	8	22
Engineering #1 (Extended 1-2-3)	8	10
Engineering #2 (Word Processor)	3	10
Signal receivers	2	2
Signal subscribers	6	14
Lotus magazine	8	9
Total revenue	$277	$364

SOURCES: *Software Access International* and Paine Webber estimates.

EXHIBIT 5   **Channel Choice: Direct versus Distribution, Distributors Volume-Purchasing Terms**

Annual Units Purchased[a]	Discount Off Retail List (%) Price[b]
50,000 and below	36%
50,001 to 100,000	37
100,001 to 150,000	38
150,001 to 200,000	39
200,001 and over	40

[a]A unit means one 1-2-3, Symphony, or Jazz program. Other Lotus programs, companion products, or upgrades did not count toward discount volumes, but were purchased at the same discount levels achieved through unit purchases.
[b]These discount levels became effective September 1985. Previously, they were each 5% higher.

EXHIBIT 6   **Channel Choice: Direct versus Distribution, House Accounts Volume-Purchasing Terms**

Annual Units Purchased	Discount Off Retail List (%) Price
2,000 to 12,000[a]	37%
12,001 to 20,000	38
20,001 to 30,000	39
30,001 to 40,000	40
40,001 and over	41

[a]All house accounts had to commit to a minimum of 2,000 units. Since a majority of such accounts were large retail chains, there never was a problem of getting this commitment.

KRAFT FOODSERVICE

In February 1985, executives of Kraft's Australian subsidiary met to discuss the future strategy and organization of the foodservice unit (KFS), which manufactured and sold Kraft products to foodservice distributors and operators for use in meals and snacks consumed away from home. KFS was currently an important supplier, but some executives believed KFS should forward integrate to become a full-fledged foodservice distributor. In the United States, Kraft's foodservice operation had evolved from being a supplier into one of the top five "superdistributors" in the U.S. foodservice business. Executives at the meeting first reviewed the U.S. foodservice industry and Kraft's U.S. strategy before turning to the Australian challenge.

U.S. Foodservice Industry

In 1983, consumer expenditures on food consumed away from home in the United States reached $164 billion, almost equal to purchases through grocery retailers (see Exhibit 1). The price paid by foodservice operators for the food consumed away from home was $65 billion, 8 percent more then in 1982. Fresh and perishable foods accounted for half of the purchases of foodservice operators, while dry and refrigerated/frozen groceries accounted for a quarter each.

The foodservice industry included a variety of commercial and noncommercial operators who purchased products from foodservice distributors and, in some cases, direct from food manufacturers. Commercial foodservice operations represented 275,000 outlets in the United States in 1983. The largest 100 foodservice operators, with 26 percent of separate eating places, accounted for 46 percent of foodservice industry purchases. Kraft executives grouped the foodservice operators listed in Exhibit 1 into six segments according to their buying behavior:

Truckload buyers, such as Marriott and ARA Services, bought in large quantities at the lowest possible prices and both had foodservice businesses of over $1 billion. They were "contract feeders," hired, for example, by corporations to provide meal services for their employees and by airlines to prepare meals for passengers. They accounted for 6 percent of U.S. foodservice purchases by operators in 1983.

This case was prepared by Associate Professor John A. Quelch with the assistance of Associates Fellow Mary L. Shelman. Copyright © 1988 by the President and Fellows of Harvard College.
Harvard Business School case 9-589-041.

Chains with controlled distribution, such as McDonald's, with 6,000 units and 1983 sales of $7.7 billion, designated national suppliers of their foodservice products to ensure quality control and consistency. They preferred the administrative convenience of dealing with a few national or large regional foodservice distributors. Increasingly, they were pressing for private label foodservice products carrying their own chain names. They accounted for 22 percent of total operator purchases.

Chains without controlled distribution, such as A&W, designated several approved suppliers of foodservice products and permitted individual franchisees to obtain them from their own locally selected foodservice distributors. They accounted for 32 percent of purchases.

Large accounts with unit procurement included public and private organizations, such as hospitals and schools, that required submission of competitive bids by foodservice suppliers and distributors. They were increasingly trying to consolidate their foodservice purchases with fewer suppliers. They accounted for 27 percent of volume.

Small independents, including single-unit family restaurants, accounted for 10 percent of purchases. Because they needed frequent deliveries of small order quantities, the prices that they had to pay foodservice distributors for their products tended to be higher.

Retail buyers. Three percent of purchases were made by small operators direct from grocery retailers and cash-and-carry centers.

Most operators preferred to deal with more than one distributor. A 1980 survey found that foodservice operators in Dallas purchased from an average of six distributors, but that half of the purchases were typically made from the principal distributor. As indicated in Exhibit 2, the primary distributor was typically selected on the basis of price, secondary distributors on the basis of delivery speed and reliability. On average, foodservice operators received four calls a month from the salesperson representing the primary distributor. Personal relationships between distributor salespeople and their customers were considered critical, particularly in the case of smaller foodservice operators.

Foodservice Distributors

In 1983, foodservice distribution in the United States remained fragmented, but consolidation was leading to the emergence of superdistributors. The 50 largest of the 6,000 distributors in the United States accounted for 30 percent of sales. Distributors averaged a 16 percent margin on sales to operators. A typical distributor carried about 7,000 items. Four types of distributors accounted for the $71.5 billion of foodservice distributors' sales in 1983:[1]

Superdistributors	7%
Other broad line distributors	22
Account specialists	14
All other (including specialty distributors)	57

Superdistributors included five companies: SYSCO, CFS Continental (a division of Staley), PYA Monarch (a division of Sara Lee), Kraft, and Rykoff-Sexton. These companies sold a full line of foodservice products including, in addition to food, kitchenware, paper products, chemicals, and equipment, to all types of foodservice operators. Through acquisitions of family owned local distributors, they were aiming for equally strong representation in all geographic regions and product lines. CFS and Rykoff-Sexton as well as Kraft had their own manufacturing facilities and between one quarter and one third of their sales were of their own brands. A KFS executive explained the benefits of being a superdistributor:

> We can obtain the maximum quantity discounts from suppliers. Our superior credit rating lowers the cost of debt. Our national coverage is valued by the national fast food chains because they can designate us as their primary supplier nationwide and be sure of consistent product and service quality. Through a sophisticated management information system linking headquarters and the branches and permitting direct order entry by our customers, we can minimize the inventories in our system, optimize the routing of our trucks, and provide product usage reports to our customers. The small distributor just can't afford the investment needed for this type of system.

On the other hand, an independent local distributor commented:

> The superdistributors are rapidly becoming dinosaurs. They are too large to be customer-responsive and their branches provide inconsistent service. Their salespeople and marketing programs are no better than those provided by smaller, independent distributors. They are more interested in pushing their private label products—which are no better in quality—than searching out the best product value for the customer. The foodservice business is still a local business—dealing with a nationwide superdistributor offers no advantage. In fact, most foodservice operators do not want to be dependent on a single large distributor.

Nevertheless, the five superdistributors' average growth rate of 13.5 percent in 1983 was almost twice that for foodservice distribution as a whole.

---

[1]This figure exceeds the $65 billion operator purchases from distributors in Exhibit 1 due to the inclusion of nonfood items sold to operators by some distributors.

Broad line distributors carried almost as many items as superdistributors but were local, rather than national, typically concentrating on one or two major metropolitan areas. As a result, they often could achieve a higher volume throughput per distribution center than the superdistributors.

Multiunit account specialists. These distributors specialized in serving the needs of large fast-food chains. As such, they competed with the multiunit account divisions of the superdistributors. The largest, Martin Brower, supplied many of McDonald's 6,000 outlets; its sales grew 16 percent in 1983. It aimed to maximize its percentage of each account's purchases to compensate through volume for the narrow margin it was able to obtain from the powerful chains. Some multiunit account specialists were owned by individual fast-food chains yet served other customers. Other fast-food chains like Hardees had their own captive distribution networks.

Specialty distributors included smaller, local distributors who often specialized in a product line (e.g., "center of the plate," beverages, or produce) or in serving the full range of product needs of a particular type of restaurant. Specialty distributors were especially strong in serving ethnic restaurants, concession stands, and vending outlets. About 1,000 distributors accounting for $12 billion in purchases from suppliers in 1983 were members of 1 of 10 major buying groups. These groups obtained quantity discounts from suppliers as a result of their buying power—sufficient to enable their members to compete with superdistributors. In addition, they supplied nationally advertised private labels (accounting for 25 percent of their members' sales) and sales training programs.

As foodservice distribution became more concentrated, the largest foodservice distributors were increasingly developing lines of private label products. About 30 percent of items carried by a typical large distributor was private label. One distributor explained the increase in distributor private labels as follows:

> Private labels help you control an account. Direct price comparisons with competing distributors are not as easy as they are in the case of national brands. Because private label items are exclusive to the distributor, salespeople are more motivated and the distributor's relationship with the operator is strengthened. In addition, we can usually earn a higher unit margin on our private label than on national brands, particularly in shelf-stable commodity-type products like flour and oil.

Foodservice Suppliers

Most food processors attempted to sell their products through foodservice as well as retail channels. A few, such as McCain's, had tailored their products and packaging to the requirements of the foodservice industry and enjoyed an even balance of foodservice and retail sales. However, most food processors' sales through foodservice distributors and direct to foodservice operators were about one third of their retail volume sales.

Many food processors still regarded foodservice sales as "plus business," rather than as a profit source of equivalent importance to retail sales. Traditionally, the best management talent had been assigned to the retail business, partly because of the investment risk associated with the heavy advertising expenditures required to "pull" consumer demand. However, this was changing as the public consumed more food away from home and as an increasingly powerful grocery trade put pressure on manufacturer margins. Moreover, such companies as H. J. Heinz and Kraft regarded the presence of their products on restaurant tables as highly credible low-cost advertising that helped their retail sales.

Motivated by a strategic objective to take advantage of the shift to away-from-home food consumption, several of the largest food processors, including RJR Nabisco, Pepsico, and Pillsbury, also operated restaurant chains. Kraft, on the other hand, had not invested in the restaurant business.

Kraft's U.S. Foodservice Business

In 1903, J. L. Kraft started a wholesale cheese business in Chicago. He delivered cheese to retail stores on a wagon drawn by a rented horse named Paddy. By 1984, Kraft was one of the best-recognized international brand names in the food processing industry. In that year, Kraft's U.S. foodservice sales were $773 million out of Dart and Kraft, Inc.,'s[2] total sales of $9.8 billion. Kraft food sales through grocery channels were about $3.1 billion. About one quarter of Kraft's total sales were outside the United States.

In 1960, 150 items were in Kraft's foodservice product line, some of which were co-packed (i.e., produced and packaged on Kraft's behalf by other manufacturers). Kraft was especially strong in cheese, mayonnaise, and portion-control packets of condiments, which the company had introduced in 1952. In each product category, Kraft faced a different set of competitors. Kraft's foodservice products were distributed through the "institutional departments" of Kraft-owned distribution centers, from which van salespeople delivered Kraft products primarily to grocery stores and other retail customers, but also to restaurants and other foodservice outlets. The foodservice line also was sold through more than 1,000 independent foodservice distributors, who valued the strength of the Kraft brand name as a point of differentiation and credibility in soliciting business from foodservice operators.

Beginning in the 1970s, the largest grocery chains increasingly asked manufacturers to ship direct from the

plant to their own warehouses, rather than through manufacturer distribution centers. As a result, capacity utilization in the distribution centers declined and they became less economical. Responding to the growth in food away-from-home purchases (a third of all consumer food purchases by 1973), Kraft management attempted to increase the throughput of foodservice products to take up the slack.

A 1974 consultants' study recommended that Kraft expand its foodservice product line from 600 items to 1,300 dry, frozen, and refrigerated products as well as to 300 disposables (paper cups and plates) and other nonfood items. Twelve of Kraft's 35 distribution centers would stock the complete line, while the others would continue to carry just the 600 Kraft-manufactured items. Under the plan, Kraft products would account for only 65 percent of sales as Kraft would offer to act as a foodservice distributor for other manufacturers of branded products. In 1976, Kraft executed this strategy, attracting many small- and medium-sized manufacturers. Several major manufacturers declined to sign up, not wishing to offend their existing independent foodservice distributors. However, Kraft began operations with all of the purchased items it needed to implement the broad line strategy. During the next four years, Kraft foodservice sales remained around $700 million at a time when the foodservice industry was expanding rapidly. Kraft executives estimated that $300 million in sales were lost during this period as a result of the foray into distribution. Much of the lost business was in sales of the more profitable Kraft-manufactured rather than co-packed products, as long-time distributor customers resigned the Kraft product line rather than compete with Kraft in the distribution arena.

By 1982, the poor profitability of Kraft's foodservice operation resulted in the closure of three distribution centers and in substantial reductions in headquarters staff. Kraft executives determined that they had three options: cease to be a distributor; retrench to remain a distributor mainly to smaller, less price-sensitive accounts; or find an effective way to add enough products to achieve necessary scale economies and become a full-line distributor. Following a strategic audit, Kraft decided to aim to become through internal growth and acquisition the first truly national distributor. In addition, the following changes in policy were put into effect:

- The sales organization was given much more latitude to deviate from the national price list to meet local competition and to reward large customers with appropriate quantity discounts.

- Kraft's 1,500 salespeople and their managers, hitherto compensated on salary, were all put on commission based on account profitability.

- A much leaner headquarters staff was charged with supporting the needs of field sales, where decision-making authority was now focused.

---

[2]In 1980, Kraft, Inc., merged with Dart Industries, Inc. In 1986, Kraft again became an independent company.

- Investment in computerized customer ordering and delivery route scheduling aimed to improve the speed and efficiency with which orders were delivered to customers.
- A new team of procurement managers, specializing by product segment, was charged with expanding the line of private-labeled products, setting appropriate product specifications, and ensuring Kraft's costs were the lowest in the industry.

By 1984, sales and profitability had improved considerably. Sales increased 12 percent over 1983. The Kraft foodservice line had expanded to 30,000 food and nonfood items sourced from 250 suppliers. The 600 Kraft manufactured items in the line accounted for 40 percent of sales volume. Kraft applied its brand name to co-packed items once they achieved significant volume in the line and once quality control was assured. Kraft did not aim to be a product innovator in foodservice but, rather, to use its distribution muscle to bring an improved version to market before the innovator took hold.

Kraft salespeople called on their accounts twice a week, taking inventory and orders and presenting information on new products and merchandising events. The sales force included specialists in the needs of particular types of outlet, such as vending, and in particular product lines, such as foodservice equipment, nonfood supplies, and fresh produce, in addition to the core group of salespeople who handled Kraft's dry, refrigerated, and frozen products. National account teams serviced the largest operators, while telemarketing was used to solicit orders from small accounts. Independent distributors continued to be used to supplement the Kraft distribution system in remote areas.

Kraft's sales force was highly regarded by operators as one of the most sophisticated and best trained in the industry. Headquarters provided salespeople with hand-held computers to monitor operator inventories and enter orders automatically; the speed and accuracy of deliveries to customers increased as a result. Inventory turnover data collected in this manner could be analyzed and used by salespeople to emphasize the highest volume items in presentations to their accounts. Added value services that Kraft provided operators included: assistance in restaurant site selection and interior design; dieticians who provided recipes and assisted operators in product preparation and menu planning using computerized nutrition programs; and merchandising aids for display at the point of sale.

The Australian Foodservice Industry

The Australian population in 1984 was 16 million, one-16th of the United States, yet the Australian land mass was bigger than that of the continental United States. Australia was a federation of six states plus the Northern Territory. A map is presented in Exhibit 3. About 68 percent of the population lived in the nine principal urban areas; Sydney and Melbourne were the largest cities. Each state's foodservice sales and the number of foodservice outlets were roughly proportionate to population, though fast-food sales in South Australia, Western Australia, and Queensland were growing more rapidly than in the largest states, Victoria and New South Wales, where fast-food penetration was more established.

Expenditures on food purchased away from home were 25 percent of total Australian food expenditures in 1984. This figure was expected to grow to 33 percent by 1987 due to the rising percentage of women in the work force, expansion of the tourist trade, increased leisure time, the liberalization of hotel, club, and restaurant licensing hours, and union demands for on-site catering facilities for workers.

As shown in Exhibit 4, there were about 45,000 catering establishments in Australia serving over 4 billion meals a year. Sales by these establishments to consumers totaled A\$2.24 billion in 1983.[3] Thirty percent of outlets accounted for 70 percent of sales; but, at the operator level, the foodservice industry was fragmented. Single-outlet independent operators accounted for 85 percent of retail foodservice establishments. Because they lacked storage facilities, their chefs or catering managers typically made frequent irregular purchases from cash-and-carry outlets, retail grocers, and markets. Some of the independent operators were organized into buying groups, but they were less powerful than in the United States.

Foodservice tonnage had grown at an annual rate of 2.7 percent between 1976 and 1983. Growth in fast-food chain volume was especially pronounced, reaching an 8.6 percent annual rate in 1983. By 1984, there were 1,100 fast-food outlets in Australia, compared to 52,000 in the United States. The leading fast-food chains, McDonald's and Kentucky Fried Chicken, had only entered Australia in 1971 and 1968, respectively. By 1983, McDonald's had 120 outlets. The growth of the fast-food chains and family restaurant chains, such as Pizza Hut, was occurring primarily at the expense of independent fast-food outlets and hotels/motels.

Fast-food chains typically purchased from foodservice distributors or direct from manufacturers. McDonald's purchased through a different foodservice distributor in each state but specified certain suppliers, including Kraft, on a nationwide basis. Only one fast-food chain—Denny's—operated its own warehouse.

Foodservice Distributors in Australia

The relative importance of various distributor channels in the supply of food to operators is shown in Exhibit 5.

---

[3]In 1984, an Australian dollar was worth 70 percent of a U.S. dollar.

Given the geographical size of Australia, foodservice distribution was fragmented, with many local distributors, often former truck drivers, serving the needs of outlets in a single urban area. A large Australian foodservice distributor might have $10 million annual turnover and sell 2,000 items. Foodservice distributors obtained an average 15 percent margin on their sales to foodservice operators. The typical foodservice outlet supplied by a distributor received 36 deliveries a year. Distributors were mostly unsophisticated entrepreneurs who provided few added value services in addition to physical distribution.

Grocery retailing was much more concentrated than in the United States, and the major retail supermarket chains played an especially important role in foodservice distribution, using their warehouse facilities to supply foodservice establishments as well as retail stores. About 23 percent of Kraft's 1984 foodservice volume and 34 percent of its retail volume were sold through five major supermarket chains performing this dual role.

Kraft Foodservice in Australia

As in the United States, the principal manufacturers of foodservice products also served the retail market through grocery stores. With 1984 sales of $45 million, Kraft's foodservice operation was similar in size to those of Nestlé and Unigate (the Australian subsidiary of Unilever). Only the Australian firm Allied had substantially higher foodservice sales, at around $75 million.

Outside the United States, KFS was the third largest Kraft foodservice operation in sales. Yet, despite being a major player in the Australian market, KFS accounted for only 2.5 percent of all foodservice sales by manufacturers in Australia in 1983.

As in the United States, the evolution of Kraft's foodservice business in Australia was linked to changes in grocery retailing. By the early 1980s, grocery retailing in Australia had become so concentrated that five competitors accounted for 80 percent of all commodity volume. These chains had built their own distribution centers to which manufacturers shipped direct. As a result, manufacturer-owned warehouses, which had serviced foodservice as well as retail customers, had become progressively uneconomical. By 1984, Kraft operated just one warehouse, located in Melbourne, to serve retail and foodservice customers in the entire country. Partly as a result, KFS's return on assets, a principal criterion against which all Kraft units were evaluated, had risen to 25 percent.

In 1984, KFS competed in 10 of 32 foodservice product categories. Exhibit 6 shows KFS's 1984 dollar sales, gross margins, and market shares by category. Kraft was especially strong in portion controls, accounting for 20 percent of the items, salad dressings and processed cheese. KFS accounted for 10 percent of combined tonnage in the 10 categories in which it competed.

The KFS product line comprised 75 items. About 16 percent of KFS products were contract packed but all carried the Kraft brand name. KFS earned a 15 percent contribution margin on contract-packed goods, compared to 30 percent on products it manufactured itself. Kraft Australia earned an average 40 percent margin on nonfoodservice sales to grocery retailers. The lower margin on foodservice versus retail was due to intense price competition among suppliers, who often viewed foodservice sales as "plus business" over retail sales, and due to lower advertising costs. The contract packers often sold the same product that they delivered to KFS under their own labels at substantially lower prices. However, KFS management viewed contract packing as a way to extend the product line without investing in additional production capacity.

KFS shipments accounted for 26 percent of Kraft's total tonnage and 20 percent of total dollar sales, a mix similar to that of other packaged goods companies in Australia like Nestlé. KFS, like Nestlé, relied on the strength of its brand name to minimize competing on price and to enforce tight payment terms on its customers.

KFS shipped 30 percent of its tonnage direct to foodservice operators and 70 percent via 320 wholesale distributors and grocery wholesalers/retailers. Seventy accounts—of which 52 were wholesale distributors—accounted for about three quarters of KFS tonnage. KFS's largest account, Amalgamated Wholesalers, accounted for 15 percent of the volume. KFS products were carried by 9 of the top 10 largest distributors, and at least one Kraft product was used by over 80 percent of Australian foodservice operators.

KFS was especially strong with the grocery wholesalers and retailers who doubled as foodservice distributors. On the other hand, KFS was weak in the vending channel and on bid business, including government contracts.

Consultant's Survey of KFS

A recent survey of foodservice operators and distributors by an independent consultant commissioned by Kraft concluded that:

- KFS provided poor service (only 88 percent on-time order fulfillment), slow delivery and out-of-stocks partly because of inadequate interstate buffer inventories. Lead times on orders of major items were especially long. In addition, KFS salespeople were said to be "inflexible, slow to act, retail-oriented, and elitist."

- KFS's product quality and product innovation lead over competitive brands was thought to have diminished. KFS had not responded to operators' requests for customized package sizes and increased shelf life on portion controls. According to one distributor, "KFS was once a leader but now is too arrogant."

- KFS did not provide enough training and trade show support to distributors.
- Many distributors preferred annual volume rebates over the periodic retail-type trade deals that KFS offered. In addition, KFS ran too few joint promotions with operators users and did not take enough initiative in developing them.
- Smaller distributors suggested that the KFS quantity discount structure should have seven price brackets, not four. As one distributor put it, "We often stretch to achieve a better quantity discount, stock more than we need, and jeopardize product freshness." At the same time, the distributors did not want steeper quantity discount schedules, which tended to advantage the large retail grocers and foodservice operators who wanted to buy direct from manufacturer.
- Just because they had to be shipped separately, dry and refrigerated goods ordered by an account were treated separately for purposes of calculating quantity discounts.
- The KFS pricing schedule discouraged small emergency fill-in shipments. KFS aimed for less-frequent, higher-volume deliveries even if this weakened its customer service image.
- KFS did not delegate enough pricing latitude to its district sales offices in each state so they could match local competition.

Following the survey, KFS studied various distribution options to improve customer service and delivery performance:

- To be able to provide one-day-after order delivery in the five major cities, KFS would have to set up warehouses in Perth and Brisbane and establish a fast haulage capability from its Melbourne warehouse to serve Adelaide and Sydney. The extra cost in facilities, buffer inventories, and inventory handling would be 1.05 percent of total KFS sales. Some KFS executives questioned whether customers would pay extra for 24-hour delivery or whether they "would expect KFS to provide it free because that's what they get from everyone else they deal with." Others questioned establishing warehouses in Brisbane and Perth, cities which together accounted for only 15 percent of KFS sales.
- If KFS forward integrated to become a distributor for, say, 60 percent of its current foodservice sales, the cost of warehousing and delivery was estimated at 10 percent of sales, and the cost of selling, order processing, and administration at 7 percent. To be profitable, KFS as a distributor would have to establish a minimum drop size of $200.

Strategy Meeting

In February 1985, senior Kraft Australia executives met to discuss the growth strategy options open in KFS. These included remaining a supplier, becoming a distributor as in the United States, or becoming an operator.

Several executives believed KFS's strengths were as a supplier and that substantial growth was possible if KFS "stuck to its knitting." Expansion opportunities included the following:

1. KFS could contract to sell for a fee the products of food manufacturers, such as Campbell's, that did not have their own foodservice sales forces. According to one marketing manager: "This could help us round out our product line and improve our sales force productivity without requiring further investments in wholesaling and distribution."

2. KFS could expand its sales and marketing efforts to penetrate further foodservice accounts, particularly the largest ones; KFS could add product formulations and packages that were more closely adapted to foodservice distributor and operator needs.

3. KFS could expand its own product line, thereby increasing the average customer order size and, hence, the call frequency and efficiency of its sales force. According to one manager: "We should add more imported products from Kraft USA and redouble our new product development efforts in Australia."

4. KFS could use its excess manufacturing capacity to contract-pack for small specialty manufacturers. Alternatively, or in addition, KFS could pack private label brands for foodservice distributors. According to one manager: "The private label threat is increasing; we need to get a piece of the action now." Another retorted: "Private labels so far have been of poor quality. Most distributors and operators aren't interested." A third queried: "We currently have a distributor who's selling private label product in direct competition with our line. Should we cut him off?"

5. KFS could "rent" an underutilized sales and distribution network of a food or even a nonfood company without directly competitive products in order to penetrate accounts in outlying areas on which the KFS sales force could not cost-justify calling.

Some executives argued that KFS should become a distributor as well as a supplier. As one put it:

Foodservice distribution is going to evolve in Australia as it did in the United States. That means suppliers are going to be under pressure eventually from distributor private labels. To ensure our long-term influence with the operator, we need to establish ourselves as a distributor now.

There were two key issues if KFS went ahead. First, should KFS be a distributor to all types of foodservice operators or specialize in contract distribution to the major fast-food chains (as Martin Brower had done in the United States)?[4] Second, should KFS be a full-line distributor—in which case the existing product line would have to be rounded out—or a limited-line distributor of its own products over which it would be able to ensure quality control?

A minority group of executives argued that Kraft Australia should become an operator as well as a distributor. The executives believed that the U.S. company had missed out by not participating directly in the growth of away-from-home food consumption; that operator margins—in the ice cream parlor business, for example—were very attractive; and that experience as an operator would increase KFS's understanding of operator and end-user needs. Others argued that the investment risk was too great and that KFS could participate profitably in industry growth by being the most progressive supplier serving the needs of the fast-food chains.

The strategic role of KFS was not the only subject for discussion. There was also debate over how the foodservice function should be organized within Kraft Australia. Currently, the same 100-person sales force called on both retail and foodservice customers, though 10 salespeople and 10

---

[4]In 1984, contract distributors accounted for 5 percent of total foodservice volume in Australia.

executives at headquarters were dedicated exclusively to key foodservice accounts. With this background, the following debate occurred at the planning meeting:

Manager—Foodservice

In setting product shipment priorities, foodservice always seems to take a back seat to retail. We need a separate foodservice organization with our own sales force, our own financial reporting system, and our own P+L. This would boost morale, send a "we care" signal to our foodservice customers, and enable us to service them better. In addition, we'll be able to offer a career path to our people specializing in foodservice. That means we'll attract a higher caliber of salesperson who'll be able to call on the top people in the largest firms.

Marketing Manager—Retail

I disagree. Selling retail and foodservice customers is pretty similar. Most of the products are the same. And many of the foodservice distributors are, in fact, the retail grocery chains. Right now, our lean foodservice operation helps absorb overhead. A separate foodservice organization would add overhead, result in duplication of effort. Outside the major cities, it's impossible to justify two sales forces.

Manager—Foodservice

In the past, we've looked at foodservice as an additional channel for our retail products. What we have to realize now is that selling foodservice is not the same as selling retail. That's why we need a separate organization.

EXHIBIT 1   1983 U.S. Foodservice Industry[a]

	Equivalent Consumer Expenditures for Food ($ billions)	Food Purchases ($ billions)	Increase over 1982
Commercial	$105.2	$36.8	10%
Separate eating places	89.2	30.7	11
Refreshment places (fast food)	41.5	12.9	13
Restaurants and lunchrooms	44.8	16.6	8
Commercial cafeterias	2.9	1.2	6
Lodging	6.2	2.5	2
Recreation	4.9	1.9	7
Retail hosts	3.9	1.5	9
Separate drinking places	1.1	0.4	2
Noncommercial	58.6	28.2	4
In-plant/in-office	10.6	5.3	5
Health care (hospitals and nursing homes)	13.1	6.6	1
Vending	10.3	4.6	3
Primary/secondary schools	11.0	5.5	5
Colleges/universities	4.9	2.1	4
Military	2.4	2.3	5
Airlines	2.4	0.9	12
Other captive	1.7	0.9	4
Total	163.8	65.0	8

[a] Excluding alcoholic beverages and sales taxes.

SOURCE: Technomic Consultants.

EXHIBIT 2   Key Findings of Foodservice Operator Survey

1. The percentages of respondents rating certain services other than price "most important" in their selection of a foodservice distributor:
   - Reliable on-time delivery   51%
   - Professional/knowledgeable sales representatives   39
   - Consistent in-stock availability   33
   - Broad line   29
   - Offers a selection of quality/price levels   27

2. Most respondents believe their primary foodservice distributors offer the lowest prices. Reasons for changing primary distributors were:
   - Price   50%
   - Better service/delivery   24
   - Product quality   16
   - Change in sales representative   13
   - In-stock availability   11

3. Kraft customers offered the following reasons for choosing Kraft as their primary foodservice distributor:
   - Product quality   86%
   - Good prices   43
   - Broad line   29

4. On-time delivery is relatively more important and price less important in the selection of a secondary versus primary distributor.

5. Kraft customers rated Kraft sales representatives high on "product familiarity" and "understands menu matching of his or her products to my operation." Kraft sales representatives were rated less favorably on "responds to emergency orders" and "handling of damaged/spoiled products."

NOTE: Findings based on a survey of 1,200 Kraft foodservice customers and 1,800 noncustomers in the Dallas area.

EXHIBIT 3

Australia: Principal population centers

EXHIBIT 4   1983 Australian Foodservice Industry

	Number of Establishments		Food Purchases ($ millions)		Growth in Purchases versus 1982
Commercial					
Separate eating places:					
Fast-food chains	724	(2)%	$ 164.9	(9)%	13%
Fast-food independents	13,189	(29)	332.7	(18)	6
Restaurants and cafes	8,108	(18)	307.3	(17)	8
Lodging	6,003	(13)	264.6	(15)	2
Venue caterers	1,486	(3)	86.7	(5)	5
Clubs	3,242	(7)	201.5	(11)	3
Noncommercial					
In-plant/in-office	1,000	(2)	52.5	(3)	5
Health care	1,140	(3)	174.9	(10)	10
Schools and colleges	9,934	(23)	83.2	(4)	5
Travel operators	15		88.0	(5)	4
Prisons	67		37.0	(2)	4
Military	NA		16.7	(1)	5
Total	44,818		$1,810.0		

NA means not available.

SOURCE: Biz-Shrapnel pty, 1983.

EXHIBIT 5   Foodservice Distribution Channels in Australia

	Percentage of Food Service Volume Moving from Manufacturers to Operators via . . .
Direct from manufacturer	26%
Specialist foodservice distributor	17
Wholesale grocer delivered	20
Wholesale grocer cash and carry	3
Retail outlet	9
Markets	10
Van	4
Other	2

SOURCE: Biz-Shrapnel pty, 1982

EXHIBIT 6 **Kraft Foodservice Australia Sales, 1984**

	Dollars (000s)[a]	Sales (%)	Gross Margin (%)	Category Growth Rate (%)	Kraft Market Share (%)
Portion controls	$10,345	23.1%	24.6%	2%	26%
Processed cheese	14,377	32.1	27.1	4	12
Natural cheese	5,580	12.5	30.0	4	11
Soft white cheese	2,258	5.0	NA	4	10
Salad dressings	3,707	8.3	34.9	7	16
Pickles and sauces	1,512	3.4	27.7	1	11
Oils and shortenings	2,231	5.0	13.6	5	4
Other[b]	4,746	10.6	23.0	NA	NA
Total	$44,756	100.0%			

NA means not available.

[a]In Australian dollars.

[b]Includes coffee, milk, spices, and flavor enhancers.

MURRAYHILL, INC.

C. Gifford Davis, president of Murrayhill, Inc., a privately held manufacturer of high-quality men's shoes, carefully studied the sales forecasts for 1986. The problem the company now faced was very different from that of the previous decade. During the 1970s, Murrayhill's sales had dropped as the company's retail accounts were undergoing basic structural changes. Double-digit inflation had resulted in a retail industry move from full-priced outlets to discount stores, leading to less service for Murrayhill customers. Traditional Murrayhill retail accounts were faced with stiffer competition, and the company's total reliance on nonproprietary retail distribution had resulted in excess capacity problems at the factory, which had increased per item costs and lowered company profits. Direct mail distribution through proprietary catalog sales and a broader-based product offering had solved the problem; it also enabled Murrayhill to exploit market niches that were less exposed to competition from imports or other U.S. manufacturers. In fact, strengthening of traditional retail business from 1983 to 1985 and the rapid growth of direct mail cataloging presented Davis with another difficult problem: how to manage Murrayhill's growth with its only factory approaching full capacity.

Edward Wilson, executive vice president, reviewed Murrayhill's alternatives. Expanding capacity would be the most logical action, yet Wilson knew that skilled craftsmen were difficult to find and training "green" labor would be prohibitively expensive. Murrayhill could subcontract manufacturing or acquire a small U.S. manufacturer, but in either case, it would be two years before workers at another company could be trained in the complexities of welt shoe construction.[1] Other responses included raising prices further or restricting distribution through either retail or direct channels, or both.

The irony of this situation was not lost on Christopher Hill, manager of Lynn Shoes, the Murrayhill direct mail catalog operation. His objective with the catalog had been to fill excess plant capacity profitably, and this had been accomplished. The speed of Lynn Shoes' growth had been greater than anticipated, however. Now that excess capacity was no longer a problem, there was debate about how aggressively the Lynn Shoes operation should be promoted and what percentages of the shoes made in Murrayhill's single factory should be made available to Lynn Shoes and to Murrayhill's nonproprietary retail outlets.[2]

This case was prepared by Research Associate Melanie D. Spencer under the direction of Associate Professor John A. Quelch.
Copyright © 1986 by the President and Fellows of Harvard College.
Harvard Business School case 1-586-047 (Rev. 6/24/91).

[1]Goodyear welt construction was a costly and time-consuming process by which a leather strip, or welt, was sewn to a channeled insole of a shoe to bond the shoe's upper and its sole. The welt gave lateral support around the forepart of the shoe and helped the shoe hold its shape. The result was a durable, heavy-grade shoe.

[2]Nonproprietary retail stores were not owned by any manufacturer and carried multiple brands and product lines.

Company Background

Thomas Murray and Mitchell Hill began manufacturing men's dress shoes in Lynn, Massachusetts, in 1926. In 1930, they incorporated their business as Murrayhill, Inc. Throughout its history, the company maintained a reputation for exceptional quality and comfort. Integral to this reputation was Murrayhill's special contour footbeds, developed in 1933. This concept was based on the belief that a sole molded in the shape of a footprint would be comfortable and provide orthopedic benefits. In addition, Murrayhill employed a costly manufacturing process, the Goodyear welt construction, that securely bonded the shoe and sole to ensure exceptional durability.

Commitment to customer comfort and adherence to high-quality standards, both in raw materials and construction, built strong customer loyalty, which sustained demand for Murrayhill shoes through economic downturns. Commitment to quality meant that in 1985 each pair of Murrayhill shoes still required over 100 separate hand operations and 20 formal inspections; one pair of shoes took a full month to make. Manufacturing had kept pace with technological developments but remained highly labor-intensive. In addition, many manufacturing processes required skilled and experienced craftsmen, who were increasingly hard to replace in the 1980s.

Despite the market pressures, Murrayhill remained profitable and had even diversified its distribution channels by establishing direct mail cataloging in the late 1970s. In 1985, the company made a pretax operating profit of 9 percent on sales of $27 million.

The Evolution of the Shoe Industry

From 1900 until the 1940s, approximately 400 shoe manufacturers were operating in New England; by 1985, only 10 percent remained. The continued labor intensity of shoe manufacturing made the industry vulnerable to lower-priced imports.

Murrayhill survived by producing a premium-quality product that was difficult to duplicate and that appealed to a narrow market segment willing to pay high prices for Murrayhill quality. As fashion became a more important component of men's shoe purchasing behavior and casual styles became more popular, the company broadened its product line to include several fashionable and lightweight styles that retained the famous Murrayhill quality. Nonetheless, Murrayhill faced several strong domestic competitors and unrelenting price competition from imports.

In 1985, the men's premium shoe market was considered to include brands with a price range of $75 or higher. Murrayhill, Inc., Johnston & Murphy, E. T. Wright & Company, Allen Edmonds, and Florsheim were the major domestic manufacturers producing premium shoes. Measuring market share within the industry was difficult because so many of the manufacturers were private companies, like Murrayhill; in addition, these companies were not always in direct competition because distribution channels differed.

Allen Edmonds and E. T. Wright & Company were considered to be Murrayhill's closest domestic competitors, with an estimated market share of 8 percent each, compared with Murrayhill's dollar market share of approximately 12 percent. Allen Edmonds, headquartered in Wisconsin, relied primarily on nonproprietary retail outlets for its distribution. Its advertising was sizable, with expenditures in the $1 million to $2 million range. Most of this was spent promoting brand name awareness to consumers. Allen Edmonds also operated a small direct mail catalog business, the majority of whose costs were handled by Edmonds' retail accounts. E. T. Wright & Company, headquartered in Massachusetts, operated an extensive direct mail business and, like Murrayhill, relied on nonproprietary distribution. Johnston & Murphy, on the other hand, operated proprietary retail outlets and experimented in the mail order business for both men's and ladies' premium shoes. Florsheim's product line covered several price points, including those in the premium market. Florsheim was, by far, the strongest competitor, with an estimated market share of 18 percent and both nonproprietary and proprietary retail distribution channels. Hanover, a medium-priced shoe manufacturer, also was noted for its direct distribution system. The company owned over 100 proprietary retail stores, operated a successful mail order business, and produced private label footwear for J. C. Penney and Sears, Roebuck department stores.

Imports accounted for a 50 percent share of sales of premium men's shoes; this compared with a 77 percent share of the total men's shoe market. Bally, the strongest competitor, was the leading imported brand in this market before 1975 and maintained a market share of close to 25 percent at that time. By 1985, other imported brands included Baker Benjes, Cole Hahn, Ferragamo, Bruno Magli, and Church's. The imported products differed from the domestic premium brands, however: most were lighter in weight and designed to appeal to more fashion-conscious consumers.

The Retail Shoe Business

Murrayhill's principal distribution channel until 1979 was a network of approximately 450 nonproprietary retail outlets throughout the United States, many of which also sold other brands of men's premium shoes. Murrayhill's shoes were sold wholesale to retailers at approximately 50 percent of the suggested retail price. Price increases usually were announced in February or August. The company did not offer its retail accounts quantity discounts.

Because producing high-quality men's dress shoes demanded highly skilled labor and specialized facilities, Murrayhill's entire product line had been manufactured at the company's facility in Lynn, Massachusetts, throughout most of the company's history. As consumer preferences changed and fashion became more important in men's shoes during the 1970s, Murrayhill began contracting with outside manufacturers to produce casual shoes that matched Murrayhill's quality and feature specifications yet could extend the brand's franchise to a younger age group. Murrayhill's executives labeled these styles "outside" shoes, while those manufactured at the Lynn plant were called "inside" shoes. In 1985, the average prices the retailer paid Murrayhill for a pair of inside shoes was $52 and, for a pair of outside shoes, $34. Variable manufacturing costs per pair of inside shoes were $40. The average cost of a pair of outside shoes to Murrayhill was $28.

Murrayhill sold approximately 160 inside shoe styles and 56 styles made by outside manufacturers. Since there were 80 sizes to each style, Murrayhill's total SKUs numbered around 17,280, and it carried an inventory in stock of over 64,000 pairs. Both internal and external production schedules for each style were set in advance, based on sales projections. Murrayhill rarely did "make-ups" (styles not included in its regular product line, manufactured to the specifications of a retailer) for a particular retail account.

Each of Murrayhill's 16 salespeople was assigned a geographic territory and was responsible for retailer sales and service within the area. Salespeople also were expected to perform "previews" at the beginning of the fall and spring seasons as a method of increasing both consumer and trade sales. Previews consisted of a sales presentation at a retail store, where the Murrayhill salesperson would display and explain the company's entire line to store customers. During the preview, the consumer was offered a price promotion of $10 off any pair of Murrayhill shoes. The retailer was responsible for absorbing the cost of the promotion, while the cost of advertising placed to stimulate retail traffic during the preview was shared between Murrayhill and the retailer. The Murrayhill salesperson would spend time with the retailer's salespeople and customers describing the quality and comfort of Murrayhill shoes. Company management believed that consumers were likely to "trade-up" to a higher-priced brand if they understood the features and benefits of premium shoes. The managers believed that retail salespeople often missed sales opportunities by assuming that casually dressed customers would not buy expensive high-quality shoes, and one of Murrayhill's goals was to have retail salespeople try a pair of Murrayhill shoes on every customer. For some Murrayhill retail accounts, close to 30 percent of annual sales were made during the fall and spring previews.

Murrayhill management tracked the sales of every shoe style. If sales of a particular style slowed, management might elect to replace only the middle sizes, ensuring that Murrayhill would end up with the most popular sizes of a style before the style was terminated or "closed out." Established retail accounts had the option of purchasing close-outs at a 30 percent discount from the regular wholesale price. A list of close-outs was sent to retail accounts twice each year. Retailers would often try to sell these styles at full retail price to increase their unit margins, then mark them down, as necessary. Close-outs accounted for unit sales of 5,500 to 6,500 pairs of Murrayhill shoes per year.

Traditional Murrayhill retail outlets, included department stores, clothing stores, family shoe stores, and men's shoe stores. The economic conditions of the 1970s, however, resulted in changes in Murrayhill's retail account mix. The channel mix and unit sales by type of retailer for 1978–79 and 1984–85 are shown in Exhibit 1. Between these two periods, sales through clothing stores and department stores dramatically decreased as Murrayhill lost several accounts while others reduced their orders. However, the percentage of sales through specialty shoe discount stores rose from 13.9 percent to 33.1 percent as this channel grew in importance. Murrayhill also became increasingly reliant on Hartwell, a large East Coast chain, for a sizable percentage of unit sales.

Partly in response to the loss of some accounts, Murrayhill established a program to attract additional retail accounts. Any new account that purchased at least 150 pairs of shoes was allowed to pay 20 percent in each of the five months following a 30-day period. A dedicated dealer could sell the 150 pairs before the first invoice payment was due. Forty new accounts were opened under this policy in 1984.

Problems with Retail Distribution

Murrayhill's selective distribution system performed well during the early 1970s. With the 1973 recession, however, the retail trade began to undergo change. Consumers' limited purchasing power made them increasingly price-sensitive and value-conscious, and, because of a sales downturn during this period, retailers were under pressure to cut their inventory carrying expense. Orders of high inventory, low turnover items including shoes, particularly top-of-the-line products, were reduced or eliminated. Since a wide range of shoe sizes had to be inventoried to ensure that a store could provide any customer with a proper fit, some stores responded by reducing the number of styles they carried. Murrayhill shoes, and other premium brands, such as Johnston & Murphy and E. T. Wright & Company, achieved a retail turnover of only 1.7 times per year, compared to an inventory turnover of 3 times per year for moderately priced brands.

Around 1975, traditional full-price retail outlets came under growing pressure. Consumer purchasing trends, the effects of the recession, and inflation laid the groundwork for the emergence of off-price retailing. Off-price retailers typically sold shoes and other apparel below suggested retail prices, accomplished by eliminating expensive fixtures and displays, locating stores in areas with lower rents, and minimizing personnel. The result was a "warehouse" atmosphere—yet the purchase savings overcame consumer resistance and the concept became increasingly popular. To Murrayhill, many off-price retailers were unappealing since they lacked the customer service that company executives considered especially important to stimulate sales of higher-priced shoes. Some executives also believed that distributing Murrayhill shoes to discounters might result in retail price erosion that would hurt relations with full-price outlets and perhaps put pressure on Murrayhill to lower wholesale prices. The growth of off-price retailing, however, convinced the company that it had to do business with these types of stores. It selected only those off-price accounts that would carry substantial inventories and provide good in-store service.

Partly in response to population shifts and emerging competition from discounters, many department stores expanded their operations from city business districts to the suburbs. Because the primary target for premium men's shoes, the businessman, remained in the business district, the better-quality men's shoe business did not follow. As a result, premium-quality men's shoes became a less important component of department store sales.

The economic pressures placed on retailers during the late 1970s and the stiff competition from discounters caused Murrayhill's sales to suffer. Exhibit 2 shows sales trends through the 1970s. As consumer sales through traditional retail outlets declined, less-well-capitalized retailers were forced to eliminate many low-turnover items, such as Murrayhill shoes. The company lost several accounts. Management became concerned about Murrayhill's exclusive reliance on nonproprietary retail distribution.

Competition from other manufacturers exacerbated problems with retail accounts. Some shoe companies introduced exchange privileges to stimulate retailers to place larger orders. Retailers were allowed to exchange styles that did not sell for new inventory, placing the burden of retail sales risk on manufacturers. Murrayhill refused to adopt this policy. Although exchanges might boost short-term sales, profitability would suffer because production schedules would be difficult to predict and returned shoes probably would have to be sold at a discount. Murrayhill executives also believed that such a policy would make the retailer less concerned about the size and mix of the order he or she placed. One manager remarked, "Personally, I think that the retailer must take some responsibility for sales. If we ship record numbers of shoes only to have them dribbling back later, we'll soon go out of business."

A few retailers ceased placing orders with Murrayhill because of its position. Management felt that the policy resulted in a stronger distribution network, but sales lost during the 1970s resulted in underutilization of plant capacity. By 1978, the factory was operating at only 80 percent of capacity.

Murrayhill management considered several options to increase sales. One was to open proprietary retail outlets where Murrayhill could maintain complete control over distribution. This choice was rejected because of the investment costs, Murrayhill's lack of retail experience, and the likelihood that the proprietary outlets would face the same problems that had troubled Murrayhill's retail accounts.

Manufacturing ladies' shoes was another alternative. Because women purchased a large portion of men's apparel, executives advocating this option believed that women were already familiar with the Murrayhill name. The quality and comfort associated with Murrayhill's men's footwear could be transferred easily to a ladies' product line. Ladies' shoe styles however, were highly influenced by fashion and changed each season. Manufacturing economies were hard to realize: as soon as a shoe craftsman would learn how to handle one style efficiently, the style might be changed or deleted. In addition, Murrayhill personnel had little experience either manufacturing or selling ladies' footwear. These problems led management to pursue other options.

Direct Distribution

In the mid-1970s, C. Gifford Davis received a call from a direct marketer of ladies' shoes. He was interested in expanding his distribution to include men's shoes and proposed that Murrayhill include several styles in his catalog. Murrayhill had been receiving complaints from customers who could no longer find its shoes in retail outlets. Davis concluded that adding a direct distribution system could help retain customers and use excess plant capacity with little risk to regular operations. Murrayhill accepted the proposal.

When the catalog was published a few months later, Murrayhill executives were disappointed. To increase his margins, the direct marketer had priced Murrayhill shoes far above what they sold for at retail. Styles in the catalog were poorly displayed, and customers complained about the lack of service provided on orders. Although Davis held little hope for the venture's success, the catalog sold hundreds of pairs of Murrayhill shoes.

Management, therefore, continued to explore this form of distribution. With proper display and good service, Murrayhill executives believed direct mail catalog sales could alleviate the excess capacity problem. To gain control of the catalog operation, Murrayhill discontinued the initial catalog venture and hired two consultants to experiment with a proprietary direct mail catalog. In January 1977, Murrayhill ran its first advertisement in *The Wall Street Journal*. The copy described Murrayhill shoes and provided an inquiry form for consumers who were interested in receiving a catalog of Murrayhill men's shoes. The advertisement cost was approximately $2,400 and generated 1,120 inquiries and sales of 585 pairs of shoes in the year after it was run.

During the early 1980s, direct sales through mail order catalogs became an increasingly important method of distributing a wide variety of products, from specialty foods to camping equipment. As gas prices increased and two-career families had less time to devote to shopping in stores, purchases through catalogs became more popular as a convenient and cost-effective alternative. Many industry analysts credited the successful L. L. Bean catalog, which featured quality outdoor apparel and equipment, with developing the consumer's habit of purchasing by mail.

Direct mail shoe sales began in the nineteenth century. Sears, Roebuck & Company and Spiegel both marketed shoes through their catalogs. In 1985, Spiegel still offered premium men's shoes in its catalogs, featuring such brands as Bally and Johnston & Murphy. Hanover, E. T. Wright, and Murrayhill were among the few manufacturers that operated successful proprietary catalogs. Estimates of premium men's shoes sold in 1985 through direct mail for seven leading companies are shown below:

Catalog Company	Brands Sold	Estimated Units Sold
Spiegel	J&M, Bally	150,000
Murrayhill	Murrayhill	110,000
E. T. Wright	Wright	40,000
Norm Thompson	Allen Edmonds, Bally, J&M	35,000
Hanover	Hanover, Bostonian	20,000
Luxury Leather	Nettleton	15,000
Brooks Brothers	Brooks's own brand	15,000
Total		385,000

Some executives questioned whether Hanover was in direct competition with Murrayhill, because its shoes were typically sold at somewhat lower price points. In addition to the seven companies listed, other direct mail houses, such as L. L. Bean, sold lower-priced shoes through the mail.

The Direct Mail Operation

Murrayhill named its catalog operation Lynn Shoes. Murrayhill management was concerned about its retail accounts' possible reactions to the new venture. For this reason, Murrayhill was not included in the catalog name, although it was clear to the catalog reader that the shoes being offered were Murrayhill brand. Lynn Shoes "purchased" shoes at transfer prices equal to those paid by Murrayhill's retail customers.

Before 1982, Lynn Shoes used a simple approach to operating the catalog business. Advertisements were placed in magazines and newspapers, such as *The Wall Street Journal, Smithsonian, Yankee,* and fraternal magazines, that were likely to be read by potential Murrayhill customers. An inquiry from these advertisements would result in Murrayhill sending seven catalog mailings in the course of one year. Shoe styles varied by season, and promoted items differed for each mailing. Nearly all the advertising budget was used to generate inquiry names for the catalog mailings. Half of the expenses of the catalog operation were for catalog production and mailings. The majority of the promotions featured reduced prices, but some also offered premiums, such as a shoe care kit, with a purchase.

The primary focus of Lynn Shoes for close to three years was regaining lost retail sales. As the cataloging business evolved, however, Murrayhill executives found that the catalog was becoming particularly important to customers who needed uncommon-sized shoes, such as narrow or wide widths. Cost-control pressure on retailers had forced them to keep lower inventories, which included primarily the more common sizes, making less popular sizes hard to find. Murrayhill expanded the focus of the catalog to include this market niche. By 1985, nearly one half of catalog sales were in sizes not normally carried in retail stores, and the availability of uncommon sizes became a prerequisite for any style to be included in the catalog.

Other changes in the product line Lynn Shoes offered were the result of shifts in company objectives. The more casual life-styles that consumers adopted in the late 1970s resulted in the increased popularity of casual shoes, particularly among younger consumers. Murrayhill expanded its product line to include lightweight dress and casual shoe styles. Because a major objective of catalog operations was to provide a source of supply to Murrayhill customers who could no longer locate a retailer who sold Murrayhill shoes, the initial customer base consisted primarily of these individuals; research had shown that the Lynn Shoes customer was an older, affluent man. As the catalog operation became increasingly successful, however, Murrayhill executives saw an opportunity to broaden Lynn Shoes' customer base by including casual styles in the catalog. This move, initiated in 1982, dramatically changed the customer base. In 1985, almost 60 percent of Lynn Shoes' sales were from customers who had never purchased Murrayhill shoes before they made their first catalog purchase. Outside-produced casual styles constituted the fastest growing area of both Murrayhill's and Lynn Shoes' product lines.

The success of the catalog venture was far beyond expectations: after the first year, annual sales growth exceeded 25 percent. By 1982, the catalog operation had grown to the point where a full-time manager was needed to handle the business. Davis hired Christopher Hill.

In 1984, Lynn Shoes expanded its sources of names for catalog mailings. Advertisements were continued in the publications read by Lynn Shoes' target audience; but direct mail lists of consumers who had previously purchased through the mail were also purchased. With advertising space growing more expensive, these lists offered a cost-effective alternative for obtaining names of prospects. By 1985, Hill estimated that 85 percent of the $481,000 Lynn Shoes advertising budget paid for print space, while 15 percent was spent on purchasing lists of direct mail purchasers.[3]

In addition, Hill decided that the catalog mailings needed a more focused approach to soliciting business. In 1982, Murrayhill set up a system of sequential mailings, with one mailing every other month, that aimed to persuade prospects to buy from the catalog. Because the sequential mailings were initiated by a customer inquiry, which could occur at any time, Lynn Shoes could, in any given month, be mailing seven different catalogs to seven different groups of consumers. Each subsequent mailing offered the potential customer a more powerful price incentive to purchase Murrayhill shoes. Once a customer made a purchase, the sequence of promotional mailings would cease and the customer's name would be added to a list that received retention catalog mailings.

All seven promotional catalogs, except the last, were 40 pages long and included a brief history of shoemaking, a letter from the Lynn Shoes marketing manager, and the Murrayhill shoes unconditional guarantee of satisfaction. The center 32 pages of the catalog changed every six months, while the 8-page "wrapper" around the center of the catalog changed every 60 days. Generally, 80 styles of shoes were included in each catalog, which fell into three groups: 52 styles of "inside-made" shoes that were also available through retail; 12 styles of inside shoes made exclusively for the catalog; and 16 styles of casual shoes made by other manufacturers under contract to Murrayhill that could be purchased only through the catalog. Retail accounts were allowed to purchase styles exclusive to the catalog on special request but paid standard markups, regardless of whether the style was promoted in the catalog. Catalog prices were slightly higher than suggested retail prices on shared styles to cover possible price increases during the run of a catalog. Shoes shared by the catalog and the wholesale business were never promoted in the catalog

to ensure that the selling prices of retail accounts would not be undercut. All of the promotions offered in the catalog carried an expiration date to motivate purchase decisions that might otherwise be postponed. Exceptions to this policy might be made if a new customer ordered shortly after the expiration date. The promotional focus and the customer purchase rate for each of the catalogs are described and summarized in Exhibit 3.

Mailing 1. The first mailing attempted to stimulate sales through persuasion rather than price promotion. Each customer purchasing two pairs of Murrayhill shoes was offered two pairs of cashmere socks. A $2 handling fee was charged for the socks to partially offset the $10 total cost of the premium. Approximately 2.8 percent of consumers receiving catalogs purchased shoes. The average order size was 1.45 pairs.

Mailing 2. Price promotions began with the second mailing. The catalog offered $15 off each pair of shoes purchased and an additional $15 off for every two pairs ordered. This promotional offer was surprisingly weak in impact, registering a closure rate of only 2.5 percent and an average order size of 1.45 pairs. On subsequent mailings, the $15 off promotion became a standard offer on any full-priced item displayed in each catalog.

Mailing 3. The third mailing offered specific styles at reduced prices, displayed on the cover of the catalog. One of the basic "traditional lace-up" inside-made dress styles not available to retailers was shown at 35 percent off the regular price. One other inside-made shoe also was promoted. Five outside-made casual styles, with factory costs of around $28, were offered at $55. When the sequential mailings were first developed, only the dress style was offered, and closure rates were about 3 percent. The addition of the casual styles increased the closure rate to 6.2 percent.

Mailing 4. The promotions in the fourth mailing were similar to those in the third. Six dress styles were featured at a discount; one inside-made dress shoe and one outside-made casual were featured on the cover of the catalog. The standard $15 off on the purchase of any full-priced style was strengthened by an offer of a shoe shine kit for a $2 handling fee; the kit cost Murrayhill $4. For every two pairs of shoes purchased, a leather wallet would be provided free. Each wallet cost Lynn Shoes $8. The wallets were not considered to be a very effective sales incentive, with 25 percent of orders receiving the item. Around 4.3 percent of individuals receiving the fourth mailing ordered Murrayhill shoes.

Mailing 5. Four dress styles were discounted on the cover of this mailing, from $149 to $99. Three casual styles were promoted on the inside of the catalog, with one featured at

---

[3]Murrayhill spent an additional $340,000 in 1985 on print advertisements for Murrayhill shoes that were not intended to generate inquiries for Lynn Shoes.

a very low price of $49. The highly discounted casual style did not appear on the cover, which Hill believed accounted for the relatively low 2.4 percent closure rate.

Mailing 6. The sixth mailing offered deeper price cuts on inside dress shoes, with four styles of $149 shoes at $89. Seven casual styles by outside manufacturers were promoted at $59. Closure rates for this mailing averaged slightly over 3.6 percent.

Mailing 7. The seventh mailing did not include the 32-page center section and displayed Lynn Shoes exclusively. All the shoes featured in the catalog were priced at "half price or less," with some casuals priced as low as $49. The closure rate for this catalog was 7.9 percent.

The overall response rate to solicitation mailings was 4.1 percent. The average pair of inside shoes sold through these mailings for $88 and the average pair of outside shoes for $60. On the earlier mailings, half the responses were received by telephone and half by mail. With the later mailings, the ratio changed to 35 percent by telephone and 65 percent by mail. Of all items purchased, 80 percent were promoted shoes. Inside-made styles accounted for two thirds of all shoes purchased at regular price. If a consumer who had inquired had not purchased by the seventh mailing, Lynn Shoes would send a "drop dead" letter informing customers that they would receive no further catalogs unless they returned an enclosed card. Close to 15 percent responded and, as a group, displayed closure rates to the seven sequential mailings that were very similar to those of initial inquiries. Hill believed this high response rate was due to impulse purchasing and to some consumers simply waiting for shoes to wear out before purchasing a replacement pair.

In 1985, each catalog cost 50 cents to produce and mail. Premium costs totaled $230,000, of which $88,000 was offset by handling charges to consumers. Lynn Shoes also incurred variable processing costs of $1.50 per order and delivery costs of $1.75 per order. Customers were charged $3.50 to cover handling and delivery of each order.

A mailing's success was judged not only by its initial response rate but also by its repeat rate: the percentage of customers responding to any given mailing who also purchased Murrayhill shoes again. This repeat rate varied for each mailing from a high of 33 percent from respondents to the first catalog to a low of 11 percent from respondents to the last mailing. Christopher Hill explained Murrayhill's direct mail catalog philosophy this way: "We sell such a high-quality, comfortable shoe that we have a very high customer retention rate. We can afford to run a break-even catalog operation to attract new customers because these customers are likely to continue to purchase Murrayhill shoes."

This philosophy was the basis for Lynn Shoes' retention mailing program. Once a consumer purchased from one of

the sequential catalogs, he or she would be placed on the retention mailing list. Catalogs were mailed every 75 days with the objective of maximizing profit, rather than attracting new customers. Lynn Shoes mailed 700,000 retention catalogs and 1,020,000 solicitation catalogs in 1985. The retention catalogs were similar to the solicitation catalogs: each had 40 pages with a 32-page core that remained the same and an 8-page "wrapper" that changed for each mailing. While the retention mailings included price promotions, discounts were not as deep and premiums always included the $2 handling charge. Catalog merchandise was also seasonally adjusted, with one spring mailing devoted to white shoes. Lynn Shoes maintained a retention list of 156,300 customers in 1985. The typical response rate was 5.9 percent. The size of an order averaged 1.2 pairs and $111, compared with 1.45 pairs and $111 for a response to a solicitation mailing.

Hill conducted two pricing tests with the retention mailings. The first attempted to determine the price sensitivity of Murrayhill customers by implementing a $10 price increase for each style in the retention catalog. Response from this mailing showed lower unit sales but a higher dollar volume, indicating to Hill that such price increases might be a way of dealing with the capacity issue without lowering dollar sales. The second test was mailed to four randomly chosen groups of 10,000 customers from the retention list. The test catalog featured a handcrafted imported shoe made of a specialty leather, lizard skin, that Murrayhill purchased for $89 per pair. The shoe included Murrayhill product features, such as the molded shoe sole. The four groups of customers were offered the shoe at price points shown below:

	Group 1	Group 2	Group 3	Group 4
Price	$210	$189	$179	$169
Units sold	58	212	220	383

Lynn Shoes had a consistently impressive record. Exhibit 4 shows key operating statistics for 1979 to 1985. In 1985, the catalog business handled approximately 136,000 inquiries, an increase of 16,000 inquiries over 1984. It filled 83,050 orders accounting for 110,000 pairs of shoes in 1985, with 20 percent of respondents ordering more than one pair. Response from retention mailings accounted for 50,000 of these pairs. Lynn Shoes accounted for 35 percent of Murrayhill's total dollar sales and 17 percent of the pairs produced in the factory. Exhibit 5 compares sales for Lynn Shoes and Murrayhill's wholesale business from 1981 to 1985. The earlier program had solved Murrayhill's problem of excess capacity and had opened up new markets for Murrayhill shoes.

The Problem

In 1985, full production at the plant was 1,600 pairs per day, or 400,000 pairs per year. Some executives estimated that an additional 30,000 pairs of inside shoes could be sold if they were able to be produced. With the factory's capacity limitations, further sales growth of inside-made shoes would pressure both manufacturing and customer service (i.e., speed of order fulfillment). While purchasing additional capacity was an option, preliminary research on space availability, equipment, and labor resources had shown that this was not a viable short-term solution. Some executives believed that in the long run Murrayhill could negotiate additional capacity through joint ventures with U.S. or foreign manufacturers, but that in the short run they had to consider other methods of managing the company's growth. The two primary strategic alternatives were to slow the growth of Lynn Shoes, which had 156,300 customers by the end of 1985 and 197,000 customers expected by the end of 1986, or to reduce sales to retail accounts.

Slowing Lynn Shoes' growth was controversial. The catalog offered Murrayhill a distribution method over which it had complete control. Despite assertions that catalog promotions lowered unit contribution, tests Hill conducted showed that increases in sales generated by the promotions more than made up for the cost of the discounts. The higher prices of the unpromoted items balanced the cost of promoted items, so Hill believed direct sales were more profitable for the company than those through traditional channels. Nevertheless, of the four options being considered, three involved controlling the number of Lynn Shoes customers:

1. Lynn Shoes could reduce the number of initial inquiries by reducing advertising. The promotions the seven catalogs offered would remain the same. Hill believed that this option offered the greatest flexibility; any demand reduction in Murrayhill's retail accounts could easily be made up by stepping up advertising. Hill also felt that the importance of promotions in attracting new business argued for their continuation.

2. Prices could be raised or promotions eliminated, or both, thereby increasing margins and discouraging sales. Advertising expenditures would remain the same. Several executives supported this option, believing that excessive Lynn Shoes' price promotions could create an antagonistic relationship with some of Murrayhill's retail accounts and detract from Murrayhill's reputation for quality. Price increases also had been used effectively in the past to curb demand and bolster profits. Nevertheless, pricing tests conducted by count on promoted styles resulted in little change in unit sales volumes, although the ratio of higher-priced nonsale pairs sold to sales pairs sold increased.

3. The catalogs could include fewer inside-made styles. However, if there was any reduction in sales of inside-made shoes to retailers, catalogs with fewer inside-made styles would not so easily make up the difference. Therefore, the catalog operation would become less effective as an alternative channel for Murrayhill.

4. Murrayhill could allow Lynn Shoes to grow at the expense of the wholesale business. One manager suggested that, by no longer opening new accounts, eliminating marginal accounts, and increasing stocking requirements, Murrayhill could free up additional pairage to allow for the growth of the direct mail operation.

Reducing sales to retail accounts was not a popular option. Most managers believed that curtailing the new account program could ease capacity pressure slightly without disrupting relations with established retail accounts. Such measures as placing existing retailers on allocation met strong resistance from Murrayhill executives, however. They argued that wholesaling to retail outlets was the business that Murrayhill knew best, and that most consumer shoe purchases would continue to be made in stores. Edward Wilson also was concerned about the larger ramifications of such a sales reduction: "Retail distribution is vital to brand awareness for shoe manufacturers. Without the retailer, the consumers' view of Murrayhill shoes would be little more than a picture on a page."

By the end of 1985, the capacity problem at Murrayhill had become critical: orders were increasingly backlogged and the company's retail accounts were complaining of delays. In light of industry and environmental trends, Murrayhill executives were uncertain how to balance the wholesale and direct mail business and whether to emphasize one over the other. The issue of balance was not only a short-term tactical challenge—it was also central to determining Murrayhill's long-term strategy. Davis realized that an action plan to manage Murrayhill's growth would have to be implemented early in 1986.

EXHIBIT 1   Unit Purchases of Key Retail Accounts

September 1978–August 1979		September 1984–August 1985	
Account	*Pairs*	*Account*	*Pairs*
Hartwell's	39,685	Hartwell's	54,550
Discount Stores		**Discount Stores**	
Store 1	9,522	Store 2	23,429
Store 2	8,728	Store 3	9,928
Store 3	5,870	Store 34	7,584
Store 4	3,570	Store 1	6,325
Store 5	1,645	Store 4	5,115
Discount store total	29,335	Store 35	5,176
		Store 36	3,792
Family Shoe Stores		Store 5	2,722
Store 6	7,997	Store 37	2,363
Store 7	7,482	Store 38	1,915
Store 8	3,542	Discount store total	68,349
Store 9	2,762		
Store 10	2,581	**Family Shoe Stores**	
Store 11	2,414	Store 6	7,242
Store 12	2,216	Store 39	3,698
Store 13	2,200	Store 10	2,502
Store 14	2,190	Store 9	2,459
Store 15	1,726	Store 14	2,163
Store 16	1,691	Store 40	1,923
Family shoe total	36,801	Store 41	1,787
		Store 42	1,749
Clothing stores		Store 12	1,738
Store 17	12,512	Store 16	1,667
Store 18	8,566	Store 43	1,662
Store 19	6,339	Family shoe total	28,590
Store 20	3,347		
Store 21	1,770	**Clothing Stores**	
Store 22	1,661	Store 20	4,789
Clothing store total	34,195	Store 44	3,424
		Clothing store total	8,213
Department stores			
Store 23	12,211	**Department stores**	
Store 24	4,933	Store 23	3,528
Store 25	3,480	Store 24	3,014
Store 26	2,976	Store 26	1,638
Store 27	2,934	Department store total	8,180
Department store total	26,534		
		Men's Shoe Stores	
Men's Shoe Stores		Store 28	11,110
Store 28	14,070	Store 29	10,254
Store 29	12,483	Store 30	6,202
Store 30	9,554	Store 31	3,424
Store 31	3,309	Store 32	3,013
Store 32	2,878	Store 33	2,418
Store 33	1,965	Store 45	1,907
Men's shoe store total	44,259	Men's shoe store total	38,328
Total account and stores	210,809	Total account and stores	206,210

EXHIBIT 2   **Sales in Units and Dollars for 1970–1980**

Year	Pairs Shipped	Dollar Shipments	Average Price
1970	444,747	$9,233,418	$20.76
1971	481,875	10,326,280	21.43
1972	556,590	12,430,848	22.33
1973	572,806	14,400,942	25.14
1974	485,194	13,255,635	27.32
1975	471,755	13,517,534	28.65
1976	516,760	16,035,339	31.03
1977	443,149	15,015,605	33.88
1978	436,288	16,315,626	37.40
1979	376,318	16,288,598	43.28
1980	353,795	16,097,558	45.49

EXHIBIT 3   **Summary of Lynn Shoes Promotion Offers and Results**

Mailing	1	2	3	4	5	6	7
Timing	On Receipt	2 Months	4 Months	6 Months	8 Months	10 Months	12 Months
No. sale styles	0	0	7	9	10	13	25
Regular price offer	0	$15 of each pair	$15 off each pair	Shoe shine kit and $15 off	Shoe shine kit and $15 off	Shoe shine kit and $15 off	1 pair at half price
Two pair offer	2 pair cashmere socks for $2 handling fee	$15 off order	2 pair cashmere socks for $2 handling fee	Free wallet each 2 pairs	$15 off order	$15 off order	None
Response percent	2.8%	2.5%	6.2%	4.3%	2.4%	3.6%	7.9%
Average order	$154	$118	$110	$104	$113	$95	$58
Pair/order	1.4	1.45	1.55	1.56	1.54	1.35	1.11
Dollar/pair	$110	$81	$71	$67	$73	$70	$52
Repeat factor (8 mo.)	33%	26%	23%	21%	18%	25%	11%
1985 merchandise breakdown:							
Regular price inside-made	72%	68%	15%	12%	19%	12%	0%
Promotion price inside-made	0%	0%	30%	41%	59%	57%	58%
Total inside-made	72%	68%	45%	53%	78%	69%	58%
Regular price outside-made	28%	32%	5%	8%	8%	4%	0%
Promotion price outside-made	0%	0%	50%	39%	14%	27%	42%
Total outside-made	28%	32%	55%	47%	22%	31%	42%

NOTE: Data in this exhibit may not reconcile precisely with other case data due to differences in the number of catalogs distributed with each mailing.

EXHIBIT 4   Key Operating Statistics for Lynn Shoes (figures in 000s)

	1979	1980	1981	1982	1983	1984	1985
New customers	6.4	16.0	17.6	19.2	25.6	25.6	45.9
List size	6.4	22.4	40.0	59.2	84.8	110.4	156.3
Orders	4.8	20.8	27.2	40.0	56.0	67.2	84.42
Percent repeat orders	14%	18%	24%	32%	36%	42%	46%
Net sales	$445	$1,856	$2,864	$4,088	$5,570	$7,190	$9,120
Net pair inside	8.0	24.0	33.6	40.0	52.0	57.6	70.0
Net pair outside	0.0	0.0	0.0	8.0	14.4	28.8	40.0
Total	8.0	24.0	33.6	48.0	66.4	86.4	110.0
Gross margin %	37%	47%	49%	47%	47%	53%	48%
Nonmerchandise Expenses as Percent of Sales							
Advertising/materials	33	23	27	31	19	19	18
All other expenses[b]	13	17	17	20	19	22	18
Total expenses	46	40	44	51	38	41	36
Contribution	−9	7	6	−5[a]	9	12	12

[a]In 1982, Murrayhill invested heavily in media advertising to acquire names of new prospects. Payoff occurred in later years.
[b]Includes proportional allocations of Murrayhill overhead.

EXHIBIT 5   Comparison of Wholesale and Catalog Operations

Year	Pairs Shipped	Percent Inside Shoes	Percent Outside Shoes	Percent Wholesale Shoes	Percent Lynn Shoes	Shipments ($millions)	Percent Wholesale Shoes	Percent Lynn Shoes
1981	376,000	98%	2%	91%	9%	$18.0	86%	14%
1982	374,400	97	3	87	13	19.5	80	20
1983	401,600	95	5	83	17	21.4	76	24
1984	430,000	92	8	80	20	23.8	73	27
1985	456,000	89	11	76	24	27.1	65	35

U.S. Pioneer Electronics Corporation

In fall 1977, Bernie Mitchell, president of U.S. Pioneer Electronics, placed an ad featuring a portrait of William Shakespeare in several trade magazines. The ad was an open letter from Shakespeare and Mitchell to several dissident dealers franchised to sell Japanese-made Pioneer products in the United States.[1] It alleged that a few dealers had resorted to "disparagement of Pioneer products and 'bait and switch' advertising" and threatened dealer investigations to protect Pioneer's reputation (see Exhibit 1).

Mitchell hoped these "unjustifiable practices" were the sporadic misconduct of only "an unwise few" and could be dealt with individually. If, however, they represented an overall erosion of dealer support for Pioneer products, he was determined (1) to take immediate steps to prevent further erosion and (2) to establish a new long-run distribution strategy to ensure U.S. Pioneer's continued leadership in the hi-fi industry.

Industry Background

The U.S. hi-fi industry was started in the 1960s by a few engineers who, according to industry legend, left their positions (mostly in the aerospace industry) to pursue their hobby of building amplifiers and speakers in their garages and basements. By the late 1960s, larger component manufacturers were beginning to broaden their product lines.[2] For instance, Scott, previously identified solely with electronics, was building its reputation in the speaker business. Sherwood, also an electronics manufacturer, introduced an automatic turntable in 1969. KLH, which had started out making speakers, turned to stereo compacts about the same time.[3]

Japanese hi-fi manufacturers, such as Pioneer, Kenwood, Sansui, and Teac, also entered the U.S. market in the late 1960s while most original founders of the hi-fi companies, who had operated in a club-like business atmosphere, were leaving the industry.

The 1970s saw a new attitude among hi-fi manufacturers. As Mitchell told one trade magazine reporter:

Six years ago . . . we only wanted to sell our product to a certain select group of people who had to qualify somehow intellectually and technologically. We didn't want to sell . . . to kids or to ordinary people, only to superpeople. It was a real elitist attitude, and terribly dangerous. We've changed it from an elitist business that didn't really want to grow to an industry that has some pride in itself and its products and says, "These products are so good we won't be happy until we tell everybody." (*Crawdaddy,* July 1976)

Company Background

Pioneer Electronics Corporation was founded in Tokyo in 1938. It started with capital of $235 and by 1977 had expanded to $843 million in worldwide sales. Overseas sales surpassed domestic sales in 1974 and, in 1977, accounted for 65 percent of the total. Net income (pretax) in 1977 was nearly $61 million.

U.S. Pioneer was established in March 1966 under Ken Kai, vice president, then 26 years old. He had joined the parent company in Tokyo after graduating from college and was sent to New York a year later as Pioneer's U.S. liaison. In 1966, U.S. Pioneer had less than $200,000 in sales and fewer than 30 dealers.

Bernie Mitchell joined the company in 1970. An economist by training and a music buff, as well as a member of the boards of directors of the New Jersey Symphony and the Metropolitan Opera, he had worked previously with Westinghouse, Toshiba, and Concord Electronics.

To help U.S. Pioneer grow, Mitchell and Kai took on the task of developing the market—making more people aware of and knowledgeable about hi-fi products. U.S. Pioneer sponsored hi-fi shows on college campuses and became the first hi-fi company to advertise in such magazines as *Playboy, National Lampoon,* and the *New Yorker.* These ads featured music, sports, and other celebrities.

The company also strengthened its distribution network. U.S. Pioneer was supplied by its parent in Japan.

This case was prepared by Assistant Professor Hirotaka Takeuchi with the assistance of William Falkson.

Copyright © 1978 by the President and Fellows of Harvard College.

Harvard Business School case 579-079 (Rev. 7/15/91).

[1]The words *retailers* and *dealers* are used interchangeably in this case.

[2]Components were combinations of different audio equipment, which reproduced sound highly faithful (i.e., high-fidelity or hi-fi sound) to the original record or tape. Consumers created component systems of their choice by combining (*a*) an inlet source, such as a turntable, tape deck, or FM tuner; (*b*) a control center, such as an amplifier or receiver, which was an amplifier and FM tuner combined into one unit; and (*c*) an outlet, such as speakers. In audio terminology, receivers and amplifiers were called "electronics."

[3]Compacts were preassembled audio systems, usually consisting of two units—one containing a turntable, receiver, and/or tape

player and the other a pair of speakers. A compact system usually cost less and was smaller than a component system. It reproduced stereo sound (i.e., sound reproduced through two separate channels) but not necessarily high-fidelity sound.

Commission sales representatives sold to its retail dealers. In 1972, U.S. Pioneer had six independent sales representative offices, which sold only Pioneer products (with the exception of accessories, complementary items, and very high-priced lines of electronics that did not directly compete with Pioneer). Each office served a given region and had from four to seven salespeople, each earning an average annual salary of $20,000. The sales force assisted retailers with merchandising and display, store operations, and sales training. By 1975, U.S. Pioneer had added 10 independent sales representative offices and 4 company-owned offices—in New York, Washington, D.C., Florida, and Missouri. These "captive" offices were paid the same commission as the independents, but were not allowed to carry product lines of direct or indirect competitors.[4]

By 1977 the number of retail outlets carrying Pioneer products had grown to almost 3,600 from approximately 500 in 1970. Retailers had to sign franchise agreements with U.S. Pioneer. Mitchell believed they did so unhesitatingly because the company's strong national and local cooperative advertising created considerable consumer pull. U.S. Pioneer allocated 5 percent of its sales to local ads featuring its products. In addition, the firm offered dealers attractive gross margins and credit terms.

Fair Trade[5] versus Free Market

FTC Action.   Just as market expansion and distribution building were starting to generate higher net sales ($80 million in 1974), the Federal Trade Commission (FTC) issued a complaint against U.S. Pioneer and three other competitors. It alleged that Sansui, Sherwood, Teac, and U.S. Pioneer (1) granted dealerships to retailers only if they agreed to maintain suggested retail prices, (2) directed

their sales representatives to report on retailers who failed to maintain such prices, and (3) delayed shipments to retailers who cut prices. These practices violated Section 5 of the Federal Trade Commission Act, which prohibited "unfair methods of competition . . . and unfair or deceptive acts or practices in commerce." Their effect, the FTC charged, was to inflate consumer prices.

Consent Decree.   In August 1975, the four companies signed consent decrees with the FTC. They did not admit guilt, but did promise not to engage in the alleged practices. Specifically, they were prohibited from fair-trading their products for five years in the 21 states where this practice was still permitted and from using suggested list prices for two years in any part of the country. They also could not ask consumers the price of purchased products on warranty registration forms. Finally, the companies were required to distribute copies of the consent order to all their dealers and to give any dealer whose franchise had been terminated an opportunity to regain it.

U.S. Pioneer's Response.   Asked why U.S. Pioneer decided not to contest the FTC decree, Mitchell replied:

> I don't mind being a crusader. In fact, I kind of enjoy it. But I like to crusade for something that makes some long-term sense.
> The FTC is asking us not to violate the law. It has never been our intention to violate the law. They are asking that we no longer fair trade our products. We had already unilaterally made the decision that fair trade wasn't viable anymore anyhow. . . . The third thing they are asking us is that we not conspire to fix prices, either among dealers or among ourselves, and we had no intention of doing that.
> We did try to fix retail prices at the dealer level as long as fair trade lasted; that was the purpose of fair-trade statutes. When we fair-traded, we did it pretty darn well. But when we decided to go off fair trade, we decided we were going to be the best there was at free market practices. (*Electronics Retailing*, October 1975)

To implement this new goal, Pioneer replaced the price sheet in effect during fair trade (see Exhibit 2) with a list that replaced the words "fair-trade resale price" with "approximate nationally advertised value" and added optional retail prices under gross margins of these percentages: 15, 20, 25, 30, 35, 40, and 45 (see Exhibit 3).

According to *Home Furnishings Daily* (August 27, 1975), "Most of the dealers and manufacturers contacted scorned [Pioneer's] list because they felt it was, in the words of one manufacturer, 'an open invitation to cut the hell out of prices.' " Mitchell said in the same article that the initial response was fear and that dealers did not understand the significance of the change from fair-trade to free-market prices.

> Too often, under the fair-trade environment, dealers felt, "If we have a very fine mix of products, and people come in and we tell them wonderful stories about each of those products, they will

---

[4]Before 1974, U.S. Pioneer sales representative offices received a 10 percent commission. In 1974 the rate was reduced to 5 percent, comparable with that of other manufacturers.

[5]Fair-trade (or resale price maintenance) laws permitted a manufacturer or distributor of trademarked products to determine their resale prices. Although on the surface such laws seemed to support a manufacturer's desire to influence retail prices, they had initially been advocated by small, independent retailers seeking protection from direct price competition by large chains. The first such state law was passed in 1931, and by 1941 all but three states had such laws. In 13 states a nonsigner clause bound all retailers selling a fair-traded product to the contract if one retailer in the state signed an agreement. The Miller-Tydings Act, passed in 1937, applied resale price maintenance to interstate commerce.

Fair-trade practice and enforcement began to decline steadily in the early 1950s. By 1975, fair trade was being used only for certain brands of hi-fi equipment, television sets, jewelry, bicycles, clothing, cosmetics, and kitchenware. Major efforts to repeal state laws started in 1974. In December 1975, the Consumer Goods Pricing Act terminated interstate fair-trade regulations.

tell us which products they want. They'll sort of self-sell in an enlightened environment."

I don't really think that's a very good way to run a business. Dealers have to identify what needs the consumer has, acquaint him very quickly with options, suggest an option they think he ought to take, and bear down very hard to lead him to take that option. That's called selling.

Effects of Consent Decree on Sales and Prices.   The immediate impact of the consent decree, according to *Home Furnishings Daily,* was a "price war which lowered dealer profit margins to 5 or 6 percent in many parts of the country." The newspaper also said that "many retailers began to criticize manufacturers for 'abandoning' them and called for them to control the fluctuating markets." Some softening of the market, according to an FTC spokesperson, was expected as a backlash. But "prices won't stay as low as they are now and higher margins will eventually return. [In the meantime] I expect to see greater sales at discount prices and the good dealers will survive."

In 1976, retail dollar sales jumped 12.6 percent and unit sales increased 9.4 percent over the previous year (see Exhibit 4). In 1975, on the other hand, the increases had been 1.6 and 2.2 percent, respectively. According to Kai, the much smaller percentage increase between 1974 and 1975 probably resulted from the recession and consumer decisions to delay purchases until fair-trade laws were repealed. In New York and New Jersey repeal had been rumored as early as August 1975.

In the meantime, U.S. Pioneer net sales increased from $80 million in 1974 to $87 million in 1975. In addition, its market share increased between 1974 and 1975 in all hi-fi product categories except turntables and speakers (see Exhibit 5). All Pioneer's market share percentages in 1976 were equal to or higher than those of 1974.

Market Growth and Changes

The hi-fi market was growing, and there was evidence that buyer profiles for component parts were changing. As shown in Exhibit 6, there were fewer women, more young adults (ages 18 to 24), more Pacific area residents, more college graduates, and more households with incomes of $25,000 and over purchasing stereo component parts in 1975 than in the previous year.

Realizing a shift in buyer demographics, U.S. Pioneer undertook extensive research to determine (1) the market potential of hi-fi products compared with low-fi products, such as compacts or consoles;[6] and (2) the purchasing behavior of hi-fi component buyers.

---

[6]Consoles were preassembled all-in-one audio systems that were larger, cost more, and had generally poorer sound reproduction than most component systems.

An independent research firm found that sales of components were growing faster than sales of compacts and consoles. In sheer volume, however, compacts outsold components and consoles by a wide margin. In 1975, 3.5 million units of compacts were sold in the United States, compared with 1.5 million component systems and 400,000 consoles. To Mitchell, this meant that 3.9 million U.S. buyers were taken off the hi-fi market. Once they had purchased compacts and consoles, these customers were not expected to consider replacing them with hi-fi components for several years.

"Also, every time a compact or console is sold, you lose the potential of an additional speaker, add-on tape deck, upgraded receiver, tuner, turntable, and more," said Mitchell. The research revealed that this add-on market was larger than expected. In 1975, add-on sales accounted for 55 percent of total dollars spent on hi-fi components. New system sales made up the remaining 45 percent.

Buying Influences.   Consumer research showed that buyers of different audio systems were influenced by different factors, in order of importance:

Component Buyers
1. Lifelike sound reproduction.
2. Superior electronics.
3. Add-on capability.
4. Status symbol.

Console Buyers
1. Esthetics.
2. Adequate electronics.
3. No involved hookup.
4. A lot for the money.

Compact Buyers
1. Lower price.
2. Small size.
3. No involved hookup.
4. Ease of operation.

The research also found that component buyers:

- Depended heavily on advice of family and friends.
- Thought they knew just enough about hi-fi components to get by (only 8 percent thought they knew "a lot").
- Shopped around, especially for the initial purchase.
- Paid either $350–400 or $650–750 for initial purchase of system.
- Replaced or upgraded components approximately one to two yeas after their initial purchase.

New Marketing Strategy.   On the basis of this research, Mitchell established the goal of "doubling the number of people owning and buying *any* brand of hi-fi components next year." He said, "We'd rather see a consumer buy a Marantz, Sansui . . . yes, and even a Technics, than a fancy fruitwood console or plastic compact, both of which deliver less than true high fidelity."

To implement this goal, he asked dealers to persuade prospective compact or console buyers to consider lower-priced hi-fi components. He argued that this could be best accomplished by prominently displaying low-end components and explaining their advantages over compacts and consoles. To support this dealer effort, Pioneer introduced lower-priced components. It also allocated $6 million national advertising for 1976. Of this, $2 million was earmarked for persuading consumers that only hi-fi components produced true high-fidelity sound. Head copy for one of the ads read, "BAD SOUND IS AN UNNECESSARY EVIL." The ad referred by name to some of Pioneer's competitors—Marantz, Kenwood, and Sansui—as dedicated companies trying to reproduce high-quality sound.

Mitchell also asked dealers to use direct mail to tap the replacement and add-on markets. Ads were mailed to customers who had purchased audio systems one and two years before.

Results. Mitchell and Kai were very satisfied with their new strategy as Pioneer's sales increased from $87 million in 1975 to $135 million in 1976. Although their goal of doubling the number of hi-fi owners and buyers was not achieved, they felt that more people were buying components than compacts and consoles. The number of compact systems sold in the United States increased from 3.5 million in 1975 to 3.6 million in 1976, whereas component *unit* (not system) sales increased from 8.0 million in 1975 to 8.7 million in 1976 (see Exhibit 7).

They were also impressed by the findings of a Gallup Organization[7] consumer survey for U.S. Pioneer. This survey, conducted in the first half of 1977, measured consumer brand preference for different hi-fi component categories (receiver, FM tuner, amplifier, turntable, speaker, and tape deck). As shown in Exhibit 8, prospective component purchasers preferred Pioneer over all other brands in every category except tape decks.

Retailer Dissidence

Just as Pioneer's "franchise" with consumers was strengthening, Mitchell came across a number of reports suggesting that relationships with its franchised dealers were starting to deteriorate. His particular concern was with sales representatives' reports about dealers (1) disparaging Pioneer

products by misrepresenting product specification sheets or manipulating sound demonstrations and (2) using an illegal and unethical tactic known as "bait and switch."[8]

Pioneer Field Investigation

Disparagement of Pioneer products was spotted in continuous field work by employees (mostly part-time) who, posing as interested shoppers for Pioneer products, visited Pioneer's franchised stores, interacted with store personnel, and then prepared "shopping reports" for the company (see Exhibit 9).

In one report, a U.S. Pioneer employee visited a midwestern hi-fi specialty store and asked for a Pioneer tape deck, but was persuaded by the salesperson to buy a competing brand (see Exhibit 9). The report noted that (1) the store salesperson made a comment on how he "could produce copies of letters that dealers had written to Pioneer complaining about service"; (2) Pioneer's tape deck (CT-F7272) was missing from its display area; (3) the store salesperson, when asked for a CT-F7272 specification sheet, handed over that of a competing brand but did not have one for Pioneer; and (4) the store salesperson set the playback sound control at maximum volume for the competing brand but at less than maximum for Pioneer.

To counter these objectionable practices, Pioneer placed the Shakespeare ad (Exhibit 1) in major trade publications to appeal to dealers. The company also asked the presidents of all its sales representative offices to identify the offenders in their territories who used the most blatant, most persistent disparagement and bait-and-switch tactics.

Audio Warehouse Suit. In July 1977, U.S. Pioneer filed a suit against Audio Warehouse, a five-store chain with 1977 sales of $10 million, and its advertising agency, both of Akron, Ohio. It charged them with using bait-and-switch tactics, advertising without sufficient inventory, and disparaging Pioneer products to customers. A temporary restraining order barred Audio Warehouse from engaging in these practices.

Ed Radford, the 34-year-old president of Audio Warehouse, told *Retail Home Furnishings* (September 26, 1977):

> Yeah, we're being sued [by U.S. Pioneer], but we're not taking this lying down—we're going to fight it. Pioneer surprised me because they got a temporary restraining order, and, within one

---

[7]Gallup Organization was an independent research firm that specialized in survey research and had gained its reputation through political polls.

[8]"Bait and switch" refers to advertising a product at a bargain price to draw customers into the store, then selling them something similar to, but more expensive than, the advertised item. Pioneer products were good baits because of their strong consumer pull—created through national advertising and favorable word-of-mouth communication. In one Pioneer survey, 98 percent of Pioneer component owners interviewed said they were satisfied and would buy the brand again.

day, they had it in every newspaper in my state. As far as I'm concerned, Pioneer's trying to make me look bad. The public doesn't understand that a temporary restraining order doesn't mean anything. Anybody who puts up a bond can get one.

To prove his point, Radford (who was called "Fast Eddie" because of his hurried speech and quick rise to fortune)[9] placed a full-page advertisement in two Ohio newspapers (see Exhibit 10). The ad contained Audio Warehouse's version of the suit filed by U.S. Pioneer and offered sharply reduced prices on several Pioneer products.

Radford contended that "many dealers around the country were having difficulty maintaining margins on Pioneer equipment" and charged that Pioneer didn't "seem to care whether we make a profit or not" (*Retail Home Furnishings*).

Although Mitchell was confident that the suit would be settled in Pioneer's favor (especially because the attorney general of Ohio became a co-plaintiff), he was concerned about the impact of Audio Warehouse's publicity on Pioneer's dealer outlets. At the same time he wondered whether to initiate legal action against other offenders or terminate their franchises, or both.[10]

Dealer Communication Program

Sales representatives suggested that U.S. Pioneer organize an extensive communication program to convince dealers that the company was concerned about their well-being and to demonstrate how effective selling of Pioneer products could improve their profits. The sales reps were increasingly confronted with complaints from dealers, such as:

"Most of my customers ask for Pioneer. But I can't make money with Pioneer."

"How can we compete with discounters or mail-order guys who are selling Pioneer for as low as 10 percent above cost?"

"We'd be better off selling products of smaller manufacturers like Advent and Bose, which still sell at list prices."

"I'm making 50 percent to 60 percent margin on house brands; why should I push Pioneer?"

Such comments concerned Mitchell, because he thought dealer support was crucial. Table A shows the results of a

---

[9]According to the Ohio *Sunday Tribune* (February 12, 1978), Ed Radford, who was orphaned at age five, was planning a "fast" retirement at age 49. He had started his business in 1973 with his life savings of $10,000. In 1978, "Fast Eddie" was a millionaire who still came to work in jeans and an "exploding blond Afro."

[10]Most of these dealer franchise agreements (see Exhibit 11) had been signed during the fair-trade days and did not fully reflect the changes resulting from the FTC consent order.

TABLE A   **Factors Influencing Purchase of Hi-fi Products**

	Percent of Respondents[a]
Recommendations of friends	29%
Dealers/salespeople	27
Advertising by manufacturers	15
Recommendations of family members	12
Advertising by dealers	8
Store display	7
All others	14
No answer	(n = 1,290)

[a]Percentages total over 100 because of multiple answers.

---

consumer survey that asked "What factors had the greatest influence in your most recent purchase of hi-fi products?"

In a sales representatives' meeting, Bob Gundick, president of the company sales office in Florida, displayed a presentation package he had used successfully. A set of flip charts was shown to dealers during regular visits, and handouts (similar in content) were left after the presentations. As shown in Exhibit 12, the package suggested ways the dealers could (a) cope with their competitors, (b) determine their product mixes, (c) creatively sell Pioneer products in combination with other brands, and (d) improve their businesses in general. Gundick offered his package for nationwide use.

Other suggestions during the meeting included (1) direct mail brochures to all dealers; (2) more salespeople to increase the frequency of dealer visits; (3) cash rebates or other incentive programs (such as a contest for dealers); and (4) organizing a "national dealers' conference" at a resort.

Although the format of the sales communication program was yet to be determined, Mitchell felt it justified a budget of $3 million. He was uncertain, however, whether the budget should be incremental or whether some funds should be transferred from consumer advertising.

Long-run Strategy Options

Citing the broad changes occurring in the industry, several sales reps argued that the existing situation provided a timely opportunity to reconsider U.S. Pioneer's long-run distribution strategy.

Distribution Shift.   One possibility was to shift retail distribution away from specialty stores to department stores and catalog showrooms. In 1977, 75 percent of U.S. Pioneer's dollar sales were accounted for by hi-fi specialty stores, 5 percent by department stores, 7 percent by catalog showrooms, and 13 percent by appliance/TV/hardware/furniture stores.[11] Department stores and catalog showrooms did not generally offer the extensive customer services provided by specialty stores, including professional sales assistance, demonstration, extended store warranty,[12] on-the-premises repair, home delivery and installation, and loaner component programs. They usually had, however, extensive credit facilities, strong consumer "pull" advertising, and lower prices. Industry sources predicted a substantial increase in the market shares of department stores and catalog showrooms.

Multiple Branding

Some sales reps suggested that one way to take advantage of the trend toward more mass-oriented retail outlets and, at the same time, "keep specialty stores reasonably happy" would be multiple branding. U.S. Pioneer would offer several product lines of varying quality and price points under separate brand names. Different product lines would be carried by different types of retail outlets. The department-store line would presumably be of lower quality and price than a regular line. Supporters pointed out that multiple branding had been used in other industries,[13] and that it would enable U.S. Pioneer to adapt most effectively to future changes in retail distribution.[14] Others were more

concerned that such a strategy would tarnish Pioneer's reputation for selling only top-of-the-line products.

Company-owned Stores. Another strategic option for U.S. Pioneer was to move toward operating its own retail stores. Some retailers in the low-fi market (such as Radio Shack and Sears) had been selling their own house brands for some time. More recently, house brands were starting to make inroads in the hi-fi market. For example, house brand sales by Pacific Stereo (a chain of 80 West Coast stores) were estimated to be 25 percent (unit basis). In other hi-fi specialty stores, house brands accounted for 5 to 10 percent of unit sales.

Some sales reps felt that house brands would seriously threaten U.S. Pioneer. Because the primary promoters of house brands were large specialty store chains, Pioneer risked being squeezed out of them. One way to counter this prospective threat would be to start Pioneer retail stores by acquiring existing one- or two-unit family-owned stores or converting nonaudio stores into Pioneer shops.

The estimated U.S. Pioneer initial fixed investment for starting up, say, a 5,000-square foot hi-fi store was about $50,000. Given the operating data for a comparable existing specialty store, shown in Exhibit 13, the initial investment appeared to be recoverable in a short time. (U.S. Pioneer's income statement is provided in Exhibit 14.)

---

[11]In terms of the number of existing U.S. Pioneer retail outlets, 69 percent were hi-fi specialty stores, 2 percent department stores, 3 percent catalog showrooms, and 26 percent other stores.

[12]Many specialty stores extended the two-year Pioneer guarantee on parts and labor on its electronics to three years.

[13]For example, multiple branding was used in the watch industry. The Bulova Watch Company had three brand names: Bulova (intended for jewelry and department stores), Accutron (for best stores), and Caravelle (for quality drugstores and specialty gift

---

shops). In fact, Bulova had experienced considerable difficulty maintaining discrete channels for these lines.

[14]Should discount stores become a major force in hi-fi components sales, a new line with a new brand name could be added. (Pioneer Electronics of America, a separate, wholly owned subsidiary of Pioneer Electronics Corporation of Japan, currently sold compacts and car stereos to discount stores under the Centrex brand name.)

EXHIBIT 1

U.S. Pioneer advertisement

AN IMPORTANT MESSAGE FROM WILLIAM SHAKESPEARE AND PIONEER.

"Who steals my purse steals trash . . .
But he that filches from me
my good name
Robs me of that which not
enriches him
And makes me poor indeed."

The Immortal Bard said it over three hundred years ago. It's still true today.

It has come to our attention at Pioneer that a few dealers of high fidelity products, acting in what they believe to be their best interest, have taken up the practice of disparagement of Pioneer products and "bait and switch" advertising, often using Pioneer's hard earned reputation in the industry as the "bait."

This tactic hurts Pioneer, hurts the consumer and ultimately hurts all dealers since it will damage the credibility of our high fidelity business in the eyes of consumers. To protect our legitimate dealers, Pioneer will conduct frequent investigations of this practice, and we will take appropriate steps to protect and defend our reputation on behalf of the great majority of our dealers against the unjustifiable practices of an unwise few.

Respectfully,

William Shakespeare, *Stratford-upon-Avon*
Bernie Mitchell, *U.S. Pioneer Electronics*

SOURCE: Trade magazines.

EXHIBIT 2 Price List of Selected Products, April 22, 1975

Stereo Receivers	Description	Fair Trade Resale	1-3 pcs.	4-more	Case	Shipping Weight (lbs.)
SX-1010	AM/FM Stereo Receiver	$699.95	$466.60	$420.00	1	60 lbs.
SX-939	AM/FM Stereo Receiver	599.95	400.00	372.00	1	51
SX-838	AM/FM Stereo Receiver	499.95	333.40	310.00	1	44
SX-737	AM/FM Stereo Receiver	399.95	266.60	248.00	1	35
SX-636	AM/FM Stereo Receiver	349.95	233.30	217.00	1	29
SX-535	AM/FM Stereo Receiver	299.95	200.00	186.00	1	27
SX-434	AM/FM Stereo Receiver	239.95	160.00	148.80	1	22

U.A. Series	Description	Fair Trade Resale	1-3 pcs.	4-more	Case	Shipping Weight (lbs.)
Spec 1	Stereo Pre-Amplifier	$499.95	$333.40	$300.00	1	30 lbs.
Spec 2	Stereo Power Amplifier	899.95	600.00	540.00	1	60
SA-9900	Integrated Stereo Amp.	749.85	500.00	450.00	1	50
SA-9500	Integrated Stereo Amp.	499.95	333.40	300.00	1	44
SA-8500	Integrated Stereo Amp.	399.95	266.60	240.00	1	32
SA-7500	Integrated Stereo Amp.	299.95	200.00	180.00	1	30
SA-5200	Integrated Stereo Amp.	138.95	93.30	84.00	1	23
TX-9500	AM/FM Stereo Tuner	399.95	266.60	240.00	1	24
TX-7500	AM/FM Stereo Tuner	249.95	166.70	150.00	1	21
TX-6200	AM/FM Stereo Tuner	139.95	93.30	84.00	1	18
RG-1	RG Dynamic Expander	179.95	120.00	108.00	1	15
SR-202W	Stereo Reverb. Amp.	139.95	93.30	84.00	1	12
SF-850	Electronic Crossover	199.95	133.30	120.00	1	16
SD-1100	Quad/Stereo Display	599.95	400.00	360.00	1	34
WC-UA1	Walnut Cabinet[a]	34.95[b]	23.30	21.00	1	11¼

[a]Walnut cabinet for SA-8500, SA-7500, TX-9500, TX-7500 only.
[b]Suggested resale.

Turntables	Description	Fair Trade Resale	1-3 pcs.	4-more	Case	Shipping Weight (lbs.)
PL-71	2-Speed, DC Brushless Servo Motor, Anti-skating Direct-drive	$299.95	$200.00	$180.00	1	33 lbs.
PL-55X	2-Speed, DC Brushless Servo Motor, Anti-skating, Direct-drive Automatic Turntable	249.95	166.60	150.00	1	31
PL-A45D	2-Speed, Automatic Turntable 2-motor, Belt-drive, Anti-skating	169.95	113.30	105.40	1	26
PL-15D/II	2-Speed, Automatic Turntable with Hysteresis Synchronous Motor, Belt-drive, Anti-skating	129.95	87.10	83.20	1	20
PL-12D & PL-12D/II	2-Speed, Hysteresis Synchronous Motor, Belt-drive, Anti-skating	99.95	70.00	66.00	1	19

SOURCE: Company data.

EXHIBIT 3   Price List of Selected Products, July 1, 1975

Stereo Receivers	Description	Dealer Cost 1-3 pcs.	Dealer Cost 4-more	Case	Shp. Wt.	Dealer's Gross Margins at Various Retail Prices 15% Margin	20% Margin	25% Margin	30% Margin	35% Margin	40% Margin	45% Margin	Approx. Nationally Adv. Value	Your Price	Model Number
SX-1010	AM/FM Stereo Rec.	$466.60	$420.00	1	60 lbs.	$494.00	$525.00	$560.00	$600.00	$646.00	$700.00	$764.00	$700.00	——	SX-1010
SX-939	AM/FM Stereo Rec.	400.00	372.00	1	51 lbs.	438.00	465.00	496.00	531.00	572.00	620.00	676.00	600.00	——	SX-939
SX-838	AM/FM Stereo Rec.	333.40	310.00	1	44 lbs.	365.00	388.00	413.00	443.00	477.00	517.00	564.00	500.00	——	SX-838
SX-737	AM/FM Stereo Rec.	266.60	248.00	1	35 lbs.	292.00	310.00	331.00	354.00	382.00	413.00	451.00	400.00	——	SX-737
SX-636	AM/FM Stereo Rec.	233.30	217.00	1	29 lbs.	255.00	217.00	289.00	310.00	334.00	362.00	395.00	350.00	——	SX-636
SX-535	AM/FM Stereo Rec.	200.00	186.00	1	27 lbs.	219.00	233.00	248.00	266.00	286.00	310.00	338.00	300.00	——	SX-535
SX-434	AM/FM Stereo Rec.	160.00	148.80	1	22 lbs.	175.00	185.00	198.00	213.00	229.00	248.00	271.00	250.00	——	SX-434

U.A. SERIES	Description	Dealer Cost 1-3 pcs.	Dealer Cost 4-more	Case	Shp. Wt.	15% Margin	20% Margin	25% Margin	30% Margin	35% Margin	40% Margin	45% Margin	Approx. Nationally Adv. Value	Your Price	Model Number
Spec 1	Stereo Pre-Amplifier	$333.40	$300.00	1	30 lbs.	$353.00	$375.00	$400.00	$429.00	$462.00	$500.00	$545.00	$500.00	——	Spec 1
Spec 2	Stereo Power Amp.	600.00	540.00	1	60 lbs.	635.00	675.00	720.00	771.00	831.00	900.00	982.00	900.00	——	Spec 2
SA-9900	Integ. Stereo Amp.	500.00	450.00	1	50 lbs.	529.00	563.00	600.00	643.00	692.00	750.00	818.00	750.00	——	SA-9900
SA-9500	Integ. Stereo Amp.	333.40	300.00	1	44 lbs.	353.00	375.00	400.00	429.00	462.00	500.00	545.00	500.00	——	SA-9500
SA-8500	Integ. Stereo Amp.	266.60	240.00	1	32 lbs.	282.00	300.00	320.00	343.00	369.00	400.00	436.00	400.00	——	SA-8500
SA-7500	Integ. Stereo Amp.	200.00	180.00	1	30 lbs.	212.00	225.00	240.00	257.00	277.00	300.00	327.00	300.00	——	SA-7500
SA-5200	Integ. Stereo Amp.	93.30	84.00	1	23 lbs.	99.00	105.00	112.00	120.00	129.00	140.00	153.00	140.00	——	SA-5200
TX-9500	AM/FM Stereo Tuner	266.60	240.00	1	24 lbs.	282.00	300.00	320.00	343.00	369.00	400.00	436.00	400.00	——	TX-9500
TX-7500	AM/FM Stereo Tuner	166.70	150.00	1	21 lbs.	176.00	189.00	200.00	214.00	231.00	250.00	273.00	250.00	——	TX-7500
TX-6200	AM/FM Stereo Tuner	93.30	84.00	1	18 lbs.	99.00	105.00	112.00	120.00	129.00	140.00	153.00	140.00	——	TX-6200
RG-1	RG Dyn. Expander	120.00	108.00	1	15 lbs.	127.00	135.00	144.00	154.00	166.00	180.00	196.00	175.00	——	RG-1
SR-202W	Stereo Reverb. Amp.	93.30	84.00	1	12 lbs.	99.00	105.00	112.00	120.00	129.00	140.00	153.00	150.00	——	SR-202W
SE-850	Electronic Crossover	133.30	120.00	1	16 lbs.	141.00	150.00	160.00	171.00	185.00	200.00	218.00	200.00	——	SF-850
SD-1100	Quad/Stereo Display	400.00	360.00	1	31 lbs.	424.00	450.00	480.00	514.00	554.00	600.00	655.00	600.00	——	DS-1100
WC-UA1	Walnut Cabinet[a]	23.30	21.00	1	11 lbs.	25.00	26.00	28.00	30.00	32.00	35.00	38.00	35.00	——	WC-UA1
WC-UA2	Walnut Cabinet[b]	26.70	24.00	1	11 lbs.	28.00	30.00	32.00	34.00	37.00	40.00	44.00	40.00	——	WC-UA2

[a] Walnut cabinet for SA-8500, SA-7500, TX-9500 & TX-7500 only.
[b] Walnut cabinet for SA-9900 & SA-9500 only.

Turntables	Description	1-3 pcs.	4-more	Case	Shp. Wt.	15% Margin	20% Margin	25% Margin	30% Margin	35% Margin	40% Margin	45% Margin	Approx. Nationally Adv. Value	Your Price	Model Number
PL-71	2-Sp., DC Brushless Servo Motor, Anti-skating, Direct drive	$200.00	$180.00	1	33 lbs.	$212.00	$225.00	$240.00	$257.00	$277.00	$300.00	$327.00	$300.00	——	PL-71
PL-55X	2-Sp., DC Brushless Servo Motor, Anti-skating, Direct drive, Auto. Turntable	166.60	150.00	1	31 lbs.	176.00	188.00	200.00	214.00	231.00	250.00	273.00	250.00	——	PL-55X
PL-A45D	2-Sp., Auto. Turntable 2-motor, Belt drive, Anti-skating	113.30	105.40	1	26 lbs.	124.00	132.00	141.00	151.00	162.00	176.00	192.00	175.00	——	PL-A45D
PL-15D/II	2-Sp., Auto. Turntable w/Hysteresis Synch. Motor, Belt drive, Anti-skating	87.10	83.20	1	20 lbs.	98.00	104.00	111.00	119.00	128.00	139.00	151.00	125.00	——	PL-15D/II
PL-12D & PL-12D/II	2-Sp., Hysteresis Synch. Motor, Belt drive, Anti-skating	70.00	66.00	1	19 lbs.	78.00	83.00	88.00	94.00	102.00	110.00	120.00	100.00	——	PL-12D PL-12D/II

Source: Company data.

365

EXHIBIT 4   Retail Unit and Dollar Sales of Hi-fi Components, 1974–1977

	1974	1975	1976	1977
Unit Sales (in thousands)				
Total components	7,799	7,971	8,719	9,539
Receivers	960	970	1,050	1,185
Amps, pre-amps, tuners	231	263	275	320
Turntables (except OEM)	1,767	1,709	1,866	2,015
Speakers	2,500	2,550	2,800	3,125
Tape decks (cassette & open reel)	341	399	428	494
Headphones	2,000	2,080	2,300	2,400
Dollar Sales (in millions)				
Total components	$1,056	$1,073	$1,208	$1,390
Receivers	336	306	341	392
Amps, pre-amps, tuners	69	76	81	97
Turntables (except OEM)	168	179	222	252
Speakers	300	319	350	416
Tape decks (cassette & open reel)	113	120	133	147
Headphones	70	73	81	86

SOURCE: *Merchandising,* March 1978, p. 51.

EXHIBIT 5   U.S. Pioneer Retail Dollar Market Share Data[a]

Hi-fi Product Category	1971	1972	1973	1974	1975	1976
Receivers	7%	15%	23%	22%	25%	25%
Tuners	3	5	25	18	23	18
Amplifiers	3	5	8	9	12	10
Turntables	3	3	3	11	10	11
Speakers	2	1	4	5	3	7
Headphones	10	5	4	7	9	9
Cassette decks	—	—	4	11	26	20
Open reel tape decks	—	—	—	5	9	9

[a]Pioneer's overall dollar market share (at retail) was about 19% in 1977, 14% in 1976, and 13% in 1975.

SOURCE: Company data.

EXHIBIT 6 Demographic Profile of Buyers of Stereo Component Parts[a]

	1974		1975	
	U.S.	Stereo Components Buyers	U.S.	Stereo Components Buyers
Population (in thousands)	(139,778)	(3,400)	(141,622)	(2,788)
Men	47.3%	73.4%	49.6%	76.4%
Women	52.7	26.6	50.4	23.6
Age				
18–24	18.1%	42.5%	18.5%	47.6%
25–34	20.6	31.8	21.2	26.9
35–49	24.6	18.0	24.2	15.0
50–64	22.4	6.8	21.7	9.9
65 or over	14.2	1.0	14.4	0.5
Residence				
New England	3.9%	4.4%	5.9%	6.6%
Mid-Atlantic	22.2	18.6	20.6	18.8
East Central	13.1	16.9	14.2	15.1
West Central	16.5	19.8	15.2	16.6
Southeast	18.0	14.0	19.1	14.9
Southwest	10.6	10.4	10.1	7.1
Pacific	15.6	15.9	14.8	20.8
Education				
Graduated college	11.9%	16.3%	12.5%	25.6%
Attended college	14.0	30.8	14.7	27.5
Graduated high school	37.7	39.5	38.0	36.2
Did not graduate high school	36.4	13.4	34.8	10.7
Household Income				
$25,000 or more	8.8%	11.5%	11.3%	20.9%
$20,000–24,999	7.5	9.3	8.4	9.1
$15,000–19,999	17.1	21.4	18.6	22.7
$10,000–14,999	24.1	21.5	23.2	21.1
$ 8,000– 9,999	9.2	9.8	8.7	8.5
$ 5,000– 7,999	14.4	10.8	13.3	11.3
Less than $5,000	18.8	15.7	16.5	6.4
Family Life Style				
Single	16.2%	38.8%	17.3%	41.9%
Married	69.5	50.4	67.9	52.2
Widowed/divorced/separated	14.3	10.8	14.9	6.0
(Parents)	(43.7)	(36.0)	(42.4)	(37.6)

[a]Buyers of stereo component parts within the past year.

SOURCE: 1975 and 1976 issues of *Target Group Index,* published by Axiom Market Research Bureau, Inc. Sample sizes were approximately 25,000 for 1974 and 30,000 for 1975.

EXHIBIT 7   **Unit Sales of Compacts and Components, 1974–1977 (in thousands)**

	1974	1975	1976	1977
Compact Systems				
Cassette tape recorder bimode	32	36	38	44
Cassette tape recorder trimode	103	190	197	233
8-track tape player bimode	652	528	525	527
8-track tape player trimode	1,234	798	843	910
8-track tape recorder bimode	549	590	555	569
8-track tape recorder trimode	480	1,024	1,100	1,183
Changer bimode	377	325	324	337
Total	3,427	3,491	3,582	3,803
Components Parts (total)	7,799	7,971	8,719	9,539

SOURCE: *Merchandising,* March 1978, p. 51.

EXHIBIT 8 **Brand Preference Data for Hi-fi Components, July 12, 1977**

	Prospective Purchasers		*Prospective Purchasers*
Brand of Receiver		**Brand of FM Tuner**	
Pioneer	26%	Pioneer	28%
Marantz	15	Marantz	18
Sony	13	Sansui	14
Sansui	12	Fisher	6
Kenwood	7	Kenwood	6
Fisher	2	Dynaco	3
Harman-Kardon	2	Technics	1
Technics	1	Sherwin	0
Sherwood	1	Rotel	0
Other	2	Other	1
Don't plan to buy	5	Don't plan to buy	5
Don't know	14	Don't know	18
Total	100%	Total	100%
Brand of Amplifier		**Brand of Turntable**	
Pioneer	29%	Pioneer	24%
Marantz	17	Garrard	19
Sansui	9	Dual	12
Kenwood	8	BSR	8
Harman-Kardon	5	Technics	6
Superscope	3	Sansui	5
Crown	1	Bang & Olufsen	2
Dynaco	1	B.I.C.	1
Technics	1	JVC	1
Other	2	Other	3
Don't plan to buy	6	Don't plan to buy	4
Don't know	18	Don't know	15
Total	100%	Total	100%
Brand of Speaker[a]		**Brand of Tape Deck**	
Pioneer	32%	Teac	21%
Jensen	11	Pioneer	17
JBL	11	Sony/Superscope	15
AR	5	Sansui	9
Infinity	5	Fisher	6
KLH	4	Akai	5
B.I.C.—Venturi	3	Bekorder	1
Technics	3	Harman-Kardon	1
Dynaco	1	Technics	0
Other	3	Other	2
Don't plan to buy	4	Don't plan to buy	9
Don't know	18	Don't know	14
Total	100%	Total	100%

NOTE: National probability sample of 196.

[a]Among the different component parts, speakers usually offered the highest gross margin to dealers. One industry source estimated the margin spread between speakers and other components (branded products) to be 10% to 20%. This spread differed by brand and by type of retail outlets.

SOURCE: Gallup Organization.

EXHIBIT 9   A U.S. Pioneer Employee's Shopping Report

---

1. *Shopper's name:* John Smith
2. *Store visited:* ABC Sounds
3. *Salesperson and/or store attitude toward Pioneer:* Store's attitude generally negative. Salesperson was not really negative but went along with negative comment by another salesperson.
4. *Products they tried to get you to buy and discouraged:* Pushed Sankyo STD-1900 (a tape deck on sale for $218) and discouraged Pioneer CT-F7272 (a tape deck on sale for $208).
5. *Unfavorable statements toward Pioneer:* The salesperson made no derogatory remarks about Pioneer to me but became involved in a conversation with another store salesperson and prospective customer in which the other salesperson stated that he could produce copies of letters dealers had written to Pioneer complaining about service.
6. *Favorable statements toward competition:* [Store salesperson claimed that] Sankyo unit had much better frequency response and much cleaner sound. Sankyo was the second largest manufacturer of tape decks and manufactured components for Teac.
7. *How were Pioneer products displayed in comparison to competition?* I did not see any of the Pioneer equipment advertised in the paper displayed in the normal manner. Specifically, CT-F7272 was missing from where all other Pioneer decks were displayed. It was in another room with a Sankyo unit sitting on top of it.
8. *Other comments:* When the salesperson set up to play the tapes back, I noted that the Sankyo playback control was set at maximum volume and that he adjusted the Pioneer control to about 6. He began playing the tapes back, switching from one deck to the other and commented on the very audible difference of sound created by the higher frequency response of the Sankyo deck. I made no comment but asked to see the spec sheets on the two units. He came back with the spec sheet on the Sankyo but not the Pioneer.

   During the time I spent in the store I overheard no less than six customers ask specifically for one of the Pioneer products advertised in the paper. In each case the customer was told that the particular item had been sold out but that they had lesser or better products in the Pioneer line or comparable products in other lines. I also heard another customer ask if ABC Sounds could order Pioneer's HMP-100s. The salesperson replied, "No, we can't." The customer dropped the idea at that point.

SOURCE: Company data.

EXHIBIT 10

Audio warehouse advertisement

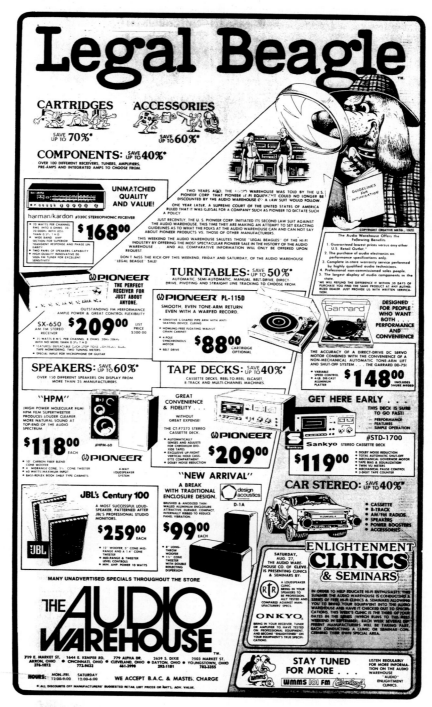

SOURCE: Ohio newspaper.

Exhibit 11

U.S. Pioneer dealer franchise agreement

Dealer Franchise Agreement

AGREEMENT made _____ this _____ day of _____ 19 ____ , by and between
U. S. PIONEER ELECTRONICS CORP. a Delaware Corporation, having its principal place of business in Moonachie, New Jersey (hereinafter called "PIONEER"), and

hereinafter called "Dealer"

Signer's name: _____

Corporate name: _____

dba _____

Address _____

City_____ State _____ Zip _____

Telephone No. (_____) _____

WITNESSETH:

WHEREAS Pioneer is the Distributor of certain quality products which are sold under the Pioneer brand name and trade marks (hereinafter referred to as "Products"); and

WHEREAS, Dealer desires to engage in the sale of Products at retail.

NOW, THEREFORE, Pioneer and Dealer mutually agree as follows:

1. Pioneer hereby appoints Dealer one of its Franchised Dealers in the continental limits of the United States only, and Dealer hereby accepts such appointment and agrees conscientiously and diligently to promote the sales of the above mentioned products.

2. Dealer shall purchase from Pioneer such Products for resale but all sales or agreements by Dealer for the resale of Pioneer Products shall be made by Dealer as principal and not as agent of Pioneer.

3. Prices to Dealer for such Products shall be set forth in the Pioneer Dealer Cost Schedules issued from time to time by Pioneer. Pioneer shall have the right to reduce or increase prices to Dealer at any time without accountability to Dealer in connection with Dealer's stock of unsold products on hand at the time of such change. When a new price schedule is issued by Pioneer it shall automatically supersede all such schedules on and after its effective date.

4. Dealer has represented to Pioneer, as an inducement to Pioneer for entering this agreement, that Dealer is at the time of entering into this agreement solvent and in a good and substantial financial position. Dealer shall from time to time when requested by Pioneer furnish such financial reports and other financial data as may be necessary to enable Pioneer to determine Dealer's financial condition.

5. Pioneer shall have the right to cancel any orders placed by Dealer or to refuse or to delay the shipment thereof if Dealer shall fail to meet payment schedules or other credit or financial requirements established by Pioneer and the cancellation of such orders or the withholding of shipments by Pioneer shall not be construed as a termination or breach of this agreement by Pioneer.

6. Pioneer will use its best efforts to make deliveries with reasonable promptness in accordance with orders accepted from Dealer, but it shall not be liable for any damages, consequential or otherwise, for its failure to fill orders or for delays in delivery or for any error in the filling of orders.

7. No territory is assigned exclusively to Dealer by Pioneer. Pioneer reserves the absolute right, for any reason whatever, to increase or decrease the number of Franchised Dealers in Dealer's locality or elsewhere, at any time without notice to Dealer.

8. Pioneer shall have the right at any time to discontinue the manufacture or sale of any or all of its Products and parts without incurring any liability to Dealer.

9. Pioneer is at liberty to change its service policies, its financial requirements and the design of its Products and parts thereof at any time without notice, and the Dealer shall have no claim on Pioneer for damage by reason of such change or changes.

10. Dealer agrees to forward promptly to Pioneer information concerning all charges, complaints or claims involving Products, by customers or accounts, that may come to its attention.

11. Dealer shall at no time engage in any unfair trade practices and shall make no false or misleading representations with regard to Pioneer or its Products. Dealer shall make no warranties or representations to customers or to the trade with respect to Products except such as may be approved in writing by Pioneer. Dealer shall hold Pioneer harmless from all damages caused by Dealer's violation of this paragraph. Any written representations respecting Pioneer products must first be submitted to Pioneer for its written approval.

12. Dealer will use its best efforts to resell Products purchased from Pioneer.

13. Dealer shall have no rights in the names or marks owned, used, promoted by Pioneer or in the names or marks of Products, except to make reference thereto in selling, advertising and promoting the sale of Products, which right shall be completely terminated upon the termination of this agreement.

14. Nothing herein contained shall be deemed to establish a relationship of principal and agent between Pioneer and Dealer, Dealer being an independent contractor, and neither Dealer nor any of its agents or employees shall be deemed to be an agent of Pioneer for any purpose, whatsoever and shall have no right or authority to assume or create any obligation of any kind, express or implied, on behalf of Pioneer except as specifically provided herein, nor any right or authority to accept service of legal process of any kind on behalf of Pioneer nor authority to bind Pioneer in any respect whatsoever.

15. All negotiations, correspondence and memoranda which have passed between Pioneer and Dealer in relation to this agreement are merged herein and this agreement constitutes the entire agreement between Pioneer and Dealer. No representations not contained herein are authorized by Pioneer and this agreement may not be altered, modified, amended, changed, rescinded or discharged, in whole or in part, except by a written memorandum executed by Pioneer and Dealer in the same manner as is provided for the execution of this agreement, except that the agreement may be terminated by either party as herein provided.

EXHIBIT 11

(*concluded*)

16. This agreement shall become effective only upon its execution by Pioneer in its executive offices at Moonachie, New Jersey, and no changes, additions or erasure of any printed portion of this agreement shall be valid and binding unless such change, addition or erasure is initialled by both Pioneer and Dealer.

17. This agreement supersedes and terminates any and all prior agreements or contracts, written or oral, if any, entered into between Pioneer and Dealer as of the effective date of this agreement with reference to all matters covered by this agreement.

18. Dealer is appointed a Franchised Pioneer Dealer by reason of Pioneer's confidence in Dealer, which appointment is personal in nature, and consequently this agreement shall not be assignable by Dealer, nor shall any of the rights granted hereunder be assignable or transferable in any manner whatsoever without the consent in writing of Pioneer.

19. This agreement shall be governed and construed in accordance with the laws of the State of Delaware. In the event of the provisions of this agreement, or the application of any such provisions to either Pioneer or Dealer with respect to its obligations hereunder, shall be held by a court of competent jurisdiction to be contrary to any State or Federal Law, the remaining portions of this agreement shall remain in full force and effect.

20. Either Dealer or Pioneer may terminate this agreement at any time by giving five days' written notice to the other and such termination may be made either with or without cause. Neither Dealer nor Pioneer shall be liable to the other for any damages of any kind or character whatsoever on account of such termination. Pioneer, at its option, shall have the right to repurchase from Dealer any or all Products in Dealer's inventory within a reasonable period from said notice of termination, at the net prices at which such Products were originally invoiced to Dealer less any allowances which Pioneer may have given Dealer on account of such Products: If such option to repurchase is exercised by Pioneer, Dealer agrees to deliver the inventory of Products so purchased to Pioneer, Moonachie, New Jersey, immediately after receipt of the exercise of such option.

21. Any notice which is required to be given hereunder shall be given in writing and shall either be delivered in person or sent by registered letter via United States mail to the respective addresses of the parties appearing above. If mailed, the date of the mailing shall be deemed to be the date such notice has been given.

22. Dealer shall not return merchandise without Pioneer's prior written authorization; and Pioneer shall assume no responsibility for returns made without prior written authorization.

IN WITNESS WHEREOF, the parties hereto have caused these presents to be executed the day and year first above written.

DEALER:

BY: _____ U. S. PIONEER ELECTRONICS CORP.

Title: _____ BY: _____

EXHIBIT 12   Sunshine Audio Sales Presentation Program

MOST OF MY CUSTOMERS ASK FOR PIONEER!!!

I CAN'T MAKE MONEY WITH PIONEER!!!

HOW OFTEN HAVE WE HEARD, OR HAVE YOU MADE, THESE VERY STATEMENTS? IF YOU ARE INTERESTED IN INCREASING YOUR OVERALL BUSINESS AND YOU WANT TO INCREASE YOUR OVERALL PROFIT DOLLARS—READ ON.

You and Your Competitor

Your business is really not that different from that of the store down the street. You both sell hi-fi, you both are after the same consumer, you both have to make a profit, you both want your business to grow, and you both are competing against each other. Why?

View your competitor as an ally and see what happens to your perspective of the business. You are both fighting to get consumers' disposable income dollars from the TV dealer, the motorcycle dealer, the travel agent, the car dealer, and any number of places they can spend that extra $300–$700. You and other hi-fi retailers should run ads to make the hi-fi market in your town grow—not to "get the other guy" with a low-ball price. Think about it—how many people in your market know that an RZ105 receiver at $136 is a good buy (cost in fact)? Much less, how many know what a receiver is?

EXHIBIT 12   *(concluded)*

You and Your Sales

Think about this for a minute. Most of your business should be in systems—about 70 percent. Single-piece sales account for the 30 percent balance. Fifteen percent are high margin pieces or accessory sales, and 15 percent are low margin promotional pieces. Now, think about the margin. If you only sell 40 percent margin products and you are not a "discount" house, how come your balance sheet only shows your gross margin between 28 and 32 percent? Interesting.

You and Pioneer

Now for the sales pitch. When you put a Pioneer piece in a system you will sell more systems (better brand name recognition) at your usual system margin. Pioneer has plenty of products that sell at full margin all the time—SG-9500, RG-1, turntables with cartridges, component ensembles, TR-2022, and so on. Of course, we have promotional pieces, too: CTF 2121, Project 60, 100A, and others. But how low a margin is a CTF 2121 at a cost of $124—with an advertised price of $139—when you sell the deck and its case for $179. This makes the margin 26 percent; sell tape and your margin is higher. I can't make money on Pioneer. Don't believe it! How about the SX1250 at $595—only a $50 profit. With the $50 rebate recently offered your real profit is $100. Sell an extra three SX1250s each week and we add over 15,000 profit dollars to your bottom line in a year. Even without the $50 rebate, the contribution to profit is $7,500 in one year.

Instead of using your energy not to sell, to down sell, or to sell off Pioneer, what would happen if you put that effort into creatively selling it?

You and Your Business

Some suggestions:

- Put together systems with brand name products that can't be duplicated by any dealer in your market.
- Sell the accessories with the promotional pieces or make them part of a system to increase profitability.
- Sell brand name goods that customers want.
- Think in terms of profit dollars, not always gross profit margin.

You and the Industry

Pioneer will spend close to $7 million in advertising. Take advantage of this tremendous support. Without advertising and without brand names your business will dry up. Most hi-fi dealers have some exclusive lines. But limited distribution can mean limited market and limited growth. Pioneer in a system will help sell more JVC receivers, Bose, JBL or Advent speakers, Technics turntables, or whatever your exclusive is, and your business will grow. Pioneer has a product and a model that will fit almost any system you can design. The quality has never been questioned. Sandy Ruby from Tech HiFi in a recent *Home Furnishings Daily* was quoted as saying, "We're actually not doing as much business in limited distribution lines as we were a few years ago. We've tried to look more toward what the market wants. We see surveys of what people are buying or what they say they plan to buy around the country . . . and then we get that equipment. You can't just look at your sales figures. Sure, you may be selling a lot of private brand equipment, but what about the people who didn't buy from you?" What brand do they want? You've got to have a handle on the customers who walked. Pretty interesting stuff. How many of your customers walked? How many did your salespeople's paranoia scare away?

We can help.

SOURCE: Company document.

EXHIBIT 13 Income Statement of a Hi-fi Specialty Store[a]

	1976
Income	$680,069
Cost of Sales	509,182
Expenses	
Advertising	34,803
Sales commissions (4 salespeople)	36,048
Payroll home office (administration)	12,875
Payroll home office (clerical)	767
Payroll taxes	1,770
Rent	18,780
Depreciation	1,831
Insurance	2,937
Taxes—other	237
Freight out	2,017
Store security	1,168
Outside labor	3,374
Travel and entertainment	1,336
Bad debts	3,313
Repairs and maintenance	579
Repairs to merchandise	57
Credit plan service charges	872
Telephone	5,318
Heat, light, and power	1,242
Bad checks	4,108
Recruiting expenses	889
Store supplies and expenses	3,055
Selling and promotion	115
Cleaning and rubbish removal	45
Cash over and short	442
Office supplies and expenses	1,058
Group insurance	257
Interest expense	857
Legal and accounting	3,648
Auto and truck expense	2,070
Rental commissions	130
Computer service expenses	44
Bank service charges	147
Officers' life insurance	193
Miscellaneous	916
Total expenses	$147,298
Operating income before federal taxes	$ 23,589

[a]One of a four-unit chain on the East Coast.

EXHIBIT 14   **Income Statement for U.S. Pioneer (dollars in 000s)**

	1976[a]		1975[a]
Total revenue		135,094	87,340
Cost of goods sold (CGS) (primarily purchases from the parent company)	91,707		60,470
Selling, general and administrative expenses (SG&A)	30,608		23,409
Income before income taxes		12,779	3,461
Provision for income taxes		6,530	1,716
Net income		6,249	1,745

[a]Fiscal year ended September 30
SOURCE: Company data.

PIZZA HUT, INC.

In May 1986, Steve Reinemund, the newly appointed president of Pizza Hut, Inc., announced that he intended to pursue vigorously the "exciting opportunities afforded by our new segment, delivery." Seven months later, the home delivery units had produced mixed results, and Reinemund met with his senior managers to decide how to respond.

Entry into the home delivery market had been a major strategic decision at Pizza Hut, and Reinemund was well aware of the difficulties it presented. Half of the 5,025 Pizza Hut system restaurants were owned by large, powerful franchisees with exclusive rights to the territories they controlled. While some franchisees saw the benefits of home delivery in their markets, others were strongly opposed. Moreover, many franchisees did not agree with the manner in which Pizza Hut would implement delivery. Nevertheless, to be successful, the delivery strategy needed the franchisees' cooperation. Attaining this cooperation in the Pizza

Hut franchise system would be, in the words of Jim Baxter, vice president of franchising, "a matter of *sell,* not *tell.*"

The Pizza Market

The rapid growth in home delivery in the mid-1980s revitalized the pizza market and was responsible for pizza's position as the fastest growing part of the $53 billion fast-food market. Three main segments comprised the pizza restaurant market: eat-in, carryout, and delivery. Below were the sales for each segment.

Many companies competed in more than one segment; for example, carryout was a significant percentage of most eat-in restaurants' business. At Pizza Hut, carryout accounted for 40 percent of the dollar volume in 1986, compared with 37 percent in 1982.

	Eat-in	Carryout	Delivery	Total
1982	$4.3 billion (57%)	$3.1 billion (41%)	$0.1 billion (1%)	$7.5 billion
1984	4.7 billion (48)	4.0 billion (41)	1.0 billion (10)	9.7 billion
1986*	5.1 billion (40)	5.0 billion (39)	2.6 billion (20)	12.7 billion
1990*	5.9 billion (27)	9.0 billion (41)	7.0 billion (32)	21.9 billion

*Projections based on limited Pizza Hut entry into delivery segment as of third-quarter 1986.
SOURCE: GDR/Crest Enterprises, Inc.

This case was prepared by Professor Patrick J. Kaufmann.
Copyright © 1987 by the President and Fellows of Harvard College.
Harvard Business School case 9-588-011 (Rev. 7/5/91).

In 1986, while the overall pizza market expanded rapidly (because of home delivery), in-restaurant consumption of pizza was not increasing significantly. Industry observers believed that the restaurant industry was seriously overbuilt; pizza parlors seemed to be on every corner in some towns. They believed that the already intense local competition in the pizza eat-in and carryout segments would soon approach all-out warfare, as evidenced by increased use of couponing, deals, and price competition.

The Pizza Consumer

Pizza was a very popular restaurant food item, second only to hamburgers in frequency of purchase. Pizza was predominantly a dinner food, although many consumers also viewed it as an evening snack. Consumers did not react casually to pizza, unlike their feelings for hamburgers, chicken, and fish. Consumer research had shown that pizza was a personal, almost sensual, experience for many people. Moreover, consumers generally did not believe that great pizza could be made by a fast-food chain.

While pizza consumption was strongest in the northern and eastern parts of the United States, pizza's appeal was broad based, with no areas exhibiting major rejection. However, tastes in pizza varied significantly by region. This presented a challenge for chains attempting to maintain product continuity while expanding into different regions.

By the early 1980s, convenience was crucial to many consumers. Two-career families often found cooking at home or eating in restaurants too time consuming, thereby increasing carryout and home delivery business. In both 1985 and 1986, consumer surveys undertaken by the *National Restaurant Association* identified pizza home delivery as the most important new fast-food concept. Another study had shown that consumers generally viewed pizza as eat-at-home food. Many analysts believed that the rapid growth of the in-home video rental market, together with the increasing number of baby-boomers with small children, would further fuel the pizza delivery segment.

Competition in the Pizza Market

Although faced with intense competition from aggressive regional chains and single-unit owner-operated local competitors, Pizza Hut had dominated the eat-in pizza segment nationwide for years (Exhibit 1). Godfather's Pizza, another eat-in/carryout chain, which competed in many of the same local markets as Pizza Hut, traditionally was perceived as Pizza Hut's most significant national competitor.

Before 1984, neither Pizza Hut nor its franchisees thought that Domino's Pizza posed a serious competitive threat to Pizza Hut's leadership position in the overall pizza market. Domino's, however, had grown from sales of $626 million in 1984 to $1.085 billion in 1985, and to $1.55 billion by the end of 1986. In 1985, the chain opened 954 new outlets (bringing the total to 2,839)—the highest one-year total ever recorded by a foodservice company. Two thirds of Domino's outlets were franchised; the company used its company-owned stores as sites for required franchisee training. Although there were several large franchi-

sees operating many units all over the United States, most of the 600 franchisees in early 1986 owned only one or two stores. While some of its outlets had carryout windows, Domino's was essentially a delivery-only chain. Domino's management believed the large percentage of carryout business in the industry was especially vulnerable to Domino's delivery strategy.

Pizza Hut first experienced the effects of Domino's expansion in its company-owned stores. While Pizza Hut's franchisees had exclusive rights to most of the smaller markets, Pizza Hut's company-owned stores controlled most of the large, densely populated metropolitan markets. Domino's initially had focused its national expansion on those large metropolitan markets. By late 1985, Pizza Hut senior management was convinced that Domino's dominance of the fast-growing delivery segment was the major threat to Pizza Hut's continued leadership of the overall pizza market. By 1986, Domino's had begun to extend its expansion into the smaller towns generally controlled by Pizza Hut franchisees. Domino's clearly intended to gain total market leadership while maintaining its dominance of the delivery segment.

Pizza Hut, Incorporated

On June 15, 1958, Dan and Frank Carney, two college students from Wichita, Kansas, opened the first Pizza Hut restaurant. It was a startling success. By the following February, the Carney brothers had opened two more restaurants and had begun to develop plans for the first franchised outlet. The chain grew rapidly, with 43 restaurants opened by 1963 and 296 by 1968. Pizza Hut went public in 1969, and in 1977 was acquired by PepsiCo, Inc. In 1971, Pizza Hut became the largest pizza restaurant chain in the world in both sales and number of restaurants. Sales reached $1 billion in 1981; by December 1986, Pizza Hut, still headquartered in Wichita, had a total of 5,025 domestic units and annual sales of almost $2 billion (Exhibit 2).

Since the 1960s, Pizza Hut restaurants were characterized by a distinctive freestanding design and familiar red roof (Exhibit 3). All Pizza Hut restaurants were full-service, eat-in/carryout family-style operations seating about 60 to 90 customers and normally open from 11 A.M. to midnight.

Although the menu had changed over the years, pizza was always the main product in Pizza Hut restaurants. The company paid careful attention to operational efficiency, and it continued to offer a high quality product at a premium price. A constant stream of new product introductions served to invigorate consumer interest, but many franchisees were concerned by the increased cost of operations caused by the expanding menu.

For more than 20 years, the Pizza Hut franchisees had taken the lead in marketing. In the early 1980s, however, the company further strengthened its corporate marketing department and began developing comprehensive national and local market strategies. By 1986, the company was developing and implementing systemwide corporate marketing programs and realizing leverage from national TV advertising.

The Franchise System at Pizza Hut

Franchising was an integral part of the Pizza Hut strategy since the corporation's founding. In 1968, there were 293 franchised restaurants and only seven company-owned restaurants. Over the next seven years, the company built new stores and acquired many more (including the acquisition of the 225 units of a large Pizza Hut franchisee). By the mid-1970s, there were almost as many company-owned as franchised units. In December 1986, 135 individuals, partnerships, and corporations operated 2,395 Pizza Hut system restaurants and 96 delivery-only units as franchisees. Meanwhile, the company itself operated 2,173 restaurants and 361 delivery-only units.

Many of the original franchisees, whose holdings had grown with the company, were still part of the system in 1986. Sixty percent of all franchised units were controlled by franchisees whose main offices were still in Wichita. In the Pizza Hut system, exclusive franchises were granted for specified market areas. Unlike franchise systems characterized by single-unit owner/operators, most Pizza Hut franchisees were large companies with diversified holdings, sometimes including other foodservice franchisor units like Kentucky Fried Chicken and Long John Silver. Of the 135 franchisees, almost two thirds operated 10 or more Pizza Hut system restaurants in 1986. Except for minority opportunity programs, no new franchise areas had been offered to the public since 1971. When a franchisee chose to sell its holdings, they were purchased by the company or another franchise holder.

Franchisee rights and obligations were specified in formal franchise agreements. Under the agreements, each franchisee was obligated to develop its exclusive market area in accordance with a five-year development schedule. Essentially, the agreement required the franchisee to open an agreed-upon number of new restaurants during the first year of the agreement, an agreed-upon number during the second year, and so on, up to year five. The development schedule represented franchisee commitment to significant continuing investment in the business. After the five-year period expired, the company could negotiate a secondary development schedule with the franchisee to open additional restaurants in the area, if the company deemed it practicable. Although franchisee failure to comply with either development schedule entitled the company to franchise others or to open company-owned restaurants in the previously exclusive area, this had never been necessary. In no case could there be a restaurant established within two miles of an existing franchisee restaurant.

Franchisees paid Pizza Hut an initial fee of $15,000 for each system restaurant they opened. Franchisees also paid the company an ongoing franchise fee of 4 percent of monthly gross sales. The company or franchisee invested about $466,000–$816,000 to open each eat-in/carryout restaurant. By contrast, delivery-only units required an estimated $128,500–$198,500 investment. However, by the time one included delivery vehicles, training, additional advertising, and the company's central order-taking computer system, the company's investment in a company-owned delivery unit was about equal to that of a traditional restaurant. Franchisees investing in delivery-only units typically did not buy vehicles and did not always adopt the company's computer-ordering system (see Exhibit 4 for expenses of company-owned delivery units).

The International Pizza Hut Franchise Holders Association

The International Pizza Hut Franchise Holders Association (IPHFHA) was formed in 1967 to "solidify the national image of Pizza Hut and to further product loyalty," and to "devise the most appropriate use of the funds available for national advertising." By 1986, its role had been extended to render many other services to franchisees (e.g., accounting services, group life insurance, workman's compensation insurance, credit union).

Franchisees were required to become members of the IPHFHA. The IPHFHA communicated with the company regularly through the IPHFHA board of directors. The IPHFHA employed a professional staff headed by Gerald Aaron, president, who acted as intermediary between the board and the company. He directed for the association the broad policy areas of marketing, finance, and administration. Joint advisory committees (with franchisee and company members) were formed in 1985 to further enhance communication between the company and the franchisees on the issues of human resources, delivery, products, and buildings and equipment.

The IPHFHA was reorganized in 1975, and the Advertising Committee was formed to "determine and control the amount, kind, and quality of national advertising and sales promotion to be provided . . . for Pizza Hut and its franchisees." (In 1981, the role of the Advertising Committee was continued under the new franchise agreement.) Four marketing professionals made up the Advertising Committee, two representing the company and two representing the franchisees. IPHFHA members voted on funding for national advertising and on other IPHFHA programs. The company, although not a member of IPHFHA, was contractually bound by the franchise agreement to contribute at the same rate as the franchisees. In 1986, the current assessment was 2 percent of the first $28,000 of monthly sales for each restaurant and 1 percent of all monthly sales above $28,000. The Advertising Committee controlled the entire advertising budget, and it was also responsible for hiring and firing the national advertising agency.

Market area advertising was managed by local co-ops comprising all of those franchisees (and the company if applicable) operating restaurants within a particular market area. All co-op members, franchisees and company alike, were required to make contributions to the co-op for advertising in their area in the amount of 2 percent of monthly gross sales (in addition to the contributions to the national advertising fund). All disputes arising within co-ops were arbitrated by the Advertising Committee.

In addition to ad hoc interaction between the company and its franchisees at regional store manager meetings, there were two general systemwide meetings each year. Franchisees set the summer meeting agenda and the company set the winter meeting agenda. Company management also regularly met with the board of IPHFHA and with the franchisees on the advisory committees.

Delivery at Pizza Hut, Inc.

For many years, the prospect of entering the delivery market worried Pizza Hut senior managers: delivery units might cannibalize the traditional restaurant business, causing reduced profit margins. In the summer of 1984, however, Pizza Hut began exploring the possibility of such an entry. Because it was believed that the addition of delivery service to traditional eat-in restaurants would create unmanageable operational bottlenecks, the solution for Pizza Hut management was to enter the delivery market with separate delivery-only units (i.e., with no eat-in or carryout facilities). These units would be considerably smaller than the traditional restaurant facilities and would not require parking space or highly visible locations (Exhibit 3); occupancy costs, therefore, would be about 2.1 percent of sales, rather than 6.0 percent for the standard eat-in restaurants.

In 1985, a small delivery task group was formed at Pizza Hut and began opening company-owned delivery units in several markets. Their idea was to open a cluster of delivery-only units in each market and keep their costs as low as possible because of the small expected margins (Exhibit 4). There was considerable resistance to the delivery concept at all levels within the company, and company restaurant managers and supervisors in the markets where delivery units had been opened complained bitterly about the adverse effect on their sales. Nevertheless, Pizza Hut management was becoming increasingly concerned about Domino's rapid expansion and deemed entry into the delivery segment necessary if the company was to maintain its market leadership position.

By August 1985, eight markets had been opened, with a total of 51 company-owned delivery-only units. In the well-developed markets—Atlanta, Georgia, and Norfolk, Virginia—customers called a single phone number. Orders were then sent by facsimile machine to the appropriate delivery unit. Although the system was relatively cheap, as the number of units grew, it became more and more unmanageable, and the "fax" machines presented a significant bottleneck. In late summer 1985, senior Pizza Hut managers visited the Norfolk market and became convinced that, with a number of operational adjustments, the delivery concept was workable, offered tremendous potential growth, and should be pursued. The company postponed further expansion into new markets while it contracted for the development of a computerized central ordering system and perfected other aspects of the delivery concept.

The computerized central ordering system, called the Customer Service Center (CSC), allowed customers in a particular market to call a single number to place an order. The caller first was asked his or her phone number, and the system ascertained whether the caller had ordered before. If so, the operator would verify the caller's name and address and ask if the customer would like the same type of pizza previously ordered. The order would then be forwarded automatically to the appropriate delivery unit where a terminal would receive the order information.

The CSC system, although expensive to develop, was designed to be capable of handling the vast number of calls generated in a large market with a large number of delivery units. It was necessary, however, that the system work perfectly. Customers in an eat-in restaurant understood and tolerated waiting a few minutes to be seated. Delivery customers expected their phone call to be answered within seconds, even though 60 percent of the daily calls for an entire market area might come in during a one-hour period. While there were substantial marketing benefits to having only one phone number for an entire market, there were significant risks in operating such a complex system. In Norfolk, initial problems with the installation of the CSC had created serious losses in a once profitable delivery market.

Although there had been some difficulties during its installation, Pizza Hut management was convinced that the CSC would be a significant competitive advantage. About 70 percent of Domino's franchisees owned only one store, and Pizza Hut believed that the costs of coordination and management of such a centralized ordering system at Domino's would be prohibitive. In the Pizza Hut system, the concentration of restaurant ownership in the hands of the company and relatively few franchisees would allow for much easier coordination and substantial cost savings. Under the company's delivery concept, the company would invest in the CSC for each market and manage it, coordinating the ordering process and providing service on a fee-per-call basis to participating franchisees and company stores (currently $0.65 per call). Pizza Hut's investment in the CSCs was expected to be large, but management believed that such systems were essential to the delivery strategy. It was expected that eventually the franchisees would purchase the necessary equipment and manage the Customer Service Centers themselves in their own markets.

Another major issue presented in developing a profitable delivery concept was whether there would be a charge for service. Pizza Hut management was convinced that for competitive reasons the company could not charge for delivery (Domino's delivered free with a 30-minute guarantee). The additional cost of providing free delivery was the same, regardless of order size. This meant that, to the extent the average check price could be increased, margins would increase. To help maintain margins when offering free delivery, therefore, it was decided that the size and price of delivered pizzas would be slightly increased over pizza in traditional restaurants (i.e., delivery sizes would be 10–14–16″ versus the 9–13–15″ sizes in the traditional restaurants, and Domino's 12–16″ sizes). Customers would pay approximately 10 percent more for a small, medium, or large pizza, but would get more as well. This "upsizing" would increase the average check price and gross margin, thereby helping to defray the cost of free delivery and the Customer Service Centers.

In early 1986, Pizza Hut was reorganized to reflect the increasing importance and autonomy of the delivery segment (Exhibit 5). A senior vice president of operations managed all traditional restaurant operations, while Senior Vice President Allan Huston was general manager of delivery. Still another senior vice president led the marketing function for the traditional restaurants. Delivery had its own separate marketing department that reported directly to Allan Huston. Even the regions into which the country was divided were different for delivery and the traditional restaurant business.

Although there was some experimentation with alternative delivery concepts (e.g., no upsizing in some markets) during the spring and summer of 1986, the marketing function for the delivery group was not fully operational until July. Huston concentrated primarily on the operational details surrounding the opening of new delivery units, rather than on refining the Pizza Hut delivery concept. In the first half of 1986, Pizza Hut doubled the number of markets where it operated delivery units and had almost quadrupled the total number of units (Exhibit 6). Those delivery units were predominately in metropolitan areas—where most of the company's markets were. The initial units opened were in markets with high levels of traditional restaurant penetration and high "per-store-average" (PSA) sales. A second group, opened later in 1986, was in low penetration and low per-store-average sales markets.

Throughout 1986, Pizza Hut managers on the traditional restaurant side of the business continued to be concerned about competition from the Pizza Hut delivery operation, as well as from Domino's. Huston and other managers in the delivery operation, however, believed that delivery was expanding the market by including people who would not go to a restaurant for pizza. They argued that consumers who ate pizza in restaurants and those who had pizza delivered sought very different benefits, and that delivery did not compete directly with traditional restaurants. Moreover, the adverse effects of Pizza Hut delivery units on traditional restaurant sales growth appeared to be most pronounced in markets where there was weak sales growth already; in strong markets the effect was short lived. As Reinemund noted in early 1986, "We do not yet know how great a factor this overlap will be. But what we do know is that in many cases our restaurant business has actually grown after our delivery units have entered the market." In the words of another senior Pizza Hut manager:

> While it is true that we often are serving the same customers, we are serving them on totally separate dining occasions. When we introduce delivery to a market, we get the business of customers who probably were ordering a competitor's pizza simply for the convenience of home delivery.

As for personnel, it was clear that needs of the delivery business were significantly different from those of the traditional restaurant business. Pizza Hut restaurant managers were trained to manage the "total customer experience" and, because of the isolation from customers, some restaurant managers did not think they would enjoy running a delivery-only unit. While many production and operation functions would overlap, store managers found it hard to see how career paths could cross over from traditional full-service restaurants to delivery units or vice versa. Moreover, moving as quickly as it had into new markets, Pizza Hut found it difficult to manage at the store level. Ninety percent of the people working in the delivery business were new, and delivery presented unfamiliar operational demands in the areas of driver management, trade area definition, and order taking.

The Franchisees' Experience with Delivery

A few Pizza Hut franchisees had been offering delivery unofficially for 20 years. In the early 1980s, the company consistently attempted to dissuade franchisees from offering delivery. Nevertheless, the number of small-town franchisees delivering pizza to college dormitories and military bases from their traditional restaurants had begun to increase. In some isolated cases, franchisees faced local competitive environments that they believed necessitated offering delivery. By 1982, about 25 franchisees operated delivery services from a total of about 75 standard eat-in restaurants.

Most franchisees that entered the delivery segment did so by retrofitting existing eat-in restaurants to allow for delivery "out the back door" (Exhibit 6 shows the number of franchisees owning retrofit and delivery-only units from

1984 to 1986). They found, however, that retrofitting significantly increased demands on the restaurant manager and required much greater local management skills. Because of operational bottlenecks, some franchisees lost money on the delivery business and ceased delivery operations. The company believed this supported its concept of opening separate delivery-only units.

Through 1985, the majority of Pizza Hut franchisees saw no reason for delivery. They faced little or no competition in their market from the major chains offering delivery, and they were less interested in overall market share battles than the company seemed to be. Sixty-five percent of all franchised restaurants were in towns, with populations under 50,000 people, and delivery in those rural areas was not as easy to justify economically as in more densely populated markets. In late 1985, when the company changed its position completely and began to encourage franchisees to open delivery-only units, most franchisees were not interested in doing so.

In November 1985, the company announced to franchisees that it interpreted franchise agreement development schedules to include delivery and, therefore, the company had the right to require franchisee development of delivery units in their markets. The company announced that it would not exercise that right for one-and-a-half years while it perfected the concept, but urged franchisees to begin developing delivery-only units immediately.

The franchise community's response was quick and clear. Most franchisees saw no reason to risk business in their eat-in restaurants by expanding into the delivery market. They denied that the development schedules allowed Pizza Hut to require them to open delivery units. They openly expressed their disagreement with the company's delivery concept, especially regarding upsizing (referred to by one franchisee as "up-pricing"). They also questioned the necessity of the computerized Customer Service Centers and the delivery-only units (some franchisees wanted to retrofit existing restaurants, and others wanted carryout allowed in the delivery units). Significant tension arose between the company and its franchisees. At a heated IPHFHA board meeting in December 1985, board members and Pizza Hut senior management recognized that they had been concentrating too much on each other and not enough on Domino's. They agreed to operate temporarily under a "yellow flag" plan (an automobile racing term referring to the period when each side continues to operate as before without either side trying to improve its relative position).

The company's upsizing concept continued to be a focal point of disagreement. Although Pizza Hut suggested prices, the franchisees were free to price their products as they pleased. The franchisees argued that, even though they had not increased prices as frequently as the company-owned restaurants had in past years, they were still at a price disadvantage when compared to the competition.

This disadvantage was especially acute in the delivery business; franchisees believed that upsizing would exacerbate the problem because customers were conscious only of the absolute price of a small, medium, or large pizza and did not calculate price per square inch of the product.

The franchisees also wanted to know why Pizza Hut needed an expensive CSC system, if Domino's didn't have one. They felt that, if delivery was necessary, the costs should be kept as low as possible. This meant simple phone ordering to each local restaurant, and delivery out of existing restaurants where feasible. It was important to franchisees that the system be as flexible as possible so they could find local solutions to local problems.

The reorganization of Pizza Hut in early 1986, which provided for the delivery business to operate autonomously from the traditional restaurant business, raised another issue in the franchise community. Franchisees were concerned that, while the company could afford to run the delivery and eat-in businesses separately, the franchisees did not have the resources for separate marketing and operations departments for the traditional restaurant and delivery business. The mismatch of organizational forms between company and franchisees was expected to create significant management difficulties. To make matters worse, the Pizza Hut national advertising account had been split in two within the advertising agency so a separate group could begin working only on delivery. Many franchisees viewed the two businesses as one and were concerned that their separation would make coordination between delivery and eat-in even more difficult.

There was little consensus of opinion among the franchisees regarding the various elements of the company's delivery concept. There was, however, virtual unanimous franchisee concurrence that the existing franchise agreement did not cover delivery. In February 1986, Jim Baxter, who had been with Pizza Hut for almost 10 years, was appointed vice president of restaurant franchising and assumed the role of liaison between the company and franchisees. In May, newly appointed president Steve Reinemund accompanied Baxter to a series of regional meetings with the franchisees, where Reinemund announced that the company no longer contended that the existing development agreement covered delivery. He also announced the company's intention to negotiate with the board of the IPHFHA to produce an amendment to the franchise agreement that would provide for systemwide entry into the delivery market. Reinemund suggested that the amendment would include incentives (e.g., reduced or no royalties for a certain time period on new delivery-only units) designed to make franchisee participation in the delivery segment more attractive. These incentives would be retroactive for any franchisee delivery-only units opened in the meantime. The amendment would take effect if franchisees representing 85 percent of the units approved it within a specified time period.

The August Franchisee Meeting

As the August 1986 franchisee meeting drew near, Pizza Hut management decided it was time to press again for the full involvement of all franchisees in systemwide entry into the delivery market. Pizza Hut operated delivery units in 16 markets, with a total of 284 company-owned units. The company had hired and trained over 10,000 people. The flagship Norfolk market, which had experienced difficulties, was now profitable. The first half-year results from the operating units were impressive, and Delivery General Manager Huston was confident that the company could make a good business case for delivery.

Huston and the delivery group gave an extremely upbeat presentation of the delivery data to franchisees at the August meeting. Their purposes included (1) to convince franchisees that the time had come to give total support to the delivery effort; (2) to "sell" the company's delivery concept to the franchisees; (3) to successfully launch the amendment negotiation process that was to begin in earnest after the meeting. While many franchisees remained adamantly opposed to delivery, others were becoming convinced that they could, in fact, increase their overall income with delivery even if they would face decreased average margins. While the idea of delivery became more acceptable, however, there was still little support for the particulars of the company's delivery concept.

The Current Situation

As the negotiations for an amendment to the franchise agreement continued into the fall of 1986, competition in the delivery market intensified tremendously. Systemwide, Domino's increased advertising 100 percent over the previous year. Moreover, much of its advertising was specifically focused on the markets Pizza Hut was attempting to open for delivery. Domino's spent an average of 68 percent more on advertising in those markets than in its other markets. Moreover, Domino's had proven to be an able competitor with satisfied customers and an inexperienced but highly enthusiastic franchise system. They met Pizza Hut head-on in each market Pizza Hut entered by focusing on execution, quality, advertising, and price.

Discounting became even more prevalent in late 1986. Fifty percent of Domino's pizzas were sold on deal. Pantera's joined Little Caesar in offering two-for-one deals; Godfather's and Pizza Inn launched their own delivery services, also with deep price discounts. Delivery proved to be much more sensitive to price, coupon, and deal than the traditional restaurant business.

Of the 19 Pizza Hut company-controlled markets open in December 1986, three were profitable. At the unit level, of the 361 company-owned operating delivery units, 194 were profitable. Company-owned delivery units that had opened early that year performed well from both a sales and profit perspective. The fierce competitive environment in markets opened later that year, however, led to slower sales growth and greater operating losses than expected for those units. For example, in one market, per-store average weekly sales rose to $6,600 after three weeks. Domino's had responded with two-for-one deals for three months, and the per-store average weekly sales dropped to around $4,850. Moreover, in markets with greater than $8,000 per-store average weekly sales in traditional restaurants, Pizza Hut delivery units averaged $7,300; in markets where traditional per store average was less than $8,000, delivery units averaged only $4,225. Overall, the average weekly sales per delivery unit in December was $6,000.

Huston believed that some of the markets were overbuilt with delivery units, and that Pizza Hut was getting all the sales that could be expected from those units. The ratio of traditional restaurants to potential customers averaged 1 restaurant to 70,000 people, while the delivery units averaged 1 unit to 40,000 people.

Consumer research had shown that the standard Pizza Hut pizza served in the traditional restaurants was not as well suited to the delivery environment, causing quality to suffer. Pizza Hut research and development managers were confident that they could solve that problem by developing a new product designed especially for delivery. This would involve an entirely different production process than that used currently in the traditional restaurants.

Meanwhile, the number of franchisees who had introduced delivery was growing rapidly. Franchisees who in August had told Aaron that delivery would be "over their dead bodies" were inviting him to visit their delivery operations. Moreover, many franchisees who had introduced delivery were doing significantly better than the company-owned stores. Eighteen franchisees opened a total of 65 delivery-only units in 1986, bringing the overall total to 96. All but two units with over seven months' experience were profitable. In addition, by December 1986, 292 traditional restaurants had been retrofitted by franchisees to provide delivery service. Because the delivery operations were co-mingled with the eat-in and carryout operation in the retrofitted restaurants, it was difficult to estimate their profitability; however, the franchisees were reported to be pleased with the results so far. The franchisees' success with delivery was attributed to the fact that they had developed markets where they were already strong and had carefully picked the trade areas with the highest potential. They also had priced more competitively, and only 20 percent had upsized. Most kept costs low by having phone orders go direct to each separate unit, instead of using Customer Service Centers.

The winter franchisee meeting was scheduled for January, and Reinemund, Huston, and Baxter had less than a month to decide how to proceed. Before deciding what to do at that meeting, they wanted to review the overall strategy and the likely profit impact on Pizza Hut of delivery.

EXHIBIT 1   Top Pizza Chains, 1986

	Systemwide Sales ($ millions)	Units	Average Check/Person	Delivery
Pizza Hut	1,934	5,025	$9.99	Separate delivery units plus franchisee add-on delivery out of restaurant.
Domino's	1,550	3,696	9.50	Delivery only.
Little Caesar	520	1,308	2.75	No delivery.
Pizza Inn	278.7	748	4.30	Separate delivery units.
Godfather's	275	650	9.75	Add-on delivery out of restaurant.
Round Table Pizza	250	535	5.00	Add-on delivery out of restaurant.
Showbiz/Chuck E. Cheese	249	268	5.20	No delivery.
Shakey's	197	386	4.25	Add-on delivery out of restaurant.
Mr. Gatti's	139.2	319	7.81	Add-on delivery out of restaurant.

SOURCE: Adapted from *Nation's Restaurant News*.

EXHIBIT 2   Pizza Hut Historical Data (U.S. domestic only)

	1979	1980	1981	1982	1983	1984	1985	1986
System net sales ($MM)	732	832	1,007	1,170	1,394	1,566	1,743	1,934
Market share[a]	14.9	15.7	17.0	17.2	18.0	17.3	16.0	15.4
Units[b]:								
Company	1,940	1,888	1,843	1,845	1,911	2,051	2,224	2,534
Franchise	1,801	1,873	1,922	1,975	2,095	2,157	2,309	2,491
Total	**3,741**	**3,761**	**3,765**	**3,820**	**4,006**	**4,208**	**4,533**	**5,025**
Company								
PSA[c] sales ($M)	182	211	258	301	355	373		
(Traditional)							395	400
(Delivery)							282	289
PSA sales growth:								
Real	(3.1)	4.7	11.8	8.0	9.8	1.8	2.0	(2.0)
Price	6.4	8.1	9.0	6.6	3.9	5.1	3.4	0.8
Total	**3.7**	**12.8**	**20.8**	**14.6**	**13.7**	**6.9**	**5.4**	**(1.2)**
Net sales ($MM)	354	399	476	556	678	766	835	929
Net sales growth (%)	—	12.7	19.2	16.8	21.9	13.0	9.0	11.3
Total revenues ($MM)	495	556	489	569	699	795	867	967
ROAE (%)[d]	3.5	6.1	8.9	16.4	21.7	16.9	15.0	12.4
Franchisees								
PSA sales ($M)	—	237	280	314	350	386	400	415
Net sales ($MM)	378	433	531	613	715	799	908	1,005

[a]Based on data from GDR/Crest Enterprises, Inc.

[b]Total number of U.S. domestic units of all kinds: restaurant, delivery, and mobile open that year.

[c]PSA—per store average: annual average computed by dividing net sales for each four-week store period by number of stores open during that period and then aggregating across all 13 store periods.

[d]Return on assets employed: calculated as earnings divided by year's average net asset base.

EXHIBIT 3

Traditional Red Roof restaurant

Delivery Unit

EXHIBIT 4   **Pro Forma Profit and Loss Statement (based on $8,000/week sales)**[a]

	Company-owned Traditional Restaurant (%)	Company-owned Delivery Unit (%)
Gross sales	100.0%	100.0%
Advertising, discounts, promotions, and allowances	16.5	18.5
Cost of sales[b] and labor	48.5	46.2
Semivariables and premiums[c]	8.7	5.2
Vehicles[d]	—	6.1
Occupancy costs	6.0	2.1
General and administrative	7.2	7.2
Customer service center costs	—	5.9
Net field contribution	13.1	8.8

[a]Percentages reflect an assumed $8,000/week store. As weekly sales decreased below $8,000, expenses as percent of sales increased significantly. At approximately $7,000/week, Delivery Unit net field contribution was 0.

[b]Cost of sales tended to be lower in the Delivery Units due to a combination of upsizing and higher prices per order. Labor costs for Delivery Units did not include order-taking expenses that were reflected in the Customer Service Center costs.

[c]Semivariables refers to utilities, uniforms, and other operating supplies. Premiums refers to items, such as special glassware or toys, that were given away or sold below cost to promote the sale of a particular menu item.

[d]Vehicle expenses reflect a mix of driver- and company-owned vehicles. Eighty percent of the delivery vehicles were owned by the drivers, who were reimbursed for their use per trip.

EXHIBIT 5
Organization Chart

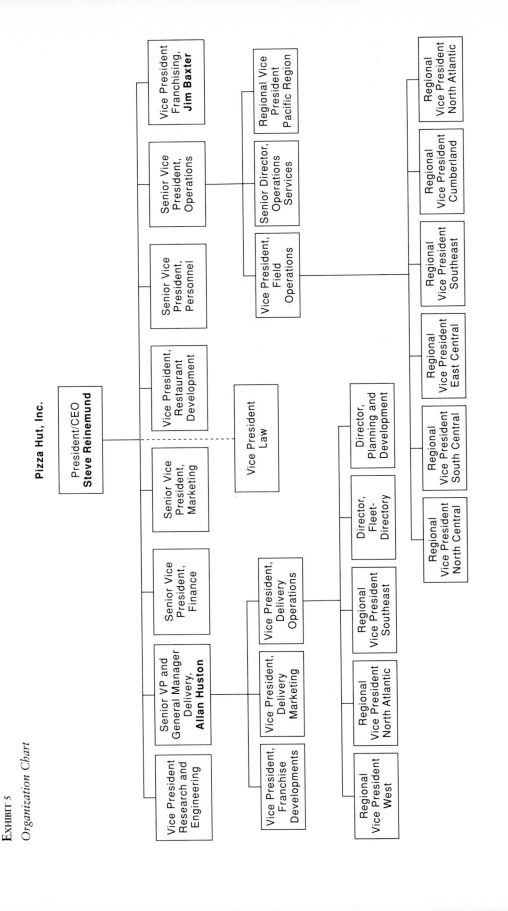

Exhibit 6   Open Pizza Hut System Traditional Restaurants and Delivery Units[a]

	Company-Owned		Franchisee-Owned		
	Traditional Restaurants	*Delivery- only Units*	*Traditional Restaurants*[b]	*Retrofit*	*Delivery- only Units*
August 1984	2,011	11	2,089	70	15
December 1984	2,025	16	2,137	98	20
August 1985	2,046	51	2,256	131	30
December 1985	2,004	78	2,352	162	46
August 1986	2,208	284	2,277	241	66
December 1986	2,173	361	2,395	292	96

[a]Domestic U.S. restaurants and delivery units only.

[b]Totals for franchisee-owned traditional restaurants include those restaurants retrofitted to provide delivery service.

P A R T

II THE MARKETING PROCESS

MARKETING RESEARCH

I. Introduction

Marketing research is an integral part of marketing management. Its function is to provide *managers* with information that assists in making decisions. The manager must be aware of the costs and benefits of alternative methods in order to select the best research program and analyze the results in the most useful way. This note presents an overview of the most widely utilized methods, which are quite diverse. For example, consider the brand manager for Quaker Oats' Life Cereal.[1] Seeking ways to increase Life's share of the Ready-to-Eat (RTE) cereal market, her review of the situation showed:

- The impetus to the development of Life had been a *motivation research study* showing that a crisp, strongly nutritional, tan-gold color cereal could appeal to all members of the family.

- After development of the product, Quaker *test marketed* Life in three different textures. The shredded biscuit form won a higher repeat purchase rate and overall share. Advertising weight tests compared a $4.1 million national equivalent budget to a $5.7 million budget. Test market shares were 2.5 percent and 2.6 percent, respectively.

- In the *test markets*, Quaker also tested alternative advertising copy: a "Most Useful Protein" campaign and "Fun of Life" campaign. Both generated less-than-hoped-for awareness and brand trial. "Most Useful Protein" generated better repeat purchase.

- Shortly after the national introduction, a *survey* profiled the Life-purchasing family as having more children and higher incomes than average.

- In the first year of national introduction, a *telephone survey* of 2,515 households using RTE cereals gathered data on the awareness, trial, and repeat purchase intention of Life and major competitors. In Year 1, 40

This note was prepared by Professor Robert J. Dolan.

Copyright © 1991 by the President and Fellows of Harvard College.

Harvard Business School note N9-592-034.

[1]This description is adapted from the "Quaker Oats Company: Life Cereal," HBS Case 513-157.

percent of households were aware of Life. Thirteen percent of those aware purchased Life. In Years 3 and 5 after the introduction, 1,692 households were surveyed. Awareness had increased to 61 percent by Year 5, and 33 percent of those aware had purchased Life. By comparison, 97 percent were aware of Kellogg Corn Flakes and 96 percent of those aware had purchased Corn Flakes. The survey also determined that nutrition was the primary reason to buy for only 13 percent of Life's buyers.

- In Year 3, a new ad campaign based on a "growing" theme was tested via an *on-the-air* test. An advertising testing service conducted telephone interviews the day after the ad appeared. Only 5 percent of consumers remembered seeing the ad, compared to a 25 percent norm for the product category.
- Later, an alternative campaign was tested. The *redemption rate* of a coupon in the ad served as a measure of effectiveness for the print media. To judge effectiveness of the TV ad, a *focus group* was held in one metropolitan area. Unfavorable reaction was found via both tests.
- In Year 5 after the introduction, a new advertising agency had taken over the Life account and conducted its own *survey research* to help in its positioning of Life. Heavy-user families were identified and targeted.
- A *consumer panel study* purchased from the Market Research Corporation of America showed consumers of RTE cereals had no clearly distinguishable characteristics.
- A company *attitudinal study* contrasted hot and RTE cereals. RTEs were seen as more tasty but less nutritious than hot cereals.
- *Industry sources* indicated that Special K had spent $4.1 million in media in the last year. Life's advertising agency was proposing a $3.1 million expenditure for the upcoming year.

The eight major research methods used by Life are shown in Table A. They differ in the following respects:

1. *Primary data vs. Secondary Data*—in primary (1,2,3,4,5,7) the data were collected solely to support Life cereal's marketing, whereas in secondary (6,8) the data were collected not specifically for Life. MRCA's Panel #6 is an example of a syndicated service which collects and formats for sale to a number of clients.
2. *Experimental versus Nonexperimental*—in the test markets (#2) Quaker manipulated the environment (e.g., by using different advertising spending levels in regions of the country, whereas most other methods generated data in the normal course of business conduct).
3. *Qualitative versus Quantitative*—the surveys (#3) used large sample sizes and summarized results in a quantitative fashion as compared to the focus group (#7), which utilized only 10 people and made no attempt to quantify the feelings people expressed in their own words.
4. *Decision Supported*—Life managers used the data to:
   a. *Identify* marketing problems (e.g., low share levels).
   b. *Diagnose* marketing problems (e.g., by showing that the low share is due to low awareness and trial levels, rather than high trial but low repeat rates).

TABLE A   **Market Research Data for Life Cereal**

Research Procedure	Data	Decision Assisted
1. Motivation research	Consumer preferences.	Product design: Ingredients. Color.
2. Test market experiment	Share. Awareness. Trial. Repeat rate.	Basic positioning. Go/no-go national. Product form. Advertising budget.
3. Surveys	Profiles of: Life buyers. Heavy RTE users. Life and competition: Awareness. Trial. Repeat. Consumers' "reason to buy." Consumer attitudes on RTEs versus hot cereals.	Advertising copy. Performance monitoring. Advertising copy.
4. On-the-air test	Advertising recall.	Advertising copy.
5. Coupon placement test	Redemption rate.	Advertising copy.
6. Panel data	Demographic profiles.	Product positioning.
7. Focus group	Reaction to advertisement.	Advertising copy.
8. Public/industry data	Competitive advertising expenditure.	Advertising budget.

    *c. **Evaluate** alternative marketing strategies (e.g., in nutrition or fun positioning).*

    *d. **Monitor** subsequent performance and indicate any need for changes in strategy (e.g., when only 13 percent of buyers say the reason to buy is nutrition).*

This note provides an overview of the major research procedures. It also provides references for each major topic, which one can consult to develop a deeper understanding of individual areas. Table B presents a taxonomy of data collection efforts. The roman numerals in Table B correspond to the section of this note in which the particular method is discussed (i.e., we begin by discussing Secondary Data in Section II). Section III covers experiments, both laboratory and field. Sections IV and V both deal with nonexperimental situations separating out methods based on the emphasis on qualitative versus quantitative data.

II. Secondary Data

For secondary data, the current issue is not the major driving force behind the data collection effort. For example, the U.S. Census is a widely used secondary source. As shown in Table B, there are two major types of secondary data: that held internal to the firm (e.g., company sales records) and that gathered external to the firm (e.g., by the Census Bureau or a syndicated research supplier, such as Nielsen or Information Resources). Secondary data offer potential advantage over primary data in their timely availability and, especially in the case of internal data, their cost.

TABLE B   **Data Collection Methods Taxonomy**

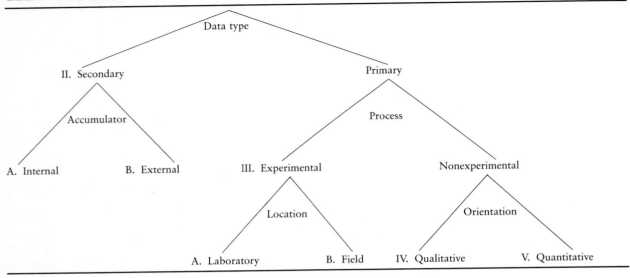

When an issue arises, the first question should be: Can it be resolved with data that have already been collected and are in the company's possession? Accounting records are the most intensively used source of internal, secondary data (e.g., cost of goods sold, unit sales broken down by product, region, or customer, and various expenditures by time period). A second important source is salesperson call reports covering such issues as account potential, account penetration, calls per account, and competitive activity. Finally, there are miscellaneous market studies, databases, and analyses purchased by other parts of the organization. The lack of an efficient mechanism for locating a relevant report outside one's own department can be very costly in terms of time and fees paid.[2]

External data relevant to market decision making are collected by a wide variety of institutions. The principal distinction between these organizations is whether they are firms whose primary business is the compilation and selling of marketing databases or not. The four largest market research firms in the United States (A.C. Nielsen, IMS, Information Resources, and Arbitron) all generate a significant portion of their revenues from the compilation and sale of statistics, such as product sales, media exposure, competitive marketing activity, and characteristics of buyers. (See the "The Marketing Information Industry," No. 588-027 for details of these firms' products.) Relevant external data can also be obtained from various trade associations, the U.S. government, and international organizations. (A list of sources is provided in "Note on External Sources of Marketing Data," No. 580-107.)

While secondary data potentially offer some advantage, they must be carefully checked to assess their accuracy and relevance. The manager must understand the data collection methods precisely. While such firms as those mentioned above have

---

[2]See "The Plugged-in Marketers at General Foods," *Marketing Communications*, March 1984, pp. C9–C13, for a description of a system for companywide use of information.

very good reputations, some "research reports" available for sale are not reliable. If one does not understand how the data were collected, it is easy to place more reliance on the data than its likely precision warrants. Second, one must check for relevance, especially how "fresh" is the information. For example, is a media habits survey of decaffeinated coffee buyers done in 1989 relevant for media buying in 1992?

III. Experiments

The primary distinguishing feature of experiments is that the researcher manipulates the environment to measure the impact. Experiments have been used to assess the effect of many marketing variables—for example, does:

1. Training in the use of computers for sales call planning increase salesperson effectiveness?
2. A full-page ad have more "drawing power" than a half-page ad?
3. A large advertising budget impact consumers' repeat purchase of the product or only awareness and trial?
4. Having a rainbow package design increase sales over that obtained from a solid red color design?
5. Distributing through factory-owned outlet stores hurt the image of the brand?
6. "Improving" the product via a formula change increase sales if not supported by advertising? If supported by advertising?
7. A price increase decrease unit sales? Sales revenue?

In short, experiments have been used to test changes in every element of the marketing mix.

In the language of experimental design, the variable the researcher manipulates is called the "treatment." The other key concept is the "measurement," the observation and recording of the level of sales, consumer awareness, or whatever the variable of interest is. Typically, one makes both a "before-treatment" and "after-treatment" measurement. For example, in judging the effect of sales force adoption of a new Marketing Sales Productivity System, we might proceed as follows:

1. Measure the unit sales generated for each salesperson during July 1990–June 1991 (call this *MB*, designating *m*easurement *b*efore the treatment).
2. Train the salespeople on Marketing-Sales Productivity Systems on June 28, 29, July 2, 3, 1991 (this is the "treatment").
3. Measure the unit sales generated for July 1991–June 1992 (call this *MA*, designating *m*easurement *a*fter the treatment).

We might then say that the effect of the treatment is MA − MB. There are perils in doing this, though. The underlying assumption of such an assessment would be that everything else in the environment is unchanged. What we would really like to compare to MA is not MB but what sales would have been in July 1990–June 1991 if the system had not been put in place. If we say the effect of the treatment is MA − MB, we are in effect saying that sales in July 1991–June 1992 would have been the same as in July 1990–June 1991 if the system were not implemented. To have a relevant benchmark to compare observed results to, it is usually a good idea to have a "control group" to compare to a "test group." In our example, we could randomly assign salespeople to a test group (to receive the system) or control group (no system). The scheme can be diagrammed as follows:

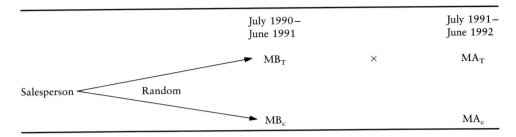

MB_T = Average sales of test group before system, July 1990–June 1991.

MB_c = Average sales of control group for June 1990–June 1991. Note that MB_T and MB_c should be approximately equal, due to random assignment to test control groups.

MA_T = After treatment measurement for test group, July 1991–June 1992.

MA_c = Comparable period measurement for control group.

Now the effect of the treatment can be more properly estimated as:

$$(MA_T - MB_T) - (MA_c - MB_c)$$

| Change in test group performance | Change in control group performance |

Changes in the economy, the company's product line, competitive actions, and the like, all influence the control group as well as the test group. The change in the control group is, therefore, to be "netted out" of the test group change to arrive at an assessment of the treatment effect.

This brief note cannot discuss all the issues of experimental design, advanced design possibilities, and data analysis procedures. These issues are covered in most marketing research textbooks.[3]

Laboratory and Field Test Markets

Market tests are of two types: laboratory tests and field tests. Laboratory tests are much less costly and time consuming as they simulate the shopping experience of the field. Most well known of these are ASSESSOR (originally developed by Management Decision Systems and now marketed by M/A/R/C) and LTM (Yankelovich, Skelley, and White). The typical procedure is for people to be intercepted at a

---

[3]An excellent elementary discussion is given in D. S. Tull and D. I. Hawkins, *Marketing Research: Measurement and Method*, 2nd ed. (New York: Macmillan Publishing, 1980). D. T. Campbell and J. C. Stanley, *Experimental and Quasi-Experimental Designs for Research* (Chicago: Rand McNally, 1969), is the seminal piece in the field.

shopping mall and prescreened for membership in the target group. After measurement of brand preference, consumers are exposed to advertising and given a chance to purchase the brand under study. After home use, a telephone interview is made to measure reaction and repeat purchase. Based on these measurements, the model makes a market share or unit sales projection.[4]

Field test markets are used to see how the consumer and the trade actually respond when the product (and marketing program for it) are placed on the market. The program anticipated for national launch (or perhaps several candidate programs) is tried in a portion of the market, as a way of reducing the risk of a marketwide introduction initially. The value of test marketing is a controversial issue. It is widely used, and some maintain that it is the most realistic test which a product can be given. Others argue, however, that the test environment is frequently not representative of the environment of a national introduction because: (1) both the salespeople and the trade give attention to the tested brand which it will not receive on a nationwide basis and (2) competitors observe the test and distort results by undertaking some atypical behavior (e.g., excessive couponing). This, together with the problems of accurately monitoring test results, has led some firms to seek other methods.

There are two major ways to do a field test market. One is the traditional "matched city pair" method, where two or more cities would be used and different marketing programs implemented. Sales from the different market areas would be attributed to the different marketing programs. The second is a "within city" test. This method has been made possible via advances in computer and telecommunications technology. The most well-known of these systems is BehaviorScan offered by Information Resources, Inc. In this system, individual households within a market area can be targeted via split cable TV systems and purchase can be monitored at the individual household level via scanners at all grocery stores in the market. This system has the advantage of better producing the "all else equal" situation assumed in comparison of two different programs.[5]

IV. Nonexperimental/Qualitative

Nonexperimental data are generated in the normal course of business. For example, when a new product is introduced, supported by the marketing plan management believes best, consumers of various demographic types become aware of the product or don't, develop attitudes toward the product, buy it or don't, and ultimately are satisfied or not. Some of these actions are captured in the secondary data of the firm (e.g., the purchase events). However, the "reason why" is typically not captured in secondary systems, and a special effort must be made to obtain that data. The major differentiating characteristic of efforts in this vein is the extent to which they rely on numerically precise measurement. This section discusses qualitative methods and the next quantitative methods.

---

[4]For a full description of such a system and evidence on its accuracy, see G. Urban and G. Katz, "Pretest-Market Models: Validation and Managerial Implications," *Journal of Marketing Research,* August 1983, pp. 221–34.

[5]See "The New Magicians of Market Research," *Fortune,* July 25, 1983, for a description of the BehaviorScan system.

Qualitative data are characterized by their lack of numerical measurement and statistical analysis. These studies typically involve an in-depth, if somewhat subjective, understanding of the consumer. The two main methods are:

- Individual depth interviews.
- Focus groups.

In the individual depth interview, the interviewer does not have a fixed set of questions to ask the respondent. Rather, the objective is for the respondent to talk freely and in detail about a product or feelings on issues. Interviews can last over an hour. The interviewer's role is a difficult one. He or she has to keep the discussion on the area of interest, but also allow the respondent to take control of the discussion to allow important feelings to surface. This unstructured discussion also requires considerable skill in interpretation. Even given the high cost and skill required, one can see the need for such a technique in some situations. For example, suppose we were interested in finding out why people buy expensive automobiles, such as a Lexus. We can imagine the responses we would get using a structured questionnaire with:

Why did you buy a Lexus? (Check one.)

☐ Good long-term investment.
☐ Road handling.
☐ Comfortable.
☐ Image it creates for me among friends.

The structured form would probably find few people checking off the image box because the respondents feel embarrassed about admitting such a motivation.

In structured interviews, the questionnaire is the dominant factor in the interview and is the same across all respondents. For depth interviews, the interviewer is a dominant factor. Time constraints sometimes make it impossible to use the same interviewer for all respondents. Because of this, the high cost per interview and the difficulty of interpretation, depth interviews are usually limited to exploratory, problem/opportunity definition stages.

The second procedure, focus group interviews, brings together a number of people, typically 8 to 10 individuals, for an open-ended discussion with a moderator. Group composition is controlled by the researcher. For example, focus groups on new telecommunications equipment might involve a number of separate groups, such as females/high education, males/blue-collar occupation, couples/both working, couples/women at home, and so on.

The moderator of the discussion attempts to have the participants engage in a free exchange of ideas on the subject of interest. Like the depth interview, its advantage over structured questionnaires lies primarily in discussion of sensitive areas. For example, the product manager for a denture adhesive commented that "it's hard to draw out of the consumer the prospect of social embarrassment. You see it come out only in focus groups."[6]

The advantage of bringing a group together, rather than just an individual, with an interviewer is that the group setting can be less threatening and more natural for the participants. This may stimulate spontaneous discussion and lead to areas that

---

[6]See the "Vicks Toiletry Products Division: Fixodent" case in B. P. Shapiro, R. S. Dolan, and J. A. Quelch, *Marketing Management: Principles, Analysis, and Applications* (Homewood, Ill.: Richard D. Irwin, 1985).

could not be uncovered in a series of individual interviews. Focus groups have many of the problems of depth interviews, viz. the moderator effect and interpretability of results. Consequently, the method is better suited to the generation of ideas, rather than systematic analysis of well-structured alternatives. A typical focus group of 10 people costs about $2,500 to run and have interpreted. The cost increases significantly with the tightness of the specification on participants (e.g., it is much more expensive to do a session with "plant engineers responsible for organic chemicals" than one with people "who play tennis").[7]

V. Primary/Quantitative

Probably the most commonly used tool in market research is the questionnaire. The design of a survey has four stages.

1. Problem Statement:	What decision is to be made?
	What information will assist in making the decision?
2. Questionnaire Design:	What information do we want to collect in interviews?
	What interview questions can get us that information from respondents?
	How should those questions be phrased?
	How are we going to contact respondents?
3. Sampling:	Who should our respondents be?
	How many should we get?
4. Data Analysis:	How do we tabulate, summarize, and draw inferences from our data?

Stage 1: Problem Statement

You must know the action alternatives to decide if survey research can be useful and, if so, exactly how to proceed. Consider a pharmaceutical firm with increasing unit sales but decreasing profits. That's the problem management wishes to address; but, before proceeding with any research, the question needs to be broken down. The question might be, "Should we increase the price of brand A by 10 percent?" This clear statement enables us to see that the answer lies in assessing consumer and competitive reaction to a specific change.

Stage 2: Questionnaire Design[8]

Fundamental Laws.   Questionnaire design deals mainly with controlling measurement error. Most of its important points can be imparted by a fundamental law:

---

[7]See P. H. Berent, "The Depth Interview," *Journal of Advertising Research,* June 1966, pp. 32–9, for details on depth interviews , and H. I. Abelson, "Focus Groups in Focus," *Marketing Communications,* February 1989, pp. 58–61 for discussion of focus groups.

[8]See A. J. Silk, "Questionnaire Design and Development," HBS Case 590-015, for a complete discussion.

Use common sense:

Corollary A: Don't ask a question unless truthful answers to it will provide useful information in making the decision at hand.

Corollary B: If there is more than one way to get a particular piece of information (and there usually is), pick the questions for which respondents are likely to—
a. Know the answer.
b. Be willing to tell you the answer.

This law and its corollaries are pretty simple. Yet, much market research collects facts that help the manager make a right decision only accidentally. Before including any question on a survey, ask yourself, "How will I use the data from this question?" If you can't be any more precise than "I'll analyze it," it's unlikely the data will be worth anything to you. (There are a few exceptions to Corollary A; for example, you may ask some questions to get respondent involvement or to disguise the purpose or sponsor of the study.)

Question and Answer Format. Each question passing the "information test" should be examined for the burden it places on the respondent: Does he or she have the information you are looking for; will giving a truthful answer embarrass the respondent? How can we deal with "little" differences in question form making "big" differences in response?

Pretest. Mentally putting yourself in the respondent's position helps to uncover questionnaire problems, but a pretest of the questionnaire is usually warranted. In a pretest, the questionnaire is administered to a small group of people *like the group to be sampled in the survey.* While filling out the questionnaire, and after they complete it, respondents are asked to explain responses, discuss any ambiguities, and so on. This can reveal unclear or sensitive questions.

Communication Mode. Finally, there are a number of ways to communicate with questionnaire respondents. These are generally personal interview, telephone, or mail. Many criteria are used in selecting the proper mode. Each mode offers obvious relative advantages. For example, in personal interviews we can show things to respondents, ask and explain complicated questions, and generally hold attention, allowing longer questionnaires. Telephone survey results are obtained quickly. Mail surveys are cheap. Most researchers, however, feel that *well-constructed* and *well-administered* questionnaires yield similar results, regardless of the form of interview.

Stage 3: Sampling

After the questionnaire is designed, pretested, and printed, the question is: Whom do we want as respondents? This question breaks down into a number of parts; the first is designation of the target population.

The target population is the group of people to which estimates will be projected. Once the target population is specified, the issue is that of selecting the *sampling frame,* a means of representing the members of the target population. A perfect frame is one in which every member of the population is represented once and only once. It is something of a tautology, but the listing of the Fortune 500 in *Fortune* magazine is a perfect frame for the population, Fortune 500 firms. The Fortune 500 would be an imperfect frame for U.S. business in general, however. Other examples of imperfect frames are a telephone book as the frame for households in a community (because of unlisted numbers and households without telephones) or a voter registration list for individuals over 18 years of age. If we use an imperfect frame, we err in projecting results to the target population (unless we redefine our target population). This infrequently acknowledged error is *frame error*. In many cases, we accept some frame error because the money spent developing a perfect frame could be better spent in other ways, such as in obtaining more respondents.

Sample Selection. After population and frame selection, we must specify the mechanism for selecting the members of the population to be included. The many ways of selecting a sample can be grouped into two categories:

1. Probability sampling.
2. Nonprobability sampling.

In probability sampling, each unit of the population has a predetermined chance of being included. For example, if in assessing the percentage of first-year MBA students at Harvard Business School owning a graphics printer, we bought a student directory, cut its relevant parts into 800 equal-size slips, each containing the name of one student, put them in a hat, and randomly selected 200 slips, each student would have a 0.25 chance of being selected. The result is a probability sample.

If, instead, we stood in front of the library and intercepted people on their way by until we caught 200 students, we would ultimately have polled the same percentage of the population. However, before we went out, we could not state the probability that any given individual would be included in the sample. Why? Because we don't know the chance that each individual walks by the library, and clearly we'd be wrong if we said everybody had an equal opportunity of being selected. Married students may go out the back door of the classroom building to the parking lot to drive home, some single students head right by the library on their way to the fitness facility, and so forth. This is nonprobability sampling. A common nonprobability sampling procedure is the *convenience sample,* where sampled units are selected not for a representative population but for ease in getting their response.

The distinction between probability and nonprobability methods is important. The key difference is this: Only probability sampling methods yield raw data from which we can both (1) derive estimates that get closer to the true value in the population as we increase the sample size (we call these consistent estimates) and (2) objectively determine the likely accuracy of our estimates. With nonprobability methods, we cannot objectively measure our accuracy.

This is a pretty strong argument for probability sampling. With nonprobability sampling we get possibly biased estimates; but, to make matters worse, we can't even figure out from the data how big the bias is likely to be, or in which direction. The argument for nonprobability methods is if they provide superior control of measurement error. Nonprobability methods are probably most useful in exploratory stages of research; the objectivity of probability methods is usually required in later stages of the research process.

Sample Size. Having decided whom to have as respondents and how to select the sample, we can determine how many respondents we should have, or what we are entitled to predict given a specified number of respondents. In practice, the second form of the question may be more relevant, because in many cases sample size determination is rather ad hoc. Specifically, the sample size is determined by dividing the negotiated budget by the cost of obtaining a respondent. Sample size determination is, however, an economic question that should be analyzed.

Sampling Distribution.   Procedures for sample size determination utilize the notion of sampling distribution. For example, let's define the population as the 800 first-year MBA students at Harvard Business School. Suppose a perfect frame exists for this target population, there is no measurement error, and the underlying truth is that half of these individuals have graphics printers and half don't. Now, if we took a random sample of 2 of the 800 individuals, we would observe one of three things, as shown in the following table:

	Sampled person 2	
Sampled person 1	Printer	No printer
Printer	2 Ps	1 P, 1 NP
No printer	1 P, 1 NP	2 NPs

In terms of printer owners, we would either observe two (top left box), one (top right and bottom left), or none (bottom right). With some simple calculations, we can figure out the chance that each of the above would occur. For example, if the population in reality has 400 "printers" and 400 "non," it's clear that if we sample randomly the odds that the first person we select as "printer" is one half. Now, leaving the first person out, we have 799 people, and the probability that the second individual we pick is "printer" can be determined. If the first sampled person was printer, then 399 of the 799 remaining are "printers." Hence, the probability of the top left box with both "samplees" being printers is $\frac{1}{2} \times 399/799 = 0.2497$. Similarly, if we calculated the other probabilities, we'd find:

	Sampled person 2	
Sampled person 1	Printer	No printer
Printer	2 Ps (0.2497)	1 P, 1 NP ($\frac{1}{2} \times 400/799 = 0.2503$)
No printer	1 P, 1 NP ($\frac{1}{2} \times 400/799 = 0.2503$)	2 NPs (0.2497)

Now, in the traditional method of sampling we assume that the sample information is the whole story; in other words, we have no a priori notions about the extent of printers. Consequently, if we wound up in the top left box, out best guess at the printer-owning percentage for first-year MBA students would be 100 percent. If we were in the top right or bottom left, we'd say 50 percent. Last, in the bottom right we'd say 0 percent.

This is a rather laborious way to reach what may be an obvious point: different samples lead to different estimates of the population value. Unless we get all members of our target population as respondents, we inevitably have some risk that the portion in our sample is not perfectly representative. Depending on the sample we draw, we may guess different values for the population as a whole. With no other information available to us, we guess that the value for the target population is the value observed in our sample.

Increased Sample Size.   As we increase the size of our sample, we tend to make better estimates of the value in the population. We just saw what happened when we drew samples of two from the target population of 800 — 400 owning graphics printers and 400 not. Now let's see what happens if we increase our samples to 5 and then to 10.

For samples of 5, our observed sample percentage of graphics printer owners will be 0, 20, 40, 60, 80, or 100 percent. With the aid of the computer, we can do the equivalent of putting the 800 names in a hat, drawing out 5, checking the number of these having programmables, throwing their names back, and drawing another sample of 5. Simulating a total of 50 samples of 5 yielded the observed sample proportions shown below.

Percent of Printers in Sample of 5	Number of Times Observed
0%	2
20	10
40	21
60	9
80	7
100	1
Total	50

The observed or sample proportions tend to bunch up around the true value. Note that because all our samples are of size 5, it is impossible for us to observe the true target population proportion of 50 percent in any one sample. We get within $\pm$ 10% of the true value in 30 of the 50 cases (21 times we observed 2 graphics printers and 9 times we observed 3). That seems reasonable for sampling only 5 people, but on occasion we really botch it—there is a 6 percent chance we would say everybody has graphics printers (we observed 5 in the sample of 5 once) or nobody has graphics printers (we observed none in the sample of 5 twice).

It seems intuitive that we would "do better" the more students we sampled and, in fact, that's right. Simulating in the same way, but with a sample size of 10 yielded:

Percent of Printers in Sample of 10	Number of Times Observed
0%	0
10	1
20	0
30	7
40	12
50	16
60	6
70	5
80	3
90	0
100	0
Total	50

We were within 10 percent on 34 (12 + 16 + 6) of 50 trials for 68 percent (as opposed to 60 percent before). Now we never say that everybody has one or nobody has one. The observed proportions from the larger sample are bunched more tightly around the true proportion.

If sample sizes are "big enough," the distribution of their sample means follows the normal distribution. ("Big enough" means about 100 in cases with yes/no, do/don't, or binary data, but as little as 30 with continuous data.) We know the probability that a given observation will fall within a particular range of values of the normal distribution. These ranges usually are counted in units called standard deviations, denoted by σ (sigma). For example, we know that 68.3 percent of the observations are within one σ of the mean; 95.5 percent are within 2 σ's; and 99.7 percent are within 3 σ's. Graphically, we show this as:

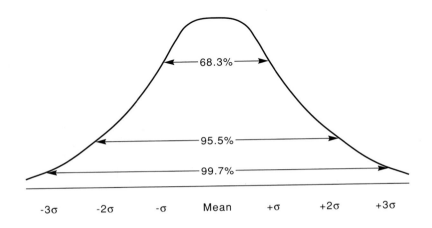

Because sample means are approximately normally distributed about the population mean, we can make such statements as the following: "About 95 percent of sample proportions fall within two standard errors of the population proportion." (We don't want to get bogged down in terminology here, but, when the standard deviation we are talking about is the standard deviation of sample means, we call it the standard error.) Thus, if we estimate the population proportion, we can express our confidence in that estimate by constructing intervals around it. For example, the 95 percent *confidence interval* CI is [L, U] where L = our estimate minus 2 σ's and U = our estimate plus 2 σ's. All we need to know now is how to figure out σ, our counting unit or standard error. For samples of sizes n from large populations and data on binary questions:[9]

$$\text{Standard error: } \sigma_p = \sqrt{\frac{p(1 - p)}{n}}$$

where, theoretically, p is the true proportion in the population. Of course, the whole point is to find out what p is, so a formula that assumes we already know it isn't too

---

[9]Similar logic applies to continuous-type data with some change in the specifics of computations.

helpful. We used the observed frequency in our sample as an estimate of population proportion, so we do the same here and estimate σ_p by:

$$\hat{\sigma}_p = \sqrt{\frac{(Observed\ probability)(1 - Observed\ probability)}{n}}$$

Note that n, the sample size, is in the denominator. This means as n gets bigger we expect our standard error to get smaller; in other words, we expect our sample estimates if we drew repeated samples to get tighter around the true mean. This is what we saw in our earlier example; now the reason is mathematically clear.

Prediction of Accuracy. These results are used primarily to assess the likely accuracy of an estimate based on given sample size or, conversely, to determine how large a sample is required to obtain a specified level of accuracy. Let's consider an example. An automobile dealer wants to know what proportion of customers consults *Consumer Reports* before shopping for a car. He draws a random sample of 100, and 43 say they consult *Consumer Reports*, 57 say they do not.

Implications:

1. The auto dealer's best guess at the percentage of all customers consulting *CR* is 43 percent.
2. How good is this best guess?

    We answer by constructing CIs. We know that approximately 95 percent of the observations in the normal distribution fall within 2 σ's of the mean.

    Based on the sample information, our estimate of σ_p is:

$$\hat{\sigma}_p = \sqrt{\frac{(0.43)(0.57)}{100}} = 0.0495$$

    Using this, we are "95 percent confident" that the true percentage for the population is within $0.0495 \times 2 = 0.099$ of the sample percentage of 0.43. We are 95 percent confident the true percentage for the population is in the range 0.331 to 0.529. (This assumes we have not committed any measurement error.)

    If we want to be "99 percent confident" that our range contains the true mean, we have to expand the range from ± 2 σ's to ± 3 σ's. Specifically, the 99 percent range is 0.2815 to 0.5785.

3. Better guesses can be obtained by increasing the sample size.

    If the auto dealer sampled 400 people instead of 100 and found 172 *CR* consulters and 228 nonconsulters, the best guess would again be 43 percent, but the standard error reduced to:

$$\sqrt{\frac{(0.43)(0.57)}{400}} = 0.0275$$

so our 95 percent CI contracts to 0.3805 to 0.4795. We can collect these results in a figure showing confidence intervals for different degrees of confidence and sample size. Note that all the CIs for $n = 400$ are exactly one-half as wide as their counterparts for $n = 100$. Mathematically, this occurs because the standard error is related to the sample size by a square root rule. Therefore we do not achieve a 50 percent reduction in the standard error by doubling the sample size; we have to quadruple it.

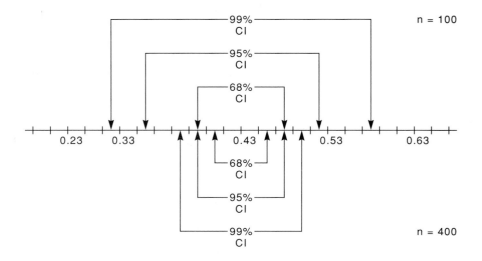

Sample Size and Confidence.   The other way we can use our knowledge of properties of the normal distribution is in determining the sample size required for given levels of precision and confidence. For example, if we want to be accurate within X percentage points at the 95 percent confidence level, we solve for *n* in:

$$X = 2 \sqrt{\frac{p(1 - p)}{n}}$$

Again, we have *p,* the true proportion, in our formula, so we have to estimate it. This time we are without the assistance of sample observations. A saving grace, however, is the fact that $p(1 - p)$ can never be bigger than 0.25. So, if we use that value, the *n* determined provides at least the desired level of precision, more if *p* is radically different from 0.5. Sample sizes required for 95 percent levels of confidence are:

CI (in percentage points)	Sample Size Required
±2.0	2,500
±3.0	1,111
±4.0	625
±5.0	400
±7.5	178
±10.0	100

Permissible Error.   There is no general rule on how big an error is permissible. By tradition, many national surveys have sample sizes of 2,000 or so to get 2 to 3 percent accuracy. However, the reliability required depends very much on the economic stakes of the decision being made.

Stage 4: Data Analysis

While this step is listed last, one should determine how one will analyze the data before they are collected. Depending on the research question, the appropriate data analysis may be:

1. Simple counts (e.g., the number of people in the survey who never hear of a product).
2. Graphical displays.
3. Assessment of association between two variables.
4. Assessment of the impact a set of independent variables has on a "dependent variable."

The important point is that the analysis be conducted in a way to reveal true relationships, rather than biased to support some preconceived idea.

VI. Conclusion

A wide variety of market research techniques is available. Each is capable of contributing to a certain set of issues. Each also is capable of leading the manager astray if not executed properly and interpreted in light of its limitation.

If market research is to be useful, the manager must take an active role in:

1. Initiating the research effort (i.e., a managerial decision to be made must drive the data collection and analysis).
2. Working with the research specialists to define the problem and determine how information will be used.
3. Reviewing the proposed research design about potential benefit versus cost.
4. Ensuring that the data are analyzed in the most useful way, and any uncertainty about the validity of the data is made clear.
5. Selecting the format for the presentation of the research results to other members of the management team.

While there is a great deal of debate on the best research procedure to follow for any given problem, there is a general agreement among managers that the quality of research information has a major impact on the quality of marketing decisions. Consequently, it is a part of the marketing process that the effective marketing manager must understand and direct.

XEROX CORPORATION:
THE CUSTOMER SATISFACTION PROGRAM

We achieve customer satisfaction through dedication to quality in everything we do.

—Xerox Corporation 1987 Annual Report Cover

In both our businesses, customer satisfaction is the key to our success.

—Xerox Corporation 1988 Annual Report Cover

The Malcolm Baldrige National Quality Award.

—Xerox Corporation 1989 Annual Report Cover

Xerox people are on a crusade to be the industry leader in all aspects of customer satisfaction. And we're making good progress. We have improved customer satisfaction by 35 percent. Dataquest now rates our products as number one in five out of six market segments. Datapro has named our 1090 copier the "best overall copier in the world."

—President Paul Allaire, Xerox 1989 Annual Report

Xerox embarked on an ambitious program in the early 1980s to regain its eroded leadership in the copier industry—an industry it virtually created with the introduction of its model 914 in 1959. During the 1970s, Xerox customers had become disappointed with Xerox quality and service, and the company lost significant market share to domestic and Japanese competitors.

An obsession with quality and customer satisfaction, cost reductions, restructurings, and new products helped Xerox stem its eroding market share and regain market leadership in multiple markets and multiple market seg-

---

This case was prepared by Professor Melvyn A. J. Menezes and Research Associate Jon Serbin.
Copyright © 1991 by the President and Fellows of Harvard College.
Harvard Business School case 9-591-055.

ments. Xerox gained 1 to 1.5 points in market share every year since 1983.

The "Leadership through Quality" strategy had been in place since 1983 and customer satisfaction had become the first corporate priority since 1987. All this appeared to have paid off with Xerox Business Products and Systems winning of the prestigious "Malcolm Baldrige National Quality Award" in 1989, the nation's highest award for quality. Established by an Act of Congress in 1987, this highly competitive award was given annually to outstanding American companies that had implemented total quality strategies and had significantly improved customer satisfaction.

In July 1990, President Paul Allaire and Wayland Hicks, executive vice president and head of Xerox Marketing and Customer Operations, decided to take some time off their otherwise hectic schedule to review the progress on customer satisfaction. They wondered whether it needed any changes or the introduction of some new programs.

The Copier Industry

The worldwide copier market was mature and intensely competitive. In the United States, copier placements (sales and rentals) had grown at a slow rate of 2.9 percent CAGR (compound annual growth rate) between 1984 and 1989; service and supplies were the rapidly growing sources of revenue in the industry (see Table A).

Xerox categorized the copier industry into three product markets:

Low-volume market. Copiers in this market were designed to make fewer than 5,000 copies per month and cost less than $4,000. Over time these machines were becoming more reliable, and users were performing more of their own maintenance. This market witnessed explosive growth in the late 1970s and was the fastest growing market until the late 1980s. By 1990, that growth flattened. Due to intense

---

TABLE A   Estimated Revenues in the U.S. Copier Industry (in billions of dollars)

	1984	*1989*	*1994 (Expected)*
Sales	$ 3.9	$ 4.7	$ 4.6
Rentals	3.3	3.6	4.6
Service	3.1	5.4	5.8
Supplies	3.0	4.3	4.9
Total	$13.3	$18.0	$19.9

competition, copier prices and margins in most markets declined steadily through the 1980s, but especially in this low-volume market. Canon, Sharp, Xerox, Mita, and Ricoh were the major players.

Mid-volume market. These copiers were designed to make up to 100,000 copies per month and cost between $4,000 and $60,000. This market, which had the highest overall growth in 1989, was where Xerox had always earned the most revenue and profit. At the lower end, there was intense price pressure, while at the top end, there was relatively less price cutting. Xerox, Canon, Mita, Ricoh, and Konica were the major players.

High-volume market. These copiers cost over $60,000. This market, primarily because of the high product-development costs, was a high-margin business. As you moved from the low-volume to the high-volume market, more machines were leased and fewer bought outright. In the high-volume market, the lease to sale ratio, although declining, was 80:20 in 1990. Competition was based primarily on service and product features. Xerox and Kodak (which purchased IBM's copier business in 1988 when IBM retreated from the business) were the major competitors; Canon, Konica, and Lanier competed in the lower end of this market.

The major producers were developing new products that utilized digital copying technology as opposed to light/lens technology. Some analysts expected that market growth in the 90s would be driven by "smart" multifunction devices that combined copying, faxing, scanning, and electronic printing functions. Competitors with direct sales forces would have an advantage, because the complexity and pricing of these machines was too high for effective dealer distribution. Color copying represented another potential growth area. The color copier market was expected to grow from about 6,000 units ($354 million in revenues) in 1989 to almost 60,000 units ($2 billion in revenues) by 1994.

Competition. The copier market was extremely competitive, with 23 companies battling for market share. However, Xerox was the only full-line supplier, with products ranging from the low end of the low-volume to the high end of the high-volume. Based on total number of unit placements, Canon was the market leader, followed by Xerox and Sharp (see Exhibit 1). Canon's placements were primarily low-volume, low-priced personal copiers, though Canon did have a presence in the mid- and high-volume markets. In terms of copier industry revenues, Xerox was the market leader, with a high market share in the higher priced mid- and high-volume markets, which also provided significant service and supplies revenues. Xerox had by far the largest service organization in the industry and was the largest paper and supplies distributor as well.

Company Background

In 1989, Xerox Corporation, headquartered in Stamford, Connecticut, had revenues of $17.6 billion and net income of $704 million. It had two divisions: (1) Business Products and Systems, which handled all document-processing businesses (1989 revenues: $12.4 billion, net income: $488 million); and (2) Xerox Financial Services, which handled insurance and other financial services (1989 revenues: $5.2 billion, net income: $216 million).

History. In 1959, the Haloid Company launched its model 914 office copier, the first viable xerographic office copier and considered by many to be one of the most successful single products ever made. Haloid renamed itself Xerox in 1961.

Protected by a ring of patents, Xerox achieved phenomenal growth and completely dominated the world copier market through the 1960s and into the early 1970s. After settling antitrust actions with the FTC, Xerox agreed to license its technology to competitors and to end pending patent suits. IBM and Kodak entered the business in 1970 and 1975, respectively, focusing on the high-margin, high- and mid-volume markets. Japanese companies concentrated on mass producing low-volume machines. By the early 1980s, IBM and Kodak gained significant market share in the high-volume market, and Japanese companies created and began to dominate the emerging low-volume market. Also, Japanese producers began to compete in the mid-volume market, and, by 1990, some of them were offering or announcing products to compete in the high-volume market.

During the 1960s and 1970s, Xerox diversified into a number of new businesses. It purchased mainframe-maker Scientific Data Systems in 1969. A decade later, the business, a large-scale failure; was sold. Other diversification efforts included entry into a range of office computing businesses, including word processors and document-processing workstations, networks, facsimile equipment, electronic typewriters, scanners, impact and laser printers, software, and medical imaging systems. In the early 80s, Xerox diversified in a new direction through its financial services acquisitions.

Xerox with its monopoly culture, its large bureaucracy, and its forays into new businesses had difficulty responding to the new competitive pressures in its flagship copier business. Costs and product prices were higher than the competition's, quality and perceived quality had declined, and market share and return on assets had fallen to alarming levels.

Around 1980, Xerox realized that the Japanese had a 40–50 percent cost advantage in the copier business and that they were selling machines for almost what it cost Xerox to produce a machine. Despite the emerging competition, Xerox continued to grow, but net income declined as a percentage of revenues. By 1980, Xerox's market share was severely eroded in all product segments of the copier business. Its share dropped from almost 100 percent in the 1960s to under 40 percent in 1980.

Turnaround. Beginning in 1980, Xerox undertook a number of initiatives to respond to the increased competition and the company's declining market share. The company was restructured and developed a philosophy emphasizing quality, led by Chairman and CEO David Kearns. He instigated a strong quality movement, in the belief that quality would drive costs down, and that getting it right the first time would eliminate costly repairs and replacements and would prevent the unnecessary breakdowns that drove customers away. Kearns and top management strove to drive the quest for quality throughout the organization.

Quality at Xerox was defined as "meeting the customer's existing and latent requirements." Xerox believed that becoming more customer and competitor oriented was critical. It began to use competitive "benchmarking" (the continuous process of measuring products, services, and practices against the toughest competitors and those companies renowned as leaders with respect to reliability, cost, and service), to improve quality and achieve cost reductions. By 1983, it developed a corporatewide quality program called Leadership Through Quality (LTQ), which emphasized preventing defects and meeting customers' expectations. Training all employees in quality tools and processes was a major part of the plan, and quality-related goals were set for each year through 1987.

The effort led to some successes. The ratio of support staff to manufacturing worker was reduced from 4.5 in 1980 to 1.5 in 1987, smaller product development teams helped shorten the product development cycle by 30 percent and reduce the amount of labor required to bring out a new machine by 40 percent, and the number of parts vendors was reduced from 5,000 in 1980 to 400 by 1987, resulting in higher quality standards, better pricing, and 99.2 percent of parts arriving defect-free. By some estimates these efforts helped Xerox save as much as $2 billion in the document-processing business.

Xerox underwent another major restructuring in 1988, refocusing its document-processing line on its core copying business. It also focused on new technologies, including color copiers and "smart" multifunction copiers. Xerox Medical Imaging was closed, the electronic-typewriter production capacity was cut back, and the workstation business was closed. Xerox expected to achieve a payback on the 1988 restructuring within three years and to position itself to achieve its goal of 15 percent pretax ROA by 1990. Xerox's ROA, which peaked at 19 percent in 1980, was 11.1 percent in 1988 and 12.6 percent in 1989.

Business Products and Systems (BP&S). BP&S developed, manufactured, marketed, and serviced a broad range of document-processing equipment. BP&S products and systems were produced in 15 countries on 5 continents and marketed in 140 countries by a direct sales force of about 15,000 and a growing network of dealers and distributors. It maintained a worldwide service force of about 30,000 technical representatives.

BP&S's three largest product lines, Copier/Duplicators, Printing Systems, and Document Systems, were sold and serviced by the three general sales and service operating companies: United States Marketing Group (USMG), Americas Operations (handling Canada, Latin America, the Middle East, and North Africa), and Rank Xerox (handling 80 countries including the European Community).

United States Marketing Group (USMG)

USMG, which handled the marketing of BP&S's main products in the United States consisted of nine functional areas, including sales, service, business operations, marketing support, services support, finance, information management, personnel, and administration. The first three functions managed the field organization, which consisted of 5 regions and 65 districts.

Starting January 1, 1990, the regions and districts were managed as partnerships of the three functional areas (sales, service, and business operations) with the district partnership reporting to the regional partnership, which in turn reported to headquarters functional managers. The heads of sales, service, and operations at the district (and regional) level operated as equal partners on management decisions and planning processes.

Decision-making authority was decentralized down to the regional and district partnerships. District partnerships were given increased responsibility to resolve customer problems and to take advantage of business opportunities, but were accountable to corporate policies and inspection. Districts had authority to allocate manpower resources among the functional areas within the overall district head count limit. Regions and districts also had flexibility in advertising investments, though they had to chose from a menu of headquarter options that they could customize to local markets. Profit and expense planning (including revenue growth, profit growth, and expense targets) were generated from the district level upward.

In 1990, USMG had four goals:

1. To become an organization with which customers were eager to do business.

2. To create an environment where every employee could take pride in the organization and feel responsible for its success.

3. To grow profits and increase Xerox presence at a rate faster than the markets in which it competed.

4. To use Leadership Through Quality principles in everything it did.

Customers. Xerox categorized its customers into four segments:

1. Commercial Major Accounts (CMA): These were Fortune 500 firms and, although accounting for only 5 percent of Xerox's customers, they accounted for about 32 percent of its copier revenues.
2. Named Accounts: These were large commercial accounts that were non-Fortune 500 firms. They accounted for about 18 percent of Xerox's customers and 28 percent of its copier revenues.
3. General Markets: These were all other commercial accounts, and they accounted for 62 percent of Xerox's customers and about 15 percent of its copier revenues.
4. Government/Education: These customers accounted for 15 percent of Xerox's customers and 25 percent of its copier revenues.

The first two groups were segmented further into large and small accounts. The average large Named Account provided the same revenues as the average small Commercial Major Account (CMA), and there were a larger number of large Named Accounts than small CMAs.

For most customers, product reliability was the top priority. As one Xerox executive put it, "Copiers are not exciting. Most customers don't notice copiers until they break down. Like toasters, they are just a convenience; they should be reliable and look reliable as well."

Apart from product reliability, purchase criteria varied by segment. In the low-volume segment, the emphasis was more on price than on service. These customers wanted the best possible quality at the lowest possible price. In the mid- and high-volume segments, service was a critical purchase consideration. (The relative importance of various purchase criteria for equipment and service purchase decisions for the mid- and high-volume segments is given in Exhibit 2.) Xerox and Kodak maintained their own national service organizations. Equipment service for other vendors was handled by dealer service organizations or by third-party service organizations, a significant emerging trend. Large service organizations, such as TRW, offered service either directly to customers or via exclusive relationships with producers or dealer organizations. Hicks saw an opportunity for Xerox to gain, through its service capabilities, a competitive advantage over its rivals in the U.S. and global markets.

Distribution. Historically, all Xerox products were sold directly by the Xerox sales force. However, the company recently began to distribute low-volume and low-priced mid-volume machines through dealer networks, and the lowest priced machines through consumer retail channels.

For the copier industry as a whole, dealers were the primary distribution channel. In 1989, according to industry specialist Dataquest, 54 percent of placements went through the dealer channel, 26 percent via the direct sales force, 10 percent via the retail channel, 9 percent via national or regional distributors, and 1 percent via alternate channels (mail order, agents, telemarketing, and so on). Dataquest estimated that, in 1994, dealers would account for 42 percent, the direct sales force for 27 percent, retail channels for 16 percent, distributors for 10 percent, and alternate channels for 5 percent of copier sales.

Product Line and Pricing. Although a copier appeared to be a dull, boring, and simple product, it contained some very sophisticated technology: chemical, electronic, optical, and mechanical science all wrapped in one box. For engineers, it was a tremendous technical and intellectual challenge to combine these different technologies and at the same time ensure that the product was easy to use.

In 1990, Xerox had two lines of copiers—the 10 series and the 50 series. The 10 series of Xerox copiers, introduced in 1982, helped Xerox regain significant market share. It also helped revitalize the company's financial outlook and rejuvenate its morale and fighting spirit. In 1988, Xerox introduced the 50 series of copiers. In 1990, Xerox had 18 copiers, 4 in the low-end (1020,1025,5012,5014), 9 in the mid-range (1040,1045,1048,1055,5018,5028,5042, 5046,5052), and 5 in the high-end (1065,1075,1090,9900, 5090). It regained market share in the low- and mid-volume segments, and preserved its high share of the high-end market. Xerox copiers ranged in list price (base unit) from $2,440 for the 5012 to $154,000 for the 5090.

Most Xerox copiers carried a 30-day warranty, in line with industry practice. Some of the high-volume machines carried a 90-day warranty. The new 50 series low- and mid-volume copiers (5012, 5014, 5018, and 5028) were launched with a three-year warranty. The longer warranty was an aggressive marketing tool to accelerate new product acceptance and to communicate the products' higher reliability to customers, dealers, and the Xerox sales force. These copiers utilized user-replaceable cartridges, which replaced many of the parts that were likely to need frequent servicing.

Customer Service. USMG provided maintenance and installation of Xerox as well as third-party products, including PCs and printers. Revenues from customer service were approximately $2 billion in 1989, making Xerox the country's third-largest service business (behind IBM and DEC). Customer service employed 18,000 people, with 15,000 in the field and additional staff of about 3,000, including a telephone support staff of 1,000.

Customer service at Xerox had several dimensions: fixing/repairing of units; providing operating systems support, interface, and integration; communicating with customers;

resolving customer issues after installation; providing technical product support; selling of services; and giving feedback to manufacturing, sales, marketing, and administration.

Customer service was run as a cost center, with cost as a percentage of revenue being a very important consideration. Some managers believed that customer service should operate as a stand-alone operation and be a profit center.

The quality of customer service was measured on the following criteria: (1) customer satisfaction, based on customer surveys; (2) the expense to revenue ratio; (3) reliability; and (4) service billing errors. The focus on customer satisfaction, originally initiated in customer service, continued to be championed by customer service. Centralized parts support enabled customer service engineers to order parts on-line and improved the availability of parts in local inventory. In 1985, service marketing was established as a separate organization to focus on the growth of service revenues.

As a result of these kinds of efforts, customer service improved Xerox's service delivery capabilities and reduced service costs. Actual average response time improved from about 5.75 hours in 1987 to 4.75 hours in 1989. Customer satisfaction with service equipment repair had improved to 96 percent. Customers' wait time on the phone when calling the Service Support Centers improved more than 40 percent (and was 20 percent better than the industry average), with most customers waiting fewer than 20 seconds.

Customer Satisfaction at Xerox

During the period 1980 to 1986, Xerox had three corporate priorities: return on assets (ROA), market share, and customer satisfaction. There was no particular order to the three priorities, yet most people focused on ROA, which had a goal of 15 percent. No specific quantitative corporate goals were set for market share and customer satisfaction.

Studies conducted in 1987 concluded that customer satisfaction was not a top priority in the day-to-day management of Xerox's businesses. The senior management team at Xerox was convinced that success in customer satisfaction would lead to successes in the other two priorities. Customer satisfaction, the team believed, would drive an external focus and give the voice of the customer a critical role. It decided that customer satisfaction should become the number one corporate priority, which, in September 1987, it announced in a series of management communications meetings and published materials. As President Allaire put it:

> We can be the industry leader in all aspects of customer satisfaction. That is our goal. It is our strong conviction that, if we meet our customers' expectations, we will improve market share, and, if we improve market share, we will improve our financial performance and shareholder value.

In November 1987, the senior management team issued to the operating units a set of requirements and guidelines to ensure that customer satisfaction (CS) became their first priority. These requirements and guidelines focused on reorienting the company at every level to CS as the first priority, and were used by the units to prepare their own operating strategies and plans to meet CS goals and business objectives. Operating units were given the authority and options to respond to their customers' requirements with a range of approved products, services, or solutions that would maximize CS for their markets. They were to delegate those authorities and options to the appropriate organizational level, allowing it to respond easily to customers' requirements.

In March 1988, President Allaire asked that a common, core system of measures for managing and improving customer satisfaction be established for use by all operating units worldwide. Each operating unit had been using its own method for surveying customers, asking different questions, and using different scales. In Brazil, for example, customer satisfaction was measured on a two-point scale, while Canada used a five-point scale. Hence, it was difficult to do any cross-comparisons or determine whether a particular dissatisfaction problem was endemic to one office, a region, an operating company, or the entire organization.

Based on the best methods in use, a common set of guidelines was formulated for tracking and measuring customer satisfaction. In August 1988, the senior management team approved the proposed framework of measures and issued a complete set of requirements and guidelines to all operating units for measuring, managing, and improving customer satisfaction. The units could customize their systems so long as they complied with the mandatory requirements and stayed within the guidelines. The common, core system was implemented by all operating units by January 1, 1989.

Vision and Goals. In 1990, Xerox's vision for customer satisfaction was "100 percent of Xerox's customers are very satisfied or satisfied with our products and services through the elimination of defects and errors in our work processes and the achievement of world-class benchmark quality and value in our products and other deliveries to the customer."

The corporate goal was that by 1993 Xerox should be recognized as the industry benchmark in customer satisfaction in all business areas. This goal had two components: For the external world, the goal was to exceed competitive benchmarks for customer satisfaction in all major business areas and to exceed competitive benchmark quality and reliability in all services to the customer by 1993. For the internal world, the goal was that, by 1993, Xerox products should meet customer requirements and exceed competitive benchmarks in quality; there should be fourfold improvements in reliability, a tenfold reduction in defects and errors in the work processes and deliverables that impact the customer, a 50 percent improvement in cost, and time to market should be reduced by 12 months.

Top management believed that to achieve the vision and goals it needed market-driven business strategies, product strategies, and investments that were determined by customer requirements and expectations. Top management also believed it was critical that the vision and goals be communicated systematically through each level in the organization to ensure understanding, capability, and commitment. Fundamental to success was the assurance of quality by problem diagnosis, identification of root causes, and corrective actions.

Action Steps. Several actions were taken to enhance customer satisfaction. Management leadership was particularly important. Senior managers in the operating units became role models for appropriate behaviors relative to the customer, by personally taking the lead in acting to totally satisfy customer requirements and resolving customer complaints. They promoted and participated in programs that placed them in direct contact with customers.

Another action was ensuring that all employees developed a proactive attitude, role, and work emphasis focused on customer satisfaction. Every customer contact by a Xerox employee was viewed as an opportunity to manage the customer's experience with and perception of Xerox. Employees who had no direct customer contact focused on supporting those who did.

A customer satisfaction code of conduct was developed for all employees. CS was introduced into all training curricula, where employees learned about the Leadership Through Quality tools and processes. CS training was provided to all front-line employees.

At the end of 1988, customer relations groups (CRG) were initiated at headquarters and at the regions and districts. At each district, the CRG consisted of two to six people. Its objective was to have direct customer contact so it could follow up on dissatisfied customers and customer complaints and to resolve issues better and faster. Problems reached the CRG in one of the following ways: customer surveys, internal sales or service problem referrals, customer losses or contract cancellations, and nonconformance costs such as machine replacement, accommodation, and sales refusals or reversals.

The perceived benefits of the customer relations group were in staying close to the customer, having a cross-functional focus on customer issues, and having a customer closed-loop process that identified problems, resolved them, conducted root-cause analyses, and provided recommendations for avoidance or elimination. The group hoped to be predictive, rather than purely reactive. It hoped to resolve issues before receiving negative feedback and to identify po-

tentially dissatisfied customers based on frequency of service, changes in billing history, changes in service contracts, deteriorating supply purchases, and so on.

The regions and districts were reorganized in 1990 as partnerships of sales, service, and business operations. Previously, the sales, service, and business operations used to report to the regional and headquarters levels, and there was not much teamwork at the local district level.

Local empowerment was another tool for increasing customer satisfaction. Processes and systems were developed and authorities were modified to enable first-line sales, service, and administration teams in the branches and districts to rapidly and effectively respond to customers and resolve complaints. All employees were made to feel accountable for CS and to act accordingly. Rewards and recognition programs were modified to ensure that they supported the CS objectives. The bonus plan for general managers, for example, included CS criteria.

Other major steps included the establishment of customer support teams for post-sale follow-up, establishment of a Customer Complaints Management System, improvements in technical service, information systems, and telephone systems. "Zero defects" programs were implemented for continuing quality improvement of those internal processes that directly impacted external customers.

Measurement of Customer Satisfaction. Xerox believed that a critical aspect for achieving CS was the development of tools to continuously measure, manage, and improve customer satisfaction. Two major sets of data were developed and utilized: (1) external customer feedback data, which included a series of customer satisfaction surveys as well a Customer Complaint Management System; and (2) internal quality and quantity measures of Xerox work processes and outputs that delivered products and services (see Exhibit 3).

The External Measurement System. Customer perceptions and market outcomes that resulted from implementing the strategies and action plans were monitored through the external measures of customer satisfaction. The external customer feedback data system consisted of surveys (to solicit from customers their satisfaction with all areas of their interaction with Xerox) and the Customer Complaint Management System, which captured any unsolicited feedback from customers. Four sets of surveys were used: (1) a periodic survey of a random sample of Xerox customers; (2) a post-installation survey of all Xerox customers within 90 days of a new installation; (3) a new-product postinstallation survey of a random sample of customers with new products during the launch phase; and (4) a blind survey of Xerox's and competitors' customers to establish benchmark levels of customer satisfaction and to determine Xerox's competitive position.

Periodic survey. Each month, USMG mailed surveys to 40,000 randomly selected customers; 50 percent were sent to key operators, 25 percent to decision makers, and 25 percent to administrators. About 10,000 surveys were returned to Xerox. The surveys queried customers about satisfaction on a number of levels: overall satisfaction with Xerox, likelihood of acquiring another product from Xerox, likelihood of recommending Xerox to a business associate, and satisfaction with several different aspects of the products, services, and support (see Exhibit 4).

The key measure tracked was the overall satisfaction. Customer satisfaction was measured on a 5-point semantic differential scale (very satisfied—very dissatisfied). Each month, the percentage satisfied (those who marked either very satisfied or somewhat satisfied) was analyzed in terms of a three-month rolling average, the prior month, the current month, actual year to date, and percent of planned target. Results were tracked by district, region, product, product type, and customer segment.

The results of the periodic surveys were used to flag problem areas and measure the effect of corrective actions for individual products, districts, and customer segments. The results were used quite extensively by product managers (to set product, district, and function targets), product development teams, customer relations groups, and various functional areas.

Post-installation survey. This survey was administered 7 to 90 days after installation of a machine and enabled the respondent to register any problem, enabled the local field unit to respond rapidly with corrective actions, and allowed Xerox to collect data for work process improvement. Often more than one survey was required: one as soon as possible after the installation, and another within 90 days to cover different interactions and aspects of the transaction.

The operator received the survey, which focused on the product (product performance against expectations, copy quality, ease of use), the sales process (responsiveness of the sales representative, fulfillment of commitments), the order process (availability of product, ease of understanding the options), the delivery process (timing, correctness, attitude of crew), the installation process (time to install, time lag between delivery and installation), and the support activities (user training, manuals and documentation, ease of contacting Xerox). Any dissatisfaction detected was followed up for quick resolution.

New-products post-installation survey. This survey was sent to a random sample of customers just after the launch of a new product to help identify any problems that customers might face with the new product. It served as an early warning system for new-product performance.

Competitive benchmarking customer satisfaction survey. This was a critical tool for comparing Xerox to its key

only blind survey)

competitors in terms of customer satisfaction and perceptions of the products and services. Other purposes of this survey were to identify which suppliers were the benchmarks in satisfying the customer, and what were customers' requirements and preferences in the quality of products and services. This annual survey focused on the various vendors and brands and used the same core questions as the periodic survey. However, in this survey, the identity of the sponsor was not disclosed.

Internal Measurement process. The common, core system of measures also required matching external customer assessments of Xerox products and services to the appropriate internal quality measures and standards for the work processes and outputs that produced those deliverables. Xerox management could routinely monitor and inspect internal performance as a leading indicator of CS and as leverage in acting to improve output quality and CS. The process included setting and monitoring quality measures of the internal work processes and deliverables that impact the customer and parallel the customer satisfaction measures. The objective was to provide leading indicators of Xerox performance and improvement opportunities.

Xerox processes that impacted each area of customer interaction were determined and systems were put in place to measure and monitor these internal processes. For every diagnostic question asked in the periodic and post-installation surveys, there was one or more internal standards and measures that indicated Xerox performance in the applicable work processes or deliverables. Examples of internal measures included service response time, number of billing errors, and number of training hours per sales rep. Benchmark standards were set for all processes (i.e., response time should be less than four hours, or billing errors should be less than 2 percent, or all sales reps should have four hours of training with a new product).

Data Analyses, Review, and Follow-up. Information on customer satisfaction was received from various sources, such as the surveys, the customer complaint management system, the district partners, and the field reports. The data were analyzed to identify segment-specific satisfiers (factors that increased customer satisfaction) and dissatisfiers (factors that when not available in the right amount led to customer dissatisfaction).

Customer satisfaction was reviewed frequently and at various levels in the organization. A Customer Satisfaction Improvement meeting attended by the president of USMG, the president of Development and Manufacturing, the senior vice president of World Wide Marketing, and their direct reports was held once a quarter for one day. This meeting covered CS results, strategic enablers, CS corrective actions, new-product status, and future-product customer requirements. Cross-functional teams were assigned to follow up and to initiate Quality Improvement Teams (QITs).

A Customer Satisfaction Improvement Network meeting of representatives from all major operating units worldwide met once a quarter for one to two days. On the agenda were customer satisfaction issues that included survey processes, targeting methodology, benchmark studies, CS results and targets, business results and targets, and best practices. On a regular basis, data were distributed to regions and districts for use by all functional areas so corrective measures could be taken and results tracked.

At USMG, the senior management team met once every two months for two hours to review customer satisfaction. This group focused on the "top 10" dissatisfiers, the progress made on achieving the CS targets, and the actions to be taken to improve customer satisfaction.

In addition, the USMG Customer Satisfaction team met for two hours twice a month to follow up on the actions initiated at the Customer Satisfaction Improvement meeting and the USMG senior staff meeting. This was a cross-functional team and consisted of members from service, marketing, administration, the headquarters customer relations group, development and manufacturing, and worldwide marketing.

The next step in the customer satisfaction process was to manage a corrective action process that responded to customer dissatisfaction indicators, off-standard internal measures, and performance improvement opportunities. All concerns, including those from customers who indicated through the survey that they were somewhat or very dissatisfied, were acted upon very quickly. About 10,000 complaints per month (150 per district) were followed up. About 35 percent came from the surveys, while the balance were from letters or telephone calls. Personal contact was made with the customer and the problem resolved within 48 hours with a closed-loop follow-up system. The districts' customer relations teams did the callbacks. Planned head-count reductions were likely to reduce the size of the customer relations team by one rep per district, unless a district decided to reallocate personnel from another function.

Root causes of problems were categorized and tracked. The most significant problems involved equipment performance and service, where surveys had revealed that customer expectations were higher than Xerox performance. Corrective measures included setting higher reliability requirements (less than one call per month) on new products, providing dissatisfied customers with better machines, and improving response time for service.

Actions were taken to improve customer satisfaction in weak market segments, such as General Markets, which constantly had the worst CS performance and was furthest from the 1990 target at 84.2 percent in the first quarter. This segment was targeted at 87.3 percent, which was needed to reach the overall target of 1990 by year-end and represented 11,000 machines that needed to move from "dissatisfied" to "satisfied." Likely causes of the problems encountered by General Markets were: (a) lack of account ownership, (b) frequent account rep changes, (c) time and material prices perceived as excessive, and (d) low priority in the service call queue.

Specific actions also were taken for products with below-target CS ratings. For example, retrofit programs were in place to improve the performance of some problem 50 series copiers. Mid-Volume copiers as a group were below customer satisfaction performance targets, mainly because these machines were generally treated with less care by customers. Mid-Volume machines were the orphans of the copier world, generally placed in common areas for use by a large group of people, as opposed to a low-volume or high-volume machine that had one or a few operators who took good care of the machine.

Results. Xerox set year-by-year overall customer satisfaction targets: 90 percent in 1990, 94 percent in 1991, 97 percent in 1992, and 100 percent in 1993. These targets were broken down by customer segment and product line. The percentage of satisfied customers increased significantly in all customer segments (see Exhibit 5).

Overall customer satisfaction targets also were set for each partnership. These were typically based on the overall improvement required and the previous performance of the partnership relative to internal and competitive benchmarks. Partnerships with the largest variance were expected to improve the most.

The management leadership actions and the focus on changing employee attitudes began to pay off. Prior to these actions, customer satisfaction was the responsibility of the service organization, while sales and business operations did not have much of a customer focus. Customers had complained about lack of follow-up and post-sale support by sales reps who seemed to disappear as soon as the order was signed. Sales reps had focused on new business and had an attitude of "sales at any cost." Many customers were frustrated with inaccurate billing and the difficulty of doing business with Xerox. When a customer problem had involved cross-functional areas, as many did, it seemed as though the sales, service, and administration people did not talk to one another, making it difficult and frustrating to find a solution.

With the district offices as partnerships, their empowerment to resolve customer issues without getting approvals at multiple levels, and the use of customer satisfaction measurements for performance appraisal changed the day-to-day customer interactions. All partners and employees felt responsible for customer satisfaction. Here are the comments of the three partners of one East Coast district:

District Service manager: "Three years ago I never went on a sales call; now I go on about three per month. We were not always focused on listening to the customer. We focused on fixing a machine, rather than fixing a broken customer who happened to have a Xerox equipment."

District Business manager: "Every customer contact—'the 1,000 moments of truth'—is now considered an opportunity to improve customer satisfaction with and perception of Xerox."

District Sales manager: "We are more customer-focused than ever before. Five years ago, there was not that much excitement about customer satisfaction. Today, customer satisfaction is everything."

Customer Guarantee

In November 1987, top management of Xerox had considered offering a satisfaction guarantee, because it expected that a guarantee would lead to greater customer satisfaction and would also drive the organization to higher levels of performance. It wanted to come up with a guarantee that would be difficult for Xerox's competitors, especially those in the mid- and low-volume segments who distributed through dealers, to emulate. However, it thought that such a guarantee should be offered only after ensuring that the Leadership Through Quality tools and processes as well as the focus on "The Customer" were implemented, and that Xerox was able to consistently perform and deliver on the guarantee. By February 1990, it believed that Xerox had achieved those targets and that the organization was ready to guarantee satisfaction.

Most senior managers believed that a money-back guarantee was the way to go. Based on brainstorming and exploratory research, however, they decided to examine four types of guarantees: (1) a service guarantee (e.g., "If your machine is not operating 98 percent of the time, you will receive 10 percent off your next invoice"); (2) a money-back guarantee (e.g., "If you are not satisfied with the product or vendor, you can return your machine, no questions asked"); (3) a product performance guarantee (e.g., "If your machine does not perform at its original specifications or better for at least three years, we will replace your unit at no charge"); and (4) a product-fit guarantee (e.g., "If the product does not meet your needs, you can trade it in for full credit toward any other product").

During May–June 1990, Xerox conducted market research to gather inputs from various customer segments to develop a unique guarantee. The research was done in two phases: focus groups and a telephone survey. First, focus groups were conducted in three cities to test reactions to the four broad categories of guarantees. Several key messages came from the groups:

- The credibility of a guarantee was tied to the reputation of the vendor.

- The length of the guarantee was critical; less than a year was viewed as a normal warranty at best, and, at worst, a desperate sales ploy. If a guarantee was for unlimited time, respondents believed that the customer paid a premium.
- Any guarantee could be significantly strengthened by making the customer the sole arbiter.
- For the service guarantee, response time (how quickly a firm responded to a call) was viewed as more appropriate than machine up-time.
- The money-back guarantee was viewed by some as low vendor commitment (i.e., being too easy for the vendor to walk away from).
- The product performance guarantee should be at the customer's request, with no questions asked, for the life of the contract.
- The product-fit guarantee was considered by many to be inappropriate. Many focus group members indicated that customers did not want to switch equipment but only wanted the equipment to work well and be right for their needs.

Based on the focus groups research, Xerox decided (1) to drop the product-fit guarantee from further consideration, (2) to substitute response time for up-time in the service guarantee, and (3) to change the product performance guarantee to "If your machine does not perform up to your satisfaction for at least three years, we will replace it at no charge at your request." Thus, the three guarantees tested in the second phase of the study were:

1. A response-time guarantee, which involved a commitment to send a service person to the customer site within a specified time after the service call was received.
2. A performance guarantee, under which Xerox would commit to a certain customer determined level of service or product satisfaction. Xerox would replace the machine with another of equal or greater capability at the sole discretion of the customer.
3. A money-back guarantee under which the customer would receive a refund if dissatisfied.

In the second phase of the research, 560 customers (Xerox and non-Xerox), selected from all five customer segments, were surveyed by telephone. The focus group results were used to develop a questionnaire for the telephone survey. The major findings from the survey are presented in Exhibit 6.

Some competitors already offered a guarantee. Kodak had just begun a new campaign touting its "Bend Over Backwards" customer guarantee. Advertised in *Time, Busi-*

ness Week, and other highly visible publications. Kodak's guarantee of product replacement was at Kodak's discretion and covered a three-year period. Canon also offered a performance guarantee, while Pitney Bowes guaranteed response time, performance, and a parts and supplies price protection. Lanier offered a 98 percent up-time guarantee.

Whichever guarantee alternative was chosen, Xerox planned an extensive marketing and advertising campaign, its biggest in 10 years, around the new guarantee. The guarantee would apply to all Xerox products for a period of three years or for the term of Xerox financing, whichever was longer, and the machines had to be serviced by Xerox (and not by third parties) throughout the guarantee period. Though Xerox executives believed that it would be difficult to link sales specifically to the guarantee, they expected that the guarantee would increase sales by 5–10 percent.

Current Situation.   Supporters of the money-back guarantee thought it was the only option strong enough to achieve the desired effects—to mobilize the organization and differentiate Xerox's offering from competitors. As one Xerox manager said, "Kodak already offers a performance guarantee, and any competitor could match the rather amorphous 'performance guarantee.' Significant results require a dramatic offering."

Other managers thought that a money-back guarantee carried negative connotations and was a "low commitment" alternative. They thought that a performance guarantee was a better option because it required a higher commitment from Xerox, which customers really wanted. They thought the offering could be differentiated on the basis of who determined whether performance met the customer's requirements. Under existing industry practice, the vendor determined whether the product met the performance criteria. Letting the customer make this decision would be a significantly different, value-added offering to the customer.

Supporters of the response-time guarantee pointed out that competitors had already made response time a critical attribute and that Xerox had to compete on that. Other managers believed that a response time guarantee would not provide enough incentive for all functional areas of the company. Some thought that Xerox did not have the process capacity to guarantee response time and that the option would be too complicated because it would require different response times and pricing based on geographic location (i.e., rural versus large city), among other factors.

Hicks and the other top executives had to decide what type of guarantee Xerox ought to offer.

EXHIBIT 1   Placement of Copiers (in units), 1989

| | Product Market | | | |
	Low-Volume	Mid-Volume	High-Volume	Total
Canon	28.6%	9.7%	12.5%	23.0%
Xerox	11.3	26.5	45.1	15.2
Sharp	18.6	7.4	—	14.6
Mita	8.4	9.0	—	8.4
Ricoh	5.0	8.5	—	5.7
Konica	4.8	8.0	7.7	5.3
Minolta	3.3	2.7	—	5.1
Lanier	4.8	3.7	3.7	4.4
Savin	1.6	7.3	—	3.2
Kodak	—	2.2	31.0	1.1
Others	13.6	15.0	—	14.0
Total	100.0%	100.0%	100.0%	100.0%
Proportion of total units	80.5%	17.0%	2.5%	100.0%
Proportion of revenues	38.7	31.3	30.0	100.0
Proportion of total copies	28.9	31.1	40.0	100.0

EXHIBIT 2   Relative Importance of Major Criteria in Equipment and Service
Purchase Decisions

| | Commercial Major Accounts | | | Named Accounts | | |
	Small	Large	Overall	Small	Large	Overall
Equipment Purchase Decision						
Reliability	0.30	0.34	0.32	0.41	0.38	0.40
Ease of operation	0.17	0.24	0.21	0.20	0.07	0.13
Completeness of product line	0.21	0.11	0.16	0.10	0.20	0.15
Service quality	0.29	0.30	0.29	0.18	0.27	0.23
Price	0.03	0.01	0.02	0.11	0.08	0.09
Service Purchase Decision						
Technical expertise	0.35	0.45	0.40	0.33	0.45	0.39
Professionalism	0.26	0.10	0.18	0.18	0.10	0.14
Guaranteed response time	0.23	0.34	0.28	0.35	0.29	0.32
Variety of contract offerings	0.09	0.10	0.10	0.05	0.11	0.08
Price	0.07	0.01	0.04	0.09	0.05	0.07

EXHIBIT 3

Customer satisfaction improvement model

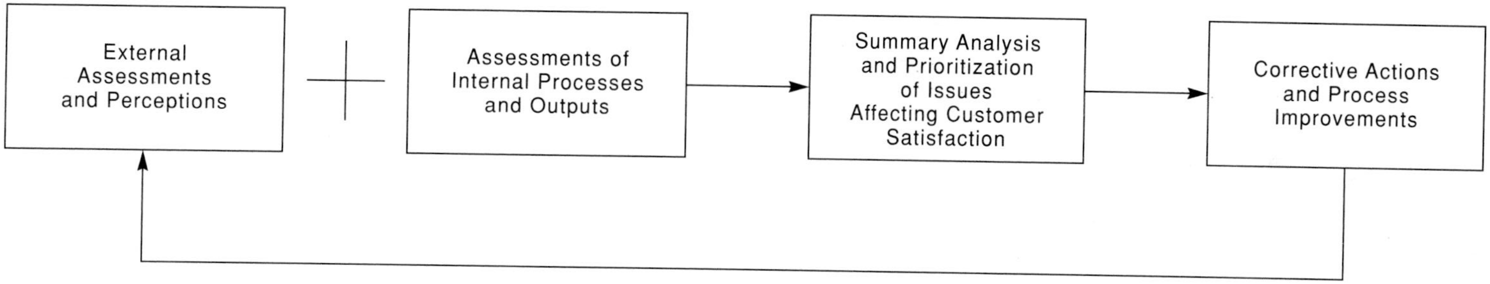

| External Assessments and Perceptions | + | Assessments of Internal Processes and Outputs | → | Summary Analysis and Prioritization of Issues Affecting Customer Satisfaction | → | Corrective Actions and Process Improvements |

DATA ELEMENTS:

- Periodic Xerox customer surveys

- Periodic Xerox and competitive customer surveys

- Post-installation customer surveys

- New product post-installation customer surveys

- Customer complaint data

- Internal measures of work processes and outputs

- Employee surveys/ roundtables

- Benchmarking studies

- Systemic national and local issues

- Cost of quality

- Input into functional plans

- Leadership through quality tools

- Tracking of solutions and improvements

- Inspection

- Closed loop with customer corrective actions

- Feedback to and from employees

EXHIBIT 4   Xerox Customer Satisfaction Survey: Decision Makers

This questionnaire should be completed by the individual who makes decisions about the acquisition of _____ .
Please focus on your experiences in the product areas mentioned as you complete the questionnaire.

SECTION I: GENERAL SATISFACTION

	Very Satisfied	Somewhat Satisfied	Neither Satisfied nor Dissatisfied	Somewhat Dissatisfied	Very Dissatisfied
1. Based on your recent experience, how satisfied are you with Xerox?	☐	☐	☐	☐	☐

	Definitely	Probably	Might or Might Not	Probably Not	Definitely Not
2. Based on your recent experience, would you acquire another product from Xerox?	☐	☐	☐	☐	☐
3. Based on your recent experience, would you recommend Xerox to a business associate?	☐	☐	☐	☐	☐

	Very Satisfied	Somewhat Satisfied	Neither Satisfied nor Dissatisfied	Somewhat Dissatisfied	Very Dissatisfied
4. How satisfied are you overall with the quality of:					
(a) Your Xerox product(s)	☐	☐	☐	☐	☐
(b) Sales support you receive	☐	☐	☐	☐	☐
(c) Technical service you receive	☐	☐	☐	☐	☐
(d) Administrative support you receive	☐	☐	☐	☐	☐
(e) Handling of inquiries	☐	☐	☐	☐	☐
(f) Supplies support you receive	☐	☐	☐	☐	☐
(g) Xerox-user training	☐	☐	☐	☐	☐
(h) Xerox-supplied documentation	☐	☐	☐	☐	☐

Please complete 4i and 4j only if you are the decision maker for systems products (printers, workstations, personal computers and wordprocessors)

	Very Satisfied	Somewhat Satisfied	Neither Satisfied nor Dissatisfied	Somewhat Dissatisfied	Very Dissatisfied
(i) Your Xerox-supplied software	☐	☐	☐	☐	☐
(j) Xerox systems analyst support	☐	☐	☐	☐	☐
(k) Telephone hotline support	☐	☐	☐	☐	☐

SECTION II: SALES SUPPORT

	Very Satisfied	Somewhat Satisfied	Neither Satisfied nor Dissatisfied	Somewhat Dissatisfied	Very Dissatisfied	Not Applicable
5. How satisfied are you with Xerox Sales Representatives with regard to:						
(a) Timeliness of response to your inquiries	☐	☐	☐	☐	☐	☐
(b) Frequency of contact to review your needs	☐	☐	☐	☐	☐	☐
(c) Frequency of contact to provide information about new Xerox products and services	☐	☐	☐	☐	☐	☐
(d) Product knowledge	☐	☐	☐	☐	☐	☐
(e) Application knowledge	☐	☐	☐	☐	☐	☐
(f) Understanding of your business needs	☐	☐	☐	☐	☐	☐
(g) Accuracy in explaining terms/conditions	☐	☐	☐	☐	☐	☐
(h) Ability to resolve problems	☐	☐	☐	☐	☐	☐
(i) Professionalism	☐	☐	☐	☐	☐	☐

Exhibit 4   (*concluded*)

SECTION III: CUSTOMER SUPPORT

---

6. What was the purpose of your most recent call to Xerox?   ☐ Inquiry   ☐ Problem   ☐ Haven't called, can't answer (skip to Question 10)

7. How long ago did you make this call?   ☐ less than 3 months   ☐ 3–6 months   ☐ 6–12 months   ☐ Greater than 12 months

8. What Xerox function did you contact?   ☐ Sales   ☐ Service   ☐ Billing   ☐ Collection   ☐ Supplies   ☐ Telephone Hotline Support   ☐ Systems Analyst   ☐ Customer Relations Group

---

	Very Satisfied	Somewhat Satisfied	Neither Satisfied nor Dissatisfied	Somewhat Dissatisfied	Very Dissatisfied
9. How satisfied are you with the support you received?					
(a) Ability to get to the right person(s) quickly	☐	☐	☐	☐	☐
(b) Attitude of Xerox personnel who assisted you	☐	☐	☐	☐	☐
(c) Ability to provide a solution	☐	☐	☐	☐	☐
(d) Time required to provide a solution	☐	☐	☐	☐	☐
(e) Effectiveness of the solution	☐	☐	☐	☐	☐
(f) Overall satisfaction with support received	☐	☐	☐	☐	☐

10. What specific things can we do to increase your satisfaction with Xerox, our products and our services? Thank you for your feedback!

Your Name _____

Position   _____

Tel #   _____

Date   _____

Account #
123456789

Exhibit 5

Percentage satisfied by customer segment (three-month rolling average reported quarterly)

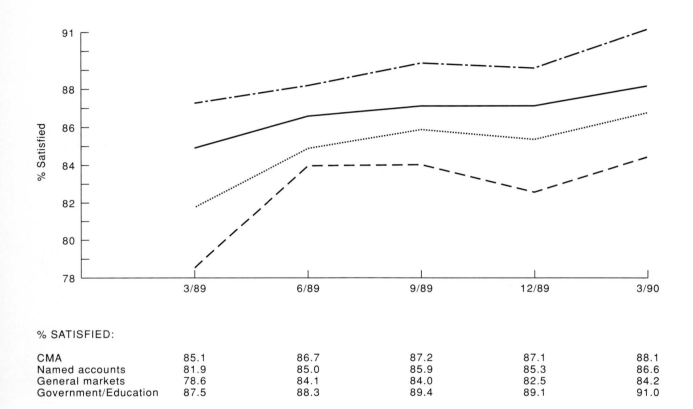

**Percent Satisfied by Customer Segment
(three-month rolling avg. reported quarterly)**

CMA ─────────
Named accounts ·············
General markets ─ ─ ─ ─ ─
Government/Education ─·─·─·─·─

% SATISFIED:

	3/89	6/89	9/89	12/89	3/90
CMA	85.1	86.7	87.2	87.1	88.1
Named accounts	81.9	85.0	85.9	85.3	86.6
General markets	78.6	84.1	84.0	82.5	84.2
Government/Education	87.5	88.3	89.4	89.1	91.0

EXHIBIT 6   Feedback from the Telephone Survey of Customers, 1990

• **General**	Agree (%)	Disagree (%)
• Guarantees are a meaningful way to protect the customer	90%	10%
• All guarantees are pretty much the same	30	70
• A company that offers a better guarantee makes a superior product	35	65
• A better guarantee on a quality product does not increase cost	45	55

• **Consideration**

• About 63% of those who heard about a guarantee took some action such as calling for more information, asking for a demo or trial, considering a new vendor or switching vendors. Thirty-seven percent did nothing on hearing about a guarantee.

• Almost half of those who took some action on hearing about a guarantee switched vendors (63% took action, 29% switched vendors).

• Named Accounts were most likely to respond to guarantees in the consideration process, exceeding the average by 5–10%. General Markets were the least responsive.

• **Decision Factors**

• In terms of the decision process, the percentage of respondents who thought that guarantees were equal to or more important than the following major criteria were: price (46%), features (42%), vendor reputation (50%), and experience with the vendor (46%).

• General Markets and Government/Education were most sensitive to price and features. Among them, 35% view guarantees as equally or more important than price.

• Guarantees were equal to or more important than prior experience or vendor reputation for all segments except General Markets where prior experience was more important.

• **Preferences**

• Customers allocated 10 points over the three guarantee offerings as follows:

	Service Response	Product Performance	Money Back
Customer segments:			
CMA	3.7	3.6	2.7
Named accounts	3.4	3.6	3.0
General markets	3.6	3.2	3.2
Government/education	3.3	3.5	3.2
Total	3.4	3.6	3.0
Product markets:			
High-volume	3.7	3.3	3.0
Low- and mid-volume	3.3	3.7	3.0

EXHIBIT 6   *(continued)*

● **Believability**
• The percentage of respondents who said that such a guarantee was believable was:

	Service Response (%)	Product Performance (%)	Money Back (%)
Customer segments:			
CMA	73%	78%	58%
Named accounts	62	73	61
General markets	63	70	61
Government/education	59	75	68
Total	63	74	62

• The top "Do Not Believe" reasons were (numbers represent percentage of respondents who indicated this):

Too open-ended	28%	12%	
Never seen it happen	14		13%
Unrealistic/ineffective	15		24
Company will try to disregard the guarantee		11	14
Will try to repair, not replace		17	
Company sets rules or specs		13	

● **Expectations**
• Who would you expect to offer a guarantee? (Numbers represent the percentage of respondents who said they would expect that company to offer a guarantee.)

	Canon	Kodak	Xerox	Other Manufacturers
High-Volume:				
Xerox users	9	35	76	10
Xerox nonusers	9	30	47	15
Total	9	33	63	12
Low- and Mid-Volume:				
Xerox users	16	5	59	23
Xerox nonusers	19	6	32	17
Total	18	6	38	18
All respondents	15	12	42	16

Exhibit 6 (*concluded*)

- **Current Practices**
- Guarantees typically covered the following items (numbers represent percentage of respondents who indicated this):

	Parts & Labor	Response Time	Uptime	Copy Quality
CMA	83	42	36	22
Named accounts	78	38	34	21
General markets	82	36	31	16
Government/education	83	47	46	19
Total	80	40	38	20

- Response time guarantees typically guaranteed response times of 4 hours (46%), 2 hours (21%), same day (20%), or next day (13%).

- **Response Time Needs**
- What response time will really satisfy you? (Numbers represent the percentage of respondents who indicated that particular amount of time.)

	1 Hour	2 Hours	3 Hours	4 Hours	Same Day	Next Day	Total
Customer segments:							
CMA	7	22	9	32	22	8	100
Named accounts	10	17	11	25	28	9	100
General markets	2	11	6	12	52	17	100
Government/education	9	12	7	20	34	18	100
Total	8	16	9	24	31	12	100
Product categories:							
High-volume	9	27	13	29	17	5	100
Low and mid-volume	8	11	7	22	37	15	100
Total	8	16	9	24	31	12	100

Boston Fights Drugs (A)*

Designing Communications Research

It was May 1, 1987, and four members of Harvard Business School's field study group were assessing the validity and usefulness of their research findings. One of them even wondered if the basic research design was effective in the first place. There were questions regarding sample size and selection, the appropriateness of the focus group method, the usefulness of the screening questionnaire, and the role of the moderator. The group's report was due to Boston's Mayor Raymond Flynn by June 15, 1987. Since the group already had spent a little over two thirds of the $20,000 budget, there wasn't much time or money left for completing the project.

Four months earlier, in January, the project had been initiated by Neil Sullivan, the mayor's policy advisor, and Marc Zegans, a key member of the mayor's policy staff. Sullivan had said, "The mayor wants your help in determining what we should do to curtail drug use among Boston's school-going population." Zegans had added, "He's interested in demand-side strategies; basically, what kind of communication the city should send to its young people." Zegans explained, "You should create a communications program which offers guidelines on the most effective messages and delivery channels for reaching our city's school-going population. Also, your plan should be ready for us to implement immediately."

Drugs in Boston

With its population of over 620,000, Boston ranked as the 19th largest city in the United States. However, with almost three million people spread over the 83 cities and towns that comprised Greater Boston, the city's influence far exceeded its size.

Along with other large American cities, Boston housed a burgeoning illicit substances market. (See Exhibit 1.) In the distribution of illegal drugs, it served as New England's hub. During 1986, law enforcement agencies made almost 1,000 drug trafficking arrests in Boston, and the Justice Department's Drug Enforcement Agency confiscated approximately 80 kilograms of cocaine, 6.4 kilograms of heroin, 47 tons of marijuana, and 2,100,000 dosage units of synthetic drugs, for an aggregate street value of over $250 million. Experts estimated that these arrests unearthed 5 to 10 percent of the total drug volume being trafficked through Boston at any one time, though they emphasized that any effort to characterize the market size was at best a guess.

Typically, drug products reached the Boston market a year after being introduced in New York City; and 1985 and 1986 marked the beginning of a new type of cocaine epidemic in New York based on "crack," a drug manufactured by mixing street cocaine, typically 20 percent pure, with baking soda and water. Boiling the mixture produced tiny chunks of 90 percent pure cocaine, small enough for teenagers to purchase for $10 apiece but potent enough, when lit with a butane lighter, to cause an immediate and intense high—and many deaths. In the summer of 1986, fear that the crack epidemic would spread to Boston prompted Mayor Flynn to make curtailing drug abuse a top priority.

"We need a comprehensive, integrated approach to the drug problem," Mayor Flynn had told Sullivan and Zegans, "and that means using every method at our disposal to decrease both the supply of and the demand for illicit drugs." Local, state, and federal agencies, as well as Boston's business community, would all be involved. As part of the initiative, the Mayor's Policy Office approached Harvard Business School and asked students to create a plan to "de-market" drugs to youth within the city.

Boston's Drug Programs

Enforcement. In 1986, the Boston area housed a variety of antidrug programs, including enforcement activities run through the city's police departments, the local arm of the Federal Drug Enforcement Administration, and the Commonwealth of Massachusetts. But quick and substantial profits were increasingly attracting drug traffickers. Said Lieutenant James Wood, head of the Drug Enforcement Division for the Boston Police Department, "We've doubled trafficking arrests since last year. That means that more weight is out there." Yet most experts agreed that America's drug problem would never be stopped by enforcement efforts alone. According to one law enforcement expert, "The most that we can do is prevent them from selling drugs on

---

*This case is based on a Creative Marketing Study (CMS) done by Dina Boufides, Paul Crnkovich, Kim Finnerty, Jennifer Lawrence, and Nancy Madoff. CMS is a second-year field study elective course in the MBA program at the Harvard Business School. Typically, student groups of three to five sign up for one of several projects sponsored by outside clients.

This case was prepared by Research Associate Jennifer F. Lawrence under the direction of Assistant Professor V. Kasturi Rangan.
Copyright © 1987 by the President and Fellows of Harvard College.
Harvard Business School case 9-588-031.

the street like newspapers. Convincing citizens to decrease their demand for illicit substances is essential."

Education. In Boston, drug education was part of the school curriculum, with programs fashioned for each age group. Fifth and sixth graders took part in a self-awareness module called "SPECDA" (School Program to Educate and Control Drug Abuse), led by trained policemen with teachers playing an advisory role. The curriculum addressed issues of self-confidence and peer pressure as well as the consequences of drug use. High school students learned about drugs in health classes, and peer programs led by teenage role models informed elementary school students of the dangers of drugs.

In addition, numerous public agencies provided counseling, detoxification centers, awareness bulletins, and educational aids. The business community underwrote public service announcements and sponsored "Drug-Free Days" throughout the city. These promotional efforts were coordinated by an alliance called "BAD," or "Boston Against Drugs," consisting of the Chamber of Commerce, the mayor's office, the Boston Police Department, and numerous corporate leaders. Finally, neighborhood groups often took the initiative, whether through community centers or as individuals, to keep their city blocks drug-free. One such prominent leader, Georgette Watson, created Boston's "Drop a Dime" program, which asked citizens to call and report drug users or pushers in their area.

Communications Programs. Boston's mass media had access to a wide array of public service announcements on the subject of drug abuse, and advertising agencies regularly volunteered to produce antidrug commercials at no charge. Typical of the genre was the close-up shot of a teenage celebrity, such as Nancy McKeon, star of a popular television comedy, who directly addressed the viewer with an admonition that "Drugs are bad for you. Be cool, like me. Don't do drugs." Another advertising campaign primarily featured sports stars, who stated that they had been cocaine addicts but had quit. They referred to cocaine as "the big lie" and told the audience not to make the same mistake that they had.

One local advertisement, which received a lot of airtime in Boston, featured a slow-motion study of a teenage girl, drawn from actual news footage. She was shown first taking drugs with her friends and then being wheeled on a gurney into a hospital emergency room to the tune of the song:

Take me out of the ballgame,
Take me out of the crowd;
Buy me some pieces of crack, Jack;
I don't care if I never come back . . .

The ad ended with Mayor Flynn urging that Boston should turn in the pushers. A final example of current advertising

featured a teenage boy in his bedroom, obviously strung out on drugs. He told the viewer that his parents were "dumb" and that they didn't understand him and his need for help. At the ad's conclusion, a voice announced a toll-free hotline number to call if a friend or child needed help for a drug problem.

The Boston Against Drugs alliance had commissioned a local advertising agency, Harold Cabot, Inc., to study Boston's teenagers and create an ad to reach them. The agency talked to six groups of five to seven high school students each, in school classrooms, to ask their opinions on drug abuse. Parents signed release forms, and each participant was paid $50 for his or her time. The results indicated that peer pressure to use drugs was intense, and that drug availability and usage were pervasive throughout the school system. The study also indicated that use of celebrities in antidrug advertising scored low with young people.

The Creative Marketing Field Study

The mayor's office made available to the student group several published studies on the drug abuse problems nationwide. Most of these studies were based on qualitative impressions of counselors, teachers, and social workers who had extensively worked with youngsters needing help. A common theme running across these studies indicated a growing drug abuse behavior; increasingly, younger children seemed to be getting involved. School-going children by and large had no sense of their own mortality, and peer pressure often was mentioned as an important reason for drug induction.

Though excited by the prospect of working with the City of Boston, the research group was somewhat daunted by the size and nature of the mayor's request to determine what messages the city should send to its young people and how these should be packaged and delivered to reach the target audience. First, the group had to limit the scope of the study to complete the project in five months of part-time work. Next, the group needed to select a research methodology that would meet its budget constraint of $20,000 and provide relevant information. Finally, the group needed to choose appropriate research questions for study. What, actually, did it wish to find out? How best to do it? And what would the group do with the information it obtained?

Market Research Options. As the group saw, it could limit the study by age, by neighborhood, or by socioeconomic bracket, it could include all Bostonians, or it could attempt some combination of the above. Further, a number of research options seemed plausible.

Quantitative surveys. A large-scale, citywide survey covering 750 to 1,000 individuals could be done by telephone for about $15,000 or by mail for about $10,000. It would take about two months to implement once the questionnaire was developed. The questionnaire normally was structured and the order of questions predetermined. Several pretesting runs would be required to perfect the details and wording of the questions. An established market research firm would search its database for respondents fitting given characteristics and would administer the questionnaire. Response rates for such surveys averaged between 5 to 20 percent. Descriptive tables and statistical correlations between background, behavior, and attitudes could be developed. Popularly referred to as an awareness and usage study, it had the advantage of generating "objective data," not biased by interviewer's interpretations.

Qualitative surveys.   Focus groups consisting of 8 to 10 persons per group would cost between $500 and $1,500 per session. The sessions normally lasted an hour to an hour and a half, and participants were paid $25 to $50 for their time. Participants would be motivated to discuss their attitudes and behavior toward drugs. The focus group moderator, operating from a "protocol" of research questions, would lead the group to discuss each of the topics, but the order and detail were basically an outcome of the group process. The moderator only loosely guided the flow of the discussion. When the dynamics were right, focus groups could act as brainstorming sessions and provide creative ideas and insights to the researchers. Focus group moderation normally required training and experience, but the discussion itself could be taped and interpreted by the researchers themselves. Professional psychologists were, at times, hired to interpret focus group data, and that would cost additional money.

One-on-one interviews.   Consumers could be interviewed individually in a more open-ended and unstructured format than surveys. Often led by trained counselors, these would cost between $50 and $100 per person, depending on the customer segment selected and the training of the interviewer. Usually, participants were paid for their time in this process as well, with fees ranging from $25 to $50. A market research firm might schedule four or five interviews daily per available interviewer. Interviewer reports were largely relied upon for interpreting the data. In addition, for sensitive topics, professional psychologists often added depth to the interpretation.

Method Selection

The field study group chose the focus group method. The survey method was rejected, because several members of the group felt that a questionnaire approach implicitly required them to have several testable propositions, when they had none. The one-on-one interview method was considered too slow and too subjective. The group briefly considered proceeding with abbreviated one-on-one interviews, obtained by intercepting teenagers at random on different street corners in the city, but it rejected this idea as being unworkable. (Called the Mall Intercept Study, such an approach was used by many marketing research firms to elicit consumer responses in shopping malls.) Given the subject matter, a simple five-minute discussion would not suffice. Furthermore, potential subjects might balk at being abruptly stopped and queried by strangers about drug use among their peer group. As one member put it, "We were keen to get started, we wanted to muddy our hands and get a feel for the problem quickly. Focus groups seemed to provide the best compromise."

Sampling.   As the field study members contemplated the key research questions, a new problem emerged: how should they recruit participants to obtain accurate market information? None of the researchers felt that interviewing students in school was ideal. With such a personal and controversial topic under study, teenagers could feel pressured to give less than accurate portrayals of their drug use, which would bias results. Additionally, much red tape was involved in using the school system, ranging from parental release forms to the requirement that the school board's legal counsel be consulted. The field study group did not think it wise to engage in such a lengthy process.

A number of area market research firms specialized in recruiting young people for focus groups; but the field study group learned that typical databases targeted upscale, predominantly white youngsters whose family members tended to be purchasers of expensive consumer products. These databases were not representative of the Boston school-going population.

In addition, most firms were not accessible by public transportation. Even if the group utilized a market research firm's database, where would the focus group participants meet? One company suggested holding sessions in restaurants or pizza parlors across the city, but the students felt that the atmosphere would be noisy and disruptive and too public for participants to divulge their attitudes concerning drug use.

Finally, the researchers hit upon a plan. In the course of interviewing Boston officials about the city's drug programs, they had learned that many activities at the neighborhood level took place in various recreational centers known as "community schools." The community centers did not substitute the local school system. They served as supplementary facilities for youngsters to socialize and play, under the supervision of qualified adults. The centers' facilities usually included a gym, classrooms, or play space. Perhaps administrators of the community schools would permit the group to talk with neighborhood kids as part of the centers' scheduled activities. Charles Rose, director of the Boston Community Schools program, endorsed the idea. "Anything that focuses attention on the needs of our kids is fine with me. You'll have to okay your plans with each director, but I don't think that will be a problem, since I'll tell them I'm in favor of cooperating with you."

With Mr. Rose's assistance, the field study group targeted four neighborhoods that were representative of the city in terms of ethnic and socioeconomic distribution: Roxbury, Mission Hill, Charlestown, and Dorchester. (Another neighborhood, the South End, was the source of two adult groups. See Exhibit 2.) A field study member met with recreational directors at each community school and explained the purpose of the study. The directors volunteered space and promised to ask local children if they wished to participate.

Meanwhile, the group had retained a market research firm to lead the focus group discussions. Since the groups would be held "off-site," and the market research firm would not be responsible for participant selection, the field study was required to pay only for the moderator's time, the cost of transcribing tapes of the proceedings, and stipends for the participants. (Though Cabot's study had provided $50 stipends, the community schools leaders felt that $10 or $15 would be more than adequate to encourage participation.) The group also would provide refreshments. As Emmett Folgert, coordinator of the Dorchester Youth Collaborative commented, "If you feed them, my kids would love to talk to you. Besides, they rarely get asked their opinions on anything."

The researchers' next step was to decide what age groups to study. The Cabot focus groups had included 14-to 18-year-olds who, everyone agreed, tended to be aware of and had experimented with drugs, and for whom drug products were an accepted part of daily life. The field study group felt that it would gain more insights into why drug use was pervasive in this group if it studied an additional age group for contrast.

Some members wanted to study adults, particularly those with young children of their own. Others made a case for studying younger children. The group agreed that both arguments had merit; but a pragmatic consideration directed their final decision: the community schools had unlimited access to children and adolescents. Finding young adults would mean relying on market research firms to solicit participants and, again selecting a meeting place. Further, the Mayor's Policy Office had stated that young people should be the primary target of inquiry. The field study members decided to concentrate on two age levels: 10-to-13-year-olds and 14-to-18-year-olds. However, time and budget permitting, they agreed to hold one or two focus groups with young adults to see if any specific trends emerged.

Drug use model. Next, the researchers tried to fashion a model of drug use, which would provide structure for data collection. They thought about ways to segment the population and talked to various experts. In the words of a team member:

> Our study divided the public into four general groups by drug awareness and abuse: nonusers, experimental users, regular users, and drug-dependent individuals. Nonusers tended to have little exposure to drugs. As drug awareness increased, nonusers had to decide whether or not to try drugs. Experimental users included people who had had an opportunity to try illicit drugs and were familiar with their names, characteristics, and availability. Although they experimented with drugs, people in this group did not actively seek out drugs or use them routinely. Regular users were people who had developed a pattern of continuing abuse. The regular user actively sought out and used drugs at predictable intervals. Drug-dependent individuals were that small minority of the drug-using population for whom life revolved around the pursuit and consumption of one or several drug products.

The field study members knew that they did not have the resources to track individuals over time to see which stages they entered, a process that would take years to investigate. So they decided that 10-to-13-year-olds could serve as a proxy for the first two stages, nonusers and experimental users, while the 14-to-18-year-olds would shed light on the third stage, regular users, in addition to the first two. The group agreed that study of stage four was beyond the scope of their project, but that talks with adults might shed some light on this segment.

Screening. "Focus groups provide insightful discussion if a broad range of opinions and experiences are represented," argued a team member. The group, therefore, devised a simple screening questionnaire to ensure that volunteers would be broadly representative of the population. (See Exhibit 3.) As an incentive for completing the questionnaire, volunteers would receive $3. If chosen for the hour-long discussion, the participant would receive $12. The researchers agreed that single-sex groups would be most candid.

The questionnaires were constructed to disguise partially the purpose of the focus group. Young people answered a question on street violence and also provided needed information about their favorite TV commercials. Questions 2 and 4 were the critical questions that addressed attitudes about drug use directly. Question 2 inquired if the respondent thought that drug use was a problem. Question 4 was so designed that respondents could reflect personal habits under the guise of providing third-party information, a less-threatening approach.

To the group's surprise, many volunteers were unable to read and interpret the questionnaire without assistance. Luckily, the recreational leaders agreed to read out the questions and write down the responses. (See Exhibit 4.) All questionnaires were coded by number and neighborhood. Only the community school leader in each neighborhood knew the young people's identities. Of the 154 who participated, 44 were screened out *(a)* because of the doubtful validity of their responses (e.g., identical answers to a previous respondent), and *(b)* overrepresentation of certain demographic segments. Of the 110 invited to participate in focus groups, about 20 percent did not show up at the announced times.

Resource constraints.   Simultaneously, the field study group members also decided how to divide age groups among neighborhoods. They did not have the resources to study 10-to-13-year-old boys in every neighborhood, for example, so they split ages and sex among the various community schools. Eventually, they held five focus groups for 10-to-13-year-olds and four focus groups for 14-to-18-year-olds. They also spoke with two groups of adults. However, the participants much preferred to discuss adolescent drug use, rather than their own, so the discussions were not of much use. (See Table A.)

Protocols.   The field study members created a series of questions for the focus group moderator. This "interview protocol" was a guide to help the moderator direct discussion to topics of interest to the researchers. In one brainstorming session, the group listed many questions. These were divided into five categories and so arranged that easier, or less controversial, subjects would be discussed first. (See Exhibit 5.) After a series of focus groups had been held, the group modified the protocol to permit the final focus group discussions to target unanswered questions from earlier group sessions. This version was shorter and more pointed.

Dynamics.   At the start of each session, the moderator wrote each participant's first name on a card, so she could address each person directly. Meanwhile, the participants munched on cookies and soda provided by the field study group. At the end of each session, a field study member handed out stipends with an explanatory note to parents, who might wonder how the youngster had obtained the money. After a few sessions led by the market research firm's moderator, the group members felt confident that they could lead sessions on their own. This approach worked particularly well, since teenagers seemed more willing to speak freely with someone nearer their age.

Though the field study group initially believed that the topic of drugs was too sensitive to discuss directly ("Let's imagine that you had a friend who took drugs . . ."), participants seemed willing and eager to talk about the topic. Virtually all the focus groups extended over one hour, and kids had to be cautioned to speak one at a time so the microphone could pick up their comments clearly.

Data Analysis

Finally, after all the focus groups had been completed, and typed transcripts of each session obtained, the team summarized the points made in each focus group under topic headings, such as "feelings about family" or "advertising recall." (See Exhibits 6 through 13.) The data analysis procedure consisted of organizing the information into 14 topics under two broad headings: advertising and community programs. The selected topics frequently were mentioned in the focus group discussions, and, in the judgment of the field study members, directly relevant to the design of communication strategies for "de-marketing" drugs. The advertising topics included attitudes toward celebrities, the use of teenagers in advertising, the use of rules to convey an antidrug message (such as "Just Say No"), storytelling's place in teenage advertising, the role of realism, feelings about family, the presentation of strategies for coping with drug use situations, questioning drug use behavior, and the usefulness of a "talking head" format. The community programs topics included discussion groups, recreational activities, SPECDA (School Program to Educate and Control Drug Abuse), work with the neighborhood, and educational movies.

Exhibit 14 shows a frequency distribution of the comments, summarizing the number of statements mentioned under each topic. The research group carefully analyzed each statement under each topic and also across the two age groups. They arrived at the following conclusions:

TABLE A   Focus Group Segmentation

	10–13 Years Male/Female		14–18 Years Male/Female		20–30 Years Both Sexes	Totals
Dorchester	1		1		1	3
Roxbury	1			1		2
Mission Hill	1	1		1		3
Charlestown		1	1			2
South End					1	1
Total	3	2	2	2	2	11

Advertising:

1. Young people do not recall drug facts or statistics.

2. Nonusers avoid both friends and strangers who use drugs, rather than confronting them with persuasive reasons to discontinue use.

3. Young people resent being told what to do and may in fact do the opposite to prove their independence.

4. Family is an important influence on drug use and attitudes. Younger respondents view older relatives as role models on the subject, while older respondents try to convince younger relatives not to experiment with drugs. While the family's influence on younger respondents was expected, the group was surprised at the strong influence of family on older respondents as well.

5. Young people vividly relate stories about drugs and drug users. While some of the younger respondents' statements seemed far-fetched, the stories had great impact on them. Older respondents also were influenced greatly by stories that they had heard. These, however, tended to be more realistic, perhaps because they came from personal experience, rather than hearsay.

6. Current drug advertising is unrealistic and does not elicit strong recall, with the major exception of "Take Me Out of the Ballgame," the antidrug commercial produced by Arnold and Company for Mayor Flynn.

7. Celebrities are not viewed as credible spokespeople about drugs, because so many use drugs, because their lives are perceived as different, and because respondents think that they are paid to read a script.

Community Programs:

8. Neighborhood programs are crucial in decreasing demand for drugs, because they provide needed diversion for younger respondents and alternatives to drug use for older respondents. Younger respondents indicated a need for recreational activity, while older respondents more often mentioned a need for peer-group support and counseling for existing drug problems.

9. Educational programs that provide realistic information in an adult manner are effective in communicating an antidrug message.

Focus Group Findings

Based on these findings, the group crafted advertising strategies for Boston's young people. All agreed that **storytelling** was crucial: the ads should present a situation, not simply recount information. The field study members agreed further that the action should appear to take place in Boston neighborhoods with **realistic local characters,** since teenagers scoffed at antidrug ads that were exaggerated or that involved celebrity endorsements. The group felt that including **family members** in the scenes was important as well, since young people appeared heavily influenced by siblings or parents in attitudes toward drug usage.

Perhaps most important, the field study members felt strongly that advertising should **question behavior or present strategies** for changing behavior, rather than command young people what to do. An overwhelming number of respondents had said that even if they agreed with the intent of a command, such as "Just Say No" (and for many, proscribed behavior prompted rebellion), determining *how to follow through* with the intention was difficult when faced with peer pressure.

One member of the group, however, was quite frustrated at how little the data seemed to add to existing knowledge. "If we salvage anything out of this confusion, it'll be purely because we have very little time or money left. I think we have made fundamental mistakes in the research design!"

<u>EXHIBIT 1</u>   **The Drug Abuse Problem**

According to the Drug Enforcement Administration and the National Institute on Drug Abuse, Americans spent over $125 billion for approximately 4 tons of heroin, 120 tons of cocaine, and 14,000 tons of marijuana in 1986. Additionally, Americans were thought to annually consume over 3 billion dosage units of synthetic drugs, such as stimulants, depressants, and hallucinogens. More than one third of the drugs smuggled into the United States were distributed via New York City, while another third reached the western half of the United States through Los Angeles. The remainder reached retailers through networks in other metropolitan regions.

Heroin: the "Worst" Drug

The more than 500,000 heroin users in the United States provided organized crime with over $6 billion annually; an ounce of pure heroin, extracted from opium poppies, was about 10 times more expensive than an ounce of pure gold. Heroin's worst-drug status developed because its addiction and withdrawal symptoms were dramatic, and because the effects of an overdose were relatively quick and lethal. A dosage just 10 to 15 times stronger than normal was fatal, yet the risk of sudden death did not deter the regular user: withdrawal symptoms were so intense that the user would go to any extreme to remain high.

Cocaine: the Fashionable Drug

Cocaine, a stimulant derived from the leaves of the coca plant, was one of the most powerfully addictive substances known. Tolerance and addiction drove the user's steadily increasing demand for the product—generating vast revenues for organized crime. The more than 120 tons of cocaine that entered the United States each year provided illicit income of greater than $14 billion.

At least 30 million Americans had tried cocaine, of which 6 or 7 million used it at least once a month. Cocaine was considered a "trendy" drug, particularly among white-collar workers. Alarmingly, adolescent use of the drug had increased in the past five years. Repeated usage caused chronic fatigue, convulsions, depressions, loss of sex drive, memory problems, nasal bleeding, paranoia, increased body temperature, and death, caused by cerebral hemorrhage, cardiac arrest, and respiratory failure.

Marijuana: the Democratic Drug

Marijuana included any part of the plant *Cannabis sativa*. Because its effects varied among users, the drug was variously classified as a stimulant, depressant, or hallucinogen. Marijuana had 50 percent more cancer-causing hydrocarbons than tobacco and was linked to fetal abnormalities and reproductive problems. Behavioral changes included a decrease in short-term memory and a loss of concentration and logical thinking. Marijuana also acted as a "gateway" to more dangerous drugs, particularly cocaine. Surveys indicated that at least 25 percent of the American population has tried marijuana, and that more than 25 million people used the drug at least once a month.

Synthetics: the Invisible Drugs

While cocaine, heroin, and marijuana were derived from plants, synthetic drugs were produced solely from chemicals. They included hallucinogens like PCP, or "angel dust," such stimulants as dexedrine and abused prescription drugs, including tranquilizers (Valium) and painkillers (Percodan). Tolerance to many synthetic drugs occurred quickly, necessitating larger and more frequent dosages.

People from all walks of life abused synthetic drugs. Often users ingested an array of drugs in which one drug compensated for the effects of another. The synthetic drug in pill or capsule form was more likely to be part of an individual's daily routine than other drugs, both because many brands were tacitly accepted by society (diet pills, sleeping pills) and, thus, readily available, and because administration was easy. Abuse over a long time was common and often seemingly easy to conceal.

SOURCE: The President's Commission on Organized Crime and Drug Abuse, December 1985, Washington, D.C.

EXHIBIT 2 Boston Community School Districts: School-Age Children (5–17 years)

District	Number of School-Age Children[a]	Race of School-Age Children[b]			
		White	Black	Hispanic	Other
1. East Boston	5,771				
2. Charlestown	2,574	94%	0%	5%	1%
3. South Boston	5,409				
4. North End					
	2,871				
5. Chinatown					
6. South End	4,053	22	24	19	25
7. Allston-Brighton	5,396				
8. Mission Hill					
	6,962	26	34	40	0
9. Jamaica Plain					
10. Roxbury	16,851	5	76	11	8
11. Dorchester	19,263	36	36	20	7
12. West Roxbury	4,830				
		98	0	2	0
13. Roslindale	6,060				
14. Mattapan	10,249	4	85	7	4
15. Hyde Park	5,918	55	29	11	5
Boston Totals	96,207	43%	36%	14%	7%

Ethnic Composition by Age Group (%)[b]

11–13 years		43%	37%	14%	6%
14–17 years		45	38	7	8

[a]SOURCE: 1980 Census of Population and Housing, Boston Redevelopment Authority Research Department.
[b]SOURCE: Boston Redevelopment Authority and Neighborhood Development and Employment Agency Household Survey, 1985.

Exhibit 3   Screening Questionnaire

Hi! We're a group of students working on a research project. We would like to know your opinion on a wide range of issues. In fact, we would like to get a group of you together to talk about some of these issues—and we'll pay you to hear what you have to say! We're hoping to use the information to develop some new advertising for kids and teenagers. But first, we need you to answer a couple of simple questions. Thanks a lot!

1. How concerned are you about street violence? (circle one)
   not at all concerned   moderately concerned   very concerned

2. In general, drug use today is: (circle one)
   not a problem   moderate problem   big problem

3. Please check the three things below that are most important to you:
   _____ getting a good job   _____ religion
   _____ family   _____ having a good time
   _____ music   _____ friends
   _____ money   _____ school
   _____ sports   _____ other (please specify below)

4. I know friends/acquaintances who: (check as many that apply)
   _____ never use drugs
   _____ sometimes use drugs
   _____ always use drugs
   _____ are addicted to drugs

5. About how many hours of television do you watch each day? (circle one)
   0–1 hours   1–2 hours   2–4 hours   more than 4 hours

6. To which commercials do you pay attention?
   _____ food commercials   _____ funny commercials
   _____ commercials with good music   _____ commercials about products I use
   _____ commercials with kids   _____ commercials about products I like
   _____ sports commercials   _____ other (please give an example below)

7. I am now ____ years old.

8. My sex is: (please circle)   male   female

9. I live in the _____ neighborhood. (give name)

10. My race is: black   white   Hispanic   Asian   other _____
    (please circle)   (please specify)

EXHIBIT 4 Screening Questionnaire Tally for 10 to 13-Year-Olds (80 respondents)

Street Violence

	Not Concerned	Moderately Concerned	Very Concerned
Boys	4	4	38
Girls	6	10	18

Drug Use

	Not a Problem	Moderate Problem	Big Problem
Boys	0	0	46
Girls	0	2	32

I Know Friends or Acquaintances Who

	Never Use Drugs	Sometimes Use Drugs	Always Use Drugs	Are Addicted to Drugs
Boys	30	16	4	6
Girls	20	16	6	10

Hours of TV Watched per Day

	0–1	1–2	2–4	4+
Boys	2	12	16	16
Girls	2	10	8	10

Important Things

	Boys	Girls
Family	40	26
Job	38	22
School	24	22
Money	14	4
Sports	12	2
Friends	8	14
Good Time	8	4
Other	0	2
Music	2	0
Religion	0	6

Commercials Paid Attention to

	Boys	Girls
Sports	24	0
Funny	12	20
Kids	14	18
Food	10	8
Products I like	6	10
Music	2	12
Other	2	0
Products I use	0	6

EXHIBIT 4   *(concluded)*
Screening Questionnaire Tally for 14 to 18-Year-Olds (74 respondents)

Street Violence

	Not Concerned	*Moderately Concerned*	*Very Concerned*
Boys	0	24	16
Girls	4	12	18

Drug Use

	Not a Problem	*Moderate Problem*	*Big Problem*
Boys	0	10	30
Girls	2	0	32

I Know Friends or Acquaintances Who

	Never Use Drugs	*Sometimes Use Drugs*	*Always Use Drugs*	*Are Addicted to Drugs*
Boys	20	30	8	10
Girls	8	20	6	6

Hours of TV Watched per Day

	0–1	*1–2*	*2–4*	*4+*
Boys	6	18	12	4
Girls	0	10	14	10

Important Things

	Boys	*Girls*
Family	38	26
Job	22	24
School	14	20
Money	6	10
Sports	18	8
Friends	12	4
Good time	8	4
Other	0	0
Music	8	0
Religion	10	2

Commercials Paid Attention to

	Boys	*Girls*
Sports	22	2
Funny	20	20
Kids	8	10
Food	8	4
Products I like	4	6
Music	18	4
Other	0	4
Products I use	2	0

EXHIBIT 5   Interviewing Protocols

I. Attitudes toward the Future

What do you want to be when you grow up?

Who do you want most to be like?

Do you plan to finish school? What do you plan to do then?

Do you plan to have a family?

Do you plan to continue living in Boston?

Do you think most kids who use drugs now will still be using them when they are 25 or 30?   Why?

Do you think it is possible to (a) have a good job or (b) raise a family, if you are a drug user?

II. Impressions of Advertising

What are some products like? How important was their advertising in your decision to try/buy them?

What are some good ads? Why are they good?

Who are some spokespeople you trust on ads?

Where do you pay the most attention to ads: radio? TV? billboards? subway placards? buses? magazines? newspapers?

What is your opinion of advertisers?

Antidrug advertising in particular:

Do you ever see antidrug ads? Where? Can you think of any good ones?

Why are they good or bad?

Do you think ads ever make people stop taking drugs? Do they make people think more about stopping drug use? Why or why not?

III. Drug Awareness

How do people learn about drugs?

How do you find out what they do to you?

How do you find out where to buy them?

How do you find out whether they are dangerous?

Of the following list of drugs, which are dangerous and which are not?

Are there any you have never heard of? Which are the most popular?

Which are easiest to get? Which are best?

When does someone have a drug problem—at what usage level?

IV. Motivations for Drug Use

What does using drugs mean to you?

Why do people first use drugs?

Why do people keep using drugs?

Why do people use more and more drugs? or more dangerous drugs?

Do you know anyone who has stopped using drugs—why? Or why do you think people would stop?

Is there any difference between kids who do and don't use drugs?

Why do people get high at parties? Why do they get high all day?

Are there any drawbacks to being high? What are they?

Have you ever seen people lose control? How do you feel about that?

Can you think of anything that, if drug users knew it or were convinced of it, would make them stop using?

What are some fun things to do besides getting high? Do many people do those things?

V. Influences on Actions/Opinions

Who do you talk to about your problems? Who would you go to if you had a drug problem?

Who advises/teaches you about drugs?

Who has an influence on your opinions—peers? parents? sports figures or other heroes? older siblings? pushers?

EXHIBIT 6   Focus Group Summaries

Dorchester Boys, ages 10–13
Roxbury Boys, ages 10–13

1. Kids are aware of the drug problem; they see it all around, know people who use drugs, where they do drugs, and what drugs look like.

    "I see them everywhere. They have needle marks on their arms and legs. They carry briefcases around with cocaine and crack. They even stuff it in their hats."
    "In my school lots of people do it in the bathroom. What are you supposed to do when they ask if you want some?"
    "In my house, right in my hallway, they have people that sell drugs. People hang around trying to sell drugs to each other."
    "All those basketball players do it. They have the money."

2. They think people do drugs because they're messed up or because friends are doing them.

    "In my school, it's kids who have nothing else to do, or with problems at home."
    "It's like, you want to show off in front of your friends."
    "Like if Robert was starting drugs, I would do it. But if Robert did it for real, I wouldn't do it anymore."

3. Kids listen to family members' opinions about drugs.

    "Like, if my brother told me drugs were bad, I'd believe him."
    "I'd tell my mother if I saw people doing drugs around me. She'd yell at 'em."
    "First you tell their mother, then you go call the Drug Hotline."
    "Yeah, but what if the mother knows they're doing it, and the mother is doing it, too?"

4. Kids know adults or relatives who are heavy drug users.

    "My older brother plays basketball a lot, but he does drugs, too."
    "My stepfather does drugs. Crack is all over the place. I worry about him."
    "I know this kid who knew another kid, and his mother was on drugs. And he tricked her and said that it was her birthday and that he was taking her out to go give her a party. But it wasn't really her birthday and when she got up he took her to a drug place to help her."

5. Education programs generated a high level of recall.

    "We had a policeman come into school and talk to us about drugs. And he listened to our ideas and talked with us for a while."
    "In school we saw movies about what drugs do. It told a story about this boy taking crack and he dies."
    "Yeah, we have a police guy who teaches us about drugs and stuff. Yeah, I liked it a lot."

Note
The kids were all talking at once, particularly when asked to tell personal experiences with drug use.

EXHIBIT 7   Charlestown Girls, Ages 10–13

1. What do you want to do when you grow up?

   "I want to be a fashion designer. I buy all the magazines, *Vogue*, stuff like that."
   "Have a family—lots of kids."
   "Be a teacher, and help people learn things."

2. Why do people do drugs?

   "To go along with their friends, you know, it's like, let's get high."
   "To forget your problems. Like if you're mad at your parents."
   "Because they have no one to talk to about people hasslin' them and they want to forget."

3. How would you treat a friend who does drugs?

   "I'd tell them to stop because it affects your brain."
   "If they're really addicted, they can't do it themselves. You have to help them help themselves."
   "I'd just walk away from her. She ain't no friend of mine, gettin' in stuff like that. Besides, I wouldn't want to get in a fight with her about it."

4. What's your opinion of drug advertising on TV?

   " 'Take me out of the ballgame' was scary. Like that could happen."
   "When they use movie stars, it's not believable, because you read about them taking drugs in all the magazines, and then the next day they're on TV telling you not to do it."
   "If they had kids on, instead of movie stars, I'd listen as long as it's not a stupid commercial, like the guy in the clouds, and people are pushing pills down his throat. It's not real."
   "Music helps you remember the message, like with Burger King or Pepsi. But when it's adults just yapping at you, I tune out. Who cares what they think? They don't know about my problems."
   "I listen to Talkabout Radio, where you call up and talk with other kids. No one has to know who you are."
   "Commercials always get it wrong—like the one with the guy in a dark hallway and someone tries to sell him drugs, and the word 'No' keeps echoing. People don't try to sell you drugs in places like that. They're people you know just trying to make a fast buck. And the echoing stuff was dumb."

5. What do you do for fun?

   "We go swimming. Or shopping at Faneuil Hall, or the Somerville Mall."
   "We hang out at the boys and girls' clubs. It costs $8 to join and they have game rooms."
   "Go to the movies."

6. Do lots of kids your age do drugs?

   "Yeah, a lot."
   "You can get people to buy you liquor pretty easily. And I know where to get joints."
   "Lots of people don't do drugs, though. Some are normal, some are nerds."
   "Like, some of my friends pretend they do 'em if people ask, but they really don't. They just want to seem cool."

7. Whom do you trust to talk to?

   "My older sister. She can keep a secret. She was the same as me when she was younger."
   "You can trust your friends. But sometimes I don't tell them everything. I don't want people to tell me what to do."
   "I talk to my friends on the phone—all the time!"

Notes

Many girls mentioned using the Teenline, a for-profit party line, as a recreational activity. Their parents get mad when large phone bills arrive.

EXHIBIT 8   Mission Hill Boys, Ages 10–13

1. Boys avoid family members or strangers with drug problems.

   "If I saw someone with drugs, I'd walk away. I don't want to get hassled, or shot at for my money."

   "Why get hit? Like, if I tried to tell my older brother to stop, he'd smack me around and tell me to mind my own business. Then he'd go in his room and lock the door like he always does."

2. People do drugs because they have nothing else in their lives.

   "Some kids I know are just bored. They don't get no attention at home, and they're just curious about what drugs will do."

   "Real addicts are no good. They're drop-outs who don't want to learn anything or do anything with their lives."

3. What works to keep people off drugs?

   "You have to scare them. Like arrest them and throw them in jail. They won't like that."

   "Tell people that drugs hurt you, make you die. Then they'll figure it out for themselves not to do drugs."

   "I don't pay attention to advertising about drugs. It's just a bunch of adults telling you what to do. I don't have to listen to that."

   "You gotta hear it from other people you know, like your friends, people like yourself."

   "We had a talk with a drug specialist, a policeman, who told us what'll happen to you. And he wasn't making it up, either."

   "I saw this movie where this guy did a lot of drugs and he got into all this bad stuff like robbing people and getting shot. Then he died."

Note

In this neighborhood, selling drugs for profit is more of a problem than regular drug usage.

EXHIBIT 9 Mission Hill Girls, Ages 10–13

1. Why do people do drugs?

   "It makes you happier, for five minutes anyway, if you're mad or bored."
   "Drugs are only bad all the time. Once in a while to try it is okay."
   "Because there's nothing else to do!"
   "I don't know. What do you think?"

2. What are some bad things about drugs?

   "They make you act gross, you get all sweaty and itchy."
   "It makes you want to steal things for the money."
   "It makes you hate your parents and steal from them."

3. Who influences you about drugs and other things?

   "My mother. She tells me stories about drugs users, like my aunt, and she says, 'If you were her daughter, you'd be dead already.'"
   "My mom tells me stuff, like don't hold drugs for your friends, because the police won't believe you."
   "My grandmother. She spoils me and helps me with school."
   "Some school counselors are good. They listen to you and get you jobs and stuff. But others are just nosy and hassle you."
   "People I talk to; my friends tell me stuff, and I tell them stuff."

4. What do you do for fun?

   "I hang out at the Dedham Mall with my friends."
   "We go roller-skating or bowling or out for a hamburger."
   "We listen to WILD and KISS 108. And we call in our favorite songs and enter the phone-in contests."
   "I watch TV or read magazines—like *Teen Beat, Fresh*."

5. What would you do if you had a friend who did drugs?

   "I'd leave them alone or stay away."
   "You can't say anything to their family, because the friend would find out and get mad and beat you up."
   "If a girl had a straight boyfriend who found out she did drugs, he'd quit her. I know someone that happened to."

6. What do you think would work to keep kids off drugs?

   "More discussions like this, where we could talk about our feelings."
   "Clean up the neighborhoods, get rid of the pushers."
   "Give people something to do, a job, a place to hang."
   "Put shows on TV about drugs. With kids, like us."
   "Tell people what drugs do to you. How they mess you up."

Notes

From many of their comments, it seemed clear that the girls were speaking about drugs from personal experience, their own or close friends' or relatives'. They talked for almost two hours and loved the idea that someone was listening to their opinions.

EXHIBIT 10   Dorchester Boys, Ages 14–18

1. Older children are a big influence on younger siblings' drug attitudes.

> "I wouldn't beat up my younger brother; I'd just talk to him."
> "It depends on the neighborhood. If you live in a real bad drug neighborhood, you're gonna start when you're young. I know girls and boys who are, like, eight and nine years old who are smoking already and drinking."
> "They get it from older brothers and uncles, stuff like that. When they've got an 18-year-old uncle, they say, well, he's doing it, so why can't I."
> "Kids look up to their older brothers.' Cause they think, 'Hey, he knows what he's talking about.' "

2. Doing drugs or getting drunk on weekends was not necessarily bad. Sometimes adults will purchase liquor for them.

> "Like my brother, he's my age, he just does 'caine once in a while. He's not addicted."
> "You gotta get somebody to buy the beer for you, like a liquor store cop—it'd be about two dollars."

3. Drugs are so prevalent that going to any corner with $20 will get you some.

> "The pushers take it up to the bus stop in the morning."
> "You see pushers every day. You know them."
> "Like yesterday I was in this store with my mother, and this dude walks in and has a paper with the daily number, and he just pulled it out and went (sniffing), and I was like, oh brother!"
> "Doing drugs is like something to do when you ain't got nothing to do."

4. Peer pressure to do drugs is high.

> "A lot of people know a lot of friends that do drugs, and then their friends say, 'What are you, yellow? Why don't you just do this with me? It ain't gonna hurt.' So they say, well, I guess I'll go do it with him. But if I know someone who wants to get high every time I walk, he ain't gonna be my friend."
> "They don't force you. They just pass it to you. If you don't take it, they just say, give me your share!"
> "The way they probably started was smoking weed and then they wanted something stronger, so they started 'caine. And after 'caine, they want to try something more strong."

5. However, doing a lot of drugs is perceived as stupid.

> "Cocaine is only a 15-minute high. Not worth it."
> "Once you blow your money on it, then you want to go and get some more money, and it just keeps you going around and around."

6. Being addicted to drugs presents a financial problem.

> "Every time they use it, they've got to go out and get money. All they think about is what time it is."
> "I used to hang with this kid, and he was doing it for about a year. He tried to hide it, but then he starts asking me for money."
> "The way they started out, they probably could've been selling for somebody."

7. If a friend gets into drugs, they'll avoid that person.

> "Stay away from me. Go hang out with Crazy Jane (cocaine)!"
> "I'd say, you walk this way, I'll walk that way."
> "We try to calm them down, but we get rid of them when they start getting on our nerves."
> "It's their business, it's their body."

8. This age group reacts to radio and direct mail advertising.

> "People listen to music, they listen to a good song that they like."
> "If it's a real rapper, not some stupid guy faking it, people would listen. Like on 104.9 FM."
> "I read my mail, if it's just one page. I check it out. You get a good deal on stuff from *Newsweek*."
> "I wouldn't pay attention to no adults. They all sound alike. Just trying to tell you how to run your life. Hey, it ain't none of their business!"

9. If treated like adults, kids are more likely to listen.

> "Our teacher, he goes right to the point. Drugs ain't healthy. He didn't waste no time, he went right into it."
> "You know what works, those documentaries when they show people getting killed doing it. That shakes people up. But they won't show drug movies in school. They say it ain't appropriate."
> "If you do a commercial, don't tell them, 'don't do drugs.' Show them how it's really done on the street, what it really does."
> "Yeah, and what causes it. Not just like, 'don't do drugs.' If somebody wants to do drugs, they're gonna be saying, 'Don't tell me don't do drugs.' But if you show them what really happens to you, they'll pay attention."
> "Make them think, I don't want to end up like that! To reach kids, you gotta use kids. That's it."

Notes

This focus group took place on the Harvard Business School campus because gang turf battles made the local center an unsafe meeting place. The discussion lasted two hours.

EXHIBIT 11   Charlestown Boys, Ages 14–18

1. Why do drugs?

   "It's something to do. You know, when you're bored."
   "It makes you seem cool."
   "What else is there to do around here?"

2. Who do you know who does drugs?

   "Lots of athletes, man. Like boxers, basketball players."
   "I know cops who do drugs. And I have an uncle who's an alcoholic."

3. How do you treat a friend who does drugs?

   "I don't say anything. It's their problem."
   "If it was my girlfriend, I'd tell her to stop, or else break up."
   "I stop calling them. They ain't my friend no more."

4. What do drugs do to you?

   "They mess you up. You could die. I know people who OD'd."
   "Gets in the way. You can't do the things you want to."
   "Crack, dust, coke, they're bad for you. Valium, grass, beer, they're okay to do."

5. Whom do you admire?

   "My mom, she works so hard for us."
   "The sports director at our community center, he helps us a lot."
   "My dad, my uncle."

6. What do you like to do for fun?

   "Hang out with my friends."
   "Watch TV, listen to KISS 108."
   "Me and the guys, we go shopping on the corner, downtown, hang out."

7. What do you think is a good way to convince kids not to use drugs?

   "Get other kids to tell 'em about it, what happens to you."
   "Show them that there's more in life than that; it's an escape."
   "Give 'em other ways to make a buck—job training and programs."
   "Kill the pushers. That'll scare people off."
   "You need alternatives to fill the day, give you a plan."

Note
Recall of antidrug advertising was nonexistent.

EXHIBIT 12   Roxbury Girls, Ages 14–18

1. Why do people do drugs?

"If they've got problems, you know, like with school or their parents."

"Some parents push kids. It's cool in some families to smoke a joint every once in a while. Or they get their kids to sell them. And lots of parents take pills to relax and stuff."

"Sometimes you're just used to doing it, and it's too late to change."

"Everyone does it. Not just street people or low-class people, but people who have money, like businessmen, or society people at clubs."

2. Why shouldn't people do drugs?

"If you have goals, it will pull you down and make you nothing."

"It ruins your body. Your face puffs up and you get all ugly."

"My mom would kill me. She'd be so embarrassed and upset. I wouldn't be able to look her in the eye anymore."

"It's a waste of time. You spend all this money and what do you have to show for it?"

3. What would help people not do drugs?

"Lots of programs, in school, at all grade levels. Start early telling little kids about the dangers."

"We need recreation centers around here, more stuff to do."

"Like if there were a place you could go and just talk about your problems, that would be great. Not formal or anything. Just if you wanted to."

"Parents should be more aware of what their kids are doing."

"These kinds of discussion groups are great. You have to be able to talk about your problems. Billboards don't do anything. And those people on them probably do drugs, anyway."

"Show me REALITY. That gets through. Show a family breaking up or something. The networks are afraid to show that stuff on TV. Like Richard Pryor getting burned from freebasing."

"Don't hang with a bad crowd. Stay busy, find a talent or sport."

Notes

From the comments, this group appeared to have personal experience with drug use. The girls did not think that advertising would be effective in preventing drug use.

EXHIBIT 13   **Mission Hill Girls, Ages 14–18**

1. Drug use is related to self-esteem

   "You're smart if you don't do drugs. You're dumb to risk your life on it, waste your money and everything."

   "A guy in my class, he got kicked out of school for doing crack. He's gonna end up dying or drop dead in the street one of these days. When the teachers tried to tell him, he didn't care about getting an education. Everyone tried to tell him."

   "If someone sat with them to see how they feel, maybe that would change their life."

2. Drug use is related to boredom, and emotional pressure.

   "You could have a little center down here, and have people come to talk if they have problems at home, work it out."

   "If my friends and me are busy, we don't even think about doing any."

   "Some people don't have anyone to talk to about things, and nothing to do except get high."

3. Girls are concerned about their neighborhoods. They relate this to drugs.

   "You can't live in peace here. You're always in a fight, or you can get hit by a car or robbed by a junkie."

   "People get killed over drugs around here. And in school they sell drugs everywhere, in the hallways. They fight over them."

   "At Mission Park, they had a clean-up day, and they gave us rakes, towels, gloves for our hands. And then we just cleaned up, got the graffiti off the walls, moved the junkies."

   "People should stop being dirty and leaving stuff in the hallways. Find a trashcan."

4. They think that almost everyone does drugs.

   "Drug dealers make one person do it, and then they try to make the next person do it, too. Monkey see, monkey do."

   "They do what their friends did, and they try it out and get used to it."

   "Around here, everybody's tried them, at least."

5. Kids think adults are part of the problem.

   "Too much attention is putting it on the kids, the teenagers, because they ain't the only ones doing it. Hey, those grownups out there do the same thing, and they just slap it on the kids."

   "Like the grownups come home with their problems, and start hitting you and that makes you want to go out and do something to feel better."

   "These people think they know everything. Like, having famous people telling you what to do on TV. Big deal. They're just getting paid to say it."

Note

Most of the group was very talkative, particularly on the subject of drug use being related to boredom or lack of goals.

EXHIBIT 14   **Concepts Mentioned Most Frequently in Focus Groups
(by number of mentions)**

	10–13- Year-Olds	14–18- Year-Olds
Advertising Themes		
1. Attitudes toward celebrities	4	3
2. Use of teenagers	3	3
3. Use of rules	4	4
4. Storytelling	7	4
5. Role of realism	3	5
6. Feelings about family	10	11
7. Presenting strategies	4	5
8. Questioning behavior	5	6
9. Talking heads	2	—
Community Programs		
1. Discussion groups	4	4
2. Recreational activities	4	11
3. SPECDA	3	2
4. Work with neighborhood	—	3
5. Educational movies	3	1

ARCHDIOCESE OF NEW YORK

Father Terence Attridge, director of vocations of the Catholic Archdiocese of New York, was reviewing the results of a 13-week advertising campaign during the winter of 1973–74. The campaign had been intended to improve the image of the priesthood and thereby to encourage vocations (i.e., young men entering training for the priesthood). The campaign was believed to be the first of its kind in the United States and, as such, Father Attridge and other archdiocesan officials were interested in assessing the impacts of the campaign to determine whether it should be extended, amended, or discontinued.

Priest Training in the Archdiocese

The Catholic Archdiocese of New York incorporated 398 parishes, which served a population of almost 2 million Catholics. Details on the percentage of Catholics in the total population, and on the number of religious personnel working in the archdiocese appear in Exhibit 1.

This case was prepared by Professors Stephen A. Greyser and John A. Quelch.
Copyright © 1978 by the President and Fellows of Harvard College.
Harvard Business School case 9-579-123 (Rev. 7/2/91).

Through its educational institutions the archdiocesan administration aimed to provide a steady flow of qualified priests to assume responsibilities within the archdiocese. There were three educational institutions through which the majority of candidates for the priesthood characteristically passed in sequence. Cathedral Preparatory School provided students of high school age with a four-year college preparatory education. Cathedral College of the Immaculate Conception offered a four-year liberal arts college education. Graduates of Cathedral College could enter St. Joseph's Seminary, a four-year professional school of theology. The average age of students entering the seminary was 25 years. Data on the number of entering freshmen at these three institutions in recent years are presented in Exhibit 2. Like many other religious denominations, the Catholic Church in general and the Archdiocese of New York, in particular, were finding it harder to attract a sufficient number of qualified applicants.

Development of the Pilot Campaign

The Catholic Archdiocese of New York was concerned that the image of the priesthood seemed to have declined over recent years. It was believed that this decline partially resulted from a lack of definition and understanding of the role of the priest and the challenge of the priesthood in modern society.

Traditionally, vocational appeals to potential candidates for the priesthood were limited to diocesan school programs with local parish support. Young men were influenced to train for the priesthood primarily by individual priests in their schools or parishes. By 1973, recruitment of priests had fallen to a level that was considered critical by diocesan officials. The Archdiocesan Advocation Committee decided that a mass media advertising campaign, although unlikely to increase recruitment of candidates for the priesthood per se, might be able to increase awareness of the priest's role in society and improve attitudes toward the priesthood, and, thus, over time exert a favorable impact upon recruitment levels.

The primary audience for such a campaign was defined as young Catholic men of high school and college age attending either Catholic or public schools. In addition, it was believed that the advertising campaign could reach the parents of these young men; the parents were defined as constituting a secondary audience in light of their potential influence in a vocational decision.

The novelty lay in using all the elements of a mass media advertising campaign. Thus, the committee concluded that time and effort should be invested both in pretesting the ads and in monitoring the campaign results. There was a possibility that the campaign, if successful, might become the basis of a national advertising program; in such a case, measurements of the advertising effectiveness of the New York archdiocese pilot campaign would be particularly valuable. Whether or not any national program materialized, the Advocation Committee believed that assessment of the campaign's effectiveness would be necessary to justify the investment in its continuation for a one-year or two-year period even within the New York archdiocese. Committee members believed that the campaign would have to continue for this length of time if favorable awareness and attitude shifts were eventually going to be translated into increased recruitment to the priesthood.

Consequently, it was decided that the campaign should be introduced on a test basis in five areas of the New York archdiocese that were representative of the social, economic, and ethnic profile of the archdiocese as a whole.

Area 1	Upper Manhattan/West Bronx
Area 2	Staten Island
Area 3	Rockland County
Area 4	Lower Westchester
Area 5	South Bronx

Funding for the campaign was raised privately. Archdiocesan funds were not used. A budget of $100,000 was set, allowing $77,500 for media purchase, $9,500 for research, $5,000 for promotion and publicity, and $8,000 for production. The archdiocese was able to draw on the advice of the Advocation Committee, consisting of professional Catholic laymen who specialized in various aspects of the advertising function and whose voluntary efforts developed the campaign. To provide objectivity an independent market research firm, Penthouse U, conducted pretesting and posttesting as well as the initial focus group interviews.

Advertising Content

The Advocation Committee's creative group developed the campaign theme "The New York Priest—God knows what he does for a living." The creative committee decided that the campaign should center on the variety of roles and challenges facing individual priests. Hence, interviews with selected archdiocesan priests were conducted. Prototype print advertisements were developed, describing the work of six individual priests. The five advertisements that were subsequently used in the campaign are presented in Exhibits 3–7, as modified in light of the focus group interviews with Catholic boys and parents (described below).

Focus group interviews were conducted to serve a twofold purpose:

1. To secure information on negative attitudes toward the priesthood, which would serve as a frame of reference in which to assess the reactions to the advertisements, both in the focus groups and in subsequent research.
2. To elicit reactions toward the concept of a diocesan vocational advertising campaign generally, and toward specific prototype advertisements. In particular, these interviews were designed to:
   a. Obtain critical reactions to the advertisements and an indication of the degree to which the main and subsidiary copy ideas were communicated.
   b. Test for the presence of negatives (if any) toward the proposed advertising.
   c. Provide guidelines for the language to be used in attitudinal statements, which would constitute the basic measuring tool for subsequent evaluation of the campaign's effectiveness.

Four focus group interview sessions were conducted with groups of 9 to 11 participants in October 1973. The composition of the four groups was as follows:

Group	
1	Catholic high school boys
2	Catholic college boys
3	Mothers of Catholic boys in high school or college
4	Fathers of Catholic boys in high school or college

The interviews indicated that the major influences upon the vocational choice of the primary target group were teachers and priests, rather than parents. Parents apparently believed that their sons *think* that they know what they want to do and that they resent any parental interference. A summary of the principal negative reactions toward priests and the Church which the interviews generated is presented in Exhibit 8. Exhibit 9 summarizes the perceived strengths and weaknesses of each of the advertisements tested. Reactions to the anticipated campaign as a whole were considered positive; especially appealing was the complementary nature of the advertisements, each showing different aspects of the priesthood.

Media Strategy

Two media objectives were set for the five test areas:

1. Reach 80 percent or more of the adult population in each area. The planning group considered this level of net reach to be warranted to ensure adequate coverage of the Catholic population segments key to this campaign, for which segments no adequate coverage data existed.

2. Reach this percentage of the population with a frequency of at least five advertising messages during the campaign. It was decided that this frequency level was necessary if the diversity of roles undertaken by priests was to be conveyed.

Print media were selected for the campaign, because the "case history" nature of the advertisements was considered to be so complex that broadcast media, with their time limitations would be insufficient to the informational task. In addition, print media provided coverage coinciding more closely with the geographic boundaries of the five test areas. Fewer advertising impressions, therefore, would be "wasted" in the test phase.

The newspaper advertising schedule aimed to achieve broad reach and frequency of the target groups through 10 black-and-white insertions in local daily newspapers (such as the *Staten Island Advance*), in the archdiocese's own weekly *Catholic News*, and in special editions of the *New York Daily News* (Westchester, Manhattan, and Manhattan–Bronx editions). The newspaper media schedule for the campaign is presented in Exhibit 10. Advertising space in special editions of major national magazines also was available in one area (Westchester County). Accordingly, black-and-white advertisements were placed in a combination of magazines (*Time, Newsweek, Sports Illustrated, New York,* and *U.S. News and World Report*) appearing in the special Westchester County editions with an average individual magazine circulation of 97,700 copies.

The pilot campaign lasted over a 13-week period and had a potential gross total of 55 million advertising impressions. Of these, 41 million were adult impressions and 14 million were impressions to teenagers (13–19 years of age).

Beyond media advertising, the campaign also included promotion and publicity efforts conducted through the Archdiocesan Office of Communication. The pastors of parishes in the five test areas were supplied with publicity kits, including poster reprints of the advertisements for prospective display in church vestibules, schools, and retail stores. In addition to these efforts to obtain extra impressions on the audience, pulpit announcements were encouraged. Also, the campaign received extensive media publicity in New York City.

Measurement of Campaign Effectiveness

Following the campaign, research was undertaken to determine the impact which the New York Priest campaign had on its primary and secondary audiences. Specifically, the study aimed to identify:

- The levels of recall achieved by the advertising.
- Changes in attitudes toward the priesthood generated by the campaign.
- Specific strengths and weaknesses of the advertising.
- Population segments to which the advertising campaign appealed to a greater or lesser degree.

To accomplish these research objectives, a two-phase research design was used. Wave I consisted of 441 telephone interviews conducted in the five selected areas of the Metropolitan New York City region prior to the campaign. This part of the study provided "normal" levels of awareness and attitudes toward the priesthood. Wave II consisted of 443 telephone interviews conducted at the conclusion of the campaign. There was no overlapping of respondents between the two research phases. The sample was generated through the cooperation of priests of the parishes in the five test areas who provided the names and telephone numbers of parishioners who had young sons. The overall sample was skewed toward the primary target (489 young men); it also included a roughly balanced number of fathers (178) and mothers (217). A breakdown of each wave of the interview sample by target group membership and location of residence is present in Exhibit 11.

In Wave I, respondents were asked to express their agreement or disagreement with each of 13 attitude statements regarding the priesthood. Results confirmed the expectations of the researchers that the primary prospects (young men themselves) less frequently expressed favorable attitudes toward the priesthood than did secondary prospects (parents). Attitudes did not vary significantly according to ethnic groups.

After 13 weeks of advertising the New York Priest campaign, the second wave of interviews was conducted to determine levels of advertising recall and changes in attitudes brought about by the advertisements.

Exhibit 12 reports levels of recall for the campaign. Generally, recall of the campaign was highest among mothers, among Catholic school students, and among families classified as religious in culture.[1] Working young men were significantly below other primary prospect respondents in advertising recall. Lower recall levels were evident among the lower socioeconomic classes. This was not considered surprising, in that these groups were believed to show generally lower recall levels for *any* kind of advertising campaign. Recall levels were also lower among families of foreign stock and among respondents residing in the South Bronx.

As shown in Exhibit 13, the visual impact of the advertising campaign emerged as the major stimulus for advertising recall. The second most memorable element of the campaign appeared to be the diversity of jobs that defined the modern priesthood.

Exhibit 14 presents data on the main points of the advertising recalled by respondents. Primary prospects demonstrated a lower level of advertising recall and also a lower ability than did the secondary prospects to communicate the main points of the campaign. Residents of the South Bronx, along with families of foreign stock, were less able to recall that the main point of the advertising campaign was to generate interest among young men to enter priesthood. They did, however, recognize the social commitment that priests display in their work.

Beyond general advertising recall, the committee was particularly interested in the basic attitudinal shifts generated by this campaign and among which population segments they occurred. Exhibits 15–19 present the percentages of respondents from both Wave I and Wave II of the

research study who agreed with the 13 attitude statements regarding the priesthood. These data are broken down by target group membership, degree of religious culture, ethnicity, and residence. It appeared that the most noticeable attitude shifts took place within the "religious culture" segment.

Campaign Evaluation

The Advocation Committee was aware that an evaluation of the test results should take account of the variations in the weight of the media advertising among the five areas. For example, it had been possible to use magazines only in the Westchester area. The employment of promotion and publicity techniques in addition to advertising increased the difficulty of factoring out the contribution of advertising alone to the attitudinal shifts that had occurred. And the budgetary constraints that limited the duration of the campaign prevented any assessment of how effectively such attitudinal shifts as did result from the advertising might be translated into raising the level of recruitment of priests at a later date.

Nevertheless, the results suggested to the Advocation Committee that, regardless of primary or secondary audience, geographical locale, ethnic background, Catholic or secular persuasion, respondents were impressed with the campaign. This was particularly so for respondents in the "religious culture" group; with this group positive, statistically significant attitudinal shifts were achieved on 10 of the 13 basic attitudinal statements.

The committee had to decide whether to recommend a second phase campaign in the five test areas (perhaps geared specifically to religious culture families), an extension of the campaign to other areas of the New York archdiocese, and/or consideration of a national campaign along the same lines. If a continuation of the campaign were to be approved, a further decision had to be made on whether to use the same copy and media strategies, or to modify either or both.

---

[1]Classification as "religious culture" or "nonreligious culture" depended upon four criteria: whether family members belonged to a parish society, whether they could name a parish priest, whether they had been visited by a priest, and whether they said "Grace."

Exhibit 1   Archdiocesan Church Membership and Personnel

Total population (1970 U.S. Census)	5,124,853
Estimated number of Catholics (1970)	1,880,788
Number of parishes	398
Priests:[a]	
Diocesan	911
Religious order	897
Religious:[a]	
Brothers	832
Sisters	7,014

NOTE: The Brooklyn area was not part of the New York archdiocese.

[a]From *1975 Catholic Telephone Guide (The Catholic News)*.

Exhibit 2   Numbers of Entering Freshman in Archdiocesan Educational Institutions

Year	Cathedral Prep	Cathedral College	St. Joseph's Seminary
1970	45	17	22
1971	48	12	13
1972	39	22	15
1973	38	16	13

EXHIBIT 3

*Campaign print
advertisement*

Father Patrick Dunne has had five jobs in the last three years—all at the same time.

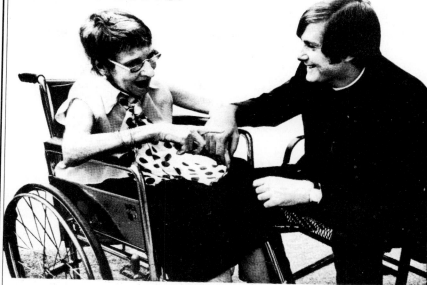

Patrick Dunne is a parish priest. Which also makes him a social worker, a youth counselor, a teacher, a spiritual adviser and a comforter of the sick.

The place in the North Bronx where Patrick Dunne works is called St. Gabriel's Church. It's not really a church because they didn't have enough money to build one. But there's a grammar school and that's where he celebrates Mass.

In the course of his six-day week he might take a call from somebody having a nervous breakdown. Or talk to the police about a kid in trouble. Or try to straighten out a dispute between a husband and wife.

He also runs an adult education program, a basketball league, and a teen-age center. Then there's the five classes a week he teaches in the grammar school. Plus his job as chaplain at a home for the terminally ill.

"You've got to be prepared for everything," he says of his job. "You're the one who has to field so many questions for which there are no answers. Whatever I need, I always hope God gives it to me on the spot."

You have to do a job like that for love. You'd be crazy to do it just for money.

But there is so much more work to do in the New York Archdiocese—and too few priests. Could you do what Patrick Dunne is doing? Have you ever thought about it? There's a phone number where you can reach him. Just dial P-R-I-E-S-T-S (774-3787). Or write: PRIESTS, 555 West End Avenue, New York, N.Y. 10024.

He'll be happy to talk to you about his vocation. And yours too.

THE NEW YORK PRIEST. GOD KNOWS WHAT HE DOES FOR A LIVING.

Father Emerson Moore. And the miracles on 134th Street.

Harlem's Joseph P. Kennedy Center is where over 700 people go when there's no place else to turn.

There's day-care if you're very small. Sports and social activities if you're bigger. Counseling if you're troubled. Company if you're old and lonely.

There's also never enough money, too few staff workers, a shortage of equipment, and not enough time.

And there's Emerson Moore. He's the Catholic priest who runs the Center, concentrating on your average, everyday kind of miracles. Nothing spectacular.

Instead of parting the waters, he may try to keep a family together. Instead of raising the dead, he may help teach a kid a new life.

As if that weren't enough, he also works in a nearby Catholic Charities office and performs other priestly duties at the parish house where he lives.

In other words, after celebrating daily Mass, he starts work at nine in the morning and finishes up at ten at night. Six hard-to-believe days a week.

And just to keep in shape, he plans to start work soon on a degree in psychology to back up his master's in public administration.

How does he do it? Easy. Besides having the constitution and serenity of a rock, he has his own personal miracle going for him. His priesthood.

And that's what makes Emerson Moore do for love what he could never do for money.

But there's so much more work to do in the New York Archdiocese—and too few priests. Could you do what Emerson Moore is doing? Have you ever thought about it? There's a phone number where you can reach him. Just dial P-R-I-E-S-T-S (774-3787). Or write: PRIESTS, 555 West End Avenue, New York, N.Y. 10024.

He'll be happy to talk to you about his vocation. And yours too.

THE NEW YORK PRIEST. GOD KNOWS WHAT HE DOES FOR A LIVING.

EXHIBIT 5

Campaign print advertisement

Father Neil Connolly isn't out to change the world. Just the South Bronx.

Neil Connolly was assigned to St. Athanasius Church on Tiffany Street shortly after he was ordained. It's a neighborhood most people leave as soon as they can.

He's been there for 15 years.

"I can't really say we're changing things," he admits. "But I think we're a sign of hope, or at least support. And that's very important."

The people he serves are mostly Latins, which he isn't, and poor, which he is. And Neil's work isn't just in church, but out on the streets where the big problems are.

There are spiritual problems, of course. And welfare problems, housing problems, immigration problems, drug problems.

In fact, he and the other three Catholic priests in the parish share most of the problems of over 2500 church-goers. Plus countless others who maybe don't go to church, but don't get turned away either.

There's also a storefront church where he celebrates Sunday Mass to help make Christ's presence more visible in the neighborhood.

It's obvious that whatever Neil Connolly does he does for love, not money.

But there's so much more work to do in the New York Archdiocese—and too few priests. Could you do what Neil Connolly is doing? Have you ever thought about it? There's a phone number where you can reach him. Just dial P-R-I-E-S-T-S (774-3787). Or write: PRIESTS, 555 West End Avenue, New York, N.Y. 10024.

He'll be happy to talk to you, in Spanish or English, about his vocation. And yours too.

THE NEW YORK PRIEST.
GOD KNOWS WHAT HE DOES FOR A LIVING.

EXHIBIT 6
*Campaign print
advertisement*

Father John O'Leary.

If he's not in church, he's probably in jail.

He was put in for good behavior.

His work as a counselor to
high school youths brought him to
the attention of Catholic authorities
when they needed a new chaplain for
the Manhattan House of Detention.
(You may have heard it referred to as
"The Tombs.")

So several months ago,
John O'Leary's world changed from
classrooms to cell blocks.

His 'flock' is an ever-changing
group of 1400 men who are waiting for
trial or sentencing. They're packed in,
two men to a cell barely big enough
for one, and from where they sit God
can seem to be very far away.

But what can one priest do?

A prisoner put it pretty well: "He brings
you your freedom." It's that simple and
that complicated. It's exactly what Christ
brought to a world of prisoners 2000
years ago.

At first glance, the dedicated
social workers and psychologists
at The Tombs might seem to be doing
the same work. But what makes
John O'Leary special in the eyes of
many of the men is his priesthood.

It's both the outward sign of
commitment and the inward source of
strength he uses to do a difficult job.

The kind of job you do for love,
not for money.

But there's so much more work to do
in the New York Archdiocese—and
too few priests. Could you do what
John O'Leary does? Have you ever
thought about it? There's a phone
number where you can reach him.
Just dial P-R-I-E-S-T-S (774-3787).
Or write: PRIESTS, 555 West End Avenue,
New York, N.Y. 10024.

He'll be happy to talk to you about
his vocation. And yours too.

THE NEW YORK PRIEST.
GOD KNOWS WHAT HE DOES FOR A LIVING.

EXHIBIT 7

Campaign print advertisement

Monsignor John Gillen has been a priest for 28 years. He's not doing it for the pension.

You're looking at a man who is hard at work.

John Gillen's most important job as a Catholic priest is to celebrate the Mass. When he does that, he celebrates the presence of God in the world.

And if he did nothing else but that, he could consider himself a success even though it takes barely an hour of his time.

But John Gillen has also accepted other duties which somewhat extend his working day. By about 11 more hours.

As pastor of Holy Spirit Church in Peekskill, he serves a congregation of over 1700 people, plus the patients of a nearby community hospital and a home for the aged and chronically ill.

He and his assistant average over 2700 visits a year to those who need them. No matter how you do the arithmetic, it all breaks down to a lot of long hours at a job that is not famous for its big paychecks.

For Monsignor Gillen the reward comes from somewhere else. "The love of God has called me to the priesthood," he says, "to praise and preach his word and give service to his people."

"A big part of the reward is in seeing the dignity and holiness of each person. I don't deal with mobs. I deal with individuals. The ministry of a parish priest is very personal and very fulfilling."

It's simply a matter of realizing that you can never do for money what you can do for love.

There's so much more work to do in the New York Archdiocese—and too few priests. Could you do what John Gillen is doing? Have you ever thought about it? There's a phone number where you can reach him. Just dial P-R-I-E-S-T-S (774-3787). Or write: PRIESTS, 555 West End Avenue, New York, N.Y. 10024.

He'll be happy to talk to you about his vocation. And yours too.

THE NEW YORK PRIEST. GOD KNOWS WHAT HE DOES FOR A LIVING.

EXHIBIT 8   **Focus Group Interviews—Summary of Negative Attitudes toward Priesthood**

- Most priests maintain too high a lifestyle.
- Most priests don't work very hard.
- Priests are not around when you need them.
- Priests don't have enough freedom and opportunity to do the type of church work they want to do.
- The childhood, home life, and family of a priest are different from those of the average family.
- A lack of communal allocation of funds between rich and poor parishes.
- Some parents blame priests for their sons' general rebelliousness.

EXHIBIT 9 Weaknesses and Strengths of Individual Advertisements

The major weaknesses and strengths of each of the six ads are summarized below.

1. **Father Patrick Dunne Ad**
   Weaknesses

   • The very hard work and courage of Father Dunne were viewed as unbelievable and discouraging.

   Strengths

   • The great humaneness, warmth, and dedication, as well as the fulfillment of the priest.

2. **Father Emerson Moore Ad**
   Weaknesses

   • None.

   Strengths

   • Humanistic—showing a human being, not a super human—and the ability to broaden his knowledge by working toward an advanced degree.

3. **Father Neil Connolly Ad**
   Weaknesses

   • Disbelief that Father Connolly would really not prefer having a cathedral to a store-front church.
   • Incongruity of the statement "most of his work isn't really in church."

   Strengths

   • Down-to-earth, showing how priests help and work with the people and get personal satisfaction.
   • More religious than previous ads.

4. **Father George Valastro Ad** (Note: This advertisement was not employed in the campaign; it was based on the focus group findings.)
   Weaknesses

   • Contradiction between "all" in headline and "50 percent" in the text.
   • Childishness of the idol image.
   • Implied slur about the students *looking* like other high school students.
   • Appeals more to high school boys.

   Strengths

   • Young men, especially those who have met Father Valastro, appear to identify strongly with him and like the ad.

5. **Father John O'Leary Ad**
   Weaknesses

   • Some few found the humor ("called the Tombs by those who know and love it" and "a murderously difficult job") offensive.

   Strengths

   • Humanizing the priest yet more Christ-like in not condemning anybody.
   • Reality oriented.
   • Shows idealism appealing to young men.

6. **Monsignor John Gillen Ad**
   Weaknesses

   • 2,700 visits-a-year figure hard to believe and inconsistent with later mention of dealing with individuals.
   • Not as meaningful as the previous social, humanistic, modern church approaches.
   • Young men might not be able to relate so well to the picture of an older priest.

   Strengths

   • Some liked the stress on the Mass and spiritual aspect of the Catholic church instead of the social aspect stressed in the prior ads.

EXHIBIT 10 Newspaper Media Schedule

	Week Commencing														
	11/11/73	11/18	11/25	12/02	12/09	12/16	12/23	12/30	1/6/74	1/13	1/20	1/27	2/03	2/10	2/17
Westchester–Rockland newspapers		G	M	C	L				D	M		L	D	C	G
Bronxville Review Press Reporter		G	D	L	C				L	M		D	M	C	G
Staten Island Advance		D	G	C	L				M	D		C	G	L	M
Catholic News		M	L	C	D				G	D		M	C	L	G
New York Daily News:															
A. Manhattan section		M	D	C	G				L	D		G	L	M	C
B. Manhattan–Bronx section				M	L	G			D	M	C		G	L	D
C. Westchester section	C		G	C	M	L			D	C	G		D	M	L

NOTE: Letters designate advertisements used in the campaign and illustrated in Exhibits 1 through 5 (i.e., G = Gillen, M = Moore, C = Connolly, L = O'Leary, D = Dunne).

EXHIBIT 11 **Demographics of Interview Sample**

| | Prime Prospects | | Secondary Prospects | | | |
| | Young Men | | Mothers | | Fathers | |
Areas	Wave I	Wave II	I	II	I	II
Upper Manhattan/West Bronx	44	53	12	20	13	11
Staten Island	50	51	29	24	25	11
Rockland County	39	51	25	26	25	21
Lower Westchester	51	49	24	25	24	24
South Bronx	46	55	21	11	13	11
Total	230	259	111	106	100	78

EXHIBIT 12 **Advertising Recall**

Wave II Data	(Base = 100%)	Recallers
Total sample	(443)	48%
Among young men	(259)	36
Among mothers	(106)	72
Among fathers	(78)	53
Among parents whose sons are in:		
Catholic schools	(92)	67
Other schools	(92)	60
Among young men who are:		
In Catholic schools	(129)	46
In other schools	(106)	26
Working, not in school	(24)	29
Among residents of:		
Upper Manhattan/West Bronx	(84)	55
Staten Island	(86)	52
Rockland County	(98)	44
Lower Westchester	(98)	47
South Bronx	(77)	40
Ethnic groups:		
Foreign stock	(106)	44
Nonforeign stock	(337)	49
Religious culture groups:		
Religious culture families	(228)	62
Nonreligious culture families	(215)	32
Social class scale:		
I (Upper)	(28)	57
II	(55)	58
III	(121)	54
IV	(131)	44
V (Lower)	(71)	34
Undetermined	(37)	40

NOTE: Advertising recall is defined as a positive reply to a question asking respondents if they recalled seeing any advertising for the priesthood by the Archdiocese of New York, and confirmation of respondent recall with playback of visual or copy points.

EXHIBIT 13   **Recall of Content of Ads among Primary and Secondary Prospects**

(Base Is Recallers = 100%)	*Total* (211)	*Young Men* (94)	*Mothers* (76)	*Fathers* (41)
Reference to visual elements (net)	47%	40%	57%	46%
Priest visiting jail	12	11	16	7
Pictures of priests (unspecified)	9	12	4	12
Priests helping children	8	4	17	2
Priest helping old people	8	3	17	2
Priest helping underprivileged	6	4	9	2
Black priest in Harlem	4	2	9	—
Priest on steps with Puerto Rican children	3	—	5	5
Older priest	1	—	1	2
Other visual	6	7	3	12
Role diversification of priests (net)	31%	31%	41%	15%
Three jobs in one	16	19	21	—
Working in slums/ghettos	6	5	10	—
More in community than church	5	4	7	5
Missionary workers	2	4	1	—
Social workers	2	—	5	2
Older priests in parish/younger in community	1	—	4	—
All other diversified role	2	2	—	7
Priests are dedicated (net)	7%	7%	8%	2%

EXHIBIT 14   **Main Points of Advertising Recalled by Respondents**

(Base Is Recallers = 100%)	Total (211)	Young Men (94)	Mothers (76)	Fathers (41)
The Church encourages vocation (net)	43%	33%	58%	37%
The Church wants to encourage vocation (net)	25	21	32	22
Encouraging young men to enter the priesthood	18	12	26	15
Social commitment (net)	41%	33%	43%	54%
There is more to priesthood than Mass/parish duties	22	12	26	39
Priests are concerned with helping people	13	15	14	7
Priests are involved in community affairs	11	8	13	15
Other social commitment responses	6	4	9	5
Other responses				
Make public aware of priests' different jobs	7	5	8	7
They need more priests	8	7	13	—
Shows what a priest's life is like	6	6	5	5
Other mentions	17	23	8	17

(Base Is Recallers = 100%)	Upper Manhattan/ West Bronx (46)	Staten Island (45)	Rockland County (43)	Lower Westchester (46)	South Bronx (31)
The Church encourages vocation (net)	48%	42%	37%	59%	19%
The Church encourages vocation unspecified	34	20	21	39	3
Encouraging young men to be priests	13	22	16	20	16
Social commitment (net)	41%	36%	51%	33%	45%
There is more to priesthood than Mass/parish duties	20	20	33	24	13
Priests are concerned with helping people	24	11	9	2	23
Priests are involved in community affairs	9	7	16	6	23
Other social commitment responses	2	7	2	2	—
Other responses					
Make public aware of priests' different jobs	2	2	12	9	10
They need more priests	13	11	7	4	3
Shows what a priest's life is like	4	4	9	5	7
Other mentions	17	20	9	20	16

EXHIBIT 15 **Attitudes toward Priesthood before and after Advertising among Primary Prospects**

(Base = 100%)	Total		Young Men	
	Wave I (441)	*Wave II*[a] (221)	*Wave I* (230)	*Wave II*[a] (94)
Agree with Statement				
Most priests are really dedicated to their work	92%	91%	88%	84%
With the way our society is going today, we need more priests	87	92	80	90
The priesthood is an extremely challenging vocation	87	94	81	88
Most priests are kind, warm, and sympathetic	85	82	80	72
The priesthood is a rewarding life	85	91	78	85
Today's priest gets more involved in social problems than priests used to	84	91	82	87
Priests are always on hand when you need them	80	81	73	78
Most priests work very long hours	79	81	77	74
Priests today are more likely to specialize in certain fields than years ago	78	87	79	93
The most important job of the priest is to celebrate the Mass	56	54	47	39
Priests don't have enough freedom and opportunity to do the type of church work they want	47	48	51	53
The Church asks for too much money from the people	34	30	39	38
Most priests maintain too high a lifestyle	21	22	26	27

[a]Based on recallers of advertising.

EXHIBIT 16 **Attitudes toward Priesthood before and after Advertising among Secondary Prospects**

(Base = 100%)	Mothers		Fathers	
	Wave I (111)	*Wave II*[a] (76)	*Wave I* (100)	*Wave II*[a] (41)
Agree with Statement				
Most priests are really dedicated to their work	97%	97%	93%	95%
With the way our society is going today, we need more priests	96	92	91	98
The priesthood is an extremely challenging vocation	93	97	94	100
Most priests are kind, warm, and sympathetic	89	91	90	85
The priesthood is a rewarding life	96	95	90	98
Today's priest gets more involved in social problems than priests used to	90	97	82	88
Priests are always on hand when you need them	89	80	85	88
Most priests work very long hours	85	86	76	88
Priests today are more likely to specialize in certain fields than years ago	80	84	72	80
The most important job of the priest is to celebrate the Mass	75	71	54	56
Priests don't have enough freedom and opportunity to do the type of church work they want	40	49	43	37
The Church asks for too much money from the people	28	29	32	15
Most priests maintain too high a lifestyle	16	17	15	22

[a]Based on recallers of advertising.

EXHIBIT 17   Attitudes toward Priesthood before and after Advertising Related to Degree of Religious Culture

(Base = 100%)	Religious Culture		Nonreligious Culture	
	Wave I (192)	Wave II[a] (142)	Wave I (249)	Wave II[a] (69)
Agree with Statement				
Most priests are really dedicated to their work	87%	95%	95%	88%
With the way our society is going today, we need more priests	78	93	93	91
The priesthood is an extremely challenging vocation	81	96	92	88
Most priests are kind, warm, and sympathetic	83	84	86	77
The priesthood is a rewarding life	76	94	92	84
Today's priest gets more involved in social problems than priests used to	78	90	88	93
Priests are always on hand when you need them	75	84	83	74
Most priests work very long hours	77	87	80	68
Priests today are more likely to specialize in certain fields than years ago	78	87	78	87
The most important job of the priest is to celebrate the Mass	50	60	61	42
Priests don't have enough freedom and opportunity to do the type of church work they want	51	44	43	58
The Church asks for too much money from the people	46	25	26	41
Most priests maintain too high a lifestyle	22	22	20	22

[a]Based on recallers of advertising.

EXHIBIT 18   Attitudes toward Priesthood before and after Advertising Related to Ethnicity

(Base = 100%)	Foreign Stock		Nonforeign Stock	
	Wave I (94)	Wave II[a] (46)	Wave I (347)	Wave II[a] (165)
Agree with Statement				
Most priests are really dedicated to their work	96%	87%	90%	92%
With the way our society is going today, we need more priests	90	91	86	93
The priesthood is an extremely challenging vocation	83	89	88	95
Most priests are kind, warm, and sympathetic	86	80	84	82
The priesthood is a rewarding life	78	91	87	91
Today's priest gets more involved in social problems than priests used to	82	96	84	90
Priests are always on hand when you need them	77	78	80	81
Most priests work very long hours	79	83	79	81
Priests today are more likely to specialize in certain fields than years ago	81	96	77	85
The most important job of the priest is to celebrate the Mass	54	46	56	56
Priests don't have enough freedom and opportunity to do the type of church work they want	48	52	46	47
The Church asks for too much money from the people	37	41	34	27
Most priests maintain too high a lifestyle	32	33	18	19

[a]Based on recallers of advertising.

EXHIBIT 19 Attitudes toward Priesthood before and after Advertising Related to Area of Residence

(Base = 100%)	Upper Manhattan/West Bronx		Staten Island		Rockland County		Lower Westchester		South Bronx	
	Wave I (69)	Wave II[a] (46)	Wave I (104)	Wave II[a] (45)	Wave I (89)	Wave II[a] (43)	Wave I (99)	Wave II[a] (46)	Wave I (80)	Wave II[a] (31)
Agree with Statement										
Most priests are really dedicated to their work	88%	85%	88%	91%	97%	98%	93%	96%	92%	84%
With the way our society is going today, we need more priests	86	89	88	96	88	95	85	91	88	90
The priesthood is an extremely challenging vocation	87	96	90	93	87	98	87	100	82	77
Most priests are kind, warm, and sympathetic	75	74	84	84	93	93	86	80	84	74
The priesthood is a rewarding life	81	89	88	87	86	93	84	94	85	94
Today's priest gets more involved in social problems than priests used to	78	94	84	89	90	91	80	91	88	90
Priests are always on hand when you need them	70	74	79	82	85	95	83	78	79	71
Most priests work very long hours	80	76	77	82	88	88	79	80	70	77
Priests today are more likely to specialize in certain fields than years ago	80	89	78	89	72	81	78	85	82	94
The most important job of the priest is to celebrate the Mass	56	52	64	58	55	54	50	65	52	36
Priests don't have enough freedom and opportunity to do the type of church work they want	51	48	51	42	45	42	36	50	52	64
The Church asks for too much money from the people	42	24	27	36	32	28	34	28	41	39
Most priests maintain too high a lifestyle	22	17	22	18	18	19	14	22	30	42

[a] Based on recallers of advertising.

Chemical Bank: The Pronto System

In September 1983, Graham Parker and Ronald Lacey, both vice presidents of Chemical Bank, met on the 23rd floor of the New York headquarters to discuss Chemical's Pronto home banking system. Parker had worked on the Pronto system for almost three years within the Electronic Banking Division, helping to develop the software and subsequently supervising the implementation of a pilot test. His immediate concerns were how to market Pronto successfully to other banks as a franchise and how to develop Pronto so it would be even more attractive to potential licensees.

Lacey was responsible for the forthcoming market introduction of Pronto in New York City. The Financial Services Group within the Metropolitan Banking Division for which he worked was, in effect, the first of Parker's licensees to launch Pronto commercially. With the launch just a few weeks away, Lacey and Parker—as they had done many times during the past year—reviewed the challenges and opportunities facing them.

Banking in the 1980s

Chemical Bank, headquartered in New York City, was the nation's sixth-largest bank in 1982 with assets of over $50 billion. Known for its aggressive new-product development, Chemical provided a full range of commercial banking services to corporate and retail customers. Over 1 million households in New York City held accounts at one of its 250 retail branches. Chemical's retail banking penetration was second only to that of Citibank, which held accounts for about 1.5 million New York City households.

Chemical competed in an increasingly turbulent banking environment. Deregulation, particularly the removal of ceilings on the interest rates that banks could charge and the relaxation of interstate banking restrictions, had heightened competition among banks for consumer deposits. Moreover, the competitive arena had broadened to include various less-regulated, nationally known institutions. These included stock brokerage firms, such as Merrill Lynch, which had pioneered the introduction of money market accounts against which consumers could write checks. In the longer term, national retailers, such as Sears Roebuck and J. C. Penney, were thought likely to take advantage of their national bases of credit card customers to offer a full range of financial services nationwide.

Partly because of increased competition from outside the traditional banking industry, deposit growth rates in commercial banks for both corporate and retail customers were declining. However, deposits by individual consumers (58 percent of the total in 1980) represented an increasing percentage of total deposits. Industry analysts pointed out that 96 percent of U.S. households had a relationship with a bank and that banks enjoyed a level of trust with many consumers that other institutions could not match.

Banks responded to these trends by improving services, by broadening product lines, and by attempting to reduce costs. The retail banking industry was both labor-intensive and paper-intensive. In 1980, 1.5 million employees processed 47.7 billion items at an average cost of 37 cents. To reduce costs, many banks took one or more of the following steps:

- Provided tellers with on-line terminals to access customer records, permitting faster balance checking and improved customer service.

- Automated the back offices of branches to reduce paper processing, improve account record keeping, and cut the number of account errors and adjustments.

- Subcontracted the processing of checks and credit card transactions to other banks and financial service firms, such as American Express, which operated automated clearinghouses. Having invested in the facilities required to process high volumes of transactions at minimal cost, these clearinghouses were able to charge their bank customers less than the per-unit cost if each ran its own dedicated processing operation.

- Developed on-line cash management systems for corporate customers, permitting them to move cash among accounts within a single bank and among accounts held at several participating banks. Chemical had pioneered corporate cash management with the development of software for its BankLink system, introduced in 1977. By 1983, the BankLink system had been franchised to 65 other banks, a quarter of all those that offered a cash management system in the United States.[1]

---

[1] The Financial Services Group within the Metropolitan Banking Division for which Lacey worked marketed the corporate cash management system together with payroll management systems and, most recently, Pronto, to Chemical's own corporate and retail customers. The Electronic Banking Division for which Parker worked marketed all of these products to other banks.

- Introduced automated teller machines (ATMs), which reduced labor costs and the pressure on tellers, permitted banks to offer uniform service around the clock, and enabled banks to expand their market reach for much less than the cost of building new branches. One study forecasted that there would be 62,000 ATMs attached to bank branches or in remote locations by 1986. The same study estimated that unit transaction processing costs for an ATM (processing 6,000 transactions monthly) versus a human teller were 54 percent less in 1982 and would be 63 percent less by 1986.

- Offered a telephone-bill-paying service to retail customers. The number of banks providing this service was forecasted to grow from 425 in 1983 to 2,000 by 1985. However, an average of only 3 percent of retail banking customers were using the service where it was available. Some industry analysts attributed this to insufficient marketing; others attributed it to the fact that consumers using the service had no visual record of their transactions until they received their monthly statements.

Home Banking

Electronic home banking systems permitted consumers to execute various banking tasks, including balance inquiry, interaccount funds transfer, and bill paying from the comfort of their homes. Compared with the approaches listed above, the cost savings and service improvements associated with home banking were seen by most analysts as further in the future. These benefits included the following:

- The elimination of the "float" that customers received when writing paper checks.
- The lower cost of processing a customer's electronic bill payment than of processing a paper check.
- The lower cost of sending the customer an electronic statement rather than printing and mailing one.
- The lower cost of advertising new services to customers by reaching them through electronic ads on the home banking system.
- The ability of banks offering home banking to serve their customers with fewer branch offices.
- The increased revenues from customers attracted from other banks by the availability of a competitive home banking service.

One industry study estimated that, by 1985, 250 banks would be providing home banking services to 1,250,000 accounts, displacing 105 million paper-based transactions each year. This figure, however, represented less than half of

1 percent of the total paper-based transactions forecast for 1985. Higher percentages of transactions were expected to be displaced by ATMs (3.9 percent) and automated clearinghouses (2.4 percent) and telephone bill payment (0.6 percent).

The study indicated that a home banking bill-payment system would reduce costs for the payer, the biller, and the bank. The cost of postage, envelopes, and paper checks would be eliminated for the payer. The biller would incur no bank deposit charge, would lose less on float, and would avoid the problem of bounced checks. The study estimated that the bank's costs of processing a check were 9 percent less using home banking in 1983 and would be 47 percent less by 1986.

In September 1983, about 45 U.S. banks experimented with home banking. The only commercially available home banking service in the United States, however, was available to subscribers of Compuserve, a national computer information network. At a cost of $4 per month[2] over and above the $5 monthly Compuserve fee, a consumer with a home computer, telephone, and modem[3] could conduct simple banking transactions, such as balance inquiry and account transfers, with any of four participating banks. These banks were medium-sized and included the First Tennessee Bank in Knoxville, Tennessee, and the Huntington National Bank in Columbus, Ohio.

Among the leading banks in the nation, Chemical and Citibank had invested heavily in developing software for their home banking systems. Both had recently completed extensive pilot tests. The range of services offered on Chemical's Pronto system is summarized in Exhibit 1. Chemical began licensing Pronto to other banks that were not interested in developing their own systems either individually or as a joint venture. Citibank apparently had no such intention. Noting Citibank's aggressive nationwide marketing of credit cards, traveler's checks, and money market funds, some industry analysts believed that Citibank viewed its Homebase home banking system as a vehicle to build a national base of Citibank checking account customers. These analysts further forecasted that no more than 10 banks would independently develop their own software.

The software had to be tailored to fit each home computer. Parker explained, "The Pronto software grabs the menus we send down and stores them in your computer's memory. When you return to a menu during a home banking session, it appears on the screen much faster."

---

[2] Additional telephone connect time charges were also incurred when the consumer accessed the home banking network.

[3] A modem converted computer signals into tones that traveled over telephone lines.

Another technology for delivering home banking services was videotex, which could link a consumer's home television set to a central computer via the telephone (or cable in households with cable television) and a videotex terminal (costing about $600 in 1983). The consumer interacted with a videotex system either by punching a hand-held keypad or by typing on a full alphanumeric keyboard.

Unlike information networks, such as Compuserve, which transmitted only black-and-white text, videotex data pages were in color and included graphics. The videotex terminal was necessary to decode the color and graphics signals relayed by the videotex central computer, tasks that a standard home computer could not perform. However, software packages costing $100, which would convert home computers with modems to videotex terminals, were under development.

By September 1983, over 25 videotex field trials were in progress in the United States. Banks and other financial institutions, such as Merrill Lynch, were involved as partners in most of these experiments along with communications companies, such as Time, Inc., Knight-Ridder Newspapers, and Times-Mirror; network providers, such as AT&T; and national retailers, such as Sears Roebuck and Federated Department Stores. In one such field trial in Ridgewood, New Jersey, funded by AT&T and CBS, AT&T provided the computer facilities and home terminals. CBS provided various information services, including continuously updated news, weather, sports, education, games, advertising, and tele-shopping. A home banking service was provided by ADP Telephone Computing Service, Inc., a division of Automatic Data Processing, and The Treasurer, a consortium of New Jersey banks. The service included balance inquiry, funds transfer, and bill-payment capabilities.

Banks participating in videotex experiments assumed the role of information suppliers and financial partners rather than system operators. The financial arrangements governing the relationships between home banking suppliers and system operators in commercial videotex systems were yet to be determined.[4]

Research Studies on Home Banking

Besides their in-house research, Parker and his colleagues had the benefit of two research studies conducted during 1982 by Booz, Allen and Hamilton (BAH) and by Reymer Gersin Associates.

The BAH study estimated that between 16 million (worst case) and 29 million (best case) of the 106 million households in the United States in 1995 would be users of home information services (HIS) and that, of these, 40 percent definitely would pay and 49 percent were somewhat likely to pay. Regarding home banking, the BAH study concluded that 75 percent of HIS users would have a "high propensity" to pay $2.50 per month for a home banking and bill-paying service; at $7.50 and $15.00, the numbers interested dropped to 60 percent and 25 percent, respectively. A home banking service including bill paying was one of two services registering the highest interest among respondents, the other being an entertainment-ticket-ordering service. Among those interested in the home banking service, a majority preferred a flat monthly rate to a monthly charge dependent upon level of use. According to BAH estimates, by 1995 home banking might replace between 5 percent (worst case) and 14 percent (best case) of personal check volume.

In 1982, Reymer Gersin Associates surveyed over 6,000 consumers to establish the appeal of different videotex services and the prices that consumers would willingly pay for them. The total sample was split into five groups of 1,240 respondents spread among 14 markets. The price per service presented to respondents before they were asked to express their level of interest in a standard set of videotex services varied across each of the five groups from no charge to $16 a month. The study identified six segments of respondents differing not only in their enthusiasm about videotex (from "all-around enthusiasts" to "anti-videotexers") but also in their interest in different services. Some consumers expressed more interest or exclusive interest in information-oriented services but not in transaction services. These segments were named "information-oriented enthusiasts" and "information onlies." As a result, the study recommended that videotex system operators allow customers to choose their own combination of services, while requiring them to take at least two services, each priced at $12 a month.

Exhibit 2 shows the percentage of respondents in total and in the six segments who would purchase each of six videotex services at various prices. Consumers who favored transaction services appeared to be less price sensitive than those who favored information services. Interest in home banking appeared to be particularly strong. The survey also asked respondents whether they agreed or disagreed with several statements about home banking. The results appear in Exhibit 3. In addition, interest in home banking was greater among those respondents who subscribed to pay cable services, those who frequently used ATMs and credit cards, those who wrote more checks, those who spent more on monthly telephone bills, those who more often purchased by mail order, and those who owned or intended to buy a personal computer or video game equipment, or both.

---

[4]For further information on the videotex industry, see Caroline Brainard and George S. Yip, "Note on the Consumer Videotex Industry," HBS case no. 9-584-029.

Chemical's Consumer Research on Pronto

The Field Trial.   Chemical's consumer research program began in February 1982, when a field trial of Pronto was initiated. The pilot program had the following objectives:

- Identify potential market segments.
- Determine user preferences for services offered within the Pronto package.
- Monitor customer usage to identify problem areas, help develop staffing requirements, and project operating costs.
- Develop positions on marketing issues including pricing, promotion, and product development.
- Gain operational experience relating to maintaining and upgrading applications software, the Tandem operating system, and the interfaces between the bank's mainframe accounting systems and Pronto.

Four hundred prospective participants were identified from among a random sample of 23,000 existing Chemical checking account customers. The criteria for participation included having a modular telephone jack in the same room as a working television, having some interest in home banking, and not owning a personal computer. The 200 households in the final test sample received an Atari 400 computer on loan as well as three video games. (At the time, IBM and Apple were seen as more involved in the business end of the personal computer market. Atari had the largest market share in the consumer segment of the market.) They also were mailed a welcoming letter, brochures, and information on Pronto and on how to use the system, and a list of 300 merchants to whom electronic payments could be made through Pronto. Half the participants were aged 25 to 34, and half had completed a four-year-degree. Their average household income was $34,500, and their average household size was 2.6 members. Fifty percent of the participants had used a computer terminal before the Pronto trial.

In July 1982, three focus groups were held in New York with heavy, moderate, and light field trial users of Pronto. The purpose was to assess the participants' attitudes toward Pronto, to identify concerns, and to explore post-trial purchase intentions. Group members indicated that they had participated either because they were interested in home banking or because the pilot test provided them with an opportunity to practice with a personal computer at no expense. Few respondents participated in order to change their banking behavior, but one claimed, "I feel a closeness with the bank now, that I probably wouldn't have if I didn't have the system."

In September 1982, a telephone survey of field trial participants was conducted to assess their attitudes toward the system and to determine their reasons for and methods of using Pronto services. A high percentage of respondents stated that they "regularly accessed" the balance inquiry service. The bill-paying and electronic checkbook services also scored high, followed by the electronic statement, funds transfer, and home budgeting services.

Although the home budgeting service was widely viewed as "hard to understand," many respondents also expressed concerns over the bill-paying service. The principal concern was that the service did not permit payments to be electronically transferred instantly to the account of the payee; time still had to be allowed for a transfer on paper to occur through Chemical headquarters. Other concerns were that the number of merchants was too limited, that it took Chemical too long to approve an additional merchant account suggested by a customer, and that the current system for scheduling multiple payments to a single merchant was cumbersome.

Respondents suggested that the instruction manual could be made clearer, that more "help" screens could be provided for new users, and that a test program could be provided for new users to practice on. Some of the more experienced users complained that they could not take shortcuts through the system to access more quickly the screens they required, and that the time lag between transaction entry and execution was too long. As one respondent put it, "Pronto implies speed, but this system doesn't deliver."

Respondents also were tested on their price sensitivity and willingness to pay for Pronto once the pilot test ended. Sixty-five percent were willing to pay $8 per month, 43 percent would pay $12, and 33 percent would pay $16. Regarding the personal computer and modem, 25 percent said $300 was the maximum price that they would willingly pay Chemical, 40 percent said $400, and 33 percent said $500. Half the respondents preferred to purchase this equipment through a retailer, rather than through a bank, even if they could receive it in lieu of interest on a high-balance deposit account. Management concluded from these and other comments that consumers who already owned personal computers would be less price sensitive regarding monthly usage fees.

The research program also included the collection and analysis of Pronto usage data from participants in the field trial. The findings were as follows:

- In June a daily average of 27 participants accessed Pronto. In December the average was 16.
- Throughout the trial period, Pronto users accessed an average of 25 screens per session. In June users spent 1.21 minutes per screen. In December they spent 0.35 minutes per screen.
- In a typical session before September, participants accessed three Pronto services. After September they typically accessed two.

- The most popular time for sessions was after work on weekdays. The lowest number of sessions occurred on Saturdays and Sundays.
- An average of four bills was paid during any session that included bill paying.

By the end of April 1983, one third of the original pilot participants already had ceased using the system (10 households had moved). Another one third had used Pronto at least 10 times in the previous 90 days, and the other one third had used the system 1 to 9 times during the same period. Among the group of more frequent users, 60 percent were between the ages of 25 and 34, and 75 percent were men. Although households with annual incomes over $50,000 represented almost one third of Pronto's pilot users, they accounted for only 15% of those who were positive about the existing Pronto system.

In April 1983, the pilot test ended. The participants received a letter giving them the option of continuing to receive Pronto at $8 a month and a payment of $240 for the computer, modem, and games.

One half of the pilot households discontinued the service. A telephone survey of these households revealed that 78 percent were, in fact, very or somewhat satisfied with Pronto, and only 17 percent expressed operational concerns about the system, primarily that the computer was too slow. Reasons for discontinuing the service are summarized in Exhibit 4. Although the most frequent objection was the price of the Atari computer, several households stated that their banking needs were not sufficiently complex to justify paying for Pronto, while some regarded transactions via Pronto as no easier than writing checks. Interestingly, 70 percent of the households that discontinued the service expected to buy a similar home banking service within two years; only one respondent expected never to purchase such a service.

Respondents were asked to name their single most important selection criterion in deciding to use a service such as Pronto. The results follow:

Price	20%
Variety of services	26%
Reputation/experience	9%
Ease of use	24%
Services save time	17%

Additional Research. In February and March 1983, two waves of three focus groups each were conducted in New York City by Lacey's group. Two group discussions were held with Atari home computer owners, two with Apple and IBM home computer owners, and two with nonowners of home computers. Group members were exposed to each of the five advertising concepts that management was considering for Pronto's introductory promotional campaign in New York City. The five concepts were as follows:

- Introducing Pronto, the 24-Hour Money Management System.
- Pronto Is the Computer That Makes Banking More Human.
- You're the Only One with a Key to Pronto.
- With Pronto, You Can Do Your Banking at Home 24 Hours a Day.
- Pronto, State-of-the-Art Banking.

Participants were shown a storyboard and a description of each concept. The descriptions are presented in Exhibit 5. The preferences of the focus groups' participants are reported in Table A.

Besides testing participants' reactions to the five advertising concepts, the focus groups were also used to elicit reactions to Pronto and to various pricing options following a demonstration of the system. Although the proposed $8-per-month fixed fee was regarded as reasonable, some participants expressed skepticism about how long the fee would remain at $8. Those not owning a personal computer saw the cost of both the computer and modem along

TABLE A **Focus Group Results: Pronto Concept Preferences**

	Number of Focus Group Participants Who . . .					
	Ranked First		Ranked Second		Ranked Third	
Concept	Feb.	March	Feb.	March	Feb.	March
Money management	12	17	6	3	1	0
Banking more human	8	7	9	8	2	7
Twenty-four hours a day	7	4	5	15	3	3
Key to Pronto	3	2	8	2	10	5
State-of-the-art	0	1	2	3	14	10

with the likely decline in personal computer prices and changes in technology as major barriers to adoption. Several thought, however, that the availability of Pronto might tip the scales and prompt them to buy personal computers. The participants enthusiastically supported the idea that Chemical Bank might provide modems to consumers who purchased a certificate of deposit or maintained a minimum checking account balance.

The comments of focus group participants confirmed management's belief that the convenience of home banking and the 24-hour access to a consumer's financial status were Pronto's principal benefits. The system would also help consumers to organize their financial records better and could be a status symbol. However, some additional questions were raised:

- What if I have accounts at different branches of Chemical?
- Will someone train me to use the system?
- What if someone somehow obtains my ID numbers and tries to wipe me out?
- How many banking transactions do I need to do to make it worthwhile?
- Can I store the information in my home computer or print a hard copy?
- Will I receive a paper record of my transactions? What if I make an error?
- How far back can I call up my banking information?
- Does the telephone line have to be tied up when I am using the system? (AT&T and others were close to completing the technology to provide a telephone line with simultaneous dual-call capacity.)

The participants' principal fears concerned confidentiality, security, and computer theft. Several consumers pointed out that, since not all checks could be paid electronically, dual paper and electronic checkbooks would have to be maintained.[5] Others noted that the convenience of home banking was limited by the necessity of visiting their banks to obtain cash.

Pronto Licensing Efforts

Because it had successfully franchised the BankLink cash management system, Chemical decided early on to license Pronto to other banks. Thus, the software was designed to be adaptable, with minimal additional programming, to the product lines and procedures of other banks. Parker estimated that three to six person-months would be required to

develop the necessary programming interfaces for a particular licensee bank, depending on the size and complexity of its operations.

By September 1983 seven banks, including Crocker National in California, the 12th-largest in assets in the United States, had made commitments to purchase Pronto. Some signed licensing agreements for defensive reasons, viewing it as a cheaper means of staking a position in the home banking arena, rather than investing in the development of their own systems. Other licensees viewed Pronto as a vehicle to build their market shares. Parker was uncertain whether large, medium, or small banks would be the most promising licensees, and whether banks with well-developed retail branch and ATM networks would be better or worse prospects than those banks with weaker retail positions that might see home banking as a means of regaining market share.

The terms of the licensing agreement permitted the licensee to offer Pronto as its own home banking system, although the name *Pronto* had to be used, and the logo had to be presented in a prescribed manner. No minimum commitment of expenditures to marketing Pronto was required. Licensees received all present and future Pronto home banking software developed by Chemical and access to Chemical's cumulative expertise in marketing Pronto and knowledge of the videotex industry. Chemical also provided technical assistance to develop the necessary interfaces between Pronto and the licensee bank's systems along with some marketing consulting assistance. Parker hoped that, as more and more banks signed up, Chemical would be able to reduce the level of assistance that it was agreeing to provide.

Parker developed two pricing schedules for potential licensee banks interested in conducting pilot tests of Pronto over a two-year period with a maximum of 200 customers. If a licensee wished to process its electronic home banking transactions internally, Pronto was available for a signing fee of $100,000 plus $10,000 annually for software support plus $1 per month per home banking customer. Alternatively, if the bank wished Chemical to process these transactions, the signing fee was $25,000 while the processing fee was $1,500 per month plus $4 per month per home banking customer. These rates applied only to pilot tests; Chemical executives had not yet settled on a pricing structure for full-fledged systems. The pilot-test licensing agreement contained a clause permitting Chemical to raise fees as new services requiring additional software development were incorporated into Pronto.

Some executives of the Electronic Banking Division believed that licensing might not be the best marketing strategy. As one commented, "We have developed a leading-edge product. We should take it to the nation ourselves as Citibank is going to do with Homebase, and not give half the profits away by licensing the system to banks that may not

---

[5]Only 300 merchants had agreed to accept electronic payments.

aggressively market it." This argument was bolstered by the fact that only seven banks had signed commitments, although efforts to secure licensing agreements had been in progress for almost two years. Parker believed that many bankers did not view home banking as an urgent issue. Knowing that they would always be able to obtain a franchise from Chemical or one of its competitors, they saw no need to make an immediate commitment. Reinforcing this conservatism was the estimated cost of $250,000 to $500,000, exclusive of marketing expenditures, to organize and launch a commercially viable system. In addition, industry analysts believed that the implementation of a home banking system would result in higher per transaction costs until between 5 and 10 percent of a bank's customers regularly used the system.

Parker was preoccupied with how to increase the number of banks signing licensing agreements. He believed that he had to develop ways to demonstrate Chemical's long-term commitment to home banking. He knew that much would depend upon Chemical's success in launching Pronto to its own retail customers in the fourth quarter of 1983. Several banks were awaiting the preliminary results of this launch. Other banks indicated their willingness to sign licensing agreements but only if they received exclusive rights to Pronto within their market areas. Parker saw several disadvantages to such an arrangement but wondered whether he should consider it and, if so, how geographical exclusivity should change the other terms of the licensing agreement.

Future Pronto Product Development

Since the launch of the pilot field trial, Parker's group of 35 programmers had been working to upgrade Pronto. (This programming staff also worked on BankLink. About half of the staff worked principally on Pronto.) In response to concerns highlighted during the focus groups, the security system had been improved. Each subscriber had to type two passwords to gain access to his or her account information and to make transactions. In addition, a second level of security was encoded in the software that was not even known to the valid user, such that a thief could not readily use a stolen or copied home banking disk to access an account.

The programming team also had worked on improving the user-friendliness of the software. Both the bill-paying service and the home-budgeting service had been revised although, subsequently, the use of the latter had not increased. In improving these services, Parker commented that he and his programmers frequently faced the problem of trading off the need for completeness with the desire to avoid complexity. Efforts also were made to adapt Pronto's software so it could be used by owners of IBM, Apple, and Commodore home computers, as well as Atari models. By September this task was completed for IBM and Apple, but the introduction of new home computers would probably require continuing effort in this area.

Parker believed that home banking services, such as Pronto and Homebase, would come under increasing pressure from videotex system operators offering a full package of services of which home banking was but one. For example, Knight-Ridder's Viewtron system, scheduled to be launched commercially in southern Florida by the end of 1983, offered various transaction services including teleshopping; telebanking; and airline, entertainment, and restaurant reservations as well as news- and education-oriented information services. Viewtron reached the consumer in alphageometric format with colorful graphics, whereas Pronto used the simpler alphanumeric format that was satisfactory for home banking but was lacking in other applications.

Parker ruled out reprogramming Pronto in alphageometric format, especially since the videotex decoder that a consumer would then have to buy cost at least six times that of the modem required by the current technology. Parker, however, believed that one or more services would have to be added to Pronto in 1984. There were two reasons for this conviction. First, the focus groups suggested that, once consumers mastered home banking, they wanted and expected more for their monthly fees. Parker believed such feelings would be especially strong among consumers who bought home computers primarily to use the Pronto home banking system. Second, Parker believed both existing and prospective Pronto licensees were waiting to see whether Chemical would be able to further develop Pronto. Even existing licensees could defect to competitive systems if they were not satisfied. Parker estimated that the research and development investment needed to create a comprehensive package of transaction and information services was $12 million, equivalent to Chemical's investment in Pronto to date.

Some of Parker's colleagues advised him that Pronto should stick to home banking alone or, at most, add other financial services such as financial tips, investment advice, tax planning and preparation information, portfolio management, and discount stock brokerage, which they believed would be especially appealing to Pronto's potential licensees.

Parker knew that transaction services, such as stock trading and teleshopping, were more expensive and complex to develop and operate than one-way information services, such as the delivery of news. Development costs would be lower and Chemical's merchant customers less annoyed if the bank added a teleshopping service via a gateway link to, perhaps, Sears Roebuck. However, in such a situation, consumers would not be able to pay for purchases directly from their bank accounts and have the transactions immediately recorded in their Pronto files. Besides, if Pronto added services using the gateway approach, it would earn considerably less than if it was able to earn money on the transaction processing and credit authorization as well. In fact, Pronto would earn only the equivalent of a finder's fee and would risk loss of control and a blurring of its overall image.

Parker hesitated to add services that required frequent updating and that, therefore, were costly to provide (such as weather) and information services that few consumers were willing to pay much for, being used to obtaining them for free.

The Pronto Launch in New York City

Pronto was scheduled to be offered to Chemical customers in New York City at the end of September. A two-month advertising blitz was planned during October and November to build awareness and knowledge of the Pronto system. The campaign targeted college-educated professionals aged 25 to 49 with household incomes over $30,000. As indicated in Exhibit 6, the media plan called for print and television advertising at a cost of $760,000. The schedule attempted to maximize reach to target group members who would be exposed to a Pronto advertisement at least three times during the campaign (see Table B).

The proposed campaign would deliver 62 million impressions at a cost per thousand of $12.24. (A sample print advertisement is presented in Exhibit 7.) Looking ahead to 1984, Lacey tentatively budgeted $1 million for advertising for the entire year.

Besides the introductory advertising campaign, display centers demonstrating the system were to be installed initially in 15 of Chemical's largest branches throughout the metropolitan area. These branches together served about 150,000 retail banking customers. Each display booth (see Exhibit 8) cost about $15,000 installed; a one-screen minicenter cost $5,000. These display centers were to be staffed by specially trained sales coordinators who would demonstrate Pronto, answer customer questions, and distribute brochures. Lacey planned to initially hire 20 sales coordinators for a six-month probationary period at a monthly salary of $1,500. He believed that additional sales help

could be obtained from an outside agency when needed at $10 per hour. Besides placing display centers in the branches, Lacey was also considering approaching Bloomingdale's electronics department, Computerland, and Crazy Eddie's (an electronics discount chain) to place Pronto display centers in their high-traffic stores. He thought that Pronto could be sold when a customer purchased a home computer. He was uncertain, however, whether to offer these retailers Chemical sales coordinators to staff the display centers, a cooperative advertising program, or a straight commission of, perhaps, $15 on each Pronto sale.

Lacey knew that he had to stimulate the enthusiasm of the branch managers and employees besides recruiting and training the right type of sales coordinator. Accordingly, he planned to encourage the branches to identify the customers who matched the Pronto target market profile and to invite them to cocktail parties at which Pronto would be demonstrated by a sales coordinator. The cost of holding such an event outside of regular banking hours attended by 30 people would be about $250. Lacey also was considering a recognition program for branch personnel, other than the sales coordinators, to motivate them to identify Pronto prospects and close sales.

Lacey had decided to develop three brochures describing Pronto in varying degrees of detail that would be available to consumers according to their degree of interest in the system. He had initially ordered 75,000 fliers at 7 cents each, 75,000 six-page brochures at 57 cents each, and 35,000 brochures costing $3.00, each of which contained application forms and a starter kit. (A short application form was available to current Chemical customers. Non-Chemical customers had to complete a longer application form.) Lacey estimated that 25 percent of the retail customers visiting the 15 branches might pick up a flier and that 5 percent might be seriously interested enough to justify being given the application form. (Lacey originally had hoped to have customers complete application forms in the branches after they visited the display booths. However, logistical constraints plus the fact that many customers did not carry with them all the information necessary to complete the application form prevented this approach. The application form took about 15 minutes to complete.) In

TABLE B   Advertising Agency's Reach and Frequency Estimates

	Target Group Reach	Average Frequency	Target Gross Rating Points	Reach to Those Exposed at Least Three Times
Print	81%	4.5 times	365	51%
Television	83%	3.4 times	282	41%

addition, depending upon their levels of interest, consumers would be mailed either a brochure or a starter kit after calling the 800 number listed in Pronto's advertising.

Lacey had set the price of Pronto service at $12 per month, plus normal banking charges. He estimated the monthly cost of providing Pronto, exclusive of marketing expenditures, at $10 per customer during the first year. Pronto subscribers could purchase a modem from Chemical for $75. Four hundred merchants (who collectively accounted for 70 percent of all bills mailed to consumers in the United States) had agreed to participate in the bill-paying service. (All home banking bill-paying services except Pronto's required subscribers to allow five days from the date they authorized withdrawals from their accounts to pay bills. By September 1983 Chemical had arranged for about 200 merchants to be listed as "instant pay" or "one-day pay.")

Lacey hoped that this marketing program would generate 2,000 subscribers by year-end and at least 15,000 by the end of 1984. He was uncertain how many home computers there were in New York City but estimated the number in September 1983 at 225,000, based on a list of Atari owners drawn from warranty cards. (By the end of 1984, industry analysts estimated that there would be over 600,000 home computers in New York City.) Because software permitting IBM, Apple, and Commodore owners to access Pronto would be available by early November, Lacey believed that he would then be able to appeal to 90 percent of all home computer owners.

Lacey had been informed by Chemical operations executives that the bank's Tandem computer could handle 300 consumers accessing Pronto at the same time before delays in response time or a computer breakdown would occur. Lacey estimated that the average Chemical retail banking customer would use the system for home banking for two hours during the first week, falling to half an hour by the end of the fourth week. (The average Chemical retail banking customer wrote about 120 checks each year, inquired about his or her balance 20 times, and made 30 transfers between savings and checking accounts). Installing a second Tandem computer equivalent in capacity to the first would cost about $250,000.

Assuming the Pronto introduction proved successful, Lacey believed that an adaptation of Pronto targeted at small businesses with annual sales of $2 million to $5 million should be considered for 1984. This system would incorporate additional features, such as a preauthorized line of credit, that could be drawn down on Pronto, discount brokerage service, Treasury bill and certificate of deposit rate information, a general ledger, and consolidated monthly and year-end statements. Customers would be charged according to usage, rather than a flat monthly fee.

EXHIBIT 1   Services Provided to Pronto Consumers

Balance Inquiry

- Daily balances of all accounts (including Chemical credit card and money market accounts).
- Details of check activity (to establish, for example, whether a particular check has cleared).

Electronic Statements

- Statements on-line before mailing.
- Available for current month and previous month.

Funds Transfer

- Shifts funds between accounts.
- Cash advances from revolving credit accounts.

Bill Paying

- Bills paid directly from accounts without writing checks.
- Payments recorded directly into home budgets.
- Value-dated payments, up to 90 days in advance.
- Recurring bills paid automatically.
- Payments can be renewed, changed, or canceled until they are made.

Electronic Checkbook

- Records checks as written.
- Monitors dates that checks clear.
- Checks recorded directly into home budget.
- Information concerning checks stored for printed monthly statements.

Home Budgeting

- Organizes income and expenditures in 50 categories.
- As many as five separate budgets.
- Multiple entries.
- Instant totals for any budget.
- Monthly summary for budget activity with regular monthly statement.
- Categorizes tax-deductible items as they occur.

Electronic Mail

- Permits user to send messages to other Pronto users.
- Customer can add accounts and ask the bank questions (and receive a reply from the customer service agent within 24 hours).

Exhibit 2 Members of Six Videotex Segments Who Would Order Videotex Services at Different Prices (%)

Segments	Total Respondents					All-Around Enthusiasts			Transaction-Oriented Enthusiasts		
	Free	$4/mo.	$8/mo.	$12/mo.	$16/mo.	Free	$4/mo.	$16/mo.	Free	$4/mo.	$16/mo.
Pay Services	100%	100%	100%	100%	100%	31%	20%	9%	8%	14%	15%
News service	64%	43%	37%	32%	26%	95%	93%	82%	68%	49%	47%
Special interest information	55	39	32	28	24	90	76	48	39	26	15
Electronic mail	50	24	20	15	13	76	53	50	9	14	11
Home banking	31	16	13	11	8	45	36	25	95	96	90
Free Services											
Shopping guide	62	54	51	46	45	93	94	86	92	99	96
Shopping at home	47	48	46	42	44	80	90	84	88	97	97
Monthly revenue-generated/HH[a]	0	$ 7	$ 10	$ 15	$ 20	0	$10	$33	0	$ 7	$25

Segments	Information-Oriented Enthusiasts			Transaction Onlies			Information Onlies			Anti-Videotexers		
	Free	$4/mo.	$16/mo.	Free	$4/mo.	$16/mo.	Free	$4/mo.	$16/mo.	Free	$4/mo.	$16/mo.
Pay Services	16%	6%	2%	5%	10%	14%	6%	4%	2%	34%	43%	56%
News service	100%	100%	100%	21%	13%	13%	95%	88%	80%	20%	14%	14%
Special interest information	97	77	73	6	1	0	60	36	35	13	6	7
Electronic mail	83	66	54	1	4	4	24	15	24	5	4	3
Home banking	79	38	35	53	42	28	20	6	16	9	3	2
Free Services												
Shopping guide	90	93	76	40	45	63	58	38	35	18	14	19
Shopping at home	76	85	88	21	45	63	8	9	0	5	11	16
Monthly revenue-generated/HH[a]	0	$ 6	$ 40	0	$10	$17	0	$ 4	$30	0	$ 5	$17

NOTE: To be read, for example, "Among the 1,240 respondents who were offered all pay services free, 95% of the all-around enthusiasts (representing 31% of the group that was offered all pay services free) would obtain the news service. The monthly revenue generated for the average household in this group would be zero since all services were free."

[a]HH signifies per household.

SOURCE: Reymer Gersin Associates.

EXHIBIT 3 Reasons for Getting or Not Getting Home Banking: Average Rating Summary by Segment

	Total Sample	All Around Videotex Enthusiasts	Transaction-Oriented Videotex Enthusiasts	Information-Oriented Videotex Enthusiasts	Transaction Onlies	Information Onlies	Anti-Video-texers
Disagree A Lot 1.0 — Agree A Lot 6.0							
How Do You Feel about the Following Statements?							
Having banking at home isn't worth it, because I'll still have to go to the bank in person to get cash.	3.9	3.0	2.9	3.3	3.9	4.9	4.5
I want banking at home, because it'll be easier than paying bills by writing checks and mailing them.	3.5	4.6	5.0	3.9	4.1	2.6	2.7
I'm so used to paying my bills the way I do now that I'll never switch to banking at home.	3.6	2.4	2.0	3.9	3.5	3.9	4.4
I'll never take a chance paying bills at home, because something might go wrong with it and the bills might not get paid.	3.6	2.8	2.5	3.3	3.7	4.0	4.2
I'll never bank or shop at home, because I prefer dealing face-to-face with a person, rather than a machine.	3.5	2.4	2.3	2.9	3.3	3.9	4.3
I want banking at home, because it won't let me bounce a check; it won't pay bills unless there's enough money or credit in my account.	3.3	4.2	4.5	3.7	3.1	2.6	2.7
I'll enjoy shopping and banking at home, because I have such a busy life; I don't always have time to shop or bank in person.	3.1	4.5	4.4	3.9	3.4	2.0	2.3
Banking at home will help me keep better track of my checking, savings, and charge accounts, since right now I'm never sure what my balances are.	2.7	3.8	4.1	2.7	2.8	2.0	2.1
I often forget to pay bills on time, so I'll worry less with banking at home paying bills for me on time automatically.	2.4	3.5	3.5	2.8	2.5	2.0	1.8

NOTE: Average ratings calculated only among those who had an opinion.

SOURCE: Reymer Gersin Associates.

▄▄▄
Exhibit 4   Reasons for Dropping Pronto Service among Pilot Users

Reasons for Dropping Pronto Service	Percent Citing as Very Important	Percent Citing as Primary	Comments: To Continue with Pronto, What Changes Do We Need to Make?
Atari too expensive	52%	22%	9% Mention lower computer cost.
			9% Want it free.
			7% Want a rental option.
Monthly service charge too high	33	7	13% Want a lower monthly charge.
Atari too awkward	39	15	
Atari too limited but would be interested if another were used	50	13	17% Want more powerful computer.
			33% Want to be compatible with other systems.
Home banking services are not timely enough	46	4	11% Want more merchants.
			17% Want quicker access time.
			7% Speed up bill payment time.
I did not find electronic banking useful	28	4	
Chemical Bank is not my principal bank	7	4	
Pronto services are too limited	54	15	11% Want more merchants.
			7% Want more noncredit service.
Pronto is too difficult to use	22	4	7% Want it easier to use.
			17% Want a single ledger or sole recordkeeping device.

Exhibit 5   Texts of Five Pronto Advertising Concepts

1. Introducing Pronto, the 24-Hour Money Management System

Pronto takes the mystery out of banking. Using Pronto and your computer, you can be on-line with Chemical—24 hours a day. You'll know everything you need to know about all your accounts—checking, savings, money market, Mastercard and Visa, and more. Pronto gives you an incredible amount of detail on every aspect of your various accounts.

Pronto's bill-paying service lets you arrange for payments of piles of bills in minutes, scheduling them for up to 90 days in advance.

You can also use balance inquiry to get daily, up-to-date reports on all your balances—by account.

You can watch your accounts—see when deposited funds are in float and when they have cleared. And you won't have to guess about how long it takes for that check you wrote to clear—Pronto keeps track of the dates checks clear and keeps track of those that are outstanding. For Mastercard and Visa, you can see the amount you owe and your credit availability, on a daily basis.

Pronto does the work for you automatically and is the perfect complement to your regular Chemical services—the bank branches and cash machines.

2. Pronto Is the Computer That Makes Banking More Human

With Pronto's home banking system, you don't have to know anything about computer programming. It's easy and practical to use, because when you "sign on" to Pronto, instructions appear on your television screen. They tell you how to select the services you need and how to use them. You just pick numbers from the list and fill in the blanks.

It's like having your own personal bank branch at your fingertips.

You'll feel closer to the bank, because it's easy for you to keep in touch with your money. You can even send electronic messages to your friends who have Pronto.

Instead of just being another customer at your branch, you'll have a close personal link between you and Chemical.

3. With Pronto, You Can Do Your Banking at Home, 24 Hours a Day

Pronto offers you the convenience of doing most of your banking transactions at any time—in the privacy of your own home. Whenever you want to, without leaving home, you can pay bills, get daily balances in your accounts, keep an electronic checkbook, find out which checks have cleared, transfer funds from one account to another, and organize and review your expenses through the home budgeting service.

You can even send electronic messages to the bank when you have inquiries about your account, and Pronto will give you a quick answer. Having Pronto is like having the branch open in your own home—24 hours a day.

4. You're the Only One with a Key to Pronto

Financial transactions are a private matter. Pronto was designed with several layers of security to ensure that only *you* can perform transactions or see information regarding your accounts.

Each user selects his or her own security codes in addition to the one assigned by the bank. Pronto will not deliver information or perform transactions without confirming these codes.

Another Pronto security feature is transactions verification. Pronto verifies every transaction you request to make sure that the information is correct. Once the information is verified, you get a reference number for each transaction.

5. Pronto, State-of-the-Art Banking

Now you can participate in not only the computer revolution but in the banking revolution, too, by subscribing to Chemical's new electronic banking system, Pronto.

Today with your computer, you can play games such as Pac Man, do programming, and enjoy lots of other educational programs.

Pronto expands the uses of your computer. It's a dynamic system built to move with the technology of the future. With the Pronto system, you can bank in an entirely new way—pay bills electronically, check all your account balances, see statements, and more—24 hours a day. You can even send electronic messages to your friends who have Pronto.

EXHIBIT 6   Media Schedule for Pronto New York Introduction Advertising Campaign

	Week Beginning Monday												
	AUG	SEP				OCT					NOV		
	29	5	12	19	26	3	10	17	24	31	7	14	21
Newspapers													
New York Times				X	X		X		X		X	X	X
Wall Street Journal (Eastern edition)				X	X		X		X				
Consumer magazines (full page)													
Business Week (N.Y. metro)					X				X				X
Fortune (N.Y. metro)			◄	►				◄	►			◄	►
Money (N.Y. metro)				◄	—	—	—	—	►		◄	—	►
National Geographic (N.Y. metro)				◄	—	—	—	—	►		◄	—	►
New York					X			X				X	
NYT Magazine (national)				X		X				X			
Newsweek (N.Y. metro)					X		X				X		X
Signature (N.Y. metro)									X		X		X
Time (N.Y. metro)						X	X			X		X	
Computer magazines (full page)													
Antic				◄	—	—	—	—	►	◄	—	—	►
Atari Connection	◄	—	—	—	—	—	—	—	—	—	—	—	►
Local cable TV (30-second spots)													
CNN (Cable News Network)				◄	—	—	—	—	►				
ESPN (Entertainment and Sports Programming Network)													
Spot TV (30-second spots)													
AM, Early, and Late News, Prime Time				◄	—	—	—	—	►				

Exhibit 7

Pronto magazine advertisement

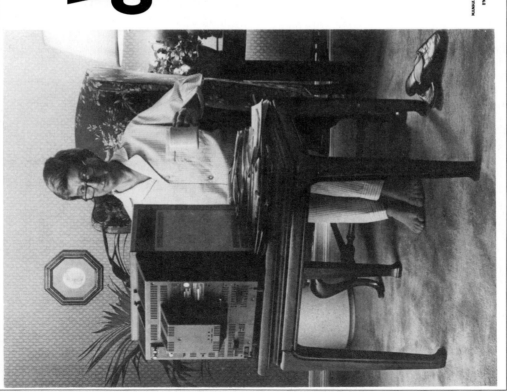

EXHIBIT 8

Pronto display center

Marketing Strategy Formulation

MARKETING STRATEGY FORMULATION

Introduction

For the last two decades, there has been increased pressure on marketing managers to rise above the details of day-to-day operating decisions about the Four Ps and think strategically about several key marketing questions:

- Who (which customer segments) should we serve?
- What differentiates us from our competitors in meeting the needs of our target customer segments?
- Where is our product in its life cycle?
- When should we introduce new products or services or enter new market segments? When should we cut back our products and services or withdraw from a market segment?
- Why are we pursuing a particular marketing strategy? What is our strategic vision for our marketing efforts, and what are the values we hold sacred in carrying out this vision?
- How will our competitors react to our marketing strategy decisions? How should we anticipate or respond to theirs?

As an applied discipline, marketing has borrowed liberally from research and leading practice in strategy and business policy to help answer these questions. However, this note will not address these more general strategic frameworks, as they are covered in detail in other sources.[1] The purpose of this note is to discuss several emerging frameworks that are marketing's contribution in the strategy formulation process. These frameworks address each of the five strategic questions above. They

---

This note was prepared by Professors Minette E. Drumwright and Thomas J. Kosnik.
Copyright © 1989 by the President and Fellows of Harvard College.
Harvard Business School note 9-590-001.

[1]See, for example, Michael E. Porter, *Competitive Strategy* (New York: Free Press, 1980), and George Stalk, Jr., "Time—The Next Source of Competitive Advantage," *Harvard Business Review,* July–August 1988, pp. 41–53.

complement the broader analytical frameworks that have been developed for competitive strategy at the cross-functional, business unit or corporate level, by providing additional detail for strategy formulation from the marketing perspective.

What Are the Elements of an Effective Marketing Strategy?

The five strategic questions mentioned in the previous section provide the foundation for describing what a good marketing strategy ought to encompass.

- It should clearly define the **served market** that has been selected by the firm.
- It should **position** the firm and its products and services to highlight their **differential advantage** over the competition.
- It should address the **timing of market entry and exit.**
- It should provide **focus** on the **variables** that are the critical points of **leverage** for the organization, and on the **vision and values** that guide behavior in carrying out the mission.
- It should provide **flexibility** in responding to competitive actions and changes in the marketplace.
- It should **integrate** marketing efforts with the **strategies of other functions.**
- Finally, it should take a **long-term** (usually at least three to five years), rather than a short-term (usually one year) perspective.

An effective marketing strategy will inform and influence strategy formulation throughout an organization, because of marketing's unique role as a communications bridge across different functional or organizational boundaries. For example, salespeople serve as liaisons and conduits between manufacturers and distribution channels, and between buying and selling organizations. Product managers gather information from the marketplace, interpret it, and coordinate its flow to such functions as R&D, production/operations, and customer service. Thus, they serve as a hub in the communications wheel for information flow between different functions. As a result, marketing strategy can help an organization to cope with uncertainty in the external environment and, thereby, reduce the costs and risks of activities in other functions, such as R&D and manufacturing.

Frameworks for Strategic Marketing Decisions

Marketers were making decisions about market selection, positioning, differentiation, market entry/exit, and response to competitive moves long before the emergence of the frameworks that will be presented in this section. However, without the discipline and the shared language of an analytical approach, many of those decisions were not made strategically. That is, they lacked the focus on a few critical objectives and values, the patience and persistence of a long-term perspective, and the flexibility to ensure continuity of the strategy in the face of a constantly changing environment. Thus, the frameworks arose from the need for a more rigorous approach to making complex and important marketing decisions.

Market Definition and Selection

Market selection is the choice of the domain in which the firm will compete for customers. Derek Abell has suggested that market selection requires making decisions about three critical dimensions of the market:

- The **customer segments** that the firm will serve.
- The **functions** of those customer segments that will be provided or supported.
- The **technologies** that will be used to provide or support the functions.[2]

For an example of how to apply Abell's market definition framework, consider the strategic issues facing a computer services company called American Management Systems (AMS). In the early 1980s, AMS developed a software package that provided automated support for collectors, the people who attempt to collect overdue amounts on credit cards. The product initially was developed for the Wells Fargo Bank in San Francisco, using a large IBM mainframe computer. However, AMS realized that similar collection functions also were performed for consumer loans, bills, and taxes for a variety of institutions ranging from banks to department stores to state and city governments. Once the first credit card collection system was successfully installed, AMS faced decisions about how to focus its marketing strategy along the three axes in Exhibit 1.

On the market segment axis, should AMS limit its attention to large commercial banks, such as Wells Fargo, or also include smaller banks and savings and loan institutions? Should it expand beyond banking to retail stores with credit cards, like J. C. Penney and Macy's? Should the company enter the public sector to help governments to collect overdue taxes or traffic fines? What about hospitals and medical clinics with overdue bills from patients?

On the functions axis, should AMS focus only on credit collection, or other credit management functions as well? For example, should it develop computer products to support the processing of applications for credit cards? Should it develop programs to support the accounting and billing process, or the detection of credit card fraud? Should it expand beyond credit cards to support collections activities for overdue loans and taxes?

Decisions on the technologies axis were somewhat related to choices about market segments, as only very large organizations could afford to purchase the large IBM computers for which the initial software had been written. Should AMS develop credit management products to run on smaller, less-expensive machines, such as minicomputers or even microcomputers? Should it support computers from suppliers other than IBM, such as Digital Equipment Corporation, Hewlett Packard, and Tandem? Should it develop versions of the software to work with database management programs such as those provided by Oracle Corporation or Cullinet?

Changes on each of the three dimensions offered AMS the potential for future growth, but with a different mix of marketing and product development costs. Expansion along different dimensions also implied that AMS would come into

---

[2]Derek A. Abell, *Defining the Business* (Englewood Cliffs, N.J.: Prentice Hall, 1980).

contact with different groups of competitors. After weighing the costs and benefits, and projecting its position relative to the competition in the various subsegments, AMS decided to focus its energies on banks and other large organizations that could afford IBM mainframe computers or would pay the costs of conversion to another brand of computer. It also added new software products to support each of the critical functions of credit management, so over a five-year period a complete family of related products for IBM mainframes was developed and marketed to the target customer segments.

Classification schemes for variables that can be used to segment both consumer and business-to-business markets have been developed to aid in market selection. Variables commonly used to segment consumer markets are shown in Exhibit 2 and can be classified into two broad groups.[3] In the first, segments are formed by looking at consumer characteristics independent of any particular product. Examples of these variables are listed in the geographic, demographic, and psychographic categories in Exhibit 2. After selecting a segmentation variable, marketers must see if the segments show different responses to a given product. For example, consumers in the North Central United States probably will respond differently to a snowmobile than will consumers in the Southwest.

In the second group, segments are formed based on consumer responses to a given product. Examples of these variables are listed in the behavioral category in Exhibit 2 and include usage occasions (e.g., business vs. pleasure airline travel), benefits sought (e.g., economy vs. quality) and usage rate (light vs. heavy users). Many marketers assert that behavioral variables provide the most appropriate bases for market segmentation. For example, the same consumer purchasing airline tickets for business versus pleasure travel may have radically different price sensitivities, scheduling needs, and purchasing processes depending on the usage occasion (e.g., a business trip to Tokyo versus a vacation in Tokyo).

Business-to-business markets can be segmented with some of the same variables used to segment consumer markets, such as geography and benefits sought, along with other variables pertaining specifically to business markets. The classification scheme for industrial markets shown in Exhibit 3 suggests that demographic variables are the starting point for segmentation, followed by operating variables, purchasing approaches, situational factors, and personal characteristics of buyers.[4] For example, a demographic variable, such as the buying company's industry, most likely will be a more obvious segmentation variable than a personal characteristic, like the buyer's attitude toward risk. Usually marketers focus not on one but on a combination of segmentation variables.

Whatever approach is used for market segmentation and selection, it is important to have the discipline to say "no" to opportunities that fall outside the served market. Too often, a company tries to become all things to all people, chasing any marketing opportunity that comes along. A lack of focus in market definition and selection dilutes a company's resources, makes it vulnerable to more focused competitors, and damages its credibility with its customers.

---

[3]Philip Kotler, *Marketing Management: Analysis, Planning, Implementation, and Control,* 6th ed. (Englewood Cliffs, N.J.: Prentice Hall, 1988).

[4]Thomas V. Bonoma and Benson P. Shapiro, *Segmenting the Industrial Market* (Lexington, Mass.: Lexington Books, 1983).

Positioning and Differentiation

At least as important as the choice of target market is the determination of what makes the company and its products and services more attractive than those of its competitors in the minds of potential customers. Marketers over the years have used two terms to describe this decision:

- **Differentiation.** (What uniquely different benefits do we offer prospective customers?)
- **Positioning.** (What might customers perceive as the advantages and disadvantages of our position relative to our competition?)

Strategy researchers also stress the importance of differentiation and positioning. For example, Michael Porter, in *Competitive Strategy,* discusses differentiation as one of the generic strategies available to competitors.[5] While most researchers agree that differentiation is important, marketing managers in the trenches must grapple with the thorny issue of how to develop and sustain a unique position in the face of multiple competitors.

Products and product lines are most frequently positioned with respect to benefits on which they are or claim to be superior for particular market segments. This is sometimes described as establishing a "unique selling proposition."[6] In most industries, marketers also devote time and energy to **corporate positioning,** the development of a company's overall image, its reputation in the marketplace.

Exhibit 4 describes 15 differentiation strategies that are frequently attempted by companies across a broad range of industries. While some of the strategies (such as quality and value leadership) are applicable to product positioning, all of the strategies offer potential for corporate positioning.[7]

As an example of how to use the positioning framework in Exhibit 4, consider three industries: credit cards (a consumer financial service), management consulting (a business-to-business professional service), and microcomputer hardware (a high-tech product that is marketed both to individuals and to organizations). Exhibit 5 is a listing of the companies in each industry that have attained a claim to leadership using different positioning variables. The listings are based on responses from a small sample of consumers and "experts" who have worked in each of the industries. There are a number of cases in Exhibit 5 in which two firms are locked in a battle for a particular leadership position. In those situations, both firms are named. In cases where a large number of competitors are all claiming superiority but none has an edge, a pair of asterisks (**) appears. In cases where no competitor appears to be aggressively pursuing a leadership position, a pair of question marks (??) appears.

Marketers attempting to assess the competitive position of their own firms would use the framework in Exhibit 4 in the following way. First, they would ask:

- Which of the positions in Exhibit 4 are of greatest value to our target customers, given their needs and the products and services we provide?

---

[5]Michael E. Porter, *Competitive Strategy* (New York: Free Press, 1980).
[6]Rosser Reeves, *Reality in Advertising* (New York: Alfred A. Knopf, 1961).
[7]Thomas J. Kosnik, "Corporate Positioning: How to Assess—and Build—a Company's Reputation," Harvard Business School Publishing Division, No. 589-087, 1989.

- Are there points of differentiation not on the list that we should add because they are critical to our prospective customers?
- Which one or two positions most clearly differentiates our company or business unit?
- Which positions are held by our major competitors?
- Which positions are "cluttered" with many competitors claiming to hold the title? Which are relatively free of competition?
- Which of these corporate positions provide the best fit with our product and product line positioning strategies?
- Which of these positions provides the best fit with our corporate goals and values?

The objective of initial internal discussions on these questions is to develop internal consensus on the most desirable positioning strategy for the firm. In addition, the firm would conduct research among its existing customers and among noncustomers to determine their perceptions of the firm and its various competitors. Identifying the differences between the firm's view of the most desirable positioning and the current perceptions in the marketplace provides a foundation for discussions about marketing plans that will change the beliefs and attitudes of prospective customers toward the desired positioning for the company.

To develop a richer understanding of the positioning framework, consider an industry with which you have experience as a consumer. Examples include automobiles, graduate business programs, and airlines. Which of the leadership positions are occupied, vacant, or being contested? What differentiation strategies should a competitor in one of those industries follow if it wants to increase its chances of winning your business?

Product Life Cycle

One of the most pervasive concepts in marketing strategy is the product life cycle. In its simplest form, the product life cycle suggests that there is a predictable pattern of sales growth over the life of products at each level below:

Level	*Example*
Product category	Computers
Subcategory	Microcomputers
Brand	IBM PC or Apple Macintosh
Model	IBM PC AT or the Apple Macintosh II FX

Once a product is developed and launched, the five stages of the product life cycle, shown in Exhibit 6, are:

1. Market development
2. Rapid sales growth
3. Competitive turbulence
4. Saturated maturity
5. Decline

While these stages are sometimes labeled differently, the critical insights from the product life cycle are that: (1) there are distinct stages of evolution, with systematic differences in market conditions at each stage; and (2) different marketing strategies and tactics are required to compete successfully at each stage.

Market Development. The market development phase for a product category is characterized by customer uncertainty and doubt about the potential benefits of the new technology. Potential customers may ask questions like: Why do I need this product? What are its benefits over what I am currently using? Will it work as promised? Can the supplier provide timely support if things go wrong? Is it hard to learn and use? Will the product last a while, or quickly become obsolete as a better mousetrap comes along? Is it compatible with what others around me are using now, or will use in the future? What are the risks to me if this new contraption is not all it's claimed to be?

The marketing company's challenge during market development is to reduce uncertainty and barriers to adoption by educating potential customers and demonstrating successful applications, often through early adopters of the product who become exemplars and opinion leaders for others to follow.

During the market development phase, there are typically few designs of the product on offer. For example, during the late 1970s, the two dominant designs in the microcomputer market were the Apple II, from Apple computer, and a standard based on the CP/M operating system from Digital Research that was offered by competitors like Tandy (Radio Shack). Marketing communications programs during the market development stage are designed to stimulate primary demand, with less emphasis on differentiating individual brands. Personal selling is important to inform distributors and customers about the benefits of the product, to answer their questions, and to reduce their perceived risk. Some competitors may select a skim pricing strategy to generate the profits necessary to pay the costs of educating the market. Others will follow a penetration pricing strategy, lowering prices in an effort to stimulate trial, establish market share leadership, increase cumulative volume, and, thereby, drive down future production costs.

It is most important at this stage to "grow the market" by stimulating basic demand than to steal market share from competitors. Indeed, early entrants often welcome other competitors into the market, as Apple, which had been in the microcomputer market since the late 1970s, welcomed IBM into the PC market with full-page ads in 1981. Apple realized that the task of educating skeptical customers was more than the existing microcomputer firms could handle, and that IBM's marketing activities would help grow the market to the benefit of Apple.

Rapid Sales Growth. During the rapid sales growth stage, year-to-year growth rates of 30 to 50 percent for the product category are common. Why do sales grow so fast? Because large numbers of new customers enter the market for the first time during this phase, spurred in part by observing the benefits enjoyed by early adopters from the market development phase. In addition, new suppliers further stimulate demand by offering marginally better products, lower prices, or both. Word-of-mouth communication among customers and the imitation of opinion leaders by others also stimulate demand. New distribution channels are opened in this stage of the life cycle as new entrants struggle to find uncluttered paths to potential customers. Prices tend to fall as economies of scale and learning curve effects associated with increasing sales volume lower per-unit manufacturing costs, and as competitors use price discounts to wrestle share from another.

Continuing with the microcomputer example, as business professionals and students in the early 1980s noticed that their colleagues were able to write and to do quantitative analysis much faster and better with microcomputers than was possible with typewriters and calculators, they bought micros of their own. New computer retailers opened their doors, and alternative distribution channels, such as mail order, emerged. At the same time, hundreds of IBM-compatible PC-clone manufacturers entered the market, leading to rapid growth rates in unit sales for five years, and a reduction of the price for a basic machine from about $4,000 to less than $1,000 over the period.

The marketing company's challenge during rapid sales growth is to offer a product that is attractive enough, in sufficient quantities, and at competitive prices, to hold or increase its market share during the ramp up in industry sales. Interfirm competition is not as intense in this phase as it is later on, because most suppliers are struggling simply to keep up with the surge in demand. It is common for market share leaders to experience, at the same time, increased sales volume along with a drop in market share. For example, in 1983, part of the reason that IBM lost market share to COMPAQ computer and other clone manufacturers was that IBM had stimulated basic demand for its PCs beyond its ability to fill all the orders of distributors and retailers. Throughout the late 1980s, Apple computer pursued a premium price strategy, which was one reason why it lost market share to other competitors despite its rapid growth during that period.

Competitive Turbulence.   While sales volume continues to grow during the competitive turbulence phase, the rate of growth decreases, until the growth curve flattens out as shown in Exhibit 6. By this phase, most potential adopters of the product category have bought their first product, and a greater percent of sales are made to consumers who are trading up, replacing older models, or buying second or third models. During this phase, the market begins to become saturated. As growth slows, the stronger competitors increase the pressure in an effort to sustain their sales growth, and weaker entrants are caught in the crossfire.

The small number of product designs often gives way to product proliferation during this stage, as competitors attempt to customize their models to meet the needs of different market segments. The products are available through a broad range of distribution channels, and competition within the channels intensifies as manufacturers compete for shelf space, and different channels compete for consumer sales. This leads to downward pressure on prices, which hurts weaker manufacturers, and often severely depresses margins in the distribution network. The result of these patterns is that both weaker manufacturers and less efficient distribution channels withdraw from the market in what is often described as an industry shakeout.

In 1983–84, U.S. unit sales of IBM PC compatible microcomputers increased 175 percent. In 1984–85, unit sales increased only 11 percent, a very rapid leveling off of growth. In the aftermath was that several IBM-clone manufacturers were driven out of business, and a number of computer retailers went bankrupt as well. The microcomputer market enjoyed a second growth spurt in the latter part of the 1980s, but by the early 1990s it was clear that the recovery was temporary, and the PC segment of the computer industry was moving from competitive turbulence to saturated maturity.

Saturated Maturity.   In the saturated maturity phase, unit sales remain level or even decline. Most sales are to repeat purchasers and are easily postponed if economic conditions are depressed, or if other problems divert customer attention and dollars. Price competition is fierce, and attempts to differentiate may be based more on packaging and other factors, rather than major product enhancements. Distribution becomes more critical, as the ability to differentiate on product features alone declines. The cost economies and market positions of entrenched competitors make it difficult to enter a mature market without a radical breakthrough in technology that either drastically reduces a new entrant's costs or provides major new benefits to customers.

In the microcomputer example, by the late 1980s, workstation manufacturers like Sun Microsystems were threatening the PC market from above. The basic hardware for desktop machines on the IBM-compatible side remained fairly stable from 1987 through 1991, and most innovations were in the area of progressively smaller laptop and notebook-sized machines. On the Apple Macintosh side there was also relatively little product innovation. However, in 1991, Apple drastically reduced prices on its desktop machines, and then introduced a series of new notebook-sized models. The basic functionality of microcomputers did not change much from 1987–91, and the miniaturization leading to notebooks can be considered as either an example of competition through innovative packaging or the emergence of a new product subcategory. Computer companies attempted to broaden distribution by selling through mass merchants and direct mail channels. By 1991, the entire industry was waiting expectantly for the next major technological breakthrough, such as multimedia computing, which promised to allow customers to combine video, animation, and sound with the existing text and graphics capabilities of traditional microcomputers.

Decline

The maturity phase of the product life cycle may last many years, especially if manufacturing innovations allow the unit price to fall sufficiently that customers buy multiple copies for reasons of convenience (as was true for pocket calculators and Walkman-like cassette players), or for fashion (as was true for Swatch watches). Eventually, however, unit sales will turn down and the product enters the decline phase. Decline may occur either because customer needs change, rendering the product obsolete, or because a substitute technology meets the needs better than existing products. As total sales in the category decline, overcapacity leads to fierce price competition. Marketing expenditures are reduced because they are no longer effective in stimulating demand. Marginal suppliers and distributors continue to exit. (However, late in the decline stage there are opportunities for profitable operation if a core of loyal, relatively price-insensitive buyers remains and only a few producers are left (as in the case of fountain pens).

In the microcomputer industry example, it can be argued that notebook and pen-based computers are new product forms, and that the 1990s will witness the decline and demise of desktop computers as they were known in the early 1980s. They will be replaced by rapidly growing new product categories (notebook and pen-based computers), which will, in time, pass through competitive turbulence, saturated maturity, and decline, as well.

Conclusion.   Why is the product life cycle important? First, because it forces managers to think strategically about the future. By knowing that sales neither go up in a straight line nor keep growing forever, managers can better anticipate the marketing resources required and how they might best be allocated. By understanding when competitors are likely to enter and how they are likely to behave at each stage, marketers can better decide when it makes sense to drop prices, to introduce new models, or to change their marketing communications or distribution strategy. Finally, the product life cycle encourages a proactive, rather than a reactive, stance. This makes it easier to make the correct decisions with respect to the timing of market entry and exit, which is a recurring strategic issue facing marketers in an industry. One caveat, however, is important. Managers must not let themselves and their marketing creativity be held hostage to the product life cycle; the creation of each stage and the level of product sales and profitability are very much in the hands of the marketer.

Market Entry/Exit Decisions

Market entry and exit decisions are sometimes made by product managers (When should we launch this new product?) and by sales managers (Should we try to penetrate a new account, or expand into a new territory?). In other cases, the decision to enter or leave a market is made by senior executives of a corporation. For example, in the mid 1980s, the executive committee of Vestron, Inc., a distributor of videocassettes and movies, had to decide whether to: (1) withdraw from the video distribution business entirely, (2) downsize its video distribution operation, or (3) enter the video production business (the making of films) to improve its competitive position in video distribution.

A number of frameworks have been developed to analyze entry and exit decisions based on the attractiveness of the market segment and the company's positioning relative to competitors.[8] However, these models do not focus attention on the fact that some markets vary with respect to risk (uncertainty about future developments) and that managers have different preferences for risk. Continuing with the Vestron example, the decision to enter the video production business involved much greater uncertainty than the two other alternatives, because Vestron executives had much less information about it. At the same time, the chairman of Vestron was an entrepreneur, who was likely to prefer a high stakes/high reward game over one with less uncertainty but less upside potential.

The framework shown in Exhibit 6 can be used to illustrate the market attractiveness (the viability of the market for long-term profitability) and competitive position (the business strengths needed to succeed) of different strategic alternatives, with the added dimension that the options may involve either **high or low risk.**[9] Thus, the management of Vestron would be able to use Exhibit 6 to highlight the differences between the two less-risky strategies and the more-risky alternative of integrating backward into video production. Take a moment to decide where you might place each of those options on Exhibit 6. Which alternative do you think might be more attractive to Vestron's chairman? To the vice president of marketing? To the vice president of finance?

---

[8]See Richard G. Hamermesh, *Making Strategy Work: How Senior Managers Produce Results* (New York: Free Press, 1986).

[9]Kotler, *Marketing Management* (1988).

In another application, a company trying to decide what countries to enter as part of its international expansion could highlight differences in country risk by using the framework in Exhibit 6. For example, in the summer of 1989, following the suppression of political demonstrations in the People's Republic of China, a poll was taken of Western business executives' beliefs about the market outlook for both China and the Union of Soviet Socialist Republics. The survey showed that, although both the Chinese and Soviet markets offered tremendous potential, there was substantially greater uncertainty about the future prospects for China. How might that difference be illustrated on Exhibit 6, if a firm was considering new marketing initiatives in those two countries?

Selecting and Articulating the Marketing Vision and Values

In the 1980s, there was increasing emphasis on the importance of articulating a strategic marketing vision that creates passion, excitement, and commitment to the strategy. Commentators noted the need for a marketing strategy to be consistent with the shared values that serve as the foundation for a company's culture and provide continuity as management personnel change.

It is important to note there are many paths to excellence; that is, highly successful competitors in the same industry often have different corporate values. For example, IBM and Apple computer, Pepsico and Coca Cola, the Marine Corps and the Air Force, and Harvard and Stanford Business Schools are all leaders in their respective domains, yet the values of each pair of institutions are perceptibly different.

There are three key points to remember with respect to the implications of vision and values for marketing strategy. First, basing a marketing strategy on purely financial goals, such as growth in sales, profitability, or market share, is unlikely to capture the imaginations of the employees who must execute the strategy or the customers the strategy is designed to serve. To marshal commitment and support, values that address a higher purpose must be included.

Second, some strategic alternatives are fundamentally inconsistent with certain values. For example, in 1981 Hartmann Luggage, a manufacturer of high-quality, expensive luggage, traded down to introduce a line of less-expensive luggage targeted at women. The line was withdrawn from the market in part because it was a poor fit with the Hartmann culture, which put strong emphasis on product quality and durability. Care must be taken in selecting a strategy to ensure that it meshes with the beliefs of the organization that must carry it out. Alternatively, some effort will be required to change the values to fit a new strategy, if such a course is deemed necessary for the survival of the organization. However, company values, which are heavily influenced by company history and tradition over time, tend to be hard to instill and even harder to change.

Finally, some strategic marketing options may place individual employees on the horns of an ethical dilemma. For example, a company creating industrial chemicals by a process that releases ozone into the atmosphere may enjoy better profits, growth, and market share if it does not act to eliminate the ozone discharge until it is required to by law. However, a marketing manager concerned with the company's social responsibility to preserve the world ecology may have difficulty following a "wait and see" strategy.

Anticipating and Responding to Competitors' Marketing Strategies

Strategic marketing decisions are rarely, if ever, carried out in a competitive vacuum. Every marketing action may provoke a wide range of reactions from competitors, which in turn must be met by a competitive move of our own. **Competitive response analysis** is a strategic exercise in which marketing decision makers:

- Identify the range of possible competitive reactions to each strategic option they are considering.
- Forecast the likely impact of each combination of their action and the competitor's reaction.
- Redo the analysis for successive periods to examine the overall effect of each series of moves on their objectives and values.
- Select the strategy that is expected to yield the best results across the range of competitive reactions.

As an illustration of competitive response analysis, consider the dilemma facing John Deere and Company in 1976. Deere was about to launch a new tractor aimed at large industrial construction contractors, a segment that was the traditional home turf of Deere's leading competitor, Caterpillar. One key strategic decision was whether to price the Deere product aggressively, in a bid to capture a major portion of Caterpillar's market share, or to set a higher price. Caterpillar's options included lowering the price of its existing products, introducing a new product in the industrial construction segment, and, over the longer term, launching a counterattack in the agricultural tractor segment that was Deere's largest and most important market. How do you think Caterpillar might respond if Deere entered with an aggressive price? With a premium price? What would Deere's likely countermoves be in each case? What set of moves and countermoves would be in Deere's best interest? How might Deere influence its competitor by its own choice of strategy?

Analytic techniques such as multiperiod game theory, payoff tables, and decision trees can be used to add structure to competitive response analysis. But whether the approach taken is quantitative or qualitative, highly analytical or intuitive, the important point is that anticipating, preempting, and influencing competitors' reactions is a central activity in effective marketing strategy.

Conclusion: Flexibility and Focus in Marketing Strategy Formulation

Exhibit 7 suggests that effective marketing strategy can and should provide varying degrees of focus and flexibility, depending on the level of change in the marketplace.[10] On the one hand, no single company can be all things to all customers, so there must be *focus* on **who** (what segments) we will serve, **what** will be the primary source of our differential advantage, and **why** we do things in our particular way (based on our marketing vision and values). On the other hand, markets and indus-

---

[10]Thomas J. Kosnik, "The Marketing Process," in Thomas V. Bonoma and Thomas J. Kosnik, *Marketing Management: Text and Cases* (Homewood, Ill.: Richard D. Irwin, 1990).

tries are constantly changing in unpredictable ways as new technology is introduced, competitors change, regulations and external shocks redefine the playing field, and consumer preferences evolve. As a result, there must be *flexibility* on decisions about **how** we will respond to competitors, **when** we will enter and exit, and **which technologies** will be used to meet the customers' changing needs.

High focus with relatively low flexibility can lead to **lockstep,** a situation whereby everyone marches to the beat of the same drummer, no questions asked. Lockstep has the advantage of concentrating tremendous mass on a marketing strategy, which increases the chances of success in the short run. The potential risk in the long run is that it may take the organization much longer to react to changes in the environment, because the people in the trenches are busy following orders, instead of using their initiative to figure out better ways of doing things.

For example, Sears, the retailing giant, enjoyed success for decades by highly disciplined adherence to a **value leader** marketing strategy: good quality products at a relatively low price under its own store brands, such as Kenmore appliances and Craftsman tools. Sears believed that its customers were the classic middle-American households, and that its competitors for customer dollars were such stores as J. C. Penney and Montgomery Ward. However, as changing demographics eroded Sears's traditional customer base, and new retailing competitors began to discount national brands in clothing and household appliances, Sears was slow to respond. The lockstep commitment to basic value that had been the mainstay of Sears's earlier success became a point of vulnerability as the marketplace grew increasingly turbulent in the 1970s and 1980s.

A lack of focus and flexibility results in **paralysis,** where the organization and the people in it seem to drift with the current, unable to do anything to control their collective destiny. This situation is common in companies that have endured a sustained period of financial losses, turnover, and layoffs, where senior management is meeting in secret trying to figure out what to do, and everyone else is either afraid to try anything new, or so constrained by lack of resources that they can't prime the pump of innovative ideas.

Eastern Airlines provides a classic example of paralysis. Once one of the largest and proudest of the international airlines, Eastern seemed to lose its customer focus in the 1980s, with a deteriorating reputation due to inconsistent service, unreliable timetables, and increased scrutiny of its aircraft maintenance procedures by federal regulatory agencies. At the same time, Eastern was not as flexible as some of its competitors, partly due to labor-management disputes, which inhibited the ability to make rapid marketing moves and hampered the introduction of innovative work procedures and technologies. Eastern's paralysis drove the company into a hostile takeover by a competitor and finally into bankruptcy.

Lack of focus coupled with high flexibility leads to **chaos,** where numerous individuals in the organization are all pulling in different directions to try to get their personal strategies implemented. A common occurrence in accounting, consulting and law firms, investment banks, technology companies, and highly competitive product management organizations, chaos is not perceived to be a problem in periods when growth is booming and everyone is enjoying the fruits of high profitability. However, when the environment becomes more competitive, and the resources needed to support the growth dry up, chaos often turns into paralysis.

The history of Sun Microsystems in the late 1980s shows both the bright side and the dark side of a chaotic marketing strategy. Founded in 1982, Sun introduced powerful engineering workstations that quickly dominated the technical/scientific market segment. In 1985, Sun established several autonomous divisions to develop and market products for other segments, such as government agencies and universities. Sun frequently created task forces to respond aggressively to problems and opportunities. The rapid pace and high energy made the chaos at Sun Microsystems exciting for employees, but the attempt to stretch for every market opportunity that presented itself caused problems. In 1989, several key executives departed; there were delays in product shipments; and the company reported a quarterly operating loss. Industry observers suggested that Sun needed to focus its marketing efforts to regain momentum.

The seemingly contradictory combination of high focus and high flexibility results in **perennial renaissance,** a constant renewal of marketing strategy that seems magically to keep the organization out in front of changing competitors, technology, and customer needs. *Perennial* suggests consistent, enduring, and constant change; *renaissance* implies creativity and a rebirth of the ideals of an earlier age.

American Express provides an example of perennial renaissance in action. It has long focused its marketing strategy on customers who were more financially stable and, hence, more responsible in their use of credit. It also has maintained a steady focus in its differentiation strategy: impeccable service and the prestige of membership. Equally important, American Express has been steadfast in articulating its vision and values to employees, thereby ensuring the consistent excellence that its customers expect.

While focused on the **who, what,** and **why** questions, American Express has shown tremendous flexibility on issues of **how, when,** and **which.** It has proven a wily competitor in the financial and travel-related services arenas, nimbly responding to a broad range of formidable adversaries. It has made timely decisions to enter new markets, such as the personal financial planning market via the acquisition of IDS. It has also been willing to withdraw from ventures that were no longer attractive, as was the case with Fireman's Fund Insurance. Finally, American Express has pioneered the use of new information technologies that allow it to make better decisions about card applications and authorizing transactions, and to provide better service when customers call to inquire about their monthly bills. Understanding which variables require focus and which require flexibility has made American Express's marketing strategy much more durable than those of its competitors in a rapidly changing marketplace.

We should not conclude from this discussion that one approach to marketing strategy formulation dominates the others. In stable environments, if the company is in a leadership position, **lockstep** may be the most effective approach. In volatile environments, where the company has not yet found its distinctive relative advantage yet has enough resources to experiment, **chaos** may be the best way to encourage rapid-fire innovation under time pressure. **Perennial renaissance** combines the benefits of both focus and flexibility. However, it requires that managers at all levels be sophisticated enough to play multiple roles in the process, strong-willed enough to champion a cause when necessary, and open-minded enough to abandon an experiment that is not working or adapt a strategy in the wake of what has been learned from recent successes and failures. The only cell in Exhibit 7 that marketers should in all circumstances avoid is that of **paralysis.**

In closing, the frameworks introduced in this note are marketing's contribution to the strategy formulation process. By conducting more thoughtful analyses of market selection, of differentiation and positioning, of market entry and exit, the blending of strategies with vision and values, and competitive response, marketers can make better decisions themselves. They also can have a positive impact on the strategic processes that involve other functional managers and the chief executive officer.

EXHIBIT 1

The market definition framework

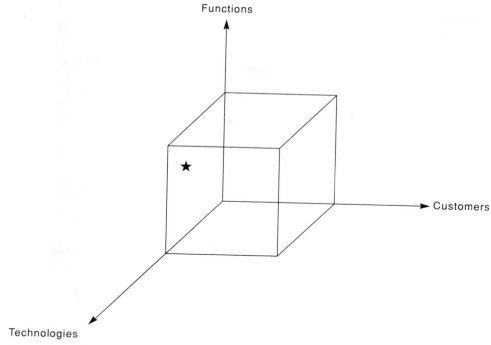

SOURCE: Adapted from Derek A. Abell, *Defining the Business* (Englewood Cliffs, N.J.: Prentice Hall, 1980).

EXHIBIT 2   **Major Segmentation Variables for Consumer Markets**

Variable

Geographic
Region
County size
City or SMSA size
Density
Climate

Demographic
Age
Sex
Family size
Family life cycle
Income
Occupation
Education
Religion
Race
Nationality

Psychographic
Social class
Lifestyle
Personality

Behavioral
Occasions
Benefits
User status
Usage rate
Loyalty status
Readiness stage
Attitude toward product

SOURCE: Adapted from Philip Kotler, *Marketing Management: Analysis, Planning, Implementation, and Control*, 6th ed. (Englewood Cliffs, N.J.: Prentice Hall, 1988), p. 287.

Exhibit 3   Segmentation Variables for Industrial Markets

Demographic
- *Industry:* Which industries that buy this product should we focus on?
- *Company size:* What size companies should we focus on?
- *Location:* What geographical areas should we focus on?

Operating Variables
- *Technology:* What customer technologies should we focus on?
- *User/nonuser status:* Should we focus on heavy, medium, light users, or nonusers?
- *Customer capabilities:* Should we focus on customers needing many services or few services?

Purchasing Approaches
- *Purchasing function organization:* Should we focus on companies with highly centralized or decentralized purchasing organizations?
- *Power structure:* Should we focus on companies that are engineering-dominated, financially-dominated, and the like?
- *Nature of existing relationships:* Should we focus on companies with which we have strong existing relationships or simply go after the most desirable companies?
- *General purchase policies:* Should we focus on companies that prefer leasing? Service contracts? Systems purchases? Sealed bidding?
- *Purchasing criteria:* Should we focus on companies that are seeking quality? Service? Price?

Situational Factors
- *Urgency:* Should we focus on companies that need quick and sudden delivery or service?
- *Specific application:* Should we focus on certain applications of our product, rather than all applications?
- *Size of order:* Should we focus on large or small orders?

Personal Characteristics
- *Buyer-seller similarity:* Should we focus on companies whose people and values are similar to ours?
- *Attitudes toward risk:* Should we focus on risk-taking or risk-avoiding customers?
- *Loyalty:* Should we focus on companies that show high loyalty to their suppliers?

SOURCE: Adapted from Thomas V. Bonoma and Benson P. Shapiro, *Segmenting the Industrial Market* (Lexington, Mass.: Lexington Books, 1983).

Exhibit 4   Alternative Strategies for Differentiation/Positioning
---

Market share leader	=	The biggest
Quality leader	=	The best/most reliable products and services
Service leader	=	The most responsive when customers have problems
Technology leader	=	The first to develop new technology
Innovation leader	=	The most creative in applying it
Variety leader	=	The largest assortment of products and services
Flexibility leader	=	The most adaptable
Relationship leader	=	The most committed to the customer's success
Prestige leader	=	The most exclusive
Knowledge leader	=	The most experience or greatest expertise
Global leader	=	The best positioned to serve world markets
Bargain leader	=	The lowest price
Value leader	=	The best price performance
Integrity leader	=	The most ethical/trustworthy
Social responsibility leader	=	The most positive force in communities it serves

EXHIBIT 5   **A Cross-Industry Comparison of Leadership Positions**

	Credit Cards	Management Consulting	Microcomputer Hardware Suppliers
Market share leader	VISA	Arthur Andersen (AA)	IBM
Quality leader	**	**	Compaq
Service leader	American Express (AMEX)	**	IBM
Technology leader	Citicorp/AMEX	AA/Booz Allen	Sun Microsystems
Innovation leader	**	BCG	Apple
Variety leader	??	**	IBM
Flexibility leader	??	??	**
Relationship leader	**	Bain & Co.	Hewlett-Packard
Prestige leader	American Express	McKinsey	Grid/Next
Knowledge leader	??	Varies by segment	??
Global leader	American Express	**	IBM/Toshiba
Bargain leader	Sears Discover	??	Tandy
Value leader	Sears Discover	SPA/Bain & Co.	Zenith/Dell
Integrity leader	??	**	??
Social responsibility leader	??	McKinsey	Xerox/IBM

NOTE: ** = many firms are vying for leadership, none dominates.
       ?? = no firm seems to be seeking leadership on the variable.

EXHIBIT 6

The product life cycle

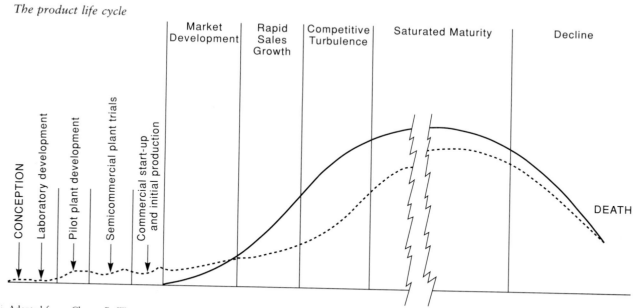

Adapted from: Chester R. Wasson, *Dynamic Competitive Strategy & Product Life Cycles* (Austin, Tex.: Austin Press, 1978), p. 4.

EXHIBIT 7

A model for analyzing market entry and exit decisions

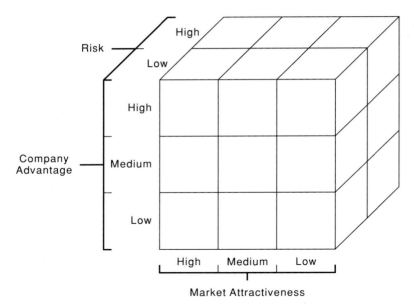

SOURCE: Adapted from Philip Kotler, *Marketing Management: Analysis, Planning, Implementation, and Control,*6th ed. (Englewood Cliffs, N.J.: Prentice Hall, 1988), p. 390.

EXHIBIT 8

Flexibility and focus: The essence of effective strategy

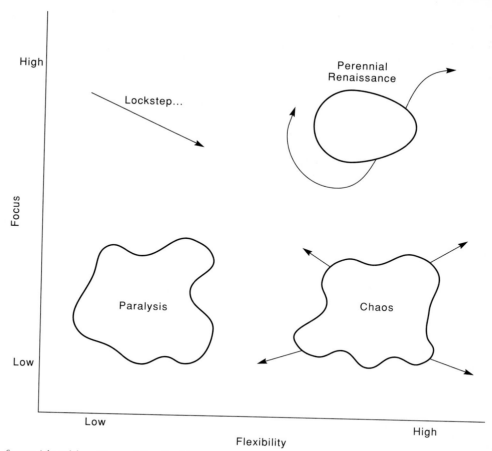

SOURCE: Adapted from Thomas J. Kosnik, "The Marketing Process," in Thomas V. Bonoma and Thomas J. Kosnik, *Marketing Management: Text and Cases* (Homewood, Ill.: Richard D. Irwin, 1990).

Note on the Motorcycle Industry—1975

In the third quarter of this century, the world motorcycle industry underwent a number of major changes. Originally used primarily for basic transport, the motorcycle became a recreational vehicle for many purchasers. Spurred largely by the increase in recreational users, the motorcycle market grew at a phenomenal pace, especially in the United States. Market leadership shifted from the established producers to the Japanese, whose exports were insignificant before 1960.

Motorcycles—Products and Production Technology

Two-wheeled motor vehicles were first produced in Germany in the 1890s. By the mid-20th century, product evolution had differentiated *mopeds* (small-engined vehicles, which also could be propelled by pedaling) and *motor scooters* (which had a shielded seating position and smaller wheels) from *motorcycles*.

Motorcycles differed along several dimensions. Some had two-stroke engines, which fired once in each cylinder for every revolution of the crankshaft; others were powered by four-stroke engines, like those of autos, which fired on every other revolution. Two-strokes gave more power at any given size and weight, and were more responsive to the throttle. On the other hand, they were less fuel-efficient and tended to wear out faster than four-stroke engines. Since two-stroke engines were less expensive, however, they were standard on many smaller motorcycles.

Motorcycle design also differed according to the type of use for which the vehicle was intended. Off-road machines (used almost exclusively for recreation) had more robust frames, with higher ground clearance, studded tires to increase traction in mud and sand, various engine modifications to ensure maximum "pulling" power, rather than speed, and unmuffled exhaust to increase power. On-road machines carried the necessary safety equipment (e.g., lights, rear-view mirrors, signals). They were designed for high cruising speeds, rider comfort, and good handling at high speeds. Combination or *enduro* machines were supposed to serve both functions; some models were designed with a bias toward on-road use, others toward off-road.

Finally, motorcycle engine sizes varied widely: displacement ranged from 50 to 1200 cubic centimeters. Motorcycles with engines smaller than 125cc were not legal for use on all roads (e.g., on interstate highways). The larger-engined motorcycles demanded both greater strength and superior skill for proper handling. Their heavier weight could make them difficult for a small person to control. Harley-Davidson's 1207cc model, for example, weighed 722 pounds while its 123cc machine weighed only 232 pounds. Moreover, since the increase in engine displacement was proportionally greater than the increase in motorcycle weight, the larger machines had much higher acceleration and, thus, required greater driver skill.

The principal production processes involved in motorcycle manufacture were metal forming ones. Two quite different approaches to this type of manufacturing operation were pursued by different competitors. One alternative was to use general-purpose, labor-intensive equipment and operate with broad ranges of tolerance in the finished-product. The other option was to adopt capital-intensive, massproduction techniques, which significantly increased productivity but required correspondingly higher capital investments. Thus, the British motorcycle producers employed £1,300 of net fixed investment per person to produce £4,200 of value added per person-year, while Honda, a Japanese producer, used £5,000 of net fixed investment to generate value added of £18,000 per person-year.

Purchased material and components, manufacturing value added, and selling and distribution expenses each represented about one third of retail value. The relative weights of purchased materials and manufacturing value added, of course, depended upon the degree of vertical integration. Similarly, the breakdown of manufacturing value added depended upon the choice of manufacturing technology. Labor cost was nearly 60 percent of manufacturing value added for the British producers but only 13 percent for Honda. Engine manufacture represented the largest part of manufacturing value added, followed by cycle parts and assembly operations.

Market Trends

Motorcycle use is closely linked with the development of a country's economic prosperity. In the first stage of the evolutionary pattern, motorcycles are purchased by lower-income consumers to provide basic transport at a fraction of the cost of a car. When they can afford to do so, however, consumers tend to replace their motorcycles with cars. Thus, as national income increases, the proportion of the

This note originally was prepared by Dev Purkayastha, research assistant under the direction of Professor Robert D. Buzzell. This revised version was prepared by Nancy Jackson under the direction of Professor Buzzell.

population using motorcycles for basic transport decreases, while automobile use rises. Eventually, as income levels continue to rise, people begin to purchase motorcycles primarily for secondary, recreational uses, rather than as a form of basic transport.

In 1974, the world motorcycle markets included countries in each of these phases. The United States and Canada were in the final phase, with recreational uses predominant. Japan and Europe were thought to be entering the second phase, with cars replacing motorcycles for basic transport. The rest of the world was either in or approaching the first phase.

United States and Canada. Between 1950 and 1960, motorcycle ownership in the United States was stagnant at about 500,000. In the next 15 years, however, sales boomed, rising from 40–50,000 units in 1960 to more than a million in 1974. Virtually all machines were imported (see Exhibit 1). Most purchasers owned a car as well as a motorcycle.

Demographic changes helped make this rapid growth possible. Between 1960 and 1970, while the overall U.S. population increased by 13 percent, the number of people aged 14 to 24 (the primary customer group for motorcycles) rose from 27 to 41 million. Per capita disposable income increased from $1,934 to $3,348 (in current dollars) over the same period.

Sales growth was not uniform over this boom period, however. In the early 1960s, an entirely new group of customers was attracted by the newly available lightweight inexpensive Japanese imports. First-time buyers accounted for 80 percent of motorcycle sales in those years. By the middle of the decade, on the other hand, sales were flattening, and 80 percent of the machines sold went to replacement buyers.

Beginning in 1968, industry sales growth again accelerated, driven by the growing popularity of off-road motorcycles—trail bikes, motocross bikes, scramblers, and desert bikes—and combination machines that also could be used on the roads. The number of off-road models offered by the major producers rose from 2 in 1968 to 38 in 1974; the number of combination models more than doubled. These new products, which generally had smaller (under 350cc) engines, drew a new kind of customer, the motorcycle hobbyist, into the market.

During this same period, sales shifted significantly toward larger motorcycles as repeat buyers traded up. "Super bikes" over 750cc grew at an annual rate of 47 percent from 1968 to 1974, while sales of bikes under 350cc remained essentially stagnant (Exhibit 2). These large-engined motorcycles were almost exclusively for on-road use. The Japanese expanded their export product line during the 1970s to include larger bikes previously available only from British and American producers.

The Japanese products matched the strengths of big British bikes—premium finish, elegant styling, superior handling, and high performance—and also added new features: electric starters, four-cylinder engines, disk brakes, and five-speed transmissions. Moreover, the Japanese producers were able to capitalize on their reputation for superior reliability.

By 1974, 2.4 percent of the U.S. population owned motorcycles. Off-road models accounted for some 20 percent of these 6 million machines; on-road and combination models accounted for 40 percent each.

The Canadian motorcycle market was similar to the U. S. markets in its essential features, although much smaller at 55,000 units in 1974.

Europe. During the 1960s, cars were superseding motorcycles as a form of basic transport in Europe. In the United Kingdom (U.K.), for example, motorcycle registrations fell from 205,000 in 1964 to 86,000 in 1969. Per capita ownership varied from country to country; 2.3 percent of the Italian population owned motorcycles in 1969, but only 0.4 percent of the West Germans.

As recreational uses began to emerge in the early 1970s, European motorcycle sales revived substantially, as shown in Table A. In 1974, 400,000 motorcycles were sold in Europe, almost 20 percent of them with engines larger than 450cc.

Japan. Between 1967 and 1974, the Japanese domestic market for motorcycles, scooters, and mopeds hovered around 1.2 million units, down from a 1961 high of 1.7 million units. In large part because of the extremely stringent regulations governing the issuance of drivers' licenses for large motorcycles, more than 90 percent of machines sold were smaller than 125cc.

Rest of the World. In the remaining countries, where motorcycles were used for primary transportation, total 1974 sales were 1.5 million units.

The Purchase Decision in a Mature Market: The U.S. Consumer

As we have seen, U.S. motorcycle demand in 1974 included a large component of recreational use. More than half of all

---

TABLE A Motorcycle Sales, 1969–1973

	Annual growth rate (%)
West Germany	45%
France	32
United Kingdom	25
Italy	22

owners were less than 25 years old, and 90 percent were men.[1] Their median income was $12,720.

Most motorcyclists (81.2 percent) were introduced to motorcycles by a family member or friend. The buying process involved extensive shopping and information gathering, lasting an average of eight weeks. The information sources used included: other motorcycle owners (consulted by 85.3 percent of purchasers), dealer visits (82.2 percent), motorcycle magazines (68.9 percent), manufacturers' literature (51.9 percent), competition results (38.6 percent), and test driving (37.8 percent). On average, 3.7 makes or models were considered.

Buyers considered a variety of factors in selecting a brand or model as shown in Table B. More than half of all first-time buyers chose a motorcycle smaller than 175cc; replacement purchasers favored larger machines, typically trading up from their previous motorcycle, as shown in Table C. Only a third of repeat purchasers chose their old brand again, although there was evidence of brand loyalty among at least some customer groups.

Nearly all motorcycles in the United States (98 percent) were used for purposes other than commuting, and 58 percent were also used for traveling to work or school. Only 38 percent were used regularly for trips of more than 10 miles one way. On-road machines, particularly the large ones,

---

[1]Except where otherwise indicated, the U.S. consumer information is based on a 1973 study of motorcycle buyers by AHF Marketing Research, Inc. The study was kindly made available to the authors by *Cycle* magazine.

TABLE B　Factors Influencing Motorcycle Buyers

Product Attributes	Percent of Buyers Rating This Attribute as Important or Very Important
Quality of workmanship	94.6%
Availability of parts	91.6
Handling/performance	88.9
Power/acceleration	85.9
Styling/appearance	84.6
Recommendation of owners/friends	81.3
Dealer's reputation	80.4
Dealer's service	76.9
Resale value	74.8
Warranty coverage	72.1
Economy of operation	63.9
Test drive	56.3
Owned same make before	34.3

Source: AHF Marketing Research, Inc., "The Market for New Motorcycles," 1973.

TABLE C　Purchasing Trends of Repeat Motorcycle Buyers

Engine Size of Buyer's Present Motorcycle	Percentage of Buyers Purchasing Larger Motorcycle
Under 90cc	73.3%
100–135cc	77.3
175–250cc	54.3
300–350cc	55.3
360–450cc	38.8
500–650cc	35.7
Over 750cc	5.4
All Owners	57.9

Source: AHF Marketing Research, Inc., "The Market for New Motorcycles," 1973.

received heaviest use. The median annual distance traveled for the 600cc-and-over classes of motorcycles was 5,441 miles, compared with 2,273 miles for off-road bikes.

Virtually all motorcycle purchasers (95 percent) bought on credit, using banks (55 percent), finance companies (20 percent), and credit unions (20 percent).

Although the price sensitivity of motorcycle buyers had not been statistically documented, the general sense of the market was that customers' purchase decisions were not significantly influenced by small price differences (up to 10 percent) between competing brands in the same displacement class. Higher premiums reduced sales, and only customers who saw a distinct advantage in a particular model would pay a premium of as much as 20 percent. Such customers were sometimes willing to pay even higher premiums. The producer that commanded the highest premium, BMW, charged roughly 30 percent more than the best-selling brands in the same size classes.

Distribution

In the United States, motorcycles moved from the manufacturer to the consumer through distributors (generally subsidiaries of the producer) and dealers. Suggested margins were 10 percent of retail price for distributors and 25 percent for dealers.

Motorcycle dealers were independent businesspeople, usually specializing in motorcycles and their accessories. Since sales required a knowledgeable and enthusiastic salesperson and adequate backup service facilities, discount stores, department stores, or service stations could not handle motorcycles effectively. Sears Roebuck, for example, withdrew from the motorcycle business because it could not provide the after-sales service needed. Similarly, attempts to sell motorcycles through car dealerships had been largely unsuccessful.

In 1960 there were only about 3,000 U.S. motorcycle dealers, many of them part-time enterprises. By 1974, that number had swelled to around 10,000; most of these were small businesses, as shown in Table D. The median annual sales per dealership was 200 new motorcycles and 35 used motorcycles. About 80 percent of these dealerships were franchised by manufacturers, and most were exclusive (i.e., the dealer had to carry a full line of the franchisor's product and could not carry competitors' brands). European dealers, in contrast, typically carried a number of brands.

As motorcycle sales leveled off, accessories (e.g., helmets, luggage racks, backrests), parts, and service became an increasingly important part of the dealer's business (see Table E).

A 1974 Yamaha dealership survey showed that average dealership net worth was about 14 percent of sales. Profit before tax averaged 35.3 percent of net worth and return on sales was 5.1 percent. On average, inventory was turned over four times a year. Dealers spent 1.2 percent of sales revenue on promotions, advertising through newspapers, yellow pages, radio, and television. Relatively little advertising was done in cooperation with manufacturers.

The Competitors—Historical Development

During the 1960s, the mix of competitors in the U.S. motorcycle market changed markedly. Earlier, the market had been served mainly by Harley-Davidson of the United States; BSA, Triumph, and Norton of the United Kingdom; and Moto-Guzzi of Italy. Harley was the market leader in 1959 with sales of $16.6 million.

In that year the first two Japanese producers, Honda Motor Company and Yamaha Motor Company, entered the American market. The Japanese motorcycle industry had expanded rapidly since World War II to meet the need for cheap transportation. In 1959, Honda, Suzuki, Yamaha, and Kawasaki together produced some 450,000 motorcycles. With sales of $55 million in that year, Honda was already the world's largest motorcycle producer.

Excerpts from a report written by the chairman of BSA/Triumph (the largest British producer at the time), following a 1960 visit to several of the Japanese producers, are reproduced in Exhibit 3.

In contrast to other foreign producers, who relied on distributors, Honda established a U.S. subsidiary, American Honda Motor Company, and began its push in the U.S. market by offering very small lightweight motorcycles. The Honda machine had a three-speed transmission, an automatic clutch, five horsepower (compared with two and a half for the lightweight motorcycle then sold by Sears Roebuck), an electric starter, and a step-through frame for female riders. Generally superior to the Sears lightweight, and easier to handle, the Honda machines sold for less than $250 retail, compared with $1,000–$1,500 for the bigger American or British machines.

Honda followed a policy of developing the market region by region, beginning on the West Coast and moving eastward over a period of four to five years. In 1961 it lined up 125 dealers and spent $150,000 on regional advertising. Honda advertising represented a concerted effort to overcome the unsavory image of motorcyclists that had developed since the 1940s, given special prominence by the 1953 movie, *The Wild One*, which starred Marlon Brando as the surly, destructive leader of a motorcycle gang. In contrast, Honda addressed its appeal primarily to middle-class consumers, and claimed "You meet the nicest people on a Honda." This marketing effort was backed by heavy advertising expenditures. In 1965 Honda was estimated to have spent $4 million on advertising, and the other Japanese exporters also invested substantial sums: $1.5 million for Yamaha and $0.7 million for Suzuki.

Honda's strategy was phenomenally successful. Its U.S. sales rose from $500,000 in 1960 to $77 million in 1965. By 1966 Honda, Yamaha, and Suzuki together had 85 per-

TABLE D **Motorcycle and Accessories Dealers: Sales Distribution**

Annual Sales ($)	Dealers (%)
Under $50,000	19.0%
$50,000–$99,999	16.2
$100,000–$299,999	33.9
$300,000–$499,999	14.9
$500,000–$999,999	10.9
$1,000,000 and over	5.0
Total	100.0

SOURCE: *Motorcycle Dealernews.*

TABLE E **Breakdown of Motorcycle Dealer's Business, 1975**

	Percent of Sales	Gross Profit (%)
Motorcycles		19.2%
New	40%	
Used	10	
Accessories	20 ⎫	
Spare parts	12 ⎬	25.9
Service	19 ⎭	
Total	100	

SOURCE: Yamaha survey.

cent of the U.S. market. From a negligible position in 1960, lightweight motorcycles had come to dominate the market (see Exhibits 1 and 2).

The transformation and expansion of the motorcycle market during the early 1960s benefited British and American producers as well as the Japanese. British exports doubled between 1960 and 1966, while Harley-Davidson's sales increased from $16.6 million in 1959 to $29.6 million in 1965. Two press reports of the mid-1960s illustrate these traditional manufacturers' interpretation of the Japanese success:

> The success of Honda, Suzuki, and Yamaha in the States has been jolly good for us," Eric Turner, chairman of the board of BSA, Ltd., told *Advertising Age*. "People here start out by buying one of the low-priced Japanese jobs. They get to enjoy the fun and exhilaration of the open road and frequently end up buying one of our more powerful and expensive machines." The British insist that they're not really in competition with the Japanese (they're on the lighter end). The Japanese have other ideas. Just two months ago Honda introduced a 444cc model to compete, at a lower price, with the Triumph 500cc. [*Advertising Age*, December 27, 1965]

> "Basically we do not believe in the lightweight market," says William H. Davidson, son of one of the founders and currently president of the company (Harley-Davidson). "We believe that motorcycles are sports vehicles, not transportation vehicles. Even if a man says he bought a motorcycle for transportation, it's generally for leisure time use. The lightweight motorcycle is only supplemental. Back around World War I, a number of companies came out with lightweight bikes. We came out with one ourselves. We came out with another one in 1947 and it just did not go anywhere. We have seen what happens to these small sizes." [*Forbes*, September 15, 1966]

Meanwhile, the Japanese producers continued to grow in other export markets. Total 1974 production of motorcycles in Japan amounted to 3.4 million units, of which 2.9 million (85 percent) were exported. In Europe, where the Japanese did not begin their thrust until the late 1960s, they had captured a commanding share of key markets by 1974, as shown in Table F.

In short, by the mid-1970s the Japanese producers had come to dominate a market shared by European and American producers 20 years earlier. More than 100 American

companies had manufactured motorcycles at one time or another during the 20th century. One by one these firms vanished; three of them—Rupp Industries, Yankee Motor Company, and Fox Corporation—ceased production in 1973–74. In mid-1975 only Harley-Davidson and one other very small producer, Rokon of Keene, New Hampshire, remained.

Common Elements in Japanese Strategy

The four major Japanese producers—Honda, Yamaha, Kawasaki, and Suzuki—pursued strategies that were similar in several important respects. All placed great emphasis on market share and sales volume. The Japanese sales companies set their objectives in terms of annual sales volume, rather than short-term profitability, and these objectives were regarded as critical.

To realize their growth goals, the Japanese producers:

1. Updated or redesigned products whenever a market threat or opportunity was perceived.
2. Set prices at levels designed to achieve market share goals, and reduced them if necessary.
3. Established effective marketing systems in all markets where serious competition was intended, regardless of short-term costs.
4. Took a long-term perspective in planning and defining objectives.

The Japanese firms' financial policies also supported their growth orientation. With characteristically lower rates of dividend payout and higher debt/equity ratios, the Japanese firms could sustain a higher growth rate at any given level of return on assets than could their British or American counterparts.

The Japanese producers' higher volume allowed them to use a number of production techniques that would not have been economic at lower volumes. Machining and assembly operations were highly mechanized. Extensive use was made of rotary index, in-line transfer machines,[2] and conveyorized assembly lines. The Japanese also used advanced techniques, such as high-pressure die casting, hot and cold forging, and sintering, which reduced processing cost and metal wastage. Intracompany demand often was sufficient to justify the design and manufacture of their own machine tools.

TABLE F   **European Motorcycle Market Shares, 1974 (percent)**

	U.K.	*France*	*Germany*
Honda	50%	37%	39%
Yamaha	12	19	20
Suzuki	9	13	6
Kawasaki	5	5	6
Total	76	74	71

[2]"A transfer machine is a composite of a number of standardized machine unit stations. Each machine station performs a set of operations, and at the conclusion of a work cycle the part is transferred to the following station in the machine. Transfer machines usually save space and result in greater production." Bolz, Young, and Carson, *Production Handbook*, 3rd ed. (New York: Ronald Press, 1972), pp. 16–50.

Because their purchases were so large, motorcycle producers in Japan enjoyed a close relationship with parts suppliers, sometimes cemented by financial cross-holdings. The large volumes involved also allowed the parts suppliers to employ the most economic production techniques. The level of service provided, in terms of new parts development, delivery, and quality control tended to be very high.

The Japanese also made substantial investments in research and development, managing R&D activities with a view to balancing engineering, production, and marketing requirements. Lead times for new product introduction were relatively short.

The Competitors in 1974

Exhibits 4–10 present summary comparisons of the major world motorcycle producers. Each manufacturer's position in 1974 is described briefly below. Honda's development is described in some detail, since it illustrates the kinds of strategies and policies adopted by the other Japanese producers as well. The briefer descriptions of the other Japanese manufacturers focus on their distinctive features.

Honda Motor Company. The largest motorcycle company in the world, Honda held leading market shares in nearly all the markets in which it chose to compete (Exhibit 4). The company's sales volume in 1974 was 519.9 billion yen (equivalent to $1.69 billion) with total motorcycle production of 2.1 million units.

Starting as a tiny operation in 1948, Honda achieved phenomenal market and financial success by providing a wide range of products at popular prices. It often was said that Honda created the market for the recreational uses of motorcycles through its extensive advertising and promotional effort.

The company achieved a significant product advantage through a heavy commitment to R&D and advanced manufacturing techniques. Honda used its productivity-based cost advantage (Exhibit 5) and R&D capability to introduce new models at prices below those of competitive machines. New products could be brought to market very quickly; the interval between conception and production was estimated to be only 18 months. Honda was also reported to have a "cold storage" of designs that could be introduced if the market developed.

In the early 1970s, Honda increased its coverage to include the larger sizes but was still not competing in the 750cc-and-over segment (Exhibit 6A). The product line had been broadened to serve the off-road market but Honda remained oriented toward on-road or combination motorcycles (Exhibit 6B). Its retail prices are compared with those of competing brands in Exhibit 7.

Since 1960, Honda had consistently outspent its competitors in advertising (Exhibit 8). It also had established the largest dealership network in the United States (Exhibit 9). On average, Honda dealers were larger than their competitors. In new markets, Honda had been willing to take short-term losses to build up an adequate selling and distribution network. In the U.K., for example, it accepted losses during 1963–70 to carry out an extensive market development program.

Since 1971, however, Honda's share of the U.S. market had fallen from 51.8 to 43 percent. Several factors contributed to this decline:

- Honda had pioneered the Japanese entry in bigger bikes in the late 1960s. More recently, Yamaha, Kawasaki, and Suzuki had entered this market and eroded Honda's share.

- Honda had always been committed to four-stroke engines, which were better suited to on-road than off-road use. The accelerating growth of the off-road market found Honda without an appropriate product.

- During 1969–74 Honda's corporate focus had been on motor cars, and motorcycles may have suffered as a result.

There were indications that Honda would try to win back any ground lost in motorcycles. The Elsinore line introduced in 1973 was helping the company regain share in the off-road market, and, in 1975, Honda introduced the 1,000cc Goldwing model, which was well received in the market. Industry observers believed that Honda would now shift its marketing thrust to Europe and the Third World countries. Assembly operations also were being moved overseas, with 30 plants already established outside Japan.

Yamaha Motor Company. The second-largest world motorcycle producer in 1974, Yamaha had been growing faster than Honda since 1962. Yamaha's particular strength was in off-road machines, and its sporting image had been supported by numerous racing successes.

Yamaha had been the last Japanese company to offer the bigger motorcycles, but its 500cc and 650cc machines were selling well in 1975. The company's future plans included upgrading the 650cc to 750cc and introducing a three-cylinder, four-stroke shaft-driven motorcycle of high displacement (perhaps 1000cc) to compete in the heavyweight touring market.

Kawasaki Heavy Industries, Ltd. For Kawasaki, which was active in shipbuilding machinery, railway rolling stock, aircraft, and structural steel, motorcycles represented a diversification move, building on the strength of its substantial industrial engine business.

The strength of Kawasaki motorcycles (as exemplified by their four-stroke 900cc Z-1 model) was their speed and performance; among all Japanese models, Kawasakis were rated closest to British motorcycles.

Kawasaki's corporate plan projected above-average growth in the motorcycle business between 1975 and 1979. Specifically, it planned to upgrade the Z-1 to 1000cc and launch a 750cc machine at the very low price of $1,800 retail. An assembly plant had been established in Lincoln, Nebraska. In Europe, which Kawasaki reportedly saw as the main future growth market for large motorcycles, its market development program concentrated on developing a relatively small number of exclusive dealerships.

Suzuki.   Like Yamaha, Suzuki had tended to be stronger in off-road than on-road machines, had concentrated even more exclusively on two-stroke machines, and had done well in competition racing. Suzuki's stock models had not performed particularly well, however, and the brand's appeal had stressed comfort and solid design more than speed and a sporting image. In on-road machines, Suzuki had recently been offering machines (380cc, 550cc) with engine displacement slightly higher than those of competing models. These models had had some success but had not won significant volume from the market leaders.

Suzuki's next development was expected to be a 1000cc four-stroke, three-cylinder, water-cooled machine.

Norton Villiers Triumph Limited (NVT).   Created in 1973 by a merger of the collapsing BSA Company with Norton Villiers, NVT was the only major British motorcycle manufacturer in 1975.

NVT and its predecessor firms had traditionally focused on larger motorcycles. During the early 1970s, these were increasingly threatened by newly introduced Japanese models in the 450cc-and-over class, which offered equivalent or superior quality and features at lower prices. Thus challenged, the British had tended to withdraw from direct competition and to move to higher displacement classes.

The retreat to bigger bikes was a continuation of a long-standing British strategy. Management has cited poor profitability as the reason for withdrawing from marketing 175, 250, 350, 500, and 600cc motorcycles (see Exhibit 6A). As a result, the British manufacturers' share of the 450–749cc

market fell dramatically between 1969 and 1973, as shown in Table G. And while sales of British 750cc bikes increased fivefold over the same period, other producers grew still faster. In 1975 the British had essentially exhausted the segment retreat strategy, since engines larger than 1200cc were unmanageable.

In general, the British producers had emphasized short-term financial goals. They had set prices so as to ensure that each model offered was profitable, largely ignoring the second-order effect that loss of volume might have on costs and profits. (In the United States, for example, 1975 Triumph models were selling at a $400 price premium over competitive brands.) Similarly, they had not invested in market development. In 1974, for example, NVT had been unwilling to spend £3,000 to obtain general homologation[3] for its machines, preferring to treat each machine sold as a separate case. Nor was production policy growth-oriented. BSA had for many years restrained capacity increases and produced fewer machines than the market demanded. In the short term, this tended to maintain prices and margins, a measure of exclusivity for the product, and a relatively easy match between production and demand.

In its first 20 months, NVT had incurred a loss of £7.4 million. (Equity in 1975 was £9 million.) Management had hoped that consolidating production in two facilities would yield enough savings to cover the operating losses, but union pressure had forced the company to accept a three-factory setup instead. In mid-1975 NVT was awaiting the government's decision on how production could be expanded to justify a three-factory setup; government financing to carry out such a program had been requested. In a report prepared for the Secretary of State for Industry, the Boston Consulting Group estimated that a minimum of £11 million would be required to finance NVT between mid-1975 and the end of 1978.

In 1975 NVT was producing Triumph Bonneville (750cc), Triumph Trident (750cc), and Norton Commando

---

[3]Homologation: the process of demonstrating to the authorities that a particular model meets an importing country's legal requirements.

TABLE G   British Producers' Segment Retreat

	450–749cc		750cc and over	
	1969	*1973*	*1969*	*1973*
Number of models	4	2	3	3
U.S. sales (000)	25	12	4	21
U.S. market share (%)	49%	9%	49%	19%

NOTE: British producers are BSA, Norton, Triumph.

(850cc) motorcycles, the two latter models newly updated with electric starters, rear disk brakes, and other improvements. In July 1975 the company also announced a new line of motorbikes: a 50cc moped, a 125cc lightweight motorcycle, and a 750cc machine.

Harley-Davidson.   A subsidiary of AMF, Inc., Harley produced its large motorcycles in the United States, sourcing smaller machines from an Italian subsidiary.

Harley's market appeal in the United States—its sales abroad were limited—rested on a combination of factors:

- As the only U.S. producer, Harley enjoyed a type of nationalistic loyalty in some customers, not to mention an edge in police and army contracts.
- Harley had a long-standing premium product image and had been successful in racing.
- Harley ran training courses for its dealers, who were generally rated among the best in the industry.

Like the British manufacturers, Harley had generally followed a selective production policy. Its market share had been fairly constant since 1971. While profitability data were not available, some financial hardship was suggested by Harley's recent effort to persuade the U.S. International Trade Commission that tariffs should be maintained at current levels, equivalent to about 3 percent of U.S. retail price, or raised to protect employment in the U.S. industry.

BMW.   In Germany, BMW had been producing motorcycles since 1923. Between 1950 and 1969, motorcycle sales declined from 18,000 to about 5,000 units, and automobiles dominated corporate sales.

In 1969, BMW introduced three new models—a 500cc, a 600cc, and a 750cc—and sales rose to 12,000 units in 1970, to 19,000 units in 1971. Backed by outstanding engineering, BMW was seen as the "Rolls Royce" of the motorcycle world. In keeping with this reputation, its U.S. prices were 30 percent higher than those of comparable Japanese machines.

Production and R&D for motorcycles were integrated with BMW's automotive activities, whereas a separate subsidiary handled motorcycle marketing. The production system reflected BMW's concern for quality: many components were produced in-house, and in-line transfer machines were used even though they were not economic at BMW's volume level (25,000 units in 1974.) Because all BMW motorcycles were variants on the same basic engine and frame, the company could achieve scale economies in a number of components, despite relatively low volume per model.

Although its scanty dealer network gave BMW poor coverage of the U.S. market, its market share in the 750cc-and-over class had risen from 2 percent in 1970 to 5 percent in 1974–75, presumably on the basis of high product quality and new model introductions.

In Europe, BMW was substantially stronger. It had a 55 percent share of the 500cc-and-over class in Germany and a 32 percent share of the 625cc-and-over class in France. Even in the U.K., NVT's home country, BMW had a 12 percent share of bikes over 500cc. Moreover, BMW had recently gained market share in each of these markets. Several factors contributed to BMW's success in Europe:

- The Japanese were subject to a 10.5 percent tariff.
- It was easier for BMW to secure distribution. Since dealerships were not exclusive, the dealer could carry Honda's small bikes but not its big bikes.
- BMW maintained a smaller price premium (6–19 percent) over the Japanese in Europe than it did in the United States.

BMW's plans called for expansion of motorcycle production to 45,000 units in 1980. While the profitability of the motorcycle business was not known, industry observers believed that returns on motorcycle sales were lower than in BMW's motorcar business.

Moto-Guzzi, Benelli, and Ducati.   These three Italian producers had a significant share of the Italian market, primarily because import restrictions and tariffs protected them from Japanese imports. Their share of the international market was negligible.

Other Manufacturers.   In several countries, national producers served their home markets, playing an insignificant role in international motorcycle trade. In recent years, Communist bloc producers had tried to penetrate the western European market with very inexpensive motorcycles directed primarily to the basic transportation segment.

Relative Costs of Competing Manufacturers

As we have seen, the Japanese motorcycle manufacturers rapidly gained commanding market positions by offering products equivalent or superior in quality to their American and British counterparts, and lower in price. At the same time, the Japanese producers had been consistently profitable (Exhibit 10), suggesting they enjoyed significant cost advantages over their competitors. Wage rate differences between Japan and the Western countries may have been significant at the beginning of the period of rapid Japanese growth—per capita income in 1959 was $299 in Japan, $1,019 in the U.K., and $2,232 in the United States—but they shrank over the period. As shown in Exhibit 5, the Japanese clearly excelled in manufacturing productivity, reflecting their willingness to invest in more efficient technologies. (In 1962 Honda's net fixed asset investment was $8,170 per employee, compared with $3,250 for NVT in 1974.) Similarly, the Japanese had made a greater commitment to R&D: in 1960, Honda Research and Development employed 700 designers/engineers; NVT had 100 engineers/draftsmen in 1974.

In its analysis of the motorcycle industry, the Boston Consulting Group (BCG) concluded that the Japanese cost position was a clear example of the experience curve effect observed in many industries—that is, real unit costs tend to decline by a certain percentage each time cumulative production doubles.

Since cost information over time was not available, the BCG analysts examined Honda's price and volume trends, under the assumption that price behavior closely paralleled cost behavior. The expected pattern was found. As Exhibit 11 illustrates for three large Honda bikes, real prices declined by 13–15 percent each time accumulated volume doubled. These experience-based cost reductions were the net result of economies realized in various components of cost.

As a result of their improved productivity, list prices of Honda models in the United States were virtually unchanged from 1970 to 1975 despite a rise of nearly 40 percent in the general level of consumer prices during that period.

Selling and Distribution.   As the Japanese manufacturers accumulated experience (making better management possible) and increased production volumes (realizing economies of scale), they should have been able to reduce distribution expenses—sales force, physical distribution, dealer support and training, advertising, and headquarter administration—as a percent of sales. Instead of taking those savings as profit, however, the market leaders continued to commit the same proportion of revenues to selling and distribution expenses, thus delivering greater value to the customer and solidifying their market share position.

Economies of scale were realized at the dealer level as well. A high-volume dealership could afford to discount its motorcycles, thus attracting even greater volume.

Production (factory value added).   Over time, the cumulative experience effect could influence all technological and organizational factors associated with product design and manufacture. In addition, the level of current volume (scale) affected the extent to which the most up-to-date technology could be applied and the degree to which production facilities could be specialized and focused. Growth rates had an influence beyond absolute volume levels. If volumes were increasing, the move to more efficient production technologies could be made without displacing workers. This helped to get the labor force committed to seeking out and implementing the most productive manufacturing processes.

For any manufacturing process, the choice of the most economic methodology depends on production volume. At low volumes, simple, labor-intensive technologies are most cost-effective. As production volume increases, more capital-intensive technologies become economic, since their higher fixed costs can be amortized over a larger number of units.

In motorcycle manufacture, the choice of technology had the greatest cost impact on engine part machining. When volumes reached 60,000–125,000 parts per year, it became economic to use special-purpose machinery such as rotary indexing or in-line transfer systems.

Similarly, cycle parts manufacture methods could be streamlined at high volumes. For example, painting could be automated, jigs and fixtures could be improved. And in assembly, higher volume made it possible to conveyorize the operation and increase the division of labor.

Purchased Materials and Components.   As its production volume increases, a manufacturer can typically command larger purchasing discounts from its suppliers. Large customers also get better service, in terms of deliveries, development of new parts, quality assurance and credit terms. Moreover, the supplier's own costs will be declining following the experience curve pattern.

Long-Term Future Market Growth

In 1974 the United States was the most highly developed market in the world for secondary motorcycle use. Industry observers felt there was little likelihood that new uses for the product would be developed in the future, and the market for current uses was expected to grow slowly, for several reasons:

1. The growth of the 15–24 age group was expected to decline sharply, to approximately 0.5 percent per annum between 1975 and 1980.

2. Only about a quarter of 1974 motorcycle sales were first-time purchases, indicating that market penetration was nearing its peak. Replacement sales would continue, but the total number of motorcycles owned could be expected to stabilize.

3. Some legal changes were likely to diminish motorcycle demand:

   - Environmental pressures would restrain off-road riding, which tore up topsoil and disturbed wildlife.
   - Noise control regulations might make motorcycle ownership less enjoyable for riders who equated noise with power.
   - Emission restrictions might reduce the power of motorcycles.
   - Safety regulations, such as compulsory driver education and mandatory crash helmets, might repel some potential new purchasers.

Substantial further growth seemed possible only if entirely new customer groups could be attracted to motorcycles. For years, advertising and promotion had sought to interest women and older men, but with little success. Thus, industry observers projected a modest overall growth in the U.S. motorcycle market between 1975 and 1980, with relatively faster growth for bigger motorcycles because of trade-ups (Table H).

The European market of 1974 was in the early stages of development of secondary uses. While primary transportation use was expected to decline through the end of the decade, the growth of secondary uses was expected to provide an overall increase in the market, especially in France and West Germany, where the shift away from primary transportation use was more advanced than in the U.K. and Italy. As in the United States, growth was expected to be higher in the bigger motorcycles (Table H).

In Japan, where motorcycles were used as a primary transport vehicle, the market was essentially saturated. Almost a quarter of all households owned a motorcycle. While rising national income would ordinarily be expected to trigger a substitution of automobiles for motorcycles, there were reasons to believe that the pattern might be different in Japan. That country already had the highest number of cars per mile of roadway in the world, and its traffic jams were justly famous. On balance, therefore, Japanese motorcycle sales seemed likely to stay at their 1974 level through 1980.

In the rest of the world, growth through 1980 would be primarily in the smaller machines used for primary transportation. Japan's Ministry of International Trade and Industry forecast high growth rates in the richer nations of Central and South America (18 percent per year) and the Middle East (20 percent per year), and lower growth for Southeast Asia (11 percent per year) and Africa (12 percent per year).

Short-Term Industry Prospects

In mid-1975 the development of the motorcycle market was uncertain. Retail sales in the United States had declined 21 percent from 1973 to 1974, and 1975 sales were running 30 percent lower than the 1974 levels. Inventories of Japanese motorcycles were estimated at more than 600,000 units. This huge inventory of unsold units created heavy pressure on the producers and dealers, thus discounting was rampant.

TABLE H   Projected Motorcycle Sales (thousands of units) and Annual Growth Rate, United States and Europe

	United States			Europe		
	Sales 1974 (000)	*Sales 1980 (000)*	*Annual Growth Rate (%)*	*Sales 1974 (000)*	*Sales 1980 (000)*	*Annual Growth Rate (%)*
Under 450cc	704	795	2%	307	445	6.4%
450–749cc	139	169	3	31	68	14.0
750cc	91	133	7	27	62	14.9
Over 750cc	77	108	6	16	45	18.8
Total	1,011	1,205	3	381	620	8.5

SOURCE: BCG, "Strategy Alternatives for the British Motorcycle Industry," 1975.

EXHIBIT 1   **U.S. Retail Sales, Imports, and Origin of Imports**

Year	Retail Sales ($ millions)	Retail Sales (unit 000s)	Total Imports (unit 000s)	Imports U.K. (%)	Imports Japan (%)
1960	$ 17	40–50	NA	NA	NA
1962	40	NA	94[a]	NA	60%
1963	75	170	NA	NA	NA
1964	130	300[c]	324	6.7%	71.6
1965	225	410	NA	NA	NA
1966	300	475	455	NA	90
1969	NA	670	643	5.7	82.4
1970	NA	1,010	1,092	3.6	84.7
1971	NA	1,240	1,538	3.5[b]	87.1
1972	1,025[c]	1,360	1,690	9.5[b]	86.9
1973	1,249[c]	1,520	1,206	10.7[b]	84.5
1974	1,285[c]	1,200	1,504	7.5[b]	89.8

NOTE: Import volume is frequently greater than retail sales because of inventory build-up.

NA means not available.

[a]Nine months only.

[b]European countries including U.K.

[c]Casewriter's estimates.

SOURCE: Various.

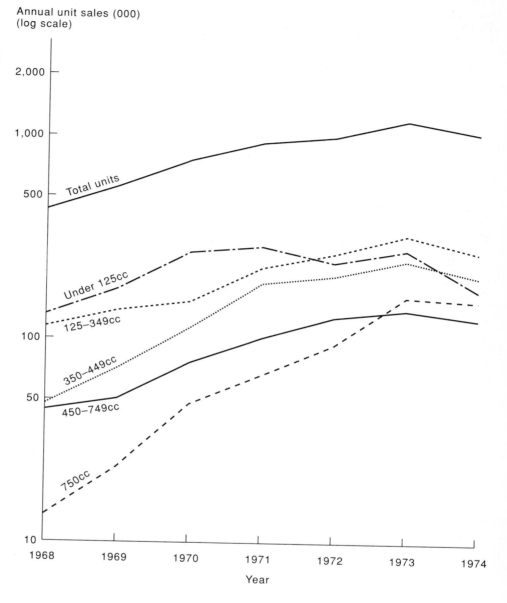

EXHIBIT 2

The U.S. motorcycle market, 1968 and 1974, distribution by size class

Annual unit sales (000)
(log scale)

Total units

Under 125cc

125–349cc

350–449cc

450–749cc

750cc

Year

	Percent of Total	
	1968	1974
Under 125cc	41	19
125–349cc	33	28
350–449cc	11	20
450–749cc	11	15
750cc and over	4	18
	100	100

SOURCE: R. L. Polk.

Exhibit 3   Excerpts from "Report on Japan" by Edward Turner

The following are excerpts from a report written by BSA/Triumph Motorcycles Chairman Edward Turner in 1960. In his report, Turner summarized a trip to Japan in which he visited several Japanese motorcycle producers.

Japan today is the largest manufacturer in the world of motorcycles, all of excellent quality. One company of this largest national producer of motorcycles produces more motorcycles than the whole of the British industry put together, and this is only one of the 20 or more motorcycle companies in full operation.

* * * * *

The speed with which the Japanese motorcycle companies can produce new designs and properly tested and developed models is startling, and the very large scientific and technical staff maintained at the principal factories is, of course, out of all proportion to anything ever visualized in this country, or for that matter in the United States. Honda alone, the largest company, has an establishment of 400 technicians engaged in studying new manufacturing techniques, new designs, new developments, and new approaches.

* * * * *

The Honda factory was everything that one could desire as an up-to-date manufacturing conception for motorcycles, and, although nothing I saw was beyond our conception or ability to bring about in our own factories, it should be borne in mind that we have not now, nor ever have had, the quantities of any one product which would justify these highly desirable methods being used. They had a large number of single-purpose, specially designed machine tools which reduce labour for any large component, such as the crankcase, to an absolute minimum. All components, except very small ones, such as gear shafts and gears more conveniently transported in trays, were moving on conveyors throughout the factory. Every section for the small, medium, and larger motorcycles being made was geared to a time cycle, all assembly was on moving bands.

* * * * *

It may appear by this report that I am inclined to emphasize and exaggerate, but I am purposely avoiding any form of exaggeration. It is essential that our industry in general and the B.S.A. Group in particular should know the facts and what we are up against in the retention of our export markets. Even our home market for motorcycles will be assailed and, although personally I do not think the Japanese motorcycle industry will eclipse the traditional type of machine that the British motorcyclist wants and buys, they are bound to make some impact on our home market by virtue of the high quality of their product and low prices.

* * * * *

Having familiarized myself with the situation as it exists, I have been giving considerable thought to what we might do, and a course to pursue to combat this situation, and I must confess that these answers are going to be hard to find. In the first place it should be borne in mind that the motorcycle industry has never been big business in Britain. Its safety has to some extent been that it has never attracted big capital and big enterprise. We have never made to date, even in these relatively boom times, 1,000 units of any one product in a week consistently, whereas many factories in Japan are currently doing this in a day. It is true that many of the large quantities in Japan are on small motorcycles, but even the larger ones (250cc/300cc) are being turned out in quantities in excess of any equivalent model in this country and, therefore, it has never been feasible—and certainly not economically sound—to lay down manufacturing lines fully mechanised with complete single-purpose machine tool equipment of special design at every stage of manufacture.

Experience has shown that the British motorcycle industry and our many export markets abroad want a range of motorcycles from each manufacturer. It may well be that we have not had the courage to reduce our variety of manufacture so as to produce larger requirements for any given model, but previous attempts in this direction have always led to a reduction in overall turnover. Therefore, with Japan they have the manifold advantages of a large requirement for a single developed article, and they have had the great courage to invest enormous sums of money with full confidence that their products will be purchased in sufficient quantities at home and abroad, and currently they are in full flight and are receiving snowball advantages from their enterprise.

* * * * *

One of the most practical thoughts in this present situation would be to visualize opening up our own motorcycle operations in Japan, thereby obtaining the full advantages of their plentiful and cheap labour and having available a window for observation on the Japanese industry. We might even, should we consider this, obtain technical help which is not to be despised, particularly in regard to our future tooling and development.

By and large the menace of Japanese motorcycles to our own export markets is that they are producing extremely refined and well finished motorcycles up to 300cc at prices which reach the public at something like 20 percent less. The machines themselves are more comprehensive than our own in regard to equipment, such as electrical starting, traffic indicators, etc., and probably better made but will not appeal to the sporting rider to anything like the same extent as our own. However, they will make very big inroads into the requirement for motorcycles for transportation.

Source: Reprinted by permission, from Ivor Davies, *It's a Triumph* (Somerset, England: Haynes Publishing Group, 1980), pp. 200–205.

EXHIBIT 4 Financial and Commercial Performance of Competitors in 1974 (figures for 1959, or another year as noted, listed in parentheses)

	Total Company Sales ($ millions)	Total Company Profits ($ millions)	Motorcycle Production (000 units)	Motorcycle Exports (000 units)	Share of U.S. Market (% units)	Share U.K. Market (% units)
Honda	(55) 1,686	(3.3) 46.5	(285) 2,118	1,497	43%	54%
Yamaha	302[b]	6.6[b]	(64) 1,162	848	20	19
Kawasaki	(225)[c] 1,484	(5.7)[c] 31.2	(10) 355	327	13	5
Suzuki	(93)[c] 555[d]	(3.2)[c] 8.1[d]	(96) 838	600	11	13
Harley-Davidson (Division of AMF)	(16.6)[e] 1,026[a]	19.0[a]	60	5.7	6	0
NVT	100[f]	loss	approx. 20	15	1.4	5
BMW	(41) 1,000	(−2) 16	(8.4) 23			

[a]Total company.
[b]Half year.
[c]1964 figure.
[d]1973 figure.
[e]Harley-Davidson only.
[f]20 months ended 3/31/75.
SOURCE: Various.

EXHIBIT 5 Motorcycle Industry Productivity Comparison

	Motorcycle Output	Motorcycles per Person/Year
Britain:		
Small Heath factory 1975	10,500	10
Wolverhampton factory 1975	18,000	18[a]
Meriden factory 1972–73	28,000	14[a]
Japan:		
Honda:		
Total company	2,000,000	106 plus 21 cars
Suzuki factory	1,500,000	350 (estimate)
Hamamatsu factory	500,000	174
Yamaha:		
Total company	1,000,000	200
Suzuki:		
Motorcycle activities[b]	800,000	114
Kawasaki:		
Akashi factory	300,000	159
Other:		
Moto-Guzzi/Benelli	40,000	13 plus 20 mopeds
BMW	25,000	20[c]
Harley-Davidson[d]	50,000	15

[a]Higher proportions of bought-in components than Small Heath.
[b]Head office and main plant (machining) plus Toyama and Toyakawa motorcycle assembly factories.
[c]Very low proportion of bought-in components.
[d]These are estimates based on actual production of 38,000 motorcycles (and 11 motorcycles per person-year) during nine months of 1974.
SOURCE: Annual reports, company histories, published articles. Plant data in Britain direct from NVT manufacturing records. Information on other non-Japanese companies partly derived from interviews with the companies concerned.

Exhibit 6   Competitors' Product Offerings in the United States, 1968 and 1975

A. Number of Models Offered by Engine Size

	Under 125cc		125–349cc		350–449cc		450–749cc		Over 750cc	
	1968	1975	1968	1975	1968	1975	1968	1975	1968	1975
Honda	10	14	9	6	2	3		3		
Yamaha	11	12	11	11		4		2		
Kawasaki	3	10	9	6		4	3	4		1
Suzuki	1	10	2	7		3	1	4		6
Harley-Davidson	3	3	2	2			1	4		10
NVT[a]				3	2		15	7		10
BMW							3	2		2

[a]Includes BSA, Triumph, and Norton.

B. Number of Models Offered by Usage Type

	On-Road		Combination		Off-Road	
	1968	1975	1968	1975	1968	1975
Honda	20	7	1	13		6
Yamaha	18	9	4	5		15
Kawasaki	10	9	3	7	2	7
Suzuki	3	7	1	9		8
Harley-Davidson	9	6	1	4		1
NVT[a]	14	15	6	1		1
BMW	3	4				

[a]Includes BSA, Triumph, and Norton.

Source: NADA Motorcycle Appraisal Guide, April–July 1975.

Exhibit 7   U.S. Motorcycle Retail Price by Engine Size Range, 1975 (U.S. $)

	Under 125cc	125–349cc	350–449cc	450–749cc	Over 750cc
Honda	304–899	897–1175	1176–1443	1555–2112	
Yamaha	454–995	965–1229	1371–1486	1749–1889	
Kawasaki	414–904	1037–1232	995–1401	1542[a]	2505
Suzuki	485–815	875–1175	1230–1295	1175–2475	
Harley-Davidson	495–749	930–1130			2675–3375
NVT[b]				1159–2519	2195–2895
BMW				2330–2730	2930–3430

[a]Price of 748cc model not shown because unknown; was $1,848 in 1974.

[b]Includes BSA, Triumph, and Norton.

Source: NADA Motorcycle Appraisal Guide, April–July 1975.

EXHIBIT 8 U.S. Advertising Expenditure of Major Competitors ($000)

	1961	1965	1970	1974
Honda	$95	$1,376	$2,365	$5,509
Yamaha		266	885	2,187
Kawasaki			258	2,932
Suzuki		129	699	1,572
Berliner—Ducati distributor		107		
Johnson Motors—Triumph distributor		29		
Harley-Davidson	75	162	539	1,508

NOTE: Does not include newspaper and motorcycle magazine advertising. Figures for 1961 and 1965 do not include spot TV, radio, and outdoor advertising. NVT's U.S. subsidiary had an $800,000 advertising and promotion budget.
SOURCE: *National Advertising Investments,* various issues.

EXHIBIT 9 U.S. Distribution Network of Major Competitors, 1974

	Estimated Total Selling and Distribution Expenditure by Sales Company[a] ($mil.)	Dealers	Unit Sales per Dealer
Honda	$90–100	1,974	220
Yamaha	40–45	1,515	135
Kawasaki	30–35	1,018	127
Suzuki	25–30	1,103	98
NVT		408	40

[a]Includes sales representation at the dealer level, physical distribution of parts and machines, warranty and service support, dealer support, advertising and promotion, market planning, and control and sales support by dealers.
SOURCE: BCG, "Strategy Alternatives for the British Motorcycle Industry," 1975.

EXHIBIT 10 Motorcycle Manufacturers: Financial Summary

	Norton		BSA/Triumph		Honda		Yamaha		Suzuki	
	Earnings (£ mil.)	ROI (%)	Earnings (£ mil.)	ROI (%)	Earnings (¥ Bil.)	ROI (%)	Earnings (¥ Bil.)	ROI (%)	Earnings (¥ Bil.)	ROI (%)
1969–70	0.37	4.5%	0.4	NA	35.0	24.6%	2.4	16.27%	8.4	18.8%
1970–71			(7.2)	loss	35.0	20.4	3.4	17.0	10.0	16.2
1971–72	0.38	7.3	(3.1)	loss	35.4	19.6	5.6	30.2	11.4	15.8
1972–73	.02	loss	(2.9)	loss	34.2	18.6	8.8	35.0	10.6	13.2
1973–74	(5.1)[a]				34.4	14.8	8.4	22.8	10.0	11.45
1974–75 (est.)					32.0	12.4	9.5	21.6	9.0	10.4

NOTES:
1. Earnings are expressed before tax and interest, and include provisions for reorganization, etc., in the case of BSA/Triumph, for which company the results of the motorcycle activities only are quoted.
2. ROI equals earnings divided by net assets at the end of the year.
3. In 1975 ¥1 billion = £1.5 million.
4. Year-ends: July for NVT, February for Honda, March for Suzuki, April for Yamaha. Data for Japanese companies are for parent company, not group.
[a]£5.1 million is the loss in earnings of NVT, which was created by a merger of Norton and BSA/Triumph.
SOURCE: Annual reports, NVT Group Accountant, BCG Tokyo.

Exhibit 11

Honda large bikes: price experience curves

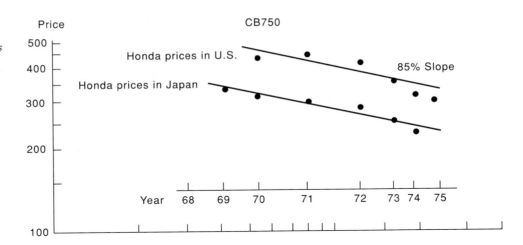

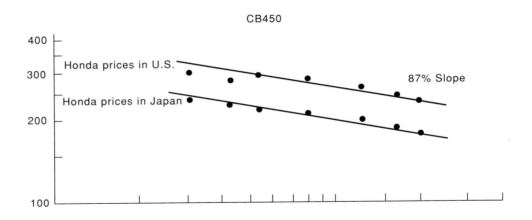

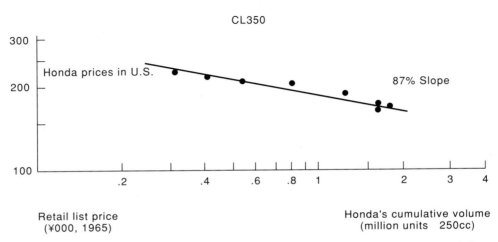

Retail list price
(¥000, 1965)

Honda's cumulative volume
(million units   250cc)

NOTE: Prices plotted above are retail prices for specific Honda models, in the United States and Japan, respectively, expressed in thousands of yen at 1965 values (i.e., adjusted for inflation).

SOURCE: BCG "Strategy Alternatives for the British Motorcycle Industry."

Deere & Company: Industrial Equipment Operations

In November 1976, Robert Gerstenberger, vice president for worldwide Industrial Equipment Operations at Deere & Company, was reviewing his unit's newly developed 1977 crawler tractor prices. Deere & Company was about to introduce a bulldozer, the JD750, substantially larger than any it had previously produced. Gerstenberger was particularly concerned with the price of the JD750.[1]

Deere & Company and Industrial Equipment Operations

Deere & Company was among the world's leading manufacturers of farm and industrial equipment. Total sales for the year ending October 31, 1976, were $3.134 billion and net income was $216 million. Industrial equipment accounted for $452 million in sales, or 14 percent of the total. Exhibit 1 shows selected financial data for Deere & Company and the Industrial Equipment Operations, as well as some comparative data for Caterpillar Tractor Company.

Deere & Company evolved from John Deere's invention of the steel plow in 1837. By the end of World War II, Deere & Company had a large business in tractors and farm implements, and it also had a strong reputation for reliability and engineering excellence in the farm community. It developed its industrial operation in five phases. The company entered the industrial equipment field (i.e., equipment designed for industrial, construction, and forestry applications as opposed to agricultural applications) soon after World War II, when a small factory in Washington State converted standard agricultural wheeled tractors to crawler tractors to meet the requirements of orchard operators who needed low-profile tractors to operate among the trees. As farmers went into the logging business to supplement their agricultural operations, Deere crawler tractors began to be used in small forestry operations. Meanwhile, during this first phase of development, industrial operators—such as small contractors—began to use agricultural equipment in nonagricultural applications.

In the second phase, Deere developed industrially oriented attachments, such as tractor-mounted backhoes, to supplement its agricultural equipment. As part of its evolution, Industrial Equipment Operations was organized in 1955 and staffed with engineers to develop a crawler tractor line designed for industrial application. In phase three, the newly developed crawler line and other product lines, each containing only one or two models, met with competitive success. By the early 1960s, Deere had perhaps a 20 to 30 percent share of the North American crawler tractor market where it operated against seven principal competitors. In the mid-1960s, phase four evolved with the introduction of the JD350 and JD450 (described in its 1976 form in Exhibit 2), and later the JD550. As these items grew in popularity, the line gained a 50 to 60 percent share of the market for small (under 100 horsepower) crawlers in North America.

Phase five began in 1976 with the introduction of the JD750 bulldozer (described in Exhibit 3) and the JD755 crawler loader. These machines competed in the market for larger units used in the heavy construction (highways, dams, airports, etc.) and mining industries. Machines in these markets were referred to as productive machines because they were often required to work for 10 to 24 hours per day, as opposed to the smaller utility machines, which were under less strain because their usage was more sporadic. The larger equipment market was dominated by the Caterpillar Tractor Company, with a crawler market share of about 45 percent worldwide. Caterpillar, or "Cat," became almost a generic term for large crawlers.

Other Deere industrial lines evolved like the crawler tractors. By late 1976, the Deere industrial line consisted of:

3 light crawler loaders

3 light bulldozers (JD350, 450, 550)

1 heavy crawler loader (JD755)

1 heavy bulldozer (JD750)

3 light-wheeled tractors with loaders, blades, and so forth, mounted on them

4 wheeled tractors with integral backhoes and loaders

2 heavy four-wheel-drive loaders

3 motor graders

3 scrapers

1 excavator

A variety of attachments and some specialized equipment for forestry and other applications (e.g., a sanitary landfill compactor).

This case was prepared by Associate Professor Benson P. Shapiro. Copyright © 1977 by the President and Fellows of Harvard College. Harvard Business School case 577-112 (Rev. 12/85).

[1]A *tractor* can be either wheeled or *crawler*—that is, running on an endless chain of tread so that it can move through mud or over rocks in the same manner as a military tank. A *bulldozer* is a crawler tractor with a flat blade for pushing dirt, sand, and so forth. A *loader* (or front-end loader) has a scoop on the front for pushing and lifting; it is often used for loading dump trucks.

Deere's major success had been in light crawler tractors. Case, another company with agricultural ancestry, had the major share (50 percent) of the North American light-wheeled industrial tractor market. Caterpillar dominated the markets for heavy construction and mining equipment. (It had worldwide construction and materials handling sales of $4.5 billion in 1975. Its domestic product line had about 60 items compared to about 40 for Deere.) Deere, however, had made substantial penetration into some of these markets, such as the one for motor graders. After introducing the articulated grader[2] in 1967, it gained 30 percent of the market for smaller graders—a market previously dominated by Caterpillar. Eighty percent of Deere's industrial sales were in the United States, compared to only about 43 percent of Caterpillar's.

Industrial Equipment Operations distributed its products through 433 dealers who operated a total of 437 outlets. These dealers were not the same as those who sold agricultural tractors—the industrial operation had its own dealer network. The dealers ranged in size from about $1 million to $16 million in sales, and they primarily offered only Deere products. In fact, 87 percent of the dealers' sales of new (not used) merchandise was in Deere industrial products. Related equipment and accessories of limited line producers were also sometimes offered. Industry sources believed that Deere had a distribution network that was second only to Caterpillar. Caterpillar, according to Deere estimates, had only 122 U.S. dealers with 219 outlets. Sales per dealer for Caterpillar ranged from about $12 million to about $70 million.

Deere had three different agreements with its dealers. Each covered one of the following: utility, construction, and forestry. Construction equipment, including the large crawler tractors, was sold by 275 dealers. While some Deere executives believed that ultimately it would be good to have dealers specialize by product line, most dealers had at least two agreements (could sell two lines) and many had three.

The typical Deere dealer had the following sales profile:

	Percent of Sales	Percent Gross Margin
New equipment	50%	15–17%
Parts	17	25–30
Service	8	(usually priced at twice direct labor cost, but varied)
Used equipment and accessories not purchased with equipment	25	(margins varied)

Deere granted 20 percent discounts from list price for construction equipment and 23 percent for utility equipment. It also offered a 4.5 percent volume discount that most dealers earned. Caterpillar offered a 20 percent discount. According to industry sources, Caterpillar dealers averaged 28 to 30 percent of their sales in parts because of: (1) the large stock of units in use, (2) their intensive use, and (3) the proportion of machines that were crawler tractors and required frequent replacement of undercarriage parts.

The Industrial Equipment Operations' sales force included 13 managers and 60 salespeople who called on dealers and major end users. It was expected that the advertising and promotion expenses for the JD750 introduction would be $300,000 over 14 months.

The Crawler Tractor Line

In 1976, the Deere crawler tractor line[3] included four tractors, each of which was the basis for both a bulldozer and a loader. Exhibit 4 contains the prices, costs, and sizes of the four bulldozers, plus the JD850 bulldozer and JD855 loader whose introductions had already been scheduled. Exhibit 5 shows the design evolution of the JD750/755, the 850/855, and competitive units.

The JD350 and 450 were very successfully introduced in the mid-1960s. The JD550—a modified version of the JD450—was added in 1975. These appealed to the utility market. The JD750 and 755 were about to be introduced to the construction market. The three smaller models were fairly standard design tractors, although each had features unique in the market. The JD350 was the only tractor of its size with a wet clutch, which provided better wear resistance than the standard dry clutch. The Caterpillar D-3, on the other hand, which was the most recent entrant in this market, had a dry clutch even though it was a 62-horsepower unit as opposed to 42-horsepower for the JD350 (and 65 for the JD450).

The JD750/755 was a truly unique product, because it had a fully automatic dual-path hydrostatic drive that would also be offered on the JD850/855. This was part of a Deere strategy to enter a market by providing superior customer benefits based on technological innovation. The articulated grader mentioned earlier was another example of this policy. In that situation, Caterpillar had responded with an articulated design of its own in seven years. Deere's market share growth continued even after the Caterpillar entry.

A Deere bulletin on the hydrostatic transmission described it as follows:

A hydrostatic drive converts mechanical engine power into high-pressure hydrostatic power and then back to mechanical power to propel a machine.

---

[2]An articulated grader has a powered hinge in the middle that enables it to turn in an area much smaller than a standard grader and substantially increases the machine's productivity.

---

[3]From this point on, except where noted, all data are for the North American market.

A hydrostatic drive can be likened to a direct gear-drive transmission in that it has the capability to transmit mechanical power to the ground without power train slippage.

The difference is that a hydrostatic drive delivers infinitely variable power and speed to match the changing demands of operating conditions.

On the JD750 and JD755 Crawlers, mechanical engine power is carried by two drive shafts (Dual Path) to two reversible, variable-displacement hydrostatic pumps. The pumps convert the mechanical power to high-pressure hydrostatic power that drives two variable-displacement hydrostatic motors—one for each track. The motors convert the hydrostatic power back to mechanical power, which is then transmitted through the final drives to the sprockets and tracks to propel the machine.

The hydrostatic drive system provides infinitely variable travel speeds and tractive effort—forward and reverse—without the use of a conventional torque converter, Power Shift transmission, ring gear and pinion, steering clutches, and steering brakes.

Most important—the unique feature about the Dual-Path hydrostatic drive system used on the JD750 and JD755 is that it is **FULLY AUTOMATIC.**

The bulletin went on to describe the benefits:

The new JD750 and JD755 have been designed to out-produce any other competitive-size crawler loader or bulldozer on the market today.

Here's why:

1. You don't have to think about upshifting or downshifting during operation. The fully automatic Dual-Path hydrostatic drive does that for you—automatically and always at the optimum moment. You just set the speed control lever, and the machine takes care of the rest. Because you're free to concentrate on operating the loader or bulldozer, you can be more productive.

2. Independent, counterrotating tracks increase overall machine production, because you can spot-turn either machine within its own length for better maneuverability in tight quarters.

3. Infinitely variable power to the tracks lets you make full-power turns under load. This simply means you have infinite control of speed and power for each track—from 0 to 6.5 miles per hour—forward or reverse. It also improves machine traction in unstable soils and increases maneuverability when you're backfilling or spreading material in and around buildings or other obstacles.

4. You don't have to adjust or replace steering clutches and steering brakes anymore. The JD750 and JD755 don't have any. Steering and braking are done hydrostatically. An automatic parking brake dynamically locks the machine into park when the engine is stopped.

5. 100 percent of engine power goes to propel the machine the moment equipment hydraulics are not in use. This means faster travel speeds and shorter cycle times. Conventional torque converter Power Shift crawlers generally offer no more than 85 to 90 percent of engine power for propel.

Deere executives believed that the transmission could lead to 10 to 15 percent higher productivity. Some field results showed it to be meeting Caterpillar D-6 results and surpassing the D-5.

The tractors were produced at Deere's Dubuque, Iowa, industrial equipment plant. The three smaller ones were produced on one production line, while the JD750/755 were produced on a second. The JD850/855 would be produced on the JD750/755 line. Many of the 350 and 450 parts were common. The designers strove for commonality between the JD750/755 and the JD850/855, but because of size differences, there was a limit to the amount that could be achieved.

The loaders and bulldozers differed in mainframe design. Large ones differed particularly, because of the high torque and strain introduced by the loader bucket, especially when it was high in the air. Each bulldozer/loader pair, however, shared most parts in common.

Factory costs, at standard operating rates, usually were 63 percent materials, 6 percent direct labor, 5 percent other variable, and 26 percent fixed. This cost distribution came about because many parts, especially on the larger units, were purchased from outsiders. Undercarriage parts—a major source of supplemental revenue—were purchased from a European vendor, and the hydrostatic transmissions were purchased domestically.

The investment in the JD750/755 and JD850/855 was gigantic. The engineering cost through the end of October 1976 was about $16 million, and the budget for the remainder of the work on the JD850/855 was $4 million. The capital expenditure for tooling and equipment was about $50 million. It took Deere almost 10 years from the original concept to engineer and tool the line. Tooling alone took three years. The largest piece of equipment in the factory, a $2 million machine to finish final drive assemblies, had to be ordered 28 months before installation. Thus, the JD850/855 designs had to be finalized three years before production, and, on common and interrelated parts, three years before production of the JD750/755.

One engineering executive stated that heavy construction equipment was expensive to produce because it "required big, very precise pieces of metal which required heavy equipment to fabricate." He went on to say that the hydrostatic transmissions were "beyond the state of the art when we began to design them into the line. Our supplier had good experience in hydrostatic drives, particularly for machine tools, but neither it nor anyone else had done what we were about to do." The hydrostatic transmission supplier was not limited to selling only to Deere, and Deere had little patent protection on its line.

Crawler Tractor Customers. Crawler loaders and bulldozers were used by a wide variety of customers including landscapers, home builders, underground contractors (electrical, sewer, etc.), paving contractors, sanitary landfills, industrial plants, general contractors, mines, foresters, sugar cane plantations, and so on. In general, bulldozers were oriented to rural areas, while loaders were oriented to urban areas because of their industrial and hole-digging applications.

The large units were purchased by large contractors (who specialized in such projects as highways, dams, and airports) and by mines. They were used for much of the day and sometimes into the night. The purchasers were sophisticated and kept detailed records concerning productivity (tons moved per hour or per dollar) and reliability. They tended to purchase crawlers on the basis of parts availability, as well as on durability and reliability. Large contractors also purchased small machines. These utility machines, however, were not used quite as intensively as the larger units.

Most small units were purchased by small contractors. The small contractor was concerned primarily with reliability. It usually relied upon the local dealer for service, while the large contractor moved its equipment from one area to another and often had its own repair facility. The small contractor also was apparently much more sensitive to initial price than the larger contractor.

The very small customer was often an owner/operator who purchased on the basis of personal experience and attitude. Operator attitude had a good deal of effect, even for the medium-sized and larger contractor, because the operator had a major impact on productivity.

The large contractors tended to buy from a new supplier in small quantities to test a line, and then, if satisfied, to purchase in larger quantities. The large contractors had traditionally not been Deere customers, so the learning process was fairly long.

Some Deere executives believed that as very large projects, such as the interstate road system and Alaska pipeline, became fewer—especially domestically—the large contractors would become involved in smaller projects and change their mix of equipment toward smaller machines.

Crawler Tractor Competitors. The market for crawler tractors could best be divided into large (over 100 horsepower) and small. In 1976, about 8,500 small bulldozers (and about 6,500 small loaders) were sold in the United States. Deere had 50 to 60 percent of the small tractor market, according to Deere managers, because of high reliability, good engineering, and dealer strength with small contractors. International Harvester, which also produced farm equipment and trucks—especially heavy trucks—was ranked as number two, with perhaps 10 percent of the market. Case, which had the strongest competitive position in small industrial wheeled tractors, was number three. Caterpillar, which many years earlier had moved out of the small tractors in favor of heavy equipment, was probably number four. It reopened its interest in the market in 1973, when it introduced the D-3, a Caterpillar-engineered product made in Japan by a joint venture with Mitsubishi. According to industry sources, the D-3 had not been very successful. Some people thought it was because the Caterpillar dealer organization was already prosperous and oriented toward larger units.

In the large tractor market, the situation was considerably different. Caterpillar led the market with a share of 50 to 60 percent. Its parts operation was viewed as excellent— superior to all competitors. Although some Deere managers praised their own as being almost equal, other Deere executives believed that to be an exaggeration. Number two was International Harvester. Other competitors included Case, Fiat-Allis (a joint venture of Fiat and Allis Chalmers), Komatsu, and the Terex Division of General Motors. Komatsu was a Japanese manufacturer that copied Caterpillar designs, and in doing so brought the designs up to the existing state of the art—its strategy was to offer an equivalent product at a lower price. According to some Deere managers, this caused dealers and customers to wonder what was wrong with the product. In addition, Komatsu apparently had gone on the assumption that list prices were firm, while in fact dealers sometimes cut their markup on the large machines. Terex was viewed as a highly innovative competitor with little impact in the market.

Terex was known to be field testing a prototype bulldozer with a hydrostatic transmission. Some Deere engineers estimated that it would take Caterpillar five years to engineer and tool for a hydrostatic transmission. Others believed that Caterpillar would move much more quickly than that because its engineering operation was considerably bigger than Deere's, which had 700 people including 220 professionals in the industrial operation. In 1975, Caterpillar introduced reengineered versions of the D-7, D-8, and D-9, which were the largest bulldozers in its line. It was rumored to be experimenting with a truly gigantic D-10. Some Deere executives believed it was notable that Caterpillar had not reengineered the D-4, D-5, and D-6. The D-5 had the oldest design in the Caterpillar line. One Deere engineer believed that the D-6 was at the practical size limit for the hydrostatic transmission. Deere managers believed the D-5 and D-6 to be the bread and butter of the Caterpillar line because of the unit volume involved. Some believed the dealers liked the D-5 less than the D-6 because of its smaller size and consequently lower dollar gross margin.

Deere management estimated that the 1977 to 1980 domestic sales of JD750- and D-5-sized machines would be 5,500 per year; those of the JD850 and D-6 machines would be 3,500 per year.

The Price-Making Process at Deere

The price-making process for new products was very complex, and that for existing products quite complete. For a new product, the initial concept of a machine and its price could come from several sources, the most likely being the field sales organization, the product engineering group that reported to the Dubuque plant general manager, or an analytical staff group. The initial basis for the design was sketched out and, if reasonable, the process began in the market development department and product engineering. (See Exhibit 6 for the organizational location of this and other relevant groups.) The engineers developed a rough cost estimate, and the market development people—given the product specifications—obtained price and volume forecasts from the four North American sales regions. One marketing development manager reported to each regional manager. Three product specialists in turn reported to the market development managers—one each for utility, construction, and forestry. The field and factory input was combined with that of the director of planning and administration for the industrial equipment operation. This material went to a corporate product council including top management, engineers, marketing people, and staff experts at both the corporate and group[4] levels. If the return on investment seemed acceptable and the product reasonable, it went into development as part of a five-year development plan, which was reviewed annually with a new year added and the current year removed.

As the product neared the point of a decision regarding manufacturing commitment, the pricing process became more complete. Each year, the market development manager gathered inputs from the corporate market economics group concerning gross economic forecasts (e.g., inflation), the field as previously described, and staff marketing groups. The market development group also performed competitive comparisons. That group, with the product engineering group, then submitted a proposal to the corporate pricing group. Corporate pricing elicited input from the director of planning and administration and developed a pricing proposal. The proposal was reviewed by the directors of manufacturing, marketing services, and sales, and then—after negotiation where necessary—it was passed on to Gerstenberger.

Regular price changes involved the corporate pricing group—which had specialists for both parts and whole products—the directors of planning and administration, manufacturing, marketing services, sales, and Gerstenberger, as well as their subordinates.

---

[4]The term *group* is used here to denote the three areas of corporate activity: agriculture, industrial, and consumer (garden tractors, snow blowers, etc.).

Pricing the Tractors. The primary issues in pricing the tractors involved the larger ones. The smaller ones were priced on an evolutionary basis, with much emphasis on competition and past Deere prices. The usual procedure was to price a representative configuration—that is, a tractor with standard, popular features and options. From this, the other options and accessories were priced. Careful attention was paid to the cost/price ratios, which one executive defined as the figure of merit reflecting the quality of engineering, manufacturing, and marketing in the customer's view. Choosing the items to be in the representative configuration was a difficult task since it had major competitive impact. As Exhibit 7 shows, different manufacturers considered different options and accessories standard. Prices had been reviewed every year, but, since the inflation surge of the mid-1970s, they were reviewed every six months.

The larger tractors were much more controversial. One engineering executive suggested three possible product strategies that implied pricing strategies:

1. Head-to-head with competition in horsepower, the product specification viewed as most important.
2. Close to competition, but slightly under in horsepower.
3. In between competitive units; if they have 150 and 200 horsepower units, we design to 175.

Another executive suggested a fourth alternative—coming in just above competition in horsepower. He believed that, because product designs were more fixed than prices, if one had a slightly superior product one could vary the price over the life cycle of the product. During the introduction, therefore, one could keep the price at the competitive level but offer better performance, features, or utility to induce the customer to try the product. As market acceptance was gained, he argued, one could raise prices more rapidly than costs to reflect the improved reputation for quality and value. He went on to argue that the other strategies forced a reactive price posture, while his enabled a proactive one.

The JD750/755 had been designed to meet competition head on. The idea was to introduce a product of the same size, but to offer features that made it superior—primarily the hydrostatic transmission. With a parity price, it was thought, the features would overcome the buyer's reluctance to try a product new to the market. Deere managers believed that, although the hydrostatic transmission was slightly more expensive to produce at the onset than a standard transmission, eventually it would be cheaper.

Gerstenberger believed that pricing was important for the success of the new JD750/755 and JD850/855, as well as for the continued success of the smaller models.

Pricing Accessories and Parts. As Exhibits 2 and 3 show, the tractors were offered with many accessories. Prices had to be developed for each of these. In general, industry practice was to attempt to obtain higher margins on accessories than on the tractors themselves. Where accessories were offered for use on only one tractor, the cost/price ratio of that tractor was the starting point for pricing. For accessories used on more than one tractor, the starting point was an average of the cost/price ratios of the tractors weighted by judgment. The competitive situation also affected pricing. Most of the analyses and recommendations for accessory pricing were done by the corporate pricing group's parts expert.

Parts were a very important part of the crawler tractor line. Because the undercarriage of the tractor was complex, carried a heavy load, experienced great stress, and was often suspended in sand or gravel, the tractor literally destroyed its own undercarriage parts. While it varied with soil conditions and usage, an industry rule of thumb stated that the average crawler needed 65 percent of its initial cost in service and parts during its first three years of operation. This percentage was even higher for units that worked more than one shift per day. An engineering executive stated that, over a life of 10,000 operating hours, the average crawler used service and parts equivalent to 90 percent of its purchase price, and fuel equivalent to 35 percent.

Deere parts faced strong competition because the company purchased undercarriage parts for its assembly operation and competed with those parts in the aftermarket.[5]

So-called will-fitters also manufactured parts, particularly undercarriage parts, for the aftermarket.[6] Industry sources believed that International Harvester and Case faced particularly intense will-fitter competition. Caterpillar, on the other hand, supposedly changed its parts frequently to make it difficult for will-fitters to copy them. The corporate parts-pricing expert was heavily involved with crawler parts pricing.

Parts were divided into three classifications: captive, competitive, and highly competitive. Captive parts were either manufactured in a Deere factory or purchased from an outside supplier. Most captive manufactured items were priced from steel schedules or casting schedules. These schedules took into account the kind of material and the amount that was used in making the part. They were so scaled that smaller parts returned a higher profit than larger pieces. The labor and overhead involved in manufacturing also were included in developing the suggested retail price. Competitive parts were generally those that were fast wearing; they could be either manufactured or purchased. Prices were developed on a cost basis or by following suggested list prices of competitive suppliers with national distribution. Highly competitive parts were priced on cost to meet many different competitors who might have sold exactly the same product.

---

[5]Deere produced most of the undercarriage parts for its small tractors internally. Undercarriage parts were purchased in Europe for the large tractors.

---

[6]Will-fitters for undercarriage parts were all foreign. Some industry executives thought that the home countries of these companies provided various forms of subsidization to encourage export.

EXHIBIT 1   Selected Financial Data

	1975		1976	
	($ millions)	*(%)*	*($ millions)*	*(%)*
Deere & Company				
Net sales	$2,955	100%	$3,134	100%
Cost of goods sold	2,273	77	2,316	74
Gross margin	682	23	818	26
Research and development	98	3	108	3
Selling, general, and administration	275	9	316	10
Income from operations (post-tax)	155	5	216	7
Worldwide sales by type of product ($ millions)				
Farm equipment	2,374		2,523	
Industrial equipment	412		452	
Consumer products	169		159	
	$2,955		$3,134	

	1975		Six months ended June 22, 1976 (unaudited)	
	($ millions)	*(%)*	*($ millions)*	*(%)*
Caterpillar Tractor Company				
Net sales	$4,964	100.0%	$2,466	100.0%
Cost of goods sold	3,859	77.7	1,875	76.0
Gross margin	1,105	22.3	591	24.0
Selling, general, and administration	451	9.1	234	9.5
Operating income (pre-tax)	654	13.2	357	14.5
These included the following research and engineering costs:	169	3.4	88	3.6
Of that, the following amounts were attributable to new product development and major improvements to present products:	$ 121	2.4	$ 61	2.5

NOTE: Data on Caterpillar Tractor Company were obtained from a prospectus dated October 28, 1976. Because of rounding, some numbers do not add or subtract correctly.

EXHIBIT 2

*JD450-C/6405
bulldozer*

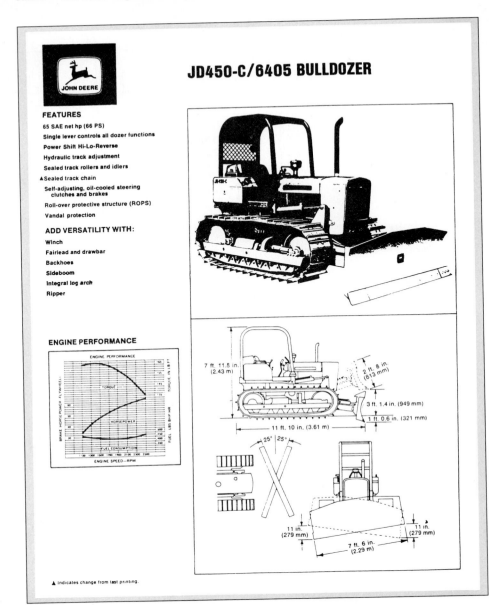

JD450-C/6405 BULLDOZER

FEATURES

65 SAE net hp (66 PS)

Single lever controls all dozer functions

Power Shift Hi-Lo-Reverse

Hydraulic track adjustment

Sealed track rollers and idlers

▲Sealed track chain

Self-adjusting, oil-cooled steering clutches and brakes

Roll-over protective structure (ROPS)

Vandal protection

ADD VERSATILITY WITH:

Winch

Fairlead and drawbar

Backhoes

Sideboom

Integral log arch

Ripper

ENGINE PERFORMANCE

▲ Indicates change from last printing.

EXHIBIT 2
(concluded)

JD450-C/6405 BULLDOZER SPECIFICATIONS

(Specifications and design subject to change without notice. Wherever applicable, specifications are in accordance with IEMC and SAE Standards. Except where otherwise noted, these specifications are based on a unit with roll-over protective structure and standard equipment.)

Power (@ 2500 engine rpm):   **SAE**
Gross .... 70 hp (52.2 kW*)
Net .... 65 hp (48.5 kW)   66 PS
Drawbar .... 48.6 hp (36.2 kW)   49.3 PS

Net engine flywheel power is for an engine equipped with fan, air cleaner water pump, lubricating oil pump, fuel pump, alternator and muffler. The gross engine power is without fan. Flywheel power ratings are under SAE standard conditions of 500-ft. altitude and 85° F. temperature, and DIN 70 020 conditions (non-corrected). No derating is required up to 10,000 feet (3000 m) altitude.
*In the international system of units (SI) power is expressed in kilowatts (kW).

Engine: John Deere 4-cylinder diesel, 4-stroke cycle
Bore and stroke .... 4.02x4.33 in. (102x110 mm)
Piston displacement .... 219 cu. in. (3588 cm³)
Compression ratio .... 16.2 to 1
Maximum torque @ 1,400 rpm ...... 164.5 lb-ft (22.74 kg-m)
NACC or AMA (U.S. Tax) horsepower 23.84
Lubrication .... Pressure system w/full-flow filter
Main bearings 5
Cooling .... Pressurized w/thermostat and fixed bypass
Fan .... Blower
Air cleaner w/restriction indicator .... Dry
Electrical system .... 12-volt w/alternator
Battery .... Reserve capacity: 180 minutes

Transmission .... H-L-R: 4 speed ranges; with high, low, and reverse speeds shifted hydraulically without clutching in each range.

Clutch .... 11-in. (279mm) single-disk

Gear:

	Travel Speeds:		Max. Drawbar Pull: (with adequate weight and traction)	
	mph	km/h	lb.	kg
Range 1				
Low	1.3	2.1	18,050	8188
High	1.8	2.9	12,600	5715
Reverse	1.7	2.7		
Range 2				
Low	2.0	3.2	10.050	4559
High	2.8	4.5	7,050	3197
Reverse	2.7	4.3		
Range 3				
Low	3.0	4.8	6,400	2903
High	4.3	6.9	4,250	1928
Reverse	4.1	6.6		
Range 4				
Low	4.7	7.6	3.500	1588
High	6.7	10.8	2,350	1066
Reverse	6.4	10.3		

Steering:
Steering clutches and brakes are controlled by a single lever for each track. A pedal provides braking, and lock-down for parking.
Clutches .... Oil-cooled, hydraulically-actuated, multiple-disk. 11-in. (279 mm) disks; 16 friction surfaces per clutch.
Brakes ... Self-adjusting, self-energizing, oil-cooled contracting band with bonded lining.

Hydraulic System: Open-Center
Control .... Single "T-bar", triple hydraulic system
Pump .... Gear, 15 or 23 gpm (57 or 87 l/min)
Pressure .... 1750 psi (123.0 kg/cm²)

Hydraulic Cylinders: **Bore**   **Stroke**
Lift, two .... 3.5 in. (88.9 mm)   15 in. (381 mm)
Angle, two .... 3.5 in. (88.9 mm)   13.375 in. (342.9 mm)
Tilt, one .... 3.5 in. (88.9 mm)   3 in. (76.1 mm)
Cylinder rods .. Ground, heat-treated, chrome-plated, polished
Cylinder pivot pins .... Hardened steel (replaceable bushings)

Tracks (5-roller track frames w/rock guards):
Grouser .... 16-in. (406 mm)
Track shoes, each side 36
Ground contact area .... 2328 sq. in. (15 019 cm²)
Ground pressure .... 6.1 psi (0.429 kg/cm²)
Length of track on ground .... 72.75 in. (1.85 m)
Track gauge .... 52 in. (1.32 m)
Carrier roller 1
Adjustment .... Hydraulic
Clearance at rear crossbar .... 14.25 in. (362 mm)

Blade: Reinforced, box-welded
Cutting edge .... 3-piece, reversible, replaceable
Center section .... 0.75 in. (19 mm)
End bits, cast steel .... 0.75 in. (19 mm)

Capacities: **U.S.**   **Liters**
Cooling system .... 4 gal.   15.1
Fuel tank .... 31 gal.   117.3
Crankcase, including filter ...... 9 qt.   8.5
Transmission .... 8 gal.   30.3
▲ Final drive (each) .... 6.5 qt.   6.2
Hydraulic reservoir .... 6.4 gal.   24.5
Hydraulic system .... 12.25 gal.   46.4
Steering clutch housing (each side) ... 14 qt. 13.2

Additional Standard Equipment:
Front/rear bottom guard
Front hitch
Lights
Trash-resistant radiator
Transistorized voltage regulator
Deluxe cushion seat w/armrests
Key switch w/pushbutton safety start
Precleaner
Electric hourmeter
Cigaret lighter
Vandal protection
Grease gun
Outer sprocket shields
▲ Tachometer
▲ Ether starting aid
▲ Altitude compensator
▲ ROPS w/canopy and seat belt

SAE Operating Weight .... 14,250 lb. (6463 kg)

Special Equipment:
PTO (1000 rpm)
Upper and lower front idler shields
Two batteries
16-in. open-center grouser shoes
16-in. triple semi-grouser, open-center shoes
Auxiliary hydraulic system w/breakaway couplings
Swinging drawbar
Remote hydraulic cylinder
Cab (includes ROPS)
Winch drive

▲Indicates change from last printing.

8 ft. 4 in. (2.54 m)

Limb risers and brush-protection assembly for roll-over protective structure

EXHIBIT 3

JD750/6525 bulldozer

JD750/6525 BULLDOZER

ENGINE PERFORMANCE

FEATURES

110 SAE net hp (111.5 PS)

Dual-path automatic hydrostatic drive with infinite speeds up to 6.5 mph (10.5 km/h)

Single lever for speed and direction control

Levers or pedals for independent track control steering

Counterrotating tracks

No steering clutches or steering brakes

Automatically engaged parking brake

Sealed track rollers and idlers

Sealed, counterbored track links and bushings

Single-lever dozer control w/hydraulic tilt and blade float position

Designed for quietness

Roll-over protective structure (ROPS)

ADD VERSATILITY WITH:

Winch

Drawbar

Ripper

EXHIBIT 3
(concluded)

JD750/6525 BULLDOZER SPECIFICATIONS

(Specifications and design subject to change without notice. Wherever applicable, specifications are in accordance with ICED and SAE Standards. Except where otherwise noted, these specifications are based on a unit equipped with roll-over protective canopy, 18 in. (457 mm) grousers and standard equipment.)

Power (@ 2100 rpm): **SAE**
Gross . . . . 122 hp (91 kW*)
Net . . . . 110 hp (82 kW)   111.5 PS

Net engine flywheel power is for an engine equipped with fan, air cleaner, water pump, lubricating oil pump, fuel pump, alternator and muffler. The gross engine power is without fan. Flywheel power ratings are under SAE standard conditions of 500-ft. altitude and 85 F. temperature, and DIN 70 020 conditions (non-corrected). No derating is required up to 10,000 feet (3000 m) altitude.

*In the International System of units (SI), power is expressed in kilowatts (kW)

Engine: John Deere 6-cylinder turbocharged diesel, valve-in-head, 4-stroke cycle.
Bore and stroke . . . . 4.19x5 in. (106.4x127 mm)
Piston displacement . . . . 414 cu. in. (6784 cm³)
Compression ratio . . . . 16.2 to 1
Maximum torque @ 1300 rpm . . 345 lb-ft (468 Nm) (47.7 kg-m)
NACC or AMA (U.S. Tax) horsepower 42
Lubrication . . . . Pressure system w/full flow filters
Main bearings 7
Cooling . . . Pressurized w/thermostat and controlled bypass
Fan . . . . Blower
Air cleaner w/restriction indicator . . . . Dry
Electrical system . . . . 24 volt w/alternator
Batteries (2 12 volt) . . . . . . Reserve capacity: 180 minutes each

Transmission:
Cold weather starting . . . . Disconnect clutch completely disengages hydrostatic drive and all hydraulics.
Splitter drive . . . . Pressure-lubricated helical gears drive both hydrostatic transmissions, main hydraulic pump, winch drive shaft and auxiliary pump drive.
Drive . . . . Dual-path, fully automatic, infinitely variable hydrostatic transmissions.
Speeds . . . . Infinite from 0 to 6.5 mph (0 to 10.5 km/h) forward or reverse.
Control . . . . Single-lever, variable speed, forward and reverse.

Drawbar pull:
Maximum drawbar pull . . . . 47,500 lb. (213 kN) (21 550 kg) at 0.30 mph (0.48 km/h)

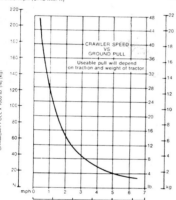

CRAWLER SPEED
VS
GROUND PULL
Useable pull will depend on traction and weight of tractor

Steering:
Fully modulated infinitely variable lever steering for live power turns and counterrotation. Pedal steering optional. No need for steering clutches or steering brakes.

Brakes:
Service . . . . Hydrostatic
Parking . . . . Wet-disk brakes are automatically applied when engine is stopped, or manually applied with center foot pedal during normal operation.

Hydraulic System: Open-center
Control . . . . Single-lever, two-function control
Pump . . . . . Vane. 46 gpm (174 l/min) @ rated engine speed
Pressure . . . . 2000 psi (137.9 bar) (140.6 kg/cm²)

Hydraulic Cylinders: **Bore**   **Stroke**
Lift, two . . . . 4.25 in. (108 mm)   31.85 in. (809 mm)
Tilt, one . . . . 5.5 in. (140 mm)   5.71 in. (145 mm)
Cylinder rods . . . . Ground, heat-treated, chrome-plated, polished
Cylinder pivot pins . . . . Hardened steel (replaceable bushings)

Tracks (6-roller track frame w/front track guides and sprocket guard):
Grouser . . . . 18 in. (457 mm)
Track shoes, each side 40
Ground contact area . . . . 3240 sq. in. (20 903 cm²)
Ground pressure . . . . 8.95 psi (0.617 bar) (0.629 kg/cm²)
Length of track on ground . . . . 90 in. (2.29 m)
Track gauge . . . . 74 in. (1.88 m)
Oscillation . . . . 10 in. (254 mm)
Carrier rollers . . . . 2 each side
Adjustment . . . . Hydraulic
Minimum ground clearance . . . . 14 in. (356 mm)

Blade:
Cutting edge . . . . 3-piece, replaceable
Center section . . . . 0.75 in. (19 mm)
End bits, boron steel . . . . 0.75 in. (19 mm)

Capacities: **U.S.**   **Liters**
Cooling system . . . . 7 gal.   26.5
Fuel tank . . . . 73 gal.   276.3
Crankcase . . . . 18 qt.   17.0
Crankcase, including filter . . . . 20 qt.   18.9
Splitter drive . . . . 1.5 gal.   5.7
Final drive, each: 1st reduction . . . . 8.5 gal.   32.2
                  2nd reduction . . . . 3.5 gal.   13.2
Hydraulic system . . . . 33 gal.   124.9
Hydrostatic drives . . . . 33 gal.   124.9

Additional Standard Equipment:
Enclosed alternator w/ solid state regulator
Bottom guards
Cushioned seat w/armrests
Key switch
Pushbutton starting
Electric hourmeter
Cigaret lighter
Vandal protection
Muffler
Ether starting aid
Front idler shields
Master electrical disconnect switch
Toolbox
Transmission neutral lock with starter safety switch
Horn
Air cleaner restriction indicator
ROPS canopy w/seat belt

SAE Operating Weight w/ROPS . . . . . . 28,985 lb. (13 148 kg)

EXHIBIT 4   **The Deere Crawler Tractor Line**

	List Price	Net Price[a]	Cost[b]	Cost/Price Ratio[c]	Net Horsepower	Weight (in pounds)
JD350-C Bulldozer	$20,923	$15,169	$11,377	75%	42	10,600
JD350-C Loader[d]					42	12,400
JD450-C Bulldozer	29,854	21,644	14,068	65	65	14,250
JD450-C Loader					65	16,700
JD550 Bulldozer	33,336	24,169	16,919	70	72	15,510
JD555 Loader					72	18,255
JD750 Bulldozer	59,785	45,138	36,110	80	110	28,985
JD755 Loader					110	32,000
JD850 Bulldozer[e]			40,717		140	36,140
JD855 Loader					190	46,060

[a]Net price is list price minus the 23% discount and the 4.5% volume discount for utility tractors. For the JD750 it is list price minus the 20% discount and the 4.5% volume discount.

[b]Costs are factory standard cost.

[c]The cost/price ratio is cost divided by net price.

[d]Loaders are listed to show the total line. Price and cost data were deleted for simplicity.

[e]The JD850 and 855 were due to be introduced in May 1977 and January 1978, respectively. Thus, costs and weights are estimated.

NOTE: All confidential company data have been disguised. Price, cost, and weight are for the representative configuration, the standard configuration of popular choices and options used for pricing purposes. For the three smaller bulldozers, a popular blade, not used in the representative configuration, was included here for simplicity.

EXHIBIT 5   **Evolving Horsepower of the 750/755, 850/855, and Competitors**

Type of Equipment	1970	1971	1972–73	1973–74	1975–76
Bulldozers					
Deere:					
750	[95]	[95]	[105]*	[110]*	110
850	[140]	[130]*	[130]	[140]*	[140]
Caterpillar:					
D-3				62	62
D-4	72	72	72	85*	85
D-5	100	100	100	105*	105
D-6	130	130	130	140*	140
Loaders					
Deere:					
755	[95]	[95]	[105]*	[110]*	110
855	[130]	[120–125]*	[160]*	[160]	[190]*
Caterpillar:					
951	90	90	90	95*	95
955	115	115	115	130*	130
977	175	175	175	195*	195

NOTE: Numbers stand for net horsepower. Brackets [ ] indicate a planned but not marketed model. Asterisks * indicate a change from previous year.

EXHIBIT 6

Location of people relevant to pricing

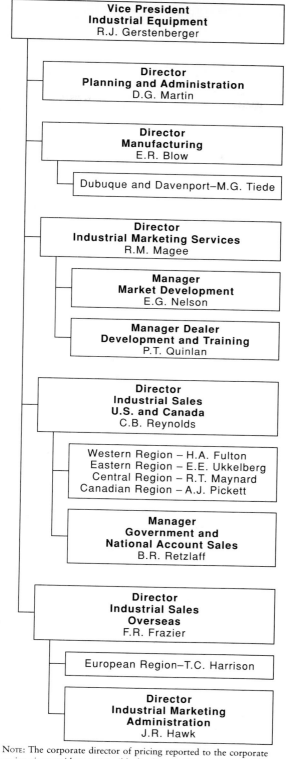

Vice President
Industrial Equipment
R.J. Gerstenberger

Director
Planning and Administration
D.G. Martin

Director
Manufacturing
E.R. Blow

Dubuque and Davenport—M.G. Tiede

Director
Industrial Marketing Services
R.M. Magee

Manager
Market Development
E.G. Nelson

Manager Dealer
Development and Training
P.T. Quinlan

Director
Industrial Sales
U.S. and Canada
C.B. Reynolds

Western Region – H.A. Fulton
Eastern Region – E.E. Ukkelberg
Central Region – R.T. Maynard
Canadian Region – A.J. Pickett

Manager
Government and
National Account Sales
B.R. Retzlaff

Director
Industrial Sales
Overseas
F.R. Frazier

European Region—T.C. Harrison

Director
Industrial Marketing
Administration
J.R. Hawk

NOTE: The corporate director of pricing reported to the corporate senior vice president responsible for finance. The corporate director of market economics reported to the vice president for corporate planning, who in turn reported to the corporate senior vice president responsible for staff activities. Product engineering reported to the Dubuque plant general manager.

EXHIBIT 7 Competitive Crawler-Dozer Price Comparisons

	JD450-C	Case 450	M.F. 300	I.H. TD7E (Stand.)	Cat D-3	JD750	Case 1150B	Cat D-5	F.A. 10-B
Crawler—diesel	$24,992	$24,816	$30,651	$32,802	$20,960	$59,059	$45,343	$48,422	$57,184
Power shift transmission	X	X	X	X	X	X	(Powershift) X	(Powershift) X	(Powershift) X
Engine side shields	X	121	X	X	143	X	X	X	X
Blower fan with trash-resistant radiator	X	208	X	X		71	699	162	X
Triple hydraulic system	X	X	X	X	1,061	X	X	X	X
16" grousers[a]	X	819	X	(15") X	145	X	X	X	(19 ¾") 1,407
90 AMP battery	X	X	X	X	X	X	X	X	X
Lights	X	X	X	X	130	X	X	X	X
Rear bottom guard for drawbar	X	X	X	X	406	313	412	453	X
Tachometer	X	NA	NA	NA	NA[a]	342	X	402	X
Ether starting aid	97	75	X	X	276	X	X	X	X
Swinging drawbar	X	127	293	(Fixed) X	1,154	X	X	2,776	X
ROPS canopy[b]	X	X	1,607	X	NA	X	874	726	X
Altitude compensator	72	NA	NA	NA	NA	X	82	638	X
90" inside hydraulic dozer	4,765	4,689	4,538	X	5,139	X	(116") 6,010	(124") 6,812	(113 ⅜") X
Winch drive	X	NA	NA	NA	443	X	132	306	Parts
Track rock guards	X	X	X	X	93	X	159	232	X
Decelerator	X	NA	X	X	47	X	148	NA	Parts
Front hitch	X	35	X	X	96	X	44	188	Parts
Vandal protection	X	133	NA	X	53	X	550	NA	NA
Horn	X	NA	NA	NA	NA	X	NA	NA	NA
Total price	$29,926	$31,023	$37,089	$32,802	$30,146	$59,785	$54,453	$61,117	$58,591
Price book date	11/1/76	8/1/76	4/1/76	10/18/76	8/28/76	11/1/76	8/1/76	8/28/76	6/1/76
Net horsepower	65	51	63	65	62	110	105	105	110
Price/horsepower	$460	$608	$589	$505	$486	$544	$519	$582	$533

[a] Grousers are to crawlers what tire chains are to tires; they aid in traction.

[b] ROPS: rollover protection system.

NOTE: All data are disguised. M.F. is Massey Ferguson, I.H. is International Harvester, and F.A. is Fiat-Allis. X means item is included in base price. NA means item is not available.

SEALED AIR CORPORATION

The president and chief executive officer of Sealed Air Corporation, T. J. Dermot Dunphy, explained the firm's 25 percent average annual growth in net sales and net earnings from 1971 to 1980:

> The company's history has been characterized by technical accomplishment and market leadership. During the last 10 years we built on our development of the *first* closed-cell, lightweight cushioning material, introduced the *first* foam-in-place packaging system, and engineered the *first* complete solar heating system for swimming pools. We intend to follow the same management guidelines in the 1980s. We intend to seek market leadership because market leadership optimizes profit, and foster technological leadership because it is the only long-term guarantee of market leadership.

In July 1981 Barrett Hauser, product manager of Sealed Air's Air Cellular Products, was reflecting on Dunphy's management philosophy as he considered how Sealed Air should respond to some unanticipated competition in the protective packaging market. As product manager, Hauser was responsible for the closed-cell, light-weight cushioning material that Dunphy had mentioned. Sealed Air's registered trademark name for this product was AirCap.[1] AirCap cushioning materials had always faced a variety of competitors in the protective packaging market. More recently, however, several small regional producers had invented around Sealed Air's manufacturing process patents and begun to market cheap imitations of AirCap in the United States.

AirCap Cushioning and Its Competitors

AirCap cushioning was a clear, laminated plastic sheet containing air bubbles of uniform size (see Exhibit 1). The feature that differentiated AirCap cushioning from all other bubble products was its "barrier-coating": each AirCap bubble was coated on the inside with saran. This greatly increased air retention, meaning less compression of the material during shipment and, consequently, better protection. Barrier-coating and its customer benefits had been the central theme of Sealed Air's AirCap cushioning selling effort for 10 years.

Between 1971 and 1980 Sealed Air and Astro Packaging of Hawthorne, New Jersey, were the only air bubble packaging material producers in the United States. Sealed Air licensed Astro to use Sealed Air's patented technology. Astro produced two types of bubbles: a barrier bubble similar to AirCap,[2] and an uncoated bubble. Its sales were split about evenly between the two. In 1980, Astro's total U.S. sales were approximately $10.5 million, compared with $25.35 million in U.S. sales for AirCap cushioning. Sealed Air's market education had made customers aware of the advantages of coated bubbles; consequently, uncoated bubbles had never achieved greater than a 15 percent dollar share of the U.S. market before 1980.

In July 1981 uncoated bubble operations were being set up in Ohio, California, and New York. GAFCEL, which served the metropolitan New York market, was the only competitor yet to achieve significant sales volume. Two GAFCEL salespeople—one full time, the other about half time—had reached a $1 million annual sales rate. Several of AirCap's distributors had taken on the GAFCEL line.

Hauser was preparing to recommend Sealed Air's reaction to these somewhat unanticipated competitors. The firm could produce an uncoated bubble as cheaply as GAFCEL within a month with no major capital investment; it could run on machines used for another Sealed Air product. If Hauser were to recommend that the historic champion of barrier-coating offer an uncoated bubble, he would have to specify timing, the marketing program for the new product, and any adjustments in policies for AirCap cushioning and Sealed Air's other products. As Hauser thought about his options, he again flipped through the training manual recently distributed to Sealed Air's sales force: "How to Sell against Uncoated Bubbles."

The Protective Packaging Market

The three major use segments of the protective packaging market were:

1. Positioning, blocking, and bracing: These protective materials had to secure large, heavy, usually semirugged items in a container. Typical applications included shipment of motors and computer peripherals.

This case was prepared by Robert J. Dolan, associate professor. Copyright © 1982 by the President and Fellows of Harvard College.
Harvard Business School case 582-103 (Rev. 9/85).

[1] Sealed Air, AirCap, and Instapak are registered ® trademarks of Sealed Air Corporation. Solar Pool Blanket is a TM trademark of the same corporation.

[2] Astro's barrier bubble and the AirCap bubble differed in both manufacturing process and coating material. Astro used nylon rather than saran. The basic idea of reinforcing the polyethylene bubbles to improve air retention was, however, the same.

2. Flexible wraps: These materials came under less pressure per square foot. Applications included glassware, small spare parts, and light medical instruments.

3. Void fill: These materials were added to prevent movement during shipping when an item and its protective wrap (if any) did not fill its carton.

The positioning, blocking, and bracing market was unique because of the heavier weights of items shipped. Flexible wrap and void fill were sometimes hard to separate because it was convenient to use the same product for both functions. The key distinction was that loose fills (for instance, polystyrene beads) dominated the void fill market but provided no cushioning protection and, hence, did not qualify as flexible wrap.

Until 1970 most materials used for protective packaging were produced primarily for other purposes. Heavy, paper-based products had dominated the market. Sealed Air was one of the first companies to approach the market with a customer orientation (i.e., it began product development with an assessment of packagers' needs). Since then a variety of products specifically designed for protective packaging had appeared.

Sealed Air served these markets with two products:

1. Instapak® foam-in-place systems (1980 worldwide sales of $38.8 million) could accommodate any application, though their most advantageous use was for heavy items. In this process two liquid chemicals were pumped into a shipping container. The chemicals rapidly expanded to form a foam cushion around the product. Instapak's comparative advantage resulted in a majority of applications in positioning, blocking, and bracing.

2. AirCap bubbles (1980 worldwide sales of $34.3 million) primarily served the flexible wrap and void fill markets.

In addition to coated and uncoated polyethylene air bubbles, there were two major competitors in these markets: paper-based products (cellulose wadding, single-face corrugated, and indented kraft), and foams (polyurethane, polypropylene, and polyethylene).

An excerpt from an AirCap promotional brochure in Exhibit 2 shows how Sealed Air positioned AirCap as a cost-effective substitute for these competitive products and loose fills. The brochure first pointed out the cost savings from AirCap cushioning, then presented results of "fatigue" and "original thickness retention" tests to demonstrate AirCap's protective superiority. Exhibit 3 compares products competitive with AirCap cushioning and Exhibit 4 gives their U.S. list prices, which represent relative costs for any order size from an end user. Quantity discounts were offered on all materials.

Buying Influences.   The proliferation of packaging products and the lack of easily demonstrable universal superiority caused confusion among end users. For example, products such as pewter mugs were shipped around the United States in AirCap cushioning, Astro coated bubbles, or even old newspapers.

Users were a varied lot. Some bought on a scientific price/performance basis. They understood "cushioning curves," such as those in Exhibit 5. Sealed Air could provide independently measured cushioning curves for competitive products as well as its own. Regardless, many firms did their own testing.

At the other end of the spectrum were firms with "a purchasing-department mentality," as some packaging materials suppliers put it. Price per square foot was their first consideration, delivery their second. As one Sealed Air executive commented, "To these people, cushioning curves are like accounting numbers. They think you can make them say anything you want."

There were no systematically collected data on the buying process or the extent to which price dominated performance in the purchase decision. Based on his experience as a district sales manager and now product manager, Hauser guessed that a packaging engineer influenced about 40 percent of the material purchase decisions.

The U.S. Market.   In 1980, dollar sales by segment in the U.S. protective packaging market were:

- Positioning, blocking, and bracing: $585 million
- Flexible wrap: $126 million
- Void fill: $15.6 million

Exhibit 6 breaks down total sales for the flexible wrap market by product type for 1975, 1978, and 1980.

AirCap cushioning annual sales in the United States since 1972 were:

Year	Gross Sales (in millions)	Year	Gross Sales (in millions)
1972	$ 7.7	1977	$16.4
1973	10.0	1978	18.4
1974	13.0	1979	21.2
1975	12.8	1980	25.3
1976	14.6		

Despite the high cost of coated bubbles relative to the uncoated product, Sealed Air had kept most of the U.S. air bubble market. Key factors were Sealed Air's patent protection and licensing of only one competitor, extensive market education, and the packaging mentality in the United States. Packaging engineers enjoyed a status in U.S. organizations not accorded them elsewhere. Packaging supplies were viewed as a productive, cost-saving resource. In contrast, recent research by Sealed Air indicated that many European firms viewed packaging supplies as "expendable commodities."

The European Market. Sealed Air had manufacturing operations in England and France and a sales organization in Germany.[3] It was the only company selling a coated product in these countries. Sales figures for 1980 were:

Country	Total Bubble Sales	AirCap Sales
England	$3,649,000	$2,488,500
France	4,480,000	592,200
Germany	7,688,000	404,600

England. Sealed Air had developed the protective packaging market here and had good distribution. Later on, Sansetsu, a Japanese firm, began marketing a high-quality uncoated product made in Germany. Prices for the uncoated bubble were 50 percent less than the cost of comparably sized AirCap cushioning. Sansetsu and other uncoated bubble manufacturers had chipped away at Sealed Air's one-time 90 percent market share. The most pessimistic Sealed Air distributors estimated that the firm would lose 50 percent of its current market share to uncoated bubbles within three years.

France. Here, Sealed Air owned an uncoated bubble manufacturer, SIBCO, with sales of $750,000 in 1980. In 1972, SIBCO was the only marketer of uncoated bubbles

---

[3]The firm also had a manufacturing facility in Canada and a sales organization in Japan. Sealed Air licensees operated manufacturing facilities in Australia, Mexico, South Africa, and Spain.

in France. Two major competitors, one with superior production facilities, had entered the market. Uncoated bubbles were priced about 40 percent lower than AirCap, and price was the key buying determinant. The major French distributor of AirCap cushioning had a 50–50 mix of coated and uncoated sales in 1978. In 1980 the mix had changed to 70–30 (uncoated over coated), with 90 percent of new bubble applications being uncoated.

Germany. AirCap cushioning was a late entrant (1973) to the German market and never held commanding share. Moreover, from 1978 to 1980, it had lost share at a rate of 20 to 30 percent per year. Sansetsu had an efficient manufacturing facility in Germany and sold approximately $6 million of uncoated product in 1980. (The price for uncoated was about 35 percent less than for coated.)

AirCap Cushioning

Grades and Sales. AirCap cushioning grades differed in bubble height and thickness of the plastic films. Bubble heights were designated by a letter code, and the plastic films came in four thicknesses (see Table A). Sealed Air produced eight different height/thickness combinations (see Table B). Some of the known end uses for each grade are shown in Exhibit 7.

Sales by grade for the last six months of 1979 and the first six months of 1980 are shown in Table C.

Pricing. All AirCap cushioning was sold through distributors. Prices reflected Sealed Air's costs and the prices of competitive products. Variable costs and prices to the distributor are shown in Table D.

Sealed Air's suggested resale price list is shown in Exhibit 8. Largely because of its selective distribution policy, distributors generally followed this list. The price schedule entailed quantity discounts for end users. Thus, distributor margins varied with the size of the customer's individual

---

TABLE A   Differing Grades of AirCap Cushioning

Bubble Heights

SB: ⅛ in. high, used for surface protection when cushioning requirements were minimal.

SC: 3/16 in. high, used primarily for wrapping small, intricate items, possibly for larger items if not very fragile.

ST: 5/16 in. high, used in same kinds of applications as SC grade, except with slightly greater cushioning requirements. Also used as a void fill.

SD: ½ in. high, used for large, heavy, or fragile items or as a void fill.

Plastic Film Thicknesses

Light duty (110): each layer of film was 1 mil (1/1,000 of an inch) thick; used for light loads.
Regular duty (120): one layer of 1 mil and one layer of 2 mils; for loads up to 50 lbs. per sq. ft.
Heavy duty (240): one layer of 2 mils and one of 4 mils; for loads up to 100 lbs. per sq. ft.
Super duty (480): one layer of 4 mils and one of 8; for loads over 100 lbs. per sq. ft.

TABLE B   **Eight Different Height/Thicknesses by Sealed Air**

Height (inches)	Thickness			
	110	120	240	480
SB-$\frac{1}{8}$	X			
SC-$\frac{3}{16}$		X	X	
ST-$\frac{5}{16}$		X	X	
SD-$\frac{1}{2}$		X	X	X

TABLE C   **AirCap Sales by Grade**

	Sales in 1,000 Square Feet	
Grade	July–December 1979	January–June 1980
$\frac{1}{8}$ in.:		
SB-110	59,128	48,513
$\frac{3}{16}$ in.:		
SC-120	76,349	81,014
SC-240	5,036	4,426
$\frac{5}{16}$ in.:		
ST-120	31,912	42,234
ST-240	4,369	3,914
$\frac{1}{2}$ in.:		
SD-120	44,252	43,624
SD-240	25,202	21,799
SD-480	3,138	1,358
Total sales	249,386	246,882

NOTE: In addition, because SB-110 could not compete in price against foams for many surface protection applications, Sealed Air introduced an A-100 grade in January 1980. The A-100 bubble was $\frac{3}{32}$ in. high—the shortest coated bubble Sealed Air could make with available technology. January to June 1980 sales of A-100 were 17,802,000 sq. ft.

order. (Quantity price was determined by the total square footage of a single order, combining all grades, ordered for shipment at one time to a single destination.) In some major metropolitan areas, up to 50 percent of AirCap business was truckload/railcar orders by end users. In this event Sealed Air shipped the material from its plant directly to the end user; the distributor received a 10 percent margin and handled user credit and technical service. In some markets the percentage of direct shipments was as low as 10 percent.

Selling Effort.   Sealed Air's U.S. operation consisted of 7 regional manufacturing operations, 62 salespeople (each selling AirCap cushioning, Instapak, and other Sealed Air products), and 370 distributors. To control the shipping cost of its bulky product, Sealed Air had regional manufacturing operations in three eastern states, Ohio, Illinois, Texas, and California. The regional presence, however, had proven to be an effective sales promotion device as well.

Before Instapak was acquired in 1976, 28 salespeople devoted 90 percent of their time to AirCap cushioning products. In 1981, the 62-person force was expected to allocate time as follows: 60 percent to Instapak systems, 35 percent to AirCap cushioning, and 5 percent to other Sealed Air products. (Exhibit 9 shows Sealed Air sales by product line and other financial data.)

Part of Sealed Air's market share leadership philosophy was a consultative selling approach. Salespeople spent about half their time making cost studies at end-user locations. With the help of Sealed Air's packaging labs, salespeople attempted to show how their products could save on material and labor cost and reduce damage in the end user's particular situation. Distributors' salespeople took orders on AirCap cushioning but did little to demonstrate AirCap use and application to customers. If a distributor's salesperson identified a potential AirCap account, he or she would inform the Sealed Air salesperson and a joint call would be arranged. In this way the potential account learned about the product and ordering procedures simultaneously.

Distributors sometimes complained to Sealed Air about the level of AirCap selling effort. Since distributor's margins on AirCap cushioning were generally higher than the 10 to 12 percent for Instapak sales, distributors were not happy with Sealed Air's greater allocation of salesperson time to Instapak. Some distributors said they would be content if the salesperson in their area really allocated 35 percent to AirCap; some claimed the actual AirCap selling effort amounted to only 20 percent. Instapak's sales growth had been impressive, but some Sealed Air executives felt this had cost them some distributor satisfaction.

Both distributors and end users regarded Sealed Air's salespeople as among the best trained and most knowledgeable in the packaging industry. Sales force salaries were above average. They were composed of a base salary plus commissions of 2 percent on net AirCap sales and 1 percent on net sales of all other products, including Instapak. (As an added incentive Sealed Air gave salespeople $75 for each Instapak dispenser placed. It took back $75 for each one removed.) In a typical week a salesperson called on 20 end users and checked in with two or three distributors.

U.S. Distributors.   During the 1970s Sealed Air invested heavily in developing a selected distributor network. The firm had 370 distributors by 1980. Sealed Air considered 135 of these their "first-line distributors" because they collectively handled over 80 percent of its business. The 20 largest AirCap distributors handled about 35 percent of the

TABLE D AirCap Variable Costs and Distributor Prices (in dollars per 1,000 sq. ft.)

Grade	Manufacturing	Freight	(1) Total Variable Cost	(2) Price to Distrib- utor for Truck- load Delivery[a]	(2) − (1) Sealed Air Dollar Margin
A-100 ($\frac{3}{32}$ in.)	$12.46	$1.32	$13.78	$ 20.60	$ 6.82
SB-110 ($\frac{1}{8}$ in.)	14.02	1.99	16.01	30.25	14.24
SC-120 ($\frac{3}{16}$ in.)	17.92	2.64	20.56	43.50	22.94
SC-240 ($\frac{3}{16}$ in.)	29.83	2.64	32.47	56.30	23.83
ST-120 ($\frac{5}{16}$ in.)	25.36	5.29	30.65	51.40	20.75
ST-240 ($\frac{5}{16}$ in.)	32.83	5.29	38.12	65.35	27.23
SD-120 ($\frac{1}{2}$ in.)	28.38	7.93	36.31	65.35	29.04
SD-240 ($\frac{1}{2}$ in.)	36.52	7.93	44.45	78.60	34.15
SD-480 ($\frac{1}{2}$ in.)	62.88	7.93	70.81	140.90	70.09

[a]Less than truckload shipments were priced 15% to 20% higher. Consequently, distributors almost always ordered in truckload quantities. They were allowed to mix grades within an order. Depending on the grade ordered, a truckload could contain 70,000 sq. ft. (all SD-480) to 420,000 sq. ft. (all A-100).

business. Larger distributors typically carried both Insta-pak foam-in-place and AirCap cushioning. The largest distributor of Sealed Air products had 1980 Sealed Air sales of approximately $2 million, just about half of which were AirCap.

Distributors traditionally tried to be full-line houses—capable of meeting each customer's complete packaging needs—so they carried a broad range of products. A survey of Sealed Air's first-line distributors showed that 83 percent carried loose fills, 65 percent carried polyethylene foam, and 29 percent carried Du Pont's polypropylene foam. Although most carried competitive products, distributors had displayed loyalty to Sealed Air and AirCap cushioning. Sealed Air, in turn, had kept to its selected distribution policy.

Competing Uncoated Bubble Cushioning

Sealed Air considered both types of bubbles made by Astro as inferior products. GAFCEL, the new regional producer, made a "decent product" in Hauser's estimation; he felt that its success to date came largely at Astro's expense.

The New York metropolitan market was ideal for the new producer. It was not customer- or distributor-loyal, and price was a key variable. Sealed Air's estimate of GAFCEL sales rates was $750,000 per year for the ½-in.-high uncoated bubble and $250,000 per year for the 3/16-in. bubble. Both had two layers of film 2 mils each.

GAFCEL's distributor prices for truckload shipments and suggested resale prices to end users for the metropoli-

tan New York market are shown in Table E. (Astro's uncoated bubble prices are in Exhibit 4.)

Sealed Air had not yet extensively tested the GAFCEL uncoated bubble. Although it was better than Astro's uncoated, its performance would not be dramatically different from that found in previous uncoated testing (see Exhibit 2). In terms of cushioning curves, the ½ - in. GAFCEL bubble was comparable to Sealed Air's ST-120 or SD-120 for very light loads, not greater than 0.15 lbs./sq. in. pressure. At greater loads, however, the acceleration curve would increase rapidly, moving above even the SB-110 by pressures of 0.25 lbs./sq. in. (see Exhibit 5).

TABLE E GAFCEL's Distributor Prices per 1,000 Sq. Ft.

	SO-22 ($\frac{3}{16}$ in.)	LO-22 ($\frac{1}{2}$ in.)
Distributor-truckload	$31.63	$36.03
Suggested resale by order size:		
1,000 sq. ft.	$56.54	$75.24
20,000 sq. ft.	47.12	62.70
40,000 sq. ft.	42.84	57.07
100,000 sq. ft.	39.40	44.68
Truckload	34.79	39.63

Sealed Air Decisions

Sealed Air had conducted a good deal of research on manufacturing uncoated bubble products. It knew the best production process would be similar to that currently used for its Solar Pool Blankets™. Thus, the firm could begin manufacture of an uncoated product quickly in its New Jersey plant. Likely distributor response to a Sealed Air uncoated product was difficult to predict. Some distributors had requested it, but others regularly complained that there were already too many coated grades.

Preliminary estimates of the variable costs for producing Sealed Air uncoated bubbles were $19 per 1,000 sq. ft. for $3/16$ in. height, $20 per 1,000 sq. ft. for $5/16$ in., and $21 per 1,000 sq. ft. for $1/2$ in. Freight cost depended on bubble height and distance shipped. Although GAFCEL's production process was completely different, its production costs were believed to be comparable.

Hauser now had to decide whether to recommend that Sealed Air enter the uncoated bubble market (with an about-face on its previous exclusive emphasis on coated bubbles), or whether to suggest some other reaction to its new competitors.

EXHIBIT 1

AirCap® product and uses

Cushioning

AirCap® air bubble cushioning protects products against shock and vibration during handling and shipping by literally floating them on a cushion of air. This material offers consistent performance because our unique *barrier-coating* guarantees air retention. AirCap withstands repeated impact since it will not fatigue or take a compression set. Cushioning applications include a range of products from lightweight retail items to delicate power supplies weighing several hundred pounds. Choose the grade that best fits *your* cushioning application!

SC-120	ST-120/ST-240	SD-120/SD-240/SD-480
Regular Duty	Regular, Heavy Duty	Regular, Heavy, Super Duty

Protective Wrap/Interleaving

AirCap is an excellent "protective wrap" material and ideal for "interleaving" between similarly shaped items. It is clean, non-abrasive, easy to use and provides superior surface protection. Lay your product on AirCap sheeting, fold it over and your product is fully protected! Typical protective wrap/interleaving applications include china, glassware, printed circuit boards, and spare parts.

SB-110	SC-120/SC-240	ST-120
Light Duty	Regular, Heavy Duty	Regular Duty

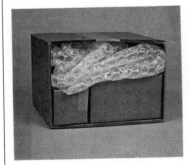

Void Fill

When a void in a package is not completely filled, the cushioned product may migrate within the shipping container. This movement is a major cause of damage in transit. Since large *regular-duty* AirCap bubbles do not compress, they fill voids effectively and eliminate product movement. Simply stuff AirCap sheeting into the carton, (left) or use an economical rolled "log". It's easy, clean, lightweight and cost efficient!

ST-120	SD-120
Regular Duty	Regular Duty

Exhibit 2

Sealed Air presents AirCap as cost-effective substitute

Typical Cost-Savings Comparisons

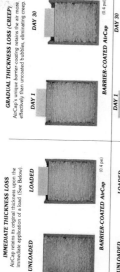

Resists Fatigue

In the transportation environment, packages are subjected to many jolts, bumps and shocks that can potentially cause damage. To function effectively, a cushioning material must retain its ability to protect over a series of repeated impacts. The loss of protective ability during repeated impact is termed "material fatigue".

This graph (left) indicates the increased shock an average product (0.25 psi) will receive during a ten-drop sequence from 24 inches. Test results show *barrier-coated* AirCap outperforms all materials tested.

BARRIER-COATING
Each individual AirCap bubble is barrier-coated to retain the air.

Retains Original Thickness

When a load is placed on a cushioning material two things occur that may contribute to a deterioration in its performance. First, is the *immediate* compression of the material. Second, is the additional, more *gradual* loss of thickness, termed "creep." Generally, excessive thickness loss of a material results in increased material usage in cushioning and dunnage applications. Creep may contribute to product damage as the loss of thickness creates a void in a package, allowing the product to move, shift or migrate.

This chart (left) demonstrates how *barrier-coated* AirCap retains its original thickness better than all materials tested and provides product protection throughout the entire packaging, shipping, handling and storage cycle.

Material Tested	Initial Thickness Loss Upon Load (0.4 psi)	Gradual Thickness Loss After 30 Days	Total Thickness Loss
AirCap® SD-240	7%	7%	14%
Polypropylene Foam	19%	11%	30%
Polyethylene Foam	16%	24%	40%
Cellulose Wadding	26%	12%	38%
Rubberized Hair IV	24%	27%	51%
Uncoated Bubbles (Large)	14%	50%	64%
Urethane Foam (1.25 pcf.)	53%	•	•
Embossed Polyethylene (Hex)	54%	•	•

*30 day evaluation not conducted due to excessive initial thickness loss.

IMMEDIATE THICKNESS LOSS

AirCap retains its original thickness upon the immediate application of a load (See Below).

BARRIER-COATED AirCap (0.4 psi)

UNLOADED   LOADED

GRADUAL THICKNESS LOSS (CREEP)

AirCap's unique barrier-coating retains the air more effectively than uncoated bubbles, eliminating creep.

BARRIER-COATED AirCap (0.4 psi)

DAY 1   DAY 30

CONVENTIONAL CELLULOSE MATERIAL

UNLOADED   LOADED

UNCOATED BUBBLES (0.4 psi)

DAY 1   DAY 30

AirCap Vs. Corrugated Inserts

A manufacturer using corrugated inserts, cellulose wadding and polyethylene bags eliminated the need to inventory many packaging components (right), and reduced labor 84% by switching to AirCap (left).

Item	Corrugated Package	AirCap Package
Carton	$ .55	$ .55
Inner packaging	.80	1.05
Labor	.83	.13
Freight	2.60	2.40
Total cost	$4.78	$4.13
Savings using AirCap		$ .65

AirCap Vs. Loose Fills

A distributing firm found that it needed an excessive amount of flowable to prevent product migration. A new AirCap package (left) using a simple criss-cross technique resulted in reduced material, shipping, labor and carton costs.

Item	Loose Fill Package	AirCap Package
Carton	$ .73	$ .47
Inner packaging	.75	.54
Labor	.42	.25
Freight	3.02	2.72
Total cost	$4.92	$3.98
Savings using AirCap		$ .94

AirCap Vs. Thin-Grade Foams

An electronic service center employing the use of a thin-grade foam (right) required many layers of wrapping to protect against shock and vibration. Large AirCap bubbles (left) provided superior performance and lower packaging costs.

Item	Foam Package	AirCap Package
Carton	$ .46	$ .38
Inner packaging	1.33	.87
Labor	.66	.33
Freight	4.09	3.94
Total cost	$6.54	$5.52
Savings using AirCap		$1.02

AirCap Vs. Cellulose Wadding

A metering firm discovered it needed only half as much AirCap to achieve the same performance that cellulose wadding provided (right). In addition to lowering material costs, AirCap (left) is clean, lint free, non-abrasive and lightweight.

Item	Cellulose Wadding Package	AirCap Package
Carton	$ .30	$ .22
Inner packaging	.22	.12
Labor	.25	.08
Freight	1.35	1.20
Total cost	$2.12	$1.62
Savings using AirCap		$ .50

EXHIBIT 3   **Competitive Product Information**

1. Cellulose wadding (a paper-based product which tries to trap air between piles of sheeting).
   - Major suppliers:
       Jiffy Packaging, Hillside, N.J.
       CelluProducts Co., Patterson, N.C.
   - Sizes available:
       Thickness of 0.17 in., 0.25 in., 0.37 in., 0.50 in.
   - Advantages/disadvantages:
       Much cheaper than AirCap in thin grades; will not mark item wrapped; heavier than AirCap (3–4 lbs. per cu. ft. vs. less than 1 lb. for AirCap) meaning higher shipping cost; excessive compression under heavy loads (see test results, Exhibit 2).
2. Corrugated products (sheets of ribbed cardboard, often cut and perforated to specific sizes).
   - Major suppliers:
       About 800 firms manufacturing in 47 states, including larger paper companies.
   - Advantages/disadvantages:
       Single face (cardboard with ribs on one side) appreciably cheaper than AirCap on square-foot basis; labor cost of using corrugated usually very high; poor cushioning.
3. Polyethylene foam (thin, smooth, rigid sheets of low-density foam).
   - Major suppliers:
       Sentinel Foam Products, Hyannis, Mass.
       CelluProducts Co., Patterson, N.C.
       Jiffy Packaging, Hillside, N.J.
   - Sizes available:
       48 or 68 in. wide rolls of thickness 1/16, 3/32, 3/16, 1/4 in.
   - Advantages/disadvantages:
       Appreciably cheaper than AirCap in thin grades on square-foot basis; does not mark item wrapped; rigid product means hard to work with; tendency to tear; cushioning inferior to AirCap; more expensive than AirCap in thicker grades.
4. Polypropylene foam (thin, coarse, rigid sheets of low-density foam).
   - Major supplier:
       Du Pont Microfoam
   - Sizes available:
       Standard 72 in. wide rolls of thickness 1/16, 3/32, 1/8, 3/16, 1/4, 3/8 in.
   - Advantages/disadvantages:
       Basically the same as for polyethylene foam.
5. Loose fills (expanded polystyrene beads, peanuts, etc.).
   - Major suppliers:
       Many small firms
   - Advantages/disadvantages:
       50% cheaper than AirCap on cubic foot basis; messy, poor cushioning.
6. Uncoated bubbles (sheets of small air bubbles made of polyethylene film).
   - Major producer:
       Astro, Hawthorne, N.J. (Sealed Air licensee)
   - Sizes available:
       48 in. wide roll standard, bubble heights 3/16, 1/4, 1/2 in. Bubbles also varied in the thickness of the films used. Generally, thicknesses were 1, 2, 3 or 4 mils with increasing film thickness giving greater strength.
   - Advantages/disadvantages:
       Cheaper than comparable height coated bubble; excessive air loss over time (about 65% height loss under 50 lbs. per sq. ft. pressure over 30 days vs. 15% for AirCap).
7. Competitive coated bubble (essentially the same as uncoated bubble except nylon film coating added).
   - Major supplier:
       Astro, Hawthorne, N.J. (Sealed Air licensee)
   - Sizes available:
       48 in. wide roll standard, bubble heights 1/8, 3/16, 1/4, 1/2, 1 in.
   - Advantages/disadvantages:
       Under heavy loading, nylon barrier holds up better than Sealed Air's saran barrier; poor quality control (bubble heights generally 13% less than specified).

EXHIBIT 4   Suggested End-User Prices (in dollars) for Major Competitive Products

1. Paper-Based

Cellulose Wadding (Jiffy Packaging)		
Thickness (in.)	*Price*	*Single-Face Corrugated*
0.17	$27.70	$22.75
0.25	37.40	
0.37	50.60	
0.50	65.00	

2. Foams

Thickness (in.)	*Jiffy Packaging (polyethylene)*	*Sentinel Products (polyethylene)*	*Du Pont Microfoam (polypropylene)*
$\frac{1}{16}$	$20.30	$18.20	$ 17.20
$\frac{3}{32}$	25.90	24.00	25.17
$\frac{1}{8}$	34.15	32.70	34.90
$\frac{3}{16}$	53.35	49.40	53.86
$\frac{3}{8}$	NA	NA	109.72

3. Competitive Bubbles (Astro)

Coated Nylon			Uncoated—Polyethylene		
Bubble Height (in.)	*Film Thickness[a] (mils)*	*Price*	*Bubble Height (in.)*	*Film Thickness[a] (mils)*	*Price*
$\frac{1}{8}$	1 and 1	$ 35.25			
$\frac{3}{16}$	1 and 2	49.50	$\frac{3}{16}$	2 and 3	$47.00
$\frac{1}{4}$	1 and 2	57.00	$\frac{1}{4}$	2 and 3	54.50
$\frac{1}{2}$	1 and 2	71.75	$\frac{1}{2}$	2 and 4	65.75
$\frac{1}{2}$	2 and 4	87.75			
1	1 and 2	90.00			
1	2 and 4	110.00			

[a]Each bubble is made of two layers of film. Thicknesses shown are for individual layers in mils. Thicker film produces a stronger product.

NA means not available.

NOTE: Prices are per 1,000 sq. ft. based on a 50,000-sq.-ft. order.

Exhibit 5

Comparative cushioning performance by grade

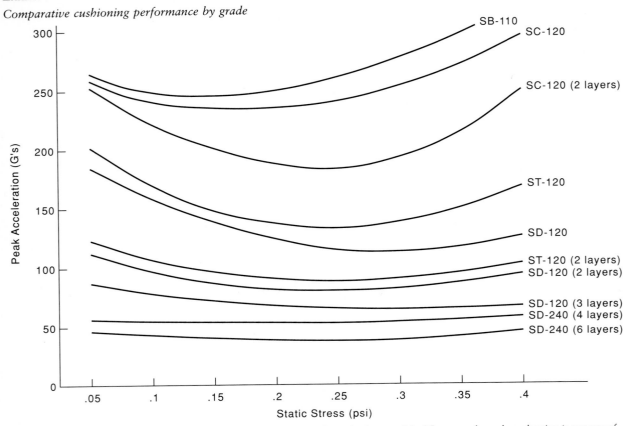

Note: To be read: For a product exerting 0.25 lbs. per sq. in. of pressure on the packaging material while at rest, the peak acceleration (a measure of shock to the product) when dropped from 2 ft. is 118 g. if SD-120 is used, 260 g. if SB-110 is used.

Source: AirCap brochure.

EXHIBIT 6 U.S. Market—Flexible Wraps by Product Type (in millions of manufacturers' dollars)

	1975	1978	1980
Paper-based			
Cellulose wadding	20	23	23
Single-face corrugated	20	25	27
Indented kraft	1	1	1
	41	49	51
Foams[a]			
Polyurethane	10	11	12
Polypropylene	4	5	7
Polyethylene	1	6	25
	15	22	44
Polyethylene air bubbles[b]			
Coated and uncoated (combined)	15	22	31
Total	71	93	126

[a]Sales figures exclude nonpackaging uses, such as construction and furniture industries.
[b]Figures are for flexible wrap market only and are, therefore, less than AirCap's and Astro's total U.S. sales.
SOURCE: Company records.

EXHIBIT 7 AirCap Applications by Grade

Grade	Package Contents	Packaging Material Displaced (if known)
SB-110	Furnace thermostats	
	Shorthand machines	
	Taco shells	Corrugated
	Tempered glass sheets	1/16-in. polypropylene foam
SC-120	Clocks	Shredded paper
SC-240	Wooden picture frames	Corrugated
ST-120	Light fixtures	Corrugated
	Overhead projector lenses	
	Computer components	
	Telephone bell ringers	Corrugated
	Amplifiers	3/32-in. polyethylene foam
	Saucepans	Corrugated
	Two-way radios	Urethane foam pads
ST-240	Exit alarms	
	Mixers	
	Fryers	
	Carbonless paper rolls	
SD-120	Oven burners	
	Pharmaceutical bottles	Shredded paper
	Candleholders	
	Recorders	
	Carburetors	Polypropylene foam
SD-240	Lamps	
	Gallon jugs	
	Computer terminals	Corrugated
	Printed circuit boards	Foam pads and corrugated
	Foil wallpaper	
	Blood coagulation timers	Corrugated
SD-480	Leaded glass windows	
	Custom motorcycle seats	Astro uncoated bubble LP-24
	Motor controls	

EXHIBIT 8   Suggested U.S. Resale Price List, Effective March 1980

Item (thickness in inches)	Sq. Ft. per Order per Single Destination	Price per 1,000 Sq. Ft.
A-100 ($\frac{3}{32}$)	1,000 or more	$ 34.30
	5,000 " "	30.85
	10,000 " "	27.45
	30,000 " "	25.70
	50,000 " "	24.75
	Truckload/railcar	22.80
SB-110 ($\frac{1}{8}$)	1,000 or more	50.00
	5,000 " "	45.40
	10,000 " "	40.90
	30,000 " "	38.10
	50,000 " "	37.05
	Truckload/railcar	33.50
SC-120 ($\frac{3}{16}$)	1,000 or more	71.70
	5,000 " "	64.55
	10,000 " "	57.40
	30,000 " "	53.75
	50,000 " "	52.60
	Truckload/railcar	47.65
SC-240 ($\frac{3}{16}$)	1,000 or more	93.40
	5,000 " "	84.40
	10,000 " "	74.95
	30,000 " "	70.20
	50,000 " "	68.60
	Truckload/railcar	62.25
ST-120 ($\frac{5}{16}$)	1,000 or more	85.30
	5,000 " "	77.10
	10,000 " "	68.50
	30,000 " "	64.25
	50,000 " "	62.75
	Truckload/railcar	57.25
ST-240 ($\frac{5}{16}$)	Same price per 1,000 sq. ft. as SD-120	
SD-120 ($\frac{1}{2}$)	1,000 or more	107.85
	5,000 " "	97.70
	10,000 " "	87.55
	30,000 " "	81.40
	50,000 " "	79.35
	Truckload/railcar	72.40
SD-240 ($\frac{1}{2}$)	1,000 or more	130.75
	5,000 " "	118.30
	10,000 " "	105.95
	30,000 " "	98.55
	50,000 " "	95.70
	Truckload/railcar	87.25
SD-480 ($\frac{1}{2}$)	1,000 or more	232.75
	5,000 " "	210.55
	10,000 " "	188.35
	30,000 " "	175.55
	50,000 " "	171.25
	Truckload/railcar	155.60

EXHIBIT 9   Selected Financial Data ($ in thousands)

	1976	1977	1978	1979	1980
Net sales by class of product:					
Air cellular packaging	$ 18,872	$21,422	$25,028	$29,996	$34,330
Foam-in-place packaging	3,049	15,489	21,133	29,056	38,802
Other packaging	4,553	3,595	3,453	3,432	3,688
Recreational and energy prod.		2,682	4,644	7,951	11,777
Total worldwide	$ 26,474	$43,188	$54,258	$70,435	$88,597
United States	—	35,765	43,410	54,325	67,344
Costs and expenses:					
Cost of sales	$ 16,451	$24,270	$31,111	$43,199	$54,125
Marketing, administration, development	6,696	12,093	14,527	16,855	21,485
Other income (expense)	32	(816)	(738)	(278)	(119)
Earnings before income tax	3,359	6,009	7,882	10,103	12,868

SOURCE: Sealed Air annual reports 1979, 1980.

SEALED AIR CORPORATION: MARKETING IMPACTS OF ELIMINATING CFCs

Manufacturing, R&D, and marketing cannot reach separate conclusions on this issue; they have to work together.

—Larry Chandler,
Sealed Air Corporation

In September 1988, Ray Meltvedt, polyethylene (PE) foam marketing manager at Sealed Air Corporation, was preparing for an important meeting with the company's executive vice president. At the meeting, he would present the commercial and environmental costs and benefits of removing chlorofluorocarbons (CFCs) from the production of PE foam.

Six months earlier, in March 1988, Meltvedt was in a hotel room in Chicago, where he was visiting one of Sealed Air's polyethylene (PE) foam production plants. He had recently been appointed PE foam marketing manager, responsible for Cell-Aire[1] and Cellu-Cushion protective

packaging products (Exhibit 1 shows examples). Meltvedt had been in sales positions with Sealed Air on the West Coast since joining the company in 1984, but had little experience of PE foam and was in Chicago to learn more. Yet it was not from the bundle of papers he'd been given and was casually reviewing that evening, but from the television that he learned most that evening.

On the news it was reported that scientists had identified a significant ozone depletion in the mid-northern hemisphere, adding to fears of major environmental damage which had grown in recent months following the discovery of an ozone "hole" over Antarctica. CFCs were said to be largely to blame. Meltvedt then realized that his products were contributing to this problem. He recalled a company confidential memo written in February 1988, by Bill Armstrong, the technical development manager, which had covered a range of environmental issues and how they affected Sealed Air. This memo had been passed to Meltvedt by Paul Hogan, Sealed Air's vice president of marketing. Meltvedt had not had a chance to study the memo, but he remembered that, across the top, Hogan had written: "Very serious and important issue. Please handle."

This case was prepared by Professor N. Craig Smith with the assistance of Professor John A. Quelch.
Copyright © 1989 by the President and Fellows of Harvard College.
Harvard Business School case 9-589-107 (Rev. 6/28/91).

[1]Cell-Aire, Cellu-Cushion, Sealed Air, Instapak, AirCap, Poly-Cap, Mail Lite, Jiffylite, Rigi Bag, Poly Mask, Bubble Mask, Kushion Kraft, and Dri-Loc are registered ® trademarks of Sealed Air Corporation. Jiffy is a ™ trademark of the same corporation.

Sealed Air Corporation

In 1988, Sealed Air was the market leader in the manufacture and sale of protective packaging materials and systems. Its sales had grown threefold since 1980 to $303 million in 1987, with a similar growth in net pretax earnings to $34 million. It had 2,400 employees. Sealed Air's principal protective packaging products were Instapak foam-in-place packaging systems; AirCap and PolyCap Plus air cellular cushioning materials; Mail Lite, Jiffy Padded, Jiffylite, Jiffy Utility, and Jiffy Rigi Bag protective shipping mailers; Cell-Aire and Cellu-Cushion polyethylene foam; Poly Mask and Bubble Mask coated masking materials; and Kushion Kraft cellulose wadding. Jiffy Packaging Corporation, a company with sales of $60 million in 1986, had been acquired in August 1987. Sealed Air also produced food packaging materials such as Dri-Loc absorbent pads for the retail packaging of meat, fish, and poultry; products that provided protection from electrostatic discharge and corrosion; and miscellaneous recreation and energy conservation products.

Sealed Air, founded in 1961, had exploited the concept of encapsulated air bubbles and eventually had come to define its business as protective packaging. Sealed Air's president and CEO, T. J. Dermot Dunphy, had brought stability to Sealed Air when he joined the company in 1971. It then had sales of $5 million. Through innovation and technological leadership (Sealed Air committed 2.3 percent of sales to R&D, compared with an industry average below 1 percent) together with sound marketing and a selective acquisition strategy, Sealed Air achieved market leadership and substantial sales and earnings growth. Dunphy was aiming for sales of around $500 million by 1990 and, excluding any possible acquisitions, growth of around 15 percent per annum to realize sales of $1 billion by 1997.

Dunphy believed that "virtue is a competitive edge" and sought to combine high principles with economic reward. The old American saying "nice guys don't win ball games" was wrong in his opinion. In 1980 he had introduced a code of conduct to Sealed Air, which was regularly updated as a result of experience. Its provisions in 1988 covered employee relations, honesty in communications, dealing with competitors, product and worker safety, financial interests, bribery, political contributions, commercial confidentiality, and the importance of a customer orientation; Exhibit 2 summarizes the code. Dunphy was keen on having an "open door," not least because employees tended to protect their subordinates or those they worked for. "Whistleblowing" was encouraged, despite fears in other companies that it undermined middle management; Dunphy had received several calls under this recent provision. Sealed Air did not recruit from competitors or interview employees with competitors and, thereby, obtain competitive information. This was prohibited by the code; it was also, in Dunphy's view, not something to be encouraged by an industry leader, because retaliation would make it a losing game. Dunphy was beginning to question the appropriateness of Sealed Air's policy of recruiting from companies with good training programs in other industries, because, for a company of Sealed Air's size, even this might be seen as "poaching."

Dunphy was actively involved in and supportive of voluntary activities. He had, for example, developed company-wide commitment to the "I Have a Dream" project, whereby a class at a local inner-city high school had been adopted, with its students visiting the company, and company employees in their spare time organizing social activities and helping the students develop study skills. The objective of the program was to prepare and encourage the students for a college education, which would be entirely funded by Dunphy and Sealed Air. Dunphy saw this as "a wonderful thing," which also had management development benefits—a good bonding activity involving people from different levels of the company. In 1986, Meltvedt had secured company support for a donation of 14 rolls of plastic (valued at $1,120) to the voluntary organization Survival. This gift was to be used to better equip the huts of Oaxacan Indians living on the Baja peninsula in California.

Dunphy's interest in social issues extended to the environment. He believed care for the environment was important—his daughter was an environmentalist by profession, working to protect the tropical rain forests. He also had identified a ground swell of opinion on these issues. His involvement with other companies had been helpful, particularly as a director of the New Jersey utility company for 10 years. Sealed Air was working on a company position statement on environmental issues and the environment was planned to be a major theme within the next annual report.

Working closely with Dunphy was Larry Chandler, executive vice president, reporting to whom were Jim Lyons, manufacturing vice president, Paul Hogan, vice president and director of marketing, and six other vice presidents. Meltvedt reported to Hogan (along with three other marketing managers).

Sealed Air and the Environment

Armstrong's memo asked marketing managers to prepare product statements, delineating the various environmental assets and liabilities of Sealed Air products. The statements were to be used to prioritize future R&D activities and to provide a prepared set of responses (after appropriate review and approval) to questions from customers and others. Solid waste disposal and resource depletion were of most importance, as the statement developed for Jiffy padded mailers indicates (shown in Exhibit 3). However, Sealed Air's environmental concerns ranged from manufacturing through customer use to disposal of the product.

Within manufacturing, emissions to the air and water and the production of hazardous as well as solid waste were the main concerns. Attached to Armstrong's memo was a note on CFC-related issues, identifying Sealed Air's Insta-pak and PE foams as responsible for CFC emissions at production plants. As early as 1981, water-blown formulations of Instapak had been developed in response to a request from Hewlett-Packard, the computer company. Few other customers were expressing an environmental interest at that time, but the development of the water-blown technology provided Sealed Air with a feasible alternative to the CFC blowing agent still largely used with the Instapak product line. A butane-based blowing agent seemed the best alternative for PE foam, Armstrong's memo suggested.

Sealed Air's problems in disposing of its own manufacturing waste had heightened awareness of environmental issues, alongside the extensive media coverage. There was a nationwide shortage of sanitary landfill. In New Jersey, there was no landfill capacity and the trash from Sealed Air's Totowa plant had to be taken to Kentucky. As the plant manager commented, "We easily ship our garbage farther than we do our products." Waste removal costs at Totowa were rising dramatically. Sealed Air also was concerned about being associated with the litter problem, though litter and waste disposal were different issues in many respects.

An early statement, developed mid-1988, indicated Sealed Air's position on the environment:

> Sealed Air Corporation recognizes that there are problems creating public concern regarding packaging materials (both plastic and nonplastic) and the environment. We are committed to become part of the solution to these problems. We will act to educate our customers and consumers regarding the proper selection, use, reuse, disposal, and recycling of our materials. We are investigating potential solid waste issues to formulate rational and workable solutions and to identify potential business opportunities for the company in these areas.

CFCs and the Ozone Layer

In July 1988, a *Newsweek* article observed: "For five decades, industrial societies have pumped potent chemicals into the atmosphere, unintentionally setting in motion the largest, longest, and most dangerous chemistry experiment in history." The unusually hot summer of 1988 brought to the fore public concerns about the environment. The greenhouse effect, depletion of the ozone layer, and other impacts on the environment of industrial pollutants, such as acid rain, received extensive media coverage. The drought in the Midwest was reminiscent of the 1930s and the sufferings of the dust-bowl states. Though this could not be blamed with any certainty on global warming due to the greenhouse effect, it had been reported that the average global temperature had risen by 0.9°F over the last century

and was set to rise more dramatically. Experts were predicting an increase of 3–8°F before 2050, at least 0.6°F every 10 years. Days over 90°F in New York would increase from 15 to 48 by 2030.

While some scientists argued that the apparent global warming could not be unequivocally attributed to the greenhouse effect—rather than natural variations—until the year 2000, few disputed that industrial pollutants acted to trap solar heat in the atmosphere like the glass roof of a greenhouse. Carbon dioxide (CO_2), from the burning of fossil fuels, was the principal cause, estimated to be responsible for 40–45 percent of the problem, with increases in CO_2 due to deforestation responsible for a further 10–15 percent. CFCs, however, were said to be 20 percent to blame, with methane and other gases, such as nitrous oxide (N_2O), released by commercial agricultural fertilizers, responsible for the remaining 20 percent of the problem. The inundation of low-lying parts of the globe—due to rising sea levels as a result of water expansion and the melting of glaciers and some sea ice—was predicted, as well as a severe disruption of world agriculture. Global warming to date was said to have increased the level of the world's oceans by six inches—enough to push back America's sandy Atlantic coastline at an average rate of two to three feet a year. Sea levels were estimated to rise at least two to three feet over the next century, which some observers reported should be taken into account in long-term business investment decisions, along with other climatic changes.

A single CFC molecule could trap 20,000 times more heat than a single CO_2 molecule; but, fortunately, CFCs were more thinly dispersed through the atmosphere. Of greater concern was their separate effect on the ozone layer, a screen in the stratosphere protecting the Earth from the sun's harmful ultraviolet (UV) rays. Ozone (O_3), a gas composed of three oxygen atoms, is produced naturally when ultraviolet light from the sun breaks up molecules of oxygen (O_2) into single atoms (atomic oxygen), which then collide and combine with other molecules of two-atom oxygen to form O_3. Destroyed by natural processes, ozone levels would remain constant without CFCs. Ozone was also found in smog at lower levels, formed as a result of a complex chemical reaction involving hydrocarbons and nitrogen oxides released by cars, factories, and other sources, in the presence of sunlight. Close to ground level, this ozone impairs pulmonary functions, may cause premature aging of the lungs, and damages crops, trees, and other plants. Unfortunately, ozone depletion in the stratosphere was not compensated for by ozone creation in smog, and industrial manufacture of replacement ozone was not a realistic alternative.

Chlorofluorocarbons, developed in the 1930s as a coolant for refrigerators, were soon found in a wide range of applications because of their valuable properties as chemically inert, nontoxic, and easily liquefiable compounds.

They were also long-lasting; CFC-12 had an atmospheric lifetime of 111 years. In 1974, however, University of California chemists Sherwood Rowland and Mario Molina theorized that ozone was being broken down by CFC chlorine atoms into chlorine monoxide (ClO) and regular oxygen (O_2). With free oxygen atoms then able to break up the chlorine monoxide, the chlorine atom could repeat the process, destroying upwards of 10,000 ozone molecules. Severe effects were predicted as a likely result of a thinner ozone layer. More UV would induce mutations in the plankton at the base of the food chain of the world's oceans, cause damage to the human immune system, and increases in skin cancer. The Environmental Protection Agency (EPA) estimated a 1 percent loss of ozone in the upper atmosphere was likely to cause 3–5 percent more skin cancer worldwide. Crop damage was also likely, as well as uncertain climatic changes. David Doniger of the Natural Resources Defense Council commented, "It is no exaggeration to say that the health and safety of millions of people around the world are at stake."

Rowland and Molina's findings had prompted environmentalists to launch a boycott of aerosol products. More than half of the worldwide production of around 800,000 metric tons of CFCs was for aerosols. In 1978, when CFC production had fallen to 650,000 metric tons, legislation in the United States, Canada, Norway, and Sweden banned nonessential aerosols propelled by CFCs. In the scientific debate and ensuing confusion about the effects of CFCs, public interest waned and CFC production increased. U.S. industry sales of CFCs were around $750 million in the mid-1980s, used under such trade names as "Freon," in refrigerants (45 percent by volume), blowing agents (30 percent), aerosols (5 percent), and cleaning agents and other applications (20 percent). This compared with worldwide use (excluding the United States) of aerosols (35 percent), blowing agents (25 percent), refrigerants (20 percent), and cleaning agents and other applications (20 percent).

In 1985, however, the British Antarctic Survey reported an ozone "hole" over the polar continent, confirmed by checks against data collected between 1978–85 by NASA's Nimbus 7 satellite. The discovery of this "hole"—technically a thinning of the ozone layer—led to unprecedented international action. In September 1987, building on negotiations under the United Nations Environment Program, agreement was reached to limit the production of five CFCs and three halons. The Montreal Protocol required ratifying governments to freeze CFC production and consumption at 1986 levels and achieve a 50 percent reduction by 1999. CFC-11, -12, -113, -114, and -115 were covered, as well as halon 1211, 1301, and 2402, the production and consumption of which were to be reduced to 1986 levels by 1992. (The bromine in halons—mainly used in fire extinguishers—acted in a similar way to the chlorine in CFCs in attacking ozone.)

However, there were problems in securing worldwide support for the Montreal Protocol, as some developing countries, particularly India and China, felt that their industrialization was likely to be hampered by the higher costs of alternatives and an agreement that limited them to a smaller use of CFCs per head of population than the developed nations. A further concern, noted by some experts in the United States, was that establishing a 50 percent reduction goal for CFC emissions by 1999 might encourage companies to hold their usage at current levels (or even increase it) in the interim so the regulation, when implemented, would have minimal impact on their operations. In addition, companies that were able to reduce their emissions more than 50 percent in 1999 would conceivably be able to market the difference between their actual and allowed emissions to other companies in the same area who could not economically reduce their emissions by the required 50 percent.

More recent findings indicated that, not only had there been an ozone depletion in the southern hemisphere of about 4 percent, but also, as 100 scientists reported in March 1988, a depletion of 1.7–3.0 percent in the mid-northern hemisphere. This cast doubt over the claim by the Alliance for Responsible CFC Policy, a group of CFC users and producers, that ozone depletion was "within the range of previously observed variability." Alternatives to CFCs were available for most applications, but not, however, without drawbacks of impaired performance, increased cost, or reduced safety. Du Pont had developed CFC-134a, for example, a chlorine-free substance that deteriorated before reaching the upper atmosphere and was intended to be a direct replacement for some refrigeration and air-conditioning systems; but the automotive industry was estimating R&D costs of more than $1 billion for an air-conditioning system using an alternative refrigerant. However, the impact of CFCs on the ozone layer was no longer questioned. As atmospheric chemist James Anderson of Harvard University put it: "It is totally unequivocal and straightforward . . . there would be no ozone hole without fluorocarbons."

Cell-Aire and Cellu-Cushion Packaging Products

The Cell-Aire and Cellu-Cushion product range, which Sealed Air added when it acquired the company Cellu in 1984, comprised rolls of a variety of lengths, widths, and thicknesses of extruded polyethylene foam. Nonabrasive, lightweight, waterproof, and providing thermal insulation, Cell-Aire foam was used for the packaging of such products as injection-molded parts for automobiles, china, circuit boards, furniture, pharmaceuticals, and optical lenses.

Cellu-Cushion foam was of greater density and offered added protection with increased cushioning and durability. It was used for packaging wine and liquor bottles, exotic fruits, and machined parts, and it was also used in non-packaging applications, such as spa covers, and as a lining for such items as attaché cases and camera bags.

Table A shows PE foam sales since 1984. Sealed Air's main foam competitors were Sentinel (part of Packaging Industries, with a 20 percent market share in 1987), Ametek (30 percent), Astro/Richter (15 percent), and Dow (6 percent). The market was expected to grow at around 8 percent a year in real terms over the next three years, with Sealed Air and Astro/Richter securing a disproportionately larger share of the market, according to Sealed Air estimates. Sealed Air had continued to sell and support the PE foam line, despite losses, because of its strategic importance as an integral part of the company's product offering. However, it was hoped that manufacturing efficiencies (providing yield and density improvements), together with price increases, would restore PE foam to profitability, as estimates for 1989 and beyond were beginning to indicate.

Sealed Air had considerable technological expertise. Armstrong had been very helpful in explaining to Meltvedt how the Cell-Aire and Cellu-Cushion product line was linked to the CFC issue, but his assessment of the situation was troubling. He explained that, from a packaging point of view, there were several alternatives to those products that depended wholly or in part on CFCs in their production:

- Extruded, thermoformable expanded polystyrene.
- Expanded polystyrene loose fills.
- Expanded polyethylene—bun and sheet.
- Polyurethane foams—prefoamed and foam-in-place.
- Expanded polypropylene sheeting.

Replacement materials were available to a packaging engineer tasked with eliminating materials containing CFCs. Twenty years ago, protective packaging was dominated by nonplastic forms: cellulose wadding, corrugated inserts, rubberized hair (and vegetable fibers), glass fiber products, neoprene/rubber foams, vermiculite, shredded paper, crumpled kraft, and excelsior (wood wool). However, packages using these materials would be bigger, heavier, more costly, and provide less protection than packages using modern high-performance plastic foam materials. At one time, IBM shipped computers individually in padded vans. Plastic packaging materials provided the electronics industries, for example, with a way of protecting delicate products, such as hard disk drives or VCRs, while in transit by air, truck, train, or ship. Armstrong believed there was a link between the ability to protect these products through their distribution cycles and their success in penetrating mass consumer markets. Packaging and shipping were exceedingly small percentages of product costs yet ensured low damage claim rates and high reliability of the delivered product. As plastic foams offered superior performance in most applications, nonplastic forms of packaging were unlikely to return.

Sealed Air's Cell-Aire and Cellu-Cushion products were blown with CFC-12 by injection during the extrusion process. A CFC-based blowing agent was used because it was safe, in terms of personnel exposure to the chemical and flammability; stable, with a long shelf life; relatively chemically inert; and cost effective. Alternatives to CFCs were available, but with cost or performance drawbacks. With aerosols, alternatives had, likewise, been available when CFC propellants were banned: other gases (nitrogen, CO_2, several hydrocarbons) or mechanical pumps. However, they only became viable when CFCs could not be used. Hydrocarbons, such as butane, presented flammability risks and reacted with ingredients used in the dispensed product. In some cases, internal mechanisms had to be designed, such as flexible pouches, to separate the propellant from the product. Mechanical dispensers could not provide control over mist sizing, and often the product had to be reformulated to compensate for this and similar problems. In nearly every case, the overall cost of the implemented alternative was more than the original CFC-based aerosol.

Armstrong was confident that Sealed Air could overcome manufacturing difficulties in switching to a non-CFC blowing agent but anticipated problems as well as increased costs and the possibility of reduced product performance. In his February 1988 memo on environmental issues, Armstrong stated that for Sealed Air's PE foams the most likely alternative to Freon would be butane, and that Sealed Air would be ahead of the competition because of in-house expertise available from its butane-based European foam lines. However, a new form of "environmentally safe" hydrochlorofluorocarbon (HCFC) recently had become available, which had, at most, only 5 percent of the ozone-depleting potential of CFCs, was nonregulated, and was being widely adopted as an alternative.

TABLE A **PE Foam Sales**

Year	Sales ($000)[a]	Market Share (%)	Net Income (Loss)[b]
1984	$15,600	29%	$ 50,400
1985	17,550	30	(339,300)
1986	24,050	27	(405,900)
1987	25,610	27	(674,100)
1988E	29,900	29	(351,000)

[a]Includes Jiffy sales from 1986.
[b]Fully costed.

First and foremost among product performance concerns was cushioning properties; the packaging had to reduce external impact forces to levels below those which would cause product damage. Cushioning materials act as damped spring systems within the package to control the rate of deceleration of the packaged product during impacts, such as those that occur when the package is dropped. The required protection at minimal cushion thickness reduced package size requirements. Nonplastic forms of packaging needed to be two to three times thicker than plastic foam to provide the same performance, which would not only increase the package size and associated costs but also the amount of material to be disposed of after unpacking. Other performance concerns were:

- Vibration transmissibility.
- General physical properties (tensile, tear, and the like).
- Compatibility with the product to be packaged (i.e., corrosivity, tarnishing, abrasion, and so on).
- Creep (loss of thickness over time, under load).
- Aging properties.
- Safety (flammability, off-gassing, and so on).
- Aesthetic appearance.

Replacement alternatives had to be "transparent" to the user, replicating all significant properties of the original materials so no package redesign was required. They might, however, still need to be tested against military, industrial, or corporate standards and specifications, as required of the original material.

Armstrong's prognosis was that "customers will give preference to those materials and manufacturers that present them with the fewest problems." The Montreal Protocol was a factor but legislation also was at federal, state, and particularly local levels, where there had been proposals to ban the sale or use of materials manufactured with CFCs. The Los Angeles mayor, for example, had directed city departments to stop buying products made of polystyrene foam, known as styrofoam, and asked attorneys to identify ways by which vendors leasing space from the city could be similarly prohibited. Armstrong was convinced that 100 percent elimination of CFCs would mean that "somewhere, someone will have to forfeit specific product attributes."

Options for Sealed Air on CFCs

There were five options that Sealed Air could pursue on the CFC issue and the possible removal of CFCs from the manufacture of PE foam:

1. Do nothing: This would probably be the cheapest option. Sealed Air could wait for its suppliers of blowing agents (principally Du Pont) to develop a proven alternative or, indeed, for the theory on the cause of damage to the ozone layer to be shown to be wrong and public concern about CFCs to subside.

2. Sit tight, but commit some resources to R&D: This option would involve some costs in monitoring the situation, learning from suppliers, and conducting some exploratory research.

3. Incremental change: Develop an alternative, but only employ it gradually, seeking a reduction in the CFC content of the blowing agent rather than its elimination.

4. Aggressive push: All-out commitment to develop and employ a non-CFC blowing agent as soon as possible. This would be costly but might provide commercial advantages.

5. Use known alternatives: Switch to butane-based blowing agent, as used in Europe, but which had other known environmental problems and safety hazards.

Sealed Air was not, as yet, facing any restrictions on its use of CFCs. However, price increases in the existing blowing agent were foreseen in the years to come as suppliers passed on increases resulting from the reduced availability of CFCs in line with the Montreal Protocol. The PE foam mixture currently comprised 70 percent resin and 30 percent blowing agent by weight. R&D estimates indicated that an alternative blowing agent (SA-1), with an 85 percent reduction in CFCs, would require a PE foam mixture comprising 80 percent resin, 20 percent SA-1; it, therefore, would have an improved usage efficiency. Resin cost $0.52/lb., the existing blowing agent $0.54/lb., and SA-1 $0.81/lb. One pound of PE foam comprised 100 percent resin after the blowing agent had been injected and "aged out" of the foam (escaped). Labor inputs required would remain the same, but product densities were likely to be increased by 6–10 percent using SA-1; this would increase costs and affect product performance. Production output of PE foam in the 12 months to August 1988 was just over 18 million pounds.

In order to use butane in Europe, manufacturing facilities had to be "explosion-proofed." So, for example, rapid evacuation from the facility in the event of a leak had to be ensured; though some Sealed Air employees still were doubtful about whether a plant could be fully evacuated in the 30 seconds allowed. Butane-based extrusion was dependable, the technology certainly worked, and was largely viewed as safe. Additional safety equipment was required, consisting of a butane monitoring system for each plant at $75,000, a CO_2 fire extinguishing system ($20,000), and building conversion work in venting, automatic doors, rewiring, and so on ($100,000). On the other hand, there was a 21 percent cost saving in comparison with the cost of goods using the existing blowing agent plus resin. Additional factors to consider in a switch to butane were:

- Only Hanover and Salem extruders would work on butane (new, compatible extruders would cost $800,000 each; conversion of other extruders would cost $400,000 each).
- Employee reluctance to work in a butane plant.
- Difficulty in getting V.O.C. (volatile organic compounds) permits in most states, due to filled capacities.
- Butane contribution to air pollution (smog and the greenhouse effect).
- Increased insurance rates, estimated to rise from $400,000 a year for all plants to $600,000 (and as much as $800,000 if other producers in the industry did not also switch to butane).
- More complex safety problems relating to fires or employees.
- Extra supervisory personnel and safety engineers required on staff.
- Estimated additional scrap on conversion/acquisition of new extruders of 30 percent for first 30 days, 15 percent for second 30 days, budget thereafter.
- Costs (time and money) of obtaining appropriate permits from local fire departments.

Sealed Air produced PE foam on eight extruders located in seven different plants throughout the United States. Exhibit 4 shows extruder capacity and utilization in the year to August 1988, labor requirement, whether the extruder was capable of using SA-1, and the associated costs. Changeover costs include extruder conversion and the costs of scrapping output of inferior quality as extruder operators learn to use the new blowing agent. The Salem and Hanover extruders could not be converted to CFC-free blowing agents. Based on scrap rates in a previous change of blowing agent, Meltvedt estimated total scrap costs at $557,000 for the other five plants, assuming the scrap would have no value and assuming the continuation of 1988 capacity utilization levels. As Hanover would no longer produce PE foam, there would be additional freight costs by shipping from Totowa of $55,000 a year, storage costs of $10,000 a year, mothballing costs (extruder removal for storage) of $25,000, and a requirement to absorb the overhead costs of the plant over the remaining products produced there. Six employees also would have to go. Costs incurred at Salem would be $10,000 for mothballing (at the plant). PE foam employees could be allocated to other duties.

Advantages to the use of SA-1 were seen as:

- Marketing benefits, demonstrating environmental concern to customers.

- Avoid possible increases in cost of regulated blowing agent.
- Initial step to having a completely environmentally safe blowing agent.
- Improved employee morale, in the knowledge that Sealed Air was leading the industry on this issue.

The SA-1 blowing agent had been developed by Sealed Air by replacing a large proportion of the chlorofluorocarbon with a hydrochlorofluorocarbon (HCFC), known to be environmentally safe. A blowing agent known as SA-2 was under development, which would entirely replace the CFC with HCFC and would, as a result, have only 5 percent of the ozone-depleting potential of CFC. The use of SA-2 would allow Sealed Air to claim its PE foam was 100 percent "CFC-free" and would protect the company against any outright bans on packaging applications of CFCs. However, the more volatile SA-2 would prove considerably more difficult to use and, while not involving further equipment costs after conversion to SA-1, would probably entail additional scrap rates of 15 percent, on average, over the first 30 days. SA-2 cost $0.81/lb. and would have the same usage efficiency as SA-1 (i.e., require a mixture of 80 percent resin, 20 percent blowing agent). An immediate switch to SA-2 was viewed as too problematic by R&D.

Price increases to cover the higher costs of alternative blowing agents would not be welcomed by customers. Resin cost increases had led to two price increases already in 1988 (9 percent in May, 7 percent in August), with a third price increase of 7 percent likely toward the end of the year. Price increases prompted some customers to trade down to a thinner foam. Sealed Air's competitors were generally price followers, raising their prices in line with increases by Sealed Air, the market leader.

Changes in product performance using SA-1 and SA-2 were not likely to be substantial. However, differences would be noticed, specifically the larger cell size of the foam, a rougher surface, and greater variations in thickness (the greater volatility of the blowing agent made quality control more difficult). Some specialty applications might be excluded as a consequence. The concern would be principally with consumer perceptions of differences and the requirement to reassure customers of continued performance standards and to encourage acceptance in the light of reduced environmental harm.

No customers as yet had to have CFC-free PE foam, but state legislation requiring this was a possibility in Vermont, Massachusetts, and Rhode Island. With PE foam often viewed as a commodity product, it could prove advantageous for the sales force to claim Sealed Air's product was ozone friendly—providing a selling benefit in appeals to the good nature of customers. Positive PR stories in support were also likely, promoting a good public image of Sealed

Air as a company that cares about the environment. However, the code of conduct prohibited competitive disparagement.

All of Sealed Air's competitors were using CFC-based blowing agents, with the exception of Astro, which was using butane. Ametek employed a CFC recovery system, but Sealed Air had doubts about its effectiveness in the Sealed Air manufacturing process. Sealed Air had inherited a similar system with the Jiffy acquisition, but found it would not work satisfactorily and, for this reason, had ruled out recovery systems as a possible solution to the CFC issue. No Sealed Air PE foam competitors were claiming, as yet, to be CFC-free—Astro, Ametek or, indeed, indirect competitors supplying nonplastic forms of packaging. There were no indications that this claim would be forthcoming from these or other competitors. Instapak, the only other Sealed Air product manufactured using CFCs, was gradually, and without too much difficulty or expense, being switched to the water-blown technology. Instapak competitors had also yet to indicate any interest in CFC-free claims, where these could already be made or, in other cases, in developing alternatives to CFCs.

Initial discussions with major distributors of PE foam had met with little enthusiasm for a CFC-free solution. Some were skeptical about its importance and commented: "We're supposed to be partners in this business." There was a concern about further price increases, which some viewed as "unnecessary and unjust." One distributor said, "We don't care whether it is safe for the environment or not, we can't survive further price increases."

"When Are We Going to Do Something?"

As Meltvedt settled into his job as PE foam marketing manager, he had become increasingly frustrated by the lack of progress on the CFC issue. His July response to Armstrong's memo commented on Cell-Aire and Cellu-Cushion product disposability and recycling but said little about CFCs. He did report that a competitor (Packaging Industries of Hyannis, Massachusetts) had been charged with violating state CFC emission standards.

In June, Hogan asked the marketing managers to produce an R&D "wish list." At the top of Meltvedt's list of help requests from R&D was the request "switch to 100 percent nonregulated blowing agent at all plants." Meltvedt believed this was the right thing to do. R&D, in response, had been supportive but cited difficulties. Some plant managers, meanwhile, were expressing grave doubts about using alternative blowing agents that would present production problems and be more expensive on lines which were already losing money. As one regional plant manager put it in a meeting involving marketing production and R&D: "PE foam is losing enough money—don't you know that switching blowing agents will cost us dollars and disrupt service to our customers? We can't afford that." Meltvedt sensed that he was being viewed as "the guy from California who was constantly trying to change things."

Industry delegates at a packaging association conference, which Meltvedt attended in September 1988, urged that a special case be made for the industry so it could continue its use of CFCs. One delegate, having explained that CFC-based blowing agents were the safest and most efficient available, urged that the industry wait until government forced a change or chemical companies developed equally satisfactory alternatives. Meltvedt had come across a similar argument being made by another packaging trade association and was again unimpressed. On his return, and following a meeting involving R&D and production, where yet again obstacles to CFC elimination seemed insurmountable, Meltvedt decided to approach Chandler on the issue. R&D had estimated that total elimination of CFCs could be achieved by mid-1989 with sufficient commitment. Preparing for his meeting with Chandler that afternoon, Meltvedt went over the commercial and environmental costs and benefits of removing CFCs from the production of PE foam, including the marketing impacts of a likely price increase set against a "CFC-free" claim. He would ask Chandler, "How big a commitment to this issue is Sealed Air prepared to make?"

EXHIBIT 1

Sample applications of Cell-Aire and Cellu-Cushion packaging products

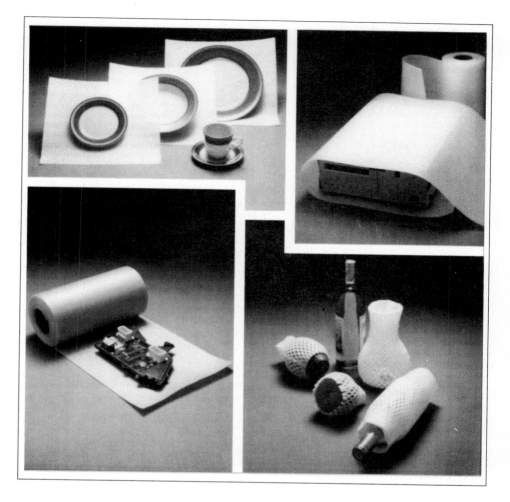

Exhibit 2   Summary of Code of Conduct

Preamble

- Reputation: "Sealed Air Corporation has a reputation for conducting its business on a highly ethical level. It is important that we continue this record of integrity in the future." All employees are responsible for maintaining this reputation.
- List of rules: No substitute for "basic morality, common decency, high ethical standards, and respect for the law."
- Test to apply if in doubt: "Assuming full public disclosure of the action, should both the employee and the company feel comfortable from a moral, ethical, and legal standpoint? If the answer is 'yes,' then the action is very probably consistent with our corporate philosophy."
- Whistleblowing: "Communication and 'whistleblowing' perform a valuable function in maintaining high ethical standards." If aware of circumstances or instructed to act contrary to the code, review with supervisor and, if matter not resolved, contact company's law department or president. Whistleblower protection ensured.
- Code violations: Subject to disciplinary action, including dismissal.
- Guidelines apply worldwide.

Guidelines

- Equal opportunity employer.
- Customer-oriented: "Everything a Sealed Air employee does on the job is ultimately related to satisfying a customer need within the framework of our Code of Conduct. Our advancement and job security, both as a company and as individuals, depend on our ability to satisfy properly the needs of our customers."
- High professional standards: In relationships with other employees, suppliers, customers, stockholders, and others having dealings with the company.
- Employee relations: Treat each other with dignity and respect. Confidential employee information is used only for proper purposes and is available on "need to know" basis.
- Premium on honesty and fair dealing: Information provided internally and externally is "expected to be truthful, accurate, and not misleading in any way."
- With competitors: Compete vigorously and fairly, affording competitors the respect we expect of them. Not using improper/illegal methods to obtain competitor information. Not encouraging actual/prospective employees to divulge confidential information gained as result of associations with other companies.
- Safety: Committed to safe working conditions, product safety, and compliance with laws relating to the protection of the environment.
- The law: Policy to comply with laws affecting conduct of the business.
- Confidentiality: Company assets, including confidential business information, are not to be misused or made available to outsiders in ways detrimental to company interests.
- Employee financial interests: No divided loyalties through financial interests in competitors, suppliers, or customers.
- Bribery: Illegal bribes or kickbacks intended to secure favored treatment for the company are forbidden. Consult with supervisor if requested. Modest gratuities and tips are not encouraged but permissible if not violating local laws and expediting action, rather than securing influence.
- Gifts: Acceptance of gifts "may involve a conflict of interest or create an appearance of impropriety." Acceptance of cash gifts is forbidden; noncash gifts of token or nominal value may be accepted if not intended/cannot be construed as a bribe, kickback, or other form of compensation. Entertainment is to be given or accepted in a manner customary and necessary for business.
- Political contributions: None made worldwide. Employees are encouraged to exercise individual rights to be active in local or national politics.
- Insider trading: Employees are reminded this is a violation of U.S. law.

Source: Based on Sealed Air *Code of Conduct,* June 1988.

Exhibit 3 Jiffy Padded Mailers: Environmental Statement

1. How much recycled material is used to manufacture this product? How much can be used?

The Jiffy Padded Mailer is made with a 60 percent recycled content. This is believed to be the maximum content of recycled materials usable in this product because a recycled Kraft exterior and/or interior liners would not have sufficient strength to encapsulate the macerated padding.

2. How recyclable is the product itself?

- Is it sortable from the general waste stream?

- Are there sufficient quantities of this or like products to make segregation, accumulation, and recycling viable?

The Jiffy Padded Mailer could be sortable from the general waste stream along with newspapers and other paper products, such as paper grocery sacks and corrugated boxes. Segregation of this product for recycling is viable only where there are programs to recycle newspaper and other recyclable paper products.

3. What advantages does this product have over more recyclable alternatives?

This product is the most recyclable alternative available for a cushioned mailer. The disadvantage of this product is its relatively greater weight. As recycling becomes a more important issue throughout the community, the recyclable nature of the Jiffy Padded Mailer can be used greatly to our advantage.

4. What disposability assets does this product have, other than recyclability (i.e., reusable, compressible, bio- or photo-degradable, easily incineratable, and so on)?

The Jiffy Padded Mailer is biodegradable and is easily incinerated.

5. How can this product be made more: Recyclable, Reusable, Degradable, and the like?

The Jiffy Padded Mailer can be made more recyclable through better education of the general public to include this product in the waste paper recycling stream. Many (most?) households are now recycling newspapers and this product should be included in that waste stream.

6. What are the recommended means by which this product should be properly disposed after use?

The best alternative for disposal is to recycle with the waste paper stream but other means, such as disposal in landfills and incineration, are acceptable.

EXHIBIT 4   PE Foam Production Plants

Plant[a]	Output M Lbs./Yr.	Extruder Capacity Lbs./Hr.	Percent 5-Day Week Filled, Year to August 1988[b]	Hourly Number of Employees[c]	Capable of SA-1 or SA-2 Blowing Agent	If Yes—Cost of Conversion: Scrap and Equipment[d]	Employee Lay-Offs if Any
Totowa, New Jersey	1,950	650	50%	9	Yes	Scrap rate 25% 1st 30 days 20% 2nd 30 days Budget thereafter Equipment cost: negligible	No
Hodgkins, Illinois	3,432	715	80	14	Yes	Scrap rate 15% 1st 30 days Budget thereafter Equipment cost: negligible	No
Hanover, Pennsylvania	1,800	300	100	8	No	NA	Yes
Warrior, North Carolina	4,914	585 x2[e]	70	25	Yes	Scrap rate 15% 1st 30 days Budget thereafter Equipment cost: negligible	No
Grenada, Mississippi	3,334	585	95	12	Yes	Scrap rate 25% 1st 30 days 15% 2nd 30 days Budget thereafter Equipment cost: negligible	No
Salem, Illinois	1,800	300	100	7	No	NA	No
C.O.I. (City of Industry), California	819	455	30	11	Yes, but at high conversion cost.	Scrap rate 15% 1st 30 days 10% 2nd 30 days Budget thereafter Equipment cost: $80,000	No

[a]The location of extruders was a result of historical factors (largely the result of acquisitions), rather than logistical demands; it was important to have a West Coast facility (COI), however.

[b]Average capacity utilization was 75%; extruders operate during all three shifts (24 hours a day).

[c]Different labor inputs reflect product differences in the output of the various extruders (specialty treatments, for example), as well as efficiency differences.

[d]R&D and labor costs excluded.

[e]Two extruders.

SOURCE: Internal data, Sealed Air Corporation.

MICROSOFT CORPORATION: THE INTRODUCTION OF MICROSOFT WORKS

In July 1987, Bruce Jacobsen, the product manager for Microsoft Works for the IBM PC and Compatibles (Works), and Ida Cole, the director of Microsoft's International Products Group, were preparing for a presentation to Microsoft's country managers. Works was a new, integrated software product that included a spreadsheet, word processor, graphics program, database, and communications program. The country managers were the chief operating officers of Microsoft's international subsidiaries. The purpose of the presentation was to outline Works' design and tentative positioning strategy and to ask for questions and suggestions from the field.

The upcoming meeting was an important one for Works. In 1986, over 41 percent of Microsoft's sales dollars were to countries outside the United States. It was critical to win the support of the country managers for the marketing strategy to increase the chances of the new product's success.

Cole and Jacobsen were aware that two issues were likely to fuel a lively debate during the meeting. The first issue was Works' product positioning strategy. Jacobsen was planning to position Works as an easy-to-learn, easy-to-sell product for the home and small business market. Ida Cole believed that the U.S. positioning strategy might not be appropriate in a number of countries. The second issue involved requests to modify the design of Works. Microsoft's strategy was for a standard version of Works to meet a set of common needs around the world. That philosophy allowed for limited "localization," whereby the program and the documentation were translated into local languages, and small changes were made to accommodate local conventions for currency, time and date formats, and so on. However, the programs that provided spreadsheet, word processing, and other functions remained unchanged. Several country managers had asked for features to meet the needs of their markets that would require redesign of Works' programs. Microsoft had to decide how to respond to the requests.

The trade-offs in viewing the target market segments for Works globally, rather than on a country-by-country basis, were significant. Establishing a worldwide standard product, with only minor variations to accommodate national differences, reduced the time required to develop localized versions of the software. In an industry where early entrants in a product category enjoyed a substantial advantage over latecomers, the benefits of reducing the localization timetable were potentially great. A global standard also reduced the cost and time needed to develop enhanced versions of a software product, which were typically rolled out every 12 to 18 months after the initial product launch.

On the other hand, if the standardized software did not meet the needs of a particular country, the product was unlikely to succeed in that market. Moreover, it generally took longer to design a global product than it did to develop a product for the U.S. market. The relentless pressure to launch a new product in the United States, either to preempt competition or to ensure availability during the heavy year-end buying season, often caused Microsoft development teams to resist requests for features that were important for global markets but unnecessary for the United States.

Jacobsen sent an electronic message to Jabe Blumenthal, the program manager and designer for Works, inviting him to drop in on the discussion. Then he turned to Ida Cole.

"Well, Ida, what are we going to say to the country managers?"

The Worldwide Market for Microcomputer Software

The microcomputer software industry emerged in the United States during the mid 1970s, as a number of enterprising individuals left more conventional pursuits to develop programs for the first generation of microcomputers. Bill Gates, chairman of Microsoft, was among those industry pioneers. As a freshman at Harvard University, Gates developed a BASIC programming language for micros. He dropped out of Harvard to found Microsoft in 1975.

Microcomputer Software Categories. By 1987, most observers divided the fledgling industry into different segments based on the products sold. The first category was *systems software*. One group of systems software products included operating systems such as Microsoft's Disk Operating System (MS-DOS). Operating systems provided a layer of communication between individual software programs and the computer itself. Another type of systems software included programming languages, such as BASIC, PASCAL, and COBOL. Such high-level languages were used to write programs to perform functions for the computer user.

The second software category was *application software*. It included horizontal applications and vertical applications. Horizontal application software performed broad

---

This case was prepared by Assistant Professor Thomas J. Kosnik. Copyright © 1987 by the President and Fellows of Harvard College. Harvard Business School case 9-588-028 (Rev. 10/17/89).

functions that were used by different customers for a variety of tasks. Microsoft Works and Lotus 1-2-3 were examples of horizontal applications. Vertical applications performed a narrower set of functions to support a specific set of tasks. Examples included accounting software for law firms and sales force management systems.

In 1986, the microcomputer software industry was over $5 billion in retail sales, with 14,000 companies offering over 27,000 different products around the world. Industry observers divided the $5 billion total into sales of $250 million for systems software, $2.25 billion for horizontal applications, and $2.5 billion for vertical application software.

Leading Competitors in the Microcomputer Software Market.   Microcomputer software was sold both by hardware companies, such as IBM and Apple, and by "independent" software companies whose products ran on a variety of computer hardware. The leading independent microcomputer software companies in 1986 are shown in Exhibit 1. All of the largest microcomputer software companies were headquartered in the United States. However, two of Microsoft's largest competitors were aggressively expanding their international sales. Twenty-four percent of Lotus Development Corporation's 1986 sales were outside the United States, compared with 14 percent a year earlier. Ashton-Tate international sales comprised 20 percent of its 1986 total.

Two companies were the most likely to compete with a product like Works on the IBM PC. Software Publishing, which had dominated the market for easy-to-learn inexpensive products with its PFS series, had recently introduced an integrated product called "First Choice." It was priced at $179 and included word processing, spreadsheet, communications, and limited database functions for the first-time computer user. Some industry watchers predicted that Software Publishing would have an improved version of the product ready for release by the autumn of 1987. Borland, which had a reputation for clever easy-to-use products at very low prices, marketed a best-selling product called "Sidekick" for $59, to support telephone lists, light calculations, and other tasks. It was rumored that Borland might enhance Sidekick to compete with Works.

Microsoft Corporation

Overall Leadership.   Microsoft was a leader in the microsoftware industry. The company chairman, Bill Gates, was an avid programmer-turned-entrepreneur whose vision for Microsoft was "to make the software that will permit there to be a computer on every desk and in every home." His hard-driving style pervaded the company. Microsoft's president, Jon Shirley, a former executive at Tandy Corporation (Radio Shack), brought a wealth of experience about

marketing of microcomputer products to the top management team. Both men were hands-on managers who delegated responsibility but demanded outstanding performance and attention to detail.

Much of Microsoft's success had come through a combination of timing and skill in managing alliances with leading hardware manufacturers. One example of timing had become an industry legend. In 1980, IBM approached Gates to have Microsoft design the operating system for the new personal computer it was planning. Gates first sent IBM to Digital Research, who already had an operating system. When IBM was rebuffed by Digital Research's attorney, it called Gates back, and he seized the opportunity. Microsoft's Disk Operating System (MS-DOS) became an industry standard. As other hardware manufacturers introduced PC clones, they turned to Microsoft to develop a version of MS-DOS for their machines. By 1986, Microsoft had supplied operating systems for over 300 different models of microcomputers.

Microsoft also made an early commitment to the emerging "second standard" in microcomputers, the Macintosh computer from Apple. Several Microsoft application software products, including Word, Excel, and Works for the Macintosh, enjoyed a leadership position among Macintosh users.

International Marketing Strategy.   Timing and hardware alliances were important facets of Microsoft's international marketing strategy as well. The company began its efforts in the international arena in 1982. Microsoft entered a number of countries with local language versions of its products a year or two before most of its competitors. In addition to being first with local language software, Microsoft formed alliances with leading computer companies in Europe and Asia. Through a series of original equipment manufacturer (OEM) arrangements, the sales forces of hardware OEMs sold Microsoft products like Multiplan (spreadsheet) and Word (word processing) along with their microcomputers to large corporations in many countries.

As a result of early entry and strong OEM alliances, Microsoft's Word and Multiplan products were market leaders in a number of countries in Europe and Asia. In 1986, the International Division had over 350 employees, and international sales were over $106 million. However, that leadership position was being challenged by Lotus, which had recently introduced a local version of 1-2-3 in Japan, and had 200 employees outside the United States and over $67 million in international sales in 1986.

Organization.   Exhibit 2 shows part of Microsoft's corporate organization chart. In addition to serving as chairman, Bill Gates was also the acting vice president of Applications Software, the division where Bruce Jacobsen worked as a product manager. Gates's keen interest in the application software side of Microsoft's business had led him to assume that role until the right person could be found to fill the position. Bruce Jacobsen reported to Mike Slade, the Works group product manager, who reported to Jeff Raikes, the director of Applications Marketing, who in turn reported to Gates. However, the informal management style and heavy use of electronic mail in decision making led to a great deal of direct communication among product managers like Jacobsen, Bill Gates, and Jon Shirley.

Exhibit 3 shows the organization of the International Division. Jeremy Butler had responsibility for International. Ida Cole reported to Butler, as did three other directors responsible for international operations in Europe, Asia, and Intercontinental (the rest of the world).

Financial Performance. Exhibit 4 contains a five-year summary of Microsoft's financial performance. The company's growth and earnings record had made it a favorite of many Wall Street analysts. Its 1986 return on sales was the highest of any company in the *Datamation 100,* an annual review of the largest companies in the computer hardware and software industries. In the first half of 1987, Microsoft's sales surpassed Lotus Development's sales, making it the largest microcomputer software company in the world. Microsoft's 1986 sales by product line were: systems software and languages = 53 percent; applications software = 37 percent; hardware and books = 10 percent.

Segmenting the Software Market

At Microsoft, four dimensions were considered in analyzing market segments for software products: the computer hardware environment; the usage situation; the level of the customer's needs; and the country-language.

Segmenting by Computer Hardware Environment. Microsoft developed application software products to meet the needs of customers who bought the most popular "standard" types of computer hardware. The first major standard in IBM-compatible microcomputer technology was established with the introduction of the IBM PC in 1981 and extended with the more powerful IBM AT in 1984. A number of companies around the world introduced PC-compatible computers—also known as "PC clones"—that used the same software and functioned the same way as the IBM PC but offered slight enhancements and lower prices. These "clone makers" moved even more quickly to imitate the IBM AT.

The average price of a PC-compatible dropped from almost $3,000 in 1983 to below $1,000 in 1987. IBM lowered its prices as well, but continued to lose market share to the "act-alike" vendors. Exhibit 5 shows unit sales from IBM and the clone makers. In 1987, IBM introduced the Personal System 2 (PS/2) family—a "second generation" of IBM machines with greater power and graphics capabilities

that had the potential to overthrow the standards it had created with the IBM PC and AT.

Although Microsoft Works was technically capable of running on both the old and new generations of IBM computers, its primary target hardware was any IBM PC or PC-compatible. The more mature, "low end" IBM-compatible hardware was selected for Works because simple inexpensive software was needed for the millions of customers who were planning to purchase inexpensive machines for use in homes and small businesses. Other Microsoft products, including Word (word processing) and Excel (spreadsheets) were targeted at the purchasers of AT-compatibles and PS/2 computers.

Exhibit 6 is a forecast of the unit sales of low-end IBM machines and PC clones in selected country markets. There was considerable controversy about the potential impact of the new IBM PS/2 computers on the sales of the older models of IBM-compatible PCs. Some experts speculated that the market for the less-powerful models would decline as customers migrated to newer easier-to-use models. Others argued that most new computer users would purchase the older less-expensive products, because in most situations the benefits of the new technology were not worth the cost. The debate heightened uncertainty about the future growth of the older IBM products, PC clones, and the software that ran on them.

Segmenting by Usage Situation. Microsoft, following most commercial market research reports, identified four major segments by customer usage of microcomputer products: business/professional, home/hobby, scientific/technical, and education.

The business/professional segment consisted of people who used microcomputers for a variety of functions in organizations. While the specialized applications depended on the industry in which a company operated, the general applications of word processing, spreadsheet, graphics, database, and communications were used in most businesses to provide automated support for office functions. Within Microsoft, the business professional market was further divided into large and small organizations. Large companies tended to have extensive data processing capabilities, more formal buying procedures for computer products, and more sophisticated requirements for computer support. Small businesses tended to have few, if any, employees with data processing expertise, a less-structured buying process, and simpler needs.

The home/hobby segment was composed of individuals and families who used computers for practical and recreational purposes in the home. Customers in the home/hobby segment tended to buy smaller less-expensive computer systems than did those in the business professional marketplace.

The scientific/technical segment consisted of scientists and engineers who used computers for tasks that ranged from analysis of laboratory experiments to computer-aided design (CAD) and computer-aided engineering (CAE). Members of this segment often needed powerful expensive computer hardware for special scientific programs. They also used word processing, spreadsheet, database, graphics, and communications software.

The education segment included students, teachers, and administrators in schools, colleges, and universities. Administrators used microcomputers for planning and fundraising, and faculty were introducing computers into their curricula. Students used word processing, spreadsheet, and graphics for term papers, presentations, and examinations. Many customers in this segment needed simple inexpensive computers, but some required the power and sophistication typically demanded in scientific/technical environments.

Segmenting by Customers' Depth and Clarity of Software Needs.   Jeff Raikes divided the office productivity software market into "breadth customers" and "depth customers." Breadth customers were professionals or managers who did a little bit of everything and needed a combination of spreadsheet, word processing, database, graphics, and communications. They were likely to want low price and simplicity in software that supported those functions, as well as "integration," which provided the ability to move information between spreadsheets, databases, and word processing documents. Depth customers were specialists who made heavy use of at least one function, like writers using word processing or financial analysts using spreadsheets. They were likely to be less price-sensitive, more willing to learn a complex product, and driven by the need for power and sophistication to do all that they demanded.

Raikes believed that people buying low-end PC-compatibles in the future, especially first-time buyers, were likely to be breadth customers: "The kind of people who come into a store to buy a computer but aren't sure why." In his mind, Works was ideal for breadth customers, because it met a variety of needs at a relatively low price. Bill Gates agreed, calling Works "the macho integrated product for the first-time user."

Segmenting by Country and Language.   It was necessary to translate software into the local language to establish a significant presence in any particular country. At Microsoft, the process of creating a local-language version was called "localization."

A major distinction existed between countries with languages based on an alphabet, like the United States or Western European countries, and those that used hieroglyphic symbols, like Japan and other Asian countries. One letter in the alphabet required a single byte of computer memory for storage purposes. However, a character in a language like Japanese Kanji required two bytes of computer memory. As a result of this difference, programs written in "two-byte"

languages like Japanese had to be designed differently from those written in "one-byte" languages like English, French, and German.

Ida Cole stressed that there were differences among one-byte languages as well:

> German is 29 percent longer than English. That means it takes 29 percent more space to translate a phrase from English to German. As a result, messages in English that might fit on one line of an 80-character computer screen might be too long for the line when translated into German. That could change the way the screen looks to the users. Programs that might fit onto one diskette in English might require two diskettes in German. If that happens, it requires writing a different user's manual, because German users need to insert different disks for various functions. The ripple effects can be enormous. Germany isn't alone. French is 10 percent longer than English, and there are problems in other languages, too. We in International try to get the program managers to think of these differences between languages when they first design a product so what the user sees on the screen or in the manual is essentially the same around the world.

Some people at Microsoft believed that, other than translating into the native language, very little was needed for "localization" in various countries. Jeff Raikes asserted: "The office productivity market is pretty similar worldwide." However, many people in Microsoft's International Division believed there were substantial differences among countries. Profiles of several European-country markets are summarized in Exhibit 7.

Differences in hardware.   Because "compatible" rarely meant identical, the hardware sold by leading PC-clone manufacturers in various countries had implications for localization. For example, there were slight differences in the keyboard layouts to accommodate the use of non-English characters such as tildes and accent marks. As a result, software documentation that showed a diagram of the keyboards from leading PC-clone manufacturers in France was different from the documentation for Italy, Holland, or Germany. The leading printers used in each country also varied, leading to slight differences in the set of printing programs (called "printer drivers") and user manuals.

Differences in Microsoft's competitive position and corporate image.   There were also differences in the relative position of competing software products in various countries. For example, in countries like Italy and Holland, where Lotus 1-2-3 was the market share leader for spreadsheet software, Microsoft country managers wanted to label Works spreadsheet columns with letters and rows with numbers, creating an "A1" reference number for the cell in the first row and column. That labeling made it easier for those familiar with 1-2-3 to use Works. However, in France and Germany, Microsoft's Multiplan was the leading spreadsheet product. Those countries wanted Works' cell in the first row and column to be labeled "R1 C1," making it easier for Multiplan users to learn Works.

Even in countries like France and Germany, in which Microsoft products were market leaders, the positioning of Microsoft as a company—which might affect how customers perceived its products—was not the same. For example, in France, much had been made of the "ease of use" of Microsoft application products. French advertisements had a corporate "tag line" after the Microsoft name that roughly translated as "software for the simple life." A butterfly was displayed as the Microsoft logo in French ads.

In Germany, the Microsoft corporate tag line was "Software with a Future." According to International, the German customer was not worried about ease of learning so much as ensuring that the software would not become technologically obsolete as new generations of hardware made it possible for the software to become more powerful. Microsoft's corporate logo in Germany was a series of cartoons by the German poet Wilhelm Busch. The cartoons were quite popular in Germany, but meant nothing to people in other countries who were unfamiliar with Busch's work.

Differences in the importance of target market segments. Data on the relative potential of market segments in various countries were difficult to obtain. Exhibit 7 contains the results of a survey of retail dealers of Microsoft software in France, Germany, Holland, and Italy. Each dealer was asked whether it sold a significant number of Microsoft office productivity products in each of 10 market segments.

Differences in price sensitivity.   Some people at Microsoft believed there were national differences in price sensitivity. The suggested retail prices for localized versions of Microsoft products varied from 10 percent higher to 40 percent higher than the price of the U.S. version. England was the lowest, with a 10 percent increase. Holland was 15 percent higher and Italy averaged 25 percent higher. France was 30 percent more and Germany 40 percent higher. Since Microsoft headquarters charged the same price per unit of software to each subsidiary, some speculated that the variation was due to country-by-country differences in the perceived relationship between price and quality. One European country manager explained: "In England, customers want the lowest possible price for software. They are always shopping for a bargain. In France and Germany, people look at software the way they do wine. If it doesn't cost a lot, it can't be good quality."

Others argued that the price differences arose because the channels of distribution varied by country. Price discounting of software occurred in countries that had a well-developed direct mail channel, or that had mass merchandisers (discount department stores) carrying computer software. For

example, while Bruce Jacobsen was planning a recommended retail price of $195 for Works in the United States, he estimated that discounting activities due to direct mail software distributors was likely to drive down the "street price" of the product to around $140. England had both a direct mail and a mass merchandiser channel, with some retailers offering computers at very low prices. International believed that the "street price" for Works in England might go as low as $110. In Germany, which had no direct mail distribution channel for software, and a higher proportion of sales via an OEM channel to large companies, the street price was rarely more than 20 percent lower than the recommended retail price.

Other differences among countries.   Some intercountry differences were the result of local habits and customs. For example, countries like France and Germany used the metric scale for distance, while England used feet and inches. This affected the spacing when printing text from a word processor or spreadsheet. The standard size of paper also changed from country to country. The formats for currencies and for time and date varied around the world.

National attitudes about copyright restrictions caused software copy protection to be essential in some countries to keep unauthorized pirating of software to an acceptable level. Microsoft did not use copy protection in the United States. The aggravation it caused customers and the added cost and quality problems it raised in the production process were a bigger headache than the loss of revenues from "pirated" copies. But some country managers demanded copy protection. One electronic mail message to Jacobsen said:

> We may need a copy protection scheme applied for certain countries. We don't need it in Germany and Switzerland, and, hopefully, we can talk France out of it. But Italy and South America will probably insist, as they would only sell one copy in each language otherwise.

While some cross-cultural differences required a change in the software itself, others affected the packaging and documentation. Mary Oksas, the localization manager for Works, recounted an example:

> We were trying to come up with a good story line to use in the training manual for Works around the world. First the U.S. documentation team suggested a "health club" theme . . . figuring that the potential market for Works were young, affluent, and would probably be into fitness and health. That was before we told them that, in a number of European countries, dieting and health clubs have a very negative connotation. Then the U.S. team decided to go with a "stockbroker" theme, until we let them know that stockbrokers in London and in Japan don't perform exactly the same functions as their counterparts in the States. Now they are suggesting a travel agency or a pet shop theme, in hopes that attitudes about vacations and animals are pretty similar around the world. The jury's still out on that suggestion.

Key Roles and Activities in the Development of Works

The U.S. version of Works was being developed through the cooperative efforts of Bruce Jacobsen, the product manager responsible for marketing, Jabe Blumenthal, the program manager responsible for product design, and Tony Cockburn, the development manager, who led the team of programmers who wrote the software. In addition, a team from User Education was responsible for developing the manuals and Computer-Based Training (CBT) for Works.

The International Product Group. The International Product Group, located in Microsoft headquarters in Redmond, Washington, was responsible for creating localized versions of Works. Ida Cole maintained liaison with the country managers, provided information about Works, solicited their requests for product features, and developed the suggested international strategy for pricing, positioning, and advertising. Michel Perrin, Microsoft's international marketing manager, was responsible for coordinating the efforts of the marketing managers in the international subsidiaries, who reported directly to their respective country managers. Mary Oksas, Works' localization manager, ensured that the software, documentation, and computer-based training were translated into various languages, oversaw testing of the local language versions of the software, and designed the packaging for each country.

The International Product Group was planning to develop localized versions in seven non-English languages: French, German, Swedish, Italian, Dutch, Spanish, and Portuguese. The investment to localize Works was estimated at $84,000 per country, assuming there were no major changes to the programs. Microsoft planned to charge the same price per unit ($68) to subsidiaries for localized versions of the product. Exhibit 8 is a forecast of unit sales and retail prices of Works in each country.

While the International Products Group was developing the localized versions of Works for Europe, Japan was responsible for its own localization. Technical complexities of the two-byte architecture and the unique issues in adapting products for the Japanese market led Microsoft to establish a separate group in the Japanese subsidiary to develop its own products and localize software developed in Redmond for Japan.

Country Managers in Microsoft's International Subsidiaries. Soon after his arrival at Microsoft, Bruce Jacobsen had been told by another product manager about how the international subsidiaries operated:

> The country managers are kings. They and the marketing managers who work for them exercise a lot of autonomy in most marketing decisions. For example, Microsoft Redmond typi-

cally recommends a worldwide retail selling price for a product and suggests a positioning strategy and communications theme. But the management in each subsidiary ultimately decides what price to charge, what distribution channels to use, what advertising to employ, and what market segments to attack.

When Jacobsen recounted the conversation to Ida Cole, she reminded him of the ways in which they really could have an impact:

> The country managers and their marketing managers are focused on tactical issues in their day-to-day operations. They are driven by the goals of selling existing Microsoft products. As a result, during a new product launch, they tend to rely on us to conduct market research, think about the longer-term issues, and present an overall marketing strategy. They won't go along with everything we suggest. . . . They'll use it as a starting point, and tell us the things that don't make sense based on the realities of their local markets.

The Debate over the Design of Works

Microsoft planned to develop the U.S. version of Works, incorporating as many of the features required for other countries as possible, given limited programmer availability and project deadlines. The U.S. version would be launched in mid-September. One month later, after minor changes, the International English version would be released. That version was the baseline product that would be translated into different languages.

Microsoft had received requests from country managers for two additional features in Works. First, France and Germany wanted a software "toggle switch" that would let the customer choose whether Works' cell references appeared as "A1," like Lotus 1-2-3, or as "R1 C1," like Multiplan. This feature would let a customer decide whether he or she wanted the spreadsheet in Works to "look like" either Lotus 1-2-3 (A1) or Multiplan (R1 C1). That way, a person who used Lotus at the office and was buying a home computer could make Works look like 1-2-3, greatly reducing the time required to learn Works. Someone who had used Multiplan at the office could choose to make the Works spreadsheet look like Multiplan, thereby minimizing learning time. In the United States, where 1-2-3 had a dominant market share position and very few customers had seen Multiplan, Microsoft planned to make Works look like Lotus 1-2-3 (A1 format), and the toggle switch feature was not important. In Europe, where both Multiplan and 1-2-3 were widely used, the toggle switch might have particular value to customers.

Second, country managers had asked that additional programs be written so Works files could be converted to the Multiplan file format. Conversion programs allowed the exchange of information between Works and other spreadsheet products. If a person made a spreadsheet using Multiplan at the office, and wanted to bring it home to continue working on evenings or weekends, he or she could convert it to use on Works and then back again. Conversion programs also allowed a person with Works to share data with colleagues using Multiplan. Works was originally designed only to allow data exchange with Lotus 1-2-3. Like the toggle switch option, file conversion programs might be particularly useful in some European countries due to the widespread use of Multiplan.

If Microsoft incorporated the two changes in the U.S. version, the introduction of Works in the United States would be delayed by two months. The additional time was needed to develop documentation and CBT showing both the A1 and R1 C1 displays and to write several new programs. It would still take one month to go from the U.S. to the International English version.

If the programmers developed the U.S. version without the two requested changes, and then tried to add the features to the International version, a major redesign would be required. Substantial portions of the programs for the U.S. version would have to be rewritten, and the elapsed time required for the International version would increase from one month to five months.

Several country managers had informed Ida Cole that, without the toggle switch and conversion programs, Works was unlikely to be successful in their markets. They also were concerned that, without the changes, Works might even undermine the market position of Multiplan by promoting the Lotus 1-2-3 user interface and file formats.

However, Jabe Blumenthal argued strongly against changing the design because of the adverse effects of missing the target U.S. launch date. The introduction of Works was set for mid-September, which allowed retailers just enough time to order the product and train their people how to sell it before the end of October. That timetable was critical, because November–December was a period of heavy buying activity for computer products, since the home market made purchases for Christmas and some businesses bought at the end of the year for tax reasons. Retailers were likely to resist or ignore a new product launch in the midst of their busiest season. Missing the September launch date also would increase the risk that Software Publishing's First Choice or a new product from Borland might establish a leadership position in the segment targeted for Works.

The labor and direct overhead cost of keeping the development team on Works was $50,000 per month. However, there was also an opportunity cost. A month spent on Works was a month that was unavailable for other software products, and programmers were in critically short supply. Assessing the impact of the decision on future sales was difficult, since unit sales forecasts for the United States were based on a September 15 launch date, and because the other countries assumed that Microsoft would make the two modifications.

Works' Positioning

Jacobsen was planning to position Works as an easy-to-learn, easy-to-sell integrated solution to the productivity needs of "breadth users" in homes and small businesses, who were buying their first computer. Tentative advertising plans were to use a Swiss Army Knife as an internationally recognizable symbol of an easy-to-use tool with multiple functions.

Microsoft had a family of application software designed to meet the needs of "depth users" and "breadth users" on IBM-compatible computers and on the Apple Macintosh. Exhibit 9 identifies a few of those products. One of the challenges in positioning Works was to distinguish it from the other Microsoft products, thereby minimizing customer confusion and the risk that Works might cannibalize sales of other software.

In discussing Jacobsen's positioning, Ida Cole pointed out the concerns of several country managers. First, throughout most of the world, the home and small business markets for IBM compatible machines were much smaller than in the United States, making his positioning difficult to execute on a global basis. Second, in European countries where Multiplan and Word were market leaders, the financial risk of cannibalization was greater than in the United States.

Plans for the Launch

Jacobsen was developing the details for an introductory U.S. marketing communications campaign with a price tag of $2.8 million and a target launch date of September 15. With a suggested list price of $195, trade margins averaging 50 percent of retail selling price, and cost of goods just over $18, Microsoft's unit contribution for Works was approximately $79. Jacobsen was confident that the projected U.S. volume of 6,000 units a month would more than offset the costs of the introductory campaign.

Conclusion

As they continued working on the presentation, Jacobsen silently wondered how he should respond to country managers' suggestions about design changes to make Works more attractive for their local markets. He saw merit in both Blumenthal's and the country managers' arguments, and knew he needed to formulate a position on that topic for the meeting. In addition, there might well be other requests for design modifications, and he and Ida Cole needed to develop an approach for handling them if they arose.

Jacobsen also pondered how, if at all, he could modify his product positioning for Works to make it more effective as the foundation for communications strategy for the product around the world.

Cole interrupted his reverie: "Earth to Bruce . . . let's put together a slide or two with our major recommendations, and then brainstorm about the reactions we're likely to get from the country managers."

EXHIBIT 1   **Leading Independent Microcomputer Software Vendors (sales dollars in millions)**

Company Name	*Worldwide Sales in 1986[a]*	*Name(s) of a Few Leading Products*	*Category of Software Products[b]*
Lotus Development Corporation	$283	1-2-3 GP Spreadsheet	GP Integrated
		Symphony	
		Jazz	GP Integrated
Microsoft Corp.	260	DOS	SS Operating system
		Excel GP Spreadsheet	
		Microsoft Word	GP Word processor
Ashton-Tate	203	DBase III	GP Database
		Framework	GP Integrated
		Multimate	GP Word processor
Word Perfect	52	WordPerfect	GP Word processor
		WordPerfect Executive	GP Integrated
Autodesk	50	AudoCad	SP Computer-assisted Design
		CAD Camera	products
Borland	38	SideKick	GP Organizer
		TurboPascal	SS Language
Micropro	36	Wordstar	GP Word processor
		Wordstar 2000	GP Word processor
Digital Research	26	CP/M	SS Operating system
		GEM	SS Operating environment
Software Publishing	26	PFS: Write	GP Word processor
		PFS: File	GP Database
		First Choice	GP Integrated

[a]Sales based on the period from January 1 to December 31, 1986. In the first half of 1987, Microsoft sales exceeded Lotus Development Corporation's.
[b]GP = General purpose application software.
  SP = Special purpose.
  SS = System software.

Exhibit 2

Microsoft's corporate organization chart

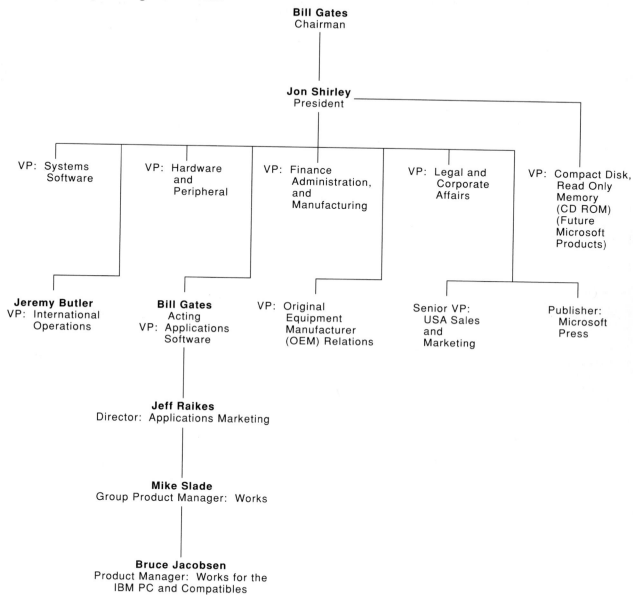

Source: Microsoft Corporation internal records.

EXHIBIT 3

Organizational chart for Microsoft's international operations

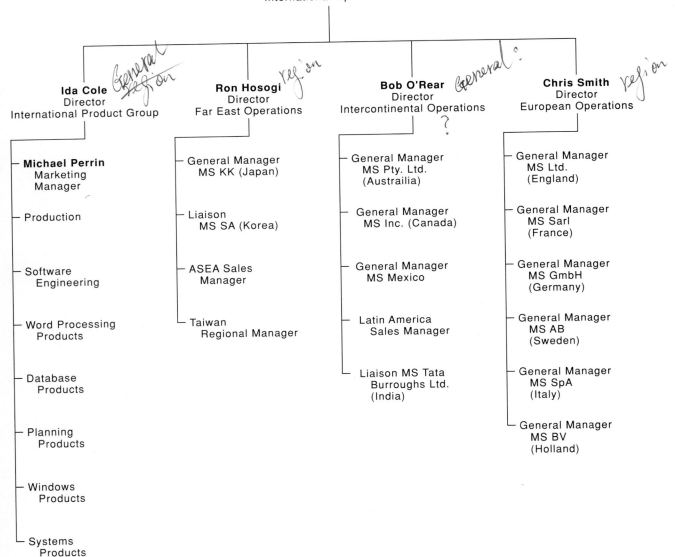

Jeremy Butler
Vice President
International Operations

Ida Cole
Director
International Product Group

General region

Ron Hosogi
Director
Far East Operations

region

Bob O'Rear
Director
Intercontinental Operations

General

?

Chris Smith
Director
European Operations

region

Michael Perrin
Marketing
Manager

- Production

- Software
  Engineering

- Word Processing
  Products

- Database
  Products

- Planning
  Products

- Windows
  Products

- Systems
  Products

- General Manager
  MS KK (Japan)

- Liaison
  MS SA (Korea)

- ASEA Sales
  Manager

- Taiwan
  Regional Manager

- General Manager
  MS Pty. Ltd.
  (Austrailia)

- General Manager
  MS Inc. (Canada)

- General Manager
  MS Mexico

- Latin America
  Sales Manager

- Liaison MS Tata
  Burroughs Ltd.
  (India)

- General Manager
  MS Ltd.
  (England)

- General Manager
  MS Sarl
  (France)

- General Manager
  MS GmbH
  (Germany)

- General Manager
  MS AB
  (Sweden)

- General Manager
  MS SpA
  (Italy)

- General Manager
  MS BV
  (Holland)

SOURCE: Microsoft Corporation internal records.

Exhibit 4 A Summary of Microsoft's Financial Performance: 1983–1987[a]

	1983	1984	1985	1986	1987
Net revenues	$ 50,065	$ 97,479	$ 140,417	$ 197,514	$ 345,890
Cost of revenues	15,773	22,900	30,447	40,862	73,854
Gross margin	34,292	74,579	109,970	156,652	272,036
Research and development	7,021	10,665	17,108	20,523	38,076
Sales/marketing	11,916	26,027	42,512	57,668	85,070
General and administrative	4,698	8,784	9,443	17,555	22,003
Income from operations	10,657	29,103	40,907	60,906	126,887
Nonoperating income (loss)	407	(1,073)	1,936	5,078	8,638
Stock option bonus					(14,187)
Income before tax	11,064	28,030	42,843	65,984	121,338
Income tax	4,577	12,150	18,742	26,730	49,460
Net income	$ 6,487	$ 15,880	$ 24,101	$ 39,254	$ 71,878
Total assets	$ 24,328	$ 47,637	$ 65,064	$ 170,739	$ 287,754
Stockholders' equity	14,639	30,712	54,440	139,332	239,105
Earnings per share	0.15	0.35	0.52	0.78	1.30
Number of employees	367	608	910	1,153	1,816

(handwritten annotations: 73,854 — 21.35%; 38,076 — 11.01%; 85,070 — 24.59%; 22,003 — 6.36%; 71,878 — 20.78%)

[a] Microsoft's fiscal year ran from July 1–June 30.

SOURCE: Microsoft Corporation financial statements.

Exhibit 5 Unit Sales of IBM PC Compatible Microcomputers in Two Technology Families (in thousands of units)

Type of Technology	1981	1982	1983	1984	1985	1986
U.S. Market Only						
IBM PC and XT	35	190	590	1,553	1,287	1,009
PC Compatibles from clone makers	0	2	108	367	839	1,270
Total PC compatible	35	192	698	1,920	2,126	2,279
IBM AT				22	261	384
AT compatibles from clone makers					132	490
Total AT compatible	0	0	0	22	393	874
Worldwide Market (includes U.S.)						
IBM PC and XT	35	195	670	1,855	1,961	1,538
PC compatibles from clone makers		2	113	427	1,069	1,610
Total PC compatible	35	197	783	2,282	3,030	3,148
IBM AT				22	330	572
AT compatibles from clone makers					151	641
Total AT compatible	0	0	0	22	481	1,213

SOURCE: International Data Corporation reports on the microcomputer market.

EXHIBIT 6   Forecast Sales of Low-End IBM-Compatible Microcomputers in Selected Countries (thousands of units)

Country	1986 Population (in 000s)	1986 Estimated Unit Sales	1987 Forecast Unit Sales	1988 Forecast Unit Sales
United States	240,856	2,279	2,000	1,500
England	56,458	170	225	220
Canada	25,625	106	120	110
Australia/New Zealand	19,098	34	45	40
France	55,239	139	160	155
West Germany	60,734	136	145	120
Italy	57,226	83	115	130
Netherlands	14,536	46	60	55
Portugal	10,095	2	5	10
Sweden	8,357	39	45	40
Spain	39,975	16	30	50
Japan	121,402	50	50	30
Total	708,701	3,100	3,000	2,460

NOTE: The figures above include IBM PCs, XTs, and computers from other manufacturers that were compatible with those IBM microcomputers. They do NOT include IBM ATs, IBM PS/2s, or computers from other manufacturers that were compatible with those IBM microcomputers.

SOURCES: A variety of International Data Corporation (IDC) market research studies from 1986 and 1987. Data have been disguised.

EXHIBIT 7   A Comparison of Market Conditions in Selected Country-Markets

Comparative Criteria	France	Germany	Holland	Italy
Leading IBM-compatible hardware manufacturers ranked roughly in descending order of 1986 unit sales of low-end PC clones	IBM Bull Goupil Olivetti	IBM Schneider/Amstrad Olivetti Siemens	IBM Olivetti Tulip Phillips	Olivetti IBM Sperry Commodore

Estimated position of Microsoft products:
  Multiplan Spreadsheet
  Microsoft Word
Microsoft corporate
  advertising theme
	
	Market leader
	Market leader
	"The software of the simple life"
		
		Market leader
		Market leader
		"Software with a future"
			
			In the top 4
			In the top 5
			"Pioneers in compatibility"
				
				In the top 3
				Tied for #2
				"Power and simplicity together"

Number of dealers surveyed reporting sales of Microsoft products to the following market segments:				
Public accounting	15	47	21	22
Banking	35	27	12	
Financial services	36	23	19	
Architecture	8	40	18	
Construction	38	50	14	
Engineering	29	47	20	
Medical/dental	5	44	8	
Legal	9	39	5	
Home	19	46	8	1
Other	66	52	15	4
Total number of dealers responding to the survey	71	70	32	27
Total market segments	260	415	140	27
How important is a low price for success of software like Works?	Somewhat important	Not very important	Very important	Very important

SOURCES: Information on leading hardware manufacturers is from International Data Corporation. All other information is from Microsoft internal records.

Country	Forecast of Monthly Unit Sales of PC Works English Version (1)	Forecast of Monthly Unit Sales of PC Works Localized Version (1)	Forecast Suggested Retail Price per Unit of Localized Version (2)
United States	6,000	0	$195
England	1,000	0	215
Canada	500	0	215
Australia and New Zealand	380	0	215
France	0	650	254
West Germany	200	500	273
Italy	50	160	244
Netherlands	80	200	224
Portugal	25	80	220
Sweden	100	200	234
Spain	50	200	234
Total	8,385	1,990	

NOTES: For planning purposes, it was assumed that Microsoft subsidiaries' selling prices to the channels of distribution would be approximately 50% of the suggested retail prices in their respective countries.

Localized versions for subsidiaries were manufactured in Ireland and sold to all subsidiaries for 35% of the U.S. suggested retail price. Import tariffs were not considered in the analysis.

SOURCES: (1) Preliminary forecasts by country managers of Microsoft's International subsidiaries made in June 1987.

(2) Estimates by Microsoft International Product Support Group based on past experience with other products.

EXHIBIT 9   Selected Products in the Microsoft Family of Software

Product Name	Description	U.S. Recommended Retail Selling Price[a] of the Products on the		
		Apple Macintosh	IBM PC/XT/AT & Compatibles	IBM PS/2 & Compatibles
Products for Depth Users				
Multiplan	Sophisticated spreadsheet for quantitative analysis. Graphics available as a separate product. Key competitor: Lotus 1-2-3 ($495)	$295	$195	NA
Word	Sophisticated word processor. Key competitor: Word Perfect ($495)	395	450	$450
Excel	New and very advanced product for spreadsheet, graphics, and data management. Key competitor: Lotus 1-2-3 ($495)	395	395 (only on IBM ATs & compatibles)	395 (Launch was planned for one month after Works)
Products for Breadth Users				
Works	Integrated, easy-to-use product for: • Spreadsheet. • Word processing. • Graphics. • Data management. • Communications. Key competitor: Software Publishing's First Choice ($179)	$295	$195	$195

NA means not available.

[a]It was anticipated that the "street price" for both Microsoft Works and Software Publishing's First Choice would fall to about $140. The comparable price for Lotus 1-2-3 was $330.

CIGNA WORLDWIDE

On a gray day in Frankfurt, Germany, in November 1988, Bruce Howson, president of CIGNA Worldwide, Inc. (CWW), convened a strategy meeting of the company's European country directors and key functional managers to discuss how CWW should respond to the European Community's (EC)[1] plan to remove existing internal barriers and restrictions to the free flow of goods and services in 1992.

At this meeting, Howson announced the establishment of a 1992 task force to define the opportunities, threats, and critical issues posed by the 1992 program, and to identify its implications for CWW's European marketing strategy and organization. The task force would report its findings to the Philadelphia home-office by December 15, 1988. Exhibit 1 summarizes the CWW organization and lists the 1992 task force members.

Herman Nieuwenhuizen, senior vice president for the Northern European area, was appointed director of the task force. He believed that it should first ask each CWW country manager to assess his or her nation's insurance market and the anticipated impact of the 1992 measures. CWW concentrated on selling commercial property and casualty (P&C) insurance, which represented over 85 percent of the premiums generated by CWW in Europe in 1987. The task force would use the country managers' appraisals to develop an overall marketing strategy for CWW's European division.

The Insurance Market

An insurance policy was a contract that bound the insurer, for a paid premium, to indemnify an insured party against a specified loss. The insurance industry sold three types of insurance: reinsurance, life, and nonlife insurance. Reinsurance and coinsurance were financial agreements between two or more insurance carriers to share the risks of particular policies; premium income was likewise shared. Life insurance covered the financial risks associated with a policyholder's death. Nonlife insurance, also known as property and casualty (P&C) insurance, included coverages for individual consumers, known as mass risk insurance (car,

home, and liability policies) and coverages for companies, known as large risk insurance (workers' compensation, fire, and business interruption policies).

In 1986, the EC was the second-largest insurance market worldwide, accounting for 22 percent of total world premiums. Exhibit 2 summarizes selected insurance market and economic data for the countries of the EC, the United States, and Japan.

The major participants in the European insurance industry were insurance carriers, brokers and agents, and customers.

Insurance Carriers. Primary insurance carriers underwrote policies, assuming an insuree's liability in the case of a specified financial loss. Some insurers specialized in one type of insurance, while others handled multiple categories. An insurer gained profits by (1) earning premiums in excess of its losses; (2) earning investment income on the premiums it received; and (3) controlling its operating expenses, which included sales, marketing, commissions, claims adjustments, and backroom operations. While all three elements contributed to a firm's financial performance, most industry experts agreed that the overall long-term viability of a company depended on its underwriting success. Since the early 1980s, however, insurance firms had derived the bulk of their profits from investment income. Smart investing of premium income, rather than income sharing with reinsurers, could cushion underwriting losses.

The industry applied two performance measures when writing P&C business: the expense ratio and the loss ratio. The expense ratio divided all expenses by net written premiums (NWP).[2] The loss ratio summed all claim losses, claim reserves, and associated administrative costs and divided this sum by net earned premiums.[3] The combined ratio (expense ratio + loss ratio) represented the total cost of underwriting as a percentage of premiums generated. A combined ratio of less than 100 percent indicated that underwriting efforts were profitable.

Sales and marketing, along with claims adjustments, were the two largest cost factors for an insurance carrier. Sales and marketing were performed through a number of channels, including dedicated agents, independent brokers, and direct marketing to customers. Claims adjustment de-

---

This case was prepared by Jonathan D. Hibbard under the direction of Professor John A. Quelch.
Copyright © 1989 by the President and Fellows of Harvard College.
Harvard Business School case 9-589-098 (Rev. 4/8/92).

[1]The EC comprised 12 member states: Belgium, Denmark, France, Greece, Ireland, Italy, Luxembourg, the Netherlands, Portugal, Spain, the United Kingdom, and West Germany.

---

[2]NWP equaled the total premiums earned (GWP) minus the portion of GWP reinsured.

[3]Net earned premiums were net written premiums amortized over the policy's life. For example, a 12-month policy commencing in January 1988 would have a net earned premium equal to 50 percent of its NWP by July 1988.

partments handled customer claims; they had to maintain good client relations while tightly controlling claims costs.

Underwriting and claims processing were both considered backroom operations expenses. Underwriters evaluated the risks customers wished to have covered, and often specialized in a particular insurance category and/or specific industry or geographic region. Claims processing was technology-intensive, and was the one cost area that could benefit from scale economies.

Insurance Brokers and Agents.   Insurance brokers and agents were intermediaries between insurance carriers and insurance buyers. They accounted for 80 percent of the P&C business placed in Europe. Most agents were involved full time in the insurance business and usually represented one carrier's product line.

Unlike agents, brokers were insurance specialists who represented several different carriers. They offered their clients impartial advice in arranging the best insurance terms possible. Brokers often relieved the carriers of such administrative tasks as premium collection and claims handling. Brokers earned commissions of 15–20 percent of the GWP; agents averaged 10–15 percent commission. In evaluating insurance companies, brokers scrutinized both claims service and price.

Because they did not have ties to particular carriers, brokers could recommend to their customers that policies be moved to other carriers. Broker power varied by country. In the United Kingdom brokers wrote over 70 percent of the total P&C business, whereas in France, Italy, and Germany they wrote, respectively, 50, 45, and 25 percent. In most EC countries, the larger brokers did not aggressively seek to switch each other's principal customers.

Industry analysts identified three tiers of brokers. The first tier included international network brokers, such as Marsh & McLennan and Johnson & Higgins. Most European brokerage revenues were concentrated in this top tier. The second tier included large national and regional brokers, while the third tier comprised small local brokers and large insurers with their own exclusive agent networks.

European brokers generated income from three basic sources: commissions, fixed fees, and investment income. Brokers received commissions on policy premiums they wrote for each carrier. They also received an annual profit-sharing commission from these insurers. Brokers sometimes received negotiated fixed fees from larger clients in lieu of commissions from carriers. Investment income was earned when brokers collected policy premiums from clients and earned interest while holding this money for 90 days or more before remitting it to the carrier. Over half of a typical broker's operating expenses were salaries and benefits.

Insurance Buyers.   Most large companies employed risk managers to place their insurance. When a company shopped for a carrier or broker, a reputation for prompt claims service was especially important. As one risk manager stated, "The capability of an insurer to provide local claims handling service is critical to my carrier decision, especially with multiple sites and multiple languages in my business." Because of the large numbers of brokers and agents, insurance buyers were accustomed to a high level of personal contact.

Once established, the relationship among client, broker, and carrier was fairly stable. The size and complexity of the P&C relationship made it difficult for a client to change carriers. In a typical year, analysts estimated that 10 percent of the total P&C policies in Europe might change hands. Companies sometimes relied on several carriers for different insurance products but usually kept a particular type of coverage with a single carrier.

Marketing Impact of 1992

Recognizing the economic value of facilitating free flows of people, goods, services and capital, the governments of the EC member countries agreed to remove their internal trade barriers by December 31, 1992. Many believed that these barriers made European firms less competitive than their United States and Japanese counterparts, which benefited from serving much larger domestic markets than those available in any single European nation. The economic integration of the EC, which accounted for 20 percent of all world trade flows, would create a single market of 325 million consumers, surpassing the United States' 226 million and Japan's 121 million consumers.

The EC believed that, in many industries, market integration also would create economies of scale, leading to lower prices, greater investment, and faster economic growth. Less-efficient companies would be driven to increase productivity, merge, or go out of business. However, leaders of some nations outside the EC were disturbed by the prospect of an increasingly protectionist "fortress Europe." The United States and Japan, the largest trading partners of the EC, exported over $110 billion in goods and services to the EC in 1987.

Background to the 1992 Program.   The European Economic Community, often called the "Common Market," was created in 1957 by the Treaty of Rome as a devastated Europe sought to rebuild its economy after World War II. Initially the EC made progress in eliminating customs duties in trade between member states, but progress slowed because of the economic recession in the mid-1970s.

Following this slow growth period, the prime ministers of the EC countries pledged to complete the common market at an EC meeting in 1982. A White Paper, published in June 1985, delineated a plan for achieving a single market. This plan was approved by the member nations and ratified in the Single European Act of 1986, which amended the original Treaty of Rome.

The Single European Act became effective on July 1, 1987. After that date, member states began considering regulations developed at the EC headquarters to remove the physical, technical, and fiscal barriers to a unified market. Exhibit 3 lists the barriers and proposed legislation. Quicker agreement was now expected because majority voting of member nations had replaced a previous requirement for unanimity. Many EC experts, however, believed that there still remained major obstacles to realizing the 1992 program; these hurdles included difficulties in harmonizing technical standards, regulations, and the value-added tax (VAT) rate.

By November 1988, one third of the 285 legislative reforms detailed in the 1985 White Paper had been adopted by the EC, and over 100 others had been sent to the Council of Ministers for approval. About 90 percent of the measures were expected to be ready for adoption by the end of 1988. Directives already adopted included common toy safety regulations, a single document for border crossings, abolition of customs formalities, mutual recognition of higher education diplomas, and permission to sell P&C insurance across borders.

Effects of the 1992 Program on the European Insurance Market. Although the Treaty of Rome called for the progressive elimination of national regulations that impeded cross-border trade in insurance services, such barriers only fell in the reinsurance market. Lack of progress prompted the nonlife establishment directive of 1973, which provided *freedom of establishment* rights and, thus, allowed insurance companies based in any single EC country to set up agencies or branches in other EC states. It also set common EC standards for granting operating licenses and calculating minimum solvency margins required for insurers.[4] A U.K. insurer, for example, thus, was entitled to establish a Paris branch, provided that its operations complied with local French insurance regulations.

Freedom of services, however, had not been realized. *Freedom of services* permitted an insurance company to market a full range of products throughout the EC even if only located in one EC member country. Hence, a U.K. insurer could directly service a French client without the need for an authorized French branch or agency. Many EC countries, including France and Germany, did not permit

freedom of services. This prompted the EC to issue the second nonlife insurance directive of 1988, allowing insurance firms to market P&C policies freely to large-risk customers beginning January 1, 1990. Qualifying customers had to meet two of the following three criteria: 500 or more employees, $29 million minimum in annual revenues, or $14 million minimum in assets. Industry experts estimated that this directive would apply to 70 percent of the commercial and industrial insurance written in the U.K. and to 50 percent of that written in Germany, France, and Italy.

Most analysts predicted that the scope of freedom of services would not be broadened to cover other types of insurable risks, such as life insurance, until the mid-1990s.

In 1992, freedom of services also would apply to independent brokers. Any intermediary based in one EC country would be able to sell policies to clients throughout the EC without having to hold a license in other EC nations.

Opportunities in the European Insurance Market. The gradual breakdown of barriers to selling insurance across national boundaries was expected to intensify the marketing of P&C insurance. In addition, cross-border trade, stimulated by the removal of trade barriers, was expected to increase dramatically and expand demand for insurance services. New insurance product lines would be needed as a result. As one marketing director noted, "Client companies will want consolidated insurance packages for their subsidiaries throughout Europe."

Many analysts predicted that the second nonlife directive would intensify competition, encourage insurance buyers to shop around, and lead to both lower overheads for insurers and lower premiums for policyholders. One industry executive explained, "Companies must become more efficient and cost-effective; premium margins will become razor-thin in some nations, with only the strong surviving." High service expectations by customers, however, could restrict the ability of insurance companies to write commercial insurance policies across borders. Only international insurance companies having their own operations within a country, or being closely associated with local brokers, could provide the necessary service on policies providing international coverage.

The sizes of the nonlife insurance markets in EC member countries are presented in Exhibit 2. Premium growth potential was considered greatest in Italy, Spain, and Portugal, where per capita premium levels were very low. Exhibit 4 summarizes the growth rates of nonlife insurance within the EC. Exhibit 5 highlights the variation in insurance prices found between countries.

Because of their open and competitively priced markets, insurers in the United Kingdom and the Netherlands were expected to be better prepared for the 1992 plan. However, in 1988, insurers in these two nations received only 10 percent of their insurance business from the rest of the EC.

---

[4]Solvency margins helped ensure that an insurance company could meet its future obligations toward the insured; these requirements varied by country. Under the 1973 directive, the solvency margin could be maintained only at the head office; branches and agencies needed only to possess sufficient assets to cover liabilities arising out of their own activities.

Insurers in the tightly regulated markets of West Germany and Italy, together with France, a country burdened with high premium taxes, were thought likely to lose business in the face of more open competition.

Increasing industry regulation at the state level during the 1960s and 1970s had made it more difficult for non-EC insurance companies to operate throughout Europe; consequently, the number of non-EC insurance firms had declined. In addition, many analysts believed that EC subsidiaries of foreign insurers were currently at a competitive disadvantage because they were obliged to meet the solvency margin requirements of each country with local assets rather than corporate assets. Many insurance companies, however, were now expected to enhance their European operations to take advantage of the more open EC insurance market.

A Swiss insurance executive offered the following options for U.S. insurers: "U.S. carriers can either make an outright acquisition, or they can set up a strategic alliance with an EC-based insurance company. Acquisitions are more difficult and expensive to carry out than they were in past years because Europeans are snapping up most available takeover targets. A strategic alliance will enable a U.S. company to obtain help from its EC partner in adjusting its products to ensure that they meet local needs."

Many analysts believed several large insurance companies would dominate the newly integrated EC market. One industry CEO stated: "After 1992, all European insurance companies will feel additional pressure with respect to premiums and commissions. As a result, economies of scale will become decisive. Mergers and acquisitions will, therefore, increase." The CEO of a British insurer noted: "In 10 years, we will see a concentration of 10–15 large European insurers. The rest will be niche players." According to one European insurance association, EC insurers were involved in 121 mergers and acquisitions between June 1984 and September 1988.

Brokers, like insurers, had to consider the impacts of the 1992 program on their businesses. "The opportunities in the large risk market must first be exploited by brokers," commented an executive of the EC's Insurance Directorate. "If national habits are going to be broken down, brokers will do the job." A Belgian broker stated: "To take advantage of 1992 opportunities, brokers will need to be more informed about conditions, prices, and regulations in other member states, so they can better advise their clients. To properly serve multinational accounts, brokers will need to import favorable foreign rates and conditions and export home advantages to foreign clients." Another broker noted: "Our clients will look for Japanese-style, zero-defect service. Price will not be the driving issue; it will be taken for granted. The business will go to the broker who gets the right price, issues documentation instantly, and, above all, obtains timely payment of claims."

Company Background

CIGNA, Inc., the parent company of CWW, was one of the largest publicly owned financial services companies in the world. Its subsidiaries were leading providers of insurance, health care, employee benefits, and financial services to businesses and individuals worldwide. CIGNA was formed in March 1982 by the merger of Connecticut General Life Insurance Company and INA Corporation. Innovation and new products were the hallmark of both predecessor companies. Connecticut General was a pioneer in group life insurance and offered the first major group medical coverage. INA sold the first automobile fire and theft policy and developed the first homeowner's package insurance policy.

CIGNA's International Operations.   Connecticut General entered the international market through its acquisition of Aetna Insurance Company in 1962. Aetna was a member of the American Foreign Insurance Association (AFIA), a consortium of insurance carriers based in the United States and doing business overseas. CIGNA acquired AFIA in 1984 for $215 million and merged it into its own international business to form CWW, one of the largest international insurance operations headquartered in the United States.

Before the acquisition, AFIA and CIGNA both maintained area offices in Belgium and had established operations throughout most of the EC. After acquiring AFIA, CIGNA consolidated the two insurance portfolios and personnel into one office in Brussels. The acquisition increased the percentage of CIGNA revenues derived from multinational corporations from 6 percent in 1984 to 12 percent in 1987. Exhibit 6 summarizes information from the CIGNA/AFIA merger.

CIGNA Insurance Company of Europe (CIGNA Europe) was a CIGNA, Inc. subsidiary and part of the CWW organization. In 1987, CWW's sales comprised 10 percent of CIGNA, Inc.'s total revenues (13 percent of CIGNA, Inc.'s total revenue and 7 percent of its operating income was foreign-based). CIGNA Europe's revenues, in turn, represented 54 percent of CWW's total revenue in 1987. Within the EC, the U.K. and France accounted for 64 percent of CIGNA Europe's net premiums. Recent financial results and information for CIGNA Europe and CWW are summarized in Exhibit 7 and Exhibit 8, respectively. Product mix information for CIGNA Europe is summarized in Exhibit 9.

Hoping to keep more of its business in-house, CWW was reinsuring fewer policies with other carriers than previously. This increased CIGNA's risk exposure but also enlarged its upside profit potential. As a result, CWW's net premiums were growing faster than gross premiums.

Over 75 percent of the CWW premiums in each nation was derived from business closely associated with the country in which it was written. The broker and agent system accounted for 95 percent of CIGNA Europe's premiums, compared to an 80 percent average for other European carriers. CWW worked almost exclusively with the largest brokers writing policies for multinationals and large risk companies. The top 10 brokerage firms in Europe wrote 80 percent of CIGNA Europe's policies.

Corporate customers could be segmented according to size. A major multinational would typically generate over $5 million in annual P&C insurance premiums. Large-, medium-, and small-sized companies would generate $1 million, $500,000, and $100,000 respectively.

CIGNA Europe competed with the major European insurers, several of which were expanding their presence in the U.S. market. In 1987, the largest European insurers were Allianz (Germany) with $10.1 billion in net written premiums; Generali (Italy) $6.3; Zurich (Switzerland) $6.2; Royal (U.K.) $5.8; and Prudential Corporation (U.K.) $5.6. Allianz had the largest dedicated agent sales force in the European insurance industry and was acquiring and building strategic alliances with insurance companies throughout Europe. Analysts expected that these factors would give the firm a distinct competitive edge within a barrier-free EC market.

Among CWW's principal competitors in Europe was the New York–based American International Group (AIG). In 1988, AIG announced that it would merge most of its European operations into a single company based in Paris, replacing 13 different national companies that had used six separate computer centers, with no central cash control and no corporate identity.[5] AIG had recently announced plans to invest $200 million in its European operations by 1992. AIG had a stronger reputation than CIGNA as a product innovator, particularly in P&C insurance.

Most CWW employees were nationals of the country in which they worked and, therefore, were well versed in the local languages and customs, familiar with local laws governing contracts, and attuned to the needs of the local insurance community. CWW supported its salespeople with direct marketing (13 million pieces mailed in 1987 versus 9 million in 1985) to generate leads.

CWW's international marketing programs were sometimes tailored to meet local insurance needs. With strong support from the home office in Philadelphia, CWW tried to delegate as much authority as possible at the point of sale by giving country managers the final say in writing a policy. Most country offices were self-sufficient, with their own underwriters, clerical staff, and data-processing operations. However, local underwriters often contacted the home office for assistance when writing complex commercial and industrial policies.

---

[5] "Who's That Knocking on Foreign Doors? U.S. Insurance Salesmen," *Business Week*, March 6, 1989, pp. 84–85.

CWW's 1992 Challenge

CWW executives believed their company was already well-placed to meet the 1992 challenge. As Steve DeBrovner, senior vice president of marketing, pointed out, "We're much better positioned than are companies that are not yet even in the EC. Because of our experience with the 1984 CIGNA/AFIA merger, we know how long it takes for a company to become fully operational after an acquisition. The merging of two insurance sales networks can create many more problems than solutions. How to reconcile computer systems, design new policies, and deal with overlapping sales agents are among the problems that arise. Many competent people will be 'on the street' after some of these mergers, and we hope to add some of these quality producers to our staff."

According to analysts, other major U.S. insurers were poorly positioned to take advantage of the 1992 plan. In the past, many of them had participated in international insurance through the AFIA insurance pool, which had been acquired by CIGNA. Bruce Howson, president of CWW, noted: "Most U.S. insurers without international penetration will have difficulty if they begin now to try to take advantage of developments in the EC. It would mean the investment of millions of dollars and a 10-year process to deal with licensing requirements."

Many CWW executives believed the company's main strength was the large volume of business CWW transacted throughout Europe and the fact that it had fully staffed offices in every EC nation. Other strengths included CWW's capacity to write large risks, good name recognition, and a strong reputation for claims service among company risk managers. One country manager stated, "We know that our local service and our tailored products are of utmost importance to our present customers." CWW spread the word about its large capacity through an advertising campaign built around the message, "Size has its advantages." Exhibit 10 shows a recent advertisement that CIGNA Europe ran in selected print media. Exhibit 11 summarizes expenditures on advertising and marketing.

CWW had excellent relationships with major U.S. insurance brokers. As a result, CIGNA Europe could rely upon its U.S.-based brokers to provide high-quality insurance packages for its customers needing insurance coverage within the EC. CWW was also expert in writing large policies (especially for P&C coverage) designed for the international market. A CWW country manager pointed out, "We are the only U.S. carrier with an established European flagship, backed by the resources of a large parent company." According to many analysts, European markets were nationalistic, and U.S. insurance firms had a reputation for entering and exiting markets at "the drop of a hat" because of the cyclical nature of the business. CWW did not have this reputation, at least in its P&C business. Most brokers and risk managers considered CWW to be a "national" company in each country in which it operated.

CWW executives believed the company's strengths outweighed its weaknesses. However, they knew improvements were needed in order for CWW to remain competitive. CIGNA's different computer systems in EC countries were not compatible and, of course, outputs were in different national languages. CWW country managers operated as independent business people and shared little information about product revenues, expenses, successes, and failures; any communication among them was purely informal. One country manager commented, "The ability to exchange product, research and development, and financial information will become critical as 1992 approaches. We need a marketing information system that will allow us to do that. Also, we don't have enough intelligence on our leading competitors."

P&C insurance comprised a proportionately greater share of CIGNA Europe's total business (60 percent) compared to CIGNA, Inc. (40 percent). CWW executives estimated that 50 percent of its P&C business would be opened to new competitors by the 1988 nonlife directive. P&C policies were relatively easy for competition to pursue because of the large volume written and rewritten each year. Some CIGNA Europe managers felt that CWW was perhaps too focused on large accounts, while many of its competitors had systems in place to service medium-size P&C accounts. CWW's EC managers also maintained that the CWW management team was conservative and slow to implement change. One of the managers noted: "CWW's organizational reporting structure is not flexible enough to allow for the quick decisions needed to take advantage of country-level opportunities."

Although CWW was already highly regarded by other European insurers, CWW wanted to develop a corporate identity with brokers, agents, and clients in Europe as strong as that which it enjoyed in the United States. In a recent survey focusing on CIGNA's U.S. image, 63 percent of risk managers and 79 percent of brokers indicated that CIGNA provided "high-quality service." CWW also wanted to emulate the cost structure of its parent, CIGNA, Inc., because the expense side of the financial statement was critical to increasing CWW's competitiveness in Europe. As Howson stated, "Currently we have too many cooks and clerks supporting our salespeople."

Commenting on the fact that only 200 out of 1,700 CWW employees were underwriters, Howson noted: "CIGNA Europe's expense ratio is running at 40 percent, but our European competitors have 35 percent expense ratios. Some German and French insurance firms are even showing expense ratios of 27–30 percent. If we can't remedy this five-point (or more) cost differential, we'll be at a disadvantage as insurance product prices fall in 1990. However, we need to decide what our goals are before we start cutting heads to lower expenses. Our 66 percent loss ratio for CWW is a great loss ratio and we can't expect to improve on it by much, but we need to focus on other key performance ratios." Table A summarizes key performance ratios for CIGNA Europe.

Howson continued: "It is up to the country managers to grow the business and bring these ratios into line. Our responsibility as European managers is to get on with our 1992 changes now and not wait until 1992, or even until 1990. We can't wait for directives from the home office on these issues."

CWW executives understood the need for coordinated effort in Europe. However, they also realized there were vast differences among the insurance markets of the EC countries. As one CWW European country manager stated, "Some companies will make the mistake of looking at the EC as a whole, offering 'Euro-insurance' products when there are still tremendous differences among nations. If these disparities are not recognized through niche product offerings, these companies might fail to satisfy any of the 325 million consumers in the EC. The key is to continue to think globally but to act in a manner that addresses local needs."

The Task Force Meeting

Nieuwenhuizen opened the task force meeting by outlining some key questions for his country managers: "How should CWW react to the changes occurring in its environment? What changes in market structure and competition are likely? What will happen to distribution channels? What countries will be most affected by the transformation? What are CWW's marketing options and how can CWW exploit its strengths to better position itself for 1992?"

After six hours of discussion, the task force emerged with an outline of the critical issues, opportunities, and threats that the 1992 integration program posed for CIGNA Eu-

TABLE A   **CIGNA Europe Performance Ratios**

	1988	*Objective for January 1, 1993*
Underwriting ratio[a]	14.0%	9.0%
Commission ratio[b]	18.0	19.0
Area office expense ratio[c]	3.2	2.0
Home office expense ratio[d]	5.0	2.5
Total expense ratio	40.2%	32.5%

[a]Underwriting expenses as a percent of sales.
[b]Commissions paid as a percent of sales.
[c]Allocated EC area office expenses as a percent of sales.
[d]Allocated U.S. home office expenses as a percent of sales.

rope. The country managers felt the important issues for CWW in Europe were its sales effectiveness (marketing, distribution, and product mix) and cost effectiveness (cost containment, economies of scale, and technology).

At least four strategic options, not necessarily mutually exclusive, had been discussed at the meeting:

1. Focus on large multinational accounts. CWW could take advantage of its size, global reach and industry expertise to develop and sell complex, customized products to this relatively narrow target market. Although the value of each policy would be high and servicing costs as a percent of net written premiums would be low, profit margins would be under pressure. Most multinationals were price-sensitive and many insurance carriers were competing for their business.

2. Focus on profitable insurance products. Most CWW revenues in Europe came from sales to national, rather than multinational, companies. Some CWW executives argued that the national subsidiaries should focus more tightly on profitable lines of business rather than trying to be all things to all people in order to grow their national revenues to cover overhead. In addition, to control the expense ratio, they argued for focusing on writing larger policies for larger companies, which could also serve as useful references when Cigna pitched other prospects. However, the "opening" of the large-risk market to competition and government subsidies to state-owned insurance companies both meant that prices and profit margins would remain low.

3. Focus on second-tier companies. While most insurance carriers pursued the largest accounts, few specialized products had been developed for medium-sized businesses that were often underinsured. Price sensitivity and service needs were lower, although claims processing costs as a percent of net written premiums might be higher than for the larger companies. Some CWW executives thought they could leverage industry-specific insurance products throughout their European network; for example, a property and casualty insurance policy developed for wineries in France also could be offered in Spain and Italy. In addition, in some cases, CWW could target efficiently multiple companies through their common industry or trade associations. Banks were increasingly targeting medium-sized companies with insurance products but they focused on personal insurance products more than property and casualty policies.

4. Explore direct marketing. Though attempting to bypass brokers risked retaliation, direct marketing was becoming increasingly important in the selling of personal insurance products. One reason was that the insurer's financial exposure was more predictable for personal insurance products (with the benefit of actuarial tables) than for property and casualty policies. Because servicing costs as a percentage of net premiums written were higher for personal insurance products, the direct marketer's profitability depended on achieving a high volume of sales over which these servicing costs could be spread.

Many managers thought product research and development could play a vital role in driving CIGNA Europe's future market share and revenue. One manager stated: "We need to develop new products to meet this fast-changing market. We need to look at what is changing technologically within various industries and then target products and services to meet the needs of a specific segment. In this way we can build our business."

The challenges posed by the 1992 program stemmed from the probability of intense price competition and the possibility of delay in reducing the expense ratio handicap. Another threat was voiced by one country manager as follows: "If the EC changes the definition of 'capital' in a future insurance directive, CWW might have to maintain dramatically increased monetary reserves in each country. Such a situation would put a real kink into our 1992 plans."

As they left the task force meeting, CWW executives could not be sure how broad the EC's future insurance directives would be or how these directives would influence the way CWW did business. One executive commented: "The firms that will do well in the EC will be those with enough patience and capital to stay in for the long haul." The managers were certain, however, that 1990 would be an important year for insurance services and an opportunity for CWW to gain a stronger foothold in the European insurance marketplace.

EXHIBIT 1
Organization chart

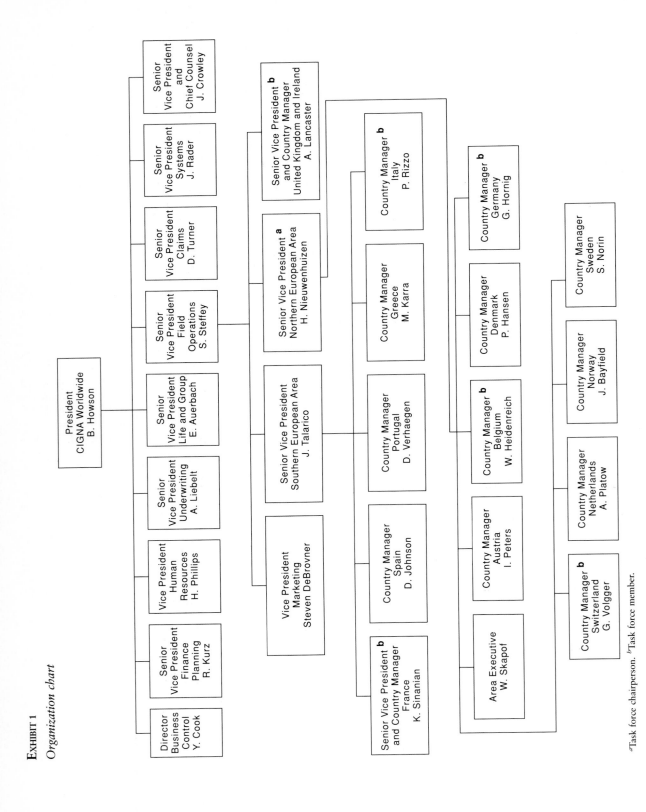

[a]Task force chairperson. [b]Task force member.

EXHIBIT 2   Selected Insurance Information for 1986

	Population (MM)	Insurance per Capita	Total Premiums ($ billion)[a]	Premiums as percent GNP	Nonlife Premiums ($ billion)	Percent Nonlife Premiums of Total	Nonlife World Share	Nonlife EC share	Number of Operating Companies
West Germany	61	$ 978	$ 60	6%	$34.4	57%	7.7%	32.5%	516
United Kingdom	56	807	46	8	18.6	40	4.2	17.6	712
France	55	658	36	5	22.3	62	5.0	21.1	462
Italy	57	253	15	2	11.8	79	2.6	11.2	207
Netherlands	15	788	11	6	6.2	56	1.4	5.9	439
Spain	38	138	5	2	4.3	86	1.0	4.1	520
Belgium and Luxembourg	10	510	5	4	3.7	74	0.8	3.5	302
Denmark	5	743	4	5	2.2	55	0.5	2.1	235
Ireland	4	616	2	8	0.9	45	0.2	0.9	63
Portugal	10	76	1	3	0.7	70	0.2	0.7	231
Greece	10	46	1	2	0.3	30	0.07	0.3	154
EC	325	468	186	5					
United States	226	1,746	395	9					
Japan	121	1,399	170	8					

[a]Premium income was an imperfect indicator of size of a nation's insurance market because, to varying degrees, national governments helped to satisfy insurance requirements through social security benefits. Such benefits were not reported in market estimates of premium income. In addition, many national governments set premium prices, thereby helping to determine the structure of each country's insurance market.

SOURCES: Swiss Reinsurance Company and EC Commission.

Barriers	Proposal	Intended Result
Physical: • Restrictions on free movement of labor and goods.	**Eliminate:** • Customs posts. • Frontier control. • Immigration checkpoints.	• Reduce salary costs, administration, and wasted time. • Increase industry efficiency through lower transportation costs and free movement of labor.
Technical: • Preventing goods and services legally manufactured and sold in one member state from competing in another state, due to disparate national technical standards on product, health, and environmental regulations.	• Mutual recognition: any product legally salable in one member country could be sold throughout the EC.	• Reduce costly modifications. • Increase length of production runs. • Decrease manufacturing costs. • Reduce prices.
Fiscal: • Restrictions on capital movements. • Disparities in value-added tax levels and excise duties.	• Two-rate value-added tax system for EC (politically impossible to agree on one rate for all goods).	• Reduce price variations across markets.

EXHIBIT 4   **EC Insurance Premium Growth Rates**

	Growth in Premium Income (%)[a]			
	Total Business		**Nonlife Insurance**	
	1985–1986	*1984–1985*	*1985–1986*	*1984–1985*
West Germany	6.4%	4.2%	4.0%	4.2%
United Kingdom	19.4	6.3	20.6	7.4
France	11.0	6.1	3.3	−0.6
Italy	11.2	7.8	7.6	5.4
Netherlands	8.7	3.3	11.2	0.2
Spain	22.0	4.7	14.0	3.3
Belgium	10.1	1.3	10.3	1.2
Luxembourg	10.6	7.4	10.6	6.8
Denmark	−2.7	21.8	7.6	6.2
Ireland	4.9	−6.9	17.3	10.3
Portugal	12.1	1.8	12.5	0.1
Greece	NA	NA	NA	NA

NA means not available.

[a]Growth has been adjusted for inflation.

Forecast of Nonlife Premium Income Growth (Index 1987 = 100)						
	1987	*1988*	*1989*	*1990*	*1991*	*1992*
West Germany	100	104	109	113	118	124
United Kingdom	100	110	118	126	134	142
France	100	105	112	118	125	133
Italy	100	110	118	127	137	148

SOURCE: Swiss Reinsurance Company.

EXHIBIT 5   **Insurance Price Comparisons**
Percentage Differences in Prices of Standard Insurance Products Compared
with the Average of the Four Lowest National Prices in 1986

	Home[a]	*Motor*[b]	*Commercial Fire, Theft*[c]	*Public Liability*[d]
West Germany	+3	+15	+43	+47
United Kingdom	+90	−17	+27	−7
France	+39	+9	+153	+117
Italy	+81	+148	+245	+77
Netherlands	+17	−7	−1	−16
Spain	−4	+100	+24	+60
Belgium	−16	+30	−9	+13

[a]Home insurance—Annual cost of fire and theft coverage for a house valued at 70,000 ECU. Contents were valued at 28,000 ECU.
[b]Motor insurance—Annual cost of comprehensive insurance for a 1.6 liter car. Driver had 10 years' experience.
[c]Commercial fire and theft—Annual coverage for premises valued at 387,000 ECU and stock valued at 232,000 ECU.
[d]Public liability—Annual premium for engineering company with 20 employees and an annual turnover of 1.29 million ECU.
SOURCE: EC Commission Study.

EXHIBIT 6   **Selected Information on CIGNA/AFIA Merger**

	1983 Headcount			1983 Net Written Premiums ($ millions)			1988 CIGNA Europe	
	CIGNA	*AFIA*	*Combined*	*CIGNA*	*AFIA*	*Combined*	*Headcount*	*Net Written Premiums ($ millions)*
West Germany	57	81	138	$ 8.9	$ 19.1	$ 28.0	113	$ 48.1
United Kingdom	355	363	718	129.7	96.4	226.1	575	267.0
France	105	339	444	35.0	54.8	89.8	360	123.7
Italy	81	248	329	9.1	26.4	35.5	254	53.2
Netherlands	68	59	127	17.8	27.8	45.6	81	49.7
Spain	34	104	138	1.7	5.8	7.5	89	22.3
Belgium and Luxembourg	93	86	179	4.6	9.7	14.3	80	25.7
Denmark	17	16	33	1.4	3.6	5.0	13	6.8
Ireland	9	34	43	5.9	11.0	16.9	42	16.5
Portugal	0	0	0	0.0	0.0	0.0	5	0.1
Greece	1	42	43	0.2	4.0	4.2	23	3.3
Total	820	1,372	2,192	$214.3	$258.6	$472.9	1,632	$616.4

EXHIBIT 7   CIGNA Europe: Selected Financial Information[a]

	West Germany		U.K.		France		Italy		Netherlands	
	1987	1985	1987	1985	1987	1985	1987	1985	1987	1985
Premiums written										
Gross written premiums	81.1	88.8	454.6	582.1	166.5	160.6	72.5	89.2	65.1	102.9
Net written premiums	47.1	32.9	267.0	227.6	123.7	106.5	52.2	60.2	48.7	58.4
Earned premiums (EP)	48.7	32.5	270.2	234.4	125.4	109.7	53.4	60.3	56.0	55.6
Losses incurred	31.1	12.1	217.3	177.2	74.5	84.0	26.2	50.2	57.5	49.8
Commissions (Comm)[b]	8.5	2.4	48.3	30.7	22.5	13.9	9.7	11.6	10.5	7.3
Taxes	0.8	1.7	0.9	2.5	2.4	5.5	2.7	3.4	0.4	0.5
Local overhead	5.9	6.5	24.3	32.8	17.9	18.7	7.1	10.9	4.4	6.9
Underwriting results	2.4	9.8	(20.6)	(8.8)	8.1	(12.4)	7.7	(15.8)	(16.8)	(8.9)
Investment income (IIN)	5.8	3.5	29.8	24.6	14.7	11.2	13.9	6.3	1.4	6.1
Operating profit	8.2	13.3	9.2	15.8	22.8	(1.2)	21.6	(9.5)	(15.4)	(2.8)
Share of EC profit (%)	15.3%	172.7%	17.2%	205.2%	42.6%	−15.6%	40.4%	−123.4%	−28.8%	−36.4%
Loss ratio										
(Losses/EP)	63.9	37.2	80.4	75.6	59.4	76.6	49.1	83.3	102.7	89.6
Commission ratio										
(Comm/NWP)	18.0	7.3	18.1	13.5	18.2	13.1	18.6	19.3	21.6	12.5
Expenses + taxes ratio										
(Expenses + taxes/NWP)	14.2	24.9	9.4	15.5	16.4	22.7	18.8	23.8	9.9	12.7
Combined ratio	96.1	69.4	107.9	104.6	94.0	112.3	86.4	126.3	134.1	114.7
Retention rate										
(NWP/GWP)	58.1	37.0	58.7	39.1	74.3	66.3	72.0	67.5	74.8	56.8
Expense ratio										
(Expenses + taxes + Comm/NWP)	32.2	32.2	27.5	29.0	34.6	35.8	37.4	43.0	31.4	25.2
Investment ratio										
(IIN/NWP)	12.3	10.6	11.2	10.8	11.9	10.5	26.6	10.5	2.9	10.4

[a]CIGNA Europe's recent financial growth was partially due to devaluation of the U.S. dollar and CWW's retention of a higher percentage of its own policies.

[b]Commissions included fees paid to brokers and agents, as well as commissions received from other insurance companies as part of reinsurance agreements.

	Spain		Belgium/Lux.		Denmark		Ireland		Portugal		Greece		Total	
	1987	*1985*	*1987*	*1985*	*1987*	*1985*	*1987*	*1985*	*1987*	*1985*	*1987*	*1985*	*1987*	*1985*
	33.5	35.5	37.0	53.8	8.8	10.2	20.3	20.8	0.2	0.0	7.7	3.0	947.3	1,146.9
	21.3	19.7	25.7	28.0	6.2	3.5	15.5	8.6	0.1	0.0	3.3	1.5	610.8	546.9
	18.9	19.9	25.8	26.2	6.3	3.0	13.6	7.8	0.1	0.0	3.0	0.7	621.4	550.1
	14.2	25.3	17.2	19.5	2.7	2.1	9.9	5.1	0.0	0.0	1.4	0.9	452.0	426.2
	3.4	3.1	4.5	3.7	1.3	0.1	2.2	−0.3	0.0	0.0	0.9	0.5	112.0	73.0
	0.8	0.7	0.8	0.9	0.0	0.0	0.1	0.1	0.0	0.0	0.1	0.1	9.0	15.4
	2.9	3.1	3.1	4.1	1.4	1.0	1.6	1.7	0.4	0.1	0.4	0.2	69.2	86.0
	(2.4)	(12.3)	0.2	(2.0)	0.9	(0.2)	(0.2)	1.2	(0.3)	(0.1)	0.2	(1.0)	(20.8)	(50.5)
	2.3	2.1	2.9	2.9	0.4	0.4	2.7	0.9	0.0	0.0	0.4	0.2	74.3	58.1
	(0.1)	(10.2)	3.1	0.9	1.3	0.2	2.5	2.1	(0.3)	(0.1)	0.6	(0.8)	53.5	7.7
	−0.2%	−132.5%	5.8%	11.7%	2.4%	2.6%	4.7%	27.3%	−0.6%	−1.3%	1.1%	−10.4%	100.0%	100.0%
	75.1	127.1	66.7	74.4	42.9	70.0	72.8	65.4	0.0	0.0	46.7	128.6	72.7	77.5
	16.0	15.7	17.5	13.2	21.0	2.9	14.2	−3.5	0.0	0.0	27.3	33.3	18.3	13.3
	17.4	19.3	15.2	17.9	22.6	28.6	11.0	20.9	400.0	0.0	15.2	20.0	12.8	18.5
	108.5	162.2	99.4	105.5	86.4	101.4	98.0	82.8	400.0	0.0	89.1	181.9	103.9	109.4
	63.6	55.5	69.5	52.0	70.5	34.3	76.4	41.3	50.0	0.0	42.9	50.0	64.5	47.7
	33.3	35.0	32.7	31.1	43.5	31.4	25.2	17.4	400.0	0.0	45.4	53.3	31.1	31.9
	10.8	10.7	11.3	10.4	6.5	11.4	17.4	10.5	0.0	0.0	12.1	13.3	12.2	10.6

Ехнівіт 8   **Selected Financial Information for CWW Consolidated Results for Years Ended December 31, 1985–87 (U.S.$ in thousands)**

	1985	*1986*	*1987*
Property and Casualty			
Gross written premiums	$1,730,871	$1,623,586	$1,603,734
Net written premiums	948,896	1,052,194	1,081,604
Net earned premiums	955,657	1,022,543	1,110,307
Losses and expenses	1,061,820	1,088,183	1,164,799
Underwriting results	(106,163)	(65,640)	(54,492)
Investment and other income	99,395	101,298	106,900
Life			
Premiums	143,067	213,772	311,937
Earned premiums	139,289	209,435	300,268
Investment and other income	69,414	129,799	183,035
Benefits and expenses	202,636	328,646	473,869
Operating income	6,067	10,588	9,434
Combined operating income (loss) before noninsurance expenses and income taxes	(701)	46,246	61,800
Property and Casualty			
Statutory Ratios			
Loss	71.7%	66.6%	65.5%
Expense	39.4	39.8	39.4
Combined	111.1	106.4	104.9

EXHIBIT 9 Selected Information for Product Mix, Product Growth, in 1985 and 1988 for CIGNA Europe

	Property	Casualty	Marine	Health and Accident
1985 Product Mix[a]				
West Germany	48.3%	15.7%	24.6%	11.4%
United Kingdom	24.2	12.6	45.9	17.2
France	53.4	21.2	7.1	18.4
Italy	38.3	15.9	14.8	31.0
Netherlands	61.3	11.5	23.6	4.0
Spain	44.8	26.7	13.7	15.0
Belgium/Luxembourg	58.7	15.9	17.2	8.2
Denmark	53.3	11.1	15.4	20.2
Ireland	47.1	31.2	1.0	20.8
Portugal	0.0	0.0	0.0	0.0
Greece	43.7	32.5	22.0	1.8
Total	37.3	15.1	30.5	17.1
1988 Product Mix[a]				
West Germany	64.6%	7.7%	12.5%	18.0%
United Kingdom	50.7	4.1	31.4	13.8
France	59.0	15.1	5.4	20.5
Italy	46.8	15.8	13.1	24.3
Netherlands	49.3	8.1	36.5	6.2
Spain	56.6	8.5	13.1	21.8
Belgium/Luxembourg	65.0	14.5	10.6	9.9
Denmark	42.1	3.5	3.5	50.9
Ireland	54.9	23.2	0.4	21.5
Portugal	96.0	0.8	1.1	2.1
Greece	62.4	22.1	15.0	0.5
Total	54.1	10.3	18.6	16.8

[a]Product mix represents each line of business as a percentage of net written premiums.

EXHIBIT 10

CIGNA Europe—recent print advertisement

SIZE DOES HAVE ITS ADVANTAGES.

When you're navigating the unsure waters of today's insurance market, you need stability.

You need a provider backed by the resources of a worldwide company. One with experience to match. As Insurance Company of North America and former AFIA-member companies, we accumulated nearly a century of experience in the property and casualty market in Europe. Now that we've become *CIGNA Insurance Company of Europe S.A.-N.V.,* we also have all the resources you're likely to need. Of course, we've always had an extensive range of services.

Our Marine and Aviation Divisions lead the industry with innovative products and a unique underwriting capability.

At CIGNA, we can meet the needs of all kinds of businesses by offering specialized property and marine coverages as well as comprehensive commercial casualty products. We specialize in developing worldwide insurance programs.

Clearly, we're not just bigger. We're better. And you can learn how much better we are by writing to CIGNA Insurance Company of Europe, S.A.-N.V., CIGNA House, 8 Lime St., London EC3M 7NA, England or to the CIGNA office in your country (listed below).

An insurer with the ability *and* stability you're looking for. It's one more example of CIGNA's commitment to personalized service to business.

Vienna, Austria • Brussels, Belgium • Copenhagen, Denmark • Paris, France • Frankfurt, Federal Republic of Germany • Athens, Greece • Dublin, Ireland • Rome, Italy
Rotterdam, The Netherlands • Oslo, Norway • Lisbon, Portugal • Madrid, Spain • Stockholm, Sweden • Zurich, Switzerland • Istanbul, Turkey • London, United Kingdom

MARKETING PLANNING

MARKETING PLANNING

A firm's marketing success depends on many factors. For instance, the size of various consumer segments, the preferences of those consumers, and the actions of competitors and distributors all interact to produce the results of a given marketing program. These factors are subject to change and uncertainty. For example, in developing its videodisc technology, RCA was uncertain about the advances that would be made by manufacturers of a competitive technology, videocassette recorders. According to reports in the press at the time of RCA's withdrawal from the market—at a loss of $580 million—RCA had not correctly anticipated the price decline of videocassette recorders, or measured accurately consumers' preference for dual-function machines—those that could record as well as play back material produced elsewhere.

Because of the number and uncertainty of factors influencing market success, a firm must have a systematic way of analyzing these factors, determining the impact of trends on its business, and designing a marketing program to meet present and future market conditions. The marketing planning process is the mechanism by which many firms accomplish these tasks.

The Marketing Plan—Contents

There are many possible formats for a marketing plan; a 1981 Conference Board Report cites 38 examples of planning formats from consumer, industrial, and service companies.[1] While differences based on company type and competitive situations are appropriate, there is a common thread running through marketing planning documents. At their most general level, all plans require that the firm ask itself three questions: (1) Where are we now? (2) Where do we want to go? (3) How do we get there?

Essentially, the planning process forces the planner to imagine the desired future for the product (or service), recognizing the realities of the marketplace, and then to

This note was prepared by Professors Robert J. Dolan and Alvin J. Silk.
Copyright © 1985 by the President and Fellows of Harvard College.
Harvard Business School case 9-585-106 (Rev. 4/2/92).
    [1]David S. Hopkins, *The Marketing Plan* (New York: Conference Board, 1981).

propose an action plan to reach the desired future. In structuring this effort, the following five-step format is useful:

1. Situation analysis.
2. Problem and opportunity statement.
3. Statement of objectives.
4. Action plan recommendation.
5. Statement of expected results, key risks.

Step 1, the situation analysis, is the "Where are we now?" question. It is factual or descriptive, rather than normative—that is, it says how things are, not how they ought to be. It identifies key company strengths to be exploited, deficiencies to be remedied, or both. Exhibit 1 illustrates graphically the components of the situation analysis.

In the external-factors analysis (Step 1a), the firm examines potential consumers to determine trends in primary demand, key market segments, and buyer behavior within various segments.

The second part of the external analysis is competitor analysis and asks such questions as the following:

- What segments do they serve?
- What products do they offer?
- What channels do they use?
- What pricing strategies have they pursued?
- What management resources do they have?
- What financial resources do they have?
- What are their objectives?
- What are their core competencies?
- What alliances are they pursuing, and for what purpose?
- How successful are they in the marketplace?

Finally, external analysis considers the other major environmental variables that may affect consumption behavior. These variables include: economic factors, such as interest rates; demographic factors, such as aging of the population; political factors, such as trade barriers; ecological factors, such as pollution or recycling; and technological factors that may bring in new competitors. All external analysis is directed at understanding both the current situation and trends that may predict future positions.

Simultaneously, the firm completes the situation analysis by examining its own resources, skills, and capabilities in much the same way it analyzes competitors (Step 1b). Although the internal assessment is easier, because key data are more accessible, it is often difficult to be objective when looking inward. It may be hard, for example, to recognize that earlier new-product development efforts have failed to produce a viable product. Some firms find outside consultants particularly useful at this stage.

Step 2, the problem and opportunity statement, is largely a summary of step 1 analysis, except that management judgment is used to prioritize issues. There is real virtue in brevity at this point; a listing of 50 opportunities is foolish and wasteful if the firm has the money and staff to pursue only two or three. This stage might produce the following list for the hypothetical HAL Company:

Opportunity

1. The market for personal computers in the home is growing at 35 percent per year.
2. Consumers are confused by the proliferation of available brands and the types of retail outlets.
3. HAL Company has a microcomputer that is compatible with the IBM PC but, because it has a 32-bit processor, it is much faster than the IBM.

Problems

1. HAL has no marketing expertise, either in the sales force or at staff level.
2. HAL's financial resources are very limited.

Step 3, the statement of objectives, the "Where do we want to go?" phase, is the basis of the action plan in step 4. Objectives should be quantitative, in that they can be compared to actual performance and may be stated at both an overall marketing level and a function level. For example:

Primary Objectives

1. Increase to 70 percent by December the target consumers' awareness of HAL as a producer of personal computers for the home.
2. Ship first units to retail outlets by September. Ship 2,000 units between September and December.
3. Improve the market orientation of the entire HAL organization.

Function Objectives

1. Hire a marketing and sales manager by June.
2. Select an advertising agency by August.
3. Recruit 15 sales-representative organizations by December; set up program to monitor sales representatives' performance.

The first two primary objectives are quantitative; eventually, the actual performance results will be compared against these goals. The firm also must be willing to track data that are not generated through sales activities. Consumer awareness, for example, cannot be ascertained from shipping data; market research is needed to assess it. The next round of the planning cycle should include an audit of the firm's performance compared to its goals. The third primary objective (improve market orientation of entire HAL organization) is not easily quantified, since market orientation measurements are ambiguous. Incorporating this objective into the plan is worthwhile, nonetheless, for the message it sends to all employees.

Step 4, action plan recommendation, is the "How do we get there?" phase based on the groundwork laid by steps 1–3. It states how the firm plans to remedy problems and achieve objectives by taking advantage of identified opportunities. Depending on industry characteristics, this plan may take from one year up to five years (or in rare cases even longer) to fulfill. For example, if a high-tech organization is undertaking a research and development effort, it may be five years before a product emerges.

This step details the actions, priorities, and time schedule needed to attain objectives. For example, if one objective is to ship 2,000 units to distributors by the end of the year, the action plan section assigns responsibilities to people, sets intermediate deadlines, specifies distributors to call on, and details such necessary marketing-support objectives as:

• Print and mail HAL brochure to all computer retail chains of more than 50 stores by July 15.

- Offer exclusive distribution of HAL personal computers to these chains, emphasizing that the product will be available only in full-service outlets.
- Produce factory inventory of 2,500 units on September 1, with production capacity of 500 units per month by September 1.

Stating the action steps prompts an estimate of the resources required to achieve the goals. In step 5, statement of expected results and key risks, the firm assesses the plan's financial impact. Step 5 anticipates the impact of step 4 actions on the firm. It calculates key resource uses and costs, expected revenues, and, often, a pro forma or estimated income statement for the upcoming time period. Typical performance measures cited at this stage are:

- Unit sales.
- Sales revenue.
- Cost of goods sold by product.
- Gross margins by product.
- Key account penetration.
- Market share by segment.

Since the plan of action is predicated on certain assumptions about uncertain events—competitive moves, for example—key risks should be noted, along with contingency plans to either prevent potential problems or respond to them if they arise.

Although this five-step outline is typical, there is no one best way for all firms to put together a market plan. If a firm adopts a given format without thinking, it is unlikely that going through the motions of mechanically filling in prespecified forms will accomplish anything of value. The firm also must tailor the specific contents of the plan to its own needs.

The Marketing Plan—Process

Many newcomers to marketing planning think the major job in getting started is to specify the contents of the plan. Much has been written on this issue. Little has been written, however, on the equally important issue of how the planning is to get done.[2] There are four major questions to consider in structuring the planning job.

1. Participation.   Who has overall responsibility for seeing that the planning gets done? Who does each segment of the job? Who acts as an advisor or information source for planners?

2. Scheduling.   How often is planning done? Should planning be done on a fixed time schedule or as market developments warrant?

3. Scope.   What is the planning time horizon? One, three, five, or ten years? How detailed are the plans?

---

[2] One exception is Stanley Stach and Patricia Lanktree, "Can Your Marketing Plan Procedure Be Improved?" *Journal of Marketing*, Summer 1980, pp. 79–90. This article considers the debt the contents and process issues in six large consumer goods organizations and traces the full process for one organization believed to be obtaining good results from its planning.

4. Review.   Who reviews and approves proposed plans?

5. Monitoring.   What is the best mechanism for ensuring that the plan is executed and desired results are achieved?

An important principle of issue 1 ("Who does what?") is that the people involved in the planning process are more committed to the plan once it is adopted than those who were not involved. Thus, if possible, people who will implement the plan should be involved in its development. This sounds clear enough, but in many organizations implementers feel that the plan is something imposed on them by top management and people in staff positions. If they consider the plan's goals or resource allocation to be unrealistic they will not be motivated to carry it out. To be effective, planning must be an integral part of managing the business; it should not be something to be got through as quickly as possible in order to get back to "real" work.

Issue 2, scheduling, is often not considered explicitly by planners. To fit in with the cycles for other reports, such as taxes and reports to stockholders, marketing planning is usually done annually. Although an annual marketing plan may indeed be the correct choice for the majority of firms, the planner should evaluate that choice in terms of the rhythms of a particular marketplace. Should the planning cycle for a producer of laundry detergents, for example, be the same as for the HAL Company, the hypothetical manufacturer of personal computers?

Most people argue that having a fixed, inflexible time schedule ensures that planning gets done. The major problem here is that requiring too much information in too little time may have unexpected consequences. Asking people to adhere to a strict schedule can encourage "filling in the form," regardless of the quality of the input.

The scope of a marketing plan has two major dimensions: the planning horizon and the level of detail. The planning horizon, or length of time encompassed by the market plan, varies widely across companies and industries. Many North American companies develop plans for one- to three-year horizons, under the assumption that the future is too uncertain for longer time horizons to be worthwhile. The plan for the first year is typically more detailed than those for later years. However, many global companies, including such large Japanese firms as Nippon Electric Corporation (NEC), and European firms like Royal Dutch Shell, engage in planning over horizons of 10 years, 20 years, or more. Uncertainty over these longer horizons often is taken into account by identifying different future scenarios and developing plans for each scenario.

The level of detail in a plan reflects the degree of specificity about who is responsible for doing what, when, where, how, and under what budget constraints. There is a wide range of intention, with some firms favoring short, crisp plans, which give general guidelines, and others insisting on a great deal of specificity. One benefit of more detailed planning is that potential problems, bottlenecks, and resource constraints are more likely to surface during the planning process. Another is that the people doing the planning may develop deeper substantive knowledge of the business by hammering out the fine points. The disadvantages of more detailed planning are that it takes longer, may make it difficult to planners and managers to see the forest for the trees, and results in large documents less likely to be read by busy executives.

There is no one right answer about the optimal time horizon and level of detail for a marketing plan. It is obviously harder to plan in volatile markets, yet a company operating in such a market may benefit from a plan as a handrail to guide it through an unpredictable environment. Regardless, one ought to ask the question: "What is the right scope?" before undertaking any planning effort. The reason for thinking deeply about scope is because too long a time horizon or too much detail may reduce the efficiency of the planning process, while too short a horizon or too little detail may compromise its effectiveness.

Review and approval, issue 4, concerns the role of top management. Practice suggests that senior management be involved at a number of points in the process, rather than just to say "yea or nay" at the end. This ensures harmoniousness with management's overall conception of the business.

Finally, issue 5, monitoring, concerns how the plan is made a living document rather than an entry on an out-of-the-way bookshelf. To be effective, the plan documentation should provide guidelines for actions and checkpoints on performance. Moreover, channels will need to be in place to allow for midcourse corrections in case an unexpected event occurs or inputs just do not yield desired outputs in spite of correct assessments of conditions.

Desired Benefits

According to David Hopkins,[3] the broad objective of planning is to encourage thinking about the future, improve performance, and keep the firm alive. But what specific benefits do companies derive from structuring their analysis of the market and writing everything down in a formal way?

First of all, a plan can be a very effective communication device (see Exhibit 2). The planning unit's document facilitates three kinds of communication flow: (1) up to superiors for their concurrence with the plan; (2) down to subordinates so they understand more clearly the mission of the unit; and (3) laterally to other planning units.

Second, the collection of plans from all planning units allows top management to check the consistency of the actions and synergies across units. A plan also can aid in evaluating managers. Since managers have asked for resources to perform activities in anticipation of certain results, they have produced a formal record of their "promises made, promises kept."

Third, the plan focuses people on the right questions. This is especially helpful when there are a number of new managers in the organization. Participation in the planning process can be an effective training device. Drawing up the plan provides an opportunity for many people to contribute facts. It also encourages constructive debate about alternative action plans in much the same way a good case study does.

Fourth, the plan helps to prevent the urgent from driving out of the important. In most firms, there are constant pressures to deal with unexpected problems that arise in a fast-changing marketplace. A plan helps to set priorities and serves as a reminder of activities that must be accomplished to achieve long-term objectives. Without it, people may drift into fire-fighting activities that are not critical to the long-term success of the organization.

Finally, the existence of a written plan with quantified objectives is a prerequisite to accurate assessment of the firm's performance. It serves as an audit and can (1) yield diagnostic information when objectives are not achieved and (2) provide better understanding of how the market performs.

---

[3]David Hopkins, "Plan or Perish," *Sales Marketing Management*, May 18, 1981, pp. 45–46.

Threats to Benefits

Marketing planning is not a universally acclaimed activity. In some firms, the line people who implement the plan view it as a burdensome overload imposed by staffers trying to justify their existence. Some top managers view it in similar terms. In the words of the chief executive officer of a multibillion-dollar company: "Get rid of those planners and put in somebody who will *do* something." To a large extent, the criticism is unfair, for what is generally at fault is not the concept of marketing planning but the firm's execution of the planning function.

Charles Ames[4] found three major pitfalls in effective marketing planning:

1. Failure to fit the concept to the company.
2. Overemphasis on the system and formats at the expense of content.
3. Failure to recognize and consider alternative, creative plans of action (i.e., the tendency to base future plans on continuation of current policies with minor changes).

Although Ames's study was of industrial products, many failures in consumer goods and service industries also can be traced to the company's attempt to borrow intact the marketing planning procedures of another organization. Procedures must be based on specific market characteristics; required interfaces between the marketing, manufacturing, and finance functions; size of the organization; breadth of the product line; and so forth.

Ames's second point concerns separating planners of the process from implementers. Some organizations have planning-input requirements that appear to be based on the principle of "the more, the merrier." The forms are overly structured and detailed. They ask implementers to provide information that is totally useless for effective management. Some managers find that planning documents direct them to provide information about unimportant factors but allocate no space to write about critical areas.

Marketing Organization

Marketing plans establish objectives and recommend actions for achieving them. The plans' execution falls to the marketing organization where planning and organizing are inexorably intertwined. Thomas V. Bonoma describes the interrelation between strategy and implementation as a "cascade phenomenon," whereby goals and decisions flow down an organization hierarchy "much like water does from pool to pool in a Japanese garden."[5] Strategic plans formulated at one level in an organization are communicated to the level below, where they are interpreted and translated into actions undertaken to achieve the broader strategy. Thus, an organization's design and management become critical factors in the successful implementation of any strategy.

---

[4]Charles Ames, "Marketing Planning for Industrial Products," *Harvard Business Review,* September–October 1968, pp. 100–11.

[5]Thomas V. Bonoma, *The Marketing Edge* (New York: Free Press, 1985), p. 9.

Strategy, Structure, and Performance

The premise that organization matters to economic performance and is realized through efforts to implement a chosen strategy is depicted in Exhibit 3, which also identifies the major classes of organization-design variables.

A key issue in appraising a marketing plan is the fit between the strategy embodied in the plan and the organization's design. In his landmark study of the evolution of large industrial corporations in the United States, Alfred Chandler shows how the pursuit of alternative product/market growth strategies posed special administrative challenges and, therefore, gave rise to distinct organization forms or structures. He summarizes his findings and thesis as follows:

> Strategic growth resulted from an awareness of the opportunities and needs—created by changing population, income, and technology—to employ existing or expanding resources more profitably. A new strategy required a new or at least a refashioned structure if the enlarged enterprise was to be operated efficiently. The failure to develop a new internal structure, like the failure to respond to new external opportunities and needs, was a consequence of overconcentration on operational activities by the executives responsible for the destiny of their enterprises, or from their inability, because of past training and education and present position, to develop an entrepreneurial outlook.[6]

Note that Chandler sees environmental change as the source of "new opportunities and needs." New strategies are adopted in response to shifts in external conditions, which leads to Chandler's famous proposition that "structure follows strategy" and to its corollary—that without structural adjustments, changes in growth strategy can lead to economic inefficiency.

A large body of empirical evidence supports these concepts. For example, after investigating the organizational practices of 10 large firms in different industries, Corey and Star concluded that "in successful companies, organization structure responds to market environment." At the same time, Corey and Star remind us, strategies do not grow out of an organizational vacuum: "Today's organization is an important influence molding tomorrow's strategy, which in turn shapes tomorrow's organization."[7]

Chandler's work provides the rationale for the strategy–organization–performance linkage shown in Galbraith and Nathanson's model (Exhibit 3). A firm's internal organization is represented by the large circle encompassing the five principle design variables that define an organization's structure and processes.

Task refers to the basic activities performed by employees and reflects the technology available for doing the organization's work. *Structure* denotes the arrangements among people for getting work done and can be conceptualized along two basic dimensions: differentiation and integration. Differentiation involves the division of labor or combining of tasks into roles and the assignment of roles to organizational units, such as departments and divisions. Differentiation, however, gives rise to the need for integration, or means for achieving control and coordination of specialized roles and units so as to accomplish both specific and general organizational goals.

Two other mechanisms for effecting control and coordination in marketing organizations are *reward systems* and *information/decision processes*. These mech-

---

[6] Alfred D. Chandler, Jr., *Strategy and Structures: Chapters in the History of American Industrial Enterprise* (Cambridge, Mass.: MIT Press, 1962), pp. 15–16.

[7] E. Raymond Corey and Steven H. Star, *Organization Strategy: A Marketing Approach* (Boston: Division of Research, Graduate School of Business Administration, Harvard University, 1971), pp. 4, 5.

anisms may be thought of as relating to both the fundamental rationale for organizing and the basic limitation of organizations. As Herbert Simon observes: "It is only because individual human beings are limited in knowledge, foresight, skill, and time that organizations are useful instruments for the achievement of human purpose; and it is only because organized groups of human beings are limited in ability to agree on goals, to communicate, and to cooperate that organizing becomes for them a 'problem.' "[8]

Information and decision processes affect communication flows, decision making, and the distribution of influence within an organization. Decision processes may be designed to be more or less formalized in terms of who participates, how the search for and analysis of alternatives is conducted, and what criteria are invoked in selecting among them. Choices about the collection, maintenance, processing, and distribution of data determine the nature, quality, and timeliness of information available to support decision making. These choices, thus, have an important bearing on how an organization responds to environmental feedback and manages internal interdependencies.

Reward systems serve to motivate individuals to perform routine and nonroutine tasks essential for the functioning of the organization. Rewards include policies relating to compensation, performance appraisal, promotion, job design, and leadership style.

People, the final organization-design variable, are invariably a company's scarcest resource when developing an organization well matched to its strategic needs and opportunities. The time-honored maxim of "find good people and turn them loose" leads to a focus on policies relating to recruitment, selection, training and development, promotion, and transfer.

The challenge for management in setting these design variables is a dual one: the choices made with respect to tasks, structure, people, rewards, and decision/information systems should not only fit the strategy being pursued but also must be internally consistent. The latter point is reflected in Exhibit 3 by the interconnecting lines of the five design variables.

Two implications of this condition deserve emphasis. First, while performance, in principle, may be affected by a change in any of these design variables, their flexibility and leverage are likely to be dissimilar and situational. A design modification that works in one circumstance may be ineffective or even dysfunctional in another. Within a short planning horizon, certain design alterations may not be feasible and will constrain implementation of a new strategy. Second, the design variables are interdependent and a change in one may require changes in others, thereby making a piecemeal approach to organization design suspect if not hazardous. Thus, the problem of organization design is highly complex, requiring continuing attention and frequent adjustment.

Generic Marketing Organization Structures

The structure of marketing organizations, like the units of a multiproduct/service firm, can be differentiated either vertically or horizontally. Vertical differentiation is reflected in the number of different levels within an organizational hierarchy, while horizontal differentiation refers to differences in task and orientation among units at the same organizational level.

---

[8] Herbert A. Simon, *Models of Man* (New York: John Wiley & Sons, 1957), p. 199.

An important property of vertical organization is the extent to which decision-making authority is centralized or decentralized. The more discretion and participation in decision making granted to members at lower organization levels, the more decentralized is the organization structure.

Marketing organizations tend to be differentiated (or centralized) by product, market, geography, and function. With respect to function, there is a distinction between the internal activities of marketing management and related support services (advertising, sales promotion, new-product development, and market research) and external activities (sales force and customer services). These internal and external functions are typically further differentiated on the basis of product or market.

The three types of structures for marketing organizations are based on these dimensions of differentiation. The first, a product-based organization, differentiates both internal and external functions by product lines. Differentiation by markets characterizes a market-based structure. For example, many sales organizations are subdivided by geography (North America, Europe, Japan, Rest of World). Another market-based structure is by the industries served (insurance, manufacturing, health care).

The hybrid form combines a product-based structure for internal functions with a market-based organization of the sales force and other external activities. Although these generic structures represent ideal types, they can help us understand the more complex organizational forms observed in practice. They also can serve as tools for analyzing organization-design problems.

In general, the more complex or diverse an organization's environment, the more differentiated will be its marketing structure. Hence, businesses producing diverse products for relatively homogeneous markets, such as consumer packaged goods and pharmaceutical firms, tend to adopt a product-based form of organization. Conversely, businesses producing a relatively homogeneous product line for diverse end-use markets, such as materials suppliers or equipment manufacturers, are more likely to operate through market-based structures. Finally, firms selling diverse products to a diverse set of markets, such as computer manufacturers, often will develop hybrid structures to cope with environmental complexity.

Consider, for example, the three-pronged hybrid structure IBM introduced in the mid-1960s for its Data Products Division, which was responsible for the firm's intermediate-to-large computer business.[9] Product marketing managers were assigned for each system in the division's product line; they had responsibility for identifying marketplace applications, working with engineering personnel on product design, and coordinating production scheduling with manufacturing people. They also participated in pricing decisions and in training the field sales force.

In addition, market managers, known as industry directors, were appointed for each of several end-user market segments. They planned strategy—including communications programs and sales force deployment—and were involved in hardware and software development.

Geographically, the division also created market regions and operated a number of branches within each, headed, respectively, by region managers and branch managers. The latter were specialized by end-user/industry market segments and were responsible for managing both sales and customer service personnel in their branches and for providing market intelligence to division management.

---

[9]This example is taken from E. Raymond Corey, Christopher H. Lovelock, and Scott Ward, *Problems in Marketing*, 6th ed. (New York: McGraw-Hill, 1981), pp. 716–17.

Organization Design and Change

The approach to organization design represented in Exhibit 3 is known as "contingency theory." As summarized by Galbraith and Nathanson, "the theory states that there is no one best way of organizing, but all ways of organizing are not equally effective. That is, the choice of organization form makes a difference in terms of economic performance. The choice depends, however, on the situation."[10]

As the above discussion stresses, the key contingency that must be addressed to design an effective organization is environmental complexity and diversity. Hence, a basic requirement of organization design is that one begin analysis of such problems with an explicit segmentation of the firm's relevant markets. Marshall states it concisely when he advises: "Design your business from the outside to the inside."[11] A second key principle is "fit." Businesses are organized to execute strategies; therefore, the problem of organization design is to match strategy with the key dimensions of organization structure and process.

Clearly, the search for an organization design that balances the interdependencies depicted in Exhibit 3 is an ongoing pursuit. Organizational changes initiated at Procter & Gamble serve to underscore this point. In 1988, P&G, a pioneer of the brand-management system, modified the structure of its decades-old marketing organization. John G. Smale, P&G's chair, announced to employees in a company newsletter that "our historical way of managing Procter and Gamble's business no longer fits the company we are today nor the business environment in which we must compete."[12]

Faced with slow growth, fragmentation of markets, and powerful retailers, P&G sought to shift its strategic focus toward management of product categories, rather than individual brands. Traditionally, brand managers had been encouraged to compete with one another in the same category. (For example, P&G markets numerous brands of bar soaps.) Under the restructured marketing management organization, brands were grouped into 39 categories, each with its own manager. The latter served as a general manager to whom brand managers reported, along with advertising, sales, manufacturing, research, and engineering.

In addition to this structural realignment, new performance measurement and compensation policies were introduced. Whereas volume and market share criteria had been emphasized under the previous brand-management system, category managers were given direct profit responsibility, and part of their compensation depended on the financial performance of their categories. P&G was apparently seeking better interfunctional coordination and reduction in the conflicts and inefficiencies resulting from brand managers' competition for the same resources.

P&G's restructuring illustrates the process of mutual adjustment of a firm's strategy and organizational design in response to a changing environment. Thus, market forces test the adaptability of even the most dominant and successful organizational forms, such as the brand-management system.

---

[10]Jay R. Galbraith and Daniel A. Nathanson, *Strategy Implementation: The Role of Structure and Process* (St. Paul, Minn.: West Publishing, 1978), p. 54; see also, Jay R. Galbraith, *Organization Design* (Reading, Mass.: Addison-Wesley, 1977).

[11]Martin V. Marshall, "Short Notes on Marketing," Harvard Business School, May 1988, p. 23 (unpublished).

[12]This discussion draws on Zachary Schiller, "The Marketing Revolution at Procter and Gamble," *Business Week* 3062 (July 25, 1988), pp. 72–76; quote, p. 73.

Conclusions

Marketing planning has made a fundamental contribution to the success of many firms. However, there are significant challenges in designing a plan's contents and development process so as to avoid the pitfalls noted here. There is no cookbook solution to planning; successful firms go beyond an understanding of the concept of planning to custom tailoring a plan to their own situation.

Once a strategy and a marketing plan to pursue it have been formulated, attention must turn to the design of the organization responsible for executing the plan. Like marketing planning, organization design defies cookbook solutions. There are no simple answers to the question: What is the right organization structure? However, two principles to guide design choices are implicit in the above discussion. First, a marketing organization should be designed from the outside to the inside; hence, the foundation for any effective organizational design is segmentation of the markets served by the firm. Second, businesses are organized to execute strategies and, therefore, must seek a fit between strategy and the entire set of key design variables that define an organization's form and processes: tasks, structure, information/decision systems, reward systems, and people.

Exhibit 1
Situation analysis

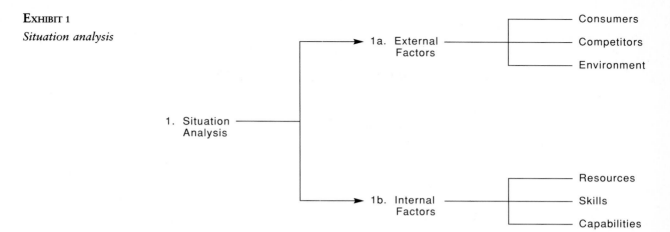

Exhibit 2
Intraorganization communications

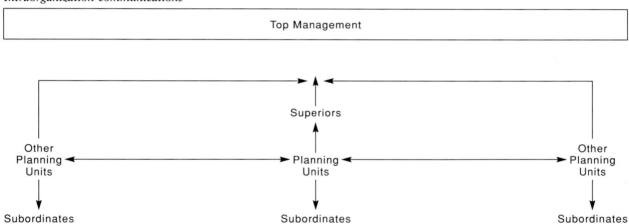

EXHIBIT 3

Strategy, organization design, and performance

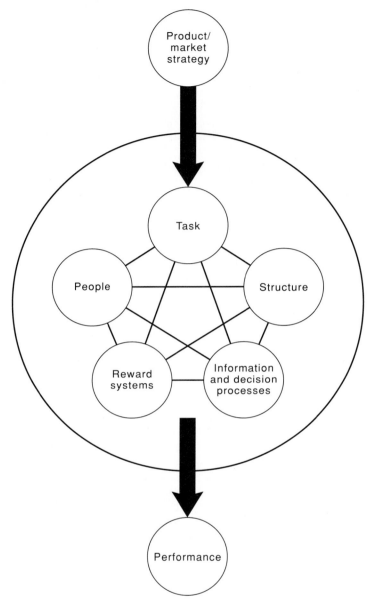

SOURCE: From Jay R. Galbraith and Daniel A. Nathanson, *Strategy Implementation: The Role of Structure and Process* (St. Paul, Minn.: West Publishing, 1978) p. 2.

PERKIN-ELMER: DATA SYSTEMS GROUP

Perkin-Elmer: The Persistent Planner"—so read the article title in the December 1980 issue of *Dun's Business Monthly* selecting Perkin-Elmer as one of the five best-managed companies in the United States. This case specifically examines the planning activities of the Data Systems Group (DSG). After a brief description of Perkin-Elmer, the case (1) describes the minicomputer business in which DSG operated; (2) details the planning process and its operation within DSG; and (3) provides comments from senior DSG executives on their perceptions of the market planning process as of December 1981.

Company Background

Incorporated in 1939 as a high-precision optics firm, Perkin-Elmer registered its twenty-fifth consecutive year of sales and earning growth in the fiscal year ending July 31, 1981. Acquisitions were a significant factor in Perkin-Elmer's growth, and in 1981 it had five businesses (or groups) pursuing the corporate objective: "Management of technology for profitable growth." (See Exhibit 1 for financial data for each business.)

Three of the Perkin-Elmer groups were leaders in their markets. The Optical Group was the world leader in equipment for semiconductor manufacturing; the Instrument Group, in measurement and analysis devices; and METCO, in flame spraying.[1]

Gerätetechnik, a West German affiliate, supplied control and navigation systems for such vehicles as the Airbus commercial airliner and military tanks. The Data Systems Group competed in the high-performance end of the minicomputer business. Perkin-Elmer entered this business with its 1974 acquisition of Interdata.

The Minicomputer Business

Important characteristics of the minicomputer business included (1) rapid industry growth; (2) rapid technological advance; (3) importance of original equipment manufacturers (OEMs); and (4) customer loyalty to vendors.[2]

Most industry sources mark the emergence of minicomputers as a significant factor in the data processing market with Digital Equipment Corporation's (DEC) introduction of its PDP-8 line in 1964. Competitors soon followed. Interdata was formed in 1966, and, by 1968, major firms in the business included Data General, Hewlett-Packard, Honeywell, and Varian.

Although time would make the distinction between minicomputers and mainframes difficult to state in terms of price/performance, there were clear differences in the late 1960s. First, minicomputers were relatively cheap. The DEC PDP-8 sold for less than $20,000. Generally, manufacturers were able to produce low-cost machines with acceptable speeds by designing products for single applications. This was in contrast to the mainframes, which were general-purpose devices. Second, minicomputer manufacturers typically "sold iron"—in other words, they provided computer hardware but little associated software. Most minicomputer sales were to OEMs, who designed the minis into their own products for sale to end users. Minis also were sold to sophisticated end users, who could customize them or incorporate them into a system to serve a particular need. Because of this OEM focus, minicomputer manufacturers were little concerned with end-user needs and concentrated instead on technical performance features.

During the 1970s, the minicomputer market grew at over 35 percent annually. The decade saw increased competition, with Prime entering in 1972 and IBM in 1976. Product proliferation occurred. Both lower- and higher-priced machines were introduced. In 1974, Perkin-Elmer's Interdata Division (the unit which would eventually become DSG) introduced the first *super-mini*—so termed because its word length of 32 bits was the same as that of mainframes.[3] Previously, all minicomputer word lengths were 8 or 16 bits, which limited their computing speed and processing complexity. Spurred largely by DEC's introduction of the 32-bit VAX-11/780 in 1977, the supermini segment grew at a faster rate than the traditional mini segment. By 1981, industry sources estimated that superminis accounted for over 60 percent of the dollar share of the total minicomputer market. The growth rate of the supermini segment was predicted to be 25 percent annually through 1985. In contrast, Perkin-Elmer executives expected no growth in the traditional mini segment.

This case was prepared by Associate Professor Robert J. Dolan. Copyright © 1982 by the President and Fellows of Harvard College. Harvard Business School case 582-101.

[1] In flame spraying, metal or other materials were melted and then sprayed to form a surface coating that improved the material's resistance to wear, heat, or corrosion. Major markets were the automotive and aircraft industries.

[2] "Note on the Minicomputer Industry in 1978" (HBS case 579-177) was helpful in preparing this section.

---

[3] Word length was measured in the number of binary digits (bits) and indicated the amount of information that could be stored in a memory location. It corresponded to how much information could be processed in a machine cycle.

Competitors varied in the importance they placed on OEM versus end-user markets, but almost all manufacturers became increasingly end-user oriented over time. For example, Interdata sold almost exclusively to OEMs in 1970; DSG sales to end users were 30 percent by 1980 and were planned to be 70 percent by 1985. Early adopters of minis were typically firms with scientific and industrial control applications. In the 1970s, mini manufacturers recognized the large potential market represented by relatively unsophisticated business data processing. Selling to this market required a problem solution rather than a technical product focus.

In 1981, the fast pace of technological advance continued. Major product announcements were expected within the year by IBM, DEC, and Prime. Despite technological change, *Datamation's* Annual Minicomputer Survey in 1979 and 1980 showed high levels of vendor loyalty; few users anticipated changing their mini suppliers in the next year. Users resisted change because either large software investments had been incurred or the mini had been incorporated into a system that would have to be redesigned if vendors were changed. For example, in the aircraft flight simulator market, the customer selected a mini supplier on the basis of a rigorous analysis of developmental systems. Once selected, the vendor was virtually assured of production run business for the next two to five years. The extent of captive business in the simulator market caused available new business to be only one quarter of total sales.

In 1981, for the minicomputer market as a whole, dollar market shares were estimated to be:

DEC	38%
Hewlett-Packard	16
Data General	11
Honeywell	7
IBM	6
Prime	4
Texas Instruments	4
Perkin-Elmer	3
All others	11

In all, over 40 firms participated in the market, with estimated sales of $6.5 billion.

The Data Systems Group

The Data Systems Group was formed in 1976 as the federation of three recent Perkin-Elmer acquisitions: Interdata (computer processors), I/O Devices (terminals), and Wangco (memory devices). Problems in the group's early operation led to decreasing profitability, as shown in Exhibit 1. In the midst of these difficulties, William Chorske became senior vice president and general manager of DSG in March 1978.

Shortly after Chorske's appointment, the group decided to concentrate on computers and divest the terminals and memory operations. In 1981, DSG had three principal product lines: 16-bit computers; 32-bit computers with ferrite core memories; and 32-bit computers with MOS memories (designated Series 3200).[4]

DSG computer sales during fiscal year 1980 (August 1, 1979–July 31, 1980) were $138.7 million, divided as follows: 16-bit—less than 20 percent; ferrite core 32-bit—about 40 percent; and the balance, Series 3200. The 16-bit machines no longer received substantial R&D support.

The Series 3200, introduced in 1979, effectively made the 32-bit ferrite core machines obsolete. Business for them continued primarily because some OEMs were contractually unable to upgrade to the Series 3200, and some longer-term programs—such as training simulators—were locked into specific configurations utilizing the ferrite core products. For all intents and purposes, DSG's future was in the Series 3200.

Series 3200 was composed of four processor models: 3210, 3220, 3230, and 3240. (See Exhibits 2 and 3 for sample advertisements for these models.) The 3210 was the most recent model (introduced September 1981); it was positioned as a low-cost entry to 32-bit computing. A basic system cost about $70,000. In 1982, DSG planned to introduce a 3250, which would be its highest-price/performance machine. The 3250 would offer roughly three times the performance of the 3210 at a price of $220,000.

The DSG's installed base of 32-bit machines was 4,500 units at the end of 1981—second only to that of DEC. Among others, DSG had been successful in the transportation systems, environmental monitoring, scientific computation, and industrial process control markets.

Planning at Perkin-Elmer

The Data Systems Group followed essentially the same planning process as all other Perkin-Elmer groups. It consisted of financial planning (using a system in place for over 15 years) and a related business planning cycle.

The business planning system was installed in DSG because of the difficulty of dealing with the group's rapidly changing environment. According to one senior Perkin-Elmer executive, the fast but irregular growth made it "easy to lose your way"; a good planning system could serve as a "handrail to find your way in the dark" by specifying and communicating the organization's goals to all its members. The following sections outline the DSG planning cycle for fiscal year '82 (August 1, 1981 to July 31, 1982). Exhibit 4 shows a calendar of planning activities and their interrelationships.

---

[4]Memories were of two basic types: ferrite core and metal oxide semiconductor (MOS). Rapid cost declines in semiconductor technology had made MOS more cost efficient.

Financial Planning. Financial planning had five steps:

Step 1: January 1981 —Phase 0 Financial Plan.
Based on examination of historical data, proposed group strategies, sales force opinions, and other pertinent data, this document provided:

- Orders forecast by quarter for FY '81.[5]
- Projected detailed income statement for FY '81.
- Orders and shipments forecast for FY '82.
- "Rough" projection of FY '82 income statement.

Step 2: April 1981 —Phase I Financial Plan.
Based on corporate and group management reaction to the Phase 0 plan and data available after January, this plan adjusted Phase 0 estimates to include:

- Detailed monthly forecast of orders, shipments, and profit for FY '81.
- Quarterly projection of orders, shipments, and profit for FY '82.
- "Rough" projection of orders, shipments, and profit for FY '83 and FY '84.

Step 3: June 1981 —Corporate Planning Conference.
All groups' Phase I plans were given corporate level review.

Step 4: July 1981 —Phase II Financial Plan.
This document incorporated any changes specified by the planning conference. Otherwise, Phase II matched Phase I estimates. Sales and order forecasts were given by month for entire FY '82, and by year for FY '83 and FY '84. Monthly budgets were established.

Step 5: October 1981 —October Reforecast.
This step identified any deviation from the Phase II plan, which had been in effect for three months, and identified the cause of the deviation and its impact. Reforecasts for the current year were also done at Phases 0 and I of FY '83 planning.

Business Planning. In 1978, the business planning process was instituted to provide better market-based planning. It

was integrated with financial planning and involved four documents: a guidance statement, target market profiles, summary of project status and plans (referred to as an "SP-squared"), and a business plan (see Exhibit 4).

The unit of analysis in the business planning cycle was the strategic business segment (SBS); documents were prepared by each SBS in a group. Chorske's first task in business planning was to partition the DSG into SBSs. Two teams would be associated with each SBS. The regular SBS line management organization was the Green Team. The Red Team, a group of senior executives (drawn from within and outside the SBS group), advised the Green Team and Chorske. The Green Team prepared all documents and held full profit and loss responsibility. The Red Team met regularly to provide a structured, independent review of Green Team plans but had no line authority.

Filing of the four documents of the business planning cycle was done in five steps:

Step 1: August 1980 —Guidance Statement.
This was a two- to three-page statement of the mission, objectives, and key strategies of the SBS for the four fiscal years that followed (see Exhibit 5 for outline).

Step 2: October 1980 —Target Market Profiles.
Required for each target market, these profiles characterized the markets served and stated alternative means of approaching them (see Exhibit 6).

Step 3: January 1981 —SP^2 (Draft).
This document gave a product-oriented overview of the SBS, specified product development plans, and proposed allocation of R&D sources. It provided basic input to the Phase 0 financial plan because it specified the potential sources of revenue (see Exhibit 7).

Step 4: March 1981 —SP^2 (Final).

Step 5: April 1981 —Business Plan.
This plan merged previous business planning documents with the Phase I financial plan and extended only for FY '82. It included a complete income statement by market and allocated primary resources of R&D, sales effort, and marketing resources to markets (see Exhibit 8).

The financial plan and the business plan related at two points each year. First, the draft SP^2 and Phase 0 financial plan had to agree in January. Second, the business plans when consolidated across all SBSs in a group had to agree with the pro formas in the group's Phase I financial plan in April.

---

[5]Shipments could be quite different from orders received in a quarter because of manufacturer's backlog or early ordering by buyers.

Planning Process Implementation in the Data Systems Group

In 1978 Chorske partitioned the DSG into three SBSs:

1. Small Computer SBS — 16-bit machines costing less than $40,000
2. Medium Computer SBS — 32-bit machines costing less than $100,000
3. Large Computer SBS — 32-bit machines costing more than $100,000

A Red Team was assigned to each SBS. Subsequent Red Team reviews of their SBSs' planning documents revealed a problem in defining SBSs on a product basis. As set up, SBSs overlapped in some markets, so it was difficult to judge the logic of one SBS's plans without knowledge of the others' plans.

In November 1979, Chorske "reoriented" the Red Teams (also known as advisory boards) in a memorandum that read in part:

> As a result of a need expressed by the Advisory Board Chairmen, we have decided to change the orientation of the Advisory Boards. The changes reflect a more market-driven approach and emphasize the target market concept in a tangible way.
>
> Two things have been done to pursue this goal: (1) the names of the Advisory Boards have been changed and (2) the standard agenda has been modified. The name changes, while largely symbolic, should serve to focus attention and emphasize the target market approach. The changes are [shown in Table A.]
>
> As noted . . . , each Advisory Board has responsibility for at least one Target Market. Perhaps the most graphic way to illustrate this is through the . . . Planning Matrix [see Exhibit 9], which shows the new Advisory Board headings along the top. . . .
>
> The standard agenda change is a straightforward shift to including, up front, a target market review. . . .
>
> These changes, I think, can contribute significantly to helping DSG and the planning system focus on target markets.

The DSG's organization chart at the time of this reorientation is shown in Exhibit 10. Planning for FY '81 was conducted under this structure.

Planning for FY '82 was affected by an organizational revision in March 1981, shown in Exhibit 11. The essential change was the creation of the Technical Systems and business Systems divisions out of the Computer Systems Division. The Computer Manufacturing Division would serve both new divisions. Sales and service functions remained separate as before.

The advisory board structure was reconciled with the new organization structure in September 1981. First, the Business and Technical Systems divisions became SBSs. Second, the old Business Market Advisory Board became the Business Systems Advisory Board. The old Industrial and Scientific Market boards merged to become the Technical Systems Advisory Board. Positions of individuals serving on the two new advisory boards are shown in Table B.

The reorganization caused some changes in filing dates of individual division planning documents for FY '82; for instance, guidance statements were filed in November 1981. Planning for FY '83 would follow the calendar shown in Exhibit 4.

In addition to the four planning documents filed by each SBS of the DSG (i.e., Technical Systems Division and Business Systems Division), FY '83 plans called for business plans from each functional organization — Sales and Customer Service. These plans, filed by general managers of Sales and Customer Service for deployment of their resources, were to concur with the resource uses stated in the business plans of the two SBSs.

Perceptions of the Planning Process

In December 1981 senior DSG executives reflected on the planning process within their group. (See the organization chart in Exhibit 11.)

William Chorske.   Bill Chorske, senior vice president and general manager of DSG, had been with Perkin-Elmer since receiving his MBA from Harvard Business School in 1965. Before becoming general manager of the Data Systems Group, he served as a deputy director in the Instrument Group. His experience was in manufacturing, control, and sales management.

> Before the planning process went in in 1978, we didn't have a strategy. We just built fast computers. Now we have a strategy and it's pretty well communicated throughout the organization, so I'm pretty happy with the basic approach to planning that we have.

TABLE A   Name Changes of Advisory Boards and Target Markets

Present Name	New Name	Major Target Market(s)
Small Computer Advisory Board	Industrial Market Advisory Board	Process Control
Medium Computer Advisory Board	Business Market Advisory Board	Office Automation
Large Computer Advisory Board	Simulation and Scientific Market Advisory Board	Environmental Monitoring and Transportation Systems

TABLE B   New Advisory Boards' Composition

Technical Systems Advisory Board	*Business Systems Advisory Board*

Chairperson
General Manager,
  Customer Service Division
	Chairperson
	General Manager,
	  Sales Division

Members
1. General Manager,
   Technical Systems Division
2. Director of Marketing,
   Business Systems Division
3. Director of Program Management,
   Technical Systems Division
4. Managing Director,
   Perkin-Elmer, France
5. Vice President of Manufacturing,
   Computer Manufacturing Division
6. Director,
   Perkin-Elmer, Instrument Group
7. Vertical Sales Manager,
   Technical Markets
8. National Sales Manager, U.S.
	Members
	1. General Manager,
	   Business Systems Division
	2. Director of Engineering,
	   Technical Systems Division
	3. Director of Corporate Computing,
	   Perkin-Elmer, Corporate
	4. Managing Director,
	   Perkin-Elmer, U.K.
	5. General Manager,
	   Terminal Division
	6. Outside Consultant
	   (independent consultant on data processing, formerly in IBM sales force)
	7. Director of Product Management and Planning,
	   Technical Systems Division

In 1978, DSG was a $145 million business. We had grown over 25 percent in each of the past two years—but we were in danger of being pushed out of the business because we were trying to do everything. Everywhere you looked there were opportunities and it's hard to keep yourself from going after all of them. But you have to stop yourself. If you don't, the big guys like DEC and those focused little guys will kill you. We had a clear idea: *narrow our focus.* But how do you make that happen? We always built the best and fastest computers for everybody. I'm convinced that to change that culture and to get people thinking and talking about markets, you need a formal planning system.

We still have a way to go with this planning system. Right now, not everybody works as hard at the planning process as they should. We've got to get it into the organization and have it take hold there. First we have to have a structured system with things on a scheduled basis to get the planners doing their job. Then, they have to get the right feedback; people have to execute against the plan.

In a sense, the plan is nothing. The process is everything. This is a big, complicated business. I have to depend on the process to focus people on the right problems. We have smart people here, and we just have to keep them looking at the right things.

It's a time-consuming process. When we're coming up to one of those corporate planning conferences, I'm spending half my time on it. Overall, I spend at least 25 percent of my time on it. Across the organization, I'd guess managers spend about a day a week on it.

You have to spend the time on it—you have to focus somehow. You focus or you're not in business.

Charles Hogan.   Charles Hogan was previously manager of software development at Interdata when Perkin-Elmer acquired it. He subsequently held positions in product planning and marketing services. In 1980, he became director of business development for DSG, reporting directly to Chorske. In this position he was responsible for preparing the DSG Planning Manual.

We were a product-oriented group and that was a problem. I think we really made a mistake when we set up the original advisory boards. They were product oriented and that held us back a couple of years, but now we are a two-dimensional business—one dimension being products, the other, markets. We still don't drive the business off serving markets, but the planning process is a way for us to get to the target market dimension of the planning matrix. We have to do that because we are growth oriented and, therefore, we must ask ourselves how we are going to achieve that growth. In the business we are in, any user problem has lots of feasible solutions. So, to answer the growth question, we have to turn to market considerations as well as product considerations.

There are a lot of difficulties in planning in a business like this. It's a fast-paced industry—multiple markets, multiple products, multiple-user needs, both bottom-up and top-down approaches. For a planning system to work in this environment you've got to have structure, a rigid schedule, and perseverance. You have to have a formal system with a specific schedule of what must be done by whom, when. Then you have to keep at it, making adjustments and improvements as you go.

We spread the planning job out over a number of months because it's a big job and, therefore, if you do it in one shot, the staff people will do it. That's not what you want. The line people should do most of it. So, we spread the job so people can digest it. The risk here is that you'll have a front end that doesn't jibe with the tail end. For example, we file guidance statements in August and business plans in April; sometimes the game changes in between.

George Larsen. George Larsen came to DSG from another computer firm in 1980. An engineer, he was vice president, director of development until the reorganization of March 1981, when he became general manager of the Technical Systems Division.

I have a theorem which says that any process will work if you work at it long enough. That's the way I feel about the planning process—it's fine, reasonable. One of the most important things about it is that people understand it because it hasn't changed that much since 1978. You say SP^2 and everybody knows what it is, what's in it.

Last year's plans were really terrible. Our marketing guys put some numbers together, just looking at the past. It was really superficial. But then reality intruded and showed us how wrong we were—that we were logically inconsistent. I guess

you have to get bit—really feel it emotionally; then you say to yourself, "Look at how this thinking hurt us. How can we have been so wrong?" But now, because of being bitten, I'm asking new questions; I know what I need to focus on.

We originally had the small-, medium-, and large-computer advisory boards. But thinking that way gives you no leverage. When I'm thinking about product development, there are maybe 20 or 30 things we as engineers could do. Now I know I have to say to my marketing people, "Go talk to somebody; find out what those people in that market want—what two or three things will get me sales."

We are institutionalizing the process. It does not generate good decisions today, but it gives you a little insight and lots of raw material. Having a specified process will be good training for when we have less-experienced people making the decisions.

Conclusion

It had been three years since the business planning process had been instituted at DSG. Chorske agreed with Hogan that "you have to keep at it, making adjustments and improvements as you go." He wondered what might be done to make the process more productive and less time consuming.

Exhibit 1   Selected Financial Data by Group, Fiscal Years 1977–1981 (dollar amounts in millions)

	Years Ended July 31				
	1981	*1980*	*1979*	*1978*	*1977*
Net Sales					
Optical Group	$ 353.7	$ 303.9	$199.3	$145.6	$105.0
Instrument Group	328.7	293.3	238.8	199.4	159.3
Data Systems Group	232.5	214.7	168.3	144.7	111.0
Gerätetechnik	111.5	92.6	52.7	32.1	26.3
METCO	100.9	100.3	79.6	64.0	53.0
	1,127.3	1,004.8	738.7	585.8	454.6
InterGroup	(11.5)	(8.7)	(5.7)	(4.4)	(2.9)
Total	$1,115.8	$ 996.1	$733.0	$581.4	$451.7
Income before Taxes					
Operating profit:					
Optical Group	$ 65.5	$ 49.1	$ 37.9	$ 26.4	$ 14.2
Instrument Group	45.8	42.5	35.9	24.9	20.7
Data Systems Group	23.5	26.3	15.5	10.4	12.2
Gerätetechnik	11.1	11.8	5.9	3.2	2.3
METCO	18.3	16.6	14.0	11.0	7.7
	164.2	146.3	109.2	75.9	57.1
Inter Group	(1.3)	(0.5)	(0.6)	(0.2)	(0.1)
	162.9	145.8	108.6	75.7	57.0
Interest income and (expense)—net	(0.8)	(6.6)	(4.1)	(3.7)	(0.8)
General corporate expense	(16.5)	(16.1)	(11.3)	(7.6)	(6.3)
Total	$ 145.6	$ 123.1	$ 93.2	$ 64.4	$ 49.9

EXHIBIT 2

Computer journal advertisement

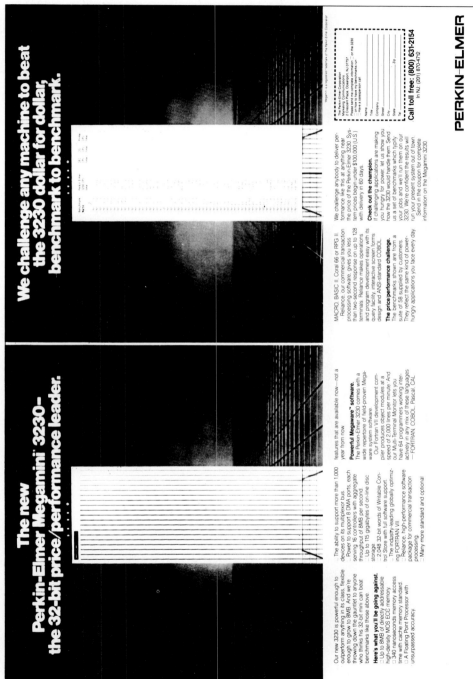

EXHIBIT 3
Geophysics magazine advertisement

The search for energy can take you anywhere.

Your search for high-powered seismic processing ends with Perkin-Elmer computers.

To date, ten oil companies and major seismic contractors have selected Perkin-Elmer minicomputers. They have the speed and power you need for both field and central site processing of seismic data.

In the field, the economy of our Perkin-Elmer 3220 minicomputer stretches your budget. You can have many more systems providing on-site intelligence, acquiring data from seismic shots and analyzing its quality and validity.

At your processing center, the large-scale, high-throughput Perkin-Elmer 3240 Megamini* delivers a unique combination of 40 MB bandwidth and 16 MB addressable memory. With that kind of bandwidth you can run large numbers of peripherals in parallel – for example, high-speed tapes to speed reports and relieve array processors and disks – to relieve data analysis bottlenecks.

And the Perkin-Elmer 3240's memory size allows large numbers of data arrays to be resident in memory – immediately available for accessing – without paging delays.

Additionally, a Perkin-Elmer telemetric interface can put the in-van processor in direct satellite communication with the high-performance computer at your processing center.

A switch to Perkin-Elmer minis will not obsolete your existing application programs. Our 32-bit Megaminis utilize FORTRAN VII compilers. Conversion is fast and easy. And no matter how far afield your explorations take you, you're never far from Perkin-Elmer service. We're a worldwide Fortune 500 company with seismic customers around the globe.

For complete information, send the coupon or call toll free.

Perkin-Elmer Corporation, Marketing Communications
Two Crescent Place, Oceanport, NJ 07757

Name:
Tel:
Title:
Company:
Street:
City: State: Zip:
Present equipment used:
Array processor used (brand):

Call toll free (800) 631-2154.
In N.J. (201) 229-6800.

PERKIN-ELMER

Exhibit 4

Perkin-Elmer fiscal year 1982 planning calendar

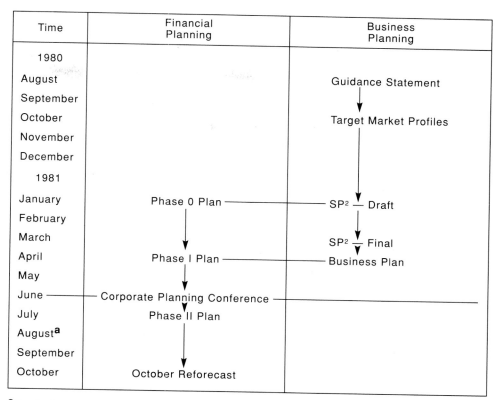

Time	Financial Planning	Business Planning
1980		
August		Guidance Statement
September		
October		Target Market Profiles
November		
December		
1981		
January	Phase 0 Plan ————————	SP² — Draft
February		
March		SP² — Final
April	Phase I Plan ————————	Business Plan
May		
June ———	Corporate Planning Conference ———	
July	Phase II Plan	
August[a]		
September		
October	October Reforecast	

[a]Beginning of fiscal year 1982

EXHIBIT 5 Outline of Guidance Statement

I. Mission Statement
II. Objectives
   - qualitative statement of intentions
III. Goals
   - major quantitative, measurable objectives over a four-year period
IV. Assumptions
   - major assumptions related to accomplishment of objectives and goals
V. Strengths/Weaknesses
   - statement of key internal strengths to be exploited, weaknesses to be corrected
VI. Opportunities/Threats
   - summary of market factors, competitive threats, and technological changes relevant to accomplishment of objectives and goals
VII. Strategies
   - definition of most important and promising actions required to achieve objectives
VIII. Segmentation
   - definition of subdivision of the business (what is offered to what market) for use in subsequent planning

SOURCE: Data Systems Group planning manual.

EXHIBIT 6 Outline of Target Market Profile for Each Target Market

I. Name
II. Definition
   - user needs to be served
   - channels of distribution used to reach
   - type of product/service needed
III. Key Accounts
   - current Perkin-Elmer customers
   - future prospects
   - description of each account
IV. Size and Character of Market
   - domestic vs. international vs. intra-Perkin-Elmer
   - OEM vs. end user
   - captive vs. noncaptive
   - old accounts vs. new
V. Buying Influences
   - major issues in vendor selection
   - perceived needs of buyers
VI. Competition
   - who
   - relative market shares
   - buying influences' evaluation of competitors
VII. Market Share
   - potential Perkin-Elmer share
   - available market
   - projected Perkin-Elmer share vs. resources required
   - risk assessment
VIII. Strategy Alternative
   - product offered
   - marketing approach
   - sales approach
   - cost estimate
   - risks
IX. Potential Unique Selling Propositions

SOURCE: Data Systems Group planning manual.

EXHIBIT 7   Outline of Summary of Project Status and Plans (SP²)

I. Introduction
   - assumptions

II. Current Business Position and Outlook
   - industry structure and trends
   - Perkin-Elmer position by target market
   - competition
   - technology trends
   - risks/uncertainties

III. Product Line Overview
   - existing products/modifications
   - new products
   - order projection by product line over next five fiscal years
   - order projection by target market for next fiscal year

IV. Developmental Projects
   - overall rate of investment
   - areas of emphasis
   - R&D budget allocations for:
       current products
       products under development
       proposed new products for next five fiscal years

SOURCE: Data Systems Group planning manual.

EXHIBIT 8   Outline of Business Plan

For each division, define the marketing plan for the following fiscal year consisting of:

I. Opportunity
   - definition of market
   - reference to relevant target market profiles

II. Current Business Position
   - environment (competition, economy, technology)
   - goals and objectives in terms of Perkin-Elmer growth, share, profit

III. Strategy in Market
   - distribution channel used
   - advertising theme
   - sales force approach
   - pricing policy

IV. Resources
   - requirements for the division
   - deployment of resources by:
       marketing staff
       promotion/advertising expense
       sales expense
       development

V. Pro Forma Income Statements
   - actual for this fiscal year
   - projection for next fiscal year

VI. Summary
   - key issues
   - risks
   - contingencies

SOURCE: Data Systems Group planning manual.

EXHIBIT 9 **Planning Matrix of Bill Chorske's Memorandum on Advisory Boards**

	Industrial Market Advisory Board		Business Market Advisory Board			Simulation and Scientific Market Advisory Board				Total
	Process control	Other	Office automation	Data communication	Other	Environmental monitoring	Transportation systems	Lab automation	Other	
Small computers < $40,000										
Medium computers < $100,000										
Large computers > $100,000										
Total										

NOTE: Matrix would specify order value in dollars for prior and current fiscal years and the planned volume for the upcoming year.

EXHIBIT 10

Organization chart, 1980

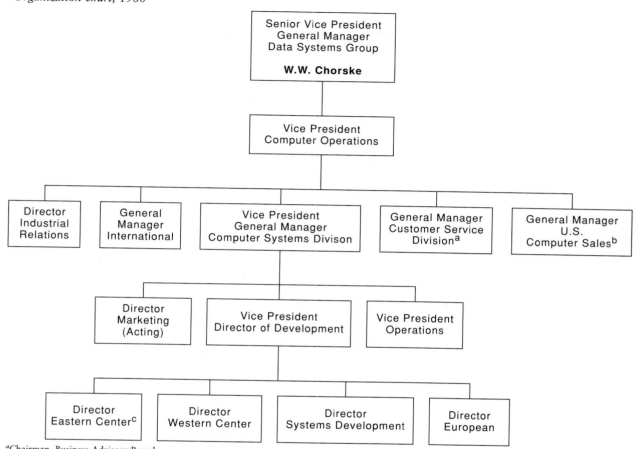

[a]Chairman, Business Advisory Board.
[b]Chairman, Simulation and Scientific Advisory Board.
[c]Chairman, Industrial Advisory Board.
SOURCE: Company data.

EXHIBIT 11
Organization chart, effective March 1981

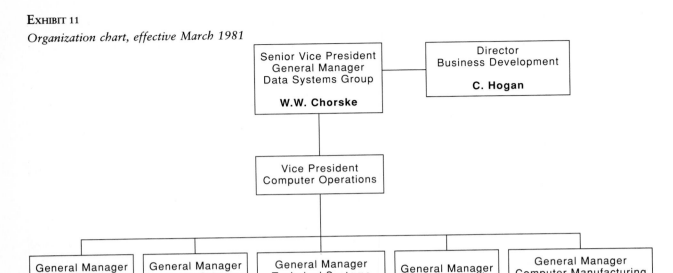

[a]Chairman, Technical Systems Division Advisory Board.
[b]Chairman, Business Systems Division Advisory Board.
SOURCE: Company data.

SCANDINAVIAN AIRLINES SYSTEM SAS (A)

The First Wave

In its corporate heart every airline knows that its essential product, an airline seat, is no different from any other's, give or take a couple of inches of width or height or a bit of extra padding.

—Survey Airlines
The Economist

Our business is not flying airplanes, it's serving the travel needs of our public. If we can do better than the other companies, we'll get the business. If we can't, we won't get the business and we don't deserve to.

—Jan Carlzon
Scandinavian Airlines

This case was prepared by Dr. Sandra Vandermerwe of the International Management Institute, Geneva.
Copyright © 1984 by the International Management Institute. Harvard Business School case 8-388-162 (Rev. 11/88).

In 1981, Scandinavian Airline Systems—SAS as it is known in the industry—was struggling with a severe downturn in business and an accumulated two-year deficit of $30 (Skr 150) million after 17 consecutive profitable years. The worldwide recession had cut deeply into the airline industry and the multinational board of directors of SAS was understandably concerned.

The company president, Knut Hagrup, had resigned in 1978 and had been replaced by Carl-Olov Munkberg. Munkberg resorted to drastic cost cutting, including the elimination of 1,300 jobs through attrition. Expenditure dropped, but so did SAS's reputation. Then Curt Nicolin, a SAS director and chairman of ASEA, Sweden's huge electrical equipment manufacturer, persuaded the board to bring in Jan Carlzon. Young and energetic, Carlzon had a flair for marketing that had made him a public figure in Scandinavia, where his views on business and government financing had been sought by press and television.

His philosophy that the public would respond to creatively positive solutions and less bureaucracy had struck a popular chord and he had two success stories behind him to prove it. In his first year as head of Vigressor, a wholly owned tourist subsidiary of SAS, Carlzon had turned the company's results from deficit to profit. During the four years of his tenure, he expanded retail outlets through Sweden and Norway, added a hotel division, and created holiday areas in 20 countries.

In 1978 Carlzon became president of Linjeflyg, the Swedish domestic airline that owned 50 percent of SAS. Within a year he restored the airline to profitability by launching price differentiation, low fare innovation, and boosting schedules to double passenger traffic. This he did despite stiff opposition from his management, which he later replaced. Nicolin had calmed the SAS board's bears that Carlzon was too much of a publicity hound and late in 1980 they placed Carlzon in charge of the airline division, retaining Munkberg as president. The arrangement caused conflict and confusion and Nicolin lobbied to put an end to the situation. By mid-1981 Carlzon replaced Munkberg.

Company and Industry Background

SAS is the national carrier of Denmark, Norway, and Sweden. Born in 1946, when the owners of the three flag carriers merged their fleets into a single airline, it comprises a consortium of three companies, Danish Airlines (DDL), with 2/7 ownership; Norwegian Airlines (DNL), with 2/7 ownership; and Swedish Airlines (ABA), with 3/7 ownership. Each parent airline is a limited company owned 50 percent by its government. The remaining 50 percent is held by more than 4,000 private and industrial investors. The SAS group includes this consortium of companies plus some 20 subsidiary and affiliated ones in transport-related sectors: catering, restaurants and hotels, travel agencies and tour operators, domestic and charter airlines, cargo forwarders, and insurance. The airline accounts for about 80 percent of the group's business both in turnover and profit.

SAS is in a unique situation compared with its European counterparts in that it has three domestic markets—Norway, Sweden, and Denmark. Competing airlines tend to have a simple star-like routing system from one central airport but SAS has the same star-like structure with a triangle in the center representing the three airports of Kastrup (Copenhagen), Arlanda (Stockholm), and Fornebu (Oslo).

The Scandinavian market is small, geographically dispersed, and somewhat on the periphery of the mainstream of airline traffic. The cost level, the rate of inflation, and government user charges are generally high in Scandinavia and labor unions are strong.

The company's three basic route networks operate in totally different competitive environments: Domestic, which runs the five most important local routes and has access to the major slice of the market; European and inter-Scandinavia, where joint agreements and regulations imply that SAS should have a 50 percent share of any routes it operates; and intercontinental where its market share of the world traffic is low and competitive.

Being a tri-country airline creates some built-in inefficiencies. For example, although Sweden dominates the consortium, a balance in numbers has to be kept on all levels, from management to crew in flight. Certain complementary head-office functions are split. The large main computer frames are located in Copenhagen, whereas the data division is in Stockholm. SAS has to retain three crew bases, one in each of the major cities, and often crews have to be moved around as passengers in order to pick up a flight from another airport. A large proportion of the flights, particularly in Denmark, cover very short distances. There are also more maintenance bases than is justified by traffic volume.

Most nations have their own national carriers. Ownership varies from full government control to entirely private ownership. International aviation is governed by more than 2,000 bilateral agreements among the nations involved. These agreements determine capacity that may be offered and the destinations that may be served. They also prescribe that fares and rates be approved by the authorities in the countries involved.

Until about 1975, when the first oil crisis made its impact on the airline business, the industry had been stable and growing. After 1975, the picture changed dramatically. The world market was stagnating. Oil prices rose fast. President Carter introduced deregulation policies in America. England followed. Then the Common Market came out in favor of more liberal aviation. Newly licensed airlines began to compete on price, and the accelerating rate of growth in "package deals" exploded. The airlines continued to share the market with pool agreements and other arrangements. This new competition, however, didn't affect the final customer (in Europe). Rather, the travel agents, forwarders, and other middlemen benefited.

During this time and up to 1981, SAS had all the negative traits associated with deficits: declining productivity, overcapacity, poor punctuality, and a bad service image on the ground. Kastrup, the main hub in the SAS system, was not looked upon, especially by Swedish and Norwegian customers, as a good airport. In fact, these passengers tried actively to avoid landing there.

But as far as most of the staff were concerned, the fact that SAS had lost Skr 150 million didn't seem to concern them. As one executive recalls: "Life went on quite normally. People who join an airline business tend to stay forever. Most people had been here 10, 15, even 20 years. They couldn't have cared less whether we were in the black or red. . . ."

The Carlzon Philosophy

Carlzon believed that SAS had become an "introverted" organization that had lost its fix on the customers' needs. He felt that management had been putting almost all its attention on the mundane aspects of flying airplanes and not enough on the quality of the customers' experience.

In contrast to the conservative and stately Scandinavian tradition, he wanted to change the airline from a technical and production-oriented company to a market-focused one, by making all personnel obsessively aware of customer service. He believed he could force attitudinal and structural changes in SAS that would bring the delivery system into harmony with the customers' needs. This, he reasoned, would get the market to recognize a significant difference between SAS and all other airline choices.

A service company, he argued, needed a different approach to the customer from other manufacturers. SAS, he pointed out, is not the airline, or head office, or an overhaul station; it's the contact between one customer in the market and one SAS employee in the front line. He demonstrated this by an idea that he called "the moment of truth," an episode in which a customer comes into contact with any aspect of the company, however remote, and thereby has an opportunity to form an impression. "SAS," he declared, "had 50,000 moments of truth out in the market every day."

The marketing concept was new to SAS. The international airline had been shaped by a strong heritage of engineering. The former president, Knut Hagrup, an aeronautical engineer, was reputed once to have said to an executive, "I know all about airplanes. I have good people on finance. I don't know anything about marketing. . . ."

Executives had regarded the buying of even larger and faster airplanes as their most important responsibility. Said Carlzon: "We used to think our biggest assets were aircraft, overhaul stations, and technical resources. But we have only one real asset, and that is a satisfied customer prepared to come back to SAS and pay for our costs once more. That's why the assets in our balance sheet should show the number of satisfied customers who flew SAS during the year, and not the number of airplanes, which are not worth one single cent as long as there is no secondhand market in the world for used aircraft, and nobody wants to pay for a flight in those airplanes. So it's really fooling the banks to use these as the assets."

The Project Team Approach

Carlzon's immediate priority early in 1981 was to find a way to change the SAS situation in the shortest possible time. He took a different approach from his days at Linjeflyg. There he had planned and executed the turnaround within the existing line organization. This time, he decided to arrange the process of change from outside the formal SAS culture and structure, creating for a five-month period a parallel management system.

He delegated total responsibility for operating the airline day-to-day to one of his existing managers, Helge Lindberg, leaving himself free to head a small project team of hand-picked people, a few trusted executives, and new recruits, who would become key players once implementation began, and a group of individuals from an outside consulting company and an advertising agency.

The project team's task was to analyze the historical background outside and inside the company, the organizational climate and functioning of SAS. It took a week for them to isolate the major characteristics of the business and its main weaknesses and come up with the direction the change should take. Then they defined the goals and formal strategies. This lasted from December 1, 1980, to March 2, 1981, followed by a few months of discussion and refining, before the full plan was presented to the board in June 1981.

"In the beginning," recalls Carlzon, "we had to decide what part of the market SAS should do business with, so that all our services could be designed to meet that specific market need and no other. This included reducing costs for which this market was not prepared to pay and eliminating them eventually so that every resource of expense was a profitable one. In the past we had hurt ourselves a little more every year by cutting away at services that customers were prepared to pay for. And we got stuck with administration overheads where they were unprepared to pay."

The plan for the project team was that it would eventually spearhead the execution of the various tasks. Executives would either create new departments or take over old ones in the new mode, as strategies came on-stream in a kind of feeder system. Carlzon felt that the new concept would require radical redirection in thinking and energy, and that if handled in the traditional way would take too long to diffuse down the organization. He and his task force personally, therefore, spread the word to all levels of management in an intensive campaign he referred to as "visible management."

The SAS Strategy

The goal set by the project team was: "To be profitable in flight operations even in a zero-growth market." This formed the basis for a medium-term plan, aimed to solve both the revenue and cost problem (see Exhibit 1 for cost/revenue relationship).

The Main Marketing Strategy

The main strategy was aimed at boosting revenues by luring more passengers to SAS, particularly business travelers at full economy fares, as opposed to heavily discounted tourist fares. This was to be achieved by increasing service levels (see Exhibit 2). First Class was abolished within Europe and replaced with Euro-Class at no extra cost to the full-fare business traveler. This was followed by the introduction of First Business Class on long-haul flights, where First Class was retained.

By positioning SAS as the "businessman's airline," Carlzon hoped to steal passengers from the other carriers like Air France and British Airways, who were upgrading their service but charging for it. Air France, who was selling "classe d'affaires" at a 17 percent surcharge, demanded that SAS change its strategy and do likewise. When Carlzon, refused, Air France retaliated and stopped sales of SAS tickets through its travel agents. Finally the conflict had to be resolved at a government level and Air France matched the SAS price.

On the basis of research conducted to establish what the business traveler regarded as the important parts of a travel experience both before and during flying (see Exhibits 3A–3D), the plan for a businessman's airline was put into action.

The new concept was communicated and distributed to the new profit units. Carlzon had made it clear that he wanted SAS to be better in a hundred details, rather than 100 percent better in only one detail. He asked management to find ideas for new services for business travelers. They came back and recommended 150 projects to implement the new concept, with an estimated investment cost of about $40 million and an extra $10 million needed annually in operating costs.

What followed was the development and introduction of a series of new services in rapid succession. While competitors were cutting back on new product development and promotions, SAS invested heavily in the Businessman's Airline Programme (see Exhibits 4A to 4C and 5).

Some of the first features were separate checking counters for full-fare passengers, who were guaranteed that they would wait not longer than six minutes. Full-fare passengers were segregated from economy travelers and given special seat assignments. Airport lounges were improved with relaxation areas, refreshments, newspapers and magazines, TV, reservation assistance, work and meeting areas, telephone and telex facilities. Service on-board improvements included hot meal menus, new tray settings, free newspapers, increased cabin attendants, fewer seats for more legroom, improved seat pitch, and flexible cabin dividers.

Arriving on time was found to be the business traveler's most important consideration. Carlzon, therefore, instituted a punctuality drive that he largely supervised himself. In his office he had installed a viewing screen, which gave him details of all flights, their departure and arrival times, and delays. Sometimes on a late flight he would phone through to the pilot to find out what had gone wrong. A special function was established in Copenhagen to monitor and analyze the punctuality performance of flights worldwide.

In the rush to reduce costs per seat mile, many of the world's airlines acquired large wide-bodied aircraft. These Boeing 747s, airbuses, and the McDonnell DC-10s performed well but airlines found that, if seats could not be filled, their costs per passenger seat mile often produced higher than expected expenses. Since business travelers, who dominated the world's air traffic, demanded proper departure times and frequent flights, using these wide-bodied airplanes effectively worked against the strategy of increasing traffic.

Carlzon reckoned that SAS would sell even more seats if it ceased straining to fly the unsuitable aircraft that got in the way of giving more nonstop flights. The DC-9s were stopping at the airline's hub in Copenhagen just to funnel passengers onto the large wide-bodied aircraft. These planes, therefore, were grounded or relegated to charter work.

Other Markets and Marginal Strategy

Marginal sales also were regarded as significant to the airline since the business person's travel pattern, with its seasonal variations and preferences on departure times and days, was expected to lead to excess aircraft capacity and crews at other times.

A marginal strategy was designed, therefore, to sell to the leisure travel market whatever capacity the business traveler could not use. As one executive put it: "We in services cannot build up stock as other manufacturers do and then sell it—once the aircraft has left, our production is gone forever."

The major thrust of this effort was geared to low-fare tickets on scheduled services departing at times not favored by business travelers. SAS wanted, however, to avoid marginal sales reaching a level where it needed an increase in resources or where low-fare tickets would compete with full-fare sales.

The business traveler and the leisure traveler are often the same person in different guises, and, depending on their role at the time, their demands and expectations vary. Also, the pattern of leisure travel is different. Business travel usually follows general economic trends. During recession, the frequency of travel declines and price sensitivity increases. For the business travelers, travel is frequently part of the job. Their travel is the best way to create and maintain contacts, survey new markets, pick up new business ideas, and carry out and finalize deals. Trips are an investment in present and future business.

For the leisure traveler, travel is nearly always associated with recreation and escape from everyday life—a chance to see new places and make new acquaintances. In contrast to business trips, vacations are planned far in advance and are seldom changed. For the tourist, the price is a very important factor. The trip itself is part of the pleasure. The pattern of leisure travel is somewhat different, too.

Demand often rises during recessions, possibly because households reduce investments in capital goods and spend their money instead on leisure pursuits. Business and tourist travel patterns show wide seasonal variations by month, week, and day. The businessperson prefers to travel between Monday and Friday, while tourists plan their excursions for weekends and holiday periods. Destinations also vary by customer category.

The cargo market is very sensitive to general economic developments and usually reflects overall industrial trends. Cargo services are a part of the customer's production resources in the field of logistics. The customer makes a precise estimate of the cost of materials handling, inventories, and capital in the purchasing process. Speed gives air cargo a competitive edge.

Three other complementary strategies formed part of the marginal strategy:

- Concentration—a traffic program focusing on destinations where SAS was strong, eliminating unprofitable or unpromising routes.
- Selective marketing—promoting vigorously in selected markets domestically and internationally. Budget directed at the business traveler.
- Trading—trading services with other airlines on a cooperative basis to offer a product bigger and better than SAS could with its own resources.
- Cargo—using research to emulate the passenger-service approach.

Trim 82 Cost Reduction Program

Part of the new venture was a cost-cutting campaign called "Trim 82." Its goals were to reduce administration costs by $30 million a year, primarily in overhead functions. Carlzon refused to engage in a general centralized cost-cutting exercise, pointing out that this would only become a pointless exercise if departments would have the same percentage of costs taken out of them irrespective of their importance to the new business strategy.

Therefore, rather than simply hand down an across-the-board instruction calling for a percentage cut in budgets, the implementation team launched a search for opportunities to do more with less. Overheads were cut mainly in administration. Redundant staff either left, were given an opportunity to retire early, or filled newly created jobs on the front line.

As part of the trim exercise, 10 aircraft were leased or sold; three 747s, three DC-8s, and four A300 airbuses. This was coupled with a reduction in pilots; "the surplus list," as it was referred to, amounting to "enough people to man an entire minor carrier fleet."

The Culture Revolution

Carlzon's "little red book," as it came to be known, was the first step in involving all employees within the company in the new wave of thinking. He wanted to find a way to communicate to all levels in the organization that SAS was in a serious crisis, fighting for its life, and get them to understand what he wanted to do about it.

The strategic plan was handed over to the advertising agency to put in more creative terms, and what came out was a booklet in cartoon form called "Let's Get in There and Fight" that detailed the airline's financial condition, the vision for the future, and the plan for delegating responsibility to front-line employees.

People were somewhat surprised in the beginning at the unusual form of the communication but in time they got used to it and came to expect it. Resistance was mainly on the technical side of the operation, especially from the older pilots. Expectations were lifted and morale improved. And this internal PR was reinforced by interest in the project taken up by the mass media.

Carlzon and his team personally visited front-liners all over the SAS system. A training company was hired to put 20,000 managers and employees through a two-day training program designed to give them a sense of the organization's purpose and their role in the new concept.

It became clear, quite early on, that culturally for many Scandinavians the service idea was not regarded as professional. The concept of differentiating service for different customers was particularly foreign to their "jamlikhet" feelings of egalitarianism.

Before launching the mass training phase, Carlzon had hosted an intensive three-week gathering of his top 120 executives and 30 of the senior union representatives. Training for middle managers proceeded more or less in tandem with the front-liner program, with supervisors joining performance-level people at large sessions of 100 people or more.

In the organization structure introduced in August 1981 (see Exhibits 6A–6C), Carlzon erased the pyramid and redrew his concept of the new organization as a kind of wheel with the CEO at the hub and operating departments revolving around him. Front-line workers with the most customer contact had formally been at the bottom of the chart. Carlzon put them on top. It became everyone else's responsibility, including his, to "serve" those who directly served the customer.

Strong emphasis was given in the new organization to delegating responsibility down the line where Carlzon believed competent result-oriented managers should be well-informed personnel who could work without supervision. In his own words, he wanted to put workers in charge and management to serve as consultant to the organization. An internal consulting group was set up and asked to work directly with management all over the company to help overcome obstacles and move ahead the various projects.

The company was divided into various profit centers, varying in size from the airline division down to the particular route. A route manager was regarded as an entrepreneur who was free to decide the time and number of flights between two cities, contingent on the approval of the governments involved, and who could lease the airplanes and flight crews from other divisions.

Carlzon actively tried to encourage initiative on the part of staff. For example, as one of the stories goes, he applauded a pilot, whose plane was grounded by a sit-down strike on the Copenhagen runway, who responded by opening the bar, taking the passengers on a guided tour of the airport perimeter, and pointing out interesting sights.

"Instructions," Carlzon said, "only succeed in providing employees with knowledge of their own limitations. Information, on the other hand, provides them with a knowledge of their opportunities and possibilities. . . . To free someone from rigorous control by instructions, policies, and orders, and to give that person freedom to take responsibility for his ideas, decisions, and actions, is to release hidden resources which would otherwise remain inaccessible to both the individual and the company. . . . A person who has information cannot avoid taking responsibility."

Carlzon, reputed to be strongly influenced by what he had read in Peters and Waterman's *In Search of Excellence,* sometime during 1983, started to think about the need to formalize a new corporate culture for SAS. Remarks one executive: "He had introduced lots of projects to change results, but he knew it wouldn't last forever. He wanted something more to cement the program. But the culture had already changed the attitudes to service and the customer in particular. It was too theoretical. We didn't want to be professors of philosophy, and the culture program finally petered out."

New Corporate Identity Program

In April 1983, the New Corporate Identity Program was launched at Oslo's Fornebu airport with a presentation of a DC-9 in the carrier's new livery. A proposal to change the name to "Royal Scandinavia," emphasizing the monarchical element of the three nations rather than the socialist, had been rejected by the SAS board; but the dragon that had been on the side of the SAS aircraft since 1946 had vanished. Likewise, the Viking image SAS had nurtured for years had been put to rest as it was felt that too many people outside Scandinavia associated Vikings with violence.

Consultants were called in to help formulate and design the new image. Calvin Klein, known for his universal appeal, was asked to come up with a sophisticated restyling for uniforms that would fit with the business passenger (see Exhibit 7).

The old familiar logotype was essentially retained because it was so well-known, but bold shapes in colors of the three nations' flags were added. Airplanes were painted white "to make them look larger than life and bigger than

the competition." All execution elements of the exercise were coordinated in a corporate identity manual, from logo to baggage labels, seating to ticket offices, to standardize SAS's visual expression worldwide. Management announced that the exercise was more than a graphic facelift. There was also, they reasoned, a good economic reason for the physical changes in the SAS image, since the exercise had saved the company many millions of kroner by extending the working life of its DC-9 fleet into the 1990s.

New Marketing Projects

To compete more vigorously, new ways of expanding its range of products through more extensive coordination among the various units of the SAS Group were developed. In addition, SAS emphasized the need for ongoing and new approaches to the products and services the company should market.

Total Travel Package

The focus on the business target market during 1982 led to a new idea—the extension of the concept to include a total travel package of all services needed by business travelers from point A to point B. The object was to cater not only to the customers' needs on the air journey itself but also on the trip to and from the airport, at the airport while waiting for the flight, and on the journey to the hotel at the other end: "an unbroken chain of services."

In 1983, when the first airline check-in in a hotel was tested in the Hotel Scandinavia in Copenhagen, consumers responded with enthusiasm. Then the concept was formally introduced to management. Either SAS owned or else appointed hotels to be involved in the scheme. A limousine service was introduced to and from airports.

Distribution

A distribution program was begun in 1985. The main objective was to allocate resources to ensure that SAS could keep up technologically with what was starting to take place in the market. This meant finding ways to control the distribution network either via travel agents, SAS's own ticket offices, or home and office computer terminals.

In Search of a New Aircraft

Carlzon announced in mid-1983 in Los Angeles that his company and American Airlines were negotiating with McDonnell-Douglas, Boeing, and Airbus Industrie of Europe to design a 120-passenger jetliner to carry business travelers in the early 1990s.

Carlzon's vision was a craft which he called a "passenger pleasing plane" of an unorthodox design, with 75–80 percent of the interior volume of the fuselage allocated to passenger comfort and in-cabin baggage storage, compared to the 35 percent allocated then. He said: "For the 1990s, our starting point is that we need an aircraft which the passenger wants. Then we can add on engines and the cockpit, not the other way around."

In a news conference prior to an address to Scandinavian businessmen, Carlzon picked up a model of a narrow-bodied plane, turned it on its side, and said: "This is what I see. The floor is lower; the roof higher. Seating would be no more than two seats abreast with an aisle. Belly space for the baggage would be reduced because there would be wardrobes for the traveler. Businessmen don't want to wait for luggage." He said he was looking beyond what was being built and what was on the drawing board for the business traveler. Unconcerned about the age of his fleet, his view was that, when SAS was ready to introduce new planes, the competition would have to go on using their old ones, because planes must last for at least 10 years.

Results

By the end of 1982, SAS presented an almost unrecognizable picture (see Exhibits 8–13). The airline had become the most punctual in Europe, as well as the number 1 choice for Scandinavian business travelers. Its full-fare passengers had increased by 8 percent in Europe and 16 percent in the zero-growth intercontinental market.

In the process, corporate overheads had been reduced by 25 percent. This resulted in a before-tax turnaround of $80 million, from a $10 million loss to a $70 million profit. With allowances made for extraordinary capital gain in 1982 from the sale of surplus aircraft, profits for 1982–83 increased by 65 percent.

At that point SAS was flying between Scandinavia and 30 destinations in European capitals, a market worth 8–10 million passengers annually. Their share was just over 50 percent. The total passenger revenue had risen by 31 percent, compared to 1981-1982, and the European network accounted for 40 percent of the airline's total traffic revenue. Intercontinental accounted for 27 percent of the revenue and domestic passengers 16 percent of overall revenue. Share of the intercontinental market amounted to 50 percent.

Fortune magazine in the summer of 1983 (see Exhibit 14) tested all the airlines in the world with business class and rated SAS highest. A few months later, SAS won the Airline of the Year award at a special ceremony in New York. The award was made by *Air Transport World*, the international trade and consumer magazine, for SAS's "overall excellence" and its "outstanding service to the traveling public." The magazine stressed SAS's marketing innovations "and its quest for dominance in business travel markets" as well as its financial and technical management.

EXHIBIT 1

*Revenues and
expenses—1980–81*

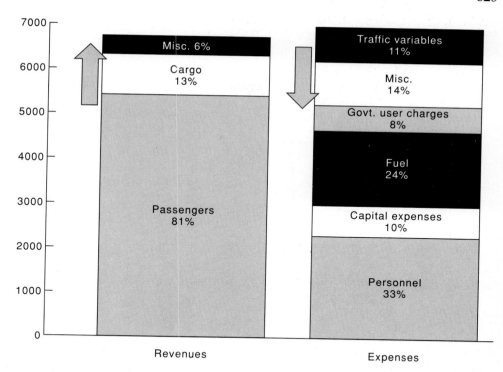

Old System   New System

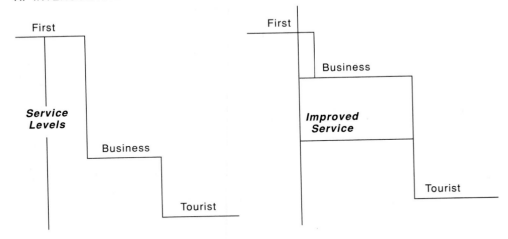

A. INTERCONTINENTAL

B. EUROPE

Nᴏᴛᴇ: Elimination of first class travel (Europe only). Euroclass is not equivalent to the old first class.

Exhibit 3A Ranking of Services at Time of Reservation

	Very Important	Important	Less Important	Not Important	No Answer
Nonstop	67	31	1	0	2
Time of departure/arrival	73	23	2	0	3
Seat reservation	12	13	39	23	15
Aircraft type	3	19	46	17	16

Exhibit 3B Ranking of Services at the Airport

	Very Important	Important	Less Important	Not Important	No Answer
Punctuality	88	11	0	0	2
Time at check-in	45	46	5	0	5
Separate check-in	31	38	21	4	8
Separate lounge	14	19	42	14	13

Exhibit 3C Ranking of Services on Board

	Very Important	Important	Less Important	Not Important	No Answer
Seating comfort	63	34	2	0	3
Cabin attendants	34	57	5	0	3
Separate cabin	34	38	18	5	7
Working possibilities	27	45	17	3	10
Meals	17	57	14	3	10
Choice of meals	5	11	54	15	17
Newspapers	12	35	28	13	13
China and cutlery	4	33	32	18	14
Free drinks	3	11	42	28	18
Professional magazines	1	6	43	32	18

Exhibit 3D Ranking of Services for Cargo Shipments

	Most Important
Contact Service	
• Information feedback	63%
• Acceptance and delivery of shipments	42
• Fast documentation	31
• Cooperation ability	31
• Telephone service	24
• Confirmed booking	22
• Handling time of claims	21
Regularity, Safety	
• Reliable delivery times	40%
• Speedy terminal handling	25
• Frequent departures	20

Note: Figures do not alway add up to 100.

EXHIBIT 4A

If airline seats make you feel like this, try ours for size

If airline seats make you feel like this, try ours for size.

Our new Business Class will fit you very nicely even if you're pushing six feet or more.

Your seat is in a truly separate Business Class cabin.

You get lots of room to stretch your legs in and a seat that you can tilt back that little bit extra when you want to take a nap.

But this is just the beginning of our story.

Listen.

We have hired six of Europe's most famous chefs to compose your meals. And believe us, they will be a pleasant surprise. Just as pleasant as our new wine cellar.

On the ground we have opened Business Service Lounges for you. Here you can relax with a cup of tea, perk yourself up with a cup of strong coffee or have a cocktail.

In some you can even sit down to work with a phone at your elbow, borrow a typewriter, send a telex or get copies made.

Why do we go to all this trouble?

We're the Businessman's Airline, that's why.

And as we travel quite a lot ourselves, we know how nice it is when someone bothers to take the bugs out of travelling.

And as we don't want you to have to go hunting for small change in your coat up above your head, all drinks, wine and beer are on the house.

All you have to do is fly full fare economy.

Then it's all yours.

SAS
SCANDINAVIAN AIRLINES
The Businessman's Airline

629

EXHIBIT 5

Task and timing map

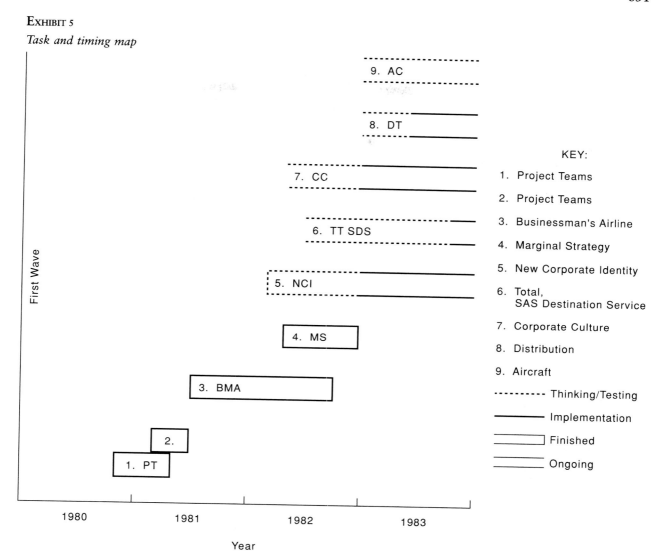

KEY:

1. Project Teams
2. Project Teams
3. Businessman's Airline
4. Marginal Strategy
5. New Corporate Identity
6. Total,
   SAS Destination Service
7. Corporate Culture
8. Distribution
9. Aircraft

- - - - - Thinking/Testing

———— Implementation

Finished

Ongoing

632

EXHIBIT 6A

SAS group organization structures

1. Prior to November 1980

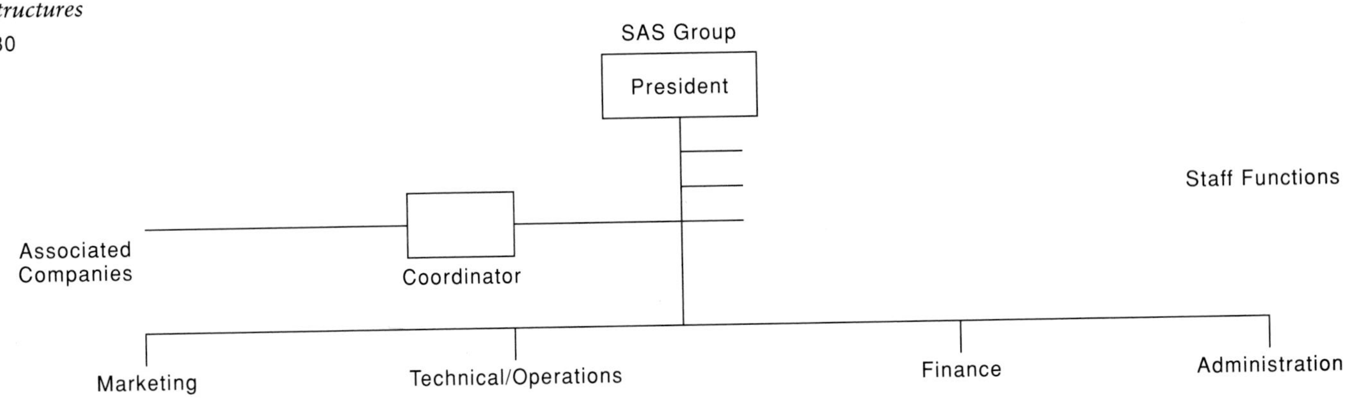

2. November 1, 1980 – March 31, 1981

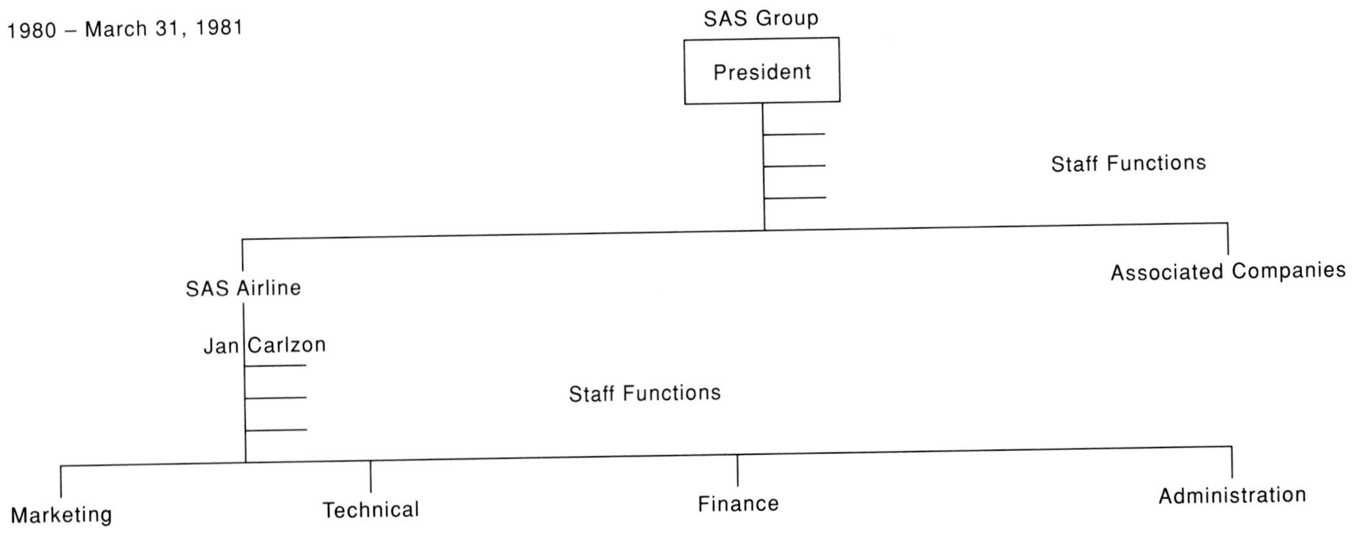

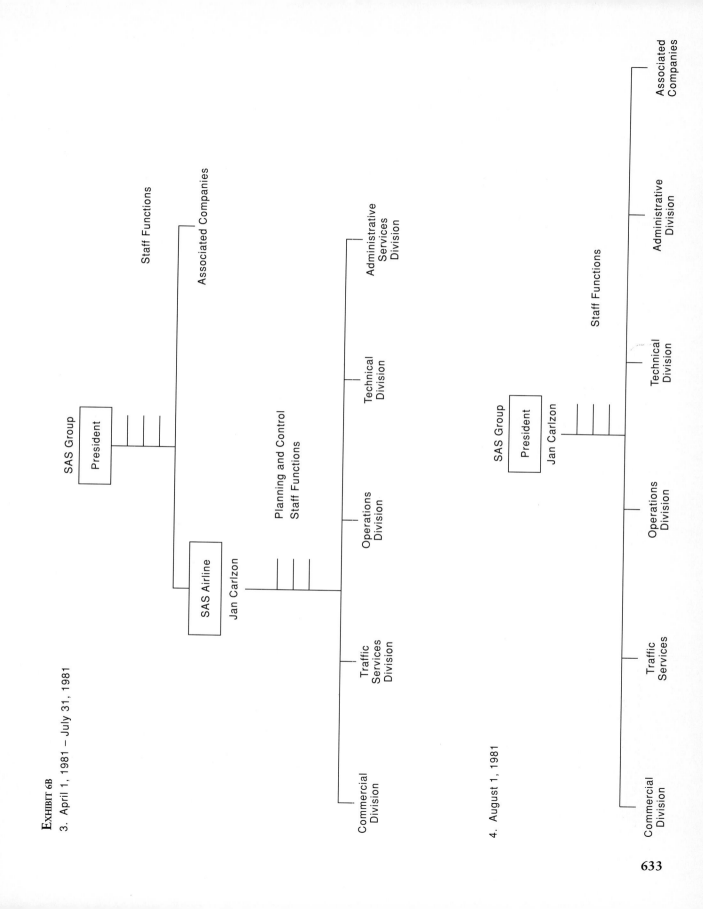

SAS Group

President

Staff Functions

Associated Companies

SAS Airline

Jan Carlzon

Commercial Division

Traffic Services Division

Operations Division

Planning and Control Staff Functions

Technical Division

Administrative Services Division

4. August 1, 1981

SAS Group

President

Jan Carlzon

Staff Functions

Commercial Division

Traffic Services

Operations Division

Technical Division

Administrative Division

Associated Companies

EXHIBIT 6C
The SAS organization—August 1981

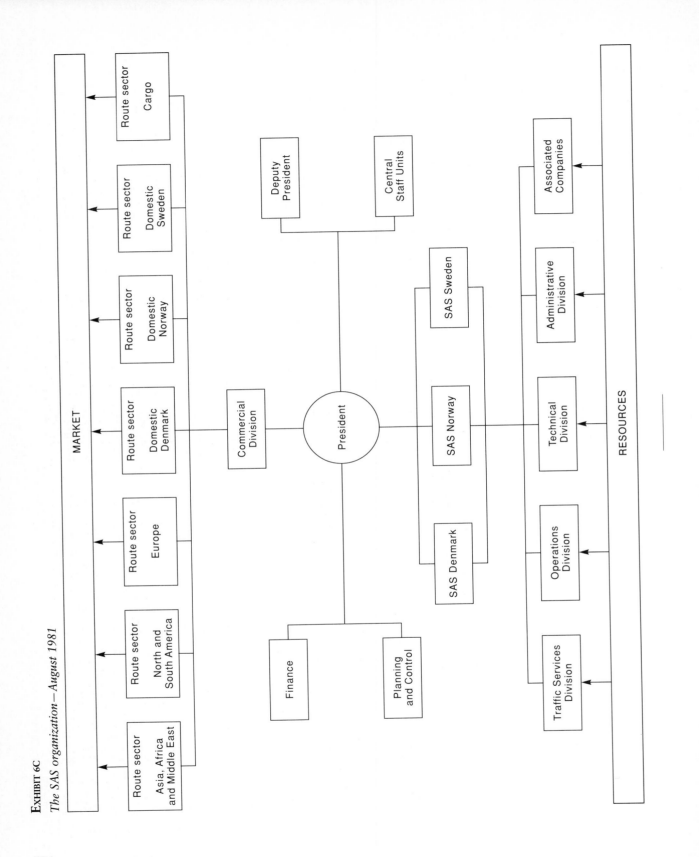

EXHIBIT 7

Newspaper accounts of the New Corporate Identity Program

CREW'S WEAR

DAILY NEWS RECORD, April 14, 1983

FLY ME, I'll CALL IN: Following in the jet stream of Halston, who did the uniforms for Braniff Airlines several years ago, Calvin Klein has announced he's designing a complete personnel wardrobe for Scandinavian Airlines System. The appropriately sleek, streamlined SAS uniforms bear the designer's unmistakably sporty signature — including poplin raincoats, gabardine overcoats, navy wool cardigan sweaters, button-lapel jackets and white stock-tie blouses, all worn with pants or skirts in navy serge or gray gabardine for summer.

WOMEN'S WEAR DAILY
April 13, 1983

SAS Kills Off Its Dragon In Unveiling New Look

Special to THE WALL STREET JOURNAL
OSLO, Norway — Scandinavian Airlines System is killing off its dragon to become a Norse of a different color.

SAS, the joint carrier for Denmark, Norway and Sweden, unveiled its new image by showing off the first plane of its fleet to be painted white with slanting stripes of red, blue and yellow – the flag colors of the three Scandinavian nations – at the front of the fuselage. The new look is part of a $13 million corporate facelift that includes new blue interiors for the aircraft and uniforms designed to make SAS pilots look a bit more military and stewardesses more stylish.

There isn't any place in the new scheme of things for the old design of the SAS viking dragon. "We discovered that people tend to regard the dragon as a snake, and that isn't a good image," said the SAS president, Jan Carlzon. "Or if they associate it with vikings, they're reminded of pirates storming ashore on missions of pillage and rape. And that isn't us."

THE WALL STREET JOURNAL,
April 14, 1983

EXHIBIT 8   Profit and Loss Statements—October 1 to September 30 (in Skr. millions)

	1982/1983	1981/1982	1980/1981
Traffic revenue	10463.1	8442.3	6823.0
Other revenue	2137.3	1559.7	1181.0
Operating revenue	12600.4	10002.0	8004.0
Operating expenses	11583.7	−9277.2	−7618.7
Operating result before depreciation	−1016.7	724.8	385.3
Depreciation	−398.8	−408.6	−370.2
Operating result after depreciation	617.9	316.2	15.1
Dividends from subsidiaries	21.6	7.4	6.7
Other dividends received	1.0	0.7	0.6
Other financial income	247.3	231.2	135.7
Financial expenses	−426.9	−362.8	−267.3
Profit/loss after financial income and expenses	460.9	192.7	−109.2
Gain on sale & retirement of equipment, etc.	11.2	59.8[b]	12.8
Extraordinary income	—	95.8[c]	103.9[a]
Extraordinary expenses	−10.3	−12.3	−12.9
Extraordinary depreciation	—	—	−103.6[a]
Profit/loss before allocations and taxes	461.8	336.0	−109.0

[a]The extraordinary income includes Skr. 103.9 million for unredeemed tickets. Simultaneously, Skr. 103.6 million was depreciated on surplus flight equipment due to excess capacity and the difficult market for used aircraft.

[b]This included half the profit made on the sale of a Boeing 747B aircraft in January 1982. The aircraft was based back for five years. At the time of sale, Skr. 53.3 million was credited, the balance of Skr. 49.6 million was deferred to be credited to income over the lease period.

[c]A pension bonus of Skr. 98.8 million was received in Denmark. This was a refund for the five-year period 1977–81.

EXHIBIT 9   Airline Results (in Skr. millions)

MSEK	1980–1981	1981–1982	1982–1983
Total revenue	8,004	10,002	12,600
Result after financial income and expenses	−109	+193	+461
Sale of equipment and extraordinary items	0	+143	+1
Result before allocations and taxes	−109	+336	+462

EXHIBIT 10

Result—punctuality

• SAS is Europe's most punctual airline!

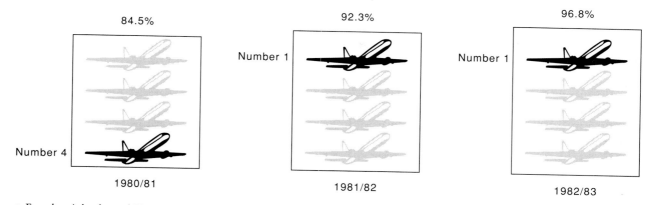

• Fornebu, Arlanda, and Kastrup—the most punctual airports in Europe, month after month.

EXHIBIT 11   Traffic Handled by European Carriers— 1980 to 1983

	Change (Percent of Last Year)		
	1980–1981	*1981–1982*	*1982–1983*
Total European Market	+4%	±0	−3%
SAS	+1	±0	+5
SAS (Euroclass)	−3	+7%	+5
SAS (Tourist Class)	+5	−5	+5

EXHIBIT 12   **Intercontinental Passengers**

	Percent Change from Previous Year Total Number Passenger Miles	Share of Total SAS Passengers	
	1982–1983	*1981–1982*	*1982–1983*
First Class	−18%	3%	3%
"First Business Class"	+11	24	27
Discounted Fares	−3	73	70

EXHIBIT 13   **Production, Traffic, and Cabin Factor**

		1982–1983 vs. 1981–1982		Cabin Factor	
		Production	*Passenger Traffic*	*1981–1982*	*1982–1983*
Europe	AEA	−0.9%	−1.4%	57.5%	57.2%
	SAS	±0	+5.8	56.9	59.8
Intercontinental	AEA	+0.1	−0.5	64.7	64.4
	SAS	−3.2	−0.5	66.6	68.4

NOTE: AEA = Association of European Airlines.

EXHIBIT 14 What You Pay, What You Get

Airline	In-flight Amenities			On-ground Amenities							Charge
	Seat Width	Distance between Seats	Choice of Entrees	Separate Check-in	Special Baggage Handling	Lounge	Open Bar	Copying Machine	Work Area		Over or (Under) Economy
Air Canada	17–18"	34"	o	o	o						0
Air One	25"	36–37"	o	NA	NA						0
American	18"	35–37"	o	o	NA						$30
Midway Metrolink	22"	34"		o	NA						($116)
Pan American	18½"	37–38"	o	o	o	o	o	o	o		7–18%
Republic	20"	36"	o	o	o	o		o	o		$10
TWA	20¼"	38"	o	o	o	o					$10–$30
United	21"	36–38"	o	o	o	o	o				40%
Aer Lingus	18"	39"	o	o	o	o					31%
Air Canada	20½"	39"	o	o	o	o					8%–18%
Air France	18"	34"	o	o	o	o	o				13%
Alitalia	19½"	35"	o	o	o	o	o				20%
American	18"	35–37"	o	o	o	o	o				42%
British Airways	24"	35"	o	o	o		o				117%
Japan Air Lines	20½–24"	34–37"	o	o	o	o					12½%
KLM	18"	37"	o	o	o						14%
Lufthansa	18"	37"	o	o	o						6%
Northwest Orient	19–21½"	34–56"	o	o	o						10%
Pan American	18½"	34–37"	o	o	o						12%–26%
Qantas	22"	38"	o	o	o	o					13%
SAS	19"	38"	o	o	o	o	o	o	o		0
Singapore	19½"	36"	o	o	o	o	o		o		10%
Thai	23"	42"	o	o	o	o	o				12½%
TWA	21"	38"	o	o	o	o	o				22%–50%
United	19"	36–38"	o	o	o	o	o				10%–12%
Varig	18"	38"	o	o	o		o				7%–12%

NA = Not applicable.

o = An amenity included in the service.

North American routes, business-class fares don't greatly exceed much – and Midway Metrolink charges less than competitors do for econo-class. On intercontinental flights, the charges listed for U.S. carriers and Canada are for frequently traveled routes. Other airline's intercontinental fares are for flights between the United States and principal cities in their home countries. British Airway's 117% surcharge is for the New York-to-London route, where economy fares are so low that all airlines tack on a large extra charge for business class. Seat widths vary a lot; by comparison, coach seats are typically 18 inches wide. The measurement between seats is from seat back to seat back, an indication of leg room.

SOURCE: *Fortune*, August 22, 1983.

Titanium Industries, Inc.: Titanium Fabrication Division (A)

In mid-June 1978, the senior management at Titanium Fabrication (TiFab) Division of Titanium Industries, Inc., was grappling with a problem unprecedented in the company's six-year history. Because of an acute shortage of capacity and increasing customer dissatisfaction with late deliveries, the company's marketing vice president, Newell Orr, and TiFab's vice president of operations, James McMaster, had to agree on which of four potential orders the company should accept and how it should bid on them. Each of the orders represented a different customer situation, mix of labor and materials, and mix of manufacturing talents, so a direct comparison among them was difficult. Robert Kane, Titanium Industries' president, had advised them to work it out themselves, but reminded them that a quick decision was necessary "if we're going to be able to fit *any* of them into our shop schedule."

Titanium Fabrication Division

Early History.   The TiFab Division was the second largest industrial fabricator of titanium in the United States. Corporate and sales offices for the company, as well as TiFab's primary fabricating facility, were located in Fairfield, New Jersey. The company had been formed from the industrial marketing group and technical laboratory people at Titanium Metals Corporation's (TIMET) Application Development Center in 1972, when the latter cut back its operations after cancellation of the American supersonic transport program.

The birth of Titanium Industries coincided with the first real growth of industrial use of titanium. Before 1972, titanium had been used almost exclusively in the aerospace industry because of its light weight and high strength. It wasn't until the price dropped (from $20 per pound for some alloys used in aerospace to $5 per pound for industrial titanium sheet and plate) and its corrosion resistance was demonstrated, however, that titanium became competitive for some applications with stainless steel, copper and nickel alloys, brick-lined steel, fiberglass, and other products used to counter corrosion. Even in 1978, titanium won the industrial applications battle only if (1) it could outlast competitive metals to such an extent that it was less expensive overall or (2) it was the only industrial metal that could

do the job. Nevertheless, Kane was enthusiastic about titanium's potential and estimated that its industrial use would grow by 15 to 20 percent per year during the foreseeable future.

Growth.   From its inception, Titanium Industries' principal business was fabrication of titanium equipment for industrial corrosion-resistant applications. The company had little involvement in the aerospace industry. Over time it added technical staff, participated in industry symposia, sponsored technical papers, and studied developing titanium markets. Active consulting and field services, such as field repairs and corrosion analysis, developed from these efforts.

In addition to the TiFab business, Titanium Industries sold titanium metal and specialty hardware (pipe fittings, bolts, nuts, pipe flanges) to the industrial market. The two organizations shared a common raw materials inventory. The corporation also purchased titanium in ingot and semi-finished form and converted it (using steel mills, which rented time on their machinery on a price-per-pound basis) to finished product forms, such as bars or plates. As business expanded, these activities were separated into a materials profit center that included metal trading, warehousing, and conversion.

In 1973, and again in 1975, capacity expansions were made in Fairfield and efforts toward geographic expansion followed. Between 1975 and 1977, a subsidiary was formed in Montreal; a branch was opened in Houston to serve the petrochemical markets; and a small, bankrupt titanium wire mill in Pennsylvania was acquired. In addition, a small subsidiary was formed in Brazil to take advantage of the rapid expansion of basic industries, such as pulp, occurring there. (Exhibit 1 provides corporate financial data.)

Organization.   TiFab's Operations was headed by James McMaster (who previously had been involved in Titanium Industries' marketing area). It consisted of two engineers who evaluated customer product designs to determine the best manufacturing processes; two drafting people; two estimators who calculated the cost of manufacture for pricing; and several administrative and clerical people. In addition, Operations' shop, which was nonunion, had 78 employees in three sections: fabrication, welding, and the machine shop. Additional fabrication capacity was available in the Houston and Montreal facilities, but these were primarily intended to serve their respective regional markets and were operating at full capacity through 1978.

This case was prepared by Research Assistant Craig E. Cline and Associate Professor Benson P. Shapiro.
Copyright © 1978 by the President and Fellows of Harvard College.
Harvard Business School case 578-208 (Rev. 1/87).

Titanium Industries' marketing organization was headed by Newell Orr; it included two regional managers located in Fairfield and Houston, the titanium metal sales group, and a customer service function. In addition, the company was represented by several manufacturers' representatives who operated both in the United States and abroad.[1] (Exhibit 2 shows the organization chart for both Titanium Industries and TiFab.)

Markets and Customers

TiFab had over 90 significant customers in 11 markets:

1. General chemicals—pressure vessels, tanks, heat exchangers, shafts and mixers, pumps, valves, piping, blowers, anodes for chlorine.
2. Pulp and paper—bleaching equipment, chemical preparation vessels, piping.
3. Basic metals—cathodes for copper, vessels for hydrometallurgy.
4. Petroleum—heat exchangers for refineries, down-hole equipment, hot-oil coolers for production.
5. Pollution—heat exchangers, vessels, and pipe for municipal waste oxidation; air scrubbers, blowers.
6. Fibers—chemical equipment for various polymer intermediate products.
7. Water desalinization—heat exchangers, tubing, piping.
8. Marine activities—high-voltage undersea electrical connectors, diver rescue chambers, research submarine components.
9. Electric power generation—tubes for surface condensers.
10. Food—corrosion-resistant equipment for pickle solutions.
11. High-performance toys—12-meter sailboat parts, race cars, golf clubs.

The majority of TiFab's customers were located within a 500-mile radius of Fairfield, but the firm also shipped worldwide. Customer orders ranged from $25 to $2 million, with $50,000 being typical. Approximately 20 percent of TiFab's customers provided 80 percent of its business.

Close business and personal relationships existed between the TiFab staff and certain customers who gave TiFab a considerable percentage of their titanium business. One customer, Refco, typically represented 15 to 20 percent of TiFab's sales each year. Two other companies ac-

counted for 10 to 15 percent of TiFab's sales on a fairly regular basis. In early 1977, TiFab's management established a corporate policy of allowing a maximum of 20 percent of its business to reside with one customer and 30 percent to be in one market area.

Competition

TiFab had five major competitors, not one of which was located in the immediate area. The largest was in Ohio and had annual sales of $16.5 million. The others were scattered across the country and had annual sales of between $2 million and $10 million in competitive titanium work, with $6 million being average. TiFab had an estimated 16 percent share of a total industrial titanium fabrication market of just under $50 million. It had a reputation for a higher quality, but also a higher price, than most of its competitors.

Forecasts

Titanium Industries' sales and equity had grown steadily from 1972 to 1975, but 1976 sales were disappointing. In 1977, despite record sales of $10.4 million, the company experienced its first net loss. Management felt that the 1976 and 1977 results were more a consequence of erratic pricing and unstable market conditions than internal problems. The titanium industry had been operating at a significantly lower level than in 1974 and 1975. Capital spending on process equipment, refinery expansion, pulp and paper projects, and chemical construction had been well below anticipated levels in 1977 and was not expected to increase significantly in 1978.

Manufacturing Process

Although titanium had several fabricating peculiarities that required special skills, some operations—such as shearing, machine work, and forming—closely paralleled those used in precision fabrication of certain stainless steels.[2] In fact, the company often was able to subcontract excess machine work to local precision machine shops. Heat treatment, thermal cutting, and especially welding were generally considered the most difficult operations. Because titanium was a "reactive" metal, it was easily embrittled by increases in its gas content (primarily oxygen and nitrogen, but also most other elements). Melting titanium, such as in welding, or heating it above 1,200°F caused it to react instantly with air, absorbing oxygen and nitrogen and becoming brittle

---

[1]A manufacturers' representative was an independent company or salesperson who sold products of related but noncompeting companies for commissions on the sales.

---

[2]Shearing was cutting titanium sheets to a specified size. Machining used lathes, mills, drills, and other chip-forming high-precision tools to obtain close tolerances. Forming, done on plate or bar rolls or on a press brake, bent the item to its ultimate shape.

and useless. Consequently, cleanliness and special inert-gas welding techniques were required to produce good welds.

TiFab used its strong competence in welding as a major selling point. One executive noted, "We feel that our expertise lies in high-quality welding. Over 80 percent of our jobs involve welding." This reputation for outstanding welding was supported routinely by radiographic, ultrasonic, and liquid penetration inspection of each weld.

The company had 33 welders who were graded from A to D, according to their ability to handle difficult work. In addition, TiFab had several automatic welding machines. Finally, various helpers and trainees assisted the welders. (TiFab's Operations' shop capacity is shown in Exhibit 3.)

Costs.   Generally a product's cost had five components, with manufacturing overhead averaging about 200 percent of direct labor cost:

Component	Range	Average
Raw material	30–65%	45%
Direct labor	5–20	9
Manufacturing overhead	10–40	18
Subcontracting	10–15	12
General and administrative costs and profit	10–25	16

The company's objective was to have cost of goods average 80 percent, with 85 percent the upper limit.

Existing Situation.   TiFab's shop backlog had reached a critical level in June 1978 (see Exhibit 4). This was the first time the company's booking exceeded its capacity by a significant margin. TiFab's delivery history for the past several months had been, in the word of one Operations executive, "horrendous." Although routine orders were going out on time, most major or complex jobs were late. Delivery times had increased from an average of 8–10 weeks in 1974 to 16–60 weeks, depending on complexity and size, in 1977. Another Operations executive added, "The main reason many customers are still coming back to us is our quality. There also aren't many other people who fabricate titanium."

According to a third Operations official, one factor underlying TiFab's capacity problem was the difficulty the company had hiring and training qualified welders.

> The labor market around Fairfield and our need for highly skilled workers make it difficult to find new people, especially because we can't offer much higher than average pay. The competition's shops are generally located in less expensive areas, and we must be careful to keep our labor costs competitive. Even hiring a new welder as part of our regular work force is difficult. If we're lucky, we can find one or two a month. Then it takes between two months and two years to train them to be

A level, depending on whether they were welders before. For many jobs the welders must also qualify under the ASME Boiler Code, which is expensive but necessary for A and B level welders. This situation is even more critical because the majority of our jobs require A and B level welding.

This official felt, however, that the major underlying factor was TiFab's lack of reliable information on the shop's actual capacity at any given moment.

> In the past, Marketing would ask us if we had capacity available for a job before they quoted on it. But in recent months late material deliveries and problems on two major jobs have swelled our backlog, which has extended delivery dates on existing jobs. These fill the capacity Marketing thought would be open for the jobs we had just bid, thereby pushing ahead *their* delivery dates. Consequently, Marketing no longer believes our capacity forecasts; they simply go ahead and book the order for the longest delivery they can get away with, which, of course, adds to our capacity problem. It's a vicious cycle.

McMaster concurred with his subordinates; he felt Marketing only recently had become realistic about the capacity limit and, thus, willing to work with Operations to improve the company's delivery schedule. He observed:

> We started TiFab because we were excited by what we could do in the industrial market. In fact, Bob Kane has made it our basic operating philosophy "to make money by moving titanium." It's been fun, and that's largely what kept us going— until now. At present we are faced with declining profits and a delivery crisis. Something has to be done, and perhaps being more selective in taking orders will do it.

From an Operations standpoint, he felt several criteria could make an order attractive to TiFab:

1. The job is technically challenging.
2. The job fits with TiFab's high-quality image and capabilities.
3. The company's engineering expertise is utilized.
4. The job is long run and repetitive.
5. The company has experience with similar products.
6. Specifications and job scope are clear.
7. For larger orders, progress payments can be negotiated (payments made on labor and material as applied, over the course of the contract, rather than all at the end).
8. Overall contribution before S.G.&A. (sales, general, and administrative expenses) is near 20 percent of the product's price.

Marketing

TiFab fabrication and titanium metal sales were under the direction of Newell Orr in Marketing. He spent an estimated 60 percent of his time on TiFab sales and the remainder on metal sales. Similarly, the two regional sales managers each devoted 10 percent of their time to TiFab sales, and a manufacturers' representative in California handled both TiFab products and titanium metal sales. Generally, however, TiFab relied on advertising in trade publications, participation in industry symposia, and trade shows for fabrication sales. Also, Kane, McMaster, Orr, and other staff people who had close relationships with customers usually handled their accounts personally. McMaster, for example, had close ties with certain Refco officials and, thus, handled all but the smallest details of this account. As one executive observed, "Most of the management people here have two or three job functions, and almost anyone can make a sale."

Bidding Process.   One of the principal tasks of the people in Marketing and Sales was to make sure that TiFab was on the bid lists of potential customers. Once a request for a quote was received, Marketing sent it to Operations for estimating (to obtain a quote as well as an estimated delivery date). Marketing then modified the quote to reflect market conditions and corporate goals.

The company had a bid success rate of 15 percent. Orr felt this percentage was somewhat low, compared with the industry average, but pointed out that only one of seven requests for quotes was "solid." He thought a more serious problem was the price competitiveness that had recently gripped the market, forcing TiFab to play pricing games.

> Our aggressive posture has been a reaction to forces in the market more than a philosophy. As the titanium market stabilizes, which I'm sure it will eventually do, we will be better able to formulate an effective, rather than a freewheeling, reactive strategy about taking orders. This is a serious concern of mine, because we haven't been able to maintain market share in the last year. We've got to pick our shots better—but we can only become more selective if we get the opportunity to call the shots.

Possible Changes.   Orr felt that the company had to become more selective about the high-risk custom jobs it took; he was also in favor of diversifying TiFab's business among customers and markets. "We have an excellent relationship with Refco, but what do we do if they represent 30 to 40 percent of our business and then suddenly stop sending us orders?" He believed TiFab would eventually move away from custom fabrication and become more involved in developing proprietary products. He also felt that the company had to pin down its costs more accurately. "We've got to target our markets better to be sure we are using our resources to their maximum potential." To do this, he felt that Marketing had to get better information out of TiFab's Operations concerning costs and capacity availability.

Orr's preferred criteria for taking an order were as follows:

1. The job is similar to what TiFab had built before.
2. The design is simple and the cost estimate reliable.

3. The job has good payment terms (progress payments on labor and material as applied).
4. The market area has potential for further development.
5. The job allows adequate delivery time.
6. Price is not the primary factor in the customer's decision.

The Four Prospective Fabrication Orders

In mid-June 1978, Orr and McMaster met to decide whether to accept each of the prospective orders: Refco, Pierce-Pike, Worldwide Paper, and Kathco. Prices were fixed for the larger two orders but still had to be determined for the smaller two. In addition, both Orr and McMaster had been uneasy about the entire bidding process and wondered if it should be changed. McMaster, for example, thought perhaps the company should expect a greater markup on labor than on materials. He went on to explain that the material cost estimates tended to be much more reliable than the labor estimates. He mused:

> I think that we should be paid more for the greater uncertainty of the labor estimates. Overruns on costs—almost solely labor costs—were a prime reason for our poor 1977 profit performance. Right now our bidding procedure makes no differentiation between labor and materials. Maybe the customer should pay for some of the uncertainty in labor costs through a higher markup.

Exhibit 5 shows cost estimates and Exhibit 6 the projected shop load for each order.

1. Refco.   Refco, TiFab's largest single customer, was one of the world's leading engineering contractors. Refco and its competitors (e.g., Bechtel, Brown and Root, and others) designed and constructed large projects around the world. Like most contractors, Refco specialized—concentrating on petroleum refineries and petrochemical plants.

Several years earlier, Refco had developed a specialized piece of machinery to perform certain refinery operations under demanding pressure, temperature, and corrosion conditions. Refco had supplied many of the units in stainless steel, but corrosion failures and increasing corrosive process requirements caused a gradual shift to titanium. The units, nicknamed *Whoppers* because of their large size and hamburger shape, had to be made to exact tolerances and with great care in welding. TiFab had worked closely with Refco in developing the design. From time to time, Refco also had come to TiFab for other titanium pieces—usually large process vessels, such as reactors, requiring a good deal of welding and fabrication. As far as TiFab's management could ascertain, TiFab was the only outside titanium fabricator in the world that Refco used. On the other hand, Refco did some in-house fabrication of superalloys and titanium at its large Rotterdam manufacturing facility.

As an engineering contractor, Refco had a trained staff of field welders and welding supervisors; however, they did little titanium work because of the unique properties of the metal. Industry rumors that Refco would set up a fabricating facility for superalloys and titanium had been circulating for the past four years. According to McMaster (who, among TiFab's managers, knew Refco best), Refco's executives were totally unwilling to discuss this possibility except with "Cheshire cat-like smiles." McMaster believed Refco was unhappy about TiFab's long delivery schedule and occasional late deliveries, and doubted its ability to handle very large requirements expected in the future.

In May 1978, Refco had come to TiFab with a request for production of an above-size Whopper, which soon became known as a *Super Whopper*. The purchasing/subcontracting specialists at Refco stated that they were willing to pay $2 million. Refco had offered to pay for 80 percent of direct "material and labor as applied" in four installments. Thus, each time 25 percent of the work was done, TiFab would receive 20 percent of the cost of materials and direct labor. Thirty days after delivery, TiFab would be paid for the completed piece. (Refco always paid its bills on time.)

To be completed on time, the Super Whopper would have to enter production at TiFab in June. It was certain that the first progress payment, and perhaps the second, would come in TiFab's 1978 fiscal year, which ended in October.

In 1977, Refco had purchased $1.5 million worth of products from TiFab. Not counting the Super Whopper order, its 1978 purchases from TiFab were expected to be $2 million (out of TiFab's projected $12 million in sales).

2. Pierce-Pike. For almost four years Orr had been pursuing business with Pierce-Pike, a company that specialized in constructing proprietary wastewater treatment plants. Pierce-Pike was the subsidiary of a large chemical company and had developed a strong position in a rapidly growing market. Until early April 1978, it had shown no interest in giving business to TiFab. All its work was shared by TiFab's largest competitor and its number-four competitor in the market.

In April, Orr had received a request for proposal on a pressurized reactor from Pierce-Pike. He was ecstatic; it represented a partial victory, or at least some interest, following a long battle. After some difficult pricing decisions, Orr quoted $1.3 million on the job, although he had some concern about whether TiFab could do the job in the hours estimated. The reactor involved some unusual fabrication with which TiFab was inexperienced. On the other hand, both Orr and McMaster had decided it was important to develop this capability.

On June 13, TiFab received the order, which it could refuse. Its original quote had contained a note indicating that TiFab might not have enough capacity to fill the order.

Orr believed Pierce-Pike's two existing sources had capacity available, but he had heard that Pierce-Pike was unhappy with the quality of both, especially the larger one. Also, Pierce-Pike was willing to make progress payments only on raw material.

3. Worldwide Paper. Worldwide Paper was a large integrated producer of pulp, paper, and fabricated paper products. In the mid-1970s, its process development laboratory had tested a new piece of equipment made entirely of titanium. The scale-up to pilot plant and small production units had gone smoothly. Now, Worldwide was putting its first full-sized production unit out for bid. Although earlier units had been made of less corrosion-resistant materials, this one was to be made of titanium. From Orr's point of view, this order had a particularly interesting facet:

> For some time we have been anxious to develop a line of proprietary items. It would ease our management task and enable us to train employees on standard work, which is less demanding than custom work. It would smooth our work flow and enable us to begin to develop a sales force. Right now we don't have a standard product line, so we can't have a regular sales force.
> Worldwide is willing to license this item to its manufacturer. If we get the bid, we can then develop it into a standard product line. There is little opportunity for customization in the primary part of the unit, so it could be a standard product.

McMaster was equally excited about acquiring or developing a standard product line. In addition, he saw the opportunity to add a new capability to TiFab's operation:

> The $150,000 subcontracting involved is for special heat treatment. It is going to cost us that much because we have to move very large parts between our plant and the subcontractor. Furthermore, this subcontractor is really taking advantage of us, because they are one of the very few facilities that can do this type of heat treating. If we made the piece as a standard product line—even at a relatively low volume—we could develop the heat-treating competence in-house with a payback of a matter of months, including the transportation savings.

Orr suspected that the cost estimators had been very conservative in their calculations. He could not be sure of the prices that competitors would offer, but he believed the $800,000 range to be about right. He stated: "Someone will come in lower—probably in the $700,000 range. A couple may be at $750,000. But we have the quality to command some sort of premium over our competitors."

This order offered no progress payments but required a penalty of 0.1 percent of the contract price for each working day that the complete order was late. There was no incentive for early delivery.

4. Kathco. The fourth order was fairly straightforward. Kathco was a metal refinery that manufactured its own titanium electrodes for purifying manganese. In the spring and summer of 1978 its sales were high. During 1978 the company had a new electrode production facility under construction. Construction was delayed, so Kathco had an important shortfall in its electrode availability.

Kathco had solicited bids from only TiFab and one competitor because it knew the companies well. TiFab had a good relationship with Kathco. But this order was clearly a "one-shot deal": Once Kathco's plant was operating, it could supply all of Kathco's needs.

Other Considerations

Titanium Industries also made money by buying, inventorying, and selling titanium. The added volume from any one of these orders would affect all metal purchases. The total effect was difficult to predict because of changes in the metal suppliers' strategy and pricing, but it was generally considered good for the company. As a rule, net profit varied from nothing to about 4 percent of material cost estimates. Gross profit was a little higher but varied substantially.

The shop capacity estimates considered only the availability of labor on a straight-time, two-shift basis (i.e., during normal working hours). It was possible to have people work overtime, although some resented it—especially in the summer. Overtime was expensive (150 percent of regular labor rates) and usually resulted in lower productivity and quality. Over the short run, however, it was the only feasible way to increase capacity. Skilled third-shift personnel were unlikely to be available, at least in the near future. More important, TiFab's limited facility size might make overtime or a third shift impractical, because there would be no room to store work in process.

EXHIBIT 1   Corporate Financial Summary, 1975–1977

	1977	1976	1975
Net Sales	$10,385,134	$8,772,509	$7,712,495
Expenses:			
Cost of sales and engineering	8,783,728	7,359,256	6,201,601
Selling, general and administrative	1,529,260	1,029,892	713,677
Interest, net	176,341	100,493	76,154
	$10,489,329	$8,489,641	$6,991,432
Income (loss) before provision (credit) for taxes on income and minority interest in subsidiary	(104,195)	282,868	721,063
Taxes on income	(59,800)	139,200	339,100
Net income before minority interest in subsidiary	($ 44,395)	$ 143,668	$ 381,963
Minority interest in subsidiary	(3,715)	7,597	—
Net income	($ 48,110)	$ 151,265	$ 381,963
Financial Position			
Current assets	$ 7,390,056	$4,500,872	4,357,560
Working capital	213,774	325,354	665,795
Property and equipment, net	709,857	503,436	282,724
Inventories:[a]			
Raw materials	2,165,450	1,738,466	1,610,722
Work in progress	2,966,248	1,427,474	1,636,485
Long-term debt	178,426	277,000	274,000
Stockholders' equity	$ 884,741	$ 932,851	$ 775,586

[a]Inventories are stated at the lower of cost (substantially on a first-in, first-out basis) or market.

Exhibit 2

Titanium Industries' organization chart

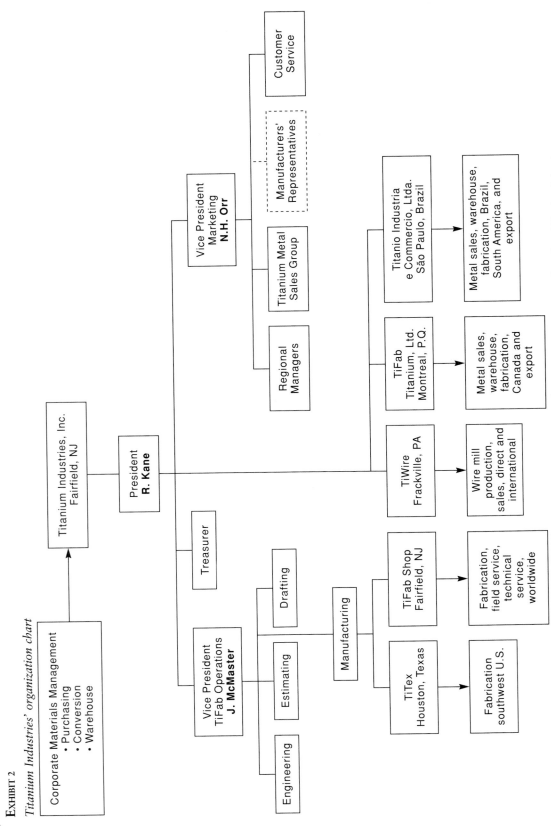

Note: The intimate ties between TiFab's Operations and the rest of the company make it impossible to separate the TiFab organization from that of Titanium Industries.

EXHIBIT 3   TiFab's Operations' Shop Capacity

	Number of People		
	Day Shift	*Night Shift*	*Total*
Welding			
Welder A	7	3	10
Welder B	3	1	4
Welder C	5	6	11
Welder D	6	2	8
Trainee	2	—	2
Helper	7	7	14
Auto A	1	1	2
Auto B	—	—	—
Auto C	2	2	4
Auto trainee	1	—	1
			56
Fabrication			
Layout mechanic	2		2
Mechanic	2		2
Fab A	1		1
Fab B	1		1
Trainee	4		4
Helper	3		3
			13
Machine shop[a]			
Machinist 1st Class	3	—	3
Machinist 2nd Class	1	—	1
Operator A	1	—	1
Operator B	2	1	3
Trainee	1	—	1
			9

[a]Additional machine capacity could be obtained through subcontracting.

Exhibit 4   TiFab's Shop Schedule as of June 1978

	June 1978			July 1978			August 1978			September 1978		
	W^a	M^a	F^a	W	M	F	W	M	F	W	M	F
Backlog	7,200	1,670	2,350	6,800	1,040	2,050	4,200	900	1,050	4,200	1,100	1,050
Capacity	6,920	1,560	2,250	6,920	1,560	2,250	6,920	1,560	2,250	6,920	1,560	2,250
Difference	(280)	(110)	(100)	120	520	200	2,720	660	1,200	2,720	460	1,200
Cumulative	(280)	(110)	(100)	(160)	410	100	2,560	1,070	1,300	5,280	1,530	2,500

	October 1978			November 1978			December 1978			January 1979		
	W	M	F	W	M	F	W	M	F	W	M	F
Backlog	5,000	1,350	1,500	4,120	1,300	1,070	4,700	700	800	5,000	400	1,350
Capacity	6,920	1,560	2,250	6,920	1,560	2,250	6,920	1,560	2,250	6,920	1,560	2,250
Difference	1,920	210	750	2,800	260	1,180	2,220	860	1,450	1,920	1,160	900
Cumulative	7,200	1,740	3,250	10,000	2,000	4,430	12,220	2,860	5,880	14,140	4,020	6,780

	February 1979			March 1979			April 1979			May 1979			Total		
	W	M	F	W	M	F	W	M	F	W	M	F	W	M	F
Backlog	4,050	560	1,150	4,220	660	1,500	4,300	750	1,350	4,300	640	1,020	58,090	11,070	16,240
Capacity	6,920	1,560	2,250	6,920	1,560	2,250	6,920	1,560	2,250	6,920	1,560	2,250	83,040	18,720	27,000
Difference	2,870	1,000	1,100	2,700	900	750	2,620	810	900	2,620	920	1,230	24,950	7,650	10,760
Cumulative	17,010	5,020	7,880	19,710	5,920	8,630	22,330	6,730	9,530	24,950	7,650	10,760	24,950	7,650	10,760

NOTE: Welding and fabrication helpers and trainees were each counted as 50% of a regular welder or fabricator for planning purposes.

^{a}Based on: $\left\{\begin{matrix} W = \text{Welders} \\ M = \text{Machinists} \\ F = \text{Fabricators} \end{matrix}\right\}$ at 2,080 hours per year per person.

EXHIBIT 5 Cost Estimates for the Four Prospective Orders

	Refco (petroleum refining)		Pierce-Pike (wastewater treatment)		Worldwide Paper (paper)	Kathco (electrodes)
Selling Price	$2,000,000		$1,300,000		≈$800,000??	≈$500,000??
Material	700,000	(35%)	750,000	(58%)	360,000	320,000
Labor:						
Welding	200,000		35,000		44,000	
Machining	52,000		6,000		5,000	10,000
Fabrication	33,000		14,000		15,000	20,000
Total labor	285,000	(14%)	55,000	(4%)	64,000	30,000
Factory overhead	570,000	(29%)	110,000	(8%)	128,000	60,000
Subcontracting	100,000	(5%)	130,000	(10%)	150,000	—
Total factory cost	1,655,000	(83%)	1,045,000	(80%)	702,000	410,000
Contribution (before S.G.&A.)[a]	$ 345,000	(17%)	$ 255,000	(20%)	≈$ 98,000??	≈$ 90,000??

NOTE: ≈ means *approximately*.
[a]Sales, general, and administrative expenses.

EXHIBIT 6 Projected Shop Load for the Four Prospective Orders

	Refco			Pierce-Pike			Worldwide Paper			Kathco		
	W[a]	M[a]	F[a]	W	M	F	W	M	F	W	M	F
1978:												
June	100	100	—	50	50	—	—	—	—	—	—	—
July	1,500	600	—	1,400	100	—	1,000	200	—	—	400	—
August	2,000	700	—	1,150	100	50	1,000	300	400	—	600	1,800
September	1,800	200	—	1,000	50	150	1,000	200	500	—	200	800
October	1,900	100	500	1,200	50	250	1,000	130	1,000	—	200	900
November	2,000	200	500	1,000	100	300	2,000	—	600	—	200	700
December	2,000	700	1,000	600	300	350	1,000	—	—	—	100	700
1979:												
January	2,000	800	1,000	500	250	500	650	—	450	—	—	—
February	2,000	600	1,000	—	—	500	—	—	—	—	—	—
March	2,500	600	1,000	—	—	500	—	—	—	—	—	—
April	2,500	800	500	—	—	150	—	—	—	—	—	—
May	2,500	500	500	—	—	—	—	—	—	—	—	—
Post-May	12,000	2,800	500	—	—	—	—	—	—	—	—	—
Total	34,800	8,700	6,500	6,900	1,000	2,750	7,650	830	2,950	—	1,700	4,900

[a]W = Welders.
M = Machinists.
F = Fabricators

CHESEBROUGH-POND'S, INC.: VASELINE PETROLEUM JELLY

On September 2, 1977, Mary Porter was appointed product manager for Vaseline petroleum jelly (VPJ) and given three weeks to prepare the 1978 budget for the brand.[1] To project 1978 sales and profits, she would have to develop a marketing plan that specified the level and nature of three types of marketing expenditures: advertising, consumer promotion, and trade promotion. Porter decided to begin by analyzing VPJ's marketing strategy over the previous five years, with particular emphasis on the nature, effectiveness, and profitability of its sales promotions.

Company Background

Vaseline petroleum jelly was the first product sold by the Chesebrough Manufacturing Company, founded by Robert Chesebrough in 1880. Chesebrough, who sold lamplighting oil, had frequently visited the oil fields of Pennsylvania, where he heard about a miraculous black jelly that formed on the rods of the oil pumps. He successfully duplicated this "rod wax" in his laboratory, lightened its color, and used a then unproven marketing technique—distribution of free samples—to introduce the product.

At the same time another entrepreneur, Theron Pond, distilled an improved kind of witch hazel from a native American shrub and sold it as a "pain-destroying and healing remedy." This product launched the Pond's Extract Company, which by the 1920s had become the leading U.S. marketer of popularly priced skin creams and cosmetics. Pond's also owed much of its early success to a marketing innovation: it was the first company to advertise with endorsements by socially prominent women.

In 1955, the two companies combined to form Chesebrough-Pond's, Inc. (CPI), and Wall Street analysts hailed it "the marriage of the aristocrats." The new firm expanded through diversification. During the fiscal year that ended December 31, 1976, CPI's six divisions recorded after-tax profits of $54 million on net sales of $747 million.

The Health and Beauty Products (HBP) Division, which accounted for 22 percent of CPI's 1977 sales, marketed VPJ. Although HBP's 1976 sales of $163 million were second only to those of the international division, HBP's five-year

average growth rate of 9.3 percent was the second lowest among CPI's divisions. The HBP Division also marketed Cutex nail-care products, Pond's creams, Q-Tips cotton swabs, and Vaseline Intensive Care moisturizing products.

The Market for Petroleum Jelly

Executives at HBP described petroleum jelly as "a household staple" used by over 90 percent of the population, but noted that both level and frequency of use varied substantially. A consumer survey indicated that heavy users were either women aged 45 years and older who viewed petroleum jelly as a multifunctional skin-care product or mothers who used petroleum jelly for baby care and did not consider it appropriate for their own skin care. Other results from this survey are reported in Exhibit 1.

Petroleum jelly sales to the consumer market at manufacturers' prices were estimated at $25 million in 1976, of which Vaseline petroleum jelly claimed a 90 percent share. (VPJ was also sold to institutions—hospitals, other medical facilities, and some industrial buyers. Porter was not responsible for these sales.) Direct competitors with VPJ were private label petroleum jellies, which sold primarily in 16-oz. jars at prices 30 percent below VPJ's through mass merchandisers, such as K mart. The Vaseline product did not appear to be losing share to these private labels, none of which was manufactured by CPI. It also competed in the broader skin-care market with special purpose products, such as hand lotions and moisturizing creams.

Vaseline petroleum jelly was available in two forms, pure and carbolated; both were packaged in several sizes of jars and tubes. Carbolated VPJ was a specialized first aid product with an active ingredient. It was priced higher than pure VPJ and distributed primarily through drugstores. It was almost never featured at a discount by the trade and was not advertised separately. For several years, carbolated VPJ had accounted for a stable 7 percent of VPJ dollar sales to consumers.

Factory shipments of each size of pure VPJ from 1974 through 1977 are reported in Exhibit 2. More than half of VPJ's ounce volume was sold in the popular 3.75- and 7.50-oz. jars.

Distribution and Pricing

Vaseline petroleum jelly was distributed primarily through grocery, drug, and mass merchandise stores; these accounted for 85 percent of Vaseline's ounce volume. Sales through variety stores and other outlets accounted for the

---

This case was prepared by Penny Pittman Merliss, research assistant under the direction of Assistant Professor John A. Quelch. Copyright © 1981 by the President and Fellows of Harvard College. Harvard Business School case 581–047 (Rev. 8/15/90).

[1]Vaseline, Pond's, Cutex, Q-Tips, Intensive Care, Ragu, Health-Tex, Adolph's, and Prince Matchabelli are registered trademarks of Chesebrough-Pond's, Inc.

remainder. However, VPJ distribution varied by size among the major channels (as shown in Exhibit 3); the 15-oz. jar, for example, was sold primarily through drugstores and mass merchandisers. Distribution penetration was high for the brand as a whole; in 1977, VPJ was carried in at least one size by 92 percent of grocery stores and 96 percent of drugstores.

All HBP products were sold by the same 130-person sales force. Salespeople focused on "headquarter accounts," rather than individual retail outlets. At least once a month, HBP salespeople visited buyers at the head offices of food, drug, variety store, and mass merchandising chains as well as buyers for wholesalers representing independent retailers in each class of trade. During 1976, chain purchases accounted for 45 percent of VPJ dollar sales to the consumer market.

Salespeople were compensated by a combination of salary and bonus based on achievement of volume quotas. Sales force management and HBP division executives negotiated quarterly volume quotas for each brand. In addition, they established a calendar of consumer and trade promotions for each brand, reflecting its need for sales force support and the number of promotion events the sales force could present to the trade at one time. Porter believed that the sales force viewed VPJ as a mature, unexciting brand, which required frequent price promotions to stimulate trade interest. Salespeople often pressed for such promotions toward the end of each quarter to help achieve their quotas.

Prices for VPJ were approved by the division general manager, whose key aim was profit improvement. (Exhibit 4 lists factory and suggested retail prices as of July 1977.) The suggested prices allowed retailers who purchased direct from CPI a 40 percent margin, but actual retail prices were often 10 percent lower, particularly in grocery stores and mass merchandise outlets. In 1974, escalating petroleum costs required price increases ranging from 37 percent on the 15-oz. size to 70 percent on the 1.75-oz. size. Annual price increases between 1975 and 1977 had added a further 18 percent to manufacturer prices. Variable manufacturing costs for VPJ were expected to rise by 5 percent in 1978.

Marketing Expenditures

The three principal areas of VPJ marketing expenditures were advertising, consumer promotion, and trade promotion. Sales force expenses were treated as division overhead and not allocated among brands. Brand budgets for VPJ from 1975 through 1977 are summarized in Exhibit 5.

Advertising.   The primary objective of VPJ advertising through the 1970s was to increase sales by suggesting new product uses. Earlier brand advertising had concentrated almost exclusively on baby care, but in 1972 the message began to include VPJ's versatility as a skin-care product for adults and children (see Exhibit 6). Some HBP executives believed that VPJ advertising should present product uses beyond skin care; others thought that emphasizing VPJ's usefulness as a shoe-shining aid or hinge lubricant might cause some consumers to stop using it for skin or baby care.

Bimonthly VPJ advertising expenditures showed substantial period-to-period fluctuations (see Table A). Porter believed these indicated a lack of sustained commitment to advertising as well as management's tendency to cut fourth-quarter advertising expenditures to meet annual profit targets.

Media selection showed greater consistency. Network television was the principal medium for VPJ advertising; print media were used primarily to announce VPJ consumer promotions. Both electronic and print media advertising rates rose on average 15 percent annually between 1974 and 1977.

Consumer Promotion.   Historically, VPJ brand management had spent little money on consumer promotion. During 1973, only one consumer promotion (a 10-cent coupon) was run; in 1974, none occurred. In 1975, however,

---

TABLE A   **Index of Bimonthly Measured Media Advertising for VPJ, 1974–1977**

	1974	*1975*	*1976*	*1977*
January–February		83	78	113
March–April		64	103	92
May–June	100	36	39	102
July–August	108	114	128	97
September–October	49	100	132	
November–December	42	11	136	

NOTE: (Base: May–June 1974 = 100.) Figures not adjusted for media cost inflation.
SOURCE: Company records.

three events were run: a free glass jar packaged with the 7.5-oz. VPJ, a 10-cent cross-ruff coupon[2] packed in 2 million boxes of Procter & Gamble's Ivory Snow, and a 50-cent refund offer for two VPJ proofs of purchase.

1976 VPJ events.   Consumer promotion expenditures continued to increase during 1976; that year marked four events, each coinciding with a promotion to the trade.

1. *February:* A $2 cash refund offer involving VPJ and four other HBP brands was announced in the February issues of *Family Circle* and *Ladies' Home Journal* and in full-page, four-color Sunday newspaper supplement advertisements on February 15 (see Exhibit 7). Consumers could also learn of the offer at the point of purchase through four-color riser cards for end-aisle and cut-case displays and shelf talkers including refund applications, which were shipped to retailers with each case of VPJ.[3]

2. *April:* To coincide with National Baby Week, one dollar's worth of coupons for five HBP brands used in baby care (including a 15-cent coupon for any size VPJ) were carried inside 4.65 million boxes of Kimbies disposable diapers. Coupons for Kimbies were carried by two participating HBP brands.

3. *June:* A shrink-wrapped twin pack of two 3.75-oz. jars of VPJ, with a label encouraging consumers to keep one jar in the kitchen and the other in the bathroom, was preticketed with a retail price of 99 cents. The pack also included a 50-cent refund offer for proofs of purchase from two 3.75-oz. jars. The twin pack was shipped only in cases of three dozen, to encourage the trade to feature it in special displays. (Exhibit 8 shows merchandising flyer.)

4. *September:* An eight-page "programmed learning" advertisement was run in *Reader's Digest* (October 1976) to educate consumers about skin care and the uses of VPJ, Vaseline Intensive Care lotion, and Vaseline Intensive Care bath beads. The reader could answer a "skin test" on a mailable pop-up card, which doubled as an entry to the Vaseline Soft-to-Touch sweepstakes. Sweepstakes prizes,

such as fur coats and cashmere sweaters, all emphasized the soft-to-touch theme. The sweepstakes was an attention-getting overlay to a $1.50 cash refund offer for a proof of purchase from each of the three participating brands. The offer also was advertised through riser cards and shelf talkers at the point of purchase (see Exhibit 9).

The principal costs to VPJ for these events are summarized in Exhibit 10. For multiple-brand promotions, costs were allocated according to each brand's share of coupon or proof-of-purchase redemptions.

1977 VPJ events.   Consumer promotion expenditures for VPJ were cut by one quarter in 1977; only three promotion events were implemented.

1. *February:* A Swiss Army multipurpose knife was offered as a self-liquidating premium[4] on the labels of 7.5-oz. jars of VPJ. The knife, a $21.00 retail value bought by CPI for $10.00, was offered to consumers for $10.50 plus one VPJ front label. The 50-cent difference between purchase and selling prices covered handling. Costs of $18,000, however, were incurred for point-of-purchase display materials and 1,500 knives used as dealer loaders.[5]

2. *April:* A 25-cent coupon for large sizes of three HBP brands, including VPJ (15-oz.), was printed on packages of the 24-oz. size of Vaseline Intensive Care bath beads. To encourage multibrand displays at the point of purchase, a self-liquidating premium, which doubled as a dealer loader, also was offered and advertised in women's magazines. Because redemption of the on-pack coupons would be delayed until purchasers had used up the contents of the boxes, HBP managers believed an additional purchase incentive was necessary to stimulate special trade merchandising activity. Thus, in selected markets, a newspaper advertisement delivered 65 cents' worth of coupons on the three participating brands (including a 15-cent coupon toward a 15- or 12-oz. jar of VPJ). In other markets, newspaper advertising featured a one dollar cash refund for proofs of purchase on two of the three brands.

---

[2]A cross-ruff coupon is carried either on or inside the package of a noncompetitive brand. It is used when the target markets of the sponsor and carrier brands are similar.

[3]Riser cards are attention-getting signs placed above a special display. Cut-case displays are shipping cartons that could double as store display units when cut to shape by store personnel; these allow retailers to display a product without unpacking it. Shelf talkers are small signs attached to the front of the shelf on which the product is regularly stocked.

[4]A self-liquidating premium requires consumers to send cash as well as proof of purchase. The cash amount covers handling, mailing, and the cost of the premium, which is usually offered at 30 to 50% below normal retail price.

[5]A dealer loader is a sample of a premium displayed at the point of purchase until the end of the promotion, when it usually becomes the property of the store or department manager.

3. *September:* A two-page advertisement in *Reader's Digest* (October 1977) and a similar advertisement in Sunday newspaper supplements delivered 50 cents' worth of coupons on three Vaseline brands, including a 10-cent coupon for VPJ. These advertisements, along with riser cards and shelf talkers at the point of purchase, also announced a $40,000 sweepstakes. To encourage potential entrants to find in-store Vaseline displays, the ads indicated that official entry forms and instructions were available at the point of purchase.

Future Considerations

After reviewing the consumer promotion history, Porter wondered how much latitude she would have in planning the 1978 VPJ consumer promotions. She thought division management would again wish to include VPJ in several multiple-brand promotions. She suspected, however, that these were of most benefit to the weaker participants and that her consumer promotion dollars might be better spent on events exclusive to VPJ.

Timing the promotions was another problem. Some HBP managers believed consumer promotions should coincide with trade promotions. Others thought they should be launched between trade promotions, arguing that promotions should be spread more evenly to avoid wide demand fluctuations, which hampered efficient production and inventory control.

Porter realized that she first had to define her objectives for consumer promotion. Some HBP executives favored it to stimulate short-term sales. Others argued that indiscriminate use of premiums, coupons, and sweepstakes further increased consumer price sensitivity and that consumer promotions were valuable only when they reinforced the brand's advertising image.

Trade Promotion.

In general practice, trade promotions temporarily offered merchandise to the trade at a discount from the regular list price. Porter characterized how trade buyers usually responded to a manufacturer's limited-time trade promotion offer:

> They weigh the financial incentive of buying an above-normal quantity of the product at a discount against the financing costs associated with the additional inventory. Of course, they can minimize these costs—and make the manufacturer happy—by accelerating the product's movement off the shelves. To do this, they have to pass all or part of our incentive on to the consumer as a retail price cut. To achieve the greatest sales increases, they should feature the price cut in store advertising and set up a special in-store display.

Manufacturers used a variety of trade promotion allowances. Case allowances on products ordered during the promotion period offered either a reduction from list price

on the invoice to the trade (e.g., 10 percent off invoice) or free goods with a specified minimum purchase (e.g., 1 case free with purchase of 10). Because manufacturers could not legally control retail prices, they had no assurance that case allowances would be fully or partially passed on to consumers as retail price reductions. (Many manufacturers, including CPI, sometimes permitted their trade accounts to take merchandise ordered during the promotion period in two shipments. Thus, the second shipment might arrive after the promotion and be sold at the manufacturer's regular suggested retail price.)

Additional merchandising allowances, also paid on a per-case basis, were sometimes offered. For example, a 10 percent allowance might be offered if the trade featured the product at a price discount in its consumer advertising. Or a special allowance might be offered to stores that set up end-aisle or off-shelf displays of prescribed size during the promotion period. Unlike off-invoice allowances,[6] these were only paid after the manufacturer received evidence of performance, such as an affidavit, advertising tear sheet, or display photograph.

In addition to case and merchandising allowances, manufacturers sometimes offered a *base contract* to the trade, by which any account buying a minimum quantity of the product received a percentage discount. A 5 percent base contract discount was offered on all VPJ orders over $75.

Past VPJ events. Given VPJ's dominance in its category, Porter was surprised to discover that over 70 percent of 1976 factory shipments were sold to the trade on promotion. The 1977 marketing plan outlined three objectives for VPJ trade promotion:

1. Stimulate cut-price feature advertising and displays, especially on larger sizes.
2. Reinforce and expand distribution of larger sizes in all trade channels.
3. Limit erosion of distribution of smaller sizes.

Porter's Analysis

Porter summarized the terms and timing of VPJ trade promotions from late 1972 through mid-1977 (see Exhibit 11). She noted that a trade promotion had been offered on at least one size during every quarter of each year. Duration of the offers varied widely, with some lasting as long as 60 days (in contrast to most retailers, who featured brands through price advertising and special displays for one week only). With one exception, VPJ's trade promotions were

---

[6]Off-invoice and free-goods allowances are deducted from the bill sent to the trade. Merchandising allowances are paid on a "bill back" basis by separate check.

national, not tailored to particular regional or city markets.[7] Porter noted that the average level of trade promotion discounts seemed to have increased over the five years. In addition, she observed that, since 1973 price increases often coincided with trade promotions, complicating evaluations of their impact.

Three questions came to Porter's mind as she reviewed the VPJ trade promotion history.

1. How extensive was inventory loading during the promotional period? Trade buyers, who could often predict the timing of a brand's trade promotion offers, could deliberately let inventory run down in anticipation of a promotion, buy heavily during the promotion period, then let orders drop again. This produced peaks and valleys in the flow of factory shipments and an artificial seasonality of demand. Porter had noted a fall-off in VPJ shipments before and after most promotions. Could HBP be selling at a discount VPJ volume that the trade would buy anyway to meet normal consumer demand?

2. Just how much merchandising support was VPJ receiving at the retail level? Comparative data on the extent of feature advertising for petroleum jelly and three other product categories, reported in Exhibit 12, suggested that the trade did not view VPJ as a traffic builder. Further, most VPJ trade promotions involved case allowances. Should the proportion of performance-based allowances be increased, and, if so, could performance requirements be enforced?

3. How effective were across-the-line promotions? Traditionally, VPJ had used line promotions across all sizes to encourage retailers to stock more than one size. However, the company typically required retailers to feature only one size in a tiny "obituary" newspaper ad to take an advertising allowance on their purchases of all VPJ sizes.

Research Evidence

During 1976, VPJ factory shipments had increased 22 percent over 1975. Unit sales to consumers had risen 11 per-

cent. During the first half of 1977, however, factory shipments and consumer sales were 11 percent and 2 percent lower than the equivalent 1976 figures. Some HBP executives suggested that heavy VPJ promotion during 1976 had overstocked the trade, the consumer, or both. To address this issue and the broader question of how much advertising, consumer promotion, and trade promotion expenditures each contributed to VPJ sales and profit performance, two research studies had been commissioned.

The first report, prepared by John Dennerlein, CPI's special projects manager, with the assistance of an independent consulting firm,[8] estimated incremental sales and contribution generated by VPJ trade promotions over a five-year period. A series of computer models estimated what the normal monthly factory shipments of each VPJ size would have been without each trade promotion, and then compared these figures with actual shipments. Similarly, the contribution from actual sales at the promotion price could be compared with the contribution normal sales would have provided at full price. The calculations of incremental unit sales and contribution took account of lost sales at full price before and after, as well as during, each promotion period.

The results of Dennerlein's investigation are presented in Exhibits 13 and 14. Exhibit 13 reports the net incremental contribution associated with each VPJ trade promotion from 1972 through June 1977, broken down by size. Dennerlein also plotted factory shipments, incremental unit sales, retail inventories, and consumer sales over time for each VPJ size. As an example, his chart for the 7.5-oz. VPJ is presented as Exhibit 14.

Dennerlein concluded that VPJ trade promotions were profitable and were "the major factor behind year-to-year changes in VPJ sales." He believed that VPJ trade promotions, especially when they coincided with consumer promotions, not only stimulated the trade to build inventories but also increased consumer sales. Dennerlein opposed any significant transfer of VPJ money from trade promotion to advertising.

A second study, conducted by the CPI market research department, measured the efficacy of VPJ advertising expenditures. It found weak correlations between quarterly VPJ advertising expenditures and factory shipments, retail inventories, and consumer sales. The researchers noted that consumer sales had declined during the first half of 1977, even though media advertising expenditures were almost 50 percent higher than during the equivalent period in 1976.

---

[7]By law, different trade promotion offers could be made at the same time in different market areas; but in any given market area an equivalent offer had to be made on a proportional basis to all competing retail outlets. Major supermarket and drug chains and mass merchandisers generally preferred that manufacturers offer the same trade promotion in all market areas.

---

[8]SPAR (Sales Promotion Analysis Reporting), a commercial service of Pan-Eval Data, Inc.

The Problem

These findings and the sales results of first-half 1977 had prompted HBP Division executives to reduce VPJ media advertising expenditures for the second half of 1977 to around $700,000, compared with $1.4 million during the same period in 1976. Porter opposed this cut. "If anything," she commented, "the 1976 promotion pumped so much VPJ into the pipeline that advertising ought to have been increased." She wanted to develop a 1978 television advertising campaign that stressed VPJ's versatility and to increase advertising expenditures at the expense of trade promotion. (Four finished commercial executions of a new television advertising campaign could be developed at an approximate cost of $200,000.) She admitted, however, that "the HBP Division's traditional orientation toward push rather than pull marketing would make this proposal tough to sell." She also expected resistance from the HBP sales force and the trade.

As she began to plan the brand budget, Porter learned that the division had scheduled several significant new product launches for the second half of 1978. Profits from established brands, such as VPJ, would cover the substantial marketing expenses for these introductions. Accordingly, the HBP general manager informed Porter that her 1978 VPJ budget should show a profit, after advertising and promotion expenses, at least 10 percent greater than the current 1977 estimate of $7.7 million.

EXHIBIT 1 Results of VPJ Consumer Survey

During March 1977 personal interviews were conducted with 500 female heads of households who qualified as users of petroleum jelly (on the basis of having used petroleum jelly during the previous month). Sixty percent of those approached qualified.

- 90 percent of petroleum jelly purchasers last bought VPJ. When asked to name a brand of petroleum jelly, 97 percent mentioned VPJ; 23 percent recalled recently seeing or hearing VPJ advertising.

- 51 percent of heavy users were aged 18 to 34 years, and three quarters of this group had a child under 4 years in their households. (Households using petroleum jelly at least once a day were considered heavy users; those using it less than twice a week were "light-using" households.)

- Heavy users made on average six purchases of petroleum jelly per year, whereas light users made on average only one purchase per year.

- 86 percent of respondents considered the size of petroleum jelly last bought their "regular" size. Heavy users were more likely than light users to purchase larger-size jars.

- 35 percent of respondents reported making their last petroleum jelly purchase in a food store, 30 percent in a drugstore, and 30 percent in a mass merchandise or discount store. Light users (46 percent) and users from households with a child under 4 years (44 percent) were more likely to have made their purchases in food stores.

- 33 percent of heavy users and 46 percent of light users could not recall the price paid for the last jar of petroleum jelly they purchased.

- 70 percent of respondents agreed strongly with the statement "petroleum jelly is economical."

- 20 percent of respondents reported having more than one jar of petroleum jelly in their households.

- 86 percent of respondents stated that they kept a jar of petroleum jelly in the bathroom; 34 percent mentioned the bedroom, 6 percent mentioned the kitchen, and 2 percent mentioned the garage, basement, or workshop.

- The average quantity of petroleum jelly applied varied significantly by use from 3.1 g (sunburn) and 2.1 g (baby use) to 0.3 g (removing makeup) and 0.1 g (chapped lips). Share of total usage occasions also varied by use: 1 percent (sunburn), 4 percent (baby use), and 12 percent (chapped lips).

- The number of households using petroleum jelly was 15 percent lower in winter than summer. However, among user households, frequency of use was 25 percent higher in winter.

- For all except household uses (such as preventing rust and lubricating hinges), both the incidence and frequency of use were higher among females than males.

SOURCE: Company records.

EXHIBIT 2   Pure VPJ Factory Shipments by Size, 1974–1977 (thousands of dozens)

Size (oz.)	1974	1975	1976	1977[a]
1.75 (jar)	1,069.5 (100)[b]	873.6 (82)	1,012.5 (95)	849.6 (79)
3.75 (jar)	997.7 (100)	973.2 (98)	1,137.5 (114)	1,116.1 (112)
7.50 (jar)	540.8 (100)	544.4 (101)	773.2 (143)	628.3 (116)
12.00 (jar)	216.7 (100)	186.3 (86)	192.7 (89)	157.5 (73)
15.00 (jar)	249.8 (100)	227.1 (91)	292.1 (117)	293.1 (117)
1.00 (tube)	114.2 (100)	104.3 (91)	120.2 (105)	106.7 (93)
3.75 (tube)	47.7 (100)	34.2 (72)	41.6 (88)	33.3 (70)
Total	3,236.4 (100)	2,943.1 (91)	3,569.8 (110)	3,184.6 (98)
Equivalent units[c]	543.6 (100)	504.5 (93)	626.9 (115)	562.3 (103)

[a]1977 sales estimated as of July 31.
[b]Numbers in parentheses are indices based on 1974 factory shipments by size (base = 100).
[c]One equivalent unit = 360,000 oz.
Source: Company records.

EXHIBIT 3   Pure VPJ Jar Sales Volume by Outlet Type, May–June 1977 (equivalent ounce basis)

Jar Size (oz.)	Outlet Type			Total
	Grocery	Drug	Mass Merchandiser	
1.75	6%	3%	0.2%	9%
3.75	18	7	2.0	28
7.50	16	8	5.0	29
12.00	8	3	2.0	13
15.00	5	11	6.0	21
Total	53%	32%	15.0%	100%

NOTE: To be read, "Of the 85% of VPJ ounce sales through the three principal channels of distribution, 6% were 1.75-oz. jars sold through grocery stores."
SOURCE: Company records.

EXHIBIT 4 Pure VPJ Price List, July 1977

Size (oz.)		Suggested Retail Price (SRP)	SRP per Ounce	Suggested Wholesale Price (SWP)	SWP per Ounce	Manufacturer's Selling Price (MSP)	MSP per Ounce	MSP per Dozen
1.75	(jar)	$0.57	$0.33	$0.403	$0.230	$0.342	$0.195	$ 4.10
3.75	(jar)	0.79	0.21	0.558	0.149	0.473	0.126	5.68
7.50	(jar)	1.19	0.16	0.840	0.112	0.713	0.095	8.56
12.00	(jar)	1.59	0.13	1.122	0.094	0.953	0.079	11.44
15.00	(jar)	1.69	0.11	1.193	0.080	1.013	0.068	12.16
1.00	(tube)	0.69	0.69	0.487	0.487	0.413	0.413	4.96
3.75	(tube)	1.25	0.33	0.883	0.235	0.750	0.200	9.00

NOTE: Suggested retail prices allowed retailers a 40.0% margin on direct purchases from the manufacturer and a 29.4% margin on purchases from wholesalers. Suggested wholesale prices allowed wholesalers a 15.1% margin on purchases from the manufacturer.

EXHIBIT 5 VPJ Brand Budgets, 1975–1977 ($000)

	1975		1976		1977[a]	
Gross sales[b]	$17,792	(100%)	$22,491	(100%)	$22,938	(100%)
Variable manufacturing costs	8,616	(48%)	10,618	(47%)	10,572	(46%)
Gross margin	9,176	(52%)	11,873	(53%)	12,366	(54%)
Advertising[c]	1,590	(9%)	2,410	(11%)	2,123	(9%)
TV: Network	1,280		1,526		1,720	
Spot	97		586			
Print: Magazine	44		141		62	
Sunday supplement			38		45	
Newspaper					97	
Consumer promotion	137	(1%)	448	(2%)	330	(1%)
Trade promotion	1,810	(10%)	2,468	(11%)	2,202	(10%)
Total marketing expenditures	3,537	(20%)	5,326	(24%)	4,655	(20%)
Profit before SG&A expenses, overhead, and taxes	$ 5,639	(32%)	$ 6,547	(29%)	$ 7,711	(34%)

[a]Revised budget as of July 31, 1977. By September 1977 it appeared that these estimates would closely match actual results.
[b]Before deductions of off-invoice and base contract allowances; includes sales of both pure and carbolated VPJ.
[c]Includes production costs and public relations expenditures as well as media costs.
Source: Company records.

EXHIBIT 6

1977 VPJ 30-second television commercial (titled "Year Round")

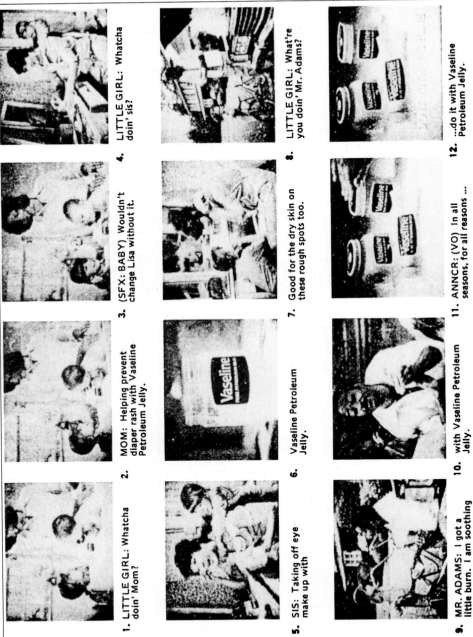

1. LITTLE GIRL: Whatcha doin' Mom?

2. MOM: Helping prevent diaper rash with Vaseline Petroleum Jelly.

3. (SFX: BABY) Wouldn't change Lisa without it.

4. LITTLE GIRL: Whatcha doin' sis?

5. SIS: Taking off eye make up with

6. Vaseline Petroleum Jelly.

7. Good for the dry skin on these rough spots too.

8. LITTLE GIRL: What're you doin' Mr. Adams?

9. MR. ADAMS: I got a little burn. I am soothing it.

10. with Vaseline Petroleum Jelly.

11. ANNCR: (VO) In all seasons, for all reasons ...

12. ...do it with Vaseline Petroleum Jelly.

SOURCE: William Esty Company, Inc., N.Y., N.Y.

EXHIBIT 7

1976 newspaper and magazine advertisement for $2 cash refund promotion

EXHIBIT 8

1976 merchandising flyer for VPJ twin-pack promotion

#1 selling baby item delivers multiple sales*

to meet increased consumer usage

* National Warehouse Withdrawal Service for 12 months ending December 1975 — Unit Sales

- Sales increased 28% with multi-usage TV advertising**

** National Retail Audit Firm-Dollar Sales - 1975

Combine

- Aggressive pricing
- 50¢ Cash Refund
- Effective Cross Merchandising

for Big Profits and Fast Sell-Through

2 free with 10
off-invoice*

5% advertising allowance
by separate check for a cut-price feature*

* One CPI salesman approved order only

Product Information:

Description	Size	Code #	Sugg. Retail	Regular Cost Per Shipper	Special Cost Per Shipper	Special Cost Per Twin Pack	Shelf Pack	Case Pack
Twin Pack Display Shipper	3¾ oz	2327-00	$1.50	$32.40	$26.99	$.749	—	3 doz. Twin Packs

Promotional Information:
Shipping Period: 6/1/76 – 6/25/76
Advertising Period: 6/1/76 – 7/23/76
Terms: 1% 30 days, net 31 days
Minimum Shipment: Regular CPI Minimums Apply
AFE #: 1-6-32-06
Display Shipper:
Case Dimensions: 11¼ x 10½ x 9¾
Case Cube: 682
Case Weight: 23 lbs. per case

HEALTH & BEAUTY PRODUCTS DIVISION
Chesebrough-Pond's Inc.
GREENWICH, CONNECTICUT 06830

EXHIBIT 9

1976 merchandising flyer for $1.50 cash refund promotion

A traffic builder reaching 1 out of 3 households

The biggest single H&BA advertising event ever run in Reader's Digest

- 18 million cash refund certificates
- 10 pages of "consumer stopping" advertising with a sweepstakes offer
- Reaching over 44 million adult readers

October issue on sale September 28

Merchandising for multiple sales

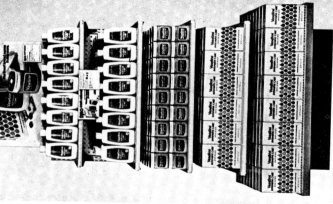

$1.50 cash refund
by mail from Chesebrough-Pond's Inc.

when you buy all 3 of these quality **Vaseline brand products**

Vaseline® Intensive Care® Lotion
Regular or Herbal, 10 oz. ___¢

Vaseline® Intensive Care® Bath Beads
Regular or Herbal, 15 oz. ___¢

Vaseline® Petroleum Jelly 7½ oz. ___¢

*Get required certificate at our stores

Riser card #2308-00
Shelf talker #2309-00

HEALTH & BEAUTY PRODUCTS DIVISION
Chesebrough-Pond's Inc.
GREENWICH, CONNECTICUT 06830

Exhibit 10   Costs to VPJ of 1976 Consumer Promotions

1. January: Allocated Cost to VPJ: $129,000

	Circulation (million)	Percent Response	Number of Responses	Cost per Response	Total Cost (five brands)
Sunday supplement	30.00	0.7%	210,000	$2.25[a]	$599,625
Magazines	14.50	0.2	29,000		
Point-of-purchase materials	2.75	1.0	27,500		
21,000 riser cards					$ 27,225
60,000 shelf talkers					$ 15,375

2. April: Allocated Cost to VPJ: $56,620

	Face Value	Circulation (million)	Redemption Rate (%)	Number of Redemptions	Cost per Redemption	Total Cost (VPJ only)
Coupon redemption	15 cents[a]	4.65	4.0%	186,000	21.05 cents[a]	$39,150
Coupon artwork and printing						$14,300
Package flagging and coupon insertion						$ 3,170

3. June: Cost to VPJ: $82,150

	Circulation (no. of twin packs)	Percent Response	Number of Responses	Cost per Response	Total Cost (VPJ only)
Refund offer	1,260,000	7.0%	88,200	75 cents[a]	$66,150
Special packaging					$16,000

4. September: Allocated Cost to VPJ: $141,200

	Circulation (million)	Percent Response	Number of Responses	Cost per Response	Total Cost (three brands)
Reader's Digest	18.0	0.5%	90,000	$1.75[a]	$315,000
Point-of-purchase materials	4.5	2.0	90,000		
30,000 riser cards					$ 27,000
75,000 shelf talkers					$ 13,000
Sweepstakes prizes, judging, handling					$ 54,000

[a]Includes face value of coupon or refund plus handling charges.

Source: Company records.

EXHIBIT 11 VPJ Trade Promotion History, 1972–1977

Year	Date of Promotion — Duration	Sales Days Promoted	Consumer Promotion Activity	1.75 oz.	3.75 oz.	7.50 oz.	12.00 oz.	15.00 oz.	Comments
1972	9/1–10/15	29	None	—	—	5% OI staple; 10% OI M/C	5% OI staple; 10% OI M/C	5% OI staple; 10% OI M/C	OI = off-invoice. A staple or standard case contained one dozen units. A master case (M/C) was a prepacked mix of sizes, usually including six dozen units.
1973	1/2–2/13	31	None	5% OI staple; 10% OI M/C + 5% OI on choice of one size	5% OI staple; 10% OI M/C + 5% OI on choice of one size	5% OI staple; 10% OI M/C + 5% OI on choice of one size	5% OI staple; 10% OI M/C + 5% OI on choice of one size	5% OI staple; 10% OI M/C + 5% OI on choice of one size	
	5/1–6/30	43	None	5% OI (SE and SW regions only)	5% OI	5% OI	—	—	
	9/4–11/2	46	10-cent coupon on any size VPJ	7% + 5% OI on choice of one size	7% + 5% OI on choice of one size	7% + 5% OI on choice of one size	7% + 5% OI on choice of one size	7% + 5% OI on choice of one size	
1974	2/1–3/15	29	None	—	—	10% OI	10%	10%	An additional 10% discount given to accounts showing evidence of feature advertising support for the brand.
	5/1–6/14	31	None	10% OI + 10% ad	—	10% OI + 10% ad	—	—	
	8/1–9/13	31	None	1 w/11	1 w/11	1 w/11	1 w/11	1 w/11	One case provided free for every 11 ordered.
	11/1–12/13	28	None	—	10% OI	—	—	10% OI	
1975	1/2–2/14	31	Container pack premium with 7.50-oz. size	1 w/11	—	1 w/11	—	—	
	3/10–4/18	32	10-cent cross-ruff coupon with P&G Ivory Snow Multibrand	—	—	1 w/11 or 2 w/10 on choice of one size	1 w/11 or 2 w/10 on choice of one size	1 w/11 or 2 w/10 on choice of one size	
	6/2–6/27	21	None	—	1 w/11 + 10% ad	—	—	—	
	9/2–9/30	21	50-cent refund offer 2 VPJ proofs of purchase	1 w/11	—	2 w/10	—	—	
	11/3–12/12	27	None	—	2 w/10 + 10% ad choice of one size	—	—	2 w/10 + 10% ad choice of one size	

(continued on next page)

Exhibit 11 *(concluded)*

Year	Duration	Sales Days Promoted	Consumer Promotion Activity	1.75 oz.	3.75 oz.	7.50 oz.	12.00 oz.	15.00 oz.	Comments
1976	1/5–2/27	41	$2 refund offer Multibrand	1 w/11	1 w/11	2 w/10	1 w/11	1 w/11	5% ad allowance for feature ad on any one size.
	4/5–4/30	21	15-cent cross-ruff coupon with Kimbies Multibrand	—	—	2 w/10 on choice of one size	2 w/10 on choice of one size	2 w/10 on choice of one size	Only one order permitted during promotion period. 10% ad allowance for ads featuring all three promoted brands.
	5/14–6/25	38	50-cent refund offer for 2 VPJ proofs of purchase		2 w/10 on twin pack + 5% ad	—	—	—	
	8/2–9/24	43	Reader's Digest sweepstakes; $1.50 refund offer and sweepstakes Multibrand	1 w/11 + 5% ad	1 w/11 + 5% ad	2 w/10 + 5% ad	1 w/11 + 5% ad	1 w/11 + 5% ad	Bonus 5% ad allowance for ads featuring all three promoted brands. Display allowance of $3 per retail outlet for an end-aisle, off-shelf display of all three brands (minimum 15 dozen per display).
	10/4–11/11	30	none	—	12% OI	—	—	—	
	10/4–12/13	50	none	—	—	—	—	15% OI	
1977	1/3–2/25	40	Swiss Army knife self-liquidating premium	—	—	10% OI	—	—	5% ad allowance if knife featured in advertising.
	4/4–4/29	20	25-cent coupon for 15-oz. VPJ Multibrand	—	10% OI on choice of one size + 5% ad	—	—	10% OI on choice of one size + 5% ad	Display allowance of $3 per retail outlet for displays of two out of three promoted brands (minimum 15 dozen per display).
	5/2–5/27	21	none	—	—	2 w/10	—	—	
	6/6–6/24	22	none	—	10% OI on twin-pack	—	—	—	

Source: Company records.

EXHIBIT 12 **Food Trade's Advertising Support for Petroleum Jelly and Other Packaged Goods**

	A Ads (> 3 in.)[a]		B Ads (1–3 in.)[a]		C Ads (< 1 in.)[a]		Total		Average Number of Ads per Account per Year
	No.	%	No.	%	No.	%	No.	%	
Petroleum Jelly									
VPJ	—	—	3	7.0%	39	93.0%	42	100%	2.63
Private label	—	—	—	—	6	100.0	6	100	0.37
Category									
Laundry detergents	109	10.1%	517	48.1%	449	41.8%	1,075	100%	67.00
Bar soaps	18	3.9	249	53.3	200	42.8	467	100	29.00
Hand lotion	2	1.2	25	14.7	143	84.1	170	100	11.00

[a]Ads are grouped by size in newspaper column inches. For example, a C ad would be one column wide and less than one inch long. In a large newspaper advertisement featuring many brands offered by a supermarket, a C ad (also known as an obituary ad or line mention) might consist of a single line giving the brand name and unit price. An A ad, in contrast, would usually appear in very large type and include a picture.

Note: Of the 42 VPJ ads counted, 2 were for the 1.75-oz. size; 12 for the 3.75-oz. size; 20 for the 7.50-oz. size; 6 for the 12-oz. size; and 2 for the 15-oz. size.

SOURCE: Company records, based on 1975 Majers data for three major metropolitan markets. Majers, an independent market research firm, monitored grocery, drug, and mass merchandiser newspaper advertising support for a wide variety of products.

EXHIBIT 13 Estimates of Trade Participation and Net Incremental Contribution (or loss) Associated with VPJ Trade Promotions, 1972–1977

Promotion Period		Sales Days Promoted	Estimated Trade Participation					Incremental Contribution (or Load) by Size					Total Net Incremental Contribution (or loss)
Year	Duration		1.75-oz.	3.75-oz.	7.50-oz	12.00-oz.	15.00-oz.	1.75-oz.	3.75-oz.	7.50-oz.	12.00-oz.	15.00-oz.	
1972	9/1–10/15	29	—	—	75%	55%	60%	—	—	$ 29,133	$ 27,246	$ 56,870	$113,249
1973	1/2–2/13	31	55%	65%	70	50	55	$ 14,522	$ 58,982	36,770	31,471	32,682	174,427
	5/1–6/30	43	55	70	75	—	—	14,054	21,795	61,066	24,970	60,730	96,915
	9/4–11/2	46	55	65	70	55	55	38,496	68,334	54,191	24,970	60,730	246,721
1974	2/1–3/15	29	—	—	75	55	60	—[a]	—[a]	26,204[a]	28,306	56,335	110,845
	5/1–6/14	31	55	—	70	—	—	11,146[a]	—[a]	24,973[a]	—[a]	—[a]	36,119
	8/1–9/13	31	55	65	70	55	55	(48,388)	25,881	(15,644)	43,808	24,533	30,190
	11/1–12/13	28	—	75	—	—	70	—[a]	8,562	—[a]	—	54,615[a]	63,177
1975	1/2–2/14	31	55	—	75	—	—	(90,623)	—	23,148	—	—	(67,475)
	3/10–4/18	32	—	—	85	65	75	—	—	46,934	39,894	49,182	136,010
	6/2–6/27	21	—	75	—	—	—	—	(18,334)	—	—	—	(18,334)
	9/2–9/30	21	55	—	75	—	—	(13,219)	—	27,652	—	—	14,433
	11/3–12/12	27	—	75	—	—	70	—	(31,115)	—	—	29,509	(1,606)
1976	1/5–2/27	41	80	90	95	80	80	32,984[a]	21,921[a]	159,265[a]	50,669[a]	65,902[a]	330,741
	4/5–4/30	21	—	—	90	75	80	—	—	8,939	(2,651)	15,693	28,581
	5/14–6/25	38	—	85	—	—	—	—	89,887	—	—	—	89,887
	8/2–9/24	43	70	80	85	70	75	48,863	59,310	102,004	40,103	41,278	291,558
	10/4–11/11	30	—	90	—	—	—	—	(39,570)	—	—	—	(39,570)
	10/4–12/13	50	—	—	—	—	85	—	—	—	—	26,932	26,932
1977	1/3–2/25	40	—	—	85	—	85	—[a]	—[a]	124,248[a]	—[a]	—[a]	124,248
	4/4–4/29	20	—	90	—	—	85	—	51,642	—	—	99,763	151,405
	5/2–5/27	21	—	—	90	—	—	—	—	11,094	—	—	11,094
	6/6–6/24	22	—	85	—	—	—	—	32,136	—	—	—	32,136
1972–77	Average	32	59	78	79	62	70	871	26,879	47,998	31,535	47,233	86,160

[a] A list-price increase on the designated size occurred simultaneously with the promotion.

Note: To be read: The trade promotion running from September 1 through October 15, 1972, generated a net incremental contribution of $29,133 on sales of the 7.50-oz. size, and a total net incremental contribution of $113,249.

Source: SPAR research commissioned by CIP.

EXHIBIT 14

Factory shipments, incremental unit sales, retail inventories, and consumer sales for 7.5-oz. VPJ, 1972–1977

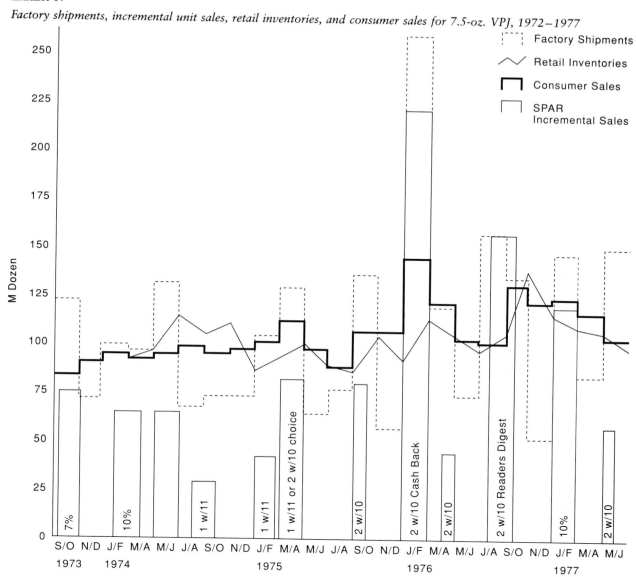

SOURCE: Company records.

MARKETING ORGANIZATION AND IMPLEMENTATION

MARKETING ORGANIZATION AND IMPLEMENTATION

During the 1970s and 1980s, marketing managers and academics, abetted by some prominent management consulting firms, became enthralled by the glamour of marketing strategy. In some circles, developing strategy has been viewed as a more creative and important activity than dealing with the nuts and bolts of implementation.

But by the late 1980s and 1990s, there were clear signs of another emerging trend: the increasing emphasis on improved performance in the *implementation* of marketing and business strategy. For example, an INSEAD survey of senior executives in companies operating in Europe[1] asked respondents to rate the relative importance of 18 different marketing issues. The issues were a comprehensive list of both strategic and implementation-oriented challenges. The top five issues were all concerned with implementation and organization, as listed below:

1. The increasing importance of product and service quality.
2. Assessing changing customers' needs.
3. Creating a "marketing culture" throughout the firm.
4. Adapting firm structure to changes in market strategies.
5. Recruiting and retaining high-quality marketing professionals.

None of the five challenges above is concerned with the strategic questions of "What should we do?" The executives knew that they *must* improve quality, assess changing needs, and create a marketing culture. The challenge is in the execution question: "How shall we do it?"

In the INSEAD survey, the executives rated strategy issues, such as developing effective international marketing strategies, corporate image strategies, and formulating strategies for mature products and services, much lower on their list of priorities.

In 1991, another survey at Stanford University[2] asked a group of senior and upper-middle managers from companies around the world to rank 16 challenges for

This note was prepared by Professor John A. Quelch.
Copyright © 1984 by the President and Fellows of Harvard College.
Harvard Business School note 9-584-024 (Rev. 4/2/92).

[1]Larréché, Powell, and Ebeling, *Key Strategic Marketing Issues for the 1990s,* (Fontainbleau, France: INSEAD, 1987).

[2]Kosnik and Montgomery, *Marketing Challenges of the 1990s,* survey of the Stanford 1991 Senior Executive Program, Stanford, California (1991).

the 1990s. The researchers used questions similar to the INSEAD study, with three exceptions. First, they asked for separate rankings of the need to improve product quality and enhance customer service, to determine the relative importance of each. Second, they added a challenge missing from the INSEAD study: building and managing alliances. Finally, they deleted several of the challenges that had been rated toward the bottom of the INSEAD survey.

The results, like those of the INSEAD study, showed the predominance of implementation-related issues. The five leading challenges were:

1. Assessing changing customer needs.
2. Adapting to changing markets.
3. Enhancing customer service.
4. Creating a marketing culture throughout the firm.
5. Ensuring product quality.

Once again, the problems facing executives were of the "how to?" variety. How exactly should a company so assess changing needs that it can adapt, enhance its service to customers, and improve continually the quality of its product? How can a company's culture be so changed that everyone from the accountants to the receptionists to the workers on the shipping dock are more marketing- and customer-oriented?

Much of the impetus for this emerging emphasis on execution has come from the remarkable success of companies that have focused on the basics: delivering high-quality products and services faster and at prices lower than their leading competitors. Such names as British Airways, Federal Express, Honda, Motorola, SAS, and Sony have come to symbolize impeccable quality and rapid innovation at reasonable prices, thereby earning the loyalty of the customers they serve around the globe. As these firms have demonstrated, although world-class quality, speed, and value may be critical to the success of a firm's *strategy,* they can only be achieved through continuous improvements in *implementation.*

Some managers are often heard to claim that a business degree is no substitute for experience. What they often are referring to is experience in dealing with day-to-day problems that arise in the process of focusing people on continually improving quality in everything they do, despite continual surprises in a fast-moving marketplace. This cannot be easily reproduced in the business school classroom. The purpose of this note is to help you understand the skills associated with good marketing implementation. With this knowledge, you will be better prepared to handle the day-to-day challenges of creating satisfied customers in a real world that will often appear to operate by Murphy's law: "Whatever can go wrong, will go wrong."

Bonoma's Framework

The most useful framework for understanding marketing implementation issues has been developed by Thomas V. Bonoma at Harvard Business School.[3] His framework, presented in Table A, sees marketing execution taking place at four levels in the organization—actions, programs, systems, and policies. He also reviews four man-

---

[3]Thomas V. Bonoma, "Making Your Marketing Strategy Work," *Harvard Business Review* 62, no. 2 (March–April 1984).

TABLE A   **Framework for Diagnosing Implementation Problems**

Functions	Skills			
	Interacting	*Allocating*	*Monitoring*	*Organizing*
Actions				
Programs				
Systems				
Policies				

SOURCE: Thomas V. Bonoma, "Making Your Marketing Strategy Work," *Harvard Business Review* 62, no. 2 (March–April 1984).

agerial skills—interacting, allocating, monitoring, and organizing—which can contribute to the quality and effectiveness of the actions, programs, systems, and policies. In the following paragraphs we review the elements of Bonoma's framework.

Levels of Execution Activities

Actions represent "the lowest level of execution." Examples include how a salesperson presents a cooperative advertising program to an account and how, when, and by whom a pricing change is announced to the trade. Too many managers are all too willing (or self-important) to assume that others will take care of implementing the details of their plans. While senior executives frequently have to do more strategic thinking and less tactical implementation than their subordinates, it is essential that executional tactics are not given short shrift or viewed as less intellectual and, therefore, less important. Many of the most successful U.S. corporations, such as Procter & Gamble, are renowned for the attention to detail paid by all their employees, including the most senior executives.

The managements of IBM, Xerox, and other companies that have made serious commitments to improving customer satisfaction have put this into practice by becoming more involved with visiting accounts and personally responding to customer complaints.

Programs are integrated sets of detailed marketing actions. A product manager will typically develop an integrated program for his or her product covering all elements of the marketing mix. In addition, a detailed program will be developed on each element of the marketing mix. For example, an integrated communications program specifying advertising, personal selling, and merchandising efforts for the coming year will often be put together. Each program must be internally consistent and mutually consistent with other programs developed by the product or market managers, or both, and by other functional groups.

Systems include "the firm's formal organizational monitoring and budgeting overlays, which foster or inhibit getting the marketing job done." Systems do not just refer to organization charts. There are systems on more focused topics, such as reward and compensation systems, and systems for monitoring quality and customer satisfaction. The importance of systems stems from their ability to influence the responses of those working within them, hopefully in positive and predictable directions. Organization structures, for example, affect the direction and speed of information flows, which can greatly influence the ability of the organization to respond swiftly to unexpected changes in the competitive environment or to manage smoothly the new product development process.

Policies prescribe whereas systems describe, according to Bonoma. Policies can, of course, be developed on a myriad of issues important to an organization's existence and functioning. These issues range from the strategic to the tactical, from focused topics, such as personnel recruitment and promotion, to more broadly based topics, such as quality and a code of ethics. These policies set high standards and help to shape the organization's marketing theme, culture, and leadership style. Policies, written and unwritten, in these latter areas given direction to the organization's systems, programs, and actions. Given the uncertainties inherent in marketing, the importance of leadership to marketing success cannot be overstated. A committed leader who can get the organization behind him or her often can execute successfully a seemingly unimplementable program.

Managerial Skills

Bonoma cites four managerial skills that can reinforce good policies, systems, programs, and actions, or partly compensate for poor ones.

Interacting. We can all recall the manager who had a great idea but could not persuade his or her superiors, peers, and subordinates to devote the time, money, and effort needed to implement it. Interacting skills are fundamental to effective implementation in a marketing context, because marketing, by its very nature, involves transactions between individuals. Interacting skills depend on the manager's understanding that he or she cannot do his or her job alone; understanding the viewpoints of those both within and outside the organization on whom his or her success depends; and understanding how to so manage the process of implementing marketing programs that the needs and motivations of all interested groups are at least taken into account if not accommodated.

The implementation challenges confronting the marketing manager are especially great, because of the diversity of groups within and beyond the organization on whose cooperation the achievement of objectives depends. The marketing manager who stays in the ivory tower of headquarters and rarely visits the field may have trouble motivating the sales force and the trade. The marketing manager who never visits the plants where the products for which he or she is responsible are made may have trouble securing the cooperation of production personnel when a sudden surge in demand requires overtime production or the installation of a new production line. The marketing manager who treats advertising agency personnel as subordinates, rather than as partners, is unlikely to motivate them to go the extra mile in developing a world-class communications campaign.

Interacting skills are especially important for the product manager, whose responsibility often extends beyond the limits of his or her authority. The product manager must persuade sales, manufacturing, and R&D to provide help in implementing his or her programs. Interestingly, relationship management problems seem to occur more frequently with these other functions within the organization than with the external groups and organizations for which the marketing function is exclusively responsible, such as advertising agencies and distributors. In the latter cases, relationship management problems are perhaps more likely to be anticipated and, therefore, avoided.

Allocating. Allocating refers to the assignation of an organization's scarce resources—principally human resources, time, and money—among competing programs, and the further allocation of these resources within each program. For example, the advertising budget must be allocated by product, by region, by media vehicle, and over time. As a managerial skill, allocating captures the concept of husbanding the resources under the manager's control for maximum productivity. Practical examples of this skill include assigning the right subordinates to the tasks that build on and develop their capabilities, and assigning marketing dollars among products to ensure that new products in particular are given a fair chance of success.

Monitoring. The measurement of performance against objectives is essential to the ongoing assessment of strategies and their implementation. Monitoring can be done at the level of the individual, the program, or the organization, and can range from a review of an individual salesperson's call reports to a periodic audit of the capabilities of the entire marketing function.

The value of monitoring in guiding the revision and improvement of strategies and programs is obvious; yet monitoring is often a weak link in implementation. Three problems can arise.

First, the performance measures used may be those that are conveniently available, rather than those that are most relevant. For example, many firms will target a specific market segment yet measure performance in terms of overall market share.

Second, many organizations' internal information and data processing systems have been designed primarily for the benefit of the accounting department, rather than to provide the marketing function with the information it needs sufficiently quickly to help decision making. Many companies cannot assess profitability by product or by major account. Even banks rarely know the profitability of their individual branches.

Third, managers can sometimes overmonitor, becoming bogged down in a surfeit of performance data leading to "analysis paralysis" or the tendency to take at face value data that should be viewed more skeptically. As associated risk is that managers may become too involved in evaluating data on past performance at the expense of thinking strategically about the future.

Good managers identify the limited number of key factors that really make the difference between success and failure in their businesses. These are the factors that they monitor and on which they build the objectives that are then communicated to their subordinates. Good managers also know the motivational importance of giving their subordinates the tools to monitor those factors for which they are responsible and the power to correct problems that are within their control. Finally, good managers tend to monitor by exception, following up primarily on cases in which performance falls short of forecast, and complimenting subordinates when performance exceeds expectations.

Organizing. Managers must work within and around the formal organization structure to implement marketing strategies and programs expeditiously and effectively. A change in marketing strategy often requires a change in the formal organization structure, but this typically cannot be implemented overnight. In the short term, therefore, managers may have to use their organizing skills to accommodate the revised strategy, perhaps developing new dotted-line relationships, reassigning personnel, or instituting ad hoc task forces. The good manager does not ignore the formal organization structure, but he or she is not obsessed with it either. Rather, the good manager has a task focus (and encourages others to adopt the same perspective) and uses his or her organizing skills to get the job done. The more complex or unusual the task, the greater the organizing skills required.

Comments on the Framework

Having presented Bonoma's framework, three points should be made.

First, marketing implementation problems can rarely be classified neatly into one of the cells of the Table A mix. As Bonoma himself points out, most problems will involve deficiencies in more than one skill area at more than one level of organizational activity.

Second, the field of marketing implementation remains so little developed that other frameworks may prove to be equally if not more valuable. Bonoma's contribution has been to attempt to identify the specific skills associated with good marketing implementation.

Third, while developed to gain insight into marketing implementation, Bonoma's framework is broadly applicable to other functional areas. Their implementation skills are often important to marketing. Manufacturing's ability to build quality products will affect the required level of customer service in the field. Research and development's ability to move new products rapidly to development will greatly influence the marketing organization's competitive advantage. In implementation, as in strategy, an organization's chain is only as strong as its weakest link.

Importance of Implementation

The importance of good implementation cannot be overstated.

First, implementation skills valued by distribution channels or end customers, or both, can be important points of competitive differentiation. Frito Lay's dominance of the salty snack market is largely attributable to the training, commitment, and effectiveness of its army of 10,000 van salespeople, who heavily influence the allocation of retail shelf space. In addition, smaller companies, which cannot afford heavy R&D or marketing expenditures, often discover that implementation skills in servicing distribution channels can be an effective point of competitive differentiation achievable at relatively low cost.

Second, the economic penalties stemming from poor execution can be substantial. To launch a national advertising campaign for a new product before sufficient distribution has been achieved is wasteful. Likewise, being unable to keep stores adequately stocked with product during periods of strong seasonal demand worsens trade relations and results in lost sales.

Poor execution in customer service is particularly costly. One study found that customers are five times more likely to switch vendors because of a customer service problem than because of price concerns or a product quality problem.[4] And a second study demonstrated that reducing customer defections by 5 percent boosts profits by 25 to 85 percent across a variety of industries![5]

Third, poor execution can be embarrassing both to the organization and to the managers responsible. General Mills recently had to cancel a sweepstakes promotion because the odds of winning had appeared incorrectly in its advertising of the offer. After an advertisement for Northwest Orient Airlines' fares from Minnesota to Europe was mistakenly run in *Boston Magazine*, a tear sheet of the correct advertisement with Boston to Europe fares had to be mailed to all the magazine's subscribers. Such errors are embarrassing and expensive to correct.

An interesting question for discussion is whether there are certain product-market circumstances under which implementation skills become relatively more important to success.

First, mature products may be more execution sensitive than new products. Grocery products manufacturers in the United States are confronting low population growth, limited opportunities for product innovation, and increasing private label and generic competition. They have to be increasingly concerned about maintaining shelf space for their brands at the point of sale. The executional skills of their sales forces or brokers in securing distribution are more essential than ever to their products' success.

Second, implementation skills may be more important when the competitive environment is turbulent. For example, list price changes or temporary price promotions may need to be implemented more frequently and rapidly than usual. Budgeted expenditures may need to be increased, reallocated, or cut back in response to competitive pressures, and these changes must be communicated throughout the headquarters and field organizations as well as to distribution channels and suppliers.

Third, implementation skills may be more or less important for companies in the same industry pursuing different strategies. For example, a computer hardware manufacturer stressing technical leadership and product innovation might appear less dependent on implementation skills than a manufacturer pursuing a follower strategy and emphasizing field service. In fact, the first manufacturer also will need implementation skills—but of a different kind. It will have to be adept at managing all the interfunctional relationships needed to bring new product concepts efficiently to market. Implementation skills are always important, but the required mix of skills may vary from one organization to another just as the appropriate mix will vary within an organization from one execution level to another.

Evaluating Performance in Marketing Implementation

Prior to the 1970s, marketing managers focused on such measures as sales volume, gross margin, and profits to assess the success of marketing programs. These measures are indicators of a firm's *efficiency*—that is, its ability to *do things right* in the process of creating and delivering value to customers at a reasonable cost.

---

[4]Forum Corporation, *Customer Focus: An Executive Briefing* (Boston, Massachusetts, 1989).

[5]F. Reichheld and E. Sasser, "Zero Defections: Quality Comes to Services," *Harvard Business Review*, September–October 1990.

There has been increased emphasis during the last 20 years on market share, and for the last 10 on quality and customer satisfaction, as measures of marketing *effectiveness*—that is, a firm's ability to *do the right things* for its customers. The underlying logic is that satisfying customers through quality will lead both to increased market share and improved profitability in the long run.

In the last five years, another criterion has emerged: *ethics*. In marketing implementation, ethics encompasses honesty, integrity, and fairness in managing a company's relationships with customers, channels, other stakeholders, and competitors.

The first challenge for anyone responsible for implementing marketing actions, programs, systems, and policies is to consciously consider efficiency, effectiveness, and ethics at each step in the process. The second is to build explicit standards and monitoring mechanisms so the people engaged in the marketing process can learn what good practice looks like, spot potential problems early, and take corrective action. The final implementation challenge is never to become complacent. World-class competitors understand that past standards of excellence in profits, quality, and ethical behavior can always be improved, and they continuously strive to do better. They are implicitly following the advice of the American humorist, Will Rogers: "Even if you're on the right track, if you sit down to rest, you'll get run over."

Conclusion: Implementation and Strategy

It is frequently a challenge to determine whether a marketing problem confronting an organization is an implementation problem or a strategy problem. Often, problems that appear to be implementation-based and are, therefore, blamed on an ineffective sales force or uncooperative distributors, reflect a basic weakness in an organization's marketing strategy. At the same time, it is equally appropriate to examine any problem situation closely for implementation deficiencies before deciding that the organization's marketing strategy must be changed.

An effective marketing manager must be both a good strategic thinker and a good implementer. The appropriate mix of strategic and implementation skills will vary according to product market circumstances and each manager's responsibilities. But it is always essential to recognize that strategies only are as good as their implementation.

GENERAL FOODS CORPORATION: THE PRODUCT MANAGEMENT SYSTEM

In February 1985, senior marketing executives from General Foods (GF) Desserts Division (DD) met over lunch to discuss the trimming of the marketing organization that had been implemented during the previous two years under the leadership of Roger Smith, general manager. The discussion turned to the broader issue of the future of the product management system in use at GF since the company was founded in the 1920s. Differences of opinion about the product manager's tasks and responsibilities were evident in the comments of two senior DD managers:

> Our product managers must have profit responsibility. Only then will they act to add to stockholder value, to manage our assets effectively, and to deliver an ROI that exceeds the cost of capital. As for advertising, that is just one aspect of their job.
>
> Product managers should not be general business managers. They should be the advertising and promotion specialists on their products, responsible for building the franchise in terms of sales volume and share. With no growth in the volume of food consumed in the United States, franchise building depends upon regional marketing and rifling more finely defined target segments. This takes time.

As Roger Smith looked at the current DD organization chart (see Exhibit 1), he wondered about the effectiveness of the product management system and what, if anything, he and his colleagues could do to improve it.

Company Background

Product Lines. Since its formation in the 1920s, GF had been a leading U.S. producer of processed food products. In 1984, with sales of $8.9 billion and operating profits of $768 million, up 12 percent from 1983, GF was still the largest U.S. company operating solely in the food business. Beatrice Foods and Dart & Kraft were larger, but only as a result of revenues from their nonfood businesses. GF marketed over 1,200 items in the United States and held the first or second market share position in three quarters of the product categories in which it competed.

GF was organized into the following six sectors, each representing a specific menu segment:

1. *Basic Foods* and *Baked Goods* included Entenmann's, Inc., and the Breakfast Foods Division, which marketed Post cereals and Log Cabin Syrup.

2. The *Oscar Mayer* sector manufactured and sold processed meats and also was responsible for the manufacture of Louis Rich turkeys and Claussen pickles.

3. *Coffee and Food Service* included the Maxwell House Division and the Food Service Products Division, which sold coffee and other GF products to institutional buyers.

4. The *Packaged Convenience Foods* sector included three divisions organized by menu segment. Each division sold products that used a variety of manufacturing processes and distribution systems:

- The Beverage Division sold powdered soft drinks, including Tang, Kool-Aid, Country Time, and Crystal Light.

- The Meals Division produced Bird's Eye frozen products, dry products, such as Minute Rice, Stove Top stuffing, Shake'n Bake seasoned coating mixes, and Ronzoni pasta.

- The Desserts Division manufactured Jell-O gelatin, Jell-O Pudding, D-Zerta, and frozen toppings like Cool Whip. In addition, DD had recently expanded into the frozen novelty category with Jell-O Pudding Pops and Jell-O Gelatin Pops. Most DD brands were share leaders in their respective subcategories. In FY 1984, the division delivered $110 million in operating profits on more than $600 million in revenues.

5. *International operations.* Organized into five geographical groups and accounting for a quarter of GF sales, the international division had subsidiaries or joint ventures in 20 countries and exported GF products to 100 more. As well as marketing products paralleling GF's U.S. lines, GF subsidiaries, as a result of acquisition, also marketed the leading ice cream in Brazil, the leading chewing gum in France, and the leading snack product line in Canada.

This case was prepared by Professors John A. Quelch and Paul W. Farris.
Copyright © 1985 by the President and Fellows of Harvard College. Harvard Business School case 9-586-057.

Evolution of Strategy. During the 1970s, the rate of U.S. population growth flattened, and volume growth in the food industry declined to 1–2 percent per year. In addition, many of the product categories that GF dominated had matured. For example, per capita consumption of coffee, which accounted for a third of GF's sales, peaked in 1962. Consumption of Jell-O gelatin topped out in 1969. As these products matured, GF had to identify new avenues for future growth.

Nevertheless, during this period, GF's financial results were strong. Earnings per share doubled between 1973 and 1979. By FY 1981, GF's return on equity and return on invested capital were among the highest in the food industry. CEO James Ferguson commented, however, that "the predominant part of the growth we've achieved has been a function of our good control of costs. What we were not doing was broadening the base of the business."

Hence, in 1981, GF shifted strategy from earnings and margin protection to volume and franchise building. Under the leadership of a new president, Philip Smith, GF managers were instructed to strive for 3–5 percent annual volume growth instead of 1 percent, and to achieve 15.0 percent return on capital instead of the 13.2 percent achieved in the previous year.

GF management responded in three ways. First, there was renewed emphasis on new product development to identify and develop new items that would appeal to a more convenience-oriented consumer. Second, continued attention was paid to achieving cost reductions on established products to build margins that could be used to fund new product development. Third, GF engaged in a selective acquisition strategy to acquire food companies that would fill gaps in GF's product menu as well as add new manufacturing processes, technologies, or distribution systems. Oscar Mayer, Entenmann's, and Ronzoni were acquired as part of this strategy. Unlike competitors, such as Quaker Oats and General Mills, which acquired nonfood businesses that made products with high margins and fast growth, GF maintained its focus on food and beverages. At the same time, the emphasis on volume growth led GF to divest operations that continued to experience volume declines, notably the pet foods division, which was sold to Anderson Clayton Foods in 1984.

Top management realized that volume growth could not be achieved without investment. Capital investment in 1984 exceeded $200 million and advertising close to $500 million made GF the second largest national advertiser after Procter & Gamble.

Philip Smith espoused three principles to guide GF's mission through the 1980s:

- GF aims to be the premier food and beverage company in the world *through providing superior customer satisfaction.*
- GF believes that *ideas* are what build business.
- GF affirms that it will reward well the people who come up with business-building ideas and *carry them successfully into action.*

The Product Management Function

Overview.   Within each operating division dealing with a particular menu segment, GF used a product management system to manage its businesses. The strength of the system was that it identified specific individuals responsible for the well-being of each business. As a result, the system encouraged individuals to develop a sense of ownership for their businesses, within the framework of a larger organization.

While the operation of the product management function varied somewhat from one division or business to another, there were elements common to all brands. Brian Harvey, DD marketing manager for frozen novelties, explained the basic organizational structure and career path:

> The product management system is like a pyramid in which individuals take on more responsibilities and brands with increased experience. At the base of the pyramid is the assistant product manager, the entry-level position for recent MBA graduates. At the top of the pyramid is the marketing manager. Along the way, an individual progresses from assistant product manager to associate product manager, product manager, product group manager or category manager, before being appointed marketing manager. Beyond this level, individuals leave the product management function to take on general management responsibilities.

The broad-based training and exposure individuals received as they progressed through the product management career path were regarded as excellent preparation for general management. All but one of GF's domestic division general managers had risen through the product management function.

Assistant Product Manager.   *Recruitment and training:* Recent business graduates entered GF as assistant product managers (assistants). Occasionally, assistants were drawn from other functions. A GF recruiting brochure profiled candidates for a product management career as people who:

- Can figure out what needs to be done and get it done without substantial supervision.
- Have leadership qualities and the ability to guide others to reach an objective.
- Have an entrepreneurial spirit, like to maintain a degree of ownership for their ideas and translate them into reality.
- Possess good instincts for the marketplace—feel empathy with consumers—and show the vision and creativity that lead to new ideas of worth and value to consumers.
- Are able to apply their intelligence in an analytic framework.
- Can demonstrate administrative skills.
- Have the potential to develop into candidates for general management.

According to one DD marketing manager:

> We want people who are at one and the same time leaders and team players; people who have an enormous amount of drive and self-confidence and are able to innovate, rather than just be the stewards of others' ideas.

Training and development began as soon as a new assistant joined GF. Training was considered fundamental to the effectiveness of the product management system. As a result, senior marketing executives were evaluated not only on their business results but also on the training of individuals within their organizations. According to Denise Rodriguez, DD product group manager for packaged desserts:

> The sound development of assistant and associate product managers is key to GF's longer-term success. After all, the product management system is our major source of candidates for general management. There is so much to be done and so few people to do it, it's critical to have everyone contributing at a maximum degree of effectiveness.

Ninety percent of a new assistant's training was on the job. In addition, GF's line management and marketing staff groups offered in-house seminars throughout the year. These seminars focused on such topics as product positioning, sales promotion, consumer research, and advertising copy development. The seminars enabled individuals to discuss their businesses with their peers who were facing similar challenges.

All new DD assistants also completed a 13-week sales training program shortly after arrival. This program was designed to improve their understanding of the changing retail environment and of how products are actually sold and distributed as well as to give them a feel for the sales representative's job. This exposure was considered essential, given the importance of sales and its role in developing longer-term brand strategies. During the 13 weeks, individuals called on accounts, observed retail and key account representatives, and undertook special projects for field personnel.

Tasks and responsibilities: The tasks and responsibilities of assistants were defined to provide as broad an exposure to an entire business in as short a time as possible. Initially, assistants were responsible for volume planning (market and share forecasting), financial budget control, production planning coordination, promotion execution, coordination with legal and purchasing functions, and business analysis. A conscious effort was made to expose new assistants to the nonmarketing functions. In addition, the assistant often assumed responsibility for national promotion strategy, planning and execution, as well as packaging strategy and execution.

When asked about the assistant's responsibilities, one product manager commented:

> A good assistant will come in, learn the fundamentals of the business during the first few months, and then generate new ideas and programs which will yield results. The most successful assistants define their job far more broadly than volume planning or forecasting.

Comments from several DD assistants reflected varying attitudes toward the nature of the job:

> The scope of the assistant's job depends on the size of the brand. The larger the brand, the more likely that the assistant will specialize. On the other hand, a new assistant assigned to a smaller brand would be part of a smaller team, so would be exposed to a broader array of issues.

* * * * *

> I felt important from day one. But it was six months before I knew what I was doing. The next six months I spent turning my ideas into actions and making something happen in the marketplace.

* * * * *

> I found volume planning to be great fun. Some people thought that projecting a brand's sales would mean spending all day at a computer. What it really involved was talking to people, interpreting data, and making judgments about what was going on. In fact, I felt enormous power because I was the one person in the organization with the most knowledge of what was happening in the marketplace.

* * * * *

> I liked being given projects for which I was responsible from day one. I was able to watch my ideas take shape and, with the guidance of my product manager, see the plan executed. In many ways, my first experiences were a microcosm of what the product manager was doing for the brand as a whole.

The need to ensure that assistants maintained a broad business perspective and did not become bogged down in numbers was a concern of some senior managers. The corporate vice president of Marketing Services commented:

> Our MBA hires are very numbers oriented when they come here. I feel that we reinforce that bias by putting them to work on volume planning and regional marketing analyses. Assistants spend more time on the personal computer than any other level of management. True, an assistant can understand the business better by running the numbers, but there's always a temptation to rely too much on the numbers. You must develop a strategy without the numbers first. It's important that the job of the assistant is not so detailed and numbers oriented that we end up merely developing detail and numbers-oriented product managers.

Typically, assistants would work on their initial brand assignment for a year or more. This provided sufficient time to enable an assistant to become familiar with a brand and make significant contributions to its growth. One assistant noted:

> It was six months before I felt in control enough to take charge of programs and to direct the organization in implementing the

programs I felt were right. Had I left my initial assignment too soon, I would have had to have started up the learning curve again.

Associate Product Manager.   Assistants who performed well could expect promotion to associate product manager (associate) within 18–20 months of arrival. However, GF managers stressed that promotion was based on performance, rather than according to a timetable. Promotion was not automatic. According to Roger Smith:

> Every new brand assistant has the intellectual ability needed to do a good job. Those that succeed derive enjoyment from building the business. We quickly separate out people who merely play the system and do formula business management from those who have ideas and initiative, seize opportunities, and show an ability to lead and manage.

Associates were given the autonomy to make things happen on a business by identifying business-building ideas, convincing others they were worthwhile, and taking them from concept to execution. Associates were often given responsibility for substantial projects on a large brand or total responsibility for managing a small brand. In addition, associates maintained day-to-day contact with personnel in operations, technical research, and market research, as well as executives at the advertising agency, particularly regarding media and copy execution.

Several DD associates commented on the position as follows:

> I've been an associate for seven months now. I've worked on a project to add Jell-O to chocolate chip cookies. It didn't work out but it was a memorable project. Many associates spend some time working on secondary line extensions for their brands. This gives an associate responsibility for a tangible product with minimal financial risk.

> * * * * *

> I've been an associate for 18 months on sugar-free Jell-O. I've had three product managers during that time. I know more about the brand than my boss, so my recommendations carry a lot of weight. I'm also effectively the product manager on D-Zerta and report directly to the category manager on issues relating to this brand.

> * * * * *

> An associate might not do a better job than an assistant would but, as a result of greater experience, would get it done faster. Another difference is that an associate would never go to his or her product manager with a problem without a suggested solution.

> * * * * *

> I've learned a lot beyond marketing at this level. In developing and introducing a line extension, I have worked on business proposals, facility plans, cost programs, and product for-

mulations in addition to advertising and promotions. It has broadened my knowledge and exposure as I prepare to run my own brand.

Product Manager.   The GF product manager (PM) was responsible for the day-to-day health of his or her franchise. This responsibility involved the development of annual plans and, once approved, ensuring their excellent execution. Since the plans were related to functions beyond marketing, PMs were responsible for leading all functional resource efforts affecting their products. The scope of the PM's responsibilities often was discussed by senior DD managers, some of whom supported a broader definition of the PM's role:

> We no longer want PMs to be just advertising and promotion managers. We want each PM to be the hub of the interfunctional decisions and activities that affect the product. PMs must provide leadership, not just coordination. They must lead and encourage the other functions in developing business-building ideas.
>
> We are moving to a business management view of product management, pushing the concept of general management further down the organization. When GF had multiple SBUs and matrix management, too many decisions were made at too high a level.

Gail Turner was product manager on Pudding Pops. She described how she spent her time:

> I've worked on all three parts of the business—packaged desserts, toppings, and now frozen novelties. They're at different life-cycle stages and use different distribution systems. I've also had assignments on both new and established products. There's a conscious effort in DD to plan an individual's career path to develop breadth and depth, while also permitting you to get to know the same team of professionals in marketing and other functions. Also, there's so much new product activity in DD that career progress can be fast.
>
> Right now, about 10 percent of my time is spent touching base with my boss, Brian Harvey, the marketing manager on frozen novelties. About 20 percent of my time is spent coaching and directing the associates and assistants in my brand group. A third of my time is spent working with our advertising agency and with other functions, such as MRD and sales planning. Daily fire fighting takes about 10 percent of my time, probably a higher percentage in the summer when Pudding Pops sales peak and retail stock-outs are more frequent. The rest of the time, I'm thinking and working on plans for the product.
>
> Increasingly, PMs in the DD are being evaluated on their ability to lead the other functions. The marketing manager is also looking to me for longer-term planning because, on a growing business, the cost and timing of incremental capacity investment is important. A good PM should have a portfolio of business-building projects at various stages of development in his or her operating plan. For me, the fun of the job is selling ideas to management and building the business by making them happen.

I have only one reservation. I think there should be bonuses for performance at the PM level to reflect the increased responsibility that management is claiming the PM should assume.

To illustrate the broadening nature of the PM job, Brian Harvey summarized several of Turner's contributions to the business in the past year:

She initiated a major review of the Pudding Pops advertising strategy, which culminated in a presentation we made to Roger Smith. She managed the technical development, marketing research, and introduction of a subline of the Pudding Pops brand. She and her team have reassessed the sales promotion strategy for Pudding Pops. Finally, she has worked with technical research to develop a research program for Pudding Pops for the next three years.

Transfers of individuals from one division to another did not typically occur before the product manager level. Management believed that each division could provide a sufficient breadth of experience during the first few years of an individual's product management career. Because DD's product line included frozen as well as dry distribution systems, and new businesses like Pudding Pops alongside old ones like Jell-O gelatin, there was a wide diversity of assignments. One DD product manager who had been in another division commented on the differences:

I found some differences when I moved to DD. The products here have high unit margins, so tend to be driven by marketing ideas and marketing spending. The previous product I worked on was more sales driven, but it gave me a different perspective. I've had fun in both assignments. In fact, now I feel I could move anywhere in GF and manage any kind of business.

Beyond Product Manager. *Product group manager and category manager:* Following the product manager level, individuals were placed in charge of a series of businesses. The product group managers (PGMs) and category managers (CMs) were responsible for the overall strategic direction and long-term financial health of the businesses they supervised. They focused on overall business management and the quality of execution of their brands' annual plans. When necessary, they were responsible for making resource trade-offs among their businesses. Typically, a PGM or CM would supervise two or more PMs and would be responsible for sales of over $200 million.

According to PGM Denise Rodriguez:

The PM focuses on brand volume, brand share, and the marketing expenditure details of the P&L. The PGM worries more about nonmarketing issues, such as capacity planning and asset management.

PGMs differ in the closeness with which they supervise their PMs, often as a function of how experienced the PMs are. If a PGM is consistently supervising too closely, that means either that the PGM is not doing his or her job or that the PM is having real problems.

In addition to his or her specific responsibilities, a PGM or CM also might be given divisionwide responsibility for coordinating training, recruiting, or the development of the divisional five-year plan. PGMs and CMs could organize their management teams as they saw fit and also frequently headed multifunctional task forces within DD.

Marketing Manager. The DD marketing manager (MM) was responsible for the direction of marketing activities, both staff and line, across the division's entire menu segment. The MM was the prime mover in shaping long-term strategies for the segment and was the ultimate determinant of the quality of near-term marketing activities. As a member of the DD general manager's (GM) staff, the MM participated in developing financial strategies to improve the overall profitability of the division's franchises.

John Day, DD MM for established products, commented on the thrust of his position and on his role in the approval process:

Idea generation and strategy are the key elements of my job. My responsibility is to have a vision of where the DD businesses under my direction should be going and then to secure the organization's commitment to that vision. I spend about 60 percent of my time on marketing-related issues, giving advice, and approving the proposals of my direct reports. As is typical in a consumer-driven business, my role as marketing manager goes beyond marketing, since I'm really responsible for the overall health and value of DD businesses. So I spend a good portion of my time with nonmarketing functions, especially finance and operations on capital investment planning.

As marketing manager, I oversee the development of and approve each product's annual marketing plan. I deliver synopses of all the plans to the GM. Any major changes in a brand's strategic direction reflected in the plan have to be approved by him. He also reviews each product's five-year strategic plan. While this sounds primarily like an approval and refinement role, a big part of this responsibility is shaping an environment in which the organization is encouraged to generate new ideas.

In the advertising area, a new execution of an existing campaign would be shown to the GM as a courtesy, but any new copy proposal would be shown to the GM at the storyboard stage. A major shift in the media budget from radio to print would need the GM's approval but not a reallocation of television dayparts.

Approvals for price changes go beyond the division general manager. On many GF products, the price-value relationship got out of line in recent years. Annual price increases on our brands, therefore, have to be approved by the group vice president for Packaged Convenience Foods.

General Manager. The DD general manager was responsible for the performance of the division and oversaw staff in all functional areas. According to Roger Smith:

My job is to prioritize business opportunities and allocate resources to ensure that the necessary long-term commitments are made to development projects, and that resources are properly allocated to achieve our quantitative division goals. I have to bring home the plan.

Retention.   GF's product management pyramid was such that almost all appointments and promotions occurred from within. Attrition occurred at all levels and for a variety of reasons. According to John Day, marketing manager, the ability to be a strong leader was the key skill where product management personnel were most likely to run into difficulty. Day recalled what happened to the 12 assistants who joined GF with him in 1974:

> Three left before the PM level, one to start his own company, another went to an advertising agency. Seven left at the PM and PGM levels. Three went into management consulting and one transferred to our corporate marketing services department. Three others left for smaller companies to gain what they hoped would be more general management responsibility faster than they thought they could get it at GF.
>
> One of the other two survivors apart from me is the marketing manager for new product development in the beverage division. His previous assignment was as GF marketing manager in Puerto Rico. The other is a category manager in the Maxwell House Division. He took a two-year stint as a district sales manager in the course of his career. This kind of cross-functional experience is being encouraged more and more.

There was concern among senior managers that GF sometimes lost marketing personnel it would rather have retained, but there was little agreement on how such losses could be prevented. One subject, however, on which there was agreement was the importance of superior-subordinate coaching, and the need to ensure that product management personnel not only had the skills to do a good job in this area but also practiced them. According to one PGM:

> It's easy to know if a product manager isn't paying enough attention to some aspect of his business. Results will either be unacceptable, or the situation will be brought to my attention. Sometimes, this isn't the case with training. We need to make sure people aren't short-changed here.

Product Management's Relations with Other Functions

As in other packaged goods companies, the product management organization at GF had traditionally been the lead function in initiating and executing product policies and programs. The other functions—such as technical research, operations, and sales—had often been viewed merely as support groups that put into effect what marketing wanted to happen.

This put a substantial burden of responsibility for the company's success on marketing. As one GF general manager put it:

> As the lead function, marketing personnel must realize that they are ultimately responsible for the well-being of the thousands of people who work for GF in the other functional areas.

By 1985, the GF product manager was being encouraged to act more as a team leader than a ringmaster. According to a DD product group manager who had begun his career in market research:

> Our product management personnel should not just approach the other functions with requests for executional and fire-fighting assistance. They should approach them with *questions* on how to grow the business and involve them in strategic as well as tactical decision making. This would enhance the morale of the people in these functional areas, ensure that GF continues to attract top quality personnel to serve in them, and add to the overall climate of creativity in the division. The world has become increasingly complex. Marketing needs the help of our functional specialists now more than ever.

As shown in Exhibit 1, the divisional heads of all non-marketing functions in the DD organization, such as technical research, operations, and sales, reported to the DD general manager. They also reported on a dotted-line basis to the corporate vice presidents responsible for their respective functions. Two marketing service groups, the Consumer Promotion Group and the Marketing Research Department, reported to the DD marketing manager.

Technical Research.   GF prided itself on the quality of its technical research staff, numbering 400 in central research and 1,200 in the divisions. Research spending was twice that of GF's nearest food industry competitor. A Technical Strategy Board, which included Phil Smith, decided and directed activity on GF's technical research priorities. Central research personnel focused on long-term basic research to address these priorities, though half their time was spent on research commissioned and paid for by the GF divisions. Applied research was conducted by the technical research staff of each division. Jeff Jones, who held a Ph.D. in organic chemistry, was the DD Technical Research manager. He described his organization and responsibilities:

> Our organization structure mirrors that of product management. We have food technologists, project leaders, group leaders, laboratory managers, and a senior laboratory manager who work with different levels of the product management organization. For example, an associate product manager who needed specific ingredient or package cost information would ask the appropriate project leader.
>
> My team comprises 100 people working in three groups that each focus on a category of products—frozen novelties, frozen whipped emulsions, and ready-to-eat desserts. The rationale here is that each group deals with a different technical process. Coincidentally, this breakdown matches the way marketing splits the category managers' responsibilities, which makes cross-functional communications easier.
>
> My primary responsibilities are to guide product and process development for new and established products, to specify all raw materials, and to ensure the technical validity of any claims marketing may wish to make about our products.
>
> I take a special interest in new product development—moving products from the laboratory benchtop through a pilot plant to full-scale production. Once a new product hits the market, the development work will often focus on achieving

cost reductions while maintaining the product quality. On Pudding Pops frozen novelties, we are currently looking at cost reductions and line extensions, such as the development of different products for each season. On Jell-O, we are investigating ways to make the product more convenient.

Each year, I oversee the development of our operating plan and budget. Technical research personnel will interface with their marketing counterparts to develop a research wish list. Then we'll screen out proposals that are technically unfeasible or require too much capital investment relative to potential profit. Next we'll estimate the man-years required to execute each of the remaining projects, allocate our limited resources, and request any additional help we need from central research. The cost of each project is charged against the budget of the relevant product.

Although marketing takes the lead, we in technical research in no way feel like second-class citizens. There is a feeling of mutual dependency. However, I do sometimes wish that our marketers were more knowledgeable about the technical characteristics and manufacturing of their products. If product managers visited the laboratories and plants more often, they'd be less likely to make ill-informed suggestions that would require major capital investment to be implemented. In addition, young product managers who want to make their mark will invariably suggest a new flavor or formulation for an established product. Our experience at technical research is that, relative to the time and money required to implement such suggestions, the incremental profits are minimal.

Operations. The DD operations manager, Dan Peterson, was responsible for operating within budget the plants that made GF desserts, meeting productivity improvement targets, delivering sufficient product to meet weeks-of-supply targets, and adhering to quality specifications. Reporting to Peterson were four plant managers, three operations service managers responsible for packaged desserts, frozen novelties, and ready-to-eat products, plus managers responsible for logistics, inventory control, scheduling and deployment, engineering, and quality assurance. These five managers also reported on a dotted-line basis to the corporate directors for their respective functions.

The operations service managers and their assistants were a key link between Operations, Marketing, and Technical Research. They were responsible for reviewing cost and quality trends for their assigned products, managing cost reduction programs, overseeing the implementation of capital projects, and providing volume and promotion planning input to the logistics manager to ensure consistent delivery of product to trade accounts.

Peterson commented on the relationships between marketing and operations:

There was a time when marketing totally dominated the other functions. That's not to say that the marketing people didn't pay attention to operations or that operations people were second-class citizens. But recently, I've seen a change, particularly with the increased focus on business management and on identifying our sources of competitive leverage. Our production processes are highly complex, and product managers need to fully understand them because, often, our source of advantage is in operations. Marketing people are waking up to this. As a result, there is more career-path interchange across functions. For example, we recently had a product manager spend time in one of our plants and he is now much more sensitive to the operations implications of his marketing decisions. Sometimes, product managers don't think of the plant layoffs involved with some decisions or forget that an organization can't always turn on a dime!

Sales. A dry grocery sales organization of 700 salespeople represented the products of the Desserts, Breakfast Foods, and Main Meal divisions. GF maintained separate sales forces for coffee (460 salespeople), refrigerated meats (470), and baked goods (250). Both GF soft drinks and frozen foods were sold primarily through brokers.

The organization of GF's separate sales forces partly reflected the different delivery systems used to distribute the products they represented. Distribution costs including transportation and warehousing were about 4 percent of sales for dry foods and 11 percent for frozen foods. Items with less than a 60-day shelf life, including Oscar Mayer and Entenmann's products, were store-door delivered, rather than distributed through warehouses. In FY 1984, GF field sales costs totaled 3.3 percent of net revenues, 3.7 percent when broker commissions were included.

A GF recruiting brochure described the qualities sought in candidates for a career in sales as:

- Professionalism—either previous professional knowledge or the frame of mind to absorb quickly the basics of professional sales.
- Good judgment.
- The ambition to perform in increasingly responsible positions.
- An orientation toward achieving results.
- Creative problem-solving ability.

Each DD sales representative covered about 50 grocery stores. DD salespeople were responsible for using market research data to develop each account; relating national advertising campaigns, shelving plans, and merchandising programs to the advertising and promotion programs of each account; gaining placement and shelf space allocation for each brand to ensure product availability in proper proportions; and maintaining regular contact with warehousing accounts on delivery schedules, promotions, and new products.

New salespeople developed their knowledge through on-the-job experience, working with their supervisors, and seminars on selling skills and account management. They could advance through a series of account, district, and regional management positions to eventually become division national sales managers. Promising individuals often were assigned to the headquarters sales planning function to expose them to product management perspectives before they were promoted to a higher level in the field sales organization.

Mr. Ed Royal was in charge of sales planning at DD headquarters. He supervised 15 executives, including 2 sales planning managers assigned to dry and frozen desserts who each led a team of four region franchise managers (RFMs). The latter spent half their time in the field. Each RFM had responsibility both for the merchandising of all DD products in a specific region and for the merchandising of one group of products across all regions. Royal explained the tasks of his group:

Broadly, our role is to serve as a link between sales and marketing. Marketing looks to us for advice on how to deal with the trade. Sales looks to us, as former salespeople, to represent their views to product management. For example, if a sales district needed an additional deal on a product to match unexpected competitive deal rates, the district manager would send a request to product management through the appropriate RFM.

In addition to communicating information back and forth between headquarters and the field, we have four key functions. First, we evaluate the operating plans developed by each product group. As early as July, we would be in discussions with each group about the merchandising support needed to achieve its volume projections for the fiscal year starting the following March.

Second, we play a very important role in trade promotion planning. We assess the promotion events proposed by the product groups, help prioritize them, and then propose a promotion calendar. Sometimes the small brands justifiably feel short-changed. Since our sales force also serves two other GF divisions, the DD's preferred calendar may be subject to negotiation. Partly to reduce the burden on the sales force, we have been trying to focus our promotion dollars behind fewer, more powerful events. Once the promotion budget for each product is approved, we develop detailed allowance allocations by calendar quarter and sales district.

Third, we develop specific annual objectives by product in the areas of distribution, shelf facings, merchandising performance, and retail pricing. With the help of syndicated research data and our own sales force, we measure our performance against these objectives.

Fourth, we provide assistance to our sales force. We recently developed a software program that uses check-out scanner information to calculate the profitability of different shelf arrangements. Salespeople can use this program in their presentations to key accounts.

Royal commented on the relations between sales and marketing:

There's a cultural difference between the field and headquarters. Most assistants have MBAs. Few sales trainees do, though many now take part-time MBAs. I wish there was more career interchange between sales and marketing. The problem is that the marketing career path moves faster than the sales career path so that a product manager moving into sales as a district

manager might have to make a short-term career sacrifice for a longer-term benefit. Also, with only 23 sales districts, how could we assign product managers to these positions—it would be demoralizing for our salespeople.

Consumer Promotion Group.   A similar review process to that conducted by the sales planning function for each product's trade promotions was conducted by a four-person Consumer Promotion Group (CPG) that reported to the DD marketing manager. It jointly reviewed the consumer promotion component of each product's operating plan and developed promotion objectives with each product group that supported the product's marketing strategy. Detailed program development and execution was to be left to the CPG with the product group operating in an approval capacity. According to Tony Taylor, a former salesperson who was now the DD consumer promotion manager:

As promotion experts, our role is to help execute innovative promotion ideas in the marketplace. The product management function used to execute promotions, but we found this cumbersome and were constantly reinventing the wheel. Now, with experts handling the task, we have freed up some of their time.

Marketing Research Department.   GF had one of the largest marketing research departments of any corporation, numbering over 100 executives throughout the company. Henry Katz, DD market research manager, supervised nine executives. Four associate managers serviced each of the four product category groups. Three other executives worked on forecasting and planning. Katz reported to the DD marketing manager and, on a dotted-line basis, to the corporate director of marketing research who, in turn, reported to the corporate vice president for information management.

MRD played an important role in the development of DD marketing strategy. According to John Day, marketing manager:

Analysis of market research data is central to our success. We have developed many new products not through brilliant creativity but by really understanding the marketplace.

Henry Katz commented on MRD's level of involvement in DD marketing decision making:

We are the business's eyes and ears for the consumer. We share responsibility with marketing for the development of a product line that delivers superior consumer satisfaction. Three quarters of my bonus depends upon the division's overall performance, and only one quarter on MRD's performance against its specific objectives.

MRD analyzes data for the product group that, at other companies, the groups would analyze for themselves. To my mind, the second approach is like putting Morris the cat in charge of a tuna fish sandwich. We in MRD provide objectivity and a sophistication that's extremely important as market research techniques become more complex. In addition, the desserts marketplace is pretty complicated, so our help is in demand among the product groups even though their budgets are charged for the services we deliver.

According to Katz, MRD's principal function was the management of market and consumer information within DD. MRD was responsible for the quality, quantity, and prioritization of information used by the division. Specifically, MRD was charged with:

- Monitoring, measuring, and projecting the results of marketing programs, changes in the environment, and competitive factors.
- Helping to identify consumer and marketplace issues and opportunities critical to short- and long-range planning.
- Conducting appropriate and cost-effective research to support strategic as well as tactical planning.
- Providing objective business counsel to marketing from a consumer perspective.

Under Katz's leadership, the MRD within DD was heavily involved in forecasting the impact of alternative advertising and pricing programs, counseling line marketing managers on the use of new marketing research techniques, and providing advice on the positioning of new and established brands. As Katz pointed out:

Brand personnel change frequently. We provide continuity and can offer a historical perspective to a new product manager. We are the knowledge leaders in this division. My one problem is that our market research staff often do not exercise the leadership that they could or should in making recommendations to push the business forward. It's very rare for a market research executive to transfer from product management. In DD, though, we are lucky to have two people in product management who started their careers in marketing research. That helps relations considerably.

New Product Development

GF had a long and proud history of new product development. Kool-Aid, Jell-O gelatin, and Bird's Eye frozen foods were all dramatic innovations. Between 1978 and 1983, GF introduced six new food products that each earned at least $40 million in annual sales. Only 25 other grocery products introduced in the United States during that period met this criterion. According to Chairman and CEO James L. Ferguson:

When we enter new categories, we are careful to select those where we see major opportunities to improve margins by taking costs out of our business or improving production capacity. Sugar-Free Kool-Aid and Crystal Light are expected to generate $300 million in annual sales. Another 15 new products in var-

ious stages of development should add almost $600 million in annual revenues when they reach national distribution.[1]

Line Extensions versus Innovatons. How to encourage the generation of new product ideas and, more importantly, their translation into commercial successes, was a subject of frequent debate at GF. Line extensions presented no problem. Product management personnel were constantly looking for new ideas that would build established businesses. Opportunities of this nature were, however, decreasing. According to the DD Technical Research manager:

Our traditional research approach has been to look for flavor improvements. But our flavor delivery system is now of such excellent quality that only minor improvements can be expected. We are increasingly taking a longer-term perspective, asking "What can we do that's different?" and "How can we add value to the consumer?"

An increasing concern was how to ensure that dramatic new product concepts were explored and commercialized. Technical research personnel were in their jobs longer than product management personnel, enjoyed working on challenging projects, and provided a measure of continuity to longer-term new product development. They typically assumed a more important role, the more radical the product innovation. On the other hand, securing the long-term commitment of marketing personnel to a new product development project could be more difficult. A DD product group manager commented:

Our product management people are very career oriented. They aren't prepared to commit three or four years without a promotion to a high-risk, new product project. Even if the product proved successful, at the end of the day their peers would have passed them by on the career ladder. In addition, when you're working on an established product, both you and your boss can assess your performance versus your predecessor's. This isn't as easy on a new product.

Managing New versus Established Products. Almost all newly hired assistant product managers worked on established brands for their two initial assignments. They, therefore, were trained in a style of management that was not necessarily applicable to new products. Two DD product managers who had worked on both new and established brands commented on the differences:

The world won't come to an end if the product manager on an established business is away for a day. His task is to manage the information flow, massage and analyze the data, and develop business-building programs. The product manager on a new product has a lonelier existence. He has to be more self-motivated and set his own time line and deadlines. He has to

---

[1]Duane L. Taylor, "New Product Analyses," *Food Engineering*, October 1984, p. 94.

collect information, not merely manage it. He has to persuade the other functions to give him their attention and buy into the product. This is especially challenging because the other functions have been involved with so many new product concepts that have never been successfully commercialized.

I started as an assistant on Jell-O gelatin, our flagship business. I used to receive lots of notes from senior managers who had worked on the business themselves. The tasks—and the deadlines—were clearly defined. Now, working on a new product, I have more freedom. I am the expert. If Phil Smith wanted a presentation on my product, I'd probably do it because I'm the only one who could field the questions.

Organizing for New Product Development. The DD tried in several ways to ensure a high level of successful, new product development activity, both in the established business groups as well as in a separate development organization. First, development of DD's established businesses focused on extending existing trademarks and building on existing strengths, through the introduction, for example, of new forms of packaged desserts or different types of frozen novelties. New product introductions within the established businesses were important in creating excitement in the marketplace and could usually be developed and implemented within one to two years. One product group manager noted:

It's important for the growth of the existing brands to develop and implement new product ideas. The prospect of new products and line extensions also excites the top agency people who are assigned to our major established brands.

Second, the DD organization included a group dedicated exclusively to new product development, which was headed by a marketing manager, Oliver Jones. Jones supervised six marketing executives working on product areas new to DD. The group had worked on the frozen novelty category prior to GF's entry into this market and was currently developing and test marketing an in-house soft ice cream similar to Dairy Queen. Typically, Jones' group developed a product to the point of expansion beyond test market and then turned it over to an established brand group. It was not unusual for the person who had managed the product in test market to continue to manage it once it was rolled out.

The new product development group included individuals who had previously worked on established products and were now broadening their experience, as well as others who wished to make a career in new product development. One such manager, Dave Feldman, had guided Pudding Pops from concept development to national expansion. He commented:

For me new product development is the core of marketing. It's exciting to figure out what the consumer wants and how we can deliver that in a way which will have long-term impact on GF profits. It's fun to nurture your project to reality and then to apply the marketing muscle to make an impact in the market place.

Third, DD was experimenting with a seven-member multifunctional venture team working on a major new product development project. Reporting to Jones and led by a product group manager, the team included representatives from each of the key promotional areas who were all working solely on the project. Team leader, Diana Morgan, described the venture team concept:

We are all making a three- to four-year commitment to seeing this project through to completion. In return for putting our career paths on hold, all team members have been offered a very attractive bonus if the product succeeds commercially. The result is that we have more senior people involved in our group than would normally work on a new product. The finance representative, for example, has 15 years' experience with GF.

New products that use the existing asset base don't require venture teams. But this one does, for three reasons. First, it involves a new technology that GF is not currently involved in. Second, because it is a short shelf life, fast-turn product, it requires a new distribution system. Third, this product will, we hope, be the basis for an entirely new product category which GF will dominate. Even though our venture team draws staff from existing product groups, we believe it's very important to the division long term.

Two Examples. DD managers provided two examples of effective product development—the revitalization of Jell-O gelatin and the successful launch of Jell-O Pudding Pops, GF's first entry in the frozen novelties category.

Sales volume on Jell-O gelatin peaked in 1969, then declined consistently so that, by 1983, volume was 35 percent less than in 1969. Not only did GF's market share dip below 70 percent but the entire category declined as increasingly health-conscious Americans cut down on sweets in general. Second, demographic shifts left fewer children in the Jell-O target group. A third problem was the fact that Jell-O took at least three hours to set and, therefore, was increasingly perceived as inconvenient by working mothers. Fourth, at a time when snacking was on the increase, 80 percent of gelatin consumption occasions were associated with traditional meals.

John Day, marketing manager, described the inadequacies of the initial response:

All our functional resources were used initially to justify why the business was declining and why we couldn't really do much about it. Then we said, "Let's stop wringing our hands! Let's fix it!"

What followed was a turnaround. Technical research developed a patented low-cost starch that delivered product quality superior to competition.[2] Manufacturing resources were focused to ensure that GF could become the low-cost producer. Marketing developed new advertising to counter

---

[2]Nabisco Brands' Royal line was GF's main competitor in this category.

Jell-O's association with traditional lifestyles and stimulate faster household usage. No price increases were taken for three consecutive years. Finally, technical research tapped into a corporate commitment to subsidize new products using aspartame to develop a newsworthy line extension, Sugar-Free Jell-O gelatin.[3] As a result, in 1983, Jell-O volume grew for the first time in 15 years.

The maturation of the Jell-O gelatin business also stimulated interest in new product development. Attention focused on frozen novelties, which were single prepackaged frozen desserts or snacks including ice cream cones, cups, bars and sandwiches, ice milk bars, and fudgesicles. The concept of a frozen Jell-O pudding had been aired as early as 1965, and a prototype product had been developed. However, no further development had been undertaken, partly because the product was viewed more as a snack than a dessert. Then, in 1975, a marketing research analyst, Dave Feldman, became enthusiastic about the product:

> Retail sales of frozen novelties were only $400 million in 1975, and volume growth was only 1 percent a year. But I believed the category was undermarketed. Most frozen novelties were produced by regional dairies, often under license from the Popsicle Division of Consolidated Foods. The challenge was to develop an appealing product that could capitalize on the Jell-O name and GF's refrigerated distribution system. The eventual result was Jell-O Pudding Pops, individual servings of frozen pudding on a stick.
>
> In 1975, I was working in marketing research and had previously analyzed several other new product opportunities, which I knew were losers. Then I looked at Pudding Pops, saw a potential winner, and decided that I wanted to manage its development. I made a presentation to the DD general manager and was appointed associate, then product manager, on Pudding Pops.
>
> I was a brand champion in the old sense. The way you sell an idea to management is what distinguishes a good product manager from a poor one. You gain authority here by what you recommend, rather than by what you decide.
>
> Technical research was enthusiastic about Pudding Pops from the start. They developed a product that would melt at zero degrees, rather than 20 below like ice cream and that could, therefore, be shipped along with Bird's Eye frozen vegetables. However, it wasn't all plain sailing. Operations and Sales were not supportive. To get the attention of Operations, I signed a $45,000 contract with a co-packer. I didn't know or care whether I was breaking any rules. I didn't want control. I just wanted the product to happen.
>
> Sales was also lukewarm. I wanted to capitalize on GF's frozen food distribution network, rather than use the store-door distribution approach employed by the regional dairies. But Sales said such a distribution system would not be effective, that Pudding Pops would be buried at the bottom of the grocer's freezer. I, therefore, had a consultant survey 200 dairies to show that GF could achieve the required distribution at lower

cost with my proposed system. I then had the data to go head-on-head with the national sales manager—and win.

Feldman took Pudding Pops to test market in 1979. Because the manufacturing process required a $75 million plant investment, the national launch did not occur until April 1982. In that month, three flavors were launched in three package sizes, backed by a $25 million advertising campaign featuring Bill Cosby. Pudding Pops was positioned as a wholesome lower-calorie alternative to frozen ice cream novelties.

Sales reached $100 million in the first year. Pudding Pops expanded the frozen novelty category by 25 percent. Market research showed, unexpectedly, that half of all Pudding Pops were eaten by adults. GF's only challenges were to ensure that Pudding Pops were placed in the ice cream, rather than the frozen food, section of the grocer's freezer and that the shelves were restocked often enough—since Pudding Pops turned much faster than other frozen novelties.

By 1985 GF was researching and test marketing additional frozen novelties, such as Gelatin Pops, whipped frozen gelatin on a stick, and a soft-serve product called Soft-Swirl.

A Leaner Organization

Partly as a result of increasing pressure for cost control, the DD Marketing Department in 1985 comprised 30 executives, compared to 50 in 1980, even though the number of products had increased and the pace of new product development was greater than ever before.

Roger Smith commented on the change:

> Until last year, the marketing function was overstaffed. We bent over to give good people career and salary advancement, and in the Desserts Division, we could afford to do so. Our margins are so good that relatively small new product ideas can seem profitable enough to justify the expense of a separate product group.
>
> The problem was, however, that we had too many people chasing a finite level of decision-making responsibility. You distinguished yourself as an assistant by coming up with the big new promotion idea for the eastern region. Now, there is more work and task diversity for each person. More than ever before, you have to be a juggler and have a general business perspective, even at the assistant and associate levels.
>
> With fewer people, the atmosphere is less bureaucratic. There is less emphasis on formal written reports. Our annual product marketing plans are much shorter now than they used to be. The depth of analysis may not be as great, but the speed of decision making is faster. Our five advertising agencies appreciate not having to make presentations to as many levels of management, and the specialist support of our staff functions, such as MRD, is more highly valued by the product groups.
>
> A leaner organization is more flexible. There are fewer turf issues. My philosophy is that the people who do the work present it, no matter what level of management it goes to. In addition, I maintain an open-door policy. Last week, for example, about three quarters of our product managers were in to see me, not for approvals but for advice.

---

[3]GF's corporate priority system provided corporate subsidies to the divisions for new product development in specific areas.

Smith's enthusiasm for the leaner organization did have some side effects. Two product managers noted:

> The breadth of tasks in this job is great. But I wish I had more time to think and to get out in the field to talk to consumers.
>
> True, a leaner organization has advantages. It forces you to focus on the actions and programs that will generate the most impact. But the world is becoming more complicated—the grocery trade is increasingly sophisticated, more precise target segmentation is needed, and there's growing interest in regional marketing. We need more people, more specialists, not less.

As Roger Smith evaluated the results of trimming the marketing organization within DD, his thoughts turned to the effectiveness of the product management system and what he could do to improve it. He jotted down some of the key questions that came to mind:

- Should our product managers have responsibility for profits as well as for volume, share, and marketing expenditures?

- Should our product managers be general business managers, rather than advertising and promotion experts? Can they be both?

- Should we have the same product management system and the same types of product manager working on new as well as established products?

- Was the traditional product management system still appropriate for GF and DD in 1985? Or would product management through formal business teams, led by marketing but including representatives of all functions, be more effective?

As he pondered these issues, Smith recalled a comment made by his former boss:

> The strength of the product management system is that it puts one person in charge of making a business plan work for each product.

Exhibit 1

General Foods Corporation: Desserts Division organization chart

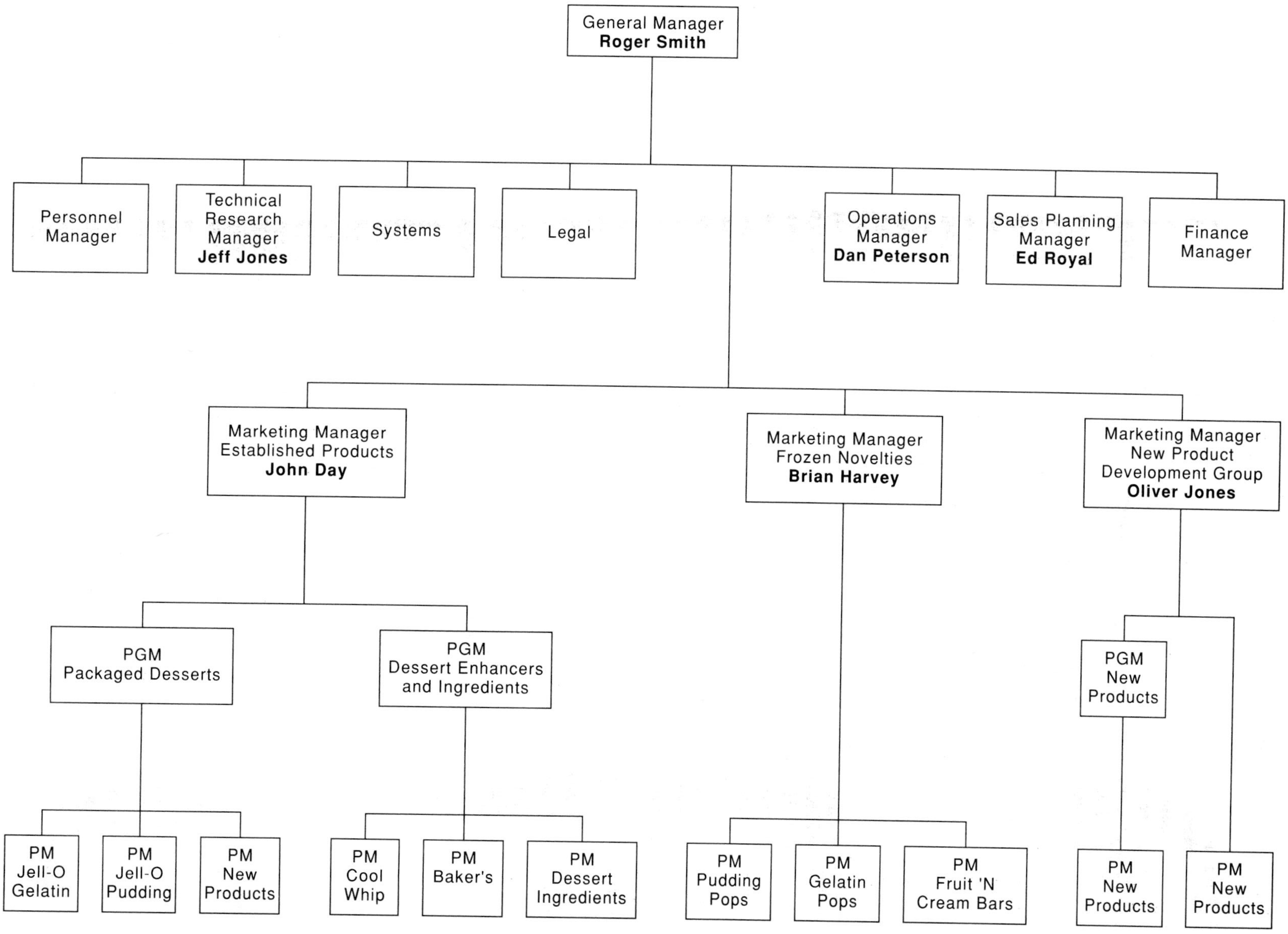

General Manager
Roger Smith

Personnel Manager

Technical Research Manager **Jeff Jones**

Systems

Legal

Operations Manager **Dan Peterson**

Sales Planning Manager **Ed Royal**

Finance Manager

Marketing Manager Established Products **John Day**

Marketing Manager Frozen Novelties **Brian Harvey**

Marketing Manager New Product Development Group **Oliver Jones**

PGM Packaged Desserts

PGM Dessert Enhancers and Ingredients

PGM New Products

PM Jell-O Gelatin

PM Jell-O Pudding

PM New Products

PM Cool Whip

PM Baker's

PM Dessert Ingredients

PM Pudding Pops

PM Gelatin Pops

PM Fruit 'N Cream Bars

PM New Products

PM New Products

REGENCY FACSIMILE, INC.

On Monday, July 2, 1990, Michael Folder, vice president of customer service for Regency Facsimile, Inc. (ReFax), was reflecting on some of the discussions he had earlier that day.

"You cannot win two races at the same time, Mr. Folder," was the comment of Jin Soo Roh, vice president of the Worldwide Customer Services Group of Regency of Japan, referring to ReFax customer service department's dual mission of (1) customer satisfaction and (2) profit making through selling service, parts, and supplies. Roh had earlier described his vision of building one service organization that would handle all Regency products sold in the United States. He hoped to fold ReFax's service organization into the three-year-old Regency Customer Services, Inc. (RCS), which was the incarnation of that vision and which handled all Regency products sold in the United States except for ReFax products.

Folder had a major task ahead of him: to prepare a plan for merging the ReFax customer service department into RCS. To do this, Folder felt that he had to assess the significance of the relationship between ReFax sales and service departments, analyze the proposed merger's impact on ReFax and RCS, and reexamine the department's dual missions of customer satisfaction and profit.

Company Background

Regency Facsimile, Inc. (ReFax), a Chicago-based U.S. corporation with a large parent company in Japan, sold and serviced Regency fax and related equipment under the Regency brand name in the United States. ReFax's total revenues were about $166 million in FY 1990, of which the customer service department accounted for $21 million and supplies for another $20 million. (ReFax's FY 1990 ran from July 1, 1989, to June 30, 1990.) ReFax employed around 700 people, including 300 in sales, 196 in service, and the rest in corporate, administrative, and other functions.

Regency Customer Service (RCS), based in Phoenix, Arizona, serviced all Regency products (such as office equipment, computers, and consumer electronics) sold in the United States, except for Regency fax equipment. In FY 1990, RCS employed around 500 people, had revenues of $47 million, and made a small profit.

The Fax Industry

Fax transmission technology was developed in 1842 by Scottish clockmaker Alexander Bain, refined in the 1920s by German inventors to send photographs overseas, and perfected in the 1940s at Bell Laboratories. But commercial production did not begin until the Japanese applied advanced circuitry technology and began producing the machines in volume in the late 1960s.[1] The machines first gained wide acceptance in Japan. A Magnavox and Xerox joint venture brought the first products to the United States in 1965. Deregulation in the telecommunications industry (use of public telephone systems by nontelephone companies) initially spurred production; but telephone-line leasing arrangements limited the profitability of the fax business, leading to consolidations and failures of U.S. entrants in this market. By the mid-1970s, U.S. fax production was all but abandoned. In 1990, nearly all fax equipment sold in the United States was manufactured in Japan, with some production in Korea and Singapore.[2]

Although it had been around for some years, the U.S. fax market did not grow much until the early 1980s, when it grew in value from less than $300 million in 1982 to over $2 billion in 1989. Unit volume sales grew from 60,000 units in 1982 to over 1.3 million units in 1989. Though it slowed somewhat in 1989, market growth was expected to remain strong well into the 1990s (see Exhibit 1).

Introduction of low-priced fax machines contributed substantially to the market growth boom, as did aggressive pricing and distribution and the general acceptance of fax usage in companies large and small. Faxes became a quicker and cheaper alternative to overnight mail for transmitting information. Rapidly escalating demand for fax equipment enabled manufacturers to achieve economical production volumes, leading to lower prices and further increases in demand. U.S. prices had dropped 10–15 percent annually since 1982 (even with yen-dollar exchange adjustment). Prices for standard products were expected to continue to drop through the early 1990s.

In 1990, most fax machines used a thermal process and thermal paper for output. "Plain paper" products had recently been introduced at about a $4,000 base list price, and prices were expected to drop as competition and demand increased for this new product category. Earlier

This case was prepared by Professor Melvyn A. J. Menezes and Research Associate Jon D. Serbin.
Copyright © 1990 by the President and Fellows of Harvard College.
Harvard Business School case 9-591-037 (Rev. 1/12/91).

[1]Pamela Ellis-Simons, "Just the Fax Please," *Marketing & Media Decisions*, July 1988, p. 118.
[2]"The U.S. Market for Business Facsimile Equipment," *Frost & Sullivan Report* (A1555), December 1985, pp. 22–23.

plain-paper machines were priced as high as $12,000 without options. These machines integrated fax, copier, and laser-printer technology into one machine. Other recent market changes included the introduction of fax boards for personal computers and mobile fax machines that fit in a briefcase and used a cellular or any standard phone line for communication.

The facsimile market attracted several players, because of its rapid expansion, excellent prospects for further growth, and the fact that no clear market leader had emerged. The fax market was intensely competitive. The number of fax suppliers grew from about 12 in 1983 to about 50 by 1989.[3] A few Japanese manufacturers produced all the fax machines offered by these suppliers; some of the manufacturers marketed fax equipment under their own names as well.[4]

Intense competition had created a buyers market, reducing margins for most participants. Competition was most intense and margins the lowest in the low end of the market.

Major Players. Seven major suppliers (including ReFax) accounted for about 67 percent of the U.S. fax market in 1988. Sharp, Canon, and Ricoh had existing distribution and service networks for other office equipment products, mainly photocopiers. Companies (as well as larger dealers) with multiple product lines (fax, copiers, laser printers, scanners, and so on) generally maintained dedicated specialists for both sales and service of the various types of products. An account rep would not sell both fax machines and copiers. Service representatives generally specialized in fax or copier service, but in some instances were cross-trained.

Sharp. Sharp (estimated market share 20 percent) ranked first in total placements for the last three years. It introduced 20 new products from 1987 to 1989 and was most effective at hitting the market first with the right features at the right price points. Sharp pursued a strategy of aggressive pricing across its product line and an aggressive national advertising campaign. It pursued the dealer channel early, in time to take advantage of the explosive growth in the low end of the market during the mid-1980s. Sharp also relied significantly on the retail channel for its low-end equipment. It had an intensive distribution strategy, and its equipment was serviced by dealers. Sharp maintained

national account fax representatives to assist dealers with large sales.

Murata. Murata (estimated market share 15 percent) sold only fax equipment and was strong in the low end and mid end of the market. Murata introduced 11 new products from 1987 to 1989. Its products were feature-rich, positioned as "deluxe" machines, and priced a little higher than Sharp's or Canon's. Murata stayed out of the price wars led by Sharp and Canon; its marketing strategy focused on a "get what you pay for" attitude. Murata sold extensively through dealers and maintained a direct sales force for national accounts. Most service was handled by dealers. Murata had also begun distributing its M series through retail channels. This series had essentially the same features as models sold directly and through dealers and was priced 40 percent lower.

Canon. Canon (estimated market share 10 percent) introduced 18 new products from 1987 to 1989, was strong in both the low and higher end, and maintained a strong national advertising campaign. It, too, aggressively used both the dealer and retail channels for distribution. Canon also maintained a national sales and newly established service organization, but most distribution and service was handled by dealers.

Ricoh. Ricoh (estimated market share 9 percent) introduced 15 new products from 1987 to 1989. Its strength was in the mid-range and high end of the market. Ricoh distributed one low-end model through the retail channel but planned to abandon this channel shortly. Its national sales and service organization helped it service national accounts. Ricoh's national direct sales organization sold fax machines only; but the national service organization serviced multiple Ricoh products, including fax machines, copiers, laser printers, and scanners. Ricoh also maintained an extensive dealer network.

Fujitsu. Fujitsu (estimated market share 4 percent) concentrated on the mid to high end of the market and introduced 13 new products from 1987 to 1989. It maintained a large sales force and service staff dedicated exclusively to fax equipment. Fujitsu sold primarily through its direct sales force and, to a lesser extent, through dealers and resellers.

Pitney Bowes. Pitney Bowes (estimated market share 4 percent) concentrated on the mid to high end of the market. Its fax business operated as a separate division and maintained a large sales force (about 250) dedicated exclusively to fax sales. Pitney Bowes did not use the dealer network. The fax division used Pitney's national service organization (for its mailing and postage equipment) of about 7,000 service reps for service, and a dedicated diagnostics center for fax repair.

Customers. Fax customers were divided into three major segments: large corporate users, small to medium-sized businesses, and home office. A potential fourth segment was consumers.

---

[3]"More Fax in Your Future," *Industry Week*, September 7, 1987, p. BC3; "Fax in '88: More models, More Features," *Industry Week*, May 16, 1988, pp. BC3–BC6; "The Fax Market Comes of Age," *Marketing Communications*, October 1988, pp. 37–43; James A. McConville, "No Cooling Seen for Hot Fax Market," *HFD*, March 20, 1989, p. 107; "Sharp Garners Top Fax-Sales Spot," *HFD*, April 3, 1989, pp. 221–22.

[4]"The U.S. Market for Business Facsimile Equipment," *Frost & Sullivan Report* (A1555), December 1985, p. 131.

Large corporate users. Loosely referred to as Fortune 1,000 firms, these companies tended to demand high-end models, state-of-the-art technology, and national service and support. They usually bought direct from the supplier. Purchase decisions were typically made by the MIS or communications director. For the first purchase, price and availability of nationwide service were important considerations; for further purchases, product features, price, and service were the main criteria.

Small and medium-sized businesses. This rapidly growing segment of the market accounted for nearly 80 percent of the fax machines sold in 1989. The office manager, controller, or principal made the purchase decision and typically used price as the main purchase criterion. Most of these firms bought the product from dealers.

Home office. Purchase decisions in this emerging segment were driven mainly by price, and the product was generally purchased from a dealer or consumer electronics outlet.

ReFax's customer base was large and concentrated. Of the over 6,000 customers, 300 major ones accounted for over 70 percent of the fax machines sold through ReFax's direct sales force.

Marketing at ReFax

Product Line. ReFax's product line of 11 models covered the range from low-end to high-end products. Industry analysts classified fax machines into four categories:

1. High-end products. Fully featured and usually console or desktop type. They usually had modular or expandable designs, data communications options, password and security controls, and large storage capacity for delayed and multiple transmissions. High-end machines typically cost $4,000 and above and were sold by the direct sales force. ReFax's *Regency A100, Regency A200,* and *Regency A300* were in this category.

2. Mid-range products. Usually desktop type and handled medium to high volume. These products typically had multiple-page automatic feeders, automatic cutters, and memory chips to store phone numbers and instructions for automatic dialing. They cost between $1,500 and $4,000 and were sold by both the direct sales force and office equipment and computer dealers. ReFax's *Regency B100, Regency B200, Regency B300, Regency B400, Regency B500,* and *Regency B600* were in this category.

3. Low-end products. These were portable or compact machines that handled low volume. They were basic units, often with autodialer, and cost between $500 and $1,500. They were sold by office-equipment and computer dealers (models above $1,000) and consumer electronics retail outlets (models under $1,000). Many of the new competitors entered the industry with low-end products. ReFax had just entered this category with its *Regency C100* and *Regency C200.*

4. Consumer/personal products. These were basic fax and answering machines. They cost less than $500 and were sold by consumer electronics retail outlets. ReFax had no models in this category.

New product introductions were critical to success. ReFax introduced 10 new products from 1987 to 1989. ReFax was relatively strong in the mid-range and high-end product categories. It was slow in taking advantage of the rapid growth of the low end of the market, and this contributed to the company's poor performance in 1989.

Regency fax machines carried a 90-day warranty covering parts and labor. But ReFax sometimes offered large customers a longer warranty as an inducement to choose Regency. On a recent sale to a large East Coast manufacturer, for example, ReFax offered a two-year parts and labor warranty and received an order for 75 fax machines.

Customers who purchased Regency fax machines called the local service branch for warranty service. ReFax customer service reps provided warranty service at the customer site for high-end and mid-range products, and at the service branch for low-end products.

Sales and Distribution. Fax machines were sold through several channels: direct sales forces, dealers (office-equipment dealers and computer dealers), retailers (mass merchandisers and consumer electronics retail outlets), and specialized resellers. This multichannel distribution of fax machines had developed in the mid-1980s. Earlier fax machines were sold mainly by the direct sales force to end customers. But the introduction of low-priced, technologically adequate fax machines caused a shift in the distribution. By 1984, office-equipment dealers and computer dealers sold fax machines economically to millions of small businesses.[5]

In 1986, a third channel of distribution, consumer electronics retail outlets, was introduced as suppliers sought new ways of reaching the small-business and home-office markets. These retailers operated at much lower margins than dealers, and this forced many dealers to cut prices or drop low-end lines. By 1990, the street prices of fax machines were often 20–25 percent below list price, leaving the dealer with less than 5 percent profit margins. Suppliers responded by segmenting their lines into separate channels to reduce price competition between dealers and retail outlets.[6]

---

[5]"The U.S. Market for Business Facsimile Equipment." *Frost & Sullivan Report* (A1555), December 1985, p. 1, p. 144; L. Conigliaro, "High Tech Notes—Industry Report," *Prudential Bache Securities Analyst Report,* October 12, 1987, p. 13.

[6]"Distribution Changes in Sight for Home Office Products," *OEP Office Equipment & Products,* June 1988, pp. 28–39; "Terminal Success: Plugging into New Markets," *OEP Office Equipment & Products,* July 1988, pp. 52–70; "Fax Makers Target Low-End Market," *High Technology Business,* March 1988, pp. 26–30.

ReFax originally relied on its direct sales force. In 1986, when industry sales were split 40:60 between dealers/retailers and direct sales force, ReFax sold only through its direct sales force. By the end of 1989, when industry sales were split 70:30 between dealers/retailers and direct sales force, ReFax's split was 40:60.

Sales force. As of March 1990, ReFax had 170 direct salespeople who sold to end customers and an additional 34 salespeople who sold to dealers. Of the 170 direct salespeople, 90 were national account representatives and 80 were territory sales representatives. National account representatives sold to national accounts (Fortune 1,000 firms and assigned large accounts) and accounted for 75 percent of ReFax's direct sales. Territory sales representatives sold to small and medium-sized businesses and accounted for 25 percent of ReFax's direct sales. They often competed with dealers focusing on small and medium-sized businesses.

ReFax direct salespeople had control over pricing to the extent that they could discount equipment up to 20 percent off list. Additional discounts needed approval from headquarters. ReFax salespeople were paid a salary plus commissions (based on the discount at which they sold the machines) and bonuses for achievement of quarterly quotas. The commissions on fax equipment averaged 7 percent and ranged from 15 percent for products sold at list price to 1 percent for products sold at maximum discount. Salespeople also earned commissions of 7 percent on sales of maintenance contracts and an average of 8 percent on supplies sales. The average annual compensation of territory sales reps was $50,000 (including $30,000 in salary); that of national account reps was $75,000 (including $40,000 in salary).

Dealers. ReFax had about 500 dealers who were office-equipment dealers. They typically sold copiers, fax machines, electronic typewriters, supplies, and service. For most dealers, copiers were their main products; fax machines were secondary. Compared to the copier business, revenues from and margins on fax machines were lower. ReFax serviced the fax machines sold through its dealers.

To increase dealer interest and loyalty, ReFax set up exclusive dealers for various geographic territories with market-share targets. Offering exclusive territories was seen as a way to compensate dealers for the absence of other product categories that most of ReFax's competitors offered.

Advertising. By 1990, with the explosion of the low and middle segments of the market, advertising was becoming an increasingly effective marketing tool. ReFax advertised in national business publications like *Fortune, Business Week, Newsweek,* and *The Wall Street Journal,* and in trade journals like *The Office* and *Office Automation.* The ads were to create awareness of Regency fax machines among small and mid-sized businesses. (Large organizations were typically aware of Regency.) The ads focused on product reliability, ReFax's service, and the depth of the product line and attempted to create an image of security.

Customer Service at ReFax

The customer service department's objectives were to ensure customer satisfaction by providing quality service to all ReFax customers (including those who purchased Regency fax machines from the dealers), to support the sales effort at ReFax, and to make a profit. As Folder put it: "My department is a 'cash cow' for ReFax. In FY 1990, we had profits of $2.5 million, revenues of $21.1 million, and sold an additional $4.0 million in supplies." Apart from sales of supplies, the department had three sources of revenue: maintenance contracts (MCs), which accounted for 80 percent of revenues; time and materials (T&M) charges, which accounted for 10 percent of revenues; and installations, which accounted for 10 percent of revenues. The gross margins were about 36 percent. Most of the department's costs were for manpower and travel.

Customer service at ReFax comprised presales support (demonstrations and trials), installation, technical support, training, and postsale support. The most important dimension, postsale support, comprised:

1. Telephone support between 8 A.M. and 5 P.M., Monday–Friday. Of the calls received, approximately one third were concerning product information and two thirds were problem related. Half the problem-related telephone calls were resolved over the telephone, while the other half required site visits (referred to as service calls) by the service reps.

2. Warranty service. Although the department serviced all warranty claims, it did not recover warranty costs (estimated at about 1 percent of equipment sales) from the sales department.

3. Service for products covered under MCs. Most MCs covered on-site service; MCs for a few low-end products were covered by depot service only.

4. Service for products not covered under MCs and for which customers were charged for time and materials (T&M). For T&M service, ReFax provided both on-site and depot options (with significant costs savings).

The department also sold supplies and MCs, provided leads for equipment sales to ReFax salespeople, and did its own invoicing and collection of receivables.

Organization. Before 1983, customer service reported to the sales department at the branch level and was viewed as an expense entity. In 1983, service was reorganized as an independent profit center. After this change, the sales department was upset at the loss of control over service and the "credits" for service revenue. But service personnel felt they were no longer treated as "stepchildren," though they still felt that salespeople were favored.

In July 1990, the customer service department was a profit center headed by Folder, who reported to the president of ReFax, Steve Davis (see Exhibit 2). The department had a total of 196 people (28 at headquarters and 168 in the field), a central parts repair facility at the Chicago headquarters, 22 branches, and a depot maintenance center in St. Louis, Missouri. The headquarters staff included a technical support staff of 10 and a logistics support staff of 11. In the field, the department had two regional service managers, 22 branch service managers, 133 service reps, and 11 clerical people. To improve profitability, Folder hoped to reduce the number of branches to 15 over the next two years. Customer service shared office space with the local sales branch in most cities.

Service Representatives.   The 133 service reps focused on satisfying customers through technical competence and speed of response. They were trained on both the technical aspects of maintenance and also on how to handle customers. Effort was made to make the customer feel like part of the team. Audio- and video-taped programs were used for customer training. The objective was to provide customers with more than just a service rep to fix a machine; it was to provide a value-added service that would also be perceived as such.

On average, a service rep made three service calls per day and spent approximately 1.9 hours (including travel time) on a call. As the population of ReFax machines increased, demand for service was expected to increase, and service reps would be expected to make more calls per day because travel time would decline.

Service representatives also were responsible for answering customer product/service queries over the telephone, and for collection of service related receivables. Most service reps saw themselves as technical experts and often felt hesitant to ask customers to pay their service bills. As one service rep noted: "Collecting money should be done by the sales reps, and not by technically qualified service reps."

Folder, the regional service managers, and the branch service managers tried very hard to instill an "ownership mentality" among the service reps. They hoped that the reps would provide the same quality of service for all Regency fax machines located within their territory, regardless of which branch sold the machine. Several reps tended to give higher service priority to units in their territory that were sold by their branch. As Folder said, "This is a major concern in branches where a significant portion of the machine population was sold by other branches. For example, over 50 percent of the machines located in the Dallas area were not sold by the sales reps in the Dallas branch."

Service reps were paid an annual salary of about $28,000, plus commissions on sales of MCs (7 percent of sales), supplies (1–12 percent depending on the discount offered, and averaging 8 percent), and 7 percent on all T&M billing. The average annual compensation of a service rep was $35,000.

Maintenance Contracts (MCs).   This was the largest source of revenues and gross margins for the service department. For machines covered under an MC, ReFax offered complete service, which included parts, labor, retraining, diagnosis, and assistance even for nonmachine-related problems.

MCs were sold by ReFax's direct sales force, service reps, dealers, and resellers, at the time of equipment sale. Renewal MCs were usually sold by service reps. Selling MCs had become an increasingly difficult task, because (1) equipment reliability was improving, (2) some large companies with maintenance departments were beginning to do fax maintenance on their own, and (3) there was increasing media attention to the profits made by providers of service contracts. In 1990, only 60 percent of machines sold by ReFax were covered by MCs, compared to 75 percent in 1987. Of the MCs sold, 60 percent were for one year, 30 percent were for two years, and 10 percent were for three years.

For products covered under MCs, the mean time between service calls was 30 weeks, although the mean time between product failures was one year. The average costs of these service calls were: labor $45/hour and parts $45 per product failure. Market research indicated that speed of response to customer requests for help was very important to customers. To be competitive, ReFax had two response time goals: (a) at least 50 percent of all service calls in less than four hours and (b) an overall average response time of five hours.

Service reps did not make special calls to customers to sell supplies for MCs; they did that on their service calls. Roh believed that service reps should not sell supplies and MCs as it would impact service quality. But Folder was convinced that, on service calls, service reps could attend to the customers' service needs and also sell supplies and MCs. He did not believe that selling MCs and supplies would detract from the quality or efficiency of service. At times Folder wondered whether it was in the best interests of the department and the company to provide sales incentives for service reps.

Pricing had become an increasingly difficult problem due to the sharp drop in equipment street prices and the fact that industry practice had led customers to expect MC prices to be about 8–10 percent of the equipment purchase price.

MC prices had ranged from $300 to $800 per year depending on the machine. But, with the decline in equipment prices, MC prices had dropped to as low as $125 per year for the *Regency C200* and averaged $300 per year. Many customers were trading up in technology at a lower price and a big savings in maintenance costs. For example, a company could replace a machine purchased in 1985 for $9,000 that had an annual MC cost of $800 with an equally good machine that cost $3,000 and had an annual service cost of $300. Thus, it could take two or even three new MCs to replace the revenue loss of one old MC.

Customer Service and Sales. Service had become an increasingly important competitive tool in the sale of fax equipment. Since fax machines were not stand-alone pieces of equipment like copiers, the availability of a strong nationwide service network was often a requirement for national accounts. Although customer service was important on the initial sale, it became an extremely important purchase criterion for repeat business.

Overall customer satisfaction was closely related to the perceived quality of customer service. Speedy responses and having the equipment working properly greatly improved customers' perceptions of service quality.

To support the sales of Regency fax machines, the customer service department worked closely with the sales department. Service reps often helped salespeople by conducting presale demonstrations and installing machines placed on a trial basis. Service reps also gave the sales department qualified leads for equipment sales. These leads accounted for 5–10 percent of fax equipment sales.

From time to time, ReFax salespeople tried to pressure the service department to discount the MCs heavily as part of a package sale. To clinch the sale, salespeople sought and often obtained discounts of up to 20 percent on the MC prices. Sometimes customer service bent over backward to help salespeople. As Folder put it, "At times we give 20 percent discounts for existing MCs to help get new sales of 30–40 machines."

Performance Evaluation. Evaluation of the service department was based on its performance in two areas: (1) revenues, margins, and expenses compared to targets; and (2) number of complaints reaching the president of the company. Branch service managers were evaluated on the following criteria: (1) revenues and margins; (2) response time; (3) sales of supplies; (4) branch administrative performance; and (5) relationship with the sales department. The first three criteria had objective measures and targets; the last two were subjectively evaluated. One branch manager noted: "We face a conflict between the margins goal of 40 percent and the response time goals." A monthly report comparing four branches on the first two criteria is shown in Table A.

Proposed Merger

In the proposed merger, ReFax's entire customer service department was to be merged into RCS. (The postmerger RCS will be referred to as RCS/ReFax in the case.) The headquarters staff of ReFax's customer service department would move to Phoenix and be merged with the RCS headquarters staff, and the field forces would be combined.

ReFax customer service reps would have to adjust to a very different working environment as RCS/ReFax customer service reps. For example:

1. They would be servicing several different product categories, not just one.
2. They would not be required (nor would there be any incentives) to provide ReFax salespeople with leads for equipment sales.
3. They would not sell MCs.
4. They would not have to sell parts and supplies.
5. Some representatives in rural areas would lose their "storefront" ReFax offices. Like RCS reps they would be given a van and would operate out of their homes.

Each ReFax branch received calls directly from customers. Under RCS/ReFax, however, customer calls would go to headquarters and be dispatched to branch offices, as was

---

TABLE A **Customer Service Branch Analysis: Fiscal Year 1990**

Branch	Revenues ($000s)	Margin (%)	Revenue per CSR[a] (dollars)	Units per CSR[a]	Percent Calls 4 Hours or Less	Average Response Time (hrs.)
Boston	$ 952	45.30%	$190,400	402	40.90%	6.20
Ft. Lauderdale	798	32.50	133,000	292	57.90	5.80
Los Angeles	1,473	48.40	184,100	480	29.50	6.90
Denver	1,130	38.00	161,400	329	42.10	6.30
Average of all 22 branches	959	39.40	158,650	335	46.60	5.50

[a]CSR signifies customer service representative.

being done by RCS. RCS/ReFax would bill ReFax for installation and warranty work.

RCS's View of the Merger.   RCS had achieved strong growth as the installed base of Regency products steadily increased. RCS's total revenues had grown over 40 percent annually since FY87, and it appeared that RCS would continue to grow steadily.

Compared to ReFax, RCS had a significant headquarters staff handling engineering and information services, marketing, field operations, support services, finance, and human resources. It developed an information system exclusively for its service operation, which tied into its parent and affiliate companies. But that information system was different from and incompatible with the information systems at ReFax.

Here are the comments of some RCS executives:

"The addition of fax machines to the present product line for service would not be difficult to accomplish."

"Economies of scale would certainly be achieved."

"We have 11 product lines, each requiring very different technical competencies. Our reps are stretched to their technical limits. We shouldn't take on fax machines—it can only hurt us."

"When we had fewer lines, our reps were technical experts on each. Gradually, they are losing that product-specific expertise. If we add fax machines, we ought to recognize the reps by product lines. No rep should handle more than six product lines."

"Having two national service networks (one for fax equipment and one for all other products) was a waste of resources and contrary to Regency's long-term customer-oriented strategy for the market."

"Separating the sales and service functions would allow ReFax to focus more effectively on its mission of sales and profits, and RCS/ReFax to concentrate on customer satisfaction."

Equally, if not more important, RCS managers believed that the quality of service would be improved under one service organization dedicated solely to providing a uniform standard of top-quality service to all Regency customers across all product lines. They believed that RCS would generate service revenues of over $26 million from fax machines. In addition, they expected to make at least a 40 percent gross margin on that, compared to ReFax's gross margin of around 36 percent.

RCS's total field headcount including headquarters service reps was 229 in FY 1991, compared to ReFax's field headcount of 168. Combined organization charts prepared by RCS indicated a consolidated field headcount of 306 and some streamlining of the headquarters organization (see Exhibit 3).

Exhibit 3 indicates a savings of 78 full-time equivalents in the combined organization for FY 1991. This represented a savings of more than $3.5 million per year, based on an average annual compensation of $30,000 per employee, plus benefits and overhead at 50 percent of salary. Additional savings would be achieved through a consolidation of office space. Several managers believed that there was no need, for example, to maintain both a ReFax and RCS office in the same town.

Exhibit 4 shows the quantitative results of the analyses done by RCS. As a result of the merger, RCS expected to generate additional revenues of $54.6 million and additional profits of $17.4 million during the two-year period FY 1991 and FY 1992.

ReFax's View of the Merger.   Folder looked at RCS's analyses of the projected savings in customer service manpower and costs as a result of the proposed merger. He focused his thoughts and analyses on the effects the proposed merger would have on various aspects of ReFax's business:

Fax equipment: The loss of the lead program is going to result in lower ReFax equipment sales. Even if some of this is made up by the salespeople, there will be a loss of at least 5 percent. Margins will be 26 percent (lower than the 27 percent with no merger) because RCS/ReFax will bill ReFax for warranty costs (estimated at 1 percent of sales).

Nonfax equipment: There is unlikely to be any effect on the sales and margins of nonfax equipment.

Supplies: Since RCS/ReFax service reps will not be selling supplies, ReFax would lose the supplies sales ($4 million) that were achieved by my service reps. ReFax could at best recover $1 million of that business through its salespeople. Expenses will be lower by $240,000 (average commission of 8 percent on $3 million).

MCs: MCs were expected to account for 80 percent of the service revenues from fax machines. Of the revenues from fax MCs, ReFax would receive 15 percent and RCS would keep 85 percent.

I can quantify all this and see what the financial implications of the merger are for ReFax.

Exhibit 5 shows the quantitative results of the analyses of Folder and other senior management at ReFax. For the two-year period FY 1991 and FY 1992, ReFax would lose revenues of $75.3 million and would lose profits of $12.8 million as a result of the merger. The senior management at ReFax felt this represented the most optimistic scenario for ReFax and that things could get worse. Folder thought:

At present, customer service is so very intertwined with the sales force and distribution. RCS/ReFax will never have that same relationship with ReFax salespeople. This merger will result in some additional drop in fax sales. Would RCS/ReFax service reps cooperate as much with ReFax salespeople with regard to demos and trial installations, and technical training of salespeople? Would the RCS/ReFax service department be willing to discount the MCs to help ReFax salespeople get an order? I doubt it!

Folder was concerned about additional expenses that would be needed to facilitate the merger of the service organizations. He was aware that the management information systems of the two organizations were different and incompatible. The merger would require RCS to accelerate the development of its new information system project, which might cost an additional $500,000 over two years. Folder wondered what financial and other effects that would have on ReFax and RCS/ReFax.

Folder also believed that the two organizations had very different cultures, and that the service reps were used to very different businesses. RCS and ReFax also differed substantially on employee benefits. Folder was convinced that the human factor added another major dimension to the troubling financial effects he had analyzed.

As he was preparing for the meeting with Roh, Folder wondered whether he had appropriately considered all the relevant factors that would affect the decision. He also was wondering how best to present his analyses, which he realized argued against what Roh wanted. He also remembered Roh's comment about ReFax customer service's dual objectives and concluded:

> I think we *can* win two races at the same time. The key is that people in the field should have the flexibility to make the trade-off between profitability and customer satisfaction.

EXHIBIT 1 **Industry Data**

| Year | Unit Sales (000s) | Industry Sales | | |
		Revenues* ($ millions)	Revenue/Unit ($)	Installed Base (000s)
1985	145	$ 623	$4,297	500
1986	191	692	3,623	645
1987	475	1,150	2,421	1,063
1988	1,125	2,016	1,792	2,114
1989	1,325	2,112	1,594	3,341
1990e	1,600	2,289	1,431	4,807
1991e	1,925	2,415	1,255	6,459
1992e	2,375	2,592	1,091	8,450
1993e	2,950	2,564	869	10,693

*End-user price.
eSignifies expected.
SOURCE: Adapted from BIS CAP International.

| Year | Percent of U.S. Placements (in units) by Product Category | | |
	Low-End	Mid-Range	High-End
1989	65%	29%	6%
1990e	70	25	5
1991e	74	22	4
1992e	74	22	4
1993e	76	21	3

eSignifies expected
SOURCE: Adapted from BIS CAP International.

Exhibit 2

Organization structure

Regency Facsimile, Inc.

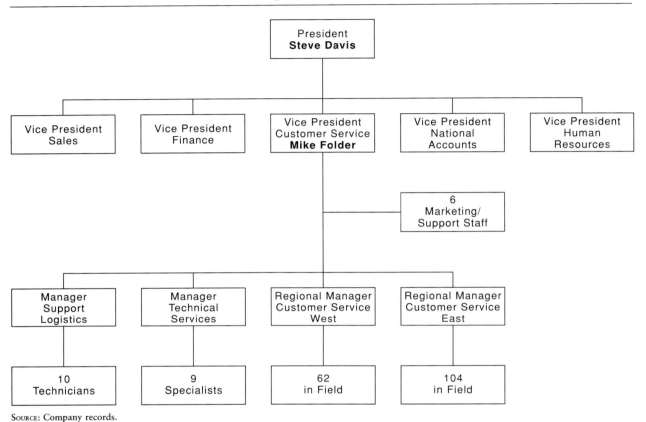

Source: Company records.

EXHIBIT 3 Headcount

	Headcount				
	RCS FY91	*ReFax Service FY91*	*Total RCS + ReFax FY91*	*Proposed Combined FY91*	*Personnel Change FY91*
Direct (cost of sales):					
Field operations					
Eastern region:					
Regional managers	1	1	2	1	−1
District managers	0	0	0	2	2
Branch managers	4	13	17	15	−2
Service representatives	111	82	193	150	−43
Clerical	2	9	11	4	−7
Total eastern region	118	105	223	172	−51
Western region:					
Regional managers	1	1	2	1	−1
District managers	0	0	0	2	2
Branch managers	4	9	13	12	−1
Service representatives	104	51	155	116	−39
Clerical	2	2	4	3	−1
Total western region	111	63	174	134	−40
Total field operations	229	168	397	306	−91
Support services:					
Customer service center	32	0	32	49	17
Technical support center	15	10	25	20	−5
Repair centers	42	0	42	42	0
Logistics	25	11	36	36	0
Systems & data processing	29	0	29	29	0
Staff	15	4	19	20	1
Total support services	158	25	183	196	13
Total direct	387	193	580	502	−78
Indirect (operating expenses):					
Management	5	1	6	6	0
Human resources	7	0	7	7	0
Finance	25	0	25	25	0
Information/engineering services	50	0	50	50	0
Marketing	17	2	19	19	0
Total indirect	104	3	107	107	0
Total	491	196	687	609	−78

SOURCE: Company records.

EXHIBIT 4   RCS Revenues and Expenses (all amounts in millions of dollars)

	RCS		RCS (No Merger)		RCS (Merger)	
	FY 1989	*FY 1990*	*FY 1991*	*FY 1992*	*FY 1991*	*FY 1992*
Revenues:						
Maintenance	$20.50	$32.50	$40.60	$48.80	$63.50	$ 77.00
Warranty	2.90	1.60	2.00	2.30	3.50	4.30
Special services	5.80	7.30	9.20	11.40	9.20	11.40
Other	4.00	5.30	6.90	7.80	6.90	7.80
Total revenues	33.20	46.70	58.70	70.30	83.10	100.50
Cost of sales	24.40	33.10	42.90	47.60	58.10	66.50
Gross margin	$ 8.80	$13.60	$15.80	$22.70	$25.00	$ 34.00
Operating expenses	$ 8.10	$10.40	$12.40	$13.60	$13.30	$ 15.80
Operating profit/loss	0.70	3.20	3.40	9.10	11.70	18.20

NOTE: FY 1990 runs July 1, 1989, to June 30, 1990.
SOURCE: Company records.

EXHIBIT 5   ReFax Revenues and Expenses (all amounts in millions of dollars)

			ReFax (No Merger)		ReFax (Merger)	
	FY 1989	*FY 1990*	*FY 1991*	*FY 1992*	*FY 1991*	*FY 1992*
Fax equipment:						
Revenue	$ 80.40	$115.60	$ 157.10	$ 206.50	$ 149.20	$ 196.20
{Unit sales}*	{53,987}	{72,238}	{140,000}	{214,000}	{133,000}	{203,500}
Gross margin	20.60	31.30	42.40	55.80	38.80	51.00
Expenses	32.20	33.00	39.00	44.00	38.40	43.30
Profit/loss	−11.60	−1.70	3.40	11.80	0.40	7.70
Nonfax equipment:						
Revenue	3.00	9.90	13.70	19.60	13.70	19.60
Gross margin	0.80	4.60	6.40	9.10	6.40	9.10
Expenses	2.50	5.30	6.00	7.00	6.00	7.00
Profit/loss	−1.70	−0.70	0.40	2.10	0.40	2.10
Supplies:						
Revenue	14.60	19.60	24.50	30.00	21.50	27.00
Gross margin	4.80	7.10	8.80	10.80	7.70	9.70
Expenses	5.30	5.40	6.20	7.00	6.00	6.80
Profit/loss	−0.50	1.70	2.60	3.80	1.70	2.90
Customer service:						
Revenue	19.70	21.10	26.00	32.00	3.10	3.80
Gross margin	6.10	7.60	9.40	11.50	3.10	3.80
Expenses	4.40	5.10	6.20	7.70	1.80	2.00
Profit/loss	1.70	2.50	3.20	3.80	1.30	1.80
Totals:						
Revenue	117.70	166.20	221.30	288.10	187.50	246.60
Gross margin	32.30	50.60	67.00	87.20	56.00	73.60
Expenses	44.40	48.80	57.40	65.70	52.20	59.10
Profit/loss	−12.10	1.80	9.60	21.50	3.80	14.50

*In units, not in millions of dollars.
SOURCE: Company records.

IBM Innovations: Introduction of the PS/2*

It was February 10, 1987. Ned Lautenbach, head of the National Distribution Division (NDD), which oversaw IBM's dealer network, and Bill Lowe, head of the Entry Systems Division (ESD), which had development and manufacturing responsibility for IBM's personal computers, were meeting with other senior managers to complete plans for the forthcoming announcement of a new personal computer line, the Personal System/2 (PS/2).

Lautenbach and Lowe had to decide whether to confirm the proposed announcement date of April 2, 1987. The announcement would be the biggest in IBM's recent history; it would be the first time IBM would introduce an entire new line of products, rather than just one new product.

Lautenbach expressed concern about the proposed date: "Bill, we really have to be sure that we can deliver when we announce; I have to fill up the channels of distribution before that. You have to assure me that you can deliver enough boxes so that the supply/demand relationship is balanced."

Lowe replied, "We can do it. I am confident production will be on schedule. I think we can easily make our proposed April 2 announcement." However, Lautenbach, having examined the proposed schedule of availability of the PS/2's various models, remained dubious. Other issues yet to be resolved were how to announce the new line to the dealers and how best to prepare the channels of distribution.

Company Background. IBM sold or leased most of its products through its worldwide marketing organizations, with selected products marketed and distributed through authorized dealers and remarketers. In 1986, "Big Blue" had more than 400,000 employees worldwide, it increased revenues from $34 billion in 1982 to more than $51 billion, and had total assets of more than $57 billion.

In its annual report, IBM described 1986 as a difficult year. Worldwide orders and shipments had not matched forecasted levels. The company attributed this decline to slow capital spending in North America, moderate economic performance in some key foreign markets, and unsatisfactory demand for some of its product line.

The 1986 annual report acknowledged the increased competition IBM was facing worldwide. To remain a successful world-class competitor, IBM felt that it had to strengthen and renew its product line, significantly increase the number of IBM people directly serving customers, and streamline its operations and redeploy resources to make the company as lean and vigorous as possible.

Believing constant innovation essential in this highly competitive industry, IBM had invested more than $5 billion in R&D and engineering in 1986. IBM felt it had unique long-term strengths in its technology base, ability to meet customer needs, and fundamental financial position.

National Distribution Division (NDD). NDD was formed in 1983 as a marketing division to sell such high-volume, low-cost products as personal computers, small computer systems, typewriters, and supplies through other channels of distribution than the direct sales force. These channels included value-added remarketers (VARs)[1] and authorized dealers. In addition to managing IBM's 2,200 authorized dealers, NDD had primary responsibility for identifying new product requirements based on customer and market surveys, and for distributing the personal computer product line and the PS/2. NDD also had its own sales representatives, who sold only to dealers, not to end users. Dealers, in turn, could sell to large, medium, or small accounts. Ned Lautenbach described his own and NDD's responsibilities:

> NDD is responsible for doing business with all IBM resellers in the United States. We select them, develop marketing plans for the products IBM sells to them, and support them with specific programs, such as education. My job as president is to make certain all sales, administration, and management teams accomplish our objectives. I'm also in charge of developing product strategies and determining our approach to working with resellers.

At the same time, IBM had a direct sales force of approximately 10,000 people unconnected to NDD who reported to other marketing divisions responsible for direct sales to users of large computer systems, as well as some small systems and typewriters.

Entry Systems Division (ESD). In 1987, ESD had worldwide development, product management, and U.S. manufacturing responsibility for IBM's general-purpose, low-cost personal-use computer systems, graphics workstations, and related software. It also had profit and loss responsibility. Bill Lowe was an IBM vice president and president of ESD.

This case was prepared by Professor Fareena Sultan.

---

[1]VARs: a VAR was a company that would take an IBM product and customize it by writing software for a specific industry or customer, such as the medical or law profession, and sell the IBM product along with this software.

IBM Personal Computers History

Early History. The microcomputer (personal computer) industry was born in the early 1970s with the development of microprocessor chips, which made it possible to pack the computing power of a huge 1950s mainframe into a desktop-sized box.

In the summer of 1981, IBM announced its first personal computer, the IBM PC, whose hardware and operating system specifications were widely published to encourage outside developers to write software. The firm also bought most of the major components from outside manufacturers; the PC had floppy disks and was based on Intel's 8088 microprocessor chip. IBM's strategy of acting as an assembler in this case guaranteed that the PC could be built quickly and reliably with industry-tested parts and with low development costs. IBM built only one basic model so all effort could be focused on making it a success.

1981 to 1983. The period 1981 to 1983 was one of rapid growth in the personal computer industry. New technologies were emerging, and standards were being developed. Personal computers grew into a $3 billion U.S. industry. In 1983, IBM announced the PC XT, which had a fixed disk drive, thus offering more convenient and increased storage of information than the PC. Increasing numbers of dealers each year were selling personal computers. Supply shortages were frequent, because demand was far greater than expected. In addition, distribution channels were still developing and, thus, were not ready to handle this explosion in demand. The challenge for manufacturers was to secure maximum shelf space.

1983 to 1985. From 1983 to 1985, personal computer sales growth slowed as consumers looked for better and more varied software. IBM announced a number of new products; by 1984, DOS (Disk Operating System), originated by IBM's business partner, Microsoft, had become an industry standard.

In 1984, IBM introduced the PC AT, which had larger storage capacity than previously existing IBM PCs and faster, more powerful processing capabilities. It was based on the new Intel 80286 microprocessing chip. However, the open architecture of IBM PCs allowed other firms to duplicate the IBM product. These IBM PC "clones," which began to appear in 1983, contributed to an oversupply. By 1984, IBM architecture was to be found in an increasing number of non-IBM personal computers. The manufacturers of IBM clones competed on price. Retail prices fell. IBM wanted to compete on the basis of product performance, software availability, and overall satisfaction of customer needs. Its share in the personal computer market declined, and many IBM dealers faced financial difficulties.

1985 and Beyond. The industry had changed substantially by 1985. Business activity was dictated no longer by price and inventory considerations but by end-user applications requirements. At the same time, an increasing number of IBM dealers continued to face financial pressure due to oversupply. Moreover, there was no protection offered them for excess inventory or unsold PCs. IBM continued to face competition from the clones. PC unit shipments as a percentage of the IBM-compatible market fell further.

In 1986, IBM decided that a new approach was required to manage the channels of distribution. It also planned to emphasize price/function trade-offs in its new product introductions.

Situation Assessment

Distribution Channels. Bill McCracken, who worked under Ned Lautenbach, was NDD director of PC channel management and head of the project office for the PS/2 announcement. In assessing the channel situation, he and others in NDD felt that things looked pretty bad for the existing line as early as 1984. Bill, extremely concerned about oversupply and falling prices, commented, "NDD was the *Chicken Little* saying 'The sky is falling.'" Others at IBM were skeptical of this assessment.

In tracing the PS/2's history, McCracken recalled that it was February 1985 when he became concerned about what was happening to IBM's existing PC line, particularly about the distribution channels. He felt that, although all personal computer dealers were facing financial pressure, IBM dealers were worse off. Besides having to compete with other manufacturers' personal computers on the basis of price and performance, they had to compete with an increasing number of clones on the basis of price. Starting in 1984, some dealers were going out of business. By mid-1985, McCracken felt strongly that urgent measures were needed to be taken to support the dealers, but first he had to sell the idea internally that oversupply and falling prices were creating a crisis situation for the entire personal computer line. It did not take McCracken long to convince NDD.

However, ESD was not as easy to convince. Bill Lowe felt that IBM dealers had problems because NDD was not doing its job as a marketing division. Even though NDD had figures to show that IBM's share of the market was down, ESD's position was that the volume of personal computers sold was up since their introduction in 1981. To assess the situation in the distribution channels, NDD looked at a variety of information. IBM had several market research firms scan the competitive environment regularly, monitoring such indicators as market share, long-term trends, volume, and profitability on a continuous basis.

They gathered some data annually and others monthly or quarterly. Exhibit 1 shows monthly sales in computer specialty stores by major manufacturers and associated market share trends. Industry sales estimates, developed for planning purposes, were monitored annually.

Exhibit 2 shows estimates of industry sales from 1984 to 1986, while Exhibit 3 shows them broken down by end-user price segments. These estimates were made by IBM's Forecasting Group. To assess its standing in the market, NDD also monitored personal computer sales. Exhibit 4 shows quarterly comparisons from 1984 to 1986.

Bill McCracken, concerned about the trends portrayed in the information, looked at prices and sales volumes for PCs with different microprocessor chips. For the 8088 microprocessor chip (the technology used for the PC), as well as for the more technologically advanced 80286 chip (used for the PC AT), IBM products were priced higher than comparable competitive models. Exhibit 5 shows dealer prices for selected models. McCracken felt that price trends were making it impossible for IBM and its dealers to remain competitive. Meetings within NDD resulted in the formation of a task force in October 1985.

Task Force. The task force, consisting of Ned Lautenbach, Bill Lowe, Bill McCracken, and other senior executives, was to assess the channels situation and then make marketing recommendations to alleviate the problem. NDD initiated tracking studies to determine how much volume was actually being shipped by dealers. Many small dealers were shipping hardly any volume. In 40 percent of stores, fewer than 10 systems per month were actually being shipped to customers.

NDD also monitored dealer productivity by geographic regions, or Metropolitan Statistical Areas (MSAs), in terms of volume shipped. From these tracking studies, NDD concluded that, in addition to external market conditions, too many dealers in some geographical areas depressed average dealer sales volume. Six weeks later, in November 1985, the task force recommended that the distribution channels be frozen. *No new dealers would be authorized.* Efforts should instead be made to enhance relationships with existing dealers.

Market Evolution: The Customer and PC Usage. When the IBM PC was announced in 1981, its primary positioning was as a personal productivity tool. By 1983, businesses also were using it as a terminal to a mainframe computer. By 1985, IBM was manufacturing and marketing a line of products comprising the PC, the PC XT, the PC AT, and a large number of option cards (e.g., memory, communications, graphics). The principal operating system was DOS.

These products were developed with heavy OEM (original equipment manufacturer) participation, which meant other vendors could easily duplicate IBM's products without incurring the same development expense. According to Dr. Pat Bowlds, technical director at ESD, "IBM tried to be first with innovations. However, at times, these distinctions were difficult to quantify to personal computer customers. A growing number of new users were not computer scientists or engineers. Rather than focusing on technical superiority, these customers' main concern was ease of use. IBM lost market share because of supply problems, price pressures from clones, and new products by competitors, such as Apple's Macintosh, which focused on ease of use."

Although the IBM products were fully application-compatible with one another, the ability to attach to or work with other IBM systems was not the primary objective. The focus was on building the best individual machine. However, over time, IBM's corporate customers demanded more capabilities. For example, they wanted to connect systems together and use the same software on personal computers as they did on mainframes.

During 1985 to 1986, it became obvious that personal computers were being used as part of integrated systems in corporations. The personal computer environment was increasingly integrated into advanced data processing and communications systems instead of remaining a stand-alone system. In addition, many software packages—such as communication packages and packages for multitasking (i.e., the ability to run more than one program at a time)—were becoming available for advanced applications and "systems solutions." By 1986, due to rapid technological progress and expanding customer needs, the personal computer also was being used as an intelligent work station (IWS) (i.e., not just as a terminal) and in local area networks (LANs) in which a series of personal computers connected to one another.

By 1987, the personal computer encompassed a whole array of uses. The business customer had grown sophisticated and was demanding a lot more function and flexibility from the personal computer. However, the architecture of existing products made it difficult, if not impossible, to perform these additional tasks.

Innovation as a Response to Situation Assessment

PS/2 Strategy. The PS/2's strategic role was to reestablish IBM's position as an innovator and, thus, revive IBM's personal computer line. Targeted primarily at business customers, the new line was technologically superior. Competitors would have to incur significant development costs to match it. For ESD, the PS/2 demonstrated technological superiority in response to growing customer sophistication. For NDD, the PS/2 addressed the turbulent situation in the dealer channels. Bill McCracken in particular saw the pending announcement of the PS/2 as involving major innovations in product and in channels.

Product Innovation: Objectives.   According to senior ESD managers, the PS/2 provided enhanced benefits, including compatibility at competitive prices across the entire product family—from beginner systems to advanced workstations.

Product development.   Although technology exploration of the PS/2 had been initiated as early as 1984, the decision to introduce a new family of products and the plans for its production were not made until the third quarter of 1985. ESD recognized that a new software system would have to be designed to deliver the features that customers were demanding. This led to the definition of the Operating System 2 (OS/2). However, the hardware needed for OS/2 was the new 80386 microprocessor chip being developed by Intel, and not available until 1987.

ESD worked on incorporating new architecture in the PS/2 hardware. IBM saw the PS/2 being used in a variety of ways: as a workstation, for personal productivity, for business/departmental productivity, in local area networks, and for multitasking. NDD advised that one of the most challenging aspects of the introduction would be to help customers (both end users and dealers) make the transition from a stand-alone personal computer system to a workstation system.

The new PS/2 product line.   With the introduction of the PS/2, IBM was planning to announce not only a new line of personal computers but also new systems software and peripherals. The new products would differ from IBM's existing systems in many ways. For one, 3½-inch disk drives would be standard, as opposed to the 5¼-inch drives of the previous line. Persuading existing customers to accept this transition switch would be a major challenge for ESD. New, advanced graphics capabilities also would be available, and a new Micro Channel architecture was proposed to allow multitasking.

The new product line would include four new computer models in a total of eight configurations. These were Model 30, 50, 60, and 80. Exhibit 6 shows the prices for the various PS/2 models. The models and their features are described in the table below.

Although all products would be announced simultaneously, only some of the machines could be available on April 2, 1987. Due to production constraints, the others, which were technologically more sophisticated, would not become available until later in the year. However, IBM executives felt that announcing all the new products at once would assist dealers in the transition from the old to the new product line.

Prototypes of the PS/2 models were ready in the second quarter of 1986. The manufacturing line was set up in December 1986, and volume production was to commence in February 1987.

Channel Innovation: Advanced Systems Dealer (ASD) network.   NDD knew that an efficient and well-trained dealer network was essential to help customers make the transition to the PS/2. Dealers would have to fulfill minimum sales quota requirements, develop business plans, and agree to send every sales representative for training and education programs. The qualifying dealers would form the Advanced Systems Dealer (ASD) network, and only they would be authorized to carry the new PS/2 line.

Chronology of actions.   Since November 1985, no new dealers had been authorized. Ned Lautenbach had to decide how long the channels should remain frozen once the PS/2 was announced. The next consideration was inventory price protection for dealers. In January 1987, a return policy was initiated so that, for a 5 percent rehandling fee, dealers could return excess PCs. IBM also considered a "buy-back" of old products when new ones were introduced.

In February 1987, PROPLAN, a program to award "points" to dealers based on sales, was to be initiated. For each $300 of sales, IBM would credit the dealer with 10 PROPLAN points redeemable for certain IBM-approved marketing support activities, including education. This system was considered preferable to giving additional discounts to dealers, because they tended to use discounts to cut prices, which would result in too much emphasis on price competition. The points, on the other hand, did not affect prices of the PC line; they were a nonprice benefit that could be redeemed for dealer training. In addition, a financing plan to provide credit to dealers was to be initiated in March 1987 through the IBM Credit Corporation.

Model	30	50	60	80
Microprocessor (computer chip)	8086	80286	80286	80386
Input/output[a] architecture	Existing (PC)	New (Micro Channel)	New (Micro Channel)	New (Micro Channel)
Operating system	DOS 3.3[b]	DOS 3.3 or OS/2[c]	DOS 3.3 or OS/2	DOS 3.3 or OS/2

[a]Mechanism by which a company communicated with input and output devices, such as keyboards and monitors.

[b]A new version of Microsoft's Disk Operating System, DOS 3.3 was expected to be available by April 1987.

[c]OS/2 was needed for some of the new features of the new PS/2 line, but was not expected to be available until after the PS/2 line was announced.

NOTE: All PS/2 models needed the new PS/2 monitors to run the advanced graphics features of the new PS/2 line.

Next, promotions and cooperative advertising were to be initiated in July 1987 to clear inventories of the old PC line. Finally, IBM planned to promise a faster, 10-day delivery program starting in October 1987.

NDD felt that the combined effect of these actions would be to help dealers manage their supply and inventory better. The cost of implementing these proposals would be about $50 million.

Dealer education. NDD proposed a dealer training and education program starting in March 1987, one month before the PS/2 announcement. Five training centers were to be set up—in San Francisco, Dallas, Chicago, Atlanta, and New York. IBM would require that every authorized dealer-salesperson attend these training sessions. The cost of 120,000 student days would be $3 million to $4 million. NDD felt that this dealer training was essential for the success of the PS/2 introduction.

Direct sales force. To compensate IBM's direct sales force, NDD recommended a compensation program under which the direct sales force would earn commissions for sales transacted via the dealer channels.

Dealer reaction. NDD anticipated opposition from some dealers who would not see the need to develop the business plans IBM would require. Furthermore, although they would not pay for the training program, they would incur the costs of salesperson time spent on the two-week training program as well as air and hotel expenses. Most dealers recognized the importance of training to enhance their selling effectiveness; a minority believed that they could train themselves.

The PS/2 Announcement

Project Office. In July 1986, Ed Lucente, Lautenbach's boss, asked him to set up a project office to handle the PS/2 announcement. The project office was founded in August 1986 and would be in place until April 1987, with Ned Lautenbach of NDD and Bill Lowe of ESD as its key executives and Bill McCracken as its head.

About 300 people were assigned full time to the project office. However, given the project's scope, the number of IBM employees involved in the PS/2 announcement in some capacity or other was about 1,000. The senior staff met weekly to review progress and also decided that any disagreements would be resolved by the division presidents within a week.

The project office was divided into subgroups (each with cross-divisional representation) to handle aspects of the PS/2 introduction, such as:

Announcement	Including press communications, the announcement meeting, and advertising.
Marketing Support	Including education, service, technical support, and replacement of the existing personal computer line.
Business Volume	Including supply, coverage, distribution, sales plan, and administration.
Product Line Support	Including competitive comparisons, benchmarks, conversion, industry support, key accounts, new business, and customer support center.
Business Relationships	Transition issues, such as conversion of existing software to a format suited for PS/2.

Other issues were to be handled by existing departments (e.g., ESD would decide on price).

Announcement Strategy. In September 1986, Bill McCracken presented to senior executives a PS/2 marketing strategy to be announced in the first quarter of 1987: a family of products focused on end-user solutions. Attributes to be emphasized included performance, capacity, application, and connectivity. The strategy deemphasized hardware speeds, chip technology, and megahertz rates in favor of addressing how these new technologies could address emerging customer needs.

Based on input from NDD and ESD, the project office recommended that 40,000 systems be built before the announcement; at an average price of $4,000 each, IBM was planning to ship goods worth $160 million. Overall, $500 million was to be invested in the PS/2 before the announcement. Once the announcement was made, approximately 7,000 computers per day would be manufactured. The Product Group, to which ESD reported, forecast the demand for the new product line. (As part of a system of checks and balances, forecasting was not left to the product manager.) Of the 40,000 total systems needed on announcement day, the need by model type was forecast as follows:

	PS/2 Model			
	30	50	60	80
Number needed on announcement day	20,000	10,000	7,000	3,000

The project office also recommended that the Advanced Systems Dealership program and other channel innovations be announced at the same time as the PS/2.

Communicating the Announcement: the Miami convention. In his September 1986 presentation, Bill McCracken proposed that the announcement would be made to the dealers and press at a convention in Miami on April 2. About 3,000 people were to be invited. A major business show, to include IBM dealers who had been selected to be part of ASD, was planned to coincide with the announcement. The presentation was to be broadcast via satellite to the rest of the distribution network and to IBM personnel and analysts at 90 sites across the United States.

A press conference, chaired by Ned Lautenbach and Bill Lowe, was to be held after the business show to announce the product to the public. The press conference would be broadcast live to New York so reporters could ask questions via a satellite hookup. However, there was debate about whether the press should be invited to the business show. NDD thought that it would result in good publicity for IBM, but some of IBM's public relations executives felt otherwise; allowing the general press to walk around the exhibits and solicit initial reactions from dealers might not be advisable, because of the dealers' unfamiliarity with the new technology. McCracken's group had to decide whom to invite to the convention. One suggestion was to invite 90 percent dealers and 10 percent press people.

Advertising the PS/2.   The project office firmly believed that advertising should emphasize solving end-user problems. The advertising message was expanded to give consumers additional reasons for purchasing the PS/2 and to address customer concerns about product obsolescence.

The advertising agency, together with many NDD executives, felt that IBM should keep the Charlie Chaplin theme then being employed to maintain a sense of continuity between the old and the new lines. The project team, particularly those with ESD backgrounds, disagreed, believing that a new image was needed to stress the technological advancement of the PS/2 over the existing line.

Full-page ads were to be run in newspapers on the announcement day, and 24-page inserts were to be included in business and professional magazines, such as *Time* and *Newsweek*. In the three months following the announcement, media expenditures would be $30 million.

Maintaining confidentiality.   In January 1987, rumors of a new IBM PC were prevalent. Buyers were, however, skeptical. In the spring of 1984, rumors had circulated of a new IBM microcomputer called the "PC2," for which some customers had delayed buying decisions. In June 1985, IBM had to announce that no such product existed.

By early 1987, the press was reporting that IBM was preparing to introduce an "astounding" new line of personal computers, and popular computer magazines reported that buyers were sitting tight until the actual announcement was made. Managing the expectations of customers without allowing the news of the PS/2 to leak to the media was a challenging task for IBM. On the one hand, to ensure in-store availability, IBM had to brief dealers in advance. On the other, the company wished to maintain strict secrecy for competitive reasons. It would reveal details of the announcement only on the announcement date, April 2. It would tell dealers in advance only that a pending announcement would be made on that date without revealing technical details.

Customer anxiety.   Many corporate buyers were concerned about software and hardware compatibility and product availability. They were anxious to know whether existing software would run on the new machines without modification and whether the new machines could use existing hardware and peripherals.

Any gap between announcement and availability represented an important issue. Dr. Pat Bowlds explained: "IBM felt that, for technologically intensive innovations, which were high-ticket items, the planning cycle of corporate buyers would allow a wider gap between announcement and availability—that is, people plan and budget for such major purchases well in advance of actual delivery."

Timing of Announcement.   In explaining how the timing of an innovation announcement is determined, one ESD executive commented:

> When you announce a new product in the retail channel, as in the case of the PS/2, certain quarters are automatically ruled out. January/February are nonmonths for announcement. The December retail activity due to holidays and end-of-year clearance keeps retail people busy through January 15. The fourth quarter of a year is excluded because of peak selling for retail. One cannot announce at this time because manufacturers and retailers do not have time to stock the shelves. Summer is downtime because many people are on vacation. One window is September or early October, but that may be too close to holiday shopping days. That leaves us the months of March, April, and May as the best times to announce.

Ned Lautenbach pointed out, "The most serious debates regarding the PS/2 announcement centered around its *timing*." He elaborated: "Bill Lowe and I are good friends and have worked together for a long time. However, throughout the PS/2's history, this issue has been one of real contention between the two divisions."

Bill McCracken added: "When and how much availability will there be is a big issue in deciding announcement of an innovation. How long the old product is available is another issue." Exhibit 7 shows the production schedule for both the old and new lines for 1986 and 1987. Exhibit 8 shows monthly production schedules from December 1986 to March 1987 for the PS/2 line.

Earlier in the fall of 1986, IBM had planned to announce the PS/2 in January 1987. ESD felt that early announcement was necessary to preempt competition. However, NDD argued for April 1987 to ensure that the channels of distribution were ready, trained, and loaded before announcement.

Bill McCracken felt that IBM could not announce early in 1987, due to anticipated supply shortages. ESD was promising 40,000 boxes for shipment in January 1987, even though it had experienced manufacturing delays in 1986. However, McCracken feared a repeat of the PC AT announcement in August 1984. At that time, IBM had announced the PC AT as "available now"; stock-outs followed the announcement, with only 40 percent of the demand being met. The first quarter of 1985 had seen severe supply shortages for the AT, which enabled clones to establish a strong foothold in the PC market.

Proposed dates for the announcement and availability of selected items in the PS/2 line are shown in Exhibit 9. Ned Lautenbach and Bill Lowe were scheduled to confirm these dates at a meeting on February 10, 1987.

Factors Affecting Timing of Announcement: competitive activity. When asked whether the PS/2 announcement was a response to competitive activity, a senior executive at NDD said: "IBM differs from its competition in that it offers a total solution, a breadth of product line. Most competitors don't have this breadth. They are optimizing one piece at a time, treating the PC as a stand-alone item. With the PS/2, IBM is emphasizing the notion of a systems network."

Another issue was whether IBM should incorporate the latest and fastest 80386 chip in its product line. IBM felt that it should focus on end-user solutions, rather than simply on speed, and decided that being first in the market with the new chip was not so critical. In addition, no personal computer manufacturer yet had the software to support the potential of the new 80386 chip. In any event, the operating system (OS/2) for the IBM PS/2 that would use this chip was still being developed. (The OS/2 could also be used with the 80286 chip. However, the 80386 was faster and had more capabilities than the 80286.) The timing of the PS/2 announcement had to take this factor into account.

Being first. In mid-1986, the industry was caught by surprise when Intel decided to deliver the new technology of the 80386 chip by the third quarter of 1986, rather than by 1987.

IBM then was faced with a major decision. Should it incorporate the new chip into the old line, as Compaq had done, or take advantage of this technology in the new line? From a technological innovation viewpoint, IBM wanted to be first with the new 80386 chips; however, there were market considerations. If IBM put the 80386 chips in the old product in September 1986, it would encourage third-party applications programmers to start designing software for the old line. Then, when IBM announced the PS/2 in 1987, all that software would have to be rewritten. To avoid this confrontation with application programmers, ESD decided to lag behind the competition by six to seven months and to introduce the new chip in the new PS/2 line in 1987.

History of previous announcements. In announcing an entire line of products, IBM would be departing from its previous history of announcing one new model at a time. Exhibit 10 shows the dates of announcement for models introduced since 1982. NDD wanted to ensure that the PS/2 would be physically available on April 2, the an-

nouncement date, whereas ESD's focus was on generating profits as fast as possible.

Hardware versus software availability. The new operating system, OS/2, being developed by Microsoft, was needed for some of the enhanced features of the PS/2 line. It was estimated that it might be six to eight months after an April 2 announcement of PS/2 before OS/2 would be available. In discussing the gap between the timing of availability of hardware versus software, Ned Lautenbach said: "You have to give time to application software writers to examine the enhanced features of the hardware and figure out what application programs should be written. Sure, the end user would want the software on the same day that the hardware is announced. However, we would not delay the announcement of the new line simply because the software was not ready. After all, existing software could be run on the new line, although it is true that some of the enhanced features of the PS/2 can be utilized only once the new operating system is written."

In further justifying the gap between hardware and software availability, Ned cited the example of IBM's mainframe: "The IBM 360-370 hardware was announced 18 to 20 months before its software became available." Bill Lowe agreed with Ned: "Announcement heightens end-user awareness. It proliferates the hardware technology and increases the development and availability of software applications. We should not delay an announcement of a new product for software reasons alone."

Phasing in new—phasing out old. According to Ned Lautenbach: "A major consideration in announcing any innovation is when the new line will be introduced and the old one phased out. One has to manage down old inventory and manage up the new; otherwise, profits could be jeopardized." Between April 1 and April 2, $5.5 billion to $6.0 billion of business would be phased in with the new line and phased out with the old.

Bill Lowe and Ned Lautenbach looked at the supply/demand forecasts, based on inputs from NDD and ESD, for the old and new line (see Exhibit 11). They had to determine a schedule for phasing out the old and phasing in the new. To facilitate the transition, IBM considered offering price reductions on its existing line. One proposal was a 35 percent cut in the PC XT dealer price to $1,395 and a 13 percent cut in the PC AT dealer price to $4,595. Other cuts of about 15 percent were proposed for the rest of the existing line to make space on store shelves for the PS/2 line.

The February 10, 1987, meeting between Ned Lautenbach and Bill Lowe was interrupted by an urgent phone call for Bill. After putting the receiver down, he looked at Ned and said: "There has been a fire in our plant in Taiwan where monitors for our computers are made. We were able to get some of the production molds for the PS/2 monitors out in time. As you know, the new PS/2 systems cannot work without the new PS/2 monitors. Although production of these monitors might be affected for at least six months, I think we can catch up on our proposed production schedule. I think we should go ahead and stick to our April 2 date for the announcement. Postponing the announcement would have a negative effect on the morale of ESD since they have been planning for this for several months."

Ned Lautenbach said: "I can understand your point about employee morale; however, we have to ensure that there is a smooth supply of products and that we have the channels of distribution ready for this announcement."

Bill Lowe reminded Ned Lautenbach that ESD already had started reducing production of the old PC line in anticipation of the announcement of the new PS/2 line. He also reminded Ned that other manufacturers already had incorporated the latest chip technology in their personal computers, and, as the market leader and innovator in the industry, ESD did not want to delay this announcement.

Ned said: "If we announce and can't deliver, the repercussions on IBM and the PC dealers will be devastating." Ned paused to ponder. "I wonder if this is the right time to announce. Perhaps we should postpone the announcement by at least six months until the production schedule becomes more predictable."

Lautenbach and Lowe focused on the following two options:

1. **Delay announcement:**

   - Instead of announcing the new PS/2 line, IBM could try to ramp up the old PC line—this would take at least six months and involve ordering parts from vendors for products that had been discontinued.

   - Even if it were possible to obtain those parts to restart the line, it would cost $100 million to do so.

   - IBM could try to contract outside vendors to build new monitors with new designs. However, it would have to pay up-front investment costs of at least $25 million. Finding vendors and putting production in place would take about nine months.

2. **Announce as planned:**

   - Arrange for IBM plants in other locations, such as Scotland, to divert production from the existing line. This action could generate only 5,000 of the estimated 40,000 monitors required on April 2 in the intervening two months. Meanwhile, ESD would try to catch up on its production schedule at the Taiwan plant.

Ned Lautenbach and Bill Lowe wondered about the pros and cons of the options. They knew that 10,000 PS/2 monitors already had been built at the Taiwan plant. They felt that they could secure an additional 5,000 new PS/2 monitors for a total of 15,000. Although they were fairly sure of having 69,000 PS/2 computers available, at best only 15,000 of these would be equipped with the new PS/2 monitors, though demand for the new line was estimated at 40,000 units on announcement day. They wondered whether they should announce as planned or delay the announcement? In either case, how should they handle it? What would they tell the media, customers, dealers, and IBM employees, and when? What was the best response to this crisis?

EXHIBIT 1

Retail unit sales of personal computers in computer specialty stores (major manufacturers)

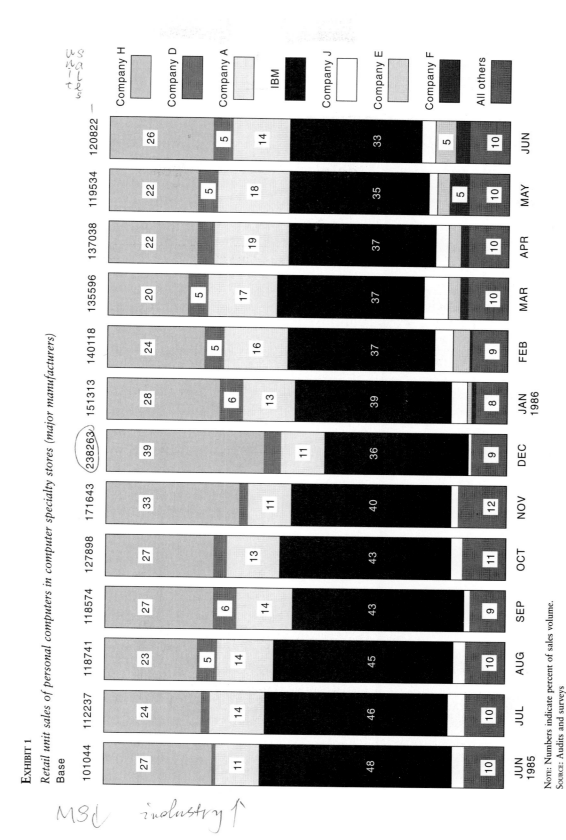

Legend:
- Company H
- Company D
- Company A
- IBM
- Company J
- Company E
- Company F
- All others

US units

Base

	JUN 1985	JUL	AUG	SEP	OCT	NOV	DEC	JAN 1986	FEB	MAR	APR	MAY	JUN
	101044	112237	118741	118574	127898	171643	238263	151313	140118	135596	137038	119534	120822

JUN 1985:
- Company H: 27
- Company A: 11
- IBM: 48
- All others: 10

JUL:
- Company H: 24
- Company A: 14
- IBM: 46
- All others: 10

AUG:
- Company H: 23
- Company D: 5
- Company A: 14
- IBM: 45
- All others: 10

SEP:
- Company H: 27
- Company D: 6
- Company A: 14
- IBM: 43
- All others: 9

OCT:
- Company H: 27
- Company A: 13
- IBM: 43
- All others: 11

NOV:
- Company H: 33
- Company A: 11
- IBM: 40
- All others: 12

DEC:
- Company H: 39
- Company A: 11
- IBM: 36
- All others: 9

JAN 1986:
- Company H: 28
- Company D: 6
- Company A: 13
- IBM: 39
- All others: 8

FEB:
- Company H: 24
- Company D: 5
- Company A: 16
- IBM: 37
- All others: 9

MAR:
- Company H: 20
- Company D: 5
- Company A: 17
- IBM: 37
- All others: 10

APR:
- Company H: 22
- Company A: 19
- IBM: 37
- All others: 10

MAY:
- Company H: 22
- Company D: 5
- Company A: 18
- IBM: 35
- Company F: 5
- All others: 10

JUN:
- Company H: 26
- Company D: 5
- Company A: 14
- IBM: 33
- Company F: 5
- All others: 10

NOTE: Numbers indicate percent of sales volume.
SOURCE: Audits and surveys

711

EXHIBIT 2   **Estimates of Industry Sales for Computers Priced $1K–$15K (in thousands of units)**

Date of Estimate	1984	1985	1986
12/84	3,504	3,753[a]	4,405
7/85	3,306	3,526	4,060
12/85	3,274	3,289	3,339
2/87	3,274	3,385	3,494

[a]To be read: in December 1984 it was estimated that 3,753,000 computers priced between $1K–$15K would be sold in 1985.
NOTE: Includes price of monitor and printer.
SOURCE: IBM.

EXHIBIT 3   **Estimates of Industry Sales by Price Segment (in thousands of units)**

Year	$1K–$3K	$3K–$6K	$6K–$15K	$1K–$15K
1984	955	1,652	667	3,274
1985	1,155	1,658	572	3,385
1986	1,644	1,318	532	3,494

NOTE: The prices refer to end-user prices and include price of monitor and printer. These were estimates available as of February 1987.
SOURCE: IBM.

EXHIBIT 4

Personal computer sales ($1K–$12K quarterly comparisons)

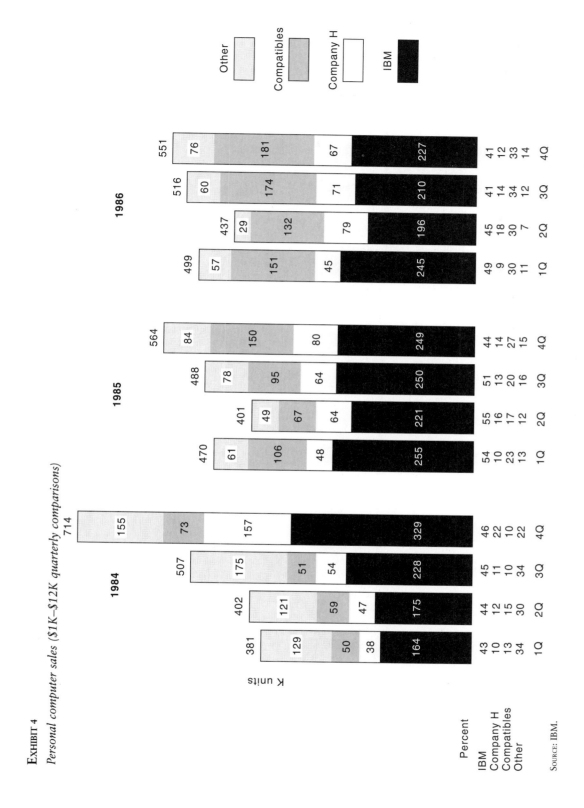

Source: IBM.

EXHIBIT 5

PC price trends for selected models

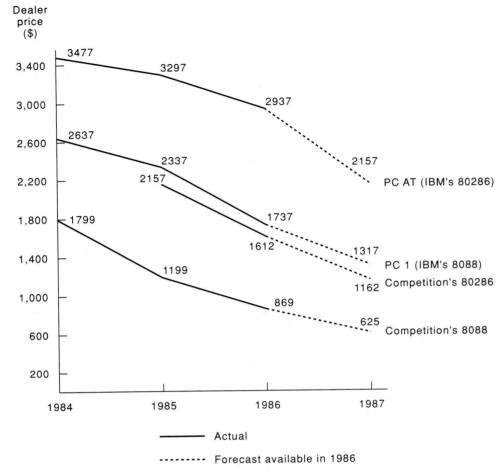

NOTE: Dealer price of CPU only.
SOURCE: IBM.

EXHIBIT 6   Ownership Costs—1987 Prices of Selected Models of Old/New Line

| | | | Retail Price | | |
| | | | Without Monitor | With Monitor | One-Year System Unit Maintenance Agreement |
	Model	Memory			
Old Line					
PC XT	5160–088	640KB	$2,660	$3,265	$432
PC AT	5170–339	512KB	5,295	5,900	455
New Line					
PS/2–30	8530–021	640KB	2,295	2,980	160
PS/2–50	8550–021	1MB	3,595	4,280	180
PS/2–60	8560–041	1MB	5,295	5,980	190
PS/2–80	8580–041	1MB	6,995	7,680	220

NOTE: MB = Megabyte. KB = Kilobyte. 1 Megabyte or 1,000 kilobytes equals approximately 500 typewritten pages of text.
SOURCE: IBM.

EXHIBIT 7   IBM PC Production Schedule (000s)

	1986				1987			
	1st	2nd	3rd	4th	1st	2nd	3rd	4th
Total old PC line	152	287	319	392	147	40	30	—
Total new PS/2 line	—	—	1	12	143	183	304	362

NOTE: 1987 demand was expected to be 10% higher than the supply. Supply could catch up to demand in 90 days under normal conditions.
SOURCE: IBM.

EXHIBIT 8   PS/2 Monthly Production Schedule (000s)

	December 1986	January 1987	February 1987	March 1987
Total new PS/2 line	12	32	49	62
Units needed internally/for testing	5	10	10	—
Units available to general public	7	10	10	—
Cumulative production of new systems	8[a]	22	39	62
		30	69[b]	131

[a] Includes 1,000 units from third quarter 1986 (see Exhibit 7).
[b] Since it would take about four weeks to fill the distribution pipeline, only 69,000 units of the 131,000 would be available for distribution to the general public by the beginning of April 1987.
SOURCE: IBM.

EXHIBIT 9   PS/2 Announcement/Availability Dates

1987	Apr.	May	June	July	Aug.	Sep.	Oct.
Model 30	‾*						
Model 50	‾*						
Model 60 (Version I, II)	‾* I — II ‾		*II				
Model 80 (Version I, II)	‾* I — II ‾		*II				
Displays	‾*						
Communication Card[a]	‾	*					
Memory Cards	‾					*	
Operating System OS/2	‾					*	
PC DOS 3.3	‾*						

‾ Announce   *Availability

[a]Communication Card for Model 30 was already available. This refers to card for Models 50, 60, and 80.

NOTE: Model 60 and Model 80 had two versions, each of which differed in storage capacity.

Model 60 and Model 80, Version I, would be announced and available in April 1987.

Model 60 and Model 80, Version II, would be announced in April but available in June 1987.

SOURCE: IBM.

EXHIBIT 10 Announcement History and Product Highlights

1981	1982	1983	1984	1985	1986	1987
September Introduction of IBM Personal Computer	**December** Announced PC in world trade	**March** PC XT	**February** • IBM Portable PC2 8088 chip	**March** New models of PC XT (diskettes only)	**April** • Enhanced PC AT	**April** Introduce PS/2 family of products
Monochrome display U.S. only		8088 chip			• IBM enhanced keyboard (101 keys)	D.T. Model 30 2 disk drives
83-key keyboard		Color display announced worldwide	**June** • 2 new models of PC1 and 1 new model of PC XT	**October** New model of PC AT (30MB hardfile)	• 30MB hardfile	D.T. " " 20MB fixed, 1 disk drive
160KB diskette		360KB diskette	• 256KB		• 1.2MB diskette	D.T. Model 50 20MB "
8088 chip		10MB fixed disk	**August** • PC AT		• 80286 chip	F.S. Model 60 40MB "
		November PC Jr.	• 1.2MB diskette		• New PC XT	F.S. " " 70MB "
		360KB diskette	• 20MB hardfile		• 20MB hardfile	F.S. " " 40MB "
		63-key keyboard (cordless)	• 80286 chip		• IBM enhanced keyboard (101 keys)	F.S. Model 80 70MB "
					August • New PC XT	F.S. " " 110MB "
					• 20MB hardfile	Highlights
					• 1.2MB diskette	Micro channel
					• IBM enhanced keyboard	Enhanced graphics with analog display
					• 80286 chip	8086 chip in Model 30
						80286 chip in Model 50, Model 60
						80386 chip in Model 80
						32-bit BUS architecture up to 2MB

NOTE: D.T. = Desk top.
F.S. = Free-standing.
SOURCE: IBM.

717

EXHIBIT 11

Cumulative available supply (inventory and build plan) vs. cumulative forecasted demand (as of 2/87)

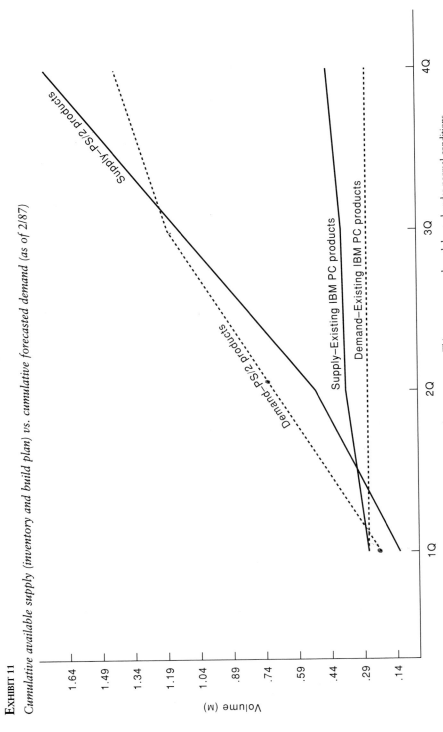

Supply–PS/2 products

Demand–PS/2 products

Supply–Existing IBM PC products

Demand–Existing IBM PC products

1Q   2Q   3Q   4Q   1987

Volume (m)

.14   .29   .44   .59   .74   .89   1.04   1.19   1.34   1.49   1.64

NOTE: Supply figures estimated by manufacturing group and demand by forecasting group. This represents supply and demand under normal conditions.

SOURCE: ESD IBM.

Black & Decker Corporation: Spacemaker Plus[1] Coffeemaker (A)

"My Black & Decker Spacemaker Plus coffeemaker has just set itself on fire," said the California caller to Black & Decker's customer service "800" number on December 1, 1988. Fortunately, as the caller calmly explained, the fire had been confined to the unit and was quickly extinguished. As he was preparing to paint his kitchen, he was not concerned about the smoke damage, though he did want a replacement coffeemaker. Black & Decker's concern was to get the unit back to the Household Product Group's (HPG) Shelton, Connecticut, headquarters as soon as possible to establish the cause of the fire in its new "Cadillac product."

With sales exceeding the same period in 1987 by more than 20 percent, 1988 Christmas orders were strong for HPG. By December, it had succeeded in shipping all it could produce of the Spacemaker Plus line, including over 80,000 coffeemakers, in time for the peak holiday buying period. Launched mid-1988, the Spacemaker Plus line was a "key introduction" for HPG in the United States, illustrating Black & Decker's commitment to innovation and the development of quality new products with design appeal. A product recall would be a big professional and personal disappointment to HPG president Dennis Heiner. It could not automatically be assumed that a product involved in a fire would need to be recalled; it would need to be established whether the product was the cause or the victim of a fire. However, customers had already reported steaming problems with the Spacemaker Plus coffeemaker prior to the December 1 fire call. One of HPG's main competitors had recently settled out of court a product liability suit involving a fire hazard in one of its coffeemakers, at a figure around $40 million. But the prospect of litigation was only one of many considerations likely to influence Heiner's decision about a recall.

Black & Decker Corporation

In 1910, Duncan Black and Alonzo Decker started their Baltimore machine shop. The name Black & Decker was soon to become synonymous with power tools after the company obtained a patent, in 1917, on the world's first portable power drill with pistol grip and trigger switch,

virtually inventing an industry. Seventy years later, Black & Decker was "a global marketer and manufacturer of quality products used in and around the home and for commercial applications." It was the world's largest producer of power tools but also had become a leading supplier of household products, such as irons and toaster ovens. Marketing its products in over 100 countries, there was worldwide recognition of its brand name and a strong reputation for quality, value, and innovation. In fiscal 1988,[2] Black & Decker sales were $2.28 billion, generating net earnings of $97 million and a return on equity of 14.1 percent. These figures constituted a turnaround after some years of poor performance and were a credit to the leadership of Nolan Archibald, CEO since 1985, and his management team. In 1987, Alonzo Decker, Jr., the 80-year-old son of the company's co-founder, was able to say to Archibald: "Nolan, I want you to know this is the best Christmas I've had in 10 years."

Much of the success of the turnaround was attributed to a transformation in the corporate culture, with a customer orientation replacing a complacent manufacturing mentality such that "being market driven is more than a catch phrase; it defines [the] entire organization." This was a vital part of Black & Decker's efforts to reverse a persistent decline in market share to foreign competition, such as Makita of Japan and Bosch of West Germany. There was also a major restructuring, involving a $215 million write-off in 1985, five plant closures and downsizing of others, streamlining of the distribution system, and a 10 percent reduction in the number of employees to 20,800 by 1988. Under this "cut and build" strategy, globalization in manufacturing and marketing also came to be emphasized. With many of its products based around small electric motors, Black & Decker had been using 100 different motors worldwide. Rationalization and globalization reduced that number to less than 20. A global product strategy allowed Black & Decker to have common products worldwide that were customized to suit individual markets.

By 1988, Black & Decker had also digested its 1984 acquisition of the General Electric (GE) Housewares Division. Under the terms of the acquisition, Black & Decker had been permitted to manufacture and market appliances under the GE name until 1987. A marketing program was developed, which successfully transferred the Black & Decker name to the GE small appliance lines, increasing market share from 27 percent to over 30 percent by 1988.

This case was prepared by Professor N. Craig Smith.
Copyright © 1990 by the President and Fellows of Harvard College.
Harvard Business School case 9-590-099 (Rev. 7/16/90).

[1]Spacemaker Plus is a trademark of the General Electric Company, U.S.A.

[2]The Black & Decker fiscal year end was September 30. A calendar fiscal year was adopted as of 1990.

The slower growth rate of the power tool market and increased foreign competition, as well as the success of its Dustbuster[3] rechargeable hand-held vacuum cleaner, had prompted Black & Decker to significantly increase its presence in the housewares market, with the GE acquisition providing greater access to housewares buyers. Further acquisitions were likely, to expand the earnings base and exploit a substantial tax loss carryforward. A hostile bid for American Standard, attractive to Black & Decker because it included a plumbing products business, had proven unsuccessful in 1987.[4]

In 1988, 52 percent of Black & Decker sales were in the United States, 33 percent European, and 15 percent in other countries. Following the GE acquisition, Black & Decker had been formed into two key business units: power tools and small household appliances. The Power Tools Group was responsible for power tools (42 percent of worldwide sales), accessories (11 percent) and outdoor products (8 percent). Power tools included portable electric and cordless electric drills, screwdrivers, saws, sanders, and grinders; car care products; Workmate[5] Workcenters (a workbench with vises), and stationary woodworking tools. Accessories included power tool accessories and fastening products. Outdoor products included hedge and lawn trimmers, electric mowers, cordless brooms, and chain saws. The Household Products Group (33 percent worldwide sales) was responsible for products used inside the home: cordless vacuums, irons, food preparation products (such as mixers), coffeemakers, toasters, toaster ovens, lighting, heating, and fire safety products. HPG sales grew by 14 percent in fiscal 1988. Supporting both groups was Black & Decker's service operation (6 percent worldwide sales), comprising 244 company-owned service centers (120 in the United States) and several hundred authorized independent outlets.

Spacemaker Plus

Industry analysts described the flow of new products as probably the single most critical factor in Black & Decker's growth equation. In 1988, 40 percent of HPG sales came

from products three years old or less. At the housewares trade exhibition in January 1989, Black & Decker planned to display 12 new small appliance lines. Archibald had said, "There are no mature markets only mature managements." Heiner believed the way to sell a product as mature as an iron was to add something like an automatic shutoff feature; similarly, blenders became cordless and Dustbuster vacuum cleaners became more powerful. Average industry returns on sales were low, at 3–4 percent, in the price-sensitive domestic appliance market. (It had yet to attract much interest from Japanese competition.) Some companies serving narrow niches in the market realized 8 percent; HPG had done better still, realizing an operating income in excess of 10 percent of sales in 1987 and 1988. But achieving growth and high levels of profitability through innovation was certainly a challenge for HPG.

Black & Decker's household product sales were $749 million worldwide in 1988, the majority of which were in the United States. Heiner aimed to significantly increase U.S. sales over the next five years by concentrating on the five core business areas where Black & Decker felt it had sustainable competitive advantage: irons, vacuum cleaners, toaster ovens, coffeemakers, and toasters. While some of this growth probably would be through acquisitions, much of it would need to be internally generated. In keeping with Black & Decker's market-driven philosophy, HPG's mission was "to provide superior customer satisfaction as the dominant brand of high-quality, innovative household products." Heiner was striving to develop a total quality culture with a commitment to customer care within HPG. He believed this approach would enable the group to realize its ambitious sales targets.

In a composite market share estimation, Black & Decker dominated the U.S. small domestic appliance market in 1988, with around a 30 percent share by volume and value, compared to the roughly 10 percent share held by each of its nearest rivals, Proctor Silex and Sunbeam. Exhibit 1 shows Black & Decker and competitor composite quarterly market shares 1987–88. Exhibit 2 shows Black & Decker and leading competitor market shares by product category for July–September 1987 and 1988. Exhibit 3 shows Black & Decker and competitor quarterly market shares for drip coffeemakers 1987–88.

The new Spacemaker Plus line was described in the annual report as a "major product highlight of 1988." As well as offering new products, this line was able to command the better profit margins HPG was keen to secure: its "contribution margin" (effectively gross profit) was substantially higher than the 40 percent average of all HPG lines. Black & Decker had inherited the Spacemaker concept from GE. An under-the-cabinet electric can opener had been launched in 1982, followed in 1983 by the addition of a toaster oven, a drip coffeemaker, a mixer, and an electric knife to the Spacemaker line. However, while off

---

[3]Dustbuster is a registered trademark of Black & Decker Corporation.

[4]In April 1989, Black & Decker acquired the larger Emhart Corporation, a diversified multinational producer of industrial and consumer products, including fastening products, and information and electronic systems. Annual revenues would be doubled; but industry analysts had doubts about the acquisition, with the more favorable commenting that this would be "an interesting story in the long term." A bid to acquire Sunbeam/Oster from the bankrupt Allegheny International had fallen through earlier in 1989.

[5]Workmate is a registered trademark of Black & Decker Corporation.

the countertop, these products remained bulky and saved little space in their vertical configuration. Lower-priced competitive imitations also had appeared.

In the product line evaluation after the GE acquisition, Black & Decker decided the Spacemaker line needed to be completely redesigned. An integrated development team, comprising former GE and Black & Decker designers, engineers, and manufacturing experts, was responsible for the project from conception to production. Focusing on the coffeemaker, the product development team sought to reduce its size and bulk, making it as horizontal as possible and a genuine spacesaver. A new "book-shaped" water reservoir that inserted like a video cassette was developed, and much of the volume of the housing of the coffeemaker was kept to the rear of the cabinet, significantly reducing actual and, from a standing position, perceived size. An innovation stemming from consumer research, the use of a thermal carafe, eliminated the requirement for a "keep-warm plate," reducing space and size but also manufacturing and assembly costs. Design featured strongly in Black & Decker's strategy of leveraging low-cost manufacturing with aggressive marketing.

Launched to praise from many quarters in June 1988, the Spacemaker Plus line comprised five models: the PDC403 coffeemaker, with digital clock for preset brewing (suggested retail price $112); the PDC401 coffeemaker, without clock ($80); the PEC90 can opener, with knife sharpener ($37); the PEC60 can opener, without knife sharpener ($32); and the PLA100 kitchen accessory light ($24). In contrast to the dark colors of the original Spacemaker line, these products were in white and together made up a cohesive visual scheme, encouraging consumers to combine units, as shown in Exhibit 4. Said to resemble a Danish stereo, Spacemaker Plus met with the approval of the Industrial Designers Society of America, winning in August 1988 its Design Excellence award; the "design's elegant restraint is exquisite" said the jurors. In October 1988, *Appliance Manufacturer* magazine named Spacemaker Plus the first place winner in its annual award competition for appliance products, based on its aesthetic appeal, functionality, ease of use, and engineering execution. Spacemaker Plus was soon "making inroads in a market that swooned over Krups and Braun," commented the *New York Times*. Until December 1988, at least, it was a Black & Decker success story.

The Fire Investigation

When the fire call came in, David Wildman, manager of the HPG Product Safety and Liability Group, had been immediately alerted. This group was responsible for safety. It had reviewed the design and initial prototype of the coffeemaker and arranged for its testing in Black & Decker's laboratories when approval had been given for the produc-

tion of larger numbers of prototypes. A Failure Mode Effect Analysis had not indicated a safety problem arising from any of the three primary causes of injury: fire, shock, or cut hazard. However, the coffeemaker's new design meant there were no established standards. The normal industry practice for small appliances was to have them certified as safe by Underwriters' Laboratory (UL), an independent testing service. This was not mandatory, but it was required of manufacturers by many retailers. It was Black & Decker company policy not to sell a product unless it met, if not exceeded, UL requirements. The Spacemaker Plus exceeded the UL requirement for coffeemakers of a single temperature cut-off (TCO), which shuts the unit off in the event of overheating. Black & Decker fitted two TCOs to all its coffeemakers, believing that the fire and consequent liability problems experienced by a competitor with one of its coffeemakers might have been avoided if a second cut-off had been included in the unit. The PDC401 and PDC403 coffeemakers were both fitted with two TCOs.

Wildman spoke with the California customer about possible causes of the fire and arranged for the immediate collection of the coffeemaker by a courier service. Within 24 hours, the damaged coffeemaker was in Shelton, and investigations began immediately. Working round the clock, it was concluded on December 3, less than 48 hours after the fire had been reported, that the unit was responsible and external sources or misuse could be ruled out. The precise cause of the fire had yet to be established. However, a laboratory test, which involved clamping the feed from the reservoir to the heater element, starving the unit of water, had produced overheating and fires in new units, despite the TCOs. Accordingly, all units could be considered potentially faulty and, therefore, fire hazards. Wildman informed Heiner, who was then in Australia and promptly curtailed his trip to return to Shelton.

A manufacturer was obligated under the United States Consumer Product Safety Act to recall a product where there was knowledge of a substantial product hazard. Although telephone calls to California had led Wildman to suspect the fire had something to do with the customer not fully inserting the water reservoir drawer, he did believe there was some prospect of a legal requirement to recall the coffeemaker. In the event any product liability claims emerged, these would have to be met by the company because Black & Decker was self-insured.

Product Recalls

Product recalls were not uncommon, with the Consumer Product Safety Commission (CPSC) overseeing more than 100 product recalls annually, involving millions of individual items. Other federal agencies with recall authority were the Food and Drug Administration (FDA), the National Highway Traffic Safety Administration (NHTSA), the

Environmental Protection Agency (EPA), and the Federal Trade Commission (FTC). The agencies relied primarily on self-reported voluntary recalls, which manufacturers had strong incentives to organize, but NHTSA could mandate recalls and had forced automobile manufacturers to undertake major recall programs. Recalls could result from poor design or manufacturing, although many arose from faults that developed in unanticipated ways. Product tampering (e.g., Tylenol case) or legal action by a competitor (e.g., in response to a breach of trademark) also could prompt recalls. As well as the costs of obtaining recalled goods and possible harm to the company's reputation, recalls could increase the prospect of product liability litigation. However, delays to a necessary recall, by not acting quickly when a problem was apparent or not responding to a federal agency request for a voluntary recall, could have severe legal consequences.

The CPSC, created in 1972, was responsible for all goods used by final consumers except those covered by the FDA, NHTSA, and EPA. The agency relied upon the legal requirement of firms to report safety problems. It would then negotiate a recall plan with the firm if needed. The firm then had to provide monthly reports on progress of the recall. Black & Decker believed CPSC could mandate a recall if necessary. According to CPSC, a dangerous defect could result from:

1. A fault, flaw, or irregularity that causes weakness, failure, or inadequacy in form or function.
2. Manufacturing or production error.
3. A product's design or materials.
4. A product's contents, construction, finish, packaging, warnings or instructions, or both.

Guidelines also helped determine whether the safety problem was substantial:

1. The nature of the risk of injury the product presents and the severity of the risk (i.e., the seriousness of the possible injury and the likelihood that an injury could occur).
2. The necessity for the product, its utility, and the ways it can be used or misused.
3. The number of defective products, and the population group exposed to the products.
4. The physical environment within which the defect manifests itself.
5. Case law involving health, safety, and product liability.
6. The CPSC's own experience and expertise as well as other relevant factors.

Recall return rates varied greatly. NHTSA recalls for automobiles reportedly achieved correction rates of 15–70 percent. Many CPSC recalls achieved return rates under 10 percent, particularly with the difficulty in contacting owners of inexpensive but harmful products. A study of CPSC recalls,[6] obtained by HPG, had examined factors influencing the three conditions necessary for a successful recall:

- Product availability—in the distribution channel or at least still in the possession of consumers (determined by the average age of the product and its average useful life).
- Distributor and consumer awareness of the recall.
- Benefits of compliance with the recall exceeding perceived costs of time, effort, and lost product services.

The CPSC study outlined a model for predicting likely recall return rates, highlighting these variables:

- The number of months separating end of distribution and the start of the recall.
- The percentage of products owned by consumers who are notified of the recall directly by mail.
- The percentage of items (produced) in retail inventory. (Distributors and retailers had strong incentives to comply with recalls, because of concern for their reputations and the prospect of liability suits; their costs of compliance were usually relatively low and they could be relatively easily reached.)
- The percentage of items (produced) in the hands of consumers. (Return rates are typically lower for products with consumers than those in the distribution channel. Factors said to influence consumer compliance include the severity of the safety hazard, the value of the product (higher benefit of compliance with more expensive products), and the type of remedy provided.)
- Whether a repair at home is offered to the consumer (relative to more inconvenient alternatives).

While the CPSC study reported an average correction/return rate of 54.4 percent over the sample of 128 recalls between 1978 and 1983, there was considerable variance, largely explained by the above variables. In the experience of Black & Decker personnel, return rates of products distributed to consumers were historically low, with a domestic appliance industry average said to be around 5 percent and anything over 22 percent "doing excellent." HPG had not previously recalled a product, though the GE Housewares Division had recalled an electric fan some years ago and Black & Decker had recalled some of its power tool products in the past. The GE fan recall also had involved a

---

[6]R. Dennis Murphy and Paul H. Rubin, "Determinants of Recall Success Rates," *Journal of Products Liability* 11 (1988), pp. 17–28.

fire hazard. The low response rate of 6 percent was attributed to the late announcement of the recall; negotiations with the CPSC had delayed the announcement to November, when few consumers were thinking about fans. Return rates on Black & Decker outdoor products had been as low as 3 percent.

In the opinion of Ken Homa, vice president of marketing at HPG, most manufacturers would try to avoid recalls but, should they arise, had few incentives to pursue high return rates. The conventional wisdom was that recalls were difficult to do effectively, they increased the possibility of product liability litigation, the regulatory agencies were cumbersome to deal with, and a high return rate would set a precedent for future recalls. The cost of recalls and the potential damage to the company's brand name were also considerations. As a consequence, established procedures were limited and, as Gael Simonson, director of brand marketing and strategy development, put it: "There was a precedent to be passive."

Heiner's Decision

On December 5, Wildman informed the CPSC that there had been a fire in a Spacemaker Plus coffeemaker, which was being investigated, and that shipments of the product had stopped. He also advised the corporate legal department. The next day at a meeting with Heiner, Homa, and other senior management, Wildman reported his investigations. While not certain of the cause of the starvation problem, he suspected it was due to incomplete closure of the reservoir drawer. "You'd have to try hard to get the reservoir in the wrong way" was one, exasperated reaction at the meeting.

Heiner was told that about 25,000 units were with consumers in virtually any of the 90 million households in the United States. About 10 percent of these owners were believed to have returned warranty cards, supplying their

names and addresses. Black & Decker had distributed 88,400 Spacemaker Plus coffeemakers, the majority through major retailing chains, such as Sears, Penney's, Best Products, and Service Merchandise, with the remainder through small local appliance and department stores and some within Black & Decker. The precise number of units sold through to consumers could not be ascertained, but was believed to be about 30–35 percent of units distributed. In some recalls, consumers were provided with a similar or superior model to replace the faulty product; but HPG did not have a suitable replacement for the Spacemaker Plus coffeemaker. Most worrying for the HPG management team was the likelihood of the safety problem arising when the product was unattended. Both versions of the coffeemaker operated automatically; the PDC403 had a 24-hour digital clock/timer so consumers could preset the machine at night to start at a selected time, in order to wake in the morning to fresh-brewed coffee. Around 40 percent of HPG sales were during the pre-Christmas season and many of these units, therefore, were wrapped up as gifts.

HPG was facing increased pressure on margins, with rising costs of raw materials. The corporate safety manager from Black & Decker's Towson, Maryland, headquarters had suggested a 15–20 percent return of units with consumers would probably meet the letter of the law. It had been estimated that, with a 25 percent consumer return rate, the recall would cost around $4 million (excluding opportunity costs of lost sales). Exhibit 5 shows recall cost estimates. The corporate safety manager explained that the normal procedure, in the event of a recall, was to notify CPSC and develop a recall program. This usually took four to six weeks, but the process could be accelerated if HPG executives wished.

Heiner had informed Archibald of the safety problem, but it was Heiner's decision about what HPG should do next.

EXHIBIT 1   **Composite Quarterly Market Shares by Volume and Value: Small Domestic Appliances, 1987–1988**

	By Volume								By Value	
Core Categories*	1987 Jan–Mar	Apr–Jun	Jul–Sep	Oct–Dec	1988 Jan–Mar	Apr–Jun	Jul–Sep	Oct–Dec^E	Jul–Sep	Oct–Dec^E
Black & Decker	25.0%	25.9%	26.1%	27.4%	27.3%	29.0%	29.0%	32.2%	28.6%	31.1%
Hamilton Beach	7.8	7.8	7.4	8.1	7.8	7.9	7.4	7.1	6.1	5.3
Proctor Silex	9.5	10.3	10.7	9.5	11.4	10.4	11.2	9.0	8.3	6.6
Sunbeam	10.7	10.1	10.5	10.7	10.0	9.8	10.2	9.4	9.4	8.4
Norelco	8.0	7.1	6.6	5.0	5.1	4.1	3.5	2.8	2.6	2.2
Toastmaster	5.5	5.2	5.5	5.3	5.4	5.4	5.3	4.6	4.5	3.7
Other	33.5	33.6	33.2	34.0	33.0	33.4	33.4	34.9	40.6	42.6

E = estimated.

*Core categories are: irons, rechargeable hand-held vacuum cleaners, rechargeable stick vacuum cleaners, toaster ovens, toasters, drip coffeemakers, food processors, food choppers, portable mixers, can openers, electric knives, and blenders.

NOTE: Columns may not total 100% due to rounding error.

SOURCE: Black & Decker Corporation.

Product Category	Company (rank ordered)	Percent Market Share by Volume	
		July–September 1987	July–September 1988
Irons	Black & Decker	47.4%	47.7%
	Proctor Silex	13.6	18.3
	Sunbeam	18.9	18.0
Can openers	Rival	30.6	29.2
	Black & Decker	22.6	23.3
	Sunbeam	11.2	11.3
Rechargeable hand-held vacuum cleaners	Black & Decker	79.8	74.4
	Hoover	2.1	15.0
	Eureka	8.6	5.6
Toaster ovens	Black & Decker	45.7	59.7
	Toastmaster	16.0	13.8
	Proctor Silex	19.9	13.4
Portable mixers	Black & Decker	27.2	35.0
	Sunbeam	28.7	23.0
	Hamilton Beach	7.9	10.0
Food choppers	Black & Decker	14.5	27.0
	Sunbeam	13.9	23.9
	Cuisinart	21.2	16.2
Food processors	Sunbeam	30.5	22.4
	Hamilton Beach	15.1	12.5
	Black & Decker	8.2	9.5
Drip coffeemakers	Mr. Coffee	21.3	21.6
	Black & Decker	11.3	16.4
	Proctor Silex	13.6	15.3
Toasters	Toastmaster	32.8	30.7
	Proctor Silex	25.7	25.9
	Black & Decker	12.0	12.6
Rechargeable stick vacuum cleaners	Black & Decker	NA	37.6
	Eureka	32.6	32.7
	Regina	62.4	29.7
Rechargeable "lites"	First Alert	35.2	31.3
	Black & Decker	34.7	24.7
	Houseworks	5.0	20.4
Smoke alarms	First Alert	38.2	38.4
	Southwest Labs	2.1	20.0
	Family Gard	23.0	17.6
	Black & Decker	7.1	11.6
Stand mixers	Sunbeam	50.0	45.7
	Kitchen Aid	15.3	34.3
	Hamilton Beach	10.6	7.1
	Waring	13.5	5.2
	Krups	8.5	5.2
	Black & Decker	0.0	0.5
Electric knives	Hamilton Beach	34.2	37.0
	Black & Decker	30.7	31.4
	Regal/Moulinex	16.9	11.1
Regular blenders (excluding hand blenders)	Oster	44.6	45.7
	Hamilton Beach	37.5	34.0
	Waring	16.0	10.4
	Black & Decker	2.0	7.1
Hot-air corn poppers	West Bend	36.8	32.1
	Presto	36.4	31.3
	Wearever	22.0	19.9
	Hamilton Beach	3.4	8.5
	Black & Decker	1.4	6.5

SOURCE: Black & Decker Corporation.

EXHIBIT 3 Drip Coffeemakers: U.S. Market Shares by Volume and Value, 1987–1988

Company (ranked order)	1987 Jan–Mar By Volume	By Value	1987 Apr–Jun By Volume	By Value	1987 Jul–Sep By Volume	By Value	1987 Oct–Dec By Volume	By Value	1988 Jan–Mar By Volume	By Value	1988 Apr–Jun By Volume	By Value	1988 Jul–Sep By Volume	By Value	1988 Oct–Dec[E] By Volume	By Value
Black & Decker	12.0	(14.9)	12.8	(15.1)	11.3	(12.8)	14.3	(14.8)	12.8	(13.6)	16.7	(16.8)	16.4	(16.2)	22.0	(23.3)
Mr. Coffee	21.9	(17.6)	19.4	(15.5)	21.3	(16.9)	21.6	(17.6)	19.0	(15.2)	19.3	(15.4)	21.6	(16.3)	20.8	(15.2)
Braun	7.8	(9.6)	9.2	(11.6)	10.5	(13.9)	12.0	(15.5)	11.7	(15.7)	11.6	(15.8)	12.2	(16.5)	13.0	(17.4)
Proctor Silex	11.4	(7.5)	13.3	(8.8)	13.6	(9.4)	14.0	(9.5)	17.7	(12.6)	16.6	(11.6)	15.3	(10.0)	11.9	(7.4)
Krups	8.3	(13.6)	9.7	(15.2)	9.4	(14.4)	6.8	(10.0)	7.1	(11.5)	8.1	(13.2)	9.3	(15.6)	9.4	(15.0)
Norelco	18.3	(14.3)	15.6	(12.2)	15.0	(11.8)	13.3	(10.7)	12.6	(10.1)	8.9	(7.1)	7.3	(5.7)	7.2	(5.8)
All other	20.3	(22.5)	20.0	(21.6)	18.9	(20.8)	18.0	(20.0)	19.1	(21.4)	18.8	(20.3)	17.9	(19.6)	15.7	(15.7)

E = estimated.

Columns may not total 100 percent due to rounding error.

SOURCE: Black & Decker Corporation.

EXHIBIT 4
Spacemaker Plus coffeemaker, can opener, and accessory light

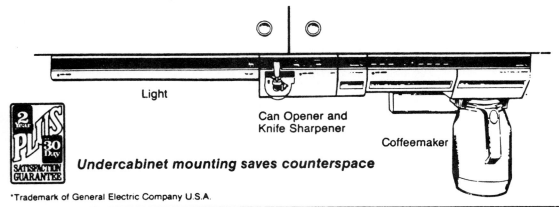

BLACK & DECKER®

Spacemaker Plus™* Appliances

THE ULTIMATE IN SPACESAVING CONVENIENCE AND CONTEMPORARY STYLING!

- **Kitchen Accessory Light** brightens up your kitchen counter, and features a handy, hidden electric outlet. PLA100
- **Can Opener and Knife Sharpener.** Opens cans — hands free — then shuts itself off. Plus, provides fail-safe sharpening of even your finest cutlery. PEC90
- **Thermal Carafe Drip Coffeemaker with Electronic Clock/Timer** offers an unique convenience feature — coffee brews THRU lid, locks in freshness, flavor. Clock/Timer lets you set brewing time in advance. Automatic Shut-Off for safety. PDC403.

Light

Can Opener and
Knife Sharpener

Coffeemaker

Undercabinet mounting saves counterspace

2 Year PLUS 30 Day SATISFACTION GUARANTEE

*Trademark of General Electric Company U.S.A.

Spacemaker Classic Line

Can Opener   Coffeemaker   Toaster Oven

SOURCE: Black & Decker Corporation.

EXHIBIT 5   Recall Cost Estimates

	Approximate $ millions

Consumer Recall

- 25,000 units sold at 25% response—6,250 units returned.

  Option 1:   Replacement coffeemaker when available at (current) manufactured cost of $40 (PDC403) and $30 (PDC401). PDC403 sales were approximately twice those of PDC401.

$$\text{PDC403 } 6,250 \times \tfrac{2}{3} \times 40 = \$166,667$$

$$\text{PDC401 } 6,250 \times \tfrac{1}{3} \times 30 = \underline{\quad 62,500}$$
$$\$229,167$$

  $0.230

  Option 2:   Cash refund at suggested retail prices:

$$\text{PDC403 } 6,250 \times \tfrac{2}{3} \times 112 = \$466,667$$

$$\text{PDC401 } 6,250 \times \tfrac{1}{3} \times 80 = \underline{\quad 166,667}$$
$$\$633,334$$

  $0.635

- Freight, labels, administration.
  Approximately $100/unit returned

  $0.625

Retail Recall

- Return of 63,400 units for refund (and to be reworked).
  Lost margin, at an average of $30/unit:

$$63,400 \times 30 = \$1,902,000$$

  $1.900

- Freight, refunds on joint promotions, administration, etc.:
  Estimated at $500,000

  $0.500

- Rework of returned units for later sale.
  Best estimate, unless major work required, of $10/unit:

$$63,400 \times 10 = \$634,000$$

  $0.635

Total cost approximately $4.3M
(with cash refund
to consumers)

NOTE: Cost and margin data have been disguised, but estimates provided here are useful for analysis.

Rossin Greenberg Seronick & Hill, Inc. (A)

Looking through the latest issue of *Computer Reseller News,* Neal Hill, president of the Boston advertising agency Rossin Greenberg Seronick and Hill (RGS&H), came across a story indicating that Microsoft Corporation was conducting an agency review. Two days later, November 5, 1987, Hill wrote to Martin Taucher, at Microsoft in Redmond, Washington, suggesting he consider RGS&H. This was an account the agency was keen to secure.

"Our Ambition is Your Opportunity"

RGS&H had been established in 1983. Four years later, it had billings of around $25 million and was described in the trade press as the "hottest agency in New England." Yet it was still comparatively small, employing 45 people. Hill would not find it easy to convince the West Coast software company, which had sales of just under $200 million in 1986, that it should transfer its $10 million account to RGS&H. The agency had, however, recently recruited two new creative people, Jamie Mambro and Jay Williams, who had computer industry experience.

In his letter, Hill posed the question: "Why should you even think about an agency in Boston that you've probably never heard of?" He gave four reasons in response:

1. We turn out a wonderful creative product (which has won much more than its share of national and regional awards) and have a tremendous fund of experience in marketing PC-related products, both hardware and software. (That means we do some great advertising, because it's both on target and creatively powerful. *One specific fact:* I've included the recent Lotus insert because *the creative team which produced it and the rest of Lotus's work over the past year joined this agency last Monday.*)

2. We're just under five years old, and billing just over $25 million annually. (Translation: we're old enough to be "real," and large enough to have terrific resources in creative, marketing, media, and production. It also means that we're young enough and small enough to move quickly and intelligently—to still be *very* hungry to do the kind of work that explodes off the page and screen. Just

a note: Lotus's agency is just down the road from us in Providence, Rhode Island, and is the same size we are.)

3. We already handle large national accounts—our clients include Hasbro, Dunkin' Donuts, Fidelity Investments, Clarks of England, and British Telecommunications—and have several concrete ideas for eliminating any problems posed by the (perceived) distance between Redmond and Boston. (This demonstrates that we know how to work with advertising needs on the scale of yours . . . and that we'd love to fly out to show you some of our work and explain some of our logistical approaches.)

4. We are intent on becoming a nationally recognized advertising agency—and doing a bang-up job with one or more Microsoft products would take us a good way down that road. (Which means that our ambition is your opportunity.)

A week later, Hill called Taucher and established that his letter should have been sent to Rob Lebow, director of corporate communications, to whom it had been forwarded. On November 16, Hill wrote to Lebow enclosing further samples of work done by the agency's staff: a Lotus direct mail brochure, an advertisement for Charles River Laboratories, and an advertisement for software by a company no longer active in the U.S. market. His key message was: "We are an awfully good agency, with a great deal of knowledge of Microsoft's industry, competition, and products. And we would kill to do even a project for you."

Follow-up calls were not returned, so Hill decided to send a further sample of artwork to Microsoft: a 12 × 9 inch brochure promoting RGS&H and containing a plane ticket for a trip to Boston. This specially produced "flier" was mailed by overnight express to Lebow on November 20. On the front, in white letters against a dark background, it simply stated: "You probably haven't thought about talking to an agency in Boston." The interior of the flier is shown in Exhibit 1.

Encouraging News

On November 23, RGS&H received a "no thanks" letter from Lebow. As this was dated November 16, Hill was not too disappointed. A call the following day established that Lebow was out of the office for the next week. On November 30, Hill was told that Lebow "certainly took notice of

This case was prepared by Professor N. Craig Smith with the assistance of Professor John A. Quelch.
Copyright © 1989 by the President and Fellows of Harvard College. Harvard Business School case 9-589-124.

the mailed piece" and that he should call back December 4, when Lebow would be available. Hill wrote a further letter to Lebow expressing his delight at securing some attention with the flyer and explaining "what we wanted to do was to demonstrate simultaneously our creative approach to messaging and our aggressive approach to marketing—in this case, marketing ourselves." He included an extract from *Adweek* (New England), which discussed RGS&H, its commitment to sophisticated office automation, and how it pitched against New York agencies for the Playskool print account. Hill also explained that the agency would be interested in a single product or limited-term project instead of the entire account: "We just want a chance to show you what we can do for you."

EXHIBIT 1
RGS&H "flier"

III   CONCLUSION

Marketing Strategy — An Overview

Strategy. (1) The science or art of military command as applied to the overall planning and conduct of large-scale combat operations. Compare *tactics*. (2) A plan of action resulting from the practice of this science. (3) The art or skill of using stratagems in politics, business, courtship, or the like.[1]

As this dictionary definition suggests, the meaning of the word *strategy* developed originally in a military context. Strategy meant a plan for the deployment and use of military forces and material over certain terrain (which might or might not be of the military commander's choosing) to achieve a certain objective. The strategy had to be based on what was known of the enemy's strength and positioning, the physical characteristics of the battleground, the friendly or hostile sentiments of those who occupied the territory, and, of course, the strength and character of the resources available to the commander. Time was a factor, too, and it also was necessary to anticipate changes that might significantly alter the balance of forces.

Strategy, then, is a plan of action carried out tactically. According to the same dictionary, a tactic is an expedient, or maneuver, for achieving a goal. Therefore, a plan of action (strategy) is carried out through a series of interrelated maneuvers that are not always planned in advance and may represent responses to the unanticipated actions of either opposing or even friendly forces.

The analogy to business strategies is direct and useful. In business, and in marketing, the terrain is the marketplace in particular and the economic, political, social, legal, ethical, and technological environments in general. The resources are people with wide-ranging skills and expertise, as well as factories, laboratories, transportation systems, financial resources, and the corporation's reputation.

This case was prepared by Professor E. Raymond Corey.
Copyright © 1979 by the President and Fellows of Harvard College.
Harvard Business School case 9-579-054 (Rev. 4/2/92).

[1] *The American Heritage Dictionary Second College Edition* (Boston: Houghton Mifflin, 1985), p. 1,203.

It is important to distinguish between objectives and strategies. A business objective is a desired end result; a strategy is a plan for getting there. Objectives may be set at various levels. For the enterprise as a whole, the objectives may be to achieve a certain rate of growth in sales and earnings, to meet a target level of customer satisfaction, or to sustain a target return on shareholders' equity. Objectives also may be imposed on managers of individual divisions so the enterprise as a whole accomplishes its mission. Division managers may see market share, profit, quality, and customer satisfaction as important measures of their own performance. Thus, a key objective might be to increase a particular product line's share of its market by X percent. Another objective might be to increase profitability while yielding a limited amount of market share. Yet another might be to increase customer satisfaction ratings by a certain percent while simultaneously increasing profits.

At the level of individual products and markets, objectives may be expressed in terms of customer satisfaction, market share, profits on sales, and return on investment. But the objectives also may be of a different order. A company's primary objective for a certain product or service, for example, might be to help support sales of other products in the line. A newspaper might publish a Sunday edition primarily to help build its circulation for weekday editions.

The importance of explicitly defining objectives to give purpose and direction to strategies cannot be overestimated. How can we develop useful strategies unless we know what we are trying to accomplish?

Overall corporate strategies are often thought of as having several components, including:

- **A financial strategy.**   What should be the debt-to-equity balance? What sources of capital should be utilized?
- **A manufacturing strategy.**   What should we make and what should we buy from outside suppliers? Should we have a few large plants or several smaller ones? How should they be designed? Where should they be located?
- **A research and development strategy (R&D).**   Will we attempt to be a technical leader in our field or should we depend on others for new technical developments? Will we undertake basic or applied research? In what fields of technology will we work? What level of spending should we sustain?
- **A quality strategy.**   What are our quality objectives for our products and services? What tools and training will we give our employees to build quality into their work processes? How will we measure quality in each function in the company? How can we best use information about customer satisfaction to enhance the quality of our products and services?

Depending on the nature of the business, strategy may have other dimensions as well. At the heart of any business strategy is a marketing strategy. Businesses exist to deliver products to markets. To the extent that they serve this purpose well and efficiently, they grow and profit. Other components of the overall strategy (financial, manufacturing, R&D, quality) must support the business's marketing mission. By the same token, the firm's marketing strategy must be appropriate to its resources and its strategies in other major areas of the business and take account of their limitations. Financial resources and manufacturing facilities, for example, typically impose certain constraints on the range of objectives set. Marketing goals and strategies have to be developed within these limitations.

Elements of a Marketing Strategy

A marketing strategy is composed of several interrelated elements. The first and most important is *market selection:* choosing the markets to be served. *Product planning* includes the specific products the company sells, the makeup of the product line, and the design of individual offerings in the line. Another element is the *distribution system:* the wholesale and retail channels through which the product moves to the people who ultimately buy it and use it. The overall *communications* strategy employs *advertising* to tell potential customers about the product through radio, television, direct mail, and public print and *personal selling* to deploy a sales force to call on potential customers, urge them to buy, and take orders. Finally, *pricing* is an important element of any marketing program. The company must set the product prices that different classes of customers will pay and determine the margins or commissions to compensate agents, wholesalers, and retailers for moving the product to ultimate users.

Depending on the nature of the product and its markets, the marketing strategy also may include other components. A company whose products need repair and maintenance must have programs for *product service.* Such programs are often businesses in themselves and require extensive repair shops, technical service personnel, and inventories of spare parts. For some companies, the nature and amount of *technical assistance* provided to customers is critical to marketing success and, therefore, an important part of strategy.

In many businesses, *customer credit* is an important element of the marketing program. Companies that operate gasoline stations, retail stores, or travel agencies, for example, must extend credit simply to compete for business. So must companies selling industrial equipment, raw materials, and supplies.

In businesses where products can be shipped only a certain distance from the plant, *plant location* determines the company's available market. A container plant, for example, can serve only a limited geographic area, because shipping costs are high in relation to the product's unit value. When transport over long distances becomes uneconomical, plant location becomes a strategic marketing decision.

Brand name also can be an important element of marketing strategy. A company may have to choose between using a family brand name (such as Kraft for cheeses, jams, jellies) or a distinct name (such as Lite for a beer made by Miller Brewing Company).

Other elements of strategy, especially for consumer goods companies, are *display* of the merchandise at the point of sale, and *promotions* to consumers (e.g., cents-off coupons, two-for-one sales, and in-package premiums), retailers, and wholesalers. The list of elements that might shape marketing strategy is long and will vary among products, markets, and companies. Moreover, emphasis on particular aspects of marketing strategy will vary considerably, even among competitors selling comparable products to the same markets. Emphasis will shift, too, over time as products mature and market conditions change. At one stage a company may gain a competitive edge through extensive new-product development; at another, it may rely on low prices.

Strategy formulation can be seen as the choice of a marketing mix:

The "marketing mixes" for different types of products vary widely, and even for the same class of product, competing companies may employ different mixes. Over time a company may change its marketing mix for a product, for in a dynamic world the marketer must adjust to changing forces of the market . . . to find a mix that will prove profitable. . . . The marketing mix refers to the apportionment of effort—the combination, the designing, and the integration of the various elements of marketing—into a program that, on the basis of an appraisal of the market forces, will best achieve the objectives of an enterprise at a given time.[2]

While the precise mix varies from one marketing plan to another, most strategies include five basic elements: market selection, product planning, pricing, distribution systems, and communications. It is useful to examine each of these elements, identifying some of the strategic options that may be open in each area, and exploring considerations that bear on managers' choices.

Market Selection

The most important choice made by any organization, whether a business, school, hospital, or government agency, is deciding what markets it will serve with what products. Market selection implies major commitments to particular customer groups, specific skills and fields of technology, and a certain competitive milieu. Many organizations, however, seem to make decisions in this important area almost by default and in hasty reaction to the market opportunities at hand.

Market Segmentation.   A first step in market selection is the division of the market into segments according to some rational scheme. A market segment may be defined as a set of potential customers that are alike in the way they perceive and value the product, in their patterns of buying, and in the way they use the product.

Market segmentation has developed as production capabilities have expanded to permit product variations, rather than a single standardized product, and as heterogeneity in income and lifestyles has fostered subsegments of demand where only a single market was thought to exist. A good example is the progression from the early standardized black automobile to the plethora of colors and options in cars today. Experience also has shown that marketing success is more likely when communications—and products—are aimed at a more narrowly defined group. A good example is the decline of mass-circulation magazines and the rise of more specialized (targeted) publications.

Markets may be segmented along several dimensions:

- **Demography.**   People in different income and age groups, occupations, and ethnic and educational backgrounds may exhibit characteristically different tastes, buying behavior, and consumption patterns.
- **Geography.**   Some products are culturally sensitive. That is, their usage, the ways in which they are promoted, and government restrictions with regard to product form, advertising, and pricing may vary considerably from one geographic area to another. An example of culturally sensitive product class is pharmaceuticals.
- **Lifestyle factors.**   Going beyond demographic differentiation, so-called psychographic typologies attempt to segment markets according to individual lifestyles and attitudes toward self, work, homes, families, and peer groups. Career-oriented women, for example, may differ in these

---

[2]Nil H. Borden, "Concept of the Marketing Mix," HBS case no. 9-502-004.

respects from those who see themselves primarily as homemakers. Marketers might usefully distinguish between the two groups in planning their product lines and advertising programs.

- **Product-use patterns.** Particularly for industrial customers, a useful segmentation scheme often can be developed on the basis of how purchasers use the product and how it fits into their processes and systems. For example, a firm that buys nylon fiber to make hosiery uses it in the manufacturing process very differently from one that buys it for use in rubber tires. Similarly, the customer who buys a small plane for crop dusting is in a different market segment from one who buys an executive jet.

There are, of course, other useful ways of segmenting markets. Industrial marketers may find it useful to distinguish between large and small accounts, or to differentiate government agencies, commercial companies, schools, and hospitals. In each category, the purchase-decision process is characteristically different and may be shaped by different rules, regulations, and measurement systems as well as by different levels of purchasing professionalism.

Consumer-goods marketers may find it valid to differentiate between those who buy something as a gift and those who purchase it for themselves, or between light and heavy users of a product.

Market segmentation is an art, not a science. The important criteria in selecting one or another dimension or combination are customers' needs and the distinctive and significant differences in their buying behavior.

It also is important to recognize that the segmentation scheme appropriate at one stage in the development of a market may be less relevant later and may need to be recast as a market grows and matures. Customers become educated in buying and using the product. Demand increases and new competitors enter. Retail and wholesale distribution channels develop in response to market growth and change in character. New product forms emerge to serve the needs of different kinds of customers. Such events change the way people buy and reshape the industry environment; as a result, the original segmentation scheme becomes obsolete.

Market Selection Criteria. The development of a market segmentation scheme is just the beginning point. The next step is to select among market segments the particular targets of opportunity that are best suited to the company. A number of issues need to be considered.

- The organization's objectives and their fit with the specific market opportunity under consideration.
- The firm's particular strengths and weaknesses vis-à-vis particular market segments (e.g., its financial strength, marketing skills and resources, technical expertise, and product advantages).
- Resource commitments required for product development, advertising, sales force development, and manufacturing and distribution systems.
- The strengths and weaknesses of competitors and their positions in the market.
- Whether demand is growing or leveling off.
- The possibility of taking a significant share of the market.

Product Planning

A product offering is the total package of benefits the customer obtains when making a purchase: the product itself; its brand name; its availability; the warranty, repair service, and technical assistance the seller may provide; the sales financing arrangements; and the personal relationships that may develop between representatives of the buyer and the seller. A watch, for example, is an instrument for telling time as well as a piece of jewelry. The purchaser may derive psychic satisfaction from its style, its content of precious metals, its brand name, the fact that it performs several time functions and has digital readout, and the prestige of the store in which it was purchased. Indeed, part of a product's meaning may be the pleasure the buyer derives from shopping for it and making a purchase selection.

Thus, product meaning must be defined in terms of the benefits the buyer obtains with purchase and use. Regardless of what the seller thinks of the product, what counts for strategic planning purposes is the purchaser's opinion and the value he or she places on alternative competitive offerings. Thus, the product package will have different meanings to different potential buyers. The technical assistance, for example, that a seller of industrial chemicals offers to customers may be especially valued by small firms with no R&D resources of their own. Large companies with extensive technical staffs may give it little weight in making a buying decision.

Product-planning Options.   Planning the product line is a key element in marketing strategy. The product is not a given, but a variable. Marketing programs are designed to develop markets and the product is a vehicle intended to serve that purpose. Some specific choices to consider are these:

- How broad or narrow should the product line be?
- Will it span a range of price points or be concentrated at the low end or at the premium-price level?
- What are the physical and performance specifications?
- Will it consist of standard off-the-shelf components or will products be designed to individual customer preferences?
- Will the company market end products ready for use or will it sell materials and components to other firms that manufacture the end products?
- Will customers be given warranties? Will field service be available for repair and product maintenance?

Other more general considerations are also relevant in planning the product line:

- First, and most important, does the proposed product line allow the seller to serve a customer need profitably?
- Does the product differ from competitive offerings in its design, quality, or performance characteristics? (Profit opportunities typically are greatest for differentiated products.)
- Can the product be manufactured in existing facilities? Can it be marketed through distribution systems now in place?
- Will the proposed offering enhance the company's reputation, its position with existing customers, and its strength in dealing with retailers and distributors? Or will the new product only cannibalize sales of existing products without increasing total profitability?

Market selection and product-planning choices often must be made together. The starting point may be the identification of a customer need not being filled as well as it might, or a new technical development that will make it possible to perform some function in a better way. Or the company simply may see an opportunity to add to the supply of available products to help satisfy a rapidly growing market.

It is useful to think of the market as a chessboard, with the squares representing market segments. Competitors are arrayed over the playing area, each seeking to occupy certain spaces with certain product offerings. The heart of marketing strategy is determining what squares to go after with what products. It may be that some spaces, previously unrecognized as market opportunities, now lie vacant and would be relatively easy to occupy. Some may be filled by weak competitors with inadequate product offerings; they can be attacked. But other squares are solidly dominated by strong competition and superior product lines; it would be risky to try to enter those spaces.

Pricing

At the simplest level, pricing is establishing the price at which a product will be sold to a customer. The true art of pricing is to make the price a quantitative expression of the value of the product to the customer. If the price is lower than the customer is willing to pay, the seller sacrifices potential profits. In addition to retail price, the price structure may need to provide for quantity discount schedules; functional discount schedules for different classes of buyers; retail and wholesale margins; and payment terms (e.g., a certain percentage off the billed price for payment within a specified period).

Price Discrimination.   Because the product may be worth more to some customers than to others, the seller might sell the same product at different prices to different groups of buyers. Many firms, for example, establish different prices in different countries or make minor modifications to differentiate product offerings to different classes of buyers. Food products sold to hotels and restaurants usually are packaged in bulk and sold at lower unit prices than the same items sold through retail stores to consumers. In such ways, a seller discriminates among market segments, attempting to maximize the revenue derived from each.

In other cases, it may not be possible to price discriminatingly either geographically or through packaging, use of different brand names, or minor (nonfunctional) design modifications. Then the price set for all customers must equal the lowest valuation placed on the product by any target customer group.

The seller also may fail to realize a price that equals the value of the product to the customer if competitors charge lower prices. Competitive prices then establish value, since the customer has the option of buying a competitive product. Hence, competition tends to set a ceiling on the price any one seller may charge.

To the extent, however, that a supplier can differentiate its product from others, it enjoys a degree of freedom in setting prices. If buyers can be persuaded that the product is superior, the seller can obtain a premium theoretically equal to the increment of value the buyer perceives.

Cost as a Factor in Pricing.   If competitive price levels set the ceiling, cost sets the floor. A supplier cannot long sell below the costs of manufacture and still stay in business. But a company may elect to sell at a loss, temporarily, in the hope of gaining a foothold in the market and realizing profits as volume increases and unit costs decline. It may even temporarily sell the product at a price that covers the direct costs of labor and material but not fixed overheads, such as plant depreciation, simply to keep the work force employed.

A manager also has some choice with regard to the time over which certain investments are amortized. Prices for a new product line, for example, may be set so as to recover the product-development costs in one, three, five, or even more years. The choice of amortization period significantly affects the product cost base and, hence, the basis for setting price.

The relative levels of fixed and variable costs also affect pricing strategy. If such fixed costs as depreciation on plant and equipment, research and development, and advertising are high relative to variable costs (labor and material), maximizing sales volume becomes an important strategic objective to spread fixed charges over as many units as possible. For example, in the airline and hotel businesses, where fixed costs are very high, managers set prices to achieve maximum utilization of capacity. Bargain rates may substantially increase profits if they result in significantly higher sales volume.

In contrast, if variable costs are a relatively high proportion of the total, maximizing unit margins is critical to profitability. In the packaged foods business, for instance, materials and packaging represent such a large part of total costs that profitability depends on increasing as much as possible the spread between these variable costs and unit selling price.

Skimming vs. Penetration Pricing.   The question of skimming versus penetration pricing often arises in developing strategy for a new product. In a skimming mode, the seller initially prices high and focuses its marketing efforts on customers who are likely to value the product highly. Then, as this pocket of opportunity is exhausted, prices are reduced to reach a larger group of potential buyers who were unwilling to pay the higher price. This process is repeated until the seller reaches all potential customers at the lowest price it is willing to charge.

Many major airlines use a skimming strategy in selling seats in their first class cabins. Initially, they offer first class tickets at prices hundreds of dollars over the coach fare to passengers who are willing to pay that much for the benefits of larger seats, better food, free drinks, and more genteel fellow travelers. Then, one or two days before flight time, they sell any remaining seats to "frequent fliers" for a coupon worth $50 to $70 over the price of coach fare. In this way, the airlines capture the additional profit from business travelers who believe first class is worth $70 extra, but not several hundred dollars more than coach.

A penetration price strategy is just the opposite. The seller first enters the market at a low price, usually with the expectation of preempting competitors and establishing a dominant market position. It also may hope to achieve significant manufacturing-cost reductions with substantial production volumes. The cost of penetration pricing is the profits sacrificed by initially charging some groups of customers considerably less than they would be willing to pay. The potential gain is large market share.

Southwest Airlines has successfully followed a penetration pricing strategy since its founding in the early 1970s. Southwest offered only coach seats (no first class), and charged the lowest possible prices to generate the highest volume of passenger traffic. The strategy of Southwest's founders was to offer one-way fares lower than $20 on high-volume routes, initially in Texas, to persuade frequent commuters between pairs of cities like Dallas and Houston as well as pleasure travelers to fly rather than drive. Penetration pricing has worked well for Southwest. It has been consistently profitable in an industry where many major carriers consistently lose money.

Despite successes like that of Southwest Airlines, penetration pricing is generally regarded as a risky strategy. If it is to succeed, several conditions must be met:

- The product must be free of any defects that might create customer dissatisfaction and incur large costs for recall, repair, or retrofitting.
- Production capacity must be in place to satisfy anticipated demand.
- Distribution channels must be available for reaching potential buyers.
- The product should not be such that potential customers would require long periods of testing before adopting it; such lags would give competitors an opportunity to react.

Price Leadership. As the foregoing discussion implies, a key factor in setting prices is competitive response. Very often sellers are forced to adjust prices because of a competitor's moves in the market. By the same token, sellers often initiate price moves in the expectation that competitors will follow. This is called price leadership. The price leader is often the industry's largest firm, respected for its economical manufacturing costs, strong distribution, and, frequently, technical leadership. Its decision to raise price levels, perhaps in the face of rising material and labor costs, may be perceived as beneficial to the entire industry and is likely to be followed. On the other hand, if competitors do not follow its lead, the initiator usually must retract its announced price rise or risk significant sales losses.

Price reductions often are initiated by smaller competitors, usually in the hope of increasing market share. If prices then decline generally as competitors move to protect sales volumes, the market leader may formally recognize the new lower levels by publishing revised price schedules.

Given the exercise of price leadership and the fundamental motivations of competitors, there is a good deal of parallel pricing in any industry. As long as competitors do not communicate with each other directly, and pricing moves cannot be construed as predatory (intended to drive smaller competitors out of business), conscious price parallelism is not only legally acceptable but may be essential to survival.

Distribution Systems

A distribution system is a complex of agents, wholesalers, and retailers through which a seller's product moves physically to its markets. For the most part, this system consists of independent middlemen, although some companies operate their own captive sales branches. For example, although Nike sells shoes through middlemen, such as the Foot Locker chain of shoe stores, it has opened a small number of company-owned stores as well to stay close to the end consumer and to dispose of excess inventory. Distribution also may be handled through a combination of owned and franchised outlets.[3]

---

[3]Franchised outlets (e.g., McDonald's, Kopy Kat, Midas Muffler) typically operate under the franchisor's brand name and performance standards, selling the products or services with which the franchising company is identified. The franchisee usually owns or leases the property, manages it, pays the franchisor a royalty based on sales, and takes the profit.

Direct vs. Indirect Selling Systems. In designing a distribution system, a manufacturer must choose between selling directly to user-customers through its own sales force or going through independent agents, wholesalers, and retailers. Initially, the decision depends on whether the manufacturer has the sales-volume base needed to support a direct sales effort. These costs are largely a function of the number of potential customers in the market, how concentrated or dispersed they are, how much each buys in a given period, and the logistical costs, such as those associated with transporting the product and maintaining field stocks.

If the balance of distribution costs and sales volume is favorable, industrial-goods manufacturers often sell directly. Consumer-goods manufacturers seldom go direct, however, because potential customers are so numerous and so widely dispersed. Most sell to retailers or through wholesalers to retailers and rely on these middlemen to take the product to the ultimate consumer. This form of distribution works because wholesalers and retailers are able to spread their operating costs over a sales base that includes the products of a great many manufacturers—often thousands.

Another consideration in planning distribution systems is how the ultimate customer wants to buy. The customer may prefer the large selection and rapid delivery offered by an industrial distributor or a retail store. Alternatively, if technical assistance and product service are important, the buyer may prefer a direct relationship with the manufacturer.

A third area affecting the choice of distribution is the degree of control the manufacturer wishes to exert over sales strategy and execution as the product moves to the ultimate customer. Motivating independent retailers and wholesalers to stock the product, promote it effectively, and, perhaps, to provide product service is often difficult. In addition, legal limitations make it difficult, if not impossible, to control the prices wholesalers and retailers charge customers or to limit where and to whom these intermediaries sell.

Selective vs. Intensive Distribution. A key issue in distribution strategy is the intensity of retail coverage in any given market area. The primary argument for selective or even exclusive distribution (i.e., one retailer or wholesaler in each market area) is that the manufacturer's one representative will enjoy a large market potential and need not compete with other dealers. Presumably, he or she will benefit from higher sales volume and unit margins and be motivated to work hard at market development. In general, exclusive or selective distribution is a good choice if (a) the unit costs of stocking and selling the product are high (as in furniture) and (b) buyers are inclined to shop for the product and will travel to outlets where they may see the product and talk to salespeople.

By contrast, intensive distribution typically is used when (a) convenience of purchase and minimal shopping effort are key considerations for potential buyers and (b) the unit costs of stocking and display are relatively low. Bally Shoes, for example, which seeks a relatively small segment of affluent, highly fashion-conscious buyers, uses very selective distribution. Thom McAn, on the other hand, attempts to cover the market with its own retail outlets to attract the mass of middle-income, convenience-oriented shoe purchasers.

It is not unusual for products to move from exclusive or selective distribution to intensive distribution over the product life cycle. In the early stages, when potential customers need to learn about the product—what to consider in making a purchase and how to use it—it may be essential that sales personnel provide extensive help at the point of sale. Such assistance adds considerably to retail sales costs and indicates the desirability of selective distribution. As the product matures and total sales volume increases, buyers need less point-of-sale education. At the same time, shopping convenience and retail price become more important to the buyer, and resellers' unit sales costs decrease markedly. In response, competitors move to establish strong market exposure by expanding their representation at the retail level. These factors typically prompt the industry leader to shift from selective to intensive distribution. Handheld calculators made this transition relatively rapidly as one large manufacturer, Texas Instruments, led the way in shifting from college bookstores and office equipment stores to mass merchandisers (discount houses) and drug chains.

Like other elements of a marketing strategy, distribution strategies should evolve in response to changing market conditions. Nonetheless, of all the elements of marketing strategy, except perhaps market selection, distribution systems, which take a long time to build and involve complex relationships with a great many independent businesspeople, are the most difficult to change. They represent the link to important groups of customers, and disturbing these relationships is at best risky. But failing to restructure the channel system as markets change may be courting disaster.

Marketing Communications

A core marketing function is communications: informing people about your product, showing them how it can be useful, persuading them to buy. Marketers can reach potential customers through such public media as radio, television, newspapers, magazines, and billboards, or by direct mail. Or, they may rely on personal messages through field salespeople calling on customers, telemarketers reaching out by phone, or sales personnel at the point of sale. These options are like a kit of tools that may be used in combination, each of which is especially useful for certain purposes under certain conditions. The optimal communications mix depends on several factors.

The Process of Decision Making. The purchase-decision process typically moves through several stages: (1) initial awareness of need, (2) identification of options, (3) a search for information, (4) selection, and (5) post-purchase reaffirmation. These stages are likely to depend on the nature of the product, the purchaser's previous buying and use experience, and the involvement of others in the buying decision. The key point for marketers is that the communications vehicles needed to reach prospective purchasers and to influence the decision-making process may be different at different stages. Television and magazine advertising may stimulate the initial desire to buy, but talking to friends, visiting stores, and reading relevant publications may be more effective when identifying options and searching for information. During the final selection, the most powerful communicator might be the clerk behind the counter or a company's sales representative.

Often several people are involved in a purchasing decision; this complex of players is called the *decision-making unit* (DMU). For a major household purchase, such as a car or a vacation, the DMU may consist of a parent and child, or a wife and husband, or indeed the whole family. In industrial companies, the DMU can include engineers; production personnel; controllers; financial, marketing, and general managers; as well as members of the procurement department. Which players are involved depends on the product being purchased, the importance of the commitment, and individuals' previous experience in buying and using similar products.

Of course, the various participants in the decision-making process have different concerns, and the marketer may need to address them separately, offering each one information that he or she believes is important and recognizing the biases that person brings to interactions among DMU members.

Media Advertising.   As marketing vehicles, media advertising may be especially effective in performing particular tasks:

- Providing information on product specifications and prices.
- Informing potential purchasers where to buy.
- Introducing new products.
- Suggesting ideas on how to use the product.
- Assuring prospective buyers of product quality, reliability of the source, and rightness of a decision to buy.
- Creating a prestige image.
- Establishing brand and packaging familiarity to facilitate product identification at point of sale.
- Developing interest among dealers.
- Positioning the product in reference to competitive offerings—that is, indicating the particular market segment for which it is best suited.

The use of media advertising, therefore, may be especially helpful in particular situations, as when (*a*) a specific medium (television, radio, newspaper, or magazine) is especially well suited for getting across the intended message; (*b*) the target audience can be most efficiently reached through the medium selected; (*c*) the volume of sales justifies advertising costs; and (*d*) prospective buyers are open to receiving and acting on promotional messages—that is, they can be persuaded to buy and are not so loyal to competitive brands that they are unwilling to try something new.

Personal Selling.   Besides performing some of the same functions as media advertising, personal selling is especially useful in identifying prospective customers; providing personalized reassurance on the rightness of a purchase decision; and developing solutions tailored to buyer needs (e.g., in clothing, furniture, computers, and machine tools). Only through personal selling can a manufacturer deal with such customer problems as late deliveries, product failure, or the need for technical assistance.

At the same time, personal selling offers a unique means of gathering vital information on product performance, competitive activity, level of market demand, and new sales opportunities. Unlike media advertising, personal selling is a two-way channel of communication between buyer and seller.

Personal selling is usually preferable to media advertising when relevant information is difficult to communicate through mass media (either the message is too complex or the target audience is difficult to reach). It also is preferable when the sales base may be too small to support the cost of media advertising, especially when arrangements must be tailored to the individual customer. Finally, in some purchasing decisions it is important for prospective purchasers to "feel the goods."

For all those reasons, marketing strategies vary considerably in the resources allocated to media advertising and personal selling. The appropriate balance hinges on the nature of the sales message and the suitability of different media to communicate that message efficiently to a target audience. It also depends on the relative costs of using alternative communications options. The cost per customer is typically much higher for personal selling than for mass media. On the other hand, the total cost of communicating a particular message to a target audience is usually much higher when advertising campaigns are used, particularly on a national scale.

Imagine that you are the managing partner of a prestigious international consulting firm. Your target clients are the senior executives of the 1,000 largest global companies. Your clients pay your firm hundreds of thousands or millions of dollars per project. What marketing communications media should you use to reach prospective clients? Now imagine that you are a publisher who is marketing a book entitled *How to Save Thousands of Dollars by Making Your Home Energy Efficient,* targeted at millions of North American home owners. The book sells for $12.95. How would your marketing media mix differ from the strategy consulting firm's and why?

Push vs. Pull Strategies.   In the push strategy, effort is concentrated on selling to the intermediate customers—say, retailers—and providing these channels of distribution with strong incentives to promote the product vigorously to the ultimate purchaser. Incentives at this level may include high retail margins, sales aids, sales contests, and sales training programs. In a pull strategy, on the other hand, the seller focuses marketing expenditures on influencing the ultimate user, typically through advertising, to go into the store to ask for the product by name. In effect it pulls the product through its distribution channels by creating demand at the consumer level. Push and pull also are relevant concepts for industrial marketers. Pursuing a pull strategy, a manufacturer of aircraft engines may concentrate its selling efforts on the airlines, who buy planes from the airframe manufacturers. It tries to persuade the airlines to specify its engines in the equipment they purchase.

In balancing marketing resources, the choice between push and pull strategies rests on many of the same considerations as the choice between emphasizing personal selling or media advertising—that is, on cost efficiency, the nature of the sales message, and volume of sales. Pull strategies, especially in consumer markets, can be tremendously costly, and only the largest companies may be able to afford them. Fundamentally, the choice depends on what kinds of messages influence people to buy, where and how they can be delivered in the buying-decision process, and at what cost.

Advertising and personal selling are, however, but two elements in the marketing mix. Effective communications cannot bring marketing success in the face of adverse economic, social, and technological trends. Nor can heavy outlays for advertising and selling assure the sale of products that do not represent good value for the customer.

Marketing Strategy and Stages of Market Growth

As product markets grow, mature, and decline over time, the marketing strategy must evolve in response to changing customer and competitive demands. For purposes of this discussion, we identify four stages of growth: the introductory period, the rapid-growth phase, the leveling-off stage, and market maturity. The customer's comprehension of the product and its uses, and the degree of competitive intensity, are different at each stage. The marketing infrastructure (the channels of distribution and the media reaching relevant customer groups) may also differ.

Introductory Phase

A new market opportunity is often based on some new technology—for example, synthetic fibers, plastics, or computers—that creates possibilities for a range of new products. In the early stages, marketing strategies typically stress market education—assisting industrial purchasers of new materials and components in end-product design and in the development of manufacturing processes. Market education also includes communicating with potential end users regarding the use of the product and its advantages over the conventional product it is intended to replace. In pricing and market selection, the strategy is typically to skim, which serves to generate high margins with which to fund the costs of research and development and technical market development. At this stage, the market tends to be relatively insensitive to price as long as the new product offers significant advantages over what it replaces.

The basic objective is to create primary demand—that is, to maximize total demand for the new product category by replacing, as fully and rapidly as possible, the market volume held by competing traditional products. At this stage, patent protection may give the manufacturer a legal monopoly, so it alone profits from the market it creates.

Rapid-Growth Phase

As the new-product concept takes hold, market conditions change markedly. Buyers become more discriminating and sophisticated in their purchasing behavior and product-use patterns. They may demand products tailored to their individual requirements. As competitors enter the market, potential customers realize they have options with regard to price, quality, product form, and brand. The need for buyer education grows, particularly at the point of purchase, where choices must ultimately be made.

The innovating firm and its new competitors may at this stage focus on expansion of primary demand, which all may enjoy. Their strategies for building demand typically take the form of product proliferation—the development of a variety of product forms to meet the specific needs of identified market segments. Market skimming continues to be profitable in this phase. As product prices gradually are reduced, the new product comes into direct competition with the lower-priced traditional products, market potential broadens, and unit manufacturing costs may decline enough to outweigh the profit impact of price reductions.

Leveling-Off Stage

At some point the strategic emphasis shifts from developing primary demand to maximizing selective demand. Having worked to make the pie as large as possible, each competitor now tries to claim as large a piece as possible for itself.

Strategies for holding or expanding a company's market shares at this stage often stress expanding distribution systems to get as wide a market exposure as possible. A supplier may try to preempt shelf space in retail stores and distributor warehouses, not only to build sales volume but also to reduce competitors' market exposure. Paralleling the grab for shelf space is the drive for consumer "share-of-mind" through increased outlays for advertising, personal selling, and promotions.

Product strategy at this stage focuses on achieving maximum differentiation to permit latitude in pricing and to provide substance for the advertising messages needed to establish brand loyalty. Product lines also tend to broaden, to fill shelf space, and to get the maximum return from investments in advertising and distribution systems. At the same time, a wide range of product variations emerges to satisfy customers' diverse needs in increasingly segmented markets.

The marketing strategy evolves and elaborates as buyers become more concerned with tailored-to-use products, ease of purchase, and product availability, and more sensitive to market communications in all forms.

Market Maturity

In the mature phase, the structure of the supply industry has taken shape. A few firms have staked out major shares of the market; other marginal firms have lost out in the race for market dominance and must adjust to follower roles. At this point, if not before, the strategies of leaders and followers typically diverge.

The goal of market leaders is primarily to preserve and, if possible, to expand their market share. Their strategies reflect an effort to increase sales volume, sometimes but not always by means of low prices. In addition, to develop a preferential position with their customer bases and gain a product edge, they stress service to their channels of distribution and user-customers, as well as technical leadership. A related objective is to optimize manufacturing and marketing costs by attaining a level of critical mass[4] in both areas.

Market leaders at this stage display a strong sense of territorial imperative. They often stake out particular accounts, channels of distribution, and customer groups and defend them aggressively, by service and pricing actions, from competitive attack. At the same time, dominant firms demonstrate a high degree of strategic interdependency. That is, each develops its own strategy in such areas as price, product, technical service, and promotion in clear recognition of its competitors' strategies. Decisions to add new plant capacity are now significantly influenced by competitors' additions, as preserving the firm's share of productive capacity is often thought necessary to retaining its market share.

At this point, leading firms are especially vulnerable to competitive developments that may make obsolete the technologies on which their product lines are based. Often new technologies are introduced from outside the industry, bringing in new competitors and new norms of industry behavior. An effective response to such threats is painful, since it often means discarding the old technology, manufacturing facilities, and distribution systems and cannibalizing profitable sales of existing products. Moreover, the rapid adoption of a new technology means abandoning psychological commitments to once-successful patterns of business in the manufacture, distribution, and marketing of the product.

By contrast, smaller companies in the industry focus primarily on survival. Since they typically lack the resources to fund extensive product development and promotional programs, they survive by picking a specific market segment and concentrating on serving it well. The target market should be one to which the company can

---

[4]The concept of critical mass is based on the idea that unit costs are, to a significant extent, a function of the total size of the operation. Up to a point, unit costs decline as plant size increases or as the marketing effort scales up. Further increases in scale beyond that theoretical point reduce costs more slowly, if at all, and may even create diseconomies as limits are reached in plant capacity and in the ability of management to implement strategies. The level of critical mass will vary considerably from one product to another, depending on process technology and the extent to which pull strategies and outlays for mass media are effective in building sales volume.

bring some particular strengths and that does not require a large critical mass of resources in manufacturing, research, and marketing. A follower's profitability is likely to depend on its ability to operate with low overheads and no frills.

For the follower, new technological developments may create new opportunities, perhaps the chance to win market share from large entrenched competitors intent on preserving their position. To the smaller firm, the risk of sacrificing investments in the old technology may not seem so great as the possible gain from moving quickly to embrace the new technology. What differentiates leaders from followers in this situation, then, is their perceptions of relative risk and gain and their ability to relinquish psychological commitments to past successes and systems.

Analytical Approaches in Formulating Marketing Strategy

The responsiveness of a firm's strategy to changing market conditions and cost factors will almost always be based on careful analysis of the following areas.

Environmental Analysis.   At the broadest level, it is useful to assess the significance of environmental elements, including growth in population and disposable income, government regulations, and interest groups, such as environmentalists or consumer advocates that may influence how the company conducts its business. Also relevant are the directions of new technological developments, the availability of critical materials and other key resources, inflation rates, and evolving lifestyles. This listing is simply illustrative; the relevant environmental factors will depend on the products and markets under consideration.

Market Analysis.   Focusing on a particular market, strategists will need to determine its size, rate of growth, stage of development, trends in the distribution systems serving it, buyer behavior patterns, seasonality of demand, segments that currently exist or could be developed, and unsatisfied opportunities that might provide a market entry. Next they will ask what levels of investment and marketing spending will be required.

Competitor Analysis.   Strategists also will need to know who the competitors are, what product/market positions they occupy, what their strategies are, their strengths and weaknesses, their cost structures (to the extent this can be determined), and their production capacity. It is critical to consider potential new entrants in this analysis as well as existing competitors.

Company Analysis.   The company's own strengths and weaknesses relative to competitors must be appraised in such areas as technology, financial resources, manufacturing skills, marketing strengths, and the existing base of customers. Strategy researchers have coined the term *core competencies* to describe those special capabilities which: (1) make significant contribution to the value of a company's product; (2) are difficult for competitors to imitate; and (3) can be applied across a wide variety of market segments.[5] For example, Honda has a core competence in devel-

---

[5]C. K. Prahalad and G. Hamel, "The Core Competence of the Corporation," *Harvard Business Review*, May–June 1990, pp. 79–91.

oping small high-performance engines, which it has successfully applied in such diverse markets as motorcycles, automobiles, lawn mowers, and outboard motors. For purposes of market selection and strategy formulation, a company's core competencies must correspond to the needs of the market. It is essential to ask: "What can *we* bring to the party? How are we uniquely qualified to add something that others do not currently offer?"

Customer Analysis. The analysis of patterns of purchasing behavior is central to product design, pricing, choice of distribution channels, and communications strategy. To a large extent we can hypothesize about buyer behavior from our own purchasing patterns and those we observe in others. Beyond that, buyer behavior can be analyzed in considerable depth with the aid of sophisticated market research tools, including survey techniques (e.g., customer interviews, questionnaires) and statistical analysis of sales patterns. Market tests can assess potential demand for a new product, the appeal of a proposed brand name, or the relative pull of different advertising messages. Market research, one of the most technical areas in marketing, is generally expensive; its cost always must be weighed against the anticipated value of the information—which often is less definitive and revealing than expected and is, at best, subject to interpretation.

One of the most promising new tools for customer analysis in the 1990s is *customer satisfaction measurement.* An outgrowth of the quality movement in the 1980s, customer satisfaction measurement identifies the gaps between customers' expectations and their perceptions of what a company is delivering. This information provides direction about where improved quality of products and services will provide the greatest impact on customer satisfaction.

Channel Analysis. To the extent that a company relies on resellers to take the product to market, its strategy must consider the availability of distribution channels as well as their requirements. What are the operating-cost structures of wholesalers and retailers? What costs are they likely to incur in stocking, selling, and servicing the products? What kinds of margins will they require? To what extent must they be relieved of competition from other resellers of the product? What sales training and promotional support will they require? What commitments might they already have to competing suppliers? What alternative opportunities do they have for utilizing limited resources, in particular shelf space?

Economic Analysis. The summation of marketing economic analysis is the profit-impact calculation. If the company goes ahead, how much profit can it earn as compared with the profitability of other opportunities for utilizing limited resources? The profit-impact calculation assesses the fixed commitments needed to make and sell a new product, and then asks what contributions each unit sold will make toward amortizing these investments and generating an acceptable level of profit. Finally, it calculates the volume of sales that must be attained and compares that figure with the market potential for the product. Needless to say, such calculations are at best based on rough estimates. They are useful, however, in identifying and isolating the relevant variables and giving the marketing manager a framework within which to apply all the available information and his or her best judgment.

Ethical Analysis. Marketing decisions also require thoughtful analysis of ethical issues involved in the exchange process. Customers rely on marketers to provide safe, reliable products at fair prices. Company leaders have an obligation to ensure that the rights of consumers are not compromised in pursuit of profit or market share targets. Three basic principles can guide the ethical analysis of any marketing strategy. The *utilitarian principle* implies that a company should not waste society's resources. For example, marketing products that harm the environment may violate the utilitarian principle. The *rights principle* admonishes marketers to treat customers and others in the marketplace in the same way that marketers would want to be treated themselves. Truth in advertising and fair pricing reflect the rights principle. The *justice principle* offers three guidelines: treat equals equally, care for those less fortunate, and honor diversity. Ensuring that products are safe and that advertising does not take advantage of children are practices consistent with the justice principle. Applying these three principles to conduct an ethical analysis should be an essential component in any marketing strategy.

Exhibit 1 depicts graphically the analytical areas and decisions relevant to developing a marketing strategy.

A model of strategic marketing activities

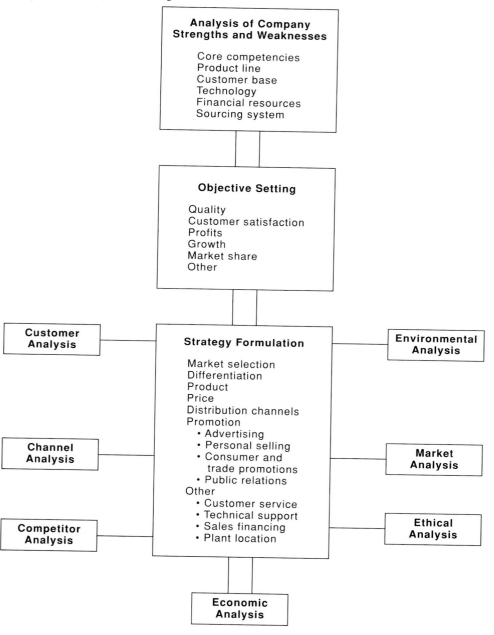

IDS FINANCIAL SERVICES

In mid-1987, Reed Saunders, senior vice president of marketing at IDS Financial Services, was reviewing IDS's position. He was pleased by IDS's performance since its acquisition by American Express in January of 1984. Between year-end 1983 and year-end 1986, revenues and net income had grown by an average of 30 percent annually. Fees from financial plans had mushroomed at an average annual rate of 174 percent. In addition, IDS had substantially exceeded its sales force expansion goals, increasing the number of financial planners by an average annual rate of 11 percent.

Despite this record-setting performance, Saunders knew that IDS field management faced significant challenges in meeting its aggressive growth goals for 1987. Although sales at midyear 1987 were 15.0 percent higher than midyear 1986, they were 10.5 percent below forecast. Likewise, while sales of financial plans to clients were 30 percent higher than midyear 1986, they were 23 percent below the forecast level. The shortfall in financial plan sales was especially disappointing in that financial planning was the company's major strategic focus for the 1990s. In addition, limited management resources threatened to constrain sales force growth. The number of district managers (who trained and supervised planners) had decreased by 5 percent from midyear 1986 to midyear 1987.

IDS's performance also was disappointing in light of the aggressive growth goals set by Harvey Golub, IDS president. In January 1987 Golub had declared as formal company goals an average annual growth of 30 percent in revenues and 24 percent in earnings between year-end 1986 and year-end 1990, while decreasing the cost of sales. Golub's plan for sales force expansion would almost double the IDS field force by year-end 1990, increasing it to more than 12,100 financial planners. To achieve its ambitious growth goals, IDS had to leverage its field force. Saunders explained:

> Because financial planning relationships must be established through our field force, distribution is the critical element in the equation. We must deliver outstanding service to more people with increased efficiency. Perhaps we should increase our marketing programs or accelerate the expansion of our field force numerically or geographically.

This case was prepared by Professor Minette E. Drumwright with assistance from Professor Thomas V. Bonoma.
Copyright © 1987 by the President and Fellows of Harvard College. Harvard Business School case 9-588-044 (Rev. 1/90).
Note: A glossary of financial terms is included in the Appendix at the end of this case.

Consumer Financial Services Industry

The consumer financial services industry encompassed all forms of managing and investing assets, providing credit, and providing financial or tax advice for consumers. At year-end 1986, the 88.5 million U.S. households had financial assets totaling $11.2 trillion and liabilities totaling $2.7 trillion. Transactions involving consumer financial services generated an estimated $200 billion in revenues for financial services providers in 1986.

Financial services providers were a large and diverse group. At one end of the spectrum, the group included major financial institutions, such as commercial banks, savings and loan associations, insurance companies, mutual fund companies, and securities firms that distributed various financial products (e.g., savings accounts, loans, stocks, bonds, life insurance). At the other end of the spectrum, the provider group encompassed accountants, lawyers, and financial planners in private practice who primarily were financial advisors.

The 1970s was a decade of increased innovation and intensified competition among financial institutions. Inflation precipitated high interest rates, which gave consumers an incentive to become more sophisticated money managers. The more sophisticated consumers demanded new financial products, and deregulation enabled firms in a variety of businesses to respond to that demand.

By the mid-1980s, the traditional boundaries between financial institutions, like commercial banks, insurance firms, and securities firms, had blurred. Many were becoming financial generalists, offering broad product lines that often included mutual funds, annuities, insurance, and limited partnerships (see the Appendix at the end of this case for a glossary of financial terms). Nonfinancial firms, such as Sears and American Can Company, which was renamed Primerica, entered the market with broad product lines as well.

The end of 1986 and the beginning of 1987 represented a particularly competitive era in the financial services marketplace. The increased competitiveness was attributed to stock market fluctuations, which made some consumers more cautious investors, and changes in tax laws, which made some investment products less appealing. In addition, some financial services firms were aggressively recruiting their competitors' personnel.

Financial Planning. In addition to broad product lines, many financial services institutions in the mid-1980s claimed to offer some form of financial planning or advice. However, the manner in which they used the term *financial planning* varied widely. Some providers used *financial plan-*

ning as a euphemism for a product sales approach, while others used it to refer to informal advice that salespeople offered. Still others used *financial planning* to refer to a comprehensive process resulting in a professionally prepared plan that would guide clients' overall investment policies.

Financial planning as a comprehensive process began with a financial planner meeting with a client to develop an understanding of his or her financial needs, assist with clarifying financial objectives, and gather financial information. Some companies had financial planners submit the information to the company home office for analysis. Typically, plans with home office analysis were designed for people with similar financial needs and objectives. For example, a company might offer a plan consisting of a standard set of analyses helpful to middle-income people planning for retirement. After the analyses were completed, formal written plans were prepared at the home office and sent to the planners, who presented them to their clients. In contrast, other companies merely recommended financial planning software to their planners, who conducted the analyses and prepared the written plans themselves.

Some companies offered the plans free in hopes of earning commissions on product sales made in implementing the plans, while others charged either an hourly or a set fee. Of those charging for financial plans, some offered both the plans and the products to implement them on a fee-plus-commission basis. Others offered only the plans and charged a fee.

Competition. With many of the major financial services industry players offering similar products, distribution was viewed as key. As one industry observer commented, "Anybody can provide the products; the difficulty is in distributing them."

Many financial services firms provided broad product lines on a nationwide basis, distributed through a sales force. Sixteen of the largest nonbank financial services companies, all of which distributed financial products through a sales force, are listed in Exhibit 1. Three of these—Merrill Lynch, Integrated Resources, and FSC Securities—were considered particularly strong competitors by IDS management.

Merrill Lynch (ML). A diversified financial services holding company, ML provided securities, mutual funds, insurance, investment management, investment banking, and real estate through its subsidiaries on a nationwide basis. It owned $64 billion in assets and managed $149 billion in assets. Its chief subsidiary, Merrill Lynch, Pierce, Fenner & Smith, was the nation's largest stockbroker. ML had the highest consumer-name recognition of any financial firm and was considered a formidable competitor because of its sheer size. Historically, ML had targeted a high-income clientele.

In 1982, ML introduced "Pathfinder," a financial plan with home office analysis.[1] The plan was designed for the middle market: households with annual incomes ranging from $36,000 to $85,000. In 1985, ML changed the title of its brokers from *account executive* to *financial consultant* and instituted a training program in consultative selling. By 1987, it provided a second middle-market program, called "Blueprint," which offered reduced investment commissions along with periodic investment advice. Typically, ML Blueprint clients paid up to 55 percent less in investment commissions on equity transactions, 30 percent less on mutual fund transactions, and 80 percent less on precious metal transactions. In 1987, the Pathfinder plan was priced at $300.

ML had never publicly adopted financial planning as its predominant strategy, and its compensation system was not perceived as particularly compatible with financial planning. Typically, financial consultants' income levels at ML depended on the number of brokerage transactions completed and the number of new accounts opened in a day. On average, financial consultants who were ML employees had approximately 600 clients and earned an annual net income (i.e., gross income less business expenses) of approximately $80,000. ML had an excellent training program stressing investments, rather than risk management and estate planning, which were considered critical to effective financial planning. It also had strong marketing and sales support.

Integrated Resources (IR). IR owned $6.2 billion in assets and managed $14 billion in assets, provided life insurance, investment management, and investment brokerage on a nationwide basis. IR publicly advocated financial planning as its driving corporate strategy. Rather than providing home office analyses, IR recommended financial planning software to its planners, who charged by the plan ($120–600 per plan) or by the hour ($75–180 per hour). IR provided investment/asset management for high-net-worth individuals, who typically were the planners' target market.

IR planned to expand its field force aggressively, doubling its size by 1990. Because the company offered little training, it hired experienced financial planners. IDS planners, who were considered among the best trained in the industry, were prime targets for IR recruitment. IR's financial planners were independent contractors, who paid a large part of their own business expenses and provided

---

[1]In this type of financial planning, brokers gathered data from clients at the beginning of the planning process and interpreted the analyses for clients after the plans were prepared. The actual plan preparation was done by analysts, computer analysis, or both, at the home office of the plan vendor.

much of their own marketing support. On average, IR planners, who served about 300 clients each, earned an annual net income of $31,000.

FSC Securities. Primarily a broker for independent financial planners, FSC provided financial products and financial planning software. Its lines of business were securities brokerage, mutual funds, limited partnerships, and life insurance. FSC offered a plan with home office analysis and recommended planning software for its planners, who determined the prices of all plans. Plan prices ranged from $300 to $4,800, but typically were under $725. FSC's target market varied considerably by planner.

In 1987, FSC was acquired by Mutual of New York (MONY) Financial Services. With $7.7 billion in assets owned and $18 billion in assets managed, MONY was expected to provide FSC with a capital infusion to finance growth. FSC planned to triple its field force by 1990.

FSC financial planners were independent contractors, who paid most of their business expenses and received little marketing or field support. Like IR, FSC primarily hired experienced planners and recruited IDS planners. On average, FSC planners served about 300 clients each and earned an annual net income of $22,400.

Consumer-Buying Patterns. According to IDS executives, consumers could be grouped into two broad segments: confident investors and advisor-dependent investors. Confident investors played an active role in managing their own financial affairs. They were often avid readers of periodicals, such as *Money Magazine* or *Sylvia Porter's Personal Financial Planning*. While confident investors might seek the counsel of advisors from time to time, they did not delegate the management of their financial affairs to any one advisor. As one confident investor explained, "I just don't trust any single advisor enough." On average confident investors were more affluent and better educated than advisor-dependent investors.

Typically, advisor-dependent investors wanted to delegate their financial affairs to trusted advisors. They did not feel well versed in financial affairs, often because they did not have either the time or the interest in developing financial expertise. As one industry participant observed, "Many people spend the bulk of their time pursuing their careers and the rest trying to keep their marriages intact. They haven't got the time to look after their financial affairs."

Advisor-dependent investors were prime candidates for financial planning. However, studies indicated that they frequently had no clear understanding of financial planning or its benefits. Sometimes they thought that financial planning was only for wealthy people and, thus, inappropriate for them. The different ways in which financial services providers used the term *financial planning*, coupled with the intangible nature of the service itself, contributed to consumer confusion.

According to a study conducted by a market research firm in early 1987, 16 percent of the 42 million U.S. households with annual incomes over $25,000 had obtained professionally prepared financial plans by year-end 1986. The factors that motivated consumers to have a plan prepared were the approach of retirement, career advancement, a financial windfall or inheritance, and purchase of a house. The benefits that they received from purchasing a plan were financial security and peace of mind, better investment strategy, and provisions for retirement. According to the study, 60 percent initiated the contact with their planners, and most selected their planners through a strong referral from a trusted friend or associate. Other factors that motivated consumers to choose a particular planner were the planner's style (low-key, rather than high-pressure), the planner's objectivity, and the reputation of the planner's firm. The planner's access to sources of information and expertise at the firm were particularly important.

Of those who had no plans (i.e., 84 percent of households with annual incomes greater than $25,000), 75 percent had heard of the concept of financial planning, 19 percent had given serious thought to having a plan prepared, and 7 percent said they were likely to have a plan prepared in the next 12 months. Factors that deterred consumers from obtaining a financial plan included procrastination, perceptions of financial planners as insurance agents in disguise, beliefs that only wealthy people benefit from financial plans, and a desire to maintain control of personal finances.

The market research firm conducting the study classified 9 million heads of households as high-potential customers for financial services, because they either already had a plan or said they were likely to obtain one in the next 12 months. Of the high-potential customers, 53 percent felt that financial planners should be compensated on a fee-only basis; 18 percent favored a commission-only arrangement; and 16 percent preferred a fee-plus-commission basis. Approximately half of the high-potential consumers said they would prefer to implement their plans themselves through their stockbrokers, insurance agents, and bankers.

Company History

After witnessing the financial hardships of the 1893–94 depression, John Tappan, a 25-year-old law student in Minneapolis, wanted to help Americans plan for the future. Tappan recognized that if he could bring together 1,000 people, each investing $5, he would have $5,000 to invest at the higher interest rates available to wealthy individuals. Tappan organized Investors Syndicate, the predecessor of IDS, to bring together small investors.

Tappan was convinced that people would not ask for financial planning, no matter how badly they needed it. To take the service directly to the people, he formed a field force. From the beginning, the field force consisted of independent business people with exclusive contracts to sell the company's only product: face value certificates—investment products with fixed interest rates. The field force embodied Tappan's entrepreneurial spirit as well as his desire to help people meet their financial goals and secure their futures.

Through the years, the company grew conservatively, expanding its product lines in response to its clients' changing needs. In the 1940s, the company organized three mutual funds, and, in 1949, changed its name to Investors' Diversified Services, Inc., to better reflect the growing diversity of its financial products. During the 1950s, IDS formed a life insurance company, and, in the 1960s, it entered the business-to-business market by managing pension funds of small and medium-sized companies.

In the early 1980s, IDS responded to the demands of increasingly sophisticated consumers, intensified competition, and deregulation by expanding its product lines to include international money management and financial planning on a fee basis. As the product lines expanded, the company's mission necessarily blurred. IDS's three major product lines—certificates, mutual funds, and life insurance—were not coordinated or marketed in a synergistic manner. As one IDS manager observed:

> Because nobody said, "This is the business we are in," financial planners were free to define our business as they wished. While many would have said that we were in business to help people manage their money, others would have said that we were primarily certificate providers, life insurance agents, or mutual funds salespeople. Thus, we missed opportunities for synergy.

In January 1984, the American Express Company acquired IDS and renamed the company IDS Financial Services. The IDS field force, which then comprised approximately 5,000 independent contractors, was among the most valuable assets that IDS brought to the combined company. The field force served approximately 1.2 million clients in the middle market. Although there were IDS representatives from coast to coast, the field force had been most successful in small towns and mid-sized communities in the Midwest, where the cost of doing business was relatively low and competition was not as strong as in metropolitan areas.

Post-Acquisition Focus: Financial Planning.

Immediately after the acquisition, Harvey Golub, a partner with McKinsey & Company in New York City and a consultant to American Express, was appointed president and chief executive officer of IDS. Golub clarified IDS's mission: to become the premier financial planning firm in the world. As Golub explained:

> Our future is not in selling products one at a time, but in selling groups of products and services through the IDS financial planning process. Through this process we hope to help individuals and small businesses achieve their goals in a prudent and ethical manner better than any other financial firm.

Through the financial planning strategy, IDS flourished during 1985 and 1986, reporting record revenues of $2.9 billion and record earnings of $129 million at year-end 1986. (The company's historical performance in terms of revenues, net income, and field force growth is summarized in Exhibit 2. Income statements for 1984 through 1986 are shown in Exhibit 3.) At year-end 1986, IDS owned assets of $12.1 billion, and managed assets of $24.2 billion. Approximately half of the assets were in mutual funds, representing a 3.7 percent market share. With $23 billion of life insurance in force, IDS had a 0.5 percent market share of ordinary life insurance.

In December 1986, the field force comprised 6,062 financial planners and 669 district managers, who offered the broad product line shown in Exhibit 4 to approximately 1.4 million clients. The client base comprised consumer households and small businesses that made purchases in 1986 or had money under management from purchases in previous years. (IDS's historical client growth is shown in Exhibit 5.)

In 1986, the average IDS consumer client purchase was approximately $17,000 in investment products, insurance, or annuities, while the average business client purchase was $43,100. Consumer households accounted for 95 percent of the client base and generated 90 percent of revenues. On average, a new consumer client was 45 years old, with a gross annual income of $50,800. (The income distribution of consumer clients purchasing financial plans in 1986, for example, is given in Exhibit 6. It was representative of the entire client base.)

The IDS Financial Planning Process.

The IDS financial planning process was a comprehensive, integrated approach to help individuals manage their financial needs over time. It was more than just another product; the financial planning process enabled IDS to provide and maintain an enhanced, ongoing relationship with clients. As Reed Saunders, senior vice president of marketing, explained:

> There is a strategic opportunity in the marketplace for someone to provide a new, value-added approach to managing relationships with clients. Through our concept of financial planning, we can offer clients better quality in a financial planning relationship than they could get elsewhere.

IDS's financial planning process began with an IDS financial planner conducting an in-depth interview with the client concerning his or her current financial position, short-term financial needs, and long-term goals. On the basis of the interview, the planner completed detailed forms, which were submitted to the IDS home office for analysis.

The simpler, less-expensive plans were computer-analyzed, while the more complicated and more expensive plans were prepared by analysts at IDS's Minneapolis home office, who often conferred with accountants, attorneys, or real estate experts. (An example of each type of plan is shown in Table A.)

Typically, financial plans consisted of at least 70 typed pages. Although the fees ranged from $180 to more than $12,000 depending on the complexity of the plan, the average charge was approximately $360. (IDS's historical growth in financial plan sales is given in Exhibit 7.)

The completed plan was sent to the planner, who presented it to the client and recommended IDS products that the client could purchase to implement the plan. Often, four to six weeks would elapse between the initial meeting with the client about the plan and the sale of any financial products.

Although the financial planning process took longer initially to generate product sales than a product-oriented sales approach, it resulted in more sales per client. An IDS buyer study in 1987 revealed that the average number of products purchased per household was 4.3 for clients who purchased a financial plan, compared with 1.9 for clients who had not. While 25 percent of the new clients in 1987 had purchased a financial plan, only 11 percent of the total client base had purchased a financial plan. Only 4.6 percent of clients who had been with the company for more than two years had purchased a financial plan.

IDS Field Force

In June 1987, IDS's 6,720 financial planners were grouped into 635 districts, which were supervised by district managers who were both managers and financial planners with active practices. Both the financial planners and the district managers were independent contractors, with the stipulation that they sell only IDS products. The districts were

TABLE A Examples of IDS Financial Plan Product Line

The *Personal Financial Profile* was a computer-prepared plan designed for people who wanted to accumulate capital toward one objective, such as retirement income or income needs in the event of premature death. An analysis of objectives for educating children was provided for an additional fee.

Fee: $180 without education analysis
    $210 with education analysis

The *Retirement Report* was an analyst-prepared plan designed for people who were either retired or planning to retire within 12 months. It was appropriate for individuals who had estate-planning concerns regarding income and estate tax reduction, estate settlement and distribution, current resource needs, and survivor-income needs.

Fee: $880

grouped into 215 divisions, each of which was supervised by a division manager, who was a full-time manager and an employee of IDS. The divisions were grouped into 16 regions, which were managed by IDS regional vice presidents. The division managers and regional vice presidents, who were IDS employees, were not considered part of the field force.

Saunders commented on the nature of IDS's relationship with its independent contractors:

> The IDS field force is a unique organization in the financial services industry. Its strength is the result of a philosophy that combines two distinctly different elements. On one hand, IDS district managers and financial planners are encouraged to take an entrepreneurial approach to building the business. On the other hand, there is a "common glue" that binds the entire company together. That glue consists of our shared values, which define how we deal with clients and each other, and a set of shared operating systems that standardize certain activities and tasks.

Most financial planners had been attracted to IDS by the opportunity to be in business for themselves, with unlimited income potential and the ability to set their own hours. Many planners had been teachers, small-business owners, or managers with no previous work experience in financial services. The field force had been described as "average people," "the get-rich-slow crowd," and "people you could trust rather than financial gurus."

People aspiring to be IDS financial planners went through an extensive selection process that lasted four to six weeks. The process included a series of personal interviews, a personality inventory, and an attitude and opinion survey. Of the 12,328 people who applied for positions as IDS financial planners during the first six months of 1987, only 1,196 were appointed. Those appointed entered a three-month program of orientation to IDS and preparation for licensing examinations. Prospective planners were not paid during the three-month period and had no assurance of being appointed by IDS.

Before they were eligible for appointment by IDS, prospective planners had to pass examinations to earn the life, accident, and health insurance, fixed annuity and variable annuity licenses required by the state in which they practiced, as well as the National Association of Securities Dealers license required to sell securities. All planners entered an 18-month self-study program focusing on financial planning, financial products, and sales skills. Some planners went on to earn the designations of Chartered Life Underwriter, Chartered Financial Consultant, and Certified Financial Planner after starting their practices.

Those appointed by IDS attended an intensive two-week training program, which was followed by a year of field training. To train each new financial planner cost IDS $20,570. During the year of field training, financial planners were employees of IDS. Historically, first-year planners had received a monthly stipend to defray their expenses (e.g., $600 a month in 1986), plus commissions. Beginning in February 1987, first-year planners received a base compensation of $29,000 plus bonuses if they sold more than the equivalent of $29,000 in commissions. Approximately 30 percent of the first-year planners qualified for bonuses. The base compensation was instituted to free new planners from the pressures of a fluctuating income while they learned the financial planning process. It was adopted after testing in only one region for 10 months, because it was viewed as vital to the introduction of the financial planning process. Without the base compensation, new planners would be sorely tempted to resort to product-oriented sales, which typically produced commissions faster than financial plans. If financial planners in their first year of employment left their IDS positions or were terminated, the division and district managers, who were responsible for selecting and training financial planners, could be penalized. A division manager was charged 40 percent of the difference between the salary paid to the planner and the commissions generated by the planner, while a district manager was charged 30 percent. Thus, division and district managers had incentives to train and manage first-year planners.

After the first year, financial planners became independent contractors. Their compensation was based on a complex system of commission schedules, bonuses, awards, and benefits. Because of the wide variety of IDS products, 150 different commission schedules were needed. The commission system was further complicated because second- and third-year planners received supplemental commissions while they were building their practices.

The timing of the commission payments depended upon how and when IDS made money on the products sold. All commission schedules except those for financial plans had two components: immediate commissions paid at the time of sale and deferred commissions paid over the years that money from the sale was under management by IDS. Deferred commissions were designed to reward planners for money remaining under management for three or more years. Typically, IDS did not profit from a new account until the fourth year. During the first three years, the money generated from the account covered IDS's costs related to opening the account, commissions paid to the planners, and commissions paid to the district and division managers. District and division managers received commissions based on the sales of the planners they supervised, which were called "overwrites." Typically, district managers received 12 percent of the commissions earned by the planners they supervised, and division managers received 17 percent.

Financial plan commission schedules were different from the other schedules in that they had no deferred commissions. Planners earned 40 percent of the fee at the time of sale, while both district managers and division managers received overwrites of 5 percent of the fee. IDS offered financial plans on a breakeven basis, expecting to make money on product sales made in implementing the plans. (Examples of the two types of commission schedules are shown in Table B.)

Another function of IDS's complex set of 150 commission schedules was to equalize commissions across products to encourage objectivity in selling. Objectivity was vital to ensuring high-quality financial planning on a fee-plus-commission basis. Calibrating the compensation program was a difficult and delicate task. As one compensation manager explained:

> Designing compensation programs is a balancing act all the time. First, we must balance the charge to the client, the payment to the field, and the company profit in a way that's fair to everybody. Second, we must balance the immediate commission, deferred commission, bonus, and benefit components of the planners' compensation. When we change one thing, everything else gets out of whack.

IDS's compensation system was not perceived as perfectly balanced by the field force; however, planners estimated that the compensation system was balanced to the point that it was 80 to 90 percent objective. Planners also perceived that Integrated Resources and FSC Securities gave planners higher and more immediate cash payouts on equivalent production, which was viewed favorably. In contrast, IDS had higher noncash components and more deferred compensation. IDS's compensation system was also considered more complicated than that of its competitors.

While some planners earned more than $350,000 in 1986, planners on average earned $47,200 in monetary compensation (i.e., commissions and bonuses) annually. (Exhibit 8 shows average monetary compensation and client base according to planners' length of service.) On average, planners received retirement and insurance benefits valued at $6,650. Planners incurred marketing expenses by

---

TABLE B Commission Schedules

Example 1
Product: $17,000 mutual fund, 5% ($850) sales load.[a]
Immediate commission: 50% of sales load, $425.
Deferred commissions:
   1st year, year-end: $1 per $1,000 of initial purchase, $17.
   2nd year, year-end: $2 per $1,000 of initial purchase, $34.
   3rd year, year-end: $3 per $1,000 of initial purchase, $51.
   4th year and on, year-end: $.50 per $1,000 of the fund's current value.

Example 2
Product: $210 personal financial plan.
Immediate commission: 40% of $210 ($84).
Deferred commission: None.

[a]A sales load was a fee that a client paid to open an account (i.e., purchase the financial product).

participating in home office marketing programs. The median annual marketing expense was $1,752.

Financial planners also paid their own operating expenses, which included rent, office furniture, secretarial support, telephone, postage, and supplies. The median operating expense for planners was $9,100 annually.

District managers were compensated like financial planners for their personal sales. The remainder of their incomes came from overwrites on the sales of the planners they supervised, bonuses on the total district production, and fees for training new financial planners. District managers earned $1,452 for training new financial planners during their first three months in the field. While the most successful district manager earned more than $240,000 in 1986, district managers on average earned $95,600 in monetary compensation annually and received $11,130 in benefits.

District managers also paid their own operating expenses, which averaged $24,200 annually. These higher operating expenses sometimes deterred planners from accepting positions as district managers, particularly in areas with high costs. The average annual marketing expense for a district manager was $14,520.

Marketing Productivity

To achieve its goals, IDS had to increase revenues dramatically while decreasing the acquisition costs by 5 percent each year. Acquisition costs were IDS's costs related to making sales, including indirect selling and marketing expenditures and excluding direct compensation. Acquisition costs had actually gone up by 4 percent from midyear 1986 to midyear 1987. (Marketing and sales expenses, along with direct compensation—that is, commissions, overwrites, and fees—are shown in Exhibit 9.)

To increase planner productivity, the IDS home office offered a variety of marketing programs. Saunders explained their purpose:

> Through the marketing programs, we provide a core set of systems for acquiring and serving clients that we believe will provide a higher level of success. Our purpose is to help new planners build a professional financial planning practice during their first three years with IDS and to assist veteran planners to expand their practices each year.

Revenues could be increased in two general ways: by increasing productivity (i.e., revenue per planner) and by increasing the sales force size. Productivity could be leveraged by increasing (1) the number of clients per planner and (2) the number of sales per client.

Planners participating in home office marketing programs often shared in the program expense individually or through contributing to their division's Marketing Operations Account (MOA). Division managers assessed planners and district managers $30 to $50 each per month for the

MOA, which they used to obtain home office marketing programs. The marketing programs were grouped in four categories: new-client marketing, existing-client marketing, sales promotions, and sales support.

New-Client Marketing Programs.   The objective of the new-client marketing programs was to optimize contact points between qualified prospects and IDS planners. (Descriptions of the new-client marketing programs and related expenses that IDS and the field force incurred are shown in Exhibit 10.) In addition to the program expenses in Exhibit 10, IDS spent approximately $11 million on national advertising, in conjunction with new-client marketing programs. Many of the programs generated sales leads, which planners purchased; however, studies indicated that planners pursued only about half of the leads purchased. Some financial planners said that they bought the leads for "insurance purposes" and pursued them only as a last resort after exhausting all their referral leads. Others complained that the quality of the leads was low. Newer planners tended to use the home office new-client marketing programs most. As a result, some veteran planners felt that they were subsidizing new planners with their MOA contributions.

Existing-Client Programs.   Existing-client programs were designed to increase the number of products purchased per client. Although IDS had the capability to manage 80 to 90 percent of its clients' financial assets, studies indicated that it typically managed about 15 percent. Other research had revealed that it was more efficient for planners to sell to existing clients, rather than to new ones. While an average of 24.3 telephone calls were needed to sell a new account[2] to prospective new clients, an average of only 5.3 telephone calls would sell a new account to existing clients. There were two existing-client marketing programs: client direct marketing and client communications.

Through the client direct marketing program, 16.5 million pieces of promotional literature were mailed to existing clients in transaction statements and monthly consolidated statements as well as through a lead-generation direct mail effort. The program generated 451,000 leads, provided to planners at no charge. The leads resulted in sales of 53,240 new accounts. IDS absorbed the entire program expense of $1,651,650 in 1986.

Through the client communications program, 72,600 letters welcoming new clients were mailed, and 1.5 million newsletters, which were mailed along with statements, were printed. Planners were not charged for the letters or the newsletters. The program also enabled planners to subscribe to a quarterly magazine, *Financial Directions*, which was mailed to their clients for an annual charge of $0.99

---

[2]A new account represented the sale of a financial product.

per client. Planners had the option of having response cards enclosed in the magazine for an additional annual charge of $0.36 per client. IDS's expense for the client communications program was $381,000 in 1986; planners paid $375,600.

Some executives suspected that new- and existing-client marketing programs merely enabled financial planners to maintain their desired incomes while decreasing their work time. That is, as marketing programs enabled planners to acquire clients more efficiently, selling more in less time, they chose to work less. These executives thought marketing dollars were better spent in sales promotion programs.

Sales Promotion Programs. To motivate the field force, IDS spent $7.9 million in 1986 on sales promotions, which included contests, awards, and campaigns. Planners attaining production and financial planning goals could qualify for the IDS national conference held in places like Hawaii, as well as for vacations and prizes. Top financial planners could qualify for the President's Advisory Council, an honorary advisory group.

Sales Support Programs. Sales support programs also were provided under the auspices of IDS home office marketing and were supported entirely by IDS. Through the product management program, 13 product managers, who specialized in specific product lines, were liaisons between the home office and the field force. They provided product line information personally as well as through literature and videotapes. The product management program cost $916,000 in 1986. Through a second sales support program, toll-free telephone hotlines were available for planners in need of sales or service information. The telephone hotline program cost $908,000 in 1986. In addition, $1,788,400 of sales literature was printed and provided to planners as sales support.

Growth: Field Force Expansion

Through dramatically expanding the field force, IDS could increase its revenues substantially. Often, IDS expanded by spinning a new division off an existing one and appointing a division manager from the ranks of the district managers in the older division. The division manager then recruited district managers, usually from the ranks of successful financial planners in the older division. District managers accepted the assignment of building a district, which required three to four years of arduous work. In expanding rapidly, district management talent could prove to be a binding constraint. (The turnover among district managers

is illustrated in Exhibit 11.) Of the 404 district managers leaving their positions from 1984 to 1986, 65 percent returned to financial-planner status, 19 percent were promoted to division management, and 16 percent resigned or retired.

Building a district was arduous because district managers had to recruit and train planners. Planner turnover, although low for the industry, made recruiting and training perpetual tasks. For example, 2,321 new planners were appointed to realize a net gain of 633 in 1986 (see Exhibit 12). Field force terminations by length of service for 1986 are presented in Exhibit 13. IDS's turnover rate had been negatively impacted by competitors who lured financial planners away (32 percent of the planners who left IDS in 1986 went to competitors).

In addition to achieving numerical expansion, IDS hoped that the field force could achieve strategic geographical expansion. Traditionally, the field force had expanded opportunistically, spinning new divisions and districts off of successful ones. Thus, the field force grew like an amoeba, becoming bigger and stronger in areas where it was already concentrated. For example, at year-end 1986, Minneapolis, St. Paul, and Rochester, Minnesota, each had nine districts. In contrast, Philadelphia had one district; Washington, D.C., had two; and Atlanta had three. In expanding the field force, IDS hoped to build districts to strengthen its position in major metropolitan areas where the company traditionally had not been strong. Fourteen key metropolitan areas with significant market potential had been targeted for growth: New York, Los Angeles, San Francisco, Washington, D.C., Philadelphia, Chicago, Dallas/Fort Worth, Houston, Atlanta, Seattle, San Diego, Denver, Stamford/Bridgeport (Connecticut), and Baltimore. Because business expenses were usually higher in major metropolitan areas, attracting district managers and financial planners to go to these areas was more difficult.

Current Situation. Saunders had a number of issues to ponder in preparing a plan to dramatically increase production to meet IDS's aggressive growth goals. He had to determine the most effective way or combination of ways to leverage IDS's field force. Among his options were increasing marketing programs, accelerating field force numerical growth, and emphasizing the expansion of the field force in major metropolitan areas. On the other hand, perhaps the most appropriate tack would be to try to revise the ambitious growth goals and ride out the difficult competitive environment of 1987, being satisfied with a more modest level of growth.

Exhibit 1   Major Nonbank Financial Services Firms (year-end 1986)

Company	Sales Force Size	Sales Status	Historical Businesses	Revenues ($ millions)	Net Income (Loss) ($ millions)	Revenue per Salesperson	Net Income per Salesperson
Merrill Lynch	13,189	E*	Securities	$11,616	$ 549	$ 880,734	$ 41,626
Metropolitan†	10,052	E	Insurance	91,960	2,196	9,148,428	218,464
Dean Witter Reynolds	10,043	E	Securities	4,132	(45)	411,431	(4,481)
E.F. Hutton	7,623	E	Securities	3,340	(109)	438,148	(14,299)
IDS Financial Services	6,731	IC	Certificates	2,910	129	432,328	19,165
Shearson Lehman	6,655	E	Securities	5,566	382	836,364	57,401
Prudential-Bache	6,292	E	Securities	1,331	NA‡	211,539	NA
PaineWebber	5,227	E	Securities	2,886	87	552,133	16,644
Integrated Resources	3,630	IC	Limited partnerships	100	47	27,548	12,948
A.G. Edwards	3,146	E	Securities	637	65	202,479	20,661
John Hancock†	3,093	E	Insurance	4,328	NA	1,399,289	NA
Smith Barney	2,420	E	Securities	957	NA	395,455	NA
FSC Securities	1,513	IC	Securities	110	NA	72,703	NA
CIGNA†	1,204	E	Insurance	20,647	989	17,148,671	821,429
Edward D. Jones	1,162	E	Securities	217	NA	186,747	NA
Aetna†	1,029	E	Insurance	24,784	1,262	24,085,520	1,226,433

NA means not available.

E* indicates an employee sales force; IC indicates a sales force of independent contractors.

†Sales force size for some insurance companies can be deceiving in that, in addition to their employee sales forces, they sold through agents, who were neither employees nor independent contractors. As a result, revenue per salesperson and net income per salesperson may be disproportionately high.

‡The net incomes for some private companies were not available.

Exhibit 2   IDS Historical Growth

	Revenues ($ millions)	Net Income ($ millions)	Field Force*	Revenue/ Field Force Member	Net Income/ Field Force Member
1980	$1,001	$ 67	3,524	$284,052	$19,013
1981	1,249	52	4,127	302,641	12,600
1982	1,422	76	4,773	297,926	15,923
1983	1,543	67	5,036	306,394	13,304
1984	1,907	75	5,337	357,317	14,053
1985	2,666	96	6,075	438,848	15,803
1986	2,910	129	6,731	432,328	19,165

*The field force consisted of financial planners and district managers.

Exhibit 3   IDS Income Statements, 1984–1986 (dollars in thousands)

	1984	*1985*	*1986*
Revenues			
Premiums	$1,062,690	$1,565,692	$1,555,882
Sales loads	102,284	153,940	219,936
Investment management and service fees	103,961	120,155	173,986
Interest and dividends	630,710	822,523	940,604
Other	6,866	4,021	19,538
Total revenues	1,906,511	2,666,331	2,909,946
Expenses			
Provisions for losses and benefits	1,474,280	2,123,883	2,174,376
Compensation and employee benefits	185,829	278,100	395,723
Amortization of intangible assets	66,469	55,096	33,418
Taxes (other than income taxes)	16,035	25,613	24,396
Depreciation and amortization	7,721	11,404	26,777
Rent	19,629	22,041	19,769
Other	21,347	15,279	53,974
Total expenses	1,791,310	2,531,416	2,728,433
Pretax income	115,201	134,915	181,513
Income tax expense	40,165	39,200	52,870
Net income	$ 75,036	$ 95,715	$ 128,643

Exhibit 4   IDS Product Lines at Year-End 1986

Product	*Percent of 1986 Sales*
Mutual funds	42.0%
Annuities	23.5
Insurance	17.8
Limited partnerships	9.0
Financial plans	4.0
Certificates	3.2
Unit investment trusts	0.5
Securities services	NA*
Total	100.0%

*Securities services, which included brokerage and portfolio management, were in the start-up phase in 1986 and accounted for a negligible percentage of sales.

EXHIBIT 5   **IDS Client Base Growth, 1984–1986**

	1984	*1985*	*1986*
Beginning client base	1,197,400	1,264,509	1,317,620
Reactivated clients*	4,158	8,266	11,529
New clients	167,086	161,769	177,693
Lost clients	(104,135)	(116,924)	(113,085)
Ending client base	1,264,509	1,317,620	1,393,757
Accounts† per client	1.99	2.14	2.34
Accounts per new client	1.71	1.91	2.07

*Reactivated clients opened an account with IDS within three years after closing all their previous accounts.

†*Accounts* refer to financial products sold to a client.

EXHIBIT 6   **Income Distribution of Clients
Purchasing IDS Financial Plans**

| *Annual Gross
Income ($000)*	*Percent of Clients*
Under $30	18.3%
$31–40	19.0
41–50	16.8
51–60	12.7
61–70	8.8
71–80	4.8
81–90	2.7
91–100	1.4
Over $100	3.4
Not given	12.1
Total	100.0%

NOTE: Although percentage of fees by income category was not available, there was evidence that fees increased with income.

EXHIBIT 7   **Financial Plans Sold**

| | *Computer-
Prepared
Plans* | *Analyst-
Prepared
Plans* | *Fees
from Plans
($000)* |
|---|---|---|---|
| 1979 | | 87 | $ 146 |
| 1980 | | 891 | 273 |
| 1981 | | 1,084 | 413 |
| 1982 | 2,229 | 307 | 734 |
| 1983 | 9,421 | 643 | 3,210 |
| 1984 | 17,189 | 1,542 | 6,393 |
| 1985 | 42,264 | 2,644 | 12,423 |
| 1986 | 70,620 | 4,429 | $20,006 |

EXHIBIT 8   IDS Financial Planner Compensation, 1986

Length of Service	Average Monetary Compensation	Active Planners*	Clients
1 year	$29,040	2,320	398,964
2 years	35,090	1,879	276,331
3–5 years	46,827	1,744	373,048
More than 5 years	82,885	1,805	345,414
Total		7,748	1,393,757

*Includes financial planners active at year-end 1986 and those who were terminated during 1986.

EXHIBIT 9   IDS Marketing/Sales Expenses (dollars in thousands)

	1984	1985	1986	1987 Plan
New-client marketing programs	$ 11,350	$ 18,709	$ 21,388	$ 15,400
Existing-client marketing programs	703	1,627	2,033	2,911
Sales promotion programs	2,061	2,736	7,921	5,859
Sales support programs	2,016	2,236	3,612	5,046
Marketing research	1,249	3,997	7,921	5,859
Education and training	6,171	7,508	10,872	21,072
Recruiting and licensing	1,516	1,572	2,369	3,237
Home office marketing/sales salaries	5,266	7,364	9,189	11,062
Division office expenses	24,349	30,219	36,678	45,162
Infrastructure*	12,278	15,820	19,626	22,982
Direct compensation†	179,141	209,846	275,158	337,873
Total	$246,100	$301,634	$396,767	$476,463

*Infrastructure included a variety of administrative expenses, such as recordkeeping, home office computer support, and legal support.

†Direct compensation included commissions, overwrites, and fees paid to the field force.

EXHIBIT 10   1986 New-Client Marketing Programs

---

1. Through the **Right-Number-of-Leads Program,** 18,918,350 pieces of promotional literature generated 539,600 new-client leads. Financial planners paid from $5 to $10 each for the leads, depending on their divisions' conversion rates (i.e., leads converted to clients). Planners in divisions with higher conversion rates were charged less per lead than planners in divisions with lower rates. The leads resulted in 21,000 new clients.

   IDS's expense: $2,533,740
   Planners' expense: $2,470,992

2. Through the **Amex Marketing Program,** 3,945,000 pieces of promotional literature were mailed to American Express cardmembers to generate 108,000 new-client leads, which were sold to planners for $5 to $10 each. The leads resulted in 5,200 new clients.

   IDS's expense: $1,201,530
   Planners' expense: $ 473,100

3. The **Seminar Program** provided field force members with materials, such as slides and scripts, for conducting consumer seminars from which leads were generated. Division managers purchased seminar materials for $180 from MOA funds. In 1986, 1,806,500 people were mailed invitations to one of 1,378 seminars. Of the 11,606 people attending seminars, 3,190 conferred with planners, and 1,913 became clients.

   IDS's expense: $ 370,000
   Planners' expense: $ 78,650

4. Through the **Pre-Retirement-Segment Marketing Program,** sales kits and a direct-mail effort were designed to target 45- to 64-year-old clients. The direct mail effort generated 31,584 leads, which resulted in 1,232 new clients.

   IDS's expense: $ 182,710
   Planners' expense: $ 187,671

5. Through the **Local Prospecting Program,** the IDS home office and the division offices equally divided the expenses of local marketing efforts, such as sales fairs and local newspaper advertising.

   IDS's expense: $ 752,600
   Planners' expense: $ 556,600

6. Through the **Yellow Pages Program,** IDS paid the entire cost of advertising in the local Yellow Pages.
   IDS's expense: $ 521,510

7. Through the **Employee Financial Planning (EFP) Program,** a corporate sales force approached companies about providing financial planning through IDS as an employee benefit. In 1986, 33 companies either sponsored seminars led by IDS financial planners or provided lists of prospects. A total of 6,240 people attended 472 seminars, and 3,504 new clients resulted from the seminar leads and the prospect lists. Planners did not participate in the expense in 1986; but, in 1987, they received only half the usual commissions on EFP financial plans. Planners received the full commissions on financial products sold in conjunction with EFP financial plans.

   IDS's expense: $4,825,480

NOTE: The costs given include only the direct expenses associated with each program and exclude the $11 million in national advertising that was included in the New-Client Programs budget.

EXHIBIT 11   District Manager Turnover

	Appointments	Net Gain	District Managers at Year End
1984	191	73	583
1985	189	55	638
1986	183	31	669

EXHIBIT 12   Historical Field Force Growth

Year	New Financial Planners Appointed	Net Gain	Planners at Year-End
1980	1,223	218	3,161
1981	1,529	560	3,721
1982	1,757	588	4,309
1983	1,980	214	4,523
1984	1,999	231	4,754
1985	2,196	675	5,429
1986	2,321	633	6,062

EXHIBIT 13   IDS Financial Planner Retention, 1986

Length of Service	Active Planners	Terminated Planners	Retention Rate
First year	2,320	327	86%
Second year	1,879	669	64
Third year	1,116	316	72
Fourth year	628	154	76
More than 4 years	1,805	220	88
Total	7,748	1,686	78%

APPENDIX   Glossary of Financial Terms

Annuity—A contract between an insurance company and an individual in which the company agrees to provide an income, which may be fixed or variable in amount, for a specific period in exchange for a stipulated amount of money.

Limited Partnership Investment—A form of business between a general partner who supplies expertise and ability to operate in a certain industry (e.g., real estate, oil and gas) and a group of limited partners who invest in capital. The partnership itself pays no taxes; instead, as partners, the investors report their pro rata share of partnership profits, losses, and deductions on their own individual tax returns.

Mutual Fund—A mutual fund pools the dollars of many people and undertakes to invest those dollars more productively than individuals could for themselves.

Permanent or Whole Life Insurance—Any type of life insurance with a cash value that can be borrowed, used as collateral, or withdrawn by surrendering the policy; and a lump sum benefit payable at death. The coverage is not limited to any particular time period.

Security—An investment of money in a common enterprise with the expectation of profit from the effort of others.

Unit Investment Trust—A limited portfolio of bonds or other securities in which investors may purchase shares. It differs from a mutual fund in that no new securities will be added to the portfolio.

LifeSpan, Inc.: Abbott Northwestern Hospital

It was Thursday, January 2, 1986. Steve Hillestad, vice president of marketing for LifeSpan, Inc. (the parent holding company of Abbott Northwestern Hospital), was thinking about the next morning's special budget meeting with the Abbott Northwestern Hospital board. Earlier that day at the regular budget meeting, Hillestad had presented what he thought was an excellent review of the progress made by Abbott Northwestern Hospital during 1985 in a number of marketing areas. He had requested a substantial increase in the 1986 advertising budget—from $717,000 to $1.25 million. But Gordon Sprenger, president of LifeSpan, had expressed some concerns:

> Steve, Abbott Northwestern Hospital has come a long way in 1985. But many of us are unconvinced about the role of marketing in this performance. Show us that marketing did in fact play a major role in our improved *performance*—not just awareness or public relations—and we will be better able to evaluate your request for a 75 percent increase in your 1986 budget. Also, while you are at it, please tell us more clearly how those increased resources might get allocated across different programs. I know you've pondered these issues, and would appreciate your presenting them to the board members tomorrow at 9 A.M.

The Health Care Industry

The health care industry was among the largest in the United States. National health expenditures had grown very rapidly, reaching $425 billion in 1985. Health care expenses as a percentage of the nation's gross national product (GNP) had doubled during the previous 25 years; by 1985, they accounted for as much as 10.7 percent of the GNP (see Exhibit 1).

Employment in the private health industry had grown three times as fast as that of the total private nonfarm economy, reaching over 7.2 million employees in 1983. The unemployment rate for health care workers was lower than rates for comparably skilled workers in other areas. Viewed over time, the data described an industry that was large, strong, and insulated from business-cycle swings.

National health expenditures were divided into the following categories: personal health care, program administration, government public health activities, noncommercial research, and construction of medical facilities.

Personal health care included a number of different goods and services: hospital care, nursing home care, physicians' services, dentists' services, drugs and medical sundries, eyeglasses and appliances, and other health services. It was the biggest category of health care expenditure—accounting for approximately 88 percent of total industry expenditures. In 1985, $371.4 billion was spent on personal health care ($166.7 billion of this went to hospital care alone).

Financing Health Care. Health care was financed either by direct patient payments or by "third-party payors," who could be classified into (1) government and (2) private insurance companies. The health care market differed from the market for most other goods and services in that it was dominated by these third-party payors. According to industry analysts, third-party coverage of health care may have contributed to a healthier population, but it had increased prices as well. The analysts believed that most consumers did not care very much about price since they did not directly pay for health services at the time of consumption.

The main third-party payor—the government (federal, state, and local)—spent $174.8 billion in 1985, accounting for 41.4 percent of all health care expenditures. The advent of Medicare and Medicaid programs had dramatically changed government funding of personal health care.[1]

Rapid growth of health care expenditures in recent years placed an increasing financial strain on government programs, such as Medicare and Medicaid. To control Medicare costs, a series of major reforms had been enacted since 1981. Despite these reforms, Medicare spent $70.5 billion in 1985. Considered together, Medicare and Medicaid financed 29 percent of the personal health care expenditures in 1985 and expended $110 billion in benefits to 48 million people (see Exhibit 2).

The other major third-party payor—the private health insurance industry—had been attracting an increasing number of consumers and paid $113.5 billion in medical benefits in 1985. The main third-party payors—government and private health insurance—were not independent but shared a complex relationship. For instance, when Medicare and Medicaid were established in 1966, hospital care spending increased dramatically, and the portion

---

This case was prepared by Assistant Professor Melvyn A. J. Menezes with special thanks to Professor Thomas V. Bonoma for his support.

Copyright © 1986 by the President and Fellows of Harvard College. Harvard Business School case 9-587-104 (Rev. 8/88).

---

[1]Medicare was a federal program that provided hospital and medical insurance benefits to persons 65 years and older and to certain disabled persons under 65. Medicaid was a joint federal-state program that provided medical assistance to certain categories of low-income people. Both programs were established in 1966.

paid by private insurance, although growing in dollar terms, dropped from 41 percent in 1965 to less than 34 percent by 1967. Since then, however, private third-party payments of hospital care had grown to 37 percent because consumers sought more depth in their hospital coverage.

Third-party payments accounted for 71.6% of the total U.S. health care expenditures, and the balance (28.4 percent) was borne by consumers paying directly for health services. However, the share of direct consumer payments varied by type of service. For example, direct payments accounted for 26.3 percent of physicians' services expenditures, but for only 9.3 percent of hospital care expenditures.

Hospital Systems.   Expenditures on hospital care had increased from $52.4 billion in 1975 to $166.7 billion in 1985—a growth rate of 13 percent per year.[2] The total supply of hospital beds had increased substantially. By 1985, there were 6,148 hospitals with about 1.3 million beds. Industry observers generally agreed that the supply of beds exceeded the demand by as much as 20 percent. The 67 percent bed-occupancy rate of hospitals in 1984 supported this contention.[3]

Hospitals could be characterized in a number of different ways, including ownership, type of patients treated, and whether they were teaching or nonteaching hospitals. According to the American Hospital Association, 305 of the 6,148 hospitals in the United States were owned by the federal government; 1,723 were owned by state and local government; 3,363 were nonprofit "voluntary" hospitals; and 757 were proprietary (investor owned).

Changes in the Industry.   Historically, the health care industry had functioned as a decentralized cottage industry with a multitude of individual operators—physicians, hospitals, pharmacies, other services—offering fairly homogeneous services, differentiated mainly by their geographic distribution. However, after World War II and more strikingly in the 1975–85 period, the industry was reshaped by social policy, technology, scarcity of capital resources, and an increased number of physicians as well as health care facilities. It resulted in the emergence of several centralized and well-structured organizations—often with regional or national scope—designed to compete effectively and efficiently with other medical organizations in the marketplace.

Health maintenance organizations (HMOs) represented one of the significant changes occurring in health care. HMOs required a fixed payment for each person enrolled and delivered comprehensive, coordinated medical services—usually with 100 percent coverage of hospital and physicians' services, including routine physicals. An attractive feature of HMOs was that they offered preventive health care services.

HMOs were priced competitively. They provided no incentive for a physician to institute extra procedures to augment his or her fee, as might occur in the "fee-for-service" cases. Many studies also showed that hospitalization rates were lower for customers of HMOs than for those of private physicians in traditional practice. As cost-consciousness increased, health planners and government payors increasingly endorsed HMOs. The number of HMOs in the United States grew from 39 in 1971 to 431 in 1985, with 16.7 million people enrolled in those 431 HMO plans. However, some consumers resisted joining because HMOs offered a limited choice of physicians and hospitals.

Toward the end of 1985, the health care industry was undergoing further restructuring. An emerging organizational structure involved the linking of doctors, hospitals, and an insurance plan. These organizations, referred to as "supermeds" or "managed health care systems," offered a full range of vertically integrated services within one structure. For example, Hospital Corporation of America had purchased an insurance company to enable it to develop managed health care systems. Industry experts believed that by 1990 there would be 10 to 20 managed health care systems delivered by very large organizations that operated on a national basis with regional affiliates.

The role of physicians also was beginning to change. Historically, there had been too few doctors for too many patients. Physicians' success depended on their reputation among their peers; they built their practices in a year or two; and information about their medical skills spread by word of mouth from one patient to another and from one doctor to another. In addition, there existed few specialists, and their offices were so crowded that they had trouble catching up with their appointments. As in many professional service organizations, advertising was taboo.

However, all this had changed in the 1980s. The supply of physicians had increased substantially, and there was no dearth of specialists. Major contributing factors were (1) the increase in medical schools (from 79 in 1950 to 126 in 1980) and (2) aid from the government in terms of grants to medical schools and loans to medical students. The number of medical students graduating each year rose from 7,000 in 1960 to 15,000 in 1980. By 1980, the consensus was that there were too many physicians.

---

[2]Hospital care included all inpatient and outpatient care in public and private hospitals, and all services and supplies provided by hospitals.

[3]Bed-occupancy rate is the percentage of total staffed beds that are actually utilized.

Company Background

LifeSpan, Inc., a Minneapolis-based, not-for-profit corporation, was the parent holding company of a diversified health services corporation consisting of three hospital corporations, a nursing home, a major rehabilitation center, two product and equipment corporations, a home health services corporation, and a foundation. It was incorporated in 1982 when Abbott Northwestern Hospital (ANH)—a regional medical center in its 100th year of operation—underwent a corporate restructuring, creating LifeSpan, Inc., as its parent corporation. The primary function of LifeSpan was to direct the overall strategic planning and new business development for members of the LifeSpan family. It also provided its members with support services, such as financial planning, marketing, human resource administration, internal audit, management, and information systems.

LifeSpan's long-range goal was to develop a comprehensive regional system of the highest-quality health care services in the Midwest, focusing both on a metropolitan area (Minneapolis/St. Paul) total care network and on referral relationships with physicians and hospitals outside Minneapolis/St. Paul. The operating revenues for LifeSpan and its combined affiliate organizations were $211 million in 1985 (see Exhibit 3). LifeSpan's net income increased by over 25 percent to $9.8 million in 1985, from $7.8 million in 1984. This increase in net income was achieved, according to Gordon Sprenger, "through a combination of cost containment and improved productivity further supported by low price increases, all strategically positioned to enhance growing market share." In its most recent debt offering, LifeSpan received an AA credit rating from Standard & Poor's. LifeSpan was a founding member of Voluntary Hospitals of America (VHA), a national organization of 650 large hospitals representing 20 percent of the country's inpatient market share. VHA was created to be a national health care delivery system of preeminent institutions; it included such organizations as Johns Hopkins and Massachusetts General Hospital.

Abbott Northwestern Hospital.   Abbott Northwestern, an 800-bed hospital in South Minneapolis, was the largest private hospital in Minneapolis/St. Paul (Twin Cities), with a high market share in many key medical services. For example, its share of medical surgeries was 18.8 percent in 1985 (see Exhibit 4); yet, in its own backyard (South Minneapolis), its share was very low.

Abbott Northwestern had seven "Centers of Excellence"—cardiovascular, neurosciences, rehabilitation (in conjunction with the Sister Kenny Institute, a LifeSpan organization), cancer, perinatal (in conjunction with another LifeSpan hospital, Minneapolis Children's Medical Center), low back, and behavioral medicine. Its cardiovascular program, for example, was unique in that it provided truly comprehensive services, from diagnostics through heart replacement. In 1985, ANH performed nearly 1,000 open heart surgeries—more than any other hospital in the area. On December 17, 1985, the first woman ever to receive an artificial heart had one (a mini Jarvik 7) implanted at ANH. The cardiovascular program at ANH was viewed as the premier one in the upper Midwest and served portions of the five-state area. This was an important market for ANH, since more than 50 percent of its cardiac patients came from other parts of Minnesota and out of state—primarily Wisconsin.

ANH's patients could be classified into inpatient and outpatient categories. Inpatients were admitted to the hospital by a physician and were resident in one of the hospital's beds. Outpatients used the services of the hospital without being admitted. The latter included both former inpatients who required follow-up treatment and patients referred by their private physicians to have day surgery or laboratory or diagnostic tests performed.

Management.   The ANH management philosophy was to render high-quality service with emphasis placed on taking care of the patient's needs. Although a not-for-profit organization, the objective of various policies was twofold: to support the corporation's long-range goal and at the same time maintain strong financial viability (represented by a fair return on equity) to finance appropriate growth of quality health care services. Therefore, in order to assure corporatewide commitment to necessary asset maintenance, enhancement, and expansion, management set key business ratio targets for liquidity, leverage, and profitability. As one executive noted: "While the party line is human service, it is vital that we meet the bottom line."

The management team was young (average age, 34), including the marketing group, which was beginning to have an increasingly high profile within ANH. Richard Kramer, executive vice president of LifeSpan, had received an M.S. degree from Syracuse University and a master's degree in hospital administration from the University of Minnesota. He had been with the organization for 15 years and was very active in developing LifeSpan's hospital mergers, physician joint ventures, and strategic plans. Kramer started the LifeSpan marketing department in 1982. He was involved in various industry associations, and, in 1985, was a member of the Government Relations Committee of the Minnesota Hospital Association.

Steven Hillestad, vice president of marketing, had a double master's degree in health administration and public administration from the University of Wisconsin. Hillestad, who had been involved in health care marketing since 1974, had served as executive director of corporate marketing for another hospital in Minneapolis prior to joining LifeSpan in October 1983. Hillestad had published several marketing articles in journals, such as *Modern Healthcare* and *Journal of Health Care Marketing*. He also was a coauthor of a book entitled *Health Care Marketing Plans: From Strategy to Action*.

The Minneapolis/St. Paul Health Care Market

The health care industry was the largest employer in Minneapolis/St. Paul. In addition, the Twin Cities had one of the most fiercely competitive health care marketplaces in the United States, with as many as 26 hospitals and 6 HMOs. During 1980–85, HMOs in the metropolitan area had experienced an annual growth rate of 80 percent, reaching a level of 865,000 members. In 1985, HMOs controlled as much as 41 percent of the Twin Cities marketplace, compared with just 11 percent on a national basis.

Industry experts believed that this dominance by HMOs had caused the inpatient market to shrink. During the five-year period 1980–84, hospital utilization had declined by approximately 29 percent (see Table A).

As inpatient days declined, many hospitals had lower occupancy rates. Richard Kramer commented on the shrinking market size:

> Some hospitals experienced declines of over 50 percent in the number of inpatient days during the 1980–1985 period. In those hospitals, occupancy was down to less than 50 percent. Many hospitals were under severe financial pressure and "business as usual" was no longer feasible.

To survive with HMOs, hospitals were undertaking cost containment measures and changing practice patterns—shifting more care to an outpatient basis. During 1981–85, ANH's outpatient surgery volume increased from 13 percent to 44 percent of all surgical procedures performed at the hospital. Hospitals also resorted to using more temporary personnel. For example, full-time permanent professional staff, such as nurses, were often replaced with part-time employees.

Despite the fact that total admissions and inpatient days were declining, the number of physicians was increasing. The result was a decline in the admissions per physician. In 1985, there was a surplus of doctors in the Twin Cities, and their average income had declined by 25 percent from 1984 to 1985. Consequently, the Twin Cities began witnessing intense rivalry between doctors. Competitive pressures were transforming the industry and pushing hospitals, HMOs, and doctors into a struggle for survival.

The Buying Process

In 1982, ANH management conducted a survey of 1,800 consumers and 400 physicians in the Twin Cities. The survey found that, increasingly of late, it was the *patients* who selected which hospital to enter, once the physician decided that hospitalization was required. Previously, the patients had depended on their physicians to select the hospital. (Table B presents the summary of the responses to the question, "Who is the key decision maker in hospital selection?")

Various factors were found to influence consumers' hospital choice. Most important among patients with recent hospital experience were proximity to home, quality-related attributes, and presence of a particular physician. The survey results also indicated that:

1. Consumers believed that most hospitals were of good and similar quality.
2. Consumers had no marked preference for any hospital—with the exception of the University of Minnesota Hospital, which was perceived as the hospital to go to if one was very sick.

With respect to ANH, the survey indicated the following:

- Two out of three consumers did not recognize the name *Abbott Northwestern Hospital*.
- Less than 10 percent of consumers had a clear image of Abbott Northwestern Hospital.
- Approximately 30 percent of ANH's patients came from outside the seven-county metropolitan area.
- Those who had used ANH were very satisfied with their experience.
- Of the consumers that did recognize the name *Abbott Northwestern Hospital*, over 80 percent believed that ANH was located in a part of Minneapolis in which a disproportionately large amount of crime took place.

TABLE A **Twin Cities' Hospital Utilization**

Year	Discharges	Inpatient Days	Average Length of Stay (in days)
1980	361,421	2,794,810	7.73
1981	353,220	2,647,065	7.49
1982	343,716	2,486,505	7.23
1983	333,933	2,298,459	6.88
1984	316,695	1,989,466	6.28

Source: LifeSpan, Inc.

TABLE B   **Key Decision Maker in Hospital Selection, 1982 Twin Cities Survey (%)**

	Consumers' Views*			Physicians' Views†	
	Men	Women	Total	Inpatient Stay	Outpatient Surgery
Patient alone	36	26	30	7	7
Patient with doctor	24	28	26	49	38
Subtotal	60	54	56	56	45
Physician alone	37	42	40	40	51
Emergency room	3	4	4	4	4
Subtotal	40	46	44	44	55
Total	100	100	100	100	100

*1,800 consumers.
†400 physicians.

Marketing at Abbott Northwestern Hospital

The goal of the marketing group at ANH was to increase ANH's market share. To achieve this goal, a three-pronged approach was adopted:

1. Provide potential customers with an incentive to visit the hospital when they were not sick. (The marketing group believed that, once consumers had contact with ANH through one of its various programs, they would be so satisfied with the service quality that they would be more likely to use ANH when they needed hospital facilities and services.)

2. Identify potential customers who did not have a physician and recommend an ANH physician to them. (This would please not only the potential customer but also the physician, who, it was hoped, would then send the patients to ANH whenever hospital facilities and services were needed.)

3. Ensure that patients were very satisfied with their experience at ANH and that they felt they were treated as individuals. The marketing group believed that patients who had a positive feeling about their experiences at ANH would probably choose ANH again if they needed a hospital. Also, in relating their hospital experiences to relatives and friends, their positive word-of-mouth would help ANH's image.

ANH management believed that this strategy was consistent with the culture at ANH, which encouraged all employees who had contact with customers to exhibit a warm, tender, and caring attitude. For example, patients who ar-

rived at ANH early in the morning for the popular one-day surgery program were received with a warm welcome between 5 A.M. and 7 A.M. by a hospital manager and a senior executive, such as Robert Spinner, executive vice president of ANH, and Steve Hillestad, vice president of marketing. Also, free valet parking was introduced, primarily to assist the elderly and handicapped. Richard Kramer felt that "all this was a customer orientation never before seen in the health care industry."

To make ANH more attractive to out-of-Minneapolis patients and their families, a 123-room hotel-like facility called Wasie Center was set up in the ANH complex. Accommodations in Wasie Center, though not fancy, were very clean, comfortable, and secure. The center was run on a break-even basis, and rooms for patients and their families were priced at $28–35 per day. This encouraged non-local patients to pick ANH when selecting a hospital in Minneapolis.

Product Management.   At ANH each medical service, such as cardiology, radiology, neurology, cancer, chemical dependency, and emergency services, was treated as a "product" or department. ANH management kept a close watch on the progress made by each product. Management felt that while some products (e.g., cardiology) were doing very well, some others (e.g., urology), though profitable, were not receiving adequate attention. To focus attention on products that were profitable but not being given much attention, product management was introduced in May 1985. Five nonphysician product managers were appointed—one for each of the following products: neurology, urology, orthopedics/rehabilitation, low back, and chemical dependency.

The primary objective of product managers was to increase the market share of their product. They interacted with concerned physicians, made sales calls, talked to patients, worked on special programs to promote the product, and were responsible for pricing. Product managers were evaluated on the basis of their performance with respect to targets that were set for gross dollar sales as well as number of operative procedures. A product manager's compensation consisted of a base salary (approximately $35,000) and a bonus linked to accomplishment of previously set targets.

Most ANH managers felt that the product management system worked very well. An indication of its success was the large number of requests for product managers received by Hillestad from various departments. For instance, emergency room services wanted a product manager to increase ANH's share of the emergency room business. As one executive put it:

> If the emergency room product manager could put together a program directed at neighborhood groups, neighborhood schools, and ambulance drivers, our emergency room business will shoot up and so will our revenues and profitability. For instance, we could have coffee and donuts provided to ambulance drivers and paramedics. This might provide them an incentive to bring patients to the ANH emergency room. After all, for each patient brought into the emergency room we make about $40 on an average revenue of $100.

Some department managers who did not have product managers were upset because they believed that departments with product managers were getting more attention and were also being allotted bigger shares of the marketing budget.

Pricing. ANH's charges for inpatients typically were divided into a daily room-and-board fee and a fixed fee each time an ancillary service was used by the patient. The impact of ANH's fee structure on its financial performance was directly affected by the mix of patients. For inpatients covered under any cost-based reimbursement program, the fee set had little impact on the revenue-generating ability. For self-paying and privately insured consumers, adjustments to the rate structure could produce meaningful changes in revenues and profits.

The continuing implementation of Medicare's Prospective Payment System (PPS) for hospital inpatient services was having a strong effect on hospitals. Under PPS, which became effective on January 1, 1984, payments to hospitals for inpatient services were set in advance by the U.S. Health Care Financing Administration through a system in which a price was fixed for each of 467 different diagnostic-related groups (DRGs). Several DRGs belonged to each of the "products" at ANH. To be more in line with the new reimbursement scheme, ANH changed its pricing policy from cost-plus to product-based. In addition, price competition was becoming very intense (see Table C). ANH management was unsure about the appropriate course of action. As Hillestad said, "We pondered over whether we should continue to price our open heart surgery at $22,000 and watch competitors [who charged $15,000] gain market share but lose money, or whether we should match the $15,000 price to retain our market share."

Outpatients tended to be more profitable than inpatients, because third-party payors reimbursed the hospital for outpatient services on a fee-for-service, rather than a cost, basis. On an average, the revenue from an outpatient was $200 and the contribution was $85, compared with $6,000 and $700, respectively, for an inpatient.

Another area of concern was pricing to HMOs. HMOs controlled access to over 40 percent of the market, and the average number of HMO patients at ANH had risen from 6 percent in 1983 to 26 percent in 1985. To protect its patient base, ANH believed it was necessary to establish contractual relationships with HMOs. However, due to intense competition among Twin Cities hospitals, bidding to HMOs had become very competitive. Besides, margins on HMO business were already lower than on the non-HMO business.

Distribution. ANH executives believed, as did most health care corporate executives, that physicians were an important part of the hospital distribution system. As Hillestad noted:

> Physicians are our retailers and are critical in getting patients to the hospital. Physicians play a dominant role in determining who should be hospitalized and the type of services that the patient should receive. Physicians influence 70 percent of all personal health care spending. Unfortunately, they view themselves as leaders of the health care team and view business terminology as repugnant. At one meeting, when they [physicians] were referred to as "our customers," two physicians walked out.

TABLE C   **Product Line Pricing**

Product	ANH's Cost	ANH's Price	Competitors' Prices
Open-heart surgery	$ 17,000	$ 22,000	$ 15,000
Delivery (1-day)	750	800	NA
Delivery (3-day)	1,200	1,400	$1,100–1,400
One-day surgery	150–500	200–900	200–900

Of the 1,125 physicians registered with ANH, approximately 400 were active (an "active" physician being one who brought at least 30 patients a year to the hospital). Most physicians wanted to be active members of a hospital, since this qualified them for policy-making positions and gave them an opportunity to participate in the hospital's malpractice insurance program. Active physicians accounted for almost 85 percent of ANH's patients.

ANH management took several steps to support its active physicians. One form of support was the physician-referral system, in which ANH referred patients who did not have a regular physician to one of its physicians. To direct referrals appropriately, ANH needed to evaluate its physicians objectively. Physicians were evaluated by peers, administrators, and patients. Some physicians who received high-quality reviews from their peers for their medical practice were not well received by patients, because they did not have the best bedside manners. Such physicians were not ANH's best "retailers" in terms of patient satisfaction and the number of patients they brought to ANH.

ANH also initiated a Medical Staff Development Program; in 1984, it helped five groups of physicians (including 31 independent practitioners in downtown Minneapolis) establish full-service suburban clinics in communities with demonstrated needs for primary-care services. Assistance was provided in terms of market research, office site selection, staff to manage the office, and legal advice. Physicians also were provided with innovative solutions to capital financing problems. For example, equipment and ambulatory care ventures were set up in conjunction with physicians and selected outside investors. More suburban clinics were set up in 1985 through joint ventures with leading Twin Cities physicians.

To strengthen its out-of-town "retail network," ANH took steps to link primary physicians and hospitals in rural areas with tertiary care support, teaching, and consultation whenever they were needed. A 24-hour toll-free phone line was set up in 1985 to link rural physicians and hospitals with ANH's subspecialty physicians.

Communications.   Historically, ANH's communications had been directed exclusively at physicians, who were viewed as the ones who brought consumers to the hospital. Since 1982, however, most of ANH's communications were being directed at the end consumer.

In 1982, ANH management took advantage of the hospital's centennial celebration to communicate ANH's name and services to a wider public than had previously been attempted. A wide variety of media (radio, television, newspapers, and billboards) was used to enhance the awareness and image of ANH. Research conducted after the campaign showed a significant increase in ANH's name recognition.

Spurred by this success, ANH management decided in 1983 to launch the first major health care advertising campaign in Minneapolis. The campaign focused on individual "products," such as heart disease, cancer, and prenatal care. Expenditure on communications continued to increase, reaching $405,900 in 1984; all the while, all other departments had budget cuts. Richard Kramer noted: "We need and like to have continuity, hence the regular advertising. It's the reinforcement of repeat messages that impacts consumer behavior."

Specific Programs

Some ANH executives felt that, although the 1983 communications program was directed at the end consumer, it did not have a "call-to-action." In addition, they felt that consumers would find it easier to deal with just one telephone number for all concerns, rather than many different numbers for different health inquiries. This led to the creation of "Medformation."

Medformation.   Medformation was set up in July 1984 as a community telephone line providing health care information and referrals to various programs, services, and physicians affiliated with ANH. Its objective was to reach consumers directly and to make it easier for them to call ANH for any health need, since the various ANH programs would be consolidated under one system.

Selling Medformation internally had been a very difficult task for the marketing group. Several physicians did not understand or appreciate the benefits of advertising and raised concerns about its high expenditures. They felt that the money could be far better utilized by purchasing new medical equipment. Also, they wondered how the physician referral system would actually work. Many expressed the fear that a few physicians would get most of the referrals while others would get none or, at best, a few. Many physicians were uncomfortable with the perceived loss of control resulting from the hospital trying to bring patients to them, instead of the traditional method of physicians getting patients to the hospital. In the words of one physician, "ANH is attempting to increase its control so that it can manipulate the physician."

A major statewide promotional campaign announced Medformation and a single phone number that connected callers to the Medformation staff. Care was taken to make sure that the ads downplayed the link between Medformation and Abbott Northwestern Hospital. Some of the consumers interviewed in a focus group revealed that they were surprised and upset to learn that Medformation was in fact linked with a hospital.

John Penrod, marketing manager responsible for Medformation, had a staff consisting of two information specialists and one registered nurse. Two on-call nurses were available to help out if necessary. Medformation staff members were trained to provide the caller with necessary information or to forward the call to the appropriate departmental and medical personnel. Medformation operators were provided with a protocol to follow for each product line or department. After the call, an appropriate follow-up letter and collateral pieces including brochures relating to the appropriate ANH programs were sent to the caller. The fixed cost of Medformation was approximately $175,000.

Early Medformation advertising focused on creating an awareness of Medformation and providing a physician referral service. In addition to all those who called in for a physician referral, almost 10 percent of consumers who called in regarding cancer, medical information, and "other" information also requested a physician referral. Hillestad estimated that 70 percent of consumers who were given a physician referral contacted the physician. Of those who contacted the referred physician, it was believed that approximately 25 percent would return within a year to the hospital (10 percent as inpatients, 10 percent as outpatients, and 5 percent in the emergency room), and that 20 percent would return during the following year (5 percent as inpatients, 10 percent as outpatients, and 5 percent in the emergency room).

In 1985, the focus of Medformation was extended to cover various other ANH programs, such as weight loss, stress management, natural fitness, heart seminars, and quit-smoking. Many who called regarding these programs actually attended the programs. For example, almost 60 percent of those who called regarding weight loss and quit-smoking attended these programs. The fee was $100–200 and gave ANH a contribution of approximately 60 percent. In many of these programs, participants were told that they should check with their physicians before adopting the recommended approach. Participants who indicated that they did not have a physician (approximately 10 percent) were referred to one of ANH's physicians.

Medformation was advertised in the two leading local newspapers; 90 percent of the insertions were quarter-page ads on weekdays and cost $700 per insertion (see Exhibit 5). The rest were full-page ads in the Sunday edition and cost $7,000 per insertion. Hillestad believed that the higher response to the Sunday ads justified the higher cost. In 1985, a total of 28,667 Medformation calls were received, with the heaviest response on the day of the ad insertion, only slightly lower response on the following day, followed by a sharp drop. (Exhibit 6 shows a breakdown of the Medformation ads and calls received in 1985.) The overall response to Medformation ads in terms of telephone calls had far exceeded management's expectations.

Commenting on Medformation, Penrod noted that "Medformation has been a phenomenal success. We have had a big increase in calls, and our research has shown a sharp improvement in consumer perception [see Exhibit 7]. We are delighted with this." Hillestad and Penrod were contemplating extending Medformation to cover outbound telemarketing as well (i.e., to have Medformation operators call people at their homes to promote specific programs), but were not sure how effective this would be. Hillestad felt that first they needed to evaluate in a better way the effectiveness of the existing Medformation programs (i.e., inbound) before pushing for extension to outbound.

Hillestad was surprised when on December 20, 1985, he received a call from the marketing director of a New York hospital who wanted to buy the 36 ads used by ANH for $100,000. He also was willing to pay ANH an additional $20,000 to learn which one of the two Medformation cancer ads worked better. Hillestad turned down that offer; but he began seriously contemplating putting together a package of the ads, including information on the ads' relative effectiveness, and selling the package to hospitals on a national basis.

ANH management also considered licensing Medformation to hospitals in the nonmetro areas of Minnesota and western Wisconsin. Under this arrangement, ANH would license the Medformation name and telephone number to a hospital in exchange for some predetermined minimum number of referrals of complicated illnesses.

WomenCare. WomenCare was a program developed by ANH, who recognized that women had a variety of specialized health care needs that went beyond obstetrics/gynecology services. The program provided a total range of services for women seeking wellness, fitness, weight control, aging, and behavioral and reproductive guidance. It encouraged women to play a more active role in their health care by becoming better informed through WomenCare seminars and classes.

WomenCare was inaugurated on March 25, 1985, by Women's Day—a day-long event that focused on the special health care needs of women. The response was outstanding: over 2,500 women attended, paying $100 each. Throughout the year, WomenCare continued to provide the community with timely seminars on various subjects. It also helped develop breast cancer diagnostic and osteoporosis prevention programs. During the year there were 12 such programs, and the average attendance was 120 people. The fee for these programs ranged from $100 to $200 each, and the contribution was 60 percent.

ANH management was surprised at the response that WomenCare programs had received. For example, a weight loss program for women, advertised under WomenCare, filled up much faster than a general weight loss program—despite the fact that over 80 percent of those who attended the general weight loss program were women and that the fee was $120, compared with $100 for the general class. (Exhibit 8 shows an ad used for WomenCare.)

Other Programs. To meet the needs of a society that had become far more fitness oriented, ANH offered a number of other programs—community courses in weight loss, quit-smoking, and stress management. Each course was presented by trained professionals, who emphasized behavior modification.

Keeping elderly people independent was another important part of LifeSpan's philosophy of care. In October 1985, ANH organized "Seniors' Day"—a free event, which included sessions on such topics as facing the crisis of illness, managing urinary incontinence, and staying in charge of life. Over 450 people attended. Wellness programs for the elderly on such topics as diabetes, medication, and exercise were offered as well.

Current Situation

In 1986, ANH's communications strategies were to broaden reach for maximum penetration of health care buyers, enlarge and reinforce the centers of excellence among consumers and physicians, and integrate the Medformation and WomenCare programs more fully with the Abbott Northwestern campaign. Projected media advertising expenditures, summarized in Exhibit 9, emphasized television and newspapers with support from radio and posters. The mix for television advertising was the same for all "products"—40 percent prime time, 30 percent news, 20 percent fringe, and 10 percent daytime.

For Medformation, television would be used in addition to newspapers. In South Minneapolis, to increase emphasis, eight outdoor posters per month would be used for four months. It was estimated that over the four-month period, approximately 74 percent of adults in South Minneapolis would be exposed to the posters an average of 15 times each.

To increase consumer reach and build awareness of the WomenCare program, a broader range of media was planned. In addition to quarter-page newspaper ads, outdoor posters would be used to carry a WomenCare-image program, and 60-second radio spots would promote special events, such as Women's Day, Spring Seminar, and Fall Seminar.

Advertising for tertiary care was aimed at adults aged 18 and above. A multimedia campaign using television and newspapers was planned. Television would be used for a total of 14 weeks with 80 GRPs per week.[4] Newspapers would carry 17 full-page ads.

The Decision.   Steve Hillestad had a little over 16 hours to think about the next morning's presentation to the ANH board. As he scanned his papers, he focused on two main issues. First, he was convinced that marketing contributed significantly to LifeSpan's 1985 performance. Sales and market share had increased, and consumer perceptions of ANH had improved. Hillestad wondered how he could measure the sales response to ANH's marketing activities—especially Medformation—in a manner he and the board would find credible. Second, if the budget was approved, he wondered how he might justify the allocation of resources to the different products and programs.

---

[4]Gross rating points (GRPs): a combined measure of reach (number of people exposed) and frequency (number of exposures per person reached) for advertising weight.

EXHIBIT 1   National Health Care Expenses and Gross National Product

| | Gross National Product ($ billions) | National Health Expenditure | |
		($ billions)	(% of GNP)
1955	$ 400.0	$ 17.7	4.4%
1965	705.1	41.9	5.9
1970	1,015.5	75.0	7.4
1975	1,598.4	132.7	8.3
1980	2,731.9	248.1	9.1
1981	3,052.6	287.0	9.4
1982	3,166.0	323.6	10.2
1983	3,401.6	357.2	10.5
1984	3,774.7	390.2	10.3
1985	3,988.5	425.0	10.7

SOURCE: Office of Statistics and Data Management, Health Care Financing Administration.

EXHIBIT 2   Health Care Expenditures

1. Financing of Personal Health Care, 1950–1985 (%)

Year	Federal	Public State and Local	Total	Private	Total Third Party	Patient Direct Payments	Total
1950	10.4%	12.0%	22.4%	12.1%	34.5%	65.5%	100%
1955	10.5	12.5	23.0	18.9	41.9	58.1	100
1960	9.3	12.5	21.8	23.4	45.2	54.8	100
1965	10.1	11.9	22.0	26.4	48.4	51.6	100
1970	22.2	12.1	34.3	25.2	59.5	40.5	100
1975	26.8	12.7	39.5	28.0	67.5	32.5	100
1980	28.5	11.0	39.5	31.9	71.4	28.6	100
1985	30.3	9.4	39.7	31.9	71.6	28.4	100

II. Sources of Funds in 1985 ($ billions)

	Total Personal Health Care	Hospital Care	Physicians' Services	Dentists' Services	Other Professional Services	Drugs and Sundries	Eyeglasses and Appliances	Nursing Home Care	Other Health Care
Total (in billions)	$371.4	$166.7	$82.8	$27.1	$12.6	$28.5	$7.5	$35.2	$11.0
Direct patient payments	105.6	15.5	21.8	17.3	6.0	21.8	5.1	18.1	—
Third parties	265.8	151.2	61.0	9.8	6.6	6.7	2.4	17.1	11.0
Private health insurance	113.5	59.3	36.9	9.2	2.9	4.0	0.9	0.3	—
Other private sources	4.9	2.1	0.0	—	0.1	—	—	0.3	2.4
Government	147.4	89.8	24.1	0.6	3.6	2.7	1.5	16.5	8.6
Federal	112.6	71.6	19.7	0.3	2.8	1.4	1.3	9.4	6.0
Medicare	70.5	48.5	17.1	—	2.0	—	1.2	0.6	1.1
Medicaid	21.9	8.1	1.9	0.3	0.7	1.3	—	8.1	1.5
Other programs	20.2	15.0	0.7	0.0	0.1	0.1	0.1	0.7	3.4
State and local	34.9	18.2	4.4	0.3	0.8	1.3	0.2	7.1	2.6
Medicaid	17.9	6.8	1.5	0.2	0.6	1.0	—	6.6	1.2
Other programs	17.0	11.4	2.9	0.1	0.2	0.3	0.2	0.5	1.4

SOURCE: Office of Statistics and Data Management, Health Care Financing Administration.

EXHIBIT 3   Income Statement and Change in Operating Fund Equity (dollars in thousands)

	1985	*1984*	*1983*
Total net revenue	$211,457	$149,941	$135,316
Operating expenses:			
Salaries	118,083	103,352	92,650
Supplies and other expenses	68,071	28,716	28,121
Depreciation	12,118	8,087	7,177
Interest	6,973	5,523	4,850
Total operating expense	205,245	145,678	132,798
Operating margin	6,212	4,263	2,518
Total other revenue (expense)	3,588	3,583	2,336
Net income (loss)	$ 9,800	$ 7,846	$ 4,854
Operating fund equity at beginning of year	56,232	47,323	42,154
Transfers from restricted funds for purchase of plant assets	0	0	315
Fund equity of new affiliates	19,691	1,063	0
Operating fund equity at end of year	85,723	56,232	47,323

SOURCE: LifeSpan, Inc.

EXHIBIT 4   Health Care Industry in Minneapolis

	*Number of Staffed Beds**	*Bed Occupancy*	Market Shares (M.S.)[†]		
			1984	*1985*	*(Expected) 1986*
Abbott Northwestern	705	71.2	17.2%	18.8%	20.5%
South Parkway	372	71.1	12.2	12.7	12.7
Presbyterian	333	68.3	13.8	13.3	12.7
Lawrence Memorial	506	57.3	12.1	11.6	11.1
Glenbrook General	396	55.6	10.8	10.2	10.9
Glenbrook Memorial	488	68.2	7.5	7.6	8.3
Glenbrook Wilson	103	47.8	—	1.9	1.9
St. Agnes	376	71.6	8.2	5.5	4.5
Trinity	223	62.6	6.9	7.4	6.5
Mt. Carmel	160	59.8	6.4	6.0	6.2
Emerson	259	60.7	4.9	5.0	4.7

*A staffed bed is one that is operational and available for use by patients.
[†]M.S.: Medical Surgical.
SOURCE: Metropolitan Health Board (January–June 1985).

EXHIBIT 5

Quarter-page newspaper ad

If you really want to quit smoking, before you pick up your next cigarette, pick up the phone and call Medformation.

Find out about the Quit Smoking Program that works. It has an 80% success rate for those difficult first 2 months.

It's a professional program—developed by Abbott Northwestern Hospital, and led by psychologists and other health professionals. Best of all, the program takes only 3 weeks to complete.

The next classes begin *January 15th* at Northland Executive Center in Bloomington and *February 5th* at Abbott Northwestern.

For more information on becoming a non-smoker, or for the answer to any health question, call Medformation.

"I give up. Help me quit."

Call 874-4444 for Medformation.

One of the loving arms of Abbott Northwestern Hospital.

EXHIBIT 6   Medformation Ads and Responses, 1985

	Weight Loss		Quit Smoking		Physician Referral		Cancer		Medical Information		Others		Total	
	Ads	Calls	Ads	Calls	Ads	Calls	Ads	Calls	Ads	Calls	Ads	Calls	Ads	Calls
January	3	113	4	124	5	119	—	0	—	205	12	1,965	24	2,526
February	2	98	3	118	3	126	—	0	—	181	10	1,745	18	2,268
March	3	147	—	18	2	163	—	0	—	176	10	1,667	15	2,171
April	3	115	3	123	6	261	7	240	—	229	4	1,829	23	2,797
May	—	19	1	53	5	202	2	81	4	256	8	1,767	20	2,378
June	—	33	1	44	6	195	2	61	4	235	12	1,577	25	2,145
July	2	66	2	49	7	265	3	1,087	1	257	4	1,444	19	3,168
August	1	46	2	53	2	218	2	1,414	—	250	5	1,378	12	3,359
September	1	26	2	21	6	220	—	57	—	260	6	1,379	15	1,963
October	—	6	2	25	5	263	—	31	3	344	4	1,393	14	2,062
November	—	9	2	21	3	160	—	3	3	240	6	1,253	14	1,686
December	—	15	—	6	2	146	—	0	—	197	4	1,780	6	2,144
Total	15	693	22	655	52	2,338	16	2,974	15	2,830	85	19,177	205	28,667

SOURCE: LifeSpan, Inc.

EXHIBIT 7   Consumer Perception of Which Hospital Provides the Best Medical Care, 1984 and 1985 (%)

	Serious Heart Problems		Stroke		Severe Pregnancy Problems		Chemical Dependency		Emergency	
	1984	1985	1984	1985	1984	1985	1984	1985	1984	1985
Abbott Northwestern	13.7%*	26.1%	12.0%	15.7%	13.7%	10.9%	5.6%	7.0%	4.7%	5.7%
South Parkway	3.0	6.1	4.7	5.7	2.1	3.5	0.4	0.9	7.3	12.2
Presbyterian	3.8	2.2	4.3	3.0	3.8	3.0	0.9	1.3	6.0	6.5
Lawrence Memorial	4.7	4.8	5.1	3.0	1.7	0.0	3.4	2.2	9.0	11.3
Glenbrook General	3.4	1.7	6.0	3.0	4.3	2.6	0.9	0.4	11.5	8.7
Glenbrook Memorial	0.4	0.4	0.4	0.0	0.4	0.0	0.9	0.9	0.4	0.0
Glenbrook Wilson	1.3	0.4	0.9	0.4	1.7	0.4	0.4	0.4	0.9	0.4
St. Agnes	0.4	2.2	1.3	2.6	5.1	3.5	42.5	38.8	0.0	0.0
University of Minnesota	28.2	26.0	16.7	12.6	9.8	7.0	3.0	0.9	2.1	2.2
Others	10.7	7.7	7.7	4.8	8.2	3.9	16.3	13.8	31.7	25.2
All the same	1.7	0.4	0.9	3.9	1.2	2.6	1.3	1.3	1.7	2.6
Don't know	28.7	22.0	40.0	45.3	48.0	62.6	24.4	32.1	24.7	25.2
Total	100.0%	100.0%	100.0%	100.0%	100.0%	100.0%	100.0%	100.0%	100.0%	100.0%

*13.7% of consumers surveyed perceived that Abbott Northwestern Hospital provided the best medical care for serious heart problems.
SOURCE: LifeSpan, Inc.

WEIGHT CONTROL: IT'S A JOB WHERE WOMEN HAVE TO WORK HARDER THAN MEN.

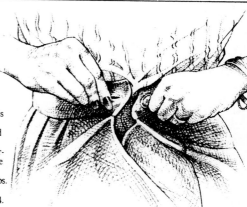

It's something women have suspected for a long time. But, until recently, no one really understood why women have a more difficult time losing and keeping weight off.

There is a physiological reason. Most women have a higher percentage of body fat while most men have more muscles. Since fat is metabolically less active than muscle, women end up burning fewer calories.

WomenCare's Lifestyle Weight Loss program focuses on these differences. This is a women's weight loss program. It's not a diet. It's a program that gives you the facts, motivation and the emotional support you need to help you control your weight…for good. There are Fitness Specialists who work with you to develop an exercise program that will reduce body fat and increase muscle mass, the key to burning more calories. How successful is this program? The average weight loss is more than 20 lbs. And, it's weight most of the people keep off for years.

For more information call Medformation 874-4444.

© 1985 LifeSpan, Inc.

WOMENCARE℠
of Abbott Northwestern Hospital ✿

EXHIBIT 9   Media Split of Communications Budget

		1985			1986		
		Prod.	*Media*	*Total*	*Prod.*	*Media*	*Total*
Medformation	TV	—	—	—	$ 79,000	$278,600	$ 357,600
	Newspaper	$ 24,000	$270,000	$294,000	9,500	98,100	107,600
	Posters	—	—	—	16,500	60,500	77,000
		24,000	270,000	294,000	105,000	437,200	542,200
Tertiary care	TV	64,000	164,000	228,000	108,000	217,350	325,350
	Newspaper	—	—	—	33,600	131,650	165,250
		64,000	164,000	228,000	141,600	349,000	490,600
WomenCare	TV	—	—	—	30,000	57,850	87,850
	Newspaper	35,000	131,400	166,400	9,600	64,850	74,450
	Posters	—	—	—	5,000	10,400	15,400
	Radio	—	—	—	4,500	34,900	39,400
		35,000	131,400	166,400	49,100	168,000	217,100
Trade	Magazine	10,400	17,700	28,100	—	—	—
Total	TV	64,000	164,100	228,100	217,000	553,800	770,800
	Radio	—	—	—	4,500	34,900	39,400
	Newspaper	59,000	401,400	460,400	52,700	294,600	347,300
	Posters	—	—	—	21,500	70,900	92,400
	Magazine	10,400	17,700	28,100	—	—	—
Total		$133,400	$583,200	$716,600	$295,700	$954,200	$1,249,900

SOURCE: LifeSpan, Inc.

LOCTITE CORPORATION: INDUSTRIAL PRODUCTS GROUP

The first place a marketing person has to sell is on the inside—and that's the hardest of all.

Jeffrey Fox, vice president for marketing of Loctite Corporation's Industrial Products Group (IPG), was commenting on the concerns of some Loctite executives regarding the proposed introduction of a simple adhesive dispensing system, tentatively named the Bond-A-Matic 2000.[1]

The system was designed to dispense instant adhesive to bond metals, plastics, rubber, and other materials in manufacturing operations. In September 1978, Fox had to de-

cide whether to recommend full-scale launch of the Bond-A-Matic in early 1979 and, if launched, what marketing strategy to employ.

Company Background

With a product line of over 300 items, Loctite Corporation, headquartered in Newington, Connecticut, was a leader in the development and marketing of high-performance adhesives and sealants for industrial and consumer applications. One of the company's principal objectives was to become the premiere worldwide marketer of instant adhesives for industrial use by 1985.

The company had three major profit centers:

1. IPG was responsible for sales of adhesives to industrial customers in the United States and Canada, both original equipment manufacturers

This case was prepared by Professor John A. Quelch.
Copyright © 1980 by the President and Fellows of Harvard College. Harvard Business School case 581-066 (Rev. 7/15/91).

[1]Permatex, Quick Set, SuperBonder, and Super Glue are registered ® trademarks, and Bond-A-Matic, Duro, Front Line, Gluematic, Tak Pak, and Vari-Drop are ™ trademarks of Loctite Corporation.

(OEMs) and companies in the business of maintenance, repair, and overhaul (MROs). IPG accounted for about 25 percent of Loctite's sales in FY 1978 and was responsible for most of the company's research and development.

2. The Woodhill Permatex Group, accounting for 34 percent of sales, reached the North American do-it-yourself market through 75,000 retail outlets with its Duro product line and Super Glue, which held the second-highest market share among consumer instant adhesives. In addition, it sold the Permatex line of gasketing and adhesive products designed for the automotive aftermarket through 20,000 wholesalers and jobbers to 800,000 professional mechanics.

3. Loctite International, accounting for 41 percent of sales, serviced industrial and consumer markets outside North America.

IPG sales had been growing 25 percent each year and in FY 1978 had reached $32 million.[2] IPG's two principal business units, both of which had profit responsibility, were General Industrial Business (GIB) and Selected Industrial Business (SIB). They accounted for 60 percent and 30 percent of IPG sales, respectively. GIB sold to industrial distributors, who resold to medium and small OEMs and the MRO market. SIB sold direct to large OEMs, such as automobile and farm equipment manufacturers. Over half of SIB's FY 1978 sales were generated by the Systems Division, which manufactured and sold equipment for applying adhesives, both direct to OEMs and through distributors.

The Market for Adhesives

A variety of technologies competed in the industrial adhesive market. They included mature technologies, such as solvent cements and epoxies, and newer technologies, such as anaerobics and cyanoacrylates (CAs). The mature technologies presented numerous problems. For example, solvent cements often were toxic, flammable, and subject to shrinkage after being applied. Epoxies were toxic and inconvenient. Furthermore, they required high-temperature ovens, energy, and significant operator training. On the other hand, 70 percent of IPG's revenues were from anaerobics and CAs.

Anaerobic Adhesives. Anaerobic adhesives were colorless and nontoxic, required no mixing, cured at room temperature, and hardened within a few minutes of application. They were intended to bond cylindrical metal parts (such as a bolt to a nut), a limited application. Increasingly, however, they were viewed as an attractive alternative to traditional mechanical locking devices, such as lock wash-

---

[2]FY 1978 ran from July 1, 1977, through June 30, 1978.

ers and crimped nuts. Through improved locking, sealing, and retaining of mechanical parts subject to stress, anaerobics could prevent leakage, loosening, wear, and corrosion; cut repair and replacement costs; improve energy efficiency; and reduce equipment downtime. Although mechanical locking devices easily could be disassembled for service and inspection, they were often more cumbersome and costly to maintain. Adhesives, however, distributed loads more evenly than mechanical joints, and so permitted more flexibility in product design.

Despite the apparent advantages of anaerobics, North American industry in 1978 still spent almost $4 on mechanical locking devices for every $1 on adhesives. One explanation was that, although metalworking firms could easily be located, considerable sales effort was required to convince mechanical engineers that adhesives could be as effective as metal lock washers. They were skeptical about a chemical solution to a mechanical problem.

As the original patent holder on anaerobic technology, Loctite held an 85 percent share of the North American anaerobic market in 1978. Low capital barriers to entry and expiration of some patents in 1978 had attracted several small European and Japanese competitors, but Loctite believed these companies lacked adequate selling expertise. A more serious threat was 3M Company, whose highly trained sales force had begun to promote anaerobics and CAs aggressively under the Scotch Weld brand name.

Cyanoacrylates. CAs, popularly known as instant adhesives, set faster than anaerobics but were less tough and durable. CAs could be used to bond a broad range of materials, including rubber, plastic, and metal. The first CA was introduced by a division of Eastman Kodak in 1958. During the 1960s, Eastman sold CAs to Loctite for repackaging under the brand name Loctite Quick Set 404. After developing its own manufacturing technology in 1971, IPG introduced its SuperBonder line of CAs. By FY 1978, Loctite was believed to have exceeded Eastman's share of the North American industrial CA market. Eastman sold a line of four CAs through its own sales force and was a particularly important supplier to the electronics industry. Loctite's other significant competitor was the Permabond Division of National Starch and Chemical, Inc., a Unilever subsidiary. Loctite, Eastman, and Permabond collectively accounted for about 75 percent of the industrial CA market, and all were manufactured in the United States. Other competitors sold CAs made in Japan under their own brand names.

Unlike anaerobics, CAs also were sold to consumers. Of the 890,000 pounds of CAs sold in North America during FY 1978, about 625,000 pounds were sold to consumers under brand names, such as Krazy Glue (manufactured by Toagosei in Japan), Super Glue (manufactured by Loctite and sold through its Woodhill Permatex subsidiary), and Elmer's Wonder Bond (marketed by Borden Chemical). The remaining 265,000 pounds were sold to industrial users. Convenience, however, prompted many industrial users, who required only small quantities of CAs, to purchase an additional 25,000 pounds from retailers serving the consumer market.

The total adhesives market was growing at about 10 percent, but CA sales were increasing twice as fast. Industrial usage was expected to outpace consumer market growth significantly, although the industrial market was more vulnerable to economic downturns. Sales of 335,000 pounds were forecast for the industrial market in 1979. CA management was determined to participate in this growth.

Information about the identity of CA's industrial users was sparse. Estimates of actual and potential use of CAs by SIC[3] industry groups during FY 1978 are presented in Exhibit 1. The market for CAs was much broader and more fragmented than that for anaerobics. The principal purchasers of anaerobics were large, easily identifiable firms concentrated in metalworking. Firm size was a poor predictor of CA demand. Small firms (with fewer employees) in such diverse products as electronic circuits, sneakers, and lipstick could be relatively heavy CA users.

SuperBonder Adhesives.   In 1976, there were 11 products in Loctite's SuperBonder line of CAs. They differed in viscosity, curing time, and the materials they were best suited to bond. (Exhibit 2 shows a 1976 sales force data sheet illustrating the line.) Beginning in 1977, IPG executives made efforts both to increase the number of SuperBonder users and to expand the volume purchased by existing users. To this end, several SuperBonder kits were developed for specific industries. The Front Line Tool Box was targeted at mechanics and engineers concerned with sealing pipes and gaskets; and the Tak Pak, a wiretacking kit, was introduced to appeal to the electronics industry. Executives hoped trial of the SuperBonder kits would stimulate brand loyalty and repeat purchases.

During 1977, IPG commissioned a market research study of CA behavior (see Exhibit 3). Partly as a result, it attempted in FY 1978 to give a stronger identity to the SuperBonder brand and to link it more closely to the well-known Loctite name. Packaging was redesigned to distinguish items in the line. The number of SuperBonder adhesives was reduced to five to minimize confusion among end users and distributor salespeople, and to make it easier for distributors to stock the full line (see Exhibit 4). A cap with a built-in applicator allowing greater dispensing control also was introduced on the standard one-ounce bottles. An advertising and promotion budget of $175,000 for FY 1978 was spent primarily on trade magazine advertisements targeted at particular industry segments. The ads (see

Exhibits 5 and 6) aimed to give visibility to instant adhesives, to increase SuperBonder brand awareness, to compare SuperBonder performance with those of competing adhesive technologies, and to highlight Loctite's ability to develop formulations customized for particular industry segments. During FY 1978, SuperBonder advertising expenditures exceeded those of all competing CAs combined.

Industrial sales of SuperBonder adhesives increased from 62,150 pounds in FY 1977 to 91,800 pounds in FY 1978. Their average sales price was $37.45 per pound during FY 1978, of which 52 percent was variable cost. Marketing and selling expenses ordinarily amounted to 30 percent of dollar sales. The rest was available for other overheads, including research and development expenditures, and profit. During FY 1978, 14,200 pounds of Quick Set 404 (Loctite's other CA) were sold at $129.40 per pound. Quick Set 404 had built substantial brand loyalty, so it commanded a premium price. SuperBonder adhesives were priced to attract new users of CAs, rather than current users of Quick Set 404; but they were priced above competitive industrial CAs, which sold at an average of $33 per pound in FY 1978. In FY 1978, Loctite sold $3.44 million of SuperBonder, $1.84 million of Quick Set 404, and $17.12 million of anaerobics.

The SuperBonder marketing plan for FY 1979 would continue the FY 1978 strategy with similar advertising and promotion efforts. Objectives included an increase in sales to $4.5 million, a market share of at least 35 percent across SICs 20 through 39, and a substantial increase in awareness and trial. To broaden the reach of SuperBonder advertising, the FY 1979 media schedule more heavily emphasized general engineering, rather than industry-specific, magazines. The principal innovation for FY 1979 was the introduction of the Gluematic Pen—a hand-held plastic disposable tube of SuperBonder adhesive connected to a spring valve designed to open when applied to a firm surface and close instantly when removed. The valve, called the Gluematic tip applicator, was to facilitate precise placement of the adhesive and prevent clogging inside the pen. The pen was expected to reduce waste, protect users' fingers, and eliminate mess. It was scheduled to be introduced in January 1979 by Woodhill Permatex in a 3-gram size for both industrial and consumer markets.

Distribution and Sales Organization

In 1978, Loctite sold selectively through 285 distributors with 1,400 outlets. Although there were about 10,000 distributors nationwide through which Loctite products could have been distributed, executives believed that their distributors provided good market coverage and superior service. Sixty percent of Loctite's distributors were bearing distributors (who supplied to machinery and equipment manufacturers a diverse range of products costing between $1 and

---

[3]Standard Industrial Classification (SIC) codes denote groups of related industries.

$10,000); 25 percent were general-line distributors; and 15 percent were specialty distributors for a particular market segment, such as the electrical and electronics industry.

Over 50 percent of SuperBonder adhesive sales were made through Loctite's distributors. A higher percentage of Loctite CAs than anaerobics was sold to industrial users through distributors, who typically expected a 25 percent margin on adhesives. They stocked products with established demand. Most distributors avoided stocking equipment that required servicing; however, a distributor might arrange a direct or drop shipment from factory to end user, in which case Loctite would usually pay the distributor 10 percent of the price to the end user.

Relationships with distributors were highly valued. The efforts of IPG salespeople were considered critical to maintaining and developing these relationships. In 1978, 20 IPG salespeople specializing by industry sold CAs and other Loctite products direct to SIB accounts, while 80 GIB salespeople, each with a geographic territory, sold the same product line to distributors. IPG salespeople earned a base salary plus commission on incremental sales over the previous year. The commission percentage was lower on equipment than on adhesives.

Most IPG salespeople were qualified engineers and highly regarded as experts in their field. They were viewed by management as problem solvers, who would work with end users, demonstrating, testing, and recommending the most appropriate adhesive for specific applications. They frequently called on end users with distributor salespeople, who also were usually compensated on a commission basis, complementing the latter's account knowledge with their technical expertise. The Loctite sales force also helped distributors plan their inventories of instant adhesives to maximize return on investment.

In addition, Loctite training programs for distributor and end-user personnel were highly regarded. During 1978, IPG trained 75,000 people in its five technical service and training facilities and its six "labmobiles," which traveled to end-users' plants. IPG also held annual distributor advisory council meetings and published a newsletter, which distributors could deliver to their customers under their own names. Together with consistently high product quality, these services enabled Loctite to command premium prices among both distributors and end users. Distributors were expected to carry a full line of Loctite adhesives, to list Loctite products in their catalogs, and to use Loctite's promotional literature and display materials.

Some IPG executives believed the company should move toward more extensive distribution. They argued that many existing or potential users of Loctite CAs were not reached by existing distributors. In addition, distributor salespeople often called on only one person at a particular firm, and this person might not be the most appropriate or indeed the only person to approach regarding CAs.

The Bond-A-Matic 2000 Dispenser

In FY 1979, IPG also was considering introduction of a unique low-cost adhesive dispensing system using the Gluematic tip. The IPG Systems Division developed the product at the request of the marketing group following the 1977 Sales Leadership Conference, in which several salespeople highlighted the difficulties of assembly line workers in dispensing CA from the standard one-ounce and smaller bottles. Because these bottles were cumbersome, the adhesive frequently clogged in the nozzle. The Systems Division developed a device that could precisely dispense dots, dashes, or lines of adhesive. (The prototype, tentatively named the Bond-A-Matic 2000 dispenser, and the Gluematic Tip are shown in Exhibit 7.) When the reservoir of the Bond-A-Matic dispenser, which held a 1 lb.-container of adhesive, was pressurized, air would force the adhesive through a feed tube to the Gluematic tip.

After extensive testing, two Bond-A-Matic dispenser models were developed: a high-pressure model, with an aluminum reservoir to dispense the more viscous adhesives, and a low-pressure model, with a plastic reservoir to dispense less-viscous adhesives.[4] Material costs were estimated at $105 for the high-pressure model and $75 for the low-pressure model, assuming annual production of at least 250 units each. Variable labor costs for in-house assembly would be $17.50 per unit for both models, or parts assembly could be subcontracted to an outside supplier at $15.75 per unit. By September 1978, prototype development costs had been $18,000 and capital investment had been $30,000. Significant additional capital investment was not anticipated.

The Gluematic tip especially was suited to dispensing adhesives onto hard surfaces. The Vari-Drop applicator was designed for soft surfaces. It dispensed adhesive through a detachable needle, which could be replaced when worn. The needle also could deliver free-falling drops where the applicator tip could not touch the part. Variable costs of each Gluematic tip and each Vari-Drop needle were 25 cents and 15 cents, respectively. Preliminary tests indicated that an operator using the Bond-A-Matic dispenser and Gluematic tip could apply a dot of adhesive every three seconds. Speed of application and durability of the tip depended on the surface and adhesive; however, tests suggested that a tip, if used properly, would be good for at least 12,000 dot applications. An ounce of SuperBonder adhesive could provide at least 850 such applications.

---

[4]The high-pressure model was designed for SuperBonder 430, 414, and 416. The low-pressure model was designed for SuperBonder 420 and 495, though SuperBonder 430 and 414 could also be used. (About half of existing sales were of SuperBonder 420 and 495.)

Fox believed the Bond-A-Matic offered many advantages to the end user, though some might view it as nothing more than an interesting gadget (see Exhibit 8); however, he was not sure how large a market might exist for it. He wondered what level of usage would be sufficient to warrant purchase of the Bond-A-Matic. A related issue was whether its anticlogging feature would stimulate increased sales of instant adhesives or merely highlight to potential users one of their principal problems.

Internal Reaction to the Bond-A-Matic.   Before planning the details of a Bond-A-Matic market introduction, Fox had to consider the likely response of the Systems Division, the IPG sales force, and Loctite's distributors.

During FY 1978, the Systems Division estimated that it secured half the dollar market for instant adhesive applicator control consoles and dispensing heads in North America. Equipment valued at $750,000, much of it customized, was sold direct to SIB customers. Standard models valued at $450,000 were sold direct to GIB customers, with an additional $250,000 worth reaching GIB customers through distributors or drop shipment. The Systems Division had built a reputation for high-quality equipment. Exhibit 9 shows two consoles and a patented pencil-type applicator dispensing head typical of the product line, together with cost and price information. The Model 200 could dispense a variety of adhesives; the more sophisticated and durable Model 205 had been specifically designed to dispense CAs. Both were more precisely engineered than the Bond-A-Matic and included adjustable pressure regulators. The cheapest system (200 console plus applicator) was priced at $725 to end users. Comparable competing equipment was priced as much as one third lower. Competitors were generally small, with limited resources, serving either regional markets or particular industries. None manufactured instant adhesives. They usually sold through independent manufacturers' representatives, rather than direct to users.

Automatic adhesive dispensing equipment generally was purchased by large firms that manufactured products not subject to frequent design changes. Although plant and production engineers often had discretionary purchasing authority on capital equipment of up to $250, the size of the dispensing equipment purchase usually meant that design engineers and the purchasing staff also became involved in the decision-making process.

The Systems Division had designed both Bond-A-Matic models to dispense a broad range of adhesives, including CAs and anaerobics, but the IPG marketing group argued that the Bond-A-Matic should be positioned primarily as a CA dispenser. Systems Division executives wondered how the new dispenser might affect the image of their existing product line, particularly if it carried the Loctite name. They were uncertain whether the Bond-A-Matic would stimulate or cannibalize sales. They doubted that they could rapidly manufacture large quantities of a standard product, and feared being inundated with customer service calls from end users inexperienced with adhesive dispensing equipment. Existing Systems Division equipment sales already required heavy account maintenance.

The Loctite sales force traditionally had not focused on selling equipment. Fox wondered whether it would be interested in learning to demonstrate the Bond-A-Matic and to determine which model and tip best fit each intended application. There was also a risk that, given the limited time of any sales call, salespeople would either ignore the new dispenser or push it at the expense of Loctite's basic products. The cost of a sales call, estimated at $120, would probably preclude visiting a distributor or end user solely to sell the Bond-A-Matic.

Fox also suspected that sales force reaction would depend on the willingness of Loctite's distributors to stock the Bond-A-Matic dispenser and necessary accessories. Distributors would have a stake in its success only if they could be persuaded to stock it.

Developing a Marketing Plan

Product, Pricing, and Quality Assurance.   If the Bond-A-Matic dispenser was introduced, Fox first had to decide which customers to pursue. Only then could he develop a detailed marketing plan and decide whether both models should be made available and whether the Vari-Drop needle as well as the Gluematic tip should be included with each unit. He also had to determine a pricing schedule for the dispenser and accessories. (Exhibit 10 presents one schedule being considered.) Some executives argued that a $175 price might jeopardize Loctite's quality image without encouraging multiple purchases for several work stations in an assembly line.

A further question was whether the Loctite name should appear prominently on each unit. Some executives argued that the Loctite name was associated with high-quality adhesives, not low-cost dispensing equipment, and questioned linking the name with the unproven Bond-A-Matic. They also suggested that the similarity between the names Bond-A-Matic and SuperBonder might jeopardize the favorable brand name recognition recent advertising had built up for SuperBonder should the Bond-A-Matic prove unsuccessful.

Fox was considering two approaches to assure potential end users and distributors of the new dispenser's quality. A 30-day free trial could be introduced, with the purchaser being invoiced at the end of the trial period if the dispenser was not returned. Or, a one-year limited warranty, valid only so long as Loctite adhesives were used in the dispenser, could be offered. A warranty registration card to be returned to Loctite's head office would be included with each unit. This also would allow Loctite to inform purchasers of future product improvements or additions. The Systems Division, however, questioned whether the costs of returned equipment and service repairs associated with these offers would be treated as a marketing or a manufacturing expense.

Advertising. Fox was uncertain whether to use advertising to assist the product launch, since he could not forecast its impact. An advertising campaign might fail; but it also might be too successful, stimulating unmanageable inquiries and orders. But Fox doubted whether advertisements for the Bond-A-Matic dispenser, even if placed in magazines directed at specific industries, could convey a message sufficiently tailored to stimulate purchase. Nevertheless, Loctite's advertising agency had developed the media schedule in Exhibit 11 on the assumption that the dispenser would be introduced early in 1979. Magazines were selected to maximize reach to production and packaging engineers of firms in SICs 35 through 39. Insertions were timed to complement the projected editorial emphasis and SuperBonder advertising in each issue. The agency also recommended that brochures on the Bond-A-Matic be included with all 1 lb.-packages of SuperBonder adhesives and with 10-packs of 1-oz. SuperBonder bottles during the launch period.

Concerns about the content of any advertising centered on whether the price of the dispenser should be included and what degree of emphasis should be placed on the Loctite name. Fox also wondered whether the advertising should be used merely to develop awareness or whether it should actively solicit inquiries and orders. In the latter case, ads could simply include the company's address or incorporate a reply coupon in the body of the advertisement, or the Bond-A-Matic could be included on the multicompany "Bingogram" information request cards included in most industrial magazines. Any inquiries could be followed up with a telephone sales call by Loctite headquarters staff, company salespeople, or an outside telephone sales organization, which would charge $12 per call. Telephone orders might be credited to the salesperson managing the territory from which they originated. If an order came from a firm already using a Loctite distributor, the distributor might receive Loctite's standard 10 percent drop shipment allowance.

Direct-Mail Program. Because of uncertainty that all potential Bond-A-Matic purchasers could be effectively reached through advertising, Fox was considering direct mail as an alternative or supplement to the advertising campaign. Three mailing lists could be purchased from different sources, containing the names and addresses of production and packaging engineers working for firms in SIC categories 35 through 39. The lists would cost as follows: $225 (containing 2,678 names), $675 (14,740 names), and $305 (5,177 names). At a unit cost of $3, a package could be produced and mailed to each individual; this would contain a letter tailored to the recipient's business, a brochure describing the Bond-A-Matic, a reply card, and a Gluematic Pen, which could highlight the dispenser's unique anticlogging feature. Fox hoped that at least 10 percent of the recipients would return the reply cards. Each might then receive a telephone sales call.

EXHIBIT 1 Actual and Potential Usage of Instant Adhesives in the Industrial Market, FY 1978

SIC Code	Industry	Number of Establishments	Instant Adhesives Usage (lbs.)	Percent of User Establishments	Additional % of Potential User Establishments
20–24	Food, textile, wood products	92,874	4,700	5.0%	7.6%
26–27	Paper and printing	62,872		14.3	6.4
25	Furniture	13,845	9,500	12.0	20.2
28–29	Chemicals, petroleum products	20,167	15,850	12.5	6.0
33–35	Metal products, machinery	102,523	48,200	14.7	7.8
36	Electrical and electronic equipment	19,610	42,000	26.7	18.3
38	Scientific instruments, photo equipment, watches	10,143	10,650	27.6	20.1
30–31	Rubber, plastic, leather products	16,332		15.3	9.7
32	Stone, clay, glass products	19,190	27,350	15.1	3.8
37	Transportation equipment	11,771		17.3	15.2
39	Jewelry, toys, sporting goods	23,904		24.6	18.7
40–49	Transportation, communications, utilities	135,657	16,000	11.8	7.1
70, 72, 73	Personal, tourist, business services	282,239	8,450	8.3	6.2
75	Motor vehicle services	89,257	58,900	36.1	10.1
76	Appliance repair	85,838	13,500	30.8	4.1
78–80	Entertainment and health services	42,001	9,900	10.1%	5.6%

SOURCE: Company records.

Exhibit 2

1976 SuperBonder line sales force data sheet

LOCTITE®
SUPERBONDER®
**Adhesives for
Product Assembly**

Loctite SuperBonders are rapid setting (fixturing in 1-30 seconds) adhesives, engineered to meet varied product assembly needs, providing advantages over conventional assembly techniques...

**SuperBonder Adhesives
Reduce Direct Costs**
• Save labor and time
• Waiting periods can be reduced between on-line assembly operations
• Mechanical fastening techniques (fasteners, keys, retaining rings, etc.) can be replaced with rapid setting bonds
• Part tolerances can be reduced
• Weight of final assembly can be reduced by eliminating mechanical components

**SuperBonder Adhesives
Reduce Indirect Costs**
• Capital investment in assembly tooling is eliminated
• Inventory carrying costs are minimized
• Handling and secondary processing costs for mechanical fastenings are eliminated.

**SuperBonder Adhesives
Improve Product Reliability**
• Sealing components as they are joined
• Tamper proofing
• "Unitizing" assembly, increasing vibration-resistance
• Distributing working stresses more evenly than mechanical fastening techniques

**SuperBonder Adhesives
Increase Finished
Product Value**
• Aesthetic advantage of colorless bonding
• Performance advantage of improved reliability

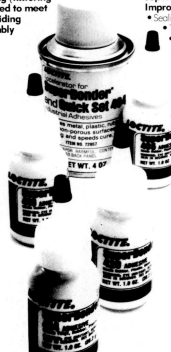

EXHIBIT 3   Selected Findings of Instant Adhesive Industrial Market Research Study

---

- 16% of all firms used instant adhesives. In only 16 SIC industry groups did more than 10% of the firms use instant adhesives.
- 55% of volume was accounted for by small firms with fewer than 20 employees.
- 71% of purchasers used the product in only one application.
- 64% of volume was used by OEMs, 36% was used by MROs. Many firms used instant adhesives in OEM applications alone.
- 62% of users purchased their instant adhesives through distributors; 3% purchased direct from manufacturers; and 35% purchased from retail stores.
- 81% of users stated that all instant adhesives were about the same price; 67% of purchasers from distributors and manufacturers and 75% of retail purchasers stated that price was not very important in instant adhesive purchase decisions.
- 72% of purchasers from distributors and manufacturers and 45% of retail purchasers stated that technical service was important in their choice of an instant adhesive supplier.
- 67% of brand purchases from distributors and manufacturers and 84% of retail purchases were specified by production, quality control, design, and plant engineers in larger firms, and by company presidents in firms with fewer than 20 employees. Employees and users specified brands on 18% and 9% of purchase occasions, and purchasing agents on 12% and 6% of purchase occasions respectively.
- 11% of firms using instant adhesives purchased 10 or more pounds annually; 29% purchased between 1 and 9 pounds; 60% purchased less than a pound. Many purchasers were uncertain about the exact volume and cost of instant adhesives they used.
- 26% of current users expected to increase their usage of instant adhesives, 51% expressed interest in improving dispensing technology.
- 64% of instant adhesive users did not have a preferred brand, though 97% were satisfied with the products they used; 21% of users could recall the SuperBonder brand name.
- 72% of nonusers of instant adhesives stated that price was not a barrier to their use; 19% stated they had an assembling/fastening operation where instant adhesives might be used; 15% had received sales calls regarding instant adhesives. Among nonusers, there was a low knowledge of instant adhesives and their capabilities.

SOURCE: Company records

EXHIBIT 4   SuperBonder Adhesives' Benefits, Characteristics, and Typical Applications

Product Benefits

Speed assembly and test
- Bond most materials in less than 30 seconds without pressure—simplifies fixturing and clamping

Easy to use
- Single component—no mixing
- No surface preparation normally required
- Bond materials to each other or in any combination

Improve product reliability
- Bonds have high strength—up to 5000 psi
- Bonds have good solvent and weather resistance

Speed production
- Loctite SuperBonder adhesives can be automatically dispensed in as small a volume as 0.001cc at a rate of 60 cycles per minute

Economical to use
- Eliminate need for costly heat and curing ovens—Loctite SuperBonder adhesives cure at room temperature
- Low cost-per-unit application—one pound contains 40,000 drops at an approximate cost of $\frac{1}{7}$ cent per drop

Preserve product attractiveness
- Bond is colorless and transparent
- Negligible shrinkage—no solvent to evaporate
- Automatic application virtually eliminates clean-up problems

Product Characteristics

SuperBonder 420 Adhesive
- Low viscosity
- Very fast setting
- Bonds rubber, plastics, or in combination with metals
- Penetrating action
- Parts should be closely matched

SuperBonder 495 (IS04E) Adhesive
- Medium-to-low viscosity
- Fast setting
- Bonds rubbers and plastics or in combination with metals
- Parts should be closely matched

SuperBonder 430 (IS06) Adhesive
- Medium viscosity
- Fast setting
- Bonds metal and plastic
- Parts should be well matched

SuperBonder 414 Adhesive
- Medium viscosity
- Fast setting
- Excellent for metal and plastic bonding or in combination to themselves
- Moderate strength on hard-to-bond plastics such as polyethylene and polypropylene

SuperBonder 416 Adhesive
- High viscosity
- Bonds irregular or porous surfaces
- Excellent for bonding rubber and plastic parts

Exhibit 5

1978 SuperBonder magazine advertisement

SuperBonder® Instant Adhesive assembly cost: 6¢

Mechanical fastener assembly cost: 30¢

Loctite® SuperBonder® Instant Adhesives cut your assembly costs. They cost less to buy than mechanical fasteners. And take less time to use. Because they reduce or eliminate the clamping, drilling, tapping, screwing, countersinking and torquing that make mechanical fasteners so time consuming, and expensive.

SuperBonder Instant Adhesives are instant setting. Instant curing. Bond almost any material in 1 to 30 seconds with a continuous, stress resistant bond.

Loctite will give you the right SuperBonder Instant Adhesive for the job, get it on line, and service what we sell better than any other adhesive manufacturer in the world.

The #1 threadlocking company is also the #1 engineering adhesive company.

For further information or a free demonstration call your local Loctite distributor. For his name and number, call 1-800-243-8810. In CT call 1-800-842-8684. In Canada call (416) 625-6511.

LOCTITE® SuperBonder® Instant Adhesives

© 1979 Loctite Corporation, Newington, CT 06111
Loctite Canada, Inc., Mississauga, Ontario L4W 2S3

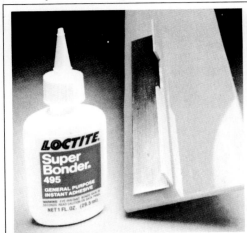
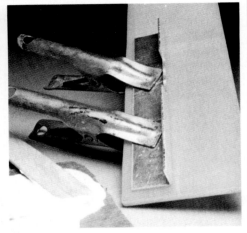

Exhibit 7

Prototype Bond-A-Matic 2000 dispenser and Gluematic tip applicator

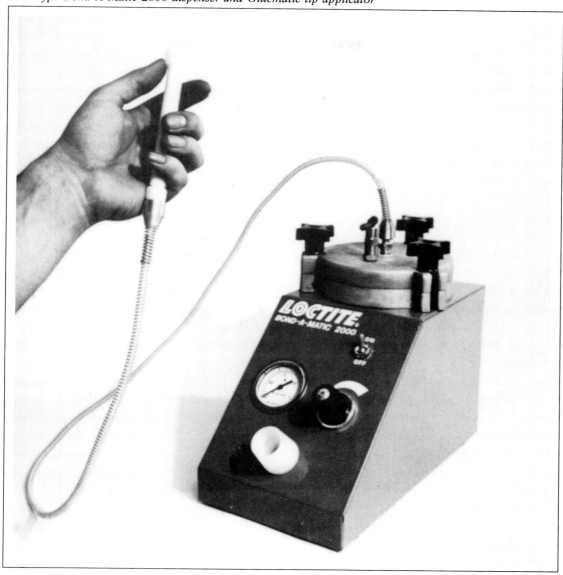

EXHIBIT 8   Features of the Bond-A-Matic 2000 Dispensing System

- Anticlog application using the Gluematic tip.
- No mess or waste.
- Simple, inexpensive maintenance.
- Short startup and shutdown time (2 minutes each).
- Average operator training time of 15 minutes.
- Easy loading of 1-lb. or 150-ml containers.
- Portable; weighs less than 10 lbs.
- Only one cubic foot of space required.

- Hand-activated; shuts off automatically when pressure is released.
- No electrical connection requirement.
- Adjustable pressure range, handling most Loctite adhesives with varying viscosities.
- Faster parts assembly.
- Decreased assembly error, increased product reliability, and reduced scrap and rework costs.
- More accurate control of labor and material costs.

SOURCE: Company records.

EXHIBIT 9

Systems Division applicator control consoles and dispensing heads

Model 200 Control Console
End-user price: $450
Drop shipment price: $405
Total manufacturing cost: $300
Variable cost: $255

Model 27A Pencil Applicator
End-user price: $275
Drop shipment price: $247.50
Total manufacturing cost: $186
Variable cost: $160

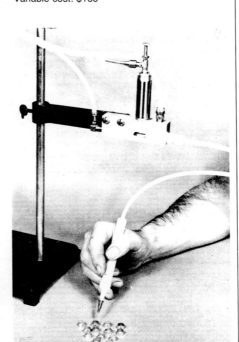

Model 205 Control Console
End-user price: $995
Drop shipment price: $895.50
Total manufacturing cost: $670
Variable cost: $570

SOURCE: Company records.

Exhibit 10   Proposed Distributor and End-User Price Schedule for Bond-A-Matic 2000 Dispenser and Replacement Parts

	Suggested Price to End User	*Loctite Price to Distributor*
Bond-A-Matic 2000 (both low- and high-pressure models)	$175.00	140.00
Gluematic tip	1.00	0.75
Vari-Drop dispensing needle	0.50	0.28
Vari-Drop applicator	22.00	15.00
Feed line replacement kit	27.00	18.75
Airline filter replacement kit	14.25	9.95

NOTE: Loctite would receive $157.50 ($175.00 less a 10% drop shipment allowance to the local distributor) on a direct sale to an end user.
SOURCE: Company records.

Exhibit 11   Proposed Media Schedule for Bond-A-Matic and SuperBonder: First Half of 1979

Magazine	*Circulation*	*January*	*February*	*March*	*April*	*May*	*June*	*Cost of BAM Advertising*
Assembly Engineering	74,570		SB		BAM	BAM	BAM	$ 9,375
Design News	149,307		SB	SB	SB	SB	SB	
Electronic Products	93,196				BAM	BAM	BAM	8,190
Industrial Equipment News	186,796		SB	SB	SB	SB	SB	
					BAM	BAM	BAM	13,320
Production Engineering	92,660				BAM	BAM	BAM	11,130
Production	80,063				BAM	BAM	BAM	9,801
Total								$51,816

NOTE: All four-color, full-page advertisements. BAM denotes an advertisement for the Bond-A-Matic, SB an advertisement for SuperBonder.
SOURCE: Mintz & Hoke, Inc.

APPENDIXES

LEGAL RESTRICTIONS ON MARKETING MANAGEMENT

Introduction

Every day marketing managers make strategy and implementation decisions that are constrained or influenced by the myriad laws and regulations designed to promote competition, protect the consumer, and enhance public welfare. Every day judges, legislators, and regulators apply, reexamine, and amend those laws and regulations in an ongoing effort to recreate a system that even better serves society's interests. While marketers may not always agree with the wisdom of the laws and regulations they face, it is vital for both their corporations and themselves that they become familiar with them.

One of the marketing managers' most frequently voiced complaints concerns the number and breadth of the legal and regulatory restrictions that impact their strategic and implementation decisions. These restrictions range from laws that deal with collusive price stabilization to celebrity endorsements, from implied warranties to discriminatory advertising allowances, and on and on. They exist at the federal and state level, and vary by state. They are derived from statutes, judicial decisions, and the charters and rule-making powers of many regulatory agencies and commissions. Even in the current era of deregulation and "free market economics," the body of law and regulation that affects marketers is enormous.

This note will introduce some of the most important aspects of the marketer's legal environment. The note is restricted to an examination of U.S. law,[1] but is by no means a complete treatment of it, nor even an extensive survey. It focuses on general laws and regulations that affect marketers in many industries. Unfortunately, the industry-specific laws and regulations that often will be most central to the marketer's decisions cannot be treated in a note of this kind. Corporations employ highly trained internal and external legal counsel, who should be consulted for answers to specific questions and for general guidance in the marketing manager's particular

---

This note was prepared by Assistant Professor Patrick J. Kaufmann.

Copyright © 1987 by the President and Fellows of Harvard College.

Harvard Business School note 9-588-009 (Rev. 1/89).

[1]The applicability of U.S. antitrust law to a case involving foreign commerce is a complex question beyond the scope of this note. The general rule is that U.S. law applies when there is an impact on U.S. commerce, but does not apply when that impact is a result of a foreign "act of state."

industry and area of responsibility. It is important, however, for the marketer to become as familiar as possible with the general issues in his or her legal environment.

The note is organized around familiar marketing decision variables: price, distribution, promotion, and product policy. Only *legal* constraints are examined; *ethical* issues represent an equally important but different dimension of the marketing manager's decision environment. While the law may offer rough guidance about the ethics of a particular decision or activity, by no means should mere legality be equated with ethical behavior.

Price

Although most managers know that agreements between competitors to fix prices are illegal, many are unaware of how far reaching pricing regulations are.

The impact of the legal environment of the pricing decision takes two basic forms. First, there are laws prohibiting certain activities that are presumed to interfere with the natural tendency of competition to push prices down toward cost plus a normal return on investment; the Sherman Act's condemnation of price fixing falls into this category. Second, there are laws that deal with a firm's decisions regarding prices charged particular customers; for example, the Robinson-Patman Act's requirement that a firm's competing customers be offered the same price (barring certain exceptions).

Price Fixing and Horizontal Market Allocation

Questions about pricing normally fall within the purview of that body of law called antitrust. The first antitrust statute, the Sherman Act, was passed in 1890 and provides that agreements between competitors to distort the natural forces of competition are illegal. Those illegal practices include not only agreements between competitors that fix, set, or stabilize prices but also agreements that allocate particular markets or customers (assumed ultimately to affect prices as well). For example, competing oil companies might agree to sell their gasoline only in particular areas of the country and not overlap into others' territories. The obvious result of that agreement would be that each could increase its prices. The argument that the real purpose of such an agreement was not anticompetitive is not an acceptable defense. An agreement that fixes prices or allocates markets between competitors is illegal per se (i.e., in and of itself) and the motives of the parties are irrelevant.[2]

Furthermore, the parties need not be successful in their endeavor in order to be prosecuted; the Sherman Act also covers mere conspiracy to restrict competition. In the example above, if some of the oil companies could not be convinced to join the market allocation scheme, the nonjoiners might put enough competitive pressure on local markets so prices couldn't be raised. Although the scheme would fail, the conspirators still would face possible prosecution.

---

[2]Agreements between competitors (e.g., to fix prices or allocate markets) are referred to as *horizontal agreements* and are per se illegal. Agreements between buyers and sellers within a channel of distribution (e.g., to set up an exclusive territory) are referred to as *vertical agreements*. Some are per se illegal while some are examined under a "Rule of Reason" to determine whether they are, in fact, anticompetitive. See the Distribution section.

Nor is there a need for direct evidence of a real "agreement" between the parties. Merely sharing pricing information about specific customers, together with subsequent price stability, could lead a court to infer an agreement. For example, competitors who meet and agree to provide each other with the names of customers and the prices at which they sold to them might be presumed to have done so to reduce the customers' ability to bargain among suppliers. The court, therefore, could draw the inference that such actions were designed to reduce price fluctuations normally caused by competition in the market.

The Sherman Act is vague and broadly interpreted. Penalties for violations can include up to $1 million fines (per violation) for the corporation, and $100,000 fines and/or three-year prison terms for individuals. The act covers not only agreements between competitors referred to above but also monopolization by a single firm. Monopolization occurs when a firm actively uses its dominant market power to manipulate the price of a product or otherwise restrain competition.

Another antitrust statute, the Clayton Act, allows injured parties to bring civil suits against antitrust violators and provides for successful plaintiffs to receive judgments of three times the damages proven to have been suffered due to the illicit agreements. For example, if the injured party proves that the damages suffered amounted to $1 million, $3 million is awarded. This is done to punish the offender and discourage such activity, as well as to encourage private enforcement of the law. In addition to the Justice Department and injured parties, the Federal Trade Commission can prosecute individuals and corporations for these kinds of practices. The FTC act, making "unfair methods of competition" illegal, has been interpreted to include violations of the Sherman and Clayton acts.

Simply stated, therefore, marketers should avoid any discussions with competitors, especially those concerning prices, markets, and specific customers. If innocent discussions with competitors are necessary (e.g., the creation of industry safety standards), the parties should seek legal advice to learn the best way to avoid legal misinterpretation.

Resale Price Maintenance

Another form of pricing agreement prohibited under the Sherman Act, but one which does not involve competitors, is resale price maintenance. Products reach the consumer through channels of distribution. The demand for the product at any level in the channel of distribution is derived from the demand at the lower levels. Assuming a two-level channel of distribution, where manufacturer sells to retailer who sells to consumer, demand at the manufacturer's level is derived from the demand at the retail level. The manufacturer may feel that a low retail price would hurt the brand's image or that high levels of retail service are indispensable to its marketing plan. Such service only may be possible if sufficiently high retail prices are available to provide the necessary distribution margins. The prevailing retail price, therefore, is of great concern to the manufacturer.

Although the manufacturer can suggest and even advertise suggested retail prices, it is illegal for the manufacturer to obtain from the retailer an agreement regarding the price at which the retailer will sell the product. A threat to cut off the retailer's supply, together with the retailer's coerced promise to maintain the desired price, can constitute such an "agreement." For example, a manufacturer finds that a retailer is constantly discounting a product for which the manufacturer wants to create a prestige image, and the manufacturer tells the retailer that it is considering not selling to the retailer any longer. If the retailer responds by saying that it won't discount the product anymore, and the manufacturer continues to supply the product, the conversation would constitute a price maintenance agreement. Legal scholars, however, do differ on whether mere compliance by the retailer in response to the manufacturer's threat (i.e., without the retailer's communication of intent) would constitute an agreement.

Sellers are generally free to choose with whom they will do business. A manufacturer, therefore, legally can choose not to sell to known price cutters, and *may* be able legally to stop selling to someone who has begun cutting prices. Such termination of a price cutter is extremely hazardous, however. If there is any attempt to use the threat of termination to curtail the price-cutting behavior, rather than merely terminating the price-cutting distributor, the manufacturer may be found to have engaged in resale price maintenance. Moreover, the termination of a price-cutting distributor for unrelated reasons often results in a law suit by the angry distributor claiming the real reason for dismissal was to maintain resale prices. For many years, complaints from full price dealers and the resulting termination of a price cutter by the supplier was found to constitute resale price maintenance and was, therefore, per se illegal. Recently the Supreme Court clarified its position, finding that, unless the supplier had entered into a specific agreement about price with the remaining dealers, such a termination was only a nonprice vertical restraint and should be judged under the Rule of Reason to determine whether it was anticompetitive.

Discriminatory Pricing

Pricing-related violations of the antitrust laws can occur without any agreement with competitors or channel members. The complex and often criticized Robinson-Patman Act (the 1936 amendment to Section 2 of the Clayton Act) precludes price discrimination (i.e., charging different customers different prices for the same product) where the effect may be to lessen competition substantially. Such an effect has generally been inferred if the customers are competing with one another. For example, if a dairy were to offer milk to a large chain at a lower price than to the mom and pop grocery store next door, the inferred effect would be to give the chain a competitive advantage over the small grocer. The defendant supplier can, however, introduce evidence of the competitive health of the industry to rebut that inference.

Discrimination between competing customers in advertising and promotion allowances also is prohibited under the act. For example, when a cosmetic firm offers a demonstration person to a department store, it must offer a proportionally equivalent promotion to a small competing drug store. The amount of the promotion is prorated on the basis of account size and probably would not include a demonstration person, but rather some point-of-purchase displays or other types of sales aid.

There are a number of defenses to charges of price discrimination. For example, sellers can offer a discriminatory price in order to meet (not beat) a competitor's offered price to the same customer. Price differences that are cost-justified because of the efficiencies realized by selling to a particular customer are also allowed (n.b., this exception has been notoriously hard to prove in court and usually requires detailed cost data unavailable in many companies). Moreover, volume discounts are permitted under the statute. However, volume discounts must be graduated to be functionally available to competing customers. For example, it might be difficult to justify a major price discount offered on such a large amount of product that the discount is available only to one customer capable of purchasing that amount. It should be noted that these defenses are applicable only to price discrimination and not to discriminatory advertising or promotional allowances.

The Robinson-Patman Act (historically called the anti-chain store act) was designed to protect small businesses from the cost advantage large chains enjoyed due to their tremendous buying power. Because it precludes sellers from offering discounts to some customers, the Robinson-Patman Act can be criticized for keeping prices higher than they would be, thereby contradicting the policy expressed in the Sherman Act. In recent years, neither the Justice Department nor the Federal Trade Commission has prosecuted actively under Robinson-Patman. Marketers should still beware, however, since civil actions by private injured parties are permitted under the act and treble damages available to those who prevail.

Predatory Pricing

Predatory pricing is another pricing practice that may precipitate prosecution or civil litigation under the antitrust laws. Essentially, predatory pricing is the attempt to enhance one's competitive position by driving a competitor from the market instead of improving one's own performance. As evidence of predatory intent, courts often use patterns of pricing below average variable cost. For example, if an established manufacturer with variable cost of $5/unit was selling its product at $4/unit in a market that a competitor was trying to enter, the court might interpret it as an intent to drive the competitor from the market. Parties engaged in predatory pricing sometimes subsidize below-cost pricing in markets where the target competition exists with profits from less-competitive markets. (This also has been called *primary line price discrimination,* because the anticompetitive effect takes place on the manufacturer's, not customer's, level.) The question becomes whether the pricing policy merely reflects fair, hard competition or an attempt specifically to injure the competitor. Commonly heard statements by marketers about "destroying this or that competitor" make corporate attorneys cringe when these are coupled with significant market power and pricing behavior that is hard to justify strictly economically.

Like price discrimination, rules against predatory pricing seem inconsistent with overall antitrust policy. Some analysts argue that rules against predatory pricing create an unwanted and unwarranted chilling effect on hard competition. Nevertheless, the marketer should be aware that pricing below variable cost under certain circumstances can expose the individual and firm to liability. Therefore, the marketer should consult the company's attorney if he or she intends to price this way, or faces a competitor who is doing so.

Distribution

As with pricing decisions, antitrust law covers the central legal issues involving distribution. Legal constraints on the marketer's decisions regarding the distribution system fall into three general categories: (1) product mix requirements or restrictions; (2) territory, location, or customer restrictions; and (3) pricing restrictions (vertical price restrictions—that is, resale price maintenance agreements—were covered in the preceding pricing section).[3]

---

[3]Although treated differently from other types of vertical restraints, resale price maintenance has much the same rationale behind it (i.e., to increase the amount of interbrand competition in a particular market). Consequently, many legal scholars have argued that it should be treated the same as territorial restrictions, instead of being per se illegal like horizontal price fixing.

Product Mix Requirements and Restrictions

Product mix issues arise when (1) a marketer refuses to sell a distributor (i.e., wholesaler, retailer) a desired product unless another brand or product is purchased, also; or (2) a marketer tries to keep competitors' products out of the marketer's distribution outlets. The first of these practices is called *tying,* and the second is called *exclusive dealing.* Tying is a violation of both the Sherman Act and the Clayton Act and is per se illegal. An exclusive dealing agreement is a violation of the Clayton Act if it may "substantially lessen competition or tend to create a monopoly."

Tying is essentially an effort to use the market power of one brand to help another. For tying to occur there must be two products (or brands), a requirement that they be bought together, and economic power in the tying product sufficient to appreciably restrain competition in the tied product. For example, if a maker of the dominant brand of toothbrushes entered the toothpaste business and refused to sell toothbrushes to any distributor who didn't also sell its toothpaste, the manufacturer could face prosecution. The central question would be whether the brand of toothbrushes had the type of market power that allowed the manufacturer to force the toothpaste on unwilling distributors.

This reasoning has been extended to include franchisor trademarks as possible tying products. Because the only source of the trademark is the franchisor, the trademark may have the same monopoly power of a patented product; when that power is used to require purchases of other products, prosecution for tying can result. For example, if a franchisor of an established chain of restaurants refuses to sell franchise rights to use that trademark unless the franchisee agrees also to buy napkins or paper cups (items for which specifications for outside sourcing could easily be written) from the franchisor, the franchisor could be prosecuted (or suited by the franchisees) for tying. It should be noted that the franchisor may be able to require the franchisee to buy from it such products as a special spice mixture because to specify the contents for outside sourcing would require the disclosure of trade secrets.

Exclusive dealing refers to an agreement between a manufacturer and distributor whereby the distributor agrees not to carry competing brands. This agreement may be illegal if the manufacturer enforces it by refusing to sell to the distributor or by refusing to grant the distributor the same price unless the distributor acquiesces. The question will be whether competitors have been foreclosed from a substantial line of distribution. If the amount of trade handled by the distributor or covered by the agreement is substantial—either in absolute or market share terms—the manufacturer may be liable under the Clayton Act.

Territory, Location, and Customer Restrictions

Another form of distribution restriction involves agreements about from where and to whom the distributor can sell. These agreements take several forms; some specify the location from which a retailer can sell, some segment customers assign segments to specific distributors, some restrict the territories in which distributors can solicit or accept business. Generally, these types of agreements are part of a market allocation system by which the marketer grants each distributor exclusive rights to a particular territory or customer group so each is shielded from "intrabrand" competition. By doing so, the marketer hopes to provide an environment wherein the distributor can engage in interbrand competition more effectively. For example, a camera retailer might wish to hire expert (and expensive) retail salespeople to provide customers with important information about the marketer's brand of camera versus other brands. The retailer may not wish to do so, however, if the benefits of providing that information are shared by other lower-cost/lower-price dealers located nearby selling the same camera. To encourage effective interbrand competition, therefore, marketers may try to limit intrabrand competition by permitting only a limited number of retailers to carry the product and limiting their ability to change location. This is sometimes referred to as *selective,* as opposed to intensive, *distribution.*

Prior to 1977, both horizontal and vertical territorial restrictions were per se illegal. In 1977, the Supreme Court decided the landmark *Sylvania* case, thereby radically changing the law concerning vertical territorial restrictions (i.e., within the channel of distribution, not between competitors). In response to increasing competition in the television market and decreasing market share, Sylvania had decided to switch to a selective distribution strategy with a limited number of distributors serving specific territories. One dealer violated the agreement by opening a new store out of its territory without Sylvania's permission. Sylvania terminated the dealer and the dealer claimed the territorial restrictions were in restraint of trade. The court found that the test of illegality for vertical territorial restrictions was to balance the restrictions' negative effects on intrabrand competition with their positive effects on interbrand competition. The restrictions are allowed if the net result is that more overall competition is in the market. This is referred to as a *Rule of Reason* test and is contrasted with the per se rule applicable to horizontal agreements. In Sylvania's case, the increase in dealer dedication produced by the selective distribution system allowed Sylvania to once again become competitive with other brands. The restrictions, therefore, had a positive effect on interbrand competition.

Promotion

Although there are many regulations and laws dealing with specific issues of promotion and advertising, the most important statute is Section 5 of the Federal Trade Commission Act. Section 5 makes "unfair or deceptive acts or practices" illegal, while other sections of the act empower the FTC to prosecute and adjudicate such violations.

Unfair Acts or Practices

The FTC's primary focus has always been on "deceptive acts or practices." In the 1970s, however, the term *unfair* allowed the FTC to venture into the regulation of unscrupulous and unethical conduct. In recent years, the FTC has been more restrained in its interpretation of "unfair acts or practices," confining it to instances of substantial consumer injury that the consumer could not avoid by acting reasonably, and balancing the injury against any positive effects the act may have on consumers and competition.

One of the prime targets of inquiry under these criteria has been advertising for children. For example, the FTC obtained a cease and desist order precluding a bicycle manufacturer from running an advertisement that showed children riding their bicycles through an intersection without stopping.

Deceptive Acts or Practices

In deciding what is deceptive, the FTC will try to determine whether an advertisement has the tendency or capability of deceiving even a small but significant number of credulous consumers. In doing so, the FTC uses both available proof and its own expertise to examine the advertisement.

The FTC has singled out some areas for special treatment. For example, in 1980 the FTC issued a guide on the types of endorsements it considers deceptive. The guide covers both celebrity and consumer endorsements and requires, among other things, that celebrities actually use the product and that there is reason to believe that they continue to use it as long as the advertisement runs.

When an advertisement has been found deceptive, the FTC can issue an order requiring the company to cease running it. It also can require that, before the advertisement runs again, it be altered with wording that removes the deception. At one time the FTC also used corrective advertising orders, compelling companies to run a specified number of additional advertisements designed to correct consumer misperceptions created by deceptive advertisements. Because FTC actions can lead to expensive legal procedures and disrupt ongoing marketing programs, marketers and their advertising agencies must be sensitive to the mere possibility for deception in their advertising. It is not enough that the marketer or other intelligent individuals would not be deceived, the advertisements must be examined from the perspective of the naive, credulous, and even ignorant consumer who also is protected under this law.

Product Policy

Four important areas of the law that impact the marketer's product policy decisions are: (1) patents, trademarks, and copyrights; (2) warranties; (3) product liability; and (4) product safety regulation. Unlike pricing and distribution issues, antitrust law does not cover these areas of the marketer's legal environment; they are, instead, the subject of a broad conglomeration of statutes, regulations, and court-made law.

Patents, Trademarks, and Copyrights

The word *patent*, meaning open, is derived from *litterea patentes*—open letters from the king bestowing monopoly rights over a product or manufacturing process to a favored subject. Subsequently, those rights were granted as a reward for a limited time only to the inventor of the product or process.

To be patentable under U.S. law, a product, process, or machines employed in that process must be new, nonobvious, useful, capable of doing what it claims, and adequately described in the documentation. All patents are granted for 17 years and cannot be renewed. If granted, a patent confers exclusive rights to the product, process, or machine. A patent holder does not need to use a patent for it to remain intact. If another marketer intentionally or inadvertently introduces the patented product or one not clearly distinguishable from it, the patent holder can sue for an injunction and for damages for patent infringement. Therefore, new products must be checked to ensure they do not infringe on existing patents.

Trademarks are similar to brands in that they embody the marketer's investment in creating a meaning or image attached to and conveyed by some mark or symbol. A trademark specifies the source of the product and provides information about the product because of its source. Trademark law, therefore, protects the consumer by ensuring the product is made by a familiar and trusted producer. Furthermore, it protects the marketer by allowing him or her to invest in quality products and by creating a reputation for quality without fear of another usurping those investments.

Trademarks do not have to be registered to be protected from infringement. Registering a trademark, however, provides procedural protections, such as dated constructive notice to the public that a trademark exists (i.e., the public is legally presumed to have been notified as of that date). Because trademarks may not always be registered, the marketer desiring to introduce a new mark should employ a specialist in trademark searches prior to investing in the trademark's development, and then register the new trademark immediately.

If a trademark becomes a general term, it can be lost by the company and become part of the public domain. This happened to cellophane and could happen to brands like Kleenex®, Xerox®, or Rollerblade®. When the trademark stops indicating the specific manufacturer and begins to be synonymous with the product, the manufacturer's exclusive right to the trademark can be lost. The manufacturer must protect the trademark by ensuring that it is always used as a reference to the source of the product and not the product itself (e.g., "Buy Kleenex® *tissue*").

In the same way that patents encourage invention, and trademarks encourage investment in a reputation for quality, copyright encourages the production of thought. The Copyright Act of 1976 provides protection for a wide range of forms of expression, from books and music to computer programs and data bases. To be protected, any publicly distributed copies must be labeled with the symbol © (℗ for sound reproduction), the author's name, and the date first published. It also is necessary to register the work with the Copyright Office.

Warranty

Warranties are based on the law of contract, and covered by the Uniform Commercial Code and the Magnuson-Moss Warranty Act. A warranty is essentially a statement about a product that the buyer relies on as true. If it is not true, the seller has not sold the buyer what was promised and has breached the contract. The buyer can then sue the seller for damages. These damages can include personal injury or economic damages as long as they were caused by the product's failure to live up to the standard promised by the seller.

If the statement about the product is expressly made by the seller, it is called an *express warranty*. Such a statement may take the form of a fact, promise, description, or model. If, and only if, the buyer has relied on its truth in purchasing the product, the seller is bound by it. The product may contain no defect whatsoever and yet may not meet the standard set by the express warranty.

Other warranties are not expressly made by the seller, but still become part of the bargain. If the seller is a merchant (i.e., someone in the business of selling a particular item), there is an implied warranty of "merchantability" for all goods sold in the course of that business. Merchantability means that the product would pass without objection in the trade, be of fair and average quality, be of reasonably even quality and quantity across all units, be adequately packaged and labeled, and conform to affirmations on the label. Whether the marketer intends to promise those things about the product or not, he or she is deemed to have done so merely by being in the business and offering the product for sale. The warranty is implied, and , if the product does not meet those standards, the buyer can sue for damages.

A marketer can avoid express warranties simply by not making the statements. A marketer can avoid implied warranties by conspicuously disclaiming the implied warranty of merchantability (using that term). Successfully disclaiming implied warranties in consumer sales is much more difficult than in sales to other businesses. Under the Magnuson-Moss Warranty Act, if a firm enters into a written warranty or service contract, implied warranties can be limited to the length of the written warranty but cannot entirely be disclaimed. Magnuson-Moss describes the specific terminology and procedures necessary to create and disclaim various warranties.

A final type of warranty ensures that the product is fit for a particular purpose. If the seller knows that the product will be used for a particular purpose (e.g., a car will be used to pull a house trailer), and the buyer is relying on the seller's knowledge of whether the product will do that job, the seller is deemed to have warranted the product fit for that purpose. As in the case with express warranty, the product may be entirely without defect (e.g., a four-cylinder subcompact that performs perfectly well under normal conditions), and yet it may not be up to the more rigorous standard of fitness for the particular purpose the buyer intended (e.g., pulling a heavy house trailer).

Product Liability

While warranties are based on contract law (i.e., express or implied promises about the product), product liability is based on tort law (i.e., the requirement that persons and companies exercise due care not to injure others). Like warranties, product liability can be divided into product disappointment cases and product defect cases. Even if the product is without defect, a marketer can be held liable if he or she makes important statements to a buyer about the product that are not true, and which the marketer knew or should have known were false. This is called the *tort of misrepresentation.*

Product defect cases arise in three ways. A manufacturer can be negligent in the way it designs, manufacturers, or markets its products. Even a product designed and manufactured with the utmost care can be made dangerous if marketed incorrectly. For example, some critics believed that one company's policy of providing free infant formula to Third World mothers while still in the hospital produced a dangerous product. The criticism was that this marketing strategy created a dependency on the product that the mother could not afford to support after leaving the hospital. This caused the mothers to dilute the formula, thereby endangering the infants' health. Negligent marketing of a product can include failure to attach warnings or instructions necessary for safe operation, use, or enjoyment of the product. For example, a chain saw without proper operating instructions and warnings is a lethal product. It is, therefore, very important for marketers to make themselves aware of the dangers inherent in each product and make certain that full and explicit warnings and instructions accompany the product to the purchaser.

Product Safety Regulation

There are numerous statutes and regulations dealing with specific issues of product safety. Some states have seat belt laws, while others outlaw the sale of fireworks. The federal government also is involved in everything from meat inspection to tamper-proof packaging. Marketers should be aware of the particular regulations pertaining to their industry.

One of the most important federal commissions with broad jurisdiction over many industries is the Consumer Product Safety Commission. The CPSC creates safety standards for individual products and bans unreasonably hazardous products. To issue a safety standard, the CPSC must find that the standard is "reasonably necessary to eliminate or reduce an unreasonable risk of injury associated with such product." In the case of banned products, it must find that no feasible safety standard could be written that could adequately protect the public from the unreasonable risk of injury. Manufacture for sale, sale, or distribution for sale of banned products or those not meeting promulgated standards is illegal. Safety standards may include requirements especially important to marketers, such as those pertaining to consumer product packaging and to the warnings and instructions accompanying the products.

The CPSC has been accused by all sides of being too aggressive or too passive. As a commission, its activity generally follows the current administration's attitude toward regulation. The CPSC seeks to identify potential threats to consumer safety and creates rules that are designed to prevent injury. Product liability law and warranty law seek to redress injury once it has occurred and indirectly encourage careful design, manufacture, and marketing through fear of potential liability.

Conclusion

Decisions made by marketing managers require attention to both the business and legal environment. In this note we have looked at some generally applicable principles of U.S. law and examined some specific issues involved in the thousands of individual cases to which these principles have been applied, each with its own facts and outcome. There are many areas that this note does not cover at all, however. Moreover, with the globalization of business, the legal environment is expanding rapidly; marketers must contend with the complexities of doing business within radically different legal systems. Although it is ultimately the corporate attorney's responsibility to guide the marketer through that maze, a basic understanding of the legal environment will prevent marketers from wasting time and effort on marketing plans, programs, and decisions that eventually are vetoed by the legal department.

This note is designed to assist the marketer in familiarizing himself or herself with some of the more important laws and regulations relevant to marketing decisions. The books listed in Appendix A provide a more thorough survey of the law as it relates to marketing decisions. Appendix B contains an excerpt of some of the most important sections of the various statutes referred to in this note. One, of course, should *not* rely on this, or the note, as a substitute for appropriate legal advice.

APPENDIX A

Bibliography

Blackburn, John D.; Elliot I. Klayman; and Martin H. Malin. *The Legal Environment of Business.* Homewood, Ill.: Richard D. Irwin, 1982.

Howard, Marshall C. *Antitrust and Trade Regulation.* Englewood Cliffs, N.J.: Prentice-Hall, 1983.

Matto, Edward A. *A Manager's Guide to the Antitrust Laws.* New York: AMACOM, 1980.

Noel, Dix W., and Jerry L. Phillips. *Products Liability in a Nutshell.* St. Paul, Minn.: West Publishing, 1980.

Posch, Robert J. *The Complete Guide to Marketing and the Law.* Englewood Cliffs, N.J.: Prentice-Hall, 1988.

Shaw, William, and Arthur Wolfe. *The Structure of the Legal Environment.* Boston: PWS-Kent Publishing, 1991.

Stern, Louis W., and Thomas L. Eovaldi. *Legal Aspects of Marketing Strategy.* Englewood Cliffs, N.J.: Prentice-Hall, 1984.

Steuer, Richard M. *A Guide to Marketing Law.* New York: Law and Business/Harcourt Brace Jovanovich, 1986.

Sullivan, Lawrence A. *Antitrust.* St. Paul, Minn.: West Publishing, 1977.

Welch, Joe L. *Marketing Law.* Tulsa, Okla.: Petroleum Publishing, 1980.

APPENDIX B

Sherman Act

Section 1. "Every contract, combination . . . , or conspiracy, in restraint of trade . . . is hereby declared to be illegal. Every person who shall make any [such] contract, or engage in any [such] combination or conspiracy, shall be deemed guilty of a felony, and . . . shall be punished by fine not exceeding one million dollars if a corporation, or, if any other person, one hundred thousand dollars, or by imprisonment not exceeding three years, or by both. . . ."

Clayton Act

Section 2(a) (Robinson-Patman Act). "That it shall be unlawful for any person . . . to discriminate in price between different purchasers of commodities of like grade and quality, . . . where the effect of such discrimination may be substantially to lessen competition or tend to create a monopoly. . . . Provided, that nothing herein contained shall prevent differentials which make only due allowance for differences in the cost of manufacture, sale, or delivery . . . to such purchasers. . . ."

Section 2(b). [If a seller is found to have discriminated in his pricing, the seller can rebut the charge by] "showing that his lower price . . . was made in good faith to meet an equally low price of a competitor. . . ."

Section 2(d). "That it shall be unlawful for any person . . . to pay or contract for . . . any thing of value . . . for the benefit of a customer . . . , unless such payment or consideration is available on proportionally equal terms to all other [competing] customers. . . ."

Section 3. "That it shall be unlawful for any person . . . to lease or make a sale . . . , or fix a price charged therefor, or discount from, or rebate upon, such price, on the condition . . . that the lessee or purchaser thereof shall not use or deal in the goods . . . of a competitor . . . of the lessor or seller, where the effect . . . may be to substantially lessen competition or tend to create a monopoly."

Section 4. "That any person who shall be injured in his business or property by reason of anything forbidden in the antitrust laws [not including the FTC Act] may sue . . . , and shall recover threefold the damages by him sustained, and the cost of suit, including a reasonable attorney's fee."

Federal Trade Commission Act

Section 5(a)(1). "Unfair methods of competition . . . and unfair or deceptive practices . . . , are hereby declared unlawful."

Uniform Commercial Code

Section 2–313. Express Warranties by Affirmation, Promise, Description, Sample

(1) "Express Warranties are created as follows:
   (a) Any affirmation of fact or promise made by a seller to the buyer which relates to the goods and becomes part of the basis of the bargain creates an express warranty that the goods shall conform to the affirmation or promise.

(2) It is not necessary to the creation of an express warranty that the seller use formal words . . . , but an affirmation merely of the value of the goods or a statement purporting to be merely the seller's opinion or commendation of the goods does not create a warranty."

Section 2–314. Implied Warranty; Usage of Trade

(1) "Unless excluded or modified, a warranty that the goods shall be merchantable is implied in a

contract for their sale if the seller is a merchant with respect to goods of that kind. . . .

(2) Goods to be merchantable must be at least such as
  (a) pass without objection in the trade . . .
  (b) . . . are of fair average quality . . .
  (c) are fit for the ordinary purpose for which such goods are used; and
  (d) [are] . . . of even kind, quality and quantity . . .
  (e) are adequately contained, packaged, and labeled . . .
  (f) conform to the promises or affirmations of fact made on the container or label if any. . . ."

Section 2–315. Implied Warranty: Fitness for Particular Purpose

"Where the seller at the time of contracting has reason to know any particular purpose for which the goods are required and that the buyer is relying on the seller's skill or judgment to select or furnish suitable goods, there is unless excluded . . . an implied warranty that the goods shall be fit for such purpose."

Magnuson-Moss Warranty Act

Section 2308. "Implied Warranties—Restrictions on Disclaimers or Modifications.

(a) No supplier may disclaim or modify (except as provided in subsection *(b)* of this section) any implied warranty to a consumer with respect to a consumer product if (1) such supplier makes any written warranty to the consumer with respect to the consumer product, or (2) at the time of sale, or within 90 days thereafter, such supplier enters into a service contract with the consumer which applies to such consumer product.

Limitation on Duration

(b) For purpose of this chapter [other than for 'Full' warranties where implied warranties cannot be limited] implied warranties may be limited in duration to the duration of a written warranty of reasonable duration, if such limitation is conscionable and is set forth in clear and unmistakable language and prominently displayed on the face of the warranty."

Consumer Product Safety Act

Section 2058(*c*). "Required considerations and findings.

(1) Prior to promulgating a consumer product safety rule [which creates a safety standard or bans a product], the Commission shall consider, and

shall make appropriate findings for inclusion in such rule with respect to
  (A) the degree and nature of the risk of injury . . . ,
  (B) the approximate number of consumer products . . . subject to the rule;
  (C) the need of the public for the consumer products subject to such rule, and the probable effect of such rule upon the utility, cost, or availability of such products to meet such need; and
  (D) any means of achieving the objective of the order while minimizing adverse effects on competition or disruption or dislocation of manufacturing and other commercial practices consistent with public safety.

(2) The Commission shall not promulgate a consumer product safety rule unless it finds (and includes such findings in the rule)
  (A) That the rule (including its effective date) is reasonably necessary to eliminate or reduce an unreasonable risk of injury associated with such product.
  (B) That the promulgation of the rule is in the public interest; and
  (C) in the case of a rule declaring the product a banned hazardous product, that no feasible consumer product safety standard . . . would adequately protect the public from the unreasonable risk of injury associated with such product."

Copyright Law

Section 401. Notice of Copyright

(a) "*General Requirement:* Whenever a work protected under this title is published in the United States or elsewhere by authority of the copyright owner, a notice of copyright . . . shall be placed on all publicly distributed copies. . . .

(b) *Form of Notice:* The notice appearing on the copies shall consist of the following three elements:
  (1) the symbol © . . . or the word 'Copyright' . . .
  (2) the year of first publication of the work . . .
  (3) the name of the owner of the copyright. . . ."

Section 408. Copyright Registration in General

(a) "Registration Permissive: At any time during the subsistence of copyright in any published or unpublished work, the owner . . . may obtain registration of the copyright claim by delivering to the Copyright Office [one copy of an unpublished work or two copies of a published work], together with the application and fee. . . ."

GLOSSARY OF MARKETING TERMS

Users of this glossary should understand that many of the terms defined below have industry-specific or situation-specific meanings. The definition and/or contextual use of a term in a case or note always takes precedence over the necessarily more general definition in the glossary.

Advertising—Any form of paid or public service presentation and promotion of ideas, goods, or services by a sponsor[17]* Though "word-of-mouth" advertising (in which consumers tell one another about their experiences with a product or service) is a well-known phenomenon, advertising usually takes the form of mass (as opposed to interpersonal) communication. That is, the advertiser buys space or time to get a message across to a large number of people whom no one from his or her organization may know or interact with. The defining characteristic of advertising can be said to be its persuasive nature. It is not disinterested dissemination of information. Rather, it is designed to convince those exposed to it of the merits of what is being sold.

Advertising Agency Commission—The percentage of advertising costs earned by advertising agencies for their services to advertisers. Standard practice has traditionally set this commission at 15 percent of gross media expenditures (time, talent, facilities, space, and so on) and 17.65 percent of net advertising production expenses for art work, photography, typesetting, engravings, and the like. [2] These "standard" figures are, however, often subject to negotiation.

Aftermarket—The market which is created by the need for new component parts for a finished product already in use. The sale of automobile tires, batteries, and air filters is an example.[18]

Agent—A person or business unit which negotiates purchases or sales or both but which does not take title to the goods in which it deals. Agents commonly receive remuneration in the form of a commission or fee. They do not usually represent both buyer and seller in the same transaction.[7] Agents are similar to brokers except that agents tend to have long-term relationships with their principals whereas brokers, in general, do not.

This glossary was prepared by Associate Professor Richard S. Tedlow.
Copyright © 1981 by the President and Fellows of Harvard College.
Harvard Business School case 9-582-044 (Rev. 7/87).

*These numbers refer to the sources of the definitions. They correspond to the list at the end of the Glossary. Some of the definitions are quoted almost directly from the sources, while others are loosely based upon them.

All-Commodity Rate—In transportation, a rate applicable regardless of the nature of the *commodities** shipped.[19]

All-Commodity Volume—One way in which manufacturers whose products are distributed through *supermarkets* and other food stores evaluate the effectiveness of their distribution systems. "Eighty-five percent of ACV," for example, means a product is distributed in stores that represent 85 percent of the sales volume of all food store products in an area. It does not mean the product is carried by 85 percent of the stores in an area.

Arbitrage—The buying and selling of the same *commodity,* security, or foreign exchange at the same time but in two or more different markets to take advantage of differences in the prices of the item in question in the markets.[19]

Arbitron—A market research service owned by *SAMI/Burke,* Arbitron specializes in measuring local radio and TV audiences through a paid, *diary panel.* Audience is estimated in 15-minute blocks of time.[15]

Auction—Offering an article to the highest of several bidders.[19]

Audits—Audits track the movement of products to give manufacturers the most current sales information possible. The two most important are *Nielsen* and *SAMI. Nielsen* monitors retail product movement through an audit of beginning and ending inventory plus purchases. *SAMI* is a middleman audit, monitoring warehouse withdrawals through estimates of shipments from warehouses to retail stores.[15]

Bait and Switch—Bait advertising is "an alluring but insincere offer to sell a product or service which the advertiser in truth does not intend or want to sell." The practice of placing such advertising and attempting to "switch" the consumer once in the store to another (more profitable) product through disparagement or various other tactics is illegal.[24]

Bargain Basement—The lowest floor of a *department store* (often, literally the basement) which specializes in merchandise priced lower than in the store as a whole.[14]

Billings (*Advertising*)—The total charges for space, time, production, and other services provided by the advertising agency to the client.[2]

Brand—A name, term, sign, symbol, or design, or a combination of them, which is intended to identify the goods or services of a seller and to differentiate them from those of competitors.[7]

Break-Even Analysis—A technique for determining the volume of sales necessary (at various prices) for the seller to cover costs or to break even between revenue and cost. Break-even analysis is used to help set prices, estimate profit or loss potential, and determine costs that should be incurred.[6]

Broker—See Agent.

Burke—Recently merged with *SAMI, Burke* is a major supplier of research and is perhaps the largest custom research supplier. Through phone interviews, personal interviews, mail surveys, group discussions, concept tests, and product tests, *Burke* conducts awareness, trial, and usage studies as well as advertising research.[15]

Business Format Franchising (as distinguished from *product* or *trademark franchising*)—A type of franchise relationship where the franchisor provides the franchisee with the total system for doing business. Not only does the franchisee receive rights to use the trademark of the franchisor but also conducts business under specific guidelines and standards covering operations, marketing, and all other as-

---

*Italicized words have their own definitions in this Glossary.

pects of the business. Some well-known examples of format franchising are fast-food restaurants, motels, and car rentals. Business format franchising accounted for approximately 26 percent of franchise sales in 1985.

Buying Allowance (Off-Invoice Allowance)—A *trade promotion* consisting of a short-term offer of a stated reduction in price for a certain quantity of a product purchased.[21]

Buying Center—The *decision-making unit* involved in a specific organizational buying decision. (See DMU.)

Buying Group (also Buying Office or Resident Buying Office)—An organization representing a group of noncompeting stores formed primarily for buying merchandise. The group may be independent, store owned, or may own the stores.[14]

C.B.D.—Abbreviation for "cash before delivery." The payment of cash for a purchase before the purchase is actually delivered.

C.I.F.—Abbreviation for "cost, insurance, and freight." These three letters signify that the items for which they stand have been included in the price quoted.[19]

C.O.D.—Abbreviation for "cash on delivery." The payment of cash for a purchase at the time of its delivery.

Cable Television—A system for delivering television programming, which relies upon a cable to connect the television set to a central antenna, rather than upon the transmission of signals through the air directly to a residence. Because cable television does not use the air waves as does the traditional transmission system, it is less subject to federal regulation. The basis for federal regulation traditionally rested upon public ownership of the air waves.

Cannibalization—Takes place when a new product gains a portion of its sales at the expense of an existing product sold by the same company.

Captive Distributor—A *distributor* owned by a manufacturer. The captive distributor provides a *channel of distribution* for products the parent company sells and also may carry related items made by other manufacturers.

Car Card—A poster type of advertisement designed for mounting inside public transportation vehicles, usually 11 inches high by 28 inches wide.[2]

Carriage Trade—The wealthy class of patrons.[14]

Cash Cow—One of four categories of business lines or products in a portfolio theory of product management. (The other three are *stars,* "*problem children,*" and *dogs.*) A cash cow is a product judged to be in the mature or decline stage of its life cycle, requiring little investment and produced at a low cost, to be "milked" for high profits in order to fund fast-growing *stars* or to invest in *stars* and more questionable "*problem children.*"[9a]

Catalogue Retailers—These merchants sell a variety of high-margin branded goods at low prices, and they rely on catalogues both in their stores and mailed to customers to inform the consumer of their product offering. The orders that customers place are filled from a backroom warehouse, which is designed as a low-cost facility. The lower prices of catalogue retailers are made possible by lower rents for the out-of-the-way locations that they use, by providing minimal service, and by featuring products that are not fashion intensive.

Caveat Emptor—A Latin phrase meaning "Let the buyer beware." The phrase describes a philosophy that it is and/or should be the responsibility of the purchaser to assure himself or herself of the value of a seller's wares, rather than relying on the seller's word.[14]

Chain Discount—A series of discounts taken on a base lessened successively by the amount of the preceding discount. For example, $100 discounted by 40 plus 10 plus 2 equals $52.92, and the total amount of the discount is $47.08 percent ($100 − 40% = $60; $60 − 10% = $54; $54 − 2% = $52.92; $100 − $52.92 = 47.08).[19]

Chain Store—A group of retail stores of essentially the same type, centrally owned and with some degree of centralized control of operation.[7]

Channel Captain or Commander—An organization in a *channel of distribution* that assumes leadership for firms from which it buys and/or to which it sells by absorbing risk on their behalf and generally engaging in actions designed to benefit its suppliers and customers as well as itself.[11] An example of a channel commander's role would be J. C. Penney's relationship with some of its apparel suppliers. Penney's volume and importance relative to these suppliers are such that it can establish the specifications of their product, conduct inspection programs at the factory, and determine the *margin* structure.

Channel of Distribution—The structure of intercompany organization units and extra-company *agents* and *dealers,* wholesale and retail, through which a product or service is marketed.[7]

Circular—Printed *advertising* matter, usually from 1 to 24 pages, widely used in sales promotion.[2]

Clayton Act—A federal statute passed in 1914, which strengthened antitrust legislation by restricting such practices as price discrimination, exclusive dealing, *tying contracts,* and interlocking directorates.[5]

Closed Circuit—A telecast fed to receivers by cable, rather than broadcast by air. Reception is controlled, limited, and not available to the public at large.

Clutter—The incidence of numerous short commercials, particularly on television, increasing the potential level of confusion on the part of the intended recipients of *advertising.*[11]

Commodity—A product category or a product that is not distinguished in the minds of potential customers from similar products produced by competitors.[11]

Commodity Exchange—An organization usually owned by the member traders, which provides facilities for bringing together buyers and sellers of specified commodities, or their *agents,* for promoting trades in these *commodities.*[7]

Comparative Advertising—*Advertising* that makes specific *brand* comparison using actual product names.[18]

Concentration Ratio—The percentage of total output of an industry manufactured by a certain number of firms. Thus, if the four-firm concentration ratio in industry X is 40 percent, four firms produce 40 percent of the output in that industry.

Consignment Sales—Sales not completed until products placed with a retailer by a supplier are sold to the consumer. Payment for goods placed on consignment is not due until such goods are resold.[11]

Consumer Behavior—The acts of individuals directly involved in obtaining and using economic goods and services, including the decision processes that precede and determine these acts.[3]

Consumers' Cooperative—A retail business owned and operated by ultimate consumers to purchase and distribute goods and services primarily to the membership.[7]

Consumer Credit—Funds borrowed or financial obligations incurred for periods of time of generally three years or less.[6]

Consumer Goods—Goods destined for use by ultimate consumers or households and in such form that they can be used without commercial processing.[7]

Consumer Panel—See Diary Panel.

Consumer Promotions—Techniques designed to attract the ultimate consumer or end user to a specific product.[21]

Consumerism—A social movement seeking to increase the rights and powers of consumers and the responsibilities of sellers.

Contests and Sweepstakes—These are important *consumer promotion* devices. They differ in that in a contest participants compete for prizes on the basis of their skill in fulfilling a certain requirement, usually analytical or creative. In sweepstakes, participants merely submit their names to have them included in a drawing of prizewinners.[21]

Contracting Out—The decision by a firm to have goods or components of a good which it assembles and/or sells manufactured by another company.

Contribution—The monetary (or percentage) difference between revenues realized and the variable costs incurred in the production and distribution of one or more units of a product.[11]

Convenience Goods—*Consumer goods* that usually are purchased frequently, immediately, and with a minimum of comparison. The articles are usually of small unit value and are bought in small quantities at any one time. Examples include tobacco products, chewing gum, and newspapers.[7]

Convenience Store—Smaller grocery stores, with limited numbers of items usually at relatively high prices, which are open long hours. These stores specialize in fill-in type items, such as bread, milk, and soft drinks and usually do not carry fresh meat or fresh produce.[14]

Cooperative—An establishment owned by an association of customers of the establishment. In general, the distinguishing features of a cooperative are patronage dividends based on the volume of expenditures by the members and a limitation of one vote per member regardless of the amount of stock owned.[14]

Cooperative Advertising—Local or regional *advertising,* the cost of which is shared by a national advertiser (manufacturer) and a *retailer* and/or *wholesaler.*[2]

Copy—In the *advertising* world, copy usually refers to the text, written or spoken, accompanying an advertisement.

Copy Testing—Preliminary trials of different copy *advertising* appeals or selling ideas to determine their effectiveness.[2]

Cost of Goods Sold—The total amount of all costs related to the acquisition and preparation of goods for sale.[25]

Cost per Thousand (often abbreviated "CPM")—The cost of *advertising* for each 1,000 homes reached in TV or radio or for each 1,000 circulation of a publication.

Coupon—A certificate which, when presented for redemption at a retail store, entitles the bearer to a stated savings on the purchase of a specific product.[21]

Credit—A loan extended, often for the purpose of facilitating the acquisition of goods and services, in advance of the payment for them.

Cumulative Audience (or "Cume")—The net unduplicated audience delivered by a specific program in a particular time slot over a measured time, usually one to four weeks.[2]

DMP—Abbreviation for "Decision-Making Process," which is the process by which a *decision-making unit* arrives at the decision to make a purchase.

DMU—Abbreviation for "Decision-Making Unit." DMU can refer to a single individual. More commonly, however, it refers to a group of individuals linked by a common organizational bond, but separated by functional specialization, trying to reach a joint decision on a purchase. Individuals tend to take on certain roles in the buying process, such as *initiator, gatekeeper, influencer, decider, purchaser,* and *user,* descriptive of their purchase involvement and predictive of their behavior.

Dating—The practice of giving *credit* beyond a stated period by forward dating of an *invoice.* For example, a buyer technically obliged to pay for a purchase within 30 days may be given a postdated *invoice* bearing a date perhaps a month later than the actual date of purchase. In effect, the buyer now has 60 days in which to make payment. Dating is often used to encourage orders for seasonal goods well in advance of need.[1]

Dealer—A firm that buys and resells merchandise at either retail or wholesale.

Dealer Loader—A premium presented to retailers for the purchase of certain quantities of merchandise. Its purpose is to gain new distribution or to move an unusually large quantity of goods from the manufacturer to the retailer and subsequently to the consumer.[21]

Deciders—Those individuals actually making the decision concerning whether a contemplated purchase should be made.[4] (See DMU.)

Demographic Segmentation—Market *segmentation* on the basis of age, sex, family size, family life cycle (e.g., young, single; young, married; young, married, youngest child under six; and so on), income, occupation, education, religion, race, nationality, and/or social class.[13]

Department Store—A large *retailing* business, which carries a wide assortment of *shopping* and *speciality goods,* usually in the medium-to-high price range. Its products are "departmentalized" or segmented by categories within the store. Each department has a discrete store space allocated to it, a cash register to record sales, and salespersons to assist customers. There are two types of department stores: "traditional" and "departmentalized speciality." The major difference is that the former carry a full line of merchandise, including consumer *durables,* such as furniture and home appliances; the latter tend not to carry such items but, rather, to focus their efforts on apparel.

Department Store Ownership Group—An aggregation of centrally owned stores in which each store continues to be merchandised and operated primarily as an individual concern with central guidance, rather than central management or direction.[14]

Diary Panel—A survey technique in which an individual or a family keeps a record of listening or viewing behavior or of product purchasing activities.[2]

Diffusion—The process through which a new product or service moves from its introduction to a wider acceptance in its potential market.

Direct Selling—The process whereby a firm responsible for production sells to the user, ultimate consumer, or retailer without intervening middlemen.[7]

Discount Store—A departmentalized retail establishment utilizing many self-service techniques to sell hard goods, health and beauty aids, apparel and other soft goods, and other general merchandise. These stores operate at low margins, have a minimum annual volume of $1 million, and are 10,000 square feet or over in size.[10]

Discretionary Income—Funds remaining after necessities are paid for out of *disposable income.*[18]

Disposable Income—Personal income remaining after the deduction of income taxes and compulsory payments, such as Social Security.[7]

Distributor—A firm (or an individual) selling manufactured products either to retail outlets (*dealers*) or direct to consumers. In common parlance, distributors often are thought of as having closer and more long-term relationships with the manufacturers from which they buy than are *wholesalers.*

Dog—One of four categories of business lines or products in a portfolio theory of product management. (The other three are *cash cows, stars,* and "*problem chil-*

dren.") Dogs are low-share products in slow-growth markets. The chances of such products becoming major cash generators are not good, and they are thus often thought of as cash traps because of the investment needed to maintain their market position.[9a]

Drawing Account—An account from which an employee is permitted to draw commissions against future sales. Deficits are accumulated and subtracted from earned commissions in later periods when there is an excess over the drawing account limit.[14]

Drop Shippers (Desk Jobbers)—*Wholesalers* who do not handle or store the goods they sell. They take customer orders and then arrange for manufacturers to ship directly to the buyers. Their role is similar to that of manufacturers' *agents* except that they take title to the merchandise they handle and assume the corresponding risks.[6]

Dry Goods—A broad term applied to textiles. It is generally used to include piece goods, narrow yard goods, and the textile items of women's accessories and men's furnishings.[14]

Dumping—The sale of goods abroad at prices well below those charged in the country of origin in order to gain the advantages of scale economies or the learning curve for the producer and/or in order to make it difficult if not impossible for foreign firms to compete in the market in question.

Durable Goods—Goods expected to last longer than three years such as appliances, furniture, and automobiles.[1]

E.O.M., R.O.G.—Abbreviation for "End of Month, Receipt of Goods." This is a form of *dating,* which indicates that the net credit period applies as though the shipment were made at the end of the month. It also indicates that the cash discount period begins on receipt of the goods by the purchaser.[14]

80–20 Rule—The common observation that 20 percent of products or customers often account for 80 percent of sales. The term also is used to express the view that 20 percent of the effort on a project often produces 80 percent of the results.

Elasticity of Demand—The relative responsiveness of sales revenue to particular changes in price. When total revenue falls as prices fall or when revenue rises as prices rise, the demand for the product is said to be relatively price inelastic. When revenue rises as prices fall or when revenue falls as prices rise, demand is said to be relatively elastic.[6]

Envelope (or Statement) Stuffer—An *advertising* leaflet, folder, or circular placed in an envelope along with its primary contents, usually an *invoice* or statement.[2]

Evoked Set—The range of *brands* of some product group that is looked on as true alternatives by the consumer.[3]

Exclusive Distribution—Selling through only one *wholesaler* and/or *retailer* in a particular trading area.[18]

Experiment—A scientific method of investigation that is used in marketing research in an attempt to establish cause-and-effect relationships. Typically, an experimenter manipulates or controls one or more independent variables and observes the effect on a dependent variable. For example, a marketer might manipulate *advertising* messages (i.e., run a different message in equivalent markets) to determine the effects of the *advertising* messages on sales. In such an experiment, the *advertising* messages are the independent variables, and sales is the dependent variable.

F.O.B.—Abbreviation for "Free-on-Board." Any agreed-upon destination to which transportation charges are paid by the vendor and at which title passes to the purchaser.[14]

Factoring—The practice by which a company sells its accounts receivable at a discount to a financial institution, which then collects them.

Fair Trade Laws—Laws permitting *resale price maintenance*. There were at one time a number of such laws on the state level, but they were determined to be unconstitutional in 1975. *Resale price maintenance* is, therefore, illegal in the United States. (See resale price maintenance.)

Family (or Umbrella) Brand—The use of a single *brand* name for several products.[18] Kellogg, for example, uses its corporate name with all its cereals, such as Kellogg's Corn Flakes, Kellogg's Rice Krispies, and the like. Procter & Gamble, by contrast, does not use its corporate name to accompany its *brands*. Thus, Crest Toothpaste is not called Procter & Gamble Toothpaste or Procter & Gamble Crest.

Fashion—The mode of dress, etiquette, furniture, style of speech, and so on—in general, the taste—of a particular segment of consumers at a particular time.

Federal Trade Commission (FTC)—Created by Congress in 1914, the Federal Trade Commission is an independent regulatory agency designed to police "unfair competition" and various corporate practices held to harm not only competitors but consumers as well. The commission's area of interest extends to pricing and *advertising* practices and their impact on industry concentration.

Flight—Part of an *advertising* campaign that is divided into segments, with lapses of time between segments.[2]

Floor Planning—The financing of display stocks for auto and appliance retailers by manufacturers or financial institutions.[18]

Focus Group—A group of 8 to 12 consumers who meet a marketer's specifications in terms of usage of or interest in a particular product category. The group is brought together with a moderator to discuss products, *promotions, advertising,* or other marketing ideas.[23]

Football Item—Merchandise used by *retailers* to attract customers through frequent price changes.[14]

Franchising—The granting of supporting services by a supplier to a reseller in return for the sale of products or services for a specified fee. Such supporting services have included the use of a *trademark* or *brand*, merchandising assistance, advice on location, financing, and limits on the number of directly competing outlets.[11]

Free-Goods Deal—An offer of a certain amount of a product to *wholesalers* or *retailers* at no cost to them but dependent on the purchase of a stated amount of the same or another product.[21]

Frequency—The average number of times an accumulated audience has been exposed to—or has had the opportunity for exposure to—the same *advertising* message within a measured period.[19]

Full Line Forcing—This is a type of tying arrangement in which the seller demands that the buyer purchase an entire line as the price of purchasing one particularly desired item in it. Full line forcing and other *tying agreements* that do not involve *patents*, copyrights, or *franchises* are normally illegal unless the tying product is neither unique nor attractive enough to restrain competition in the tied market.[24]

Functional Discount—A discount allowed a middleman from the list price to cover the middleman's *margin* (i.e., his or her costs plus his or her profit).

Gatekeepers—Those individuals, such as purchasing agents, whose responsibility it is to be knowledgeable concerning the range of vendor offerings that may be useful in satisfying needs or solving problems. They largely determine which vendors are granted the opportunity to get in touch with the decision makers involved in making a purchase.[4] (See DMU.)

General Merchandise Chain—A phrase often used to describe Sears, Ward's, and Penney's—large, nationwide *chains* selling a wide variety of *consumer goods*.

Generic Products—Products that have no other *brand* than the identification of their contents.[18]

Geographic Segmentation—*Segmentation* of a market on the basis of region, county size, city or Standard Metropolitan Statistical Area (SMSA) size, population density, and/or climate.[13]

Gestalt (in *advertising*)—The phenomenon of perceiving the whole of an advertisement to have greater impact or effectiveness than merely the sum of its parts.[2]

Gondola—A type of self-service counter with tiers of shelves back-to-back, which is free-standing between aisles of a retail store.[14]

Gross Margin—Sales revenue minus the *cost of goods sold*.

Gross Rating Points (GRPs)—The measure by which a TV time buyer or advertiser evaluates his or her impact or clout against one or more segments of the total market. It is arrived at by multiplying reach times frequency (i.e., the total number of persons exposed to an advertisement times the average number of exposures per person).[26]

Guarantee—See Warranty.

HBA—An abbreviation for the "health and beauty aid" product category.[14]

Hard Goods—This term is sometimes used synonymously with *"durable goods"* (i.e., *consumer goods* expected to last longer than three years). It also sometimes refers specifically to consumer durables made principally from metal, such as most electrical appliances, automobiles, cutlery, and tools.[1]

Horizontal Integration—The expansion of a company through the acquisition of other companies engaged in the same stage of production of the same product. An example would be the acquisition of one *chain* of apparel retailers by another.[1]

House Agency—An *advertising* agency offering full or limited service capabilities and owned wholly or in part by an advertiser who typically is the agency's only or most important client.[2]

Implementation—The effective execution of marketing strategy at the functional (e.g., *sales force management*), programmatic (e.g., *product management*), and policy levels of the firm. Implementation involves the organization, interaction, allocation, and control necessary to carry out strategic plans efficiently and effectively.

Impulse Purchase—A purchase decision made on the spur of the moment, without prior planning.

In-Stock Program—The maintenance by a vendor of an *inventory* of finished goods, which a purchaser can buy and receive delivery on virtually immediately.

Industrial Goods—Goods intended to be sold for use in producing other goods, rather than to the ultimate consumer.

Industrial Marketing—Marketing goods to companies (or the government or nonprofit groups), rather than to individual consumers.

Influencers—Managers with some voice in determining whether a purchase is to be made and what is to be bought.[4] (See DMU.)

Information Resources, Inc.—A market research firm that has developed Behavior Scan, a service in which all stores in a market are provided with scanning equipment, and data are collected at the household level.

Initiators—Those individuals who start the purchase process in motion through their recognition that a company problem can be solved or avoided through purchasing a product or service.[4] (See DMU.)

Installment Credit—Consumer credit that is repaid in periodic installments over a time period.[6]

Intensive Distribution—The sale of a product through a large percentage of the available *wholesale* or *retail* units in a defined market area.[11]

Inventory—Unsold goods, or elements of unsold goods. Finished goods inventory are products ready for sale, such as, for example, canned goods awaiting shipment from a factory to a *supermarket*. Work-in-process inventory are products in the process of production, such as, for example, an automobile engine prior to the final assembly of the vehicle. Raw material inventory are *commodities* that are still in the condition in which they were acquired from a supplier and which have not yet entered the production process. Crude oil stored at a refinery would be an example.

Invoice—A business form showing the items shipped and charges levied by the seller at the time of the shipment to the buyer.[19]

Irregulars—Merchandise containing some flaw, such as poor fit or poor workmanship.[14]

Jobber—A term with specialized meanings in various industries but which is generally synonymous with *wholesaler*.[7]

Joint Venture—An arrangement in which one company shares the risks, costs, and management of a specific business project with another.[19, 5] A joint venture differs from a partnership in that it is not necessarily conceived of as an ongoing relationship.[1]

Keystone Markup—Doubling the cost to arrive at a price. Thus, a men's clothing store that purchases a suit for $125 and retails it for $250 is "keystoning" it.[14]

Knockoff—The exact or similar reproduction of another firm's *merchandise*.[14]

Landed Cost—The total cost of imported merchandise, including price paid, transportation, and crating but prior to customs duties.[14]

Lay-Away—A method of deferred payment in which merchandise is held by the store for the customer until it is completely paid for.[14]

Lease—A contract for the possession of land, buildings, machinery, *patents*, or some other item of value in return for periodic payment of a certain sum of money.[19]

Letter of Credit—A letter authorizing the extension of *credit* or the advance of money to the bearer, who is usually named in the letter. The *credit* or advance is charged to the person issuing the letter.[19]

Licensing—The sale of the right to use some process, *trademark, patent,* or other item for a fee or royalty.[18]

Line Extension—A new product that is a variation on a product already offered. This new product is introduced to exploit the equity already built up in other product(s) in the line and/or as a competitive reaction to the strategies of other firms in a market.[10a]

List Price—The price shown on the sales list of the seller. It is used as the basis from which discounts may be computed for various classes of buyers.[19]

Local Advertising—*Advertising* appearing in one or more specific localities as distinguished from regional or national *advertising*.[2]

Locker Stock—The shipment by a manufacturer or *wholesaler* of extra *inventory*, which is held in a store's central warehouse unopened. As soon as the buyer needs any item held in locker stock, payment becomes due to the vendor for the entire shipment.[14]

Loss Leader—Merchandise sold at a loss to attract customers.[14]

Mail Order Chains—See General Merchandise Chains.

Manifest—A shipping form used by carriers for consolidation purposes, listing all pertinent information, such as consignor, consignee, commodity classification, number and weight of packages, and (sometimes) cost.[14]

Manufacturers' Agent—An individual, generally operating on an extended contractual basis, who often sells within an exclusive territory, handles noncompeting but related lines of goods, and often possesses limited authority with regard to prices and terms of sale. He or she is sometimes authorized to sell a specific portion of his or her principal's output. This term and "manufacturers' representative" are often used interchangeably.[7,5]

Manufacturers' Representative—See Manufacturers' Agent.

Margin—The difference between the selling price and the acquisition cost (manufacturing cost in the case of a manufacturer and purchase cost in the case of a *wholesaler* or *retailer*) of a unit of product.

Markdown—A reduction in the originally established price of a product, typically in a retail outlet. The reduction percentage is determined by dividing the amount of the reduction by the original price.[11]

Markdown Money—Money a manufacturer pays to a *retailer* to enable the latter to put slow-selling or obsolete merchandise on sale without absorbing the loss itself.

Market Niche—A protected segment of a market. The nature of the protection can vary. Thus, a group of buyers may be particularly sensitive to price, to quality, to appeals through *advertising* and the like. Servicing that group through the development of a special competence can enhance the competitive strength of the seller.

Market Penetration—The percentage of a target market that is purchasing a company's product or service.

Market Share—The ratio of a company's sales to total industry sales in a particular market. Market share can be measured in dollars or units.

Marketing—The process of planning and executing the conception, pricing, promotion, and distribution of ideas, goods, and services to create exchanges that satisfy individual and organizational objectives.[17a]

Marketing Management—The planning, direction, and control of the entire marketing function, specifically the formulation and execution of marketing objectives, policies, programs, and strategy. Responsibilities include product development, organization and staffing to carry out plans, supervision of marketing operations, and control of marketing performance.[7]

Marketing Mix—Usually refers to the four pillars of marketing management: *product policy, promotion (advertising* and personal selling), *pricing,* and *channels of distribution.* For the sake of alliteration, "distribution" is often referred to as "place." Thus, the "Four Ps."

Marketing Research—A systematic investigation conducted to establish facts or to solve problems relating to the marketing of goods or services.[11]

Markup—The percentage by which a seller increases the selling price of goods over the price he or she paid for them. Conventionally, markup is computed as a percentage of sales price, rather than cost. Thus, an item that a retailer purchases for $10 and sells for $15 has a 33⅓ percent ($5/$15) markup.[1]

Mass Merchandise Chains—This often-used phrase has no generally agreed-upon meaning. Sometimes it is used specifically to refer to Sears, Ward's, and Penney's. At other times it is used to refer to such national or regional retail outlets as K mart and Caldor, which are generally thought of as selling at price points below Sears, Ward's, and Penney's. Yet another use of the term has it including large discount drug chains.

Matrix Organization—In the marketing context, this phrase usually refers to the assignment of responsibilities in such a way that one group of managers (including those for sales, *advertising, marketing research*, and so on) is responsible for ensuring the contribution of specialized, differentiated, functionally oriented expertise to the marketing effort, while another (composed of product or brand managers) is responsible for integrating the functional inputs to provide effective marketing programs for products, *brands*, or product lines.[11]

Mean—This statistic is the arithmetic average of all observations in a *sample*. It is calculated by summing the values of all observations and dividing by the number of observations.[15]

Median—This statistic is the observation that is exactly in the middle of a *sample*.[15] Thus, in a sample consisting of the values 1, 5, 7, 8, 9, 11, and 13, the median is 8.

Merchandise Allowance—A short-term contractual agreement through which a manufacturer compensates *wholesalers* or *retailers* for "features" (i.e., *advertising* or in-store displays of his or her products). Proof of performance, such as an *advertising* tear sheet, is an essential component of the merchandise allowance.[21]

Merchandising—The planning and supervision involved in marketing merchandise at the places, times, and prices and in the quantities that will best serve to realize the marketing objectives of the business. The term is most often heard in the retail, especially *soft goods*, trade.[7]

Merchant—A business unit that buys, takes title to, and resells merchandise.[7]

Mode—This statistic is the most frequent observation in a *sample*.[15] Thus, in a *sample* consisting of the observations 1, 1, 1, 3, 5, 7, and 9, the mode is 1.

Model—A set of inputs (often called "parameters of the model"), an explicit system or set of relationships for combining and manipulating those inputs, and the definition of the outputs that will be used to summarize what happens when a specific set of values for the inputs is subjected to the relationship of the model.[12]

Motivation Research—A group of techniques developed by behavioral scientists, which *marketing researchers* use to study *consumer behavior*.[7] These techniques attempt to identify the underlying purchase motives of consumers.

Multivariate Analysis—A collection of procedures for analyzing the association between the values of two or more variables in a data set. For example, let us assume that a researcher undertakes to interview five people in order to evaluate the effectiveness of an advertisement. He or she might ask those people how often each saw the advertisement, what they remembered about it, and whether they felt it to be persuasive. In this case, the variables are frequency, recall, and persuasiveness. The data set is the 15 measurements (i.e., five people times three answers per person). Examples of multivariate analysis include multiple regression, discriminate analysis, factor analysis, and cluster analysis.

National Account—A large geographically diverse customer with high pre- and post-sales service needs.

National Advertising—*Advertising* in one or more media that individually or collectively provide nationwide reach or exposure opportunity.[2]

National Brand—A manufacturer's *brand*, usually enjoying wide distribution.[7]

Nielsen—The largest supplier of *marketing research*, Nielsen is most well-known for its *retail audits;* providing information on grocery products, alcoholic beverages, toiletries, proprietary drugs, and product movement from retail stores, and for its rating system for television shows. Its speciality is providing services on a syndicated basis (i.e., it recruits clients for a specified time).[15] Nielsen is owned by Dun & Bradstreet.

Non-Durable Goods—*Consumer goods* such as food or clothing, expected to last less than three years.[1]

Non-Store Marketing—*Retailing* through other means than a retail store, such as catalogs, telephone orders, mail, and, more recently, cable.

Non-Tariff Barriers—Restraints on international trade, other than *tariffs*. Examples of such restraints are quotas, domestic government purchasing policies, and safety and technical standards.[16a]

Odd Lot—An unbalanced assortment of styles, colors, sizes, fabrics, and quality.[14]

Off Price Stores—Stores that sell *brand* name merchandise, predominantly apparel, textiles, footwear, and housewares, at well under the prices at which those same *brand* names are being sold in *department* and *speciality stores*. Off price stores are able to sell at these lower prices for a variety of reasons. They usually offer little service, and ambience is not emphasized. Often they buy manufacturer overruns or end-of-season merchandise at sharp discounts.

Oligopoly—An industry in which there are few sellers.

Open-to-Buy—The amount of merchandise a buyer may order during the balance of a given period. The phrase is most common in *department store* and other *soft goods* retailing.[14]

Opinion Leader—A person who influences others.[18]

Order Entry System—Computerized systems designed to streamline order processing. Processing an order involves a number of tasks, including the transmission of the order to the firm in question; the firm's checking to see that the *inventory* is available and that the customer is creditworthy; and the preparation and shipment of the product. Computerized order entry systems are now facilitating every phase of this process.[13a, 20a]

Original Equipment Manufacturer (OEM)—A company that buys a product to incorporate into what it in turn makes and sells.[8]

Outlet Store—A store specializing in job lots and clearance merchandise; or a store owned by a manufacturer to dispose of surplus stocks.[14]

Over-the-Counter (abbreviated OTC)—A term used to identify such "proprietary drugs" as cough medicine and aspirin, which can be purchased without a prescription, as opposed to "ethical" drugs, for the purchase of which a doctor's prescription is needed.[2]

Packer's Brand—An unadvertised and unpromoted brand owned by a manufacturer, usually sold on price.

Patent—A grant of protection from would-be copiers to an inventor of a product for a definite time. Such a grant, made to persons obtaining certification from the Patent Office of originality of their product or process, currently is extended for 17 years in the United States.[11]

Penetration Pricing—A *pricing* strategy based on a low price relative to actual or potential alternatives designed to (1) stimulate purchase by several customer groups (market segments), (2) gain a large share of the market, (3) facilitate production economies, and/or (4) preempt potential competitors.[11]

Personal Selling—Oral presentation in a conversation with one or more prospective purchasers for the purpose of making sales.

Physical Distribution—The management of the physical movement and handling of goods from the point of production to the point of consumption or use.[7]

Planned Purchase—A purchase decision made in advance of exposure to or final direct contact with a particular product.[11]

Point-of-Sale Advertising (also Point-of-Purchase or P-O-P)—Displays of various kinds used in *retailing* at one or more in-store locations, such as shelf, window, counter, wall, island, over-wire, or checkout area.[2]

Positioning—The art of fitting a product to one or more segments of the broad market in such a way as to set it meaningfully apart from competition and, thus, optimize opportunity for greater sales and profits.[2] Positioning can exploit the physical and/or nonphysical attributes of a product in order to influence the customer's perception and to establish the mental space which that product is to occupy in the customer's mind. Positioning strategies can be implemented either through *advertising* and other forms of communication or through specific product attributes themselves.

Predatory Pricing—This term is used to describe a *pricing* policy that somehow restricts competition by driving out existing rivals or by excluding potential rivals from the market.[12a]

Premiums—Items of merchandise offered free or at a low cost as a bonus to purchasers of a particular product.[21]

Price Fixing—Agreements between or among vendors to set prices, including efforts to raise, stabilize, or lower them by any one of a number of means, including splitting markets by rotating bids, maintaining prices by distributing price lists to competitors, fixing certain aspects of the price mix by agreeing on markups or discounts, or various other conspiracies. All joint efforts to "raise, depress, fix, peg, or stabilize" prices are illegal.[24]

Price Leader—A firm whose *pricing* policies are followed by other companies in its industry.[7]

Price Line—Prices set by company policy to give a range for customer choice.

Price Packs—Packages that contain a stated discount on them.

Price Point—Synonym for price. In some industries, this term is used to denote prices at which some kinds of products are traditionally sold or which are thought of as having noteworthy psychological meaning to consumers.

Pricing—The art of translating into quantitative terms (monetary units) the value of a product to a customer at a point in time.[8]

Primary Demand—Demand for a product category, not just a company's own *brand*.[18]

Prime Time—The evening hours of broadcasting (from 7:30 P.M. to 11:00 P.M.), when audience potential is greatest and rates charged the advertiser are highest.[2]

Private Brands—(or Private Labels)—*Brands* (or labels) owned by merchants or *agents* as distinct from those owned by manufacturers or producers.[7]

"Problem Children"—One of the categories of business lines or products in a portfolio theory of *product management*. (The others are *cash cows, stars,* and *dogs*.) "Problem children" have small relative market shares, weak cash flow from operations, and, as a result, large needs for cash to fund fast growth.[9a] These products are thought of as problematic, because it is particularly difficult to decide whether or not the chance for fast growth and future profits justifies the cash investment that is called for.

Product Differentiation—Any difference, real or imaginary, in products that may result in a preference for one over the other even though their prices are identical or even though one may be priced higher than the other.[19]

Product Life Cycle—The progression of a product from introduction to withdrawal. The progression is sometimes thought of as encompassing five stages: introduction, early growth, late growth, maturity, and decline.

Product Management—The planning, direction, and control of all phases of the life cycle of products, including the creation of ideas for new products, the screening of such ideas, the coordination of research for physical development of products, packaging, and *branding*, introduction on the market, market development, modification, servicing, and, eventually, deletion from the product line.[7]

Product or Trademark Franchising (as distinguished from *Business Format Franchising*)—A type of *franchise* relationship where the franchisor grants to the franchisee the right to sell the franchisor's product and display or use the franchisor's *trademark*. Although the franchisee may receive training, *advertising*, and management assistance, the franchisee generally conducts business as an independent distributor. Well-known examples would be automobile and gasoline dealerships. Product or trademark franchising accounted for approximately 74 percent of *franchise* sales in 1985.

Product Policy— A product is a tangible good, a service, or an idea that satisfies a customer need. Product policy is the determination of the characteristics of that product. Included under product policy would be such issues as the actual features of the product, the number and variety of products to be offered and their relation to one another in the product line, services to be offered with the product, new product introduction and the deletion of mature products from the line, and naming, packaging, and others.[20a]

Product Portfolio—Products that a company attempts, for strategic purposes, to manage as a group.

Product Recall—The retrieval by a manufacturer of products that it has placed in the hands of *wholesalers, retailers,* or end users. Such retrieval typically is prompted by a discovery of a defect in the product.[11]

Product Testing—The solicitation of reactions to products by encouraging their actual use among a sample of typical customers, if possible in a manner that allows comparison with competing products along critical dimensions.[11]

Promotion—(1) The use of communication to persuade or convince potential customers. (2) All communication with the exception of *advertising* and personal selling. Examples here would be *contests* and sales aids. (3) A short-term price cut—that is, in certain industries the phrase "to promote a *brand*" means to cut its price.[11]

Promotional Item—In *retailing*, merchandise that has great price appeal to a customer because it appears to be a bargain.[14]

Psychographic Segmentation—The *segmentation* of a market on the basis of such aspects of the consumer as: lifestyle, personality, benefits sought (i.e., convenience, prestige), user status (i.e., non-user, user, ex-user), usage rate, loyalty status, readiness (i.e., unaware, aware, informed, interested, desirous), and/or marketing factor sensitivity (i.e., quality, price, service, *advertising*, sales promotion).[13]

Public Relations—Mass communication primarily concerned with the corporation as an institution, rather than as a vendor of specific items.

Publicity—Unpaid nonpersonal presentation of ideas or products.[7]

Pull Strategy—A marketing strategy in which the manufacturer, rather than the *channel of distribution*, assumes a great share of the burden for promotional effort, often through the use of *advertising* directed at potential end users or buyers. Such a strategy often may accompany a relatively intensive distribution program offering low percentage *margins* to channel intermediaries and most often accompanies the sale of noncomplex products at low per-unit prices.[11]

Purchaser—The individual whose responsibility it is to obtain a product or service.[4] (See DMU.)

Push Money—Payment by a manufacturer to a *wholesaler* or *retailer* in excess of the usual *margin* to provide an added incentive for greater selling effort.

Push Strategy—A marketing strategy in which the *channel of distribution*, rather than the manufacturer, assumes a great share of the burden for promotional effort, often through the use of personal selling efforts directed to customers. Such a strategy may accompany a selective distribution program offering high percentage *margins* to channel intermediaries and most often accompanies the sale of relatively complex products at high per-unit prices.[11]

Quantity Discount—See Volume Discount.

Rack Jobber (also known as Service Merchandiser)—A *wholesaler* who markets specialized lines of merchandise to certain types of retail stores and who merchandises, arranges, and stocks the racks on which these items are displayed. Rack jobbers are most prevalent in the grocery industry.[7]

Rating—The percentage expression of the size of a TV or radio program's audience. An "8" rating means that 8 percent of all homes with sets in the coverage area were tuned in to a particular program.[2]

Recall Test—A type of test whose purpose is to assess the actual communication impact of an advertisement after it has appeared in the media. Recall tests involve finding persons who are regular users of the medium in question and asking them to recall or play back everything they can remember. The administrator may or may not aid them in their recall.[13]

Reciprocity—Trading sales for sales (e.g., I'll ship my steel on your railroad if you purchase steel rails from me). Such arrangements can be anticompetitive and illegal.[24]

Reference Group—The group to which an individual looks when forming his or her attitudes.[18]

Refund—The return of part or all of a payment. A cash refund is just that; a merchandise refund stipulates that the refund be spent on other merchandise offered by the same seller.[1]

Regression—A form of *multivariate analysis* that predicts a dependent variable as a function of one or more independent variables.[15]

Relative Market Share— The *market share* of a product relative to the combined *market share* of the three leading competitors.[9a]

Reliability—A term in statistics meaning repetitive consistency. A measure is said to be reliable if it consistently obtains the same result when measuring the same observation.[15]

Replacement Market—The market for products or components of products, many of which are already in the hands of end users but which have been used up or ceased for other reasons to operate effectively.

Resale Price Maintenance—The practice, legal prior to the repeal of *Fair Trade Law* enabling legislation by Congress in 1975, of a manufacturer's requiring adherence to a prescribed price by *wholesalers* and/or *retailers* who resold its goods.[11]

Reset—The periodic reorganization of the shelves of a *retail* outlet. The reset process often involves intense competition among manufacturers and their *agents* for shelf space.

Retailing—Selling to the ultimate consumer.[7]

Robinson-Patman Act—This legislation, passed by Congress in 1936 as an amendment to the *Clayton Antitrust Act,* made it illegal to discriminate in price between competitors who purchase *commodities* of like grade and quality where the effect of the discrimination may be to lessen competition substantially. Price differentials can be justified: if it costs the seller less to transact with a particular buyer, if the price change is based on changes in market conditions or the deterioration of merchandise, or if the seller is seeking to meet the low price of a competitor. This act is enforced by the *Federal Trade Commission*.[24]

Roll-Out—The process by which a firm with a product offered for sale in a regional market, perhaps as part of a test, extends the physical distribution and promotion of the product to a much wider geographical area.[11]

Sales Management—(also known as Sales Administration or Sales Force Management)—The planning, direction, and control of the personal selling activities of a business unit, including recruiting, selecting, training, equipping, assigning, routing, supervising, paying, and motivating as these tasks apply to the personal sales force.[7]

SAMI—An abbreviation for Selling Areas—Marketing, Inc. Recently merged with *Burke,* SAMI is a commercial research service, which conducts wholesale (rather than retail, like *Nielsen) audits.* Withdrawals from grocery warehouses are monitored every four weeks.[15]

Sample—(1) In statistics, a limited or finite number of items of data selected from a universe or population. (2) In marketing, one or more units of a product given free (or sold at a price far below market) in order to induce prospective buyers to give it a trial or to enable them to determine its characteristics by inspection or analysis.[19]

Scanner—A device used at checkout counters of *supermarkets* and some other stores, which emits a laser beam to identify automatically items marked with the *Universal Product Code* as they pass over the checkstand. Scanners have speeded the checkout process, reduced personnel needs, and provided valuable data on inventory movement.[21a]

Scrambled Merchandising—The tendency for retail establishments to offer a growing number of product types, leading to an increasing duplication of assortments among various types of retail establishments. This has led to an increase in what has been termed "intertype competition" among, for example, *supermarkets* offering drug products and discount drugstores offering items previously sold principally in *supermarkets.*[11]

Segmentation—The process by which groups of potential customers are identified by geographic area, buying behavior patterns they hold in common, common perceptions they may share for a product or service, and/or common uses to which they may put a product or service for the purpose of (1) designing more efficient marketing programs that can be targeted primarily to one or more selected segments or (2) *positioning* a product in relation to competition in a particular market segment.[11]

Selective Demand—The demand for one particular *brand* as opposed to that for a product category in general.

Selective Distribution—The sale of a product or service through a carefully selected subset of all available wholesale or retail outlets in a given market area.[11]

Semidurable Goods—Goods expected to last between six months and three years, such as luggage or shoes.[1]

Served Market—That portion of the market for which a company's product is suitable and which it is presently targeting.

Share—The share of audience of a television program is the percentage of households using television during a specific time period that is tuned to the program in question.[17]

Sherman Antitrust Act—Passed by Congress in 1890 to prohibit: (1) monopolies or attempts to monopolize; and (2) various acts, including contracts, combinations, or conspiracies intended to restrain trade. The Sherman Act was aimed primarily at firms operating at one particular level in a *channel of distribution,* particularly manufacturers.[11]

Shopping Goods—Goods whose purchase entails risk perceived sufficient to warrant a search aimed at comparing price, quality, style, and so on among a number of possible purchases.

Shrinkage—In *retailing,* the value of book inventory in excess of actual physical inventory. The difference represents losses from shoplifting, employee theft, breakage, and the like.[14]

Skimming Strategy—A *pricing* strategy based on high initial price and successively lower prices designed to appeal in sequence to market segments placing successively greater emphasis on price while earning the highest possible per-unit profits.[11]

Soft Goods—This term is sometimes used as a synonym for *"non-durable goods"* (i.e., *consumer goods* expected to last less than three years, such as food or clothing). It is also sometimes used to refer specifically to goods that are literally soft to the touch, such as textiles.[1]

Source Effect—The extent to which the nature of a source influences the credibility of a message. Most citizens of the United States, for example, would be far more likely to believe a news story they read in the *New York Times* than to believe precisely the same story if it appeared in *Pravda.*[16]

Sourcing System—The complex of outside suppliers and internal manufacturing sources for all materials, component parts, supplies, machinery and equipment, facilities, and services the organization requires.[9]

Speciality Goods—Goods for which a consumer is willing to expend the effort required to purchase a most preferred item, rather than to buy a potentially acceptable substitute.[11]

Speciality Store—A retail store that makes its appeal on the basis of a restricted class of *shopping goods.* By its selection of these goods, it aims to differentiate itself from *department store* competition.[7]

Spiff—A direct payment to a wholesale or retail salesperson as an incentive to the selling effort behind a manufacturer's product.

Split Run—The running of different advertisements in alternating copies of the same issues of a publication to test the effectiveness of the copy.

Spot Advertising—The purchase of television or radio time on a station-by-station or market-by-market basis, rather than networkwide.[17]

Star—One of four categories of business lines or products in a portfolio theory of product management. (The other three are *cash cows, dogs,* and *"problem children."*) These products are share leaders in growing markets, which may need cash to sustain their strong position.[9a]

Starch—A commercial research firm, best known for its Starch Message Report, which attempts to measure the impact of advertisements in magazines and newspapers.[15]

Stockkeeping Unit (often abbreviated SKU)—The lowest level of disaggregation at which a product can be ordered. Thus, a shirt stockkeeping unit would be a particular size (collar and sleeve length) of a particular style of a particular color.

Strategic Alliance—A business arrangement more intimate and more permanent than that of preferred vendor/major customer but short of actual merger. Firms may enter into a strategic alliance to develop some new, shared technology or because the size of a contemplated transaction is extraordinarily large, the sale particularly complex, the need for ongoing technological back-up pressing, and/or the opportunity for mutual learning great. An example is the relationship between Fujitsu Fanuc, a Japanese robot vendor, and General Motors. Their *joint venture* provides an opportunity for Fanuc to learn more about robot applications in a factory than it could as a typical vendor, and for General Motors to better understand robotics and to capitalize upon its knowledge by selling factory robot technology to other companies.

Strategy—The pattern of objectives, purposes, or goals and major policies for achieving these goals, stated in such a way as to define what business the company is in or is to be in and the kind of company it is or is to be.[6]

Super Store—A store similar in general layout to a *supermarket* but much larger, averaging around 30,000 square feet, compared to 18,000 square feet for the *supermarket*. Super stores sell not only groceries but a large variety of convenience items (such as garden supplies) and even some bigger ticket durables like televisions. Some super stores offer such services as laundry and dry cleaning.[20a, 13a]

Supermarket—A large, low price, low margin, high volume, self-service retail store selling food and a limited range of household products. The supermarket has annual sales of at least $2 million and is under 30,000 square feet in size.

Survey—The organized solicitation of information or opinions from a *sample* or population of respondents for the purpose of drawing conclusions about the population.[11]

Targeted Gross Rating Points—*Gross rating points* with the base defined as a specific target group. For example, if the target market is men, ages 18–34, 100 gross rating points would mean that all the individuals in that group had been reached once, or half of them twice, or a third of them three times, and so on.

Tariff—(1) A customs duty or tax laid on goods as they enter or exit a country. These duties are either specific (i.e., according to the number or bulk of the items) or ad valorem (i.e., according to the value of the items). (2) A schedule of regulated rates and rules affecting the application of rates for specific products.[19]

Tear Sheet—An entire actual page containing an advertisement, illustration, or article clipped from a publication. Manufacturers who have *cooperative advertising* or merchandise allowance programs with retailers often demand that the retailers submit tear sheets as proof of performance.[2]

Telemarketing—The use of the telephone for selling as part of a planned and systematic effort to reduce expenditures for personal sales calls.

Test Marketing—An attempt to evaluate the nature and degree of customer acceptance of a product by actually putting it on the market in selected areas. It may involve using a full-scale marketing program in those areas; or it may use different combinations of marketing factors, such as promotional appeals, prices, or types of intensity of distribution in various areas in an attempt to determine the most effective way of marketing.[6]

Trade Association—An association of manufacturers or *dealers* engaged in a particular trade for interchange of information, establishment of standards, and other activities of common interest to the members.[19]

Trade Promotion—Devices designed to obtain special short-term merchandising and/or sales support from *distributors,* to induce retailers to promote a product through *advertising* and display, or to stimulate retailers and their sales clerks to-"push" a certain manufacturer's product, rather than that of a competitor.[21]

Trade Show—A gathering of sellers and buyers for the purpose of displaying and surveying, respectively, new products, processes, or services.[11]

Trademark— A *brand* that has been given legal protection.[5]

Trading Area—A district whose size is usually determined by the boundaries within which it is economical in terms of volume and cost for a marketing unit to sell a product.[7]

Trading Company—There are two types of trading companies. One, the specialized trading companies ("senmonshosha" in Japanese), exist all over the world. These firms specialize by product, function, and region. Thus, a firm that imports footwear to the United States from Italy is a specialized trading company. By contrast, the general trading company ("sogoshosha") is diversified in terms of product, function, and region. The largest Japanese trading companies, such as Mitsui, Mitsubishi, and Sumitomo, have a presence all over the world. They facilitate all aspects of transactions, including, for example, *physical distribution* and insurance. Their transactions are not limited to the family of firms of which they are a part. They move a great variety of products in and out of many countries.

Trading Up—An attempt to induce a current or prospective owner of a product to purchase a more expensive model or version of the same product.[11]

Transfer Price—The price charged by one unit of a corporation when it supplies a product or service to another unit of the same corporation.[19]

Turnover or **Turns**—The total number of times during the course of a year that the average *inventory* is sold.[18]

Tying Contract—An arrangement in which the seller agrees to sell one product (the tying product) only if the buyer agrees to buy the seller's other product or products (the tied products). Such arrangements are subject to prosecution if competition relative to the tied product is substantially reduced.[24]

Universal Product Code—Often abbreviated UPC, the Universal Product Code is a numerical and bar coded item identification number that can be read by a *scanner* at the checkout counter of a grocery store. These codes make possible the more efficient tracking of the store's *inventory*.[21a]

Validity—The degree to which a measure represents the object or concept which it is intended to measure.

Value Added—The extent to which an organization enhances the price customers are willing to pay for its goods or services through the creation of form, place, time, or ownership utilities. Value added is determined by subtracting the cost of materials, supplies, fuel, and contract work from the value of the shipments.[6a]

Value Pricing—*Pricing* on the basis of the buyer's perception of the value of the product to him or her, rather than on the basis of the seller's costs.[15]

Variety Store—A retail establishment offering many kinds of merchandise at low prices and with few attendant services. Woolworth's is a good example.[11]

Vertical Integration—The acquisition of firms or the development of divisions in earlier or later stages of the production process. For example, an apparel manufacturer that purchases retail stores or that establishes its own division for the building and operating of such stores is vertically integrating. In this case, the integration is forward, toward the consumer. If the apparel manufacturer purchased a textile company or established a textile division, it would be backward integrating, away from the consumer.

Volume Discount—An amount deducted in advance from payment that is due as a reward for buying in quantity.[1] There are a wide variety of such discounts. Discounts can be given on each unit above a base; or they can be established stepwise, with, for example, a 5 percent discount on units 11–20, a 6 percent discount on units 21–30, and so on. Other variants include the volume rebate (a year-end refund according to the volume purchased by the account during the year) and the growth volume rebate (given on the difference between purchases from one year to the next).

Voluntary Chain — A group of retailers each of whom owns and operates its own store and is associated with a wholesale organization.[14]

Warehouse Outlet — A large retail facility located in a warehouse-type building or with an adjoining warehouse. Warehouse outlets compete on the basis of low prices made possible by their no-frills approach. They are located in low rent areas, offer few if any services, and make maximum use of vertical space in the storage of their large inventories.

Warranty — An undertaking of responsibility by the seller of a good or service for the quality or suitability of the product. An express warranty (which can be written or verbal) is one based on express statements voluntarily made by the seller. An example of an express warranty would be an automobile manufacturer that warrants that its vehicle will perform as promised for seven years or 70,000 miles, whichever comes first. Warranties also can be implied. An implied warranty is one not made directly by the seller but implied by law, for example, that a product sold as food is fit for human consumption.

Wholesaler — A business unit that buys and resells merchandise to retailers and other merchants and/or to industrial, institutional, and commercial users but which does not sell to ultimate consumers.

SOURCES

Glossary of Marketing Terms

1. Christine Ammer and Dean S. Ammer. *Dictionary of Business and Economics.* New York: Free Press, 1984.

2. *Ayer Glossary of Advertising and Related Terms.* Philadelphia: Ayer Press, 1972.

3. Carl E. Block and Kenneth J. Roering. *Essentials of Consumer Behavior.* Hinsdale Ill.: Dryden Press, 1979.

4. Thomas V. Bonoma and Benson P. Shapiro. *Segmenting the Industrial Market.* Lexington, Mass.: D.C. Heath, 1983.

5. Louis E. Boone and David L. Kurtz. *Contemporary Marketing.* Hinsdale, Ill.: Dryden Press, 1980.

6. Robert D. Buzzell; Robert E. M. Nourse; John B. Matthews, Jr.; and Theodore Levitt. *Marketing: A Contemporary Analysis.* New York: McGraw-Hill, 1972.

6a. Census of Manufacturers', 1982.

7. Committee on Definitions of the American Marketing Association. *Marketing Definitions.* Chicago: American Marketing Association, 1963.

8. E. Raymond Corey. *Industrial Marketing: Cases and Concepts.* Englewood Cliffs, N.J.: Prentice Hall, 1976.

9. E. Raymond Corey. *Procurement Management: Strategy, Organization, and Decision-Making.* Boston: CBI Publishing, 1978.

9a. George S. Day. *Analysis for Strategic Market Decisions.* St. Paul, Minn.: West Publishing 1986.

10. *The Discount Merchandiser.* June 1987.

10a. Catherine L. Hayden. *The Handbook of Strategic Expertise.* New York: Free Press, 1986.

11. James L. Heskett. *Marketing.* New York: Macmillan, 1976.

12. Barbara Bund Jackson. *Computer Models in Management.* Homewood, Ill.: Richard D. Irwin, 1979.

12a. Paul L. Joskow and Alvin K. Klevorick. "A Framework for Analyzing Predatory Pricing Policy." *Yale Law Journal* 89, no. 2, 1979.

13. Philip Kotler. *Marketing Management.* Englewood Cliffs, N.J.: Prentice Hall, 1980.

13a. Philip Kotler. *Principles of Marketing.* Englewood Cliffs, N.J.: Prentice Hall, 1986.

14. Murray Krieger. *The Complete Dictionary of Buying and Merchandising.* New York: National Retail Merchants Association, 1980.

15. Donald R. Lehmann. *Market Research and Analysis.* Homewood, Ill.: Richard D. Irwin, 1979.

16. Theodore Levitt. *Industrial Purchasing Behavior: A Study of Communications Effects.* Boston: Division of Research, Harvard University Graduate School of Business Administration, 1965.

16a. *Macmillan Dictionary of Modern Economics.* New York: Macmillan, 1986.

17. Maurice I. Mandell. *Advertising.* Englewood Cliffs, N.J.: Prentice Hall, 1974.

17a. *Marketing News.* March 1985.

18. E. Jerome McCarthy and William D. Perreault, Jr. *Basic Marketing.* Homewood Ill.: Richard D. Irwin, 1981.

19. Erwin Esser Nemmers. *Dictionary of Economics and Business.* Totowa, N.J.: Littlefield, Adams, 1976.

20. Sidney A. Packard; Arthur A. Winters; and Nathan Axelrod. *Fashion Buying and Merchandising.* New York: Fairchild, 1980.

20a. David J. Reibstein. *Marketing: Concepts, Strategies, and Decisions.* Englewood Cliffs, N.J.: Prentice Hall, 1985.

21. Benson P. Shapiro. "Improve Distribution with Your Promotional Mix." *Harvard Business Review* 55, no. 2 (1977).

21a. Louis W. Stern and Adel I. El-Ansary. *Marketing Channels.* Englewood Cliffs, N.J.: Prentice Hall, 1982.

22. Hirotaka Takeuchi. "A Note on Retailing Institutions." Boston: HBS case no. 9-580-042.

23. "Test Marketing Sharpens the Focus." *Sales and Marketing Management.* March 16, 1981.

23a. *The Food Marketing Industry Speaks, 1986.*

24. Joe L. Welch. *Marketing Law.* Tulsa, Okla.: Petroleum Publishing, 1980.

25. Kirkland A. Wilcox and Joseph G. San Miguel. *Introduction to Financial Accounting.* New York: Harper & Row, 1980.